Handbook of Motivation at School

The *Handbook of Motivation at School* presents the first comprehensive and integrated compilation of theory and research on children's motivation at school. It covers the major theoretical perspectives in the field as well as their application to instruction, learning, and social adjustment at school. Section I surveys the major theoretical perspectives addressing children's motivation at school, its antecedents, and its development. Section II focuses directly on children's motivation in school and how it relates to both positive and negative achievement. The final section includes more recent perspectives on the role of social processes, socialization agents, and contextual factors that can promote or hinder the development of students' motivation at school.

Key Features

Comprehensive — No other book provides such a comprehensive overview of theory and research on children's motivation at school.

Theoretical & Applied — The book provides a review of current motivation theories by the developers of those theories as well as attention to the application of motivation theory and research in classrooms and schools.

Chapter Structure — Chapters within each section follow a similar structure so that there is uniformity across chapters.

Commentaries — Each section ends with a commentary that provides clear directions for future research.

Kathryn R. Wentzel (PhD Stanford University) is Professor of Human Development at the University of Maryland. Her research interests focus on parents, peers, and teachers as motivators of adolescents' classroom behavior and academic accomplishments. She is currently Co-Editor of the *Journal of Applied Developmental Psychology*, is past Vice-President of Division E of AERA, and is a Fellow of the APA, Division 15.

Allan Wigfield (PhD University of Illinois) is Professor and Chair of the Department of Human Development and Distinguished Scholar-Teacher at the University of Maryland. His research focuses on how children's motivation develops across the school years in different areas, including reading. He currently edits the Teaching, Learning, and Human Development section of the *American Educational Research Journal*. He is a Fellow of Division 15 of APA, a Fellow of the Association for Psychological Science, and a Fellow of the AERA.

EDUCATIONAL PSYCHOLOGY HANDBOOK SERIES
Series Editor: Patricia A. Alexander
University of Maryland

Handbook of Educational Psychology (2006)
Edited by Patricia A. Alexander and Philip H. Winne

Handbook of Moral and Character Education (2008)
Edited by Larry P. Nucci and Darcia Narvaez

International Handbook of Research on Conceptual Change (2008)
Edited by Stella Vosniadou

Handbook of Motivation at School (2009)
Edited by Kathryn R. Wentzel and Allan Wigfield

Handbook of Motivation at School

Edited by
Kathryn R. Wentzel
Allan Wigfield

Routledge
Taylor & Francis Group

NEW YORK AND LONDON

First published 2009
by Routledge
270 Madison Ave, New York, NY 10016

Simultaneously published in the UK
by Routledge
2 Park Square, Milton Park, Abingdon, Oxon OX14 4RN

Routledge is an imprint of the Taylor & Francis Group, an informa business

© 2009 Taylor and Francis

Typeset in Minion by EvS Communication Networx, Inc.

Library of Congress Cataloging-in-Publication Data
Wentzel, Kathryn R.
Handbook of motivation at school / Kathryn R. Wentzel, Allan Wigfield.
 p. cm. — (The psychological foundations of teaching and learning)
Includes bibliographical references and index.
Motivation in education—Handbooks, manuals, etc. I. Wigfield, Allan. II. Title.
LB1065.W46 2009
370.15'4—dc22
2008047601

ISBN 10: 0-8058-6284-6 (hbk)
ISBN 10: 0-8058-6290-0 (pbk)
ISBN 10: 0-203-87949-X (ebk)

ISBN 13: 978-0-8058-6284-3 (hbk)
ISBN 13: 978-0-8058-6290-4 (pbk)
ISBN 13: 978-0-203-87949-8 (ebk)

Contents

Acknowledgments and Dedication   ix

Contributors   xi

1. Introduction   1
    KATHRYN R. WENTZEL AND ALLAN WIGFIELD

Section I: Theories   **9**

2   An Attributional Approach to Motivation in School   11
    SANDRA GRAHAM AND CHRISTOPHER WILLIAMS

3   Self-Efficacy Theory   35
    DALE H. SCHUNK AND FRANK PAJARES

4   Expectancy-Value Theory   55
    ALLAN WIGFIELD, STEPHEN TONKS, AND SUSAN LUTZ KLAUDA

5   Achievement Goal Theory: The Past, Present, and Future   77
    MARTIN L. MAEHR AND AKANE ZUSHO

6   Goal-Directed Behavior in the Classroom   105
    MONIQUE BOEKAERTS

7   Self-Theories and Motivation: Students' Beliefs About Intelligence   123
    CAROL S. DWECK AND ALLISON MASTER

8   Self-Worth Theory: Retrospection and Prospects   141
    MARTIN COVINGTON

9   Promoting Self-Determined School Engagement: Motivation, Learning, and Well-Being   171
    RICHARD M. RYAN AND EDWARD L. DECI

10 Situational and Individual Interest   197
    ULRICH SCHIEFELE

11 Engagement and Disaffection as Organizational Constructs in the Dynamics of Motivational Development   223
ELLEN A. SKINNER, THOMAS A. KINDERMANN, JAMES P. CONNELL, AND JAMES G. WELLBORN

12 Motives to Self-Regulate Learning: A Social Cognitive Account   247
BARRY J. ZIMMERMAN AND TIMOTHY J. CLEARY

13 Commentary: Building on a Strong Foundation: Five Pathways to the Next Level of Motivational Theorizing   265
MARTIN E. FORD AND PEYTON R. SMITH

Section II: Contextual and Social Influences on Motivation   **277**

14 Parenting and Children's Motivation at School   279
WENDY S. GROLNICK, RACHEL W. FRIENDLY, AND VALERIE M. BELLAS

15 Students' Relationships with Teachers as Motivational Contexts   301
KATHRYN R. WENTZEL

16 Peers and Motivation   323
GARY W. LADD, SARAH L. HERALD-BROWN, AND KAREN P. KOCHEL

17 Teacher Expectations and Self-Fulfilling Prophecies   349
LEE JUSSIM, STACY L. ROBUSTELLI, AND THOMAS R. CAIN

18 School as a Context of Student Motivation and Achievement   381
ROBERT W. ROESER, TIMOTHY C. URDAN, AND JASON M. STEPHENS

19 Gender and Motivation   411
JUDITH L. MEECE, BEVERLY BOWER GLIENKE, AND KARYL ASKEW

20 Achievement Motivation in Racial and Ethnic Context   433
TAMERA B. MURDOCK

21 Commentary: The Role of Environment in Contextual and Social Influences on Motivation: Generalities, Specificities, and Causality   463
ADELE ESKELES GOTTFRIED

Section III: Teaching, Learning, and Motivation   **477**

22 Beliefs About Learning in Academic Domains   479
MICHELLE M. BUEHL AND PATRICIA A. ALEXANDER

23 Reading Motivation   503
JOHN T. GUTHRIE AND CASSANDRA S. CODDINGTON

24 Understanding Motivation in Mathematics: What is Happening in Classrooms?   527
JULIANNE C. TURNER AND DEBRA K. MEYER

25 Motivation and Achievement in Physical Education   553
ANG CHEN AND CATHERINE D. ENNIS

26 Emotions at School   575
REINHARD PEKRUN

27 Motivation and Learning Disabilities: Past, Present, and Future   605
GEORGIOS D. SIDERIDIS

28 Teachers' Self-Efficacy Beliefs   627
ANITA WOOLFOLK HOY, WAYNE K. HOY, AND HEATHER A. DAVIS

29 Commentary: What Can We Learn from a Synthesis of Research on Teaching,
Learning, and Motivation?   655
BARBARA L. MCCOMBS

Index   671

Acknowledgments and Dedication

We would like to extend thanks to Patricia Alexander, the series editor, for her vision and generosity that made this handbook possible. We also acknowledge with gratitude the many pioneering scholars of motivation who built the foundations for the work that is presented in this volume.

We dedicate this Handbook to Frank Pajares, who passed away in January, 2009. Frank was a prolific scholar in the motivation field who co-authored (with Dale Schunk) the chapter on self-efficacy for this volume. He also was a giving and generous colleague, mentor, and teacher. His death is a great loss to the field and to all who knew him.

Contributors

Patricia A. Alexander, Department of Human Development, University of Maryland, College Park

Karyl Askew, Department of Human Development and Psychological Studies, University of North Carolina at Chapel Hill

Valerie M. Bellas, Psychology Department, Clark University

Monique Boekaerts, Center for the Study of Education and Instruction, Leiden University, The Netherlands

Michelle M. Buehl, Program in Educational Psychology, George Mason University

Thomas R. Cain, Department of Psychology, Rutgers University

Ang Chen, Department of Exercise & Sport Science, University of North Carolina at Greensboro

Timothy J. Cleary, Department of Educational Psychology, University of Wisconsin at Milwaukee

Cassandra S. Coddington, Department of Human Development, University of Maryland, College Park

James P. Connell, Institute for Research and Reform in Education, Philadelphia, PA

Martin Covington, Department of Psychology, University of California at Berkeley

Heather A. Davis, School of Educational Policy and Leadership, The Ohio State University

Edward L. Deci, Department of Psychology, University of Rochester

Carol S. Dweck, Department of Psychology, Stanford University

Catherine D. Ennis, Department of Exercise & Sport Science, University of North Carolina at Greensboro

Martin E. Ford, College of Education and Human Development, George Mason University

Rachel W. Friendly, Psychology Department, Clark University

Beverly Bower Glienke, Department of Human Development and Psychological Studies, University of North Carolina at Chapel Hill

Adele Eskeles Gottfried, Department of Educational Psychology and Counseling, California State University, Northridge

Sandra Graham, Department of Psychological Studies in Education, University of California, Los Angeles

Wendy S. Grolnick, Department of Psychology, Clark University

John T. Guthrie, Department of Human Development, University of Maryland, College Park

Sarah L. Herald-Brown, Psychology Department, Arizona State University

Anita Woolfolk Hoy, School of Educational Policy and Leadership, The Ohio State University

Wayne K. Hoy, School of Educational Policy and Leadership, The Ohio State University

Lee Jussim, Department of Psychology, Rutgers University

Thomas A. Kindermann, Psychology Department, Portland State University

Susan Lutz Klauda, Department of Human Development, University of Maryland, College Park

Karen P. Kochel, Psychology Department, Arizona State University

Gary W. Ladd, Department of Psychology, Arizona State University

Barbara L. McCombs, Center for Motivation, Learning, and Development, University of Denver

Martin L. Maehr, Department of Psychology, University of Michigan

Allison Master, Department of Psychology, Stanford University

Judith L. Meece, Department of Human Development and Psychological Studies, University of North Carolina at Chapel Hill

Debra K. Meyer, Education Department, Elmhurst College

Tamera B. Murdock, Department of Psychology, University of Missouri-Kansas City

Frank Pajares, Division of Educational Studies, Emory University

Reinhard Pekrun, Department of Psychology, University of Munich, Germany

Stacy L. Robustelli, Educational Testing Service, Princeton, NJ

Robert W. Roeser, Department of Psychology, Portland State University

Richard M. Ryan, Department of Psychology, University of Rochester

Ulrich Schiefele, Faculty for Psychology and Sport Science, University of Bielefeld, Germany

Dale H. Schunk, School of Education, University of North Carolina at Greensboro

Georgios D. Sideridis, Department of Psychology, University of Crete, Greece

Ellen A. Skinner, Psychology Department, Portland State University

Peyton R. Smith, Madison Learning, Seattle, Washington

Jason M. Stephens, Department of Educational Psychology, University of Connecticut

Stephen Tonks, Department of Leadership, Educational Psychology & Foundations, Northern Illinois University

Julianne C. Turner, Psychology Department, University of Notre Dame

Timothy C. Urdan, Psychology Department, Santa Clara University

James G. Wellborn, Williamson County Counseling Center, Nashville, TN

Kathryn R. Wentzel, Department of Human Development, University of Maryland, College Park

Allan Wigfield, Department of Human Development, University of Maryland, College Park

Christopher Williams, Department of Psychological Studies in Education, University of California, Los Angeles

Barry J. Zimmerman, Program in Educational Psychology, Graduate School, City University of New York

Akane Zusho, Division of Psychological and Educational Services, Fordham University

1
Introduction

Kathryn R. Wentzel and Allan Wigfield

The academic lives of children are challenging and complex. In line with the mission of schooling, children are expected to engage in academic activities, learn from instruction, and meet standards of intellectual competency established by others. Each day at school children also are expected to adhere to classroom rules, maintain and establish new relationships with classmates and adults, and participate in activities as part of their school community. Central to understanding children's success at these activities is motivation, that is, the energy they bring to these tasks, the beliefs, values and goals that determine which tasks they pursue and their persistence in achieving them, and the standards they set to determine when a task has been accomplished. Given the motivational challenges inherent in accomplishing these tasks, questions concerning how and why children are motivated (or not motivated) to achieve these academic and social outcomes at various stages of their educational careers have been at the forefront of research for over 40 years.

The history of scholarship on motivation at school reflects many rich theoretical traditions encompassing a variety of constructs. Initially, motivation theorists focused on drives and needs as the basis of motivation, along with the patterns of rewards and punishments individuals received in school and in other settings. Over the last 30 years, social cognitive theories have dominated the field. For example, theoretical perspectives have focused on the motivational significance of individuals' beliefs about their abilities, self-efficacy, and expectancies for success; attributions and beliefs about intelligence; and sense of control over outcomes on students' effort, persistence, and subsequent performance. Similarly, theorists have generated a rich and extensive literature on why students choose to achieve specific outcomes, focusing on constructs such as goals, standards for performance, values, interest, and orientations toward learning and performance. In recent years, this focus on motivation as a characteristic of the individual has been extended to include frameworks specifying developmental, ecological, and socialization factors that can influence motivational beliefs and intentions. Indeed, the complex interactions of individual and contextual factors are hallmarks of much current work on motivation.

Although the study of motivation at school continues to be vibrant, we believe that it is time to take stock of where the field has been and the current challenges it is facing. Thus part of our vision for this handbook was to provide a detailed scholarly overview of the current state of theory and research in the field and of new directions and provocations for the field. Moreover, we believe that researchers and scholars of motivation at school have much to offer a larger body of stakeholders who formulate educational policy, develop school-based interventions, and teach children on a daily basis. Therefore, many of the authors in this volume discuss the application of theory and research to instruction, learning, and social adjustment at school, and corresponding implications for larger societal issues facing those concerned with educating children.

This volume is the first comprehensive, edited volume of work on motivation theory and related research as it applies to school settings. It is comprehensive with respect to its coverage of current theories, consideration of social and contextual influences, and applications of motivation to a variety of academic and non-academic domains. We believe that this compilation of work on children's motivation at school is particularly important and timely for several reasons. First, the profound significance of theoretical and empirical work on motivation for understanding the broader social and academic outcomes of schooling is reflected in its wide application to intervention efforts to improve students' academic and social outcomes by way of curricular development and classroom management strategies. Pioneers of basic research and theorizing about motivational processes began a rich tradition of applied work on educational training and instruction and laid a strong foundation for subsequent efforts (see e.g., Bandura, 1986; DeCharms, 1984; Lewin, Lippitt, & White, 1939; McClelland, 1965; Sherif, Harvey, White, Hood, & Sherif, 1988). Indeed, early intervention studies influence the field to this day in their identification of psychological and contextual processes that motivate change in student outcomes. Constructs such as social cohesion and goal setting, self-efficacy and modeling, self-determination, and needs for competence and affiliation come to mind.

Current interest and efforts in applied research have demonstrated the enduring strength of motivational concepts for improving students' engagement in learning activities, academic performance, school attendance and graduation rates, and social competencies (Wentzel & Wigfield, 2007). These efforts are also timely given the increased focus of policy makers and funding agencies on identifying "what works" to improve performance in educational settings through experimental school-based intervention research. However, we also believe that researchers need to incorporate into their work knowledge concerning the greater complexity of motivational processes and multiple levels of influence uncovered over the past four decades. This is necessary to move the field toward a more sophisticated application of motivation theory and research to practical educational issues and problems. We challenged authors in this volume to consider these complexities, and so hope that this volume will be an important source of scholarship and inspiration in this regard.

Recent developments in the areas of educational policy and testing also have moved student motivation to the level of national debate and discussion. For instance, since the passing of the No Child Left Behind legislation there has been increased focus on assessing children's achievement in school and finding ways to improve it. The persistent achievement gap between children from some minority groups and their Caucasian American and Asian American peers has also been at the forefront of national political debate concerning educational best practices. Although most prescriptions for change have focused on the development of instructional strategies to improve cognitive skills (e.g., National Reading Panel, 2000), the community of scholars who study motivation has simultaneously voiced warnings about the detrimental effects of high-stakes testing on students' motivational functioning (Deci & Ryan, 2002), as well as suggested that performance deficits might be explained in part, by motivational rather than cognitive issues (e.g., Graham & Hudley, 2005; Pintrich, 2003).

As part of this discussion, scholars also have identified the clear and substantial benefits of practices designed to promote social motivational processes such as a sense of social relatedness and belonging. Along with motivational processes that focus on the self (e.g., self-efficacy, self-determination), these social aspects of motivation appear to have potentially powerful and positive effects on students' engagement in academic pursuits (National Research Council, 2004). In contrast, the absence of positive social motivational processes, as reflected in feelings of alienation and social rejection, can have a negative impact on students' self-perceptions, interest in learning, and willingness to engage in academic activities. The systematic study of social motivational processes is relatively new to the field. However, investigating ways in which social and academic motivational processes interact and complement each other to influence academic performance might be central to understanding the comparatively low levels of achievement of many children, especially those who are members of traditionally low-performing groups. Several authors in this volume have begun to make important advances in this essential area of scholarship, and we hope their work will move the field forward.

Finally, the fields of educational and developmental psychology have seen exciting and significant advances in research methodologies that have the potential to change the way we think about and study motivation in context. Policy makers and funding agencies have increased focus on sampling strategies that yield more generalizable results and methodologists have developed sophisticated statistical strategies for parsing out the unique and nested effects of individuals and contexts on student outcomes. Use of multiple informants and mixed-methods designs have become gold standards for researchers who seek to provide a balanced portrayal of how quantitatively-derived "explained variance" reflects the unique perspectives of individuals (e.g., Greene, 2001). Many of the challenges that the study of motivation at school pose to researchers can be met with these methodological tools.

Specific to the area of motivation at school, scholars have challenged the field to define theoretical constructs more precisely and to reflect these refinements in ways that constructs are measured. The need to take domain and subject-area factors into account, along with levels of contextual complexity (dyadic, classroom-level, school-level), when developing measurement strategies also has been raised. Many of the authors in this volume address these issues directly in their chapters. We believe such discussions are timely and necessary for understanding where the field needs to move next and will provide important and new directions for the field.

Overview of the Volume

The focus of this volume is on motivation in school settings. However, our vision was to consider motivation in school as a process that supports the pursuit and accomplishment of many outcomes, not just academic achievements. Indeed, school-aged children come to school with many goals they wish to achieve that reflect learning and intellectual development, social and interpersonal concerns, and affective functioning. Educators themselves promote the successful accomplishment of these multiple goals in school-aged children. Therefore, the authors of this handbook speak not only to issues surrounding motivation to achieve academically but also to issues concerning social connectedness and competence with classmates and teachers, the development of a healthy sense of psychological and emotional well-being, and students' ability to adapt to educational contexts that often support values or interpersonal styles that are incongruent with those of their family, community, or culture.

A related goal for the handbook was to acknowledge the growing and diverse literature on contextual supports that promote motivation at school, or at times impede its growth. Historically, theoretical models and empirical studies of these supports have focused on how various aspects of teachers' instructional practices motivate learning, including discussions of how instruction is embedded in the classroom structures that teachers create and degrees of autonomy afforded to students. More recently, this focus has expanded to include consideration of instructional and other supports within particular academic subject areas, and non-academic domains such as sports. In addition, there is increasing concern for the motivational functioning of special populations of students. The field also has enjoyed a growing literature on social processes and supports with the potential to motivate students at school. This work has brought to the fore a recognition that traditional theories of motivation also have relevance for understanding students' social outcomes at school. Moreover, scholars in this area have increased awareness of how socialization processes known to promote social and affective development also can provide a foundation for the development of motivational processes associated with learning and academic outcomes. The sections of the handbook are organized around these multiple concerns.

Authors in section 1 of this book present overviews of the major theoretical perspectives that address children's motivation at school, its antecedents, and development. These theories encompass the beliefs, values, goals, and needs that have been the focus of much of the research on achievement motivation over the last several decades: attributions for success and failure; self-efficacy beliefs; expectancies and values for different achievement activities; goals for learning and achievement; beliefs about the nature of intelligence; how one's competence and performance influences overall self-worth; interest in different activities; intrinsic motivation and its relation to self-determination and the satisfaction of basic needs; and ways individuals regulate behavior and how motivation influences self-regulation. We were especially pleased that many of the originators of these theories agreed to contribute chapters to this volume. We also were pleased to include newer perspectives on motivation at school that introduce theoretical and methodological approaches to the study of goal content and multiple goal pursuit, and the notion of engagement.

We asked the authors in this section to present their theoretical perspective, how it has evolved over time, and how it applies to school-based issues. We also asked authors to discuss measurement issues with respect to the constructs in their theory, to provide their perspectives on theoretical and methodological challenges that remain, and to reflect on how they see their theory and its component constructs moving forward. We are particularly excited about the authors' thoughts about future directions both from the standpoint of their theoretical perspective but also about the motivation field more broadly. In their commentary on this set of chapters, Ford and Smith also propose intriguing new directions for motivation theorists, suggesting five pathways that can move the field ahead. The first pathway is to think about motivation from the perspective of broader evolutionary-based theories in psychology, and incorporating emotions more clearly into conceptual models. The next two pathways require additional focus on the role of personal goals in driving and organizing other motivational processes, and attention to the fundamental importance of social aspects of motivation in addition to individual characteristics. Fourth, they note the importance of having multiple constructs in different models (termed "motivational pluralism" by Ford and Smith). Finally, they urge theorists to begin the task of integration across theoretical perspective in order to have a richer and fuller understanding of the development of motivation.

The chapters in section II reflect more recent perspectives on the role of social processes, socialization agents, and contextual factors that can promote or hinder the development of students' motivation at school. In the first three chapters, authors describe empirical work and reflect on important theoretical advancements in the areas of parent, peer, and teacher influences on student motivation. Work in these areas is relatively new. Therefore, the sophisticated and rich perspectives on motivation provided by these authors is testament to the growing recognition that social processes, interactions, and relationships can have a powerful influence on student motivation, and that integration of social developmental models with more traditional approaches to motivation brings much strength to the discussion of students' motivation at school. In a fourth chapter, the specific role of teacher expectations on student motivation is reviewed and discussed. Research on teacher expectancy effects has a rich tradition in the field although few scholars have considered explicitly the impact of teacher expectations on student motivation. A chapter on school characteristics in relation to student motivation also is included in this section. This chapter reminds us of the broader contextual factors that can have profound impact on student motivation but that are frequently ignored in school-based studies of motivation. Finally, two chapters consider the role of social identities as reflected in gender, race, and ethnicity in promoting or undermining motivation at school.

In her commentary on this set of chapters, Gottfried notes the growing complexity that considerations of social and contextual influences bring to research and theorizing on motivation. In doing so, she highlights the important distinctions between proximal and distal environmental influences on motivation. She describes general findings that emerge from the body of work contained in the chapters, but also some unique ways in which the general findings and principles play out in different contexts and settings. Gottfried also reminds us of the challenges of documenting social influences on motivation and cautions the field about making premature claims of causal linkages. The importance of future researchers employing designs to get more clearly at both the nature and direction of causal influences on children's motivation is underscored.

The chapters in section III focus on teaching, learning, and motivation. This section reflects three sets of issues related to classroom teaching, additional factors that influence students' learning that are not addressed explicitly in broader theories of motivation, specifically learning difficulties and school-related emotions, and factors that influence the motivation of teachers. The chapters in this section also are concerned with how children's motivation in school relates to both positive and negative academic outcomes. The first set of chapters discusses motivation in different academic content areas and sports. These chapters reflect the growing understanding in the motivation field that children's motivation can differ markedly across the different activities in which they engage, and that the characteristics of specific activity domains can greatly influence children's motivation. We selected math, English, and sports as the domains to include in this volume because of their centrality to children's lives.

Two chapters focus on emerging areas of work on motivation. There is increasing interest in the field on how motivation links to children's emotions and how school experiences lead to different emotional reactions and also impact students' motivation. There also is growing interest in the impact of motivation on the performance in school of students who have learning challenges. Two chapters focus on these issues. Finally, the section closes with a chapter on teachers' sense of efficacy that describes the rich research tradition and established models of teacher efficacy, and its impact on students' motivation and achievement. As in the other sections of the book, we asked authors to discuss extant research in their area and identify important new directions for research.

Barbara McCombs begins her commentary on the chapters in section III by noting her own assumptions about motivation and learning. These include observations that research and common sense often are not in agreement with respect to our understanding of motivation and learning and when there is disagreement researchers must identify the source of misperceptions (i.e., tacit knowledge or empirical methods); that all humans learn in self-organizing ways and are naturally motivated to continue learning across their life spans; that formal instruction in schools often works against this natural motivation, leading to student disengagement, and therefore, provisions of choice and autonomy are essential for maintaining students' engagement in lifelong learning; and researchers must challenge their own assumptions about motivation and learning if educational reform is to take place. She returns to these assumptions as she comments on each chapter, connecting the authors' work to them. She concludes with two strong recommendations: that motivation researchers must articulate clear and straightforward messages about motivation for practitioners if these messages are to have an impact in schools, and that student engagement can be fostered by connecting formal education to lifelong learning. The chapters in this section make important contributions concerning each of these recommendations.

Looking Forward

In closing, we would like to thank the authors who contributed to this volume for their thought-provoking and forward-looking chapters on motivation at school. We are encouraged by the evolution of constructs that defined earlier work in the field into more complex motivational phenomena (e.g., new ways to define and think about school-related goals), and the integration of new constructs such as emotions and social supports with more traditional social-cognitive approaches to motivation. Increased focus on the notion of engagement is also moving the field to connect psychological processes to observable actions and outcomes in more meaningful ways. Broad consensus concerning the centrality of social motivational processes for understanding motivation at school is a relatively new phenomenon that should provide a strong impetus for much future work. The emergence of common themes concerning the roles of interpersonal relationships and learning contexts for understanding self-related aspects of motivation is also a welcomed addition to the field. We also appreciate the increasing emphasis on contextual influences on motivation and many authors' depiction of motivation as a complex interplay of individual processes and contextualized experiences. Similarly, as should be apparent from the chapters in this volume, we think the field has advanced in its understanding of the motivation of individuals from different racial and ethnic groups. Finally, we believe the application of motivation theory to practical issues, including consideration of domain- and subject-specific educational problems is an exciting and important new direction for the field. Integrating theory with practice, and coordinating models of motivation with curricular and instructional concerns are inevitable next steps that we applaud.

There is much yet to be done. We look forward to the development of more integrated models that retain the complexity of processes and constructs found in this volume but that also achieve a simplicity that is useful to practitioners and policy makers interested in educational reform. In this regard, integration of perspectives on social motivation with models that focus solely on self-processes and academic outcomes is a clear challenge. Theories that account for school-related phenomenon, ranging from issues concerning the day-to-day realities of classroom instruction and how they impact motivation, to the influence of broader administrative decision making and its impact on students' motivation also need to be developed further. Another challenge is that much of the work on motivation at school has maintained a static, snapshot view of children's lives at school. Developmental perspectives are essential to provide a more complete picture of how and why motivation changes over time and how motivational processes lead to change in students' social and academic competencies.

We also look forward to the application of a broader set of methodological tools to the study of motivation in context, and the continued development of new measurement tools. Although the measurement of motivation has improved over the past few decades, additional advances with respect to specificity, focus on process and change, and use of multiple methods are still needed. Self-report measures will remain a central tool in motivation research, but they need to be supplemented with other ways of measuring motivation and engagement. Examples include observations, ratings by teachers or other informants, and "on line" measures that move away from the static views that self-report measures provide. More attention to assessing structural aspects of schools and classrooms that influence students' motivation, and incorporating the complex and nested qualities of educational contexts into research designs also is warranted.

Finally, we anticipate future discussions of work on motivation in other domains and its relevance for understanding motivation at school. For example, exciting and provocative work is emerging from social psychological studies of motivation that examine implicit or unconscious aspects of motivation (Schultheiss & Brunstein, 2005). The interplay of conscious and implicit motivational processes and their development over time is an exciting area for future research. There also is increasing interest in the neurological and biological bases of motivation and behavioral engagement. Research on the influence of such processes on emotions and interest are examples of the relevance of this work for understanding motivation, but this work is extending to other aspects of motivation as well (Panksepp, 2003). Expanding our focus to examine more systematically the motivational processes of teachers and other adults (including parents) who work with children, more diverse samples, and to include a broader life-span perspective that considers the motivation of preschool children as well adult learners would undoubtedly bring fresh perspectives to the field.

We hope that this handbook will stimulate and provide guidance to current and future scholars of motivation in their efforts to understand more fully students' motivation at school.

References

Bandura, A. (1986). *Social foundations of thought and action: A social cognitive theory.* Englewood Cliffs, NJ: Prentice-Hall.

DeCharms, R. (1984). Motivation enhancement in educational settings. In R. Ames & C. Ames (Eds.), *Research on motivation in education: Student motivation* (pp. 275–310). New York: Academic Press.

Deci, E. L., & Ryan, R. M. (2002). The paradox of achievement: The harder you push, the worse it gets. In J. Aronson (Ed.), *Improving academic achievement: Impact of psychological factors on education* (pp. 61–87). San Diego: Academic Press.

Graham, S., & Hudley, C. (2005). Race and ethnicity in the study of motivation and competence. In A. Elliot & C. Dweck (Eds.), *Handbook of Competence and Motivation* (pp. 392–413). New York: Guilford.

Greene, J. C. (2001). Mixing social inquiry methodologies. In V. Richardson (Ed.), *Handbook on research on teaching* (4th ed., pp. 251–258). Washington DC: AERA.

Lewin, E. K., Lippitt, R., & White, R. (1939). Patterns of aggressive behavior in experimentally created social climates. *Journal of Sociology, 10,* 271–299.

McClelland, D. C. (1965). Toward a theory of motive acquisition. *American Psychologist, 20,* 321–333.

National Reading Panel (2000). *Teaching children to read: An evidence-based assessment of scientific research literature on reading and its implications for reading instruction.* (NIH Pub. No. 00-4769). Jessup, MD: National Institute for Literacy.

National Research Council (2004). *Engaging schools: Fostering high school students' motivation to learn.* Washington, DC: National Academies Press.

Panksepp, J. (2003). At the intersection of the affective, behavioral, and cognitive neurosciences: Decoding the emotional feelings of the brain. *Brain and Cognition, 52,* 4–14.

Pintrich, P. R. (2003). Motivation and classroom learning. In W. Reynolds & G. Miller (Eds.), *Handbook of psychology, Vol. 7: Educational Psychology* (pp. 103–122). New York: Wiley.

Schultheiss, O. C., & Brunstein, J. C. (2005). An implicit motive perspective on competence. In A. J. Elliot & C. S. Dweck (Eds.), *Handbook of competence and motivation* (pp. 31–51). New York: Guilford.

Sherif, M., Harvey, O. J., White, B. J., Hood, W. R., & Sherif, C. W. (1988). *The robber's cave experiment: Intergroup conflict and cooperation.* Middletown, CT: Wesleyan Press.

Wentzel, K. R., & Wigfield, A. (2007). Promoting motivation at school: Interventions that work. *Educational Psychologist, 42,* 187–194.

Section I
Theories

2

An Attributional Approach to Motivation in School

Sandra Graham and Christopher Williams

"There is nothing so practical as a good theory." These sage words have been attributed to Kurt Lewin, one of the major figures in the history of motivation. Much of the practical significance of attribution theory resides in its usefulness for understanding real-world motivational concerns that unfold every day in school settings—concerns such as emotional reactions to success and failure, self-esteem maintenance, and acceptance or rejection by peers. A handbook on motivation in school contexts is therefore a good venue for reviewing an attributional approach to motivation. While this approach shares the theoretical spotlight with the rich and varied perspectives that comprise the first section of this volume, it has remained influential in the field of motivation for at least the past 30 years. To provide some evidence of the continuing influence of attribution theory, we searched the PsycINFO database for peer-reviewed journal articles during the last three decades, using the keywords *attribution theory* or *causal attributions*. Over three 10-year periods, there were about 750 articles published from 1975–1985, 800 from 1986–1996, and 700 from 1997–2007, showing remarkable continuity of empirical activity on attribution theory even as other approaches to motivation were gaining more visibility.

Attribution theory as a field originated with the publication of Fritz Heider's now classic book, *The Psychology of Interpersonal Relations* (1958). Many theorists associated with attributional analyses followed Heider (e.g., Jones & Davis, 1965; Kelley, 1973), but in this chapter we focus on attribution theory as formulated and elaborated by Bernard Weiner (see reviews in Weiner, 1986, 1995, 2006). Weiner's model incorporates the antecedents of attributions, the dimensions or properties of causes in addition to causes per se, and the affective, cognitive, and behavioral consequences of particular causal ascriptions. That theory also distinguishes between the consequences of attributions that individuals make about their own outcomes—labeled an intrapersonal theory of motivation—and the consequences of attributions that perceivers make about the outcomes of other people—labeled an interpersonal theory of motivation. Hence, this theory is more complete than other attributional conceptions, and it remains the framework of choice for most educational psychology researchers who study motivation in school.

In the following sections, we begin with a brief overview of causal attributions and their underlying properties. This will be followed by a review of research on both the antecedents and consequences of particular attributions for both intrapersonal and interpersonal motivation. As with most chapters of this handbook, we aim for breadth rather than depth and we acknowledge that we cannot do justice to a number of attribution-related phenomena that have rich empirical literatures in their own right. In the final section, we conclude with a set of recommendations for conducting motivation research in schools that is informed by our attributional perspective.

Causal Attributions

Figure 2.1 shows a conceptual representation of Weiner's attributional theory of motivation, with the intrapersonal theory and the interpersonal theory depicted. Think of the linkages as a temporal sequence that begins with an outcome interpreted as a success or failure. Following an initial reaction of happiness or sadness, individuals then undertake a causal search to determine why that outcome occurred. Attributions are answers to those "why" questions, such as, "Why I did I fail the exam?" when the motivational domain is achievement, or "Why wasn't I invited to the party?" when the motivational domain is affiliation. Individuals make attributions about other people as well as themselves. Teachers might ask, for example, "Why did Mary fail the exam?" or "Why doesn't Johnny have any friends?" As these examples illustrate, perceivers especially seek answers to "why" questions following negative, unexpected, or unusual events (Gendolla & Koller, 2001). Causal search is therefore functional because it can help us impose order on an unpredictable environment.

In the achievement domain, which has served as a model for the study of causality in other contexts, Figure 2.1 shows that success and failure often are attributed to an ability factor that includes both aptitude and acquired skills, an effort factor that can be either temporary or sustained, the difficulty of the task, luck, mood, and help or hindrance from others. Among these causal ascriptions, in this culture at least, ability and effort are the most dominant perceived causes of success and failure. When explaining achievement outcomes, individuals attach the most importance to their perceived competence and how hard they try. That is, when someone succeeds they probably infer that, "I tried hard" or "I am smart" and, if they do not succeed, they are likely to conclude that "I did not try hard enough" or "I am not very smart."

As attribution theorists, we believe that people spontaneously engage in such causal thinking in their everyday lives (Weiner, 1985). Because that spontaneity is difficult to capture in research, most studies of attributions in the achievement domain elicit attributions by having participants respond to some stimulus. For example, participants might be induced to succeed or fail at an achievement task, asked to recall a real-life success or failure, or told to imagine that they experienced a positive or negative achievement outcome. Attributions for the real or imagined outcome are then elicited. The most common methods are a free-response format where subjects generate their own causal explanations, a forced-choice format where subjects select from an array of presented causes, or a rating-scale method where subjects rate the extent to which each cause influenced an outcome. There is no one best way to measure attributions and each of the methods has it own strengths and limitations (see Weiner, 1983, for a cogent discussion about measurement of attributions).

Because specific attributional content, however assessed, will vary between motivational domains as well as between individuals within a domain, attribution theorists have focused on the underlying dimensions or properties of causes in addition to specific causes per se. Here we ask,

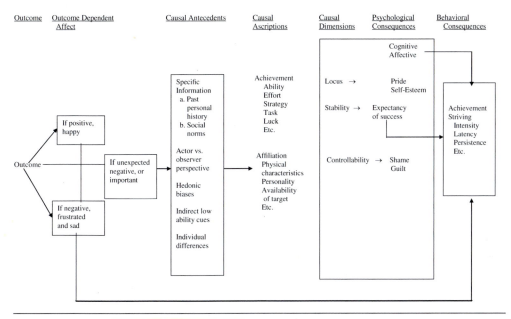

Figure 2.1a An attributional theory of intrapersonal motivation.

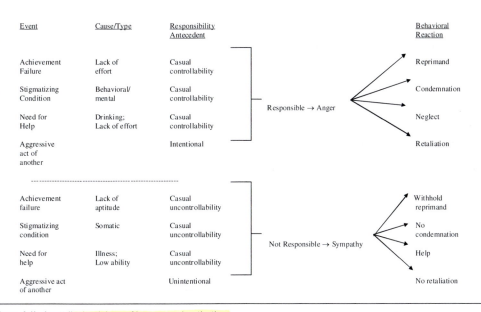

Figure 2.1b An attributional theory of interpersonal motivation.

for example, how are ability and effort similar and how are they different? Are there other attributions that share the overlapping and nonoverlapping properties of ability and effort? Three causal dimensions have been identified with some certainty. These are *locus*, or whether a cause is internal or external to the individual; *stability*, which designates a cause as constant or varying over time; and *controllability*, or whether a cause is subject to volitional influence. All causes theoretically are

causal dimensions

locus
stability
controllability

classified into one of the eight cells of a locus X stability X controllability dimensional matrix. For example, ability is typically perceived as internal, stable, and uncontrollable. When we attribute our failure to low ability, we tend to see this as a characteristic of ourselves, enduring over time, and beyond personal control. Effort, on the other hand, is also internal, but unstable and controllable. Failure attributed to insufficient effort usually indicates a personal characteristic that is modifiable by one's own volitional behavior. For attribution theorists, it is the three dimensions that are constant; the placement of a cause along a dimension will certainly vary between individuals. This is not a problem for the theory. For example, effort can be judged as quite stable when it takes on a trait-like quality (think of the attributions we make about the chronically lazy student). Similarly, ability can be perceived as unstable if perceivers believe that new learning can change one's basic abilities. Carol Dweck's research on theories of intelligence (see Dweck & Master, this volume) maps closely onto an attributional analysis of ability as stable versus unstable.

The conceptual distinctions between causes based on dimensional placements are central to an attributional theory of motivation because each dimension is uniquely related to a set of cognitive, emotional, and behavioral consequences. We return to these consequences in a later section. But first we move backward in the temporal sequence shown in Figure 2.1 to examine some of the antecedents or determinants of particular attributions.

Attributional Antecedents

How do perceivers arrive at the attributions that they make about themselves or other people? We know a good deal about these antecedents from early research on what has been called the attribution process (Kelley & Michela, 1980). That research has identified a number of antecedent cues, such as prior performance history and social norm information that influence self-ascriptions (Kelley, 1973). If I as a student have been doing poorly in a course all semester, or if I fail a test and everyone else gets an "A," both of these are very salient sources of information that I might use to infer that I have low ability. Using antecedent information in a systematic way to reach causal attributions, even when they may be unflattering, is consistent with the metaphor in early attribution research of the person as a scientist—rational and dispassionate in their search for causal understanding (Weiner, 1992). At times, however, individuals are also prone to self-enhancing biases or errors in the way they arrive at attributions. For example, people tend to take credit for success and to blame failure on external causes, a phenomenon known as the "hedonic bias" (Miller & Ross, 1975); they tend to overestimate the role of traits and underestimate the role of situational factors when making causal inferences about other people, a bias so pervasive that it has been labeled the "fundamental attribution error" (Ross, 1977); and while making trait attributions about others, people are more likely to attribute their own behavior to situational factors, a bias that has been labeled the "actor-observer effect" (Jones & Nisbett, 1971).

Indirect Attributional Cues

Another source of attributional information, particularly about effort and ability and especially relevant to motivation in school, is feedback from teachers. Teachers no doubt often directly and intentionally tell their students that they did not put forth enough effort, for trying hard has moral implications and is certainly compatible with the work ethic espoused in school. Although teachers typically do not intentionally tell their students that they are low in ability, this attributional information may be subtly, indirectly, and even unknowingly conveyed. In a series of laboratory-experimental studies, one of us (Graham, 1990) was able to draw on basic attribution principles to document that three seemingly positive teacher behaviors can indirectly function as low ability cues. The particular behaviors examined in these studies were communicated sympathy following failure; the offering of praise following success, particularly at easy tasks; and unsolicited offers of help.

In attribution research it has been documented that failure attributed to uncontrollable factors such as lack of ability elicits sympathy from others and sympathy, in turn, promotes offers of help (see review in Rudolph, Roesch, Greitemeyer, & Weiner, 2004). This is in contrast to failure attributed to controllable causes such as lack of effort, which tends to evoke anger and the withholding of help. Now suppose that a teacher does respond with sympathy as opposed to anger toward a failing student or with an unsolicited offer of help rather than neglect. It might be the case that the student will then use these affective and behavioral displays to infer, first, the teacher's attribution, and second, his or her own self-ascription for failure. In a study that manipulated failure on a novel puzzle solving task, sixth grade failing students who received sympathy from an experimenter posing as a teacher were more likely to attribute their failure on the task to low ability whereas students who received feedback from the experimenter that communicated anger were more likely to report lack of effort as the cause of failure (Graham, 1984). In other words, the students used the emotional displays of teachers to infer why they themselves failed. Using a methodology of observed rather than experienced achievement failure to study unsolicited help, Graham and Barker (1990) had 6- to 12-year-old participants watch a videotape of two students working on a challenging achievement task, where one of the students was offered unsolicited help from the teacher. All participants, including the youngest children, perceived the helped student to be lower in ability than the student who was not helped. Thus unsolicited help, like sympathy, can function as an antecedent to low ability.

Teachers can also indirectly communicate low ability cues in situations of success accompanied by positive verbal feedback such as praise. Two attribution principles are relevant here. First, praise is related to perceived effort expenditure in that the successful student who tries hard is maximally rewarded (Weiner & Kukla, 1970). Second, effort and ability are often perceived as compensatory causes of achievement: in both success and failure, the higher one's perceived effort, the lower one's perceived ability, and vice versa (Kun & Weiner, 1973; Nicholls, 1978). Thus, if two students achieve the same outcome, often the one who tries harder (and is praised) is perceived as lower in ability. Drawing on these attribution principles in studies with both college students (Meyer et al., 1979) and children (Barker & Graham, 1987), it was documented that students who were praised for success at a relatively easy task were inferred to be lower in ability than their counterparts who received neutral feedback. In other words, the offering of praise following success, like communicated sympathy following failure and unsolicited help, functioned as a low ability cue.

Although not grounded in attributional analyses per se, there are many examples in more current motivational literatures of how teacher feedback of the types described above can have unexpected ability-implicating consequences. For example, in laboratory research with both early and middle childhood participants, Dweck and her colleagues have found that praising students for their high intelligence ("you're a smart person") or their positive traits ("you're a good person") can lead to motivational deficits, such as decreased persistence or avoidance of challenging tasks, when students do encounter failure (Kamins & Dweck, 1999; Mueller & Dweck, 1998; see Dweck & Master, this volume, for further discussion). In gender research, a form of unsolicited help from men labeled as *benevolent sexism* resulted in greater self-doubt and poorer performance among female college students than did outright hostile sexism (Dardenne, Dumont, & Bollier,

2007). Benevolent statements were presented in a warm and friendly manner but conveyed the message that women were in need of men's help and therefore relatively incompetent. And in research on social stigma, African American students reported lower academic self-esteem when they received unsolicited help on an intelligence test from a White confederate than did their African American counterparts who received no such help (Schneider, Major, Luhtanen, & Crocker, 1996). Consistent with our attributional analysis, these authors proposed that help that is not requested can confirm a "suspicion of inferiority" among African Americans who regularly confront the negative stereotypes about their group's intellectual abilities. In a related program of research (Cohen, Steele, & Ross, 1999; Study 1), the motivation of African American students to revise a challenging writing assignment was weaker in a feedback condition of unbuffered praise for performance compared to feedback that communicated criticism and high expectations for improved performance.

In summary, principles from attribution theory can be enlisted to understand how some well-intentioned teacher behaviors might sometimes function as low ability cues. It has been suggested that teachers might be more likely to engage in such feedback patterns when they desire to protect the self-esteem of failure prone students, particularly ethnic minority youth (Graham, 1990). Recent findings from adult research on stigmatized groups also suggests that African American students confronting feedback on their intellectual abilities and women confronting feedback on their achievements in male-dominated fields might be particularly susceptible to evaluations from authority figures that implicate their ability.

Of course, we are not suggesting that the types of feedback that we discussed always function as indirect low ability cues. Sympathetic affect, generous praise, minimal criticism, and helping behavior are useful instructional strategies that often neutralize some of the immediate impact of failure, such as public embarrassment or frustration. The appropriateness of any teacher communications, or the achievement of what Cohen et al. (1999) label as "wise" feedback, will depend on many factors, including the characteristics of both students and teachers. Rather, the general message we wish to convey is that attribution principles can facilitate our understanding of how some well-intentioned teacher behaviors can have unexpected or even negative effects on student motivation.

Individual Differences in Causal Attributions

Historically, the study of individual differences as an antecedent to achievement-related behavior played a central role in theories of motivation. For example, characterizing people as high or low in need for achievement or internal versus external in locus of control are core distinctions in achievement theory (Atkinson, 1964) and social learning theory (Rotter, 1966), the two most prominent motivational conceptions of the 1960s and early 1970s. Although not central to the development of attribution theory, there are at least two prominent theories in the motivation literature that focus on individual differences in causal reasoning.

Explanatory Style Explanatory style emerged in the late 1970s as part of early efforts to understand the role of attributions in learned helplessness and depression (Abramson, Seligman, & Teasdale, 1978). It was argued that when people experience helplessness or depression, they often ask why. An attributional analysis of depression resulted in the development of a measure that was designed to assess individual differences in the way people habitually explain good and bad events (Peterson, 1991). Over the years, the labeling of this instrument has shifted from "attributional" to "explanatory" style as it has been applied to the achievement domain and other contexts beyond helplessness and depression.

In broad individual difference terms, explanatory style classifies respondents as pessimists versus optimists. People who explain negative outcomes as internal ("it's me"), stable ("things will always be this way"), and global ("it affects many areas of my life") are judged to have a pessimistic explanatory style. In contrast, those who typically attribute negative events to external, unstable, and specific causes are considered to have an optimistic explanatory style. Attributions for good events can also be considered as pessimistic (external, unstable, and specific) or optimistic (internal, stable, global). Thus, explanatory style incorporates two dimensions of causality from attribution theory (locus and stability) as well as a third dimension (globality) that has been more closely associated with the helplessness literature. Research on explanatory style has generated a large empirical literature that spans the clinical, academic, sports, health and work domains (see Peterson, 2000). In the achievement domain, a number of studies have documented that students with an optimistic as opposed to pessimistic explanatory style for both success and failure achieve better outcomes in school (e.g., Boyer, 2006; Rowe & Lockhart, 2005). Although the broad and sweeping claims of some explanatory style proponents are probably unwarranted (see Anderson, Jennings, & Arnoult, 1988 for a critique), it also is true that when measured at the appropriate level of specificity, how people typically explain good and bad events is related to subsequent outcomes.

Entity versus Incremental Theories of Intelligence In chapter 7 of this volume, Dweck and Master cover theories of intelligence and their relation to motivation. We briefly refer to that literature here because it captures individual differences between people in their preference for attributions that differ on the stability dimension. Dweck and her colleagues have proposed that individuals hold one of two implicit theories about intelligence (Dweck, 1999; Dweck & Molden, 2005). Some people are what Dweck labels *entity* theorists: They believe that intelligence is basically fixed and unmalleable, as when they endorse statements such as "You can learn new things, but you can't really change your basic intelligence." In contrast, other individuals appear to be *incremental* theorists: They believe that intelligence is modifiable and are more likely to agree with statements such as "Smartness is something you can increase as much as you want to." This distinction therefore highlights the underlying characteristic of constancy or change, which is captured by the stability dimension. A large empirical literature documents the motivational consequences of entity versus incremental theories that are consistent with predictions derived from attribution theory. In challenging academic situations, for example, entity theorists (intelligence is stable) display more motivational impairments than incremental theorists (intelligence is unstable). Attribution theory can accommodate the fact that people might view ability in an entity or incremental way inasmuch as the dimensional placement of any cause along the main dimensions can vary between individuals. But rather than focus on individual differences in particular causal preferences, attribution theorists are more likely to believe in the power of the situation to shape attributional interpretations and to be concerned with general principles linking the stability of attributions to particular consequences.

Summary

Both situational and dispositional factors can be antecedents to particular self-ascriptions for success and failure. Perceivers use causal rules in both unbiased and biased ways to make attributions about their own and others' behavior. Typically, well-intentioned teacher feedback, such as communicated sympathy, unbuffered praise, and unsolicited help can sometimes function as low ability cures. Furthermore, individual differences in the way people typically explain events (i.e., optimistically vs. pessimistically) or view aptitude along the stability dimension (i.e., malleable vs. unchanging) affect causal reasoning in particular achievement settings, although we suspect that these traits rarely override situational determinants.

Attributional Consequences

What difference does it make if an individual attributes success to, for example, trying hard versus "getting the right breaks" or failure to low ability versus the prejudice of others? To answer these questions, we turn to the consequences of causal ascriptions, or the implications of causal thinking for achievement-related thoughts, feelings, and actions. These are the issues of greatest concern to motivational psychologists who conduct their research in school contexts. Hence, it should come as no surprise that the study of causal consequences embodies the very heart of an attributional approach to motivation.

To examine attributional consequences, it is necessary to return to causal dimensions, or the underlying properties of causal attributions. Recall that locus, stability, and controllability are the three dimensions that have been identified with some certainty. As depicted in Figures 2.1, each dimension is linked to a set of psychological, emotional, and behavioral consequences. The locus dimension of causality is related to self-esteem and esteem-related emotions like pride and shame. We review research on self-handicapping and attributions to prejudice as illustrations of how individuals implicitly make use of the locus-esteem relation. The stability dimension affects subjective expectancy about future success and failure. This linkage is the organizing construct for reviewing the attribution retraining literature, which is one of the best examples of how changes in motivation can result in actual changes in achievement-related behavior. As the third dimension, causal controllability relates largely to perceived responsibility in *others* and therefore is linked to a set of interpersonal cognitive, emotional, and behavioral consequences that are directed toward other people (Weiner, 1995, 2006). These consequences are displayed in Figure 2.1. We review research on perceiving the other as responsible in the social domains of achievement evaluation, the endorsement of stereotypes, and peer-directed aggression.

Locus of Causality and Self-Esteem

Locus of causality, which distinguishes between internal and external causes of success and failure, is related to self-esteem and esteem-related affect. More specifically, a successful outcome that is ascribed to the self (e.g., personality, ability, effort) results in greater self-esteem and pride than does success that is attributed externally—for example, to task ease or good luck (Weiner, 1986). Similarly, failure attributed to internal causes evokes more shame or guilt than when the same outcomes are attributed to external causes. When people make use of the hedonic bias introduced earlier, which is the tendency to take credit for success and blame others for failure, they are making use of the locus-esteem relation.

Self-Handicapping Other than hedonic bias, it is possible that individuals might engage in various strategies, some of which might be quite dysfunctional, to avoid self-ascriptions for failure to low ability. Jones and Berglass (1978) first described a phenomenon, labeled *self-handicapping*, in which people create obstacles that make failure more likely, but where presumably that failure is not diagnostic of their abilities. For example, a student may avoid effort by partying all night before an important exam so that poor performance on the exam can be attributed to factors other than his or her ability. It is also possible that pride and positive self-esteem can be enhanced if success is achieved despite the handicap (i.e., the person must have very high ability to succeed in spite of lack of effort). In attributional terminology (Kelley, 1973), self-handicappers can *discount* ability attributions for failure by blaming the handicap, but can *augment* ability attributions following success.

Self-handicapping is a construct with considerable intuitive appeal; many researchers have been drawn to the study of individuals who are willing to place obstacles in the way of successful performance in order to protect themselves from the esteem-threatening implications of failure. A large number of empirical studies of self-handicapping have been conducted in the 30 years since Jones and Berglas first coined the term and that research appears to have found its niche in the larger literature on defensive self-attributions and other esteem-protecting motivational strategies (Elliot & Church, 2003; Rhodewalt & Vohs, 2005). Individuals are more likely to self-handicap when they have low self-esteem to begin with, the tasks are important, criteria for evaluation are unclear, and in the presence of an audience, which suggests that self-presentational concerns in addition to esteem protection can motivate students to create impediments to successful performance. While most research on self-handicapping has been conducted with college-aged participants, there is also a growing interest in studying the phenomenon in school-aged children who are encountering academic difficulty. Recent studies suggest that the antecedents of self-handicapping include a performance avoidant goal orientation as well as less autonomy support from the teacher, whereas the consequences of self-handicapping include lower academic achievement and more depressed affect (Maatta & Nurmi, 2007; Turner, Meyer, Midgley, & Patrick, 2003; Urdan, 2004).

Attributions for Discrimination among Stigmatized Groups A second area of research that can be incorporated within the locus-esteem linkage focuses on the esteem-protective functions of attributions about discrimination among stigmatized groups. By stigmatized we mean those groups or individuals who are perceived to possess characteristics or social identities that are devalued in certain contexts—for example, racial/ethnic minorities and women in achievement contexts and people who are obese, facially disfigured, learning disabled, mentally ill, or criminally delinquent (Crocker, Major, & Steele, 1998). There is a growing literature indicating that ethnic minority youth do experience discrimination in school settings from teachers as well as peers, that such experiences are painful, and that they can have a detrimental effect on motivation (e.g., Fisher, Wallace, & Fenton, 2000; Greene, Way, & Pahl, 2006; Rosenbloom & Way, 2004; Wong, Eccles, & Sameroff; 2003). Among the most prevalent kinds of unfair treatment reported by ethnic minority youth are receiving a lower grade than deserved from teachers, being the recipient of unusually harsh discipline from authority figures, and being the target of verbal, psychological, or physical abuse from peers. Some data indicate that African American and Latino youth are especially likely to report discrimination from adults in their school whereas Asian students feel more harshly treated by peers (Rosenbloom & Way, 2004; Fisher et al., 2000).

How are stigmatized individuals able to cope with such unfair treatment by others? In an influential theoretical review, Crocker and Major (1989) drew on attribution research to argue that attributing unfair treatment to external causes, such as to prejudice of others, is an important self-protective mechanism that members of stigmatized groups use to maintain their self-esteem in spite of disparaging treatment by others. A number of laboratory-experimental studies that followed the Crocker and Major review supported that position (see Major, Quinton, & McCoy, 2002 for a review).

The idea that external attributions can be self-protective for stigmatized groups has been quite popular because it provides a compelling theoretical account for why low status groups have positive self-views *in spite of* their disadvantaged position. However, there is almost no research on the attributions that children and adolescents make for unfair treatment that draws on the richness of the attribution literature among adults who are members of stigmatized groups (see Brown & Bigler, 2005). That is, we know that the experience of discrimination in school is common among youth of color, but we do not know whether and at what age they begin to make external attributions for unfair treatment and whether such attributions have the same esteem-protecting function that they apparently have for adults. Because discrimination in school can negatively affect achievement strivings (e.g., Wong, Eccles, & Sameroff, 2003), we believe that further research on the motivational consequences of attributions to prejudice is warranted.

Causal Stability and Expectancy of Success: Attribution Retraining

One of the most well-documented findings in attribution research is that expectancy is related to the perceived stability of causes (Weiner, 1986). When achievement failure is attributed to a stable cause, such as low aptitude, one is more likely to expect the same outcome to occur again than when the cause is an unstable factor, such as lack of effort. Thus, the failing student who believes that she did not try hard enough can be bolstered by the expectation that failure need not occur again. Failure attributed to low aptitude, in contrast, tends to lower one's expectations for future success. Attribution researchers believe that differences between ability and effort on the stability dimension, rather than the controllability dimension, account for expectancy increments and decrements (see Graham & Brown, 1988).

Guided by these known consequences of ability versus effort attributions based on the stability-expectancy linkage, a number of attribution retraining studies have attempted to change the failing student's attribution for failure from low ability to lack of effort. Most of the studies have followed a similar format. Target subjects are first selected on the basis of some maladaptive behavior or cognition. For example in the first attribution retraining study in achievement settings, Dweck (1975) selected elementary school students labeled as "helpless" on the basis of ratings by their classroom teacher and a school psychologist. Because these children were doing poorly in school, it was assumed that their maladaptive cognition was to attribute failure to low ability (or not to lack of effort). Once selected, targeted individuals then underwent a reattribution training program to teach them to attribute their failure to insufficient effort. Typically, this attributional feedback is delivered by an experimenter following induced failure on a laboratory task, although more recent studies have initiated interventions in the context of the regular school curriculum with children (e.g., Horner & Gaither, 2006) as well as college students (e.g., Struthers & Perry, 1996). Following the intervention, the cognitions and behavior of the retrained subjects are then compared to those of a nontrained comparison group with similar characteristics. For example, Dweck's helpless students who received effort retraining showed more persistence in the face of failure and better performance than their counterparts who in the training period had received success only feedback.

Some retraining studies have directly manipulated the stability dimension rather than specific causes. In one of the first achievement retraining studies with adults, Wilson and Linville (1982) manipulated the stability dimension by telling a group of anxious college freshmen that their grades would improve from the first to the second year; that is, the reasons for poor performance in the freshman year were unstable. Compared to a control group who received no attribution information, retrained students had greater expectations for success in their sophomore year, achieved higher grade point averages, and they were less likely to drop out of college at the end of the first year.

Although not necessarily framed as attribution retraining, a number of recent studies have implicitly manipulated the stability dimension by teaching students to adopt an incremental versus entity theory of intelligence (cf. Dweck, 1999). In the first study in this series, Aronson, Fried, and Good (2002) recruited African American and White college students to be "academic pen pals" with fictitious middle schools students who were purported to be at risk for school failure. College subjects were instructed to write encouraging letters that reflected on the ability needed to succeed in school. In the incremental theory condition, participants were given a script in which they were prompted to tell their pen pals about the malleability of intelligence—for example, that it expands with mental effort and is capable of growing and making new connections throughout life. Those in the control condition were given a script that prompted them to emphasize to their pen pals the notion of multiple intelligences. Results showed subjects in the incremental condition had more favorable attitudes toward college over the course of the year and achieved higher grades than did students in the control condition, and this was particularly true for African American students. In two follow-up studies with early adolescents transitioning to middle school, those in the incremental condition achieved higher grades in math than their counterparts in nonattribution information or no information control groups (Blackwell, Trzesniewski, & Dweck, 2007, Experiment 2; Good, Aronson, & Inzlicht, 2003). Focusing more on feelings of belonging than on theories of intelligence, Walton and Cohen (2007) exposed African American and White college freshmen to a condition stating that all college students worry at first about whether they fit in but that such worries dissipate over time (i.e., they are unstable). Compared to their classmates in a no-information control group, students in the retraining condition felt better about college and actually achieved higher grades in their sophomore year. Like the earlier research of Good et al. (2003), the intervention was particularly effective for African American students for whom the transition to college is often more academically and socially challenging.

As interventions designed to alter motivational tendencies, attribution retraining programs have been quite successful with both children and adults in academic settings (see reviews in Forsterling, 1985; Robertson, 2000; Wilson, Damiani, & Shelton, 2002). However, we believe that there are at least three ways in which the richness of attribution theory has not been fully utilized in these programs.

First, most attribution retraining studies begin with the dysfunctional attribution and its consequences without considering the earlier points in a motivational sequence where intervention could also occur (see Weiner, 1988, for a related discussion). Because the attributional process begins with the perception of an outcome as a success or failure, the change agent might consider ways to alter the perception of failure—for example, by developing strategies to help the student view poor performance on a test not as failure but as information about areas that need improvement. It could also be that causal cues were inaccurately processed, such that the failing student did not have adequate knowledge about the performance of others or even incorrectly recalled his or her own history of performance. In these examples the attribution change agent is not directly communicating a new attribution, such as "you did not try hard enough"; rather the goal is to help the target student re-evaluate the outcome or arrive at a new attribution by attending more closely to causal antecedents.

Second, there has been insufficient attention to the mediating mechanisms that explain how altering maladaptive attributions can lead to changes in achievement behavior. Attribution theory suggests that emotions are one such important mechanism. Failure due to lack of effort gives rise to guilt; and guilt, in turn, is believed to instigate renewed achievement behavior. Low ability attributions, on the other hand, elicit shame and humiliation, emotions that are believed to inhibit achievement strivings. Yet no attribution retraining studies have examined the relative contribution of emotions to increments and decrements in achievement behavior.

A third area of theory underutilization in the retraining studies is the almost exclusive focus on achievement failure or the threat of failure. However, attribution theory also predicts that success experiences can be accompanied by both adaptive and maladaptive attributions. For example, success attributed to good luck or unusual help from others might be maladaptive because success is external (thus mitigating feelings of pride) and unstable (thus lowering one's expectations for future success). There is evidence that "helpless" as opposed to mastery-oriented children do process success in this manner (Diener & Dweck, 1980) and that members of stigmatized groups who question their abilities are sometimes reluctant to take credit for success (Crocker et al., 1998). Hence, there is a need for change programs designed to alter maladaptive cognitions for positive as well as negative outcomes.

Causal Controllability and Interpersonal Consequences

Thus far our discussion of attributional consequences has been guided by the intrapersonal theory of motivation displayed in Figure 2.1. Within that intrapersonal theory, the controllability dimension is related to a number of self-directed emotions such as guilt versus shame. Attributions for failure to controllable factors tend to elicit guilt and the desire to alter the situation (Weiner, 1986). In contrast, individuals tend to feel shame when failures are attributed to internal, uncontrollable causes such as low aptitude or a physical handicap; the absence of control also leads people to feel helpless and depressed and to display behaviors such as passivity, escape, and withdrawal (see Skinner, 1995).

Attribution research on the consequences of perceived controllability has been especially fruitful when causal inferences are made about other people, as in the interpersonal theory of motivation depicted in Figure 2.1. Here the perceiver asks: Is the person responsible? Was it his or her fault? Are there responses in the person's repertoire that could have altered the outcome? Judgments about responsibility then lead to other-directed emotions such as sympathy and anger and a vast set of interpersonal behaviors including reward versus punishment, help versus neglect, and prosocial versus antisocial behavior. Thus, attribution theorists propose a particular thought-emotion-action sequence whereby causal thoughts determine feelings and feelings, in turn, guide behavior.

The emotional and behavioral consequences of perceiving others as responsible have been documented across a range of motivational domains; indeed, this set of principles is among the most robust in attribution theory (Weiner, 1995, 2006). Figure 2.1 shows the many phenomena to which the analysis applies. All of these phenomena are relevant to events that take place in classrooms and schools. The perceivers might be teachers making controllability attributions and responsibility inferences about their students' academic performance, or peers making similar causal judgments about the social behavior of classmates who have stigmatizing conditions. We illustrate these attribution principles in three distinct domains.

Achievement Evaluation Teachers reward the effortful student and punish the lazy and unmotivated. Attribution theory can explain this empirical fact. When a teacher attributes failure by a student to lack of effort, the student is perceived to be responsible, anger is elicited, and punishment or reprimand is meted out. In contrast, when failure is attributed to low aptitude, the student is perceived as not responsible, sympathy is aroused, and help may be offered. It is important to point out that evaluative reactions to student failure as a function of low effort versus ability attributions are more related to differences between ability and effort on the controllability dimension than on the stability dimension. For example, in a study of the punishment goals of actual high school teachers, Reyna and Weiner (2001) found that teachers were more likely to report that they punish students for low effort whether that cause is stable (e.g., the student never tries) or unstable (the student is sometimes "flaky"). Similarly, the teachers were more supportive of the student when the cause of failure was low ability, whether that cause was stable (the student always has difficulty) or unstable (the student had difficulty learning the material for this exam). Judgments of causal controllability, responsibility, anger, and sympathy were also systematically related to the severity of punishment in a manner consistent with attribution predictions. If anything, causal stability appears to be a magnifier of these linkages or more directly associated with a teacher's belief in her efficacy to change student behavior.

We partially introduced the above principles in the discussion of indirect attributional cues: When teachers express sympathy toward a failing student or offer unsolicited help, these emotions and behaviors can indirectly communicate low ability (Graham, 1990). Thus, attribution principles from the intrapersonal theory of motivation and the interpersonal theory are closely interrelated. These interrelated linkages also highlight the dilemmas that some students might face in terms of their own experiences of success and failure and managing the impressions that others have of them. For example, some students may choose to avoid the appearance of having tried too hard for fear of being perceived as low in ability, as we documented in the self-handicapping literature. The endorsement of low effort attributions also can result in more peer approval, particularly during adolescence when popularity and downplaying effort appear to go hand-in-hand (see review in Juvonen, 2000). In so doing, however, the student risks the negative reactions of evaluative agents like teachers and parents. High effort can therefore be a "double-edged sword" (Covington & Omelich, 1979), rendering approval from one's teacher and parents but at the same time possibly undermining perceived personal competence and peer approval. The complex interplay between private evaluations and self-presentational concerns in achievement settings are well-illustrated in attribution principles related to perceived controllability in others.

Causal Controllability and Stereotypes Stereotypes are culturally shared beliefs, both positive and negative, about the characteristics and behaviors of particular groups. For example, the notion that blondes have more fun or that adolescents are victims of "raging hormones" are part of our culturally endorsed beliefs about the attributes of those social groups. Attributional analyses have been applied to stereotypes about members of some socially stigmatized groups. According to Reyna (2000), stereotypes function as attributional signatures; they convey information about responsibility for a stigmatizing condition and therefore impact the way stigmatized individuals and the groups to which they belong are treated by others.

In our own attribution research, one of us has been particularly interested in the consequences of negative racial stereotypes about African American adolescent males (Graham & Lowery, 2004). Even though privately held beliefs about African Americans have become more positive over the last 50 years, studies of cultural stereotypes continue to show that respondents associate being Black (and male) with hostility, aggressiveness, violence, and danger (e.g., Correll, Park, Judd, & Wittenbrink, 2002; Devine & Elliott, 1995). Moreover, as recent research in social psychology has documented, racial stereotypes often are activated and used outside of conscious awareness (e.g., Bargh & Chartrand, 1999). By automatically categorizing people according to cultural stereotypes, perceivers can manage information overload and make social decisions more efficiently.

Using a priming methodology with police officers and probation officers in the juvenile justice system, Graham and Lowery (2004) examined the unconscious activation of racial stereotypes about adolescent males and their attributional consequences. Participants in whom racial stereotypes were unconsciously primed judged a hypothetical adolescent offender as more dangerous, responsible and blameworthy for his alleged offense, and more deserving of harsh punishment than participants in an unprimed control condition. The priming effects were documented irrespective of the respondents' gender, race/ethnicity, political orientation, or consciously held attitudes about African Americans. Hence, automatic stereotype activation does not require perceivers to endorse the stereotype, to dislike African Americans, or to hold any explicit prejudice toward that group. Even decision makers with good intentions can be vulnerable to racial stereotypes and their responsibility-related consequences.

We believe that such findings also have implications for decisions makers in our schools who make judgments about the social (mis)behavior of African American youth. Reviews of Zero Tolerance and related "get tough" policies in schools have produced racial disparities in the use of disciplinary practices such that African American youth are more likely to be suspended or expelled from school than White youth who engage in similar or even more serious transgressions (see review in Skiba, Reynolds, Graham, Sheras, Conoley, & Vasquez, 2008). Particularly among perceivers at the front end of a system, like teachers dealing with classroom disorder, decisions often must be made quickly, under conditions of cognitive and emotional overload, and where much ambiguity exists. These are the very conditions that are known to activate unconscious beliefs (Fiske, 1998).

We tend to focus in our own work on racial stereotypes about social behavior, but there are equally pervasive racial stereotypes about intelligence and academic behavior that also are amenable to attributional analyses of the type proposed here. For example, there is quite a lot of evidence that African American youth are underrepresented in programs for the gifted, while their overrepresentation in special education programs mirrors that found in the juvenile justice system (National Research Council, 2002). Because teacher referrals are often the main vehicle by which students get the opportunity to be tested as mentally retarded or gifted, it is essential that teachers be aware that referrals are subjective judgments about the behavior of other people and therefore are vulnerable to all of the known biases, both conscious and unconscious, that can be present when perceivers make inferences about other people. The underlying message here is that attributional analyses about perceived responsibility in others, in conjunction with recent thinking from social psychology on the meaning and function of stereotypes, provide an ideal context for examining the unconscious racial stereotypes of well-intentioned teachers and administrators that can have far-reaching consequences.

Peer-Directed Aggression Causal controllability and responsibility inferences have been prominent in the peer aggression literature. One very robust finding in that literature is that aggressive children display a "hostile attributional bias" to overattribute negative intent to others, particularly in situations of ambiguously caused provocation (Dodge, Coie, & Lynam, 2006). To illustrate, imagine a situation where a student experiences a negative outcome, such as being pushed by a peer while waiting in line, and it is unclear whether the peer's behavior was intended or not. When asked whether the peer's action was hostile or benign, aggressive youth are more likely than their nonaggressive counterparts to infer that the push occurred "on purpose." Attributions to hostile intent (the person is responsible) then lead to anger and the desire to retaliate. Many studies document that hostile attributional bias in aggressive youth is correlated with maladaptive outcomes including poor school achievement, conduct disorder, externalizing behavior, and peer rejection (Dodge et al., 2006). A common theme underlying this literature is that having a tendency to adopt a blameful stance toward others interferes with the processing of social information, anger management, and effective problem solving.

If attributions to hostile peer intent instigate a set of reactions that lead to aggression, then it should be possible to train aggressive-prone students to see ambiguous peer provocation as unintended. This should mitigate anger as well as the tendency to react with hostility. The notion of altering causal thinking to produce changes in behavior has been a guiding assumption of attributional change programs in the achievement domain that we reviewed earlier. Thus, there are good theoretical and empirical precedents for considering attributional change as a way to alleviate peer-directed aggression.

Hudley and Graham (1993) developed a 6-week school based attribution intervention for fourth- to sixth-grade boys labeled as aggressive. Using a variety of interactive activities, the intervention was designed to (a) strengthen aggressive boys' ability to accurately detect responsibility in others, and (b) increase the accessibility of attributions to nonresponsibility when the causal situation was portrayed as ambiguous. Later refinements incorporated a greater repertoire of social skills such as managing the impressions (attributions) of others. Across this series of studies, the intervention led to reductions in attributional bias, better attitudes about the legitimacy of aggression, and improved teacher ratings of social behavior, both concurrently and longitudinally (see review in Hudley, Graham, & Taylor, 2007). This program of research is unique in documenting the effects of specific attribution retraining on *social* behavior.

General Summary

We organized our review by conceptualizing attribution theory as a motivational sequence that includes both the antecedents and consequences of causal thinking and that distinguishes between causal beliefs about oneself and about other people. The sequence begins with an outcome perceived as a success or failure. We reviewed a number of antecedents to attributions including indirect low ability cues and individual differences in attributional tendencies. It is evident that teacher feedback to students is an important source of attributional information and that seemingly well-intended behaviors, like sympathy, unbuffered praise and unsolicited offers of help, can function as low ability cues. The reactions of *others* to students' successes and failures are just as important as the objective outcomes as sources of attributional information about the self.

Given a list of antecedents, the next important linkages in attribution theory focus on the dominant, perceived causes for success and failure and their three underlying properties, labeled causal dimensions. Once a particular cause is endorsed, it theoretically is located in dimensional space and each dimension is related to unique psychological, emotional, and behavioral consequences. The locus dimension is primarily related to self-esteem and esteem-related affect and we reviewed research on self-handicapping and attributions to discrimination as illustrations of this linkage. The stability of causes determines expectations for future success and this linkage has guided a motivation change literature on attribution retraining. Finally, perceived controllability (responsibility) in others is related to a cluster of interpersonal reactions, including achievement evaluation, stereotyping, and peer-directed aggression. Feelings of sympathy and anger play an important motivational role in these linkages because they mediate thoughts about responsibility and subsequent interpersonal reactions. Thus, at the very heart of this temporal sequence comprising an attributional model of motivation is the specification of complex interrelationships between thinking, feeling, and acting.

What Can Attribution Theory Tell Us About Motivation Research? Our Top 5 Recommendations

The editors of this volume asked us to conclude our chapter with reflections on challenges and future directions for the field of motivation. We use our attributional lens to offer five recommendations for future research. None of the recommendations is discussed in detail, and they surely reflect our biases as well as the concerns that continue to shape our own evolving research program.

On Methods and Dependent Variables

It goes without saying that the study of motivation can benefit from a multi-method approach. In an earlier section, we described the different ways that researchers can assess attributions (e.g., open-ended, force choice, rating scales) as well as the different contexts in which attributions and related judgments can be elicited (e.g., real or imagined outcomes). Although attribution researchers who study motivation in school are likely to be most interested in conducting studies of actual achievement, we believe that role-playing paradigms, in which individuals imagine that a particular outcome occurred, should also have a place in the motivation researcher's methodological toolkit. Many of the attribution principles reviewed in this chapter employ role-playing or simulation methods. For example, attribution researchers often ask about the *likelihood* of help or aggression given certain conditions rather than actual prosocial or antisocial behavior. Similarly, we ask individuals whether they would feel certain emotions if particular attributional antecedents are present rather than measuring emotions per se during their state of activation. These choices grow out of a belief among attribution theorists that simulation studies are both appropriate and valuable when testing hypotheses and developing theoretical principles that are expected to apply quite generally across individuals and contexts. For example, attempts to map out the conceptual distinctions between ability and effort attributions, which has become the cornerstone of attribution theory, was initiated with the now classic simulation studies of Weiner and Kukla (1970). In those studies, respondents imagined that they were teachers rewarding or punishing their hypothetical students based on information about students' outcome (success or failure), ability level, and effort expenditure. We believe that what individuals *say* they would think, feel, or do in a particular situation maps closely onto how they *actually* think, feel, and behave in real-world contexts—"all else being equal." Role-playing studies allow for experimental control of those elusive "all else" variable.

Although a complete test of an attributional theory of motivation should be able to relate attributional consequences to achievement-related and social behavior, starting with behavior—or a primary focus on behavior in the absence of antecedent thoughts and emotions—can place unrealistic demands on a theory. Particularly in the achievement domain, both proximal indicators of achievement, such as grade point average or exam performance, as well as distal indicators such as high school completion, are greatly overdetermined; they are influenced by many factors other than (in addition to) motivational variables. In the achievement motive literature, David McClelland and colleagues reminded us of this as early as 1953 (McClelland, Atkinson, Clark, & Lowell). Thus, inconsistency in the prediction of actual achievement behavior should not be considered a fatal flaw in any theory of motivation. What our approach highlights is that thoughts and feelings, whether imagined or real, are legitimate outcomes to study in their own right.

The Need for a Developmental Perspective

Understanding development is central to any theory of motivation for school experiences. Children develop a more complex understanding of motivation constructs as they get older, their level of motivation sometimes changes (declines?) as they approach adolescence, and it is evident that achievement strivings are influenced by the match between children's developmental stage and the ways in which instruction and schools are organized (see Wigfield & Eccles, 2002). Developmental research on attributional principles has not kept pace with the needs of the field. In the 1970s several highly influential and oft-cited studies on children's understanding of attributions were conducted. Those studies revealed, for example, that children understand the properties of effort before they understand the properties of ability. Not until middle childhood do they perceive a compensatory relation between ability and effort, where being smart means being smarter than others, but having to try less hard (e.g., Kun, 1977; Nicholls, 1978). Consistent with these earlier findings, it has also been documented that children infer that teacher anger is a cue to lack of effort attributions at a younger age than they recognize that teacher sympathy can be a cue to low ability attributions (Weiner, Graham, Stern, & Lawson, 1982) and that teacher praise as a low ability cue is not inferred before middle childhood when students understand the compensatory rule (Barker & Graham, 1987). All of these developmental findings are relevant to an intrapersonal theory of motivation and they suggests that children younger than age 9 or 10 may not be as vulnerable as their older school mates to the negative consequences of attributions to low ability.

Some of the more recent attribution research that we reviewed focuses on an interpersonal theory of motivation, but little of that research has been carried out developmentally. Weiner (1995, 2006) proposed the metaphor of the "person as judge" as an organizing construct for explaining the diversity of phenomena depicted in Figure 2.1. For example, in deciding whether to help or neglect a needy other, forgive or deride a social transgressor, reward or punish a failing student, individuals act as intuitive judges, weighing the evidence to make inferences about controllability and responsibility and then meting out judgments that entail either punishment and rejection on the one hand, or forgiveness and acceptance on the other hand.

We believe that children, too, act as intuitive judges in the classroom. More attribution research is needed on children's developing understanding of the meaning of responsibility and its everyday operational vocabulary (e.g., "on purpose," "meant to," "should have," "ought to"), and how they use this understanding to both organize their thinking about the behavior of peers and make decisions about how subsequently to interact with those peers. The closest developmental literature that we have on these topics is the early research on children's emerging understanding of the meaning of intentionality, which all but faded by 1980 (see Karniol, 1980). One related area in contemporary developmental social cognition is research on theory of mind, defined as children's abilities to infer the mental states of others. Despite its relevance to work on inferences about others' responsibility, theory of mind research is much more closely associated with cognitive development than with social motivation, and the two literatures have experienced very little cross-fertilization. Moreover, the dominant models in current motivation research are intrapersonal theories rather than interpersonal theories, so there is relatively less attention to children's social interactions in comparison to the focus on individual achievement strivings. Our position is that children's social adjustment and their achievement strivings are closely intertwined and one cannot fully understand the development of academic motivation without knowing about the social milieu. The construct of perceived responsibility in others, and its fit within a general attributional theory of motivation, has much to offer as a conceptual framework for understanding the developmental significance of peers as sources of influence on academic motivation.

Mediation and Moderation in Attribution Research

Much of the contemporary discourse in psychology around theory utility focuses on the degree to which conceptual models address *mediators*, or the mechanisms that explain the relationships between a set of predictors and their correlated outcomes, and *moderators*, or "third" variables that describe the conditions under which the predicted relations are strong versus weak. Beginning with Baron and Kenney's (1986) classic article, psychologists now have a full battery of statistical methods for detecting mediation and moderation, both separately and in the same model (Edwards & Lambert, 2007).

As a theory based on motivational sequences, attribution theory has many examples of tests of emotions as mediators of the relations between causal thoughts and subsequent behavior. A logical next step will be to test for bidirectional, cyclical, or cumulative relations over time. For example, can the subjective meaning of attributions to prejudice change over time such that there is a shift from external to internal causality and decreases in esteem-related affect? Do emotions such as sympathy and anger influence *subsequent* perceptions of responsibility in others? Such sequence questions can best be addressed with longitudinal research that tracks within-person change over time in causal beliefs about self and others. With the notable exception of research on expectancy-value approaches to motivation that has a rich longitudinal literature (Wigfield & Eccles, 2002), there are not many examples in motivation research that test continuity and discontinuity in mediating mechanisms with longitudinal analyses.

Studies including moderating variables also have a place in attributional analyses. Age might be an important moderator of thinking-feeling-action linkages and we have already argued for the importance of more developmental analyses of attribution principles. Gender, ethnicity (a topic we return to in the final recommendation), and individual differences in attributional tendencies are good third variable candidates for examining conditions under which the consequences of causal thinking are strong versus weak. As attribution theorists, we view the study of individual differences as complementing theory development as opposed to being the core element of the theory itself. Some motivational theories that preceded attributional analyses such as Atkinson's achievement theory (1964) and Rotter's social learning theory (1966) were identified with predictions based on individual differences in, respectively, the need for achievement and locus of control, neither of which has withstood the test of time. Attribution theorists believe that it is first important to document general principles of motivation that are extremely robust and only then turn to how those principles vary between individuals or contexts. In this way, the absence of individual differences can lead to theory generality and the presence of differences can lead to theory refinement.

Unconscious Motivation

As an early motivation theorist, Sigmund Freud introduced the notion of unconscious motivation. In everyday life, people are powerfully influenced by thoughts, wishes, and motives of which they have no conscious awareness. Atkinson's achievement theory (1964) further supported the role of the unconscious because individual differences in need for achievement were assessed with the Thematic Apperception Test (TAT), a projective measure that supposedly revealed unconscious achievement desires. Long after the waning of research on the achievement motive, the study of the unconscious has enjoyed a renewed vitality in the fields of social psychology and motivation. Unconscious processes have a number of characteristics. They are unintentional because they are not planned responses; involuntary, since they occur automatically in the presence of an environmental cue; and effortless, in that they do not deplete an individual's limited information processing resources. Those characteristics can be contrasted with conscious processes, or mental activities of which the person is aware and can verbally report on, that they intend, that they volitionally control, and that require mental effort. A good deal of empirical evidence has been amassed in the last two decades on how judgments and behavior can be triggered by unconscious processes (see reviews in Bargh & Chartrand, 1999; Bargh & Morsella, 2008). Automatically activated processes are as varied as racial stereotypes in contexts of interpersonal evaluation and performance goals in contexts of individual achievement strivings.

At first blush, one may wonder what relevance unconscious processes have to causal attributions about the self and others, which clearly are consciously undertaken mental activities. In research by one of us mentioned earlier (Graham & Lowery, 2004), we have proposed that unconscious racial stereotype activation can influence the attributions and attribution-related judgments that perceivers make about other people—in this case, the perceived responsibility and punishment deservingness of adolescent offenders. Thus, unconscious processes can function as attributional antecedents, particularly in the domain of interpersonal motivation. We know a good deal more about the consequences of attributions to responsibility in others than we know about the factors that lead perceivers to make that causal inferences in the first place. Given the apparent robustness of automatic influences on social life, the development of reliable experimental methods to activate and study those influences, and the availability of measurement tools to assess both explicit and implicit attitudes about social groups, the time seems right for new research that integrates conscious and unconscious thinking in the study of attributions.

Race, Ethnicity, and the Attributional Process

The changing demography of the last generation, driven largely by immigration and revealed by Census 2000, has redefined the racial and ethnic landscape in this country. Although Whites are still the majority group in the nation as a whole, African Americans have been surpassed by Latinos as the largest ethnic minority group and Latinos and Asians are now the fastest growing ethnic groups in the country. A K-12 population that was 80% White a generation ago has dropped to 57% White, and public schools will soon be the first social institution in the nation without a clear racial/ethnic majority group (Orfield & Lee, 2007). Attribution research and motivation research in general will need to cast a broader conceptual and methodological net to encompass more ethnically diverse samples in our schools.

One very direct (and theoretically less complex) way to study school motivation in different racial/ethnic groups from an attributional perspective is to examine whether there are differences in attribution content or the meaning of disparate attributions in terms of their underlying properties. For example, are African American students more likely to endorse external attributions for failure than White students? Does good luck as an attribution for success have a different subjective meaning in Asian students with recent immigrant histories compared to their more assimilated peers from the same country of origin? If differences in attributional content or subjective meaning are found, the attribution researcher must be cautious not to conclude that the theory does not "work" or that it lacks cross cultural generality. Weiner has always maintained that attributional judgments are phenomenological; they depict the causal world as perceived by the actor or the observer. Thus, attributional content as well as causal meaning will surely differ between individuals and between different racial/ethnic groups.

A more fruitful approach to studying school motivation in ethic minority youth from an attributional perspective is to embrace the full motivational sequence. For example, if a researcher is interested in motivational explanations for the achievement gap between different racial/ethnic groups, it is probably too narrow to limit one's research questions to causal attributions per se when studying antecedents and consequences in the context of both intrapersonal and interpersonal theories is conceptually so much richer. As attribution theorists, we would want to know whether low achieving students perceive poor performance as an achievement "failure," which then raises questions about achievement values and the meaning of success; how feedback from teachers is processed, which addresses antecedents; whether altering the perceived stability of causes for failure can lead to enhanced achievement strivings, whether students' public versus private attributions are concordant, and whether teachers are susceptible to unconscious biases when they assign responsibility and mete out punishment for misbehavior to ethnic minority youth.

At any point along this motivational sequence, it seems likely that attributional thinking, feeling, and acting will be influenced by important context factors such as racial identity, parental socialization about race, or immigrant history. In research on peer victimization with multi-ethnic youth from an attributional perspective, we have been arguing that the ethnic composition of classrooms and schools is an important context factor that shapes the attributions and adjustment of some victimized youth (see Graham, 2006). We found that being a victim and a member of the majority ethnic group in one's school made students particularly vulnerable to self-blaming attributions ("it must be *me*") and this attribution, in turn, was related to low self-esteem and depression. We reasoned that it may be especially hard to make an esteem-protecting attribution to the prejudice of others when most of the perpetrators are from one's own racial/ethnic group. Similarly, we hypothesize that ethnically diverse contexts where multiple racial/ethnic groups are relatively evenly represented may be particularly adaptive because they create enough attributional ambiguity to ward off self-blaming tendencies (cf. Juvonen, Nishina, & Graham, 2006). These kinds of hypotheses are guided by our belief that it is not so much ethnicity per se, but rather ethnicity within a particular context (e.g., diverse vs. nondiverse schools) that will inform attribution research with different racial/ethnic groups.

Attribution theory will never provide all of the answers to the complex problems associated with low achievement or poor peer relations among members of historically marginalized groups. These problems often involve issues of poverty and social injustice in this society that are far beyond the range and focus of attribution theory. What the theory does offer us, however, is a useful framework for asking some of the right questions.

References

Abramson, L., Seligman, M., & Teasdale, J. (1978). Learned helplessness in humans: Critique and reformulation. *Journal of Abnormal Psychology, 87*, 49–74.

Anderson, C., Jennings, D., & Arnoult, L. (1988). The validity and utility of the attributional style construct at a moderate level of specificity. *Journal of Personality and Social Psychology, 55*, 979–990.

Aronson, J., Fried, C., & Good, C. (2002). Reducing the effects of stereotype threat on African American college students by shaping theories of intelligence. *Journal of Experimental Social Psychology, 38*, 113–125.

Atkinson, J. (1964). *An introduction to motivation.* Princeton, NJ: Van Nostrand.

Bargh, J., & Chartrand, T. (1999). The unbearable automaticity of being. *American Psychologist, 54*, 462–479.

Bargh, J., & Morsella, E. (2008). The unconscious mind. *Perspectives on Psychological Science, 3*, 73–79.

Barker, G., & Graham, S. (1987). A developmental study of praise and blame as attributional cues. *Journal of Educational Psychology, 79*, 62–66.

Baron, R., & Kenney, D. (1986). The moderator-mediator variable distinction in social psychological research: Conceptual, strategic, and statistical considerations. *Journal of Personality and Social Psychology, 51*, 1173–1182.

Blackwell, L., Trzesniewski, & Dweck, C. (2007). Implicit theories of intelligence predict achievement across adolescent transition: A longitudinal study and an intervention. *Child Development, 78*, 246–263.

Boyer, W. (2006). Accentuate the positive: The relationship between positive explanatory style and academic achievement of prospective elementary teachers. *Journal of Research in Childhood Education, 212*, 53–63.

Brown, C., & Bigler, R. (2005). Children's perceptions of discrimination: A developmental model. *Child Development, 76*, 533–553.

Cohen, J., Steele, C., & Ross, L. (1999). The mentor's dilemma: Providing critical feedback across the racial divide. *Personality and Social Psychology Bulletin, 25*, 1302–1318.

Correll, J., Park B., Judd, C. M., Wittenbrink, B. (2002). The police officer's dilemma: Using ethnicity to disambiguate potentially threatening individuals. *Journal of Personality and Social Psychology, 83*, 1314–1329.

Covington, M., & Omelich, C. (1979). Effort: The double-edged sword in school achievement. *Journal of Educational Psychology, 71*, 169–182.

Crocker, J., & Major, B. (1989). Social stigma and self-esteem: The self-protective properties of stigma. *Psychological Review, 96*, 608–630.

Crocker, J., Major, B., & Steele, C. (1998). Social stigma. In D. Gilbert, S. Fiske, & G. Lindzey (Eds.), *The handbook of social psychology* (Vol. 2, pp. 504–553). Boston: McGraw-Hill.

Dardenne, B., Dumont, M., & Bollier, T. (2007). Insidious dangers of benevolent sexism: Consequences for women's performance. *Journal of Personality and Social Psychology, 93*, 764–779.

Devine, P. G., & Elliott, A. J. (1995). Are racial stereotypes really fading? The Princeton trilogy revisited. *Personality and Social Psychology Bulletin, 21*, 1139–1150.

Diener, C., & Dweck, C. (1980). An analysis of learned helplessness II: The processing of success. *Journal of Personality and Social Psychology, 39*, 940–952.

Dodge, K., Coie, J., & Lynam, D. (2006). Aggression and antisocial behavior in youth. In N. Eisenberg (Ed.), *Handbook of child psychology* (6th ed., Vol. 3, pp. 719–788). Hoboken, NJ: Wiley.

Dweck, C. (1975). The role of expectations and attributions in the alleviation of learned helplessness. *Journal of Personality and Social Psychology, 31*, 674–685.

Dweck, C. (1999). *Self-theories: Their role in motivation, personality, and development.* Philadelphia.: Psychology Press.

Dweck, C., & Molden. (2005). Self-theories: Their impact on competence motivation and acquisition. In A. Elliot & C. Dweck (Eds.), *Handbook of competence and motivation* (pp. 122–140). New York: Guilford.

Edwards, J., & Lambert, L. (2007). Methods for integrating moderation and mediation: A general analytic framework using moderated path analysis. *Psychological Methods, 12*, 1–22.

Elliot, A., & Church, M. (2003). A motivational analysis of defensive pessimism and self-handicapping. *Journal of Personality, 71*, 369–396.

Fisher, C., Wallace, S., & Fenton, R. (2000). Discrimination distress during adolescence. *Journal of Youth and Adolescence, 29*, 679–694.

Fiske, S. T. (1998). Stereotyping, prejudice, and discrimination. In D. T. Gilbert, S. T. Fiske, & G. Lindzey (Eds.), *Handbook of social psychology* (4th ed., pp. 357–411). New York: McGraw-Hill.

Forsterling, F. (1985). Attributional retraining: A review. *Psychological Bulletin, 98*, 495–512.

Gendolla, G., & Koller, M. (2001). Surprise and causal search: How are they affected by outcome valence and importance? *Motivation and Emotion, 25*, 237–250.

Good, C., Aronson, J., & Inzlicht, N. (2003). Improving adolescents' standardized test performance: An intervention to reduce the effects of stereotype threat. *Journal of Applied Developmental Psychology, 24*, 645–662.

Graham, S. (1984). Communicating sympathy and anger to black and white children: The cognitive (attributional) antecedents of affective cues. *Journal of Personality and Social Psychology, 47*, 40-54.

Graham, S. (1990). On communicating low ability in the classroom. In S. Graham & V. Folkes (Eds.), *Attribution theory: Applications to achievement, mental health, and interpersonal conflict* (pp. 17–36). Hillsdale, NJ: Erlbaum.

Graham, S. (2006). Peer victimization in school: Exploring the ethnic context. *Current Directions in Psychological Science, 15*, 317–320.

Graham, S., & Barker, G. (1990). The downside of help: An attributional-developmental analysis of help-giving as a low ability cue. *Journal of Educational Psychology, 82*, 7–14.

Graham, S., & Brown, J. (1988). Attributional mediators of expectancy, evaluation, and affect: A response time analysis. *Journal of Personality and Social Psychology, 55*, 873–881.

Graham, S., & Lowery, B. (2004). Priming unconscious racial stereotypes about adolescernt offenders. *Law and Human Behavior, 28*, 483–504.

Greene, M., Way, N., & Pahl, N. (2006). Trajectories of perceived adult and peer discrimination among Black, Latino, and Asian American adolescents: Patterns and psychological correlates. *Developmental Psychology, 42*, 218–238.

Heider, F. (1958). *The psychology of interpersonal relations.* New York: Wiley.

Horner, S., & Gaither, S. (2006). Attribution retraining with a second grade class. *Early Childhood Education Journal, 31*, 165–170.

Hudley, C., & Graham, S. (1993). An attributional intervention with African American boys labeled as aggressive. *Child Development, 64*, 124–138.

Hudley, C., Graham, S., & Taylor, A. Z. (2007) Reducing aggressive behavior and increasing motivation in school: The evolution of an intervention to strengthen school adjustment. *Educational Psychologist. 47*, 251–260.

Jones, E., & Berglas, S. (1978). Control of attributions about the self through self-handicapping strategies: The appeal of alcohol and the role of underachievement. *Personality and Social Psychology Bulletin, 4*, 200–206.

Jones, E., & Davis, K. (1965). From acts to dispositions: The attribution process in person perception. In L. Berkowitz (Ed.), *Advances in experimental social psychology* (Vol. 2, pp. 219–266). New York: Academic Press.

Jones, E., & Nisbett, R. (1971). The actor and the observer: Divergent perceptions of the causes of behavior. In E. Jones, D. Kanouse, H. Kelley, R. Nisbett, S. Valins, & B. Weiner (Eds.), *Attribution: Perceiving the causes of behavior* (pp. 79–94). Morristown, NJ: General Learning Press.

Juvonen, J. (2000). The social functions of attributional face-saving tactics among early adolescents. *Educational Psychology Review, 12*, 15–32.

Juvonen, J.. Nishina, A., & Graham, S. (2006). Ethnic diversity and perceptions of safety in urban middle schools. *Psychological Science, 17*, 393–400.

Kamins, M., & Dweck, C. (1999). Person vs process praise and criticism: Implications for contingent self-worth and coping. *Developmental Psychology, 35*, 835–847.

Karniol, R. (1980). Children's use of intention cues in evaluating behavior. *Psychological Bulletin, 85*, 76–85.

Kelley, H. (1973). The process of causal attribution. *American Psychologist, 28*, 107–128.

Kelley, H., & Michela, J. (1980). Attribution theory and research. *Annual Review of Psychology, 31*, 457–501.

Kun, A. (1977). Development of the magnitude-covariation and compensation schemata in ability and effort attributions of performance. *Child Development, 48*, 862–873.

Kun, A., & Weiner, B. (1973). Necessary versus sufficient causal schemata for success and failure. *Journal of Research in Personality, 7*, 197–207.

Maatta, S., & Nurmi, J. (2007). Achievement orientations, school adjustment, and well-being: A longitudinal study. *Journal of Research on Adolescence, 17*, 789–812.

Major, B., Quinton, W., & McCoy, S. (2002). Antecedents and consequences of attributions to discrimination: Theoretical and empirical advances. In M. Zanna (Ed.), *Advances in experimental social psychology* (Vol. 34, pp. 252–330). New York: Academic Press.

McClelland, D. Atkinson, J., Clark, J., & Lowell, E. (1953). *The achievement motive.* New York: Appleton-Century Crofts.

Meyer, W., Bachmann, M., Biermann, U., Hempelmann, M., Ploger, F., & Spiller, H. (1979). The informational value of evaluative behavior: Influence of praise and blame on perceptions of ability. *Journal of Educational Psychology, 71*, 259–268.

Miller, D., & Ross, L. (1975). Self-serving biases in the attribution of causality": Fact or fiction? *Psychological Bulletin, 82*, 213–225.

Mueller, C., & Dweck, C. (1998). Intelligence praise can undermine motivation and performance. *Journal of Personality and Social Psychology, 75*, 33–52.

National Research Council (2002). *Minority students in special and gifted education.* Washington, DC: National Academy Press.

Nicholls, J. (1978). The development of concepts of effort and ability, perception of own attainment, and the understanding that difficult tasks require more ability. *Child Development, 49*, 800–814.

Orfield, G., & Lee, C. (2007). *Historic reversals, accelerating resegregation, and the need for new integration strategies.* Los Angeles: The Civil Rights Project.

Peterson, C. (1991). Explanatory style in the classroom and on the playing field. In S. Graham & V. Folkes (Eds.), *Attribution theory: Applications to achievement, mental health, and interpersonal conflict* (pp. 53–75). Hillsdale, NJ: Erlbaum.

Peterson, C. (2000). The future of optimism. *American Psychologist, 55*, 44–55.

Reyna, C. (2000). Lazy, dumb, or industrious: When stereotypes convey attribution information in the classroom. *Educational Psychology Review, 12*, 85–110.

Reyna, C., & Weiner, B. (2001). Justice and utility in the classroom: An attributional analysis of the goals of teachers' punishment and intervention strategies. *Journal of Educational Psychology, 93*, 309–319.

Rhodewalt, F., & Vohs, K. (2005). Defensive strategies, motivation, and the self. In A. Elliot & C. Dweck (Eds.), *Handbook of competence and motivation* (pp. 548–565). New York: Guilford.

Robertson, J. (2000). Is attribution training a worthwhile classroom intervention for K-12 students with learning difficulties? *Educational Psychology Review, 12*, 111–134.

Rosenbloom, S., & Way, N. (2004). Experiences of discrimination among African American, Asian American, and Latino adolescents in an urban high school. *Youth and Society, 35*, 420–451.

Rotter, J. (1966). Generalized expectancies for internal versus external control of reinforcement. *Psychological Monographs, 80*(1, Whole No. 609).

Ross, L. (1977). The intuitive psychologist and his shortcomings: Distortions in the attribution process. In L. Berkowitz (Ed.), *Advances in experimental social psychology* (Vol. 10, pp. 173–220). New York: Academic.

Rowe, J., & Lockhart, L. (2005). Relationship of cognitive attributional style and academic performance among a predominantly Hispanic college student population. *Individual Differences Research, 3*, 136–139.

Rudolph, U., Roesch, S. C., Greitemeyer, T., & Weiner, B. (2004). A meta-analytic review of help giving and aggression from an attribution perspective. *Cognition and Emotion, 18*, 815–848.

Schneider, M., Major, B., Luhtanen, R., & Crocker, J. (1996). Social stigma and the potential cost of assumptive help. *Personality and Social Psychology Bulletin, 22*, 201–209.

Skiba, R., Reynolds, C., Graham, S., Sheras, P., Conoley, J., & Garcia-Vasquez, E. (2008). *Are Zero Tolerance policies effective in the schools? An evidentiary review and recommendations.* Manuscript under review.

Skinner, E. (1995). *Perceived control, motivation, and coping.* Thousand Oaks, CA: Sage.

Struthers, C., & Perry, R. (1996). Attributional style, attributional retraining, and inoculation against motivational deficits. *Social Psychology of Education, 1*, 171–187.

Turner, J., Meyer, D., Midgley, C., & Patrick, H. (2003). Teacher discourse and sixth graders' reported affect and achievement behaviors in two high-mastery/high performance mathematics classrooms. *The Elementary School Journal, 103*, 357–382.

Urdan, T. (2004). Predictors of academic self-handicapping and achievement: Examining achievement goals, classroom goal structures, and culture. *Journal of Educational Psychology, 96*, 251–264.

Walton, G., & Cohen, G. (2007). A question of belonging: Race, social fit, and achievement. *Journal of Personality and Social Psychology, 92*, 82–96.

Weiner, B. (1983). Some methodological pitfalls in attribution research. *Journal of Educational Psychology, 75*, 530–543.

Weiner, B. (1985). "Spontaneous" causal thinking. *Psychological Bulletin, 97*, 74–84.

Weiner, B. (1986). *An attributional theory of motivation and emotion.* New York: Springer.

Weiner, B. (1988). Attribution theory and attributional therapy: Some theoretical observations and suggestions. *British Journal of Clinical Psychology, 27*, 93–104.

Weiner, B. (1992). *Human motivation: Metaphors, theories, and research.* Newbury Park, CA: Sage.

Weiner, B. (1995). *Judgments of responsibility: A foundation for a theory of social conduct.* New York; Guilford.

Weiner, B. (2006). *Social motivation, justice, and the moral emotions.* Mahwah, NJ: Erlbaum.

Weiner, B., Graham, S., Stern, P., & Lawson, M. (1982). Using affective cues to infer causal thoughts. *Developmental Psychology, 18*, 278–286.

Weiner, B., & Kukla, A. (1970). An attributional analysis of achievement motivation. *Journal of Personality and Social Psychology, 15*, 1–20.

Wigfield, A., & Eccles, J. (Eds.). (2002). *Development of achievement motivation.* San Diego, CA: Academic Press.

Wilson, T., Damiani, M., & Shelton, N. (2002). Improving the academic performance of college students with brief attributional interventions. In J. Aronson (Ed.), *Improving academic achievement: Impact pf psychological factors on education* (pp. 91–110). New York: Academic Press.

Wilson, T., & Linville, P. (1982). Improving academic performance of college freshmen: Attribution therapy revisited. *Journal of Personality and Social Psychology, 42*, 367–376.

Wong, C., Eccles, J., & Sameroff, A. (2003). The influence of ethnic discrimination and ethnic identification on African American adolescents' school and socioemotional adjustment. *Journal of Personality, 71*, 1197–1232.

3
Self-Efficacy Theory

Dale H. Schunk and Frank Pajares

Self-efficacy refers to perceived capabilities for learning or performing actions at designated levels (Bandura, 1997). Since Bandura (1977a, 1977b) introduced the construct of self-efficacy to the psychological literature, researchers have explored its role in various domains including education, business, athletics, careers, health, and wellness. Researchers have investigated the operation of self-efficacy among different individuals, developmental levels, and cultures.

Self-efficacy has been shown to be a powerful influence on individuals' motivation, achievement, and self-regulation (Bandura, 1997; Multon, Brown, & Lent, 1991; Pajares, 1997; Stajkovic & Luthans, 1998). In education, it has been shown to affect students' choices of activities, effort expended, persistence, interest, and achievement (Pajares, 1996b, 1997; Schunk, 1995). Compared with students who doubt their capabilities to learn or to perform well, those with high self-efficacy participate more readily, work harder, persist longer, show greater interest in learning, and achieve at higher levels (Bandura, 1997).

In this chapter we initially provide background information on self-efficacy to show how it is situated in Bandura's (1986) social cognitive theory of human functioning and how it differs from other conceptions of personal competence. We discuss influences on the development of self-efficacy and summarize research on the influence of self-efficacy on students' learning, motivation, and self-regulation. We explain some challenges remaining for self-efficacy researchers, and conclude with suggestions for future research.

Social Cognitive Theory

In Bandura's (1986) social cognitive theory, human functioning results from a dynamic interplay among personal, behavioral, and environmental influences. In this conception of *reciprocal determinism*, (a) personal factors in the form of cognitions, affects, and biological events, (b) behaviors, and (c) environmental influences, create interactions that result in a triadic reciprocality.

Social cognitive theory is rooted in a view of human agency in which individuals are proactively engaged in their own development and can largely determine the outcomes of their actions. Individuals are imbued with certain capabilities that define what it is to be human. Primary among these are the capabilities to symbolize, plan alternative strategies (forethought), learn through vicarious experience, self-regulate, and self-reflect. For Bandura, however, the capability that is most distinctly human is that of self-reflection; hence it is a prominent feature of social cognitive theory. Through self-reflection, people make sense of their experiences, explore their cognitions and beliefs, engage in self-evaluation, and alter their thinking and behavior accordingly.

The reciprocal nature of the determinants of human functioning in social cognitive theory makes it possible for education, therapy, and counseling to be directed at personal, environmental, or behavioral factors. Strategies for increasing well-being can be aimed at improving emotional, cognitive, or motivational processes, increasing behavioral competencies, or altering the conditions under which people live and work. In school, teachers have the challenge of promoting the academic learning and confidence of their students. Using social cognitive theory as a framework, teachers can improve their students' emotional states and correct their faulty beliefs and habits of thinking (personal factors), raise their academic skills and self-regulation (behaviors), and alter the school and classroom structures (environmental factors) to ensure student success. The next section presents a theoretical account of self-efficacy—a key personal factor in Bandura's theory.

Self-Efficacy

Definition, Sources, and Effects

In social cognitive theory, self-efficacy is hypothesized to influence behaviors and environments and, in turn, to be affected by them (Bandura, 1986, 1997). Students who feel more efficacious about learning should be more apt to engage in self-regulation (e.g., set goals, use effective learning strategies, monitor their comprehension, evaluate their goal progress) and create effective environments for learning (e.g., eliminate or minimize distractions, find effective study partners). In turn, self-efficacy can be influenced by the outcomes of behaviors (e.g., goal progress, achievement) and by input from the environment (e.g., feedback from teachers, social comparisons with peers).

Bandura (1997) postulated that people acquire information to gauge their self-efficacy from interpretations of actual performances, vicarious (e.g., modeled) experiences, forms of social persuasion, and physiological indexes (Table 3.1). How students interpret their actual performances should provide the most reliable information for assessing self-efficacy because these interpretations are tangible indicators of one's capabilities. Performances interpreted as successful should raise self-efficacy; those interpreted as failures should lower it, although an occasional failure or success after many successes or failures should not have much impact. Later in this chapter we discuss the development of self-efficacy and the process whereby students arrive at self-efficacy judgments.

Individuals can acquire much information about their capabilities through knowledge of how others perform (Bandura, 1997). Similarity to others is a cue for gauging one's self-efficacy (Schunk, 1995). Observing similar others succeed can raise observers' self-efficacy and motivate them to try the task because they are apt to believe that if others can do it they can as well. A vicarious increase in self-efficacy, however, can be negated by subsequent performance failure. Persons who

Table 3.1 Sources of Self-Efficacy Information

- Actual performances
- Vicarious experiences
- Forms of social persuasion
- Physiological indexes

observe similar peers fail may believe they lack the competence to succeed, which can dissuade them from attempting the task. Because people often seek models with qualities they admire and capabilities to which they aspire, models can help instill beliefs that will influence the course and direction of one's life (Schunk, 1995).

Individuals also can create and develop self-efficacy beliefs as a result of social persuasions (e.g., "I know you can do it") they receive from others (Bandura, 1997). Persuaders play an important part in the development of an individual's self-efficacy. But social persuasions are not empty praise or inspirational statements. Effective persuaders must cultivate people's beliefs in their capabilities while at the same time ensuring that the envisioned success is attainable. Although positive feedback can raise individuals' self-efficacy, the increase will not endure if they subsequently perform poorly (Schunk, 1995). Just as positive persuasions may work to encourage and empower, negative persuasions can work to defeat and weaken self-efficacy.

Individuals also can acquire self-efficacy information from physiological and emotional states such as anxiety and stress (Bandura, 1997). People can gauge their self-efficacy by the emotional state they experience as they contemplate an action. Strong emotional reactions to a task provide cues about an anticipated success or failure. When they experience negative thoughts and fears about their capabilities (e.g., feeling nervous thinking about speaking in front of a large group), those affective reactions can lower self-efficacy and trigger additional stress and agitation that help ensure the inadequate performance they fear. One way to raise self-efficacy is to improve physical and emotional well-being and reduce negative emotional states. Individuals have the capability to alter their thoughts and feelings, so enhanced self-efficacy can influence their physiological states.

The sources of self-efficacy information are not directly translated into judgments of competence (Bandura, 1997). Individuals interpret the results of events, and these interpretations provide the information on which judgments are based (Pajares, 1996b). The types of information people attend to and use to make self-efficacy judgments and the rules they employ for weighting and integrating them form the basis for such interpretations. The selection, integration, interpretation, and recollection of information influence judgments of self-efficacy.

Furthermore, Bandura (1997) made it clear that self-efficacy is not the only influence on behavior. No amount of self-efficacy will produce a competent performance when students lack the needed skills to succeed (Schunk, 1995). Students' *values* (perceptions of importance and utility of learning) also can affect behavior (Wigfield, Tonks, & Eccles, 2004). Even students who feel highly efficacious in science may not take science courses that they believe are not germane to their goal of becoming a medical doctor. Also important are *outcome expectations*, or beliefs about the anticipated outcomes of actions (Bandura, 1997). Students typically engage in activities that they believe will result in positive outcomes and avoid actions that they believe may lead to negative outcomes. Efficacious students may avoid volunteering answers in class if they believe that by so doing they will be socially shunned by peers. Assuming requisite skills and positive values and outcome expectations, self-efficacy is a key determinant of individuals' motivation, learning, self-regulation, and achievement (Schunk, 1995).

Self-efficacy is predicted to enhance human accomplishment and well-being in many ways (Bandura, 1986, 1997; Table 3.2). Self-efficacy can influence the choices people make and the courses of action they pursue. Individuals tend to select tasks and activities in which they feel competent and confident and avoid those in which they do not. Unless people believe that their actions will produce the desired consequences, they have little incentive to engage in those actions.

Table 3.2 Effects of Self-Efficacy

- Motivation (task choice, effort, persistence)
- Learning
- Self-regulation
- Achievement

Self-efficacy also helps determine how much effort people will expend on an activity, how long they will persevere when confronting obstacles, and how resilient they will be in the face of adverse situations. People with a strong sense of efficacy are apt to approach difficult tasks as challenges to be mastered rather than as threats to be avoided. They set challenging goals and maintain strong commitment to them, heighten and sustain their efforts in the face of failure, and more quickly recover their sense of self-efficacy after setbacks. Conversely, people with low self-efficacy may believe that things are more difficult than they really are—a belief that can foster anxiety, stress, depression, and a narrow vision of how best to solve a problem. Self-efficacy can influence one's ultimate accomplishments and lead to a self-fulfilling prophecy in which one accomplishes what one believes one can accomplish.

Types of Self-Efficacy

In Bandura's (1977a, 1977b) early clinical studies with snake phobics, participants possessed the skills to perform the particular behaviors (e.g., touch the snake) but did not perform them because of feared consequences. Their *self-efficacy for performance* of skills they possessed was low until they overcame these fears. In school, students spend some time reviewing what they have learned, but much time is devoted to learning new skills. Thus, it is meaningful to speak of *self-efficacy for learning* skills that one does not currently possess.

Self-efficacy often refers to one's perceived capabilities, but many educational situations require that students work in teams to accomplish a task. *Collective self-efficacy* refers to the perceived capabilities of the group, team, or larger social entity (Bandura, 1997). Collective self-efficacy is not simply the average of individuals' self-efficacy but rather refers to what the members believe the group can accomplish by working together. The collective self-efficacy of school professional staff bears a positive relation to the achievement of students in the school (Bandura, 1993).

Self-efficacy has been applied to teachers as well as to students. *Teacher (or instructional) self-efficacy* refers to personal beliefs about one's capabilities to help students learn (Pajares, 1996b; Tschannen-Moran, Woolfolk Hoy, & Hoy, 1998). Social cognitive theory predicts that teacher self-efficacy should influence the same types of activities that student self-efficacy affects: choice of activities, effort, persistence, achievement (Bandura, 1997). Teachers with higher self-efficacy are apt to develop challenging activities, help students succeed, and persist with students who have difficulties.

Researchers also have begun to investigate the role of *collective teacher self-efficacy,* or teachers' beliefs that their collective capabilities can influence students' outcomes (Goddard, Hoy, & Woolfolk Hoy, 2000). As with collective self-efficacy, collective teacher self-efficacy is not the average of the individual teachers' self-efficacy but rather reflects teachers' perceptions of the capabilities of the faculty as a whole to positively affect student outcomes (Henson, 2002). Collective teacher self-efficacy bears a positive relation to teachers' job satisfaction (Caprara, Barbaranelli, Borgogni, & Steca, 2003).

Distinctions with Other Variables

There are variables that bear conceptual similarity to self-efficacy (Schunk & Zimmerman, 2006). Because self-efficacy is a belief about what one is capable of doing or learning it is not the same as knowing what to do (i.e., skill, ability; Schunk & Pajares, 2004). Although students with higher skills and abilities tend to be more self-efficacious, there is no necessary relation between self-efficacy and academic ability. In gauging self-efficacy, individuals assess their skills and capabilities to translate those skills into actions. Possessing skill positively affects self-efficacy, which in turn influences subsequent skill attainment; however, skill and self-efficacy are not synonymous in meaning (Bandura, 1997).

Collins (1982) identified high-, average-, and low-ability students in mathematics, and within each of these three levels identified students with high and low self-efficacy. Students were given problems to solve and told they could rework those they missed. Ability related positively to achievement, but, regardless of ability level, students with high self-efficacy solved more problems correctly and chose to rework more problems they missed than did learners with lower self-efficacy.

Even when children possess the skills to solve problems, those who hold strong self-efficacy are more effective problem solvers. Pajares and Kranzler (1995) tested the joint contribution of mental ability (the variable typically acknowledged as the most powerful predictor of academic outcomes) and self-efficacy to mathematics performance and found that self-efficacy made a powerful and independent contribution to the prediction of performance.

Self-efficacy also is not the same as *self-concept,* which refers to one's collective self-perceptions formed through experiences with and interpretations of the environment and influenced by reinforcements and evaluations by others (Shavelson & Bolus, 1982). There are different conceptions of self-concept, but it often is viewed as multidimensional and comprising elements such as self-confidence and self-esteem (discussed below) (Pajares & Schunk, 2001, 2002).

Although most investigators posit that individuals hold a general self-concept, research shows that self-concept is hierarchically organized with a general self-concept on top and subarea self-concepts below (Marsh & Shavelson, 1985; Pajares & Schunk, 2001, 2002). Self-perceptions of specific competencies influence subarea self-concepts (e.g., in subject areas such as history and biology), which in turn combine to form the academic self-concept. For example, Chapman and Tunmer (1995) found that students' reading self-concept included perceived competence in reading, perceived difficulty of reading, and attitudes toward reading. General self-concept may be formed by self-perceptions in the academic, social, and physical domains.

Because self-efficacy involves perceived capabilities in specific areas, it should contribute to development and change in self-concept (Pajares & Schunk, 2001, 2002). Another distinction lies in the normative nature of self-concept. Many investigators posit that self-concept heavily reflects how one views oneself relative to others (Schunk & Pajares, 2005). This idea is reflected in the *big-fish-little-pond effect* (Marsh & Hau, 2003): Students in selective schools may hold lower self-concepts than those in less selective schools. Although self-efficacy can be affected by normative experiences (e.g., comparisons with peers), the strongest influence on it comes from one's personal accomplishments (Bandura, 1997). In short, self-efficacy beliefs are cognitive, goal-referenced, relatively context-specific, and future-oriented judgments of competence that are malleable due to their task dependence. Self-concept beliefs are normative, typically aggregated, hierarchically structured, and past-oriented self-perceptions that are more stable due to their sense of generality.

According to Bong and Skaalvik (2003), self-efficacy acts as an active precursor of self-concept development. This is consistent with Covington's (1984, 1992) *self-worth theory,* which espouses a view of self-concept in which competence beliefs are central to the self system such that individuals are motivated by a need to perceive themselves as competent. Because modern society places a powerful premium on achievement, individuals want strongly to be perceived as capable, and they define self-worth in terms of such capability. The need to safeguard this mental perception of competence often gives rise to external attributions and self-handicapping strategies that protect the individual from potential feelings of incompetence (Covington, 1984).

Self-esteem is a general affective evaluation of one's self that often includes judgments of self-worth (Schunk & Pajares, 2005). Like self-concept, it differs markedly from self-efficacy. Self-efficacy beliefs revolve around questions of can (e.g., Can I write this essay? Can I solve this problem?), whereas self-esteem beliefs reflect questions of feel (e.g., Do I like myself? How do I feel about myself as a writer?). One's beliefs about what one can do may bear little relation to how one feels about oneself. Many capable students approach their academic tasks with high self-efficacy for learning despite their academic skills being a source of low self-esteem because their classmates view them as nerds or geeks.

Self-efficacy beliefs also differ from *outcome expectations* (discussed earlier). In educational settings, self-efficacy often helps to determine the outcomes one expects. Students confident in their academic skills expect high marks on exams and that the quality of their work will reap personal and professional benefits, whereas those who lack confidence in their academic skills envision a low grade before they begin an examination or enroll in a course. The expected results of these imagined performances are greater academic success and subsequent career options for the former and curtailed academic possibilities for the latter.

But self-efficacy also can be inconsistent with one's expected outcomes (Bandura, 1997). High self-efficacy may not result in behavior consistent with that belief when individuals also believe that the outcome of engaging in that behavior will have undesired effects. A student highly self-efficacious in her academic capabilities may elect not to apply to a particular university whose entrance requirements are such as to discourage all but the hardiest souls.

The notion of *perceived control* (or *personal* agency) also differs from self-efficacy. In Bandura's (1997) social cognitive theory, personal agency is the capability to control one's life events. One's system of personal agency includes self-efficacy and outcome expectations. Skinner, Wellborn, and Connell (1990) distinguished three types of beliefs that affect perceived control. Strategy beliefs are expectations about what influences success, such as, "With hard work I can earn good grades." Capacity beliefs refer to personal capabilities (e.g., "I can study hard for tests."). Control beliefs are expectations about doing well without reference to means (e.g., "I can do well if I try.").

Although self-efficacy is a key component of personal agency (Bandura, 1997), as Ryan (1993) has noted it is not the only one. People who believe they can control what they learn and perform are more apt to initiate and sustain behaviors directed toward those ends than are individuals who hold a low sense of control. However, a responsive environment is necessary for self-efficacy to be able to exert its maximal effects (Bandura, 1997). People may believe they can control their use of learning strategies, effort, and persistence, yet still hold a low sense of self-efficacy for learning because they feel that the learning is unimportant and not worth the investment of time. Or they may feel highly self-efficacious for learning yet make no effort to do so because they believe that in their present environment learning will not be rewarded.

Finally, self-efficacy differs from the lay conception of *self-confidence*: A general capability self-belief that often fails to specify the object of the belief (e.g., one who exudes self-confidence). In contrast, self-efficacy is situated within Bandura's (1986) social cognitive theory of human behavior and has a clear and specific meaning. Although self-confident individuals often are self-efficacious, there is no automatic relation between these variables. As Bandura (1997) noted, persons can be highly confident that they will fail at a particular task or activity (low self-efficacy).

Self-Efficacy in Educational Settings

Although Bandura's (1986) theoretical ideas about self-efficacy have been applied and tested in educational settings, there are a few features of learning contexts that have necessitated clarification of the operation of self-efficacy (Schunk & Pajares, 2004). Earlier we noted the educational emphasis on self-efficacy for learning, which in educational settings often is a more meaningful variable than self-efficacy for performance.

Bandura (1977a, 1977b) originally hypothesized that persons with higher self-efficacy should be more apt to choose challenging activities, expend greater effort to succeed, and persist longer on difficult tasks. These motivational effects lead to better learning and higher achievement.

These three hypothesized effects must be tempered in educational settings due to situational factors. With respect to choice, many times students engage in activities not because they choose to but rather because the teacher has told them to, because they anticipate rewarding outcomes if they do and punishment if they do not, or because they do not want to appear incompetent. Under these circumstances, self-efficacy bears little relation to choice. When teachers allow students choices (e.g., paper or project topics), we should expect to see the hypothesized relation between self-efficacy and choice (i.e., students with higher self-efficacy choose more challenging activities).

The relations of self-efficacy to effort and persistence also need clarification. In a learning situation, students initially will not possess the skills and likely will have low self-efficacy for performing them. They reasonably will have to expend some effort to succeed. As their skills become better established, their self-efficacy should increase; however, compared with the early stages of learning they should need to expend less, not more, effort to succeed.

In similar fashion, task persistence may be higher when skills are not well established, but as skills and self-efficacy develop, students should require less time to complete tasks. As students acquire skills, their effort and persistence may bear negative, rather than positive, relations to their self-efficacy. A better test of these relations is made by giving students tasks that are challenging but attainable given their skill levels. Then we should expect that students with higher self-efficacy will expend greater effort and persist longer.

Another issue that complicates the role of self-efficacy in learning settings is that there are factors that can affect students' self-efficacy differently than how they affect their learning and performance. For example, *calibration* refers to how well self-efficacy relates to actual performance on the corresponding tasks (Pajares & Kranzler, 1995). When people judge that they are capable of performing a task and then perform it, or when they judge that they are incapable of performing it and cannot perform it, they are said to be well calibrated because self-efficacy accurately predicts performance. Conversely, when people judge that they are capable of performing a task but do not perform it, or when they judge that they are incapable of performing a task but then perform it, they are said to be poorly calibrated because of the lack of correspondence between self-efficacy and performance. In his early clinical studies with adults, Bandura (1977a, 1977b) typically found high rates of calibration; however, the situation is complicated in school settings.

Calibration is educationally important. Students who overestimate their capabilities may sometimes fail, which can lower motivation. Some who underestimate what they can do may be reluctant to try the task and thereby retard their skill acquisition. Bandura (1986, 1997) argued that self-efficacy judgments that slightly exceed what one can do are desirable because such overestimation can raise effort and persistence. But recurring overestimation can lead to continued failure with resulting decrements in students' motivation to learn.

Children can be poorly calibrated because they do not fully understand the demands of the task and therefore overestimate what they can do. This is a common situation in school because students are learning skills and they may not fully understand what success at the tasks requires. Greater experience with tasks helps to inform students of the skills needed to succeed.

Calibration also can be affected by instructional and social factors (Schunk & Pajares, 2004). Although instructional practices that provide information about skills required for the task can increase calibration (Schunk, 1981), such practices also can lower it. Students in low-ability groups from which they cannot move may feel demoralized and perform poorly, even though they feel efficacious about learning. Teachers who indiscriminately encourage students (e.g., "Come on, I know you can do this.") without ensuring that they learn skills may produce highly efficacious students who lack the skills to succeed.

The social cultures of schools also may affect calibration (Schunk & Pajares, 2004). Students may perform less than their best—and lower than their self-efficacy would predict—so that they do not become socially isolated as a consequence of being perceived by their peers as overly intelligent. Research also shows that self-efficacy and performance can be related to gender differences. Girls often perform as capably as boys in various academic domains but may report lower self-efficacy, especially at higher academic levels (Pajares & Miller, 1994, 1997). Social factors may prevent girls from performing too well in mathematics and science, even though they may feel highly capable in those subjects.

Because schools are different than controlled laboratory settings, the operation of self-efficacy will be more variable and its power to predict learning and performance more complex. Researchers continue to explore how instructional and social factors affect students' learning, motivation, and self-efficacy. This focus seems important given the increasing student diversity in schools with more factors that potentially can affect achievement outcomes (Schunk & Pajares, 2004).

Development of Self-Efficacy

Self-efficacy does not arise automatically. There are many factors that influence self-efficacy, and the development of self-efficacy begins in infancy.

Family Influences

The first influences on an individual's self-efficacy occur within the family. Like other aspects of children's development and learning, self-efficacy is affected by family capital. *Capital* includes resources and assets (Bradley & Corwyn, 2002), such as financial and material resources (e.g., income, assets), human (nonmaterial) resources (e.g., education levels), and social resources (e.g., those obtained through social networks and connections). Children are motivated to learn when the home is rich in activities and materials that arouse children's curiosity and offer challenges that can be met (Schunk & Pajares, 2002). Parents who are better educated and have wide social connections are apt to stress education to their children and enroll them in programs (e.g., schools, camps) that foster their self-efficacy and learning.

Home influences that help children interact effectively with the environment positively affect self-efficacy. Parents who provide a warm, responsive, and supportive home environment, who encourage exploration and stimulate curiosity, and who provide play and learning materials accelerate their children's intellectual development. Because mastery experiences constitute the most powerful source of self-efficacy information, parents who arrange for their children to experience various forms of mastery are more apt to develop efficacious youngsters than parents who arrange fewer opportunities. Such experiences occur in homes enriched with activities and in which children have freedom to explore (Schunk & Pajares, 2002).

Family members also are important models. Those who model ways to cope with difficulties, persistence, and effort strengthen their children's self-efficacy. Family members also provide persuasive information. Parents who encourage their children to try different activities and support and encourage their efforts help to develop children who feel more capable of meeting challenges.

Social and Cultural Influences

As children develop, peers become increasingly important (Schunk & Meece, 2006). Parents who steer their children toward efficacious peers provide opportunities for vicarious increases in self-efficacy. When children observe similar peers succeed, they are likely to feel more self-efficacious and be motivated to try the task themselves.

Peer influence also operates through *peer networks*, which are large groups of peers with whom students associate. Students in networks tend to be highly similar (Cairns, Cairns, & Neckerman, 1989), which enhances the likelihood of influence by modeling. Networks help define students' opportunities for interactions and observations of others' interactions, as well as their access to activities (Dweck & Goetz, 1978). Over time network members become more similar to one another.

Peer groups promote motivational socialization. Changes in children's motivation across the school year are predicted well by their peer group membership at the start of the year (Kindermann, McCollam, & Gibson, 1996). Children affiliated with highly motivated groups change positively, whereas those in less motivated groups change negatively. Steinberg, Brown, and Dornbusch (1996) tracked students from entrance into high school until their senior year and found that students who entered high school with similar grades but affiliated with academically-oriented crowds achieved better during high school than students who became affiliated with less academically-oriented crowds. Peer group academic socialization can influence the individual member's and the group's academic self-efficacy (Schunk & Pajares, 2002).

Educational Influences

Research shows that competence beliefs such as self-efficacy, as well as academic motivation, decline as students advance through school (Eccles, Wigfield, & Schiefele, 1998; Jacobs, Lanza, Osgood, Eccles, & Wigfield, 2002). This decline has been attributed to factors such as greater competition, more norm-referenced grading, less teacher attention to individual student progress, and stresses associated with school transitions (Schunk & Meece, 2006). These and other school practices can retard the development of academic self-efficacy, especially among students who are poorly prepared to cope with ascending academic challenges. Lock-step sequences of instruction frustrate some students who fail to grasp skills and increasingly fall behind their peers (Bandura, 1997). Ability groupings can weaken the self-efficacy of students relegated to lower groups. Classrooms that allow for much social comparison tend to lower self-efficacy for students who find their performances deficient to those of peers.

Periods of transition in schooling bring other factors into play that affect self-efficacy (Schunk & Meece, 2006). Because elementary students remain with the same teacher and peers for most of the school day, the children receive much attention and individual progress is stressed. In middle school, however, children move from class to class for subjects and are grouped with peers whom they do not know. Evaluation becomes normative, and there is less teacher attention to individual progress. The widely expanded social reference group, coupled with the shift in evaluation standards, requires that students reassess their academic capabilities. As a consequence, perceptions of academic competence typically begin to decline.

We noted earlier that it is not uncommon for children to report overconfidence about accomplishing difficult tasks (Schunk & Pajares, 2004). Even when they are given feedback indicating that they have performed poorly, their self-efficacy may not decline. The incongruence between children's self-efficacy and their actual performance can arise when children lack task familiarity and do not fully understand what is required to execute a task successfully. As they gain experience, their accuracy improves. Children may also be unduly swayed by certain task features and decide based on these that they can or cannot perform the task. In subtraction, for example, children may focus on how many numbers the problems contain and judge problems with more columns as more difficult than those with fewer columns, even when the former are conceptually simpler. As children's capability to focus on multiple features improves, so does their accuracy.

Children sometimes do not know what they are capable of accomplishing. In writing, for example, it is difficult for them to know how clearly they can express themselves or whether their writing skills are improving. A teacher's feedback is intended to encourage and stress what children do well. Children may believe they can write well when in fact their writing is below normal for their grade level. As they develop, children gain task experience and engage more often in peer social comparisons, which improve the accuracy of their self-assessments. The correspondence between self-efficacy and performance also can be increased by giving children instruction and opportunities to practice self-evaluation and with instructional interventions that convey clear information about children's skills or learning progress (Schunk & Pajares, 2002).

Self-Efficacy and Learning, Motivation, and Self-Regulation

Educational researchers have investigated the relation of self-efficacy to learning, motivation, and self-regulation. In this section we discuss findings from correlational and experimental research and from studies using causal modeling.

Correlational Research

Much research shows that self-efficacy correlates with several educational outcomes including motivation, learning, and achievement. Many studies have obtained significant and positive correlations between self-efficacy for learning or performing tasks and subsequent achievement on those tasks (Pajares, 1996b; Schunk & Pajares, 2002). Correlations between academic self-efficacy and performance in investigations in which self-efficacy corresponds closely to the criterion task have ranged from .49 to .70; direct effects in path analytic studies have ranged from $\beta = .349$ to .545 (Pajares & Urdan, 2006). Self-efficacy explains approximately 25% of the variance in the prediction of academic outcomes beyond that of instructional influences. Self-efficacy is responsive to changes in instructional experiences and plays a causal role in students' development and use of academic competencies (Schunk, 1995).

Using meta-analytic procedures, Multon et al. (1991) found that self-efficacy was related to academic performance ($r_\mu = .38$) and accounted for 14% of the variance. However, effect sizes depended on characteristics of the studies. Stronger effects were obtained by researchers who compared specific self-efficacy judgments with basic cognitive skills performance measures, developed self-efficacy and skill measures that were highly congruent, and administered them at the same time. In another meta-analysis, Stajkovic and Luthans (1998) found that the average weighted correlation between self-efficacy and work-related performance was $(G)r = .38$, which translates into a 28% gain in performance due to self-efficacy.

Self-efficacy also correlates positively with indexes of self-regulation (Schunk & Pajares, 2002). Pintrich and De Groot (1990) found that self-efficacy, self-regulation, and cognitive strategy use by middle school students were positively intercorrelated and predicted achievement. Bouffard-Bouchard, Parent, and Larivee (1991) found that high school students with high self-efficacy for problem solving displayed greater performance monitoring and persisted longer than students with lower self-efficacy. Zimmerman and Bandura (1994) showed that self-efficacy for writing correlated positively with college students' goals for course achievement, self-evaluative standards (satisfaction with potential grades), and achievement.

Experimental Research

Research in diverse settings has explored the effects of instructional and other classroom processes on self-efficacy (Schunk & Pajares, 2002). Much of this research has been guided by the model shown in Table 3.3.

At the outset of an activity, students differ in their self-efficacy for learning as a function of their prior experiences, personal qualities (e.g., abilities, attitudes), and social supports. The latter include the extent that parents, coaches, and teachers encourage students to learn, facilitate their access to resources necessary for learning (e.g., materials, facilities), and teach them self-regulatory strategies that enhance skill development. In a non-experimental study, Bandura, Barbaranelli, Caprara, and Pastorelli (1996) found that parents' academic aspirations for their children affected children's academic achievements directly as well as indirectly by influencing children's self-efficacy.

As students engage in activities they are influenced by personal factors (e.g., goal setting, cognitive information processing) and situational variables (e.g., feedback, social comparisons). These influences provide students with cues about how well they are learning. Self-efficacy is

Table 3.3 Self-Efficacy Model in Achievement Settings

Influences on Self-Efficacy for Learning	Pretask	During Task	Posttask
Prior experiences			Self-efficacy
Personal qualities	Self-efficacy	Personal	Motivation
Social supports		Situational	Learning
			Self-regulation
			Achievement

enhanced when students believe they are performing well and becoming more skillful. Lack of success or slow progress will not necessarily lower self-efficacy if students believe they can perform better by adjusting their approach, such as by expending greater effort or using better learning strategies (Schunk, 1995). In turn, self-efficacy enhances motivation, learning, self-regulation, and achievement.

Experimental educational research supports the hypothesized relations shown in Table 3.3 (Schunk, 1995; Schunk & Ertmer, 2000). These studies have employed students in different grade levels (e.g., elementary, middle, high, postsecondary) and with diverse abilities (e.g., regular, remedial, gifted), and have investigated different content areas (e.g., reading, writing, mathematics, computer applications).

Some instructional and social processes that have been found to be beneficial for raising self-efficacy are having students pursue proximal and specific goals, exposing children to social models, providing students with performance and attributional feedback, teaching students learning strategies, having learners verbalize strategies while they apply them, linking students' rewards to their learning progress, and having students self-monitor and evaluate their learning progress (Schunk, 1995; Schunk & Ertmer, 2000). These processes differ in many ways but they all help to inform students of their learning progress, which raises self-efficacy.

Predictive Power of Self-Efficacy

Several researchers have used causal models to test the predictive and mediational power of self-efficacy. Using path analysis, Schunk (1981) found that self-efficacy exerted a direct effect on children's achievement and persistence in mathematics. Pajares (1996a, Pajares & Kranzler, 1995) demonstrated that mathematics self-efficacy has as powerful and direct effect on mathematics performance as does cognitive or mental ability and mediates the influence of these variables on performance. Pajares and Miller (1994) reported that mathematics self-efficacy was a better predictor of the mathematics performance of college undergraduates than were mathematics self-concept, perceived usefulness of mathematics, prior experience with mathematics, and gender, and it mediated the influence of gender and previous high school and college experience on subsequent performance.

Zimmerman and Bandura (1994) found that self-efficacy affected achievement directly as well as indirectly through its influence on goals. Schunk and Gunn (1986) found that children's long division achievement was directly influenced by use of effective strategies and self-efficacy. Relich, Debus, and Walker (1986) also found that self-efficacy exerted a direct effect on division achievement and that instructional treatment had both a direct and an indirect effect on achievement through self-efficacy. Schack (1989) found that gifted children's self-efficacy at the end of the school year was strongly affected by previous participation in independent investigations and by self-efficacy assessed after such participation. The latter measure also predicted subsequent participation in independent investigations.

Remaining Challenges

In the years since Bandura's (1977a, 1977b) introduction of self-efficacy into the literature, educational researchers have tested its operation in myriad ways such that today we know much about its role in learning, motivation, achievement, and self-regulation. Yet research and practice have shown that the complexities of educational settings present challenges that require clarification of self-efficacy's operation in those settings. Three challenges are generality, calibration, and contextual influences.

Generality of Self-Efficacy

One challenge is the extent to which self-efficacy generalizes across domains. Self-efficacy refers to perceived capabilities within specific domains (Bandura, 1997; Pajares, 1997). However, some researchers—including Bandura—have assessed self-efficacy at levels more general than subject-specific tasks (Bandura et al., 1996; Bandura, Caprara, Barbaranelli, Gerbino, & Pastorelli, 2003; Zimmerman & Bandura, 1994). These studies have assessed factors such as academic self-efficacy, self-regulatory self-efficacy, and social self-efficacy, with items such as, "How well can you get teachers to help you when you get stuck on school work?" and "How well can you study when there are other interesting things to do?" To arrive at these types of judgments students presumably must integrate their perceptions across different situations; for example, getting the teacher to help them when they get stuck in mathematics, science, social studies, and reading. These types of assessments, while not as general as the typical self-concept measure, have broadened the conceptualization of self-efficacy beyond specific domains. There is some research evidence for a generalized sense of self-efficacy (Smith, 1989).

There are certain educational conditions that might lead to a generalized sense of self-efficacy. School curricula are structured for positive transfer: New learning builds upon prior skills. Mastering long division, for example, requires that one be proficient in estimating, subtracting, and multiplying. Children who generally perform well in mathematics, especially in the prerequisite areas, might approach the study of long division with higher self-efficacy for learning than children who have encountered difficulties with the component skills and have low self-efficacy in those areas.

Even in the absence of specific curricula structure, generalization also might occur in situations where students believe that the new learning will require skills that they previously have mastered. Many college and graduate students approach writing a research paper with some trepidation. However, some students may believe that writing a research paper requires such component skills as identifying a topic, conducting a literature review, synthesizing and organizing information, and drawing conclusions. These are skills that students may have used to write essays and term papers in English class. Students who believe they are competent in the component skills are apt to approach writing a research paper with higher self-efficacy than those students who question their capabilities in the component areas.

Finding evidence of generality would not refute the subject specificity of self-efficacy, but it is important to determine how students weigh and combine efficacy information to arrive at generalized judgments. Developmental factors may be an issue, because we should expect that with development children would be better able to assess their capabilities in component areas and determine the types of skills needed in the new domain.

Calibration of Self-Efficacy with Performance

Calibration is a challenge because we do not fully understand how learners weigh and combine various sources of self-efficacy information to arrive at self-efficacy judgments and how calibration links with academic performance. Bandura (1986) argued that successful functioning is best served by reasonably accurate self-efficacy judgments, although the most functional are those that slightly exceed what one can actually accomplish because this overestimation can increase effort and persistence. But when can overconfidence be characterized as excessive and maladaptive in an academic enterprise, what factors help create inaccurate self-perceptions, and what are the likely effects of such inaccuracy? Students with learning disabilities frequently have difficulties accurately evaluating their academic skills and predicting their performance. When the self-efficacy of students with learning disabilities is so miscalibrated that it leads to insufficient preparation and poor performance, then excessive self-efficacy can be problematic and even maladaptive (Klassen, 2006).

Bandura (1997) argued that the stronger the self-efficacy, the more likely are persons to select challenging tasks, persist at them, and perform successfully. Researchers should determine to what degree high self-efficacy demonstrated in the face of incongruent performance attainments ultimately results in these benefits. Efforts to lower students' self-efficacy or interventions designed to raise already overconfident self-efficacy should be discouraged, but improving students' calibration will require helping them understand what they do and do not know so that they may more effectively deploy appropriate cognitive strategies as they perform a task.

These issues of accuracy, however, cannot easily be separated from issues of well-being, optimism, and will. Research supports the idea that as people evaluate their lives, they are more likely to regret the challenge not confronted, the contest not entered, the risk unrisked, and the road not taken as a result of underconfidence and self-doubt rather than the action taken as a result of overconfidence and optimism (Bandura, 1997).

Indeed, researchers have found that possessing an optimistic explanatory style is related to adaptive academic benefits including achievement, positive goal orientation, and use of learning strategies, whereas a pessimistic style is associated with negative outcomes and learned helplessness (Buchanan & Seligman, 1995; Peterson, 2000; Seligman, 1991). Others have reported than an optimistic outlook bears fruit not only psychologically but also physiologically, helping to protect persons from many of the effects of disease and ill-health (Bandura, 1986, 1997; Taylor, Kemeny, Reed, Bower, & Gruenewald, 2000). The challenge to educators is to make students more familiar with their own capabilities without lowering confidence, optimism, and drive.

Contextual Influences on Self-Efficacy

Bandura's (1986) model of triadic reciprocality shows that self-efficacy—a personal factor—can be affected by one's behaviors and environmental (contextual) factors. To determine how self-efficacy affects motivation, learning, achievement, and self-regulation in educational settings requires that we understand how contextual variables operate.

We noted earlier that the transition from elementary to middle school brings about many changes in contextual factors. To say that these contextual factors affect self-efficacy is not helpful unless we know how students combine their influence with that of their prior experiences in elementary school to arrive at self-efficacy judgments. For self-efficacy to predict achievement outcomes, we must be able to predict which factors will affect self-efficacy and how they will do so.

Social factors offer another example. Student retention and dropout prevention are receiving much current attention (Alexander, Entwisle, & Kabbani, 2001; Hardre & Reeve, 2003; Lee & Burkam, 2003; Rumberger & Thomas, 2000). There, undoubtedly, are many factors that contribute to dropout including poorly developed academic and social skills, lack of interest in school subjects, classrooms that stress competition and ability social comparisons, low perceived value of school learning, and little sense of belonging or relatedness to the school environment (Alexander et al., 2001; Meece, Anderman, & Anderman, 2006; Wentzel, 2005). Students' involvement and participation in school depend, in part, on how much the school environment contributes to their perceptions of autonomy and relatedness, which in turn can influence self-efficacy and achievement (Hymel, Comfort, Schonert-Reichl, & McDougall, 1996). Parents, teachers, and peers contribute to students' feelings of autonomy and relatedness, and the peer group exerts increasing influence during adolescence (Kindermann, 2007; Steinberg et al., 1996). This suggests that students with a good sense of self-efficacy for learning, but who feel disconnected from the school environment, may display low motivation and achievement. A clear challenge is to determine how self-efficacy intertwines with social influences on academic outcomes.

Future Research Directions

There is much evidence to support Bandura's contention that self-efficacy beliefs can affect virtually every aspect of people's lives—their thoughts, feelings, and actions. Self-efficacy also is a critical determinant of how individuals regulate their thinking and behavior. Self-efficacy has proven to be a more consistent predictor of educational outcomes than other motivational variables.

But much research still is needed. The preceding challenges require research attention, as do cross-cultural differences, self-efficacy in effective schools, and the measurement and analysis of self-efficacy.

Cross-Cultural Research

There is a clear need for more research studies using students from different cultures. Most self-efficacy research studies have sampled from the school population of the United States. Cross-cultural studies will expand our understanding of the operation and generality of self-efficacy. Klassen (2004b) reviewed 20 self-efficacy studies from a cross-cultural perspective and found that efficacy beliefs tended to be lower for students from non-Western cultural groups (e.g., Asian and Asian-immigrant students) than for students from Western groups (e.g., Western Europe, Canada, United States). Moreover, in some cases the more modest self-efficacy beliefs expressed by the non-Western students predicted academic outcomes better than the higher self-efficacy beliefs of the Western students. Klassen posited that immigration status and political factors also may modify the mean self-efficacy of a cultural group. Optimistic self-efficacy beliefs did not necessarily translate into higher performance for all cultural groups.

Cultural dimensions such as individualism and collectivism also influence the relationships between social and academic self-efficacy beliefs and between academic achievement and social factors (Oettingen & Zosuls, 2006). Kim and Park (2006) argued that existing psychological and educational theories that emphasize individualistic values (e.g., ability, intrinsic interest, self-esteem, self-efficacy) cannot explain the high level of achievement of East Asian students. Instead, the Confucian-based socialization practices that promote close parent-child relationships are responsible for high levels of self-regulatory, relational, and social efficacy. Self-regulatory efficacy (i.e., one's perceived capabilities for effectively engaging in activities designed to promote self-regulated learning) is a powerful predictor of students' academic performance. In these cultures, relational efficacy (i.e., the confidence that young people have in their familial and social relations) has a powerful influence on students' academic performance. In addition, the lower levels of self-efficacy found in some collectivist groups do not always signify lower subsequent performance but instead reflect differing conceptualizations of self. Self-efficacy may be more other-oriented in some non-Western (particularly Asian) cultures than in Western cultures (Klassen, 2004a).

Self-Efficacy in Effective Schools

Effective schools create a positive environment for learning and provide support to teachers and students so that that learning can occur. The literature on effective schools generally has examined their effects on student achievement and teacher satisfaction (Muncey & McQuillan, 1993; National Research Council, 2004; Sizer, 1992). We recommend that self-efficacy researchers devote attention to the issue of which features of effective schools contribute to teachers' and students' self-efficacy.

Some characteristics of effective schools that should have positive effects on self-efficacy are parental involvement, supportive learning environments, smooth transitions between grades, and integrated curricula (Maehr & Midgley, 1996; Muncey & McQuillan, 1993; Sizer, 1992). Research evidence summarized in this chapter shows that each of these factors can positively affect self-efficacy. Researchers should examine their collective influence to determine how they create and build students' and teachers' self-efficacy.

Measurement and Analysis of Self-Efficacy

Bandura (1986, 1997) argued that contextually bounded, reasonably precise judgments of capability carefully matched to a corresponding outcome afford the best prediction of behavioral outcomes because these are the sorts of judgments that individuals use when confronted with behavioral tasks. Regrettably, the mismeasurement of self-efficacy continues to be a problem in many studies in which researchers either fail to establish an appropriate correspondence between self-efficacy and the outcome with which it are compared, assess self-efficacy at inappropriate levels of specificity, use items that more closely resemble self-concept or self-esteem, or fail to heed the cautions that Bandura (2006) provided regarding self-efficacy measurement (Bong, 2006). Decontextualized or atheoretical self-efficacy assessments that lack consistency with the criterion task distort the influence of self-efficacy.

Although correspondence between self-efficacy and the task of interest is critical in studies that attempt to establish an empirical connection between them, requirements of specificity will differ depending on the substantive question of interest and the nature of the variables with which self-efficacy will be compared. To be both explanatory and predictive, self-efficacy measures should be tailored to the domain(s) of functioning being analyzed and reflect the various task demands within that domain. In the final analysis, evaluating the appropriateness and adequacy of a self-efficacy measure will require making a theoretically-informed and empirically sound judgment that reflects an understanding of the domain under investigation and its different features, the types of capabilities the domain requires, and the range of situations in which these capabilities might be applied. These understandings can then be used to evaluate a self-efficacy measure by the level of specificity of its items, the range of task demands that it includes, and its correspondence with the outcome of interest (Bandura, 2006).

We believe that we are past the point of needing to determine whether self-efficacy is correlated with academic motivation and attainments in varied domains. Studies in which these relations are investigated are becoming redundant. Rather, we need experimental research that sheds further light on the interplay between determinants and educational interventions that put into practice the policies and strategies that emanate from insights already obtained from prior research. We know a good deal about the influence of self-efficacy as it relates to motivation and achievement. What is lacking is putting that knowledge to greater use by altering school and classroom structures, the content of teacher education programs, and educational policies. Self-efficacy researchers should dedicate themselves to these paths with greater vigor.

References

Alexander, K., Entwisle, D., & Kabbani, N. (2001). The dropout process in life course perspective: Early risk factors at home and school. *Teachers College Record,103,* 760–822.

Bandura, A. (1977a). Self-efficacy: Toward a unifying theory of behavioral change. *Psychological Review, 84,* 191–215.

Bandura, A. (1977b). *Social learning theory.* Englewood Cliffs, NJ: Prentice Hall.

Bandura, A. (1986). *Social foundations of thought and action: A social cognitive theory.* Englewood Cliffs, NJ: Prentice Hall.

Bandura, A. (1993). Perceived self-efficacy in cognitive development and functioning. *Educational Psychologist, 28,* 117–148.

Bandura, A. (1997). *Self-efficacy: The exercise of control.* New York: Freeman.

Bandura, A. (2006). Guide for creating self-efficacy scales. In F. Pajares & T. Urdan (Eds.), *Self-efficacy beliefs of adolescents* (pp. 307–338). Greenwich, CT: Information Age.

Bandura, A., Barbaranelli, C., Caprara, G. V., & Pastorelli, C. (1996). Multifaceted impact of self-efficacy beliefs on academic functioning. *Child Development, 67,* 1206–1222.

Bandura, A., Caprara, G. V., Barbaranelli, C., Gerbino, M., & Pastorelli, C. (2003). Role of affective self-regulatory efficacy in diverse spheres of psychosocial functioning. *Child Development, 74,* 769–782.

Bong, M. (2006). Asking the right question: How confident are you that you could successfully perform these tasks? In F. Pajares & T. Urdan (Eds.), *Self-efficacy beliefs of adolescents* (pp. 287–306). Greenwich, CT: Information Age.

Bong, M., & Skaalvik, E. M. (2003). Academic self-concept and self-efficacy: How different are they really? *Educational Psychology Review, 15,* 1–40.

Bouffard-Bouchard, T., Parent, S., & Larivee, S. (1991). Influence of self-efficacy on self-regulation and performance among junior and senior high-school age students. *International Journal of Behavioral Development, 14,* 153–164.

Bradley, R. H., & Corwyn, R. F. (2002). Socioeconomic status and child development. *Annual Review of Psychology, 53,* 371–399.

Buchanan, G. M., & Seligman, M. E. P. (Eds.). (1995). *Explanatory style.* Hillsdale, NJ: Erlbaum.

Cairns, R. B., Cairns, B. D., & Neckerman, J. J. (1989). Early school dropout: Configurations and determinants. *Child Development, 60,* 1437–1452.

Caprara, G. V., Barbaranelli, C., Borgogni, L., & Steca, P. (2003). Efficacy beliefs as determinants of teachers' job satisfaction. *Journal of Educational Psychology, 95,* 821–832.

Chapman, J. W., & Tunmer, W. E. (1995). Development of young children's reading self-concepts: An examination of emerging subcomponents and their relationship with reading achievement. *Journal of Educational Psychology, 87,* 154–167.

Collins, J. L. (1982, March). *Self-efficacy and ability in achievement behavior.* Paper presented at the annual meeting of the American Educational Research Association, New York.

Covington, M. V. (1984). The motive for self-worth. In R. Ames & C. Ames (Eds.), *Research on motivation in education* (Vol. 1, pp. 77–113). New York: Academic Press.

Covington, M. V. (1992). *Making the grade: A self-worth perspective on motivation and school reform.* Cambridge, England: Cambridge University Press.

Dweck, C. S., & Goetz, T. (1978). Attributions and learned helplessness. In J. Harvey, W. Ickes, & R. Kidd (Eds.), *New directions in attribution research* (pp. 157–179). Hillsdale, NJ: Erlbaum.

Eccles, J. S., Wigfield, A., & Schiefele, U. (1998). Motivation to succeed. In W. Damon (Series Ed.) & N. Eisenberg (Vol. Ed.), *Handbook of child psychology: Vol. 3. Social, emotional, and personality development* (5th ed., pp. 1017–1095). New York: Wiley.

Goddard, R. D., Hoy, W. K., & Woolfolk Hoy, A. (2000). Collective teacher efficacy: Its meaning, measure, and impact on student achievement. *American Educational Research Journal, 37,* 479–507.

Hardre, P., & Reeve, J. (2003). A motivational model of rural students' intentions to persist in, versus drop out of, high school. *Journal of Educational Psychology,95,* 347–356.

Henson, R. K. (2002). From adolescent angst to adulthood: Substantive implications and measurement dilemmas in the development of teacher efficacy research. *Educational Psychologist, 37,* 127–150.

Hymel, S., Comfort, C., Schonert-Reichl, K., & McDougall, P. (1996). Academic failure and school dropout: The influence of peers. In J. Juvonen & K. R. Wentzel (Eds.), *Social motivation: Understanding children's school adjustment* (pp. 313–345). Cambridge, England: Cambridge University Press.

Jacobs, J. E., Lanza, S., Osgood, D. W., Eccles, J. S., & Wigfield, A. (2002). Changes in children's self-competence and values: Gender and domain differences across grades one to twelve. *Child Development, 73,* 509–527.

Kim, U., & Park, Y. S. (2006). Factors influencing academic achievement in collectivist societies: The role of self-, relational, and social efficacy. In F. Pajares & T. Urdan (Eds.), *Self-efficacy beliefs of adolescents* (pp. 267–286). Greenwich, CT: Information Age.

Kindermann, T. A. (2007). Effects of naturally existing peer groups on changes in academic engagement in a cohort of sixth graders. *Child Development, 78,* 1186–1203.

Kindermann, T. A., McCollam, T. L., & Gibson, E., Jr. (1996). Peer networks and students' classroom engagement during childhood and adolescence. In J. Juvonen & K. R. Wentzel (Eds.), *Social motivation: Understanding children's school adjustment* (pp. 279–312). Cambridge, England: Cambridge University Press.

Klassen, R. M. (2004a). A cross-cultural investigation of the efficacy beliefs of south Asian immigrant and Anglo Canadian nonimmigrant early adolescents. *Journal of Educational Psychology, 96,* 731–742.

Klassen, R. M. (2004b). Optimism and realism: A review of self-efficacy from a cross-cultural perspective. *International Journal of Psychology, 39,* 205–230.

Klassen, R. M. (2006). Too much confidence? The self-efficacy of adolescents with learning disabilities. In F. Pajares & T. Urdan (Eds.), *Self-efficacy beliefs of adolescents* (pp. 181–200). Greenwich, CT: Information Age.

Lee, V. E., & Burkam, D. T. (2003). Dropping out of high school: The role of school organization and structure. *American Educational Research Journal, 40,* 353–393.

Maehr, M. L., & Midgley, C. (1996). *Transforming school cultures.* Boulder, CO: Westview.

Marsh, H. W., & Hau, K. (2003). The big-fish-little-pond effect on academic self-concept: A cross-cultural (26-country) test of the negative effects of academically selective schools. *American Psychologist, 58,* 364–376.

Marsh, H. W., & Shavelson, R. (1985). Self-concept: Its multifaceted, hierarchical structure. *Educational Psychologist, 20,* 107–123.

Meece, J. L., Anderman, E. M., & Anderman, L. H. (2006). Classroom goal structure, student motivation, and academic achievement. *Annual Review of Psychology, 57,* 487–503.

Multon, K. D., Brown, S. D., & Lent, R. W. (1991). Relation of self-efficacy beliefs to academic outcomes: A meta-analytic investigation. *Journal of Counseling Psychology, 38,* 30–38.

Muncey, D., & McQuillan, P. (1993). Preliminary findings from a five-year study of the Coalition of Essential Schools. *Phi Delta Kappan, 74,* 486–489.

National Research Council (2004). *Engaging schools: Fostering high school students'motivation to learn.* Washington, DC: National Academy Press.

Oettingen, G., & Zosuls, C. (2006). Self-efficacy of adolescents across culture. In F. Pajares & T. Urdan (Eds.), *Self-efficacy beliefs of adolescents* (pp. 245–266).Greenwich, CT: Information Age.

Pajares, F. (1996a). Role of self-efficacy beliefs in the mathematical problem-solving of gifted students. *Contemporary Educational Psychology, 21,* 325–344.

Pajares, F. (1996b). Self-efficacy beliefs in achievement settings. *Review of Educational Research, 66,* 543–578.

Pajares, F. (1997). Current directions in self-efficacy research. In M. Maehr & P. R. Pintrich (Eds.), *Advances in motivation and achievement* (Vol. 10, pp. 1–49). Greenwich, CT: JAI.

Pajares, F., & Kranzler, J. (1995). Self-efficacy beliefs and general mental ability in mathematical problem-solving. *Contemporary Educational Psychology, 20,* 426–443.

Pajares, F., & Miller, M. D. (1994). The role of self-efficacy and self-concept beliefs in mathematical problem-solving: A path analysis. *Journal of Educational Psychology, 86,* 193–203.

Pajares, F., & Miller, M. D. (1997). Mathematics self-efficacy and mathematical problem-solving: Implications of using different forms of assessment. *Journal of Experimental Education, 65,* 213–228.

Pajares, F., & Schunk, D. H. (2001). Self-beliefs and school success: Self-efficacy, self-concept, and school achievement. In R. J. Riding & S. G. Rayner (Eds.), *Self-perception* (pp. 239–265). Westport, CT: Ablex.

Pajares, F., & Schunk, D. H. (2002). Self and self-belief in psychology and education:A historical perspective. In J. Aronson (Ed.), *Improving academic achievement: Impact of psychological factors on education* (pp. 3–21). San Diego: Academic Press.

Pajares, F., & Urdan, T. (Eds.) (2006). *Self-efficacy beliefs of adolescents.* Greenwich, CT: Information Age.

Peterson, C. (2000). The future of optimism. *American Psychologist, 55,* 44–45.

Pintrich, P. R., & De Groot, E. V. (1990). Motivational and self-regulated learning components of classroom academic performance. *Journal of Educational Psychology, 82,* 33–40.

Relich, J. D., Debus, R. L., & Walker, R. (1986). The mediating role of attribution and self-efficacy variables for treatment effects on achievement outcomes. *Contemporary Educational Psychology, 11,* 195–216.

Rumberger, R. W., & Thomas, S. L. (2000). The distribution of dropout and turnover rates among urban and suburban high schools. *Sociology of Education, 73*(1), 39–67.

Ryan, R. M. (1993). Agency and organization: Intrinsic motivation, autonomy, and the self in psychological development. In J. E. Jacobs (Ed.), *Nebraska Symposium on Motivation 1992* (pp. 1–56). Lincoln: University of Nebraska Press.

Schack, G. D. (1989). Self-efficacy as a mediator in the creative productivity of gifted children. *Journal for the Education of the Gifted, 12,* 231–249.

Schunk, D. H. (1981). Modeling and attributional effects on children's achievement: A self-efficacy analysis. *Journal of Educational Psychology, 73,* 93–105.

Schunk, D. H. (1995). Self-efficacy and education and instruction. In J. E. Maddux (Ed.), *Self-efficacy, adaptation, and adjustment: Theory, research, and application* (pp. 281–303). New York: Plenum.

Schunk, D. H., & Ertmer, P. A. (2000). Self-regulation and academic learning: Self-efficacy enhancing interventions. In M. Boekaerts, P. R. Pintrich, & M. Zeidner (Eds.), *Handbook of self-regulation* (pp. 631–649). San Diego: Academic Press.

Schunk, D. H., & Gunn, T. P. (1986). Self-efficacy and skill development: Influence of task strategies and attributions. *Journal of Educational Research, 79,* 238–244.

Schunk, D. H., & Meece, J. L. (2006). Self-efficacy development in adolescence. In F. Pajares & T. Urdan (Eds.), *Self-efficacy beliefs of adolescents* (pp. 71–96). Greenwich, CT: Information Age.

Schunk, D. H., & Pajares, F. (2002). The development of academic self-efficacy. In A. Wigfield & J. Eccles (Eds.), *Development of achievement motivation* (pp. 15–31). San Diego: Academic Press.

Schunk, D. H., & Pajares, F. (2004). Self-efficacy in education revisited: Empirical and applied evidence. In D. M. McInerney & S. Van Etten (Eds.), *Big theories revisited* (pp. 115–138). Greenwich, CT: Information Age.

Schunk, D. H., & Pajares, F. (2005). Competence perceptions and academic functioning. In A. J. Elliot & C. S. Dweck (Eds.), *Handbook of competence and motivation* (pp. 85–104). New York: Guilford.

Schunk, D. H., & Zimmerman, B. J. (2006). Competence and control beliefs: Distinguishing the means and ends. In P. A. Alexander & P. H. Winne (Eds.), *Handbook of educational psychology* (2nd ed., pp. 349–367). Mahwah, NJ: Erlbaum.

Seligman, M. E. P. (1991). *Learned optimism.* New York: Knopf.

Shavelson, R., & Bolus, R. (1982). Self-concept: The interplay of theory and methods. *Journal of Educational Psychology, 74,* 3–17.

Sizer, T. (1992). *Horace's compromise: Redesigning the American high school.* Boston: Houghton Mifflin.

Skinner, E. A., Wellborn, J. G., & Connell, J. P. (1990). What it takes to do well in school and whether I've got it: A process model of perceived control and children's engagement and achievement in school. *Journal of Educational Psychology, 82,* 22–32.

Smith, R. E. (1989). Effects of coping skills training on generalized self-efficacy and locus of control. *Journal of Personality and Social Psychology, 56,* 228–233.

Stajkovic, A. D., & Luthans, F. (1998). Self-efficacy and work-related performances: A meta-analysis. *Psychological Bulletin, 124,* 240–261.

Steinberg, L., Brown, B. B., & Dornbusch, S. M. (1996). *Beyond the classroom: Why school reform has failed and what parents need to do.* New York: Simon & Schuster.

Taylor, S. E., Kemeny, M. E., Reed, G. M., Bower, J. E., & Gruenewald, T. L. (2000). Psychological resources, positive illusions, and health. *American Psychologist, 55,* 99–109.

Tschannen-Moran, M., Woolfolk Hoy, A., & Hoy, W. K. (1998). Teacher efficacy: Its meaning and measure. *Review of Educational Research, 68,* 202–248.

Wentzel, K. R. (2005). Peer relationships, motivation, and academic performance at school. In A. J. Elliot & C. S. Dweck (Eds.), *Handbook of competence and motivation* (pp. 279–296). New York: Guilford.

Wigfield, A., Tonks, S., & Eccles, J. S. (2004). Expectancy value theory in cross-cultural perspective. In D. M. McInerney & S. Van Etten (Eds.), *Big theories revisited* (pp. 165–198). Greenwich, CT: Information Age.

Zimmerman, B. J., & Bandura, A. (1994). Impact of self-regulatory influences on writing course achievement. *American Educational Research Journal, 31,* 845–862.

4

Expectancy-Value Theory

Allan Wigfield, Stephen Tonks, and Susan Lutz Klauda

In this chapter we discuss expectancy-value theory and review research that has emanated from this theoretical model. We focus in particular on the expectancy-value model developed by Eccles, Wigfield, and their colleagues and research that has tested it. We pay special attention to three broad issues with respect to expectancy-value theory: how expectancies and values develop, how they are influenced by different kinds of educational contexts, and how culture impacts the development of expectancies and values.

Expectancy-Value Theory: A Brief History

The constructs of expectancy and value and theoretical models based on these constructs have a long history in the field of psychology and especially in the achievement motivation field (Eccles et al., 1983; Higgins, 2007; Rose & Sherman, 2007; Weiner, 1992; Wigfield & Eccles, 1992). The expectancy and value constructs initially were defined by theorists such as Lewin (1938) and Tolman (1932). Lewin discussed how the value (or valence) of an activity influenced its importance to the individual, and Tolman discussed how expectancies for success function in different areas. Social psychological theories of attitudes, intentions, and their relations to behavior, such as the theory of reasoned action and the theory of planned behavior, are based in part in expectancy and value constructs (Ajzen, 1991; Fishbein & Ajzen, 1975; see Rose & Sherman, 2007, and Higgins, 2007, for review). Rose and Sherman (2007) defined expectancies as our beliefs about the future. Higgins (2007) initially defined value in terms of the relative worth of a commodity, activity, or person. Later he defined value as the psychological experience of being attracted to (or repulsed by) an object or activity. Valuing something means wishing to attain it; thus for Higgins value is a motivational force and not just a belief.

In the achievement motivation field Atkinson (1957, 1964) developed the first formal, mathematical expectancy-value model in an attempt to explain different kinds of achievement-related behaviors, such as striving for success, choice among achievement tasks, and persistence. Atkinson was influenced by Murray's (1938) notion that various human needs guide behavior, and focused specifically on the need for achievement Murray included in his theory. Atkinson (1957) postulated that achievement behaviors are determined by achievement motives, expectancies for success, and incentive values. He viewed achievement motives as relatively stable dispositions, and included both a motive to approach success and a motive to avoid failure in the theory, stating that individuals can be described by the relative strength of these approach and avoidance motives. Atkinson defined expectancies for success as the individual's expected probability for success on a specific task (which can range from zero to one). He defined incentive value as the relative attractiveness of succeeding on a given achievement task, and also stated that incentive value is inversely related to the probability for success. Thus, expectancies and values were more situationally or task specific, and also tied closely (and inversely) to one another; an implication of this inverse relationship is that Atkinson argued that highly valued tasks are ones that individuals think are difficult to do. He and his colleagues did an extensive body of laboratory-based research on individuals' achievement strivings under different probabilities for success. One major conclusion from this work is that for success-oriented individuals, motivation to do an activity is strongest when the probability of success is .5 (see Atkinson, 1964; Wigfield & Eccles, 1992, for further discussion of this theory and research emanating from it).

Modern Expectancy-Value Models in Developmental and Educational Psychology

Modern expectancy-value theories (e.g., Eccles, 1987; 1993, 2005; Eccles et al., 1983; Feather, 1982; 1988; Pekrun, 2000; Wigfield & Eccles, 1992, 2000, 2002) are based in Atkinson's (1957, 1964) work in that they link achievement performance, persistence, and choice most directly to individuals' expectancy-related and task value beliefs. However, they differ from Atkinson's expectancy-value theory in several ways. First, both the expectancy and value components are defined in richer ways, and are linked to a broader array of psychological, social, and cultural determinants. Second, these models have been tested in real-world achievement situations rather than with the laboratory tasks often used to test Atkinson's theory.

The Eccles et al. Expectancy-Value Model Eccles and her colleagues' expectancy-value model proposes that these constructs are the most immediate or direct predictors of achievement performance and choice, and are themselves influenced by a variety of psychological, social, and cultural influences (e.g., Eccles, 1987, 1993, 2005; Eccles et al., 1983; Eccles & Wigfield, 1995; Meece, Wigfield, & Eccles, 1990; Wigfield, 1994; Wigfield & Eccles, 1992, 2000, 2002). In their research Eccles and her colleagues have focused on how expectancies, values, and their determinants influence choice, persistence, and performance. They also have examined the developmental course of children's expectancies and values. They initially developed the model to help explain gender differences in mathematics expectancies and values and how these influenced boys and girls' choices of mathematics courses and majors. They broadened the model to other activity areas, most notably sport and physical skill activities (e.g., Eccles & Harold, 1991).

Figure 4.1 depicts the model. Moving from right to left in the model, expectancies and values are hypothesized to influence performance and task choice directly. Expectancies and values themselves are influenced by task-specific beliefs such as perceptions of competence, perceptions of the difficulty of different tasks, and individuals' goals and self-schema, along with their affective memories for different achievement-related events. These beliefs, goals, and affective memories are influenced by individuals' perceptions of other peoples' attitudes and expectations for them, and by their own interpretations of their previous achievement outcomes. Children's perceptions and interpretations are influenced by a broad array of social and cultural factors. These include

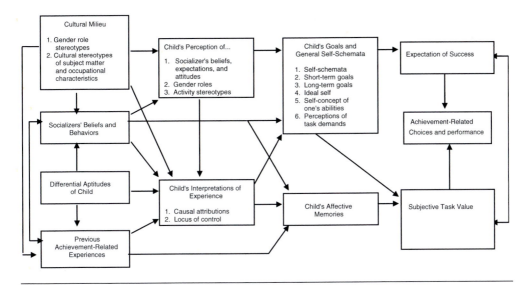

Figure 4.1 Eccles, Wigfield, and colleagues' expectancy-value model of achievement performance and choice.

socializers' (especially parents and teachers) beliefs and behaviors, children's specific achievement experiences and aptitudes, and the cultural milieu in which they live.

Defining the Expectancy, Value, and Ability Belief Constructs in This Model

Eccles and colleagues broadened Atkinson's (1957) original definitions of both the expectancy and value constructs. They defined expectancies for success as children's beliefs about how well they will do on an upcoming task (e.g., how well do you think you will do in math next year?). They distinguished conceptually expectancies for success from the individual's beliefs about competence or ability. These latter beliefs refer to children's evaluations of their current competence or ability, both in terms of their assessments of their own ability and also how they think they compare to other students. Ability beliefs are prominent in many motivation models; Wigfield and Eccles (2000) discuss different definitions of this construct in these models (see also Schunk & Pajares, this volume).

Values have both broad and task-specific definitions (see Higgins, 2007; Rohan, 2000; Wigfield & Eccles, 1992, for review of some of these definitions). In their model Eccles and her colleagues define values with respect to the qualities of different tasks and how those qualities influence the individual's desire to do the task; hence the term *task* value (Eccles, 2005; Eccles et al., 1983; Wigfield & Eccles, 1992). Like Higgins' definition, this definition stresses the motivational aspects of task value. Further, these values are *subjective* because various individuals assign different values to the same activity; math achievement is valuable to some students but not to others.

Eccles et al. (1983) proposed four major components of subjective task values: attainment value or importance, intrinsic value, utility value or usefulness of the task, and cost (see Eccles et al., 1983, and Wigfield & Eccles, 1992, for more detailed discussion of these components). Building on Battle's (1965, 1966) work, Eccles et al. defined attainment value as the importance of doing well on a given task. Attainment value incorporates identity issues; tasks are important when individuals view them as central to their own sense of themselves, or allow them to express or confirm important aspects of self.

Intrinsic value is the enjoyment one gains from doing the task. This component is similar in certain respects to notions of intrinsic motivation and interest (see Renninger, 2000; Ryan & Deci, 2000; Schiefele, 2001), but it is important to acknowledge that these constructs come from different theoretical traditions. When children intrinsically value an activity, they often become deeply engaged in it and can persist at it for a long time.

Utility value or usefulness refers to how a task fits into an individual's future plans, for instance, taking a math class to fulfill a requirement for a science degree. In certain respects utility value is similar to extrinsic motivation, because when doing an activity out of utility value, the activity is a means to an end rather than an end in itself (see Ryan & Deci, 2000). However, the activity also can reflect some important goals that the person holds deeply, such as attaining a certain occupation. In this sense utility value also connects to personal goals and sense of self, and so has some ties to intrinsic motivation.

Cost refers to what the individual has to give up to do a task (e.g., do I do my math homework or call my friend?), as well as the anticipated effort one will need to put into task completion. Is working this hard to get an A in math worth it? Eccles et al. (1983) emphasized that cost is especially important to choice. Choices are influenced by both negative and positive task characteristics and all choices are assumed to have costs associated with them because one choice often eliminates other options. For instance, choosing to major in history means that one cannot major in another field that also may have some value to the individual. Despite the theoretical importance of cost to choice, to date, cost has been the least studied of the different components of subjective values.

Measuring Ability Beliefs, Expectancies, and Values

Eccles and her colleagues have developed questionnaires to measure children's ability beliefs, expectancies for success, and subjective values in a variety of academic and non-academic domains (e.g., Eccles et al., 1983; Eccles, Wigfield, Harold, & Blumenfeld, 1993; Wigfield & Eccles, 2000; see these articles for sample items). These measures have been used with children and adolescents across the school years, and have clear factor structures, good psychometric properties, and demonstrated relations to different achievement and choice outcomes (Eccles & Wigfield, 1995; Eccles et al., 1993; Meece et al., 1990).

There also are some other measures of task value in addition to the scales developed by Eccles, Wigfield, and their colleagues. The Motivated Strategies for Learning Questionnaire developed by Pintrich, Smith, Garcia, and McKeachie (1991) includes a scale that measures the different aspects of task value defined by Eccles et al., but it does not have enough items measuring task values to create subscales for the different components. Graham and Taylor (e.g., Graham & Taylor, 2002; Graham, Taylor, & Hudley, 1998; Taylor & Graham, 2007) devised an innovative measure of task value that asks students to nominate other students whom they most admire, like, and want to be like. They also ask their participants to say who in their class tries hard and gets good grades, who doesn't try and gets poor grades, and who follows or doesn't follow school rules. Graham and her colleagues report interesting gender and ethnic differences in whom children admire, which they interpret as indicating how much the participants in their study value school.

In sum, there are available in the literature well-established measures of ability beliefs, expectancies for success, and task value. These measures can be extended to additional achievement domains that have not been studied as much as some of the academic domains have. They also can be written with more or less specificity; for instance, in the math domain children's valuing of specific kinds of math could be assessed. One of the measurement challenges for researchers is matching theoretical constructs to appropriate measurement tools. For instance, the constructs of ability beliefs, expectancies for success, and self-efficacy have some overlap in how they are defined, but also differ in important ways (see Pajares, 1996; Schunk & Pajares, this volume, for further discussion). Too often researchers state that they are measuring a certain construct but use a measure that perhaps does not capture the construct in the way it is defined theoretically. This can lead to conceptual confusion and conflicting results, and thus impede the advancement of the field.

Major Research Findings on Expectancies and Values

Expectancies, Values, Performance, and Choice There is clear evidence from a variety of studies in different domains that individuals' expectancies for success and achievement values predict their achievement outcomes, including their performance, persistence, and choices of which activities to do (e.g., Bong, 2001; Eccles, 1993; Eccles et al., 1983; Dennissen, Zarret, & Eccles 2007; Durik, Vida, & Eccles, 2006; Meece et al., 1990; Simpkins, Davis-Kean, & Eccles, 2006). Students' expectancies for success and beliefs about ability are among the strongest psychological predictors of performance. Students' subjective task values predict both intentions and actual decisions to persist at different activities, such as taking mathematics and English courses and engaging in sports activities.

The relations are evident in children as young as first grade, although they strengthen across age (Eccles, 1984; Eccles et al. 1983; Eccles & Harold, 1991; Meece et al., 1990; Wigfield, 1997). These relations also extend over time; Durik et al. (2006) reported that the importance children gave to reading in fourth grade related significantly to the number of English classes they took in high school. Also, children's interest in reading measured in fourth grade indirectly predicted (through interest measured in 10th grade) high school leisure time reading, career aspirations, and course selections. In another longitudinal study looking at relations of performance, ability beliefs and values, and choice, Simpkins et al. (2006) found that children's participation in math and science activities in late elementary school related to their subsequent expectancies and values in these areas, which in turn predicted the number of math and science courses they took through high school. Interestingly, in this study it was children's ability-related beliefs in high schools that predicted choice more strongly than did students' values; Simpkins et al. speculated that this may have occurred because students know the importance of such courses for college entrance, and are more likely to take them when they expect to do well in them.

Battle and Wigfield (2003), in one of the few studies to include the cost component of achievement values, found that attainment and utility value were positive predictors of college students' intentions to enter graduate school, but the perceived psychological cost of graduate school attendance was a negative predictor. Thus, when students value something they also report they are more likely to engage in the activity. When the activity is seen as having too great a cost, they will be less likely to engage in it.

Development of Expectancy-Related Beliefs and Values One important developmental question is how distinct the expectancy and value constructs are in children of different ages. Eccles & Wigfield (1995) and Eccles et al. (1993) factor analyzed children's responses to questionnaire measures of each construct. The major findings from these analyses were: a) children's expectancy-related beliefs and values formed distinct factors in children as young as 6 years; b) *within* a given domain (e.g., reading, math, sports) children's beliefs about their current competence, expectancies for success, and perceived performance load on the same factor, suggesting that these components comprise a single concept for children age 6–18; c) *within* a given domain the components of achievement values identified by Eccles and her colleagues can be distinguished factorially in children in fifth grade and beyond; and d) *across* activity domains competence-related beliefs form distinct factors in children as young as 6, indicating that children differentiate across domain with respect to these beliefs (e.g., expectancy-related beliefs in math are factorially distinct from expectancy-related beliefs in reading). The same is true of achievement values.

A second important developmental question is how the level of children's expectancy-related beliefs and values change across age. The general pattern is that children's competence beliefs for different tasks decline across the elementary school years and through the high school years (see Dweck & Elliott, 1983; Eccles, Wigfield, & Schiefele, 1998; Stipek & Mac Iver, 1989; Wigfield, Eccles, Schiefele, Roeser, & Davis-Kean, 2006, for review). Many young children are quite optimistic about their competencies in different areas, and this optimism changes to greater realism and (sometimes) pessimism for many children. Researchers in the United States have examined change over the entire elementary and secondary school years in children's competence beliefs for math, language arts, and sport (Jacobs, Lanza, Osgood, Eccles, & Wigfield, 2002; Fredricks & Eccles, 2002), and Watt (2004) looked at change across middle and senior high school in Australia. Jacobs et al. found that children's perceptions in each area were strongly positive early on. However, the overall pattern of change was a decline in each domain. There were some differences across domain with respect to when the strongest changes occurred, particularly in language arts and math. In language arts the strongest declines occurred during elementary school and then little change was observed after that. In sports the change accelerated during the high school years. The decline in math competence beliefs was steady over time. Fredricks and Eccles and Watt also found declines over time in competence beliefs and values, although the specific trends were somewhat different across these studies.

Two caveats about these findings should be mentioned. First, most of the research just described is normative, describing mean-level change across groups of children. Researchers have shown that these patterns do vary for children achieving at different levels (Harter, Whitesell, & Kowalski, 1992; Wigfield, Eccles, Mac Iver, Reuman, & Midgley, 1991). Second, it also has been shown that some preschool children react negatively to failure (see Dweck, 2002; Stipek, Recchia, & McClintic, 1992). Children reacting negatively to failure early on may be more likely to be pessimistic about their abilities even in the early elementary school years (Burhans & Dweck, 1995). Thus, not all children are overly optimistic about their abilities in different areas.

Relations of Expectancy-Related Beliefs and Values How do the different components of task value and expectancy-related beliefs relate to one another over time? Wigfield et al. (1997) studied change across the elementary school years in children's expectancy-related beliefs and values in several domains (measuring the usefulness and interest components of value). In contrast to Atkinson's (1957, 1964) view that expectancies and values are inversely related, in this study at all grade levels and in all domains relations among the constructs were positive. The positive relations increased in strength across age. For instance, at first-grade children's competence beliefs and values in math and reading had a median correlation of .23. By sixth grade the median correlation of these variables in these domains was .53. Thus children's task values, expectancy, and competence beliefs increasingly are positively related, suggesting that children come to value what they are good at. Indeed, Wigfield et al. (see also Wigfield & Eccles, 1992) explained the differences between their work and Atkinson's by stating that in real-world achievement situations individuals value the tasks at which they think they have a good chance of doing well. Similarly, Harter (2006) has argued that being competent at activities one thinks are important is an important positive predictor of self-esteem. When one lacks competence at activities deemed important, self-esteem can suffer.

A further interesting question from a developmental perspective is whether competence-related beliefs or achievement values begin a causal sequence in these observed relations. That is, do children come to value activities at which they are competent, or do children learn to be competent at things they value? Bandura (1997) has argued that efficacy beliefs are the prior causal factor; children learn to enjoy those activities at which they are competent. Jacobs et al. (2002) reported data that supports this claim, in their longitudinal study of first- through 12th-grade children. They found, first, that children were more likely to value math, sports, and language arts activities when they believed they were competent at those activities. Further, change in competence beliefs predicted strongly the developmental trajectory in children's subjective task values, accounting for over 40% of the variance in these trajectories.

Development of Expectancy-Related Beliefs and Values: Psychological and Experiential Influences

What psychological and experiential factors influence the development of expectancy-related beliefs and subjective values? Much has been written about how children develop beliefs about competence in different areas (e.g., Bandura, 1997; Dweck, 2002; Schunk & Pajares, 2002, this volume; Stipek & Mac Iver, 1989; Stipek et al., 1992). Children's mastery experiences during the infancy and preschool years are one important influence. When children learn to master different tasks and activities on their own (i.e., become a successful causal agent in their interactions with the world), their sense of competence can grow. Feedback from parents also is a crucial influence during these years, and beyond. Parents who encourage their children to master different things and provide appropriate feedback to them help children develop a sense of competence and control. Overly critical parents can destroy children's beliefs about their competence and expectations for the future (Dweck, 2002; Heyman, Dweck, & Cain, 1992). On the other hand, Dweck and her colleagues also have argued that parents who praise children's abilities rather than their effort and persistence may inadvertently weaken their child's sense of competence because such children do not learn how to deal with and overcome challenges and even failures.

When children begin school, they receive information from two main sources that can have strong influences on their competence beliefs. First, they are evaluated more systematically, formally, and frequently than they are at home, and these evaluations become more prevalent and important as children go through school. Receiving clear evaluations in different areas helps children develop distinct ideas about their competencies in these areas, and also to have a better understanding of their strengths and weaknesses in each area. The ways in which these evaluations are done can have either positive or negative effects on children's competence beliefs and motivation. For example, the strong push for high-stakes testing in school can weaken the competence beliefs and motivation of students doing poorly on such tests (Deci & Ryan, 2002).

Second, once they begin school children engage more systematically in social comparison with others as a way to judge their own abilities (Ruble, 1983). Being placed in a classroom with a group of same-age peers makes such comparisons easy to do, and they can alter the sense of competence children have based on their own mastery experiences in important ways. For instance, a first grader may think she is good at reading because she has mastered the alphabet; however, when she sees the child sitting next to her reading the Harry Potter series on her own, she likely will re-assess her own competencies. Schools vary with respect to how they handle social comparison information; some highlight it by posting work and grades on classrooms walls, and others minimize it to the extent possible (it can never be eliminated). Regardless of schools' and teachers' approaches to sharing information about other students' performance, all students use the information they receive about how others are doing to judge their own experiences. As Schunk and Pajares (this volume) put it, these kinds of information sources help children calibrate their ability beliefs in different areas, and likely are one reason why children's ability and expectancy beliefs relate more strongly to their performance as they get older.

Less has been written about the psychological and experiential factors influencing the development of children's task values. Some of the same factors just discussed that influence the development of expectancy-related beliefs likely influence the development of children's subjective values as well. Children's own experiences with different activities can influence how much they like or are interested in different activities; for instance, some children will find reading fascinating, and others will find it boring. Parents and teachers provide children with feedback about the importance and usefulness of different activities (e.g., doing well in school is important; you need to learn math so you can become a scientist), which can influence children's own valuing of them (Wigfield et al., 2006). Children also likely compare their interest in different activities to those of their peers, and these kinds of value-related social comparisons may influence children's own valuing of the activity. More broadly, cultural norms and ideas about what is appropriate for different children to do can influence the value children place on different activities (see Eccles, 2005). If engineering is defined as a male-dominated domain in a culture, then females may be less likely to value it and, as a consequence, choose it less as a major.

Wigfield (1994) discussed how the different components of value may develop across the childhood years. He made several points with respect to their developmental trajectory. First, given the factor analytic results reported earlier, it would appear that the components of task value are not clearly differentiated until the middle childhood years. With respect to which develops first, Wigfield argued that task value likely appears first in the form of interest in different kinds of activities, toys, and other experiences. Children are actively involved in a variety of things, and they likely become quite interested in some and less interested in others. These interests may be quite transitory at first, but over time they can develop into stable, longer lasting interests (see Guthrie, Hoa, et al., 2007; Hidi & Harackiewicz, 2000, for discussion of how immediate or situated interests in specific activities can develop into long-term personal interests). Because usefulness requires a more elaborate understanding of the purposes of different activities and because importance is defined with respect to the individual's sense of self, these task value components likely develop through middle childhood and into adolescence.

Wigfield (1994) argued further that children's conceptions or understandings of what it means to value something likely change over time as well. This is perhaps most easily illustrated with the usefulness component of task value. As discussed earlier, utility or usefulness has to do with how an activity relates to other plans the individual has, such as taking a certain math class in order to get into veterinarian school. In this instance the student may not be especially interested in the class, but is taking it for another purpose. Young children likely have a rudimentary sense of this process, as the idea of doing one thing in order to accomplish something else is complex cognitively. Further, in terms of their school experiences young children probably have a sense that one of the reasons they attend school is to learn things they will need later on, but their initial sense of exactly what skills they will need later on in life in all likelihood is murky. As they go through school and develop interest in particular school subject areas, they likely then begin to understand better how different subjects or activities can be useful in furthering these interests.

As noted earlier, attainment value or importance relates to how tasks or activities fit in with the individual's sense of themselves. Tasks gain importance when they are tied to one's identity as a person. Given this definition it is likely that importance undergoes an important developmental progression as well, perhaps (like utility) arising out of interest in different activities. As a child more clearly understands who she is and which kinds of activities relate to that emerging sense of self, the importance component of task value will become more clearly defined, and children will have a clearer sense of the importance of different tasks and activities to them. For instance, a student who finds math interesting and does well in math may begin to see math as an important part of her academic identity. Thus, math activities would take on more salience for this individual, and become increasingly important to her.

Sources of Value Recently, Higgins (2007) discussed five general sources of our value for different activities or tasks. The first is need satisfaction, where the activity satisfies some kind of biological need, such as hunger reduction. Higgins described this source as quite basic in the sense that no reflection or cognition is involved in this source of value. The second source of value is shared beliefs about what is desirable. Although this source rests in the individual because it consists of beliefs, culture and social context have a strong influence on what kinds of beliefs about the desirable are shared among a given group of individuals. Higgins discussed how standards of excellence are involved in this source of value.

The third source of value is derived from the relation of ones' current actual self to either desired or undesired end states. Higgins argued that socializers' views on what kind of person their child should turn out to be are a strong influence on the development of values, and influence the person's ideas about what appropriate end states are and how to reach them through the regulation of their behavior. He also stated that social comparison is an important source of information with respect to the self's relation to desired end states. One way of understanding how close one is to reaching the desired or ideal end state is to compare oneself to similar others. Discrepancies between where one is and where one thinks one should be (the ideal or ought self) are also crucial; when actual and ought selves are closer to congruence, then the individual is better off psychologically. Thus, activities that help promote congruence between the actual and ideal self should have more value to the individual. To continue with the example above from math, students who value math may have an "ideal self" with respect to math. Activities that help them attain aspects of this ideal self will be perceived as valuable to these individuals.

Fourth is value from evaluative inference, and Higgins (2007) focuses on Bem's (1965, 1967) self-perception theory in discussing this source of value. Bem discussed how people make inferences about themselves and attempt to judge their own actions in logical and inferential ways. Activities will be valued to the extent that they help individuals reflect on and evaluate themselves accurately. Further, individuals prefer it when the actions in which they engage come from their own volition; such actions and activities are of most value to the individual.

Fifth is value from one's experiences. Higgins (2007) tied this source of value to the long-standing distinction in both philosophy and psychology between belief and action, arguing that beliefs and cognitions are not enough to generate action and therefore cannot be the sole source of the value of something. Higgins discussed several broad types of experiences that can create value. First are experiences that create pleasure versus those that create pain, and Higgins discussed the large body of work showing that in general humans value activities that provide pleasure more than those that provide pain. Indeed, he argued that the utility of an action often is based in its production of pleasure rather than pain. Moral or ethical experiences are different from the previous type because they involve consideration of how one's action influences others, and also involve approval and disapproval rather than just pleasure or pain. Next, there are regulatory fit experiences, which have to do with how one's actions during the pursuit of a goal relate to their overall orientation to the goal. Thus, it is not the outcome itself that is the source of value for an activity, but the way in which the activity is approached. Related to this latter type are understanding experiences, or experiences having to do with making sense of the world and one's actions in it. Higgins ties these experiences to attribution theory and Festinger's (1957) cognitive dissonance theory. People like to think they understand the world and have balance and consistency in their views about their actions. When there is dissonance rather than consistency, individuals will try to overcome the dissonance. Thus activities that reduce dissonance have more value. Finally, agentic experiences refer to experiences that individuals believe they control. Following White (1959) and others (including Bandura, 1977), Higgins discussed how seeing oneself as an agent can create value irrespective of whether a particular (biological) need is being satisfied. That is, the experience of agency is valuable in and of itself, irrespective of how the ultimate action one engages in satisfies a need. Further, when faced with a challenging or difficult activity the sense of agency becomes particularly important, and actions that help the individual overcome challenges are especially valuable.

Sources of Value: Developmental Considerations How might these different sources of value play out over the course of child and adolescent development with respect to children's valuing of different academic activities? With respect to need satisfaction, in certain respects this source may not be directly relevant to the valuing of academic activities, because such activities do not directly satisfy biological needs, if need satisfaction is taken in the strict sense of the biological need satisfaction that Higgins (2007) describes. However, there are a number of needs that children have that are relevant to this source. Foremost of these is the need or desire to please important adults; most children do appear to want to do this. Because school is very important to most parents and certainly to teachers, a way to satisfy this need for approval from adults is to work hard in school and attempt to do well. Indeed, the literature on how teachers socialize children in school suggests that teachers often rely on students' desire to please the teacher as a way to socialize children into conforming to the rules and roles of school (Blumenfeld, Pintrich, Meece, & Wessels, 1982). As children get older, the desire to please parents and teachers may wane to a degree, and the desire to please peers may become more important. With respect to the valuing of school, there likely are individual differences with respect to how different peer groups approach school. Groups of children with similar levels of motivation and achievement tend to coalesce (Kindermann, 1993, 2007) and so children whose peers wish to succeed in school likely themselves value school, at least in part to get along well with the group. Peer groups who resist school may lead children in that group or who want to be in that group to devalue school.

The shared beliefs about what is desirable also takes its initial form from parents' beliefs about schooling, and then teachers' beliefs. As noted earlier, most parents state that schooling is important to their children and think of education as the major way for children to ready themselves to be productive citizens in our society (Galper, Wigfield, & Seefeldt, 1997; Stevenson, Chen, &

Uttal, 1990). They therefore likely communicate these beliefs to children as a way for children to understand that school is important. Many teachers also communicate the importance of school to children, and these messages and the ways in which teachers communicate their own enthusiasm for learning increases children's valuing of learning (Brophy, 1999, 2004). As children get older, these messages and conversations about school become more specific, as children, parents, and teachers come to understand children's academic strengths, weaknesses, and interests. It likely is the case that when parents and children's beliefs about what is important in school and its out-comes (e.g., going to medical school) are similar, children's valuing of these activities is increased in important ways. If children and parents have quite different ideas about this, problems could arise that could lead children to de-value at least some aspects of schooling.

The next two sources (connections of self-regulation to end states, making evaluative inferences) involve relatively complex cognitive judgments and so likely are not major sources of academic task value during the early school years. As children develop clearer ideas about themselves, learn to understand and regulate their behavior, and have clear ideas of who they are and who they want to be, these two sources may become more prominent. We suggest that this will begin to occur during the middle childhood years and continue through adolescence.

Higgins' (2007) final source of value is experience. There are many ways in which children's experiences with different tasks and activities can influence the development of their valuing for these activities. Examples were given earlier about how children's experiences with different toys, books, and other things may generate interest in those activities, or decrease it. A major aspect of experience as a source of value is the extent to which the activity provides pleasure or pain, and Higgins noted that most individuals are motivated to obtain pleasure and avoid pain. Children's experiences in school determine how much school is pleasurable versus painful, in a number of ways. We mention two major sets of experiences. First is children's performance in school. Chil-dren who do well in their classes, receive good grades, and otherwise do well in school are more likely to see school as pleasurable than are children who do poorly; for this latter group school attendance can become psychologically painful as their failures in school mount. Thus following Higgins, the first group of children should value school more. Second are children's experiences with different teachers and school contexts; do teachers teach in interesting ways, attempting to engage children in school and otherwise support their learning activities? Are the schools that children attend strong learning communities, or not? These kinds of contextual experiences likely have a great deal to do with how much children value schooling and learning (Brophy, 1999, 2004; Wigfield, Hoa, & Klauda, 2008). We return to a specific example of this later. Another of the experiential sources that may be present quite early is agentic experiences. When children do well in school and believe they are the ones responsible for that good performance their value for school may grow more strongly.

The other kinds of experiences Higgins (2007) described (moral or ethical experiences, "fit" experiences, understanding experiences) all may become more important as children proceed through school, in large part because of the complex cognitive demands they place on children. Truly understanding the causes or reasons for one's experiences in school or other places is some-thing that develops over the childhood years (Connell, 1985; Wigfield et al., 2006).

The Role of Educational Contexts in the Development of Expectancies and Values

Children's experiences in school have strong influences on their developing expectancy-related beliefs and values, and these influences range from broad school and classroom climate factors to the specific kinds of interactions children have with teachers and classroom activities (Eccles & Midgley, 1989; Wigfield, Eccles, & Rodriguez, 1998). Indeed, many researchers are studying how different educational contexts influence children's developing motivation (see Perry, Turner, & Meyer, 2006; Urdan, 1999; Wigfield et al., 1998 for review). We have learned much about educational contexts which support students' motivation and also those that don't (Perry et al., 2006; Stipek, 1996, 2002; Wigfield et al., 1998). Some of the principles emerging from this work are that classrooms can foster students' motivation when: a) there is a focus on learning and mastery rather than solely on performance outcomes; b) teachers hold the belief that all children can learn and have high expectations for children's learning; c) students have increasing control over their learning and many opportunities for making decisions about what they do in school; d) relationships between teachers and students are positive and emotionally supportive; e) relationships among students are collaborative and cooperative; f) public information about student performance is minimized; and g) the cognitive content of the curriculum is challenging, interesting, and focused on higher-order thinking for all children.

Although we have learned much about the kinds of educational contexts and practices that support student motivation, there still are not many instructional programs in different subject areas that directly incorporate these ideas into daily teaching practices. One reading comprehension instructional program that does this is Concept Oriented Reading Instruction (CORI). Here we describe CORI and discuss its impact on constructs related to children's expectancy-related beliefs and values, as one specific example of positive instructional influences on motivation.

The purpose of CORI is to help children become truly engaged readers, that is, strategic, knowledge-driven, motivated and socially interactive in their reading activities (Guthrie, Wigfield, & Perencevich, 2004a). To achieve this aim, CORI teachers are trained to instruct students in a variety of reading comprehension strategies for information and narrative text and to implement a set of five motivational practices grounded in achievement motivation research: hands-on activities, conceptual knowledge goals, interesting texts, autonomy support, and collaboration support.[1] Reading instruction is integrated with instruction related to a conceptual theme in science or social studies, such as "The Interdependency of Life in Communities" that provides rich content for teaching the comprehension strategies and applying the motivational practices (see Guthrie et al., 2004a; Swan, 2003, for detailed overviews of CORI). Here we focus on our recent CORI project that merged reading and science instruction during elementary school.

In the theoretical framework underlying CORI, it is the joint implementation of strategy instruction and motivational practices that fosters students' engagement in reading, and thereby their growth in comprehension (Guthrie & Wigfield, 2000). Learning specific comprehension strategies, such as activating background knowledge and making inferences, may contribute to children increasing their expectancies for success in reading and valuing of it. However, because of the nature of this Handbook we focus here on the CORI motivational practices as they were implemented in the most recent CORI intervention study conducted in elementary school because they may relate more directly to children's expectancies and values. (For more information about the comprehension strategies, see Guthrie & Taboada, 2004.)

Hands-on activities is the practice of involving students personally in experiments, observations, and simulations of processes related to the conceptual theme of the unit currently being taught (Guthrie, 2004; Guthrie, Wigfield, & Perencevich, 2004b). For example, for the "Interdependency of Life" theme, students observed pairs of horseshoe crabs and conducted a bee pollination experiment, both across multiple days (Perencevich, Guthrie, & Taboada, 2004). Teachers implement the hands-on activities, especially at the start of a unit, to stimulate students to form their own questions and interests related to the conceptual theme. The activities are designed to *not* provide all the information students need to satisfy their curiosities, but rather to encourage them to read and search for further information in books, articles, and Internet resources, that is, increase their motivation and valuing of reading. Indeed, one study of CORI showed that participation in relatively high numbers of stimulating tasks tied to hands-on activities was related to increased intrinsic reading motivation during the course of the intervention (Guthrie et al., 2006).

Second, CORI teachers emphasize *conceptual knowledge goals* and the relatedness of all activities to the one central theme throughout the instructional unit (Guthrie, 2004; Guthrie et al., 2004b). In other words, CORI teachers emphasize mastery and learning goals much more than performance goals. For example, for the "Interdependency of Life" theme, students focused on understanding such concepts as mutualism, parasitism, predation, and competition (Perencevich et al., 2004), rather than, for example, memorizing facts about numerous animals and plants. This practice aligns with the contention of Higgins (2007) that shared beliefs are an important source of value. Having teachers who frequently communicate that they want students to learn a set of concepts related to the instructional theme and who explicitly teach students about those concepts and how they can learn more about them (i.e., by using reading strategies) can influence children to espouse conceptual knowledge goals themselves and help them understand the key role that reading may play in fulfilling them.

The next motivational practice, the *provision of interesting texts*, means that rather than employing basal readers or science textbooks, CORI supplies students with a wide variety of high-quality information and literary trade books related to the conceptual theme. The information books always include features, like a table of contents, index, and glossary, that make them apt for applying the comprehension strategies taught in CORI. The literary books include novels, poetry, folk tales and legends. Numerous books of both types are selected that are appropriate for diverse reading levels. Special care is taken to find books for struggling readers that do not sacrifice depth, accuracy, or interestingness for easiness to read (Davis & Tonks, 2004). This practice, then, particularly supports students' expectancy beliefs, as it helps enable all students to frequently experience success, as well as enjoyment, in their school reading, which should lead to more positive beliefs about their future chances for success in the classroom.

A fourth CORI motivational practice is *autonomy support*, which means helping students develop control over their learning (Guthrie, 2004; Guthrie et al., 2004b). For example, students might be given choices about what books or sections of books to read or in what written or oral format they will share the knowledge they gleaned from reading. CORI teachers, however, support student autonomy not by simply letting their students make lots of choices, but by modeling decision-making processes and carefully scaffolding the choices that they give. Students' valuing of reading may increase due to autonomy support if students make decisions that reflect their personal interests, preferences, and talents, giving them more investment in the outcomes of activities when the teacher decides everything for them (Au, 1997; Guthrie et al., 2004b). In other words, the personalization of reading activities promotes the attainment value or importance that students associate with reading.

Lastly, CORI teachers enact the practice of *collaboration support* by frequently providing opportunities for students to work as pairs, teams, or a whole class (Guthrie, 2004; Guthrie et al., 2004b). They may employ several types of group sizes within even one period, and often form groups on different bases: for instance, sometimes they consist of students of similar reading levels, whereas other times they consist of mixed levels, or are formed on the basis of student interests. Some tasks on which students collaborate are conducting science experiments, generating questions for research, analyzing novels, and writing and presenting reports. Teachers give their students guidelines for interacting and sometimes assign or have students select roles within their groups. This practice is implemented in CORI because collaboration in reading has been linked to increased reading comprehension performance (Ng, Guthrie, Van Meter, McCann, & Alao, 1998) and because social interaction is intrinsically motivating for many students (Guthrie, 2004).

Much research has been conducted on CORI, and results indicate that this set of practices, implemented in conjunction with reading comprehension strategies, has significant positive effects on elementary school students' reading motivation as well as their reading comprehension and other cognitive variables. Recently, Guthrie, McRae, & Klauda (2007) meta-analyzed 11 quasi-experimental studies that investigated how CORI impacted third- through fifth-grade students, in comparison to two other types of instruction: an intervention that involved the strategy instruction but not the motivational component of CORI and traditional reading instruction employing basal readers. Most relevant to the value construct of expectancy-value theory, CORI showed moderate to strong positive effects on self-report measures of curiosity (M ES = .47; N ES = 5) and task orientation (that is, enjoying reading and reading for long periods; M ES = .29; N ES = 3) and a composite measure of intrinsic reading motivation (M ES = 1.20; N ES = 1). Most relevant to the expectancy construct, CORI showed moderate effects on self-report measures of self-efficacy (M ES = .49; N ES = 5) and perceived difficulty (M ES = .29; N ES = 2). In addition, CORI had moderate to strong positive effects on several cognitive variables, including reading comprehension (measured with both standardized and experimenter-created measures), reading strategy use, science knowledge, word recognition speed, and oral reading fluency.

Broader Cultural Influences on Expectancy-Related Beliefs and Values

Now, we turn to cultural influences on the expectancy, task value and ability belief constructs. As stated above, the Eccles et al. (1983) expectancy-value model was originally developed to explain gender differences in mathematics performance and choice, a sociocultural phenomenon in and of itself. Further, from the beginning, it has been acknowledged that cultural influences help determine expectancy beliefs and values, and their relationships with choice, persistence, and performance. Therefore this model is an exceptionally appropriate starting point for investigating motivation and behavioral choices in cultural context (Wigfield, Tonks, & Eccles, 2004).

To consider culture as a determinant, we consider cross-cultural research that has been conducted on the key constructs of the model in Figure 4.1. Included are studies comparing students who live in different countries, which is one of the many meanings of the term cross-cultural as it applies to psychological research (Poortinga, 1997). This discussion is framed in terms of the key constructs and links from the Eccles et al. model (1983) that have been addressed in cross-cultural research.

Cross-Cultural Research on Expectancy and Ability Beliefs There has been some cross-cultural research on expectancy beliefs and ability beliefs. One group of researchers looked cross-sectionally at the competence beliefs of second- and eighth-grade students in Hong Kong (Chang, McBride-Chang, Stewart, & Au, 2003), and found more positive beliefs among the younger children in the domains of academic and sports self-competence. Such results are similar to findings in the United States reviewed above. The authors wrote that similar to U.S. children, Hong Kong children face various transitions around the time of middle school that may cause competence beliefs to decrease. It would be interesting to know if such decreases occur universally and what role culture plays in this process.

A number of studies have looked at mean differences in competence beliefs across cultures, generally finding that students in the United States, Canada, and England have higher competence beliefs than students in East Asian cultures and in Russia (e.g., Elliott, Hufton, Illushin, & Lauchlan, 2001; Kwok & Lytton, 1996; Stevenson, Lee, Chen, Stigler, et al., 1990; Stigler, Smith, & Mao, 1985; for more complete review, see Hufton, Elliott, & Illushin, 2002a, and Zusho & Pintrich, 2003). Such differences between East Asian and Western cultures have been explained in terms of the psychological tendency for students from East Asia to self-criticize, whereas students from Western cultures tend to self-enhance in their presentations (e.g., Heine & Hamamura, 2007; Kitayama, Markus, Matsumoto, & Norasakkunkit, 1997). A number of researchers have investigated this phenomenon in recent years, focusing mainly on Japan and the United States, and the literature has become increasingly complex, some researchers claiming that self-enhancement is universal, and others arguing that it is not. For example, Sedikides, Gaertner, & Toguchi (2003) studied U.S. and Japanese university students and found that Japanese students do self-enhance, but that they focus on collectivistic attributes such as cooperation and responsibility to the group, whereas U.S. students tend to self-enhance on individualistic attributes such as independence and putting oneself before the group. Conversely, after conducting a meta-analysis, Heine and Hamamura concluded that compared to Westerners who self-enhance, East Asians do not self-enhance, while Asian Americans' level of self-enhancement fell in between these two groups. The authors' interpretation would seem to then explain the higher ratings of self-competence in the above studies.

Cross-Cultural Research on Task Values In general, there has been less work done on students' task values in non-western settings than on students' expectancies and ability beliefs. Nevertheless, some studies exist, and provide a good base for further research. Bong (2001) included three components of task value (importance, usefulness, and interest) in her study of motivational constructs among Korean middle and high school students. Her results were consistent with studies in Western groups of students: Task values in four different subject areas were distinct conceptually, but somewhat more differentiated among the high school students, as compared to the middle school students, implying developmental change in differentiation. In addition, task values correlated positively with academic self-efficacy and mastery goal perceptions. Notably in this study, Bong wrote very little about cultural influences, nor about differences in the task values of Korean students and Western students, perhaps due to the striking similarities in her findings.

Another study by Henderson, Marx, and Kim (1999) investigated U.S., Korean, and Japanese children's interest in numbers, words, and ideas, which they called academic activities. Using cross-sectional data and a one-item indicator of interest, they found a decrease in children's interest in numbers and words from second to fifth grade. Although preliminary, this finding is consistent with decrease in subjective values found by Eccles and colleagues (see above). Clearly, more research looking at the development of task values in various cultures is needed.

Turning now to the question of whether students in different cultures value activities differently, a handful of studies have addressed this. Stevenson, Lee, Chen, Lummis, et al. (1990) had first and fifth graders from Chicago and Beijing rate their interest in math. Although a higher percentage of Beijing students (85%) reported liking math than did Chicago students (72%), both groups were relatively high. Randel, Stevenson, and Witruk (2000) reported that 11th grade students in Germany reported liking math more than Japanese 11th graders. Findings are too few to draw any meaningful conclusions in this area. Further, interest and other aspects of task values may take on different meanings, depending on culture and language. Therefore, research assessing various aspects of task value and investigating meanings unique to different cultures is needed.

Regarding how task values relate to performance and choices cross-culturally, a few studies have shown that interest measured by items similar to those used by Eccles, Wigfield and colleagues relates to children's achievement. Stevenson, Lee, Chen, Stigler, et al. (1990) showed that relations between interest in math and achievement in math were similar among first and fifth graders in Taiwan, Japan, and the United States. Randel et al. (2000) showed a positive correlation between math attitude (interest in and liking of math) and achievement in Japanese 11th graders, but not their German counterparts. We know of no cross-cultural work relating task values to choice similar to work done by Eccles, Wigfield, and colleagues. How task values relate to students' performance and choice in different cultures is a wide open field, and we look forward to future research in this area.

Differences in the Meaning of Ability Beliefs and Balues across Cultures Central to any discussion of cross-cultural research should be the question of whether a construct has the same meaning or is perceived in the same way in different cultures. Van de Vijver (2001) wrote about the importance of ensuring that constructs are equivalent in the different cultural groups when doing cross-cultural research. Differences in construct meaning can jeopardize the equivalence of data across cultural groups. This work has not been done on expectancy beliefs per se; however, some researchers have investigated such meaning differences concerning students' ability beliefs, a belief closely connected to expectancies. Hufton, Elliott, and Illushin (2002a, 2002b) interviewed adolescents in England, Russia, and the United States, and found cultural differences in the students' notions of ability. For example, students in Russia were the most likely to see ability as the outcome of effort, and exerted the most academic effort compared to students in the other two countries. U.S. students discussed "smart" as something that that can be increased by effort, and British students saw intelligence as somewhat less changeable. The authors noted that measures of ability beliefs need to reflect such differences in meaning.

As noted earlier, very little cross-cultural work has been done on the meaning of value as conceived in expectancy-value theory. Wigfield et al. (2004) speculated about ways that each of the components of task value might differ across cultures. Utility value or usefulness is a good example. In cultures where high importance is placed on the group (i.e., collectivistic cultures), usefulness to the group may play a large role in determining an individual's utility value of a task. In addition, different adult roles may be valued differently across cultures, so then the utility value of behaviors and activities that are instrumental in achieving those adult roles will also vary across cultures. For example, school teachers may be valued more highly in East Asian countries than in the United States (Stevenson & Stigler, 1992). This respect could cause students in East Asia to value the behaviors and activities that lead to becoming a teacher more highly than students in the United States. One could speculate in similar ways for each of the value components, indicating that cross-cultural studies on the components of task values are likely to yield interesting findings.

All in all, few researchers have looked at the expectancy-value model of Eccles and colleagues in other cultures. Therefore our knowledge based on non-Western research only skims the surface of possibility. Expectancy-value theory is well-suited for cross-cultural investigations, as it affords tests of individual links within the model (see Figure 4.1), but is flexible and adaptable to change based on new findings from diverse populations. As Wigfield et al. (2004) noted, based on future research done in various cultures, additional constructs may need to be added, and existing constructs may need to be adapted to better explain linkages between constructs in different cultures.

Conclusions

Research stemming from expectancy-value models of motivation continues to thrive in various achievement domains, as researchers from across the world have used these models as theoretical frameworks for their work. We have learned much about how children's expectancy-related beliefs and values change across the elementary and secondary school years, relate to one another, and predict outcomes such as performance in different areas and choices of activities to pursue. We also have learned how different educational contexts and practices influence children's expectancies and values.

We close with two general suggestions for future research directions in this area. First, as research on expectancy-related beliefs and values continues, we think it is especially important to continue to focus on achievement values. Although research on task values has increased, it still lags behind research on expectancy-related beliefs. We think an understanding of children's valuing and de-valuing of different activities is particularly important for developing interventions to foster children's motivation, especially for children who seem apathetic or resistant to schooling. Indeed, Brophy (2004) says that student apathy is the most challenging motivational problem that teachers face. Graham and Taylors' recent work is an important step in this direction, but more work is needed.

Second, we need much more work on the development of expectancies and values in diverse groups of children. Although this work is increasing (see Wigfield et al., 2006, for review), much more needs to be done. Gender differences in expectancies and values have been a continuing focus of Eccles, Wigfield, and their colleagues work. Taylor and Graham's work suggests that there are interesting gender by ethnicity interactions with respect to children's valuing of achievement, using their nomination measure described earlier. African American, Caucasian, and Latino girls nominate high achieving girls as whom they wanted to be like. This also was true for Caucasian boys, but not for African American and Latino boys, particularly after students entered middle school. There are many other interesting questions that await research. These include whether relations of expectancies, values, performance, and choice are similar in different ethnic groups. Another interesting question is whether the developmental declines in expectancies and values found in the Eccles and Wigfield work also occur in other ethnic groups.

Acknowledgment

Much of the research on the development of children's competence beliefs and values discussed in this chapter was supported by Grant HD-17553 from the National Institute of Child Health and Human Development (NICHD). Other research discussed in this chapter was supported by Grant MH-31724 from the National Institute for Mental Health, HD-17296 from NICHD, Grant BNS-8510504 from the National Science Foundation, and grants from the Spencer Foundation.

Note

1. In recent writings Guthrie and his colleagues have re-named some of these motivational practices and added others, in an effort to generalize them to subject areas other than science and to make them more accessible to teachers (see Guthrie & Coddington, this volume; Guthrie, McRae, & Klauda, 2007). *Relevance* involves practices designed to relate instructional content to students' experience and background knowledge, through the use of hands-on activities and interesting texts. *Choices* are teachers' ways of supporting students' autonomy for their learning. *Success* involves practices that ensure that students are able to master meaningful classroom tasks in ways that enhance their self-efficacy and expectancies for success. *Collaboration* is opportunity to interact with other students around

learning, and *thematic units* means presenting the content of reading and other instructional activities in organized and conceptually connected ways, rather than in piecemeal fashion.

References

Ajzen, J. (1991). The theory of planned behavior. *Organizational Behavior and Human Decision Processes, 50,* 179–221.

Atkinson, J. W. (1957). Motivational determinants of risk taking behavior. *Psychological Review, 64,* 359–372.

Atkinson, J. W. (1964). *An introduction to motivation.* Princeton, NJ: Van Nostrand.

Au, K. H. (1997). Ownership, literacy achievement, and students of diverse cultural backgrounds. In J. T. Guthrie & A. Wigfield (Eds.), *Reading engagement: Motivating readers through integrated instruction* (pp. 168–182). Newark, DE: International Reading Association.

Bandura, A. (1977). Self-efficacy: Toward a unifying theory of behavioral change. *Psychological Review, 84,* 191–215.

Bandura, A. (1997). *Self-efficacy: The exercise of control.* New York: W. H. Freeman.

Battle, E. (1965). Motivational determinants of academic task persistence. *Journal of Personality and Social Psychology, 2,* 209–218.

Battle, E. (1966). Motivational determinants of academic competence. *Journal of Personality and Social Psychology, 4,* 534–642.

Battle, A., & Wigfield, A. (2003). College women's value orientations toward family, career, and graduate school. *Journal of Vocational Behavior, 62,* 56–75.

Bem, D. J. (1965). An experimental analysis of self-persuasion. *Journal of Experimental Social Psychology, 1,* 199–218.

Bem, D. J. (1967). Self-perception: An alternative interpretation of cognitive dissonance phenomena. *Psychological Review, 74,* 183–200.

Blumenfeld, P. C., Pintrich, P. R., Meece, J., & Wessels, K. (1982). The formation and role of self perceptions of ability in elementary classrooms. *The Elementary School Journal, 82,* 401–420.

Bong, M. (2001). Role of self-efficacy and task value in predicting college students' course enrollments and intentions. *Contemporary Educational Psychology, 26,* 553–570.

Brophy, J. E. (1999). Toward a model of the value aspects of motivation in education: Developing appreciation for particular learning domains and activities. *Educational Psychologist, 34,* 75–85.

Brophy, J. E. (2004). *Motivating students to learn* (2nd ed). Mahwah, NJ: Erlbaum.

Burhans, K. K., & Dweck, C. S. (1995). Helplessness in early childhood: The role of contingent worth. *Child Development, 66,* 1719–1738.

Chang, L., McBride-Chang, C., Stewart, S. M., & Au, E. (2003). Life satisfaction, self-concept, and family relations in Chinese adolescents and children. *International Journal of Behavioral Development, 27,* 182–189.

Connell, J. P. (1985). A new multidimensional measure of children's perception of control. *Child Development, 56,* 1018–1041.

Davis, M. H., & Tonks, S. (2004). Diverse texts and technology for reading. In J. T. Guthrie, A. Wigfield, & K. C. Perencevich (Eds.), *Motivating reading comprehension: Concept-Oriented Reading Instruction* (pp. 143–172). Mahwah, NJ: Erlbaum.

Deci, E. L., & Ryan, R. M. (2002). The paradox of achievement: The harder you push, the worse it gets. In J. Aronson (Ed.), *Improving academic achievement: Impact of psychological factors on education* (pp. 61–87). San Diego: Academic Press.

Dennissen, J. J. A., Zarret, N. R., & Eccles, J. S. (2007). I like to do it, I'm able, and I know I am: Longitudinal couplings between domain-specific achievement, self-concept, and interest. *Child Development, 78,* 430–447.

Durik, A. M., Vida, M., & Eccles, J. S. (2006). Task values and ability beliefs as predictors of high school literacy choices: A developmental analysis. *Journal of Educational Psychology, 98,* 382–393.

Dweck, C. S. (2002). The development of ability conceptions. In A. Wigfield & J. S. Eccles (Eds.), *Development of achievement motivation* (pp. 57–88). San Diego: Academic Press.

Dweck, C. S., & Elliott, E. S. (1983). Achievement motivation. In P. H. Mussen (Ed.), *Handbook of child psychology* (Vol. IV, 3rd. ed., pp. 643–691). New York: Wiley.

Eccles, J. S. (1984). Sex differences in achievement patterns. In T. Sonderegger (Ed.), *Nebraska Symposium on Motivation* (Vol. 32, pp. 97–132). Lincoln: University of Nebraska Press.

Eccles, J. S. (1987). Gender roles and women's achievement-related decisions. *Psychology of Women Quarterly, 11,* 135–172.

Eccles, J. S. (1993). School and family effects on the ontogeny of children's interests, self-perceptions, and activity choice. In J. Jacobs (Ed.), *Nebraska Symposium on Motivation, 1992: Developmental perspectives on motivation* (pp. 145–208). Lincoln: University of Nebraska Press.

Eccles, J. S. (2005). Subjective task values and the Eccles et al. model of achievement related choices. In A. J. Elliott & C. S. Dweck (Eds.), *Handbook of competence and motivation* (pp. 105–121). New York: Guilford.

Eccles, J. S., & Harold, R. D. (1991). Gender differences in sport involvement: Applying the Eccles' expectancy-value model. *Journal of Applied Sport Psychology, 3,* 7–35.

Eccles, J. S., & Midgley, C. (1989). Stage/environment fit: Developmentally appropriate classrooms for early adolescents. In R. Ames & C. Ames (Eds.), *Research on motivation in education* (Vol. 3, pp. 139–181). New York: Academic Press.

Eccles, J. S., & Wigfield, A. (1995). In the mind of the achiever: The structure of adolescents' academic achievement related-beliefs and self-perceptions. *Personality and Social Psychology Bulletin, 21*, 215–225.

Eccles, J. S., Wigfield, A., Harold, R., & Blumenfeld, P. B. (1993). Age and gender differences in children's self- and task perceptions during elementary school. *Child Development, 64*, 830–847.

Eccles, J. S., Wigfield, A., & Schiefele, U. (1998). Motivation to succeed. In W. Damon (Series Ed.) & N. Eisenberg (Vol. Ed.) *Handbook of child psychology* (5th ed., Vol. III, pp. 1017–1095). New York: Wiley.

Eccles (Parsons), J. S., Adler, T. F., Futterman, R., Goff, S. B., Kaczala, C. M., Meece, J. L., & Midgley, C. (1983). Expectancies, values, and academic behaviors. In J. T. Spence (Ed.), *Achievement and achievement motivation* (pp. 75–146). San Francisco, CA: W. H. Freeman.

Elliott, J. G., Hufton, H., Illushin, L., & Lauchlan, F. (2001). Motivation in the junior years: International perspectives on children's attitudes, expectations, and behaviour and their relationship to educational achievement. *Oxford Review of Education, 27*, 37–68.

Feather, N. T. (1982). Expectancy-value approaches: Present status and future directions. In N. T. Feather (Ed.), *Expectations and actions: Expectancy-value models in psychology* (pp. 395–420). Hillsdale, NJ: Erlbaum.

Feather, N. T. (1988). Values, valences, and course enrollment: Testing the role of personal values within an expectancy-value framework. *Journal of Educational Psychology, 80*, 381–391.

Festinger, L. (1957). *A theory of cognitive dissonance*. Evanston, IL: Row, Peterson.

Fishbein, M., & Ajzen, J. (1975). *Beliefs, attitudes, intention and behavior: An introduction to theory and research*. Reading, MA: Addison-Wesley.

Fredricks, J., & Eccles, J. S. (2002). Children's competence and value beliefs from childhood through adolescence: Growth trajectories in two male sex-typed domains. *Developmental Psychology, 38*, 519–533.

Galper, A., Wigfield, A., & Seefeldt, C. (1997). Head Start parents' beliefs about their children's abilities, task values, and performance on different activities. *Child Development, 68*, 897–907.

Graham, S., & Taylor, A. Z. (2002). Ethnicity, gender, and the development of achievement values. In A. Wigfield & J. S. Eccles (Eds.), *Development of achievement motivation* (pp. 121–146). San Diego: Academic Press.

Graham, S., Taylor, A. Z., & Hudley, C. (1998).Exploring achievement values among ethnic minority early adolescents. *Journal of Educational Psychology, 90*, 606–620.

Guthrie, J. T. (2004). Classroom contexts for engaged reading: An overview. In J. T. Guthrie, A. Wigfield, & K. C. Perencevich (Eds.), *Motivating reading comprehension: Concept-Oriented Reading Instruction* (pp. 87–112). Mahwah, NJ: Erlbaum.

Guthrie, J. T., Hoa, L., Wigfield, A., Tonks, S., Humenick, N., & Littles, E. (2007). Reading motivation and reading comprehension growth in the later elementary years. *Contemporary Educational Psychology 32*, 282–313.

Guthrie, J. T., McRae, A. C., & Klauda, S. L. (2007). Contributions of Concept-Oriented Reading Instruction to knowledge about interventions for motivations in reading. *Educational Psychologist, 42*, 237–250.

Guthrie, J. T. & Taboada, A. (2004). Fostering the cognitive strategies of reading comprehension. In J. T. Guthrie, A. Wigfield, & K. C. Perencevich (Eds.), *Motivating reading comprehension: Concept-Oriented Reading Instruction* (pp. 87–112). Mahwah, NJ: Erlbaum.

Guthrie, J. T., & Wigfield, A. (2000). Engagement and motivation in reading. In M. L. Kamil, P. B. Mosenthal, P. D. Pearson, & R. Barr (Eds.), *Handbook of reading research* (Vol. III, pp. 403–422). Mahwah, NJ: Erlbaum.

Guthrie, J. T., Wigfield, A., Humenick, N. M., Perencevich, K. C., Taboada, A., & Barbosa, P. (2006). Influences of stimulating tasks on reading motivation and comprehension. *Journal of Educational Research, 99*, 232–245.

Guthrie, J. T., Wigfield, A., & Perencevich, K. C. (Eds.). (2004a). *Motivating reading comprehension: Concept-Oriented Reading Instruction*. Mahwah, NJ: Erlbaum.

Guthrie, J. T., Wigfield, A., & Perencevich, K. C. (2004b). Scaffolding for motivation and engagement in reading. In J. T. Guthrie, A. Wigfield, & K. C. Perencevich (Eds.), *Motivating reading comprehension: Concept-Oriented Reading Instruction* (pp. 55–86). Mahwah, NJ: Erlbaum.

Harter, S., Whitesell, N. R., & Kowalski, P. (1992). Individual differences in the effects of educational transitions on young adolescents' perceptions of competence and motivational orientation. *American Educational Research Journal, 29*, 809–835.

Harter, S. (2006). The self. In W. Damon (Series Ed.) & N. Eisenberg (Vol. Ed.), *Handbook of child psychology* (6th ed., Vol. 3, pp. 505–570). New York: Wiley.

Heine, S. J., & Hamamura, T. (2007). In search of East Asian self-enhancement. *Personality and Social Psychology Review, 11*, 1–24.

Henderson, B. B., Marx, M. H., & Kim, Y. C. (1999). Academic interests and perceived competence in American, Japanese, and Korean children. *Journal of Cross-Cultural Psychology, 30*, 32–50.

Heyman, G. D., Dweck, C. S., & Cain, K. M. (1992). Young children's vulnerability to self-blame and helplessness: Relationships to beliefs about goodness. *Child Development, 63*, 401–415.

Hidi, S., & Harackiewicz, J. (2000). Motivating the academically unmotivated: A critical issue for the 21st century. *Review of Educational Research, 70*, 151–180.

Higgins, E. T. (2007). Value. In A. W. Kruglanski & E. Tory Higgins (Eds.), *Handbook of social psychology* (2nd ed., pp. 454–472). New York: Guilford.

Hufton, N., Elliott, J. G., & Illushin, L. (2002a). Achievement motivation across cultures: Some puzzles and their implications for future research. In J. Bempechat & J. G. Elliott (Eds.), *Learning in culture and context: Approaching the complexities of achievement motivation in student learning* (Vol. 96, pp. 65–86). New York: Wiley.

Hufton, N. R., Elliott, J. G., & Illushin, L. (2002b). Educational motivation and engagement: Qualitative accounts from three countries. *British Educational Research Journal, 28*, 265–289.

Jacobs, J., Lanza, S., Osgood, D. W., Eccles, J. S., & Wigfield, A. (2002). Ontogeny of children's self-beliefs: Gender and domain differences across grades one through 12. *Child Development, 73*, 509–527.

Kindermann, T. A. (1993). Natural peer groups as contexts for individual development: The case of children's motivation in school. *Developmental Psychology, 29*, 970–977.

Kindermann, T. A. (2007). Effects of naturally existing peer groups on changes in academic engagement in a cohort of sixth graders. *Child Development, 78*, 1186–1203.

Kitayama, S., Markus, H. R., Matsumoto, H., & Norasakkunkit, V. (1997). Individual and collective processes in the construction of the self: Self-enhancement in the United States and self-criticism in Japan. *Journal of Personality & Social Psychology, 72*, 1245–1267.

Kwok, D. C., & Lytton, H. (1996). Perceptions of mathematics ability versus actual mathematics performance: Canadian and Hong Kong Chinese children. *British Journal of Educational Psychology, 66*, 209–222.

Lewin, K. (1938). *The conceptual representation and the measurement of psychological forces.* Durham, NC: Duke University Press.

Meece, J. L., Wigfield, A., & Eccles, J. S. (1990). Predictors of math anxiety and its consequences for young adolescents' course enrollment intentions and performances in mathematics. *Journal of Educational Psychology, 82*, 60–70.

Murray, H. A. (1938). *Explorations in personality.* New York: Oxford University Press.

Ng, M. M., Guthrie, J. T., Van Meter, P., McCann, A., & Alao, S. (1998). How classroom characteristics influence intrinsic motivations for literacy. *Reading Psychology, 19*, 319–398.

Pajares, F. (1996). Self-efficacy beliefs in academic settings. *Review of Educational Research, 66*, 543–578.

Pekrun, R. (2000). A social-cognitive, control-value theory of achievement emotions. In J. Heckhausen (Ed.), *Motivational psychology of human development* (pp. 143–163). Oxford, UK: Elsevier.

Perencevich, K. C., Guthrie, J. T., & Taboada, A. M. (2004, August). *Fifth grade teacher's guide: Concept-Oriented Reading Instruction.* College Park: University of Maryland.

Perry, N. E., Turner, J. C., & Meyer, D. K. (2006). Classrooms as contexts for motivating learning. In P. A. Alexander & P. H. Winne (Eds.), *Handbook of educational psychology* (2nd ed., pp. 327–348). Mahwah, NJ: Erlbaum.

Pintrich, P. R., Smith, D. A., Garcia, T., & McKeachie, W. J. (1991). A manual for the use of the Motivated Strategies for Learning Questionnaire (MSLQ). Ann Arbor, MI: National Center for Research to Improve Post Secondary Teaching and Learning.

Poortinga, Y. H. (1997). Towards convergence? In J. W. Berry, Y. H. Poortinga, & J. Pandey (Eds.), *Handbook of cross-cultural psychology: Vol 1. Theory and method* (pp. 347–387). Boston: Allyn & Bacon.

Randel, B., Stevenson, H. W., & Witruk, E. (2000). Attitudes, beliefs, and mathematics achievement of German and Japanese high school students. *International Journal of Behavioral Development, 24*, 190–198.

Renninger, K. A. (2000). Individual interest and its implications for understanding intrinsic motivation. In C. Sansone & J. M. Harackiewicz (Eds.), *Intrinsic and extrinsic motivation* (pp. 373–404). San Diego, CA: Academic Press.

Rohan, M. J. (2000). A rose by any name? The values construct. *Personality and Social Psychology Review, 4*, 255–277.

Rose, N. J., & Sherman, J. W. (2007). Expectancy. In A. W. Kruglanski & E. Tory Higgins (Eds.), *Handbook of social psychology* (2nd ed., pp. 91–115). New York: Guilford.

Ruble, D. (1983). The development of social comparison processes and their role in achievement-related self-socialization. In E. T. Higgins, D. N. Ruble, & W. W. Hartup (Eds.), *Social cognition and social development: A sociocultural perspective* (pp. 134–157). New York: Cambridge University Press.

Ryan, R. M., & Deci, E. L. (2000). Intrinsic and extrinsic motivation: Classic definitions and new directions. *Contemporary Educational Psychology, 25*, 54–67.

Schiefele, U. (2001). The role of interest in motivation and learning. In J. M. Collis & S. Messick (Eds.), *Intelligence and personality: Bridging the gap in theory and measurement* (pp. 163–194). Mahwah, NJ: Erlbaum.

Schunk, D. H., & Pajares, F. (2002). The development of academic self-efficacy. In A. Wigfield & J. S. Eccles (Eds.), *Development of achievement motivation* (pp. 15–32). San Diego: Academic Press.

Sedikides, C., Gaertner, L., & Toguchi, Y. (2003). Pancultural self-enhancement. *Journal of Personality & Social Psychology, 84*, 60–79.

Simpkins, S. D., Davis-Kean, P. E., & Eccles, J. S. (2006). Math and science motivation: A longitudinal examination of the links between choice and beliefs. *Developmental Psychology, 42*, 70–83.

Stevenson, H. W., Chen, C., & Uttal, D. H. (1990). Beliefs and achievement: A study of black, white, and Hispanic children. *Child Development, 61*, 508–523.

Stevenson, H. W., Lee, S., Chen, C., Lummis, M., Stigler, J., Fan, L., & Ge, F. (1990). Mathematics achievement of children in China and the United States. *Child Development, 61*, 1053–1066.

Stevenson, H. W., Lee, S. Y., Chen, C., Stigler, J. W., Hsu, C. C., & Kitamura, S. (1990). Contexts of achievement: A study of American, Chinese, and Japanese children. *Monographs of the Society for Research in Child Development* (Vol. 55, pp. 123). London: Blackwell.

Stevenson, H. W., & Stigler, J. W. (1992). *The learning gap: Why our schools are failing and what we can learn from Japanese and Chinese education.* New York: Summit Books.

Stigler, J. W., Smith, S., & Mao, L. (1985). The self-perception of competence by Chinese children. *Child Development, 56*, 1259–1270.

Stipek, D. J. (1996). Motivation and instruction. In R. C. Calfee & D. C. Berliner (Eds.), *Handbook of educational psychology* (pp. 85–113). New York: Macmillan.

Stipek, D. J. (2002). Good instruction is motivating. In A. Wigfield & J. S. Eccles (Eds.), *Development of achievement motivation* (pp. 309–332). San Diego: Academic Press.

Stipek, D. J., & Mac Iver, D. (1989). Developmental change in children's assessment of intellectual competence. *Child Development, 60*, 521–538.

Stipek, D. J., Recchia, S., & McClintic, S. M. (1992). Self-evaluation in young children. *Monographs of the Society for Research in Child Development, 57*(2, Serial No. 226).

Swan, E. A. (2003). *Concept-oriented reading instruction: Engaging classrooms, lifelong learners.* New York: Guilford.

Taylor, A. Z., & Graham, S. (2007). An examination of the relationship between achievement values and perceptions of barriers among low-SES African American and Latino students. *Journal of Educational Psychology, 99*, 52–64.

Tolman, E. C. (1932). *Purposive behavior in animals and men.* New York: Appleton-Century-Crofts.

Urdan, T. C. (Ed.). (1999). *The role of context: Advances in motivation and achievement* (Vol. 11). Greenwich, CT: JAI Press.

Van de Vijver, F. (2001). The evolution of cross-cultural research methods. In D. Matsumoto (Ed.), *The handbook of culture and psychology* (pp. 77–97). Oxford: Oxford University Press.

Watt, H. (2004). Development of adolescents' self-perceptions, values, and task perceptions. *Child Development, 75*, 1556–1574.

Weiner, B. (1992). *Human motivation: Metaphors, theories, and research.* Newbury Park, CA: Sage.

White, R. H. (1959). Motivation reconsidered: The concept of competence. *Psychological Review, 66*, 297–333.

Wigfield, A. (1994). Expectancy-value theory of achievement motivation: A developmental perspective. *Educational Psychology Review, 6*, 49–78.

Wigfield, A. (1997, April). *Predicting children's grades from their ability beliefs and subjective task values: Developmental and domain differences.* Paper presented at the biennial meeting of the Society for Research in Child Development, Washington, DC.

Wigfield, A., & Eccles, J. (1992). The development of achievement task values: A theoretical analysis. *Developmental Review, 12*, 265–310.

Wigfield, A., & Eccles, J. S. (2000). Expectancy-value theory of motivation. *Contemporary Educational Psychology, 25*, 68–81.

Wigfield, A., & Eccles, J. S. (2002). The development of competence beliefs, expectancies for success, and achievement values from childhood through adolescence. In A. Wigfield & J. S. Eccles (Eds.), *Development of achievement motivation* (pp. 91–120). San Diego, CA: Academic Press.

Wigfield, A., Eccles, J. S., Mac Iver, D., Reuman, D., & Midgley, C. (1991). Transitions at early adolescence: Changes in children's domain-specific self-perceptions and general self-esteem across the transition to junior high school. *Developmental Psychology, 27*, 552–565.

Wigfield, A., Eccles, J. S., & Rodriguez, D. (1998). The development of children's motivation in school contexts. In. A. Iran-Nejad & P. D. Pearson (Eds.), Review *of research in education* (Vol. 23, pp. 73–118). Washington, DC: American Educational Research Association.

Wigfield, A., Eccles, J. S., Schiefele, U., Roeser, R. W., & Davis-Kean, P. (2006). Development of achievement motivation. In N. Eisenberg (Ed.), *Handbook of child psychology* (Vol. 3, pp. 933–1002). New York: Wiley.

Wigfield, A., Eccles, J. S., Yoon, K. S., Harold, R. D., Arbreton, A., Freedman-Doan, C., & Blumenfeld, P. C. (1997). Changes in children's competence beliefs and subjective task values across the elementary school years: A three-year study. *Journal of Educational Psychology, 89*, 451–469.

Wigfield, A., Hoa, L. W., & Klauda, S. L. (2008). The role of achievement values in the self-regulation of achievement behaviors. In D. H. Schunk & B. J. Zimmerman (Eds.), *Motivation and self-regulated learning: Theory, research, and applications* (pp. 169–195). Mahwah, NJ: Erlbaum.

Wigfield, A., Tonks, S., & Eccles, J. S. (2004). Expectancy-value theory in cross-cultural perspective. In D. M. McInerney & S. Van Etten (Eds.), *Research on sociocultural influences on motivation and learning, volume 4: Big theories revisited* (pp. 165–198). Greenwich, CT: Information Age.

Zusho, A., & Pintrich, P. R. (2003). A process-oriented approach to culture: Theoretical and methodological issues in the study of culture and student motivation in a multicultural context. In F. Salili & R. Hoosain (Eds.), *Teaching, learning, and motivation in a multicultural context* (pp. 33–65). Greenwich, CT: Information Age.

5

Achievement Goal Theory
The Past, Present, and Future

Martin L. Maehr and Akane Zusho

Achievement has been, and remains, a topic of continuing concern for societies, institutions, groups, and the individuals who compose them. Factors that result in achievement are many and varied, but it is widely assumed that one of its primary elements is motivation. Numerous theoretical perspectives on the nature and nurture of motivation exist; one theory that has garnered considerable attention in recent years is achievement goal theory (also referred to as goal orientation theory). We summarize here the major findings and assumptions, both past and current, of this theoretical perspective and its implications for schooling. We conclude with a commentary on remaining challenges and future directions.

What is Goal Theory?

Defining the Achievement Goal Construct

Motivation is typically defined as that which influences the initiation, direction, magnitude, perseverance, continuation, and quality of goal-directed behavior (Dweck & Elliott, 1983; Maehr & Meyer, 1997). The significance of "goals" in such a definition is clear; according to goal theory, they are essentially what give an activity purpose or meaning (Kaplan & Maehr, 2007; Maehr & Nicholls, 1980). In short, achievement goal theory specifies the kinds of goals (purposes or reasons) that direct achievement-related behaviors.

It is important to distinguish generally how the goals defined by achievement goal theory are similar to and distinct from other goal constructs (see also Urdan & Maehr, 1995). In the psychological literature, goals are most commonly defined as the incentive or outcome a person is trying to achieve, as in this statement "my goal is to get an A in this class" (Pervin, 1989). Examples of this more content-oriented approach to goals would include Klinger's (1977) notion of current concern, Locke and Latham's (1984) goal-setting theory, Cantor and Kilstrom's (1987) work on life-tasks, Bandura's (1989) discussion of proximal and distal goals as related to self-efficacy, and Wentzel's (2000) work on social goals. These goal representations vary both in terms of their level of specificity and level of importance—from the specific and mundane, (e.g., my goal is to go pick up my clothes at the dry cleaners) to the general and personal (e.g., my goal is to be a good student). Nevertheless, what is common across these approaches is the emphasis placed on what individuals are trying to achieve.

By contrast, achievement goal theory is less concerned with *what* individuals are trying to achieve and instead focuses more on understanding *why* (Urdan & Maehr, 1995). Why, for example, would a student's goal be to get an A? Two possible reasons are suggested by achievement goal theory (Ames, 1992; Dweck & Leggett, 1988; Maehr & Nicholls, 1980; Nicholls, 1984). A student may want to get an A in the class because she wants to learn and understand the material; getting the A would indicate mastery of the content. Or, a student may want the A just to demonstrate to others (namely teachers, classmates, parents) that she was smarter than others; getting the A in this instance indicates greater academic ability, but not necessarily content mastery.

According to Urdan and Maehr (1995), when goals are defined in this way, they represent a more "superordinate category" than the content goals specified earlier. Thus, achievement goals share similarities with motives (classically defined as global, diffuse, largely implicit, affect-laden, dispositional and therefore stable goal representations) (McClelland, 1961; Schultheiss & Brunstein, 2005) and personal strivings (or goals that individuals hopes to accomplish in different situations) (Emmons, 1986, 1989) in that they can serve to organize lower-level goals (e.g., tasks, concerns, projects) and direct behaviors.

Consider Figure 5.1 as an illustration of this principle. Returning to our previous example, the goal (or current concern) of "getting an A", might be associated with specific behaviors such as completing math homework, purchasing materials related to math, and searching for internship opportunities. However, these behaviors do not take on full meaning unless one begins to consider higher-level goals, such as those presented in levels 1–3. For example, one could argue that a goal to learn and understand mathematics may simply be an expression of the personal striving (Emmons, 1986, 1989) of trying to become an educated person, which in turn may be considered an expression of the achievement motive. In short, achievement goals, similar to personal strivings and motives, explain why individuals make choices toward certain outcomes or behaviors and away from others. It is important to note that the distinction between achievement goals and personal strivings is somewhat nebulous. However, since Emmons' theory is not

Hierachy of Goals	
1 Motives	1.1 Need for Achievement
2 Personal Strivings	2.1 To become an educated person
3 Achievement Goals	3.1 To learn and understand mathematics
4 Concerns, Projects, Tasks	4.1 Attend school regularly; To get an 'A' in math; investigate how math is used in the real world; work on math-related projects
5 Specific Action Units	5.1 Set alarm clock; Complete HW; Purchase math-related materials; Find internships

Figure 5.1 Hierarchical model of goals. Note: This figure builds on Emmons, 1989, Figure 3-1. Although we have depicted otherwise, the distinction between personal strivings and the achievement goal construct is not entirely clear; in certain cases, strivings and goals could be considered to be among the same class of goals.

limited to the achievement domain, it could be considered to be somewhat more general than achievement goal theory

Theoretical Assumptions of Goal Theory

There exist a number of perspectives of achievement goal theory. The aim of this section is not to make clear demarcations among these points of view—we leave that for a later section. Rather, our aim here is to outline those assumptions that intersect these various perspectives.

Assumption 1: Motivation as a Process Contemporary research in motivation in general and achievement goal theory in particular has primarily been social-cognitive in nature, with an emphasis on the role of students' beliefs, perceptions, and strategies (Dweck & Leggett, 1988; Schunk, Pintrich, & Meece, 2008). To this end, motivation is assumed to be discernable through students' reports of their beliefs about goal adoption as well as through behaviors such as choice of activities, level and quality of task engagement, persistence, and performance. This approach also underscores the multidimensional nature of such processes, and examines how goal endorsement is influenced by broader cultural and contextual factors. In other words, emphasis is placed on the process of learning, and on understanding the factors, both personal and contextual, that influence how an individual approaches, engages in, and responds to achievement-related situations. In contrast to earlier research, motivation is no longer considered to be primarily a dispositional trait, with some students being "more" or "less" motivated. Increasingly, student motivation is recognized to be a function of instruction, tasks, and activities that take place in a classroom (Ames, 1992; Hickey & McCaslin, 2001; Maehr, 1974a; Maehr & Nicholls, 1980).

Assumption 2: Competence is at the Heart of Goal Theory Goal theorists by and large assume that the goal of achievement behavior is competence, defined here as the sense of being able to deal effectively with one's environment with the skills and abilities one has developed (Elliot & Dweck, 2005; Maehr & Nicholls, 1980; Nicholls, 1984; White, 1959). This assumption is perhaps best reflected in the two major goals this theory promotes, namely *mastery* (also referred to as task-involved, learning goals) and *performance* (also known as ego-involved, ability goals) goals.

Mastery goals are, above all, goals focused on the development of competence (Kaplan & Maehr, 2002). Under such a focus, it is presumed that competence can be developed and mastery achieved through the application of effort and hard work (Ames, 1992; Dweck & Leggett, 1988). As such, value is placed on progress, which is measured in self-referential or intrapersonal terms—that is, how one's current performance compares to and improves upon one's previous performance (Ames, 1992; Nicholls, 1984). The focus here is on the process of learning and not necessarily on the outcome, per se, or as Ames (1992) simply puts it, learning for the sake of learning.

In contrast, performance goals are goals focused on the demonstration of competence (Kaplan & Maehr, 2002). Central to this goal is the aim to show others that one is capable. Evidence to this effect would include outperforming other students (e.g., getting the highest grade), surpassing normative-based standards, or achieving success with minimal effort (Ames, 1992). Success, in this case, is defined primarily in terms of the extent to which one's performance compares to and exceeds others. Preserving and maintaining one's sense of ego is of utmost concern to performance-oriented students (Maehr & Nicholls, 1980); in this way, impression management is the primary focus. Learning, therefore, is considered more a means to an end.

Competence, then, is central to both mastery- and performance-goal foci; at the same time, personal definitions of competence vary under these two goal orientations. With mastery-oriented students, competence is viewed incrementally in reference to self-set standards of excellence. Performance-oriented students, on the other hand, typically view competence as a characteristic of the privileged few; thus being able to demonstrate that one has competence indicates that one is more able than others (Dweck & Leggett, 1988).

Assumption 3: Goals Create Motivational Systems In their seminal article, Elliott and Dweck (1988) lay the foundation for achievement goal theory. Included in their analysis is the following statement:

> Our research suggests that each of the achievement goals runs off a different "program" with different commands, decision rules, and inference rules, and hence, with different cognitive, affective, and behavioral consequences. Each goal, in a sense, creates and organizes its own world—each evoking different thoughts and emotions and calling forth different behaviors. (p. 11)

Similarly, Maehr (2001) presents goals as schemas, or "broader interpretative frames" (p. 183). Inherent in such a portrayal is the assumption that goals are, in essence, the unifying construct or the motivational linchpin of cognition, affect, and behavior. Goals allow us to identify how certain behaviors, thoughts, and emotions are linked and function as coordinated systems (Dweck, 1992). In this way, achievement goal theory shares similarities with Ford's (1992) Motivational Systems Theory, which specifies how personal goals including goal orientations are related to cognitive and emotional arousal processes.

The testing of this assumption has proved fruitful, resulting in a wide number of empirical studies investigating the patterns of relation between achievement goals and assorted cognitive, affective, and behavioral measures (details of these relations are outlined in subsequent sections). In terms of cognition, studies have demonstrated how achievement goals lead to differential patterns of self-regulation and cognitive and metacognitive strategy-use (Elliot, McGregor, & Gable, 1999; Graham & Golan, 1991; Pintrich, 2000b; Wolters, 2004). As for affect, studies have primarily investigated how goals are related to measures such as interest (Harackiewicz, Barron, Carter, Lehto, & Elliot, 1997; Harackiewicz, Barron, Tauer, Carter, & Elliot, 2000; Harackiewicz, Barron, Tauer, & Elliot, 2002b; Harackiewicz & Elliot, 1993), anxiety (Elliot & McGregor, 1999; Zusho, Pintrich, & Cortina, 2005) and, to a lesser extent, specific emotions (Linnenbrink & Pintrich, 2002; Pekrun, Elliot, & Maier, 2006). Finally, in terms of behavioral outcomes, efforts have been focused on how goals are associated with adaptive and maladaptive patterns of help-seeking (Butler, 1993; Butler & Neuman, 1995; Karabenick, 2004; Ryan & Pintrich, 1997), task choice (Elliott & Dweck, 1988), and academic performance (Harackiewicz et al., 2000; Harackiewicz et al., 2002b; Pintrich, 2000a). Across these studies, there is growing consensus that the pursuit of mastery goals is generally adaptive in terms of facilitating interest, persistence, adaptive patterns of help-seeking, and achievement. The findings concerning performance goals, as we shall see, are a bit more complicated (Linnenbrink-Garcia, Tyson, & Patall, 2008).

Assumption 4: Goals and Self-Related Processes Are Intertwined As reflected in earlier (and perhaps more conceptually faithful) appellations of achievement goal theory, achievement goals differ in terms of the extent to which "the self" is made salient. Nicholls (1984), for example, referred to performance goals as "ego-involved" goals, alluding to the notion that these goals heighten one's awareness of the self, or make individuals more mindful of their abilities—what they can and cannot do (Kaplan & Maehr, 2007). With mastery goals, however, the focus is not necessarily on the self but rather the task at hand.

There is also reason to believe that certain self-representations might also be related to differential patterns of goal endorsement (Kaplan & Maehr, in press; Nicholls, 1984). Specifically, it has been theorized that mastery goals, given its emphasis on intrapersonal or self-referential standards, would be associated more with a private self whereas performance goals, given its emphasis on normative or interpersonal standards, would be associated more with a public self.

Finally, there is some evidence to suggest that achievement goals may be related to how individuals view themselves (or would like to view themselves) in certain situations (Kaplan & Maehr, 2007). For example, possible selves—represented by individuals' thoughts about what they might become, what they would like to become, and what they might be afraid of becoming (Markus & Nurius, 1986)—have been associated with the adoption of certain achievement goals (Anderman, Anderman, & Griesinger, 1999). In particular, positive relations between mastery goals and constructive present selves have been noted.

A Conceptual History of Goal Theory

Previously, we alluded to there being a number of contrasting yet in some ways complementary perspectives within the achievement goal theory framework. The purpose of this section is to provide an overview of these approaches, tracing their development over time. To understand these current perspectives of goal theory, however, it is important to first consider where this theory originated, and the various motivational frameworks that inspired its development. It is their influences and assumptions, after all, that have given rise to these differing approaches to goal theory. We begin, therefore, with an overview of these origins.

Origins of Goal Theory

Achievement goal theory was influenced by and grew out of three major motivational frameworks, namely, social-cognitive theory, the achievement motive tradition, and attribution theory. First and foremost, goal theory is a social-cognitive approach to motivation. It recognizes and emphasizes the reciprocal influences of personal and environmental factors on goal endorsement, and underscores the importance of perception (Dweck & Leggett, 1988).

In many ways, goal theory is also indebted to the pioneering work on needs and motives by McClelland and Atkinson (McClelland, 1961). The primary assumption of goals as organizers and energizers of action comes from this historic area of inquiry (Elliott & Dweck, 1988), with achievement goals representing a perhaps more finer-grained, and therefore potentially more predictive, unit of analysis (Dweck & Leggett, 1988). Furthermore, many of the defining features of contemporary goal frameworks, chiefly the approach-avoidance distinction, grew out of the work on motives (see Elliot, 1999). Indeed, some theorists have suggested that achievement goals have their basis, in part, in the two achievement motives (Barron & Harackiewicz, 2001; Elliot & Church, 1997; Zusho et al., 2005). Elliot & Church's (1997) hierarchical model of achievement motivation, for example, outlines the idea that the motive to approach success (*nAch*) and the motive to avoid failure may effect the endorsement of approach and avoidance goals, respectively.

Across these three traditions, however, attribution theory has arguably been the most influential. Traces of this theory can be seen in the early writings of all the major originators of goal theory (i.e., Ames, Dweck, Maehr, and Nicholls). Maehr and Nicholls (1980), for instance, discuss how expectations of future outcomes play a pivotal role in both theories. Ultimately, goal theory is a theory concerned with the source of attributional styles; it is a theory governed by a quest to identify why students, often of equal academic ability, respond so differently to the same academic task. Why, for example, do some students exhibit what Dweck and her colleagues called a "helpless" orientation while others display a "mastery" orientation (Dweck & Leggett, 1988; Elliott & Dweck, 1988)? When faced with an academic task, why do some students make more ability attributions (e.g., "was I smart?") than effort (e.g., "did I try hard?") attributions (Ames, 1984)? The answer, according to goal theory, is the two primary goals of mastery and performance. Nevertheless, questions remain and differing opinions exist about the nature and origins of these goals. Let us turn to these perspectives now.

Perspectives of Goal Theory

A quick reading of the literature on goal theory will reveal two main perspectives—the traditional and/or normative perspective, reflected primarily in the writings of Ames, Dweck, Maehr, and Nicholls, and the revised, or what is now referred to as the multiple goals perspective, which was popularized by Harackiewicz, Elliot, and their colleagues (Harackiewicz et al., 2002; Midgley, Kaplan, & Middleton, 2001; Roeser, 2004). However, it is our contention that there are more than just these two perspectives of goal theory. In general, we see perspectives emerge according to differing assumptions about (a) the origins of goals, and (see also Kaplan & Maehr, 2007), (b) the issue of motivational equity and the role of performance goals (Harackiewicz et al., 2002; Midgley et al., 2001; Roeser, 2004), and (c) the appetitive and aversive nature of goals and the possibility of multiple goal endorsement (Elliot, 1999, 2005). We summarize the key distinctions between the various models of achievement goal theory according to these three dimensions in Table 5.1.

Where Do Goals Come From? As a rule, goal theory represents a social-cognitive approach to motivation; as such most, if not all, frameworks recognize the reciprocal influences of both person and contextual variables. Yet, there remain differing opinions about whether achievement goals have their origin more in the person, the situation, or both (Maehr, 1974a; Maehr & Nicholls, 1980). In general, perspectives differ in terms of the relative emphasis placed on one or the other and the degree to which and under what circumstances the immediate context is more "powerful" than enduring personal predispositions or traits.

Some, especially those who have been influenced by the work on attribution theory and the achievement motive tradition, argue that individuals have *goal tendencies* (Atkinson & Feather, 1966, as cited in Dweck & Elliott, 1983) that guide and determine, more or less, which goals they are likely to endorse in a given situation. These models of achievement goal theory typically present goals as based in self-schemas, focusing on how personality and/or self-related constructs play a major role in goal adoption (Kaplan & Maehr, 2007). In this case, motivation is viewed as a personal trait exhibited to varying degrees by individuals, much as intelligence. It is typically also assumed that it is a relatively stable trait: a pattern of feeling, personal orientation and behavior that is hypothesized to be a disposition acquired in early childhood and retained to a substantial degree across the course of development.

Dweck's model of achievement goals, for the most part, is representative of this approach. She argues that goals have their basis in an individual's implicit theory of intelligence. Although implicit theories have been shown to be amenable to change (Thompson & Musket, 2005), in general they are considered to be somewhat stable beliefs that can explain individual differences in goal

Table 5.1 Perspectives on Achievement Goal Theory

Goal Theorist	Representative Publication(s)	Origins of Goals	Theoretical Model	Role of Performance Goals	Unique Contributions
Ames	Ames & Archer, 1988; Ames, 1992	Situation	Two Goal: Mastery (approach), Performance (approach)	Maladaptive to the extent that performance goal classroom structures emphasize social comparative processes	Research on classroom goal structures
Dweck	Dweck & Leggett, 1988; Elliot & Dweck, 1988	Person	Two Goal: Learning (approach), Performance (implicit combination of approach & avoidance)	Maladaptive to the extent that performance goals have their basis in entity views of intelligence; Performance goals also maladaptive with low perceptions of competence	Theories of intelligence as antecedents of goals
Elliot	Elliot, 1999, 2005; Elliot & McGregor, 2003	Mostly Person	Three & Four Goal: Mastery-approach, Mastery-avoidance, Performance-approach, Performance-avoidance	Adaptive if focused on outperforming others and emerge from within (as opposed to imposed from outside)	Reintroduction of approach/avoidance distinction; Achievement motives as antecedents of goals
Harackiewicz	Harackiewicz, Barron, & Elliot, 1998; Harackiewicz et al, 2002; Barron & Harackiewicz, 2001	Mostly Person	Two Goal: Mastery-approach; Performance-approach	Adaptive in certain contexts if focused on outperforming others	Distinction between purpose and target goals; Multiple goal adoption; Development of interest
Maehr	Maehr & Braskamp, 1986; Maehr & Midgley, 1991, 1996	Person x Situation	Two Goal: Task/Mastery (approach); Ability/Performance (approach)	Maladaptive to the extent that performance goals are more likely to heighten negative self-perceptions	Role of self-processes, sociocultural factors in motivation
Midgley	Midgley, Middleton, & Kaplan, 2001; Maehr & Midgley, 1996	Mostly Situation	Three Goal: Mastery (approach), Performance-approach, Performance-avoidance	Maladaptive since the cost of endorsing performance goals outweighs any potential benefits	Classroom applications; Emphasis on motivational equity
Nicholls	Nicholls, 1984; 1990	Person x Situation	Two Goal: Task-involved (approach), Ego-involved (approach)	Maladaptive since performance goals are more likely to lead to ability attributions	Development of ability conceptions; Focus on motivational equity
Pintrich	Pintrich, 2000a,b	Person	Four Goal: Mastery-approach, Mastery-avoidance, Performance-approach, Performance-avoidance	Adaptive in certain contexts if focused on outperforming others	Interplay between motivation x cognition (SRL); Reintroduction of approach-avoidance distinction

endorsement (Dweck & Leggett, 1988; Kaplan & Maehr, 2007). Specifically, Dweck suggests that individuals who hold a more malleable or incremental view of intelligence and therefore, who view ability as something that can be improved over time, would be more likely to adopt mastery goals whereas students with low perceptions of competence who typically view intelligence as fixed and innate, or possess an entity view, would be more likely to endorse performance goals.

Another perhaps more direct example of this person-oriented approach is reflected in studies that have explored the link between motives and achievement goals (Barron & Harackiewicz, 2001; Elliot & Church, 1997; Zusho et al., 2005). As mentioned earlier, there is empirical evidence to suggest that the two achievement motives—namely, the motive to approach success and the motive to avoid failure—are related to the endorsement of certain achievement goals. Particularly, Elliot and Church (1997) suggest that the motive to approach success is related to the endorsement of mastery goals and the goal to outperform others, referred to now in the literature as performance-approach goals, since they both focus on the demonstration of competence. In contrast, they suggest that the motive to avoid failure is related to a focus on avoiding the demonstration of incompetence, or what is now more commonly referred to as performance-avoidance goals (we will return to this distinction between approach and avoidance forms of motivation subsequently). Correspondingly, Harackiewicz, Barron, and Elliot (1998) suggest that a work mastery orientation might precede the endorsement of mastery goals, while a competitive orientation might facilitate the adoption of performance-approach goals.

In direct contrast to the person-centered view of goals is the situated perspective, which essentially argues that goals are more often a function of the situation or context. Recognizing that students are not always highly motivated across all school contexts, this perspective places more weight on the activation of goal endorsement based on schemas arising from the situation (Hickey, 1997; Kaplan & Maehr, in press). In particular, this approach calls attention to the role of environmental cues. To the extent that students perceive there to be more cues focused on learning and understanding, it is hypothesized that they will be more likely to adopt mastery goals in that context. Correspondingly, it is suggested that the likelihood of students adopting performance-oriented goals would increase based upon the strength of cues emphasizing social comparison or competition in the environment. Such notions are also apparent in the supposition that students who typically endorse high levels of both mastery and performance goals may have the best academic prospects because they can selectively choose the most appropriate goal to pursue at a given time based on the perceived demands of the classroom (Barron & Harackiewicz, 2001).

This perspective has resulted in programs of research focused on understanding students' perceptions of the classroom environment and their relation to specific achievement goals. Prototypical of this approach is the work by Carole Ames (Ames, 1992; Ames & Archer, 1988; Ames, Schunk, & Meece, 1992) who largely initiated this more applied approach to the study of goals. Her work has been instrumental in outlining how cooperative classroom goal structures rather than competitive goal structures lead students to adopt more adaptive motivational profiles such as the endorsement of mastery goals. Understanding that the best efforts on the part of a classroom teacher to promote a mastery-oriented climate could be undermined by school-level policies emphasizing social comparison and performance goals, Ames's work was further extended by Maehr and Midgley (1991, 1996), who focused on applying achievement goal theory to the level of the school (we discuss this line of research in a following section).

So far, we have presented two contrasting perspectives of goal theory—one that emphasizes the origin of achievement goals in the person and one that stresses contextual factors as the more important determinant of goals. Again, it is important to note that both of these perspectives recognize that goals have their origin both in the person and context; nevertheless, very few models of achievement goals can be considered to be truly transactional in nature (Kaplan & Maehr, 2002). Moreover, studies that empirically test this assumption, for example, those that examine how goals are both stable and mutable across time and context, remain scant (cf. Fryer & Elliot, 2007; Wolters, Yu, & Pintrich, 1996). Notable exceptions include the theoretical models advanced by Nicholls and Maehr, which represent a more interactionist view of achievement goals.

Nicholls' (1984, 1990) framework is fundamentally developmental in nature and places conceptions of ability at the heart of achievement goals, with emphasis on the differentiation (or lack thereof) between effort and ability. More specifically, he proposed that students who hold a differentiated view understand that exerting effort is not necessarily indicative of a lack of ability and therefore, would be more likely to endorse mastery goals, whereas students who equate effort with a lack of ability would be more likely to adopt performance goals. Furthermore, he presupposed that certain situations (e.g., evaluative settings, emphasis on interpersonal competition) would make us more "mindful" of our ability, which could also enhance the endorsement of performance (or what he termed ego-involvement) goals.

Similarly, Maehr's Personal Investment Theory (Maehr & Braskamp, 1986), also outlines how situational constructs, such as one's perceived purpose of the situation and the accompanying options or alternatives that a person perceives to be legitimate in that situation, together with self-related processes underlie the adoption of achievement goals (Kaplan & Maehr, 2002). This approach portrays goals as emerging from both the situation and the person; specifically, drawing on work on stereotype threat, we hypothesized that performance goals represent a heightened awareness of the self that arises from situational cues, such as the extent to which the situation makes one aware of what one is, or what one can be (Kaplan & Maehr, 2007). We will revisit personal investment theory and the notion of goals as "situated meaning in action" in the final section of this chapter.

The Dilemma of Performance Goals Much has been made of the differing views about the role of performance goals in the recent literature (Harackiewicz et al., 2002; Linnenbrink, 2005; Midgley et al., 2001). On the one hand is what has been coined the normative perspective (championed primarily by theorists such as Nicholls, Ames, Maehr, Midgley, and to a certain extent Dweck), which suggests that performance goals under certain conditions, are essentially inimical to learning. On the other hand is the multiple goals perspective (forwarded primarily by Harackiewicz, Elliot, and colleagues), which, pointing to evidence of positive associations between performance-approach goals and achievement, proposes that performance goals are not entirely detrimental to learning.

As Elliot and his colleagues have suggested, the primary objective of the multiple goals perspective was never to champion performance goals, per se, but rather to document for whom and under what conditions performance goals resulted in enhanced academic performance (Elliot, 2005; Harackiewicz et al., 1998; Harackiewicz et al., 2002). Indeed, proponents of this perspective fell just short of advocating that performance goals should, in fact, be enhanced or encouraged. After all, their focus was on documenting the effects of performance goals, whether good or bad, and not necessarily on how such findings could be applied to the classroom. Ultimately, it was hoped that such findings would lead to a more nuanced view of performance goals than previously suggested.

It is important to note that theoretically, even "normative" goal theorists recognized the potential benefits of performance goals. For example, Nicholls (1984) stated in reference to clearly articulated experimental tasks of relatively short duration, "in these cases, the fact that (in ego involvement) learning is a means to an end is unlikely to impair performance. Indeed, a concern with scoring as high as possible could lead to item-selection strategies that would increase scores..." (p. 341). However, it is also apparent that such short-term gains were not reason enough to endorse performance goals.

The ideals of democratic education and motivational equity permeate the writings of Nicholls who argued passionately for the role of motivational theory, particularly achievement goal theory, to facilitate educational change and provide equal learning opportunities for all (Nicholls, 1979, 1984). Specifically, he suggested that learning situations that heighten social comparison (i.e., those that are performance-focused) inevitably result in a kind of motivational hierarchy that only benefit a select few. In contrast, mastery-oriented learning environments, he argued, would be more likely to produce optimal motivation in all students.

Similar concerns were also voiced by Ames, whose research extended to classroom applications. For example, in an essay on what teachers should know about motivation, Ames (1990) exhorted that achievement should not be viewed as the sole educational outcome and warned of the dangers of doing so:

> If we evaluate our schools and classrooms strictly by how much students achieve, we can easily lose sight of these other educational goals and values. We not only want students to achieve, we want them to value the process of learning and improvement of their skills, we want them to willingly put forth the necessary effort to develop and apply their skills and knowledge, and we want them to develop a long-term commitment to learning. It is in this sense that motivation is an outcome of education. (p. 410)

Even Dweck, whose initial approach could be considered the least reform-minded, was reluctant to advocate for performance goals. Like Nicholls, Dweck recognized that any potential gain that ensued from the endorsement of performance goals was not likely to be long-lasting and what is more, could easily turn to avoidance behaviors in the face of obstacles such as ambiguous or confusing tasks (Dweck & Elliott, 1983; Licht & Dweck, 1984).

In short, there seem to be two underlying perspectives of achievement goal theory. One that is focused purely on the description and documentation of differential patterns of goal endorsement, even if the goals being described are less than ideal and, another more utilitarian approach that openly considers the costs and benefits of endorsing certain types of achievement goals, particularly in terms of its implications for schooling.

Approach and Avoidance Goals Another distinguishing point of departure is the extent to which perspectives incorporate the approach and avoidance distinction, a hallmark of later goal frameworks. Related to this, we believe, is the notion of multiple goals, or whether or not it is possible to adopt more than one goal at a time. Since the term multiple goals is used in varying ways, it is important to note that in this instance, we refer to the concomitant endorsement of mastery and performance goals (and their variants) and not the adoption of different classes of goals, such as achievement- and socially-oriented goals.

There are essentially three basic models of achievement goals; the two-goal model, the three-goal model, and the four-goal model. There are three variations to the two-goal model. There is the traditional two goal model, initially advanced by Nicholls, Maehr, and Ames, which promotes two "approach tendencies"—one focused on learning and understanding (i.e., mastery approach) and one focused on the maintenance of favorable judgments (i.e., performance-approach). A key assumption of this earlier model was that students are generally either mastery- or performance-oriented. This stands in contrast to the contemporary two-goal model, favored mainly by Barron and Harackiewicz (2001), who suggest that the concurrent adoption of the two approach forms of mastery and performance goals is possible and should even be encouraged.

Then, there is Dweck's two-goal model, which shares many of the features of the traditional model. Like the traditional model, her model of achievement goals distinguishes between mastery and performance goals and also assumes, for the most part, students to be either mastery- or performance-oriented (in some of her early work, Dweck acknowledged the possibility of multiple goal endorsement—see Elliot and Dweck, 1983). However, her definition of performance goals stands in contrast to her contemporaries. Elliott and Dweck (1988), for example, define performance goals as those goals in which "individuals seek to maintain positive judgments of their ability *and* avoid negative judgments by seeking to prove, validate, or document their ability and not discredit it" (emphasis added; p. 645). In this way, Dweck's definition recognizes the appetitive and aversive nature of performance goals. According to Dweck, students who endorse performance goals are not just concerned with seeking positive judgments; they are striving to avoid negative judgments as well.

Dweck's model was clearly influential as it paved the way for the three-goal and four-goal models currently in favor today. What distinguishes these models from earlier conceptualizations is the clear demarcation between approach and avoidance forms of motivation. Both the three-goal and four-goal models are subsumed under the multiple goals perspective; as such, they generally maintain that the effects of performance goals are not entirely negative, and they do not assume mastery and performance goals to represent two ends of a continuum. The four-goal model, also referred to as the 2×2 model of achievement goals (Elliot & McGregor, 2001; Pintrich, 2000b), incorporates the trichotomous goal framework (Elliot, 1999) and is presented in Figure 5.2.

Briefly, Figure 5.2 depicts the dimension of valence, which distinguishes between approach goals focused on promotion or the pursuit of individual gains and avoidance goals focused on prevention or on the avoidance of losses. Crossed with the mastery-performance dimension, this results in four achievement goals: (a) Mastery-approach goals, which represent a focus on learning and understanding the course material; (b) mastery-avoidance goals, which represent a focus on not losing one's skills or competence; (c) performance-approach goals, generally defined as goals oriented toward outperforming others; and (d) performance-avoidance goals, where students are focused on not looking incompetent to others (Elliot & McGregor, 2001; Pintrich, 2000b).

The empirical work exploring the validity of this framework with college students has demonstrated that students can distinguish between these four goals, although questions related to the utility of the framework remain. Although confirmatory factor analyses generally support the four-goal structure over variations of two- or even three-goal models (Elliot & McGregor, 2001; Zusho, Karabenick, Bonney, & Sims, 2007), the 2×2 framework has been the least tested empirically. In particular, questions have been raised as to the conceptual overlap of the mastery-avoidance goal construct with other goals, especially performance-avoidance goals, and other related constructs such as fear of failure (Zusho et al., 2007).

Elliot (1999) frequently refers to Michael Jordan as an example of an individual who may have endorsed mastery-avoidance goals, particularly during the time of his protracted retirement. Jordan's achievements as a basketball player are legendary; he remains one of the best, if not the

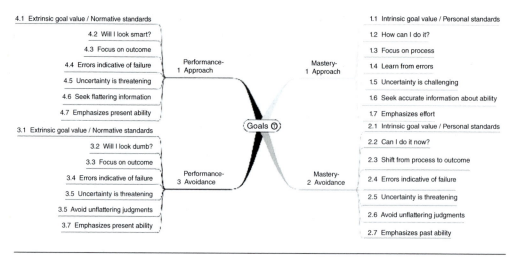

Figure 5.2 The 2 x 2 model of achievement goals.

best basketball player of his generation. One could assume that mastery-approach goals played some role—even at his prime it is conceivable that Jordan was still focused on developing his competence and skill as a basketball player. However, as he approached retirement, it is likely that his focus may have shifted from mastery-approach to mastery-avoidance goals; from developing his abilities to a focus on not losing whatever skills he had already developed.

A number of contrasts can be made between Jordan's example and the typical performance-avoidance oriented student. Perhaps the most striking difference concerns the standards for goal attainment. With performance-avoidance goals, the standards are typically normative— as such these students are more concerned with how their performance compares to others. With mastery-avoidance goals, however, the overriding concern is not necessarily how one's performance compares to others, but how one's present performance compares to one's personal standards for achievement based on past accomplishments.

There is also an implicit assumption that perceptions of competence may be an important moderator. In some ways, students who adopt mastery-avoidance goals may have higher perceptions of academic competence than students who endorse performance-avoidance goals. Although vulnerable, it is assumed that mastery-avoidance oriented students, unlike performance-avoidance oriented students, have achieved some success in the past, especially since it is against these criteria that they measure their present performance.

In examining how the four goals are related to academic and motivational outcomes, the data are most clear-cut for mastery-approach and performance-avoidance goals. In general, studies typically find benefits of pursuing mastery-approach goals, particularly in terms of its role in fostering interest in academics (Harackiewicz et al., 1997; Harackiewicz et al., 2000) and facilitating use of deeper-processing cognitive and metacognitive strategies (Elliot et al., 1999; Pintrich, 2000b). It is interesting to note that mastery-approach goals typically do not predict academic performance in regression analyses, especially when prior achievement is taken into account (Church, Elliot, & Gable, 2001; Zusho, Karabenick, Bonney, & Sims, 2007); yet, a substantial number of studies report positive correlations between mastery goals and achievement (Linnenbrink-Garica et al., 2008). It is possible to attribute the lack of such findings to the fact that the majority of studies that survey students' goal orientations to date have been conducted in classrooms emphasizing normative grading standards (Elliot & Church, 1997; Elliot & McGregor, 1999, 2001; Elliot et al., 1999; Harackiewicz, Barron, Carter, Lehto, & Elliot, 1997; Harackiewicz et al., 2002; Harackiewicz et al., 2000; Harackiewicz et al., 2002b; McGregor & Elliot, 2002), thus underscoring how contextual factors can influence students' goal endorsement. Alternatively, there is also a question as to whether the attainment of high grades necessarily indicates competence, especially since it is questionable as to whether mastery-oriented students are motivated toward high grades.

There is also almost unequivocal evidence to suggest that the endorsement of performance-avoidance goals is inimical to learning. We have found, as have others, that students who report a focus on not looking incompetent relative to others have higher levels of anxiety, and lower levels of both interest and achievement (Church et al., 2001; Elliot & Church, 1997; Elliot & McGregor, 1999, 2001; Skaalvik, 1997).

In short, the research on mastery-approach and performance-avoidance goals has been fairly consistent; in line with the traditional or normative perspective, the pursuit of mastery-approach goals has been demonstrated to be largely positive, while the adoption of performance-avoidance goals has been shown to be detrimental to most important outcomes of learning. On the other hand, the findings concerning performance-approach and mastery-avoidance goals are decidedly more uneven. Such findings may seem puzzling at first, but it is important to keep in mind that both of these goals are believed to represent a hybrid of both potentially positive (i.e., the approach and/or mastery components) and negative (i.e., the avoidance and/or performance components) motivations. To this end, it may be reasonable to expect these goals to predict both positive and negative outcomes (Elliot, 1999).

In terms of performance-approach goals, modest positive correlations between performance-approach goals and indices of achievement (e.g., final course performance, exam scores) have been found (Harackiewicz et al., 2002). Some studies have also found students who endorse performance-approach goals to report higher levels of emotionality (Elliot & McGregor, 1999), threat affect (McGregor & Elliot, 2002), and test anxiety (Middleton & Midgley, 1997). Despite the claims that have been made about performance-approach goals and achievement, it may be somewhat surprising to note that the relation of performance-approach goals and achievement are almost identical to that of mastery-approach goals (Linnenbrink-Garcia et al., 2008). Across 90 peer-reviewed journal articles, Linnenbrink-Garcia and her colleagues found positive relations between performance-approach goals and achievement in 40% of the studies, and negative relations in approximately 5% of studies. Interestingly, in experimental studies, more mastery goal effects were observed than performance-approach goal effects.

In comparison to performance-approach goals, the mastery-avoidance construct has only received limited attention in the literature thus far. However, Elliot & McGregor (2001) found mastery-avoidance goals to positively predict anxiety (both worry and emotionality components) as well as the subsequent adoption of mastery-approach, mastery-avoidance, and performance-approach goals. There is also evidence to suggest that mastery-avoidance goals may also be a positive predictor of measures of anxiety and strategy-use, as well as a negative predictor of course performance (Zusho et al., 2007). Taken together, these findings suggest that students who adopt such goals are typically more anxious, and report using more cognitive and metacognitive strategies, but that this does not necessarily translate to higher levels of achievement.

In examining the three basic models of achievement goals, it is difficult to say whether one specific model is favored more than another as preference for a particular goal framework is also tied to the other assumptions outlined previously (i.e., role of performance goals, origins of goals). Arguably, however, the four-goal model remains the most controversial, and the mastery-avoidance goal construct the least accepted (Linnenbrink-Garica et al., 2008; Zusho et al., 2007). For what it is worth, the majority of researchers have seemingly embraced the trichotomous goal framework.

Nevertheless, there is some disagreement as to whether or not the approach/avoidance distinction has led to conceptual clarity or ambiguity. Some argue that this distinction has been instrumental in understanding the divergent effects of performance goals (Elliot, 2005). Yet, others have questioned the utility of this new framework, suggesting that we may have sacrificed precision for complexity (Maehr, 2001). At issue here are the assumptions related to multiple goal endorsement, particularly as it relates to how the achievement goal construct is defined and represented cognitively.

In our opinion, the recent discussion about multiple goal endorsement has highlighted varying assumptions about the nature of the achievement goal construct, with some using a perhaps narrower definition of achievement goals than others. It is important to note that conceptually, there is very little variation in how goal theorists define achievement goals. As outlined in the first section of this chapter, the majority of researchers, no matter what their theoretical perspective, typically define goals as reasons or purposes underlying achievement-related behavior. Nevertheless, the operationalization of the goal construct has been shown to vary across studies.

More specifically, Elliot (2005) suggests that achievement goals have been defined in three primary ways: (a) as an aim, (b) as a combination of reason and aim, and (c) as an overarching orientation. A definition of goals as an aim or objective (also referred to in the literature as target goals, see Harackiewicz & Sansone, 1991), is perhaps the most specific as it relates to what individuals are trying to accomplish, as in the example, "I am striving to demonstrate my competence relative to others." To this end, such a definition would overlap with goal content theories and would be in keeping with the general literature on goals (Elliot, 1999). In most cases, Elliot's program of research has espoused this definition of achievement goals (Elliot & Thrash, 2001).

The majority of studies on achievement goals, however, have defined goals as a combination of reason and aim. For example, the performance-avoidance goal scale from the original Patterns of Adaptive Learning Scales (PALS; Midgley et al., 2000) includes items that relate to both reason (e.g., "An important reason why I do my class work is so that I don't embarrass myself") and aim (e.g., "One of my main goals is to avoid looking like I can't do my work"). This intermingling of items is also not always uniform across scales. In the case of PALS, it is most noticeable in the original performance goal scales; the mastery goal scale is almost wholly comprised of items related to reason. It is interesting to note, too, that the revised version of the PALS no longer includes many of the items that relate to reason.

Finally, in keeping with the original conceptualization of goals as schemas that organize and provide structure and meaning to achievement-related situations (Urdan, 1997), some define achievement goals more as an orientation (Ames & Archer, 1987). Researchers who espouse this definition of achievement goals typically assume that goals will elicit a distinct, yet coherent and integrated pattern of beliefs, affect, and behavior.

We highlight these varying definitions of achievement goals, in part, because it allows us to further contrast some of the contemporary models of achievement goals with their predecessors. To be more specific, it is not only the number of goals that distinguish particular models of achievement goals, but also their stance on multiple goal endorsement. In most cases, models that recognize multiple goal adoption, that is the simultaneous endorsement of mastery and performance goals (Barron & Harackiewicz, 2001; Pintrich, 2000a), are more likely to define goals as aims or objectives. Defined in this way, one could argue that the objectives of wanting to learn and understand and wanting to outperform others are not entirely antithetical. However, when defined as overarching orientations or programs, the concomitant adoption of these goals begins to make less sense. For example, it is difficult to reconcile a mastery orientation together with a helpless orientation. Perhaps it is for this reason that the issue of multiple goals was not raised until fairly recently.

One final issue related to the multiple goals perspective deserves further comment. It is important to note that slight differences exist even among those models that fall under this perspective. For example, not all models equally embrace the approach/avoidance distinction, possibly as it complicates the issue of multiple goal endorsement. Barron and Harackiewicz (2001) outline four possible hypotheses for how mastery-approach and performance-approach goals interact to produce desirable learning outcomes. However, what is conspicuously absent is any discussion of the possibility of endorsing approach and avoidance goals simultaneously.

Summary As is hopefully apparent by now, it is possible to identify numerous perspectives under the broad umbrella of achievement goal theory. In many ways, what distinguishes one perspective from another can be subtle, as it reflects somewhat implicit assumptions about the origin and nature of goals, as well as the utility of achievement goal theory to effect educational reform. Finally, it is important to note that these models of achievement goals, be it the two-, three-, or four-goal kind, all relate to personal achievement goals. While controversy may surround models of personal goals, there is considerably less disagreement about goals at the classroom level. Let us turn to that research now.

Goal Theory in the Classroom

Reflected in familiar comments such as "my students are just not motivated," a common misconception is that motivation is wholly a trait of the learner; students either have it or they don't. While one cannot deny the influence of personality on such processes, contemporary research clearly demonstrates that the context in which a student learns may be just as important a determinant of his/her motivation, cognition, and achievement-related behaviors (Hickey, 1997).

For example, goal theorists suggest that teachers' behavior and discourse often communicate to students their beliefs about the purposes of achievement, and may influence the goals, achievement-related behaviors, cognitions, and affect that students will adopt in that class (Ames, 1992; Ames, 1992; Turner, Meyer, Midgley, & Patrick, 2003). This may take place in the form of classroom- or school-level policies that make mastery or performance goals salient to students, or it could be direct messages from the teachers that convey goal-related emphases (Kaplan, Middleton, Urdan, & Midgley, 2002). These communications, in turn, are believed to have an influence on students' subsequent personal goal adoption, and other motivation- and achievement-related outcomes.

Goal theorists frequently refer to the TARGET framework—six dimensions originally identified by Epstein (1989) of teacher practices that influence the classroom goal structure (Ames, 1992; Maehr & Midgley, 1996; Patrick, Anderman, Ryan, Edelin, & Midgley, 2001; Pintrich & Schunk, 2002): classroom task or learning activity design; distribution of authority between teachers and students; recognition by way of rewards and incentives; students' abilities and opportunities to work with others in groups; the methods of evaluation for assessing student learning; and the allotment of time for allowing students to complete work, including the pace of instruction and the appropriateness of students' workload.

Research suggests that depending on teachers' instructional practices regarding these six dimensions in their classroom, students may perceive the goal structure to be more or less mastery- or performance-oriented (Ames, 1992; Maehr & Midgley, 1996; Patrick et al., 2001; Pintrich & Schunk, 2002). Teachers, for example, can stress understanding and personal improvement (i.e., mastery-oriented climate) by recognizing students for undertaking particularly challenging academic tasks, or by grading for improvement. Teachers can also stress competition (i.e., performance-oriented climate) by recognizing only high achieving students, by encouraging students to outperform other students, and by using normative grading standards.

Empirical findings of studies that examine the influence of students' perceptions of the goal structure on various student outcomes typically find mastery goal structures to be the more facilitative of positive learning outcomes. Ames and Archer (1988), for example, found that when students perceived a mastery goal structure in their classroom, they were more likely to report using adaptive learning strategies, take risks with challenging tasks, report higher enjoyment of class, and believe that success was due to effort. Perceptions of mastery goal structures have also been linked to other adaptive outcomes as increased likelihood to seek help (Ryan, Gheen, & Midgley, 1998), and decreased likelihood of self-handicapping behavior (Midgley & Urdan, 2001).

By contrast, perceptions of a performance goal structure in the classroom have been linked to negative outcomes, including decreased rates of help-seeking (Ryan et al., 1998), increased use of self-handicapping strategies (Midgley & Urdan, 2001), lower perceptions of competence (Stipek & Daniels, 1988), and harsh evaluation standards (Church et al., 2001).

Despite these negative outcomes associated with performance goal structures, Ames and Archer (1988) found that, with younger aged children, it was the degree to which students perceived a mastery climate that was predictive of students' subsequent behaviors and beliefs, suggesting that the mere presence of performance cues many not necessarily be detrimental if mastery cues are made salient. Therefore, they suggested that simply encouraging mastery goals might be sufficient for adaptive outcomes. This argument would be consistent with the multiple goals framework of achievement goal theory. It is important to note that recent findings corroborate such claims. Adaptive motivational and learning profiles have been observed in classrooms with a high-mastery/high-performance focus (Turner et al., 2003). In addition, perceptions of a performance goal structure seem unrelated to students' reports of avoidance behaviors.

It may be interesting to note that the vast majority of studies that investigate the role of classroom goal structure use only the mastery/performance dichotomy. A limited number of studies assess perceptions of both classroom performance-approach and classroom performance-avoidance goal structures; however, in most of these studies, the performance-approach and -avoidance scales were either collapsed to a single classroom performance scale (Karabenick, Zusho, & Kempler, 2005), classroom performance-avoidance items were dropped from analyses (Wolters, 2004), or perceptions of classroom performance-avoidance goal structures were not found to vary significantly between classrooms; thus not warranting its use as a classroom-level variable in subsequent analyses (Kaplan, Gheen, & Midgley, 2002). No study to date has attempted to investigate mastery-avoidance goals at the classroom level.

In general, most of the classroom-based research based on achievement goal theory has been primarily descriptive. Rather than intervening, researchers have focused their efforts on understanding the features of the classroom that explain whether students perceive their classroom to be mastery- or performance-oriented. There is, however, one notable exception to this general trend.

In *Transforming School Cultures*, Maehr and Midgley (1996) feature their efforts to enact a school-wide intervention informed by the tenets of achievement goal theory, specifically the work of Carole Ames. Their focus was somewhat unusual and ambitious in that the intervention was aimed at both the classroom and school levels. From the beginning, they recognized that a teacher's actions are often dictated and constrained by school and district-level policies. They reasoned that a focus on classroom cultures was not enough; in order to realize sustainable change, one must also attempt to "transform" the system.

As part of this transformation process, they worked collaboratively with elementary and middle school teachers and administrators toward a shared vision of emphasizing mastery goals over performance goals. As further detailed in the numerous published studies that emerged from this endeavor (e.g., Maehr & Anderman, 1993; Maehr & Meyer, 1997; Maehr & Midgley, 1991; Midgley, Anderman, & Hicks, 1995; Midgley, Arunkumar, & Urdan, 1996; Urdan, Midgley, & Anderman, 1998), their efforts were largely successful, although not without certain setbacks. At the end of the 3 years, Maehr and Midgley observed that many, although not all, of the teachers were more likely to consider their instructional practices within the achievement goal framework. For example, they note an instance when a teacher questioned the utility of presenting trophies at a school-wide history essay competition. Nevertheless, upon returning to the school after the conclusion of the project, they found open conversations about school and classroom goal structures to be comparatively less frequent, and that a handful of teachers still held strong to their beliefs about the utility of a performance-oriented climate. Thus, their tale is one of both caution and optimism; change is possible, but is also slow.

Finally, we conclude this section with a brief commentary on the developmental trends that can be discerned through the research on classrooms. In many ways, as children progress through their schooling, the learning climate becomes increasingly performance-oriented. Much has been made of the middle school transition in the literature (Eccles et al., 1989). With this transition comes numerous opportunities for social comparison; there is generally a renewed emphasis on grades, which is often further intensified by practices such as ability tracking and normative evaluation standards. Considered alongside the research on adolescents' heightened awareness of others (i.e., imaginary audience, see also Elkind, 1985), it is hardly surprising that a general decline over time in mastery goals has been observed (Anderman, Austin, & Johnson, 2002).

For example, studies suggest that elementary students typically endorse higher levels of mastery goals than their middle school counterparts. Furthermore, there is evidence to suggest that this change in goal focus is tied to students' perceptions of the classroom goal structure (Anderman & Anderman, 1999; Anderman, Maehr, & Midgley, 1999). In short, the changes in personal goal orientations observed across this transition can be attributed, in part, to the fact that students often perceive their middle school classrooms to be more performance-oriented. Such findings again underscore how contextual factors can profoundly influence personal goal endorsements.

Surprisingly very little research has been conducted at the high school level; similarly, empirical work examining aspects of the college classrooms is not as extensive as those focused on elementary and middle school classrooms (Zusho et al., 2007). Two possible reasons for this oversight have been proposed. First, there is an assumption that the interpersonal context of the college classroom may be less important given the developmental maturity of the students. Second, the traditional image of the college classroom is arguably not one of a classroom at all, but rather a large lecture hall with a professor lecturing and students taking notes with very little interaction among the students. Thus, it is possible to conclude that college classrooms may not have the same social factors believed to influence younger students' learning and engagement (Wentzel, 1997).

Emerging evidence, however, challenges this depiction of the college classroom context, indicating high levels of student interactions, efforts at interpersonal connection and support on the part of instructors. For example, researchers found college students to report, on average, their classrooms to be mastery-focused, and their instructors to be caring and facilitative of question-asking, although more so at the beginning of the semester than at the end. What is more, correlational analyses indicated a general pattern whereby students who perceived their classroom to be mastery-oriented, their instructors to be supportive of questioning, and caring also received higher grades at the end of the semester (Zusho et al., 2007).

Taken together, these findings suggest that no matter what the age level, the benefits of mastery-oriented learning climate largely outweigh one focused on performance. More generally, studies on classroom goal structure also call attention to the power of contextual influences to effect distinct patterns of personal goal endorsement.

Remaining Challenges

Achievement goal theory is clearly at a crossroads. Over the past two decades as goal theory emerged as a dominant motivational framework, we have come to understand and appreciate how important achievement goals are to the learning process. Yet, many issues remain unresolved. We outline here, what we believe are some practical, theoretical, and methodological challenges facing this approach to motivation.

Practical Issues

Practically and metatheoretically, researchers of achievement goal theory, in particular, and motivation, in general, would benefit from a frank conversation about the utility and value of its frameworks for classroom practice, or more specifically for classroom change. Indeed, a dialogue was initiated some time ago (Ames, 1992; Blumenfeld, 1992) and revisited recently (Brophy, 2005; Harackiewicz et al., 2002; Midgley et al., 2001), but we have yet to come to terms with whether and how goal theory can be applied to the modern day classroom.

Of course, this is not to dismiss the research that has already been conducted in the classroom to date. In general, the research on classroom goal structure has clearly demonstrated the benefits of creating a mastery-oriented classroom environment. And, despite the varying perspectives that exist within achievement goal theory, there seem to be consensus that mastery goals, whether it is at the personal or classroom level, are preferable to performance goals. Nevertheless, the amount of research currently being conducted in the classroom is limited and as a result, we only have vague and imprecise recommendations to give to teachers and policy makers (Urdan & Turner, 2005). In addition, goal theory has remained mostly silent about burning issues facing the field of education (e.g., high stakes testing, accountability). If this framework is to remain vital and fruitful, this trend cannot continue.

We can, for example, proselytize to no end the benefits of a mastery-oriented learning environment. However, without a true understanding of what a mastery-oriented environment looks like, or without knowing precisely how to create such an environment, this line of research will ultimately prove futile. Encouragingly, classroom-based research (e.g., Linnenbrink, 2005) is on the rise and there is also increased recognition of the effect (or lack thereof) that motivational theories can have on educational reform efforts (Ryan, Ryan, Arbuthnot, & Samuels, 2007; Ryan & Brown, 2005). However, it is clear that this research is still very much in its infancy.

First and foremost, we need to reconcile whether goal theory is an appropriate framework to study classroom motivation. Some have argued that the mastery-performance goal dichotomy may be too narrow; Brophy (2005), for example, suggests that despite the attention given to performance goals in the literature, these goals are not commonly endorsed by students. Similarly, others have argued that achievement goal theory may not fully recognize the realities of the class-room. For example, how exactly do you get students to endorse goals centered on learning and understanding in a climate that is increasingly focused on standardized test scores? Related to this issue is whether or not classrooms can be classified as either mastery- or performance-oriented; it is conceivable that features of both orientations are represented in most classrooms.

If there is agreement that goal theory can bring about and can speak to issues of educational reform, then there is also a need to reconcile which perspective(s) of goal theory would be most appropriate in necessitating those changes. Indeed, with legislation such as No Child Left Behind (NCLB), it is difficult to deny that the classroom is becoming more and more performance-oriented (Ryan et al., 2007; Ryan & Brown, 2005). To this end, it is possible to consider those perspectives that emphasize and investigate the multiple pathways actuated by performance goals as more realistic. At the same time, it could also be argued that by recognizing any potential benefits of performance goals, we are legitimizing and encouraging controversial practices such as high-stakes testing.

In stating thus, we are not by any means suggesting that goal theory is irrelevant or should be abandoned. To be sure, goal theory has the potential to guide educational reform efforts and has done so in the past (Maehr & Midgley, 1996). For example, we see the potential of achievement goal theory to inform many of the reform efforts that emphasize collaboration, whether face-to-face or virtual, as they often do not fully consider if and how those settings encourage social comparison. Nevertheless, it is difficult to deny that goal theory at this particular point in time is presenting less than a united front on many of these hot-topic issues facing the educational community. Devoting time to reconciling these perspectives, in our opinion, should ultimately prove worthwhile.

Theoretical Issues

Clarifying the nature of the achievement goal construct, specifically how students represent these goals cognitively, remains one of the most important theoretical challenges facing achievement goal theory. Three interrelated issues are especially important to consider: first, a concerted effort should be made to identify which goals are salient to students; second, the hierarchy among these goals should be considered; and third, the coordination and conflict among and between these goals should be examined. Again, it is important to reiterate that by examining these issues, we run the risk of proposing models of achievement goals that are more complex, less parsimonious, and perhaps less predictive. Thus, we must always keep in mind whether proposed revisions will serve to enhance or hinder applications to practice.

Goal theorists have long contended that mastery and performance goals are the most impor-tant goals to consider when investigating achievement-related situations. Increasingly, however, a number of researchers have questioned this assumption, arguing instead for the need to expand goal theory to consider other kinds of goals (Urdan & Maehr, 1995). For example, work-avoidance goals, or goals focused on the minimal exertion of effort, has received some attention in the lit-erature (e.g., Harackiewicz et al., 1997). Some have also argued that extrinsic goals may be more commonplace than performance goals (Brophy, 2005). There are, too, programs of research centered on the role of social goals (Dowson & McInerney, 2003; Ryan & Shim, 2006; Urdan & Maehr, 1995; Wentzel, 2000). For example, in their qualitative investigation into the kinds of academic goals endorsed by students, Dowson and McInerney (2003) distinguished between five types of social goals (i.e., social affiliation, social approval, social responsibility, social status, and social concern).

There is also a need to establish a better understanding of the hierarchy of goals. Do mastery and performance goals represent superordinate goals, as suggested by some? And, do students represent these goals at that level? If we consider social goals, are they equally important as mastery and performance goals, or is one at a higher level than the other? Similarly, how are extrinsic goals (e.g., My goal is to get an A) related to performance goals (e.g., My goal is to outperform other students); does one predict the other? In short, at issue here is the appropriate grain-size (i.e., level of specificity) of the achievement goal construct: questions remain as to whether it is better represented as an aim (or a content goal), or as a combination of reason and aim, or as an overarching schema that serves to organize and direct behavior (Elliot, 2005). The limited evidence that we do have seems to suggest that any demarcations students make between the goals may not be as clear as theory would suggest (Dowson & McInerney, 2003). This line of research would clearly benefit from further investigation.

One point about the proliferation of goal constructs deserves further mention. In our opinion, it appears that researchers who argue for the expansion of achievement goal theory may be approaching the study of goals more from a content perspective, focusing on what individuals are trying to achieve in a specific situation instead of why. To this end, reconciling the varying operationalizations of the achievement goal construct is a necessary first step in clarifying goal theory, which could be facilitated by a renewed focus on issues of goal hierarchy and multiple goal endorsement. For example, it may be necessary to reconsider the distinction between goal (purpose) and objective (target).

Research concerning the hierarchy of goals should allow us to better understand more generally, the coordination and conflict among specific goals. Although the issue of multiple goal endorsement has received greater attention since the introduction of the three- and four-goal models, we are still unclear as to when and how goals coincide or conflict, and the consequences of such tendencies. As others have noted (Dowson & McInerney, 2003; Dweck & Elliott, 1983), when goals are deemed compatible, they can work together to bring about a certain behavior. However, there are times when goals are at odds. What happens, for instance when a student may want to do well in school but also fears reprisals from his/her peers for doing so?

Questions also remain about the coordination and conflict of approach and avoidance goals, in general. Both approach and avoidance forms of performance goals are increasingly being recognized in the literature; however, it is not entirely clear as to whether the approach and avoidance dimensions represent two sides of the same goal. When students adopt a performance goal, are they trying to demonstrate their competence relative to others and at the same time, trying to demonstrate that they are not incompetent? A promising area for future research would be to consider the research on goal gradients and the issue of time. More specifically, there is evidence to suggest that the closer an individual gets to achieving his/her goal, approach tendencies outweigh avoidance tendencies (Hull, 1932). Related to the issue of time, rates of procrastination, which could be considered to be the ultimate form of avoidance, have also been shown to decrease before a deadline (Schouwenburg & Groenewoud, 2001)

Finally, we would welcome a return to a more transactional model of goal theory that equally emphasizes and investigates the interaction of person and contextual variables (we offer in the next section an example of such an approach). Understanding how and why goals arise in a given context and develops over time remains an important area for future research.

Methodological Issues

Mirroring the trend in the field of motivation in general, research according to an achievement goal framework has primarily been quantitative in nature. Specifically, survey methodology has been the modus operandi; the customary procedure entailing the administration of self-report measures at various time points over the academic calendar or semester. In addition, experimental studies have also been conducted, with attempts made to manipulate the goals of students to varying degrees of success. Recently, however, heeding calls for more qualitative research, there has been a shift, albeit tentative, toward qualitative and idiographic methodologies (Turner & Meyer, 2000; Urdan & Mestas, 2006).

This shift toward qualitative methods, in part, represents a certain level of dissatisfaction with these more traditional approaches. Nomothetic approaches such as survey and experimental methods excel at classification and prediction. However, they often mask individual variation, and what is more, the effects are not even entirely consistent across these approaches. For example, Linnenbrink-Garcia and her colleagues observed more mastery effects with experimental as compared to survey methodology (Linnenbrink-Garica et al., 2008). Thus, trying to uncover a more nuanced understanding of the generalizablity and inimitability of goal theory, therefore, with such methodologies alone is debatable. Only with qualitative studies, for example, have we been able to elucidate the many reasons why students adopt performance goals (Urdan & Mestas, 2006). It may also be interesting to note that goal effects are not always entirely consistent across nomethetic approaches.

Perhaps, of utmost concern is both the cognitive and cultural validity of current goal measures. First, some have raised the importance of assessing whether or not students actually interpret the survey items as intended (Karabenick et al., 2007). For example, many of the mastery goal measures include the words "learning" and "understanding." But how exactly are students interpreting those words? What do "learning" and "understanding" mean to a middle school student? A high school student? A college student? Similarly, how do students of differing cultural backgrounds interpret those words? Do they mean something different?

A related issue has been raised by Zusho and Njoku (2007), who argue that current measures that assess goals as a combination of reason and aim may be culturally invalid. When discussing potential cultural variation, an argument can be made that the reasons for adopting a mastery or a performance goal might vary across groups, but that the actual goals (i.e., aims) themselves might be universal. After all, the notion of improving (i.e., mastery-approach) or the idea of doing better than others is not culturally bound. At the same time, the reasons for setting or pursuing such goals may very well vary culturally.

For example, the literature on self-criticism and self-enhancement suggests that the reasons for adopting a mastery or a performance goal may be different for Asians and Anglos. As Kitayama and Markus (1999) point out, it is interesting to note that the Japanese notion of self-criticism originates from a desire to fulfill one's obligations to significant others. Consequently, they refer to this as "relational self-criticism," emphasizing that self-criticism is embedded firmly within a social context. It would follow then, that while the constructs of self-criticism and mastery-goal orientations may seem similar at first, it differs to the extent that there is some social element in relational self-criticism, which is absent in the traditional conceptualization of mastery goals. Subsequently, this suggests that the Japanese emphasis on self-criticism is not to learn for the sake of learning but rather to learn and improve in an attempt to not let others down.

In the same way, there has also been some speculation as to whether competition might be conceptualized somewhat differently among Asians, or more specifically, individuals who espouse an interdependent view of self. Heine et al (2001), for example, suggested that for such persons, competition can be framed not as a focus on outperforming others per se, but rather as a focus on living up to socially shared standards of excellence. That is, you compete not to emphasize your unique contributions but so that the group to which you belong to will excel. It would follow, then, that the Asian version of "competition" might be associated more with the collective aspects of the social self.

Finally, some of the current measures of goals, particularly those that follow the 2×2 model, present some cause for concern. At issue are the intercorrelations between certain goal constructs and the potential for suppression effects. As noted by some (Linnenbrink-Garica et al., 2008; Zusho et al., 2007), the effects of performance goals on achievement are at times masked by suppression effects. For example, Elliot and McGregor (1999) reported a weak zero-order correlation ($r = .09$) between exam performance and performance approach goals, but a positive standard regression for performance-approach goals on exam performance ($\beta = .24$).

In short, these findings raise important questions about the future of achievement goal theory, particularly as it relates to current methodology. Confirming the validity and reliability of current goal measures and expanding the methods for studying and understanding achievement goals is an important direction for future research.

Future Directions: Toward a Decision Theory Framework of Motivation

Several decades ago the United States was waging a "war on poverty." In this war the children of the poor and their achievement in schools were often the focus. In many instances, those who were waging this war not only suggested but also concluded that these children were not only intellectually, but motivationally, deprived. When their behavior patterns were observed in school settings, they often appeared lackadaisical or lazy, not only lacking any investment in learning or schooling but exhibiting little energy for almost anything—in the school context, at least. Consequently, it was often concluded that this "laziness" was a product of a "culture of poverty," which not only framed their life style but also produced little or no motivation to succeed or excel—no achievement motivation. But a closer examination of their behavior, especially in extra-school settings, suggested a quite different interpretation. On the streets and playgrounds of their own neighborhoods, these same children not only exhibited the energy they presumably did not have in school but also creative entrepreneurship, concern with succeeding as well as excelling, although perhaps in different ways and toward different ends than those espoused and promoted by the particular culture promoted within the state sponsored schools which they attended. But context clearly made a difference in the motivation levels exhibited, in these children's willingness to accept and pursue reasonable challenge, to persist in the pursuit of excellence—and to be the best they could be—albeit oft-times in something other than tasks of a standard school curriculum (cf. Duda, 1980; Maehr, 1974b).

Such everyday examples of the situated nature of motivation are offered here, first of all, as a reminder of how motivation does change with situation and circumstance in a way that trait theories of motivation do not lead us to consider. Perhaps it is in the case of the "culturally or racially different" that we are most often likely to be misled when assessing motivation as a trait variable. But just as important is the realization that trait theories of the past, as well as the present, are limited in providing solutions to "motivational problems." Yet, simply noting that children or adults may be differentially motivated in varying contexts is not in itself a solution to the question of motivation as a problem. Nor is the observation that sociocultural background may play a role in this regard all that helpful. What is needed is a perspective that leads to systematic study and understanding of how, when, and in what ways, situations influence motivation. Just what is it about situations that make a difference? When and how do they make that difference?

Conceptualizing Motivation as Decision Making

In our reading and following a choice and decision theory framework, the research on motivation readily leads to three notions about the nature of motivation and its causes: Action alternatives, sense of competence, and purpose, each explained below.

Action Alternatives First and foremost, in acting humans and other creatures for that matter (cf. Dukas, 1998; Shettleworth, 1999) choose from the set of options that are perceived to be available. That is an obvious, but not all that seriously and fully considered, fact of motivation. Clearly, in cross-cultural work, it is, and must be, central. In earlier research on "subjective culture" Charles Osgood, Harry Triandis and their colleagues (Osgood, Miron, & May, 1975; Triandia, 1972) laid out a strong case for the role of norms, roles, and societal expectations in framing the direction and nature of the action exhibited by individuals. Earlier need-drive models of motivation, indeed, most motivation theories yet today, do not pay sufficient attention to subjective culture as a component of the "motivation equation." If and when sociocultural influences on motivation are considered, such influence is largely viewed in terms of early social learning in which durable motivational predispositions are established; that is, essentially as an acquired, stable and durable trait of the person. Choice and decision theory, however, provides a framework for representing the continuing and immediate effects of sociocultural factors in specific action situations and contexts throughout the life span.

Essentially, the operative norms, roles, and social expectations which Osgood (1964) and Triandis (1972) labeled "subjective culture," may be viewed as a portrayal of the options from which action choices are made on a regular and continuing basis. A challenge here, of course, is to unpack these perceived options from the complexity of all the variables that compose the subjective culture. But as Osgood and Triandis and colleagues showed, given the right questions, individuals can describe their "cultural options" readily and effectively.

An interesting and readily operational way of representing these Action Alternatives is quite possibly to be found in the concept of "possible selves" set forth by Markus and her colleagues (see, for example, Markus & Nurius, 1986; Markus & Kitayama, 1991). While there may be multiple ways to frame possible selves for assessment purposes, it seems reasonable to suggest that the work points to at least one important perspective in assessing perceived action alternatives from which an individual is likely to choose. And thus, an important component of the choice and decision process, we suggest, is the contextual factors that frame the behavior from which we infer motivation.

Sense of Competence A second antecedent in a choice and decision theory model of motivation is the belief that one is likely to succeed rather than fail at a particular task, in a specific situation. More generally, this may be associated with a sense of competence (Urdan & Turner, 2005) or of self-efficacy (Schunk & Pajares, 2005) vis-à-vis a particular task in a given context. While sense of competence has often been treated as an enduring trait, it need not be. Indeed, one could treat it as a situated variable that is dependent on the task at hand, which was the case in Atkinson's and other decision theory models of motivation. In any event, in our attempt to stress one's view of motivation as contextually determined we suggest just this possibility.

The Potential Role of Goals While action alternatives and a sense of competence in pursuing them are crucial, they also figure into the decision making processes differentially, depending on certain conditions. Arguably, decision rules change as purposes change. In most cases, an alternative that offers a high probability of success is likely to be pursued in making a decision regarding your child's health, but you may be more willing to take a relatively high risk of losing to a better player in a game of tennis. Of course, it is all a bit more complicated than this, but the central point is that the purpose of a course of action modifies the rules that guide decision making. Here is where the goals identified by achievement goal theory can play a significant role, as it specifies a number of different ways in which purpose modifies ways in which we act.

Suggested or implied but never fully nor systematically pursued as one might expect is the possibility that when mastery goals are held, individuals are more likely to seek challenge and tolerate, if not actually pursue, what they cannot automatically predict. That is, if, and as individuals act under a mastery rather than a performance orientation, it was likely that they would exhibit a kind of reasonable "venturesomeness" and/or a willingness to think or act "outside the box" and exhibit the kind of "challenge seeking" in thought as well as action that Atkinson implied in his decision theory model of achievement motivation.

Conclusion

The study of motivation has too often treated a single variable as primary (e.g., self-efficacy, goals). Concurrently, motivation is too seldom considered as a process in which several factors collectively and systematically contribute figure strongly in the outcome. This has been considerably true of the goal theory perspective on motivation. However, it is not inevitably the fate of goal theory. Arguably, goals can and do impact motivation in significant ways. Nevertheless, we suggest that future research would do well to consider goals as a part of a larger and situated process. Decision theory once proposed a felicitous combination of critical variables that defined motivation and specified its origins and its variation in manifestations. It may now have different and more obvious relevance today than in the past as we overwhelmingly view motivation in terms of social cognitive variables rather than in terms of needs, drives, incentives or values. At the very least, we hope that, to some small degree, we have shown how the two motivational constructs that have gathered the most attention in recent years, namely mastery and performance goals, cannot be considered apart from other motivational concepts and processes. Reviving a decision theory model might, just possibly, not only suggest a way of viewing these interconnections, but also remind us that action happens within a sociocultural matrix in which norms, roles, social positions, social identity—subjective culture—defines opportunities and limits what we can do, and when, how and where we can do it.

Acknowledgments

We would like to thank the editors for very helpful comments on a previous draft. We also thank Lisa Linnenbrink-Garcia and Andy Elliot for their help with select portions of the chapter. Of course, we take full responsibility for any inaccuracies or misrepresentations.

References

Ames, C. (1984). Achievement attributions and self-instructions under competitive and individualistic goal structures. *Journal of Educational Psychology, 76*(3), 478–487.

Ames, C. (1990). Motivation: What teachers need to know. *Teachers College Record, 91*(3), 409–421.

Ames, C. (1992). Classrooms: Goals, structures, and student motivation. *Journal of Educational Psychology, 84*, 261–271.

Ames, C., & Archer, J. (1987). Mothers' beliefs about the role of ability and effort in school learning. *Journal of Educational Psychology, 79*, 409–414.

Ames, C., & Archer, J. (1988). Achievement goals in the classroom: Students' learning strategies and motivation processes. *Journal of Educational Psychology, 80*(3), 260–267.

Ames, C., Schunk, D. H., & Meece, J. L. (1992). Achievement goals and the classroom motivational climate. In *Student perceptions in the classroom* (pp. 327–348). Mahwah, NJ: Erlbaum.

Anderman, E., & Anderman, L. H. (1999). Social predictors of changes in students' achievement goal orientations. *Contemporary Educational Psychology, 25*, 21–37.

Anderman, E. M., Anderman, L. H., & Griesinger, T. (1999). The relation of present and possible academic selves during early adolescence to grade point average and achievement goals. *Elementary School Journal, 100*(1), 3–17.

Anderman, E. M., Austin, C. C., & Johnson, D. M. (2002). The development of goal orientation. In A. Wigfield & J. S. Eccles (Eds.), *The Development of Achievement Motivation* (pp. 197–217). San Diego: Academic Press.

Anderman, E. M., Maehr, M. L., & Midgley, C. (1999). Declining motivation after the transition to middle school: Schools can make a difference. *Journal of Research & Development in Education, 32*(3), 131–147.

Atkinson, J. W., & Feather, N. T. (Eds.). (1966). *A theory of achievement motivation*. New York: Wiley.

Bandura, A. (1989). Self-regulation of motivation and action through internal standards and goal system. In L. A. Pervin (Ed.), *Goal concepts in personality and social psychology* (pp. 19–85). Hillsdale, NJ: Erlbaum.

Barron, K. E., & Harackiewicz, J. M. (2001). Achievement goals and optimal motivation: Testing multiple goal models. *Journal of Personality and Social Psychology: Special Issue, 80*, 706–722.

Blumenfeld, P. C. (1992). Classroom learning and motivation: Clarifying and expanding goal theory. *Journal of Educational Psychology, 84*, 272–281.

Brophy, J. (2005). Goal theorists should move on from performance goals. *Educational Psychologist, 40*(3), 167–176.

Butler, R. (1993). Effects of task- and ego-achievement goals on information seeking during task engagement. *Journal of Personality and Social Psychology, 65*(1), 18–31.

Butler, R., & Neuman, O. (1995). Effects of task and ego achievement goals on help-seeking behaviors and attitudes. *Journal of Educational Psychology, 87*(2), 261–271.

Cantor, N., & Kilstrom, J. F. (1987). *Personality and social intelligence*. Englewood Cliffs, NJ: Prentice-Hall.

Church, M. A., Elliot, A. J., & Gable, S. L. (2001). Perceptions of classroom environment, achievement goals, and achievement outcomes. *Journal of Educational Psychology, 93*, 43–54.

Dowson, M., & McInerney, D. M. (2003). What do students say about their motivational goals?: Towards a more complex and dynamic perspective on student motivation. *Contemporary Educational Psychology, 28*, 91–113.

Duda, J. (1980). Achievement motivation among Navajo students: A conceptual analysis with preliminary data. *Ethos, 8*(4), 316–337.

Dukas, R. (Ed.). (1998). *Cognitive ecology: The evolutionary ecology of information processing and decision making*. Chicago: University of Chicago Press.

Dweck, C. S. (1992). The study of goals in psychology. *Psychological Science, 3*(3), 165–167.

Dweck, C. S., & Elliott, E. S. (1983). Achievement motivation. In P. Mussen & E. M. Heatherington (Eds.), *Handbook of child psychology* (pp. 643–691). New York: Wiley.

Dweck, C. S., & Leggett, E. L. (1988). A social-cognitive approach to motivation and personality. *Psychological Review, 95*(2), 256–273.

Eccles, J. S., Midgley, C., Wigfield, A., Miller-Buchannan, C., Reuman, D., Flanagan, C., et al. (1989). Development during adolessccence: The impact of stage-environment fit on young adolescents' experiences in schools and families. *American Psychologist, 48*, 90–101.

Elkind, D. (1985). Egocentrism redux. *Developmental Review, 5*, 218–226.

Elliot, A. J. (1999). Approach and avoidance motivation and achievement goals. *Educational Psychologist, 34*(3), 169–189.

Elliot, A. J. (2005). A conceptual history of the achievement goal construct. In A. J. Elliot & C. S. Dweck (Eds.), *Handbook of competence and motivation* (pp. 52–72). New York: Guilford.

Elliot, A. J., & Church, M. A. (1997). A hierarchical model of approach and avoidance achievement motivation. *Journal of Personality and Social Psychology, 72*(1), 218–232.

Elliott, E. S., & Dweck, C. S. (1988). Goals: An approach to motivation and achievement. *Journal of Personality and Social Psychology, 54*(1), 5–12.

Elliot, A. J., & Dweck, C. S. (2005). Competence and motivation: Competence as the core of achievement motivation. In A. J. Elliot & C. S. Dweck (Eds.), *Handbook of competence and motivation* (pp. 3–14). New York: Guilford.

Elliot, A. J., & McGregor, H. A. (1999). Test anxiety and the hierarchical model of approach and avoidance achievement motivation. *Journal of Personality & Social Psychology, 76*(4), 628–644.

Elliot, A. J., & McGregor, H. A. (2001). A 2x2 achievement goal framework. *Journal of Personality and Social Psychology, 80*, 501–519.

Elliot, A. J., McGregor, H. A., & Gable, S. (1999). Achievement goals, study strategies, and exam performance: A mediational analysis. *Journal of Educational Psychology, 91*(3), 549–563.

Elliot, A. J., & Thrash, T. M. (2001). Achievement goals and the hierarchical model of achievement motivation. *Educational Psychology Review, 13*(2), 139–156.

Emmons, R. A. (1986). Personal strivings: An approach to personality and subjective well-being. *Journal of Personality and Social Psychology, 51*(5), 1058–1068.

Emmons, R. A. (1989). The personal striving approach to personality. In L. A. Pervin (Ed.), *Goal concepts in personality and social psychology* (pp. 87–126). Hillsdale, NJ: Erlbaum.

Epstein, J. (1989). Family structures and student motivation: A developmental perspective. In C. Ames & R. Ames (Eds.), *Research on motivation in education* (Vol. 3, pp. 259–295). San Diego, CA: Academic Press.

Ford, M. E. (1992). *Motivating humans: Goals, emotions, and personal agency beliefs.* Newbury Park, CA: Sage.

Fryer, J. W., & Elliot, A. J. (2007). Stability and change in achievement goals. *Journal of Educational Psychology, 99*(4), 700–714.

Graham, S., & Golan, S. (1991). Motivational influences on cognition: Task involvement, ego involvement, and depth of information processing. *Journal of Educational Psychology, 83*(2), 187–194.

Harackiewicz, J., Barron, K., & Elliot, A. (1998). Rethinking achievement goals: When are they adaptive for college students and why? *Educational Psychologist, 33*(1), 1–21.

Harackiewicz, J. M., Barron, K. E., Carter, S. M., Lehto, A. T., & Elliot, A. J. (1997). Predictors and consequences of achievement goals in the college classroom: Maintaining interest and making the grade. *Journal of Personality & Social Psychology, 73*(6), 1284–1295.

Harackiewicz, J. M., Barron, K. E., Pintrich, P. R., Elliot, A. J., & Thrash, T. M. (2002a). Revision of achievement goal theory: Necessary and illuminating. *Journal of Educational Psychology, 94*(3), 638–645.

Harackiewicz, J. M., Barron, K. E., Tauer, J. M., & Elliot, A. J. (2002b). Predicting success in college: A longitudinal study of achievement goals and ability measures as predictors of interest and performance from freshman year through graduation. *Journal of Educational Psychology, 94*(3), 562–575.

Harackiewicz, J. M., Barron, K. E., Tauer, J. M., Carter, S. M., & Elliot, A. J. (2000). Short-term and long-term consequences of achievement goals: Predicting interest and performance over time. *Journal of Educational Psychology, 92*(2), 316–330.

Harackiewicz, J. M., & Elliot, A. J. (1993). Achievement goals and intrinsic motivation. *Journal of Personality and Social Psychology, 65*(5), 904–915.

Harackiewicz, J. M., & Sansone, C. (1991). Goals and intrinsic motivation: You can get there from here. In M. L. Maehr & P. R. Pintrich (Eds.), *Advances in motivation and achievement* (Vol. 10, pp. 99–142). Greenwich, CT: JAI

Heine, S. J., Kitayama, S., & Lehman, D. R. (2001). Cultural differences in self-evaluation: Japanese readily accept negative self-relevant information. *Journal of Cross-Cultural Psychology, 32*(4), 434–443.

Hickey, D. T. (1997). Motivation and contemporary socio-constructivist instructional perspectives. *Educational Psychologist, 32*, 175–193.

Hickey, D. T., & McCaslin, M. (2001). A comparative, sociocultural analysis of context and motivation. In S. Volet & S. Jarvela (Eds.), *Motivation in learning contexts: Theoretical advances and methodological implications* (pp. 33–55). Elmsford, NY: Pergamon Press.

Hull, C. L. (1932). The goal gradient hypothesis and maze learning. *Psychological Review, 39*, 25–43.

Kaplan, A., Gheen, M., & Midgley, C. (2002). Classroom goal structure and student disruptive behaviour. *British Journal of Educational Psychology, 72*, 191–211.

Kaplan, A., & Maehr, M. L. (2002). Adolescents' achievement goals: Situating motivation in sociocultural contexts. In T. Urdan & F. Pajares (Eds.), *Adolescence and education* (Vol. 2, pp. 125–167). Greenwich, CT: Information Age.

Kaplan, A., & Maehr, M. L. (2007). The contributions and prospects of goal orientation theory. *Educational Psychology Review, 19*, 141–184.

Kaplan, A., Middleton, M., Urdan, T., & Midgley, C. (2002). Achievement goals and goal structures. In C. Midgley (Ed.), *Goals, goal structures, and patterns of adaptive learning* (pp. 21–53). Mahwah, NJ: Erlbaum.

Karabenick, S. A. (2004). Perceived Achievement Goal Structure and College Student Help Seeking. *Journal of Educational Psychology, 96*, 569–581.

Karabenick, S. A., Woolley, M. E., Friedel, J. M., Ammon, B. V., Blazevski, J., Bonney, C. R., et al. (2007). Cognitive processing of self-report items in educational research: Do they think what we mean? *Educational Psychologist, 42*(3), 139–151.

Karabenick, S. A., Zusho, A., & Kempler, T. M. (2005). Help seeking and perceived classroom context. *Paper presented at the biennial meeting of the European Association for Research on Learning and Instruction.*

Kitayama, S., & Markus, H. R. (1999). Yin and Yang of the Japanese self: The cultural psychology of personality coherence. In *The coherence of personality: Social-cognitive bases of consistency, variability, and organization* (pp. 242–302). New York: Guilford.

Klinger, E., & McNelly, F. W. (1976). Self states and performances of preadolescent boys carrying out leadership roles inconsistent with their social status. *Child Development, 47*(1), 126–137.

Licht, B. G., & Dweck, C. S. (1984). Determinants of academic achievement: The interaction of children's achievement orientations with skill area. *Developmental Psychology, 20*(4), 628–636.

Linnenbrink, E. A. (2005). The dilemma of performance-approach goals: The use of multiple goal contexts to promote students' motivation and learning. *Journal of Educational Psychology, 97*(2), 197–213.

Linnenbrink, E. A., & Pintrich, P. R. (2002). Achievement goal theory and affect: An asymmetrical bidirectional model. *Educational Psychologist, 37*(2), 69–78.

Linnenbrink-Garcia, L., Tyson, D. F., & Patall, E. A. (2008). When are achievement goal orientations beneficial for academic achievement? A closer look at moderating factors. *International Review of Social Psychology, 21*, 19–70.

Locke, E. A., & Latham, G. P. (1984). *Goal setting: A motivational technique that works.* Englewood Cliffs, NJ: Prentice-Hall.

Maehr, M. L. (1974a). Culture and achievement motivation. *American Psychologist, 29*(12), 887–896.

Maehr, M. L. (1974b). *Sociocultural origins of achievement.* Monterey, CA: Brooks/Cole.

Maehr, M. L. (2001). Goal theory is not dead—Not yet, anyway: A reflection on the Special Issue. *Educational Psychology Review, 13*(2), 177–185.

Maehr, M. L., & Anderman, E. M. (1993). Reinventing schools for early adolescents: Emphasizing task goals. *Elementary School Journal, 93*(5), 593–610.

Maehr, M. L., & Braskamp, L. A. (1986). *The motivation factor: A theory of personal investment.* Lexington, MA: D.C. Heath and Company.

Maehr, M. L., & Meyer, H. A. (1997). Understanding motivation and schooling: Where we've been, where we are, and where we need to go. *Educational Psychology Review, 9*(4), 371–409.

Maehr, M. L., & Midgley, C. (1991). Enhancing student motivation: A schoolwide approach. *Educational Psychologist, 26*(3), 399–427.

Maehr, M. L., & Midgley, C. (1996). *Transforming school cultures.* Boulder, CO: Westview Press.

Maehr, M. L., & Nicholls, J. G. (1980). Culture and achievement motivation: A second look. In N. Warren (Ed.), *Studies in cross-cultural psychology* (Vol. 3, pp. 221–267). New York: Academic Press.

Markus, H., & Nurius, P. (1986). Possible selves. *American Psychologist, 41*, 954–969.

Markus, H. R., & Kitayama, S. (1991). Culture and the self: Implications for cognition, emotion, and motivation. *Psychological Review, 98*, 224–253.

McClelland, D. C. (1961). *The achieving society.* New York: MacMillan.

McGregor, H. A., & Elliot, A. J. (2002). Achievement goals as predictors of achievement-relevant processes prior to task engagement. *Journal of Educational Psychology, 94*(2), 381–395.

Middleton, M. J., & Midgley, C. (1997). Avoiding the demonstration of lack of ability: An underexplored aspect of goal theory. *Journal of Educational Psychology, 89*(4), 710–718.

Midgley, C., Anderman, E., & Hicks, L. (1995). Differences between elementary and middle school teachers and students: A goal theory approach. *Journal of Early Adolescence, 15*, 90–113.

Midgley, C., Arunkumar, R., & Urdan, T. (1996). "If I don't do well tomorrow, there's a reason": Predictors of adolescents' use of academic self-handicapping strategies. *Journal of Educational Psychology, 88*, 423–434.

Midgley, C., Kaplan, A., & Middleton, M. (2001). Performance-approach goals: Good for what, for whom, under what circumstances, and at what cost? *Journal of Educational Psychology, 93*(1), 77–86.

Midgley, C., Maehr, M. L., Hruda, L. Z., Anderman, E., Anderman, L., Freeman, K. E., et al. (2000). *Manual for the Patterns of Adaptive Learning Scales (PALS).* Ann Arbor: University of Michigan.

Midgley, C., & Urdan, T. (2001). Academic self-handicapping and performance goals: A further examination. *Contemporary Educational Psychology, 26*, 61–75.

Nicholls, J. G. (1979). Quality and equality in intellectual development: The role of motivation in education. *American Psychologist, 34*(11), 1071–1084.

Nicholls, J. G. (1984). Achievement motivation: Conceptions of ability, subjective experience, task choice, and performance. *Psychological Review, 91*(3), 328–346.

Nicholls, J. G. (1990). What is ability and why are we mindful of it? A developmental perspective. In R. J. Sternberg & J. Kolligian (Eds.), *Competence considered* (pp. 11–40). New Haven, CT: Yale University Press.

Osgood, C. E. (1964). Semantic differential technique in the comparative study of cultures. *American Anthropologist, 66*, 171–201.

Osgood, C. E., Miron, M., & May, W. (1975). *Cross-cultural universals of affective meaning.* Urbana: University of Illinois Press.

Patrick, H., Anderman, L. H., Ryan, A. M., Edelin, K. C., & Midgley, C. (2001). Teachers' communication of goal orientations in four fifth-grade classrooms. *The Elementary School Journal, 102*, 35–58.

Pekrun, R., Elliot, A. J., & Maier, M. A. (2006). Achievement goals and discrete achievement emotions: A theoretical model and prospective test. *Journal of Educational Psychology, 98*(3), 583–597.

Pervin, L. A. (1989). Goal concepts in personality and social psychology: A historical introduction. In L. A. Pervin (Ed.), *Goal concepts in personality and social psychology* (pp. 1–17). Hillsdale, NJ: Erlbaum.

Pintrich, P. R. (2000a). Multiple goals, multiple pathways: The role of goal orientation in learning and achievement. *Journal of Educational Psychology, 92*(3), 544–555.

Pintrich, P. R. (2000b). The role of goal orientation in self-regulated learning. In M. Boekaerts, P. R. Pintrich, & M. Zeidner (Eds.), *Handbook of self-regulation* (pp. 452–502). San Diego, CA: Academic Press.

Pintrich, P. R., & Schunk, D. H. (2002). *Motivation in education: Theory, research, and applications* (2nd ed.). Upper Saddle River, NJ: Merrill Prentice Hall.

Roeser, R. (2004). Competing schools of thought in achievement goal theory? In P. R. Pintrich & M. L. Maehr (Eds.), *Motivating students, improving schools: The legacy of Carol Midgley* (Vol. 13, pp. 265–300): JAI.

Ryan, A., Gheen, M., & Midgley, C. (1998). Why do some students avoid asking for help? An examination of the interplay among students' academic efficacy, teachers' social-emotional role, and classroom goal structure. *Journal of Educational Psychology, 90*, 528–535.

Ryan, A. M., & Pintrich, P. R. (1997). "Should I ask for help?" The role of motivation and attitudes in adolescents' help seeking in math class. *Journal of Educational Psychology, 89*(2), 329–341.

Ryan, A. M., & Shim, S. S. (2006). Social achievement goals: The nature and consequences of different orientations toward social competence. *Personality and Social Psychology Bulletin, 32*(9), 1246–1263.

Ryan, K. E., Ryan, A. M., Arbuthnot, K., & Samuels, M. (2007). Students' motivation for standardized math exams. *Educational Researcher, 36*, 5–13.

Ryan, R. M., & Brown, K. W. (2005). Legislating competence: High-stakes testing policies and their relations with psychological theories and research. In A. J. Elliot & C. S. Dweck (Eds.), *Handbook of competence and motivation* (pp. 354–372). New York: Guilford.

Schouwenburg, H. C., & Groenewoud J., G. (2001). Study motivation under social temptation: Effects of trait procrastination. *Personality and Individual Differences, 30*, 229–240.

Schultheiss, O. C., & Brunstein, J., C. (2005). An implicit motive perspective on competence. In A. J. Elliot & C. S. Dweck (Eds.), *Handbook of competence and motivation* (pp. 31–51). New York: Guilford.

Schunk, D. H., & Pajares, F. (2005). Competence perceptions and academic functioning. In A. J. Elliot & C. S. Dweck (Eds.), *Handbook of competence and motivation* (pp. 85–104). New York: Guilford.

Schunk, D. H., Pintrich, P. R., & Meece, J. L. (2008). *Motivation in education: Theory, research, and applications.* Upper Saddle River, NJ: Pearson Education.

Shettleworth, S. J. (1999). *Cognition, evolution, and behavior.* New York: Oxford University Press.

Skaalvik, E. M. (1997). Self-enhancing and self-defeating ego orientation: Relations with task and avoidance orientation, achievement, self-perceptions, and anxiety. *Journal of Educational Psychology, 89*, 71–81.

Stipek, D. J., & Daniels, D. H. (1988). Declining perceptions of competence: A consequence of changes in the child or in the educational environment? *Journal of Educational Psychology, 80,* 352–356.

Thompson, T., & Musket, S. (2005). Does priming for mastery goals improve the performance of students with an entity view of ability? *British Journal of Educational Psychology, 75*(3), 391–409.

Triandis, H. (1972). *The analysis of subjective culture.* New York: Wiley.

Turner, J., & Meyer, D. K. (2000). Studying and understanding the instructional contexts of classrooms: Using our past to forge our future. *Educational Psychologist, 35*, 69–85.

Turner, J. C., Meyer, D. K., Midgley, C., & Patrick, H. (2003). Teacher discourse and sixth graders' reported affect and achievement behaviors in two high-mastery/high-performance mathematics classrooms. *The Elementary School Journal, 103*, 357–378.

Urdan, T. (Ed.). (1997). *Achievement goal theory: Past results, future directions* (Vol. 10). Greenwich, CT: JAI Press.

Urdan, T., & Mestas, M. (2006). The Goals Behind Performance Goals. *Journal of Educational Psychology, 98*(2), 354–365.

Urdan, T., Midgley, C., & Anderman, E. (1998). Classroom influences on self-handicapping strategies. *American Educational Research Journal, 35*, 101–122.

Urdan, T., & Turner, J. C. (2005). Competence motivation in the classroom. In A. J. Elliot & C. S. Dweck (Eds.), *Handbook of competence and motivation* (pp. 297–317). New York: Guilford.

Urdan, T. C., & Maehr, M. L. (1995). Beyond a two-goal theory of motivation and achievement: A case for social goals. *Review of Educational Research, 65*(3), 213–243.

Wentzel, K. R. (1997). Student motivation in middle school: The role of perceived pedagogical caring. *Journal of Educational Psychology, 89*, 411–419.

Wentzel, K. R. (2000). What is it that I'm trying to achieve? Classroom goals from a content perspective. *Contemporary Educational Psychology, 25*, 105–115.

White, R. W. (1959). Motivation reconsidered: The concept of competence. *Psychological Review, 66*, 297–333.

Wolters, C. A. (2004). Advancing achievement goal theory: Using goal structures and goal orientations to predict students' motivation, cognition, and achievement. *Journal of Educational Psychology, 96*, 236–250.

Wolters, C. A., Yu, S. L., & Pintrich, P. R. (1996). The relation between goal orientation and students' motivational beliefs and self-regulated learning. *Learning and Individual Differences, 8*(3), 211–238.

Zusho, A., Karabenick, S. A., Bonney, C. R., & Sims, B. C. (2007). Contextual determinants of motivation and help seeking in the college classroom. In R. Perry & J. Smart (Eds.), *The scholarship of teaching and learning in higher education: An evidence-based perspective* (pp. 611–659). New York: Springer.

Zusho, A., & Njoku, H. (2007). Culture and motivation to learn: Exploring the generalizability of achievement goal theory. In F. Salili & R. Hoosain (Eds.), *Culture, motivation, and learning: A multicultural perspective* (pp. 91–113). Greenwich, CT: Information Age.

Zusho, A., Pintrich, P. R., & Cortina, K. S. (2005). Motives, goals, and adaptive patterns of performance in Asian American and Anglo American students. *Learning and Individual Differences, 15*(2), 141–158.

6

Goal-Directed Behavior in the Classroom

Monique Boekaerts

Multiple Goals Move Students Forward

Personal goals and the emotions that successful goal pursuit evokes are the main energy sources that move people forward (i.e., give energy and direction to their life). Personal goals can relate to the home and family domain, to various social relationships, to school and work environments, to health, and spirituality. For example, a student may be motivated to learn to read for different reasons as the following examples may show. Maggie is intrigued by the symbols that she cannot decipher yet but that others can flawlessly decode. Paula views being able to read as instrumental for reaching her dream: becoming a doctor. Sammy wants to read what his grandma writes to him, and Eve wants to read well in order to establish a close relationship with her new teacher. For each of these four students reading is a meaningful and purposeful activity; they view "being able to read" as a desirable end-state and are prepared to engage in a chain of activities that will reach this end-state. Such purposeful involvement refers to a personal goal or personal project. It is essential that teachers and parents are aware of the personal goals that direct students' learning activities, because these personal projects give meaning to learning and are a source of energy that allows the students to move forward.

Elliot and Sheldon (1998) defined personal goals as the personally meaningful objectives that individuals pursue in their daily lives. They argued that personal goals play a key role in motivated action, defining its content, intensity and direction. From the moment individuals have set a personal goal, their actions have become meaningful and purposeful because that goal is used both as a desired end-state, or outcome of their actions, and as a standard for selecting the chain of actions that will lead to that desired end-state. Karoly (1999) also argued that goals are deeply and meaningfully rooted in people's everyday reality by providing a temporal anchor for thinking, feeling, and planning. He views goals as analogous to the factors in a factor analysis; they represent the latent core around which separate elements are organized. As such, goals—and the standards they imply—serve many functions; they define the cross-situational relevance and importance of settings and serve as the psychological links to the roles and social identities that are present in people's life. Most individuals have a variety of social roles that give meaning and purpose to their life. Evidence suggests that the more salient a role is to a person (e.g., I am a respected peer, good student, and excellent soccer player) the more time and energy (s)he will invest to maintain that part of his self-identity (Greenhaus & Powell, 2006).

Each student brings many goals into the classroom, but educators would like to think that learning and performance goals that students pursue are the focal goals in her multigoal environment and that they primarily draws on their limited pool of resources to realize these goals. Even though there are presently few studies available that have investigated how students allocate resources among their different personal goals, I am convinced that all students live in a multigoal environment, and that much of their daily activities concern decision making about how much of their limited resources they will invest in the many goals that they consider salient at that point in time (see Boekaerts, 2003). In other words, the multigoal environment is the rule rather than the exception in contemporary classrooms and that raises the question: how do students regulate goal pursuit in a multigoal environment?

Need to Move Beyond the Study of Single Goals in Single Goal Contexts

It is essential that motivation researchers recognize the need to focus explicitly on the *multiple goals* that students bring into the classroom and on how these goals interact. Which of these goals support each other and which ones compete for the limited resources? Goals are socially derived constructs and therefore need to be examined in light of social and cultural roles, rules, and regulations. As such, motivation researchers should also focus on the multiple contexts that may facilitate or hinder students' pursuit of multiple goals. These claims may seem obvious, because by far the largest empirical research literature on motivation in the classroom is based on studies that set out to document how multiple goals and multiple contexts interact. However, this is not at all obvious, given that researchers working in the goal theory paradigm have routinely focused on a *single type of goal*, namely achievement goals in a single type of context, namely achievement situations.

More specifically, goal theorists have studied students' lay theory of the reasons or purposes for engagement in curricular activities. Researchers working within this dominant framework split up the contextualized stream of classroom events into a limited set of components that together promote achievement in the classroom. They have identified the reasons that students give for trying to succeed on school-related tasks as "goals" or "goal orientations" (e.g., Harackiewicz, Barron, Tauer, Carter, & Elliot, 2000; Pintrich, 2000). One of the reasons (or goals) that students give for their engagement in school-related tasks is wanting to increase their competence or understanding of a task (mastery goals). Another reason is wanting to demonstrate that they are competent students (performance approach) or wanting to hide that they are not as good as their peers (performance avoidance). Goal orientation research showed that students' reasons (or purpose) for achievement may vary considerably from classroom to classroom and from culture to culture but that there are also striking similarities (McInerney, 2004).

In my opinion, these researchers described in detail what type of resources are needed to attain specific achievement standards. In fact, they advised teachers to promote and reward two types of resources, namely pursuit of mastery and performance goals. They also made students and teachers aware of a variety of contexts that may help them to fill up the tanks of their dual-energy motivation motor. As such, we know a great deal about the conditions that promote the pursuit of mastery and performance goals (e.g., Urdan, 2007) but very little about the many other non-achievement goals that students bring into the classroom and that compete for resources. In goal theory, competition between goals has typically been defined quite narrowly between mastery and performance orientations to achievement goals and most of the findings have been obtained in a single-goal context in which students are encouraged to invest effort to reduce the discrepancy between their present states (e.g., not knowing how to explain or do things in a domain) and two desirable end states (e.g., being competent in that domain and obtaining a specific grade). It is important that researchers broaden their perspective and focus on all meaningful aspects of a student's life that supply energy and not just on learning, achievement and grading. In other words, they need to study the nonachievement goals that energize a student's actions.

Students Process Cues from Multiple Sources

Today, students grow up in a variety of social settings that shape their cognitions, feelings, and actions. They have had a multitude of favorable and unfavorable experiences in these diverse settings, which have been integrated in their long-term memory schemata and their goal hierarchy. Dittmann-Kohli (1995) argued that in the course of their lives, individuals build up understanding of the world around them, of themselves as separate identities, and of the social roles they need to fulfill. Contextual and culture-specific information lead to a subjective theory of the Self-in-social-context that functions as a cognitive map for goal-directed behavior. Several researchers have linked specific styles of care-taking to the aspirations, hopes, and wishes for the future that children and adolescents express in daily life (e.g., Higgins, 1997; Phelan, Yu, & Davidson, 1994). Higgins (1997) implicated cultural patterns and early socialization processes, particularly care-taking styles, in the promotion of strong or weak "ought's" that represent obligations, duties, and responsibilities. He discussed how generalized cultural patterns and care-taking styles act as internal guides in concrete situations. This suggests that the knowledge that different students bring to bear on the learning situation is at variance and that it influences their appraisal of social settings, particularly the types of learning opportunities they value and the types of goals they want to attain in these settings. In this respect, it is important to realize that Hickey and Granade (2004) challenged the view that values and goals are resident in the hearts and minds of students. They hypothesized that values and goals that support students' engagement and disengagement patterns in a social learning setting have a reciprocal relationship with the social context.

Phelan et al. (1994) nicely illustrated this point. They described the conditions and circumstances that prevail in students' daily life (the home, peer group, and school context) and how students' perceptions of these conditions and circumstances act as pressures and constraints on their interest in academic tasks and their actual pursuit of academic goals. These researchers described the multiple worlds that students from different ethnic groups live in and how moving from one world (e.g., home) to the other world (e.g., school) may be perceived as harmonious and uncomplicated or turbulent and discordant. Phelan et al. concluded that it is not so much the perception of differences between the multiple worlds that causes problems. Instead it is the students' ability and willingness to adjust and reorient that helps them to manage the crossings successfully. They described how students may find the goals, values, beliefs, and expectations across worlds as so discordant that they consider them insurmountable and actively or passively resist transitions.

What is the Content of Students' Goals?

If we accept that students function in different worlds and bring multiple goals into the classroom, we need to know the content of their goals and examine how they coordinate their multiple goals.

I will describe two goal frameworks that help us to gain insight into the content of the goals that students pursue in their daily lives. The first framework is Schwartz's (1992) theory of human values. The second framework is Ford and Nichols (1991) taxonomy of desired intrapersonal and desired person-environment outcomes.

Schwartz's Theory of Basic Human Values

Schwartz and colleagues (Schwartz, 1992; Schwartz & Bardi, 2001) argued that 10 basic human values, or motivationally distinct trans-situational goals, serve as guiding principles in people's life. They depicted the content of these abstract goals (i.e., power, achievement, hedonism, stimulation, self-direction, universalism, benevolence, tradition, conformity, and security) in a circular structure and specified the relations between these goals in terms of the conflicts and congruities between them. As can be viewed from Figure 6.1, two orthogonal dimensions summarize the structure of the relations between the 10 value types. The vertical axis represents an asymmetry that ranges from self-transcendence to self-enhancement. The horizontal axis ranges from openness to change to the conservation of the status quo. Schwartz and Bardi (2001) assumed that the closer any two value types are located in either direction around the circle, the more similar their underlying meaning and motivation. By contrast, the more distance there is between any two values, the more antagonistic their underlying meaning and motivation.

As can be seen, achievement and power values flank the self-enhancement pole of the vertical dimension and benevolence and universalism flank the self-transcendence pole of that dimension. Schwartz and Bardi (2001) argued that power and achievement values highlight the pursuit of self-interest and are motivationally incompatible with the benevolence and universalism values that express concern for others. Self-direction and stimulation flank the openness-to-change pole of the horizontal axis and security, tradition and conformity characterize the conservation of the status quo. These investigators argued that independent thoughts, feelings, and actions, as well as

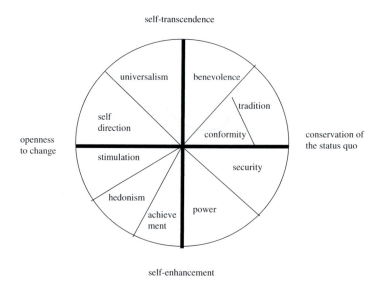

Figure 6.1 Theoretical model of the 10 values and structure of the relations between the values. (Schwartz & Bardi, 2001).

readiness for new experiences, are the hallmarks of self-direction and stimulation values (openness to change). These value types are motivationally incompatible with conformity, tradition, and security (conservation of the status quo), which typically underlie dependence, self-restriction, order, and resistance to change. Analyses in more than 200 samples from 60 countries in different continents support the circular structure and the specified relations between the 10 value types.

Boekaerts, De Koning, and Vedder (2006) used Schwartz's circular structure to inspect the literature on goals in education and concluded that not much is presently known about the relations between the 10 value types in terms of the conflicts and congruities between them in different educational settings.

Ford and Nichols' Taxonomy of 24 Content Goals

Ford (1992) presented an integrative theory of goals, namely Motivational System Theory. It is unique in that it describes personal goals as unifying constructs of human functioning. Ford's theory describes cognitive representations of goals and uses these cognitive tools to explain conceptual issues as well as empirical data from both students and clients about the goal management process (self-regulation). He described two key aspects of goals, namely goal processes and goal content. Goal processes refer to individuals' goal orientation and to how they set goals and strive for them. Goal content refers to different classes of desired and undesired outcomes.

Ford and Nichols' (1991) proposed a taxonomy of 24 content goals that are important in people's life. They split up the range of meaningful outcomes into desired outcomes that have to do with the person him or herself (desired intrapersonal outcomes) and desired outcomes that refer to the individual's interaction with the environment (desired person-environment outcomes). Ford and Nichols do not assume that any of the 24 content goals is inherently more important than any other category, although particular classes of goals may dominate the goal network empirically at certain periods in the individual's life. They divided intrapersonal goals into three main goal categories, namely affective goals, cognitive goals, and subjective organization goals. Affective goals refer to feelings, bodily sensations and well-being. This category consists of entertainment goals (e.g., I want to have fun), tranquility goals (e.g., I want to avoid stress), happiness goals (e.g., I want to feel satisfied), bodily sensations (e.g., I want to avoid unpleasant sensations), and physiological well-being goals (e.g., I want to feel healthy). Cognitive goals refer to different types of cognitive engagement and to the protection of one's self-worth. This category includes understanding goals (e.g., I want to be able to make sense of things), exploration goals (e.g., I want to have intellectual stimulation), intellectual creativity goals (e.g., I want to expand my limits) and positive self-evaluation goals (e.g., I want to feel self-efficacious). Subjective organization goals group two goal types that reflect how one perceives one's place in the world, namely unity goals (e.g., I want to live in harmony) and transcendence goals (e.g., I want to believe in an upper being).

Ford and Nichols describe person-environment goals in terms of three goal categories, namely self-assertive social relationship goals, integrative social relationship goals, and task goals. Self-assertive social relationship goals refer to how an individual wants to interact with the social environment. This category consist of individuality goals (e.g., I want to feel unique), superiority goals (e.g., I want to be better than my peers), self-determination goals (e.g., I want to experience a sense of freedom), and resource acquisition goals (e.g., I want my peers to help me). Integrative social relationship goals are in fact the mirror image of the self-assertive social relationship goals, but this category relates to how an individual looks upon social relationships. This category consist of four different types of goals, namely belongingness goals (e.g., I want to build and maintain attachments), social responsibility goals (e.g., I want to keep interpersonal commitments), equity goals (e.g., I want to promote fairness and justice), and resource provision goals (e.g., I want to help my peers). Finally, task goals include goals that refer to how individuals confront tasks and challenges that they come across during their life. This category included mastery goals (e.g., I want to meet standards of achievement), management goals (e.g., I want to be productive), material gain goals (e.g., I want to earn money), safety goals (e.g., I want to feel safe from risks), and task creativity goals (e.g., I want to invent new things).

Ford (1992) argued that any of these goals may take salience in an individual's network of goals, but that the activation of one goal does not prevent any other goal from gaining dominance in the network. Ford also argued that the location of a goal in the goal hierarchy helps individuals to set priorities in a particular situation. I will now briefly consider the properties and organization of goals.

Hierarchical Organization of Goals

Shah and Kruglanski (2000) described goals as knowledge structures about desirable and undesirable future end-states. These knowledge structures contain content, purpose, and process aspects and specify the state or standard that is desired. This standard or reference value plays an important role in goal attainment, because it allows individuals to select the chain of activities that will lead to the desired end-state as well as monitor their progress toward the goal. Goals are associated with other knowledge structures that facilitate their attainment (i.e., subgoals or means). Austin and Vancouver (1996) argued that interrelations between goals are critical and that the dominant conceptualization of the structure of goals is hierarchical. Several hierarchical frameworks have been proposed; the common view is that lower level goals are attached to multiple higher level goals, thus creating a network of goals.

Carver and Scheier (1996) explained that goals located somewhere in the goal hierarchy are not equivalent in their relevance to the person. The higher goals are located in the network, the more they contribute to an individual's sense of Self. It is generally accepted that a small set of higher order goals, or principles, should be placed at the apex of a hierarchical goal network. This set of basic principles contributes most to a person's sense of Self, because the principles represent the person's basic values and the traits that he or she considers ideal. As such, higher order goals provide general organization and orientation to a person's life and optimize personal meaning making processes. Schwartz's theory of basic human values is such a set of principles. Below principle level goals are personal projects (Little, 1983), action programs (Carver and Scheier, 2000), life tasks (Cantor & Fleeson, 1994), or self-set mid-level goals (Ford, 1992; Little, 1999).

Powers (1973) and Carver and Scheier (2000) described goal hierarchies or action networks in detail. In the Powers hierarchy, the higher order goals, or principles, are quite abstract. They give reference to several subgoals at the next level down and many of these subgoals cascade to the level of muscle tensions. Carver and Scheier (2000) explained that individuals act in line with their higher-order goals, which they labeled "I want to be goals` (e.g., I want to be sociable, successful, and honest). They stated that the personal goals or projects that individuals pursue in their daily lives (e.g., I want to speak English like my older sister, or I want to make new friends in college) have been linked to one or more higher order goals, and this connection gives meaning and value to the type of activities they engage in. The more links that exist between a personal project (mid-level goal) and the principles higher up in the goal hierarchy the more significance that project has for the person. For example, the personal project "I want to speak English like my older sister" may be linked to several higher order goals, including having intellectual achievement, being successful in life, wanting to belong, and staying out of trouble. This project will be more salient in a student's life when it has been linked to all the higher order goals mentioned above than when it has only been linked to "staying out of trouble."

Mid-level goals (personal projects or action programs) are not only linked to goals higher up in the goal hierarchy. They are also connected to a number of subgoals lower down the hierarchy. These lower order goals are more concrete, specifying in what way one may attain the goal to which it is linked higher up the hierarchy. For example, the personal project "I want to get good grades for the next math exam" may be linked to the lower order goals "I want to do all the past exam papers to prepare for the math exam" and "I want to study together with Peter who is good in math." In turn, these goals may be connected to several nonsequential scripts, specifying how one does past exam papers, how one reviews one's notes, how one encourages a fellow student to collaborate for an exam, and how one studies efficiently together. If we could glance down students' goal hierarchies, it might reveal how each of their (learning) strategies is linked to specific automatized scripts. For example, inspection of the mental representation for reading past exam papers might reveal a number of scripts lower down the goal hierarchy, such as obtaining past exam papers from the library, selecting several past exam papers for closer examination, doing and timing the tests, taking notes, summarizing and paraphrasing. Austin and Vancouver (1996) argued that well-rehearsed scripts do not require much conscious consideration and can be performed concomitantly with other scripts. In fact, once the mental representation of well-practiced goals is activated, all the knowledge necessary to realize the desired outcome (or to avoid undesired outcomes) becomes automatically available (see also Custers & Aarts, 2005).

Shah and Kruglanski (2000) explained that behavioral flexibility and choice depends on the number of links that have been established in the goal hierarchy. They assume that individuals chose the best available means for attaining their goals. At some point, individuals may opt for an action program or script that most easily comes to mind. On other occasions, they may select a subgoal that they think will help them reach the goal more efficiently or they may chose the one that costs least effort. Ford (1992) argued in this respect that lower order goals, which serve many goals located higher up in the goal hierarchy, are more significant for the person and have a better chance to be chosen as a focal goal because of their multifinality (i.e., they promote many positive outcomes). These investigators also argued that having multiple means of goal attainment is to be preferred when goal attainment is uncertain, but that it is distracting when a task is relatively easy because a great deal of time may be lost in indecision.

Content Goals Tell Us What Students Want to Attain in the Classroom?

Several educational psychologists described goals with respect to their content (e.g., Boekaerts, 1998; Boekaerts et al., 2006; Dowson & McInerney, 2001; Lemos, 1996; Lemos & Gonçalves, 2004; Wentzel, 1992, 2000). Content goals tell us *what* students want to attain in terms of specific outcomes, but, as the following example will show, it is not always obvious which outcomes students strive for in the classroom. A couple of months ago, I interviewed a group of students while they were watching a video on which they were working collaboratively. I stopped the video at specific points and asked the respective team members to write down why they thought a student had reacted in a particular way to her peers at a specific moment in time. On the clip we saw Alicia explain to Maggie how she could solve a problem. Maggie smiled and said, "Oh that is what you mean." One student responded, "Maggie said that because she wanted to understand the problem and she smiled to Alicia because she had explained it well." Another student wrote, "Maggie said that because she wanted to be friends with Alicia." Alicia reported, "Maggie said that because she wanted more help and advice from me." Maggie wrote something completely different: "I wanted to decide myself how I was going to do the problem, rather than have Alicia decide that for me. But I did not want to lose her as a friend." This example illustrates how hard it is to observe what it is exactly that students are trying to achieve in a particular episode.

Lemos' (1996) study exemplified that teachers often do not have a clue as to the goals that their students want to attain. She observed and videotaped classroom behavior and interviewed sixth-grade students and their teachers during stimulated recall sessions about the content of the students' goals during stimulated recall. Lemos proposed a categorization system of four content goals, namely complying goals, working goals, evaluation goals, and mastery goals. She reported that the students predominantly reported working goals (e.g., I wanted to finish that job), and evaluation goals (e.g., I wanted to do well on that tasks), whereas teachers, observing the same videotaped episode, thought their students were mainly pursuing mastery goals (e.g., She wanted to comprehend lesson content) and compliance goals (e.g., She wanted to follow up on teacher's instruction). More recently, Lemos and Gonçalves (2004) reported that working and complying goals are more frequently pursued in the sixth-grade classroom than evaluation and relationship goals. They also reported that there was a discrepancy between students' self-reported goals and goal pursuit observed by the researchers.

Students Espouse Distinctive Purposes for Their Academic Achievement

Wentzel (1991, 1994, 1996, 2000) argued that most goal theories focus on rather abstract aspects of goal pursuit, such as goal proximity, level of challenge, and goal specificity. Although individuals use these aspects of goals to orient on performance, to allocate effort, and to monitor against standards, these goal approaches do not take adequate account of how contextual cues influence goal pursuit. Wentzel (2000) explained that a content approach is necessary if one wants to study the effect that specific goals have on the pursuit of other content goals in the classroom. She showed that pro-social goals and social responsibility goals are instrumental to achievement while belongingness with peers and entertainment goals may hinder rather than support learning. A few researchers followed Wentzel's lead and made an inventory of the different social goals that students pursue in the classroom.

For example, Dowson and McInerney (2001) identified four distinctive purposes that middle school students espoused for their academic achievement. These include social affiliation goals (i.e., wanting to achieve academically to enhance a sense of belonging to a specific group), social responsibility goals (i.e., wanting to achieve academically to meet social role obligations), social concern goals (i.e., wanting to achieve academically to assist others in their development), and work avoidance goals (i.e., wanting to achieve academically with as little effort as possible). These researchers used inductive content analysis to analyze interviews and observations and reported that students used different action programs and scripts to attain different social goals. For example, students who wanted to attain social affiliation goals frequently interacted with peers academically outside the classroom and they wanted to assist their peers with their academic work. Action programs used in the service of social responsibility goals included being involved in extra-curricular academic activities, volunteering for classroom jobs, taking on senior roles, and making peers aware of rules and regulations. Students who aspired social concern goals got appointed to helping roles; they tried to understand the material themselves in order to be able to help their peers. Finally, work avoidance goals were reflected in a number of effort minimization strategies with respect to academic tasks. Examples are copying, asking for help too soon, engaging in off-task behavior such as chatting, negotiating less demanding tasks, and feigning incompetence or misunderstanding.

Relations Between Different Content Goals

In our own studies on goal pursuit (Hijzen, Boekaerts, & Vedder, 2006; Boekaerts et al., 2006; Boekaerts & Rozendaal, 2007), we wanted to gain insight into the mid-level goals that are meaningfully rooted in vocational students' reality. We asked students in their first year of secondary vocational school to complete a goal questionnaire based on Ford and Nichols' taxonomy of goals (1991). Nearly 2000 vocational school students indicated how salient each goal was in their life. They completed the same questionnaire 6 months later. Items were of the type: I want to master new things, I want to feel secure, and I want to be liked by my peers. We found that these students distinguished between 16 different types of goals (see Figure 6.2).

Reasoning that goals—and the standards they imply—serve many functions in the classroom, we studied the interrelations between the different content goals at the two data collection points. Ward's hierarchical cluster analysis technique allowed us to observe how the respective clusters were formed. Inspection of the dendograms at the two data collection points showed similar structures, but it also revealed some interesting differences. As can be viewed in Figures 6.2 and 6.3, vocational school students differentiated between two main goal clusters, namely ego goals (individuality and superiority goals) and all the other goals. The nonego goals split up into two main goal clusters, namely goals that concern how the Self is related to the outer world (goals 1–11) and goals that concern the relation between societal roles and opportunities and the Self (goals 12–14). The Self-outer world goals include affective goals, such as positive tranquility goals (e.g., I want to feel calm), happiness/entertainment goals (e.g., I want to enjoy my time in school), and positive self-evaluations (e.g., I want to feel confident), integrative social relationship goals (belongingness, equity, self-determination goals) and task and social support goals (management, mastery, resource acquisition and provision). Finally, the society-Self goals consist of material gain goals (e.g., I want to earn a lot of money) and social security goals, which express the intention to fulfill one's social roles and commitments and goals that express personal safety. Affective and integrative social relationship goals were amongst the most salient in these students' life and ego goals were the least salient. There were also marked gender differences. Females differed from males on 12 of the 16 goal categories. Females indicated that ego goals (individuality and superiority) were less important than males did, but they reported higher salience than males in relation to task goals, positive self-evaluations, happiness/entertainment, equity and self-determination goals. No gender differences were found with respect to the salience of tranquility, belongingness, material gain and social support goals.

Six months later, the two main goal clusters (i.e., ego and nonego goals) were again evident in the cluster analysis (see Figure 6.3). Interestingly, material gain goals had now joined the ego goals. The nonego goals split up into two core goal types, namely goals referring to the person (1–9) and social goals (7–13). Two interesting changes need to be noted. First, safety goals were now amidst the person goals, next to affective goals and task goals. Second, social support goals (resource acquisition and resource provision), which were attached to task goals in the beginning of the school year, are now firmly embedded in a social goal cluster alongside belongingness,

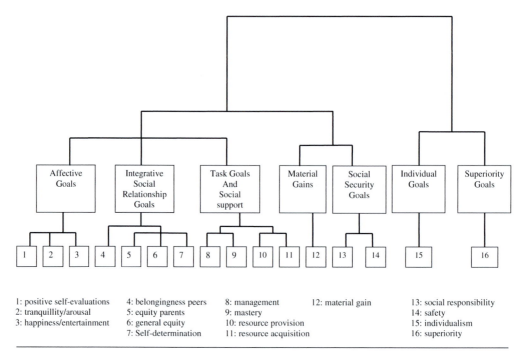

1: positive self-evaluations   4: belongingness peers   8: management   12: material gain   13: social responsibility
2: tranquillity/arousal   5: equity parents   9: mastery   14: safety
3: happiness/entertainment   6: general equity   10: resource provision   15: individualism
   7: Self-determination   11: resource acquisition   16: superiority

Figure 6.2 Clustering of the 16 mid-level goals at the first data collection point.

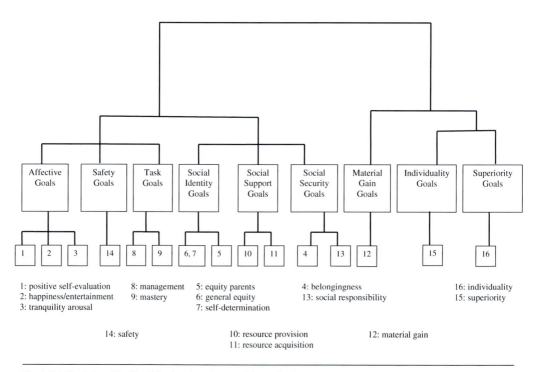

1: positive self-evaluation   8: management   5: equity parents   4: belongingness   16: individuality
2: happiness/entertainment   9: mastery   6: general equity   13: social responsibility   15: superiority
3: tranquility arousal   7: self-determination

14: safety   10: resource provision   12: material gain
   11: resource acquisition

Figure 6.3 Clustering of the 16 mid-level goals at the second data collection point.

social responsibility, and equity goals. This grouping suggests that students have come to see that striving for equity (i.e., promoting fairness, justice and reciprocity) and self-determination goals (experiencing a sense of freedom and personal control) are closely related and form an integral aspect of their social identity. Together with social support goals and social security goals, these goals help them to form integrative social relationships. Note that social responsibility goals (wanting to fulfill social roles and keeping interpersonal commitments) are now linked to belongingness goals (building and maintaining friendships with peers) rather than to personal safety. This clustering suggests that wanting to belong in the peer group and wanting to live up to social roles and expectations are closely linked in these students' every day reality.

Insight into the structure of the goals that students in different age groups pursue, may open a window on the personal and social identities that are present in their life, guiding their thinking, feeling, and acting.

Managing the Simultaneous Pursuit of Multiple Goals

Shah and Kruglanski (2000) showed that goals are rarely pursued in isolation. Pursuit of a goal always occurs in the context of pursuing other goals. For example, a student who is interested in exploring a new domain but feels insecure when she is working together with peers may activate learning and tranquility goals quasi-simultaneously in a collaborative learning context. Some cues in the social learning environment may prompt her to be more concerned with her self-esteem and well-being than with learning (see Boekaerts, 2006). Recent advances in cognitive neuroscience also revealed that situational cues (e.g., facial expressions, gender, ethnicity, and cues about cooperation, warmth and aggression) as well as subliminally presented performance words such as strive and succeed, may activate action programs and scripts automatically and without the person being aware of it. For example, a recent study by Shah (2003) showed that cognitive representations of others spontaneously prime the goals, values, and expectations that people think these persons hold for them. Consequently, it is important to consider the effect of cues that are present in the actual learning situation as well as the mental representations that students spontaneously activate in the classroom, because these actual and self-generated cues influence students' sense making processes and, as such, their engagement in the classroom.

The literature on competing goals describes what happens when students are aware that alternative goals are competing for their resources but is relatively silent about the effect that interpersonal priming may have on academic goal pursuit. Yet, under both circumstances, students may need to exercise volitional control, inhibiting those action programs and scripts that pull their energy away from the focal task. Kuhl (2000) argued that progress toward a focal goal depends on both the active pursuit of that goal and the inhibition of alternative goals. His action control theory describes state-oriented and action-oriented individuals. The former group is not able to set a goal and stick to it; they cannot ignore competing goals, are easily distracted, and cannot cognitively disengage from a failure experience. The latter group can exercise self-control by swiftly initiating goal pursuit, showing persistence during the task and disengaging from focal goal pursuit if conditions are suboptimal or when the goal is achieved. It is noteworthy that losing time in indecision, as well as the inhibition of impulses, consumes resources. Baumeister (2003) suggested that the strategies needed to control emotions interfere with active engagement and persistence on a task, unless the spent energy is restored. They showed that students who had to focus on their emotions and make an attempt to control them tended to give up faster on a successive task than those who did not have to control their emotions. They explained that the resources needed to inhibit responses (here: resist temptation in eating sweets) interacted with the effort needed to persist on the task.

How do Multiple Goals Interact in the Classroom?

I have mentioned previously that goals may be congruent or in conflict. In any situation, a unique composition of goals may come to the foreground and these goals may or may not be in harmony. If they are, they reinforce each other, thus providing extra energy that the person can invest. If these goals are in conflict, they may deplete resources, creating a shortage of energy. Wentzel (2000) highlighted that the pursuit of multiple goals in the same context implies that individuals should be able to coordinate these goals effectively. This is a critical self-regulatory skill that connects motivation to competent behavior. Argyle, Furnham, and Graham (1981) made a distinction between three types of goal coordination, namely independence (i.e., pursuing two or more goals where they neither help nor hinder each other), interference (the pursuit on one goal impedes the pursuit of other goals), and instrumentality (striving for one goal facilitates the pursuit of the other goals).

Wentzel (1996) showed that students who pursued social and mastery goals in concert are more willing to invest effort in their school work. She (Wentzel, 1989) also reported unique goal patterns for high and low-achieving students. High-achievers were inclined to focus on being successful and getting things done on time (e.g., they had salient management goals), they were also responsible and dependable students (i.e., had salient social responsibility goals) and considered making friends and having fun as less salient in their school life. Low-achieving students, on the other hand, reported that the latter two goals were salient in their life. Several researchers reported that students who strive for social and mastery goals simultaneously are more productive than students who only strive for mastery. For example, Hertz-Lazarowitz and Miller (1992) argued in this respect that much of the success of cooperative learning is because students show goal striving for the sake of the group. These researchers explained that the sense of belonging, social support, and social responsibility that is provoked when students value social goals provides an added drive for academic achievement.

Contrary to popular teacher beliefs but in line with Wentzel's findings, Hijzen et al. (2006) found that adolescents who report that belongingness goals are salient in their life (i.e., who indicated that they found it important to be liked by their peers and feel welcome in the group), reported lower perceptions of the quality of collaborative learning than students who did not attach such value to belongingness goals. Hence, it seems that belongingness with peers interferes with the pursuit of academic goals (i.e., an interference type of goal coordination). Further analysis revealed that the former students also scored lower than the latter students on perceived group cohesion and perceived quality of their cooperation skills. This result suggests that there is also an interference type of goal coordination between belongingness goals and social support goals. Järvela and Hakkinen (2002) shed some light on this type of goal coordination. They explained that not all students are convinced of the beneficial effect of group learning processes. Several students feel hindered rather than supported by collaborative knowledge construction. Järvela and Hakkinen showed that learning through collaboration is not just happening when two or more students are requested to work together. In order to profit from collaborative learning, students need to have access to essential social skills (including listening to each other, present one's opinion, reach consensus, monitor and evaluate the group learning process, support group members, and solve group conflict); they need to mindfully engage in learning *and* social interaction. In other words, an instrumental type of goal coordination between mastery goals and social support goals is needed.

Primed and Nonprimed Goal Pursuit

In order to gain more insight into the relation between various social goals and classroom engagement, Hijzen et al., (2006) conducted semistructured team interviews and stimulated recall with effective and ineffective collaborative learning teams. Effectiveness was established on the basis of students' off-task and on-task behavior as well as on their socially-oriented task engagement. Students in effective teams were more aware of the multiple goals they pursued in the classroom than were students in the ineffective teams. They also explained their task engagement in terms of their salient goals. Interestingly, both students in the effective and ineffective teams reported that certificate goals (i.e., goals that relate to obtaining a diploma) were salient goals in their lives. However, students in the effective teams also stated that mastery, social responsibility, and social support goals were important goals (instrumentality goal coordination), whereas students in the ineffective teams reported mainly that entertainment and work avoidance goals were salient alongside certificate goals (interference goal coordination). Yet, the latter students did not explain their task engagement in terms of their salient goals. Instead, they pointed to unfavorable aspects of the learning setting to account for their low task engagement. For example, they mentioned that the teacher was never there when they needed help and that tasks were boring and tedious. The verbal report of these students contrasted with students in the effective teams, who mainly pointed to favorable aspects of the learning environment when asked to account for their task engagement (e.g., "We worked really well; everybody did their fair share of the work and helped each other").

Why are the explanations of task engagement, which students in the effective teams offered, based on their salient goals in combination with a favorable perception of the learning environment? And why are the explanations that members of the less effective teams offered primarily based on their unfavorable perceptions of the learning environment and only marginally on the goals they pursue in the learning context? At the moment, I have no definite answers to these and similar questions, but I would like to speculate that students in the effective teams mainly experienced goal concordance. Their certificate goals seemed to be well integrated into their goal hierarchy, probably having many links with the action programs and scripts that served the mastery and social responsibility goals. Hence, these students may have had more than one reason to engage in the learning tasks, viewing the collaborative learning environment as an opportunity to realize both their certificate goals and their mastery and social responsibility goals.

By contrast, certificate goals may have had a more isolated position in the hierarchy of the students in the ineffective teams. Entertainment and work avoidance goals seemed to have a dominant position in their goal network, and the action programs and scripts linked to these goals may have been in conflict with the scripts to attain certificate goals (interference goal coordination). The frequency of these students' off-task behavior (here, encoded as low task engagement and low socially-oriented task engagement) seems to point in that direction. Moreover, the fact that these students explained their off-task behavior mainly in terms of unfavorable environmental cues—rather than in terms of rivaling goals—suggests that their off-task behavior was triggered by cues in the learning environment (i.e., primed behavior).

An eye-opener in this respect was that the students in our study clearly differentiated between different types of social goals, including belongingness goals, resource acquisition goals, resource provision goals, and social responsibility goals, and that these different social goals influenced their engagement in collaborative learning in unexpected ways. Students' task-relevant engagement was positively associated with their mastery and social responsibility goals and negatively related to their belongingness and tranquility goals. Task-irrelevant engagement was positively linked to belongingness, tranquility, and entertainment goals. Socially-oriented task engagement was inversely related to belongingness goals. This inversed relationship sounds paradoxical to many students, teachers, and educational researchers alike. So, we need to raise the question: What does this result imply? First of all, it implies that students, who want to master the material and strive for social responsibility goals, are qualitatively more engaged in collaborative learning than students who report that belongingness goals are salient in their goal hierarchy. The latter students are less engaged in task-relevant actions and show more task-irrelevant behavior (e.g., chatting, texting, watching the clock) and less socially-oriented task engagement (e.g., providing instrumental and emotional support to group members). Hence, our results confirm Wentzel's conclusion that there is an interference type of goal coordination between belongingness goals and academic goals. But where in the learning process does this interference take place? This question was the object of a study I conducted with Rozendaal, described in the following section.

How Are Personal Goals Related to Strategy Use?

Boekaerts (2006) argued that top down self-regulation is primed by one's own goals, values, and needs, and that it occurs without much conscious attention. Boekaerts and Rozendaal (2007) argued further that personal goals that are salient in a student's life can be viewed as a set of intrinsic demands that are posed on his or her current goal pursuit. They investigated the salience of vocational students' mid level goals and found that—apart from fundamental trust in one's ability to write and having a firm belief that the learning environment is supportive of one's writing—salience of personal goals made a unique contribution to the variance explained in metacognitive strategy use in the service of various writing activities (e.g., writing an e-mail, a term paper, an application letter). A unique and positive contribution was made by the students' perception that writing is instrumental for their mastery goals, particularly for the more serious writing activities (e.g., term paper and application letter). A unique negative contribution was made by the students' perception that writing is instrumental to the attainment of their well-being goals (e.g., positive self-evaluation, tranquility, belongingness, entertainment). Boekaerts and Rozendaal (2007) suggested that students, who believe that writing is instrumental to reach their mastery goals (well-being goals), have established a direct link between this belief and their action programs and scripts, which will help them to achieve these respective goals. In other words, means-end relationships have been established, meaning that they quasi automatically choose these scripts when presented with writing activities (primed self-regulation). By contrast, students, who do not believe that writing is instrumental to reach their mastery (well-being) goals, rely on conscious decision making when presented with a writing task (nonprimed self-regulation).

A fuller understanding of goal multiplicity will be reached when we get a better grasp of the purpose that students assign to their behavior in different domains and settings. In the meantime, it is necessary to reconsider the impact that off-task behavior may have on the way students energize and give direction to their activities in the classroom. Some teachers, parents and educators seem to think that the most direct threat to an achievement goal is—apart from not having the necessary basic resources—competing goals. They assume that the pool of personal resources (e.g., attention, time, effort) is limited and fixed and that using personal resources to attain one goal implies automatically that fewer resources are available for other goals. Recently, the assumptions underlying this theory were challenged. Greenhaus and Powell (2006) argued that engagement in one activity can buffer effects of negative emotions in a different activity. They reported that social goals pursued in a family context can bring a person to a "feeling good" state that may spill over to performance goals pursued in a works context, and vice versa. Their research demonstrated that the mere presence of alternative goals does not draw resources away from the current focal goal (thus undermining goal pursuit). Very often, competing goals strengthen the person's goal focus and intensity of engagement rather than impede it.

In summary, the simultaneous pursuit of multiple content goals is the rule in every day life rather than the exception. It requires that students find a dynamic balance between rivaling demands for their limited personal resources. Surprisingly little is known about how students coordinate their multiple goals in the classroom. In my view, we urgently need a theory that describes how students manage the competing demands that multiple goals place on their limited resources. Such a theory would allow us to answer interesting questions such as how students determine which goals are alien at a given moment and whether learning in the presence of alternative goals is beneficial or harmful for performance. We need to know whether the presence of alternative goals draws resources away from the current focal goal—thus undermining goal pursuit—or whether it strengthens the students' goal focus and intensity of learning. In order to answer these and similar questions we need to move beyond the study of the dual-energy motivation motor that is popular in educational psychology and explore how the multiple-energy motivation motor works (see Boekaerts, 2008).

Future Research on Goal Pursuit in the Classroom

In this chapter, I sketched a set of ideas that I consider important in conceptualizing about goal-directed behavior in the classroom. I argued that the goals that underlie behavior can best be conceptualized as part of a hierarchy of goals. Goals vary in concreteness and individuals have established multiple connections among their goals, as well as between environmental cues and specific action programs and scripts. These ideas have been very much part of my thinking about goal-directed behavior in the classroom.

In future research on goal pursuit in the classroom, several aspects of goal-directed behavior merit special attention. First, the restricted focus of researchers on achievement goals should be extended to include the nonachievement goals that students bring to the classroom. A fuller understanding of goal multiplicity will be achieved if we get a better grasp of the purpose that students assign to their behavior in different domains and settings and of the main action programs and scripts that they have attached to different content goals.

Second, future research should document the cues in the learning environment, particularly actors present in the social environment, that influence goal pursuit. By considering how contextual factors influence goal-directed behavior (multiple contexts), we acknowledge the role that peers and teachers play in goal-directed behavior. When the context does not encourage the students to share information and opinions, it will not be vital for the students to socially interact about the learning process, and some social goals may be put on hold. This may not be a problem for students who have learning and achievement as their primary objective but it may be a problem for students who get their energy from social and entertainment goals.

Third, we need to gain insight into the various ways that students coordinate their multiple goals, putting some on hold and making others focal. Although several studies support the notion that the presence of an alternative goal does not necessarily interfere with the pursuit of a focal goal, not much is known presently about how goals interact with each other in specific situations and how they gain dominance in the goal system. We also do not know whether the interference caused by multiple-goal pursuit is mainly due to a pulling away of resources from the focal goal or by active interference.

Fourth, motivation researchers need to consider nonconscious goal pursuit. I have recently started to integrate findings from cognitive psychology about the nonconscious pursuit of goals and the neuro-psychological basis of these findings into my theorizing about on-task and off-task behavior in the classroom. These ideas were not addressed in this chapter (I refer the interested reader to Boekaerts, 2008), but I see many ways in which these ideas can be integrated in motivation research. For example, insights from cognitive neuroscience (Custers & Aarts, 2005) locate working memory in the pre-frontal cortex. The same area that is active when solving problems is involved when people are primed with a goal. This implies that nonconscious goal pursuit uses working memory capacity. I think that this is an area of research that will certainly receive more attention over the next decade. It is my hope that many motivation researchers will become intrigued by the findings from nonconscious goal pursuit and priming studies and will begin to explore the implications of these findings for motivation in the classroom.

There are so many interesting questions that await further research, including whether students know which types of resources they can draw on when they are engaged in a task and whether they know how to compensate for temporary depletion of resources. Answers to these and similar questions will help us to explore goal coordination in the classroom. Clearly, our understanding of goal coordination is still rudimentary and not proportionate to the importance of the subject. I hope that the study of multiple goals in multiple contexts will inject fresh viewpoints into the motivation literature.

References

Argyle, M., Furnham, A., & Graham, J. A. (1981). *Social situations*. New York: Cambridge University Press.
Austin, J. T., & Vancouver, J. B. (1996). Goal constructs in psychology: Structure, process, and content. *Psychological Bulletin, 120*, 338–375.
Baumeister, R. F. (2003). Ego depletion and self-regulation failure: A resource model of self-control. *Alcoholism: Clinical and Experimental Research, 27*, 281–284.
Boekaerts, M. (1998). Boosting students' capacity to promote their own learning: A goal theory perspective. *Research in Dialogue, 1*(1), 13–22.
Boekaerts, M. (2003). Adolescence in Dutch culture: a self-regulation perspective. In F. Pajares & T. Urdan (Eds.), *Adolescence and education, vol. 3: International perspectives on adolescence* (pp. 101–124). Greenwich, Ct.: Information Age.
Boekaerts, M. (2006). Self-regulation and effort investment. In E. Sigel, & K. A. Renninger (Vol. Eds.), *Handbook of child psychology, Vol. 4, child psychology in practice* (pp. 345–377). Hoboken, NJ: Wiley.
Boekaerts, M. (2008, August). *Content goals tell us what students want to attain in the classroom*. Paper presented at the 11th International Conference on Motivation, Turku, Finland.
Boekaerts, M., De Koning, E., & Vedder, P. (2006). Goal directed behavior and contextual factors in the classroom: An innovative approach to the study of multiple goals. *Educational Psychologist, 41*, 33–51.
Boekaerts, M., & Rozendaal, J. (2007). New Insights into the self-regulation of writing skills in secondary vocational education. *Journal of Psychology, 215*, 152–163.
Cantor, N., & Fleeson, W. (1994). Social intelligence and intelligent goal pursuit: A cognitive slice of motivation. In W. D. Spaulding (Ed.), *Nebraska Symposium on Motivation* (Vol. 41, pp. 125–179). Lincoln: University of Nebraska Press.
Carver, C. S., & Scheier, M. F. (1996). *Perspectives on personality* (3rd ed.). Needham Heights, MA: Allyn & Bacon.

Carver, C. S., & Scheier, M. (2000). On the structure of behavioral self-regulation. In M. Boekaerts, P. R. Pintrich, & M. Zeidner (Eds.), *Handbook of self-regulation* (pp. 42–85). San Diego, CA: Academic Press.

Custers, R., & Aarts, H. (2005). Positive affect as implicit motivator: On the nonconscious operation of behavioral goals. *Journal of Personality and Social Psychology, 89*, 129–142.

Dittmann-Kohli, F., (1995). *Das persönliche Sinnsystem*. Hogrefe-Verlag, Göttingen, Germany.

Dowson, M., & McInerney, M. (2001). Psychological parameters of students' social and work avoidance goals: A qualitative investigation. *Journal of Educational psychology, 93*, 35–42.

Elliot, A. J., & Sheldon, K. M. (1998). Avoidance personal goals and the personality–illness relationship. *Journal of Personality and Social Psychology, 75*, 1282–1299.

Ford, M. E. (1992). *Motivating humans: goals, emotions, and personal agency*. Newbury Park, CA: Sage.

Ford, M. E., & Nichols, C. W. (1991). Using a goal assessment to identify motivational patterns and facilitate behavorial regulation and achievement. In M. Maehr & P. R. Pintrich (Eds.), *Advances in motivation and achievement: Vol 7. Goals and self-regulatory processes* (pp. 61–84). Greenwich, CT: JAI.

Greenhaus, J. H., & Powell, G. N. (2006). When work and family are allies: A theory of work-family enrichment. *Academy of Management Review, 31*, 72–92.

Harackiewicz, J. M., Barron, K. E., Tauer, J. M., Carter, S. M., & Elliot, A. J. (2000). Short-term and long-term consequences of achievement goals in college: Predicting continued interest and performance over time. *Journal of Educational Psychology, 92*, 316–330.

Hertz-Lazarowitz, R., & Miller, N. (1992). *Interaction in cooperative groups*. New York: Cambridge University Press.

Hickey, D. T., & Granade, J. B. (2004). The influence of sociocultural theory on our theories of engagement and motivation. In D. M. McInerney & S. Van Etten (Eds.), *Big theories revisited* (pp. 223–248). Greenwich, CT: Information.

Higgins, E.T. (1997). Beyond pleasure and pain. *American Psychologist, 52*, 1280–1300.

Hijzen, D., Boekaerts, M., & Vedder, P. (2006). The relationship between the quality of cooperative learning, students' goal preferences, and perceptions of contextual factors in the classroom. *Scandinavian Journal of Psychology, 47*(1), 9–21.

Järvelä, S., & Häkkinen, P. (2002). Web-based Cases in Teaching and Learning – the Quality of Discussions and a Stage of Perspective Taking in Asynchronous Communication. *Interactive Learning Environments, 10*, 1–22.

Karoly, P. (1999). A goal systems-self-regulatory perspective on personality, psychopathology, and change. *Review of General Psychology, 3*, 264–291.

Kuhl, J. (2000). A functional-design approach to motivation and volition: The dynamics of personality systems interactions. In M. Boekaerts, P. R. Pintrich & M. Zeidner (Eds.), *Self-regulation: Directions and challenges for future research* (pp. 111–169). New York: Academic Press.

Lemos, M. (1996). Students' and teachers' goals in the classroom. *Learning and Instruction, 2*, 151–171.

Lemos, M.S., & Gonçalves, T. (2004). Students' management of goals in the natural classroom setting: Methodological implications. *European Psychologist, 9*, 198–209.

Little, B. R. (1983). Personal projects: A rationale and method for investigation. *Environment and Behavior, 15*, 273–309.

Little, B. R. (1999). Personality and motivation: Personal action and the conative evolution. In L. A. Pervin & O. P. John (Eds.), *Handbook of personality: Theory and research* (pp. 501–524). New York: Guilford.

McInerney, D.M. (2004). A Discussion of Future Time Perspective. *Educational Psychology Review, 16*, 141–151.

Phelan, P., Yu, H. C., & Davidson, A. L. (1994). Navigating the psychological pressures of adolescence: The voices and experiences of high school youth. *American Educational Research Journal, 31*, 415–447.

Pintrich, P. R. (2000). The role of goal orientation in self-regulated learning. In M. Boekaerts, P. R. Pintrich, & M. Zeidner (Eds.), *Handbook of self-regulation* (pp. 451–502). San Diego, CA: Academic Press.

Powers, W. T. (1973). *Behavior: The control of perception*. Chicago: Aldine.

Schwartz, S. H. (1992). Universals in the content and structure of values: Theoretical advances and empirical tests in 20 countries. In M. P. Zanna (Ed.), *Advances in experimental social psychology, Vol. 25* (pp. 1–65). San Diego, CA: Academic Press.

Schwartz, S. H., & Bardi, A. (2001). Value hierarchies across cultures: Taking a similarities perspective. *Journal of Cross Cultural Psychology, 32*, 268–290.

Shah, J. (2003). Automatic for the people: how representations of significant others implicitly affect goal pursuit. *Journal of Personality and Social Psychology, 84*, 661–681.

Shah, J., & Kruglanski, A. (2000). Aspects of goal networks: Implications for self-regulation. In M. Boekaerts, P. R. Pintrich, & M. Zeidner (Eds.), *Handbook of self-regulation* (pp. 85–110). San Diego, CA: Academic Press.

Urdan, T. (2007, April). What are classroom goal structures and how do they matter? Paper presented at the annual conference of the American Educational Research Association, Chicago.

Wentzel, K. R. (1989). Adolescent classroom goals, standards for performance, and academic achievement: An interactionist perspective. *Journal of Educational Psychology, 81*, 131–142.

Wentzel, K. R. (1991). Social and academic goals at school: Motivation and achievement in context. In M. L. Maehr & P. R. Pintrich (Eds.), *Advances in motivation and achievement: Vol. 7. Goals and self-regulatory processes* (pp. 185–212). Greenwich, CT: JAI.

Wentzel, K. R. (1992). Motivation and achievement in adolescence: A multiple goals perspective. In D. H. Schunk & J. L. Meece (Eds.), *Student perceptions in the classroom* (pp. 287–306). Hillsdale, NJ: Erlbaum.

Wentzel, K. R. (1994). Relations of social goal pursuit to social acceptance, classroom behavior, and perceived social support. *Journal of Educational Psychology, 86,* 173–182.

Wentzel, K. R. (1996). Social and academic motivation in middle school: Concurrent and long-term relations to academic effort. *Journal of Early Adolescence, 16,* 390–406.

Wentzel, K. R. (2000). What is it that I'm trying to achieve? Classroom goals from a content perspective. *Contemporary Educational Psychology, 25,* 105–115.

7

Self-Theories and Motivation
Students' Beliefs About Intelligence

Carol S. Dweck and Allison Master

For some students, school is a struggle from the beginning. How can we keep these students motivated and prevent them from giving up? Should we praise them whenever we can, assure them of their intelligence, and, in these ways, try to build their confidence? Other students may achieve success early on, but then encounter difficulties after the transition to junior high school. This transition can be very demanding for students, due to many differences in the school environment that can lead to disengagement (Eccles et al., 1993). In elementary school, parents and teachers may constantly praise these children for how well they do, how smart they are, how quickly they learn. It might seem that these early successes would lay the foundation for a life of self-confidence and high academic achievement. Yet, many of these students struggle when they reach junior high school, and their grades begin to show a downward trajectory (Blackwell, Trzesniewski, & Dweck, 2007). Suddenly classes are challenging, and hard work is necessary for success. How do students respond when the going gets tough? Do they remind themselves that they are intelligent and capable, roll up their sleeves, and get down to work? Unfortunately, many of them do not. Instead many choose to give up, to take the easy way out, and try to get by with the minimum amount of effort. Why does this happen and what can educators do?

In this chapter, we suggest ways to keep struggling students motivated, as well as ways to remotivate students who have lost their motivation as school has become more challenging. We have long been interested in what helps children thrive in school, and years of research have led us to uncover the role of students' self-theories (beliefs about what intelligence is and how it works) in creating different patterns of student motivation (Dweck & Leggett, 1988).

We began by noticing two distinct patterns of responses to challenging situations (Diener & Dweck, 1978). One group of fifth graders showed a helpless pattern in response to difficulty (in this case, a task in which they had to problem-solve to figure out an unknown rule). They blamed their failure on lack of ability, expressed negative affect ("This isn't fun anymore"), and showed decreases in performance. In contrast, another group of fifth graders showed a mastery-oriented pattern. They remained optimistic ("I've almost got it now"), expressed positive affect ("I love a challenge"), and used more effective strategies to succeed. The differences between these two types of groups were then traced to their goals (Dweck & Elliott, 1983). Students who had performance goals (who wanted to prove their ability) were more likely to show the helpless pattern, while those who had learning goals (who wanted to improve their ability) were more likely to show the mastery-oriented pattern. Finally, the differences in these goals were traced back to differences in beliefs about the nature of intelligence (Elliott & Dweck, 1988). Again, in a sample of fifth-grade students, the belief that intelligence is fixed led to performance goals, while the belief that intelligence can be changed led to learning goals.

What are these self-theories and how do they lead to differences in motivation? Some students believe that intelligence is a fixed attribute. They believe they have only a certain amount and that's that. We call this an "entity theory." Students with an entity theory believe that intelligence is something fixed and unchanging. They believe that if individuals have a lot of it, then they are in good shape, but if they don't, there is not really anything they can do about it. Moreover, students with an entity theory may constantly worry about whether they have a lot or not. Other students see their intelligence as a changeable attribute, something that can be grown and strengthened over time. We call this an "incremental theory." These students think that the more effort they put in, the more they will learn and the better their ability will be. These beliefs about intelligence have important implications for students. They affect (a) their goals in school—whether students are interested in looking smart or learning; (b) their belief in the usefulness of effort—viewing effort as something negative or something positive, (c) the way they explain their failures—as conveying a lack of ability or simply a lack of effort or a poor strategy, and (d) the strategies they use after a setback—giving up or persevering. Their beliefs about intelligence ultimately influence students' grades and achievement test scores. Previous research using mediational analysis and structural equation modeling has shown that an incremental theory leads students to choose learning over performance goals and to believe that effort will lead to positive academic outcomes (Blackwell et al., 2007). These positive beliefs about effort lead children to make fewer ability-based, helpless attributions about failure. These in turn lead children to choose more positive, effort-based strategies, which lead to increasing grades throughout junior high school.

Although a single belief about intelligence may seem like a small thing, each of these beliefs creates a whole motivational framework. In fact, interventions that carefully target these beliefs have had a meaningful impact on how enthusiastic children are about learning and how successfully they learn (Aronson, Fried, & Good, 2002; Blackwell et al., 2007; Good, Aronson, & Inzlicht, 2003).

In this chapter, we will discuss how these self-theories create each part of this framework, how they can help students affected by stereotype threat, how they develop, how they are communicated, and finally, how they can be changed.

Self-Theories and Measurement

These "self-theories," as we have noted, are students' beliefs about the nature of their intelligence. Self-theories can be measured by asking students whether they agree or disagree with entity or incremental statements, and Dweck and her colleagues have developed questionnaires to do so (Dweck, 1999). Students who believe intelligence is fixed are the ones who agree with statements like, "You have a certain amount of intelligence, and you really can't do much to change it" or "Your intelligence is something very basic about you that you can't really change." Students who believe intelligence can grow are the ones who agree with statements like "You can always greatly change how intelligent you are" or "Everyone no matter who they are can substantially increase their intelligence" (Dweck, 1999). While students may have both beliefs to a certain extent, they tend to agree more with one set of statements or the other. Students typically mark how much they agree with several entity theory statements and several incremental theory statements on a 6-point Likert scale (Blackwell et al., 2007). Alphas for these items are typically in the .9–.96 range (Dweck, Chiu, & Hong, 1995). The questions used to assess very young children's self-theories are slightly different, and will be discussed in the later section on development.

The self-theories can also be specific to particular domains (Dweck et al., 1995). For example, some students may believe that math ability is innate, but writing ability can be improved, or vice versa. The self-theory they hold in a particular area affects their motivation in that area, including how they respond to setbacks. Self-theories can affect how people approach all kinds of situations besides intellectual settings, from athletics (Jourden, Bandura, & Banfield, 1991) to interpersonal relationships (Kammrath & Dweck, 2006) to business (Wood & Bandura, 1989). Self-theories about other domains, such as personality, may be assessed by agreement with statements such as "Everyone is a certain kind of person and there is not much that can be done to really change that" (Dweck et al., 1995).

Self-theories about intelligence tend to be relatively stable over time, with students consistently preferring one theory over the other (Robins & Pals, 2002). Among a sample of college students, the correlation in a scale assessing self-theories over a period of 2 years was high (r = .57) (Robins & Pals, 2002). In a sample of junior high school students, the test-retest reliability over a 2-week period was similarly high (.77) (Blackwell et al., 2007). However, the theories can also be induced or directly taught. Theories can be temporarily induced by having students read a scientific article supporting one theory or the other (Hong, Chiu, Dweck, Lin, & Wan, 1999; Niiya, Crocker, & Bartmess, 2004), or telling them that the task they are about to do involves a fixed or improvable ability (Martocchio, 1994; Wood & Bandura, 1989). These manipulations influence the theory with which students approach the subsequent task. In other cases, students are taught the incremental theory through movies and lectures or in multisession workshops (Aronson et al., 2002; Blackwell et al., 2007). In these cases, learning the incremental theory can have noticeable effects even months later.

Self-Theories Lead to Different Goals

These two theories steer students down two very different paths, with each theory leading to its own distinctive framework. First, the two theories lead to separate goals (Blackwell et al., 2007; Dweck, Mangels, & Good, 2004; Robins & Pals, 2002). When students believe that ability (such as intelligence) is fixed, they want to prove that they have a lot of it. They want to show off that ability, so they choose "performance goals" over "learning goals." Individuals with performance goals seek to obtain positive judgments and avoid negative judgments about their ability (i.e., prove their ability), while individuals with learning goals seek to increase their ability or gain new abilities (i.e., improve their ability) (Elliott & Dweck, 1988). For entity theorists, getting good grades and showing that they are smart come first, while learning may be incidental. In contrast, when students believe that ability can be changed, they want to improve it. They strive to increase their ability, so they choose learning goals over performance goals. Learning comes first. In this framework, students embrace challenges because challenges maximize learning.

This was illustrated in a study with seventh-grade students who were facing the difficult transition to junior high school (Blackwell et al., 2007). Those with an incremental theory were motivated to learn for the sake of learning, agreeing with statements such as "An important reason why I do my school work is because I like to learn new things." In fact, they chose learning goals even at the cost of performing poorly or having to work hard: "I like school work that I'll learn from even if I make a lot of mistakes" and "I like school work best when it makes me think hard." When students believe ability can be strengthened, their goal is to do precisely that.

In the entity framework, students show a lot of defensiveness. If they do not think they will look smart, they may avoid a task entirely—even one that may be crucial for their future success. We will now turn to this point.

Self-Theories and Learning Opportunities

Hong and colleagues (1999) examined the theories of freshmen at an elite Hong Kong university and tied this to their willingness (or unwillingness) to address a deficiency. Although fluency in English was essential for success at this university, many incoming students were not proficient. These students were asked whether they would be willing to take a remedial English class. Those with low proficiency who had an incremental theory were more likely to agree to take the course than those who had an entity theory. To students with an entity theory, taking a remedial class would mean acknowledging their current lack of ability. Furthermore, since they believed their intellectual ability could not be changed, they may have worried that their additional effort might not make much difference. Thus, rather than putting themselves on a path to future improvement and success, they chose to try to hide their shortcomings. Over time, this defensive avoidance of opportunities to learn can put students with an entity theory farther and farther behind their classmates. In contrast, students with an incremental theory realized that their abilities in this critical area were not satisfactory and were motivated to take the necessary steps to improve their abilities. Taking advantage of the opportunity to learn outweighed revealing their current limitations.

This concern over performing badly can also lead students with the entity theory to spend less time practicing, despite their greater anxiety about their performance (Cury, Da Fonseca, Zahn, & Elliot, 2008). Specifically, Cury et al. found that adolescents who believed that a task measured their ability were more likely to worry about their future performance. Ironically, these same adolescents were also less likely to take advantage of an opportunity to practice that task. Rather than taking steps to try to improve their future performance, they chose the strategy of not practicing—leaving themselves a face-saving excuse if they did poorly. Naturally, they did not do as well on the final task as the group who believed the task measured a changeable ability. Even though there was no previous struggle or deficit—just an uncertainty about future performance— the entity theory students still showed a defensive strategy and a decrease in performance. Their failure to take advantage of the opportunity to practice and improve their skills led precisely to the negative outcome they were so worried about.

Students with an entity theory may fail to take advantage of learning opportunities even when they are deeply committed to a subject. Engineering students were (temporarily) taught an entity or incremental theory (by reading a brief *Psychology Today*-style scientific article) and were told that they had performed poorly on one section of an engineering exam (Nussbaum & Dweck, 2008). The "entity theory" engineering students were less likely to choose to take a tutorial for that section of the exam. Even though they knew they needed to improve, they preferred to pass on the opportunity for improvement. Instead, they chose to review one of the sections on which they had already done well. While this may have helped them protect their self-esteem as engineering students, they missed the opportunity to repair a deficit that could impair their success in their chosen field. The incremental theory students almost all chose a tutorial for the section that they had performed poorly on. Having recognized a potentially damaging deficit in their abilities in their chosen field, they were motivated to reduce it.

Students with an entity theory may miss these learning opportunities deliberately, by deciding to turn away from remedial opportunities, or they may miss learning opportunities simply by failing to pay attention when new information is presented to them. As we have noted, students with an entity theory want to demonstrate that they have high ability, so their attention may be biased towards information that tells them about their intellectual ability, rather than toward information that could help them increase that ability. In one experiment, we measured students' brainwaves as they performed a task and thereby monitored what students were paying attention to (Dweck et al., 2004; Mangels, Butterfield, Lamb, Good, & Dweck, 2006). We found that students with an entity theory paid more attention to feedback (as indicated by EEG waveforms) about whether their answer was correct or incorrect than to feedback about what the correct answer really was, that is, feedback that could help them learn new things.

In this study, students with an entity or incremental theory were given a difficult test of general knowledge and were given feedback after each question while the electromagnetic waves of their brain were monitored (Mangels et al., 2006). First, participants were told whether their answer had been correct or incorrect (ability-relevant feedback); a short time later, they were shown the correct answer (learning-relevant feedback). While both entity and incremental theory students showed brain activity indicating anticipatory alertness before the ability-relevant feedback, only the incremental students showed the same brain activity before the learning-relevant feedback. The entity students failed to pay attention to the correct answer even when they knew they had gotten the question wrong. Because the students with an entity theory were not motivated to pay attention to the information, they missed out on this opportunity to learn. When students were later given a surprise retest on the material they missed, not surprisingly, students with an incremental theory performed significantly better.

Thus, an entity theory sets students on a path towards worrying about and protecting their image, while an incremental theory motivates students to take advantage of opportunities to learn, practice, and grow.

Self-Theories and Effort

The two theories also lead to different beliefs about the value of effort. When students believe that ability is fixed, then they often devalue the importance of effort. They believe that ability is supreme. Someone who has ability does not need effort, and effort will not help someone who lacks it. After a setback, they may think: Why should I bother? Trying harder will not change how smart they are, and even worse, *having* to try hard may further confirm that they must not be very smart (Blackwell et al., 2007). They agree with statements that say, "If you're not good at a subject, working hard won't make you good at it," and "To tell the truth, when I work hard at my schoolwork, it makes me feel like I'm not very smart." To these students, no amount of effort can bridge the gap between smart and not smart.

This may be precisely why many high-achieving students stop working when junior high school becomes difficult (Blackwell et al., 2007). They have coasted along on low effort, showing how smart they are. Now, effort is required and they are not willing to take the risk. They would prefer to do poorly and be regarded as smart but lazy than to exert the effort and feel inept.

To clarify, believing that effort is futile is already enough to put these students at a disadvantage. Even worse than that, they may believe that effort is not just useless but actively harmful. In the eyes of these entity students, the more effort they put in, the more they demonstrate and confirm that they lack ability. Thus, effort is not just futile but also dangerous—hard work is seen as a sign of low ability (Covington & Omelich, 1979; Leggett & Dweck, 1986; Nicholls, 1984). In contrast, when students believe that ability is changeable, then effort can be useful. It can help them improve, regardless of their current level of ability. These students with an incremental theory are more likely to endorse statements such as "The harder you work at something, the better you will be at it." Believing in the power of effort helps children choose the path to greater success.

Self-Theories and Reactions to Failure

Students with both theories may want to be successful in school, and, as long as they are succeeding readily, their different beliefs about intelligence may not always have much impact. However, once students begin to encounter or worry about setbacks, their theories become increasingly important in determining how they will respond to those setbacks. In particular, the two theories lead students to explain their setbacks in different ways. Failing a test is usually a sign that students need to change their behavior and study strategies in the future. But how do entity and incremental students explain their failure, and how do they choose to change?

For those with an entity theory of intelligence, failure is a sign of low ability. When they failed a test, seventh graders with an entity theory gave "helpless" explanations for their failure, claiming that they felt that they failed because "I wasn't smart enough," "I'm just not good at this subject," "The test was unfair," or "I didn't really like the subject." By attributing failure to factors outside their control, these students do not change their behavior and they set themselves up to fail again and again. When it came to choosing a strategy for the future, seventh graders with an entity theory chose negative strategies that avoided effort (Blackwell et al., 2007). Relative to the incremental students, they agreed significantly more with statements such as "I would try not to take this subject ever again," and "I would spend less time on this subject from now on." Rather than making use of a bad grade as an early warning that they needed to increase their effort, they saw it as a signal to give up on themselves and this class.

In contrast, for those with an incremental theory about intelligence, failure is an indication that that they did not try hard enough. When the incremental seventh graders failed a test, they said their failure was because "I didn't study hard enough," or "I didn't go about studying in the right way." By attributing failure to their own lack of effort, they were poised to take control of the situation and set themselves up to do better in the future. When choosing strategies for the future, the incremental students chose positive strategies based on effort. They agreed with statements such as "I would work harder in this class from now on" and "I would spend more time studying for tests." These students were motivated to work even harder so that they would do better next time.

Students with an entity theory may also react to failure in a more negative, dishonest way. For these students, once they have failed, they have demonstrated their low level of fixed ability. There is no good way for them to rebound from failure—instead, students with an entity theory may resort to other (potentially counterproductive) methods of coping with failure, such as cheating, lying, or looking for people who did worse than they did. Rather than choosing to work harder, the seventh graders with an entity theory were more likely than those with an incremental theory to say that they would try to cheat on the next test (Blackwell et al., 2007). They wanted to perform well, but failed to see better options for how to attain higher performance. Similarly, students who perceive their school to be focused on performance rather than learning are more likely to cheat (Anderman, Griesinger, & Westerfield, 1998).

Even younger students can show dishonesty. When fifth graders were told that their performance on a set of problems was due to high intelligence rather than high effort, they adopted an entity theory, and showed more helpless responses after they struggled on a subsequent set of problems (Mueller & Dweck, 1998). Like students with an entity theory, they were concerned with performing well and looking smart. When they reported their scores on the final set of problems to other fifth-grade students, these children were three times more likely to lie, claiming a higher score than they had actually earned.

Students with an entity theory also choose "downward comparison" after performing poorly (Nussbaum & Dweck, 2008). After reading an article supporting an entity or incremental view of intelligence, college students performed a highly difficult speed-reading task and were told that they had performed poorly on it. They then had the opportunity to engage in downward or upward social comparison by looking at the strategies of other participants who had gotten lower or higher scores. Students who were (temporarily) taught an entity theory chose to look at the strategies of people who had performed more poorly. Rather than using their time constructively, they opted to compare themselves to others who did less well so they would feel better about themselves. In contrast, students who were taught an incremental theory chose to look at higher performers, who were more likely to have useful strategies. When students with an entity theory fail, they do not see effort and learning as the path to success. Instead, they may choose to cheat or lie in order to perform better, or try to boost their self-esteem by feeling superior to others.

Self-Theories and Performance

We have already discussed how students with an entity theory are less concerned with learning, are less willing to put forth effort, and fail to take advantage of opportunities to learn and improve. But what does this mean for their actual performance? As expected, students with an entity theory often perform more poorly over time than students with an incremental theory. Seventh graders who entered junior high school with an incremental view of intelligence showed improvement in their math grades over time the next 2 years, whereas those with an entity theory did not (Blackwell et al., 2007). This was true even though both groups had entered seventh grade with identical achievement test scores. These effects can also emerge in the short span of a single session. Although there were no initial differences in ability between the two groups, adolescents with an entity theory performed more poorly on an IQ test than students with an incremental theory after both groups were given the chance to practice (Cury et al., 2008). These performance differences may be especially troubling given the current level of high-stakes testing, which may encourage fixed beliefs by using a single performance indicator to judge students' ability.

Theories affect performance of students of all ages in many different areas, including complex decision-making and managerial skills. Graduate business students were taught an entity or incremental theory of managerial ability before playing a simulated organization game (Wood & Bandura, 1989). Because the task was challenging, when students had an entity theory of ability their confidence in their own ability to succeed decreased over time, they set lower goals for themselves, and they used less efficient strategies. Ultimately, they performed substantially more poorly than students with an incremental theory of ability. Succeeding in this complicated task required participants to sustain attention and effort, and those with an entity theory failed to do so.

Views of ability also affect performance in negotiations. In one study, undergraduate students were told that negotiation ability was either a skill that could be developed (incremental theory) or an innate ability (entity theory) (Kray & Haselhuhn, 2007). They then completed a difficult negotiation task in which they played the role of either a job candidate or a recruiter. The negotiators who learned the incremental theory produced significantly better results than the negotiators who learned an entity theory. In a second study, they looked at how strongly MBA students believed in the incremental theory. Students who had stronger beliefs in an incremental theory gained more resources after a similar negotiation task (Kray & Haselhuhn, 2007). MBA students who held more incremental beliefs were also more successful in coming up with creative and useful solutions for extremely challenging negotiation situations. Although negotiations often involve difficult obstacles, believing that negotiation skills are malleable led students to be more willing to work hard to overcome those obstacles.

What Ability Means and How Students Judge It

Before an entity or incremental belief about intelligence develops, young children may have a very different understanding of ability from older children (Stipek & Mac Iver, 1989). Young children (ages 5 and 6 years) sometimes do not differentiate ability, effort, and outcome. (Nicholls, 1978, although see Cain & Dweck, 1989). Young children may also show less differentiation between academic ability and social competence; for example, claiming that smart children will also share more cookies and be able to jump more hurdles (Stipek & Daniels, 1990). At ages 7 through 10, children are able to distinguish effort and outcome as cause and effect, but still do not perceive ability as a capacity that causes an outcome (Nicholls, 1978). Even up through sixth grade, children are still developing the idea of ability as a possibly stable trait, yet third through sixth graders are forming a coherent set of beliefs about how intelligence relates to academic performance (Stipek & Gralinski, 1996). In one study, children who endorsed an entity theory of intelligence ("Some kids will never be smart, no matter how hard they try") also believed that intelligence was a global trait (e.g., "Kids who are not smart don't do well in any subject"), and these beliefs predicted their grades and test scores over the course of the year (Stipek & Gralinski, 1996).

Ability itself takes on a different meaning for older students in the two different frameworks. We have already discussed how students with an entity theory believe abilities such as intelligence are fixed, and students with an incremental theory believe abilities can change over time. Thus, to individuals with an entity theory, ability may mean that they succeed right away, and to individuals with an incremental theory, ability may mean that they improve over time.

Butler (2000) demonstrated this empirically. Eighth- and ninth-grade students rated the mathematical ability of another child who either showed initially high performance that declined or initially low performance that improved. The students with an entity theory believed that the student whose performance was initially high and then declined had higher math ability than the student whose performance improved. They also rated the declining student as smarter in general. In contrast, the students with an incremental theory inferred that the improving student had higher ability and was smarter. When students believe ability is fixed, then they think how well they do at first shows their true ability. When students believe ability can change, then they think that doing better over time shows that their ability is increasing.

Students' theories of intelligence also affect what type of feedback motivates students. Feedback can be either temporal (looking at the student's performance over time) or normative (comparing the student to other students) (Butler, 2000). Self-theories were measured by asking students how much they agreed with the statements, "Everyone has a certain amount of intelligence, and one can't do much to change this amount," "One's intelligence is something about oneself that one can't change very much," and "People can learn new things, but they can't really change their basic intelligence." Adolescent students with an entity theory were most motivated when they were given normative feedback that they were doing well compared to others. Students with an incremental theory were most motivated when they received feedback indicating that they were improving over time (Butler, 2000). When students believe ability is fixed, they want to know that they have a lot of ability compared to others. In contrast, when students believe ability can change, they are motivated by their own improvement and increasing success. How well these students perform compared to others is not as important to them as how much they have improved themselves.

Because performance relative to others is such a meaningful measure of ability within an entity theory, students with an entity theory may take steps to make their performance less meaningful. Specifically, they may deliberately handicap their own performance, in order to blame their failure on something besides ability. Self-handicapping is the tendency to create obstacles to performing well. Although it increases the chances of failure, poor performance can then be blamed on the obstacles, rather than on innate ability. College students who believed that their intelligence was fixed were more likely to engage in self-handicapping behaviors such withholding effort from a task, feigning or claiming sickness, and procrastination (Rhodewalt, 1994). Thus, students with an entity theory experience the double disadvantage of missing out on chances to improve while also actively sabotaging their own success.

Self-Efficacy and Self-Esteem

The beliefs that students have about intelligence and ability can affect their sense of self-efficacy and self-esteem. Self-efficacy refers to a person's belief that he or she has the resources to meet the demands of the situation (Bandura, 1982). Students who believe that a particular ability can be improved over time come to have a higher belief in their own capabilities (Martocchio, 1994; Wood & Bandura, 1989). In a training course on computers, students were induced to believe that computer abilities were fixed (entity theory) or acquirable (incremental theory; Martocchio, 1994). Because the course remained challenging, self-efficacy decreased for the entity students even though they were learning, while it increased for the incremental students as they learned. Students with an incremental theory showed less and less anxiety about computers over the course of the class, while anxiety did not change for students with an entity theory. The students who believed that they could increase their ability viewed the course as an opportunity to improve their skills even if they made mistakes as they learned, while the students who believed that their ability was fixed became frustrated and lost their confidence as a result of their mistakes.

Theories may also have implications over time for self-esteem (the general regard for oneself and the general regard for the self expected from others; Burhans & Dweck, 1995). Students with an entity theory may base their self-esteem on performing well and showing a high level of ability, while students with an incremental theory may base their self-esteem on working hard and conquering challenges (Robins & Pals, 2002). Robins and Pals followed students throughout their college years. Students with an entity theory showed a decline in self-esteem throughout college, whereas students with an incremental theory showed an increase in self-esteem over the same years. Even when their grades were similar, the two groups interpreted their academic success and failure differently. In the words of one student with an entity theory, "I feel upset, ashamed at my failure, angry that I couldn't have done better, and even a little depressed." These students saw poor grades as a reflection and indictment of their fixed abilities. In contrast, a student with an incremental theory wrote, "I feel I can do much better in school. It is still hard for me to accept the fact that I have a C on my transcript, but I look at my grades and I am inspired to do well."

When ability is viewed as fixed, any failure has negative implications for self-esteem. For these students, struggling in school means that they just do not have what it takes, which can lead to decreases in self-esteem. In contrast, when ability can be increased, setbacks, while disappointing, can serve as a signal to students that they need to do better. Instead of taking failure as an indictment of their ability, and thus their self-esteem, they were able to focus on doing better in the future. The students with an entity theory were more likely to feel distressed, ashamed, and upset about their grades, while students with an incremental theory were more likely to feel motivated, determined, enthusiastic, excited, inspired, and strong (Robins & Pals, 2002).

Self-Theories and Stereotype Threat

Theories influence how much students are impacted by negative stereotypes about their academic ability. Stereotype threat is the concern about confirming a negative stereotype about one's group (Steele & Aronson, 1995), such as the negative stereotypes about African Americans in academic settings or females in math and science settings. This concern often leads to impaired performance. However, theories can have a significant influence on this process. When students believe that ability is fixed, stereotype threat has its strongest effect (Aronson, 1998). If students have a certain level of ability and that ability is demonstrated to be low, then the stereotype has been confirmed. Having a fixed belief thus makes the stakes even higher, causing more anxiety and worse performance. On the other hand, when students believe that ability can be changed, stereotype threat has less effect. Even if performance is low right now, with more effort it can be improved, and the stereotype can be disconfirmed.

In much research, males are found to score higher on standardized math tests than females (Spencer, Steele, & Quinn, 1999). However, when we were able to look at some data more closely, this gap existed mainly for students who believe that math ability is innate (as measured by either by agreement with entity theory statements such as "You have a certain amount of intelligence, and you really can't do much to change it," or as manipulated by directly teaching students that intelligence can be expanded). When looking only at students who believed that intellectual skills can be developed, the gap disappeared almost entirely (Dweck, 2006; Good et al., 2003). Similarly, in a pre-med college chemistry course, female students who believed in the entity theory received lower grades than males, but female students who believed in the incremental theory received higher grades than males (Dweck, 2006).

Several more studies show how an incremental theory can help students improve their performance in the face of stereotype threat (Aronson et al., 2002; Good, Rattan, & Dweck, 2007). African American college students who were taught that intelligence is malleable, rather than fixed, showed greater engagement in school and earned higher grade point averages that semester (Aronson et al., 2002) despite the fact that their perception of stereotype threat did not decrease. Thus, believing that ability is malleable may take much of the pressure off evaluative situations, allowing students to start to achieve their full potential.

The entity theory can also buffer students against the threat of not belonging in an academic domain. In another study, female college students were tracked throughout a calculus class, and they were asked about the extent to which they thought people in their class held negative stereotypes about females and math (Good et al., 2007). The belief that others held negative stereotypes about females and math did not affect all students equally. Those who started the course believing that math was a gift (an innate ability) began to feel more and more uncomfortable as the course went on, and afterwards many chose not to pursue math courses in the future. In contrast, those who believed that ability could be improved were far less affected by the negative stereotypes. Thus, having an entity theory can make students more vulnerable to negative stereotypes about their group, and may even help perpetuate the stereotypes by keeping otherwise well-qualified women from pursuing careers and math and science.

Theories also affect how negatively stereotyped students receive critical feedback from a teacher (London, Downey, & Dweck, 2009). In one study, African American college students received somewhat harsh, but constructive feedback on their essay from an "arrogant" White professor. Students who endorsed an incremental theory were more likely to stay engaged with their essays, see the process as a learning opportunity, and even ask for additional help from the professor. This was even true for African American students who tended to show chronically high concern about being discriminated against on the basis of their race. Students who had an entity theory showed the opposite pattern. They were less engaged and more likely to stop working on their essays. Thus, the entity theory can lead students, especially those anxious about negative stereotypes, to react to critical feedback by disengaging and giving up. The incremental theory can lead students to take feedback, even from a source that might be biased against their group, and be motivated to use it as an opportunity for their own growth and improvement.

The Development of Self-Theories

As mentioned previously, young children do not understand intelligence as a stable trait, and fail to differentiate "smartness" from social behaviors such as sharing (Stipek & Mac Iver, 1989). Thus, their beliefs about ability are unlikely to be relevant to their motivation. However, preschool children are quite concerned with issues of goodness and badness, and their evaluations of their goodness can be tied to their performance (Heyman, Dweck, & Cain, 1992). When children see goodness/badness as global traits, they make more general inferences based on specific events, such as making a single mistake.

In one study, 5- and 6-year-old children's self-theories about goodness predicted helpless responses (Heyman et al., 1992). Their self-theories were assessed with two questions that tapped into whether children believed that goodness was a global and stable trait (with each question matched to the child's gender): "Imagine a new boy is in your class. You look over at his schoolwork and see that he did lots and lots of things wrong. Does this mean that he is bad?" and "Imagine a new boy is in your class. He steals your crayons, scribbles on your paper, then spills your juice. Then he teases you and calls you names. Will this new boy always act this way?" Next, children role-played their responses to making a mistake during several tasks. One group of children was more likely to endorse the belief that badness is a fixed entity (i.e., making a mistake means you are bad, and that you will always be bad).

After role-playing criticism from a teacher after an imaginary mistake (such as leaving the feet off a drawing), these children rated their own work more negatively. These same children were also less likely to want to persist at each task and more likely to feel sad. Believing that badness is a global trait, they also blamed themselves for the imaginary mistake, inferring from this single mistake that they were not good at the task, not smart, not a good person, and not nice. When asked what they could do to fix the situation (e.g., draw missing feet on a person), these children were less likely to come up with a constructive solution that would correct the mistake. Thus, even very young children who see goodness and badness as fixed show similar patterns to older children who see intelligence as fixed.

As children get older, they continue to respond in patterns similar to those of older students. Seven- and 8-year-olds who believed that sociomoral traits were stable were more likely to explain another child's success in terms of ability, and to believe that a teacher would be upset with a student who made lots of mistakes (Heyman & Dweck, 1998). They were also more likely to believe that a student with academic difficulties was lacking ability. While children at this age can distinguish the academic and sociomoral domains, their sociomoral beliefs still affect their judgments about the academic domain.

Thus, young children show motivational patterns similar to those of older children and adults. When they believe that a motivationally self-relevant trait is a fixed entity, they show many more helpless responses to making a mistake than when they believe the trait is malleable.

How Self-Theories Are Communicated

So, where do these theories come from? How do children develop either an entity theory or an incremental theory about intelligence? The type of praise and criticism that teachers and parents give often sends a signal regarding the nature of ability. Sometimes without realizing it, teachers may be sending subtle messages to their students supporting one theory or the other.

Although most adults believe that praising children's intelligence or ability will boost their confidence, praising children for their ability can reinforce an entity theory (Mueller & Dweck, 1998). It conveys that adults can judge children's underlying ability from their performance, and perhaps also that ability is what adults value most in them. In our research, we were so surprised by the impact of intelligence praise that we did the research over six times—with children from different regions of the country and children from different racial and ethnic groups. Each time we found the same thing (Mueller & Dweck, 1998, Studies 1–6). Indeed, previous work had suggested that ability praise led to better outcomes (including skill and self-efficacy) than effort praise (Schunk, 1983).

After working on problems from a nonverbal IQ test, fifth-grade students were either praised for their ability ("You must be really smart at these problems") or for their effort ("You must have worked hard at these problems") (Mueller & Dweck, 1998). When they had a choice, children who were given ability praise wanted to keep doing relatively easy problems so they could keep on feeling smart. Next, they were given a second, more difficult set of problems to do. These children (recently praised for their high ability) now said that they were struggling because they lacked ability. So, rather than giving them lasting confidence, praising ability made their confidence fragile. What's more, they no longer enjoyed the problems or wanted to take them home to practice. After the difficult problems, the children were given a third set of problems that were as easy as the first set. This time, the ability-praised children did significantly worse than they had on the first set of problems—their performance on this IQ test had decreased. Finally, as mentioned earlier, they were also more likely to misrepresent their actual score to a stranger, by reporting that they had solved more problems than they actually had. Having high ability was so important that they could not acknowledge their actual performance.

In contrast, the children who were given effort praise were overwhelming likely to choose opportunities to learn more. They wanted harder problems that they would learn from, even if it meant not looking smart. When they had difficulty with the hard problems, they attributed it to lack of effort. Not surprisingly, their enjoyment remained high and their scores on the final set of problems were higher than their initial scores. These children also told the truth about their difficulties on the hard problems. Praising these children's effort, rather than their ability, put them on the path towards hard work and greater success.

Criticism can have the same kinds of effects, depending on whether it expresses a judgment about the person or about the process (Kamins & Dweck, 1999). After role-playing making a mistake, 5- and 6-old children were given person criticism (e.g., "I'm very disappointed in you") or process criticism ("Maybe you could think of *another way* to do it" with a critical tone of voice). After role-playing another setback, children given criticism directed towards them as a person showed more helpless responses. They rated their performance and themselves more negatively, saying that they were not smart, not nice, and not good children. They reported feeling more sad, and were less likely to persist.

Children were also given the chance to come up with a way to solve the problem, which could be as simple as saying, "I would fix it." Despite this, children given person criticism came up with fewer constructive strategies for fixing the role-played mistake. It is interesting to note that these children had adopted an entity theory as a result of the person criticism: they were more likely to endorse the belief that children's qualities are fixed. In contrast, children who were criticized for the process itself oriented themselves towards mastering the situation. They rated themselves more positively, felt happier, and were more likely to come up with constructive strategies, such as "I can do it again better if I take my time." Moreover, as a result of the process criticism, they adopted an incremental theory, believing that children's qualities could be changed. Even at this young age, children are sensitive to the messages being communicated through praise and criticism. By focusing them on the process of learning, teachers and parents can help children learn to welcome challenges and persevere in the face of setbacks.

Children are sensitive to tiny differences in the phrasing of feedback even at an extremely young age. In one study, 4-year-old children were told either "You are a good drawer" (ability praise) or "You did a good job drawing" after role-playing four success scenarios (Cimpian, Arce, Markman, & Dweck, 2007). They then role-played two scenarios in which they made a mistake. After the mistake, children who were given the ability praise evaluated themselves more negatively and were less likely to persist at drawing. Although the difference in the two kinds of praise was made as subtle as possible, here even subtle messages communicated through praise can put young children into different theories, heading down a path towards helplessness or mastery, as described at the beginning of this chapter. While it may be challenging for parents, teachers, and coaches to completely avoid praise that fosters an entity theory, they may consciously try to give more specific and process-oriented praise to help foster an incremental theory.

Teachers may more explicitly communicate the theory that they themselves believe, in the way that they talk about ability (Good et al., 2007). For example, whether geniuses are portrayed as having innate ability or as having worked hard sends a clear signal to students about the nature of intelligence. In one study, middle school students saw one of two videos with the same math lesson on spherical geometry (Good et al., 2007). The videos were presented as a new way of teaching math with historical information integrated into the lesson, and the two videos differed on the particular historical information that they presented. The first video, designed to induce an entity theory of ability, described Euclid and Riemann as two brilliant mathematicians who were geniuses. Despite being lazy, their "natural talent" and "innate ability" led them to brilliance. The second video, designed to induce an incremental theory of ability, described them as dedicated mathematicians who were committed to math. Over time, their passion for math chose to pursue led to the development of extraordinary math skills.

How would these instructions affect female students, who are the targets of negative stereotypes in math? Students were then given a very difficult math test that they were told was a measure of their math ability. Females who had seen the video about innate math ability fell prey to stereotype threat. They did significantly worse than males on the test. However, females who had seen the video about dedication to math were buffered against this negative effect. Thus, when geniuses are presented as having innate ability, it sends the message that students either have this innate ability or do not. This can be particularly threatening for female students, who have to contend with the stereotype that females do not have innate math ability. When geniuses are presented as dedicated workers, it suggests to female students that their dedication and hard work can pay off.

Teachers can also send a message through the standards they use to evaluate their students. Teachers can compare each student's performance to the performance of other students or to the student's own previous performance (Rheinberg, Vollmeyer, & Rollett, 2000). Students have no control over the performance of other students, so comparing themselves to others can be frustrating and demotivating. Indeed, a student may improve substantially but still not yet compare well to others. However, when teachers use the students' own past performance as the standard, the students see more clearly that their effort leads to better outcomes, and that their lack of effort leads to worse outcomes. When they see the direct link between their own actions and the outcomes of their work in school, students are often more motivated to learn. So, teachers can send messages to students about the power of effort in many ways, including messages about what standard the students should be comparing themselves to. Students who are on a path towards working harder and increasing their own knowledge will continue to be motivated by the progress that they make.

Changing Self-Theories

So far, we've talked about how students' beliefs about intelligence can have important implications for their motivation. The two beliefs can lead students down two different paths, towards different goals, beliefs about effort, and reactions to difficulty. We've talked about how students can develop these beliefs based on messages from parents and teachers. We now turn to research in which students were directly taught an incremental theory. We've already mentioned how an intervention teaching African-American college students that intelligence is malleable led to increased engagement in school and higher grades (Aronson et al., 2002).

Teaching younger students an incremental theory is equally effective as they face developmental challenges of their own. In particular, the transition to middle school is difficult for many students, and their motivation and grades often suffer. In one study, seventh-grade students were mentored by college students, who taught them that intelligence was malleable (Good et al., 2003). The seventh graders met with their mentors for a 90-minute session each semester, and then communicated with them through e-mail during the rest of the year. The mentors talked about how intelligence can be expanded at any time as neurons and dendrites form new neural connections, and students also learned about expandable intelligence through a web-based computer program. This intervention led impressive increases in students' math and reading achievement test scores, with Cohen's $d = 1.13$ for females' math scores and $d = .62$ for males' math scores, and an overall Cohen's $d = .52$ for reading scores. Importantly, the intervention did not involve drilling students in test preparation or teaching them additional material that would be on the test. Instead, what students learned was that they could expand their intelligence with mental effort. Once again, this simple belief motivated students to learn and removed anxieties about doing poorly or confirming negative stereotypes. Students were freed from this pressure, allowing them to demonstrate more of their potential.

Blackwell et al. (2007), in the study mentioned above, gave two groups of seventh graders an eight-session intervention either teaching them about study skills or teaching them study skills plus an incremental theory. As one of the exercises in the incremental group, students read an article ("You Can Grow Your Brain") about research showing that the brain is like a muscle that can be developed, and how it changes and grows as it forms new connections. Part of the article read: "When you learn new things, these tiny connections in the brain actually multiply and get stronger. The more that you challenge your mind to learn, the more your brain cells can grow. Then, things that you once found very hard or even impossible to do—like speaking a foreign language or doing algebra—seem to become easy. The result is a stronger, smarter brain."

Both groups had been showing a pattern of declining math grades, and the students who learned just study skills continued to show declining math grades over the course of the year. In contrast, the students who learned the incremental theory reversed this trend and showed a significant recovery. Changes were evident in their classroom behavior as well. Their teachers (who did not know which students were in which intervention group) were far more likely to nominate students in the incremental theory group as having shown more positive change in motivation in their classrooms. These teachers made comments such as "L., who never puts in any extra effort and doesn't turn in homework on time, actually stayed up late working for hours on an assignment early so I could review it and give him a chance to revise it. He earned a B+ on the assignment (he had been getting C's and lower)," and "M. was [performing] far below grade level. During the past several weeks, she has voluntarily asked for extra help from me during her lunch period in order to improve her test-taking performance. Her grades drastically improved from failing to an 84 on her recent exam." Changing this one belief about intelligence led to changes in motivation large enough to be seen by their teachers, and the students' hard work paid off in the form of better grades.

We have also been developing a computer-based workshop called "Brainology" to teach children that intelligence can change (Blackwell & Dweck, 2008). Students go through six computer modules that explain how the brain works and how to make it work better. We pilot tested Brainology in 20 New York City schools and received virtually unanimous positive feedback from the seventh graders who went through the program. They told us how the program changed their ideas about learning and motivated them to study and work harder. "I did change my mind about how the brain works ... I will try harder because I know that the more you try the more your brain knows," "I imagine neurons making connections in my brain and I feel like I am learning something," and "My favorite thing from Brainology is the neurons part where when u learn something there are connections and they keep growing. I always picture them when I'm in school." Teaching students that they can make their brains form new connections by working hard and learning was a motivating message.

Future Directions and Conclusion

We have seen how students' beliefs about their intelligence create different frameworks for motivation and achievement. As much as we have learned already, we believe that there is still much more to learn. For example, we need to know more about *teachers'* beliefs about intelligence. If teachers believe that students' ability level cannot change, there is less motivation to help students develop. Previous research has shown that when teachers expect that certain students will improve in ability throughout the year, those students are more likely to actually improve (Rosenthal & Jacobson, 1968). Also, beliefs about intelligence may affect teachers' level of self-efficacy (whether they believe they can help their students succeed). However, whether teachers believe that intelligence itself is malleable has not yet been linked to student achievement, and this would be an excellent topic for future research. Indeed, research suggests that managers' beliefs about whether employees can change significantly affect their behavior toward their employees (Heslin, Vandewalle, & Latham, 2006). Managers who held an incremental theory were significantly more likely to provide guidance in the form of clear expectations and useful feedback. They were also more likely to facilitate their employees' problem solving, and to help inspire employees to work to their full potential. Furthermore, when managers who held an entity theory were taught the incremental theory, they became much more willing to mentor their employees. For example, they were more willing to coach an employee whose bad performance they had just witnessed. They also offered more (and better quality) suggestions to that employee. Thus, there is reason to believe that teachers with an incremental theory may help students focus on learning, and may be better mentors to those students. Teachers who are open to the possibility of change may also be more likely to notice and recognize those changes in their students.

In conclusion, when students believe that intelligence is malleable and can be grown incrementally, they want to improve their ability. In choosing learning over performance goals, they opt for more challenging tasks that they will learn from. By investing effort and working to improve, they take maximum advantage of opportunities to learn, practice, and develop their skills. This belief can even buffer students against the anxiety of confirming a negative stereotype about their group. Thus, the incremental theory puts students in a framework in which motivation and effort are rewarded by continued achievement.

As powerful as these beliefs can be, parents and teachers can readily influence students' beliefs. By praising students for their effort and giving feedback about the process of learning, adults can send the message that working hard and working smart leads to greater success. They also send the message that hard work and progress are what they value, not natural, effortless, mistake-free brilliance that involves no learning. We have seen how exquisitely sensitive children are to messages from adults. Why not send messages that move students toward a path to greater success and achievement in life?

References

Anderman, E. M., Griesinger, T., & Westerfield, G. (1998). Motivation and cheating during early adolescence. *Journal of Educational Psychology, 90,* 84–93.

Aronson, J. (1998). *The effects of conceiving ability as fixed or improvable on responses to stereotype threat.* Unpublished manuscript.

Aronson, J., Fried, C. B., & Good, C. (2002). Reducing the effects of stereotype threat on African American college students by shaping theories of intelligence. *Journal of Experimental Social Psychology, 38,* 113–125.

Bandura, A. (1982). Self-efficacy mechanism in human agency. *American Psychologist, 37,* 122–147.

Blackwell, L. S., & Dweck, C. S. (2008). *The motivational impact of a computer-based program that teaches how the brain changes with learning.* Unpublished manuscript.

Blackwell, L. S., Trzesniewski, K. H., & Dweck, C. S. (2007). Implicit theories of intelligence predict achievement across an adolescent tradition: A longitudinal study and an intervention. *Child Development, 78,* 246–263.

Burhans, K. K., & Dweck, C. S. (1995). Helplessness in early childhood: The role of contingent self-worth. *Child Development, 66,* 1719–1738.

Butler, R. (2000). Making judgments about ability: The role of implicit theories of ability in moderating inferences from temporal and social comparison information. *Journal of Personality and Social Psychology, 78,* 965–978.

Cain, K., & Dweck, C. S. (1989). Children's theories of intelligence: A developmental model. In R. J. Sternberg (Ed.), *Advances in the study of intelligence* (pp. 47–82). Hillsdale, NJ: Erlbaum.

Cimpian, A., Arce, H.-M., Markman, E. M., & Dweck, C. S. (2007). Subtle linguistic cues impact children's motivation. *Psychological Science, 18,* 314–316.

Covington, M. V., & Omelich, C. L. (1979). Effort: The double-edged sword in school achievement. *Journal of Educational Psychology, 71,* 169–182.

Cury, F., Da Fonseca, D., Zahn, I., & Elliot, A. J. (2008). Implicit theories and IQ test performance: A sequential mediational analysis. *Journal of Experimental Social Psychology, 44,* 783–791.

Diener, C. I., & Dweck, C. S. (1978). An analysis of learning helplessness: Continuous changes in performance, strategy, and achievement cognitions following failure. *Journal of Personality and Social Psychology, 36,* 451–462.

Dweck, C. S. (1999). *Self-theories.* New York: Psychology Press.

Dweck, C. S. (2006). Is math a gift? Beliefs that put females at risk. In S. J. Ceci & W. Williams (Eds.), *Why aren't more women in science? Top researchers debate the evidence* (pp. 47–55). Washington, DC: American Psychological Association.

Dweck, C. S., Chiu, C., & Hong, Y. (1995). Implicit theories and their role in judgments and reactions: A world from two perspectives. *Psychological Inquiry, 6,* 267–285.

Dweck, C. S., & Elliott, E. S. (1983). Achievement motivation. In P. H. Mussen & E. M. Hetherington (Eds.), *Handbook of child psychology: Vol. IV. Social and personality development* (pp. 643–691). New York: Wiley.

Dweck, C. S., & Leggett, E. L. (1988). A social-cognitive approach to motivation and personality. *Psychological Review, 95,* 256–273.

Dweck, C. S., Mangels, J., & Good, C. (2004). Motivational effects on attention, cognition, and performance. In D. Y. Dai & R. J. Sternberg (Eds.), *Motivation, emotion, and cognition: Integrated perspectives on intellectual functioning* (pp. 41–56). Mahwah, NJ: Erlbaum.

Eccles, J. S., Midgley, C., Wigfield, A., Buchanan, C. M., Reuman, D., Flanagan, C., et al. (1993). Development during adolescence: The impact of stage-environment fit on young adolescents' experiences in schools and in families. *American Psychologist, 48,* 90–101.

Elliott, E. S., & Dweck, C. S. (1988). Goals: An approach to motivation and achievement. *Journal of Personality and Social Psychology, 54,* 5–12.

Good, C., Aronson, J., & Inzlicht, M. (2003). Improving adolescents' standardized test performance: An intervention to reduce the effects of stereotype threat. *Applied Developmental Psychology, 24,* 645–662.

Good, C., Rattan, A., & Dweck, C. S. (2007). *Development of the sense of belonging to math survey for adults: A longitudinal study of women in calculus.* Unpublished manuscript.

Heslin, P. A., Vandewalle, D., & Latham, G. P. (2006). Keen to help? Managers' implicit person theories and their subsequent employee coaching. *Personnel Psychology, 59,* 871–902.

Heyman, G. D., & Dweck, C. S. (1998). Children's thinking about traits: Implications for judgments of the self and others. *Child Development, 64,* 391–403.

Heyman, G. D., Dweck, C. S., & Cain, K. M. (1992). Young children's vulnerability to self-blame and helplessness: Relationship to beliefs about goodness. *Child Development, 63,* 401–415.

Hong, Y. Y., Chiu, C., Dweck, C. S., Lin, D., & Wan, W. (1999). Implicit theories, attributions, and coping: A meaning system approach. *Journal of Personality and Social Psychology, 77,* 588–599.

Jourden, F. J., Bandura, A., & Banfield, J. T. (1991). The impact of conceptions of ability on self-regulatory factors and motor skill acquisition. *Journal of Sport and Exercise Psychology, 13,* 213–226.

Kamins, M., & Dweck, C. S. (1999). Person vs. process praise and criticism: Implications for contingent self-worth and coping. *Developmental Psychology, 35,* 835–847.

Kammrath, L. K., & Dweck, C. S. (2006). Voicing conflict: preferred conflict strategies among incremental and entity theorists. *Personality and Social Psychology Bulletin, 32,* 1497–1508.

Kray, L. J., & Haselhuhn, M. P. (2007). Implicit negotiation beliefs and performance: Experimental and longitudinal evidence. *Journal of Personality and Social Psychology, 93,* 49–64.

Leggett, E. L., & Dweck, C. S. (1986). *Goals and inference rules: Sources of causal judgments.* Unpublished manuscript.

London, B., Downey, G., & Dweck, C. S. (2009). *The student's dilemma: Academic engagement in the face of stereotype threat.* Unpublished manuscript.

Mangels, J. A., Butterfield, B., Lamb, J., Good, C., & Dweck, C. S. (2006). Why do beliefs about intelligence influence learning success? A social cognitive neuroscience model. *Social Cognitive and Affective Neuroscience, 1,* 75–86.

Martocchio, J. J. (1994). Effects of conceptions of ability on anxiety, self-efficacy, and learning in training. *Journal of Applied Psychology, 79,* 819–825.

Mueller, C. M., & Dweck, C. S. (1998). Intelligence praise can undermine motivation and performance. *Journal of Personality and Social Psychology, 75,* 33–52.

Nicholls, J. G. (1978). The development of the concepts of effort and ability, perception of academic attainment, and the understanding that difficult tasks require more ability. *Child Development, 49,* 800–814.

Nicholls, J. G. (1984). Achievement motivation: Conceptions of ability, subjective experience, task choice, and performance. *Psychological Review, 91,* 328–346.

Niiya, Y., Crocker, J., & Bartmess, E. N. (2004). From vulnerability to resilience: Learning orientations buffer contingent self-esteem from failure. *Psychological Science, 15,* 801–805.

Nussbaum, A. D., & Dweck, C. S. (2008). Defensiveness versus modes of self-esteem maintenance. *Personality and Social Psychology Bulletin, 34,* 599–612.

Rheinberg, F., Vollmeyer, R., & Rollett, W. (2000). Motivation and action in self-regulated learning. In M. Boekaerts, P. Pintrich & M. Zeidner (Eds.), *Handbook of self-regulation* (pp. 503–529). San Diego: Academic Press.

Rhodewalt, F. (1994). Conceptions of ability, achievement goals, and individual differences in self-handicapping behavior: On the application of implicit theories. *Journal of Personality, 62,* 67–85.

Robins, R. W., & Pals, J. L. (2002). Implicit self-theories in the academic domain: Implications for goal orientation, attributions, affect, and self-esteem change. *Self and Identity, 1,* 313–336.

Rosenthal, R., & Jacobson, L. (1968). Teachers' expectancies: Determinants of pupils' IQ gains. *Psychological Reports, 19,* 115–118.

Schunk, D. H. (1983). Ability versus effort attributional feedback: Differential effects on self-efficacy and achievement. *Journal of Educational Psychology, 75,* 848–856.

Spencer, S. J., Steele, C. M., & Quinn, D. M. (1999). Stereotype threat and women's math performance. *Journal of Experimental Social Psychology, 35,* 4–28.

Steele, C. M., & Aronson, J. (1995). Stereotype threat and the intellectual test performance of African Americans. *Journal of Personality and Social Psychology, 69,* 797–811.

Stipek, D., & Daniels, D. H. (1990). Children's use of dispositional attributions in predicting the performance and behavior of classmates. *Journal of Applied Developmental Psychology, 11,* 13–28.

Stipek, D., & Gralinski, J. H. (1996). Children's beliefs about intelligence and school performance. *Journal of Educational Psychology, 88,* 397–407.

Stipek, D., & Mac Iver, D. (1989). Developmental change in children's assessment of intellectual competence. *Child Development, 60,* 521–538.

Wood, R., & Bandura, A. (1989). Impact of conceptions of ability on self-regulatory mechanisms and complex decision making. *Journal of Personality and Social Psychology, 56,* 407–415.

8

Self-Worth Theory
Retrospection and Prospects

Martin Covington

This chapter serves a three-fold purpose: First, to acquaint the reader with the basic principles of the Self-worth Theory of Achievement Motivation; second, to provide an overview of the research conducted over the past quarter-century to validate and expand the empirical and conceptual reach of the theory; and third, to consider various practical classroom applications of Self-worth Theory for purposes of enhancing the quality of school achievement as well as encouraging those positive motivations that not only draw students to their best effort academically, but also increase their willingness to learn and profit from their learning.

Regarding the first purpose, I seek to place self-worth considerations in an historic context as only one element of the ongoing efforts of countless research colleagues and educators to identify the essential nature of human motivation, particularly as this mission applies to achievement behavior. As to the second purpose, the program of research that typifies the self-worth approach is unusual in that, for the most part, it is fully integrated into the on-going life of the college class-room. In effect, the classroom itself has become a continuous and sustaining part of our inquires. In the process, students become valued informants and highly involved participants, not simply passive or disinterested research subjects—involved because these investigations are situated in an authentic, high-stakes, grade-driven context of great personal significance for students.

As to the third purpose—that of practical applications, I believe that to be truly effective motivational theories must not only account for both the purposeful and counter-productive behaviors of individuals and groups, but they should also imply what achievement goals should be serve by these insights. In effect, a complete theory of achievement motivation should be contextualized within a set of pedagogical goals, which, it will be argued shortly, ought to include an examination by students of the yardsticks by which they measure their value to themselves and to others, and why they should care. From a self-worth perspective, this quest involves a lifetime struggle to establish and then maintain a sense of personal competence. The various obstacles that interfere with this quest are part of our story.

Theoretical Overview

Self-worth Theory (Covington, 1992, 1998; Covington & Beery, 1976) makes common cause with those philosophies—both ancient and modern—which put the sense of self at the center of human existence, that is, the central axis around which the individual's beliefs, aspirations, and personal actions circle and take on meaning (Elliot & Covington, 2001). Basically, Self-worth Theory suggests that individuals strive to give their lives meaning by seeking the approval of others. This usually means accomplishing deeds or providing services that are valued by the larger group to which one belongs or hopes to belong. Typically, such achievements depend on one being competent. Whatever form competence takes, it invariably becomes equated with one's worth with both positive and potentially negative consequences. For example, sports psychologists have shown that those high school boys who drop out of wrestling competition do so when their win-loss record no longer sustains a reputation for physical strength and agility, a special kind of ability that is often highly prized by young males (Burton & Martens, 1986). Likewise, many youngsters who have given up practicing musical instruments, despite an early history of successful training, appear to do so given increasing fears that they will play badly in public (Covington, 1982). These extra-curricular activities and the fear-of-failure dynamics they reveal are similar to the behavior of failure-avoiding students when confronted with the prospects of a disappointing grade in school.

In effect, the individual is thought to be only as worthy as her ability to achieve which typically means achieving competitively. Given this, it is understandable why ability often becomes confused with worth. This point gives rise to a powerful psychological reality: To be able is to be worthy, but to do poorly implies incompetence and reason to despair of one's worth. This dynamic has been simplified in the formula: P=A=W (Beery, 1975), that is, the quality of my Performances (e.g., grades) reveals my Ability, hence, my Worth. For those who are already insecure, anchoring their worth in ability is a risky step, particularly given the ways that schools often organize and distribute the rewards for achievement—that is to say, typically on a competitive basis. In a competitive context, there are few winners, and many losers. More about the implications of this reality later.

The basic premise of Self-worth Theory can be traced back to the notion of learned drives or psychological motives such as the need for power, approval, and achievement which have evolved as a lasting legacy of John Atkinson's Need Achievement Theory (1957) as well as its subsequent reinterpretation in cognitive, attribution terms by Bernard Weiner (1972, 1974). Atkinson holds that the tendency to achieve is the result of an emotional conflict between striving for success and the fear of failure, dispositions that are characterized in emotional terms. For example, the hope for success and the anticipation of prevailing over others is thought to encourage success-oriented persons to strive for excellence, whereas a capacity for shame drives failure-avoidant individuals to avoid achievement situations where they expect to fail. It is these emotional differences (pride vs. shame) that are suggested as answers to the *why* question which is the essential explanatory domain of motivation theory: *why*, for example, do some individuals choose easy tasks for which success is assured, and others chose challenging problems where the chances of failure are exquisitely balanced against the odds for success.

Self-worth Theory essentially accepts this two-fold proposition of emotional conflict, with the additional assumption that the larger purpose of this conflict, no matter how it is played out—to the benefit or to the detriment of the individual, represents a life-long promethean struggle to establish and maintain a sense of personal worth and value to oneself and to others. It is the strategic moves and countermoves, defensive ploys, and excuses used by individuals to these ends that are a primary focus of Self-worth Theory.

Beginning the early 1970s, Bernard Weiner and his colleagues proposed a reinterpretation of Atkinson's theory asserting that it is cognitive processes (in the form of causal attributions) rather than the emotional anticipation of achievement outcomes that are the basic activating components in achievement motivation. Specifically, Weiner (1974) suggested that how people perceive the causes of their successes and failures is more likely the causal agent in their determining which tasks to work on, and how long to persist. With this shift in the casual agents responsible for the motivation to achieve, a subtle transformation occurred. The classical question of *why*, originally answered in terms of feeling states, was now stated in terms of *how*—how individuals interpret events and attribute meaning to their emotions. For instance, if failure is attributed to insufficient effort, then students are likely to try harder the next time they have the opportunity. This kind of reasoning led to an insistence on the importance of effort attributions as a positive force in sustaining achievement motivation. Self-worth Theory also acknowledges the centrality of effort as a positive force, but only at certain times. Under some circumstances, especially for some students (e.g., Atkinson's failure-threatened students), effort expenditure can also represent a threat. This is because if a student tries hard and fails anyway, then attributions typically go to low ability, which consequently—according to Self-worth Theory—implies unworthiness. But why should students feel unworthy? It is well known that teachers from kindergarten to the college level reward effort with higher grades than students might otherwise attain, and withhold these same rewards when students do not try (Omelich, 1974; Weiner & Kukla, 1970). This strategy seems well-suited for promoting a positive view of effort. But, then why don't students always try as hard as possible? The answer involves the presence of a dilemma for students. In essence, two sources of worth are competing, one favoring effort and the other favoring the need to maintain a reputation for competence. More often than not, the need to protect one's ability status trumps the benefits of trying hard with its positive reputation for fortitude (Covington & Omelich, 1979). For example, among college students, a reputation for brilliance is the most important contributor to feelings of personal well-being in school, more important that even their GPAs (Covington & Omelich, 1984a). Moreover, students are not unmindful about how the world works. When their job is to instruct students, teachers do, indeed, recognize hard work and reward it accordingly. Yet, when teachers are asked to predict who among their students is most likely to succeed in prestigious occupations, they weight ability as the more important predictor (Kaplan & Swant, 1973).

So far, several assertions have been made in outlining the broader self-worth position. First, there is the suggestion that self-estimates of ability depend largely on the context within which success and failure occur. For instance, a combination of trying hard/failure implies low ability. Second, it is proposed that self-accusations of incompetence cause feelings of shame—the ability-linked, emotional component of feeling worthless. Third, it follows, then, that by not trying, individuals can minimize information about their ability, should they fail, and thus avoid demoralizing feelings of personal shame. Fourth, the availability of credible excuses for why one did not try—or why one did try, but to no avail, should also minimize the teacher's natural tendency to punish what appears to be student indifference, but which, according to the self-worth position, may actually mask a highly motivated state that often involves desperate attempts to avoid failure or at least the implications of failure. Fifth, and finally, the accumulation of all these arguments leads to the conclusion that in many classrooms there exists a fundamental conflict of values between teacher and students reflected in the students' preoccupation with ability status and its maintenance, especially when risking failure, and the teacher's natural tendency to reward student effort and to sanction inaction.

Each of these assertions was demonstrated in a single experiment, including evidence for a student/teacher value conflict (Covington & Omelich, 1979). We asked several hundred Berkeley undergraduates to respond to hypothetical achievement scenarios in which they were to imagine themselves as having received a disappointing grade on a test when the rest of the class had done well. A sense of public shame and personal dissatisfaction was judged to be greatest by these students when they pictured themselves as having studied hard for the test, but having failed anyway, and least when they had studied very little. This finding is contrary to the expectations of a society that values honest effort. After all, should not effort—even losing effort, compensate somewhat for the onus of failure? Actually, it does not; it made things worse. These students were less interested in the consolation that effort brings to a losing cause than they were in avoiding the implication that they lacked ability. The availability of credible excuses for why one did not try (e.g., illness) or why one did try hard, but to no effect (e.g., "the test did not cover the material I studied most") sharply reduced the shame and distress experienced in the prior condition.

In a second phase of this experiment, the same students were next asked to take on the role of teachers and administer sanctions to hypothetically failing students represented in each of the four conditions portrayed in the first phase: failure after studying hard (with and without excuses), failing after little study (with and without excuses). By considering the two phases of this study in combination, one phase representing student reactions to their failures, and the other teacher responses to student failures, we can appreciate the stark incompatibility of values. Those hypothetical students who studied hard and failed anyway were less severely reprimanded than those who did not try. Although students were reprimanded least for their failures under conditions of high effort, they nonetheless experienced the greatest personal dissatisfaction and shame compared to other students under any of the four conditions. Conversely, those failures that trigger the least shame—again, when students tried little, if at all, caused the greatest degree of teacher reprisal among any of the four conditions.

The presence of student excuses moderated both feelings of shame and the excesses of teacher sanctions. Teachers make allowance for low effort, if students had a reasonable explanation for not having tried such as illness. Likewise, explanations for why effort did not pay off have the great advantage of simultaneously protecting one's reputation for being bright, while mitigating teacher disapproval.

This study not only demonstrates the kinds of motivational dilemmas visited on students when facing the threat of failure, but also importantly, indicates how they can, and, in fact, often do, avoid the threat: in this particular instance, by not trying or at least trying, but with excuses readily available. As I have remarked elsewhere, "It is difficult to imagine a strategy better calculated to sabotage the pursuit of personal excellence" (Covington, 1992, p.78).

The results of this study illustrate the bankruptcy of any educational policy that simply increases the pressure on students to work harder in the face of failure which is virtually inevitable for most students, given the competitive context in which much of schooling is conducted. Such a strategy of intensification is flawed. It assumes that teachers can control student effort by the judicious use of rewards and reprimands. But what is most meaningful to many students are not effort-linked rewards or even the fear of reprisals for their apparent indifference, nor even the feelings of guilt that typically accompany not trying, but rather it is the struggle to avoid the devastating implications that might follow from being too energetic when risking failure.

Nor is the cause of indifferent effort simply a lack of motivation as some policy makers argue.

Many students are motivated, even overly motivated, but for the wrong reasons, that is, the avoidance of failure, a highly active proposition, not at all a passive, listless pursuit. I do not mean to minimize the importance of effort. Weiner (1974) is right when he argues that energetic commitment is a vital part of feeling worthy and also of getting the job done. But obstacles to such a commitment are part of the challenge that classroom solutions must take into account. Effort levels must not be controlled by fear, but rather controlled by the learner in nuanced ways depending on the nature and difficulty of the task at hand. Some thoughts about how to accomplish this are discussed later.

An Agenda of Systematic Research

Self-worth Theory can be summarized in a nutshell: Individuals struggle to give their lives meaning by seeking the approval of others which involves being competent and able, and avoiding the implications of failure—that one is incompetent, hence unworthy. It is this basic premise that has served as the starting point for the expansion of the theory over the years. We will examine five different interlocking lines of inquiry that taken together constitute the bulk of our long-term research agenda. First, I will document our analysis of the role played by self-serving excuses in the process of self-protection. Second, I will explore our efforts to identify the underlying personality dimensions associated with approach and avoidance tendencies among students. Third, I will describe our inquiries into the essential nature of test and performance anxiety when risking failure, and consider how such fears might be overcome. Fourth, I will report on our investigations regarding the prospects for encouraging intrinsic task engagement among students in the thrall of a powerful network of extrinsic rewards and sanctions, chiefly in the form of school grades. Fifth, and finally, I will refract all these accumulated findings through the lens of practicality by offering a broad blueprint as well as examples for how we might restructure the learning experiences of students in more effective ways from a self-worth perspective.

An Arsenal of Excuses

Little wonder that self-serving excuses are such a permanent fixture in the achievement struggle that, at base, often involves a profound conflict of values between ability and effort. Excuses allow students to repackage otherwise questionable actions like not trying in a more flattering, less blameworthy form. Our research (Covington, 1992) and that of many colleagues (e.g., Birney, Burdick, & Teevan, 1969; Snyder, 1984; Thompson, 1993,1994, 1996; Thompson, Davis, & Davidson, 1998) indicate that this self-protective drama is exceedingly complex. For one thing, it is the timing, frequency, and the sense of proportion involved in excuse-making, rather than the mere presence or absence of defensive strategies, that differentiates successful from unsuccessful students. Even successful students have their deceits, but they are used far more sparingly and in more sophisticated ways (Botkin, 1990). For another thing, self-serving tactics range from relatively innocent subterfuges to actions that represent ominous threats to one's psychological well-being. In the former case, when used with discretion, excuses allow individuals to avoid revealing their ignorance or account for lapses of responsibility. In the latter case, behaviors such as chronic procrastination can take a far more dangerous turn. Instead of merely attempting to avoid being seen as unprepared—for example, not knowing the answer to a particular question or test problem, the struggle is now to escape being perceived as stupid. But ignorance and stupidity are not the same thing. Ignorance can be corrected, but presumably not stupidity! As a result, riskier defenses are called for—riskier because they are more likely to undermine the will to learn by causing the very failures that failure-threatened students are attempting to avoid.

Finally, speaking of complexity, when individuals feel compelled to convince others of their competence or to deflect the implication of incompetence, they must not only provide a credible argument to convince others, but they must also convince themselves as well. We have been particularly interested in exploring how this trick is accomplished, identifying the difficulties in sustaining it, and documenting what happens when these fictions unravel. We believe the key to this drama is the uneasy relationship between the need for self-acceptance—on the one hand, and the need for self-accuracy and rationality of judgment, one the other. The mediator between these two forces is the credibility of the excuses and the demands for modesty. In effect, self-bolstering is limited by the need to maintain credibility both in the eyes of others and for oneself, or as Fritz Heider (1958) put it, excuses maintain their self-serving value only as long as they "fit the constraints of reason." We have explored these dynamics as they apply specifically to college classroom achievement (Covington & Omelich, 1978). It was hypothesized that in the event of a test failure, students would act egotistically to protect their self-perceived ability status, but only when plausible excuses were available. As predicted, students took advantage of any uncertainty as to the causes of failure in order to aggrandize their ability status by illogically ascribing higher levels of ability to themselves than to hypothetical peers even though everyone had exactly the same alibis. Moreover, not only did these students act egotistically, they also believed that their peers would accept these inflated self-serving views (egocentrism as defined by Jones & Nisbett, 1971).

Even though disappointing grades may be successfully explained away for a time, self-serving excuses will inevitably lose their credibility, and self-doubts about one's ability will begin to surface. We have made an extensive analysis of the natural history of the failure of defenses under actual classroom conditions. In one study (Covington & Omelich, 1981), we tracked students in my introductory psychology course who repeatedly fell short of their grade aspirations over the course of several class tests. As one failure followed another, nonability explanations for their disappointing performances grew increasing implausible. As a consequence, their self-estimates of ability to handle the course material steadily deteriorated. In effect, as failures mounted, these students rated themselves lower and lower on the very attribute—ability, that was emerging in their minds as the most important element for success. These dynamics can be found in earlier years of schooling. Our evidence from middle school samples of African American students suggests that many of these youngsters have also give up the struggle for approval via high achievement and have sought out alternative sources of worth (Teel, Parecki, & Covington, 1998).

The Quadripolar Model of Individual Differences

The dynamics of protecting a sense of personal worth is neither identical for all students—certainly not the same when it comes to the specific coping mechanisms involved, nor is the process uniform in its outcomes. Rather, these dynamics result in a virtually endless variety of adaptations, some of which are quite successful, others marginally successful, and many that are neither. Much of our research over the years has involved identifying individual differences among students regarding their motivational styles for adapting to the threats posed by potential failure. As previously noted, according to Atkinson (1957), the two individual difference dimensions along which all students can be ordered with regard to achievement dynamics are characterized—on the one hand, by a dominant tendency to approach success (high approach/low avoidance), and conversely, a

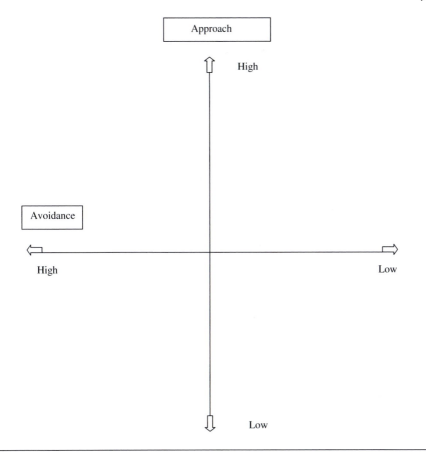

Figure 8.1 Quadripolar model of need achievement.

decided tendency to avoid failure (low approach/ high avoidance). Atkinson's point, which was not fully appreciated at the time, is that these tendencies represented two orthogonal dimensions such that the achievement process could be viewed as a conflict of opposing forces. The assumption of independence allows for four domains or quadrants occupied by four distinctive types of students as portrayed in Figure 8.1.

Our research has confirmed such a quadripolar model (Covington & Omelich, 1991). Some 400 Berkeley undergraduates were distributed into four distinct groups along a number of variables, including self-perceptions of ability, quality of study effort, and several measures of test anxiety using a series of stepwise discriminate analyses. This treatment allowed for the emergence of two hybrid groups in addition to the pure approach and pure avoidance types described above. We have labeled the first of these hybrid groups "Overstrivers" (high approach/high avoidance). These individuals are simultaneously drawn to and repelled by the prospects of achievement. In self-worth terms, these failure-threatened students have adopted a defensive posture for avoiding failure by succeeding. However, in order to guarantee repeated successes, these students must expend enormous amounts of energy studying. But because of the increasing burden of sustaining one's successes, one assignment after another, and test after test, the strategy of overpreparation is eventually bound to fall short. As a result, these students not only fail occasionally, but do so under the most threatening circumstances of all—failure after having tried hard. Because of the intolerable implications of this combination—that one lacks ability, many Overstrivers become what has been referred to as "closet" achievers (Beery, 1975). These are students who complain that they had little time to study, but who, in fact, have studied in secret. The advantage of this strategy is that, in the event of a disappointing grade, the disaster can be attributed by students to insufficient preparation, while if they succeed, a reputation for brilliance will be assured because they presumably succeeded without really trying. A number of other self-protective strategies have also been documented including *defensive pessimism* (Cantor & Harlow, 1994; Cantor & Norem, 1989) in which students maintain unrealistically low expectations for ever succeeding so that if they do exceed these expectations relief becomes the reward, and if they fail as anticipated, at least the failure had been discounted in advance.

By contrast, the hybrid group of students we have described as "failure-accepting" (low approach/low avoidance) appear largely indifferent to their mediocre record of achievement. Such passivity is open to various interpretations including using relative inaction as a defensive ploy—in effect, nothing risked, nothing lost, or even as a reflection of anger expressed in the form of passive resistance to learning. However, the weight of evidence suggests that these students have basically given up the struggle to maintain a reputation for brilliance, likely after numerous failures, and have come to content themselves in seeking approval by being helpful and a team player (Covington & Omelich, 1981)

The phenomenon of the overstriving individual explains several puzzling behaviors such as the fact that many otherwise successful students cannot endure even a single, minor setback, grade-wise, without feeling totally devastated. One might think that a superior record of noteworthy accomplishments would easily offset the single exception. No, not if those prior successes were motivated by fear in an attempt to prove one's worthiness via an outstanding GPA. A single, uncharacteristic failure serves to remind Overstrivers of their inadequacies, and of what they have feared all along, despite their accumulated successes: They are not perfect. Overstriving also make clear why there is little relationship between college GPA and satisfaction with oneself as a student. This statistic is quite puzzling. Should not a sense of student well-being depend closely on how well one is doing, grade-wise? Not necessarily. This relationship depends on the reasons for achieving. If these motives are essentially negative, as is the case of Overstrivers, then a high GPA is simply evidence of an endless struggle to avoid feelings of shame and self-doubt, a struggle that is never completely resolved. Little wonder that successful performances among Overstrivers can bring only temporary relief.

Achievement Anxiety

Anxiety is a prominent feature of the achievement process. Atkinson's Need Achievement Theory (1957) proclaims as much. In his view, failure-avoidance with its vanguard of fear and apprehension constitutes one of the twin forces that animates achievement behavior, the other force being the tendency to approach success. Anxiety is a multifaceted phenomenon. It serves many roles in the achievement process, expresses these functions through numerous avenues, and results in a variety of consequences (Covington, 1985; Zeidner & Matthews, 2005). For one thing, anxiety possesses drive-like characteristics that can mobilize some learners to greater effort, although not always effective effort. For another thing, cognitively-speaking, anxiety in the form of intrusive worry can interfere both with the initial acquisition of information as well as with its eventual retrieval from memory storage—the latter disruption being referred to as a retrieval deficit (Morris & Liebert, 1973). Likewise, emotional manifestations of anxiety such as feelings of doom along with its disruptive physiological counterparts (e.g., butterflies in the stomach) can also degrade retention.

As part of our research program, we have given a high priority to the study of anxiety. More specifically, we have sought to understand how these various facets and manifestations of anxiety become integrated as a continuous, destructive force that pervades school achievement at every turn. In effect, we ask, what is the deeper interconnectedness of the diverse manifestations of anxiety—physiological, cognitive, and affective, and is this fit invariably identical for all students? Then there is the question of the first-order of importance: What causes anxiety in the first place?

Our provisional answer to the latter question follows from Self-worth Theory. Basically, anxiety represents a failure of self. But, what can be so devastating about failure that it can result in prolonged, often paralyzing anxiety? Our earlier analysis leaves little doubt as to the answer. In attribution terms, failure especially following heightened study, implies low ability, and doubts about one's ability can be a devastating threat to one's sense of worth. In short, anxiety in its many manifestations is a reaction to failure—actual or potential, triggered by the implication of incompetence that one will be found unworthy as a person.

This proposal is buttressed by a variety of findings from several sources. First, consider the emotional component of anxiety. The evidence from our laboratory is that anxiety is an *ability-linked* reaction to failure, not an effort-linked reaction in which failure is caused by little or no effort (Covington & Omelich, 1984). The former reaction typically reflects feelings of shame, whereas the latter provokes feelings of guilt. Second, research on the cognitive component of anxiety supports the contention that anxiety is a reaction to implied low ability. More particularly, those worries that are most disruptive to learning and performance share a common theme typically concerning fears of public disclosure of incompetence (Helmke, 1988). Third, the power of many test-anxiety measures to predict school performance depend largely on items that measure self-perceived ability as compared to those items that reflect emotional arousal (Nicholls, 1976). Nicholls concluded that self-perceptions of ability are likely the main organizing principle of anxiety, while emotional upset is only one of the many consequences of believing oneself to be incompetent.

Given these arguments and the data that support them, one might conclude that anxiety is simply the creature of self-perceptions of inability. Yet, because the dynamics of anxiety are so complex and multifaceted with so many consequences, it is perhaps best understood as a distinct construct in its own right.

In order to address the question of how these components of anxiety—variously, feelings, cognitions, and physiological upset operate, singly and severally, in the achievement process through time, we undertook several studies in which students were tracked through successive study-test cycles in their actual classes. These free-running cycles can vary in duration from days to weeks, and the entire sequence is usually recursive with one test following another. The results of one study involving several hundred students in my introductory psychology course are both representative and instructive (Covington & Omelich, 1988). At the first step in this stage-wise cycle—what we referred to as the *appraisal* stage, students judged whether an upcoming test as announced by the instructor would be perceived as a challenge or a threat. Not surprisingly, failure-oriented students typically expressed doubts about their ability to do well which, during the second *test-preparation* stage, led to indifferent, ineffectual, and conflicted study which was typically accompanied by efforts to distance oneself from the meaning of potential failure either by denying the importance of the test, or by criticizing the test itself as an invalid measure of what they knew. Irrational goal setting and procrastination were also prominent ways to deflect the implication of incompetence should students fail—a kind of self-worth insurance policy that eroded further the ability of students to absorb the test material. The fact that many of these students eventually found themselves unprepared to do well has led some observers to propose a reinterpretation of the typically-accepted causal mechanism that links anxiety and poor performance (i.e., the retrieval-deficit theory). This reinterpretation of events, the so-called skill deficit theory (Culler & Holahan, 1980) suggests that rather than anxiety being the cause of poor performance due to its interference with recall, anxiety may simply reflect the realization that because of their lack of preparation, failure-threatened students judge themselves destined to fail. Here anxiety acts as a harbinger of failure, not the cause of failure which is lack of adequate preparation. After all, no one can recall things they did not learn adequately in the first place.

Meanwhile, another group of failure-threatened students, the Overstrivers, adopt a decidedly different approach to study during the *test-preparation* stage. Rather than preparing excuses against the implications of failure by studying in a half-hearted manner, Overstrivers have no choice but to study hard since their chosen self-protective strategy is to avoid failure by succeeding. In order to guarantee success, these students throw themselves in to their studies—meticulously, relentlessly, and with energy that bordered on the compulsive. They cannot afford to fail. Excuse-making is not an option.

Finally, in the *test-taking* stage, students were required to retrieve from memory what they had learned, often in the context of great turmoil and tension. As will be recalled, this stage is the focus of retrieval-deficit theories of anxiety. Consider, first, those failure-avoiding students found in the lower-left quadrant of Figure 8.1. These students are accosted simultaneously both by roiling emotions as well as subvocal worries (e.g., "Why are so many others leaving so early? Maybe the test is easier than I think. I must be dumb!") making it difficult to remember much of anything. And, it is also likely that, according to a skill-deficit view, these students have little to retrieve. The relatively low test scores earned by this group likely reflect a combination of these deficits.

Meanwhile, those super-prepared Overstrivers come to grief in the *test-taking* stage as victims of a massive retrieval-deficit. They believed they knew the material cold before the exam thanks to their obsessive overpreparation, but failed to recall much of it during the exam. Yet, once the test was over and the pressure abated, when given a second chance Overstrivers can easily recall much of what had eluded them just moments before (Covington & Omelich, 1987).

Clearly, then, from the standpoint of assisting students to overcome the destructive effects of anxiety on learning and performance, it appears that no single intervention will likely be equally effective for all (Naveh-Benjamin, 1985; Naveh-Benjamin, McKeachie, & Lin, 1987). This is because—as we have just seen—different types of students suffer different deficits. We were left wondering if the largest number of students would be best served regarding anxiety reduction if instructors would make constructive policy changes in their courses that would benefit all students, to one degree or another, rather than attempting to accommodate the particular vulnerabilities of every student individually. We will examine this proposition shortly.

Academic Engagement

Another major goal of our research agenda has been to explore the possibilities of nurturing the will to learn among students as well as encouraging their appreciation of learning for its own sake. Central to this enterprise is the concept of intrinsic motivation that assumes that the rewards for such motivation reside in the process of inquiry itself and become self-reinforcing, hence indefinitely sustainable, that is, learning for the sake of curiosity, for the pleasure of discovery, or for matters of personal enlightenment (Deci, 1975; Deci & Ryan, 1985; Ryan & Deci, this volume).

However, many observers (e.g., Kohn, 1993) have lamented the prospects of ever encouraging intrinsic motivation in a world dominated by extrinsic rewards such as praise, gold stars, and grades—extrinsic because these rewards are basically unrelated to the act of learning itself. For example, it is feared that learning may become merely the means to an end, that is, a way to get rewards, and when these tangible rewards are no longer available, the willingness to continue learning will suffer (Condry & Chambers, 1978). This view is sustained by the assumption that intrinsic and extrinsic motivation are not just separate processes, but incompatible, if not antagonistic.

Yet, despite these dire predictions, interviews with our student informants provided unmistakable evidence that much of what students learn is acquired out of personal interest and not merely for the sake of high grades. How might this apparent contradiction be understood in ways that favor the promotion of intrinsic motivation, despite the obvious fact that schools constitute an unremitting climate controlled by a host of external inducements and threats, and in particular grades?

We began our deliberations by concluding that the traditional intrinsic/extrinsic dichotomy is not a useful starting point for our inquiries, and is actually misleading by focusing attention on the wrong culprit when it comes to the undermining of intrinsic engagement (Covington, 1999). We reasoned that it is not the offering of rewards per se, nor even the tangible properties of extrinsic rewards that is to blame. The real source of disruption and reward incompatibility lies with the reasons or motives for learning. Thus, the proper dichotomy for resolving the issue of incompatibility is the classic self-worth distinction between approach goals and avoidance goals. In effect, when one's reasons for learning are defensive and avoidant-oriented, intrinsically-toned goals are the first victim of fear and anger. Striving for high grades as a way to demonstrate superior ability eclipses the inherent value of what one is learning. By this reasoning, the villain is not the tangible nature of extrinsic rewards nor even their external orientation, but rather it is the competitive *scarcity* of rewards that exacerbates fear-of-failure dynamics and intensifies the threat to one's sense of worth. By contrast, positive, approach-oriented reasons for learning provide a context compatible with the pursuit of intrinsic goals that can generate their own self-reinforcing momentum (Covington & Müeller, 2001).

The traditional intrinsic/extrinsic distinction is also misleading in that it implies that each of these motivational systems is responsive to a different class of rewards, and that no crossover is possible. Actually, however, everyday experience suggests just the opposite. A positive, additive relationship between extrinsic and intrinsic rewards is often the rule, not the exception. For example, extrinsic rewards like money frequently bolsters intrinsic interests. Consider the young thespian who is able to attend a summer stock theater workshop with the help of a financial scholarship. Although, strictly speaking, money is unrelated to the intrinsic fascination of becoming an accomplished actor—qualifying this gift as an extrinsic inducement—it is nonetheless instrumental for making a good thing happen. Thus, we can add money to a host of extrinsic rewards that can serve intrinsic goals including praise and other forms of recognition as long as they are in the service of valued goals and for positive reasons. This example clarifies the multifaceted role of extrinsic motivators in the achievement process. In effect, extrinsic payoffs such as social recognition stand in the breach between approach and avoidance goals. Extrinsic payoffs can either advance a love of learning—if they serve positive, task-oriented goals, or interfere with achievement and caring about what is being learned if they are sought after for self-aggrandizing reasons.

This reformulation of the intrinsic/extrinsic distinction explains why students can be animated simultaneously by a host of disparate motives, some intrinsic and other extrinsic in nature. And, there are variations in these relationships reflected by our student typology. For example, it is success-oriented students who are most likely to value both the intrinsic appeal of learning for its own sake while fulfilling requirements for the good grades necessary to achieve meaningful occupational goals. By contrast, for failure-threatened students the dominant animator is the fear of failure and the suppression of intrinsic pursuits.

Overall, these observations suggest that intrinsic interests can either be encouraged or discouraged by tangible rewards, depending on the kinds of motives operating. This proposition sheds new light on the long-standing debate regarding the allegedly harmful effects of tangible, extrinsic rewards on the will to learn (Cameron & Pierce, 1994; Deci, Koestner, & Ryan, 1999; Eisenberger & Cameron, 1996). In effect, it is not external rewards per se that undercut intrinsic task engagement as much as their scarcity and the absence of the kinds of tangible payoffs that encourage one's caring about learning. Examples of such payoffs and a consideration of their nature is a topic taken up shortly.

Prelude to Renewal

The reader will note that in addition to featuring the emotional components of motivation via the classic notion of motives-as-drives, we have also played host to those all-important cognitive, rational concerns that when taken together—emotions and cognitions alike, create a seamless, dynamic interplay that is responsible for our humanity. This joint emphasis is most evident in our research described above on the role that the constrains of reason play in maintaining the plausibility of self-serving excuses and in our documentation regarding the multifaceted, causal network involving both emotional and cognitive components that gives life to the phenomenon of achievement anxiety. Suspicions that these twin forces interact and jointly influence behavior as partners has long been entertained—certainly even before Freud's day. But significant progress in actually validating this presumption has had to await the advent of Achievement Goal Theory which provides a convincing theoretical basis for this rapprochement by advancing a complimentary interpretation of motives-as-goals (Covington & Pintrich, 2001; Elliot, 1999; Elliot & Dweck, 1988; Maehr & Zusho, this volume). Researchers in this tradition assume that all actions are given meaning, direction, and purpose by the goals that individuals seek out, and that the quality and intensity of behavior will change as their goals change. From this perspective, the success of goal-directed actions depends on the right reasons for learning (i.e., motives), which, by the compatible, converging arguments of both Self-worth and Achievement Goal Theory, theorists focus on non-competitive, intrinsically-oriented reasons—typically taking as their achievement vehicle a mastery learning paradigm (Covington & Omelich, 1984). Conversely, failure and its handmaiden—the fear-of-failure—prevails for both cognitive and emotional reasons when the underlying goal is one of self-aggrandizement and the need to prove one's superiority over others.

There is no incompatibility here. Neither view discounts the validity of the other; rather they are complementary. Self-worth research that draws its inspiration from the drive-theory tradition helps clarify the basic causes of school failure and its motivational roots. Likewise, the motives-as-goals approach provides a broad perspective on the kinds of educational solutions we should seek. More specifically, goal-setting stands as a practical surrogate for motives (Locke & Latham, 1984), and goal-setting control behavior, especially as it relates to the individual's future chances. Indeed, I will argue shortly that when it comes to educational reform the proper tact is to pursue a strategy of solutions-as-goals, that is, students creating solutions to problems and issues that excite both them and their teachers, and in this process of mentoring students acquire critical subject-matter skills.

Our self-worth analysis of student life has allowed us to glimpse something of the internal dynamics of learners from a motivational perspective as well as to provide an appreciation for the many learning styles that students adopt in coping with the intense pressures associated with achieving noteworthy accomplishments. We have also identified the often troublesome relationship between learners and the institutional features of learning environments, and in particular exploring how prevailing reward systems based on a philosophy of competition can exacerbate the vulnerabilities of many students who long before entering college have tied their sense of worth to a competitive yardstick.

This portrayal of events calls to mind an analogy to the college experience of a gauntlet to be run in which the rules of engagement demand that psychological survival depends on viewing peers as competitors, on lackluster effort, and on defensive strategies that can ultimately fail to protect students not only from academic failure itself, but also from the implications of failure, that one is unworthy.

This sobering portrayal has provided us a starting point for thinking about the restructuring of the college learning experience which, I believe, depends on a kind of balancing act in which instructors must seek to reduce student anxieties put in play by the threat of failure and, on the other hand, simultaneously promote contexts in which students and instructors alike can find a common basis for creating joy in learning and teaching. The development of practical guidelines for achieving and then maintaining these twin objectives has always been the ultimate goal of all our research and inquiries over the years.

But more is needed to achieve such a vision than can be drawn solely from insights gained from any given motivational theory, including Self-worth Theory. Motivation theories must make common-cause with other realities that are only partially motivational in nature. First, obviously, there are more players in this drama than just students. Instructors must play a key role in this retooling as must other staff members including graduate student instructors and even readers. What should be their part in rectifying matters from a self-worth perspective? There are no straight-forward answers here given the fact that the teaching staff itself is vulnerable to the same self-worth threats that bedevil many students.

Second, the usefulness of any guidelines for change will also depend on a thorough understanding of the nature of the beliefs and expectations that both students and instructors bring to the table. For example, this realm includes questions about how students define fairness and equity in grading—definitions that are often at odds with the views of instructors. Such potential sources of conflict add to an already contentious classroom atmosphere, made worse by fear-of-failure dynamics on both sides of the aisle.

I have referred to this confection of vexing problems as a Hidden Agenda made up of three areas of conflict (Covington, 2004). First, there is the fact that student learning is often driven by fear—fear that individuals will be proven incompetent, a point well documented so far. Second, there exists a pervasive mismatch of beliefs about the roles and responsibilities of students as learners and instructors as mentors, respectively, which invariably creates a climate of frustration and confusion for everyone. And, third there is student resentment over being subject to grade rationing policies that students argue are unfair and discriminatory.

This agenda remains largely invisible, but nonetheless is real enough in its negative impact on effective teaching and learning. Invisibility is understandable for several reasons. First, this agenda often remains eclipsed by more immediate, pressing logistic concerns in the instructor's rush to prepare for her classes on a daily basis. There just isn't enough time to concern oneself with these issues. Second, the workings of this agenda often remain obscured by the veil of common sense.

For example, who among us would think that after years of schooling college students would still not be clear about what constitutes their roles as learners? Furthermore, there is a natural reluctance to bring these issues to light, disclosures that may challenge the entrenched, but often erroneous, beliefs of even veteran instructors about the true nature of the relationship between teaching and learning. Sometimes it is more comfortable, certainly easier, just not to know. Yet, for all this, the Hidden Agenda is not inaccessible. Let's explore each element of this agenda in more detail.

Fear of Failure

We have already made a case for the fear-of-failure as a driving force in the lives of many students. Our research (Covington, von Hoene & Voge, in preparation) indicates that instructors are no less subject to these same dynamics. For many students, feelings of worth are tied to performance goals—being worthy by reason of achievement; and, for instructors, in a parallel fashion, their worth is tied to the effectiveness of their teaching. A basic revelation of Self-worth Theory is that teachers and students are linked—cheek-to-jowl, by a common need to be appreciated for their interlocking roles. Instructors are evaluated, even graded, too, by their students as well as by their academic colleagues. As a teacher, one's competency is always on public display, and often on the line when it comes to promotions and even retention in the Academy. When the fears and self-doubts of both instructors and students combine, a volatile, downward spiraling into wariness and mistrust can be the result. For instance, the unattractive, often infuriating behaviors of some students, say, procrastination and indifferent effort, often go unappreciated by instructors for what they really are: fear-driven strategies, not necessarily defiance or the disrespectful challenging of authority. Yet, it is all too easy for instructors to attribute such actions to a moral lapse of undeserving individuals. As a consequence, instructors often react with resentment, blaming students rather than searching for the true culprit in the relationship. These reactions of instructors, in turn, simply confirm what many students have feared all along—that their teachers are uncaring and insensitive to their apprehensions and concerns. In short, the worth of one group is held hostage by the worth of the other, to the disadvantage of both.

Instructors, too, have an arsenal of self-protective strategies by which they can deflect the causes of half-filled lecture halls and slumping teaching ratings. For example, some instructors may fancy themselves as the defenders of rigorous academic standards which, if students are unwilling to accept, are unworthy of consideration or help. Then there is the argument that teachers can't always be appreciated by their students in the near term, but hopefully at least respected, retrospectively, as one's former students gain the longer perspective provided later on by the exigencies of life.

These troublesome dynamics that set students and teachers at odds can develop more quickly, are triggered more easily, and ultimately made worse in large lecture courses where students already tend to feel isolated and anonymous anyway, and where instructors already stand remote from students due in part to overwhelming class sizes.

Other members of the teaching staff are no less vulnerable when self-worth concerns go awry, in particular Graduate Student Instructors (GSIs) or Teaching Assistants. We have characterized this group as the players in the middle. On the one hand, GSIs are typically seen by their students as protectors—buffers between themselves and their instructors as well as guides through their labors as learners. On the other hand, GSIs act as surrogate instructors-in-charge when it comes to administering course policy, discharging weekly teaching obligations, and giving grades. This position can quickly become precarious when, for example, GSIs are expected to administer grading policies with which they themselves disagree, and which may have been created unilaterally by instructors with little or no input from the staff.

This position is made all the more difficult by the fact that typically GSIs are still very much beginning students themselves, often only 1 or 2 years beyond their own undergraduate days. Yet, they are thought of as subject-matter experts by their students. Moreover, GSIs typically know little as yet about the art of teaching. Such inexperience on all these fronts was well described by one of our GSI informants who lamented that she "did not know enough content to teach, and did not yet know enough about how to teach." Moreover, because of GSI shortages in some fields, many graduate students are hired to teach in fields related to, but nonetheless different from, their home departments. Little wonder that GSIs are often fearful of having their ignorance exposed both in matters of *how* to teach and *what* to teach as well as fearing a loss of control over their classrooms. It is not only inexperience that is problematic. If it is students who are absolutely powerless, then GSIs are relatively so. The role of GSIs as merely part of the supporting cast makes their power over teaching and policy decisions tenuous and uncertain.

Efforts to improve teaching effectiveness must give equal attention to the vulnerability of all the players in the educational drama, and to the inevitable conflicts, frustrations, and fears that can arise, none of which are unexpected from the perspective of Self-worth Theory.

Instructor/Student Mismatches

Our research (Covington et al. in preparation) has also identified a problem so massive and potentially disruptive that it threatens the best intentions of reform-minded educators, and yet typically goes unaddressed, again because it is largely hidden, lurking just below the radar screen. I refer to a pervasive mismatch between instructors and students regarding beliefs about their respective roles and responsibilities to one another. The standoff can be simply stated: Many students assume that their role as learners is to absorb information and that instructors are expected to provide that information is a clear, simple, and accessible manner. Moreover, students expect instructors to provide the motivational impetus for learning by providing information in entertaining, enjoyable, and memorable ways. Generally, this describes a passive mind set on the part of many students, typified by the analogy of learning as a vessel that simply gets filled with information—the accumulation of inert facts and figures that have no impact on the shape, character, or size of the vessel itself.

By contrast, instructors assume (rightly so) that ultimately it is students who are responsible for their own learning and meaning-making. Additionally, instructors typically champion intellectual independence of thought and action as the ultimate goal of a college education. Yet despite these noble sentiments, we have identified several ways that instructors can become unwitting codependents by reinforcing the very passivity that they abhor in their students. For example, some instructors assume that the problem-solving skills necessary for the effective expression of independent thought will occur more or less automatically once sufficient factual information is provided students. Yet, all the available evidence belies this view (Covington, 1986). The possession of information alone—even if it is salient to the problem at hand, is no guarantee that proper conclusions will be drawn or that the best decisions will be reached. Problem-solving strategies are not only trainable, but must be trained and in their own right in order to maximize the possibilities for productive thinking to mature. Moreover, the assumption that productive thought is primarily the consequence of merely acquiring sufficient information strengthens the unfortunate implication that teaching is fairly easy. By this reckoning, teachers need only present information smoothly, and in meaningful and economic ways. Once this is done, the teaching act is complete. This belief also makes it easier for instructors to locate the causes of the failure of students to learn within students themselves. If students can't make sense of things on their own—the argument runs, then instructors may feel more justified in tailoring their teaching to those relatively few most promising individuals who "get it" without all the extra preparation and effort needed to remediate those falling behind.

Fear and Loathing of Grades

The central educational implications of Self-worth Theory concern the fact that grades often carry excess meaning for students that cuts to the heart of their struggle for self-approval. High grades imply personal worthiness, while poor marks imply worthlessness. These dynamics are perpetuated not because the act of learning itself is inherently threatening—we know that it is not, but because many students have come to tie their sense of worth to competitive achievement (Covington, 1998). Nor do students object to being evaluated; they do not. According to the results of our structured interviews, what students do object to are potential inequities thought by them to create an essential unfairness regarding some grading policies. The widespread use of a competitive yardstick—often referred to as grade rationing—is the primary ignition point for much of the anger that sets students against students as competitors for an insufficient supply of rewards as well as resentment of instructors as the instigators of such policies. Students believe they should be judged on the absolute quality of their individual work based on standards of excellence derived independently of how many other students are doing well or poorly.

From a self-worth perspective, the essential predicament facing many students is that the tests of worth they have adopted depend on a game in which there can be only a few winners, and that to rise to the top of the competitive heap, they must expend extraordinary effort that, given the likelihood of failure, becomes all the more evidence of incompetence. Grading is no less an agonizing ordeal for instructors and their staff. They are not unmindful of the high stake involved for students, but struggle nonetheless to maintain proper academic standards.

Reinventing the Teaching/Learning Process: Solutions as Goals

Overall, our approach to rethinking the teaching/learning process in light of the Hidden Agenda can be stated simply. Basically, it involves organizing student learning and problem solving around significant discipline-related problems or questions—issues whose solutions are the ultimate goal of any given course. The variety of educationally significant problem themes exemplifies virtually every subject-matter discipline. To mention only a few classic themes: Addressing a conundrum that has long stifled intellectual progress in a field; investigating the contrary finding that nags at conventional wisdom; addressing a paradox or an enduring mystery; or reframing old problems in new and novel ways that are more amenable to answers.

We envision such issues and the intellectual strategies and skills necessary for their solution as the curricular key to unraveling the tangled skein of complexities we have described—both motivational and cognitive as well as the social complications that inhabit the Hidden Agenda. We recommend that everything be harnessed to the notion of solutions as goals, from the first day of class to the last, and, hopefully, beyond for years to come.

More specifically, what is our reasoning regarding the value of this problem-based approach to teaching and learning for addressing and, hopefully, overturning the Hidden Agenda, and in the process making way for a more positive climate for learning? Our reasoning consists of three interlocking and mutually reinforcing elements: transparency of goals; redressing the mismatch of roles and responsibilities, and the use of criterion-referenced grading.

Transparency and Coherence

Let's start by considering those aspects of course design that serve to trump the fear-of-failure among students, and which in the process can also stimulate noteworthy academic performance. In the first rank of these ingredients is a sense of clarity, coherence, and purpose regarding the intellectual journey ahead. Unfortunately, all too often, students labor in the absence of the big picture that otherwise would bring meaning to their studies. Moreover, the absence of sufficient course structure and clarity regarding what one must do well to succeed creates anxiety that fosters the fear-of-failure particularly when ambiguity occurs in an atmosphere of public evaluation where one's ability status is on display and potentially in jeopardy.

The notion of solutions as goals provides academic purpose as well as a much needed perspective for students. This is accomplished in several ways. First, solutions define the purposes to which subject-matter material is put, that is, the solving of problems. In a problem-solving context, course content is no longer likely to be seen as unrelated, disembodied bits of information, cut adrift from higher purpose, things merely to be memorized and passively stored. Facts now become things to think *with* in addition to being things to think *about*.

Second, problems automatically place reasonable constraints on the scope and content coverage of courses by focusing attention on the subject-matter knowledge needed to address the problem at hand. In effect, the nature of the problem determines what information must be acquired, how well it must be learned, and when, and in what order, it must be mastered—thus, likening the problem-solving process to a progressive unfolding of a scaffolding of skill applications and information gathering. These considerations provide a logical, internally consistent rationale for why the course is arranged the way it is, not concocted arbitrarily, or on a whim—as is often perceived by students to be the case. It is this curricular reasoning that need be shared with students in advance of actual problem solving and occasionally reinforced along the way as courses unfold. This process of enlightenment provides a climate of meaningful clarity as contrasted to rules that might be clear enough, but seem devoid of rational justification.

Third, solving problems require plans of action that, in turn, depend largely on the internal structure of the problem in question and of the content field in which it is embedded. Some problems are best pursued by means of a spiral lesson plan in which the same or similar problems are reintroduced over time, but in increasingly more complex forms. Other problems are best analyzed in terms of hierarchical structures where material presented early on is considered foundational for the understanding of later material. Then there are those means-ends structures in which ideal end states (solutions) can be envisioned in advance with the students' task that of creating and carrying out the means that will move participants from currently inadequate or undesirable conditions toward the desired ends. The organizational structure of problems becomes the backbone of courses around which all curricular and instructional decisions should be made, decisions that also should be shared with students. The structures mentioned here are broadly applicable across many subject-matter disciplines, while still flexible enough to accommodate differences in specific content areas within a given discipline.

Ultimately, all the potential benefits of clarity for reducing fear and uncertainty rest on the sense of purpose brought to the table by a problem-based approach. Purpose and the sense of meaning it creates is everything when it comes to being task-engaged. The purpose implied by solutions as goals suggests direction, intent, and eventually, destination—attributes whose nurturing is critical to proper motivation, that is, the desire for success in the form of seeking answers and moving toward new horizons.

Redressing the Mismatch of Roles and Responsibilities

We have documented the ways that a misunderstanding among students regarding the true nature of intellectual inquiry can cause them to approach their studies in atomistic ways—often missing the forest for the trees, as well as producing intellectual timidity and passivity, attributes that, when combined with the expectations of students that it is their instructors who have failed in their responsibility to animate the inquiry process, further undercut the motives to approach success. As we have argued, instructors are sometimes complicit in creating this undesirable state of affairs by unwittingly fostering the very passivity they detest. Ultimately, however, it is students who must take responsibility for their learning with the teaching staff providing the guidance and support necessary to this end.

This relationship is best achieved through the creation of an alliance among all the players in the learning game for the purpose of addressing a common academic challenge represented by problems of the kinds we advocate. For students, the tasks involved in problem solving should be just difficult enough that the odds of success and failure are in delicate balance, only to be resolved satisfactorily by informed, productive effort. Regarding instructors, ideally the same challenges should hold a personal or professional fascination for them so that together—for teachers and students alike, the achievement goals of all the players will be compatible, if not at times, synonymous. Whenever solutions and the strengthening of the intellectual processes by which solutions are fashioned become the highest priority, students will find themselves immersed in a community of scholarship. They will come to learn the limits of a discipline—what kinds of problems it can reasonably address, and those it cannot; the history of its successes and shortfalls; what counts as evidence in scholarly debates; and, how to conduct inquiries consistent with the mission of the discipline. In the face of messy, ill-defined problems students can witness and then come to appreciate what it truly means to be an expert—not knowing all the answers, nor even having an encyclopedic knowledge of all the relevant facts and figures, but rather knowing how to acquire the information needed, and—of equal importance, knowing *which* information is needed given one's intuitive grasp of what make the problem so recalcitrant in the first place.

We have observed a number of demonstrations designed by instructors that encourage students to model the thinking of real-life practitioners (Covington et al. in preparation). For example, one social science instructor illustrated the many steps involved in the development of her ideas for creating a journal article by sharing with her students all her notes in a progressive fashion, beginning with tentative scribbles on the backs of envelopes and on scraps of paper (with spattered coffee stains added to boot) to the final typeset pages covered with editorial corrections. Such memorable exercises dramatize something of the hard-won, often frustrating processes by which ideas are conceived, tested, revised—revised again, and finally brought to the academic marketplace. In essence, these are invitations for students to enter into the community of scholarship largely through a process of apprenticeship. No small part of the apprentice process involves group collaboration. Indeed, the kinds of problems we have in mind are problems largely because they can only be solved through a coordinated, collective effort that often proves difficult to sustain unless the art of cooperation itself is made a process goal.

Once students have the assurances of a supportive alliance as well as sufficient clarity and transparency regarding their destination, they are released to attend to the larger purposes of their studies, not simply trying to determine how to get the best grade with the least effort. Moreover, students will be in a position to enjoy one of the greatest positive motivator of all: the realization that they are being trusted enough by their mentors to be given an opportunity to struggle along beside them.

Criterion-referenced Grading

The transformational process needed here requires that the meaning of grades be altered from being viewed by students as a potential threat to accepting grades as information necessary to become a better, more productive learner. This extraordinary challenge requires a reconsideration of the very meaning of the concept of academic excellence and of the standards by which it is assessed.

By adopting the notion of solutions as goals, the task of defining excellence is put on the proper footing. What counts as excellence in student work becomes defined by the nature and difficulty of the problem at hand. It is the quality of one's struggles to solve problems, not the unworthy, destructive efforts of students to outperform others, that becomes the yardstick by which excellence should be measured. Here the evaluation of student work, either of individuals or of groups, becomes tied to measurable progress toward answers. Real problems require absolute, criterion-based rules, or rubrics, for judging the quality of one's progress toward answers, not a relativistic yardstick that pits students against students in a race animated by a scarcity of rewards. In effect, when solutions are the goals, it is the absolute quality of one's ideas that count, independent of the relative number of students who also achieve them.

In the early years of our research, the arguments favoring absolute, criterion-referenced grading were based largely on anecdotal evidence. In order to put our position on a firmer footing, we undertook a more systematic program of research to assess the motivational and achievement benefits of various grading practices. To begin, we identified three attributes we believed should be components of any grading policy in order to maximize positive reasons for learning as well as to offset negative, fear-driven motives (Covington, 2004): (a) strengthening an effort/outcome linkage in the minds of students, (b) insuring student feelings of equity and fairness, and (c) promoting a positive instructor/student alliance.

We then developed what we judged to be an ideal prototypic grading policy that satisfied these criteria, and that could be employed as a benchmark against which to compare other extant grading policies, especially those featuring grade rationing. We referred to this prototypic system as a grade-choice arrangement (Covington & Omelich, 1984b). Under this system students can work for any grade they choose by amassing grade credits or points against a predetermined schedule of excellence (i.e., so many points for an A, so many for a B, etc.) with the requirement that the better the grades students seek, the more they must do and the better they must do it. This formula embodies several of the essential ingredients mentioned above for battling the Hidden Agenda, including transparency regarding the rules by which students must play the achievement game as well as providing reassurances that students will never get a lower grade than the number of points earned.

Over the years, we employed this grading prototype in a number of my large-enrollment introductory psychology courses. At various points in these courses, students were asked to evaluate their learning experiences against the three criteria described above. In some cases, students were asked to make absolute ratings, focusing specifically on the motivational costs and benefits to them of the grade-choice arrangement as employed in my course alone without reference to grading policies in other courses. In yet other instances, students were asked to make comparative judgments with other courses that featured various forms of grade rationing.

The overall findings of this research are easily summarized. A strong preference emerged in favor of grade-choice policies, preferences stemming largely from satisfying the three ideal grading characteristics described above.

Effort/Outcome Linkage As to the matter of an effort/outcome linkage, under a grade-choice arrangement students typically described their successes as caused by their own efforts and their shortfalls caused largely by insufficient effort because as they often pointed out, effort can be most purposely directed and calibrated when attempting to satisfy known criteria. With clear standards, students said they were willing to spend more time and energy, and ultimately believe themselves more deserving of a good grade because as one informant put it, "I earned it myself!" Contrariwise, although students agreed that classes featuring relative grading practices could also arouse great energy, the quality of effort expenditure was perceived as decidedly different. In these cases, students explained that they were driven largely by the unknown consequences of not trying, sometimes relentlessly, and as hard as possible for fear of not keeping up. As another informant stated, "I never knew what it took to do well, other than try to outperform my peers." Such effort is largely fear-driven, and, as a result, less likely to be as effective as expenditures of effort that are closely linked to absolute, criterion-referenced standards.

Perceived Equity Next, consider the issue of perceived equity or an equal opportunity for all students to do well, grade-wise, as long as each student meets the criteria for excellence set forth by the instructor. Students reported that they were reassured by the fact that they needed only to meet the standards set by the instructor without regard for the performances of others, even when those standards were seen as difficult to attain. Once again, because of such benchmarks students tended to see themselves as architects of their own fate, and came to rely more on personal effort and initiative.

Positive Alliances Finally, regarding the promotion of alliances, positive feelings were more often reported under a grade-choice arrangement owing to the fact that students were no longer in competition with other students for a limited supply of good grades. Rather, good grades were in sufficient supply for anyone who met the criteria that constituted excellence.

Nonetheless, despite the overwhelmingly positive reactions to a grade-choice arrangement, students did have some misgivings. For example, believing that one's successes are the product of one's own efforts can cut two ways. As one student put it with alarm: "But what if I fail? Must I own my failures too?" The more a grading system favors transparency and equity of opportunity, the fewer the legitimate excuses available to deflect the implications of failure. Of course, there are always intellectual risks in the pursuit of excellence, but when setbacks occur in the context of defined standards, they are more likely to be accepted as an inevitable, even beneficial aspect learning—part of a feedback loop, and not necessarily an indictment of the individual's competency (Kennedy & Willcutt, 1964).

The use of absolute grading standards also prompted some students to wonder why they would ever do more work than absolutely necessary. Once a minimally-acceptable grade is attained, the prudent strategy would be to turn one's attention to those courses where additional effort may pay off in higher grades. This is scarcely an issue under a competitive arrangement. Here the demands for relentless effort are built into the system because one never knows when enough work is enough, since the grade targets are indeterminate and ultimately depend on the performances of others. Yet, this *is* a legitimate concern for our proposed grading system. Why, indeed, should students do more than the minimums required? Our answer is comes in two parts. First, make no mistake. Minimums are not synonymous with mediocrity. Sometimes minimums are highly complex and extraordinarily demanding as in the case of the competencies necessary to pass state licensing examinations for the certification of physicians, attorneys, and pharmacists. Standards of excellence are not necessarily placed at risk when they are stated as minimums.

Second, the fundamental issue here is how to encourage extra student effort and continued engagement beyond what is absolutely necessary for the mere accumulation of grade credits. This is the realm of intrinsic motivation. The solution is that incentives other than grade points are needed. Recall our argument that it is not the external nature of rewards per se that undercuts intrinsic task engagement as much as it is the absence of the kinds of payoffs that encourage further learning and involvement beyond the minimums. These are the personally-meaningful payoffs that include, say, opportunities for students to put their knowledge to work in the case of creating educational materials such as new bibliographies or instructional manuals for the class, or being given the change to explain to the instructor and/or to fellow students just why what they are learning is important to them. And, incidentally, we have found that actually paying students to act in intrinsic ways—by, for example, consulting supplementary source material intended merely to peak their curiosity, by awarding them small amounts of extra credit does nothing to diminish their excitement and caring about what they learned in order to achieve the credit (Covington, 2002).

A Self-Worth Reformulation

So far, all our recommendations require that changes be initiated by instructors through the mechanism of course redesign. Indeed, it is the responsibility of the teaching staff to set the structure, climate, and context for student learning. Yet, students must be willing to take advantage of enriched opportunities to learn. Clearly, however, offering students the opportunity to approach success does not mean that they will always accept the invitation, especially those students we have described as failure-threatened. What, then, is the task for learners? The self-worth perspective provides a clear answer: Students need come to grips with the P=A=W formulation that implies a dependency of one's worth on competitive success. It is our view that students must struggle with the implications of this formula as it might apply to them, and if they find themselves complicit, to consider alternative or at least additional sources for self-approval. Without this struggle, all the efforts of instructors to provide a rich, healthy, and inviting climate for learning may come to naught.

Obviously, reevaluating the basis for one's sense of worth is an exceedingly difficult and potentially threatening proposition in part because of the paradoxical nature of the task—paradoxical, because despite all the negative baggage that can trail in their wake, the issue of grades must be confronted; grades can neither be ignored nor dismissed. Grades *are* important, especially in the short run as gatekeepers for prestigious future occupations. It is not enough for instructors simply to argue that in the long-term the importance of grades is sharply limited. For example, students are always surprised to learn that college GPA is virtually worthless as a predictor of lifetime income compared to predictions based simply on the number of years students stay in school, irrespective of the grades they received or the kinds of institutions that awarded them. But such impersonal statistics are not enough. Statistics do not speak to the individual case. What is needed is a mental and emotional restructuring of the issues—a new formulation more powerful than the one that describes the predicament in which many students find themselves.

Over the past few years, we have initiated a number of small focus groups in which students are challenged to struggle with this restructuring task once they have been made aware of Self-worth Theory and its potential meaning for their lives as students. Our informants easily intuited the dynamics involved and the motivational nature of the issues at stake as reflected in the P=A=W formula. Many personal insights are generated from these discussions which, when taken in the aggregate, create a potential hedge against the proposition that grades determine one's worth, yet without denying the importance of grades. First, these students submit that grades can *best* be viewed as a by-product of learning, but learning for the right reasons—to satisfy one's curiosity, to prepare for helping others, and for the sake of self- improvement. Second, this perspective is also *best*, because far from dismissing grades, the elevation of intrinsic learning goals to prominence and the redirecting of the causal linkage in which grades now follow learning—not eclipse learning, increases the chances for attaining even better grades than would otherwise be the case in an atmosphere of anxiety and self-doubt. Third, this view is *best*, because grades can now assume their rightful, constructive place as feedback for how students can improve their future chances; and, finally, this reformulation is *best*, because the intrinsic rewards of learning are not a scare commodity, limited by competitive rules, but open to all.

What are the prospects for successfully challenging students to consider this alternative self-worth reformulation as potentially applicable to their lives as students? This question rests on the assumption that—at their best, omnibus motivation theories must not only possess a sufficient conceptual reach to satisfy the theoretician's need to explain various aspects of human behavior including puzzling misbehaviors, but also that the reasoning and logic involved in these models need be readily understood by lay-persons with insights anchored securely in personal and common-sense experience. Moreover, motivation theories should imply a pedagogical purpose as to the goals and true meaning of the labor of students. In the case of Self-worth Theory, the purpose is to promote a love of learning and to seek out those personal satisfactions that fuel this commitment.

We determined that this challenge is best offered in the context of actual, ongoing classrooms that have been explicitly designed by instructors to disassemble the negative dynamics associated with the Hidden Agenda. The class we choose to overhaul was—once again, the large enrollment introductory psychology course that I offer each year on the Berkeley campus. Following our earlier recommendations urging a problem-solving approach, I cast the course in the form of a classic story/line drama in which students developed a case study of an imaginary, fantasy child of their own creation. The child's life-chances were placed in jeopardy from conception, given either a genetic disposition to a mental illness, a potential incapacity, or some other handicap of the student's choice. The central challenge of this semester-long project involved the student acting as a psychological advisor to the child's parent (s), caretakers, or guardians in a progressive effort to assist the child to thread his/her way through a series of childhood and early adolescent developmental crises, by avoiding or overcoming psychological obstacles and mental traps, while marshalling positive, compensatory resources given the child's special vulnerabilities. Solutions to each crisis depended on information drawn from lectures, discussion sections, and outside readings as well as from student-initiated research conducted individually and in small groups. The very nature of the overall task maximized transparency of action and of destination—which in the end, was to maximize the odds that the child would lead a healthy, productive post adolescent life. At times, the roles of instructor/teaching staff/students were deliberately merged when all parties combined forces to create joint solutions. In the early weeks, the quality of student solutions were evaluated against preannounced, instructor-generated criteria that allowed all ideas to be graded against a common denominator. In later weeks, as new problems were confronted, it became the students' turn to create and then agree among themselves on a common set of criteria for assigning grade credits.

The first two class meetings of the course were devoted to a description of the Hidden Agenda along with a lecture presentation on Self-worth Theory, which treats grades as by-products of learning, and how the grading policies of this course supported these reformulations. From that point on in the semester, interventions consisted solely of brief overhead messages presented weekly at the beginning of lectures to make the self-worth perspective a reality in the midst of the academic stresses and demands of the course. For example, several days prior each midterm exam, the following message was displayed: "Reflect on the lectures about Self-worth Theory and the possibilities of reframing the meaning of grades for yourself. What one idea is most likely to increase your personal confidence, feelings of support, trust and safety as you prepare for the exam?"

Immediately following the first two lecture presentations, we administered open-ended questionnaires designed to assess the initial reactions of student on hearing this frank, practical, yet theory-driven presentation about issues of vital concern to them. In summary of these findings, it was clear that on initial exposure students readily appreciated the essence of self-worth principles and were quite able—often spontaneously willing—to apply these principles to an understanding of the factors that drove many of their personal conflicts and fears associated with college achievement. Additionally, almost universally students valued these disclosures for putting them at ease regarding the upcoming course as well as conveying a sense of caring and support by the teaching staff, and for establishing a sense of academic community, especially the potential for transforming their views of fellow students, from being adversaries to becoming helpful advocates for learning.

What were the longer term consequences of disclosing the motivational rationale underlying the course structure as well as the self-insights that it might engender? Both exit interviews and anonymous questionnaire data provided a decidedly positive picture regarding the value of Self-worth Theory for promoting serviceable insights that endured throughout the term. This phenomenon was reflected in the diversity of ways in which students appropriated the motivational information. Students seized on different aspects of the theory, sometimes focusing on mere fragments of the message, but always in ways meaningful to them. At its most valuable, the theory stimulated a personal dialogue of self-questioning regarding the role that grades play in defining their worth among a near-majority of students. As one informant put it: "The information is important because I realize that sometimes I am driven by fear." And, another student: "It [the theory] made me realize how engulfed [I was]…, feeling worthy only in times of success." Some student reported taking action for positive change based on these insights. For example, "The theory has taught me which behaviors and actions trigger the feeling of unworthiness, and as a result I try my best to steer clear of those behaviors and actions."

Naturally, not all students were positive. Although they were few in number, the observations of these students were nonetheless useful in gauging the troublesome nature of the challenge presented them. Some took exception to our implied idealism, occasionally amounting to a fierce defiance in which they stated indignantly that for them idealism would always be trumped by grade pressures, no matter what anyone said. And, sometimes students would actually misremember our message, charging that we dismissed the importance of grades which, in fact, was untrue. Our intention was to challenge students to relocate the meaning of grades—to decatastrophize grades and put them in a constructive alignment with learning goals, not to dismiss them. Such misreadings of our intentions simply demonstrate the extent to which some students are in the thrall of P=A=W dynamics.

A Broader Perspective

Overall, the results of these field experiments encouraged us to believe that theories of motivation can, indeed, motivate people and that the rationale behind motivation theories can be understood sufficiently by students to provide guidance for their own educational goals as well as being of personal value in providing alternative perspectives regarding their sense of self. Yet, as affirming as these findings were, they raise several fundamental issues, each of which offers challenges to future research.

Generalizability

First, there is the question of the generalizability of the achievement dynamics portrayed by Self-worth Theory. Are these dynamics essentially identical, or perhaps parallel, or do they share little in common with those dynamics that characterize populations other than our highly-selected college samples? Until we learn otherwise, ascribing college dynamics wholesale to other groups differing by age, ethnic and cultural membership, experience, and ability must be avoided. However, at present, what we do know makes the proposition of a broad representativeness of self-worth dynamics more than merely plausible. For one thing, the same kinds of self-handicapping behaviors found in our college samples have also been documented among younger children, ranging from the elementary years through high school (Urdan, Ryan, Anderman, & Gheen, 2002). Moreover, these behaviors are thought to be linked to avoidance motives. For another thing, developmental studies beginning in the earliest years of schooling reveal a progressive shift in children's explanations for failure—initially being perceived at the preschool level as caused by a lack of effort, to eventually attributing failure to a lack of ability by the late elementary and middle school years (Nicholls, 1978, 1984). Paralleling this shift is the strengthening of a perceived reciprocal relationship between effort expenditure and self-estimates of ability in which children reason that the more effort needed to succeed, the less able one is, and that to try hard and fail anyway is convincing evidence of inability (Harari & Covington, 1981). Moreover, during this protracted time period an increasing value is being placed on the importance of ability by children—not only academically, but also as a source of social capital and popularity, to the detriment of effort as a redeeming virtue.

Taken together, these developmental findings highlight most of the essential ingredients needed to create an irresistible vortex that can draw students inexorably into the snare of tying their sense of worth to outperforming others. All that is needed now is an ignition source to trigger this process, most likely being the kinds of unhealthy, child-rearing practices discussed below. But, clearly, not all students succumb to this fate, and instead thrive for positive reasons, despite pressures to the contrary. It is these sources of resistance we need identify more fully as surely as we need to understand better the dynamics of those students who eventually become failure-threatened. In the long view, the potentially good news is that by seeking some degree of universal causality among all these individual learner differences, we can hope to identify more clearly the dynamics involved in all learning as well as the many causes of the failure to learn, and thereby establish a sounder basis for creating pedagogical solutions that will be responsive to a broad array of learning styles and a wide range of learner circumstances.

Range of Applicability

A second question raised by our demonstration studies concerns contextual issues or what we might call the "range of applicability" of motivation theories. Once again, consider Self-worth Theory as our example. Are students always threatened, no matter how learning is contextualized? What happens when students fail in contexts where failure does not necessarily reflect on ability? Basically, our answer is that those dynamics associated with the fear-of-failure materialize whenever the dominant test of one's worth depends on grade-driven, competitive success—where only a few players can win—when failure to succeed competitively implies incompetence, and where individuals have little or no voice in establishing the rules of engagement. It is these rules of the learning game that contextualize the meaning of success and failure, and thereby control the implications for self-definition.

By contrast, whenever learning goals are contextualized as positive ends in themselves and rewards are unlimited, say, in the case of accumulating the satisfactions that come from exploring or enlarging on one's own personal interests, then the reasons for learning change for the better, and with these changes so, too, does the meaning of failure change in constructive directions. In this context, occasional failures are accepted as an inevitable part of the learning process. Interestingly, when individuals pursue their own interests, observers interpret requests for help as the result of students being novices—that is, being ignorant, rather than being stupid (Newman, 1990). In effect, in self-worth terms, it is not ignorance or an initial lack of skills that is so threatening, but rather it is feeling stupid that triggers ability-linked anxiety and shame with the implication that one can never become competent. At its core, a deeply-held, abiding interest possesses a private, protected side in which the rewards that sustain it are largely undiminished by occasional setbacks, rewards that include the sense of pride in surpassing one's own idiosyncratic standards of excellence and the playful discovery of hidden talents or capabilities. These are the kinds of rewards that support a vibrant interior architecture of the self.

The larger point here is that—psychologically speaking—context accounts for a great deal, including how one interprets one's own actions and those of others, which motives prevail for the moment as well as over the long-term, and even controls the goals that induce individuals either to persevere and endure setbacks or, conversely, to sabotage one's own efforts in order to obscure the meaning of failure. As educators, we need contextualize the learning game in ways that favor positive motivational dynamics.

A Matter of Timing

A third critical issue raised by our field studies involves the matter of timing. We need ask if it is too late by the college years to challenge students successfully to undertake the kinds of personal reappraisals advocated here. The conventional reply is "its never too late," a sentiment likely true for some students if we can judge from the kinds of positive, self-insightful quotes cited earlier. But, clearly, it is not true for many other students—perhaps even a majority, for whom the challenge of reframing the meaning of grades clearly represents a threat. This is not surprising. Many students have staked their sense of worth largely on an unbroken string of academic successes, starting in the earliest years of schooling. Now, at this late date for instructors to question the wisdom of placing competitive achievement at the heart of one's value system can lead to confusion, to the willful misperception of the message, and sometimes even to a sense of betrayal. Nor is it a surprise that such resistance is typical of failure-avoiding students given their particular child-rearing histories. We asked Berkeley students to describe retrospectively the quality of the achievement climate in their homes as they were growing up (Tomiki, 1997). Success-oriented students perceived their parents as employing praise more often in success, and reprimands were fewer for failing work compared with the recollections of failure-oriented students who recalled the opposite pattern. In this latter instance, disappointing performances were often perceived by our failure-threatened informants as violations of adult expectations which were often punished severely, whereas success was met with faint praise. Most ominous were fears that parental love and caring would be withheld should they fail to perform well, which they often felt incapable of doing. These and other findings at the college level (Tomiki, 1997) closely parallel the findings of Virginia Crandall and her colleagues (e.g., Crandall, Katkovsky, & Crandall, 1965; Crandall, Preston, & Rabson, 1960) who studied youngsters in the earlier years of family life. Given the apparent consistency of such child-rearing practices over time as well as their early onset, one gains the impression that the tendencies to approach success and to avoid failure found among adults likely reflect fundamental personality structures laid down at the deepest levels.

Additionally, the transition from high school to college is an extremely turbulent, confusing time for many students, academically speaking—again, particularly among failure-threatened individuals. In a companion study, we (Covington & Dray, 2001) observed a marked decrease in student academic self-confidence in the early college years due largely to the fact that the kinds of learning styles that favored high grades in high school—what has been referred to as "achievement by conformance" (Gough, 1966), that is, achieving in conventional ways defined by authority, are no longer particularly effective in college where the dominant academic emphasis typically shifts—often without warning or transitional support by instructors, to learning styles associated with achievement by independence, that is, exploring topics and issues on one's own terms and figuring things out for oneself (Gough, 1966, 1968). This is one reason we have emphasized transparency in teaching, not only to indicate what students are expected to do, but leading them to realize that often old intellectual habits, even though previously effective, must now given way to more sophisticated, productive ways of thinking.

Taking these findings as a whole, it is clear that the odds lengthen against failure-threatened students as they work their way through the gauntlet that is schooling, and the prospects of their caring about learning grow dim. Moreover, thinking about the role of grades as the essential architecture of one's sense of worth is difficult enough in the relative safety of situations that have been deliberately designed to encourage a process of self-examination. But what about the likelihood of such an examination occurring when students encounter less forgiving environments in which instructors may deliberately encourage competition for grades as a part of their pedagogical philosophy or because of the competitive realities of a particular occupational marketplace? Ultimately, hope lies with the vast majority of teachers at all educational levels who honor motivational objectives as much as content objectives. It will be the success of the efforts of these individuals to project motivational messages of the kind we envision beyond the limits of a given place, time, or a particular subject-matter field that will be the measure by which we may answer the question of whether or not our theories of motivation can actually motivate students to higher purpose.

Finally, there remains the question of what are the active ingredients shared by all contemporary theories of achievement motivation that might account for the promotion of positive outcomes in the classroom? Whatever the eventual answer, we suspect that a fundamental element for success is not only sharing the rationale of motivation theories per se, but also conducting a candid, open discussion with students regarding the motivational issues that affect them. Also, critical is the willingness of instructors themselves to be candid about their own vulnerability from a self-worth perspective. Instructors are graded, too, and our evidence is that their fears are similar to those of students as well as the kinds of dynamics involved.

In Conclusion

This brings me to the broadest, and possibly most significant of all our conclusions, not only those derived from any particular inquiry, but arguably, from all the work and research that has sustained the development of Self-worth Theory over the years: The likelihood of motivating students to their best efforts while promoting a willingness to remain intellectually engaged for a lifetime, depends closely on the ability of institutions and individual teachers to help students discover and nurture the true purposes of their labors, that is, satisfying their personal goals and long-term aspirations. The struggle to forge personal values and meaning making is the ultimate of all human motivators. It is for this reason that future directions of research should give priority to the further study of the goal-oriented basis of motivation, and in particular to how the sharing of our theories with students can help them to create their own futures.

References

Atkinson, J. W. (1957). Motivational determinants of risk-taking behavior. *Psychological Review, 64*, 359–372.

Beery, R. G. (1975). Fear of failure in the student experience. *Personnel and Guidance Journal, 54*, 190–203.

Birney, R. C., Burdick, H., & Teevan, R. C. (1969). *Fear of failure.* New York: Van Nostrand.

Botkin, M. J. (1990). *Differential teacher treatment and ego functioning: The relationship between perceived competence and defense.* Unpublished doctoral dissertation, University of California at Berkeley.

Burton, D., & Martens, R. (1986). Pinned by their own goals: An exploratory investigation into why kids drop out of wrestling. *Journal of Sport Psychology, 8*, 1983–1997.

Cameron, J., & Pierce, W. D. (1994). Reinforcement, reward, and intrinsic motivation: A meta-analysis. *Review of Education Research, 64*, 363–423.

Cantor, N., & Harlow, R. E. (1994). Personality, strategic behavior, and daily life problem solving. *Current Directions in Psychological Science, 3*, 169–172.

Cantor, N., & Norem, J. K. (1989). Defensive pessimism and stress and coping. *Social Cognition, 7*, 92–112.

Condry, J. D., & Chambers, J. (1978). Intrinsic motivation and the process of learning. In M. R. Lepper & D. Greene (Eds.), *The hidden costs of reward: New perspectives on the psychology of human motivation* (pp. 61–84). Hillsdale, NJ: Erlbaum.

Covington, M. V. (1982, August). *Musical chairs: Who drops out of music instruction and why?* Proceedings of the National Symposium on the Applications of Psychology to the Teaching and Learning of Music: The Ann Arbor Symposium. Session III: Motivation and Creativity. Ann Arbor: University of Michigan.

Covington, M. V. (1985). Text anxiety: Causes and effects over time. In H. M. Vander Ploeg, R. Schwarzer, & C. D. Spielberger (Eds.), *Advances in test anxiety research* (Vol. 4, pp. 55–68). Hillsdale, NJ: Erlbaum.

Covington, M. V. (1986). Instruction in problem-solving planning. In S. L. Friedman, E. K. Scholnick, & R. R. Cocking (Eds.), *Blueprint for thinking: The role of planning in cognitive development* (pp. 469–511). New York: Cambridge University Press.

Covington, M. V. (1992). *Making the grade: A self-worth perspective on motivation and school reform.* New York: Cambridge University Press.

Covington, M. V. (1998). *The will to learn: A guide for motivating young people.* New York: Cambridge University Press.

Covington, M. V. (1999). Caring about learning: The nature and nurturing of subject-matter appreciation. *Educational Psychologist, 34*, 127–136.

Covington, M. V. (2002). Rewards and intrinsic motivation: A needs-based developmental perspective. In T. Urdan & F. Pajares (Eds.), *Motivation of adolescents* (pp. 169–192). New York: Academic Press.

Covington, M. V. (2004). Self-worth theory goes to college: Or do our motivation theories motivate? In D. McInerney & S. Van Etten (Eds.), *Big theories revisited* (pp. 91–114). Greenwich, CT: Information Age.

Covington, M. V., & Beery, R. G. (1976). *Self-worth and school learning.* New York: Holt, Rinehart & Winston.

Covington, M. V., & Dray, E. (2001). The developmental course of achievement motivation: A need-based approach. In A. Wigfield, & P. Eccles (Eds.), *Development of achievement motivation* (pp. 33–56). New York: Academic Press.

Covington, M. V., & Müeller, K. J. (2001). Intrinsic versus extrinsic motivation: An approach/avoidance reformulation. In M. V. Covington, & A. J. Elliot (Eds.), Special issue of *Educational Psychology Review* (pp. 111–130). New York: Plenum Press.

Covington, M. V., & Omelich, C. L. (1978). *Sex differences in self-aggrandizing tendencies.* Unpublished manuscript, Department of Psychology, University of California at Berkeley.

Covington, M. V., & Omelich. C. L. (1979). Effort: The double-edged sword in school achievement. *Journal of Educational Psychology, 71*, 169–182.

Covington, M. V., & Omelich, C. L. (1981). As failures mount: Affective and cognitive consequences of ability demotion in the classroom. *Journal of Educational Psychology, 73*, 796–808.

Covington, M. V., & Omelich, C. L. (1984a). Controversies or consistencies: A reply to Brown and Weiner. *Journal of Educational Psychology, 76*, 159–168.

Covington, M. V., & Omelich, C. L. (1984b). Task-oriented vs. competitive learning structures: Motivational and performance consequences. *Journal of Educational Psychology, 76*, 1038–1050.

Covington, M. V., & Omelich, C. L. (1985). Ability and effort valuation among failure-avoiding and failure-accepting students. *Journal of Educational Psychology, 77*, 446–459.

Covington, M. V., & Omelich, C. L. (1987). "I knew it cold before the exam": A test of the anxiety-blockage hypothesis. *Journal of Educational Psychology, 79*, 393–400.

Covington, M. V., & Omelich, C. L. (1988). Achievement dynamics: The interaction of motives, cognitions and emotions over time. *Anxiety Journal, 1*, 165–183.

Covington, M. V., & Omelich, C. L. (1991). Need achievement revisited: Verification of Atkinson's original 2 x 2 model. In C. D. Spielberger, I. G. Sarason, Z. Kulcsár, & G. L. van Heck (Eds.), *Stress and emotion: Anxiety, anger, and curiosity* (pp. 85–105). Washington, DC: Hemisphere.

Covington, M. V. & Pintrich, P. R. (April, 2001). Symposium: Goals, Motives and School Achievement: Toward an Integration. Presented at Annual Meeting of the American Educational Research Association, Seattle.

Covington, M. V., von Hoene, L. & Voge, N. (n.d.). *Intrinsic motivation in college classrooms.* New York: Cambridge University Press. Manuscript in preparation.

Crandall, V. C., Katkovsky, W., & Crandall, V. J. (1965). Children's beliefs in their own control of reinforcements in intellectual-academic achievement situations. *Child Development, 36*, 91–109.

Crandall, V. J., Preston, A., & Rabson, A. (1960). Maternal reactions and the development of independence and achievement behavior in young children. *Child Development, 31*, 243–251.

Culler, R. E., & Holahan, C. J. (1980). Test anxiety and academic performance: The effects of study-related behaviors. *Journal of Educational Psychology, 72*, 16–20.

Deci, E. L. (1975). *Intrinsic motivation.* New York: Plenum.

Deci, E. L., & Ryan, R. M. (1985). *Intrinsic motivation and self-determination in human behavior.* New York: Plenum.

Deci, E.L., Koestner, R., & Ryan, R. M. (1999). A meta-analytic review of experiments examining the effects of extrinsic rewards on intrinsic motivation. *Psychological Bulletin, 125*, 627–668.

Eisenberger, R., & Cameron, J. (1996). Detrimental effects of reward: Reality or myth? *American Psychologist, 51*, 1153–1166.

Elliot, A. J. (1999). Approach and avoidance motivation and achievement goals. *Educational Psychologist, 34*, 169–189.

Elliot, A. J., & Covington, M. V. (2001). Approach and avoidance motivation. In M. V. Covington, & A. J. Elliot (Eds.), Special issue of *Educational Psychology Review* (pp. 73–92). New York: Plenum.

Elliot, E., & Dweck, C. (1988). Goals: An approach to motivation and achievement. *Journal of Personality and Social Psychology, 54*, 5–12.

Gough, G. H. (1966). Graduation from high school as predicted from the California Psychological Inventory. *Psychology in the Schools, 3*, 208–216.

Gough, G. H. (1968). College attendance among high-aptitude students as predicted from the California Psychological Inventory. *Journal of Counseling Psychology, 15*, 269–278.

Harari, O., & Covington, M. V. (1981). Reactions to achievement behavior from a teacher and student perspective: A developmental analysis. *American Educational Research Journal, 18*, 15–28.

Heider, F. (1958). *The psychology of interpersonal relations.* New York: Wiley.

Helmke, A. (1988). The role of classroom context factors for the achievement-impairing effect of test anxiety. *Anxiety Research, 1*, 37–52.

Jones, E. E., & Nisbett, R. E. (1971). The actor and the observer: Divergent perceptions of the causes of behavior. In E. E. Jones, D. E. Kanouse, H. H. Kelley, R. E. Nisbett, S. Valins, & B. Weiner (Eds.), *Attribution: Perceiving the causes of behavior* (pp. 79–94). Morristown, NJ: General Learning Press.

Kaplan, R. M., & Swant, S. G. (1973). Reward characteristics in appraisal of achievement behavior. *Representative Research in Social Psychology, 4*, 11–17.

Kennedy, W. A., & Willcutt, H. C. (1964). Praise and blame as incentives. *Psychology Bulletin, 62*, 323–332.

Kohn, A. (1993). *Punished by rewards*. New York: Houghton Mifflin.

Locke, E. A., & Latham, G. P. (1984). *Goal setting: A motivational technique that works!* Englewood Cliffs, NJ: Prentice-Hall.

Morris, L. W., & Liebert, R. M. (1973). Effects of negative feedback, threat of shock, and level of trait anxiety on the arousal of two components of anxiety. *Journal of Counseling Psychology, 20*, 321–326.

Naveh-Benjamin, M. (1985). *A comparison of training programs intended for different types of test-anxious students*. Paper presented at symposium on information processing and motivation, American Psychological Association, Los Angeles.

Naveh-Benjamin, M., McKeachie, W. J., & Lin, Y. G. (1987). Two types of test-anxious students: Support for an information processing model. *Journal of Educational Psychology, 79*, 131–136.

Newman, R. S. (1990). Children's help-seeking in the classroom: The role of motivational factors and attitudes. *Journal of Educational Psychology, 82*, 71–80.

Nicholls, J. G. (1976). When a scale measures more than its name denotes: The case of the Test Anxiety Scale for Children. *Journal of Consulting and Clinical Psychology, 44*, 976–985.

Nicholls, J. G. (1978). The development of the conceptions of effort and ability perception of academic attainment, and the understanding that difficult tasks require more ability. *Child Development, 49*, 800–814.

Nicholls, J. G. (1984). Achievement motivation: Concepts of ability, subjective experience, task choice, and performance. *Psychological Review, 91*, 328–346.

Omelich, C. L. (1974). *Attribution and achievement in the classroom: The self-fulfilling prophecy*. Paper presented at the meeting of the California Personnel and Guidance Association, San Francisco.

Snyder, C. R. (1984, September). Excuses, excuses: They sometimes actually work to relieve the burden of blame. *Psychology Today, 18*, 50–55.

Teel, K., Parecki, A., & Covington, M. V. (1998). Teaching strategies that honor and motivate inner-city African-American students: A school/university collaboration. *Teaching and Teacher Education, 14*(5), 479–495.

Thompson, T. (1993). Characteristics of self-worth protection in achievement behavior. *British Journal of Educational Psychology, 63*, 496–488.

Thompson, T. (1994). Self-worth protection: Implications for the classroom. *Educational Review, 46*, 259–74.

Thompson, T. (1996). Self-worth protection in achievement behavior: A review and implications for counseling. *Australian Psychologist, 31*, 41–51.

Thompson, T., Davis, H., & Davidson, JA. (1998). Attributional and affective responses of impostors to academic success and failure feedback. *Personality & Individual Differences, 25*, 381–396.

Tomiki, K. (1997). *Influences of cultural values and perceived family environments on achievement motivation among college students*. Unpublished masters thesis, University of California at Berkeley.

Urdan, T., Ryan, A. M., Anderman, E. M., & Gheen, M. H. (2002). Goals, goal structures, and avoidance behavior. In C. Midgley (Ed.), *Goals, goal structures, and patterns of adaptive learning* (pp. 55–83). Mahwah, NJ: Erlbaum.

Weiner, B. (1972). *Theories of motivation: From mechanism to cognition*. Chicago: Markham.

Weiner, B. (1974). *Achievement motivation and attribution theory*. Morristown, NJ: General Learning Press.

Weiner, B., & Kukla. A. (1970). An attributional analysis of achievement motivation. *Journal of Personality and Social Psychology, 15*(1), 1–20.

Zeidner, M., & Matthews, G. (2005). Evaluation anxiety: Current theory and research. In A. J. Elliot & C. S. Dweck (Eds.), *Handbook of competence and motivation* (pp.141–163). New York: Guilford.

9

Promoting Self-Determined School Engagement
Motivation, Learning, and Well-Being

Richard M. Ryan and Edward L. Deci

Built deeply into human nature is a robust propensity to learn and to actively assimilate knowledge and cultural practices (Rogoff, 2003; Ryan, 1995). We have evolved to be both curious and social, with strong epistemic motives to understand our surroundings and ourselves. Yet, rather than capitalizing on this inherently active and curious nature, educational institutions too often attempt to replace it with strategies of external control, monitoring, evaluation, and artificial rewards to foster learning. As a result learning becomes a chore rather than a joy—an activity to be avoided rather than sought out, at least in the context of schools. At the same time, some individual educators creatively manage to carve out niches within these institutions in which they allow their students' inner tendency to learn to become manifest, and in rare cases (usually outside of the mainstream) whole schools create islands upon which natural desires to grow and learn flourish.

In this chapter, we review theory and research based upon the organismic perspective of self-determination theory (SDT; Deci & Ryan, 2000; Ryan & Deci, 2000). SDT begins with the presumption that human beings are inherently proactive and endowed with a natural tendency to learn and develop as they engage not only their outer environments, but also their inner world of drives, needs, and experiences. The inherent motivation to learn and develop is discussed within SDT in terms of the dual tendencies toward *intrinsic motivation* and *integration*. Most importantly, SDT focuses on the social conditions that either support or thwart these inherent tendencies. Because of this, SDT has strong implications for educational practice and policies, especially in the pressured, outcome-focused context of schools today (Ryan & Brown, 2005).

Some may doubt the assumption that children were "built to learn," but it seems to us simply self-evident. Just watch young children when they are not under pressure, but rather are free to follow their interests. They manipulate and explore their environments, imitate others' actions, invent games and rules, exercise their muscles in rough and tumble ways, and count, arrange, and display collections of prized objects. These kinds of activities provide rich opportunities for learning and development. Children learn from doing, and in so doing they develop evermore elaborate and unified internal representations of themselves and their surrounding world.

Play and active learning are *intrinsically motivated* activities: They are engaged in because they are inherently interesting and enjoyable. Although intrinsically motivated activities result in adaptive learning and competencies, they are not done for those aims (Reeve, Deci, & Ryan, 2004). Instead, intrinsically motivated activities are enjoyable because they satisfy deep psychological needs to feel competence and autonomy. When these needs are satisfied, people experience enjoyment, and it is a side benefit that in enjoying such activities people also learn, grow, and create. So this evolved, inherent tendency to act out of interest provides a remarkable engine for learning, when supported by the right opportunities and social nutriment.

Yet, intrinsic motivation, as represented in play and the pursuit of interests, is not the only manifestation of our species-inherent integrative tendency. Humans also have a readiness to take in or assimilate ambient practices and values from the cultures in which they are embedded. Often these practices are not in themselves enjoyable or interesting, and indeed often they can be arduous or uninteresting, but they are nonetheless motivated. The process of assimilating these nonintrinsically motivated activities and values from one's social environment is described within SDT as *internalization* (Deci & Ryan, 1985; Ryan & Deci, 2000).

Like intrinsic motivation, within SDT the process of internalization is expected to occur spontaneously under the right social conditions. When students of any age are in social contexts where they feel secure, important, and cared for, they *want* to internalize the knowledge and practices of those around them. This of course has always, throughout history, been the "secret" basis for all cultural transmission—offspring adopt, internalize, and inherit the world of the adults who love or care for them (Rogoff, 2003; Ryan & Powelson, 1991). When such supports for *relatedness* are combined with supports for autonomy and competence, then internalization goes beyond mere adoption of new practices, to the child's ownership of them—what we describe as the *integration* of extrinsically motivated activities (Ryan & La Guardia, 1999). But again, too often in schools today we see the natural basis for internalization being supplanted with artificial and controlling devices for promoting compliance that fail to reach far too many learners.

Motivation, Learning, and Schools

As we noted above, although intrinsically motivated learning and internalization are theorized to be life-long processes, these processes can be greatly influenced by social environments. As children grow beyond infancy, they face an increasing number of exogenous structures and controls as they participate in daycare, preschools, elementary school, and secondary school. Schools have always provided structures and controls, although the intensity of the control has increased in recent years with the strong emphasis on educational accountability and high-stakes testing (Ryan & Brown, 2005). These structures and controls influence students' intrinsic motivation and influence, often negatively, the quality of internalization of transmitted values, attitudes, rules, and regulations. SDT has devoted a great deal of attention to the ways in which aspects of the social environments—structures, rewards, controls, supports—that students encounter in schools and homes, affect their intrinsic motivation and internalization, and thus their learning, performance, and well-being. In this chapter we present a discussion of SDT as it relates to those important processes.

Self-Determination Theory

Whereas many theories of motivation such as expectancy-value theories or social cognitive theories (e.g., Bandura, 1996) have treated motivation as a concept that varies in amount but not kind, SDT has placed primary emphasis on the type of motivation rather than the amount. First, SDT differentiates between intrinsic and extrinsic motivation as general classes of motivation, and then it distinguishes various types of extrinsic motivation, which vary in their relative autonomy (Ryan & Deci, 2000). We begin by discussing these differentiations.

Intrinsic and Extrinsic Motivation

Early work within SDT examined whether offering people extrinsic rewards for doing intrinsically motivated activities would affect their level of intrinsic motivation. If the two types of motivation were independent and thus additive, the addition of extrinsic rewards would not have an effect on intrinsic motivation. If, however, the addition of rewards either enhanced or decreased intrinsic motivation it would mean that the two types of motivation are neither independent nor additive but are instead interactive. Deci (1971) found that providing monetary rewards to college students for working on interesting puzzle problems decreased their intrinsic motivation, measured as behavioral persistence, for doing the puzzles. In short, working on an interesting activity in order to earn a reward decreased intrinsic motivation, implying that tangible, monetary rewards were not additive but were instead negatively interactive with intrinsic motivation. Deci also found that providing participants positive feedback about performance led to enhancements in intrinsic motivation relative to no feedback. Dozens of laboratory experiments have replicated both of these initial results, as summarized in narrative (Ryan, Mims, & Koestner, 1983) and meta-analytic (Deci, Koestner, & Ryan, 1999) reviews, and the results have been consistent—namely tangible rewards tend to diminish intrinsic motivation, while positive, performance-relevant feedback tends to either maintain or enhance it.

Needs for Autonomy and Competence To provide a meaningful interpretation of these results, we (Deci & Ryan, 1980, 1985) proposed that people have basic psychological needs for competence and autonomy—an idea that was consistent with previous theorizing by White (1959) and de Charms (1968). When people experience satisfaction of these needs within a situation, they tend to become more intrinsically motivated, whereas when they experience thwarting of the needs they tend to become less intrinsically motivated. For example, Deci and Ryan (1980) suggested that when others use rewards to prompt activities, people lose their experience of autonomy in doing it, perceiving the locus of causality for the behavior to be external (de Charms, 1968). This is also the case when the others use evaluations, social pressure, surveillance, and other motivators so common in schools. In contrast, when people experiences choice about acting and an absence of external pressure, they can maintain an internal perceived locus of causality and maintain intrinsic motivation. Similarly, we theorized that whereas positive feedback helps maintain feelings of competence, and thus supports intrinsic motivation, negative feedback, especially when embedded in a controlling context, thwarts people's sense of competence and undermines their intrinsic motivation.

Additional research has confirmed these interpretations. For example, external events such as threats of punishment, deadlines, imposed goals, competition, and evaluations—all events that might be expected to control behavior rather than encourage self-initiation—were found to undermine intrinsic motivation, presumably by thwarting people's need for autonomy (see Deci & Ryan, 1985, 2000). In addition, pressure toward performance stemming from grade contingencies tends to undermine intrinsic motivation in the learner (e.g., Grolnick & Ryan, 1987). Moreover, considerable research in SDT has shown that settings that foster ego-involvement, or the hinging of self-esteem to performance, not only undermine intrinsic motivation (Ryan, 1982), but also often lead to a withdrawal of effort and persistence (Nicholls, 1984; Ryan, Koestner, & Deci, 1991).

In contrast, research has shown that providing students of all ages with choice typically increases intrinsic motivation (Bao & Lam, 2008; Reeve, Nix, & Hamm, 2003; Zuckerman, Porac, Lathin, Smith, & Deci, 1978). SDT suggests that providing people the opportunity for choice can allow them to satisfy their need for autonomy, resulting in an internal perceived locus of causality and enhanced intrinsic motivation. Of course, not all forms of choice are associated with the experience of autonomy. There can be meaningless choices, and choices that people find irrelevant (e.g., Assor, Kaplan, & Roth, 2002; Schwartz, 2004). But a recent meta-analysis of choice studies strongly supported the SDT-based hypothesis that there is a positive effect of choice on intrinsic motivation (Patall, Cooper, & Robinson, 2008). In addition, recent experimental work showed that actions that are experienced as truly chosen do not drain psychological energy—that is, they are not "ego-depleting" (Moller, Deci, & Ryan, 2006; Ryan & Deci, 2008).

Other studies have examined the relations of external events to the need for competence. For example, early research by Vallerand and Reid (1984) showed both increases in intrinsic motivation following positive feedback and decreases in intrinsic motivation following negative feedback, with these effects being mediated by perceived competence. This important role for competence supports in intrinsic motivation has been widely sustained in the subsequent literature across domains and age groups (see Deci & Moller, 2005).

To summarize, various external events such as rewards, deadlines, and feedback have been found to affect intrinsic motivation, implying that intrinsic and extrinsic motivation tend to be interactive. The research suggests that attempts to control students' performance or efforts, even through positive incentives, can undermine their sense of autonomy and interest, and thus their intrinsic motivation. Further, the suggestion that people have basic needs, which can be understood as essential nutriments for growth, integrity, and well-being, proved very useful in providing an account of the effects of various external events on intrinsic motivation. Intrinsic motivation flourishes under conditions supporting autonomy and competence and wanes when these needs are thwarted. Thus, even though humans are intrinsically motivated to learn, we can now see clearly that social contexts can either support or stifle that natural basis for learning.

Intrinsic Motivation in the Classroom: Motivation and Learning

A large number of studies has investigated the relevance to actual school settings of the experimental literature reviewed above. In one of the first, Deci, Schwartz, Sheinman, and Ryan (1981) examined the intrinsic motivation of students in late elementary-school classrooms. They reasoned that if teachers were oriented toward controlling students' behavior, they would focus on the use of rewards, evaluations, and other controlling events to make their students behave appropriately; whereas, if the teachers were oriented toward supporting students' autonomy and self-regulation, they would refrain from using rewards and controls and would instead offer more choice and supportive feedback. Deci et al. assessed teachers' reports of the degree to which they were oriented toward controlling students' behavior versus supporting their autonomy at the beginning of a school year. Then, in the first week of school, and again 2 months later, the researchers assessed the students' intrinsic motivation, perceived competence, and self-esteem. They found that in classrooms where teachers were more autonomy supportive, students tended to become more intrinsically motivated, to perceive themselves to be more competent, and to feel better about themselves, whereas in classrooms where teachers were more controlling, students tended to lose intrinsic motivation, perceived competence, and self-esteem. Ryan & Grolnick (1986) assessed students' perceptions of autonomy support and control in the classroom and found similar results. Since these early field studies this relation between teacher autonomy support and intrinsic motivation has been widely confirmed, not only in North America (e.g., Pelletier, Séguin-Lévesque, & Legault, 2002; Reeve & Jang, 2006), but also in a variety of other cultures from Scandinavia (e.g., Ommundsen & Kvalø, 2007) to the Mideast (Roth, Assor, Kanat-Maymon, & Kaplan, 2007) to Asia (e.g. Hardre, Chen, Huang, Chiang, Jen, & Warden, 2006). It has also been supported at every level of education from elementary (e.g., Assor, Kaplan, Kanat-Maymon & Roth, 2005) through professional schools (e.g., Williams & Deci, 1996; Sheldon & Krieger, 2007).

This relation between the autonomy support provided by a teacher and students' interest and intrinsic motivation suggests that intrinsic motivation is not just a person variable but also a response to what the social environment affords. As SDT has always argued, in conditions of need support natural tendencies toward interest and growth emerge. A recent study of German seventh graders by Tsai, Kunter, Ludtke, Trautwein, and Ryan (2008) supported this conceptualization. Using a multilevel modeling strategy, these investigators measured students' experience of interest and perceived autonomy support and control during instruction over a 3-week period in multiple subject areas. Perceived teacher autonomy support and control during lessons, as well as individual differences in interest, predicted the students' interest experiences in the classroom, showing that for any given student, an autonomy supportive atmosphere enhanced interest relative to his or her own baseline, whereas controlling teacher behavior undermined it.

Intrinsic Motivation and Learning An important question concerns the relation of intrinsic motivation to learning outcomes, and various studies have examined this issue. For example, Ryan, Connell, and Plant (1990) asked college students to read text material in a nondirected learning situation. They found that students who reported finding the material more interesting and enjoyable subsequently did better on an unexpected test about the material than did those who found the material less interesting. In an experiment by Benware and Deci (1984), college students spent about 3 hours learning material from a neurophysiology text. Half were told that they would be tested on their learning, and the other half were told they would have the opportunity to put their learning to active use by teaching it to other students. The first condition was expected to prompt low intrinsic motivation because students who were told they would be tested would likely feel controlled. In contrast, those told they would be learning to teach others were expected to evidence higher intrinsic motivation because they had an opportunity to experience both autonomy and competence. Results showed that students who learned in order to be tested found the material less intrinsically interesting. Further, those who expected to be tested performed more poorly on the conceptual questions than did those who learned expecting to put the material to active use, although the two groups did not differ on rote-memorization.

Grolnick and Ryan (1987) conducted an experiment in a public school with fifth-grade students who read grade-appropriate passages drawn from textbooks. Some students were told that the experimenter wanted to know their opinions about the written material whereas others were told the experimenter would test them on the material. Those in the former group were expected to be more intrinsically motivated for learning whereas those in the latter group were expected to be more controlled. The results indicated, as expected, that students who read the passages not expecting to be tested found the material more interesting than those expecting to be tested. Further, those who learned not expecting to be tested scored better on questions that assessed conceptual understanding and deep learning than students expecting to be tested.

A study by Kage and Namiki (1990) in Japanese schools also found a link between intrinsic motivation and learning. They found that students who learned in order to take tests that would count toward the semester grade (controlling condition) rather than learned in order to take tests that were used only to provide feedback (autonomy-supportive condition), were both less intrinsically motivated, and ultimately, in final examinations, performed less well.

Indeed, there is a large literature at this point on such effects of controlling versus autonomy-supportive approaches to learning. These four studies and others like them (see Deci & Moller, 2005; Fortier, Vallerand, & Guay, 1995; Ryan & La Guardia, 1999) indicate that students tend to learn better when they are intrinsically motivated, especially on heuristic tasks or those requiring conceptual development and understanding.

Extrinsic Motivation and the Continuum of Internalization

The research showing that tangible rewards and various other extrinsic motivators tend to undermine intrinsic motivation led many authors to proclaim that intrinsic and extrinsic motivation are inherently antagonistic or negatively interactive, thus implying that people cannot be autonomous when they are extrinsically motivated. SDT has maintained, however, that although extrinsic motivators are generally detrimental to autonomy and intrinsic motivation when used to control behavior, it is possible for extrinsically motivated behaviors to be autonomous. Internalization is the process that leads to this phenomenon (Ryan, Connell, & Deci, 1985).

SDT specifies four types of extrinsic motivation that vary in the degree to which they have been fully internalized and thus in the degree to which they underlie autonomous regulation. The least autonomous is *externally regulated*; for example doing something to get a reward or avoid a punishment. Such behaviors are initiated and regulated by external contingencies and are experienced as relatively controlled. The next type of extrinsic motivation is referred to as *introjected regulation*. This concerns extrinsic motivation or regulation that has been partially internalized—behavior is regulated by anxiety and the avoidance of shame or guilt for failing, and by rewards of pride and ego-inflation for success. Introjected regulation often takes the form of *ego-involvement* (Nicholls, 1984; Ryan, 1982) in which self-esteem is contingent on outcomes, resulting in a pressured, internally-controlling state of mind. Thus, people will be controlling or pressuring themselves to behave or achieve by using internal contingencies that function in much the same way that external controls operate when behaviors are externally regulated. As such, introjected regulation, like external regulation, is relatively controlled.

The next type of extrinsic motivation is *identified regulation*. When people have succeeded in identifying with the value of the target behavior they will have more fully accepted it as their own. Identification is a relatively autonomous form of regulation, because people feel volition and self-endorsement when acting in accord with identified behaviors or values. Finally, the most autonomous form of extrinsic motivation is *integrated regulation* in which people will not only have identified with the value and regulation of the behavior but will also have brought it into coherence with other aspects of their core sense of self. Integrated extrinsic motivation shares many qualities with intrinsic motivation, for people experience both as freely chosen, volitional, and

Amotivation	Extrinsic Motivation				Intrinsic Motivation
Nonregulation	External Regulation	Introjected Regulation	Identified Regulation	Integrated Regulation	Intrinsic Regulation
Lack of Motivation	Controlled Motivation		Autonomous Motivation		
Lowest Relative Autonomy	←————————————————————————————→				*Highest Relative Autonomy*

Figure 9.1 The SDT continuum of relative autonomy, showing types of motivation, types of regulation, and the degree of relative autonomy for each type of motivation. Movement from left to right within any row represents an increase in relative autonomy or self-determination.

engaging. Yet, these motivations do differ in that the basis of intrinsic motivation is *interest*—that is, people do these behaviors because they are engaging and fascinating—whereas with integrated extrinsic motivation people do the behaviors because they are *valued*, or viewed as personally important and relevant to attaining self-selected goals.

Figure 9.1 shows these four types of extrinsic motivation, along with intrinsic motivation and amotivation, the latter of which refers to a lack of intentionality and motivation. These six concepts are arranged along a continuum of relative autonomy reflecting the degree to which they represent autonomous regulation of behavior. Amotivation is totally lacking in autonomy, intrinsic motivation is invariantly autonomous, and the four types of extrinsic motivation are ordered between amotivation and intrinsic motivation.

Measuring the SDT Motivation Categories There are many ways of operationally defining and assessing these different types of extrinsic motivation. For example, Ryan et al. (1991) experimentally induced introjected motivation for a learning task by linking performance outcomes to self-esteem, and intrinsic motivation by creating a context conducive to interest and task involvement. Recently Katz, Assor, & Kanat-Maymon (2008) designed a projective tool in which children tell stories that are coded for SDT's categories of motivation. The most widely used approach to measuring these varied forms of motivation is through questionnaires that simply ask students why they engage in classroom activities, complete homework, or do other academic tasks.

The first of these instruments was developed by Ryan and Connell (1989) and since then various adaptations have emerged (e.g., Hayamizu, 1997; Vallerand et al., 1992). As reviewed by Vallerand (1997), investigators in multiple domains have shown that these self-reports of motivation form a simplex-like pattern, meaning that subscales conceptually closer to each other along the continuum are more highly correlated than those farther away. This supports SDT's characterizations of these extrinsic motivations as systematically varying along a gradation of autonomy. Similarly, Roth, Kanat-Maymon, Assor, and Kaplan (2006) applied Smallest Space Analysis (SSA) to model students' reasons for doing schoolwork, and found evidence for this underlying continuum of motives. Research also confirms that each type of motivation has a distinct character and predicts different outcomes. For example, Burton, Lydon, D'Alessandro, and Koestner (2006) showed that whereas intrinsic motivation in school predicted well-being, identified motivation was more reliably related to performance outcomes. Ryan and Connell (1989) showed that introjected motivation, unlike external motivation, was associated with effort, but also was characterized by anxiety. Thus, a value of the simplex model is in organizing the relations of motives along a continuum of autonomy, while still having a differentiated view of the types of motives students manifest and the distinct dynamics that foster them.

Need Satisfaction and Internalization According to SDT, basic psychological need satisfaction plays a critical role in promoting the internalization of extrinsic motivation, just as it does in maintaining intrinsic motivation. Yet, whereas the needs for autonomy and competence are the most critical needs in maintaining and enhancing intrinsic motivation, the need for relatedness is a very important supplement to autonomy and competence in explaining the internalization of extrinsic motivation. Specifically, an individual takes in behavioral regulations modeled or transmitted by those to whom he or she feels or would like to feel attached and connected. Of course, the individual must also feel some competence and autonomy in relation to the behaviors in order to fully internalize their regulation.

Various experiments have examined the conditions that promote a relatively full internalization. For example, Deci, Eghrari, Patrick, and Leone (1994) manipulated the amount of support for internalization provided to college students who were working on an uninteresting, extrinsically motivated task. The researchers found that the amount of autonomy support—operationalized as providing a meaningful rationale, acknowledging the participants' perspective, and providing choice—predicted the amount of internalization as reflected in the participants choosing to engage in the behavior when they had a subsequent opportunity to do so. Further, the results showed that some, though less, internalization occurred when there was relatively little autonomy support—when there was no rationale, acknowledgment, or choice—but the internalization that occurred under these conditions was merely introjected. Thus, autonomy support not only led to more internalization, it ensured that the internalization was integrated rather than just introjected. In other research, Reeve, Jang, Hardre, and Omura (2002) conducted two experiments in which college students who would be studying conversational Chinese either were or were not given an autonomy-supportive rationale for engaging in the learning activity. The researchers found that the autonomy-supportive rationale led students to more fully internalize the regulation of and put more effort into this learning.

Numerous field studies in schools and homes have also examined factors that influence the internalization of school-related motivation. The primary hypothesis that has guided this work is that supports for autonomy, competence, and relatedness from both teachers and parents facilitate internalization of motivation and, in turn, students' engagement, achievement, and adjustment. For example, Black and Deci (2000) followed college students participating in organic chemistry labs. They had students rate the degree to which their lab instructors were autonomy supportive. Results showed that students who found their instructors to be more autonomy supportive evidenced increased autonomous regulation for course learning over the semester. As well, they showed increases in perceived competence and decreases in anxiety. Finally, students who displayed increases in autonomous motivation for course learning received higher grades, controlling for their prior GPAs and standardized test scores. In short, when students had autonomy supportive instructors, they internalized the importance of the course more fully and, in turn, performed better.

Studies in medical schools have found comparable results. One found that the autonomy supportiveness of instructors in a medical interviewing course predicted students' internalization of the values inherent in the interviewing and also predicted students being judged more effective at patient interviewing 6 months after the course ended (Williams & Deci, 1996). Another study (Williams, Saizow, Ross, & Deci, 1997) showed that the autonomy support provided by preceptors in medical student rotations predicted the specialties students selected for their residencies—for example, if the surgery preceptor had been highly autonomy supportive, students were more likely to select a surgery residency than if the preceptor had been controlling.

A study with American and German college students (Levesque, Zuehlke, Stanek, & Ryan, 2004) explored students' experiences of the degree to which their learning context was externally pressuring, as opposed to autonomy supportive, and found, as expected, that external pressure negatively predicted both autonomous motivation and perceived competence and that these latter variables, in turn, positively predicted well-being in both countries.

Various studies of elementary and high school students (e.g., Hardre & Reeve, 2003; Jang, Reeve, & Deci, 2007; Skinner & Belmont, 1993) have shown that teachers' autonomy support is related to students' autonomous motivation and engagement. Similarly, in the realm of physical education, studies by Hagger and colleagues (Hagger, Chatzisarantis, Barkoukis, Wang, & Baranowski, 2005; Hagger, Chatzisarantis, Culverhouse, & Biddle, 2003) have revealed that autonomy supportive teaching is related to students' having more autonomous motivation for physical activity and to increases in activity outside of school, bespeaking internalization. Standage, Duda, and Ntoumanis (2006) extended this by showing that this relation was mediated by the students' experience of basic psychological need satisfaction.

Parent effects on internalization are similarly in evidence. Grolnick and Ryan (1989) studied parental autonomy support for late-elementary school children using in-home interviews. Each parent was interviewed separately, with the focus being on how the parents dealt with their child's school grades, homework, and chores around the house. Children and teachers were independently surveyed at school. Results indicated that when parents were rated by interviewers as more autonomy supportive, their children reported more well-internalized regulation for schoolwork and more perceived competence, and their teachers rated them as having greater self-motivation, competence, and classroom adjustment. Children of more autonomy-supportive parents also achieved better outcomes in terms of school grades. In a subsequent study, Grolnick, Ryan, and Deci (1991) found that students who perceived their parents to be more autonomy supportive evidenced greater internalization and felt more competent than did those who saw their parents as more controlling. In turn, the students who were more autonomous and felt more competent received higher year-end grades and they performed better on standardized tests.

Other studies of students' perceptions of their parents have indicated that parental involvement—that is, parents devoting time, attention, and resources to their children's learning-related activities—contributed to the children's school achievement and psychological adjustment, but largely only when it was accompanied by autonomy-support (e.g., Grolnick & Slowiaczek, 1994; Ratelle, Larose, Guay, & Senecal, 2005; Soenens & Vansteenkiste, 2005).

High school students participated in a series of studies reported by Niemiec, Lynch, Vansteenkiste, Bernstein, Deci, and Ryan (2006). Results showed that when students perceived their parents as more autonomy supportive, the students were more autonomously motivated for pursuing their learning—that is, they had more fully internalized the regulation of learning activities—which, in turn, was associated with greater psychological well-being.

A common way that parents motivate their children to learn is by conveying *conditional regard* in relation to their schoolwork This approach involves parents providing more attention and affection when their children do well at their academics (*positive conditional regard*) and providing less attention and affection when the children do poorly (*negative conditional regard*). In an initial study, Assor, Roth, and Deci (2004) found conditional regard to have negative psychological consequences. Subsequently Roth, Assor, Niemiec, Ryan, and Deci (2008) reported that even positive conditional regard has dangers. In their study, positive conditional regard promoted introjected regulation of schoolwork, which, in turn, predicted grade-focused school engagement. In contrast, children subjected to a high degree of autonomy support reported greater choice and autonomy, which, in turn, predicted interest-focused school engagement. In short, then, even the use of positive conditional regard as a socializing strategy impairs the internalization process compared to the use of autonomy support, which promotes fuller internalization and a more authentic engagement with school.

Chirkov and Ryan (2001) reported a study of Russian and U.S. high school students who rated the degree of autonomy support provided by their parents and teachers. As expected based on ethnographic studies, Russian teenagers saw both their parents and teachers as more controlling than did their American counterparts. Yet, the study also revealed that in each culture, the autonomy support of parents and teachers both promoted greater internalization and psychological health. In Canada, Legault, Green-Demers, and Pelletier (2006) assessed the perception of support for the three basic psychological needs that high school students experienced from teachers, parents, and friends. The researchers found that lack of support for the three needs contributed to amotivation, which, in turn, contributed to poor school performance, low academic self-esteem, problem behaviors, and intentions to dropout of school.

School Dropout Vallerand, Fortier, and Guay (1997) studied specific contextual and motivational predictors of high school dropout. Specifically, in October of a school year the researchers assessed the degree to which more than 4,000 students perceived their teachers and parents as autonomy supportive and also the degree to which these students were themselves autonomous in doing their schoolwork. A year later, the researchers obtained a list of all students from their sample who were still enrolled in a high school. The study indicated that students who perceived their parents and teachers as more autonomy supportive also perceived themselves to be more competent at academic work and were more autonomous in doing it. In turn, these students were also more likely to still be in school a year later than were those who were lower in autonomy support and autonomy.

In related work, Guay and Vallerand (1997) found that autonomy support from parents and teachers was positively related to students' perceived competence and autonomous motivation, which predicted year-end grades months later. Hardre and Reeve (2003) confirmed a model of rural high school students' intentions to persist at (vs. dropout of) school in which perceptions of teacher autonomy support predicted perceived autonomy and competence, and, in turn, both school performance and the intention to stay in school. Finally, Vallerand and Bissonnette (1992) found similar results with junior-college students. It is clear from such studies that autonomous motivation and perceived competence are important for preventing school dropout and that satisfaction of the basic needs in school facilitates persistence and performance.

As discussed by Ryan and LaGuardia (1999), the evidence that controlling environments contribute to academic failure and dropout is noteworthy, because a frequent response of adults to student failure is to add more controls and additional pressures rather than more autonomy support. This too often deepens the cycle of alienation for these at-risk students, increasing the probability that they will withdraw effort and decrease their engagement in school.

To summarize, research in educational settings ranging from elementary schools to medical schools have shown that autonomy supportive contexts at home and in school relate to students' autonomous motivation and perceived competence for doing schoolwork, which then predicts greater engagement, conceptual learning, and psychological well-being and adjustment.

Autonomy in Special Populations: Gifted and Delayed

A few studies have applied SDT to students who are considered gifted, learning disabled, or emotionally handicapped. In one study, Grolnick and Ryan (1990) assessed the perceived competence and autonomy of elementary school students who either did or did not have learning disabilities. Results indicated that those who had learning disabilities were lower on both autonomous motivation and perceived competence than the nondisabled students. Yet, when the students with learning disabilities were compared to the low achieving students from the nonlabeled group, there were no differences in motivation or perceived competence. This study suggests that perhaps too often poor skills or performance are assumed to be due to low motivation, leading teachers to exert more control, rather than more autonomy support.

Deci, Hodges, Pierson, and Tomassone (1992) examined over 450 students aged 8 to 21 who attended self-contained special-education schools and whose primary disability codes were either learning disability (LD) or emotional handicap (EH). The researchers assessed students' perceptions of the autonomy support of their teachers and mothers, as well as their perceived competence, autonomous motivation, self-esteem, and style of coping with failure. Results indicated that both autonomy support and autonomous motivation predicted perceived competence, self-esteem, and more positive styles of coping with failure. Further, the autonomy variables tended to be stronger predictors of well-being (i.e., self-esteem and positive coping) for the students with EH, whereas the competence variables tended to be stronger predictors of well-being for the students with LD. In other words, it appears that EH is a disability that tends to have autonomy deficiencies as a primary element whereas LD is a disability that tends to have competence deficiencies as a more central element. Further, the results showed that mother variables tended to be stronger than teacher variables in predicting motivation and well-being of elementary school students, whereas teacher variables tended to be stronger than mother variables in predicting motivation and well-being of junior and senior high school students.

Other studies have examined motivation, achievement, and well-being variables of students considered gifted. For example, Vallerand, Gagné, Senécal, and Pelletier (1994) gathered data from late-elementary school students and found that gifted students perceived themselves to be more competent and were also more intrinsically motivated for school activities than regular classroom students, indicating that perceived competence, autonomous motivation, and a high level of achievement are all interrelated concepts for students. Miserandino (1996) studied students with high academic ability and found that those within this group who were higher in perceived competence and autonomous motivation were more engaged and positive in school than were those lower on these motivation variables. Further, both perceived competence and autonomous motivation predicted school grades even after controlling for prior standardized achievement scores.

In sum, both the social-contextual and personal motivation variables central to SDT have been found to predict engagement, performance, and well-being among special population students who tend to be either quite low or quite high in their abilities, as well as students diagnosed with emotional problems. This is especially noteworthy insofar as many interventions targeting those with special needs tend to take the form of increased monitoring and control rather than autonomy support.

Goals, Aspirations, and Need Satisfaction

The concept of *needs* within psychology has had two quite different definitions. One concerns individual differences in the strength of needs, particularly the need for achievement (Atkinson, 1964; McClelland, 1985; Murray, 1938). From this perspective, needs are learned as the outcome of a developmental process that is influenced by parental practices, and the strength of the needs is then used to predict outcomes. An alternative approach to needs defines them as *universal necessities* for healthy development and psychological well-being. From this view, the important focus is not on individual differences but is instead on the degree to which the basic needs, which are essential for all people, are being been satisfied versus thwarted in particular situations or over time (Deci & Ryan, 2000). SDT uses the latter definition of needs.

Within SDT this approach to needs has led to questions about whether all goals or aspirations people pursue are equally likely to satisfy needs and thus be "good for" the person (Ryan, Sheldon, Kasser, & Deci, 1996). Specifically, research by Kasser and Ryan (1993, 1996) has shown that people's life goals tend to fall into two factor-analytically described categories—namely *extrinsic goals* (such as wealth, fame, and image) and *intrinsic goals* (such as personal growth, affiliation, and community). According to SDT, the type of goals people hold as most important is influenced by the satisfaction versus thwarting of the basic psychological needs. Research has shown that the development of strong extrinsic goals tends to result from the thwarting of basic needs for autonomy and relatedness, whereas the development of strong intrinsic goals tends to result from the satisfaction all three of these needs (Kasser, Ryan, Zax, & Sameroff, 1995; Williams, Cox, Hedberg, & Deci, 2000). Further, using a broad range of indicators, studies have linked strong extrinsic aspirations to poorer psychological well-being and strong intrinsic aspirations to greater psychological well-being (see Kasser, 2002).

More recent research has specifically applied this conceptualization of goals within the realm of education and achievement. In doing so, it changed the basic approach from assessing extrinsic and intrinsic goals as individual differences to manipulating them in an experimental format. For example, in studies by Vansteenkiste, Simons, Lens, Sheldon, and Deci (2004) high school and junior college students were told that doing an activity would help them achieve a particular goal. Half were given an extrinsic goal (saving money by recycling, making money by learning about communication, or becoming attractive by learning a physical activity) and the other half were given an intrinsic goal (saving the environment by recycling, developing as a person by learning about communication, or becoming more healthy by learning the physical activity). Using a factorial design, these intrinsic-versus-extrinsic goal-framing conditions were crossed with presenting the goals using an autonomy-supportive versus controlling communication style in three experiments that examined the hypotheses that intrinsic goal framing and an autonomy supportive context would both enhance learning and performance and that the goal-framing effect would be even stronger in the autonomy-supportive condition. Results confirmed the hypotheses by showing that students given an intrinsic goal had learned the material more deeply, taken additional opportunities to learn more about the topics, and performed better when tested, compared with students given extrinsic goal framing. Further, students given the intrinsic goal induction in an autonomy-supportive way showed greater learning and performance than would be expected from two main effects, thus confirming the synergistic effects of intrinsic goal framing and autonomy support. Additional studies by Vansteenkiste, Simons, Lens, Soenens, and Matos (2005) expanded on these results.

Important additional research with elementary school students done by Vansteenkiste, Lens, Soenens, and Van den Broeck (in press) examined the so-called *match hypothesis*—namely, the idea that students who, as individuals, were more extrinsically oriented would benefit from extrinsic goal framing, implying that the effects isolated in the three Vansteenkiste et al. (2004) studies were relevant primarily to students with intrinsic orientations. This newer research confirmed, in fact, that the positive intrinsic goal-framing effects applied to all students whether their goal orientations were intrinsic or extrinsic, thus failing to find support for the match hypothesis. Such findings suggest that stressing the extrinsic benefits of school does not enhance motivation even for those prone to such goals and values. Just as being more controlling with externally regulated students has been found to only further undermine their self-motivation, it appears that adding salience to extrinsic goals in the teaching of extrinsically oriented students only further takes them away from being personally engaged in learning.

These studies of intrinsic versus extrinsic goals, whether conducted with individual differences in the importance people place on the goals or with intrinsic versus extrinsic goal framing, indicate that being oriented toward more intrinsic goals is associated with more positive learning, performance, and well-being outcomes. This is provocative in an age when a primary message from educators is that learning is primarily instrumental to achieving extrinsic outcomes such as high test scores, high income, or future prestige. Instead, it seems, educators would do better to frame the goals of learning in terms of personal growth or social meaning.

Autonomy-Supportive Teaching: More on What It Is

It is a pleasure to visit some classrooms. Teachers and students interact freely and respectfully, students spend time focused on their own work in an interested way; students take initiative, and teachers respond to students' initiations. In short, the classroom climate feels accepting, supportive, and encouraging, and students respond positively. Many things affect the climate of classrooms, but among the most important is the teachers' style of engaging with the students. Within SDT we have examined teachers' styles in terms of the degree to which they are autonomy-supportive versus controlling, an analysis that can be meaningfully applied no matter what the grade level or subject matter of classrooms.

Theoretically, autonomy-supportive teachers begin by understanding and relating to their students from the students' perspectives. The teachers provide relevant information while providing plenty of opportunity for students to find information for themselves; they provide choices and options where possible and give students opportunities to take initiative in directing aspects of their own learning; and they encourage students to take greater responsibility for their own education (see, e.g., Ryan & La Guardia, 1999; Williams & Deci, 1998). When they set limits, they do so in ways that acknowledge the students' perspective and provide alternatives and choices, while still maintaining standards (Koestner, Ryan, Bernieri, & Holt, 1984). In contrast, controlling teachers pressure students to think, feel, or behave in particular ways while relating to the students from their own (the teachers') perspectives rather than from the students' perspectives. They use evaluations to motivate, rather than facilitating volition and internal motivation. When they set limits, they do so through external controls, with less attention to how the students being disciplined understand the situation.

Reeve and colleagues have taken an empirical approach to examining what autonomy-supportive teachers do and say. In the first studies (Reeve, Bolt, & Cai, 1999), the investigators had teachers complete the Problems in Schools Questionnaire (Deci et al., 1981) to assess teachers' self-reports of autonomy support versus control. Then, the teachers taught a brief session that was videotaped, and researchers coded and rated these teaching sessions. Finally, the teachers were separated into an autonomy-support group and a controlling group (based on the questionnaire responses) and the behaviors of the two groups were compared. Teachers who had been classified as more autonomy supportive were found to listen more, made fewer directives, responded more to students' questions, attended more to the students' wants, resisted giving problem solutions to the students, made more statements that implied perspective taking, and were generally more supportive of the students' initiatives.

In a subsequent study, Reeve and Jang (2006) identified specific teacher behaviors that were autonomy supportive and others that were controlling. They then related these various behaviors, observed during teaching sessions, to the autonomous motivation of the students they were teaching. Results indicated that eight teacher behaviors that had previously been categorized as autonomy supportive—namely, listening, creating time for students' independent work, giving students an opportunity to talk, acknowledging signs of improvement and mastery, encouraging students' effort, offering progress-enabling hints when students seemed stuck, being responsive to students' comments and questions, and acknowledging students' experiences and perspectives— were correlated with students' autonomous motivation, thus validating that the behaviors are indeed autonomy supportive. Further, six behaviors that had previously been categorized as controlling—namely, monopolizing the learning materials, providing solutions to problems before the students had time to work independently, telling students answers without giving them an opportunity to formulate answers, making directives, using controlling words such as "should" and "have to," and using directed questions as a way of controlling the flow of conversation—were negatively correlated with students' autonomy, thus confirming that these behaviors do have the functional significance of being controlling for students. A study of Israeli elementary students also showed that these types of specific controlling behaviors from teachers were associated with less student autonomy (Assor, Kaplan, Kanat-Maymon, & Roth, 2005).

High-Stakes Tests: Undermining Student and Teacher Autonomy

Our investigations into motivation for learning have led us to the conclusion that excellent educational systems must be organized in ways that promote as much autonomous motivation as possible, both in teachers and in students, because the research has continually indicated that both learning outcomes and healthy adjustment are facilitated by autonomous motivation. Yet, a current systemic threat to teachers' freedom to support the learners need satisfaction is represented by the *high-stakes testing* (HST) movement that has become ubiquitous in many countries (see Ryan & Sapp, 2005).

Although as we will discuss below, testing can be useful for gathering intervention-relevant information, self-determination theory has long suggested that HST—testing in which rewards and sanctions for schools, teachers, and/or individual students are made contingent upon test outcomes—would have deleterious effects on classroom practice, student motivation, and ultimately learning outcomes (Ryan & La Guardia, 1999; Ryan & Stiller, 1991). Specifically, it has been argued that applying rewards and sanctions to outcomes is an inherently controlling intervention. It is thus likely to decrease teacher's experience of autonomy and their satisfaction. Moreover, in accord with the principles of SDT, controlling motivation leads actors to focus on getting to rewards (or avoiding sanctions) in the most direct way possible. We thus predicted that HST policies would foster teaching to the test, the narrowing of curricula, more drill and redundancy, less hands-on practice, lower intrinsic motivation, more cheating at the level of teachers, poor transfer of gains on "rewarded" test outcomes to any other indicator of learning, and increased dropout of at-risk students. Sadly, as the actual data have come in from this large social experiment, these predictions appear to have been borne out in districts where HST are salient (see below, as well as a more comprehensive review by Ryan & Brown, 2005).

It was during an earlier era of HST policies that Deci, Speigel, Ryan, Koestner, and Kauffman (1982) tested this reasoning by examining the effects of controlling pressures on the behavior of individuals who were teaching problem-solving skills to students. Half of the participants were told that it was their responsibility to ensure that their students performed up to standards. Nothing was said about performance standards to the other half of those doing the teaching. Each of the teaching sessions was recorded and the teaching behaviors analyzed for indicators of autonomy support versus control. Results showed that teachers for whom standards were highlighted talked approximately five times as much as the other teachers and, further, that what they said was much more controlling—that is, involved many more directives and words such as "should" and "have to." Results further indicated that students of the teachers for whom standards had been emphasized completed more problems, but independently solved far fewer.

Working in elementary schools, Flink, Boggiano, and Barrett (1990) similarly showed that when late-elementary teachers were pressured toward high standards they became more controlling and directive with students. Specifically, in a prospective study, they contrasted teachers under pressure to enhance objective-test outcomes with teachers using the same curriculum who did not receive explicit pressure to raise scores. Those under pressure were found to exhibit more controlling behaviors. Paradoxically, those teachers who under pressure applied controlling techniques yielded lower objective test outcomes than those who were more autonomy supportive. Yet, interestingly, although the teachers who were pressured were more controlling with students, they were judged by naive observers to be better teachers. They appeared to these outside raters to be more active and involved.

Pelletier et al. (2002) took a different approach to studying this issue. They suggested that teachers experience pressure from above (e.g., from accountability standards) and from below (e.g., from students who are nonattentive and nonengaged). Surveys of teachers revealed that both pressure from above and pressure from below were negatively associated with teachers' autonomous motivation for teaching and that these pressures, in turn, predicted the teachers' degree of autonomy support in dealing with their students. These results, then, complement the work by Deci et al. (1982) and Flink et al. (1990).

We saw, first, that a strong emphasis on accountability results in greater control and a central focus on getting the rewarded outcomes rather than the activity per se (e.g., Deci et al., 1982). In the case of HST programs, school administrators are likely to experience the tests as pressuring, which will lead them to be more controlling with teachers. That, in turn, will lead teachers to be more controlling with students, which tends to undermine rather than enhance students' autonomous motivation and learning. Data from McNeil and Valenzuela (2000) confirm that the pressure on teachers has indeed narrowed what is taught and led to elimination of the kinds of investigatory, hands-on creative work through which students can become really engaged in school. Moreover, students in the lower end of the achievement range may be especially affected. Based on analyses from 15 states, Jacob (2001) suggested that HST greatly increased the likelihood of poorer students dropping out. Reardon and Galindo (2002) reported similar results. Moreover, even when the test-prep focus increases test scores, these gains do not seem to be reflected in broader assessments of learning or achievement as documented by Armein and Berliner (2002), McNeil & Valenzuela (2000), and others. That is, whereas test-focused teaching improves scores on local tests, such gains are not reflected in nontargeted tests like the NEAP.

Additionally, high-stakes tests either directly or indirectly have rewards or the avoidance of punishments associated with them and a plethora of studies have confirmed that working to earn rewards or avoid punishments has negative effects on autonomous motivation, learning, and psychological well-being. Further, people who work for rewards but fail to receive those sought after outcomes tend to evidence even greater decrements than those who get the rewards they work for. In the case of high-stakes tests, there is a reasonable percentage of districts, schools, and classrooms that fail to live up to standards and experience the negative consequences associated with the negative performance feedback.

There is a further consideration that is important regarding high-stakes tests. Shapira (1976) found that when extrinsic rewards were introduced into a situation, people became focused on the rewards and thus, not only was their autonomous motivation undermined, but also they tended to choose a short path to the desired reward. This can result in diminished quality of performance and even cheating. Lonky and Reihman (1989) found, for example, that students who were in a controlling context, which is surely created by high-stakes tests, were more likely to cheat on a verbal reasoning task. Thus, it is unsurprising that Hoff (2000) and others have documented many incidents of such cheating at all level of educational systems on the mandated achievement tests, as would be expected based on the SDT-related research.

Tests, of course, can serve a very useful *informational function*, helping students, administrators, or policy makers know where they need to devote more effort. Further, there are many instances in life where tests play a role in the gate-keeping function associated with such things as licensing and certification of professionals. Yet, when high stakes (i.e., salient rewards and sanctions) are added to tests as a *motivational* strategy, as has been done by recent federal and state legislation, the tests take on a strongly *controlling function*, and, as would be expected from SDT research, lead to a wide range of negative consequences (Ryan & Brown, 2005).

Making Schools a Place for Teaching and Learning

Gradually, in the wake of the testing movement, more and more people are recognizing that approaches to reforming schools that are built around high-stakes tests alone are failing (Hursh, 2008; Ryan & Sapp, 2005). Their core dynamic is control and their function turns out to be basic need thwarting of the teachers and students. What then is an alternative for improving all schools, but especially the more dysfunctional ones? We briefly mention two different reform efforts built on SDT principles that have begun by recognizing that the most effective reform will be organized in ways that will promote basic need satisfaction for teachers and students.

A Bottom-Up Approach One reform approach was introduced into three Israeli elementary schools that were concerned about reducing violence and increasing positive interactions among culturally and economically diverse urban students (Feinberg, Kaplan, Assor, & Kanat-Maymon, 2007). It began with didactic meetings for the school administrators and teachers focused on the principles of SDT. Then, an assessment was done of the degree of need satisfaction among teachers and students in the schools as a basis for planning changes. The plan was unique to each school and resulted from problem solving meetings of teachers and administrators with the change agents. The final step involved supporting the staff's basic needs during implementation. This represents a very bottom-up approach, with the school staff members formulating their own plan, based on their understanding of SDT. As such, it involves a high degree of staff ownership from the start, and the staff can continue to make changes as problems arise.

Research conducted in the intervention and comparison schools over a 3-year period showed significant differences. Teachers in the intervention schools reported feeling more empathic toward their students and feeling better about themselves as teachers. They also displayed increased limit setting on violence. Further, there was reduced violence among the students, and increases in students' perceptions of the friendliness and caring in the schools.

A Top-Down Approach First Things First (FTF) is a model of comprehensive school reform that has been used primarily in American inner-city school districts, although it has also been used in some rural districts. It was intended as a district-wide reform and in Kansas City, Kansas, it was implemented in the elementary, middle, and high schools. In other districts it has been implemented in subsets of schools, predominately in secondary schools or just high schools.

The reform is quite structured and has three critical features that are intended to facilitate greater need satisfaction among teachers and students (Connell & Klem, 2000). First, it involves dividing the large schools into small learning communities (SLCs) of about 20 teachers and 350 students who stay in the same SLC over time. The SLCs function relatively independently even though there are typically several in the same building. Second, there is a student and family advocate system within SLCs in which one teacher and 15 to 18 students meet weekly and stay together throughout their years in the school. The teacher is not only the advocate for these students but is also the liaison to the students' families. Third, there is a major focus on instructional improvement, with considerable professional development and many activities designed to help improve teaching. The aim of the improved teaching is to make the instruction, materials, and assignments more engaging and optimally challenging. Through these and other structures and activities, teachers and students are able to develop meaningful relationships even within the context of large urban schools with a few thousand students, and both students and teachers are able to develop greater competencies and feel greater autonomy and ownership of their own teaching and learning.

Two quasi-experiments examining the efficacy of FTF in intervention schools relative to comparable nonintervention control-group schools (Gambone, Klem, Summers, Akey, & Sipe, 2004; Quint, Bloom, Black, Stephens, & Akey, 2005) indicated that FTF impacted key policy-relevant student processes (e.g., perceived autonomy support from teachers, student engagement) and educational outcomes (e.g., increased attendance, improved graduation rates, and higher state-tested proficiency scores in reading and math). For example, in the first 5 years that FTF was implemented in all Kansas City, Kansas, schools, graduation rates increased from 49% to 82%, according to the independent evaluators who reported these outcomes.

Obviously, school reform initiatives based on SDT are only in their infancy. Moreover, to date this area of research lacks the kinds of large-scale controlled clinical trial studies that would be most compelling. However, as the failure of high-stakes testing strategies to improve schools becomes more salient, investigating reforms based on more empirically supported motivational perspectives will, one would hope, become more of a priority.

The Universality Question: SDT Across Development and Cultures

Among the biggest controversies surrounding SDT is concern about its generalizability across periods of development and across cultures. Questions center particularly on the centrality of autonomy, competence, and relatedness needs over time and context, and particularly the universality of autonomy as a need.

Basic Needs in Intellectual and Social Development

It is generally foreign to developmentalists to posit strong continuity across time, as so much of the terrain of development is ever changing and new. Yet, SDT posits that certain fundamental processes associated with needs for competence, autonomy, and relatedness needs are invariant across the lifespan. This is to say, whether we are looking at the exploratory learning of the infant, the classroom learning of youth, or the education of an older adult, we will find that elements of the environment that function to satisfy or support these three needs will have predictably positive effects on the individuals' motivation to actively learn and (especially in complex, heuristic tasks) on learning and performance outcomes.

Although supports for autonomy, competence, and relatedness all have a functional impact on motivation across ages, both developmental and age-related social-contextual changes impact the psychological dynamics of need satisfaction, and the specific ways in which parents and teachers support versus thwart the children's needs. Clearly, the kinds of activities and the forms of feedback that promote competence satisfactions and optimal motivation differ with age, in concert with the changing intellectual interests and capacities of the learner. Similarly, the verbal and nonverbal behaviors through which adults foster a sense of relatedness differ with the age and social roles of youth. Finally, dynamics concerning autonomy also change with development. For example, the unilateral versus reciprocal nature of autonomy support changes as children mature, as does the areas for which children are held responsible for self-regulating.

A critical distinction within SDT is between independence and autonomy (Ryan, 1993), a distinction that is often confused in some developmental perspectives. Within SDT independence concerns not relying on others for support or guidance, whereas autonomy concerns volition and self-regulation. Thus, in the SDT view one can be autonomously dependent, as when an adolescent volitionally follows the lead or guidance of adults, or one can be heteronomously independent, as when adults "force" children to act without help. In fact, we have found that adolescents who can safely depend on their parents and teachers often develop the most autonomy, or capacity for healthy self-regulation (e.g., Ryan & Lynch, 1989).

Inherent developmental changes also precipitate new autonomy dynamics. Examples of this are myriad, and thus we select just one illustration, the onset of *adolescent egocentrism*. This cognitive developmental achievement concerns the emerging capacity to understand that there are varied perspectives on the self. One becomes "self-conscious," and during this period various social others are more likely to be experienced as critically viewing or judging the individual, thus prompting both increased social anxiety, pressured conformity, and proneness to introjection (Ryan & Kuczkowski, 1994). Thus, this natural developmental stage brings with it a new vulnerability to loss of autonomy, even as it represents a new set of skills that ultimately can enhance social awareness and the capacity for self-regulation. Interestingly, it is precisely during this period when early adolescents become more peer-focused that adults too often respond with increased control rather than autonomy support (Eccles, 1993), which can lead to disengagement and even rebelliousness in the school environment. This example thus illustrates how developmental maturation interfaces with the social environment in catalyzing new autonomy/control dynamics (Ryan, 1993).

Yet, in spite of such age-related changes, the functional importance of autonomy, competence, and relatedness has proven to be invariantly profound (Ryan, Deci, Grolnick, & La Guardia, 2006). Each of the three basic needs has its own developmental trajectory that can be more or less disrupted by social-contextual and/or biological factors. For example, Ryan (2005) discussed how early traumatic experiences disrupt the developmental line of autonomy, creating cascading effects on both neurological and psychological functioning that show up in compromised self-regulation later in development. Similarly, Ryan et al. (2006) provide a detailed review of the developmental perspective within SDT, including an account of the relations of basic need deprivations or supports in the etiology of various internalizing and externalizing problems. Unfortunately, a comprehensive review of this developmental literature is beyond the scope of the present chapter, but the central idea is that the dynamics of need satisfaction and thwarting are salient across the lifespan. Moreover, it is the SDT view that at all stages of life the individual operates most effectively and experiences the greatest wellness when their psychological needs are fulfilled and supported.

Does SDT Apply Across Cultures?

An even more controversial aspect of SDT for various researchers (e.g., Markus, Kitayama, & Heiman, 1996; McInerney & Van Etten, 2004) concerns the cross-cultural importance of autonomy and autonomy support. For example, Markus et al. maintained that autonomy is not important in traditionalist, collectivist cultures, basing their view on a cultural relativist perspective in which people's needs are assumed to be learned from their cultures rather than being innate. Although we do agree with Markus and other cultural relativists that cultures vary in their values and practices, including their explicit values for autonomy, our contention is a functional one. We argue that regardless of surface values, the function of autonomy support in enhancing motivation, engagement, and learning will be evident cross-culturally. The empirical evidence for this universalist position is ever growing.

Earlier we reviewed research by Chirkov and Ryan (2001) showing that autonomous motivation was important for the well-being of adolescents in Russia as well as the United States, and we mentioned a study by Kage and Namiki (1990) that linked autonomy-support to course performance in middle school students in Japan. Yamauchi and Tanaka (1998) and Hayamizu (1997) also reported studies of Japanese elementary school students attesting to the importance of autonomy, using measures of SDT's internalization continuum. Their results showed less interest, more superficial learning strategies, and more negative attitudes and affect in those with lower autonomy. Most recently, Jang, Reeve, Ryan, and Kim (2008) showed that all three of SDT's basic needs, including autonomy, were implicated in South Korean high school students' accounts of satisfying learning experiences. Moreover, several additional studies confirmed an SDT-based model in which support for autonomy led to need satisfaction, which, in turn, was associated with greater engagement and school achievement.

Other studies have also examined the importance of autonomy in cultures that are collectivist and do not emphasize autonomy. For example, Chirkov, Ryan, Kim, and Kaplan (2003) examined the degree to which college students in South Korea, Russia, Turkey, and the United States had internalized cultural practices related to collectivism and individualism. As expected, these countries differed in terms of the practices perceived to be dominant in their cultures. Yet, in spite of these mean-level differences in cultural practices, greater internalization of all the practices predicted, to comparable degrees, greater psychological well-being in all four countries. In other words, having more fully internalized either collectivism or individualism, and thus being more autonomous, yielded positive well-being outcomes, whereas having merely introjected either collectivism or individualism resulted in more negative outcomes. These results indicated that in all four nations, and for men and women alike, autonomy with respect to enacting culturally ambient behaviors mattered greatly for psychological health.

Vansteenkiste, Zhou, Lens, and Soenens (2005) found among young adult students in China that greater autonomous motivation for studying led to more adaptive learning attitudes, greater academic success, and higher well-being. Further, autonomy support from the students' parents promoted these positive educational outcomes, mediated by autonomous motivation. Jang et al. (2008) recently found similar results in Korean high school students, in which autonomy-support predicted internalization and enhanced school outcomes.

Recent research by Bao and Lam (2008) examined the importance of choice in the lives of Chinese children living in Hong Kong. The researchers found that, in general, children making their own choices, relative to having the choices made by their mothers or teachers, enhanced the children's intrinsic motivation; however, there was also an interaction with how close the children felt to the adults. Specifically, children who did *not* feel close to their mothers and teachers evidenced significantly more intrinsic motivation when they made their own choice than when the adult made the choice for them, but children who felt very close to their mothers and teachers showed no difference in intrinsic motivation between the two choice conditions. Presumably, if they felt close to the adults, the children more readily internalized the adults' decisions and enacted them autonomously just as they had done when they chose for themselves. In an additional study, Bao and Lam assessed Chinese children's feelings of autonomy for schoolwork using an SDT-based measure of internalization. They also assessed the students' feelings of closeness to their teachers. Results indicated that both autonomous motivation and closeness to the teachers contributed to the students' classroom engagement. There was no interaction, suggesting that autonomy has a positive effect regardless of the level of closeness with parents or teachers.

In sum, these and other studies provide evidence that satisfaction of the need for autonomy, like the needs for relatedness and competence, is important across cultures whether the cultures tend to be collectivist or individualist. Thus, relevant evidence is consistent with the idea that SDT's basic psychological needs are universal.

Summary and Conclusions

An enormous amount of research has been done to test the principles of self-determination theory in schools ranging from elementary schools to medical schools, only a portion of which we have been able to review in this chapter. The research has shown that autonomy support from both teachers and parents facilitate students' intrinsic motivation and internalization. This, in turn, has promoted improvements in conceptual learning as well as psychological well-being. These positive effects of autonomy-supportive climates on learning and well-being have been found to be mediated by satisfaction of the basic psychological needs for autonomy, competence, and relatedness, and these various relations have been found in many cultures including western cultures that are more individualist and egalitarian as well as eastern cultures that are more collectivist and traditional.

Other studies have drawn a link between individual differences in the strength of one's intrinsic relative to extrinsic goals and psychological health and well-being. Studies have also shown that framing students' goals to be more intrinsic rather than extrinsic has led to better learning and performance on a variety of learning activities.

Because teachers play a critical role in creating a classroom climate in which students' basic needs for autonomy, competence, and relatedness will be either supported or thwarted, studies have examined how pressures that are brought to bear on teachers, for example by emphasizing accountability, tend to make teachers more controlling, with negative ramifications for the students. High-stakes tests were used as an example of the kinds of pressures on teachers and students that predictably have an array of negative effects. We also reviewed two recent approaches to school reform that have utilized principles from SDT. By paying attention to what structures and policies facilitate basic need satisfaction of teachers and students, reform efforts can create positive changes not only in the motivations and feelings of teachers and students, but also in the educational outcomes of school attendance and persistence, school violence, graduate rates, and achievement.

In sum, SDT emphasizes the inherent resources embedded in human nature that can be facilitated by educational environments to support the learner's (as well as the teacher's) experiences of autonomy, competence, and relatedness. Need-supportive contexts enhance intrinsic motivation, internalization, and engagement, yielding enhanced emotional well-being and cognitive growth. The study of both facilitating and undermining environments is thus relevant at the level of individual interactions between teachers and students, including the nature of the communications, feedback, and rewards conveyed. SDT analyses are also relevant at the level of institutional and governmental policies as they support or impede teachers' and students' capacities to engage in a rich, responsive and facilitating process of learning. Finally, these considerations have application across life-span development and diverse cultures, which only bespeaks the centrality of basic psychological needs in the processes of human growth in all contexts, and the importance of educators being allowed to work with rather than fight against our active human natures.

References

Armein, A. L., & Berliner, D. C. (2002, March 28). High-stakes testing, uncertainty, and student learning. *Education Policy Analysis Archives, 10*(18). Retrieved September 3, 2006, from http://epaa.asu.edu/epaa/v10n18/

Assor, A., Kaplan, H., Kanat-Maymon, Y., & Roth, G. (2005). Directly controlling teacher behaviors as predictors of poor motivation and engagement in girls and boys: The role of anger and anxiety. *Learning and Instruction, 15*, 397–413.

Assor, A., Kaplan, H., & Roth, G. (2002). Choice is good, but relevance is excellent: Autonomy-enhancing and suppressing teacher behaviours in predicting student's engagement in school work. *British Journal of Educational Psychology, 72*, 261–278.

Assor, A., Roth, G., & Deci, E. L. (2004). The emotional costs of parents' conditional regard: A self-determination theory analysis. *Journal of Personality, 72*, 47–88.

Atkinson, J. W. (1964). *An introduction to motivation.* Princeton, NJ: Van Nostrand.

Bandura, A. (1996). *Self-efficacy: The exercise of control.* New York: Freeman.

Bao, X. H., & Lam, S.-f (2008). Who makes the choice? Rethinking the role of autonomy and relatedness in Chinese children's motivation. *Child Development, 79*, 269–283.

Benware, C., & Deci, E. L. (1984). Quality of learning with an active versus passive motivational set. *American Educational Research Journal, 21*, 755–765.

Black, A. E., & Deci, E. L. (2000). The effects of student self-regulation and instructor autonomy support on learning in a college-level natural science course: A self-determination theory perspective. *Science Education, 84*, 740–756.

Burton, K. D., Lydon, J. E., D'Alessandro, D. U., & Koestner, R. (2006). The differential effects of intrinsic and identified motivation on well-being and performance: Prospective, experimental and implicit approaches to self-determination theory. *Journal of Personality and Social Psychology, 91*, 750–762.

Chirkov, V. I., & Ryan, R. M. (2001). Parent and teacher autonomy-support in Russian and U.S. adolescents: Common effects on well-being and academic motivation. *Journal of Cross Cultural Psychology, 32,* 618–635.

Chirkov, V., Ryan, R. M., Kim, Y., & Kaplan, U. (2003). Differentiating autonomy from individualism and independence: A self-determination theory perspective on internalization of cultural orientations and well-being. *Journal of Personality and Social Psychology, 84,* 97–110.

Connell, J. P., & Klem, A. M. (2000). You can get there from here: Using a theory of change approach to plan urban education reform. *Journal of Educational and Psychological Consulting, 11,* 93–120.

de Charms, R. (1968). *Personal causation: The internal affective determinants of behavior.* New York: Academic Press.

Deci, E. L. (1971). Effects of externally mediated rewards on intrinsic motivation. *Journal of Personality and Social Psychology, 18,* 105–115.

Deci, E. L., Eghrari, H., Patrick, B. C., & Leone, D. R. (1994). Facilitating internalization: The self-determination theory perspective. *Journal of Personality, 62,* 119–142.

Deci, E. L., Hodges, R., Pierson, L., & Tomassone, J. (1992). Autonomy and competence as motivational factors in students with learning disabilities and emotional handicaps. *Journal of Learning Disabilities, 25,* 457–471.

Deci, E. L., Koestner, R., & Ryan, R. M. (1999). A meta-analytic review of experiments examining the effects of extrinsic rewards on intrinsic motivation. *Psychological Bulletin, 125.* 627–668.

Deci, E. L., & Moller, A. C. (2005). The concept of competence: A starting place for understanding intrinsic motivation and self-determined extrinsic motivation. In A. J. Elliot, & C. J. Dweck (Eds.), *Handbook of competence and motivation* (pp. 579–597). New York: Guilford.

Deci, E. L., & Ryan, R. M. (1980). The empirical exploration of intrinsic motivational processes. In L. Berkowitz (Ed.), *Advances in experimental social psychology* (Vol. 13, pp. 39–80). New York: Academic Press.

Deci, E. L., & Ryan, R. M. (1985). *Intrinsic motivation and self-determination in human behavior.* New York: Plenum.

Deci, E. L., & Ryan, R. M. (2000). The "what" and "why" of goal pursuits: Human needs and the self-determination of behavior. *Psychological Inquiry, 11,* 227–268.

Deci, E. L., Schwartz, A. J., Sheinman, L., & Ryan, R. M. (1981). An Instrument to assess adults' orientations toward control versus autonomy with children: Reflections on intrinsic motivation and perceived competence. *Journal of Educational Psychology, 73,* 642–650.

Deci, E. L., Spiegel, N. H., Ryan, R. M., Koestner, R., & Kauffman, M. (1982). Effects of performance standards on teaching styles: Behavior of controlling teachers. *Journal of Educational Psychology, 74,* 852–859.

Eccles, J. S. (1993). School and family effects on the ontogeny of children's interests, self-perceptions, and activity choice. In J. E. Jacobs & R. Dienstbier (Eds.), *Nebraska symposium on motivation: Developmental perspectives on motivation* (Vol. 40 pp. 145–208). Lincoln: University of Nebraska Press.

Feinberg, O., Kaplan, H., Assor, A., & Kanat-Maymon, Y. (2007, May). *The concept of "internalization" (based on SDT) as a guide for a school reform program.* Paper presented at the Third International Conference on Self-Determination Theory, Toronto, Canada.

Flink, C., Boggiano, A. K., & Barrett, M. (1990). Controlling teaching strategies: Undermining children's self-determination and performance. *Journal of Personality and Social Psychology, 59,* 916–924.

Fortier, M. S., Vallerand, R. J., & Guay, F. (1995). Academic motivation and school performance: Toward a structural model. *Contemporary Educational Psychology, 20,* 257–274.

Gambone, M. A., Klem, A. M., Summers, J. A., Akey, T. A., & Sipe, C. L. (2004). *Turning the tide: The achievements of the First Things First education reform in the Kansas City, Kansas Public School District.* Philadelphia: Youth Development Strategies, Inc.

Grolnick, W. S., & Ryan, R. M. (1987). Autonomy in children's learning: An experimental and individual difference investigation. *Journal of Personality and Social Psychology, 52,* 890–898.

Grolnick, W. S., & Ryan, R. M. (1989). Parent styles associated with children's self-regulation and competence in school. *Journal of Educational Psychology, 81,* 143–154.

Grolnick, W. S., & Ryan, R. M. (1990). Self-perceptions, motivation, and adjustment in children with learning disabilities: A multiple group comparison study. *Journal of Learning Disabilities, 23,* 177–184.

Grolnick, W. S., Ryan, R. M., & Deci, E. L. (1991). The inner resources for school achievement: Motivational mediators of children's perceptions of their parents. *Journal of Educational Psychology, 83,* 508–517.

Grolnick, W. S., & Slowiaczek, M. L. (1994). Parents' involvement in children's schooling: A multidimensional conceptualization and motivational model. *Child Development, 65,* 237–252.

Guay, F., & Vallerand, R. J. (1997). Social context, student's motivation, and academic achievement: Toward a process model. *Social Psychology of Education, 1,* 211–233.

Hagger, M. S., Chatzisarantis, N.L.D., Barkoukis, V., Wang, C. K. J., & Baranowski, J. (2005). Perceived autonomy support in physical education and leisure-time physical activity: A cross-cultural evaluation of the trans-contextual model. *Journal of Educational Psychology, 97,* 287–301.

Hagger, M. S., Chatzisarantis, N. L. D., Culverhouse, T., & Biddle, S. J .H. (2003). The process by which perceived autonomy support in physical education promotes leisure-time physical activity intentions and behavior: A trans-contextual model. *Journal of Educational Psychology, 95,* 784–795.

Hardre, P. L., Chen, C., Huang, S., Chiang, C., Jen, F., & Warden, L. (2006). Factors affecting high school students' academic motivation in Taiwan. *Asia Pacific Journal of Education, 26,* 198–207.

Hardre, P. L., & Reeve, J. (2003). A motivational model of rural students' intentions to persist in, versus drop out of, high school. *Journal of Educational Psychology, 95,* 347–356.

Hayamizu, T. (1997). Between intrinsic and extrinsic motivation: Examination of reasons for academic study based on the theory of internalization. *Japanese Psychological Research, 39*, 98–108.

Hoff, D. J. (2000). As stakes rise, definition of cheating blurs. *Education Week, 19*, 1–4.

Hursh, D. (2008). *High-stakes testing and the decline of teaching and learning: The real crisis in education.* Lanham, MD: Rowman & Littlefield.

Jacob, B. A. (2001). Getting tough? The impact of high school graduation exams. *Educational Evaluation and Policy Analysis, 23*, 99–121.

Jang, H., Reeve, J., & Deci, E. L. (2007). *Engaging students in learning activities: It's not autonomy support or structure, but autonomy support and structure.* Manuscript submitted for publication.

Jang, H., Reeve, J., Ryan, R. M., & Kim, A. (2008). *Can self-determination theory explain what underlies the productive, satisfying learning experiences of collectivistically-oriented Korean students?* Manuscript submitted for publication.

Kage, M., & Namiki, H. (1990). The effects of evaluation structure on children's intrinsic motivation and learning. *Japanese Journal of Educational Psychology, 38*, 36–45.

Kasser, T. (2002). *The high price of materialism.* Cambridge, MA: MIT Press.

Kasser, T., & Ryan, R. M. (1993). A dark side of the American dream: Correlates of financial success as a central life aspiration. *Journal of Personality and Social Psychology, 65*, 410–422.

Kasser, T., & Ryan, R. M. (1996). Further examining the American dream: Differential correlates of intrinsic and extrinsic goals. *Personality and Social Psychology Bulletin 22*, 80–87.

Kasser, T., Ryan, R. M., Zax, M., & Sameroff, A. J. (1995). The relations of maternal and social environments to late adolescents' materialistic and prosocial values. *Developmental Psychology, 31*, 907–914.

Katz, I., Assor, A., Kanat-Maymon, Y. (2008). A projective assessment of autonomous motivation in children: Correlational and experimental evidence. *Motivation and Emotion, 32*, 199–208.

Koestner, R., Ryan, R. M., Bernieri, F., & Holt, K. (1984). Setting limits on children's behavior: The differential effects of controlling versus informational styles on children's intrinsic motivation and creativity. *Journal of Personality, 54*, 233–248.

Legault, L., Green-Demers, I., & Pelletier, L. G. (2006). Why do high school students lack motivation in the classroom? Toward an understanding of academic motivation and social support. *Journal of Educational Psychology, 98*, 567–582.

Levesque, C., Zuehlke, N., Stanek, L., & Ryan, R. M. (2004). Autonomy and competence in German and U.S. university students: A comparative study based on self-determination theory. *Journal of Educational Psychology, 96*, 68–84.

Lonky, E., & Reihman, J. (1989, August). *Moral reasoning and regulatory style as mediators of moral behavior.* Paper presented at the annual meeting of the American Psychological Association, New Orleans, LA.

Markus, H. R., Kitayama, S., & Heiman, R. J. (1996). Culture and basic psychological principles. In E. T. Higgins & A. W. Kruglanski (Eds.), *Social psychology: Handbook of basic principles* (pp. 857–913). New York: Guilford.

McClelland, D. C. (1985). *Human motivation.* Glenview, IL: Scott, Foresman.

McInerney, D. M., & Van Etten, S. (2004). Setting the stage. In D. McInerney & S. Van Etten (Eds.), *Big theories revisited* (pp. 1–11). Greenwich, CT: Information Age.

McNeil, L., & Valenzuela, A. (2000). *The harmful effects of the TAAS system of testing in Texas: Beneath the accountability rhetoric.* Cambridge, MA: Harvard Civil Rights Project.

Miserandino, M. (1996). Children who do well in school: Individual differences in perceived competence and autonomy in above average children. *Journal of Educational Psychology, 88*, 203–214.

Moller, A. C., Deci, E. L., & Ryan, R. M. (2006). Choice and ego-depletion: The moderating role of autonomy. *Personality and Social Psychology Bulletin, 32*, 1024–1036.

Murray, H. A. (1938). *Explorations in personality.* New York: Oxford University Press.

Nicholls, J. G. (1984). Achievement motivation: Conceptions of ability, subjective experience, task choice, and performance. *Psychological Review, 91*, 328–346.

Niemiec, C. P., Lynch, M. F., Vansteenkiste, M., Bernstein, J., Deci, E. L., & Ryan, R. M. (2006). The antecedents and consequences of autonomous self-regulation for college: A self-determination theory perspective on socialization. *Journal of Adolescence, 29*, 761–775.

Ommundsen, Y., & Kvalø, S. E. (2007). Autonomy-mastery supportive or performance focused? Different teacher behaviors and pupil's outcomes in physical education. *Scandinavian Journal of Educational Research, 51*, 386–413.

Patall, E. A., Cooper, H., & Robinson, J. C. (2008). The effects of choice on intrinsic motivation and related outcomes: A meta-analysis of research findings. *Psychological Bulletin, 134*, 270–300.

Pelletier, L. G., Séguin-Lévesque, C., & Legault, L. (2002). Pressure from above and pressure from below as determinants of teachers' motivation and teaching behavior. *Journal of Educational Psychology, 94*, 186–196.

Quint, J., Bloom, H. S., Black, A. R., Stephens, L., & Akey, T. M. (2005). *The challenge of scaling up educational reform, findings and lessons from First Things First, final report.* New York: MDRC.

Ratelle, C. F., Larose, S., Guay, F., & Senecal, C. (2005). Perceptions of Parental Involvement and Support as Predictors of College Students' Persistence in a Science Curriculum. *Journal of Family Psychology, 19*, 286–293.

Reardon, S. F., & Galindo, C. (2002, April). *Do high-stakes tests affect students' decisions to drop out of school? [Evidence from NELS].* Paper presented at the Annual Meeting of the American Educational Research Association, New Orleans, LA.

Reeve, J., Bolt, E., & Cai, Y. (1999). Autonomy-supportive teachers: How they teach and motivate students. *Journal of Educational Psychology, 91*, 537–548.

Reeve, J., Deci, E. L., & Ryan, R. M. (2004). Self-determination theory: A dialectical framework for understanding socio-cultural influences on student motivation. In D. M. McInerney & S. Van Etten (Eds.), *Big theories revisited* (pp. 31–60). Greenwich, CT: Information Age.

Reeve, J., & Jang, H. (2006). What teachers say and do to support students' autonomy during a learning activity. *Journal of Educational Psychology, 98,* 209–218.

Reeve, J., Jang, H., Hardre, P., & Omura, M. (2002). Providing a rationale in an autonomy-supportive way as a strategy to motivate others during an uninteresting activity. *Motivation and Emotion, 26,* 183–207.

Reeve, J., Nix, G., & Hamm, D. (2003). Testing models of the experience of self-determination in intrinsic motivation and the conundrum of choice. *Journal of Educational Psychology, 95,* 375–392.

Rogoff, B. (2003). *The cultural nature of human development.* New York: Oxford University.

Roth, G., Assor, A., Kanat-Maymon, Y., & Kaplan, H. (2007). Autonomous motivation for teaching: How self-determined teaching may lead to self-determined learning. *Journal of Educational Psychology, 99,* 761–774.

Roth, G., Assor, A., Niemiec, C. P., Ryan, R. M., & Deci, E. L. (2008). *The negative emotional and academic consequences of parental conditional regard: Comparing positive conditional regard, negative conditional regard, and autonomy support as parenting practices.* Unpublished manuscript, Ben Gurion University of the Negev, Israel.

Roth, G., Kanat-Maymon, Y, Assor, A., & Kaplan, A. (2006). Assessing the experience of autonomy in new cultures and contexts. *Motivation and Emotion, 30,* 365–376.

Ryan, R. M. (1982). Control and information in the intrapersonal sphere: An extension of cognitive evaluation theory. *Journal of Personality and Social Psychology, 43,* 450–461.

Ryan, R. M. (1993). Agency and organization: Intrinsic motivation, autonomy and the self in psychological development. In J. Jacobs (Ed.), *Nebraska symposium on motivation: Developmental perspectives on motivation* (Vol. 40, pp. 1–56). Lincoln: University of Nebraska Press.

Ryan, R. M. (1995). Psychological needs and the facilitation of integrative processes. *Journal of Personality, 63,* 397–427.

Ryan, R. M. (2005). The developmental line of autonomy in the etiology, dynamics, and treatment of borderline personality disorders. *Development and Psychopathology, 17,* 987–1006.

Ryan, R. M., & Brown, K. W. (2005). Legislating competence: The motivational impact of high stakes testing as an educational reform. In C. Dweck & A. E. Elliot (Eds.), *Handbook of competence* (pp. 354–374). New York: Guilford.

Ryan, R. M., & Connell, J. P. (1989). Perceived locus of causality and internalization: Examining reasons for acting in two domains. *Journal of Personality and Social Psychology, 57,* 749–761.

Ryan, R. M., Connell, J. P., & Deci, E. L. (1985). A motivational analysis of self-determination and self-regulation in education. In C. Ames & R. E. Ames (Eds.), *Research on motivation in education: The classroom milieu* (pp. 13–51). New York: Academic Press.

Ryan, R. M., Connell, J. P., & Plant, R. W. (1990). Emotions in non-directed text learning. *Learning and Individual Differences, 2,* 1–17.

Ryan, R. M., & Deci, E. L. (2000). Self-determination theory and the facilitation of intrinsic motivation, social development, and well-being. *American Psychologist, 55,* 68–78.

Ryan, R. M., & Deci, E. L. (2008). From ego-depletion to vitality: Theory and findings concerning the facilitation of energy available to the self. *Social and Personality Psychology Compass, 2,* 702–717.

Ryan, R. M., Deci, E. L., Grolnick, W. S., & La Guardia, J. G. (2006). The significance of autonomy and autonomy support in psychological development and psychopathology. In D. Cicchetti & D. J. Cohen (Eds.), *Developmental psychopathology: Vol 1. Theory and method* (2nd ed., pp. 795–849). Hoboken, NJ: Wiley.

Ryan, R. M., & Grolnick, W. S. (1986). Origins and pawns in the classroom: Self-report and projective assessments of children's perceptions. *Journal of Personality and Social Psychology, 50,* 550–558.

Ryan, R. M., Koestner, R., & Deci, E. L. (1991). Ego-involved persistence: When free-choice behavior is not intrinsically motivated. *Motivation and Emotion, 15,* 185–205.

Ryan, R. M., & Kuczkowski, R. (1994). The imaginary audience, self-consciousness, and public individuation in adolescence. *Journal of Personality, 62,* 219–238.

Ryan, R. M., & La Guardia, J. G. (1999). Achievement motivation within a pressured society: Intrinsic and extrinsic motivations to learn and the politics of school reform. In T. Urdan (Ed.), *Advances in motivation and achievement: Vol 11* (pp. 45–85). Greenwich, CT: JAI.

Ryan, R. M., & Lynch, J. (1989). Emotional autonomy versus detachment: Revisiting the vicissitudes of adolescence and young adulthood. *Child Development, 60,* 340–356

Ryan, R. M., Mims, V., & Koestner, R. (1983). Relation of reward contingency and interpersonal context to intrinsic motivation: A review and test using cognitive evaluation theory. *Journal of Personality and Social Psychology, 45,* 736–750.

Ryan, R. M., & Powelson, C. L. (1991). Autonomy and relatedness as fundamental to motivation in education. *Journal of Experimental Education, 60,* 49–66.

Ryan, R. M., & Sapp, A. R. (2005). Considering the impact of test-based reforms: A self-determination theory perspective on high stakes testing and student motivation and performance. *Unterrichtswissenschaft, 33,* 143–159.

Ryan, R. M., Sheldon, K. M., Kasser, T., & Deci, E. L. (1996). All goals are not created equal: An organismic perspective on the nature of goals and their regulation. In P. M. Gollwitzer & J. A. Bargh (Eds.), *The psychology of action: Linking cognition and motivation to behavior* (pp. 7–26). New York: Guilford.

Ryan, R. M., & Stiller, J. (1991). The social contexts of internalization: Parent and teacher influences on autonomy, motivation and learning. In P. R. Pintrich & M. L. Maehr (Eds.), *Advances in motivation and achievement: Vol. 7. Goals and self-regulatory processes* (pp. 115–149). Greenwich, CT: JAI.

Schwartz, B. (2004). *The paradox of choice: Why more is less*. New York: Harper & Collins.

Shapira, Z. (1976). Expectancy determinants of intrinsically motivated behavior. *Journal of Personality and Social Psychology, 34,* 1235–1244.

Sheldon, K. M., & Krieger, L. S. (2007). Understanding the negative effects of legal education on law students: A longitudinal test of self-determination theory. *Personality and Soical Psychology Bulletin, 33,* 883–897.

Skinner, E. A., & Belmont, M. J. (1993). Motivation in the classroom: Reciprocal effects of teacher behavior and student engagement across the school year. *Journal of Educational Psychology, 85,* 571–581.

Soenens, B., & Vansteenkiste, M. (2005). Antecedents and outcomes of self-determination in three life domains: The role of parents' and teachers' autonomy support. *Journal of Youth and Adolescence, 34,* 589–604.

Standage, M., Duda, J. L., & Ntoumanis, N. (2006). Students' motivational processes and their relationships to teacher ratings in school physical education: A self-determination theory approach. *Research Quarterly for Exercise and Sport, 77,* 100–110.

Tsai, Y., Kunter, M., Lüdtke, O., Trautwein, U., & Ryan, R. M. (2008). What makes lessons interesting? The role of situational and individual factors in three school subjects. *Journal of Educational Psychology, 100,* 460–472.

Vallerand, R. J. (1997). Toward a hierarchical model of intrinsic and extrinsic motivation. In M. P. Zanna (Ed.), *Advances in experimental social psychology* (Vol. 29, pp. 271–360). San Diego: Academic Press.

Vallerand, R. J., & Bissonnette, R. (1992). Intrinsic, extrinsic, and amotivational styles as predictors of behavior: A prospective study. *Journal of Personality, 60,* 599–620.

Vallerand, R. J., Fortier, M. S., & Guay, F. (1997). Self-determination and persistence in a real-life setting: Toward a motivational model of high school dropout. *Journal of Personality and Social Psychology, 72,* 1161–1176.

Vallerand, R. J., Gagné, F., Senécal, C., & Pelletier, L. G. (1994). A comparison of the school intrinsic motivation and perceived competence of gifted and regular students. *Gifted Child Quarterly, 38,* 172–175.

Vallerand, R. J., Pelletier, L. G., Blais, M. R., Brière, N. M., Senécal, C. B., & Vallières, E. F. (1992). The Academic Motivation Scale: A measure of intrinsic, extrinsic, and amotivation in education. *Educational and Psychological Measurement, 52,* 1003–1017.

Vallerand, R. J., & Reid, G. (1984). On the causal effects of perceived competence on intrinsic motivation: A test of cognitive evaluation theory. *Journal of Sport Psychology, 6,* 94–102.

Vansteenkiste, M., Lens, W., Soenens, B., & Van den Broeck, A. (in press). Does extrinsic goal framing enhance extrinsic goal oriented individuals' learning and performance? An experimental test of the match perspective versus self-determination theory. *Journal of Educational Psychology.*

Vansteenkiste, M., Simons, J., Lens, W., Sheldon, K. M., & Deci, E. L. (2004). Motivating learning, performance, and persistence: The synergistic effects of intrinsic goal contents and autonomy-supportive contexts. *Journal of Personality and Social Psychology, 87,* 246–260.

Vansteenkiste, M., Simons, J., Lens, W., Soenens, B., & Matos, L. (2005). Examining the motivational impact of intrinsic versus extrinsic goal framing and autonomy-supportive versus internally controlling communication style on early adolescents' academic achievement. *Child Development, 2,* 483–501.

Vansteenkiste, M., Zhou, M., Lens, W., & Soenens, B. (2005). Experiences of autonomy and control among Chinese learners: Vitalizing or immobilizing? *Journal of Educational Psychology, 96,* 755–764.

White, R. W. (1959). Motivation reconsidered: The concept of competence. *Psychological Review, 66,* 297–333.

Williams, G. C., Cox, E. M., Hedberg, V., & Deci, E. L. (2000). Extrinsic life goals and health risk behaviors in adolescents. *Journal of Applied Social Psychology, 30,* 1756–1771.

Williams, G. C., & Deci, E. L. (1996). Internalization of biopsychosocial values by medical students: A test of self-determination theory. *Journal of Personality and Social Psychology, 70,* 767–779.

Williams, G. C., & Deci, E. L. (1998). The importance of supporting autonomy in medical education. *Annals of Internal Medicine, 129,* 303–308.

Williams, G. C., Saizow, R., Ross, L., & Deci, E. L. (1997). Motivation underlying career choice for internal medicine and surgery. *Social Science and Medicine, 45,* 1705–1713.

Yamauchi, H., & Tanaka, K. (1998). Relations of autonomy, self-referenced beliefs and self-regulated learning among Japanese children. *Psychological Reports, 82,* 803–816.

Zuckerman, M., Porac, J., Lathin, D., Smith, R., & Deci, E. L. (1978). On the importance of self-determination for intrinsically motivated behavior. *Personality and Social Psychology Bulletin, 4,* 443–446.

10
Situational and Individual Interest

Ulrich Schiefele

With the publication of *The Role of Interest in Learning and Development* in 1992, Ann Renninger, Suzanne Hidi, and Andreas Krapp directed the attention of educational and motivational scientists to the concept of interest. For the first time, this book brought together authors from various fields who had conducted empirical studies involving interest. Since then, an increasing number of researchers studied interest and theorized about it (see Hidi, 2001; Hidi, Renninger, & Krapp, 2004; Renninger & Hidi, 2001). As a consequence, interest is now well established as a motivational construct in education (cf. Schunk, Pintrich, & Meece, 2008).

In everyday language, "interest" and "motivation" are often used synonymously. This mirrors the history of the concept of interest. Long before the term "motivation" became prevalent in psychology and education, many motivational phenomena have been dealt with under the label of "interest" (cf. Hidi et al., 2004). Therefore, it is important to start by clearly distinguishing these terms. *Motivation* is commonly understood as the state of wanting to perform a specific activity in a given situation (e.g., Schunk et al., 2008; Wigfield, Eccles, Schiefele, Roeser, & Davis-Kean, 2006). The determinants of the strength of a specific, current motivation have been identified by various approaches, including the expectancy-value theories of motivation (e.g., expectancy of success) and self-efficacy theory. In addition, the process of forming a specific motivation is influenced by enduring motivational characteristics of the person, such as motives or goal orientations.

Interest also represents a possible antecedent of motivation. A relatively unique feature of interest is its strong emphasis on the *content of learning*. Unlike many other motivational constructs, such as motives, needs, self-concepts, or goal-orientations, interest is always related to a *specific* object, activity, or subject area. In his person-object theory of interest, Krapp (2002) described interest as a *relational construct* that consists of a more or less enduring relationship between a person and an object. This relationship is realized by specific activities, which may comprise concrete or hands-on actions and abstract mental operations.

In addition, the meaning of interest may range from a single, situation-specific person-object relation (e.g., reading a stimulating text) towards the development of enduring value beliefs with respect to particular domains (e.g., interest in physics). Accordingly, two major conceptions of interest have been suggested: situational and individual interest (e.g., Hidi, 2000; Hidi et al. 2004; Krapp, 1999, 2002). *Situational interest* is a temporary state aroused by specific features of a situation, task, or object (e.g., vividness of a text passage). This state has been described as focused and effortless attention accompanied by a positive emotional tone (Krapp, Hidi, & Renninger, 1992). Experiencing situational interest may facilitate specific motivations to act. For example, after lively and expressive introductions of new topics by teachers, some students are highly concentrated and eager to learn more about it.

Individual interest is conceptualized as a relatively stable affective-evaluative orientation toward certain subject areas or objects. A high level of interest in a particular subject area involves close associations between that subject area and positive feeling- and value-related attributes (e.g., excitement). When an individual interest becomes activated (e.g., by external cues), it also potentially affects the formation of specific motivations (e.g., to buy a book related to one's interest).

In this chapter, I will first present conceptualizations of situational and individual interest in more detail and address the relation between interest and intrinsic motivation. This is followed by a brief overview of interest measurement. The next sections refer to interest development and the effects of interest on learning. Finally, contextual influences on interest are discussed. The focus of the present chapter is on academic and text-related interests as opposed, for example, to leisure or vocational interests.

Situational Interest

Definitions of Situational Interest

Situational interest describes a short-term psychological state that involves focused attention, increased cognitive functioning, persistence, enjoyment or affective involvement, and curiosity (Hidi, 2000; Ainley & Hidi, 2002; Renninger, 2000). In addition, when interest is high, focusing attention and cognitive activity feel relatively effortless. According to Hidi (1995), automatic attention may explain the facilitative effect of interest on cognitive functioning.

Theoretically, situational interest is created in two different ways (Hidi, 2000; Krapp, 2002). On the one hand, it may be caused by particular conditions or factors in the environment that focus attention and lead to an affective reaction. On the other hand, the experience of interest may be aroused through the activation of enduring individual interests. In the first case, the psychological state of interest is called *situational interest* and in the second case *actualized individual interest*. However, it remains unclear whether these two states are different or the same. Because of the lack of empirical evidence, it seems more parsimonious to assume only one state of interest that may be caused by different factors.

Silvia (2005, 2006) proposed that situational interest should be conceptualized as an emotion. He argued that interest involves all components that characterize emotions: typical facial expression, physiological parameters (e.g., level of activation), subjective experience (engaged, caught-up, fascinated, and curious; cf. Izard, 1977), behaviors (e.g., time spent reading a text), and goals (e.g., wanting to explore an object). Empirical studies confirm that these components are relatively coherent and predict each other (e.g., Reeve & Nix, 1997).

Based on an appraisal theory perspective, Silvia (2005, 2006) identified those appraisals that are most relevant for evoking interest. Appraisal theories assume that emotions are caused by cognitive appraisals of events (e.g., judging the goal relevance of an event; cf. Lazarus, 1991). According to Silvia, the appraisal structure of interest involves two components: an appraisal of novelty or complexity (including uncertainty and conflict) and an appraisal of coping potential. The novelty check includes appraising something as new, ambiguous, complex, obscure, unexpected, or otherwise not understood. Numerous studies confirm that judgements of novelty and complexity affect interest (cf. Silvia, 2006). However, both too low and too high levels of novelty or complexity may reduce interest. Therefore, at least one other variable is interacting with novelty to predict interest. A likely candidate for that variable seems to be *coping potential*. This second appraisal component refers to estimates of being able to understand a (new, complex, or surprising) event. In accordance with earlier research findings (e.g., Millis, 2001), Silvia (2005) was able to show that appraisals of novelty-complexity and coping potential interacted in expected ways to predict interest. In addition, the findings revealed that ratings of *pleasantness* did not influence interest. The latter finding is in line with several studies showing that interest and similar positive emotions such as happiness or enjoyment are distinct with respect to their antecedents (Silvia, 2006). For example, complex stimuli are rated as interesting, whereas simple stimuli are rated as enjoyable. Presumably, enjoyment serves a rewarding function, to reinforce goal attainment or attachments to familiar things. In contrast, interest motivates exploration of new and complex domains or objects.

A comparison between definitions of situational interest provided by Hidi (2000; see also Renninger, 2000) and Silvia (2006) reveals a substantial overlap. In both cases, the subjective experience of situational interest is characterized by attention and persistence (being engaged and caught-up), positive affective involvement (being fascinated), and curiosity. Only the role of enjoyment as a defining aspect of situational interest (Hidi, 2000) seems doubtful. However, Silvia's position is more strongly based on an elaborated theory that, in addition, allows us to deduce relevant determinants of situational interest (see also next section). Therefore, it may be more preferable to conceptualize situational interest as an emotion and not as a more vaguely defined psychological state.

Sources of Text-Based Interest

Because of reading's importance to achievement, there has been a great deal of work on interest that focuses on the domain of reading. The literature on situational interest with respect to reading mainly refers to factors that make text materials interesting (e.g., Hidi, 1990, 2001). Consequently, *text-based interest* and situational interest are often used synonymously. A multitude of text-based factors facilitating interest have been suggested (cf. Schraw, 1997; Schraw & Lehman, 2001; Silvia, 2006). These factors often seem to be closely related or redundant (e.g., factors like surprisingness and unexpectedness). The following examples may represent more or less unique sources of interest: surprisingness, coherence, concreteness, vividness, emotiveness, ease of comprehension, simple vocabulary, and engaging themes (death, power, sex). Only a few of the many possible interest sources have been extensively evaluated by research. Relatively strong empirical support exists for surprisingness, coherence, concreteness, vividness, and ease of comprehension (Schraw & Lehman, 2001; Silvia, 2006). Accordingly, well-organized and comprehensible texts with concrete, surprising, and vivid information enhance text-based interest.

Silvia (2006) proposed that most of the potential sources of text-based interest can be integrated in his appraisal model. The different sources of interest should refer to either one of the two appraisal components (novelty-complexity or coping potential). Thus, the sources of interest are to be understood as *facets* of the appraisal components underlying interest. According to Silvia (2006), interest sources that exemplify the novelty-complexity dimension are: surprisingness, vividness, emotiveness, and engaging themes. In contrast, interest sources thought to reflect the coping dimension are: coherence, concreteness, ease of comprehension, and simple vocabulary.

This assignment of interest sources to appraisal components, however, is preliminary and needs to be supported by empirical research.

Triggered vs. Maintained Situational Interest

Both Hidi and Baird (1986) and Mitchell (1993) distinguished two phases or forms of situational interest: triggered and maintained interest. Triggering (or catching, in Mitchell's terms) interest describes the induction of attention and arousal for only a short term. According to a qualitative study by Mitchell (1992), appropriate methods to catch interest in the mathematics classroom include puzzles (and other tools for arousing students' curiosity, such as mind-teasers or starters), group work (social exchange among students enhances the interestingness of the classroom environment), and computers (because they provide cognitive stimulation and allow exploration and testing of conjectures). Mitchell suggests that these "catch facets" are not effective for holding interest over a longer period of time. In order to hold or maintain interest, it is necessary to emphasize the meaningfulness of subject content and facilitate students' involvement ("hold facets"). Meaningfulness refers to students' perception of subject content as being relevant to their daily lives. Involvement refers to students' experience of active participation in learning. Both facets are facilitated when students are allowed to realize projects that are personally meaningful and include a high level of active engagement.

Based on her own and Mitchell's work, Hidi (2000) proposed a two-phase model of situational interest in which triggered situational interest is considered as the first phase and maintained situational interest is considered as the second phase. In addition, only maintained situational interest potentially contributes to the development of long-term individual interest (see also Hidi & Renninger, 2006; Krapp, 1998; Renninger, 2000).

The descriptions given by Hidi (2000) and Mitchell (1993) do not suggest that triggered and maintained interest represent qualitatively distinct experiential states. Instead, triggered interest differs from maintained interest mainly with respect to its duration. However, there is no empirical evidence so far that maintained situational interest—incited, for example, by enhancing the meaningfulness of learning materials—lasts for longer periods of time than situational interest triggered, for example, by vivid text elements. Although it is probable that hold facets (e.g., meaningfulness) create more extensive periods of situational interest, the case of longer lasting triggered interest seems also conceivable. The latter may take place, for example, when a given text contains *numerous* vivid, concrete, and emotive sentences or paragraphs. In addition, episodes of triggered interest with respect to a particular subject area may be experienced repeatedly. Therefore, the duration of situational interest may be not as critical for the development of individual interest as proposed by Hidi (2000). It can be argued, instead, that catch and hold facets differ with respect to their effects on *cognitions being related to an object of interest*. Catch facets, such as puzzles, group work, or use of computers only have an arbitrary relation with a given subject content. Thus, it seems likely that these facets only elicit temporary and short-lived feelings of engagement or curiosity and do not contribute to object-related value cognitions. In contrast, hold facets (e.g., emphasizing the relevance of a topic for students' daily lives) are more directly related to a potential object of interest. They enhance the meaningfulness of subject content and the active involvement with it. As such, these factors facilitate positive *value-* and *feeling-related cognitions* that may turn (especially when they occur repeatedly) into more stable beliefs being characteristic of individual interest (see below).

An interesting task for future research pertains to the question whether only hold facets or maintained interest may lead to an individual interest. It seems also possible to envision a process in which the repeated experience of triggered situational interest transforms into an individual interest. If a teacher, for example, succeeds in eliciting situational interest repeatedly by using catch facets such as puzzles, group work, or coherent text materials with concrete and vivid examples, it may become more likely that students associate their positive experience with a particular subject content and increasingly exhibit positive content-related value cognitions. Through repeated engagement with that subject content, these associations will become stronger and more stable and eventually form an individual interest.

To summarize, it seems plausible to assume two different developmental trajectories from situational to individual interest, one based on catch facets or triggered interest and one based on hold facets or maintained interest. In addition, it is hypothesized that both pathways to individual interest are mediated by the occurrence of positive content-related value cognitions. These assumptions could be tested experimentally by exposing students to subject content they find uninteresting (e.g., statistics). Then, for one group of students, catch facets should be introduced during several sessions, whereas the other group receives instructions in order to enhance the meaningfulness of subject content. After each session, the strength of situational interest and the occurrence of value cognitions must to be tested. By means of a follow-up assessment, the strength of individual interest (also tested at the beginning of the experiment) can be determined.

Individual Interest

Two different conceptions of individual interest have been proposed. The first conception describes interest as a relatively stable affective-evaluative orientation toward certain domains (i.e., subject areas, objects, events; e.g., Hidi et al., 2004; Krapp, 1998; Schiefele, 2001). That orientation is conceived of as a quantitative variable ranging from low to high levels. The second conception favors a qualitative distinction between interests and noninterests or—more recently—between well-developed and less-developed interests (Renninger, 2000; Renninger, Ewen, & Lasher, 2002). Well-developed interest is characterized by high levels of content-related knowledge and value, whereas less-developed interest includes a high level of knowledge but low value. Research related to this conception is focused on differences between well-developed and less-developed interests, whereas research related to the first conception is mainly directed at the strength of associations between interest and learning or achievement.

Individual Interest as an Affective-Evaluative Orientation

Individual interest is defined as a relatively stable set of *valence beliefs* (Schiefele, 1996, 2001). Valence beliefs are a subgroup of motivationally relevant beliefs, such as expectancies, attributions, and self-concepts. All of these beliefs are important antecedents of specific motivations to act. Valences denote cognitively represented relations between a domain (e.g., physics) and evaluative attributes. These attributes may be either feeling- or value-related. Feeling-related attributes refer to feelings that are associated with a domain, whereas value-related attributes refer to the personal significance of a domain. Theoretically, there are as many feeling-related valences as there are feelings that are possibly related to a knowledge domain (e.g., excitement, stimulation, flow). Similarly, different value-related valence beliefs are to be distinguished depending on the underlying reasons for the personal importance of a domain (e.g., self-realization, centrality within one's self-concept).

Because individual interest is conceptualized as a relatively stable characteristic, feeling- and value-related valences take the form of *enduring* domain-attribute-relations stored in long-term memory. Enduring valences are called valence beliefs, whereas temporary, current valences are referred to as valence cognitions (cf. Schiefele, 2001). It is possible to think of interest as a specific part of the network of knowledge stored in long-term memory (see also Hannover, 1998). The basic idea is that the representation of the interest domain, which itself may constitute a complex network, is related to a number of feeling- or value-related attributes (see above).

It is important to note that both feeling- and value-related valence beliefs are intrinsic in nature. Both types of beliefs are directly related to a certain interest object and are not based on the relation of this object to other objects or domains. For example, if a student highly values mathematics because competence in that domain helps him or her to get a prestigious job, then this student holds extrinsic valence beliefs which result in extrinsic motivation but not in interest (cf. Pekrun, 1988). However, it is possible that a person holds both intrinsic and extrinsic valence beliefs simultaneously with respect to the same interest object. This assumption is in line with research findings showing that intrinsic and extrinsic motivation may be present within individuals at the same time (e.g., Buff, 2001; Pintrich, 2000).

According to Krapp's (2002, 2005) person-object theory of interest, the two components of individual interest represent two fundamental regulation systems, namely a rational (or explicit) and an experiential (or implicit) system (cf. Epstein, 1990). The rational system operates at the conscious, cognitive level, whereas the experiential system operates at the subconscious, emotional level. Value-related valence beliefs are associated with the rational system, feeling-related valences result from emotional experiences. The development and maintenance of individual interests are only facilitated if both forms of valences are positive and coincide. In fact, empirical data confirm that feeling- and value-related valence beliefs tend to be highly correlated (Schiefele, 1996). Despite this close relation, it seems reasonable to expect that some individual interests are based stronger either on the experience of feelings or on the attribution of personal significance (see also Wigfield & Eccles, 1992). A similar argument may apply at the personal level: some persons are more guided by emotions when they develop interests, whereas others more strongly refer to their (conscious) values and goals.

Individual interest as a value concept resembles the notion of task value as it is proposed by Eccles, Wigfield and their colleagues (e.g., Eccles, 1983; Wigfield et al., 2006). Four motivational components of task value were defined: attainment value (importance of doing well on the task), intrinsic value (enjoyment while working on the task, or subjective interest in the task), utility value (instrumentality of the task to reach important current or future goals, engaging in the task for confirming or disconfirming salient aspects of one's self-schema), and cost (negative aspects of engaging in the task, such as amount of invested effort). Obviously, there is a conceptual overlap between feeling-related valence beliefs and intrinsic task value. In addition, individual interest seems to cover an aspect of utility value, namely the function of a task (or interest object) for confirming crucial aspects of one's self. This aspect of utility value appears to be more intrinsic than extrinsic or instrumental and coincides with the definition of value-related valence beliefs which refer to reasons for the personal importance of a domain.

Several studies have investigated the effects of *topic interest* on text learning (e.g., Alexander, Kulikowich, & Jetton, 1994; Schiefele, 1999; Schiefele & Krapp, 1996). In these studies, topic interest was used as an example of individual interest. However, this may be criticized when using interest ratings of unfamiliar topics, which do not represent enduring individual interests. As such, ratings of topic interest provide at best approximate indices for enduring individual interests. If interest is measured, for example, with respect to university students' major, then, clearly, individual interests are addressed. However, when students are asked to rate their interest in a relatively unfamiliar but appealing topic, such as Black Holes and Quasars, then these ratings can be regarded as examples of situational interest (cf. Hidi, 2000). In the latter case, the title may, for example, represent novel or incongruous information and, thus, facilitate situational interest (see above). Ainley, Hidi, and Berndorff (2002) have suggested that topic interest may be both influenced by enduring individual interests and situational factors.

Individual Interest as a Combination of Knowledge and Value

A somewhat different definition of individual interest has been offered by Renninger (2000; Renninger et al., 2002). In her view, individual interest includes two interrelated components: stored knowledge and stored value. The stored-knowledge component refers to a person's "understanding of the procedures and discourse (structural) knowledge of subject content" (Renninger, 2000, p. 376). According to Renninger (2000), individual interest only develops if a person has enough knowledge to organize new content information and, thus, becomes able to raise curiosity questions. These questions are important for creating new challenges that result in knowledge gains.

Stored value refers to feelings of competence and other positive or negative feelings that derive from the engagement with a particular subject content. More specifically, the feelings related to stored value are the result of figuring out what is understood and what still needs to be clarified (Renninger et al., 2002). As such, the stored-value component seems to be largely dependent on the process of (successfully) creating stored knowledge. When compared with the concept of feeling- and value-related valence beliefs, it becomes obvious that Renninger's value component focuses on feeling-related valence beliefs and seems to neglect value-related valence beliefs.

As noted earlier, in their qualitative empirical work, Renninger et al. (2002) distinguished between well-developed and less-developed interests. Well-developed interests involve high levels of both stored knowledge and value, whereas less-developed interests are characterized by high levels of stored knowledge and low value. This distinction seems useful when research aims at testing the role of value (or interest) by controlling for amount of knowledge. However, this approach fails to acknowledge that people vary widely with respect to the strength of their subject-related value and knowledge components and neglects combinations of low knowledge with either low or high value (Alexander et al., 1994; Tobias, 1994).

A major disadvantage of Renninger et al.'s (2002) position refers to the measurement of interest and the analysis of linear relations between individual interest and learning or achievement. Based on Renninger's approach, the measurement of interest as a continuous variable becomes difficult for two reasons. First, the construction of knowledge tests requires extensive work. Second, Renninger's work implies the exclusion of individuals with low knowledge because she has solely focused on differences among students exhibiting high knowledge and either high or low value scores. Therefore, a (continuous) measure of individual interest can only be provided for persons with high knowledge and varying levels of value. It remains unclear how individuals with low knowledge (and low or high levels of value) are to be treated within that research approach. The analysis of linear interest-achievement relations is further obscured because knowledge and value are differently related to achievement. It is to be expected that knowledge contributes more strongly than value to later achievement. In addition, different processes mediating the effects of knowledge and value have to be assumed (e.g., quality of information processing vs. investment of effort). Thus, it seems to be more parsimonious and straightforward to conceptualize interest as a value concept and to treat content-related knowledge as a separate variable. This coincides with prior research and allows for clearer research findings with respect to the influence or effectiveness of motivational vs. cognitive variables (cf. Alexander et al., 1994; Tobias, 1994).

Relations Between Situational Interest, Individual Interest, and Intrinsic Motivation

Several authors have made the attempt to clarify the relations between interest-arousing situational characteristics, situational interest, individual interest, and intrinsic motivation (cf. Byman, 1995; Deci, 1998; Hidi, 2000; Krapp, 1999; Renninger, 2000). Based on this literature and the conceptualizations presented above, a model of interrelations is proposed (see Figure 10.1). The model assumes that situational characteristics involving novel and/or complex stimuli with moderate or high coping potential generate situational interest. For example, a person with no particular individual interest in art photography reads an exciting report about a famous photographer and starts feeling stimulated, absorbed, or excited. Situational interest, in turn, facilitates intrinsic motivation to learn more about the subject content being involved in that situation (e.g., to learn more about the photographer and his art or about art photography in general).

In case of an already existing individual interest (e.g., interest in biology), it is assumed that novel or complex information (e.g., reading about the discovery of a new species) not only arouses situational interest but also activates the respective individual interest. The latter presumably contributes to the strength of experienced situational interest. The model takes into account that individual interest can also be activated by internal cues (e.g., thoughts about an interest-related event) or external cues (e.g., reading the announcement of a new book about one's interest domain) that do not involve novel or complex information and, thus, are not able to create situational interest. When an individual interest is activated, it may either indirectly (via situational interest) or directly lead to intrinsic motivation (e.g., intending to buy the new book about one's interest domain).

In addition, three reciprocal paths are included in the model. Two of these paths are based on the assumption that both situational and individual interest may lead the person to actively look for situations with novel and/or complex stimuli referring to his or her situational or individual interest. For example, a person with an individual interest in philosophy intends to watch a philo-

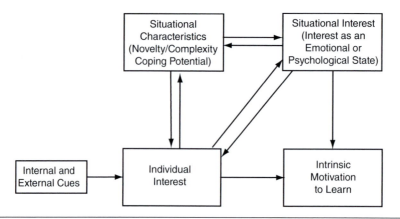

Figure 10.1 Interplay between situational interest, individual interest, and intrinsic motivation.

sophical debate on TV because he or she expects some new and exciting viewpoints. Similarly, a person who has experienced situational interest while viewing an inspiring talk show on television may decide to watch that show again because he or she expects the same interest-arousing features, even though a different topic is being discussed. Finally, the third reciprocal path refers to individual and situational interest. As was outlined above, the repeated experience of situational interest may affect object-related value cognitions and, thus, contributes to the development of individual interest.

Measurement of Interest

A review of current methods to measure interest suggests that there is a great need to develop reliable and valid instruments for assessing *situational* interest. Studies on situational interest usually asked their respondents to rate the interestingness of text segments (see below). Thus, in this work no direct measures of situational interest were taken. Instead, it was assumed that ratings of interestingness correspond with the experience of situational interest. To develop elaborated and more direct measures of situational interest, existing theories about the nature of situational interest should be used. According to Silvia's (2006) and Hidi's (2000) definitions of situational interest, an instrument measuring situational interest should include ratings of attention and persistence, positive affective involvement, and curiosity.

As pointed out already, a large part of interest research has been conducted with respect to text learning. In that area, usually quite simple measures of individual or topic interest were used (e.g., rating one's interest in a given topic on a single response scale). Only a few studies have employed more differentiated measures. For example, in our own research (e.g., Schiefele & Krapp, 1996) we have measured topic interest by means of a highly reliable scale including 10 items referring to feeling- and value-related valences (e.g., While reading the text on topic A, I expect to feel stimulated; To me personally, the topic A is meaningful).

In the past, individual interests were usually assessed by means of questionnaires. The existing inventories fall into two major categories: vocational interest and academic interest measures. The first category consists of instruments such as the Strong-Campbell-Interest-Inventory or the Kuder Preference Record (see overview by Walsh & Osipow, 1986). In these inventories, respondents are asked to indicate how much they like or prefer particular vocations, vocational activities, school subjects, or leisure activities. Individual items are allocated to subscales that represent domains of vocational interest, such as scientific, artistic, engineering, or social interests. Vocational interest inventories are designed to facilitate decisions with respect to one's vocational choice. In fact, they are well-suited for identifying broad interest domains that are preferred over other domains by a particular person. However, they are less appropriate for measuring the strength of a *specific* individual interest. This goal is better accomplished by academic interest questionnaires. Typical instruments are designed to assess individual interests in school or university subjects, such as science (Harty & Beall, 1984), physics (Hoffmann & Lehrke, 1986), biology (Tamir & Gardner, 1989), or social studies (Ataya & Kulikowich, 2002).

In developing the Study Interest Questionnaire (SIQ), we made the attempt to apply our concept of interest, as presented above, to the assessment of interest in one's university subject (Schiefele, Krapp, Wild, & Winteler, 1993). Consequently, the items of the questionnaire were supposed to measure one of three different aspects of interest: feeling-related valences (e.g., Being involved with the subject matter of my major affects my mood positively), value-related valences (e.g., It is of great personal importance to me to be able to study this particular subject), and intrinsic character of valence beliefs (e.g., I chose my major primarily because of the interesting subject matter involved). These three aspects of interest do not form separate factors. Instead, the SIQ proved to be a highly homogeneous and consistent instrument. It is noteworthy that the SIQ is not restricted to a particular subject area but may be applied to all kinds of subjects taught at the university.

Instead of referring to broad subject areas, such as mathematics or biology, and regarding them as unitary domains, some have argued that we should conceptualize interest in school subjects as being multidimensional (e.g., Gardner, 1985). In fact, most instruments designed to assess interest in a specific subject area (see above) distinguish between several dimensions. For example, Tamir and Gardner (1989) developed a questionnaire to assess interest in biology that consists of nine topical dimensions (e.g., molecular biology and biotechnology, maintaining human health) and four activity dimensions (e.g., intellectual inquiry activities, observing natural phenomena). Similarly, Hoffmann and Lehrke (1986) have measured interest in physics by differentiating between eight domains (e.g., optics, acoustics, electronics) and four activity dimensions (e.g., practical-constructive activities). In addition, these authors proposed seven different contexts for engaging with physics topics (e.g., physics as a science, physics in everyday life). Items were constructed for each combination of topic, activity, and context (e.g., I am interested in learning more about how the colors in the sky develop), thus enabling a highly differentiated picture of students' physics interest.

Although these multidimensional instruments are more differentiated than the SIQ (or similar instruments) with respect to the number of aspects of the interest domain, they are less differentiated with respect to the assessment of *interest intensity*. The SIQ uses 18 items referring to different intrinsic feeling-related and value-related valences in order to measure interest in a specific domain. In contrast, multidimensional instruments usually ask respondents to rate a variety of topics or activities on a single rating scale (e.g., How much are you interested in topic A?). The choice for a specific assessment method should depend on the nature of the domain to be investigated (e.g., simple vs. complex structured domains) and the purpose of the respective study (e.g., examining the effects of a specific interest on learning vs. the effects of instruction on interest in various aspects of a school subject). It would be also possible, of course, to combine the two methods.

In the past, only a few multidimensional instruments have been developed in order to assess school-related interests. Most of these instruments were published about two decades ago, and revised or updated versions are lacking. Instead of using multidimensional interest questionnaires, many studies that have measured interest in school subjects have employed self-constructed simple ratings of interest (Schiefele, Krapp, & Winteler, 1992). Therefore, it could be useful to intensify research on the development of multidimensional interest questionnaires. In addition, researchers who consider including interest variables in their research should not use simple or single-item measures but use more sophisticated existing instruments.

Development of Individual Interest

Past research on the development of individual interest has focused on three major issues: (a) ontogenetic development of occupational interests, (b) changes of interest in school subjects during the course of schooling, and (c) the transition from situational to individual interest. In the following section, we focus on academic interests and, thus, deal with changes in school-related interests and the transition from situational to individual interest. With respect to the development of occupational interests, see also Gottfredson (2002), Krapp (2002, 2005), Todt and Schreiber (1998), and Tracey (2001).

Changes of Interest in School Subjects

Several studies have investigated changes of (individual) interest in school subjects. The existing evidence suggests that interest in most school subjects decreases continuously during the course of schooling (cf. Hidi, 2000; Krapp, 2002). This coincides with research showing that attitudes toward school, task-value beliefs, and intrinsic motivation tend to deteriorate when children get older (e.g., Anderman & Maehr, 1994; Gottfried, Marcoulides, Gottfried, Oliver, & Guerin, 2007; Harter, 1981; Watt, 2004; see Wigfield et al., 2006, for a review). As has been summarized by Krapp (2002), the decrease of interests is particularly strong in the natural sciences (mathematics, physics, chemistry). It should be noted, however, that a decrease in interest is not always found for all topics within a given subject area. In addition, the development of interests depends on context conditions, school type, and gender. Todt, Arbinger, Seitz, and Wildgrube (1974) report that girls' decreasing interest in biology during secondary school only refers to zoological and botanical topics, whereas biology interest increases for topics related to human beings and ecology. Hoffmann, Lehrke, and Todt (1985; Hoffmann & Lehrke, 1986) showed that interest in physics is low for both girls and boys when physics is taught primarily within a scientific context (with an emphasis on the validity of general physical laws). In contrast, physics interest is rather strong (for both girls and boys) when the teacher is able to relate physical principles and facts to practical problems and the students' everyday life.

There are several possible reasons for the general decline of interest in school subjects (cf. Baumert & Köller, 1998). One attempt to explain this decline refers to a mismatch between the curriculum and the general interests of students. With respect to science education, for example, it is assumed that the strong scientific emphasis of instruction neglects students' everyday life experiences (see above). Other explanations maintain that interest development outside of school becomes increasingly important with students' age and that students' increasing desire for self-determination conflicts with the restrictive learning environment of schools (Eccles et al., 1991).

Baumert and Köller (1998) proposed that the decline of interest in academic domains over the course of secondary level I (grades 5 to 9) may also result from a process of differentiation (Todt, 1990; Todt & Schreiber, 1998). In late childhood and early adolescence, students become more and more aware of their specific strengths and weaknesses. The process of comparing one's strengths and weaknesses affects the development of interests. Students tend to show stronger interest in those domains for which they have a higher self-concept of ability (cf. Denissen, Zarrett, & Eccles, 2007; Köller, Schnabel, & Baumert, 1998; Rottinghaus, Larson, & Borgen, 2003). In addition, the transition from school to vocational education and the labor market leads students to select and intensify specific interests while abandoning others. In line with these considerations, it was found that correlations between different interest domains (e.g., English, mathematics) decrease over time (Köller et al., 1998).

In line with Baumert and Köller's (1998) proposition, Krapp and Lewalter (2001) were able to demonstrate both a general decline of interest in vocational education and the selective development of new and specific job- or training-related interests. In a longitudinal study with insurance business students, Krapp and Lewalter found that students' general interest in vocational training contents dropped significantly during the 2-year training program. However, interview data revealed a positive developmental trend: all students in the sample reported that they had discovered new areas of training-related interest. The authors concluded that a process of selection or differentiation was taking place. Probably, the students were focusing only on few selected aspects of their vocational training and, thus, reduced their interest in other training contents. This process results in a decline of students' general interest in the training program and, at the same time, in the development of new specific interests.

Although the decline of school-related interests is well-documented, the reasons for this negative development still need to be clarified. The present evidence suggests two different processes. On the one hand, a number of factors such as the neglect of students' everyday life experiences, the development of interests outside of school, and the restrictive character of learning environments contribute to low interest levels. Thus, instructional programs to increase interest in school subjects emphasized students' everyday life experience, referred to their general interests, and allowed for self-determination (e.g., Hoffmann, 2002; see also below). On the other hand, average interest scores may decrease because of a process of interest differentiation. From that point of view, the decline of interests at least in part reflects a positive development, namely the selective focusing on specific interests. However, more direct evidence for the effect of interest differentiation on the development of school-related interests is needed.

From Situational to Individual Interest

Research on general stages of interest development (e.g., Gottfredson, 2002) and on changes in school-related interests does not explain how a particular individual interest develops. Hidi and Renninger (2006; see also Krapp, 2002) described the development of an individual interest as a four-phase process that starts with a first experience of situational interest and results in a well-developed individual interest.

The *first phase* of interest development consists of triggered situational interest and is defined as an emotional state (see above). Typically, situational interest is initiated by external factors in a given learning environment. In school, for example, situational interest may be created by an exciting and vivid lesson that contains novel and surprising information. In addition, the triggering of situational interest can be supported by instructional conditions that include group work, puzzles, or computers (Mitchell, 1993).

The *second phase* of interest development—maintained situational interest—involves the repeated and increasingly persistent experience of situational interest. Maintained situational interest is facilitated by tasks that are personally meaningful and involving. In addition, project-based learning, cooperative group work, or one-to-one tutoring contribute to the maintenance of situational interest.

Maintained situational interest may initiate the development of an individual interest. Therefore, the *third phase* of interest development is characterized by emerging individual interest. From the theoretical perspective expressed in the present chapter, it is assumed that the repeated and persistent experience of situational interest only leads to emerging individual interest when value cognitions referring to feeling- and value-related attributes are involved and when these repeatedly occurring cognitions transform into enduring valence beliefs (see above). For example, when a student repeatedly experiences situational interest in the science classroom, he or she will form associations between science and positive feelings and values. The emerging formation of stored valence beliefs may motivate the person to seek out opportunities to reengage in science activities providing the experience of interest.

The *fourth phase* refers to well-developed individual interest. According to Hidi and Renninger's (2006) definition, a well-developed individual interest is characterized by stronger valence beliefs and more stored knowledge as compared to an emerging interest. As has been argued above, stored knowledge should not be an integral part of the interest concept. However, it is likely, that content knowledge increases with interest development (Tobias, 1994). In my view, the most important feature of a well-developed interest refers to the intensity and variety of valence beliefs. It is to be assumed that a well-developed interest consists of strong associations between the interest object and several feeling- and value-related attributes. Compared to an emerging interest, these associations are presumably easier to activate by internal or external cues and, consequently, exert more influence on the regulation of behavior. For example, individuals with a well-developed interest more often than others choose interest-related activities, sustain long-term constructive and creative endeavors, and persist when interest-related tasks or activities are difficult (cf. Hidi & Renninger, 2006).

The four-phase model of interest development offers a useful framework for research on the transition from situational to individual interest. However, past research on interest development has been mostly descriptive and, thus, empirical support for the proposed four-phase model is limited. Recently, Guthrie et al. (2006) have provided evidence that a high number of stimulating tasks related to reading (during several weeks of integrated reading and science instruction for third-grade students) increased longer term intrinsic reading motivation. Stimulating tasks involved mainly hands-on observations and experiments and were supposed to create situational interest (which was not directly measured, however.) Although intrinsic reading motivation should not be equated with individual interest in a particular subject content, the findings of Guthrie et al. are in line with Hidi and Renninger's (2006) assumption that the repeated experience of situational interest may lead to individual interest.

Interest and Learning

Interest and Text Learning

The greatest amount of research on academic interest concerns studies on the relation between interest and learning from text. Given the long tradition of that research and the multitude of studies (cf. Schiefele, 1996, 1999), it seems obvious that interest has been considered to be a major motivational condition of text learning (Alexander et al., 1994; Tobias, 1994).

Prior studies have either investigated the effects of *interestingness* of text materials (as an indicator of situational interest) or *topic interest* (as an indicator of individual interest) on text learning (cf. Schiefele, 1996, 1999). In studies on situational interest, subjects usually were asked to rate the interestingness of text segments (sentences or paragraphs). In most cases, intraindividual comparisons between lowly and highly interesting sentences were performed (e.g., Anderson, 1982). Although empirical tests are lacking, this research assumes that ratings of interestingness correspond with the experience of situational interest.

In order to measure topic interest, respondents had to rate their level of interest in the text topic before reading the text. However, as was mentioned above, topic interest may not always be equated with individual interest. This is especially true when individuals have to rate their interest in unfamiliar topics. In this case, their ratings are not based on stable valence beliefs.

Situational Interest Earlier reviews of the literature on situational interest (e.g., Alexander & Jetton,

1996; Hidi, 1990; Schiefele, 1996, 1999; Wade, 1992) yielded similar results as were obtained for individual or topic interest (see below). Schiefele (1996) analyzed 14 relevant studies and found an average correlation of .33 between situational interest and text learning. Findings suggested that the relation between situational interest and text learning is independent of factors such as text length, readability, importance of text or text segments, unit of analysis (sentence vs. passage vs. whole text), nature of text (narrative vs. expository), method of learning (e.g., recognition vs. recall), age (or grade level), and reading ability (or intelligence).

In a recent study, Guthrie et al. (2006; see also above) compared four classes with high versus low numbers of stimulating tasks that were designed to increase situational interest. All four classes were part of an intervention program (Concept-Oriented Reading Instruction) in which teachers linked reading fiction and nonfiction books to science activities. The number of stimulating hands-on science activities varied between classes. This enabled the authors to select two classes with high numbers and two classes with low numbers of interesting activities. A comparison between the students in the two types of classes not only revealed differences in students' intrinsic reading motivation (see above) but also in their reading comprehension. Students in the two classes with high numbers of stimulating activities exhibited significantly higher means in a standardized reading comprehension test than the students in the other two classes.

An important research issue refers to the role of attention as a mediator of the effect of situational interest on text learning. In a sample of school children, Anderson (1982) found that interestingness ratings of sentences were positively associated with persistence of attention (reading time), intensity of attention (secondary task reaction time), and sentence recall. Only reading time, in contrast to reaction time, was positively related to sentence recall. Contrary to expectations, neither indicator of attention could mediate a significant portion of the effect of interest on learning.

Shirey and Reynolds (1988) obtained different results by using a sample of university students. In their study, interestingness of sentences was *positively* correlated with learning and *negatively* with both persistence and intensity of attention (see also Bernstein, 1955; Wild & Schiefele, 1994). In accordance with Anderson (1982), a mediating effect of attention could be ruled out. Based on interview data, Shirey and Reynolds (1988) assumed that adult readers are more strategic and efficient than younger readers. They tend to allocate more attention to less interesting information because this information is harder to learn. An alternative explanation has been offered by Hidi (1990, 1995). She argued that attention may be either understood as automatic and spontaneous or controlled and effortful. Hidi suggested that interesting learning materials evoke spontaneous, involuntary, and effortless engagement with these materials, whereas less interesting materials require voluntary, active, and effortful engagement. Therefore, learning less interesting text elements leads to stronger involvement of attentional resources. According to Hidi, situational interest should increase spontaneous, involuntary attention and, thus, result in faster reading and secondary task reaction times. In fact, McDaniel, Waddill, Finstad, and Bourg (2000) were able demonstrate that secondary task reaction times were significantly slower for low interest narratives than for high interest narratives.

Topic Interest In an earlier meta-analysis (Schiefele, 1996), an average correlation of .27 between topic interest and text learning was found. Furthermore, the findings suggested that the relation between topic interest and text learning is not affected by factors such as text length, nature of text, method of learning test, age (or grade level), reading ability, and text difficulty. In addition, the reviewed studies support the conclusion that interest and prior knowledge do have independent effects on text learning. However, the effects of prior knowledge were stronger than those of topic interest. Usually, only low to moderate correlations between topic interest and prior knowledge were found.

There is some evidence that topic interest better predicts indicators of deep-level than of surface-level learning. For example, Groff (1962) was able to show that topic interest was more strongly related to outcomes from a multiple-choice test referring to text organization, inferences, and conclusions than to outcomes from a multiple-choice test referring to explicit details in the text. In accordance with these findings, Kunz, Drewniak, Hatalak, and Schön (1992) found higher correlations between topic interest and performance at an application task (transfer of text content to a concrete example) than between interest and standard indicators of text learning (free recall and multiple-choice comprehension questions). Both studies reported higher correlations for prior knowledge and ability factors than for interest and all indicators of text learning.

In two of our own studies, the attempt was made to test the differential effect of topic interest on deep-level and surface-level indicators of text learning (Schiefele, 1990; Schiefele & Krapp, 1996). In the first study (Schiefele, 1990), three different indicators of levels of learning were assessed (by means of free-response questions): recall of simple facts, recall of complex facts, and deep (or inference-based) comprehension. Schiefele and Krapp (1996) created several different indicators of free recall, such as number of main ideas, elaborations, and coherence of recall (of idea units and main ideas). The findings of both studies showed that topic interest was most highly related to outcome measures indicating deep levels of learning, such as deep comprehension, recall of main ideas, elaborations, and coherence of recall of main ideas. The associations between topic interest and other indicators of learning were lower or not significant. All of the relations between topic interest and learning were independent of prior knowledge and cognitive ability. The stronger associations between interest and deep-level text learning as opposed to surface-level text learning may be explained by two assumptions: (1) deep-level indicators require more cognitive effort than surface-level measures, and (2) interested readers are more willing than less interested readers to invest effort in order to answer challenging and complex questions.

Andre and Windschitl (2003) reported a number of studies that were aimed at facilitating the understanding of electric current flow. In these studies, college students received either a conceptual change text (designed to challenge alternative conceptions and promote conceptual change) or a regular science text (or, alternatively, an augmented science text with additional explanatory diagrams). Across various studies, conceptual change texts led to superior conceptual understanding. The authors also assessed students' interest and prior experience with physics and electricity as well as their verbal ability. By means of multiple regression analyses, a significant relation between interest and conceptual understanding was revealed. That relation proved to be independent of text type, gender, verbal ability, and prior experience. Moreover, interest was found to affect posttest understanding even when a measure of pretest understanding was taken into account. Thus, in line with earlier findings, Andre and Windschitl (2003) were able to demonstrate significant effects of interest on conceptual understanding that were independent of ability and prior knowledge. As an explanation of the effects of interest on conceptual change, the authors argued that interest facilitates the degree of involvement that leads to deeper processing.

The measures of levels of learning used in earlier studies (see above) were not based on a specific theory. Therefore, we created theoretically based text learning indicators by referring to the text processing theory of van Dijk and Kintsch (1983; Kintsch, 1998). This theory assumes that a given text is processed and represented at different levels: the verbatim, the propositional, and the situational level. The verbatim representation contains the text's superficial structure. The propositional representation refers to the meaning of the text, and the situational component is a model of the situation described by the text (e.g., people, objects, actions) that may also include analogical or pictorial information. The situation model represents the deepest level of text learning. The strength of the different types of text representation is usually determined by means of sentence recognition or sentence verification tests. For example, a strong situational representation is indicated by a good differentiation between correct and false inferences (e.g., Schmalhofer & Glavanov, 1986).

The attempt to demonstrate effects of topic interest on the situational text representation was not particularly successful. In two earlier studies (Schiefele, 1991, 1996), no significant relation between topic interest and situational text representation was found. The same result was obtained in a more recent study (Schaffner & Schiefele, 2008) with a large sample of 15-year-old students. A complex model was tested that revealed direct and significant effects of prior knowledge, intrinsic reading motivation, cognitive ability, and metacognitive strategy knowledge on the situational text representation. However, topic interest was not found to be a significant predictor of text learning.

Schaffner, Schiefele, and Schneider (2004) reported similar results. However, they used different text materials and different measures of text learning. For two of the texts, standard comprehension tests were administered consisting of several multiple-choice and free-response questions. The two tests were used as manifest indicators for a latent variable. In accordance with prior studies, this standard measure of reading comprehension was significantly and directly predicted by topic interest, although relevant cognitive predictors (see above) were part of the structural equation model.

In sum, these findings suggest that topic interest will not exert effects on the situational text representation, at least not if relevant cognitive predictors are taken into account. Obviously, text learning indicators based on multiple-choice or free-response comprehension items are more predictable and more strongly affected by motivational variables such as interest.

There is almost no *experimental* research on the effects of topic interest on text learning. This is in contrast to studies on intrinsic motivation which have demonstrated that it is possible to induce intrinsic and extrinsic motivation through appropriate instructions (cf. Schaffner & Schiefele, 2007). Recently, we conducted an experiment (with ninth-grade students) and examined the effects of experimentally induced intrinsic and extrinsic motivation (as compared to a neutral condition) on topic interest, test anxiety, and text learning (Schaffner & Schiefele, 2007). The intrinsic motivation instruction was aimed at increasing interest in the text's topic, whereas the extrinsic motivation instruction emphasized the evaluation of students' learning skills. Text-related interest and test anxiety were assessed before and after the experimental instruction as well as after the text has been read. An inference verification test was administered to assess students' situational text representation. The results showed the expected effects of type of instruction on interest and test anxiety when measured directly after the treatment. With respect to the situational text representation, no significant main effects were obtained. Instead, an interesting interaction between type of instruction and pretest interest was observed: Only students with high pretest interest exhibited the expected difference between the intrinsic and the extrinsic motivation instruction, i.e. they showed stronger situational text representations when they received an interest-enhancing instruction as compared to the neutral and the extrinsic motivation instruction. The reported interaction effect can be explained by Sansone's *goal congruence model* (Sansone, Sachau, & Weir, 1989; Sansone & Thoman, 2006). According to that model, a specific motivational context affects intrinsic motivation or interest positively only if that context is congruent with a person's goal orientation. In our study, obviously, the intrinsic motivation instruction was congruent with high interest students' motivational orientation. Therefore, only high interest students' learning from text was enhanced by the intrinsic motivation instruction.

Interest, School Achievement, and Academic Choices

There is ample evidence that individual or subject matter interest and school achievement (grades, standardized tests) are positively correlated. In a review of relevant research, Schiefele et al. (1992) reported that, on average, the strength of subject area interest accounts for about 10% of observed achievement variance. Both grade level and nature of subject area did not influence that relation. However, it was found that male students' achievement is more strongly associated with their interest level than was the case for female students. Schiefele et al. (1992) concluded that the strength and causal nature of the interest-achievement relation cannot be definitively determined unless other relevant predictors are taken into account and unless longitudinal data are available. For example, most of the reviewed studies did not include indicators of cognitive ability or prior achievement. Earlier studies, however, suggest that interest and ability are not strongly interrelated and contribute independently of each other to the prediction of achievement (cf. Schiefele et al., 1992; Schiefele & Csikszentmihalyi, 1995).

Another unresolved issue pertains to the causal relation between interest and achievement. On the one hand, it may be argued that the perception of successful performance leads to positive affect and enhanced interest. On the other hand, interest may contribute to high levels of achievement because it facilitates effort, elaborative processes, and strategy use (e.g., McWhaw & Abrami, 2001). In a longitudinal study, Köller, Baumert, and Schnabel (2001) were able to show that a reciprocal relation between interest and achievement is likely. A large sample of students from academically selected schools (*gymnasium*) in Germany was tested at three time points: end of Grade 7, end of Grade 10, and middle of Grade 12. The focus of measurement was on interest and achievement in mathematics (as measured by a standardized test based on items from the TIMSS study). In the German *gymnasium*, students have the opportunity at the end of Grade 10 to either choose a basic or an advanced mathematics course. Structural equation analyses showed that interest in Grade 7 had no significant effects on achievement in either Grade 10 or Grade 12. In contrast, achievement at the end of Grade 7 did significantly affect interest in Grade 10. High achievers expressed more interest in mathematics than low achievers. There were, however, significant direct and indirect effects of Grade 10 interest on Grade 12 achievement, although Grade 10 achievement was taken into account. The indirect effect of interest was mediated by *course selection*: Highly interested students were more likely to choose an advanced course (ß = .54). Course selection, in turn, affected Grade 12 achievement significantly (ß = .20). The direct effect of Grade 10 interest on Grade 12 achievement (ß = .19) was somewhat weaker than the direct effect of Grade 10 achievement (ß = .43).

The findings from this study, as well as those from other studies (see Baumert & Köller, 1998; Marsh, Trautwein, Lüdtke, Köller, & Baumert, 2005), suggest that at least at the lower secondary school level interest is either a nonsignificant or weak antecedent of achievement. Köller et al. (2001) argue that in German lower secondary schools students' motivation is mostly regulated by extrinsic incentives and values (e.g., regular written tests, parental reinforcements). Consequently, interest only plays a marginal role in initiating and maintaining academic activities. In upper secondary school classes, the frequency of written examination and, thus, the impact of extrinsic incentives decreases. Therefore, interest is gaining more influence on the regulation of learning activities. This assumption is supported by the significant direct effect of Grade 10 interest on Grade 12 achievement. Moreover, highly interested students more often chose an advanced mathematics course, resulting in higher achievement levels at the end of Grade 12. This is in line with research on academic choices by Eccles (1983) who presented evidence that the effects of motivational characteristics on academic choices are more substantial than those on achievement or learning (see also Schiefele & Csikszentmihalyi, 1995). Moreover, in Köller et al.'s (2001) study, earlier achievement (as measured by a standardized test) did not predict choice behavior. This corresponds to findings by Wigfield and Eccles (2000) and Marsh and Yeung (1997) suggesting that academic choices are mainly influenced by subjective measures such as self-concept of ability and interest (see also Bong, 2001; Lapan, Shaughnessy, & Boggs, 1996).

Contextual Influences on Interest

In the past, motivation theory and research has helped to develop instructional practices and programs that foster student motivation. Most of this research was based on the different constructs tied to achievement motivation (e.g., self-efficacy, achievement goals, values), and intrinsic motivation (cf. Brophy, 2004; Maehr & Midgley, 1991; Stipek, 1996). According to Stipek (1996), "although different factors have been emphasized at different times in the history of research on achievement motivation, all are assumed to play a role. Thus, teachers who want to provide an educational program that maximizes student motivation must attend to all of these sets of factors" (p. 86). In my view, the same applies to interest: most of the factors that have been found to increase motivation to learn and to achieve, should also—more or less—exert influence on interest. For example, programs to enhance achievement motivation typically focus on realistic goal setting, effort attributions, positive self-evaluation, and expectation of success (or self-efficacy). Such interventions strongly support a person's need for competence and, as such, represent also effective means to increase individual interest (e.g., Krapp, 2005). Despite these associations between various instructional methods and interest development, I will put a focus here on methods that have been more closely linked to the enhancement of *individual* interest or habitual intrinsic motivation. Conditions to promote *situational* interest mostly referred to text-related characteristics and will not be reiterated here.

Prior research on fostering interest and intrinsic motivation (e.g., Bergin, 1999; Deci, Vallerand, Pelletier, & Ryan, 1991; Prenzel & Lankes, 1989; Stipek, 1996) suggests four categories of interest-enhancing interventions: competence, self-determination, social relatedness, and personal meaning (cf. Schiefele, 2004). Interest-enhancing interventions are directed at the formation of subject-related valence beliefs. By means of facilitating the experience of competence, self-determination, and social relatedness, this goal is reached only *indirectly*, through satisfaction of basic psychological needs (see also Eccles et al., 1991, and Krapp, 2005). Contrastingly, interest is more *directly* facilitated by interventions addressing the meaningfulness of a given subject area (e.g., by emphasizing its significance for everyday life).

The advancement of *competence perceptions* aims at emphasizing the relation between competence gains and one's effort and strategic behavior. Thus, the major goal involves strengthening students' confidence in their abilities. This goal may be accomplished by means of positive competence feedback and encouragement (e.g., reinforcing even small progress, evaluation based on mastery rather than on social norms), active participation (e.g., hands-on activities, transforming a short story into a play), well-structured and concrete presentations (e.g., using examples), and appropriate task difficulty (i.e. challenging tasks that can be completed with a reasonable amount of effort; e.g., Bergin, 1999; Guthrie et al., 2006; Hannover, 1998).

The positive association between perceptions of competence and motivation has long been established (e.g., Schunk, 1991). Recently, strong evidence was presented for a positive relation between self-concept of ability and individual interest. Denissen et al. (2007) conducted a longitudinal study in which they examined the intraindividual coupling between academic achievement, interest, and self-concept of ability in a large sample of school students between grades 1 and 12. They found the strongest coupling between interest and self-concept of ability. In addition, the degree of coupling increased across time. The results from Marsh et al.'s (2005) longitudinal study suggest reciprocal effects between interest and academic self-concept. However, the causal path from interest to self-concept was found to be lower than the reverse path (see also Mac Iver, Stipek, & Daniels, 1991, and Rottinghaus et al., 2003).

The facilitation of *self-determination* aims at increasing feelings of autonomy. Intrinsic motivation and interest can only be developed when individuals have choice and perceive themselves as the cause of their own behavior (cf. Assor, Kaplan, & Roth, 2002; deCharms, 1984; Deci & Ryan, 1985). In order to increase autonomy, students need to have more control over their learning activities. Several methods are available to achieve this goal. First, students may participate in determining the goals and content of what is being taught in school (e.g., at the beginning of a school week, students and teachers agree on topics, tasks, goals, and a time- and work-schedule). Second, students should be given more flexibility for determining when and how they complete assignments. This may be realized by instructional methods that allow for more self-regulation (e.g., project-method, cooperative learning). Third, students are taught techniques for assessment and documentation of their learning progress (e.g., scoring their own written work, constructing learning curves).

Recently, Kunter, Baumert, and Köller (2007) examined the effects of classroom management strategies (rule clarity and teacher monitoring) on the development of interest in mathematics. The authors argued that pre-structured and well-organized learning environments should foster the experience of autonomy and competence in class and, thus, support students' interest. Accordingly, the results showed that both rule clarity and monitoring affected subject matter interest, and these effects were partially mediated by the experience of autonomy and competence (need satisfaction).

Social relatedness encompasses the need to feel securely connected to other persons in the social context and to be "worthy and capable of love and respect" (Connell & Wellborn, 1991, p. 51). The facilitation of social relatedness aims at increasing students' feelings of relatedness to their teachers and classmates. Presumably, this helps to make these activities and the related subject content more meaningful. Skinner and Belmont (1993), for example, proposed teamwork and involvement with teachers as appropriate methods to enhance social relatedness. Teamwork is characterized by small groups of students working on a personally meaningful project, having extensive social exchange, and taking responsibility for one's own contribution to the project. Involvement with teachers is facilitated when the teacher expresses liking, understanding, or sympathy for his or her students, shows interest in their learning progress, and is available in case of need (Skinner & Belmont, 1993).

The factors discussed so far affect students' interests indirectly, primarily by influencing their perceptions of competence, self-determination, and social relatedness. Even when students feel competent, self-determined, or socially related, however, they will not be interested in subject content that is boring, repetitive, or meaningless (Stipek, 1996). Therefore, we now turn to interventions that are apt to influence individual interest more directly. The main goal of these interventions is to enhance the *meaningfulness and value of subject content* for the learner. Several methods have been proposed and discussed in the past (e.g., Bergin, 1999; Krapp, 2005; Stipek, 1996; see also Guthrie, Wigfield, & Perencevich, 2004, for discussion of a reading comprehension instruction program that focuses on enhancing students' motivation for reading along with their comprehension):

1. Meaningfulness may be facilitated when the teacher expresses his or her own interest in the subject being taught (Bergin, 1999; Schunk et al., 2008). It is assumed that interest is contagious and can best be conveyed if the teacher functions as an interested model and expresses enthusiasm about a given topic or domain. For example, the teacher may tell students how he or she became interested in his or her subject area, what he or she feels when working on a task or a problem in his or her domain, or how excited he or she is about a particular topic. This may be further supported by expressive teacher behaviors, such as physical movement, eye contact, and humor (Perry, Magnusson, Parsonson, & Dickens, 1986).

2. Probably one of the most important and effective means to induce individual interest consists in highlighting the practical implications of subject content and its relation to students' everyday life. As has been mentioned above, Hoffmann and her collaborators (Häussler & Hoffmann, 2002; Hoffmann et al., 1985; Hoffmann & Lehrke, 1986) found evidence that interest in physics is strengthened by relating physical principles and facts to practical problems or activities (e.g., constructing a technical device, exploring something). Therefore, problem-based and constructivist teaching methods should help to increase students' interest (Hickey, 1997).

3. New subject content may become more interesting to students if that content is associated with already existing individual interests (e.g., Assor et al., Meece, 1991). Thus, it is to be recommended to assess students' interests or to refer to surveys of students' interests. For example, girls' interest in physics could be heightened by relating physical laws to examples which refer to girls' natural interests (e.g., explaining the principles of a pump by referring to the human heart; cf. Hoffmann, 2002). Also with respect to physics lessons, it has been found that those topics that are most interesting to students (e.g., astrophysics, aviation, electronics, nuclear energy) are rarely dealt with in school (Hoffmann & Lehrke, 1986). Including these topics to a larger degree could help to foster students' general interest in physics. Similarly, students are interested in certain contexts of physics, such as particular technical applications, but they dislike contexts favored by the standard curriculum (e.g., the description and explanation of physical experiments and phenomena). Again, taking into account students' already existing interests to a larger degree could help to maintain or even increase their interests in school subjects across time.

In a recent study, Durik and Harackiewicz (2007) were able to show that catch facets (e.g., appealing visual stimuli, cartoons) designed to increase situational interest in a specific math technique were only effective for students with low individual interest in math, whereas task interest of students high on individual interest was undermined. In addition, the authors tested the effects of a hold facet on task interest by emphasizing personal utility. Here, they found that task interest was promoted among participants with high individual interest and reduced among those with low individual interest. These findings are important because they suggest that strategies to increase interest depend on the already existing interest levels. A similar conclusion was drawn by Schaffner and Schiefele (2007; see above). Obviously, students with low individual interest respond positively to catch facets fostering immediate involvement with a task. Students with higher individual interest do not require external stimulation in order to become involved with the task. For them, information pertaining to the personal utility of the task strengthens already existing valence beliefs. In contrast, individuals with low interest "might be especially cautious when presented with the opportunity to become personally invested in a domain that is new or threatening" (Durik & Harackiewicz, 2007, p. 608). Consequently, information designed to infuse a task with personal meaning threatens these individuals und causes them to reduce their interest.

Concluding Comments

The present chapter reviewed conceptualizations and measuring instruments of interest, aspects of interest development, the role of interest in learning, and contextual influences on interest. The literature proved to be relatively consistent with respect to the distinction between a temporary, state-like and an enduring, dispositional form of interest. However, there is some disagreement as to how these forms of interest should be defined. It was argued to conceptualize situational interest as an emotion for three reasons: First, situational interest can be defined according to empirically validated components that are typical for emotions, namely facial expression, physiological state, subjective experience, behaviors, and goals. Second, Silvia's (2005) proposed appraisal structure of interest provides a straightforward theoretical framework for integrating the multitude of assumed sources of situational interest. Third, by defining situational interest as an emotion, it can be distinguished more clearly from intrinsic motivation (see also Fig. 10.1).

The different conceptions of individual interest disagree mainly with respect to the role of knowledge. Renninger (2000) maintains that individual interest is evoked only when a person has both high value and high knowledge of an activity or subject area, whereas others (e.g., Tobias, 1994) argued that value is orthogonal to prior knowledge and that individual interest may be accompanied with both lower and higher levels of knowledge. Although the disagreement on conceptualizing individual interest is of considerable theoretical importance, it may be less relevant with respect to its practical, research-related consequences. As far as concrete research is concerned, the two conceptions possibly complement each other. For example, Renninger's (2000) construct of individual interest is appropriate when research aims at examining the specific effect of value (or interest) on learning processes *when learners exhibit high levels of knowledge*. It is most likely that only a terminology problem will remain: Renninger theorizes about value when others speak of interest. A fruitful coexistence of these deviating approaches depends, however, on the use of separate and both reliable and valid measures of knowledge and value. As long as high quality measures of the involved variables are available, the findings may be interpretable within different theoretical frameworks.

The model presented in Figure 10. 1 represents the attempt to clarify the relations among situational interest, individual interest, and intrinsic motivation. For the sake of simplicity, only one state of interest is proposed. Thus, it is assumed that the experience of interest is basically the same, no matter how it is created (through situational characteristics or the activation of individual interest). However, empirical research is needed to justify this assumption. The model further implies that intrinsic motivation plays a key role in mediating the effects of both situational and individual interest on learning and achievement. Another important implication of the model relates to the development of interests. As was outlined above, situational interest may result in (intrinsic) motivation to seek conditions that again lead to the experience of situational interest.

If this cycle of causal interrelations is repeated and value cognitions are involved, the development of an individual interest becomes more likely.

Past research on the development of individual interests was focused on temporal changes with respect to interest in school subjects. Because of the general decline of interests during the school years, numerous studies analyzed the potential causes of that negative developmental trend. Some authors argued that the well-documented decline of subject matter interests does not necessarily represent a negative outcome. By contrast, it may be the result of a process of differentiation. This process happens because adolescents adapt their interests to their abilities. In addition, they face occupational decisions and are forced to select and intensify specific interests while eliminating others. More research on the relative importance of the different causes of the decline of school-related interests is needed.

Hidi and Renninger's (2006) four-phase model of interest development represents the attempt to describe the process from the first experience of situational interest to the development of a well-developed individual interest. As such, the model is not restricted to a particular category of interests (e.g., interest in school subjects) but applies to all possible forms of interest. Although the model has high plausibility, direct empirical tests of its validity have not been accomplished yet. Illustrations of the model by individual cases (see Hidi & Renninger, 2006, pp. 116–117) only provide preliminary evidence. Future work in that area should address, for example, the following questions: Is the assumption of four phases sufficient to describe the process of interest development? What are the relevant conditions that facilitate the transformation from repeated experience of situational interest to emerging individual interest? How does the model account for the finding of a strong coupling between interest and self-concept of ability?

There is relatively strong evidence for a substantive relation between both situational and individual interest and indicators of learning, particularly with respect to text learning. Although interest effects on learning are on the average only of small or medium size, it is noteworthy that interest effects are even observable when relevant cognitive variables are taken into account. Despite these positive findings, there is a need for more experimental research, for clarifying the relation between interest and different learning indicators within more complex models, and for identifying relevant mediator variables.

A particularly interesting and important finding refers to the impact of interest on academic choices. Köller et al. (2001) suggested that interest becomes more influential if students are allowed to self-regulate their learning activities to a larger degree. This influence becomes even larger when students have choices, such as the choice between regular and advanced courses (see also Wigfield & Eccles, 2000; Schiefele & Csikszentmihalyi, 1995). It follows, that an important task for future research would be to further substantiate Köller et al.'s proposition that choice and self-regulation enhance the importance of (individual) interests (see also Deci, 1998).

Finally, contextual influences on individual interest were reviewed. Indirect and direct effects on interest facilitation were distinguished. Indirect effects occur mainly through satisfaction of basic psychological needs, such as competence, autonomy, and relatedness. Direct effects are based on enhancing the meaningfulness of subject content, e.g., by expression of teacher interest, emphasis on practical implications, and reference to existing or natural interests of students. Future research on the facilitation of interest should take into account, that (a) specific interventions may interact with pre-existing levels of individual interest (e.g., Durik & Harackiewicz, 2007; Schaffner & Schiefele, 2007), and that (b) instructional practices depend on each other and are more effective in combination (Stipek, 1996). Thus, an important goal for the future development of interest enhancing environments consists in designing comprehensive approaches to classroom intervention that include both indirect and direct methods to promote individual interest.

References

Ainley, M. & Hidi, S. (2002). Dynamic measures for studying interest and learning. In P. R. Pintrich & M. L. Maehr (Eds.), *New directions in measures and methods* (pp. 43–76). Amsterdam: Elsevier.

Ainley, M., Hidi, S., & Berndorff, D. (2002). Interest, learning, and the psychological process that mediate their relationship. *Journal of Educational Psychology, 94*, 545–561.

Alexander, P. A., & Jetton, T. L. (1996). The role of importance and interest in the processing of text. *Educational Psychology Review, 8*, 89–121.

Alexander, P. A., Kulikowich, J. M., & Jetton, T. L. (1994). The role of subject-matter knowledge and interest in the processing of linear and nonlinear texts. *Review of Educational Research, 64*, 201–252.

Anderman, E. M., & Maehr, M. L. (1994). Motivation and schooling in the middle grades. *Review of Educational Research, 64*, 287–309.

Anderson, R. C. (1982). Allocation of attention during reading. In A. Flammer & W. Kintsch (Eds.), *Discourse processing* (pp. 292–313). Amsterdam: North-Holland.

Andre, T., & Windschitl, M. (2003). Interest, epistemological belief, and intentional conceptual change. In G. M. Sinatra & P. R. Pintrich (Eds.), *Intentional conceptual change* (pp. 173–197). Mahwah, NJ: Erlbaum.

Assor, A., Kaplan, H., & Roth, G. (2002). Choice is good, but relevance is excellent: Autonomy-enhancing and suppressing teacher behaviours predicting students' engagement in schoolwork. *British Journal of Educational Psychology, 72*, 261–278.

Ataya, R. L., & Kulikowich, J. M. (2002). Measuring interest in reading social studies materials. *Educational and Psychological Measurement, 62*, 1028–1041.

Baumert, J., & Köller, O. (1998). Interest research in secondary level I: An overview. In L. Hoffmann, A. Krapp, K. A. Renninger, & J. Baumert (Eds.), *Interest and learning* (pp. 241–156). Kiel, Germany: Institute for Science Education.

Bergin, D. A. (1999). Influences on classroom interest. *Educational Psychologist, 34*, 87–98.

Bernstein, M. R. (1955). Relationship between interest and reading comprehension. *Journal of Educational Research, 49*, 283–288.

Bong, M. (2001). Role of self-efficacy and task-value in predicting college students' course performance and future enrollment intentions. *Contemporary Educational Psychology, 26*, 553–570.

Brophy, J. E. (2004). *Motivating students to learn*. Mahwah, NJ: Erlbaum.

Buff, A. (2001). Warum lernen Schülerinnen und Schüler? Eine explorative Studie zur Lernmotivation auf der Basis qualitativer Daten [Reasons for students' learning: An exploratory and qualitative study of motivation to learn]. *Zeitschrift für Entwicklungspsychologie und Pädagogische Psychologie, 33*, 157–164.

Byman, R. (1995). Curiosity, interest and intrinsic motivation: A conceptual analysis. In P. Kansanen (Ed.), *Discussions on some educational issues IV* (Research Report, No. 145, pp. 35–62). Helsinki: Yliopistopaino.

Connell, J. P., & Wellborn, J. G. (1991). Competence, autonomy and relatedness: A motivational analysis of self-system processes. In M. R. Gunnar & Sroufe (Eds.), *Self-processes and development: The Minnesota symposium on child psychology* (Vol. 23, pp. 43–77). Hillsdale, NJ: Erlbaum.

deCharms, R. (1984). Motivating enhancement in educational settings. In R. Ames & C. Ames (Eds.), *Research on motivation in education. Vol. 1: Student motivation* (pp. 275–310). New York: Academic Press.

Deci, E. L. (1998). The relation of interest to motivation and human needs—The self-determination theory viewpoint. In L. Hoffmann, A. Krapp, K. A. Renninger, & J. Baumert (Eds.), *Interest and learning* (pp. 146–162). Kiel, Germany: Institute for Science Education.

Deci, E. L., & Ryan, R. M. (1985). *Intrinsic motivation and self-determination in human behavior*. New York: Plenum Press.

Deci, E. L., Vallerand, R. J., Pelletier, L. G., & Ryan, R. M. (1991). Motivation and education: The self-determination perspective. *Educational Psychologist, 26*, 325–346.

Denissen, J. J. A., Zarrett, N. R., & Eccles, J. S. (2007). I like to do it, I'm able, and I know I am: Longitudinal couplings between domain-specific achievement, self-concept, and interest. *Child Development, 78*, 430–447.

Durik, A. M., & Harackiewicz, J. M. (2007). Different strokes for different folks: How individual interest moderates the effects of situational factors on task interest. *Journal of Educational Psychology, 99*, 597–610.

Eccles, J. S. (1983). Expectancies, values, and academic behaviors. In J. T. Spence (Ed.), *Achievement and achievement motives* (pp. 75–146). San Francisco: Freeman.

Eccles, J. S., Buchanan, C. M., Flanagan, C., Fuligni, A., Midgley, C. M., & Lee, D. (1991). Control versus autonomy during early adolescence. *Journal of Social Issues, 47*, 53–68.

Epstein, S. (1990). Cognitive-experiential self-theory. In L. Pervin (Ed.), *Handbook of personality: Theory and research* (pp. 165–192). New York: Guilford.

Gardner, P. L. (1985). Students' interest in science and technology: An international overview. In M. Lehrke, L. Hoffmann, & P. L. Gardner (Eds.), *Interests in science and technology education*. Kiel: Institute for Science Education.

Gottfredson, L. S. (2002). Gottfredson's theory of circumscription, compromise, and self-creation. In D. Brown (Ed.), *Career choice and development* (pp. 85–148). San Francisco: Jossey-Bass.

Gottfried, A. E., Marcoulides, G. A., Gottfried, A. W., Oliver, P. H., & Guerin, D. W. (2007). Multivariate latent change modeling of developmental decline in academic intrinsic math motivation and achievement: Childhood through adolescence. *International Journal of Behavioral Development, 31*, 317–327.

Groff, P. J. (1962). Children's attitudes toward reading and their critical reading abilities in four content-type materials. *Journal of Educational Research, 55*, 313–317.

Guthrie, J. T., Wigfield, A., Humenick, N. M., Perencevich, K. C., Taboada, A., & Barbosa, P. (2006). Influences of stimulating tasks on reading motivation and comprehension. *Journal of Educational Research, 99*, 232–245.

Guthrie, J. T., Wigfield, A., & Perencevich, K. C. (2004). Scaffolding for motivation and engagement in reading. In J. T. Guthrie, A. Wigfield, & K. C. Perencevich, *Motivating reading comprehension: Concept-Oriented Reading Instruction* (pp. 55–86). Mahwah, NJ: Erlbaum.

Häussler, P., & Hoffmann, L. (2002). An intervention study to enhance girls' interest, self-concept, and achievement in physics classes. *Journal of Research in Science Teaching, 39*, 870–888.

Hannover, B. (1998). The development of self-concept and interests. In L. Hoffmann, A. Krapp, K. A. Renninger, & J. Baumert (Eds.), *Interest and learning* (pp. 105–125). Kiel: IPN.

Harter, S. (1981). A new self-report scale of intrinsic versus extrinsic orientation in the classroom: Motivational and informational components. *Developmental Psychology, 17*, 300–312.

Harty, H., & Beall, D. (1984). Toward the development of a children's science curiosity measure. *Journal of Research in Science Teaching, 21*, 425–436.

Hickey, D. T. (1997). Motivation and contemporary socio-constructivist instructional perspectives. *Educational Psychologist, 32*, 175–193.

Hidi, S. (1990). Interest and its contrubution as a mental resource for learning. *Review of Educational Research, 60*, 549–571.

Hidi, S. (1995). A reexamination of the role of attention in learning from text. *Educational Psychology Review, 7*, 323–350.

Hidi, S. (2000). An interest researcher's perspective: The effects of extrinsic and intrinsic factors on motivation. In C. Sansone & J. M. Harackiewicz (Eds.), *Intrinsic and extrinsic motivation* (pp. 309–339). San Diego: Academic Press.

Hidi, S. (2001). Interest, reading, and learning: Theoretical and practical considerations. *Educational Psychology Review, 13*, 191–209.

Hidi, S., & Ainley, M. (2002). Interest and adolescence. In F. Pajares & T. Urdan (Eds.), *Academic motivation of adolescents* (pp. 247–275). Greenwich, CT: Information Age.

Hidi, S., & Baird, W. (1986). Interestingness—A neglected variable in discourse processing. *Cognitive Science, 10*, 179–194.

Hidi, S., & Renninger, K. A. (2006). The four-phase model of interest development. *Educational Psychologist, 41*, 111–127.

Hidi, S., Renninger, K. A., & Krapp, A. (2004). Interest, a motivational variable that combines affective and cognitive functioning. In D. Y. Dai & R. J. Sternberg (Eds.), *Motivation, emotion, and cognition* (pp. 89–115). Mahwah, NJ: Erlbaum.

Hoffmann, L. (2002). Promoting girls' interest and achievement in physics classes for beginners. *Learning and Instruction, 12*, 447–465.

Hoffmann, L., & Lehrke, M. (1986). Eine Untersuchung über Schülerinteressen an Physik und Technik [An investigation of students' interest in physics and technics]. *Zeitschrift für Pädagogik, 32*, 189–204.

Hoffmann, L., Lehrke, M., & Todt, E. (1985). Development and change of pupils' interest in physics: Design of longitudinal study (grade 5–10). In M. Lehrke, L. Hoffmann, & P. L. Gardner (Eds.), *Interests in science and technology* (pp. 71–80). Kiel: Institute for Science Education.

Izard, C. E. (1977). *Human emotions*. New York: Plenum.

Kintsch, W. (1998). *Comprehension*. Cambridge, England: Cambridge University Press.

Köller, O., Baumert, J., & Schnabel, K. U. (2001). Does interest matter? The relationship between academic interest and achievement in mathematics. *Journal of Research in Mathematics Education, 32*, 448–470.

Köller, O., Schnabel, K. U., & Baumert, J. (1998, April). *The impact of academic self-concepts of ability on the development of interests during adolescence.* Paper presented at the annual meeting of the American Educational Research Association, San Diego.

Krapp, A. (1998). Entwicklung und Förderung von Interessen im Unterricht [Development and enhancement of interests in school]. *Psychologie in Erziehung und Unterricht, 44*, 185–201.

Krapp, A. (1999). Interest, motivation and learning: An educational-psychological perspective. *European Journal of Psychology of Education, 14*, 23–40.

Krapp, A. (2002). Structural and dynamic aspects of interest development: Theoretical considerations from an ontogenetic perspective. *Learning and Instruction, 12*, 383–409.

Krapp, A. (2005). Basic needs and the development of interest and intrinsic motivational orientations. *Learning and Instruction, 15*, 381–395.

Krapp, A., Hidi, S., & Renninger, K. A. (1992). Interest, learning, and development. In K. A. Renninger, S. Hidi, & A. Krapp (Eds.), *The role of interest in learning and development* (pp. 3–25). Hillsdale, NJ: Erlbaum.

Krapp, A., & Lewalter, D. (2001). Development of interests and interest-based motivational orientations: A longitudinal study in vocational school and work settings. In S. Volet & S. Järvelä (Eds.), *Motivation in learning contexts* (pp. 201–232). Amsterdam: Pergamon.

Kunter, M., Baumert, J., & Köller, O. (2007). Effective classroom management and the development of subject-related interest. *Learning and Instruction, 17,* 494–509.

Kunz, G. C., Drewniak, U., Hatalak, A., & Schön, A. (1992). Zur differentiellen Bedeutung kognitiver, metakognitiver und motivationaler Variablen für das effektive Lernen mit Instruktionstexten und Bildern [The differential role of cognitive, metacognitive, and motivational factors for effective learning with instructional texts and pictures]. In H. Mandl & H. F. Friedrich (Eds.), *Lern- und Denkstrategien* (pp. 213–229). Göttingen: Hogrefe.

Lapan, R. T., Shaughnessy, P., & Boggs, K. (1996). Efficacy expectations and vocational interests as mediators between sex and choice of math/science college majors: A longitudinal study. *Journal of Vocational Behavior, 49,* 277–291.

Lazarus, R. S. (1991). *Emotion and adaption.* New York: Oxford University Press.

Mac Iver, D., Stipek, D. J., & Daniels, D. (1991). Explaining within-semester changes in student effort in junior high school and senior high school courses. *Journal of Educational Psychology, 83,* 201–211.

Maehr, M. L., & Midgley, C. (1991). Enhancing student motivation: A school-wide approach. *Educational Psychologist, 26,* 399–427.

Marsh, H. W., & Yeung, A. S. (1997). Coursework selection: Relations to academic self-concept and achievement. *American Educational Research Journal, 34,* 691–720.

Marsh, H. W., Trautwein, U., Lüdtke, O., Köller, O., & Baumert, J. (2005). Academic self-concept, interest, grades, and standardized test scores: Reciprocal effects models of causal ordering. *Child Development, 76,* 397–416.

McDaniel, M. A., Waddill, P. J., Finstad, K., & Bourg, T. (2000). The effects of text-based interest on attention and recall. *Journal of Educational Psychology, 92,* 492–502.

McWhaw, K. & Abrami, P. C. (2001). Student goal orientation and interest: Effects on students' use of self-regulated learning strategies. *Contemporary Educational Psychology, 26,* 311–329.

Meece, J. (1991). The classroom context and students' motivational goals. In M. L. Maehr & P. R. Pintrich (Eds.), *Advances in motivation and achievement* (Vol. 7, pp. 261–285). Greenwich, CT: JAI Press.

Millis, K. (2001). Making meaning brings pleasure: The influence of titles on aesthetic experience. *Emotion, 1,* 320–329.

Mitchell, M. (1992). *A multifaceted model of situational interest in the secondary mathematics classroom.* Unpublished doctoral dissertation, University of California at Santa Barbara, CA.

Mitchell, M. (1993). Situational interest: Its multifaceted structure in the secondary school mathematics classroom. *Journal of Educational Psychology, 85,* 424–436.

Pekrun, R. (1988). *Emotion, Motivation und Persönlichkeit* [Emotion, motivation and personality]. München/Weinheim: Psychologie Verlags Union.

Perry, R. P., Magnusson, J. L., Parsonson, K. L., & Dickens, W. J. (1986). Perceived control in the college classroom: Limitations in instructor expressiveness due to noncontingent feedback and lecture content. *Journal of Educational Psychology, 78,* 96–107.

Pintrich, P. R. (2000). Multiple goals, multiple pathways: The role of goal orientation in learning and achievement. *Journal of Educational Psychology, 92,* 544–555.

Prenzel, M., & Lankes, E.-M. (1989). Wie Lehrer Interesse wecken und fördern können [How teachers can arouse and foster interest]. In S. Bäuerle (Ed.), *Der gute Lehrer* (pp. 66–81). Stuttgart: Metzlar.

Reeve, J., & Nix, G. (1997). Expressing intrinsic motivation through acts of exploration and facial displays of interest. *Motivation and Emotion, 21,* 237–250.

Renninger, K. A. (2000). Individual interest and its implications for understanding intrinsic motivation. In C. Sansone & J. M. Harackiewicz (Eds.), *Intrinsic and extrinsic motivation* (pp. 373–404). San Diego, CA: Academic Press.

Renninger, K. A., Ewen, L., & Lasher, A. K. (2002). Individual interest as context in expository text and mathematical word problems. *Learning and Instruction, 12,* 467–491.

Renninger, K. A., & Hidi, S. (Eds.). (2001). Student interest and engagement [Special issue]. *Educational Psychology Review, 13*(3).

Renninger, K. A., Hidi, S., & Krapp, A. (Eds.). (1992). *The role of interest in learning and development.* Hillsdale, NJ: Erlbaum.

Rottinghaus, P. J., Larson, L. M., & Borgen, F. H. (2003). The relation of self-efficacy and interests: A meta-analysis of 60 samples. *Journal of Vocational Behavior, 62,* 221–236.

Sansone, C., Sachau, D. A., & Weir, C. (1989). Effects of instruction on intrinsic interest: The importance of context. *Journal of Personality and Social Psychology, 57,* 819–829.

Sansone, C., & Thoman, D. B. (2006). Maintaining activity engagement: Individual differences in the process of self-regulating motivation. *Journal of Personality, 74,* 1697–1720.

Schaffner, E., & Schiefele, U. (2007). The effect of experimental manipulation of student motivation on the situational representation of text. *Learning and Instruction, 17,* 755–772.

Schaffner, E. & Schiefele, U. (2008). Familiäre und individuelle Bedingungen des Textlernens [Familial and individual conditions of text learning]. *Psychologie in Erziehung und Unterricht, 55,* 238–252.

Schaffner, E., Schiefele, U., & Schneider, W. (2004). Ein erweitertes Verständnis der Lesekompetenz: Die Ergebnisse des nationalen Ergänzungstests [An extended understanding of reading competence: Results from the national tests]. In U. Schiefele, C. Artelt, W. Schneider, & P. Stanat (Eds.), *Struktur, Entwicklung und Förderung von Lesekompetenz. Vertiefende Analysen im Rahmen von PISA 2000* (pp. 197–242). Wiesbaden: VS Verlag für Sozialwissenschaften.

Schiefele, U. (1990). The influence of topic interest, prior knowledge and cognitive capabilities on text comprehension. In J. M. Pieters, K. Breuer, & P. R. J. Simons (Eds.), *Learning environments* (pp. 323–338). Berlin: Springer.

Schiefele, U. (1991). Interest, learning, and motivation. *Educational Psychologist, 26,* 299–323.

Schiefele, U. (1996). *Motivation und Lernen mit Texten* [Motivation and text learning]. Göttingen: Hogrefe.

Schiefele, U. (1999). Interest and learning from text. *Scientific Studies of Reading, 3,* 257–279.

Schiefele, U. (2001). The role of interest in motivation and learning. In J. M. Collis & S. Messick (Eds.), *Intelligence and personality: Bridging the gap in theory and measurement* (pp. 163–194). Mahwah, NJ: Erlbaum.

Schiefele, U. (2004). Förderung von Interessen [Facilitation of interest]. In G. W. Lauth, M. Grünke, & J. C. Brunstein (Eds.), *Interventionen bei Lernstörungen* (pp. 134–144). Göttingen: Hogrefe.

Schiefele, U., & Csikszentmihalyi, M. (1995). Motivation and ability as factors in mathematics experience and achievement. *Journal for Research in Mathematics Education, 26,* 163–181.

Schiefele, U., & Krapp, A. (1996). Topic interest and free recall of expository text. *Learning and Individual Differences, 8,* 141–160.

Schiefele, U., Krapp, A., Wild, K.-P., & Winteler, A. (1993). Der "Fragebogen zum Studieninteresse" (FSI) [The "Study Interest Questionnaire" (SIQ)]. *Diagnostica, 39,* 335–351.

Schiefele, U., Krapp, A., & Winteler, A. (1992). Interest as a predictor of academic achievement: A meta-analysis of research. In K. A. Renninger, S. Hidi, & A. Krapp (Eds.), *The role of interest in learning and development* (pp. 183–212). Hillsdale, NJ: Erlbaum.

Schmalhofer, F., & Glavanov, D. (1986). Three components of understanding a programmer's manual: Verbatim, propositional, and situational representations. *Journal of Memory and Language, 25,* 279–294.

Schraw, G. (1997). Situational interest in literary text. *Contemporary Educational Psychology, 22,* 436–456.

Schraw, G., & Lehman, S. (2001). Situational interest: A review of the literature and directions for future research. *Educational Psychology Review, 13,* 23–52.

Schunk, D. H. (1991). Self-efficacy and academic motivation. *Educational Psychologist, 26,* 207–231.

Schunk, D. H., Pintrich, P. R., & Meece, J. L. (2008). *Motivation in education.* Upper Saddle River, NJ: Pearson Education.

Shirey, L. L., & Reynolds, R. E. (1988). Effect of interest on attention and learning. *Journal of Educational Psychology, 80,* 159–166.

Silvia, P. J. (2005). What is interesting? Exploring the appraisal structure of interest. *Emotion, 5,* 89–102.

Silvia, P. J. (2006). *Exploring the psychology of interest.* New York: Oxford University Press.

Skinner, E. A., & Belmont, M. J. (1993). Motivation in the classroom: Reciprocal effects of teacher behavior and student engagement across the school year. *Journal of Educational Psychology, 85,* 571–581.

Stipek, D. J. (1996). Motivation and instruction. In D. C. Berliner & R. C. Calfee (Eds.), *Handbook of educational psychology* (pp. 85–113). New York: Macmillan.

Tamir, P., & Gardner, P. (1989). The structure of interest in high school biology. *Research in Science & Technological Education, 7,* 113–140.

Tobias, S. (1994). Interest, prior knowledge, and learning. *Review of Educational Research, 64,* 37–54.

Todt, E. (1990). Entwicklung des Interesses. In H. Hetzer (Ed.), *Angewandte Entwicklungspsychologie des Kindes- und Jugendalters* [Development of interest] (pp. 213–264). Wiesbaden: Quelle & Meyer.

Todt, E., Arbinger, R., Seitz, H., & Wildgrube, W. (1974). *Untersuchungen über die Motivation zur Beschäftigung mit naturwissenschaftlichen Problemen (Sekundarstufe I: Klassen 5–9)* [Studies on the motivation to work with science problems (secondary level: Grades 5–9)]. Giessen: Universität, Psychologisches Institut.

Todt, E., & Schreiber, S. (1998). Development of interests. In L. Hoffmann, A. Krapp, K. A. Renninger, & J. Baumert (Eds.), *Interest and learning* (pp. 25–40). Kiel: Institute for Science Education.

Tracey, T. J. G. (2001). The development of structure of interests in children: Setting the stage. *Journal of Vocational Behavior, 59,* 89–104.

van Dijk, T. A., & Kintsch, W. (1983). *Strategies of discourse comprehension.* Orlando, FL: Academic Press.

Wade, S. E. (1992). How interest affects learning from text. In K. A. Renninger, S. Hidi, & A. Krapp (Eds.), *The role of interest in learning and development* (pp. 255–277). Hillsdale, NJ: Erlbaum.

Walsh, W. B., & Osipow, S. H. (Eds.). (1986). *Advances in vocational psychology. Vol. 1: The assessment of interests.* Hillsdale, NJ: Erlbaum.

Watt, H. M. G. (2004). Development of adolescents' self-perceptions, values, and task perceptions according to gender and domain in 7th- through 11th-grade Australian students. *Child Development, 75,* 1556–1574.

Wigfield, A., & Eccles, J. S. (1992). The development of achievement task values: A theoretical analysis. *Developmental Review, 12,* 265–310.

Wigfield, A., & Eccles, J. S. (2000). Expectancy-value theory of achievement motivation. *Contemporary Educational Psychology, 25,* 68–81.

Wigfield, A., Eccles, J. S., Schiefele, U., Roeser, R. W., & Davis-Kean, P. (2006). Development of achievement motivation. In N. Eisenberg (Ed.), *Handbook of child psychology. Vol. 3: Social, emotional, and personality development* (pp. 933–1002). Hoboken, NJ: Wiley.

Wild, K.-P., & Schiefele, U. (1994). Aufmerksamkeit als Mediator des Einflusses von Interesse auf die Lernleistung [Attention as a mediator of the effect of interest on learning]. *Sprache und Kognition, 13,* 138–145.

11
Engagement and Disaffection as Organizational Constructs in the Dynamics of Motivational Development

Ellen A. Skinner, Thomas A. Kindermann,
James P. Connell, and James G. Wellborn

The study of children's motivation in school is a vibrant area of research, replete with rich theories and complex constructs (Eccles, Wigfield, & Schiefele, 1998; Wigfield, Eccles, Schiefele, Roeser, & Davis-Kean., 2006). The lion's share of this work focuses on individual differences, attempting to identify the forces, originating from many levels, that shape student motivation. A wide array of factors have been identified (Deci, 1992; Eccles et al., 1998; Heckhausen, 1991; Pintrich, 2003; Pintrich & Schunk, 2003; Reeve, 2005; Weiner, 1986), including individual factors such as self-efficacy, values, achievement goals, self-regulatory style, identification, and feelings of belonging. Moreover, factors outside the person, from their social contexts, have also been found to shape motivation, factors such as contingencies, rewards, goal structures, the nature of academic tasks, autonomy support, involvement of authority figures and peers, school climate, warmth, structure, psychological control, and relationship style. General process models have guided the study of how subsets of these factors are linked to each other, examining their unique and interactive effects and exploring how they mediate each other in predicting academic success.

This work has a strong developmental bent, with the expressed goal of documenting age differences and changes in motivation itself and in each of the contributing factors, tracing their trajectories across a student's entire academic career (Eccles & Wigfield, 2002; Wigfield et al., 2006). The resulting picture is clear but not encouraging. Research reveals that children's interest, enthusiasm, and intrinsic motivation for learning in school deteriorate continuously from their entry into kindergarten until they complete high school (or drop-out), with striking losses during the transitions to middle school and high school (for reviews, see Eccles et al., 1998; Wigfield et al., 2006). The erosion of motivation is especially severe for boys and for students from low socioeconomic, minority, and immigrant backgrounds (Finn, 1989; Meece & Kurtz-Costes, 2001; Spencer, 2006; Taylor, Casten, Flickinger, Roberts, & Fulmore, 1994; Wigfield et al., 2006; Wooley & Bowen, 2007).

Researchers have succeeded in identifying many of the factors responsible for these developments. They appear to reflect normative age changes (e.g., puberty, cognitive developments, increasing interest in other activities, such as peers and romantic relationships) as well as social institutional decisions (e.g., changes in schools so that they become more bureaucratic, impersonal, and controlling). The most complete accounts are provided by explanatory theories of stage-environment fit, in which it is argued that systemic social changes in schools, especially during middle school and high school, are in direct opposition to changing developmental needs of youth for increasing autonomy, self-regulation, and connection (Eccles, 2004; Jackson & Davis, 2000; National Research Council, 2004; Wigfield et al., 2006).

Implicit in much of this work is the idea that academic motivation is not a reflection of a fixed characteristic of the child, but instead is a product of the interaction among a host of internal and external factors, many of which are changing across time (Dornyei, 2000; Ford, 1992). In other words, it may be useful to consider these elements part of a motivational system, which gives rise to the quality of a student's academic beliefs, values, and actions in school. The goal of this chapter is to bring into focus a view of the motivational system as dynamic, iterative, and changing over time. To do so, we argue that the constructs of *engagement and disaffection* must be more fully articulated and integrated into theories of motivational development, because they play a critical role in organizing the dynamics of the system.

We make our case in three sections. First, we present a motivational conceptualization grounded in action theory that depicts engagement and disaffection as a set of proximal processes (Bronfenbrenner & Morris, 1998) describing the quality of children's interactions with academic activities. We identify the defining features of engagement and disaffection, and argue that they represent the outward manifestation of motivation. Second, to support the argument that engagement and disaffection are central to an understanding of motivation, we briefly review major theories of motivation and point out that every one of them contains constructs corresponding to engagement. Third, we show how engagement itself, because of its reciprocal relations with the intrapsychic and interpersonal factors that shape motivation, organizes the motivational system and is responsible for the dynamics of its differential development. We explore how key motivational resources and vulnerabilities may emerge from these dynamics at different points in development, and conclude by enumerating the challenges to studying and promoting the development of the entire motivational system.

As subtext throughout this chapter is the conviction that a focus on engagement offers researchers the opportunity to construct a comprehensive conceptualization of motivation which integrates the many individual and interpersonal factors studied to date. We believe that the explicit inclusion of engagement has the potential to move the field forward: to move beyond theories and research implying that motivation is the product of static (mostly intrapsychic) characteristics, such as self-perceptions, and toward conceptualizations that have the potential to begin integrating individual difference, process, and developmental views of motivation, eventually leading to studies that explicitly investigate their dynamics.

A Motivational Perspective on Engagement and Disaffection

There is, of course, no single correct definition of *engagement*. In recent years, the concept has emerged as a leitmotif in research attempting to identify the factors that promote academic achievement and resilience, and protect adolescents from drop-out and delinquency (Fredricks, Blumenfeld, & Paris, 2004; Jimerson, Campos, & Greif, 2003; Maddox & Prinz, 2003). For educational psychologists, a focus on engagement represents a shift away from research showing that the personal status characteristics of students (such as ethnicity or socioeconomic status) are the primary predictors of their achievement and school completion, and towards the investigation of potentially malleable processes that schools can target in interventions (Finn & Voelkl, 1993; Newmann, Wehlage, & Lamborn, 1992). As underscored by Sinclair, Christenson, Lehr, and Anderson (2003), "engagement is not conceptualized as an attribute of the student, but rather as a state of being that is highly influenced by contextual factors, such as policies and practices of the school and family or peer interactions" (p. 31).

Engagement as a Motivational Construct

Of most interest to motivational researchers are conceptualizations that target the core features of motivation. The study of motivation is most fundamentally concerned with psychological processes that underlie the energy (vigor, intensity, arousal), purpose (initiation, direction, channeling, choice), and durability (persistence, maintenance, endurance, sustenance) of human activity. Hence, motivational conceptualizations of engagement are ones that capture the target definitional manifestations of motivation—namely, energized, directed, and sustained action. A core argument of this chapter is that "action" is *the* reflection of human motivation, with engagement versus disaffection perhaps the central manifestations of ongoing motivated actions (Wellborn, 1991). That is why constructs of engagement and disaffection should be (and always have been) central to theories of motivation.

The Concept of Action

In asserting that engagement, and "actions" more generally, are a reflection of human motivation and are energized and directed by motivational processes, the term "action" does not refer to its common language usage, as a synonym for "behavior." Instead, it refers to the notion of "action schema" from the long European theoretical tradition of action theories (Boesch, 1976; Brandtstädter, 1998; Chapman, 1984; Frese & Sabini, 1985). Compared to behavior, "action" is a more complex construct: It incorporates behavior (or physical gestures), but also requires simultaneous consideration of emotions, attention, and goals. Actions are goal-directed and the same behavior is part of different actions if it is deployed in the service of different goals. For example, the behavior of clapping, depending on the intention, can be part of "expressing appreciation," "a request for silence," or "getting rid of a mosquito." By the same token, very different behaviors, if they serve the same function, can belong to the same type of action. For example, breathing deeply, counting to 10, and taking a walk, since they all exert a calming function, can be considered part of the same action category.

Action theories are based on the idea that the natural unit of analysis for conceptualizing transactions between people and their social contexts is not "behavior" but "action." The main idea is that goals and emotions energize and direct attention and behavior, and it is this amalgam that reflects an individual's motivation. Action theories deal with motivated actions that are not expressed overtly by using the concept of "action tendencies" or "action readiness;" these are defined as desires, urges, or wishes to act, that unless constrained by internal or external regulatory forces, will be expressed as actions. Actions are available to many levels of regulation, from automatized action tendencies to reflective conscious voluntary processes.

A key tenet of action theories is that actions (and not behaviors) are the features of individuals to which the social context responds (Brandtstädter, 1998). For example, perceivers infer actor's intentions in order to distinguish actions that are "accidents" from those that are "on purpose." Likewise, teachers and parents respond differently to willing versus unwilling compliance with requests (Kochanska, Aksan, & Carlson, 2005), favoring, of course, willing cooperation. Passivity based on fear and anxiety is treated differently than passivity based on defiance or boredom (Furrer, Kelly, & Skinner, 2003). Even homework assignments "respond" differently to efforts that are fully-focused versus half-hearted. Basing conceptualizations of engagement in action theories allows the integration of intensity of behavior with emotion, attention, and intention as constitutive elements of the qualities of motivation.

Motivational Conceptualizations of Engagement

From these definitional features of action follow the idea that motivational constructs of engagement should include not only behavior, but also attention and emotions; that engagement should describe an individual's interactions with important features of the environment; and that engagement should include both the initiation of motivated action and its durability in the face of obstacles or difficulties. Hence, for motivational theorists, of most interest are conceptualizations of engagement that have at their core definitions that encompass students' constructive, enthusiastic, willing, cognitively-focused participation in learning activities. From this perspective, the behavioral dimension of engagement includes effort, intensity, persistence, determination, and perseverance in the face of obstacles and difficulties; emotional or affective engagement includes enthusiasm, enjoyment, fun, and satisfaction; and cognitive engagement encompasses attention, focus, "heads-on" participation, and willingness to go beyond what is required (see Table 11.1).

The Opposite of Engagement

Motivational conceptualizations sometimes incorporate the opposite of engagement, which is variously referred to as disengagement, alienation, helplessness, passivity, or disaffection (Miceli & Castelfranchi, 2000). The link to motivation is most clear in theories that refer to this state as "amotivation" (Vallerand et al., 1993). Conceptually, the opposite of engagement is *disengagement*, which implies the *absence* of engagement, including the absence of effort or persistence. Hence, disengagement is typically operationalized as passivity, lack of initiation, and giving up, sometimes accompanied by the emotions of dejection, discouragement, or apathy. The best known account of these actions is contained in theories of learned helplessness (e.g., Peterson, Maier, & Seligman, 1993).

However, there are other pathways to disengagement besides helplessness. For example, *alienation* has been used loosely to refer to students' lack of belonging in school. It has also been used more specifically to refer to "low motivation for schooling," which is characterized by low effort and persistence in the classroom, inattention, truancy, and behavioral problems (Murdock, 1999). Theories of self-determination posit that controlling social contexts can also lead people toward opposition, which is a nonautonomous form of withdrawing participation from an activity (Deci & Ryan, 1985). Theories of interest imply that boredom may also be a sufficient condition for lack of effortful involvement. Moreover, sociological theories (Merton, 1953) point out that the experience of being excluded from important realms of participation does not simply produce disengagement or passivity, it results in frustration and alienation (Newmann, 1991). Hence, a full account of engagement deserves a broader conceptualization of its opposite than simply absence

Table 11.1 A Motivational Conceptualization of Engagement and Disaffection.

	Engagement	Disaffection
Behavior	Action initiation	Passivity, Procrastination
Initiation	Effort, Exertion	Giving up, Withdrawal
Ongoing participation	Working hard	Restlessness
Re-engagement	Attempts	Half-hearted
	Persistence	Unfocused, Inattentive
	Intensity	Distracted
	Focus, Attention	Mentally disengaged
	Concentration	Burned out
	Absorption	Unprepared
	Involvement	Absent
Emotion	Enthusiasm	Boredom
Initiation	Interest	Disinterest
Ongoing participation	Enjoyment	Frustration/anger
Re-engagement	Satisfaction	Sadness
	Pride	Worry/anxiety
	Vitality	Shame
	Zest	Self-blame
Cognitive Orientation	Purposeful	Aimless
Initiation	Approach	Helpless
Ongoing participation	Goal strivings	Resigned
Re-engagement	Strategy search	Unwilling
	Willing participation	Opposition
	Preference for challenge	Avoidance
	Mastery	Apathy
	Follow-through, care	Hopeless
	Thoroughness	Pressured

of engagement. We use the term "disaffection," which contains a wider range of reactions and includes those stemming from exclusion, helplessness, boredom, and coercion (see Table 11.1; Connell & Wellborn, 1991; Finn, Pannozzo & Voelkl, 1995; Newmann, 1991).

Summary

An action-theoretical account of motivation conceptualizes engagement as the quality of participation with academic activities. Its positive pole encompasses enthusiastic willing effortful exertion, interest, concentrated attention, and persistence in the face of difficulties and challenge, sometimes referred to as active "hands-on" and "heads-on" learning. Motivational conceptualizations of disaffection depict ways in which students' withdraw their involvement from learning activities, including physical withdrawal of effort, such as passivity, lack of exertion, simply going through the motions, or avoidance as well as their mental counterparts, such as inattention, lack of concentration, apathy, or daydreaming. Emotional reactions are critical to descriptions of disaffection, because patterns of action differ depending on whether withdrawal is based on anxiety, boredom, shame, frustration, or sadness.

Engagement and Disaffection as Common Constructs among Motivational Theories

A central argument of this chapter is that all major theories of motivation include as a target some facet of engagement or disaffection. Perhaps surprisingly, however, these constructs are rarely in the theoretical foreground (Murphy & Alexander, 2000). Although extensive efforts have been devoted to differentiating the factors that *influence* human motivation, much less attention has been paid to explicitly identifying the factors that *reflect* human motivation. However, each framework has its own set of preferred motivational outcomes, and we argue that, because all theories focus on motivation, every set includes descriptors of the kind of durable, energized, and directed actions that can be described as engaged. Although a review of each of these theories is beyond the scope of this chapter (see Eccles & Wigfield, 2002; Heckhausen, 1991; Pintrich & Schunk, 2003; Reeve, 2005; Weiner, 1986; or Wigfield et al., 2006), brief descriptions of the features that correspond most closely to engagement and disaffection are highlighted for a selection of major theories. Examples are provided in Table 11.2.

Perceived Control, Efficacy, and Causal Attributions

Motivational theories organized around constructs of control, include theories of self-efficacy, perceived control, and causal attributions (for overviews, see Elliot & Dweck, 2005; Skinner, 1996). These theories have as their goal to predict intentional behavior and affect, most especially action initiation and goal strivings, including active attempts, effort, attention, concentration, and persistence in the face of obstacles versus passivity, giving up, and withdrawal of effort. For example, the major behavioral outcomes of attribution theory are effort and persistence, and causal attributions are considered important predictors of emotions, such as anger and shame (Weiner, 1985, 2005). The primary outcomes of self-efficacy are initiation of action, expenditure of effort, and performance attempts (Bandura, 1977, 1997; Schunk & Pajares, 2005). High perceived control predicts enjoyment, interest, and enthusiasm (Patrick, Skinner, & Connell, 1993) whereas low self-efficacy predicts anxiety and resignation (Bandura, 1977, 1997).

Learned Helplessness

Theories of learned helplessness (Abramson, Seligman, & Teasdale, 1978; Seligman, 1975) have as a major goal to examine the role of expectancies and attributions in the creation of motivational deficits, including passivity, apathy, avoidance, giving up, and failure to respond. The emotional consequences of perceived noncontingency, including sadness and hopelessness, are also defining features of the syndrome of learned helplessness (Peterson et al., 1993). The concept of mastery, as the opposite of learned helplessness (Dweck, 1975, 1999, 2002; Dweck & Molden, 2005), includes effort, persistence, concentration, enthusiasm, and enjoyment.

Achievement Expectancies and Value

Expectancy-value models of achievement (Eccles et al., 1983; Eccles & Wigfield, 1995, 2002; Wigfield & Eccles, 2000, 2002) focus on social psychological influences on achievement strivings, most especially effort, choice, and persistence. Much of this work has focused on elaborating and refining the proximal predictors of motivation, specifically, expectancies for success and task value, to incorporate task-specific beliefs, ability beliefs, and different components of task value. Researchers using these models have been particularly interested in predicting individuals' decision-making and choice (e.g., about what activities to pursue, courses to select, careers to seek).

Table 11.2 Motivational Theories and Examples of the Constructs that Correspond to Engagement and Disaffection

Motivational Theory (in alphabetical order)	Examples of Behavioral Engagement	Examples of Emotional Engagement	Examples of Engaged Orientation
Achievement Goal Orientations (Elliot, 2005; Meece et al., 2006)	Effort, Exertion, Persistence, Task involvement, Procrastination	Enthusiasm, Enjoyment Anxiety	Selection of challenging tasks
Causal attributions (Weiner, 1985, 2005)	Effort, Persistence Vs. Giving up, Withdrawal	Joy, Anger, Pride, Shame, Guilt	
Effectance motivation (Harter, 1978; White, 1959)	Energized participation	Enthusiasm Joy	Preference for challenge
Engagement in Academic Work (Newmann et al., 1992)	Effort to learn, Active involvement, Participation	Enthusiasm Interest	Concentrated attention Psychological investment
Flow (Shernoff et al., 2003)		Enjoyment Interest	Concentration Absorption
Intrinsic Motivation (Gottfried, 1985; Gottfried et al., 2001)	Task involvement Persistence	Enjoyment Interest	Curiosity Preference for challenging, difficult, novel tasks
Learned helplessness (Abramson et al. 1978; Peterson et al., 1993; Seligman, 1977)	Passivity, Apathy Avoidance Giving up, Failure to respond	Sadness Dejection	Hopelessness
Mastery (Dweck, 1975, 1999, 2002; Dweck & Molden, 2005)	Effort, Persistence Concentration Determination	Enthusiasm Enjoyment	Preference for challenge, Hypothesis testing, Optimism
Participation/Identification (Finn, 1989)	Active behavioral involvement Time and effort expended Initiate interactions	Display of enthusiasm	Expending more time and effort than required
Perceived control (Skinner et al., 1990, 1998)	Initiation of action, Effort, Determination, Persistence	Enjoyment, Interest Enthusiasm	Attention
Self-determination (Deci, 1975; Deci & Ryan, 1985, 2000; Deci et al., 1999)	Participation Persistence Vs. Withdrawal	Enthusiastic, Joyful, Energetic Vs. Anxious, Angry, Rote	Willing, Flexible, Spontaneous Vs. Rigid, pressured
Self-efficacy (Bandura, 1977, 1997; Schunk & Pajares, 2005)	Initiation of action Expenditure of effort Performance attempts	Anxiety Resignation	
Self-system Model of Motivational development (Connell, 1990; Connell & Wellborn, 1991)	Effort, Hard work Persistence Vs. Withdrawal, passivity	Enthusiasm, interest. liking Vs. Boredom, sadness, frustration	Attention Concentration Preference for challenge Beyond the call
Value-expectancy (Eccles et al., 1983; Eccles & Wigfield, 1995, 2002; Wigfield & Eccles, 2000, 2002)	Achievement strivings Effort exertion Persistence		

Self-Determination

Organismic theories of motivation assume that people are born with the capacity to engage in activities for their own sake in ways that are spontaneous, flexible, creative, joyful, and energized. "Intrinsic motivation" is used as a term to describe both the source of motivation and its manifestation (Deci, 1975; Harter, 1978). The source of motivation is intrinsic to the person in the sense that all humans are assumed to possess inborn psychological needs, and activities in which these needs can be met are intrinsically motivating. The quality of enthusiastic, flexible, joyful involvement is a hallmark of intrinsic motivation (Deci, Koestner, & Ryan, 1999; Deci & Ryan, 1985, 2000). Recent advances have also investigated the developmental processes by which motivation for activities that were originally extrinsic can be internalized and transformed, thereby allowing it to become more autonomous (Ryan & Connell, 1989; Ryan & Deci, 2000). Target motivational outcomes include the quality of an individual's participation in learning tasks, as marked by effort, persistence, interest, enjoyment, enthusiasm, and, especially emotional tone (e.g., willing, pressured, or anxious).

Achievement Goal Orientations

Theories of goal orientation focus on individuals' reasons for engaging in academic tasks, that is, what an individual is attempting to accomplish while involved in a learning activity (Ames, 1992; Blumenfeld, 1992; Dweck & Leggett, 1988; Maehr & Midgley, 1996; Meece, Anderman, & Anderman, 2006; Nicholls, 1984). Although combining the work of several distinct traditions (see Elliot, 2005; Harackiewicz, Baron, Pintrich, Elliot, & Thrash, 2002; Pintrich, 2000; Thorkildsen & Nicholls, 1998), there seems to be consensus about the consequences that should be considered in determining their effects: In addition to levels of processing in learning and performance, motivational outcomes include task involvement, effort, exertion, persistence on difficult tasks, selection of challenging tasks, intrinsic motivation, strategy use, passivity, procrastination, and emotions such as anxiety, enjoyment, and enthusiasm.

Individual Differences in Intrinsic Motivation

Theories of academic intrinsic motivation have also been proposed that focus on individual differences between children (Gottfried, 1985; Gottfried, Fleming, & Gottfried, 2001). The target construct concerns enjoyment of school learning characterized by a high degree of task involvement, mastery orientation, curiosity, persistence, and the preference for challenging, difficult, and novel tasks.

Student Engagement in Academic Work

The construct of engagement is featured prominently in some attempts to provide a conceptual framework for planning educational reforms. In this work, as summarized by Newmann and colleagues (1992), "engagement stands for active involvement, commitment, and concentrated attention" (p. 11). These researchers define "student engagement in academic work as the student's psychological investment in and effort directed toward learning, understanding, or mastering the knowledge, skills, or crafts that academic work is intended to promote" (p. 12). Because engagement depicts an "inner quality of concentration and effort to learn…", "[l]evels of engagement must be estimated or inferred from indirect indicators such as the amount of participation in academic work (attendance, portion of task completed, amount of time spent on academic work), the intensity of student concentration, the enthusiasm and interest expressed, and the degree of care in completing the work" (p. 13).

Participation and Identification

Participation-identification models of school success emphasize "students' active *participation* in school and classroom activities and a concomitant feeling of *identification* with school" (Finn, 1989, p. 123). Students' behavioral involvement in the classroom (e.g., attending, reading, studying, responding to questions), referred to as "level one participation," is considered the minimal essential ingredient for formal learning to occur; hence, its absence in the early grades is considered a risk factor for school withdrawal. As students continue in school, "level two participation" involves initiation of interactions with the teacher and the display of enthusiasm by expending more time and effort than required.

Self-System Model of Motivational Development

One of the most explicit conceptualizations of engagement can be found in the Self-System Model of Motivational Development (Connell, 1990; Connell & Wellborn, 1991; Deci & Ryan, 1985). This integrative motivational model is based on fundamental human needs and assumes that engagement reflects the extent to which a particular context has been able to tap the underlying reservoir of a student's intrinsic motivation and to foster the internalization of motivation for activities that were originally extrinsically motivated. The model holds that if schools provide children with opportunities to meet their needs for relatedness, competence, and autonomy, then students will be more engaged with the activities and people in that enterprise (Connell, 1990; Connell & Wellborn, 1991). At the same time, if school is experienced as uncaring, unfair, or coercive, students will feel they are not welcome in school, and that they are not capable of or interested in reaching the goals schools set for them. They will become disaffected and alienated, eventually withdrawing their participation, and when old enough to do so, they will leave, either through absenteeism or by dropping out.

Summary

We argue that all major models of motivation have a set of target actions in common that include initiation, exertion, concentrated attention, and persistence as well as feeling states, such as interest, enthusiasm, and enjoyment. Some theories also include their opposites, such as passivity, apathy, procrastination, giving up, going through the motions, anxiety, frustration, and boredom. Taken together, these actions, referred to as engagement and disaffection, capture an important set of descriptors of energized, directed, and persistent actions (and their opposites), and hence, can be considered core foci of all theories of motivation.

Engagement and Disaffection as Key Components of the Motivational System

Despite apparent differences among the target phenomena of models of motivation, the promise of a common thread, embodied by the constructs of engagement and disaffection, has the potential to allow meaningful integration across conceptual systems (Ford, 1992; Wigfield & Eccles, 2002). If all models have in common certain classes of constructs, this allows for the creation of a general framework organized around the general classes of action (engagement) as well as its antecedents, namely, context (interpersonal factors) and self (intrapsychic factors), and its outcomes (learning and development; Connell, 1990; Connell & Wellborn, 1991; Skinner, 1995). Despite the fact that each of these elements is itself multidimensional, a general framework can be used to collect from motivational theories the many constructs that depict the kinds of contextual supports that should facilitate engagement and the many intrapsychic processes hypothesized to mediate their effects. A selection of these is included in Figure 11.1.

Context

The social contexts that shape motivational development (like the contexts that shape all aspects of children's development) consist of a collection of partially nested settings, filled with social partners and activities (Ames, 1992; Anderman & Anderman, 2000; Bronfenbrenner & Morris, 1998). For academic engagement, the microsystem of greatest interest is the classroom, which contains important social partners (the teacher, friends, peers, and classmates) and learning activities, along with the rules and routines that regulate them, such as task assignments, group projects, authority relations, rules of conduct, norms of participation, recognition systems, and instructional and grading practices (Turner & Meyer, 2000). Children usually move between multiple classrooms, and classrooms are nested within schools which contain additional social

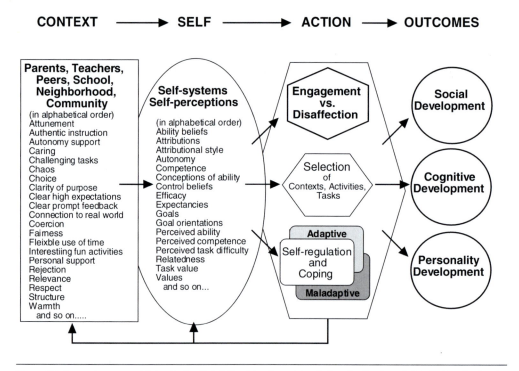

Figure 11.1 A general process model of motivation that distinguishes the social contexts and self-systems that facilitate and undermine motivation from engagement vs. disaffection and other indicators of motivated action, such as selection and self-regulation, and developmental outcomes.

partners, activities, and rules, as well as higher-order properties such as school climate or racial composition. The school in turn is embedded in a community, with its own economic and cultural attributes. Other settings, most particularly the home and neighborhood (e.g., block or street), also contain important social partners and activities.

Of great interest is the depiction of the specific motivational supports or hindrances that these social partners and activities provide. For example, the Self-system Model of Motivational Development posits that involvement, caring, structure, and autonomy support promote engagement whereas hostility, inconsistency, coercion, and neglect fuel disaffection. In a similar vein, work on goal structures has suggested multiple channels (through the use of various instructional, recognition, evaluation, and group strategies) by which teachers create classroom environments that communicate to students the purposes of learning. Since engagement depicts a child's interactions with learning activities, a critical social partner to scrutinize is the nature of the academic work itself (Wigfield et al., 2006). Engagement is facilitated by learning activities that are challenging, fun, meaningful, relevant, connected to that child's interests and real life, socially embedded (e.g., group- or dyadically-based), cumulative (e.g., project-based learning), and result in tangible share-able outcomes (e.g., books, exhibits, demonstrations).

The idea of a motivational system suggests that these different features of classrooms and relational contexts cannot be considered in isolation from each other. Instead, they work together to create a holistic message to students (Turner & Meyer, 2000), the meanings of which can be deciphered with reference to the relevant self-system processes. To what extent do teachers and classrooms communicate to students that the purpose of school is mastery versus the appearance (demonstration or protection) of ability? To what extent do they communicate to children and youth that they belong? That they are capable of academic success? That learning is fun, relevant, important, and connected to their own long-term goals? The general model in Figure 11.1 emphasizes the cumulative effects of these various inputs from multiple social partners, suggesting that contexts can be synergistically positive or negative in their effects, and that inputs from one context may cancel out, compensate for, or amplify the effects of another.

Self

Because most major theories of motivation today focus on cognitions as proximal predictors of motivation (Murphy & Alexander, 2000; Pintrich, 2003; Wigfield, et al., 2006), the most elaborated components of the motivational system are cognitive appraisals, beliefs, and self-perceptions. These appraisals are actively constructed from a history of interactions with the social context, and so are "hot" cognitions, durable and potent internal representations of apparent reality, imbued with emotion and meaning (Skinner, 1995). They are key parts of the motivational system because they filter an individual's experiences of their social interactions and they reveal whether children find the activities or tasks at school to be meaningful, possible, desirable, or fulfilling their psychological needs. Attitudes, values, and beliefs about the self and activities are among the most important proximal predictors of engagement and disaffection.

Action

The constructs of engagement and disaffection are central to all motivational models, but they do not necessarily capture the full range of possible motivational targets (Fredricks et al., 2004). Many of the theories described previously emphasize additional components as well: For example, self-determination theory accentuates flexible and creative versus pressured and unwilling involvement (Deci & Ryan, 1985); theories of learned helplessness often underscore the volitional deficits that accompany experiences of noncontingency (Dweck, 1999; Kuhl, 1984); and some educational theories highlight the development of a psychological or orientation component that includes identification, commitment, and psychological investment (Finn, 1989; Newmann, 1991).

In fact, at least two entire classes of motivated actions can be identified that are not typically included in definitions of engagement (but see Fredricks et al., 2004): (a) choice or selection of tasks, activities, or goals (Eccles, 1993, 2005; Eccles et al., 1998; Wigfield, et al., 2006), which is a key manifestation of the direction of action; and (b) action regulation or the intentional management and guidance of action in the face of (anticipated) obstacles or difficulties, which is studied in the academic domain as self-regulated learning (Schunk & Zimmerman, 1994) or academic coping (Skinner & Wellborn, 1994, 1997). In general, strategies of self-regulated learning reflect the intentional deployment of constructive engagement, and coping can be considered processes of re-engagement or disaffection in the face of challenges and threats. As depicted in Figure 11.1, the general motivational model creates a place for additional classes of motivated actions, including choice, action regulation, and coping, whether or not they are collectively referred to as engagement and disaffection.

The Dynamics of Motivational Systems

A key argument of this chapter is that engagement and disaffection not only reflect motivation but they also play a causal role in the motivational system. As can be seen in Figure 11.1, engagement: (a) contributes directly to learning and development, (b) mediates the effects of individual and contextual factors on short- and long-term outcomes, and (c) exerts an impact on changes in subsequent contextual (and perhaps even individual) factors. Empirical evidence supports the role of engagement in each of these causal processes.

Engagement and Disaffection as Proximal Processes

In their discussion of bioecological systems perspectives on development, Bronfenbrenner and Morris (1998) argue that the primary engine of all development are "proximal processes," which they define as "progressively more complex reciprocal interaction between an active, evolving biopsychological human organism and the persons, objects, and symbols in its immediate external environment" (p. 996). Engagement and disaffection, which describe children's and youth's daily interactions with academic activities, are proximal processes.

Over time, they are the process mechanisms through which development occurs in schools—most obviously, cognitive development or learning. It is through sustained high quality participation with academic materials, tasks, teachers, and classmates that children learn. For this reason, motivational researchers have begun to focus on the nature of academic work (such as classroom activities, projects, homework) as a critical factor in children's motivation (e.g., Lepper & Cordova, 1992; see Wigfield et al., 2006 for a review). If engagement is to contribute to high quality learning, it needs to be with tasks, activities, and people from whom the student can learn something. In keeping with this analysis, research has shown that students' active effortful engagement in learning activities predicts important academic outcomes, including school grades and achievement test scores (Connell, Halpern-Felsher, Clifford, Crichlow, & Usinger, 1995; Jimerson et al., 2003; Ryan, 2000; Skinner, Zimmer-Gembeck, & Connell, 1998; Wentzel, 1993), attendance and retention (Connell, Spencer, & Aber, 1994; Pierson & Connell, 1992; Sinclair et al., 2003), and academic resilience (Finn & Rock, 1997; for a review, see Fredricks et al., 2004).

Engagement as a Mediator of the Effects of Motivational Processes

A second way in which engagement and disaffection organize the motivational system is that they are the action outcomes of motivational processes, and as such they are critical mediators in all theories of motivation in school. It is possible to take the position that no intrapsychic process or interpersonal condition can have an effect on learning or development, unless it first has an impact on engagement. For example, no matter how competent a child perceives herself to be, these perceptions will not have an impact on that child's development unless they lead the child to constructively engage in activities in ways that produce actual learning. Correspondingly, no matter how autonomy supportive a teacher may be, this support will not contribute to learning and development unless it shapes student engagement. From this reasoning, it follows that all process theories of motivational development require an action component, like engagement and disaffection, task choice, or strategies of self-regulated learning and coping (Dornyei, 2000). A growing body of research has shown that these action components mediate the effects of self-system processes and contextual conditions on performance and achievement (e.g., Connell et al., 1994, 1995; Covington & Dray, 2002; Eccles & Wigfield, 2002; Furrer & Skinner, 2003; Patrick et al., 1993; Skinner, Wellborn, & Connell, 1990; Skinner et al., 1998).

Engagement as a Contributor to the Reactions of Social Partners

A third way in which engagement and disaffection organize the motivational system is through their feedback effects on social partners, especially teachers. The central idea is that students' engagement in the classroom is a valued energetic resource that teachers notice and to which they respond with warmth and involvement. In contrast, student disaffection is aversive and tends to elicit criticism or withdrawal of attention. The few studies that have used experimental or longitudinal designs to examine these reciprocal effects have typically found them, in kindergarten (Ladd, Birch, & Buhs, 1999), elementary (Skinner & Belmont, 1993) and middle school (Altermatt, Jovanovic, & Perry, 1998; see Furrer Skinner, & Kindermann, 2007, for a review). Students who are more highly engaged solicit increased attention, autonomy support, and high quality teaching from their teachers (Birch & Ladd, 1996; Reeve, 2005). At the same time, students who are more disaffected tend to lose their teachers' involvement over time (Furrer et al., 2003; Pelletier & Vallerand, 1996; Schutz & DeCuir, 2002). It should be noted that the effects of engagement on social partners extend beyond teachers to include parents and peers. For example, research shows that students who are more engaged select and are selected by more engaged peer groups (Kindermann, 1993, 2007).

Differential Development of Motivational Systems

Taken together, these links form a system organized around cycles, bouts, or episodes of engagement with academic activities in the classroom (Ford, 1992; Skinner, 1995). In these cycles, children who start school rich in motivational resources, through their engagement, become richer as they progress through school, whereas children poor in motivational resources through their disengagement with learning activities become progressively poorer. Such cycles have been documented most clearly in work on perceived control. For example, in our own research (e.g., Schmitz & Skinner, 1993; Skinner, 1995; Skinner et al., 1990, 1998), time series and longitudinal studies have shown that children who evince high levels of efficacy and confidence are more likely to engage with learning tasks and cope with difficulties in ways (referred to as "mastery-oriented") that allow them to be more successful and to learn more, thereby verifying their initially high perceptions of control. At the same time, students who doubt their capacities are more likely to participate in learning tasks and deal with challenges and obstacles in ways (referred to as "helpless" or avoidant) that interfere with their success in schoolwork and the development of competencies, thereby cementing their initially low sense of control. Over time, these amplifying loops (or virtuous and vicious cycles) can contribute to patterns of differential motivational development that increase the gap between the haves and have-nots (Dweck, 1999; Dweck & Molden, 2005; Skinner, 1995).

Hence, engagement is a critical construct organizing the development of the entire motivational system (Connell, 1990; Connell & Wellborn, 1991; Finn, 1989; Finn & Voelkl, 1993; Marks, 2000; Newmann, 1991; Ryan & Patrick, 2001; Skinner, 1995; Skinner et al., 2008; Wigfield, Eccles, & Rodriguez, 1998). The arc of an individual's trajectory of engagement over their school career is one indicator of motivational development, and individual differences in these trajectories are strong predictors of withdrawal and eventual dropout from school (Connell et al., 1994, 1995; Jimerson et al., 2000; Marks, 2000). Underlying (and creating) these trajectories are the dynamics of motivational development. The support provided by social contexts and partners, through its effects on children's appraisals, shapes children's engagement in academic activities; this engagement has a feed-forward effect on children's own learning and eventual development, as well as a feed-back effect on their self-systems and social partners. These motivational cycles, reinforcing and amplifying themselves over time, are responsible for the motivationally rich becoming richer, and to some extent, may help explain the ever tightening links among social support, self-perceptions, motivation, performance, and development.

Emergence of Motivational Resources and Liabilities

These engagement episodes or cycles have the effect of maintaining themselves at a steady state (Ford, 1992) or of creating successive increments and decrements in their components over time, as suggested by research that documents strong interindividual stability of motivational processes as well as parallel trajectories of teacher support, children's self-perceptions, engagement, and achievement over the school year and over many years (e.g., Hamre & Pianta, 2001; Jacobs, Lanza, Osgood, Eccles, & Wigfield, 2002; Kowaleski-Jones & Duncan, 1999; Roeser, Strobel, & Quihuis, 2002; Skinner et al., 1998; Trautwein, Lüdtke, Kastens, & Köller, 2006).

Cumulatively, these cycles may explain how, over developmental time, children's energized and focused interactions with academic activities and social partners become part of a process that shapes the emergence of durable energetic resources and liabilities, including actual competencies and enduring social relationships, that eventually lead youth to construct the kind of personal identity that involves lasting commitments to educational goals and taking ownership for their own learning (Finn, 1989; Roeser, Peck, & Nasir, 2006; Voelkl, 1997). Motivational researchers have documented the effects of some of these resources and vulnerabilities in early adolescence, especially during school transitions (Wigfield et al., 2006). However, we know relatively little about their emergence, the timing of their appearance, or their earlier forms. Detailed programs of research on the development of goals (Dweck, 2002), values (Wigfield & Eccles, 1992, 2002), perceived control (Skinner et al, 1998), and self-regulated learning (Pintrich & Zusho, 2002) may help guide research attempting to explore qualitative developmental changes in other key assets, such as a sense of solidarity, ownership, and identity within the academic community. These motivational resources, although they likely emerge at successive ages, can all be seen as protective factors, fostering academic coping and resilience.

Challenges to Studying and Promoting the Entire Motivational System

A focus on motivational development makes clear that research and interventions must attempt to examine and then take into consideration the dynamic interactions between engagement and the explanatory forces (such as discipline practices or relationships with teachers) that shape its quality over time, and that also shape the emergence of other important motivational outcomes (such as taking responsibility for one's own learning) that arise at later developmental levels. Figure 11.2 depicts a process model of the differential development of the motivational system that distinguishes short-term action outcomes (such as choice and participation) from long-term motivational resources and liabilities (such as self-regulated learning and identification). This general motivational framework, although useful in guiding research and interventions, also presents significant challenges. We enumerate five.

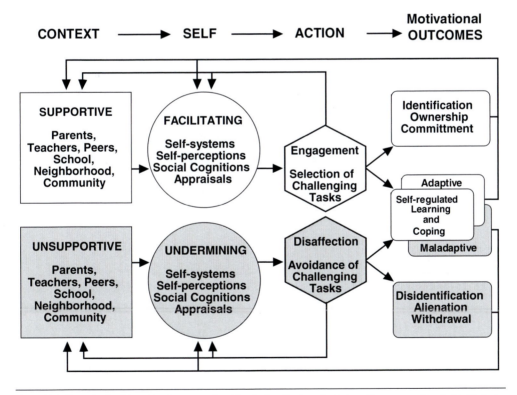

Figure 11.2 The motivational dynamics of engagement and disaffection. The dynamics that amplify engagement are depicted in the top portion, and those that fuel disaffection are depicted in the bottom portion.

Rich Conceptualizations of Engagement and Disaffection

A major challenge to researchers and practitioners is to realize the full richness promised by constructs of engagement and disaffection. Motivational conceptualizations, attempting to capture energized and directed action, suggest that the quality of children's ongoing participation in academic activities encompasses multiple components, including behavior, emotion, and cognitive orientation. A time perspective is also implied, including choice of future activities, initiation of involvement, ongoing participation, and responses to (anticipated and actual) obstacles and difficulties.

Such multidimensional constructs raise thorny conceptual and measurement issues (e.g., O'Farrell & Morrison, 2003). The construction of explicitly multidimensional assessments of engagement and disaffection (Appleton, Christenson, Kim, & Reschly, 2006; Skinner et al., in press; Wellborn, 1991), including ones with hierarchical structures, is needed to clarify and elaborate these constructs. Moreover, in identifying patterns of action, both variable-centered and person-centered approaches (e.g., Patrick et al., 1993; Roeser et al., 2002) are useful strategies. That is, combinations of dimensions may be needed to fully capture the presentation of engagement and disaffection in individual students. For example, a student who is anxiously trying hard has a different quality of engagement from one who is enthusiastically involved in a task (e.g., Patrick et al., 1993). Or a student who is behaviorally passive because of boredom has a different quality of engagement than one who is angry (e.g., Finn et al., 1995). Consistent with the view of action as an inherently multifaceted concept, conceptualizations and assessments may move toward typologies or prototypes of engagement (e.g., Connell & Wellborn, 1991; Wellborn, 1991).

For practitioners and interventionists, a complex construct like engagement and disaffection has benefits and drawbacks. On the one hand, it places more demands on teachers and evaluators: They will need to attend to multiple dimensions of students' participation in class, including ones that are not as obvious as behavioral engagement and disaffection, such as engaged and disaffected emotions. Moreover, teachers (and researchers) will need to be mindful of teachers' own reactions to students, and the unrolling of reciprocal dynamics over time. On the other hand, a full conceptualization of engagement identifies a worthy adversary, that is, a motivational outcome worth working toward, and it also specifies a motivational resource that must be safe-guarded when improvements in other outcomes (e.g., cognitive or social) are the target. No matter what the gains, if teaching practices or intervention efforts undermine any of the features of engagement or foster disaffection, they cannot have lasting positive effects.

Distinguishing and Integrating Constructs from Different Motivational Theories

The identification of a common construct that taps key motivational processes has a huge potential benefit to the motivational area: In principle, it allows theorists to compare, contrast, and begin to integrate major models of motivation, that for too long have occupied separate territories (Ford, 1992; Wigfield & Eccles, 2002). However, it will be a slow and challenging process. As first steps, researchers can examine the effects of a broad range of motivational factors (both interpersonal or individual) on a common set of important motivational processes, thus allowing for the detection of factors that have similar patterns of effects and the discovery of factors that boost one aspect of engagement (e.g., persistence) while undermining another (e.g., enjoyment).

However, progress will also involve theoretical disputes and dueling structural analyses. Because of the field's current focus on social cognitive predictors of motivation, one of the most contentious tasks will be to determine which intrapsychic processes are part of the same underlying self-systems. For example, a thicket of concepts has grown up around the issue of competence or control (Elliot & Dweck, 2005; Skinner, 1996), and the clear structural differentiation of these constructs (e.g., Bong & Skaalvik, 2003) as well as their functional integration (e.g., Skinner et al., 1998) would represent a major step forward (Eccles & Wigfield, 2002). In a similar vein, the convergence of multiple versions of achievement goal theory (Elliot, 2005) has been very useful to the motivation area, but the conceptual and empirical links of these constructs to self-determination theory have yet to be fully recognized (e.g., Ryan & Deci, 1989).

Similar care and effort will be needed to integrate work on the contextual contributors to motivational development. Because of the relative lack of attention to context (Anderman & Anderman, 2000; Urdan, 1999), initial work may focus on surfacing and collecting the many candidate factors from theories of the antecedents of self-systems (e.g., Flammer, 1995), or theories of teaching (Reeve, Bolt, & Cai, 1999), parenting (Skinner, Johnson, & Snyder, 2005), and peer relations (Hymel, Comfort, Schonert-Reichl, & McDougall, 1996). Thoughtful conversations and careful studies will be needed to tease apart whether the features depicted by one theory (e.g., the kinds of authority relations found to promote learning goals) are the same or different from the active ingredients specified by other theories (e.g., autonomy support as depicted in self-determination theory). These dialogues are an opportunity to acknowledge real overlap as well as to sharpen real differences among major theories of motivation.

Engagement as a Diagnostic Tool

Patterns of engagement and disaffection, if they are core indictors of student motivation, may also have the potential to provide teachers and parents a window into the contextual and intrapsychic obstacles students are dealing with as they tackle school-related activities (Skinner et al., 2008). However, it will be a major challenge to theorists and researchers to provide an empirical map detailed enough to justify its use in the field. A few examples may illustrate the potential of this approach: If a child shows a pattern of disaffection characterized by low participation and boredom, and the strongest predictor of such actions is a lack of autonomy, then teachers may consider the antidote of more autonomy support—that is providing students with more interesting academic tasks, more choice in selecting approaches, or activities with more apparent relevance to their daily lives (Reeve et al., 1999).

In contrast, patterns of disaffection dominated by anxiety may point to a sense of helplessness and incompetence as a likely vulnerability. Research on the facilitators of a sense of control, in turn, suggest that provision of involvement and structure, including information about strategies and support for enacting them, may begin to build self-efficacy (Bandura, 1997; Skinner et al., 1998). Research on the psychological and interpersonal predictors of other common patterns, such as self-handicapping and procrastination, or passive-withdrawn or disruptive disaffection (Covington & Dray, 2002; Finn et al., 1995; Roeser, et al., 2002), may likewise reveal both the self-perceptions that typically underlie them and the teacher and parent responses effective in counteracting them (Furrer et al., 2003). Studies investigating the progression of qualitatively different patterns of engagement and disaffection may eventually reveal warning signs early enough to allow preventative actions.

Capturing Process, Episodes, and Dynamics

A major challenge to researchers and interventionists will be to explore the directions of effects in process models and to detect feedback loops (Dornyei, 2000; Ford, 1992). To accomplish this, of course, studies will need to include markers of change over time. So far, longitudinal, time series, and experimental studies suggest that influence flows in both directions. In general, research suggests that amplifying loops are the most typical, reinforcing virtuous or vicious cycles of motivation and achievement. Additional research is needed which documents teachers' and parents' typical reactions to student engagement and disaffection at different ages and over different time windows. Of greatest interest would be studies which help to identify the conditions under which disaffection is met with *countervailing* teacher and parent reactions that lead students back toward engagement.

In general, the intelligent inclusion of time, whether real-time, episodic time, or developmental time, is in its infancy in research on motivation (Ford, 1992), just as it is in the field of psychology more generally. Process models (Dornyei, 2000; Heckhausen, 1991) and dynamic systems theories of motivation (Ford, 1992) will provide some initial guidelines for these endeavors. For example, in a time series study of perceived control and engagement, the design was organized around episodes of naturally-occurring graded homework and tests: Information about expectations and effort was collected prior to completing each assignment, whereas actual performance and attributions for success and failure were assessed only after assignments or tests were graded (Schmitz & Skinner, 1993). This allowed for the examination of the role of perceived control in sequential intraindividual cycles of effort and performance.

What is Developing in Motivational Development?

For motivational researchers, it will be a challenge to examine how motivational dynamics give rise, not just to differential trajectories of engagement, but also to qualitative shifts in important motivational resources and liabilities. For example, as children enter concrete operational thought between third and fifth grades, they may accumulate experiences and beliefs that will crystallize and consolidate as they enter middle school and beyond. Models of participation and identification provide one example of what may be at stake (e.g., Finn, 1989). These models hold that children's participation at school can lead them to identify with its values and goals, and to internalize the sense that they belong there. Other developmental models emphasize the eventual emergence of a sense of pride, ownership, and responsibility for one's own learning (Wolters, 2003), the desire to become a self-regulated learner (Schunk & Zimmerman, 1994), and the acquisition of a repertoire of constructive strategies for coping with challenges, setbacks, and failures (Skinner & Wellborn, 1997).

These models also highlight what is at risk for students who are not fully engaged or who lose their eagerness during the early school years. They paint a picture of disaffection that leads to withdrawal or disruptive classroom behavior, which if unchecked produces the kinds of disidentification, resistance to taking responsibility, and opposition to the values and goals of schooling, that eventually promises friction with teachers and parents, absenteeism, academic failure, and leaving school. These trajectories of escalating disaffection and eventual drop-out are much too familiar to researchers and educators, and as previously mentioned, are especially prevalent among boys and adolescents from low income, ethnic minority, and immigrant groups.

Conclusion

Enthusiasm about engagement has led researchers and practitioners to entrust the idea with a variety of meanings and messages. It has come to symbolize the notion that neither children's academic achievement nor their chances of completing high school are predetermined by their racial, economic, or social status, but instead depend on the extent to which teachers and educational institutions, along with parents and communities, can make schools a welcoming place where students *want* to come and, when present, where they are willing and able to do the hard work that is learning. It allows us to describe what success looks like: enthusiastic effort, concentration, determination in the face of difficulty, fun. The idea of engagement focuses researchers and practitioners on relationships and social interactions, between the student and teachers, principal, classmates, friends, family members, and importantly, the academic activities themselves, and on the disciplinary practices and organizational structures that shape these interactions and relationships.

We argue that engagement and disaffection are central players in the dynamics of motivational development: because they directly influence learning and performance, because they mediate the effects of individual and interpersonal factors, and because they shape reactions from the social context. Taken together, these feedforward and feedback effects place engagement at the heart of motivational cycles that amplify initial individual differences in such a way that the motivationally rich get richer and the poor get poorer as students progress through their academic careers. Cumulatively, such episodes give rise, not only to learning, but also to bonding, commitments, and identifications that function as social glue when the going gets tough, promoting self-regulated learning and resilience and, eventually, allowing children and youth to take responsibility for their own academic progress and development.

References

Abramson, L. Y., Seligman, M. E. P., & Teasdale, J. D. (1978). Learned helplessness in humans. *Journal of Abnormal Psychology, 87*, 49–74.

Altermatt, E. R., Jovanovic, J., & Perry, M. (1998). Bias or responsivity? Sex and achievement-level effects on teachers' classroom questioning practices. *Journal of Educational Psychology, 90*, 516–527.

Ames, C. (1992). Classrooms: Goals, structures, and student motivation. *Journal of Educational Psychology, 84*, 261–271.

Anderman, L. H., & Anderman, E. M. (Eds.). (2000). The role of social context in educational psychology: Substantive and methodological issues [Special issue]. *Educational Psychologist, 35*(2).

Appleton, J. J., Christenson, S. L., Kim, D., & Reschly, A. L. (2006). Measuring cognitive and psychological engagement: Validation of the Student Engagement instrument. *Journal of School Psychology, 44*(5), 427–445.

Bandura, A. (1977). Self-efficacy: Toward a unified theory of behavioral change. *Psychological Review, 84*, 191–215.

Bandura, A. (1997). *Self-efficacy: The exercise of control*. New York: Freeman.

Birch, S. H., & Ladd, G. W. (1996). Interpersonal relationships in the school environment and children's early school adjustment: The role of teachers and peers. In J. Juvonen & K. R. Wentzel (Eds.), *Social motivation: Understanding children's school adjustment* (pp. 199–225). New York: Cambridge University Press.

Blumenfeld, P. C. (1992). Classroom learning and motivation: Clarifying an expanding goal theory. *Journal of Educational Psychology, 84*, 272–281.

Boesch, E. E. (1976). *Psychopathologie des alltags* [Everyday psychopathology]. Bern, Switzerland: Huber.

Bong, M., & Skaalvik, E. M. (2003). Academic self-concept and self-efficacy: How different are they really? *Educational Psychology Review, 13*, 1–40.

Brandtstädter, J. (1998). Action perspectives on human development. In W. Damon (Series Ed.) & R. M. Lerner (Vol. Ed.), *Handbook of child psychology: Vol. 1. Theoretical models of human development* (5th ed., pp. 807–863). New York: Wiley.

Bronfenbrenner, U., & Morris, P. A. (1998). The ecology of developmental processes. In W. Damon (Series Ed.) & R. M. Lerner (Vol. Ed.), *Handbook of child psychology: Vol. 1: Theoretical models of human development* (5th ed., pp. 993–1028). New York: Wiley.

Chapman, M. (1984). Intentional action as a paradigm for developmental psychology: A Symposium. *Human Development, 27,* 113–114.

Connell, J. P. (1990). Context, self, and action: A motivational analysis of self-system processes across the life-span. In D. Cicchetti & M. Beeghly (Eds.), *The self in transition: From infancy to childhood* (pp. 61–97). Chicago: University of Chicago Press.

Connell, J. P., Halpern-Felsher, B. L., Clifford, E., Crichlow, W., & Usinger, P. (1995). Hanging in there: Behavioral, psychological, and contextual factors affecting whether African-American adolescents stay in high school. *Journal of Adolescent Research, 10,* 41–63.

Connell, J. P., Spencer, M. B., & Aber, J. L. (1994). Educational risk and resilience in African-American youth: Context, self, action, and outcomes in school. *Child Development, 65,* 493–506.

Connell, J. P., & Wellborn, J. G. (1991). Competence, autonomy and relatedness: A motivational analysis of self-system processes. In M. Gunnar & L. A. Sroufe (Eds.), *Minnesota Symposium on Child Psychology: Vol. 23. Self processes in development* (pp. 43–77). Chicago: University of Chicago Press.

Covington, M. V., & Dray, E. (2002). The developmental course of achievement motivation: A need-based approach. In A. Wigfield & J. S. Eccles (Eds.), *Development of achievement motivation* (pp. 33–56). San Diego: Academic Press.

Deci, E. L. (1975). *Intrinsic motivation.* New York: Plenum.

Deci, E. L. (1992). On the nature and function of motivational theories. *Psychological Science, 3,* 167–171.

Deci, E. L., & Ryan, R. M. (1985). *Intrinsic motivation and self-determination in human behavior.* New York: Plenum Press.

Deci, E. L., Koestner, R., & Ryan, R. M. (1999). A meta-analytic review of experiments examining the effects of extrinsic rewards on intrinsic motivation. *Psychological Bulletin, 125,* 627–668.

Deci, E. L., & Ryan, R. M. (2000). The "what" and "why" of goal pursuits: Human needs and the self-determination of behavior. *Psychological Inquiry, 11,* 227–268.

Dornyei, Z. (2000). Motivation in action: Towards a process-oriented conceptualization of student motivation. *British Journal of Educational Psychology, 70,* 519–538.

Dweck, C. S. (1975). The role of expectations and attributions in the alleviation of learned helplessness. *Journal of Personality and Social Psychology, 31,* 674–685.

Dweck, C. S. (1999). *Self-theories: Their role in motivation, personality, and development.* Philadelphia: Psychology Press.

Dweck, C. S. (2002). The development of ability conceptions. In A. Wigfield & J. S. Eccles (Eds.), *Development of achievement motivation* (pp. 57–88). San Diego: Academic Press.

Dweck, C. S., & Leggett, E. L. (1988). A social-cognitive approach to motivation and personality. *Psychological Review, 95,* 256–273.

Dweck, C. S., & Molden, D. C. (2005). Self-theories: Their impact on competence motivation and acquisition In A. J. Elliot & C. S. Dweck (Eds.), *Handbook of competence and motivation* (pp. 12–140). New York: Guilford.

Eccles, J. S. (1993). School and family effects on the ontogeny of children's interests, self-perceptions, and activity choice. In J. Jacobs (Ed.), *Nebraska Symposium on Motivation, 1992: Developmental perspectives on motivation* (pp. 145–208) Lincoln: University of Nebraska Press.

Eccles, J. S. (2004). Schools, academic motivation, and stage-environment fit. In R. M. Lerner & L. Steinberg (Eds.), *Handbook of adolescent psychology* (2nd ed., pp. 125–153). New York: Wiley.

Eccles, J. S. (2005). Subjective task values and the Eccles et al. model of achievement-related choices. In A. J. Elliot & C. S. Dweck (Eds.), *Handbook of competence and motivation* (pp. 105–121). New York: Guilford.

Eccles, J. S., Adler, T. F., Futterman, R., Goff, S. B., Kaczala, C. M., Meece, J., & Midgley, C. (1983). Expectancies, values and academic behaviors. In J. T. Spence (Ed.), *Achievement and achievement motives* (pp. 75–146). San Francisco: Freeman.

Eccles, J. S., & Wigfield, A. (1995). In the mind of the achiever: The structure of adolescents' academic achievement related-beliefs and self-perceptions. *Personality and Social Psychology Bulletin, 21,* 215–225.

Eccles, J. S., & Wigfield, A. (2002). Motivational beliefs, values, and goals. *Annual Review of Psychology, 53,* 109–132.

Eccles, J. S., Wigfield, A., & Schiefele, U. (1998). Motivation to succeed. In W. Damon (Series Ed.) & N. Eisenberg (Vol. Ed.), *Handbook of child psychology: Vol. 3. Social, emotional, and personality development* (5th ed., pp. 1017–1095). New York: Wiley.

Elliot, A. J. (2005). A conceptual history of the achievement goal construct. In A. J. Elliot & C. S. Dweck (Eds.), *Handbook of competence and motivation* (pp. 52–72). New York: Guilford.

Elliot, A. J., & Dweck, C. S. (Eds.). (2005). *Handbook of competence and motivation.* New York: Guilford.

Finn, J. D. (1989). Withdrawing from school. *Review of Educational Research, 59,* 117–142.

Finn, J. D., Pannozzo, G., & Voelkl, K. E. (1995). Disruptive and inattentive-withdrawn behavior and achievement among fourth graders. *The Elementary School Journal, 95,* 421–454.

Finn, J. D., & Rock, D. A. (1997). Academic success among students at risk for school failure. *Journal of Applied Psychology, 82,* 221–234.

Finn, J. D., & Voelkl, K. E. (1993). School characteristics related to school engagement. *Journal of Negro Education, 62,* 249–268.

Flammer, A. (1995). Developmental analysis of control beliefs. In A. Bandura (Ed.), *Self-efficacy in changing societies* (pp. 69–113). New York: Cambridge University Press.

Ford, M. E. (1992). *Motivating humans: Goals, emotions, and personal agency beliefs.* Newbury Park, CA: Sage.

Fredricks, J. A., Blumenfeld, P. C., & Paris, A. H. (2004). School engagement: Potential of the concept, state of the evidence. *Review of Educational Research, 74*(1) 59–109.

Frese, M., & Sabini, J. (1985). *Goal-directed behavior: The concept of action in psychology.* Hillsdale, NJ: Erlbaum.

Furrer, C., Kelly, G., & Skinner, E. (2003, April). *Can teachers use children's emotions in the classroom to diagnose and treat underlying motivational problems?* Poster presented at the biennial meetings of the Society for Research in Child Development, Tampa, FL.

Furrer, C., & Skinner, E. (2003). Sense of relatedness as a factor in children's academic engagement and performance. *Journal of Educational Psychology, 95*, 148–162.

Furrer, C., Skinner, E., & Kindermann, T. (2007). *How the motivationally "rich" get "richer": Reciprocal effects of student engagement in the classroom on changes in teacher support over the school year.* Unpublished manuscript. Portland State University.

Gottfried, A. E. (1985). Academic intrinsic motivation in elementary and junior high school students. *Journal of Educational Psychology, 77*(6), 631–645.

Gottfried, A. E., Fleming, J. S., & Gottfried, A. W. (2001). Continuity academic intrinsic motivation from childhood through late adolescence: A longitudinal study. *Journal of Educational Psychology, 93*, 3–13.

Hamre, B. K., & Pianta, R. C. (2001). Early teacher-child relationships and the trajectory of children's school outcomes through eighth grade. *Child Development, 72*, 625–638.

Harackiewicz, J. M., Baron, K. E., Pintrich, P. R., Elliot, A. J., & Thrash, T. M. (2002). Revision of achievement goal theory: Necessary and illuminating. *Journal of Educational Psychology, 94*, 638–645.

Harter, S. (1978). Effectance motivation reconsidered: Toward a developmental model. *Human Development, 21*, 36–64.

Heckhausen, H. (1991). *Motivation and action* (P. K. Leppmann, Trans.). Berlin: Springer.

Hymel, S., Comfort, C., Schonert-Reichl, K.,. & McDougall, P. (1996). Academic failure and school dropout: The influence of peers. In J. Juvonen & K .R. Wentzel (Eds.), *Social motivation: Understanding children's school adjustment* (pp. 313–345). New York: Cambridge University Press.

Jackson, A. & Davis, G. (2000). *Turning points: Educating adolescents for the 21st century.* New York: Teachers College Press.

Jacobs, J., Lanza, S., Osgood, D. W., Eccles, J. S., & Wigfield, A. (2002). Ontogeny of children's self-beliefs: Gender and domain differences across grades one through 12. *Child Development, 73*, 509–527.

Jimerson, S. J., Campos, E., & Greif, J. L. (2003). Towards an understanding of definitions and meures of school engagement and related terms. *California School Psychologist, 8*, 7–27.

Jimerson, S., Egeland, B., Sroufe, L. A., & Carlson, E. (2000). A prospective longitudinal study of high school dropouts: Examining multiple predictors across development. *Journal of School Psychology, 38*, 525–549.

Kindermann, T. A. (1993). Natural peer groups as contexts for individual development: The case of children's motivation in school. *Developmental Psychology, 29*, 970–977.

Kindermann, T. A. (2007). Effects of naturally-existing peer groups on changes in academic engagement in a cohort of sixth graders. *Child Development, 78*, 1186–1203.

Kochanska, G., Aksan, N., & Carlson (2005). Temperament, relationships, and young children's receptive cooperation with their parents. *Developmental Psychology, 41*, 648–660.

Kowaleski-Jones, L., & Duncan, G. J. (1999). The structure of achievement and behavior across middle childhood. *Child Development, 70*, 930–943.

Kuhl, J. (1984). Volitional aspects of achievement motivation and learned helplessness: Toward a comprehensive theory of action control. In B. A. Maher & W. A. Maher (Eds.), *Progress in experimental personalities research* (pp. 99–171). New York: Academic Press.

Ladd, G. W., Birch, S. H., & Buhs, E. S. (1999). Children's social and scholastic lives in kindergarten: Related spheres of influence? *Child Development, 70*, 1373–1400.

Lepper, M. R., & Cordova, D. I. (1992). A desire to be taught: Instructional consequences of intrinsic motivation. *Motivation and Emotion, 16*, 187–208.

Maddox, S. J., & Prinz, R. J. (2003). School bonding in children and adolescents: Conceptualization, assessment, and associated variables. *Clinical Child and Family Psychology Review, 6*, 31–49.

Maehr, M. L., & Midgley, C. (1996). *Transforming school cultures.* Boulder, CO: Westview Press.

Marks, H. M. (2000). Student engagement in instructional activity: Patterns in the elementary, middle, and high school years. *American Educational Research Journal, 37*, 153–184.

Meece, J. L., Anderman, E. M., & Anderman, L. H. (2006). Classroom goal structures, student motivation, and academic achievement. *Annual Review of Psychology* (Vol. 57, pp. 487–504). Chippewa Falls, WI: Annual Reviews.

Meece, J. L., & Kurtz-Costes, B. (2001). Introduction: The schooling of ethnic minority children and youth. *Educational Psychologist, 36*, 1–7.

Merton, R. K. (1953). *Social theory and social structure.* London: The Free Press of Glencoe.

Miceli, M., & Castelfranchi, C. (2000). Nature and mechanisms of loss of motivation. *Review of General Psychology, 4*(3), 238–263.

Murdock, T. B. (1999). The social context of risk: Status and motivational predictors of alienation in middle school. *Journal of Educational Psychology, 91*, 62–76.

Murphy, P. K., & Alexander, P. A. (2000). A motivated exploration of motivation terminology. *Contemporary Educational Psychology, 25*, 3–53.

National Research Council. (2004). *Engaging schools: Fostering high school students' motivation to learn.* Washington, DC: National Academic Press.

Newmann, F. (1991). Student engagement in academic work: Expanding the perspective of secondary school effectiveness. In J. R. Bliss & W. A. Firestone (Eds.), *Rethinking effective schools: Research and practice* (pp. 58–76). New York: Teachers College Press.

Newmann, F., Wehlage, G. G., & Lamborn, S. D. (1992). The significance and sources of student engagement. In F. Newmann (Ed.), *Student engagement and achievement in secondary schools* (pp. 11–39). New York: Teachers College Press.

Nicholls, J. G. (1984). Achievement motivation: Conceptions of ability, subjective experience, task choice, and performance. *Psychological Review, 91*, 328–346.

O'Farrell, S. L., & Morrison, G. M. (2003). A factor analysis exploring school bonding and related constructs among upper elementary students. *The California School Psychologist, 8*, 53–72.

Patrick, B. C., Skinner, E. A., & Connell, J. P. (1993). What motivates children's behavior and emotion? The joint effects of perceived control and autonomy in the academic domain. *Journal of Personality and Social Psychology, 65*(4), 781–791.

Pelletier, L. G., & Vallerand, R. J. (1996). Supervisors' beliefs and subordinates intrinsic motivation: A behavioral confirmation analysis. *Journal of Personality and Social Psychology, 71*, 331–340.

Peterson, C., Maier, S. F., & Seligman, M. E. P. (1993). *Learned helplessness: A theory for the age of personal control.* New York: Oxford University Press.

Pierson, L. H., & Connell, J. P. (1992). Effect of grade retention on self-system processes, school engagement, and academic performance. *Journal of Educational Psychology, 84*, 300–307.

Pintrich, P. R. (2000). An achievement goal theory perspective on issues in motivation terminology, theory, and research. *Contemporary Educational Psychology, 25*, 92–104.

Pintrich, P. R. (2003). A motivational science perspective of the role of student motivation in learning and teaching contexts. *Journal of Educational Psychology, 95*, 667–686.

Pintrich, P. R., & Schunk, D. H. (2003). *Motivation in education: Theory, research, and application* (2nd ed.). Englewood Cliffs, NJ: Merrill-Prentice Hall.

Pintrich, P. R., & Zusho, A. (2002). The development of academic self-regulation: The role of cognitive and motivational factors. In A. Wigfield & J. S. Eccles (Eds.), *Development of achievement motivation* (pp. 250–284). San Diego: Academic Press.

Reeve, J. (2005). *Understanding motivation and emotion* (4th ed.). Hoboken, NJ: Wiley.

Reeve, J., Bolt, E., & Cai, Y. (1999). Autonomy supportive teachers: How they teach and motivate students. *Journal of Educational Psychology, 91*, 537–548.

Roeser, R.W., Peck, S. C., & Nasir, N. S. (2006). Self and identity processes in school motivation, learning, and achievement. In P. Alexander & P. H. Winne (Eds.), *Handbook of educational psychology* (2nd ed., pp. 391–424). Mahwah, NJ: Erlbaum.

Roeser, R., Strobel, K. R., & Quihuis, G. (2002). Studying early adolescents' academic motivation, social-emotional functioning, and engagement in learning: Variable- and person-centered approaches. *Anxiety, Stress, and Coping, 15*, 345–368.

Ryan, A. M. (2000). Peer groups as a context for the socialization of adolescents' motivation, engagement, and achievement in school. *Educational Psychologist, 35*, 101–111.

Ryan, R. M., & Connell, P. (1989). Perceived locus of causality and internalization: Examining reasons for acting in two domains. *Journal of Personality and Social Psychology, 57*, 749–761.

Ryan, R. M., & Deci. E. L. (1989). Bridging the research traditions of task/ego involvement and intrinsic/extrinsic motivation: A commentary on Butler (1987). *Journal of Educational Psychology, 81*, 265–268.

Ryan R. M., & Deci, E. L. (2000). Intrinsic and extrinsic motivations: Classic definitions and new directions. *Contemporary Educational Psychology, 25*, 54–67.

Ryan, A. M., & Patrick, H. (2001). The classroom social environment and changes in adolescents' motivation and engagement during middle school. *American Educational Research Journal, 38*, 437–460.

Schmitz, B., & Skinner, E. (1993). Perceived control, effort, and academic performance: Interindividual, intraindividual, and multivariate time-series analyses. *Journal of Personality and Social Psychology, 64*(6), 1010–1028.

Schunk, D. H., & Pajares, F. (2005). Competence perceptions and academic functioning. In A. J. Elliot & C. S. Dweck (Eds.), *Handbook of competence and motivation* (pp. 85–104). New York: Guilford.

Schunk, D. H., & Zimmerman, B. J. (Eds.). (1994). *Self-regulation of learning and performance.* Hillsdale, NJ:Erlbaum.

Schutz, P. A., & DeCuir, J. T. (2002). Inquiry on emotions in education. *Educational Psychologist, 37*, 125–134.

Seligman, M. E. P. (1975). *Helplessness: On depression, development, and death.* San Francisco: Freeman.

Shernoff, D. J., Csikszentmihalyi, M., Schneider, B., & Shernoff, E. S. (2003). Student engagement in high school classrooms from the perspective of flow theory, *School Psychology Quarterly, 18*, 158–176.

Sinclair, M. F., Christenson, S. L., Lehr, C. A., & Anderson, A. R. (2003). Facilitating student learning and engagement: Lessons learned form Check & Connect longitudinal studies. *The California School Psychologist, 8*, 29–41.

Skinner, E. A. (1995). *Perceived control, motivation, and coping.* Newbury Park, CA: Sage.

Skinner, E. A. (1996). A guide to constructs of control. *Journal of Personality and Social Psychology, 71*, 549–570.

Skinner, E. A., & Belmont, M. J. (1993). Motivation in the classroom: Reciprocal effects of teacher behavior and student engagement across the school year. *Journal of Educational Psychology, 85,* 571–581.

Skinner, E. A., Furrer, C., Marchand, G., & Kindermann, T. (2008). Engagement and disaffection in the classroom: Part of a larger motivational dynamic? *Journal of Educational Psychology, 100,* 765–781.

Skinner, E. A., Johnson, S., & Snyder, T. (2005). Six dimensions of parenting: A motivational model. *Parenting: Science and Practice, 5,* 175–236.

Skinner, E. A., Kindermann, T. A., & Furrer, C. (in press). A motivational perspective on engagement and disaffection: Conceptualization and assessment of children's behavioral and emotional participation in academic activities in the classroom. *Educational and Psychological Measurement.*

Skinner, E. A., & Wellborn, J. G. (1994). Coping during childhood and adolescence: A motivational perspective. In D. Featherman, R. Lerner, & M. Perlmutter (Eds.), *Life-span development and behavior* (Vol. 12, pp. 91–133). Hillsdale, NJ: Erlbaum.

Skinner, E. A., & Wellborn, J. G. (1997). Children's coping in the academic domain. In S. A. Wolchik & I. N. Sandler (Eds.), *Handbook of children's coping with common stressors: Linking theory and intervention* (pp. 387–422). New York: Plenum.

Skinner, E. A., Wellborn, J. G., & Connell, J. P. (1990). What it takes to do well in school and whether I've got it: The role of perceived control in children's engagement and school achievement. *Journal of Educational Psychology, 82,* 22–32.

Skinner, E. A., Zimmer-Gembeck, M. J., & Connell, J. P. (1998). Individual differences and the development of perceived control. *Monographs of the Society for Research in Child Development, 63*(nos. 2 and 3) whole no. 254.

Spencer, M. B. (2006). Phenomenology and ecological systems theory: Development of diverse groups. In W. Damon (Series Ed.) & R. Lerner (Vol. Ed.), *Handbook of child psychology, vol. 1: Theoretical models of human development* (6th ed., pp. 829–893). New York: Wiley.

Taylor, R. D., Casten, R., Flickinger, S., Roberts, D., & Fulmore, C. D. (1994). Explaining the school performance of African-American adolescents. *Journal of Research on Adolescence, 4,* 21–44.

Thorkildsen, T., & Nicholls, J. G. (1998). Fifth graders' achievement orientations and beliefs: Individual and classroom differences. *Journal of Educational Psychology, 90,* 179–201.

Trautwein, U., Lüdtke, O., Kastens, C. & Köller, O. (2006). Effort on homework in grades 5 through 9: Development, motivational antecedents, and the association with effort on classwork. *Child Development, 77,* 1094–1111.

Turner, J. C., & Meyer, D. K. (2000). Studying and understanding the instructional contexts of classrooms: Using our past to forge our future. *Educational Psychologist, 35,* 69–85.

Urdan, T. C. (Ed.). (1999). *The role of context: Advances in motivation and achievement* (Vol. 11). Greenwich, CT: JAI.

Vallerand, R. J., Pelletier, L. G., Blais, M. R., Brière, N. M., Senécal, C. B. & Vallières, E. F. (1993). On the assessment of intrinsic, extrinsic, and amotivation in education: Evidence on the concurrent and construct validity of the Academic Motivation Scale. *Educational and Psychological Measurement, 53,* 159–172.

Voelkl, K. (1997). Identification with school. *American Journal of Education, 105,* 294–318.

Weiner, B. (1985). An attributional theory of achievement motivation and emotion. *Psychological Review, 92,* 548–573.

Weiner, B. (1986). *An attributional theory of motivation and emotion.* New York: Springer.

Weiner, B. (2005). Motivation from an attributional perspective and the social psychology of perceived competence. In A. J. Elliot & C. S. Dweck (Eds.), *Handbook of competence and motivation* (pp. 73–84). New York: Guilford.

Wellborn, J. G. (1991). *Engaged and disaffected action: The conceptualization and measurement of motivation in the academic domain.* Unpublished doctoral dissertation, University of Rochester, New York.

Wentzel, K. R. (1993). Does being good make the grade? Social behavior and academic competence in middle school. *Journal of Educational Psychology, 85,* 357–364.

White, R. W. (1959). Motivation reconsidered: The concept of competence. *Psychological Review, 66,* 297–333.

Wigfield, A., & Eccles, J. (1992). The development of achievement task values: A theoretical analysis. *Developmental Review, 12,* 265–310.

Wigfield, A., & Eccles, J. S. (2000). Expectancy–value theory of motivation. *Contemporary Educational Psychology, 25,* 68–81.

Wigfield, A., & Eccles, J. S. (2002). Students' motivation during the middle school years. In J. Aronson (Ed.), *Improving academic achievement: Impact of psychological factors in education* (pp. 159–184). San Diego: Academic Press.

Wigfield, A., Eccles, J. S., & Rodriguez, D. (1998). The development of children's motivation in school contexts. *Review of Research in Educational Psychology, 23,* 73–118.

Wigfield, A., Eccles, J. S., Schiefele, U., Roeser, R., & Davis-Kean, P. (2006). Development of achievement motivation. In W. Damon (Ser. Ed.) & N. Eisenberg (Vol. Ed.), *Handbook of child psychology, 6th Ed. Vol.3. Social, emotional, and personality development* (pp. 933–1002). New York: Wiley.

Wooley, M. E., & Bowen, G. L. (2007). In the context of risk: Supportive adults and the school engagement of middle-school students. *Family Relations, 56,* 92–104.

Wolters, C. A. (2003). Regulation of motivation: Evaluating an underemphasized aspect of self-regulated learning. *Educational Psychologist, 38,* 189–206.

12
Motives to Self-Regulate Learning
A Social Cognitive Account

Barry J. Zimmerman and Timothy J. Cleary

When students enter the primary grades in school, they must make a number of adaptations that are pivotal to their academic success, such as learning to follow directions, work cooperatively with other children, and ask for help when it is needed. As students move through the elementary grades, they are expected to function increasingly on their own, such as completing assigned homework outside class, and eventually in middle school and beyond, to engage in self-initiated and self-sustained studying and practicing. What can explain students' growing capacity to adapt successfully to the increasing demands of schools, and how can these competencies be taught more effectively? In this chapter, we will consider the defining features of students' efforts to self-regulate their learning, a cyclical phase conceptualization of Self-Regulated Learning (SRL) and self-motivation, microanalytic and other event measures of SRL and motivation, the development of self-regulatory sources of motivation from social learning experiences, and a cyclical social cognitive intervention to empower students with self-regulatory deficiencies.

Defining Self-Regulated Learning

SRL has been defined as self-generated thoughts, feelings, and actions that are planned and cyclically adapted to the attainment of personal goals (Schunk & Zimmerman, 1994).[1] This definition involves goals and motivational feelings or beliefs about attaining those goals as well as self-initiated learning processes. The purpose of self-regulatory accounts of human functioning is to explain how one adapts to changing conditions as a result of personal feedback. A *feedback loop* is a central feature of all self-regulatory accounts, including those designed to explain academic learning (Butler & Winne, 1995; Zimmerman, 1989). This loop refers to information provided as a consequence of one's behavior or understanding that has relevance to subsequent adaptations (Hattie & Timperley, 2007). The sources of feedback can be social (e.g. such as praise or guidance from a teacher, peer, or a parent), environmental (e.g., task, micro-environment, or computer outcomes), or personal (e.g., awareness of covert, physiological, or behavioral outcomes).

Researchers' understanding of the nature and functioning of feedback loops has become more detailed and complete over time.

In classic accounts of self-regulation (Miller, Galanter, & Pribham, 1960; Powers, 1973, 1998), the feedback loop is linked to *control* decisions based on an intended target, goal state, or reference standard. According to this formulation, a person's initial performance level is first tested against a standard. If the feedback indicates that his or her performance is insufficient, control shifts to a self-corrective operation, which is continued recursively until the feedback indicates one's performance meets the standard. At that point, control shifts and the corrective operation ceases, much like a thermostat shuts off a furnace when the room temperature reaches a preset level. The source of self-regulation during recursive cycles to learn has been labeled "negative" feedback because it is based on a discrepancy between one's current level of performance and a desired state. This discrepancy is viewed as noxious, which is assumed to motivate learners to reduce it. This classic view of self-regulatory feedback has been widely embraced, especially by information processing researchers.

In the mid-1980s, Bandura (1986) offered a social cognitive perspective of self-regulatory feedback loops based on three closely-linked recursive *processes*: self-observation, judgment, and self-reactions. He hypothesized that each of these processes is influenced by social variables (e.g., self-regulatory efforts by peer models) as well as by self-reactions to personal feedback. *Self-observation* refers to tracking specific aspects of one's performance and outcomes, such as one's academic grades, whereas *judgment* refers to comparing those outcomes to a standard, such as one's grade goals or the performance of other students. *Self-reaction* refers to the reactions of learners to these judgments, such as positive personal feelings and continued efforts to learn.

Social cognitive researchers have cautioned against narrow conceptions of learners' self-reactions. Classic views of feedback (i.e., as having a negative function) limit learners' self-regulatory reactions to reducing performance discrepancies against an unchanging standard (Locke, 1991). That account has also been described as "closed-loop" because the standard that controls the recursive cycles was viewed as unchanging and the learner as desisting after the standard is attained. In contrast, social cognitive researchers view feedback also in open-loop terms, wherein learners can respond to success or failure by raising or lowering their goals or by undertaking more or less challenging tasks. Social cognitive researchers assume that a comprehensive account of self-reactions involves both open and closed loop reactions to feedback. For example, when devotees of crossword puzzles decide to move to a higher level of challenge, they make success more difficult to achieve, but they continue to use outcome discrepancies as a way to motivate themselves to succeed at each level of skill. Thus, Bandura's (1986) social cognitive view emphasizes both social and personal processes in the interpretation of feedback.

A Cyclical Phase Model of Self-Regulatory Feedback

During the late 1990s, Zimmerman (2000) expanded prior social cognitive conceptions of students' feedback loops to include three cyclical phases: forethought, performance, and self-reflection (see Figure 12.1). Forethought refers to self-regulatory processes that precede efforts to act and set the stage for it, such as goal setting and strategic planning (Bandura, 1991). Performance involves self-regulatory processes that occur during motoric efforts and affect attention and action, such as strategy use and self-recording. Self-reflection includes self-regulatory processes that occur after performance efforts and influence a person's response to that experience, such as self-evaluative judgments and adaptive self-reactions. These self-reflections, in turn, influence

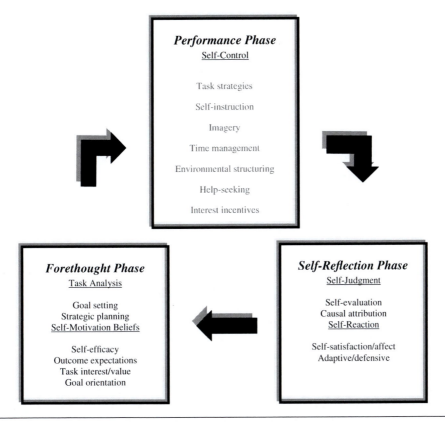

Figure 12.1 Phases and subprocesses of self-regulation. From "Motivating self-regulated problem solvers" by B. J Zimmerman, & M. Campillo (2003), in *The nature of problem solving* (p. 239). J. E. Davidson & R. J. Sternberg (Eds.). New York: Cambridge University Press. Copyright (2003) by Cambridge University Press. Reprinted with permission.

forethought processes and beliefs regarding subsequent efforts to learn—thus completing a self-regulatory feedback cycle.

It will be noted that processes of earlier social cognitive models of feedback, namely self-observation, self-judgment, and self-reactions, were expanded to include subprocesses, such as self-observation incorporating metacognitive monitoring and record keeping. Furthermore, proactive processes, such as task analysis, goal setting, and strategic planning were included in a forethought phase. These additions were made to the earlier model because of a growing body of research on the importance of these self-regulatory processes, such as Schunk and Swartz's (1993) demonstration of the effectiveness of process goals, Lodewyk and Winne's (2005) findings on the importance of task analysis, and Zimmerman & Kitsantas' (1999) research on self-regulatory strategies.

Self-Regulatory Subprocesses Designed to Enhance Personal Feedback Our discussion of these additional processes will focus initially on two forms of self-observation: metacognitive (or self-) monitoring and record keeping. Recall that self-observation was the first of three self-regulatory processes in Bandura's 1986 view of self-regulation. *Metacognitive monitoring* refers to a person's mental tracking of specific aspects of their own performance, the conditions that surround it, and the effects that it produces (Zimmerman & Paulsen, 1995). Although skill in directing one's attention may seem elementary, it is not—because the amount of information involved in complex performances can overwhelm novice self-observers and lead to cursory self-monitoring. *Self-recording* refers to keeping tangible records of one's functioning to improve his/her effectiveness. When advantageous forms of recording are used, this strategy can enhance behavioral and environmental determinants as well as metacognitive ones. For example, personal records of one's functioning can greatly increase the proximity, informativeness, and accuracy of one's feedback (Zimmerman & Kitsantas, 1997, 1999). Records are proximal in the sense that they can capture personal information at the point it occurs; records are informative in that they structure personal feedback to be most meaningful; records are accurate in that they preserve personal data to discern evidence of progress.

Both metacognitive monitoring and record keeping processes can lead to improved cycles of self-experimentation (Bandura, 1991). For example, when records of natural variations in a learner's behavior reveal confounded evidence of causality, he or she can systematically test various hypotheses. For example, when a struggling student's test score in biology suddenly improves, she or she can test various hypotheses, such as whether particular memory strategy is working or whether this success is due merely to increases in study time. In this way, systematic metacognitive monitoring and self-recording can lead to greater personal understanding and better academic performance.

Turning next to forethought phase processes, the quality of one's feedback can be improved by superior forms of task analysis and preparation, such as goal setting and strategic planning. *Goal setting* refers to deciding to attain specific outcomes of learning or performance (Locke & Latham, 1990, 2002), such as solving decimal problems in mathematics during a study session. Goals that are specific, proximal, and challenging are more effective than general goals to "do your best" or no goals (Bandura & Schunk, 1981). For example, a student who sets a specific study goal of completing a math homework assignment by the end of an evening would be more effective than a student who studies in a desultory manner. The goal systems of proactive learners are often organized in hierarchical feedback loops wherein subordinate goals operate as proximal regulators of more distant outcome goals. These subordinate goals become check points for metacognitively monitoring the attainment of highly valued outcomes. For example, a pupil learning to use metaphors to write more effectively will feel an increasing sense of efficacy as various components of this strategy are mastered, such as using the word "like" to form a comparison.

In addition to goal setting, students can improve the quality of their feedback by engaging in other methods of forethought such as *strategic planning*, the selection of advantageous methods for enhancing learning processes. Self-regulatory *strategies* refer to planned sequences of activities designed to improve the effectiveness of a specific process, such as imagining objects interacting to improve one's memory of their association (Pressley, 1977; Zimmerman & Rocha, 1987). Ideal self-regulatory strategies are powerful, parsimonious, and transferable. They are powerful in the sense that they can produce major changes in functioning in relatively brief periods of time. Strategies are parsimonious in the sense that they require minimal memory space to be stored for recall. Strategies are transferable because they can be used with a class of tasks.

Effective planning involves selecting strategies that are appropriate for the task and setting. A self-regulatory strategy seldom works optimally for a person on all tasks or occasions. As a skill develops, the effectiveness of an initial acquisition strategy often declines to the point where another strategy becomes necessary, such as when an aspiring writer shifts his or her text revision *task strategy* from editing an essay for conceptual clarity to editing it for grammar. Thus, as a result of diverse and changing intrapersonal, interpersonal, and contextual feedback, self-regulated individuals must adapt their goals and choice of strategies cyclically.

Other self-regulatory strategies have been developed to improve the quality of one's feedback during the performance phase, such as self-instruction and imagery. *Self-instruction* involves overtly or covertly describing how to proceed as one executes a task, such as articulating steps for computing gas pressure in science, and research has shown that such verbalizations can improve students' learning (Schunk, 1982b). Meichenbaum (1977) has been at the forefront of efforts to enhance students' self-instruction during learning efforts, especially with learning disabled children. *Imagery* involves forming mental pictures to assist learning and retention, such as forming an image of a person's face to help remember his name. These images can be dynamic as well as static, such as when skaters, divers, or gymnasts form images of successful executions of their planned routines in order to enhance their performance (Garfield & Bennett, 1985). Among the strategies that have been used to enhance one's cyclical control of his or her physical and social environment during the performance phase are environmental structuring and help seeking. *Environmental structuring* refers to methods for optimizing the effectiveness of one's micro-environments, such as seating oneself at a desk in order to take notes when reading assigned texts. *Help-seeking* involves asking for assistance when learning or performing. Help-seeking may seem to be the opposite of self-regulation because assistance is sought from others. However, knowing what to ask for, when to ask it, and to whom to approach involves proactive efforts on the part of learners. Help-seeking can be classified as a social form of information seeking (Zimmerman & Martinez-Pons, 1986), and research has revealed that low achievers are very reluctant to seek information (Karabenick, 1998; Newman, 1994, 2007).

Time management is another performance process that has been improved through the use of strategies, such as setting specific task goals, estimating time requirements for those tasks, and monitoring progress in the attainment of those goals (Zimmerman, Greenberg, & Weinstein, 1994). Students who procrastinate lack time management skills but can profit from training in time management strategies (Schmitz & Wiese, 2006). Clearly, a variety of creative and effective self-regulatory strategies have been used to enhance students' academic learning and performance. We turn next to the question of what motivates students to adopt and deploy these strategies.

Forethought Phase Sources of Motivation Students' decision to regulate their academic functioning strategically depends on their beliefs about the effectiveness of these strategies and their personal skill in implementing them during each phase of self-regulation. During the forethought phase, self-efficacy beliefs, outcome expectations, task interest or valuing, and goal orientation have been found to affect the strategic choices that students make (see Figure 12.1). These four sources of self-motivation also affect students' effort and persistence during the performance phase as well as their self-evaluative judgments during the self-reflection phase. For example, *self-efficacy* is defined as beliefs about one's capabilities to learn or perform at designated levels, and these beliefs have been shown to have motivational implication by increasing one's effort, persistence, and choice of activities (Bandura, 1986; 1997; Schunk & Pajares, 2004; Zimmerman, 1995). Students' self-efficacy beliefs play a major role in motivating not only their forethought phase goal setting and choice of strategies (Zimmerman & Bandura, 1994; Zimmerman, Bandura, & Martinez-Pons, 1992), but also their performance phase efforts to write (Schunk & Swartz, 1993), manage study time (Britton & Tessor, 1991), resist adverse peer pressures volitionally (Bandura, Barbaranelli, Caprara, & Pastorelli, 1996), and self-monitor (Bouffard-Bouchard, Parent, & Larivee, 1991).

By contrast, *outcome expectations* refer to beliefs about the ultimate ends of one's performance, ranging from social acclaim and a desirable job to failure or the loss of a position. Of course, students' outcome expectations depend in part on their perceptions of self-efficacy because beliefs about the effectiveness of learning processes are linked closely to beliefs about outcomes (Schunk & Zimmerman, 2006), and there is evidence that when self-efficacy and outcome beliefs are combined as predictors, self-efficacy beliefs account for the greatest variance in student achievement (Shell, Murphy, & Bruning, 1989). However, it is also possible for a student to feel efficacious about a skill, such as learning a foreign language, but not be motivated to enroll in language courses if this skill is not expected to be useful.

A third source of forethought phase motivation to self-regulate is students' *task interest or valuing,* which refers to appreciating a task for its inherent properties rather than for its instrumental qualities in gaining other outcomes (Deci & Ryan, 1985; Lepper & Hodell, 1989). Wigfield and Eccles (1992, 2002) refer to this motive as interest value and define it as enjoyment from doing an activity, such as learning to solve crossword puzzles for the pleasure of the task rather than as a way to build vocabulary to advance one's career.

A fourth motive to self-regulate involves students' goal orientation, which involves their beliefs or feelings about the purpose of learning rather then the act of goal setting (Pintrich, 2003). For example, a mastery goal orientation commits one to learning in order to improve one's academic competence without reference to a specific academic event. By contrast, setting a proximal goal commits oneself to a specific academic event at a particular point in time, such as completing a term paper in three weeks. This type of goal produces a definite feedback loop that requires self-evaluation on that date (Zimmerman, 2007).

Although there are some variations in the names and number of goal orientations by such prominent theorists as Ames, Dweck, Elliot, Harackiewiez, Midgley and their colleagues, there is consensus that the purpose of a *performance goal orientation* is to gain positive judgments of personal competence whereas the purpose of a *learning goal orientation* is to increase one's competence. According to Dweck and her colleagues (Dweck, 1988; Dweck & Master, 2007), a performance goal orientation assumes that one's ability is a fixed entity whereas a learning goal orientation assumes that one's ability can be modified incrementally. The former goal orientation will motivate confident (i.e., self-efficacious) learners to seek opportunities to demonstrate their prowess but will discourage unconfident learners and lead to feelings of helplessness. In contrast, a learning goal orientation, which is also called a mastery or task goal orientation, will motivate both confident and unconfident learners to seek opportunities to improve their abilities. Thus, a student's goal orientation has clear implications for his or her SRL: Incremental theorists seek self-improvement rather than favorable social comparisons with others.

Research shows (Grant & Dweck, 2003) that college students with a strong learning goal orientation used deep learning strategies more frequently when they studied for a pre-med course than students with a weak learning goal orientation. The former students also recovered more quickly from poor performance on the first exam in the course and displayed higher performance by the end of that course than students with a performance goal orientation. Clearly, students' goal orientation is a key precursor of their use of SRL processes.

Performance Phase Sources of Motivation Research by Wolters and his colleagues has focused on strategies that students use to enhance their motivation to learn or perform more effectively (Wolters, 1999, 2003; Wolters & Pintrich, 1998). For example, Wolters and Rosenthal (2000) studied the effectiveness of five strategies that students' can use to increase their effort and persistence in overcoming obstacles to learning using a self-report questionnaire. One of these strategies is *self-consequences*, which involved setting rewarding or punishing contingencies for oneself, such as putting off a refreshing drink until after one's homework is completed (Zimmerman & Martinez-Pons, 1986). A second motivational strategy involves *environmental control* wherein students make their physical surroundings more attractive for task completion, such as high school students' hanging a picture of their favorite college in their bedroom to motivate them to study hard enough to be admitted. A third and fourth strategy that students use to motivate themselves involves self-talk regarding either the benefits of task mastery (i.e., learning goal orientation) or performance phase outcomes (i.e., performance goal orientations). These performance phase *self-instructions* are closely linked to students' forethought phase goal orientations. The final strategy that was included in the questionnaire is *interest enhancement*, such as when a student makes learning geographic location of each American state into a game of surpassing one's previous record.

Wolters and Rosenthal (2000) assessed eighth-grade students' motivational strategies using a questionnaire and found that several performance phase strategy ratings (i.e., self-consequences, environmental control, mastery self-talk, and interest enhancement) were predicted by their forethought phase task values. In research with 9th- and 10th-grade students, Wolters (1999) discovered that mastery self-talk predicted two motivational outcomes (i.e., students' expenditure of effort and persistence) better than performance self-talk. Mastery self-talk was predicted by students' engagement in forethought planning and performance phase monitoring. Interestingly, Wolters also found that students who focused on obtaining good grades increased their motivation more than students who focused on an inner desire to learn or make the material more interesting. Thus, when students value an academic activity, whether for personal mastery or obtaining academic grades, they are motivated to increase their effort and persistence in using learning strategies, such as planning and monitoring. Zimmerman and Martinez-Pons (1986) also studied self-consequences and environmental structuring using a structured interview methodology along with 12 other forms of SRL in response to hypothetical academic tasks. These two forms discriminated significantly between advanced academic track and regular track high school students.

Metacognitive or self-monitoring has implications for motivation as well as learning. Tracking changes in one's learning outcomes can produce reactive motivational effects by inspiring learners to expend greater effort. For example, Lan (1998) studied the effects of record keeping on college students' learning during a course in statistics. The students were given specific content goals for the course and were asked to monitor their studying of each goal and their perceived levels of self-efficacy. He found that students who kept records reported higher use of nearly all SRL strategies assessed by Zimmerman and Martinez-Pons' (1986, 1988) structured interview. The motivational impact of self-recording was particularly evident in the students' informal comments as well as the learning impact of self-recording. One student expressed the feeling that self-recording "pushed" him to spend extra time study on the course. Another student commented, "The protocol helped me to realize how much time I should be spending on preparations of the course" (Lan, 1998, p. 99). Clearly, monitoring and record keeping had a strong effect on students' expenditure of time and effort.

Self-Reflection Phase Sources of Motivation What are the sources of students' motivation to persist and adapt rather than to avoid future opportunities to learn during self-reflection? One source of motivation, *self-evaluative judgments,* depends not only on the physical properties of one's feedback (e.g., the degree of praise or criticism from others), but also on one's self-regulatory standards, such as setting an absolute standard versus a graduated standard for success (Kitsantas & Zimmerman, 2006).

A second source of motivation, *causal attribution judgments,* can also have a major impact on students' motivation to learn (Weiner, 1979). The results of one's efforts to learn are often difficult to interpret because they may be due to a variety of causes, such as one's ability, expenditure of effort, and various environmental affordances or limitations. Because learners appraise the role of these factors subjectively, they can attribute their results erroneously to uncontrollable causes, such as low ability. Fortunately, students' attributions of causality depend in significant part on self-regulatory processes and beliefs from prior phases. For example, learners who plan to use a specific strategy during the forethought phase and implement its use during the performance phase are more likely to attribute failures to that strategy rather than low ability, which can sustain motivation (Zimmerman & Kitsantas, 1997). Because strategies are perceived as a controllable cause, attributions to their use protect learners against negative self-reactions and foster an adaptive course of subsequent action (Corno, 1993; Kuhl, 1985). There is extensive evidence that student attributions of learning outcomes to controllable processes, such as effort or strategy use are more motivating than attributions to uncontrollable factors, such as fixed mental or physical ability (Schunk, 1982a; Zimmerman & Kitsantas, 1997).

Learners' self-judgments are linked to key self-reactions. *Self-satisfaction* reactions refer to feelings of satisfaction or dissatisfaction (and associated affect) regarding one's performance. These emotions can range from elation to anxiety, and there is evidence that students' perceptions of satisfaction and positive affect motivate them to continue efforts to learn (Zimmerman & Kitsantas, 1999). A closely associated self-reaction involves adaptive or defensive inferences, which are conclusions about whether one needs to alter his or her approach during subsequent efforts to learn. Students displaying a high level of self-satisfaction are more likely to make *adaptive inferences* for errors, such as by choosing a more effective strategy when negative consequences occur (Zimmerman & Bandura, 1994). Conversely, students who are dissatisfied with their performance resort to *defensive inferences* to avoid further aversive affect. Garcia and Pintrich (1994) have discussed the adverse effects of defensive inferences, such as helplessness, procrastination, task avoidance, cognitive disengagement, and apathy. These self-reactions are closely linked to self-judgments. For example, learners' who attribute errors to uncontrollable causes will feel dissatisfied, which in turn discourages them from engaging in further efforts to learn. By contrast, learners who attribute errors to controllable causes feel satisfied, which in turn sustains further cyclical efforts to learn.

These self-reactions influence forethought processes regarding further solution efforts, thus completing the self-regulatory feedback cycle. For example, students who experience a high level of self-satisfaction display increases in various sources of forethought motivation, such as increased self-efficacy or valuing of the learning task (Zimmerman & Kitsantas, 1999). In addition to these motivational benefits, advantageous adaptive inferences have led to improved strategic planning and to advantageous shifts in goals when necessary (Cleary & Zimmerman, 2001). By contrast, a high level of dissatisfaction reduces students' motivation to continue, and their lack of adaptation greatly undermines the quality of further efforts to learn. It should be noted that the length of each self-regulatory cycle can vary from minutes to years depending on learners' goals and feedback as well as other self-regulatory processes. Thus, the frequency and quality of one's feedback can be self-regulated to a significant degree. The cyclical nature of self-regulatory models enables them to explain rapid shifts in learning as well as gradual shifts over protracted periods of time.

Microanalytic and Other Event Measures of SRL

An important feature of a cyclical model is its suitability to explain changes in self-regulatory functioning as they occur in real time across the three phases. Social cognitive researchers have developed a *microanalytic* methodology for assessing self-regulatory processes and motivational beliefs before, during and after each cyclical effort to learn from personal feedback (Bandura, 1997; Kitsantas & Zimmerman, 2002). According to this methodology, each student is separately queried and observed as he or she attempts to learn an authentic skill, such as mathematical computation or writing. Simple open- or closed-ended questions are asked about strategies and motivational beliefs, such as students' grade goals or sense of self-efficacy while studying for an English test on Shakespeare. Microanalytic questions are brief, which minimizes their disruptiveness of ongoing efforts to learn, and they are contextually-specific, which can increase their validity. For example, there is research indicating that these measures of self-regulation are highly predictive of performance differences between expert, non-expert, and novice athletes (Cleary & Zimmerman, 2001; Kitsantas & Zimmerman, 2002). Novices in these studies displayed deficiencies in not only the quantity and quality of self-regulatory processes but also their motivational beliefs. This result led us (Cleary & Zimmerman, 2004) to study whether microanalytic measures can be used to diagnose and remediate deficiencies in students' academic self-regulation. This issue will be discussed later in this chapter. This microanalytic methodology is an example of an *event* measure of SRL, which is defined as a temporal entity that has a beginning and an end (Zimmerman, 2008). Because a self regulation event, such use of a strategy, occurs in sequence to events that precede and follow it, these measures are sensitive to change and can capture causal relations between events. This focus on events stands in contrast to considerable research on SRL that has involved *aptitude* measures, which assess relatively enduring characteristics of a person that predicts his or her future behavior (Winne & Perry, 2000). Aptitude measures aggregate a learner's SRL over time, which is evident in the format of the questionnaire items. For example, the item stem, "I make good use of my study time in this course," is followed by the aptitude options that range from "not at all true of me" to "very true of me" (Pintrich, Smith, Garcia, & McKeachie, 1991). Among the most well known aptitude measures of self-regulation, are the *Learning and Study Strategies Inventory* (LASSI; Weinstein, Schulte, & Palmer, 1987), the *Motivated Strategies for Learning Questionnaire* (MSLQ; Pintrich et al., 1991), and *Self-regulated Learning Interview Schedule* (SRLIS; Zimmerman & Martinez-Pons, 1986, 1988). These aptitude measures have been reliable predictors of academic performance.

To assess shifts in students' use of self-regulatory processes online as they studied, a number of event measures of self-regulation have been developed (Zimmerman, 2008). In addition to microanalytic measures (Kitsantas & Zimmerman, 2002; Cleary & Zimmerman 2001), they include traces, think-alouds, diary logs, and direct observations. *Trace* measures (e.g., use of highlighter) are unobtrusively registered when studying, such as in a computer supported environment (Winne et al., 2006). *Think-aloud* measures require students to verbalize their spontaneous thoughts, such as reasons for choosing a hyperlink when learning in a hypermedia environment (Azevedo & Cromley, 2004; Greene & Azevedo, 2007). *Diary logs* require students to record SRL information, such as the frequency and successfulness of daily studying episodes (Schmitz & Wiese, 2006; Stoeger & Zigler, 2007). *Direct observations* of students' SRL behavior during classroom interactions usually involve trained observers (Perry, 1998; Perry, Vandekamp, Mercer, & Nordby, 2002).

Event measures have proven effective in revealing changes in and causal links among SRL processes and academic outcomes, but these online measures have also uncovered unexpected results (Zimmerman, 2008). One example involves the accuracy or calibration of students' self-judgments of their learning processes and outcomes when compared with objective measures of performance. Winne and Jamieson-Noel (2002) found low accuracy between students' self-reports of self-regulation processes when compared to trace measures of actual use in a computer studying environment. Is calibration accuracy of process measures greater in noncomputerized settings, and if so, is it predictive of academic success? Further research is needed. Interestingly, Winne and Jamieson-Noel found a high level of accuracy in college students' judgments of their achievement outcomes, a finding that was corroborated in research conducted in noncomputerized environments (Stone, 2000). Do students self-monitor their achievement outcomes more accurately than their use of SRL processes? This topic will also require further research in the years to come.

The effectiveness of microanalytic diary measures in assessing changes in SRL classroom interventions has been demonstrated in two recent studies. Stoeger and Zigler (2007) reported that regular classroom teachers could be trained to teach specific SRL skills to fourth grade children as part of their regular math assignments during a five week intervention. Schmitz and Wiese (2006) reported similar results with college students majoring in engineering. In both studies, self-regulatory training also enhanced several forms of self-motivation, but could these interventions motivate students who have no interest in changing their method of studying?

Developing Self-Regulatory Sources of Motivation through Social Learning

There is growing evidence that self-sustaining sources of learning and motivation can be developed from social sources, such as parental or instructors' modeling, praise, or academic rewards. Although some people view these social resources as external to a learner's control, social cognitive researchers (e.g., Schunk & Zimmerman, 1997; Zimmerman, 2000) and Vygotskian researchers (e.g., McCaslin & Hickey, 2001), view social sources of motivation as linked closely to self-sources.

Dale Schunk and I (Schunk & Zimmerman, 1997; Zimmerman, 2000) have proposed a four level developmental model that systematically shifts a student's learning from social to self sources of regulation (see Table 12.1). To acquire a skill at an *observational level*, learners must induce (or discriminate) a skill from a proficient model's performance, such as when a student learns to multiply fractions from watching a teacher's demonstration. Complete induction of a skill seldom emerges from a single exposure to a model's performance but rather usually requires repeated observations across variations in task, such as different fractions. In addition to conveying task skills, models convey associated self-regulatory processes, such as performance standards and motivational orientations. A student's motivation to learn at an observational level can be greatly enhanced by positive vicarious consequences to the model, such as a teacher's praise for a fellow student's solution of a problem.

To acquire skill at an *emulation level*, learners must duplicate a model's response on a correspondent task with social assistance. Learners seldom copy the exact actions of the model but rather his or her general pattern or style of responding. During efforts to emulate, learners can improve their accuracy and motivation if a social agent provides guidance, feedback, and reinforcement, such as higher grades or praise. Emulative performance requires students to integrate motoric cues with vicarious ones. The source of learning for the first two levels of the developmental model is primarily social but for the next two levels, the locus shifts to self sources.

The third level in this multilevel model involves *self-control* of a skill, in which learners must practice it in structured settings outside the presence of models, such as when an aspiring mathematician practices multiplying fractions during homework assignments. To optimize learning at this level, learners should regulate their practice by using a mental recollection of the solution strategy of a model (Bandura & Jeffery, 1973). Learners' success in matching a covert process standard during practice will determine the amount of self-reinforcement they will experience, which is an important source of motivation. Bandura (1986) describes its self-reinforcement benefits as follows: "By making self-satisfaction conditional on a selected level of performance, individuals create their own incentives to persist in their efforts until their performances match internal standards" (p. 467).

To achieve a *self-regulated level* of task skill, a learner should practice it in unstructured settings involving dynamic personal and contextual conditions. At this fourth level of skill, learners must learn to make adjustments in their skill based on the outcomes of practice, such as when multiplication of fractions problems are embedded in a test involving many other types of problems. These adaptations are made on the basis of self-monitored outcomes rather than prior modeling experiences. Learners' perceived efficacy in making these adjustments influences their motivation to continue. At level four, learners can practice with minimal SRL process monitoring, and their attention can be shifted toward performance outcomes without detrimental consequences.

This multilevel analysis of the development of self-regulatory competence begins with most extensive social guidance at the first level, but this social support is systematically reduced as learners acquire underlying self-regulatory skill. However, level four self-regulatory functioning still relies in part on self-initiated use of social resources. Because self-regulatory skill depends on context and outcomes, new performance tasks can uncover limitations in existing skills and require additional social learning experiences. This multilevel formulation does not assume that learners must advance through the four levels in an invariant sequence as developmental stage models assume, or that once the highest level is attained, it will be used universally. Instead, a multilevel model assumes that students who master each skill level in sequence will learn more easily and effectively.

To test the sequential validity of the first and second of levels of the model, Anastasia Kitsantas and I (Zimmerman & Kitsantas, 2002) compared the two primary sources of regulation for each level (i.e., modeling for observation level and social feedback for the emulation level (see column two in Table 12.1). High school girls were asked to revise a series of sentences from commercially available sentence-combining workbooks. These exercises involved transforming a series of simple and often redundant sentences into a single nonredundant sentence. For example, the sentences: "It was a ball. The ball was striped. The ball rolled across the room" could be rewritten as "The striped ball rolled across the room." A model demonstrated a three step strategy for revising the sentences.

Microanalytic measures of SRL revealed that adolescent girls exposed to a strategic model significantly surpassed the writing revision of those who attempted to learn from only verbal description and performance outcomes. During emulation, girls who received social feedback learned better than those who practiced without this feedback. However, the impact of this social feedback was insufficient to make up for the absence of prior exposure to a model, which validates the sequential importance of engaging in observational learning before emulation. Finally, girls exposed to observational learning from modeling also showed higher levels of self-motivation, such as self-efficacy beliefs, than did students in a control group.

To test the sequential ordering of the third and fourth levels of skill in the developmental model (i.e., self-control and self-regulation), the two primary sources of regulation for these levels (i.e., process and outcome goals) were compared (see the second column in Table 12.1) with high school

Table 12.1 Social and Self-Sources of Regulation.

Levels of Regulation	Features of Regulation			
	Sources of Regulation	**Sources of Motivation**	**Task Conditions**	**Performance Indices**
1. Observation	Modeling	Vicarious reinforcement	Presence of models	Discrimination
2. Emulation	Performance and social feedback	Direct/social reinforcement	Correspond to Model's	Stylistic Duplication
3. Self-control	Representation of process standards	Self-reinforcement	Structured	Automatization
4. Self-regulation	Performance Outcomes	Self-efficacy beliefs	Dynamic	Adaptation

From: "Achieving self-regulation: The trial and triumph of adolescence" by B. J Zimmerman (2003). In F. Pajares & T. Urdan (Eds.), *Academic motivation of adolescents* (vol. 2, pp. 1-27). Greenwich, CT: Information Age. Copyright (2003) by Information Age Press. Reprinted with permission.

girls using the same writing revision task (Zimmerman & Kitsantas, 1999). All of the adolescent girls in this study were initially taught the three steps of the revision strategy through observation and emulation (i.e., regulatory levels one and two) that was described previously. During a practice session following training, girls in the process goal group focused on strategic steps for revising each writing task, whereas girls in the outcome goal focused on decreasing the number of words in the revised passage. The inclusion of unnecessary words reduced the posttest writing revision scores. Girls in a shifting goal group started with process goals and changed to outcome goals after automatization occurred, which would confirm the sequential shift from level three to four. Half of the girls in each goal group were ask to self-record their processes or outcomes.

Microanalytic measures of SRL revealed that girls who shifted goals from processes to outcomes after reaching level four (i.e., having achieved automatization) surpassed the writing revision skill of girls who adhered exclusively to process goals or to outcome goals. Girls who focused on outcomes exclusively displayed the least writing skill, and self-recording enhanced writing acquisition for all goal setting groups. In addition to their acquisition of superior writing skill, girls who shifted their goals displayed advantageous forms of self-motivation, such as enhanced self-efficacy beliefs and task interest.

In summary, there is a growing body of evidence indicating that social processes play an important role in students' development and maintenance of a high level of self-regulation and supportive motivational beliefs, especially when training followed a multilevel sequential regulatory approach. Virtually identical results to these two writing revision studies were found in two parallel studies involving acquisition of a motoric skill (Zimmerman & Kitsantas, 1997; Kitsantas, Zimmerman, & Cleary, 2000). Collectively, these studies indicate that even passive students could be taught to use self-regulatory processes by a social change agent.

Empowering Students with Self-Regulation and Motivation Deficiencies

Recently, a self-regulatory intervention program has been developed in which microanalytic measures of self-regulation and motivation are used to diagnose and treat specific learning problems with underachieving at-risk students. The Self-Regulation Empowerment Program (SREP; Cleary & Zimmerman, 2004; Cleary, Platten, & Nelson, 2007a,b) is designed to help a self-regulation coach (SRC), such as a teacher, a school psychologist, or member of a child study team, evaluate and improve the quality of students' self-regulatory processes and motivational feelings and beliefs and ultimately their academic performance. SREP instruction adheres to a standard protocol format, which involves using explicit modules to teach students' specific learning tactics (e.g., concept maps) as well as cyclical self-regulatory thought and action. Both its assessment and intervention components are presented in a manual that has been used with students that have ranged in age from middle school to high school (Cleary et al., 2007b). However, this approach does afford a SRC the opportunity to make modifications or adaptations to specific learning modules in order to meet individual student needs as well as particular task demands, such as studying, test performance, or writing.

In terms of assessment, the SREP utilizes a multitiered approach consisting of both traditional (e.g., review of records, self-report/rating scales and interviews) and alternative measures (e.g., microanalytic protocols; Cleary & Zimmerman, 2004; Cleary et al., 2007b). The purpose of the assessment protocols are: (a) to help the SRC diagnose motivational and self-regulatory strengths and deficiencies, (b) to guide planning of an effective intervention, (c) to provide dependent measures that can be studied over time, and (d) to analyze changes in key self-regulation processes and motivational feelings and beliefs (e.g., self-efficacy, attributions) during the course of treatment. Microanalytic assessment protocols assume a key role in SREP activities because they address each of these objectives and link self-regulation processes and motivational feelings or beliefs directly to specific outcomes across the three cyclical phases.

In a recent study, researchers examined the effectiveness of SREP training in a small-group setting with urban high school youth who were experiencing significant problems on their biology unit exams (Cleary et al., 2007b). Two groups of four students participated in the project, with each group receiving approximately 22 SREP sessions from a SRC to help them self-regulate their performance on biology tests. SREP instruction consisted of two general components, training in self-regulation processes and learning tactics. Thus, each SRC taught students to set goals and make strategic plans (forethought), to self-monitor performance outcomes and processes (performance), and to make adaptive self-judgments and reactions following test performance. Instruction in these metacognitive processes occurred concurrently with training in tactics to learn and remember biology concepts. Following a social-cognitive instructional approach (Gettinger & Seibert, 2002; Zimmerman, 2000), the SRC's used behavioral and cognitive modeling techniques to enhance students' skill in developing mnemonic devices and concept maps and then conducted several guided practice sessions to help the students refine their use of these maps.

A graphing procedure was developed to facilitate the integration of students' use of specific study tactics and their metacognitive and regulatory thought processes. All students in the training groups completed a self-regulation graph during the intervention, but for illustration purposes, we will consider the graph of one student (who will be called Jake; see Figure 12.2). Jake was asked to plot both his short-term and long-term grade goals as well as the strategies that he employed when preparing for each test. Jake plotted a total of four biology test scores during the intervention project. The first test was given prior to the intervention, whereas the second test was administered several weeks after the intervention began but prior to any strategy instruction— that is, concept maps. The initial training sessions focused on restructuring student maladaptive beliefs' from focusing on uncontrollable sources as the primary determinant of their failures, such as poor teaching or poor personal ability, to focusing on strategies as the key factor in their learning and success. The third and four tests were administered approximately 5 and 10 weeks after the second test, respectively.

The strategies that were listed on the graph included not only concept mapping, which was the

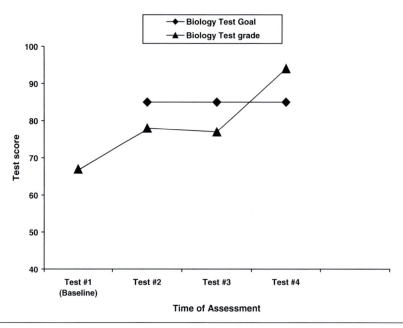

Figure 12. 2 An example of a self-regulation graph used during SREP assessment and intervention activities.

key learning strategy, but also other strategies that Jake had used during studying, such as studying notes and making up self-tests to monitoring learning. In the context of this research study, the SRC engaged Jake in the self-reflection module on two occasions—after the third and fourth tests. As an example, following his fourth test, the SRC instructed him to plot this score on the SRG and then complete the self-reflection microanalytic worksheet discussed previously. On this form, Jake and his fellow group members were instructed to self-evaluate their progress toward their grade goals, to rate their level of satisfaction with this progress, to write their attributions for their performance, and to specify the adaptive inferences that may improve performance on future tests. It should be noted that following this microanalytic assessment, the SRC engaged the group in a discussion about their perceptions and responses. Specifically regarding Jake, the SRC sought to help to establish the link between his improved test performance (i.e., from 77 to 94) and the study strategies that he used, such as self-quizzing and concept maps. Making strategic attributions is widely considered one of the most adaptive types of evaluative judgments because it sustains one's motivation and perceptions of controls and directs one's attention on essential processes and techniques which are predictive of success (Kitsantas, Zimmerman, & Cleary, 2000; Cleary, Zimmerman, & Keating, 2006).

Although the SRC was able to administer the self-reflection module on two occasions during the SREP project, it is beneficial for practitioners to provide students with several opportunities to practice and engage in the dynamic cyclical feedback loop throughout a semester. Unfortunately, in the context of classrooms across many school districts, teachers who give exams on an infrequent basis often diminish students' opportunities to develop their skills in analyzing and understanding the causes of their learning struggles and in making strategic adjustments that will improve future learning.

Conclusions

The question of what motivates students' use of self-regulatory processes to learn is central because these processes often require additional anticipation, time, and effort. What can explain the self-initiative and persistence of these proactive learners? To answer these questions, researchers have studied the role of a variety of motivational constructs, such as self-efficacy beliefs, outcome expectations, goal orientations, task values, attributions, and perceptions of self-satisfaction (Zimmerman & Schunk, 2007). Interestingly, virtually all of these constructs refer to the causes and outcomes of personal efforts to learn.

In this chapter, we have described the role of these sources of motivation in terms of a three phase model of self-regulatory feedback and adaptation, and we have reported evidence of significant correlations between specific self-regulatory processes and motivational feelings and beliefs. Microanalytic measures of these processes and beliefs have been highly predictive of differences in performance. Recent educational interventions, such as the SREP, have been successful in empowering SRCs' use of feedback to diagnose self-regulatory deficits and in providing adaptive training. Clearly, our understanding of the nature and functioning of self-regulatory feedback loops has advanced steadily during the last fifty years. Multiphase analyses of feedback and adaptation have enhanced not only the quality of students' learning but also their motivation to continue learning on their own.

Acknowledgment

We would like to express our appreciation to Kathryn Wentzel & Allan Wigfield for their helpful comments on an earlier draft of this chapter.

Notes

1. This definition of self-regulation includes components that are widely embraced by researchers from diverse theoretical perspectives. For example, after noting considerable diversity in definitions of self-regulation among chapters in their *Handbook of Self-Regulation*, the editors (Zeidner, Boekaerts, & Pintrich, 2000) identified the following common features among the definitions: "cognitive, affective, motivational, and behavioral components that provide the individual with the capacity to adjust his or her actions and goals to achieve desired results" (p. 751).

References

Ames, C. (1992). Achievement goals and the classroom motivational climate. In D. H. Schunk & J. L. Meece (Eds.), *Student perceptions in the classroom* (pp. 327–348). Hillsdale, NJ: Erlbaum.

Azevedo, R., & Cromley, J. G. (2004). Does training on self-regulated learning facilitate students' learning with hypermedia. *Journal of Educational Psychology, 96*, 523–535.

Bandura, A. (1986). *Social foundations of thought and action: A social cognitive theory.* Englewood Cliffs, NJ: Prentice-Hall.

Bandura, A. (1991). Self-regulation of motivation through anticipatory and self-reactive mechanisms. In R. A. Dienstbier (Ed.), *Perspectives on Motivation: Nebraska symposium on motivation* (Vol. 38, pp. 69–164). Lincoln: University of Nebraska Press.

Bandura, A. (1997). *Self-efficacy: The exercise of control.* New York: Freeman.

Bandura, A., Barbaranelli, C., Caprara, G. V., & Pastorelli, C. (1996). Multifaceted impact of self-efficacy beliefs on academic functioning. *Child Development, 67*, 1206–1222.

Bandura, A., & Jeffery, R. W. (1973). Role of symbolic coding and rehearsal processes in observational learning. *Journal of Personality and Social Psychology, 26*, 122–130.

Bandura, A., & Schunk, D. H. (1981). Cultivating competence, self-efficacy, and intrinsic interest through proximal self-motivation. *Journal of Personality and Social Psychology 41*, 586–598.

Bouffard-Bouchard, T., Parent, S., & Larivee, S. (1991). Influence of self-efficacy on self-regulation and performance among junior and senior high-school age students. *International Journal of Behavioral Development, 14*, 153–164.

Britton, B. K., & Tessor, A. (1991). Effects of time management practices on college grades. *Educational Psychology, 83,* 405–410.

Butler, D. L., & Winne, P. H. (1995). Feedback and self-regulated learning: A theoretical synthesis. *Review of Educational Research, 65,* 245–281.

Cleary, T. J., Platten, P., & Nelson, A.C. (2007a, March). *Implementation of the self-regulation empowerment program (SREP) in an urban school.* Poster session presented at the 2007 Annual Convention of the National Association of School Psychologists, New York, NY.

Cleary, T. J., Platten, P., & Nelson, A. (2007b). *Implementation and initial efficacy of the Self-Regulation Empowerment Program (SREP): Academic and strategic behavior change in urban minority youth.* Manuscript in preparation.

Cleary, T. J., & Zimmerman, B. J. (2001). Self-regulation differences during athletic practice by experts, non-experts, and novices. *Journal of Applied Sport Psychology, 13,* 61–82.

Cleary, T. J., & Zimmerman, B. J. (2004) Self-regulation empowerment program: A school-based program to enhance self-regulated and self-motivated cycles of student learning. *Psychology in the Schools, 41,* 537–550.

Cleary, T. J., Zimmerman, B. J., & Keating, T. (2006). Training physical education students to self-regulate during basketball free-throw practice. *Research Quarterly for Exercise and Sport, 77,* 251–262.

Corno, L. (1993). The best laid plans: Modern conceptions of volition and educational research. *Educational Researcher, 22,* 14–22.

Deci, E., & Ryan, R. M. (1985). *Intrinsic motivation and self-determination in human behavior.* New York: Plenum.

Dweck, C. S. (1988). Motivational processes affecting learning. *America Psychologist, 41,* 1040–1048.

Dweck, C. S., & Master, A. (2007). Self theories motivate self-regulated learning. In D. H. Schunk & B. J. Zimmerman (Eds.), *Motivation and self-regulated learning: Theory, research, and applications* (pp. 31–51). Boca Raton, FL: Erlbaum/Taylor & Francis Group.

Garcia, T., & Pintrich, P. R. (1994). Regulating motivation and cognition in the classroom: The role of self-schemas and self-regulatory strategies. In D. H. Schunk & B. J. Zimmerman (Eds.), *Self-regulation of learning and performance: Issues and educational applications* (p. 127–53). Hillsdale, NJ: Erlbaum.

Garfield, C. A., & Bennett, Z. H. (1985). *Peak performance: Mental training techniques of the world's greatest athletes.* New York: Warner Books.

Gettinger, M., & Seibert, J. K. (2002). Contributions of study skills to academic competence. *School Psychology Review, 31,* 350–365.

Grant, H., & Dweck, C. S. (2003). Clarifying achievement goals and their impact. *Journal of Personality and Social Psychology, 85,* 541–553.

Greene, J. A., & Azevedo, R. (2007). Adolescents' use of self-regulatory processes and their relation to qualitative mental model shifts while using hypermedia. *Journal of Educational Computing Research, 36,* 125–148.

Hattie, J., & Timperley, H. (2007). The power of feedback. *Review of Educational Research, 77,* 81–112.

Karabenick, S. A. (Ed.). (1998). *Strategic help seeking: Implications for learning and teaching.* Hillsdale, NJ: Erlbaum.

Kitsantas, A., & Zimmerman, B. J. (2002). Comparing self-regulatory processes among novice, non-expert, and expert volleyball players: A microanalytic study. *Journal of Applied Sport Psychology, 14,* 91–105.

Kitsantas, A., & Zimmerman, B. J. (2006). Enhancing self-regulation of practice: The influence of graphing and self-evaluative standards. *Metacognition and Learning 1*(3), 201–212.

Kitsantas, A., Zimmerman, B. J., & Cleary, T. (2000). The role of observation and emulation in the development of athletic self-regulation. *Journal of Educational Psychology, 91,* 241–250.

Kuhl, J. (1985). Volitional mediators of cognitive behavior consistency: Self-regulatory processes and action versus state orientation. In J. Kuhl & J. Beckman (Eds.), *Action control* (pp. 101–128). New York: Springer.

Lan, W. Y. (1998). Teaching self-monitoring skills in statistics. In D. H. Schunk & B. J. Zimmerman (Eds.), *Self-regulated learning: From teaching to self-reflective practice* (pp. 86–105). New York: Guilford.

Lepper, M. R., & Hodell, M. (1989). Intrinsic motivation in the classroom. In C. Ames & R. Ames (Eds.), *Research on motivation in education* (Vol. E, pp. 255–296). Hillsdale, NJ: Erlbaum.

Locke, E. A. (1991). Goal theory vs. control theory: Contrasting approaches to understanding work motivation. *Motivation and Emotion, 15,* 9–28.

Locke, E. A., & Latham, G. P. (1990). *A theory of goal setting and task performance.* Englewood Cliffs, NJ: Prentice-Hall.

Locke, E. A., & Latham, G. P. (2002). Building a practically useful theory of goal setting and task motivation: A 35-year odyssey. *American Psychology, 57,* 705–717.

Lodewyk, K. R., & Winne, P. H. (2005). Relations among the structure of learning tasks, achievement, and changes in self-efficacy in secondary students. *Journal of Educational Psychology, 97,* 3–12.

McCaslin, M., & Hickey, D. T. (2001). Self-regulated learning and academic achievement: A Vygotskian view. In B. J. Zimmerman & D. H. Schunk (Eds.), *Self-Regulated learning and academic achievement* (2nd ed., pp. 227–252). Mahwah, NJ: Erlbaum.

Meichenbaum, D. (1977). *Cognitive-behavior modification: An integrative approach.* New York: Plenum.

Miller, G. A., Galanter, E., & Pribham, K. (1960). *Plans and the structure of behavior.* New York: Holt, Rinehart and Winston.

Newman, R. (1994). Academic help-seeking: A strategy of self-regulated learning. In D. H. Schunk & B. J. Zimmerman (Eds.), *Self-regulation of learning and performance: Issues and educational applications* (pp. 283–301). Hillsdale, NJ: Erlbaum.

Newman, R. S. (2007). The motivational role of adaptive help seeking in self-regulated learning. In D. Schunk & B. Zimmerman (Eds.), *Motivation and self-regulated learning: Theory, research, and applications* (pp. 315–338). Mahwah, NJ: Erlbaum.

Perry, N. E., (1998). Young children's self-regulated learning and contexts that support it. *Journal of Educational Psychology, 90,* 715–729.

Perry, N. E., Vandekamp, K. O., Mercer, L. K., & Nordby, C. J. (2002). Investigating teacher-student interactions that foster self-regulated learning *Educational Psychologist, 37,* 5–15.

Pintrich, P. R. (2003). A motivational science perspective on the role of student motivation in learning and teaching contexts. *Journal of Educational Psychology, 95,* 667–686.

Pintrich, P. R., Smith, D. A., Garcia, T., & McKeachie, W. J. (1991) *A manual for the use of the Motivated Strategies for Learning Questionnaire (MSLQ).* Ann Arbor, MI: National Center for Research to Improve Post Secondary Teaching and Learning.

Pressley, M. (1977). Imagery and children's learning: Putting the picture in developmental perspective. *Review of Educational Research, 47,* 586–622.

Powers, W. T. (1973). *Behavior: The control of perception.* Chicago: Aldine.

Powers, W. T. (1998). *Making sense of behavior: The meaning of control.* New Canaan, CT: Benchmark.

Schmitz, B., & Wiese, B. S. (2006). New perspectives for the evaluation of training session in self-regulated learning: Time-series analyses of diary data. *Contemporary Educational Psychology, 31,* 64–96.

Schunk, D. H. (1982a). Effects of effort attributional feedback on children's perceived self-efficacy and achievement. *Journal of Educational Psychology, 74,* 548–556.

Schunk, D. H. (1982b). Verbal self-regulation as a facilitator of children's achievement and self-efficacy. *Human learning, 1,* 265–277.

Schunk, D. H., & Pajares, F. (2004). Self-efficacy in education revisited: Empirical and applied evidence. In D. M. McInerney & S. Van Etten (Eds.), *Big theories revisited* (Vol. 4, pp. 115–138). Greenwich, CT: Information Age.

Schunk, D. H., & Swartz, C. W. (1993). Goals and progressive feedback: Effects on self-efficacy and writing achievement. *Contemporary Educational Psychology, 18,* 337–354.

Schunk, D. H., & Zimmerman, B. J. (1994). Preface. In D. H. Schunk & B. J. Zimmerman (Eds.), *Self-regulation of learning and performance: Issues and educational applications* (pp. ix–xi). Hillsdale, NJ: Erlbaum.

Schunk, D. H., & Zimmerman, B. J. (1997). Social origins of self-regulatory competence. *Educational Psychologist, 32,* 195–208.

Schunk, D. H., & Zimmerman, B. J. (2006). Competence and Control Beliefs: Distinguishing the means and ends. In P. Alexander, P. Winne, & G. Phye (Eds.), *Handbook of Research in Educational Psychology* (2nd ed., pp. 349–367). Mahwah, NJ: Erlbaum.

Shell, D. F., Murphy, C. C., & Bruning, R. H. (1989). Self-efficacy and outcome expectancy mechanisms in reading and writing achievement. *Journal of Educational Psychology, 81,* 91–100.

Stoeger, H., & Ziegler, A. (2008). Evaluation of a classroom based training to improve self-regulation in time management tasks during homework activities with fourth graders. *Metacognition and Learning, 3,* 207–230.

Stone, N. J. (2000). Exploring the relationship between calibration and self-regulated learning. *Educational Psychology Review, 12,* 437–475.

Weiner, B. (1979). A theory of motivation for some classroom experiences. *Journal of Educational Psychology, 71,* 3–25.

Weinstein, C. E., Schulte, A. C., & Palmer, D. R. (1987). *LASSI: Learning and study strategies inventory.* Clearwater, FL: H. & H. Publishing.

Wigfield, A., & Eccles, J. S. (1992). The development of competence achievement task values: A theoretical analysis. *Developmental Review, 12,* 265–310.

Wigfield, A., & Eccles, J. S. (2002). The development of competence beliefs and values from childhood through adolescence. In A. Wigfield & J. S. Eccles (Eds.), *Development of achievement motivation* (pp. 92–120). San Diego: Academic Press.

Winne, P. H., & Jamieson-Noel, D. (2002) Exploring students; calibration of self reports about study tactics and achievement. *Contemporary Educational Psychology, 27,* 551–572.

Winne, P. H., Nesbit, J. C., Kumar, V. Hadwin, A. F., Lajoie, S. P., Azevedo, R., & Perry, N. E. (2006). Supporting self-regulated learning with gStudy software: The learning kit project. *Technology, Instruction, Cognition and Learning, 3,* 105–113.

Winne, P. H., & Perry, N. E. (2000). Measuring self-regulated learning. In M. Boekaerts, P. Pintrich, & M. Zeidner (Eds.), *Handbook of self-regulation* (pp. 532–566). Orlando, FL: Academic Press.

Wolters, C. A. (1999). The relation between high school students' motivational regulation and their use of learning strategies, effort, and classroom performance. *Learning & Individual Differences, 11,* 281–301.

Wolters, C. A. (2003). Regulation of motivation: Evaluating an underemphasized aspect of self-regulated learning. *Educational Psychologist, 38,* 189–205.

Wolters, C. A., & Pintrich, P. R. (1998). Contextual differences in student motivation and self-regulated learning in mathematics, English, and social studies classrooms. *Instructional Science, 26,* 27–47.

Wolters, C. A., & Rosenthal, H. (2000). The relation between students' motivational beliefs and their use of motivational regulation strategies. *International Journal of Educational Research, 33,* 801–820.

Zeidner, M., Boekaerts, M., & Pintrich, P. R. (2000). Self-regulation: Directions and challenges for future research. In

M. Boekaerts, P. Pintrich, & M. Zeidner (Eds.), *Handbook* of *self-regulation* (pp. 49–768). Orlando, FL: Academic Press

Zimmerman, B. J. (1989). A social cognitive view of self-regulated academic learning. *Journal of Educational Psychology, 81,* 329–339.

Zimmerman, B. J. (1995). Self-efficacy and educational development. In A. Bandura (Ed.), *Self-efficacy in changing societies* (pp. 202–231). New York: Cambridge University Press.

Zimmerman, B. J. (2000). Attainment of self-regulation: A social cognitive perspective. In M. Boekaerts, P. Pintrich, & M. Zeidner (Eds.), *Handbook of self-regulation* (pp. 13–39). Orlando, FL: Academic Press.

Zimmerman, B. J. (2007). Goal setting: A key proactive source of academic self-regulation. In D. H. Schunk & B. J. Zimmerman (Eds.), *Motivation and self-regulated learning: Theory, research, and applications* (pp. 267–295). Mahwah, NJ: Erlbaum.

Zimmerman, B. J. (2008). Investigating self-regulation and motivation: Historical background, methodological developments, and future prospects. *American Educational Research Journal, 45*(1), 166–183.

Zimmerman, B. J., & Bandura, A. (1994). Impact of self-regulatory influences on writing course attainment. *American Educational Research Journal, 31,* 845–862.

Zimmerman, B. J., Bandura, A., & Martinez-Pons, M. (1992). Self-motivation for academic attainment: The role of self-efficacy beliefs and personal goal setting. *American Educational Research Journal, 29,* 663–676.

Zimmerman, B. J., Greenberg, D., & Weinstein, C. E. (1994). Self-regulating academic study time: A strategy approach. In D. H. Schunk & B. J. Zimmerman (Eds.), *Self-regulation of learning and performance: Issues and educational application* (pp. 181–199). Hillsdale, NJ: Erlbaum.

Zimmerman, B. J., & Kitsantas, A. (1997). Developmental phases in self-regulation: Shifting from process to outcome goals. *Journal of Educational Psychology, 89,* 29–36.

Zimmerman, B. J., & Kitsantas, A. (1999). Acquiring writing revision skill: Shifting from process to outcome self-regulatory goals. *Journal of Educational Psychology, 91,* 1–10.

Zimmerman, B. J. & Kitsantas, A. (2002). Acquiring writing revision and self-regulatory Skill through observation and emulation. *Journal of Educational Psychology, 94,* 660–668.

Zimmerman, B. J., & Martinez-Pons, M. (1986). Development of a structured interview for assessing students' use of self-regulated learning strategies. *American Educational Research Journal, 23,* 614–628.

Zimmerman, B. J., & Martinez-Pons, M. (1988). Construct validation of a strategy model of student self-regulated learning. *Journal of Educational Psychology, 80,* 284–290.

Zimmerman, B. J., & Paulsen, A. S. (1995). Self-monitoring during collegiate studying: An invaluable tool for academic self-regulation. In P. Pintrich (Ed.), *New directions in college teaching and learning: Understanding self-regulated learning* (No. 63, Fall, pp. 13–27). San Francisco: Jossey-Bass.

Zimmerman, B. J., & Rocha, J. (1987). Mode and type of toy elaboration strategy training on kindergartners' retention and transfer. *Journal of Applied Developmental Psychology, 8,* 67–78.

Zimmerman, B. J., & Schunk, D. H. (2007). Motivation: An essential dimension of self-regulated learning. In D. H. Schunk & B. J. Zimmerman (Eds.), *Motivation and self-regulated learning: Theory, research, and applications* (pp. 1–30). Boca Raton, FL: Erlbaum/Taylor & Francis Group.

13

Commentary: Building on
a Strong Foundation
Five Pathways to the Next Level
of Motivational Theorizing

Martin E. Ford and Peyton R. Smith

The conceptual and empirical accomplishments represented in the 11 major theoretical contributions to this handbook are truly remarkable. Indeed, it was the transformative thinking represented in these theories that drew us into the field of motivation. We did not begin our careers with motivational concepts at the center of our work. But we naturally gravitated to those concepts as we discovered that motivational processes play a leadership role in virtually every aspect of education and human development. The research documenting the critical role of motivational processes in school success includes some of the most exciting and consequential work being done in any domain of psychology or education.

Part of what attracted us to this literature was the clarity and simplicity of some of the field's most important concepts. Nothing is more compelling to a scientist looking for elegant explanations or to an educator looking for practical solutions than a "big idea" that can be succinctly summarized in a few powerful words. Concepts such as self-efficacy (Schunk & Pajares, chapter 3), self-worth (Covington, chapter 8), self-determination (Ryan & Deci, chapter 9), causal attributions (Graham & Williams, chapter 2), mastery versus performance goals (Maehr & Zusho, chapter 5), entity versus incremental theories of intelligence (Dweck & Master, chapter 7) and many other constructs from the different motivation theories discussed in this section have captured the attention and respect of scholars and professionals all the way from the ivory towers of academe to the trenches of K–12 and adult education. These concepts have stimulated literally thousands of studies and collectively have led to the development of a strong theoretical and empirical foundation for education practitioners and policy makers looking for sound science to guide their methods and decisions.

The motivation theories highlighted in this volume have also effectively emphasized the importance of viewing student motivation not just as a means to learning and academic achievement, but also as an important outcome of education in its own right. Indeed, since motivation is an essential prerequisite for competence development (Ford, 1992), one might argue that there is nothing more important to school success than the development of enduring motivational habits that facilitate *engagement* rather than *disaffection* in the face of life challenges and opportunities (Skinner, Kindermann, Connell, & Wellborn, chapter 11). When such habits—for example, an active approach orientation, personal optimism, mindful tenacity, and emotional wisdom (Ford & Smith, 2007)—are in place, learning and achievement tend to naturally "flow" (Csikszentmihalyi, Abuhamdeh, & Nakamura, 2005) from that strong motivational foundation.

The major theoretical contributors to this volume should take great pride in what they have accomplished and in what they have encouraged others to accomplish. But they should not be satisfied. The trajectory of conceptual progress, which for many years was accelerating at a breathtaking pace, appears to have slowed down considerably in recent years, at least with respect to the introduction of new theories and new concepts. That is a clear signal that there is a need to identify new catalysts that can help move the field to the next level of motivational theorizing. There also seems to be a feeling that current theories should be more directly relevant to contemporary educational problems. Indeed, several contributors have expressed concerns along these lines. For example, Schunk and Pajares (chapter 3) express concern about the lack of intervention-oriented self-efficacy studies. Maehr and Zusho (chapter 5 raise a similar concern with regard to achievement goal theory, and suggest that all motivation researchers "would benefit from a frank conversation about the utility and value of its frameworks for classroom practice, or more specifically, for classroom change" (p. 94).

In the remainder of this commentary, we nominate several themes that could potentially serve as catalysts for motivation scholars seeking to construct useful new conceptual frameworks or to expand existing frameworks. These themes are not mutually exclusive. Multiple catalysts may be needed to address different theoretical needs. For example, conceptual clarity and precision are essential prerequisites for scientific progress. Catalysts may also be needed to focus attention on motivational processes that are important for school success but not highlighted in current theories. Finally, while several contributors recognize the need to synthesize the "big ideas" that have fueled the explosive growth in motivation theory and research during the past four decades, it is unclear if that can happen without conceptual catalysts that explicitly promote collaboration, translation, and integration.

Five Pathways to the Next Level of Motivational Theorizing

Evolutionary Theory

Among the "big ideas" in the behavioral sciences, none is bigger than Darwin's resilient hypothesis that the existence and persistence of species-typical structures and functions are closely related to the survival value of those attributes (Wilson, 2007). This proposition is playing an increasingly important role in many sub-disciplines of psychology (Buss, 2005, 2007); however, it is not yet prominent in the motivation literature. That is a missed opportunity. Although evolutionary theory does not directly provide the content needed for a theory of motivation, it provides an organizing principle for understanding what processes motivation theorists should focus on and for appreciating why those processes are important.

Natural selection is an enlightening lens through which to view motivation because it is such a parsimonious process. Adaptations only endure if they are essential for some very significant purpose. That is why we can learn so much by studying how a particular quality or process evolved. That is not to say that the outcomes of those adaptations will always be positive. "Evolutionary psychology does not claim that observable human behavior is adaptive, but rather that it is produced by psychological mechanisms that are adaptations" (Joyce, 2006, p. 5). Indeed, one of the most important ways that evolutionary theory can contribute to our understanding of motivation at school is by helping us understand why certain educationally maladaptive patterns of motivation are so prevalent and persistent. When such patterns endure, it must be because they are (or were at one time) important in some way for the well-being of the individual or people in close relationships with that individual. For example, paying close attention to one's image or reputation might have been a life-saving skill for our ancestors given the environmental perils associated with group rejection.

Is contemporary motivational theorizing well aligned with evolutionary principles? In our judgment there is substantial room for improvement in this regard. Evolutionary theory suggests a focus on action-oriented processes (Skinner et al., chapter 11) that direct and energize behavior. The most prominent processes in this regard are personal goals and emotions (Boekaerts, chapter 6; Klinger & Cox, 2004). And yet, "…most major theories of motivation today focus on… cognitive appraisals, beliefs, and self-perceptions" (Skinner et al., p. 233). Such processes are clearly influential, but they are only part of what a comprehensive theory of motivation would need to encompass.

The field's lack of emphasis on personal goals is particularly problematic. When the first creatures emerged from the ancient oceans, a new organizing principle began to take hold in the evolution of the species. Life was no longer just about living in the present; now organisms had to be able to envision and pursue desired future outcomes (i.e., personal goals) that, when attained, would facilitate their well-being and survival.

> If animals evolved with a motile strategy to go after the substances and conditions they need, the most basic requirement for their survival is successful goal-striving. In that case, all animal evolution, right up to humans, must have centered on natural selection of whatever facilitated attaining goals. This must mean that everything about humans evolved in the service of successful goal-striving—including human anatomy, physiology, cognition, and emotion. (Klinger & Cox, 2004, p. 5)

Thus, one direct implication of adopting an evolutionary perspective is that personal goals must play a central role in theories of human motivation. The role of cognitive appraisals, beliefs, and self-perceptions can only be understood if they are studied in the context of the personal goals they serve and influence (e.g., Dweck & Master, chapter 7). Such goals may include mastery and performance goals (Maehr & Zusho, chapter 5), but that is only a small fraction of the potentially relevant goal content in school contexts (Boekaerts, chapter 6; Ford, & Nichols, 1991).

When, in our evolutionary history, good outcomes such as finding water or escaping a predator became possible only through self-directed activity, some method was needed not only to mentally represent desired future outcomes, but also to provoke timely action as different goals became priority concerns. The evolutionary solution to this problem was the development of several motivational mechanisms linked to the emergence of conscious experience as a property of mental activity. Consciousness provides a method for selectively energizing perceptions, thoughts, and feelings. Although this capability has functional utility for many aspects of mental processing, it is of paramount importance for motivational systems.

One function of consciousness in this regard is reflected in the emergence of *emotion* patterns as tools for energizing and regulating behavior (see Pekrun, chapter 26, for a discussion of educational issues related to motivation and emotion). Emotion patterns include supporting biological and behavioral components linked to a characteristic affective state (the conscious "feeling" part of the emotion) that commands attention and, when sufficiently strong, communicates a sense of behavioral urgency (Frijda, 1988). Emotions evolved to help organisms deal with a variety of prototypical life challenges and opportunities. For example, interest (Schiefele, chapter 10) fuels exploration of the environment for information of potential relevance to personal goals we are currently pursuing or considering. Feelings associated with happiness (e.g., satisfaction, pleasure, joy) motivate us to "keep going" or to repeat what we're doing when things seem to be going well in our goal pursuits. Anger encourages us to confront obstacles to goal attainment, whereas fear motivates us to avoid threats to our well-being. Sadness, boredom, and disgust are also included in most lists of basic, evolutionary built-in emotion patterns (Ekman, 2003; Izard, 1991).

The under-researched status of emotions in the school motivation literature is even more apparent when one considers the potential relevance of *social emotions* in school success and failure. Some of these emotions evolved to support goals related to social bonding (e.g., affection, love, loneliness). Others evolved to facilitate altruistic actions among those with whom we feel a meaningful connection (e.g., empathic distress, contempt for those who victimize others). In addition, several emotions evolved to support goals related to fairness and social responsibility (e.g., resentment, shame, guilt, embarrassment). Since schooling occurs in social contexts and education is an intrinsically social process, these emotions must be incorporated more fully into motivational frameworks attempting to explain school success and failure (Juvonen & Wentzel, 1996).

Emotions evolved to help motivate action in particular kinds of circumstances. This was a critical step in insuring the survival and continued evolution of the species. However, perhaps the most important way that conscious experience supports successful goal pursuit is by giving us a conscious feeling of personal control and effectiveness when we sense that our actions are causing the outcomes we have envisioned. The emergence of this feeling of *personal agency* was one of the most pivotal events in our evolutionary history, as it provided a general motivational mechanism supporting the ongoing pursuit of personal goals to go along with the special purpose mechanisms represented in our repertoire of instrumental and social emotions.

The importance of this mechanism is well understood by contemporary motivation theorists, as illustrated by many of the chapters in this volume. For example, it is clear that students who experience high self-efficacy have elevated levels of classroom participation, show more effort and persistence, and reach higher levels of achievement (Schunk & Pajares, chapter 3). The experience of feeling capable and effective is so empowering that it is often regarded as an important personal goal in its own right, as emphasized by Ryan and Deci (chapter 9) when they point to deep psychological needs to experience a sense or autonomy and competence. However, the primary function of the evolved capacity to consciously experience a sense of personal agency is to support ongoing learning and development of self and others—a crucial prerequisite for survival of the species. When self-evaluative thoughts become an individual's primary concern rather than informative inputs to decision making about goals related to learning and development, a variety of motivational distortions and distractions are likely to follow, especially in contexts specifically designed to promote learning and development (e.g., schools). This is particularly likely when the self-evaluative thoughts focus primarily on reputational concerns (e.g., social approval or social status). Such concerns are understandable and quite appropriate in some contexts, as they are derived, at least in part, from evolution-based "indirect reciprocity" mechanisms that motivate people to help others not because of any expectation of a return favor, but rather in order to uphold their reputation and thus maintain group membership and inclusion in future cooperative efforts within that group (Alexander, 1987). Nevertheless, when reputational concerns take center stage in education settings, the resulting motivational trajectories are likely to suppress rather than support learning and self-improvement efforts.

> …an entity theory sets students on a path towards worrying about and protecting their image, while an incremental theory motivates students to take advantage of opportunities to learn, practice, and grow. (Dweck & Master, chapter 7, p. 127)

> Individuals struggle to give their lives meaning by seeking the approval of others which involves being competent and able, and avoiding the implications of failure—that one is incompetent, hence unworthy. (Covington, chapter 8, p. 145)

In sum, an evolutionary perspective on motivation suggests that personal goals, emotions, capability beliefs, and context beliefs must all be incorporated into theoretical frameworks focused on motivation at school, with personal goals playing a central role in any such framework. This will likely require a substantial investment in integrative motivational theorizing, as most current frameworks emphasize just one or two of these motivational components. Moreover, those that focus on personal goals and emotions generally only cover a narrow subset of the goals and emotion patterns relevant to education and human development.

Personal Goals

Personal goals are thoughts about desired (and undesired) future states. Such thoughts may be represented in consciousness where they can be evaluated and manipulated, but like other cognitions most goal processing operates at an unconscious level (Bargh & Chartrand, 1999). Either way, personal goals have two basic properties: they mentally represent outcomes to be achieved (or avoided), and they direct the other components of the person system to try to produce those outcomes (or prevent them from occurring; Ford, 1992). Goal cognitions are the central organizing force in human experience as they provide a focus for attention and action as well as criteria for evaluating the effectiveness of the resulting activity. They organize both current action (through contextualized representations of desired and undesired outcomes in the immediate future) and broader patterns of goal pursuit over time (through more distal representations of desired and undesired outcomes).

Downplaying personal goals in theoretical accounts of school motivation is problematic because personal goals are the leaders (directive function) in "motivational headquarters" (Ford, 1992). The "advisors" in the motivational system (i.e., emotions and personal agency beliefs) may be very informative and persuasive, but their advice only makes sense in the context of what the "leader" has proposed. For example, causal attributions will only matter if the outcome of concern is something a student might want to cause. Self-efficacy expectations will only matter if the student has a desire to use or learn the capabilities being assessed. Interest in an activity will not be sustained after the novelty wears off unless it leads to the activation of an enduring personal goal.

The need to place more emphasis on personal goal constructs to advance motivational theorizing to the next level is explicitly recognized in the chapter on expectancy-value theories of school motivation.

As research on expectancy-related beliefs and values continues, we think it is especially important to continue to focus on achievement values. Although research on this important construct has increased, it still lags behind research on expectancy-related beliefs. We think an understanding of children's valuing and de-valuing of different activities is particularly important for developing interventions to foster children's motivation, especially for children who seem apathetic or resistant to schooling. (Wigfield, Tonks, & Klauda, chapter 4, p. 71)

Focusing on "achievement values" and other goal-related constructs does not in any way diminish the importance of expectancy-related beliefs (i.e., personal agency beliefs) or emotions in school motivation. As key advisors to the leader in "motivational headquarters," emotions and personal agency beliefs play a critical role in energizing, amplifying, inhibiting, and regulating the timing of any actions associated with the directives represented in an individual's goal cognitions. Nevertheless, personal goals are the core around which motivational decision making and subsequent behavior is organized. This is clearly recognized in Maehr and Zusho's conceptualization of goals as broad "interpretive frames" for engaging life challenges and opportunities. "Inherent in such a portrayal is the assumption that goals are, in essence, the unifying construct or the motivational linchpin of cognition, affect, and behavior. Goals allow us to identify how certain behaviors, thoughts, and emotions are linked and function as coordinated systems" (Maehr & Zusho, chapter 5, p. 80).

As the preceding description implies, it is quite difficult to understand the meaning of a behavior pattern without knowing the content of the personal goals directing and organizing that behavior. That is why Boekaerts asserts that "it is essential that teachers and parents are aware of the personal goals that direct students' learning activities." Unfortunately, "teachers often do not have a clue as to the goals that their students want to attain" (chapter 6, p. 112). Too often they simply assume that their students will automatically adopt whatever goal the teacher has in mind. But motivation is rarely that simple. Each student brings a unique, pre-existing repertoire of personal goals to school and to each learning experience. Educators must therefore align their goals with those of their students before significant progress can be made (Boekaerts). The results can be particularly powerful and long-lasting when educational goals are linked in meaningful ways to an individual's core personal goals.

> The likelihood of motivating students to their best efforts while promoting a willingness to remain intellectually engaged for a lifetime, depends closely on the ability of institutions and individual teachers to help students discover and nurture the true purpose of their labors, that is, satisfying their personal goals and long-term aspirations… It is for this reason that future directions of research should give priority to the further study of the goal-oriented basis of motivation. (Covington, chapter 8, p. 167)

Because each individual's profile of personal goals and long-term aspirations will be somewhat unique (Boekaerts, chapter 6), it will be especially important for motivation researchers to develop idiographic methods for studying core personal goals and how they develop (e.g., Ford & Nichols, 2008; Little, 1999; Nichols, 1994).

Social Purpose Hypothesis

A third possible pathway to the next level of motivational theorizing is systematic study of the role of "helping goals" (i.e., integrative social relationship goals; Ford & Nichols, 1991) in supporting academic learning and achievement. There is a tendency for both scholars and educators to think of academic work as an individualistic enterprise. And yet there is ample evidence demonstrating that learning is facilitated by personal goals focused on social responsibility and prosocial behavior (e.g., Wentzel, 1991, 1996a) and by the use of cooperative ("win-win") goal structures in the classroom (e.g., Slavin, 1983, 1989). There is also a strong developmental connection between academic and social success at school.

> ...children who display socially competent behavior in elementary school are more likely to excel academically throughout their middle and high school years than those who do not... children must be socially as well as intellectually adept if they are to be successful students. (Wentzel, 1996b, pp. 1–2)

Ryan and Deci's (chapter 9) concept of *relatedness* as a fundamental human need that amplifies motivation across many different content areas provides one avenue for addressing the hypothesized link between helping goals and school success. Boekaerts' (chapter 6) *multiple goals* perspective offers another promising approach along these lines. Ford and Smith's (2007) description of a *thriving with social purpose* (TSP) motivational pattern and its role in optimal human functioning suggests yet another starting point for addressing this proposition. Four different kinds of helping goals are subsumed under the construct of social purpose in the TSP framework: belongingness, social responsibility, equity, and resource provision (Ford & Nichols, 1991; see also Boekaerts, chapter 6).

Regardless of what framework is used to anchor research on helping goals, it is essential that motivation scholars enrich their understanding of the role that social motivation plays in education and human development. Our *social purpose hypothesis,* which is based on and supported by recent advances in social neuroscience (e.g., Bechara & Bar-On, 2006; Cheney & Seyfarth, 2007; Stone, 2006), is that social purpose (i.e., the targeted activation of helping goals) is an essential prerequisite for enhanced development of the innate social intelligence capabilities that enable us to predict and influence the behavior, emotions, and thoughts of those with whom we collaborate. These capabilities are, in turn, an essential ingredient in the success of collaborations such as those involved in effective teaching and learning. Indeed, Cheney and Seyfarth (2007) argue that the evolution of social intelligence is what has made advanced technical and creative accomplishments possible over the course of human history. In other words, social intelligence, if sufficiently "exercised" through the selective, contextually appropriate activation of helping goals (Brown & Brown, 2006), can support the accumulation of new knowledge and skills within individuals as well as within cultures.

Social purpose does appear to be a critical element in the confluence of forces that contribute to successful classroom experiences for both students and teachers. Students who pursue prosocial and social responsibility goals are more likely to be accepted by peers and teachers and to have higher grades than students who are less invested in helping goals (Ford, 1996; Wentzel, 1989, 1991, 1994). Teachers who manifest qualities associated with social purpose and social intelligence foster a supportive classroom climate and high levels of student cooperation and engagement (Ryan & Deci, chapter 9; Wentzel, chapter 15). Indeed, some of the most salient features of high functioning classrooms are social and motivational qualities consistent with the social purpose hypothesis—teachers helping students while supporting their autonomy, students encouraging their classmates rather than judging or competing against them, and students feeling psychologically safe and socially supported within the classroom context. This suggests that there is an urgent need for motivation theorists to better understand the causal mechanisms underlying the relationships between social and academic motivation and social and academic intelligence. If social intelligence is more "basic" in human development (at both the individual and species levels) than academic intelligence, and social purpose is indeed the key mechanism for actualizing one's potential for socially intelligent functioning, the implications for schooling are enormous.

Motivational Pluralism

Historically, when goal-related concepts have been highlighted in school-based motivation theories, the tendency has been to pose research questions involving those concepts in "either-or" terms. Is motivation intrinsic or extrinsic? Are students motivated by mastery or performance goals? Do students hold an entity or incremental theory of intelligence?

When these theories were new, this was a useful tactic. The validity and implications of the key propositions highlighted in each theory could be seen in their most vivid form using group contrast research designs. However, we are now at the point where we need to focus more on typical cases than on "pure" or extreme cases. In the typical case, "students live in a multigoal environment" in which "pursuit of a goal always occurs in the context of pursuing other goals" (Boekaerts, chapter 6, p. 115). Elements of both intrinsic and extrinsic motivation are likely to be present (Covington, chapter 8). Similarly, mastery and performance goals will often coexist and reinforce one another. Thinking of them as automatic competitors rather than as potential collaborators is likely to be counterproductive, as classrooms that focus on both mastery and performance are the ones most likely to facilitate adaptive learning outcomes (Maehr & Zusho, chapter 5). In short, it is essential that motivation researchers recognize the need to focus explicitly on the *multiple goals* that students bring to the classroom and on how these goals interact (Boekaerts, chapter 6).

A multiple goals perspective may not be sufficient by itself, however, to move to the next level of motivational theorizing. There is also a need to better understand *motivational pluralism* at the level of individual goals. To simplify and standardize the process of conducting research on personal goals, motivational scholars have been quick to classify goals as falling into a prototypical or "pure" rendition of a goal concept. But in reality, individual goal thoughts are more likely to represent a personalized mix of several different goal themes. For example, when a student thinks "I really want to get good grade on this test," that single thought may include both mastery and performance themes. To use a food analogy, if you are thinking "I want macaroni and cheese," that thought is not going to be reducible to macaroni alone plus cheese alone. Your actual goal represents a blend or merging of multiple goal themes, not a desire to attain multiple, different goals.

The concept of motivational pluralism has been most commonly used in the context of altruism and self-interest comingling within a single motivational state (e.g., Batson & Shaw, 1991; Kagan, 2002; Sober & Wilson, 1998). In fact, our social purpose hypothesis includes an important corollary along these lines. Specifically, we propose that the beneficial effects of social purpose on social intelligence will be undiminished by positive self-evaluation personal goals that may be activated in conjunction with helping goals. In other words, wanting to think of yourself in a positive light, as a fair or helpful or responsible person, is unlikely to compromise the authenticity or strength of your desire to promote the well-being of others (i.e., integrative social relationship goals), assuming that other self-enhancing goals such as establishing superiority over others are not present in more than "trace" amounts. But the concept of motivational pluralism has implications for all kinds of goal content (see Boekaerts, chapter 6) and for the methods used to assess and classify goal content. Do students tend to activate many different kinds of goals in the classroom, or do they have only a few goals with multifaceted content? Are some goals more likely than others to be mentally represented in a relatively "pure" form? What are the implications if motivational pluralism is the rule rather than the exception? Is it possible, given the intrinsically social nature of motivation at school, that achievement goals will usually be mixed together with social goals in some sort of motivational stew? For example, the high achieving students in Wentzel's (1989) study appear to have achievement goals that might best be labeled "mastery-management-responsibility" goals. Such findings suggest a need for greater use of idiographic research methods as well as a need to develop conceptual frameworks that capture more of the variability and individuality in motivational profiles.

Theoretical Integration

In the early 1990s several individuals (e.g., Ford, 1992; McCombs, 1991; Pintrich, 1994) made an effort to encourage educational psychologists to construct conceptual models that integrated theory and research on motivation. These scholars envisioned that such models would ultimately be necessary to significantly increase the impact of motivation theory and research on education policy and practice. Unfortunately, to date only incremental progress has been made in this regard. That is why Maehr and Zusho lament that "motivation is too seldom considered as a process in which several factors collectively and systematically figure strongly in the classroom" (chapter 5, p. 100). However, the readiness of leading scholars to invest more effort in developing integrative theoretical frameworks does seem to be increasing. Zimmerman and Cleary (chapter 12) discuss how a variety of motivation concepts can be linked to their conceptually rich model of self-regulated learning. Skinner et al. (chapter 11) suggest that a general framework could be constructed from "certain classes of constructs" that "all models have in common." Toward this end, they offer the concept of engagement as a starting point.

> A common thread runs through these diverse bodies of research…a focus on engagement offers researchers the opportunity to construct a comprehensive conceptualization of motivation which integrates the many individual and interpersonal factors studied to date. (Skinner et al., chapter 11, p. 224)

There are two different kinds of theoretical integration that need to be explored and cultivated. The first reflects the need to include all four components of human motivation—personal goals, emotions, capability beliefs (e.g., self-efficacy), and context beliefs (i.e., beliefs about whether goal pursuits will be supported)—in theories whose intended "range of applicability" (Covington, chapter 8) goes beyond specialized motivational topics. For example, Ford's Motivational Systems Theory explicitly defines motivation as "the organized patterning of an individual's personal goals, emotions, and personal agency beliefs" (Ford, 1992, p. 78), with emotions, capability beliefs, and context beliefs serving as "advisors" (regulatory/evaluative function) to the personal goal "leaders" (directive function) in "motivational headquarters" (p. 205). In this same vein, decision making conceptualizations of motivation (e.g., Maehr & Zusho, chapter 5) have the potential to serve as integrative frameworks if they include all of the relevant motivational inputs. Identifying organizing constructs that incorporate elements from all four motivational components is another approach that could encourage integrative theorizing. For example, "motivational conceptualizations of engagement are ones that capture the target definitional manifestations of motivation—namely, energized, directed, and sustained action" (Skinner et al., chapter 11, p. 225).

Another type of theoretical integration reflects the need to identify dynamic patterns of motivational functioning that are associated with optimal and sub-optimal functioning and with positive and negative developmental outcomes. For example, Skinner et al. (chapter 11) emphasize the importance of "virtuous and vicious cycles" in which motivational patterns of engagement or disaffection are amplified over time, thus resulting in developmental trajectories that are increasingly likely to produce academic success or withdrawal. Our proposed "thriving with social purpose" motivational pattern (Ford & Smith, 2007) integrates several qualities that have been linked to academic and social competence in the classroom (i.e., an active approach orientation, personal optimism, mindful tenacity, emotional wisdom, and concern for others). We have also begun to look at an integrative pattern of motivational functioning related to goal balance that we call *equipoise*. This effort is consistent with Boekaerts' concern that we do not know enough about how students find a "dynamic balance between rivaling demands for their limited personal resources" (chapter 6, p. 119). Equipoise might be seen, for example, in a student who skillfully and flexibly balances mastery and performance goals or intrinsic and extrinsic motivational orientations in situationally appropriate ways (Covington, chapter 8; Maehr & Zusho, chapter 5).

Conclusion

The outpouring of creative and empirically sound motivation theories over the past 40 years has produced a strong foundation for researchers and practitioners seeking guidance regarding significant educational challenges and opportunities. However, theoretical progress has slowed considerably in recent years, suggesting a need for new theoretical catalysts. In this commentary, we have suggested five catalysts that have the potential to move the field to the next level of motivational theorizing: (a) a greater appreciation of the motivational implications of *evolutionary theory*, (b) a stronger focus on *personal goals*, (c) creative exploration of our "*social purpose hypothesis*," (d) deeper theoretical and empirical analysis of *motivational pluralism*, and (e) increased efforts to achieve *theoretical integration*. The ultimate goal is the construction of a unified theory of motivation that can either replace existing theories or, at the very least, provide a general framework within which a diversity of specialized theories can collaboratively inform efforts to enhance education and human development.

References

Alexander, R. D. (1987). *The biology of moral systems.* New York: Aldine de Gruyter.

Bargh, J. A., & Chartrand, T. L. (1999). The unbearable automaticity of being. *American Psychologist, 54,* 462–479.

Batson, C. D., & Shaw, L. L. (1991). Evidence for altruism: Toward a pluralism of prosocial motives. *Psychological Inquiry, 2,* 107–122.

Bechara, A., & Bar-On, R. (2006). Neurological substrates of emotional and social intelligence: Evidence from patients with focal brain lesions. In J. T. Cacioppo, P. S. Visser, & C. L. Pickett (Eds.), *Social neuroscience: People thinking about thinking people* (pp. 13–40). Cambridge, MA: MIT Press.

Brown, S. L., & Brown, R. M. (2006). Selective investment theory: Recasting the functional significance of close relationships. *Psychological Inquiry, 17,* 1–29.

Buss, D. M. (Ed.). (2005). *The handbook of evolutionary psychology.* Hoboken, NJ: Wiley.

Buss, D. M. (2007). *Evolutionary psychology: The new science of mind.* Boston: Allyn & Bacon.

Cheney, D. L., & Seyfarth, R. M. (2007). *Baboon metaphysics: The evolution of a social mind.* Chicago: University of Chicago Press.

Csikszentmihalyi, M., Abuhamdeh, S., & Nakamura, J. (2005). Flow. In A. J. Elliot & C. S. Dweck (Eds.), *Handbook of competence and motivation* (pp. 598–608). New York: Guilford.

Ekman, P. (2003). *Emotions revealed: Recognizing faces and feelings to improve communication and emotional life.* New York: Times Books.

Ford, M. E. (1992). *Motivating humans.* Newbury Park, CA: Sage.

Ford, M. E. (1996). Motivational opportunities and obstacles associated with social responsibility and caring behavior in school contexts. In J. Juvonen & K. Wentzel (Eds.), *Social motivation: Understanding children's school adjustment* (pp. 126–153). New York: Cambridge University Press.

Ford, M. E., & Nichols, C. W. (1991). Using goal assessments to identify motivational patterns and facilitate behavioral regulation. In M. Maehr & P. Pintrich (Eds.), *Advances in motivation and achievement, Vol. 7: Goals and self-regulatory processes* (pp. 57–84). Greenwich, CT: JAI.

Ford, M. E., & Nichols, C. W. (2008). *Assessment of Personal Goals.* Retrieved July 30, 2008, from www.implicitself.com/

Ford, M. E., & Smith, P. R. (2007). Thriving with social purpose: An integrative approach to the development of optimal functioning. *Educational Psychologist, 42*, 153–171.

Frijda, N. H. (1988). The laws of emotion. *American Psychologist, 43*, 349–358.

Izard, C. (1991). *The psychology of emotions.* New York: Plenum.

Joyce, R. (2006). *The evolution of morality.* Cambridge, MA: MIT Press.

Juvonen, J., & Wentzel, K. R. (Eds.). (1996). *Social motivation: Understanding children's school adjustment.* Cambridge, England: Cambridge University Press.

Kagan, J. (2002). Morality, altruism, and love. In S. G. Post, L. G. Underwood, J. P. Schloss, & W. B. Hurlbut (Eds.), *Altruism and altruistic love: Science, philosophy, & religion in dialogue* (pp. 40–50). New York: Oxford University Press.

Klinger, E., & Cox, W. M. (2004). Motivation and the theory of current concerns. In W. M. Cox & E. Klinger (Eds.), *Handbook of motivational counseling: Concepts, approaches, and assessment* (pp. 3–27). West Sussex, England: Wiley.

Little, B. R. (1999). Persons, contexts, and personal projects: Assumptive themes of a methodological transactionalism. In S. Wapner, J. Demick, C. T. Yamamoto, & H. Minami (Eds.), *Theoretical perspectives in environment-behavior research: Underlying assumptions, research problems and methodologies* (pp. 79–88). New York: Springer.

McCombs, B. L. (1991). Motivation and lifelong learning. *Educational Psychologist, 26*, 117–127.

Nichols, C. W. (1994). *Manual: Assessment of core goals.* (Available from C. W. Nichols, 7687 Winfield Road, Appling, GA 30802)

Pintrich, P. R. (1994). Continuities and discontinuities: Future directions for research in educational psychology. *Educational Psychologist, 29*, 137–148.

Slavin, R. (1983). When does cooperative learning increase student achievement? *Psychological Bulletin, 94*, 429–445.

Slavin, R. (1989). Cooperative learning and student achievement: Six theoretical perspectives. In M. L. Maehr & C. Ames (Eds.), *Advances in motivation and achievement, Vol. 6: Motivation enhancing environments* (pp. 161–177). Greenwich, CT: JAI.

Sober, E., & Wilson, D. S. (1998). *Unto others: The evolution and psychology of unselfish behavior.* Cambridge, MA: Harvard University Press.

Stone, V. E. (2006). Theory of mind and the evolution of social intelligence. In J. T. Cacioppo, P. S. Visser, & C. L. Pickett (Eds.), *Social neuroscience: People thinking about thinking people* (pp. 103–129). Cambridge, MA: MIT Press.

Wentzel, K. R. (1989). Adolescent classroom goals, standards for performance, and academic achievement: An interactionist perspective. *Journal of Educational Psychology, 81*, 131–142.

Wentzel, K. R. (1991). Social competence at school: The relation between social responsibility and academic achievement. *Review of Educational Research, 61*, 1–24.

Wentzel, K. R. (1994). Relations of social goal pursuit to social acceptance, classroom behavior, and perceived social support. *Journal of Educational Psychology, 86*, 173–182.

Wentzel, K. R. (1996a). Social and academic motivation in middle school: Concurrent and long-term relations to academic effort. *Journal of Early Adolescence, 16*, 390–406.

Wentzel, K. R. (1996b). Introduction: New perspectives on motivation at school. In J. Juvonen & K. R. Wentzel (Eds.), *Social motivation: Understanding children's school adjustment* (pp. 1–8). Cambridge, England: Cambridge University Press.

Wilson, D. S. (2007). *Evolution for everyone: How Darwin's theory can change the way we think about our lives.* New York: Bantam Dell.

Section II
Contextual and Social Influences on Motivation

14
Parenting and Children's Motivation at School

Wendy S. Grolnick, Rachel W. Friendly, and Valerie M. Bellas

Families and teachers might wish that the school could do the job alone. But today's school needs families, and today's families need the school. In many ways, this mutual need may be the greatest hope for change. (Dorothy Rich, 1987, p. 62)

There are 27 students in Ms. Douglas' third-grade classroom, each with his or her own temperament, learning style, and motivation to engage in academic and social activities. Ms. Douglas has ideas about how to motivate children to learn, based on her training and her many years of teaching experience. We can begin to understand the way motivation operates in Ms. Douglas' classroom by looking at Ms. Douglas and her students, but this is not the whole picture. Although they may not be sitting in the classroom, there are 43 parents, 4 grandparents, and 1 aunt raising the 27 students. Each caregiver has his or her own background, parenting style, values, and beliefs about education that significantly influence the day-to-day experience of each of the 27 children in Ms. Douglas' classroom. Further, Ms. Douglas also has her own ideas about how parents contribute to their children's motivation and achievement in the classroom. Most research in motivation in the academic domain has focused on child and teacher factors, however, parenting attitudes and behaviors have proven to play a central role in these areas of children's development. In order to gain a more comprehensive understanding of children's academic motivation, we clearly need to consider the role that parents play.

In the search for factors that affect children's school success, the family has long been known to be a crucial factor. Since Coleman et al.'s (1966) conclusion that family background is the strongest predictor of school success, researchers have been exploring parent and family factors associated with school achievement. The field has now progressed so that family factors amenable to change have been identified, motivational processes through which they affect achievement recognized, and complexities that make the work applicable to diverse families uncovered. This has been made possible by a number of trends in the research conducted on families and school motivation.

A first trend, begun as early as the 1980s was to move beyond background or "social address" (Bronfenbrenner, 1986) factors, such as parent education and socioeconomic status (SES), to focus on proximal factors that may explain some of the predictive power of family background variables (e.g., Davis-Kean, 2005). Researchers began to ask questions such as What parent attitudes and beliefs predict student school success? How do parents' behaviors and interactions with their children and with the school affect children's school achievement? How do relationships between parents and children affect children's motivation and achievement? This work has been highly fruitful, and we can now identify a multitude of parenting factors such as parents' beliefs and expectations about their children's competence (e.g., Alexander & Entwisle, 1988; Jodl, Michael, Malanchuk, Eccles, & Sameroff, 2001; Parsons, Adler, & Kaczala, 1982), parents' attributions for their children's successes and failures (e.g., Hokoda & Fincham, 1995), and parent behaviors including involvement, autonomy support, and structure in school-related activities and events (e.g., Grolnick & Ryan, 1989; Grolnick & Slowiaczek, 1994) that are connected to success in school.

A second trend is identifying the processes through which parents affect children's school outcomes. It is increasingly apparent that children's motivation—why they engage in school endeavors and how they experience themselves with regard to school behaviors, activities, and emotions—is crucial to children's school success. Included in these processes are children's beliefs about their abilities (e.g., Harter, 1982) and about the value of school activities and endeavors (Wigfield & Eccles, 2002), children's perceptions of control over school outcomes (Skinner, Wellborn, & Connell, 1990), children's self-regulation (Ryan & Connell, 1989), and the goals children bring to their class and homework (Dweck & Elliott, 1983). Such key motivational variables are likely mediators of relations between parenting and children's school performance. A focus on motivation is consistent with an active model of children, whereby they are not passive recipients of inputs from the social context, but active interpreters of the context as they develop motives and concepts of themselves that they then bring to achievement settings.

Another key direction for research is understanding the factors that make it possible for parents to provide resources to their children that will facilitate school motivation. Parents do not interact with their children in a vacuum—they do so within their larger social and cultural contexts. Recognizing this, researchers have begun to identify factors in parents' social surrounds that enable them to provide facilitative resources to their children. Included in such characteristics are factors within other institutions, especially schools, that make facilitative parent behavior, such as involvement, more possible (e.g., Eccles & Harold, 1996; Stone, 2006). In addition, factors within parents, such as their perceived pressure to have their children succeed (e.g., Grolnick, Price, Beiswenger, & Sauck, 2007), as well as factors within children themselves, such as their temperaments and competence levels (e.g., Pomerantz & Dong, 2006), may also affect facilitative parenting behaviors.

In addressing ways in which parents influence motivation and achievement in children, it is important to take a theoretical viewpoint specifying what children need to develop, thrive, and engage fully with their environments. While many theories of motivation are available, in this chapter we focus on three that have generated important research on parenting. For each of these theories—Self-determination Theory (Deci & Ryan, 1985), Expectancy-Value theory (e.g., Eccles-Parsons et al., 1983), and Goal Orientation Theory (e.g., Dweck & Elliott, 1983)—we first describe the motivational constructs that have been shown to be crucial to school success and then describe the parenting variables that have been linked to them.

Self-Determination Theory

Self-Determination Theory (SDT; Deci & Ryan, 1985) posits that individuals have three psychological needs, the fulfillment of which is necessary for well-being, and which, when unsatisfied, can result in maladjustment and lack of motivation. These needs are for relatedness, autonomy, and competence.

According to SDT, the need for relatedness concerns a need to be connected with, loved, and valued by others. Such an experience is associated with feelings of security that allow one to venture out and pursue goals, making a sense of relatedness necessary for taking on challenges. In addition to the need for relatedness, the need for autonomy refers to a person's need to feel agentic, to feel like the author of his or her actions. As such, autonomy as defined by SDT is not equivalent to independence (which refers to lack of dependency on others), but rather describes the need to feel one has a choice regarding one's actions. In the school domain, autonomy is exhibited when children's academic behaviors are self-initiated and managed, rather than externally controlled, and when the behaviors are initiated for internalized rather than external reasons (Ryan & Connell, 1989; Ryan, Connell, & Grolnick, 1992). Lastly, the need for competence is the need to feel effective in navigating one's environment and creating successful outcomes. When this need is satisfied, children feel both in control of their successes and failures (i.e., have a sense of perceived control; Skinner, Wellborn, & Connell, 1990) and believe in their own competence to achieve desired outcomes (i.e., have a sense of perceived competence; Harter, 1982).

We now turn to parenting behaviors that, within Self-determination Theory, facilitate the fulfillment of the three needs.

Involvement

Parents help facilitate the need for relatedness through positive involvement, which includes both the provision of tangible resources (e.g., time, attention) as well as relationship characteristics (e.g., emotional support, warmth) that provide children with the psychological resources essential for motivation in school (Grolnick & Ryan, 1989).

The area of parent involvement in children's schooling is a burgeoning one—with researchers from a variety of disciplines and viewpoints including academics, education, and public policy showing strong interest in this area (Fan & Chen, 2001). Parent involvement in children's education has been conceived as a key to decreasing the achievement gap between disadvantaged or minority children and their more advantaged peers and as a road to educational equality (U.S. Department of Health and Human Services, 2005). A variety of questions have been asked in the literature—questions to which we now have some relatively clear answers. Importantly, what is the evidence that parent involvement is associated with achievement outcomes? And what do we know about *how* parent involvement affects student outcomes?

With regard to the first question, there is now little doubt that parent involvement is positively associated with educational outcomes across a broad range of students (Fan & Chen, 2001). Bolstering this conclusion are the results of Jeynes' (2005) meta-analyses of 42 studies of urban elementary children and 52 studies of secondary school children (Jeynes, 2007), though the effect size was somewhat smaller for the secondary than the elementary school children. Parent involvement has also been linked to fewer behavior problems (Comer, 1984) and lower drop-out rates (e.g., Barnard, 2004; NCES, 1992).

Interestingly, research indicates that broader indices of parental support show higher correlations with school outcomes than more specific types of behaviors such as helping with homework at home or participating at school. In both of Jeynes' meta-analyses, measures assessing involvement as parents' supportive overall style had the strongest effects on achievement. In second through fifth graders observed interacting with their parents, a supportive style (warmth, clarity of communication, and positivity) was a stronger predictor of achievement than parent involvement at the school (Zellman & Waterman, 1998). These results support the idea that parents' positive and supportive involvement helps children to feel connected and valued, a conclusion that is reinforced by work reviewed later showing that involvement has its effect largely by helping to build motivational resources that children then bring to their school experiences (Grolnick & Slowiaczek, 1994).

Finding relations between parent involvement and children's school outcomes is important, but does not explain why these relations exist. In order to understand parent involvement, we need to determine *how* it is related to these outcomes, in other words, what are the mechanisms through which parent involvement has its impact? Children's motivational processes, including their thoughts and emotions about themselves as individuals and learners and the degree of autonomy they have for engaging in school related behaviors, have been addressed as such mechanisms.

Dearing, McCartney, Weiss, Kreider, and Simpkins (2004) found support that parent involvement at school during kindergarten affected children's literacy through its effects on children's confidence in themselves with regard to literacy activities, which then resulted in greater competence. Hill and Craft (2003) looked at social competence and academic behavior (e.g., staying on task and being a self-starter) as possible mediators of the relation between parent involvement at school and children's school achievement. Interestingly, social competence mediated the relation for European American but not for African American families. Academic behavior was a mediator for both groups of families.

In a more comprehensive study, Grolnick, Ryan, and Deci (1991) posited a motivational model whereby parenting behavior would facilitate children's school performance by building the motivational resources children need to succeed in school. They found that both mother and father involvement contributed to children feeling more competent and in control of school successes and more autonomous in their activities, each of which were, in turn, related to children's school performance.

Grolnick and Slowiaczek (1994) further examined this motivational model by examining the ways in which three types of parent involvement: behavioral involvement (i.e., going to open houses, attending parent-teacher conferences, and participating in other school activities), cognitive/intellectual involvement (i.e., exposing children to cognitively stimulating activities such as books and current events), and personal involvement (children's reports that their parents care about school and have and enjoy interactions with them around school) affected children's motivational resources of perceived competence, perceived control, and self-regulation. Results indicated that, for mothers, two of the involvement factors, behavior and cognitive/intellectual, were uniquely related to school grades through their relations with children's enhanced feelings of academic competence and beliefs that they could control their successes and failures in school (i.e., control understanding). There was also a direct effect of parent behavior on school grades. For fathers, behavioral and intellectual/cognitive involvement were associated with children's perceived competence, which was then associated with children's grades. The results for both parents thus support a model whereby parent involvement is related to children's academic achievement by way of children's motivational resources.

Finally, closely connected to parental involvement are positive and caring relationships that can lead children to have secure relations with their parents. Such secure relations or attachments have been found to be strongly connected to children's school motivation. For example, securely attached elementary school children reported a more mastery-oriented approach to learning 2 years later than did insecurely attached children (Moss & St. Laurent, 2001). Feelings of closeness to parents predict greater engagement in school (Furrer & Skinner, 2003; Learner & Kruger, 1997). Such findings underscore the importance of relationships with parents for children.

Summary

The literature on parent involvement unequivocally supports its strong relations with academic outcomes. Further, there is evidence that involvement has its effects by facilitating motivational processes such as perceived competence, perceived control, and positive feelings about academic endeavors. If motivation is a potent mediator of involvement, it can be concluded that parents can have a strong impact on children's school success, whether or not they are able to provide assistance with specific skills such as those in math or social studies. Attachment work supports the idea that involvement may have much of its impact through the feelings of connectedness and value for the child that it conveys.

Autonomy-Support versus Control

Parents support children's need for autonomy by taking children's perspectives, encouraging their initiations, and supporting their autonomous problem solving. Controlling parenting behaviors, by contrast, involve parents taking their own perspectives, pressuring children toward particular ends, and solving problems for them (Grolnick & Ryan, 1989).

As with parental involvement, the association between parental autonomy-support and child well-being outcomes is well supported in the literature. Research has demonstrated positive effects of parental support of child/adolescent autonomy for many outcomes, including internalizing and externalizing psychopathology (e.g., Barber, 1992; Barber, Olsen, & Shagle, 1994; Ryan, Deci, Grolnick, & LaGuardia, 2006; Soenens, Elliot, Goossens, Vansteenkiste, Luyten, & Duriez, 2005), social and job search contexts (Soenens & Vansteenkiste, 2005), and health risk behaviors (e.g., Turner, Irwin, Tschann, & Millstein, 1993). Additionally, one of the key areas of interest in autonomy-support research has been in the domain of academic motivation.

Research spanning more than three decades provides ample evidence connecting parental autonomy-support with academic achievement motivation for children and adolescents. Although work on autonomy support has been primarily conducted with older children or adolescents, SDT research has illustrated that autonomy-support is associated with motivation in infants and young children, possibly setting the stage for academic motivation in the later years. For example, Grolnick, Frodi, and Bridges (1984) showed positive correlations between mothers' autonomy support and the mastery motivation of 1-year-olds. Deci, Driver, Hotchkiss, Robbins, and Wilson (1993) similarly showed that mothers who were more autonomy supportive versus controlling during play showed more intrinsic motivation to pursue challenges presented by toys when on their own.

With elementary school children, multiple studies support the relationship between autonomy-supportive parenting and positive academic outcomes. In the study discussed previously, Grolnick and Ryan (1989) showed that maternal autonomy support was associated with children's more autonomous self-regulation in school. In a subsequent study using children's reports of parenting, Grolnick, Ryan, and Deci (1991) replicated this finding, with both maternal and paternal autonomy-support predicting both autonomous academic self-regulation, as well as perceived competence (Harter, 1982), and maternal autonomy-support predicting control understanding (i.e., perceived control; Connell, 1985). Though these results are compelling, the authors caution that the results are likely bidirectional. In fact, Self-Determination Theory readily acknowledges the complexity of the relationship between parent and child factors, and research suggests that these variables most likely represent a reciprocal, transactional process of influence between parent and child (Bronstein, Ginsburg, & Herrera, 2005; Grolnick & Ryan, 1989). For example, parents may respond to children they consider more competent by being autonomy-supportive and children they consider less competent with a more controlling parenting style.

Research has also examined parent autonomy support and adolescents' motivation. For example, Soenens and Vansteenkiste (2005) found self-determination in the school domain to be an intervening variable between maternal autonomy-support and academic achievement outcomes (e.g., GPA, scholastic competence ratings) in Belgian high school students. Steinberg and colleagues (1992) found that authoritative parenting (adolescent report of parental acceptance/involvement, supervision/strictness, and psychological autonomy granting; Baumrind, 1971) at Time 1 predicted greater increases in adolescent engagement in school than nonauthoritative parenting over the course of 1 year. Further, in a study of the transition to junior high, Grolnick and colleagues (2000) found that maternal autonomy-support in the sixth grade buffered against increases in learning problems and acting-out behaviors in school in the seventh grade, and that increases in maternal autonomy-support between sixth and seventh grades protected against the declines in self-worth and control understanding that were evident in other children. These findings highlight the importance of parental autonomy-support, especially in times of transition, during which children may be vulnerable.

Importantly, student drop-out has been linked to parental autonomy support. Vallerand, Fortier, and Guay's (1997) examination of a motivational model revealed a chain of effects whereby low perceived parental autonomy-support was linked to low feelings of competence and autonomy about school, which predicted less self-determined school motivation, which in turn led first to intentions to drop out, and finally, to actually dropping out of school. In addition, although perceived autonomy-support from teachers and school administrators were significant in the model, parents had by far the strongest impact on these outcomes, a reflection of the depth of influence that parents have on their children's lives.

Summary

Substantial research over the past few decades points to parental autonomy-support as a key element in facilitating children's academic motivation. When children's need for autonomy is supported, they are more likely to be intrinsically motivated to learn, to be autonomously self-regulated in academic contexts, and to be more engaged in school. In contrast, when children perceive their parents as controlling, they are more likely to experience extrinsic motivation for learning, which is related to more negative motivational and academic outcomes. That the results are consistent across such a wide range of ages and indicators of school motivation speaks to the importance of this parenting dimension.

Structure

While parent involvement and autonomy support are both key to children's motivation, work on parenting has suggested a third dimension that is crucial to a variety of child outcomes. In particular, this third dimension involves the way parents set up and organize the environment to facilitate success for children. We have labeled this dimension structure. Structure refers to the consistent rules, guidelines, and expectations parents have for their children. Theoretically, these guidelines give children the knowledge they need about how to attain desirable outcomes and avoid undesirable ones. In particular, when expectations and consequences are clear and support for following these guidelines is provided, children are expected to develop a sense of perceived control and perceived competence that will allow them to pursue desirable ends.

In the parenting literature, there has been acknowledgement of this third dimension. However, the dimension has been variously conceptualized and operationalized. For example, some researchers have referred to the dimension as firm vs. lax control, with lax control representing allowing extreme independence and using lax discipline (Schaefer, 1965). Others have referred to the dimension with terms like demandingness or strictness, though often these constructs have included elements of both structure and control. SDT makes a clear distinction between structure, which involves the provision of information, rules and expectations that facilitate competence, and autonomy support versus control, which concerns how such structures are implemented (i.e., in a manner that is pressuring and coercive or one which allows input and child problem solving). Rather than reviewing all of the literature on the third dimension, we focus on work that refers specifically to parents' provision of guidelines, expectations, and rules with regard to school or cognitively-related activities and interactions.

Some of the work relevant to the structure dimension, especially that involving young children, has addressed the ways in which parents facilitate competence during parent-child task interaction. In much of this work, the parenting dimension has been labeled quality of assistance. For example, Englund, Luckner, Whaley, and Egeland (2004) rated quality of assistance as how well mothers structured task situations with their children and coordinated their activities to the children's during a problem solving activity. Quality of assistance was associated with IQ, which then predicted higher achievement in first and third grade. Similarly, Pianta, Nimetz, and Bennett (1997) showed that quality of assistance during a block design task, including providing orienting instructions and well-timed hints, as well as autonomy support, predicted children's competence in kindergarten. With somewhat older children, Mattanah (2001) rated how well the parent established, maintained and followed through with limits during a 40-minute interaction with their fourth grader. This rating was positively correlated with teacher ratings of academic competence.

Less work has focused on the effects of structure on motivation per se. Based on interviews of parents of third- through sixth-grade children, Grolnick and Ryan (1989) rated parents on two dimensions of structure: (a) parents' provision of clear rules, expectations, and guidelines for behavior and the stipulation of consequences for not meeting expectations, and (b) the degree to which rules and guidelines were consistently applied or promoted. Children of parents high on these dimensions reported more knowledge of how to succeed and how to avoid failure (control understanding) both in school and in general, than children of parents rated low on these dimensions.

In their review of work on parenting and school performance, Christenson, Rounds, and Gorney (1992) suggested a larger dimension called structure for learning and stated that there is no study that has addressed this concept comprehensively. They noted the importance of variables such as providing an appropriate space for homework, establishing a schedule, and providing adequate lighting and materials. Though there is little empirical work on such factors, Cooper, Lindsay, and Nye (2000) identified elimination of distraction as a key parenting dimension that impacts on homework.

In order to address the effects of parental structure more comprehensively, Farkas and Grolnick (2009) identified six key components of structure that would be relevant to children's school functioning. The first, clear and consistent communication of expectations, includes clearly provided and consistently endorsed rules, guidelines, and expectations. The second, opportunities to meet or exceed expectations includes opportunities to behave within guidelines such as necessary materials or support. This might include some of the aspects that Christenson and Cooper and colleagues describe, including provision of adequate lighting and time to complete homework in the allotted time. The third component, predictability, is clearly conveyed and consistent consequences for actions. Fourth, informational feedback is feedback provided for meeting expectations. The fifth component, provision of rationales, involves providing reasons for rules and expectations. Finally, authority involves parents taking an active role in guidance and decision making and serving as ultimate authorities.

In a first study of these six components of structure, Farkas and Grolnick (2006) interviewed 75 seventh- and eighth-grade students and their mothers. Their findings suggest important links between components of structure and children's motivation. In particular, provision of clear and consistent guidelines were positively correlated with children's control understanding and perceived competence, indicating that when parents provide clear rules and expectations in a consistent fashion, children report that they know how to attain success and avoid failure in school and that they feel competent to obtain desired outcomes.

Summary

While there is little research directly addressing structure, this dimension has the potential to organize research on what parents can provide to facilitate competence in children. The existing evidence supports the importance of providing rules and expectations, and opportunities to meet them, for children's perceptions of competence and control. Clearly more research is necessary to delineate the ways parents can use structuring behaviors to facilitate competence.

Modern Expectancy-Value Theories

Modern expectancy-value theories (e.g. Eccles-Parsons et al., 1983; Feather, 1992, Heckhausen, 1977; Wigfield & Eccles, 2002) take a social-cognitive perspective on motivation and achievement. More specifically, in the tradition of Atkinson's original expectancy-value model (1957, 1964), such theories link an individual's persistence, task choice, and performance to their expectancy-related and task-value beliefs.

Expectancy-related beliefs are beliefs about how well an individual will do on upcoming tasks (Eccles-Parsons et al., 1983) or their perceived efficacy. Task-value beliefs include the individual's positive and negative assessment of the task. Eccles-Parsons and her colleagues (1983) have outlined four motivational components of task value: (a) attainment value (personal importance linked to self-schema, gender, ethnicity etc.); (b) intrinsic value (enjoyment and subjective interest); (c) utility value (usefulness in relation to current and future goals); and (d) cost (the negative aspects of engaging in task performance, including performance anxiety, expenditure of effort and lost opportunities as a result of task participation).

Children's expectancy and task-value beliefs have been shown to be strong predictors of performance and persistence in different domains, including math, reading and sports (see Wigfield & Eccles, 2002 for a review). For example, Meece, Wigfield, and Eccles (1990), in a study of 250 seventh-through ninth-graders, found that students' performance expectancies predicted math grades and their value perceptions predicted course enrollment intentions. In another study, Simpkins, Fredricks, Davis-Kean, and Eccles (2006) found that children's self-perceptions of competence, importance and interest in sports in sixth grade were positively related to adolescents' sport participation in 10th grade. These relationships have been shown empirically as young as first grade and strengthen across age (e.g., Eccles, 1984; Eccles & Harold, 1991; Eccles-Parsons et al., 1983; Meece, Wigfield, & Eccles, 1990; Wigfield, 1994).

Within the expectancy–value model, parents influence children's achievement motivation through their general beliefs and behaviors (which include gender-role stereotypes, locus of control, efficacy beliefs, child-rearing beliefs and interpretive biases), their parent-specific behaviors (teaching strategies, encouragement to participate in various activities, training of specific personal values, and explicit causal attributions), and their child-specific beliefs (which include expectations for children's performance, perception of talents, temperament and interests and socialization goals; Eccles, 2007). These parental beliefs and behaviors have been shown to predict children's self and task beliefs in a variety of studies (e.g., Fredricks & Eccles, 2002, 2005; Frome & Eccles, 1998; Miller & Davis, 1992; Pallas, Entwisle, Alexander, & Stluka, 1994; Stevenson, Chen, & Uttal, 1990).

With the understanding that parental beliefs regarding the child's ability to successfully complete the task may have the most targeted influence on a child's perceived competence, motivation, and achievement, the largest set of expectancy-value studies has focused specifically on parents' beliefs about their children's competence. In one such study, Parsons, Adler, and Kaczala (1982) found that the more parents expected their children to do well at math, the more positive the children felt about their own math competence. Notably, the relations between parents' and children's beliefs were stronger than those between children's beliefs and their own performance.

Findings for parents' expectations and aspirations for their children's achievement mirror these results and extend them to children's own expectations and values. For example, parents' expectations for their children's educational attainment have been linked to children's own expectations of how far they will go in school (Halle, Kurtz-Costes, & Mahoney, 1997; Phillips, 1987). In a study of adolescents' occupational aspirations, children of mothers and fathers who viewed their children as having a greater chance to obtain positive academic outcomes and who held high educational expectations/aspirations valued school as being important for their future and had higher educational aspirations. Children's educational aspirations in turn predicted their professional career aspirations (Jodl et al., 2001). In the longitudinal study referenced above, Simpkins et al. (2006) found that parents who reported more sport and math promoting beliefs and behaviors, such as high ratings of their children's competence, valuing of the activity, encouragement, provision of materials, and time involvement with their children in the activities, had children with higher sport and math ability self-concepts, interest, importance and participation in both domains concurrently and across time.

Because expectations for achievement in different academic domains may vary according to the child's gender, in particular, that boys may be viewed as more competent in math and girls as more competent in language tasks, the role of parents' gender-based beliefs in the development of children's achievement motivation has been a focus of study. For example, Jacobs and Eccles (1992) found that parents' gender-based stereotypes directly influenced their perceptions of their children's abilities in math, English and sports, which in turn influenced the children's performance and self-perceptions of their abilities across these domains, even after controlling for the child's previous performance.

Summary

Modern expectancy-value studies provide a model of the manner by which parent and family characteristics are transmitted via parents' general and child-specific beliefs and parental role modeling and activity specific behaviors (Eccles, 2007). Consistent with the theory, parents' expectancies of their children's competence and parents' valuing of the task in which the child is engaging appear to have strong influences on children's motivation across childhood and adolescence (Wigfield & Eccles, 2002). Further research is needed to address the development of children's achievement values, the link between expectancies and values and achievement and motivation across ages, and the manner in which expectancies and values themselves are linked with these developmental processes (Wigfield, Eccles, Schiefele, Roeser, & Davis-Kean, 2006).

Goal Orientation Theory

In the realm of academic achievement, Goal Orientation theorists (e.g., Dweck & Leggett, 1988; Nicholls, 1984) distinguish among children's different approaches to learning. Children with a *mastery orientation, learning, or mastery goals* focus in their achievement pursuits on learning new things and mastering new skills. Children with a *performance orientation, or performance goals* tend to focus on external outcomes such as grades or "looking smart" (as judged by themselves and others), with an ultimate goal of maximizing the likelihood of being evaluated as competent and minimizing evaluations of incompetence. Within the category of performance goals, some researchers argue that it is necessary to further differentiate between approach and avoidance components (e.g., Elliot, 1999, 2005; Elliot & Harackiewicz, 1996; Pintrich, 2000). For example, performance-approach would involve appearing competent and outperforming peers, and performance-avoidance goals would involve avoiding any evaluations of incompetence.

In general, the research has been fairly clear about the consequences for children of adopting these various orientations to learning. Children with a mastery orientation or learning goals tend to be more intrinsically motivated to learn, leading them to be more engaged in the learning process, and thus to have more positive achievement outcomes (Gutman, 2006; Matos, Lens, & Vansteenkiste, 2007). Children with performance-approach-oriented goals have been shown to have positive academic self-concepts and often perform well, but do not tend to exhibit intrinsic motivation to learn. In contrast, children with performance-avoidant goals tend to be low on measures of learning and achievement motivation (Harackiewicz, Barron, Pintrich, Elliot, & Thrash, 2002; Matos, Lens, & Vansteenkiste, 2007).

Given the significance of children's achievement orientations for academic motivation and success, researchers have begun to examine how these orientations may develop in children. Classroom contexts (e.g., Gutman, 2006; Midgley, 2002), peer and other social relationships (e.g., Nelson & DeBacker, 2008), and parental influences (e.g., Boon, 2007; deBruyn, Dekovic, & Meijnen, 2003; Gonzalez & Wolters, 2006; Gonzalez-DeHass, Willems, & Holbein, 2005; Gurland & Grolnick, 2005) have all been addressed.

In an effort to examine children's development of goal orientations, Gutman (2006) conducted a study of African American adolescents transitioning to high school. Notably for our discussion of parenting influences, results indicated that adolescents whose parents endorsed mastery goals had higher grades than peers whose parents did not endorse mastery goals. However, these authors did not include motivational outcomes in children so it is not clear how parents' goals had their effect.

In support of the hypothesis that goal orientations are at least in part socialized by parents, Hokoda and Fincham (1995) conducted a laboratory study of mastery-oriented and "helpless" third-grade children doing solvable and unsolvable tasks with their mothers. They found that, compared with mothers of "helpless" children, mothers of mastery-oriented children were more sensitive and responsive to their children's requests for help, were warmer in their interactions with their children, and were more likely to respond to their children's low-ability attributions and performance goal statements with mastery-oriented responses. In contrast, mothers of "helpless" children were more likely to respond to their children's performance goal statements with performance goal statements of their own, to respond to low-ability attribution statements with suggestions to quit the task, and to respond to negative child affect with negative affect.

Several studies lend support to the central role that parenting styles play in children's goal orientations. In particular, both Boon (2007) and Gonzalez and Wolters (2006) found that an authoritative parenting style, in which the child's perspective is elicited and respected, but appropriate rules and boundaries are enforced (Baumrind, 1967), was related to enhanced mastery goals in children. Further, Gonzalez and Wolters (2006) found that authoritarian parenting (a parenting style focused on conformity, obedience, and respect for authority; Baumrind, 1967) was associated with a performance-approach orientation in children, whereas permissive parenting (a parenting style involving little to no provision of rules, boundaries, or limitations; Baumrind, 1967) was negatively related to children's mastery orientations and positively related to children's performance-approach orientations. Similarly, in a laboratory task, Gurland and Grolnick (2005) found that controlling parenting behaviors (see the discussion of Self-Determination Theory) were associated with children's endorsement of performance goals.

Summary

Goal Orientation Theory provides a useful lens through which a greater understanding of children's academic achievement motivation can be reached. Abundant research has shown the positive motivational and academic outcomes associated with having mastery, as opposed to performance, goals. While some research links parenting to goal orientations, much of this work includes broad parenting constructs such as authoritative parenting. Although the Gurland and Grolnick (2005) and Hokoda and Fincham (1995) studies have offered a first step towards describing more specific parenting behaviors that are associated with mastery goal orientations, more research in this area is needed. It is interesting that several of the key parenting constructs identified as important for facilitating learning versus performance goals such as authoritativeness, responsiveness, and autonomy support overlap with facilitative dimensions identified within Self-Determination Theory. Such work highlights the need for research on parenting and motivation that crosses theoretical areas.

Diversity and Parenting—Age, SES, and Cultural Background

Much of the research presented above assumes that the effects of parenting are consistent across populations. However, there is reason to believe that, not only is parenting affected by background factors, but the ways in which key parenting behaviors are expressed differs for different populations and ages. For example, while the effects of parent involvement are consistent across populations, the types of involvement that are facilitative vary with age, with involvement at the school more important for younger ages (Grolnick et al., 2000; Jeynes, 2007). Further, while parent involvement affects families across background and culture; the ways parents from different cultural groups become involved may differ (Kerbow & Bernhardt, 1993). For example, Asian American families may be more involved in educational activities outside the school while European American and African American families tend to be more involved at school (Lee & Bowen, 2006).

Given the ways in which parents from various ethnic/racial groups tend to be involved, it is not surprising that the effects of different types of involvement have sometimes been found to vary for these groups. For example, involvement at home was found to be more predictive of European American children's scores on quantitative concepts (math readiness) while involvement at school was more important for African American children's math readiness scores (Hill, 2001). With regard to SES, Cooper and Crosnoe (2007) found that reports of parent involvement at school were positively correlated with economically disadvantaged children's academic orientation but were negatively correlated for nondisadvantaged children. These authors concluded that while parents of nondisadvantaged children become involved when their children are achieving poorly, those of disadvantaged children may be involved regardless of achievement level; thus for disadvantaged children parent involvement is a resource that can facilitate academic progress. Clearly, it is important to consider the meaning of and goals for involvement behaviors for different groups.

While such complexities in the types of specific behaviors and practices that affect motivation in diverse families do not challenge overall theories of parenting and motivation, more controversial is the idea that some parenting dimensions themselves may have different effects in different cultures or groups. For example, some authors have questioned the assumption that autonomy-support is universally beneficial, positing that the need for autonomy is merely a western phenomenon (e.g., Markus, Kitayama, & Heiman, 1996). In an effort to demonstrate the applicability of the construct of autonomy-support cross culturally, Chirkov and Ryan (2001) studied 236 high school students in the United States and Russia. They discovered that the construct of autonomy-support was interpreted similarly by Russian and U.S. students. In addition, the findings that autonomy-supportive parenting was associated with more intrinsic motivation in school, less extrinsic motivation in school, and more general well-being were almost identical for the two groups. Thus, there is at least some evidence that the motivational model appears to be supported across a variety of settings (see also Chen, Dong, & Zhou [1997] for complementary work with Chinese students). However, additional work in more cultures and with other key parenting constructs is crucial to determine how parenting and motivation may play out across cultures.

Factors that Build and Limit Parents' Capacities to Support Children's Motivation

A number of parent beliefs, orientations, and behaviors have been identified as facilitating children's school motivation. Nonetheless, just as children's environments affect their motivation, parents themselves are affected by factors that influence their abilities to provide facilitative environments for their children's motivation. External stresses and available resources, including socioeconomic factors, contribute to the parental context for motivation, as does the more proximal context of the parent-school relationship. Furthermore, parents experience internal pressures (e.g., concerns about the competition that children may face, and their sense of their own worth as a reflection of their children's achievements) and individual perspectives and beliefs (e.g., ideas about children's motivation) that may affect the manner in which they provide support for their children overall and particularly in relation to children's motivation in school.

External Stresses and Resources: The Broader Context for Parenting

As with any parental behavior, parental support for children's motivation in school must be understood within the context within which the parents and family live (Belsky, 1984; Bronfenbrenner, 1986). High levels of stress have been found to be negatively related to parental characteristics such as warmth and responsiveness (Belsky, 1984; Roberts, 1989), whereas social support has been positively associated with provision of a nurturant family environment (Crnic, Greenberg, Ragozin, Robinson, & Basham, 1983). In many research models, parenting has been conceived as mediating the relationship between socioeconomic context and children's developmental outcomes (e.g., Conger & Conger, 2002; Duncan & Brooks-Gunn, 1997; Keating & Hertzman, 1999). McLoyd (1990) proposed a family stress model, suggesting that parenting behaviors are mediating processes through which socioeconomic inequalities and financial stressors influence child outcomes. Evidence for this relationship has been found in European American, African American, and Latino families (Gutman & Eccles, 1999; Mistry, Vandewater, Huston, & McLoyd 2002). Conger and Donnellan (2007) proposed an interactionist model of SES and human development. In this model, parental "positive characteristics," which include attributes such as cognitive abilities, social competence, persistence, planfulness, and ambition, affect SES. Further, SES affects these parental characteristics, and it is this reciprocal dynamic process that affects children's development. Longitudinal investigations of these transactional relationships have shown support for the model (e.g. Capaldi, Conger, Hops, & Thornberry, 2003).

Less work has specifically examined the manner in which such contextual factors influence the three dimensions identified as facilitative within SDT, i.e., autonomy support, involvement, and structure. Grolnick, Weiss, McKenzie, and Wrightman (1996) interviewed parents about how they motivate their adolescents to do their homework, do well in school and other behaviors, whether they have expectations or rules for these behaviors, how they respond to positive or negative outcomes, and how they respond to conflicts in these areas. They also collected information about the stressful events parents had recently endured and the availability of social supports to them. For mothers, the more stressful events they had experienced, the less they tended to provide structure and autonomy support. These results suggest stressful events may interfere with mothers' abilities to provide resources, such as time and energy, and to developing and enforcing rules and guidelines overall, and may serve to undermine mothers' tendencies to take children's perspectives and support their initiations, which likely require emotional availability. The study found, however, that the number of stressful events endured was not related to fathers' behaviors. Instead, for fathers, reports of social support were related to greater levels of involvement. It is possible that daily stresses do not interfere with fathers' manners of interacting with their children as much as they may for mothers. Nevertheless, when fathers have extra support, they may be more able to extend their capacities to spend time and energy with their children. These results demonstrate the complex relationships between external pressures and parenting behaviors associated with child motivation.

Although Grolnick et al. (1996) examined the relationship of contextual factors to parenting behaviors from a Self-Determination Theory perspective, they did not look at these factors in relation to parenting behaviors with regard to school more specifically. In a subsequent study, Grolnick, Benjet, Kurowski, and Apostoleris (1997) examined relations between contextual factors and parental involvement in children's schooling. The researchers identified three hierarchically organized sets of factors influencing parental involvement, namely parent and child characteristics, family context, and teacher behavior and attitudes. They found that mothers who felt efficacious, who saw their roles as that of teacher and who viewed their children as less difficult were more involved in cognitive activities. Parental social support was associated with both school and personal involvement. While this study found that SES did predict involvement, especially school and cognitive involvement, SES was not associated with parents' personal involvement in children's schooling. Similarly, single parents were also less likely to be involved in school activities than parents from two-parent families; however no relationship was found between family configuration and cognitive-intellectual or personal involvement. Thus, not all types of parental involvement are equally susceptible to external stress. These results lend support to the findings of Chavkin and Williams (1989) which dispute the idea that low-income parents lack interest in their children's schooling, by showing that parents with fewer resources may participate less than their more resourced counterparts in school activities, but are fully involved with supporting and knowing about their children's progress in school. Overall, research in this area calls for a complex understanding of the manner in which context influences the kinds of support parents may provide for their children's motivation in school.

School Factors: Schools Can Make a Difference

The parent-school relationship is a particularly salient context for parents' support of children's motivation at school. Both exogenous and process variables have been shown to influence parents' relationship with their children's schools (Eccles & Harold, 1996; Stone, 2006). Exogenous variables include background characteristics of the school staff (e.g., experience and race), school structural and compositional variables (e.g., student body characteristics, size), and resources and general school practices (Stone, 2006). Process characteristics consist of teacher beliefs about parents and students and practices that are instituted to influence the relationship families have with the schools (e.g., parent involvement, parent outreach, parent-teacher communications; Stone, 2006).

Research has provided some information regarding the role of exogenous factors in parent-school relationships. For example, schools with a high proportion of minority and low-income students have been found to have poorer teacher-parent relationships (Metropolitan Life Survey of the American Teacher, 2001), while smaller schools have higher levels of parent involvement (Gardner, Riblatt, & Beatty, 2000).

Likewise, teacher characteristics have been related to parent-school relationships. Thus, teachers who reported more negative beliefs and lower expectations of students were less likely to reach out to parents and reported more distrust of parents (Stone, 2003). In the study of factors associated with parent involvement in children's schooling discussed earlier (Grolnick et al., 1997) teachers reported on their beliefs about parent involvement and the degree to which they used practices to involve parents in their classrooms. Teachers' active efforts to include parents in classroom activities fostered parental involvement, but this was the case only when parental attitudes and social context were facilitative. In particular, teacher practices were positively associated with parent involvement for parents who saw themselves as efficacious and viewed their roles as that of teacher, and those who experienced less difficult contexts, but were not associated with parent involvement for parents low on these attitudes or high in stress. This indicates that, at least with the types of practices teachers used in this study, teachers may not be reaching parents who are in the most difficult circumstances or whose beliefs may not match those of the teacher. Such findings suggest that schools may need to think especially creatively about involving parents who are traditionally hard to reach.

In addition to these classroom level factors, system-wide attention to enhancing family-school partnerships can provide parents environments that are favorable to involvement in children's education. One approach to fostering family school relationships is the National Network of Partnership Schools (Sanders & Epstein, 2000), which provides states, districts, and schools assistance to improve family-school relationships through comprehensive development strategies, including the creation of "action teams," explicit attention to goal-oriented system-wide planning, ongoing assessment of the quality and progress of development of partnerships and each school's participation in networking activities. Studies have indicated that when schools devote these types of attention and resources to family-school relationships, family and community involvement in schools improve (Epstein, 2001; Sanders & Simon, 2002; Sheldon & Van Voorhis, 2004). A longitudinal study of one such partnership school demonstrated increased connections with families on seven out of eight indicators of family involvement and commitment to family involvement over time (Epstein, 2005). These results demonstrate the role of school-family partnerships in providing parents the contexts they need to more fully support their children in school.

Parents' Experiences of Internal Pressure

In the same way that social-contextual and school factors may provide a context for parenting practices, the psychological processes which parents bring to their efforts to support their children overall and in relation to their schooling may influence parental motivational attitudes and behaviors.

To understand how pressure and individual difference factors predict autonomy supportive versus controlling parental behaviors, Grolnick, Gurland, DeCourcey, and Jacob (2002) observed mother-child dyads completing homework like tasks (poem and map task) in a laboratory setting. Dyads were placed in either a high-pressure condition with a focus on the child being tested on the task and their parents responsible to prepare them for this evaluation, or a low-pressure condition with no mention of performance standards. Mothers also completed questionnaires about their attitudes toward supporting children's autonomy versus controlling their behavior. Mothers who endorsed controlling attitudes before the laboratory manipulation were more controlling during the homework-like tasks, marking the role of parent factors in their interactional styles. In addition, mothers in the high-pressure condition were more controlling overall on the poem task. However, on the map task mothers who had controlling attitudes were more controlling in the high- than the low-pressure condition, whereas mothers who endorsed more autonomy supportive attitudes were not affected by the condition. These results highlight the role of evaluative pressure, motivational style, and task type in predicting controlling parental behaviors.

To further explore the role of internal factors in parental practices, Gurland and Grolnick (2005) examined the role of worry and perception of threat in parents' behavior in interacting with their children. They hypothesized that mothers' anxiety about their child's performance and their perceptions of competition, and scarcity of resources for their children would increase their controlling behaviors which might, in turn, predict children's goal orientations. They found that mothers who perceived higher threat in their children's current and future environments used more controlling behaviors and endorsed more controlling attitudes than mothers who reported a greater sense of security, predictability, and resources available to their child. Furthermore, controlling parenting was associated with children's endorsement of performance rather than learning goals (Dweck & Leggett, 1988) with some support for a mediational model for these relationships, whereby threat was associated with controlling behavior which then predicted more performance-oriented goals.

Grolnick, Price, Beiswenger, and Sauck (2007) broadened this exploration of the factors that might contribute to controlling behavior in mothers by examining the effects of situation, maternal and child characteristics on maternal autonomy supportive versus controlling behavior. In this study, mothers were placed either in a socially evaluative condition in which they were told that their child would be rated for how much they were liked or accepted by other children, or a no-evaluation condition in which they were told that their child would simply meet and play with other children. Mothers reported on their attitudes toward supporting or controlling children's behavior and the degree to which they tended to hinge their self-worth on how successful their children were socially or social contingent self-worth (Crocker & Park, 2004; Eaton & Pomerantz, 2004). Results showed that mothers in the evaluation condition spent more time giving their children answers (a controlling behavior), mothers with controlling attitudes exhibited more controlling behaviors, and mothers high in social contingent self-worth who were in the evaluation condition were most controlling. Thus, situational pressures combined with parental attitudes and psychological processes may set the stage for controlling parental behaviors. More research on the nature of parental internal pressures and the manner in which they affect children's motivation in school is needed to understand the complex relations among situational, child, and parental characteristics at play in these relationships.

Child Characteristics

A final factor that may help explain parents' controlling behavior is characteristics of the children themselves. Parenting is clearly a bidirectional process, with children as active participants in their parenting environments (Lollis & Kuczynski, 1997). It makes sense that it would be far easier to provide autonomy support to a child who is well-behaved and cooperative than one who is constantly testing boundaries. Further, involvement with a child who is positive and appreciative may be much more rewarding than that with a child who is more negative. Supporting this reasoning, Grolnick, Weiss, McKenzie, and Wrightman (1996) found that parents who saw their adolescents as more difficult tended to report less involvement and more controlling behavior than parents who saw their adolescents as easier. Similarly, in the Grolnick et al. (1997) study described earlier, parents who viewed their children as more difficult were less likely to be involved in school activities.

Just as parents' perceptions of children's difficulty may be associated with parental attitudes and behavior, so may parents' perceptions of their children's competence be related to parental attitudes and practices. Grolnick et al. (2007) showed that mothers who perceived their children as more fearful of negative evaluation in social situations tended to have more controlling attitudes regarding children's behavior. Similarly, Pomerantz and Eaton (2001) found that parents who worried about their child's academic performance reported more controlling attitudes and using more controlling practices. Following up on this, Pomerantz and Dong (2006) found that mothers with negative perceptions of their child's competence who also endorsed the stability of these child characteristics were most likely to pass on this pressure, thus affecting children's academic and affective functioning over time.

Conclusions and Future Directions

Children's motivation and achievement in school are clearly the result of the interplay of many factors at multiple levels. Our review of the literature suggests that the family, and in particular parenting, is an important influence on school outcomes at all levels including school readiness, the transition to school, developing and maintaining positive motivation in elementary and secondary school, and preventing drop-out. In particular, when parents believe in children's competence and have high expectations for them, provide the resources that children need to feel connected to others, and facilitate a sense of autonomy by supporting children's initiations and problem-solving, children's motivation is most likely to thrive. Unfortunately, there are many factors that interfere with parents' abilities to provide such resources to their children. While one promising direction is for schools to use practices for involving parents, there is some evidence that such strategies may not be effective for reaching the most stressed parents and those whose ideas about their roles do not match those of the school (Grolnick et al., 1997). Certainly there are challenges ahead for helping all parents to support their children's educations.

There are a number of promising research directions that may help to advance the area of parenting and children's motivation. Here, we identify three that we are pursuing.

First, more attention needs to be paid to transactional processes among children, parents, and schools in understanding children's motivation. Though children's active role in their own socialization has been recognized since the 1960s (e.g., Bell, 1968), the majority of research still assumes parent to child directionality. In our own work, we have identified child to parent pathways in which parents appear to be responding in their behavior to children's levels of competence (e.g., Grolnick & Slowiaczek, 1994). Stattin and Kerr's (2006) work showing that adolescent problem behavior largely drives parents' monitoring efforts, with more problem behavior predicting decreased monitoring over time, is a good example of work in this area. Longitudinal studies employing cross-lagged correlations and structural modeling techniques will be useful avenues for assessing bidirectional relations.

While most research in the academic domain examines cognitive processes, children's school success depends on emotional competence as well. Children's emotional competence, including being able to identify and understand emotions and to regulate emotional responses, have been linked to both academic and social outcomes (Howse, Calkins, Anastopoulos, Keane, & Shelton, 2003; Shields et al., 2001). In a recent study (Bellas & Grolnick, 2007), we are using classroom observations and teacher interviews to understand how teachers think about and respond to children's emotions in their classrooms. Preliminary results show that teachers acknowledge the importance of emotions in supporting children's motivation, often emphasizing that children's emotional reactions may influence their ability to attend and persist in challenging academic situations. Further, teachers emphasize the role of parents and parent-teacher relationships in supporting children's emotional development and providing an environment for children's emotional well-being and motivation in school. More research is needed to understand the role of teachers and parents individually, as well as teacher-parent relationships, in supporting children's emotional development both overall and in school.

A third area of research involves the expectations about adults that children bring to the school setting. We have been studying the effects of children's expectations about how autonomy supportive vs. controlling adults are likely to be on their experiences of rapport with new adults. Gurland and Grolnick (2003) used a videotape procedure in which children were shown a video of an unfamiliar adult taking them through a task. Results showed that children who expected the adult to be more autonomy-supportive before seeing the video reported higher levels of rapport with the adult.

In our current work, we are attempting to provide information to children before encounters with new adults to determine whether we can increase the development of rapport (Friendly, Grolnick, & Gurland, 2007). With regard to parents, there are several promising directions for this work. First, it would be important to understand how experiences with parents might shape expectations of new adults. Second, parents may play an important role in helping children to develop and maintain positive expectations of teachers and other adults in the school setting. The area of children's expectations is one of several that require effective exchanges between parent and teacher.

Clearly, the area of parenting and motivation is a ripe one for research in the next decades. As Dr. Rich stated in her wise comment with which we began this chapter, parents and schools must work together to assure student success.

References

Alexander, K. L., & Entwisle, D. R. (1988). Achievement in the first two years of school: Patterns and processes. *Monographs of the Society for Research in Child Development, 53*(2, Serial No. 218).

Atkinson, J. W. (1957). Motivational determinants of risk taking behavior. *Psychological Review, 64*, 359–372.

Atkinson, J. W. (1964). *An introduction to motivation.* Princeton, NJ: Van Nostrand.

Barber, B. (1992). Family, personality, and adolescent problem behaviors. *Journal of Marriage & the Family, 54*(1), 69–79.

Barber, B., Olsen, J., & Shagle, S. (1994). Associations between parental psychological and behavioral control and youth internalized and externalized behaviors. *Child Development, 65*(4), 1120–1136.

Barnard, W. M. (2004). Parent involvement in elementary school and educational attainment. *Children and Youth Services Review, 26*, 39–62.

Baumrind, D. (1967). Child care practices anteceding three patterns of preschool behavior. *Genetic Psychology Monographs, 75*(1), 43–88.

Baumrind, D. (1971). Current patterns of parental authority. *Developmental Psychology, 4*, 1–103.

Bell, R. Q. (1968). A reinterpretation of the direction of effects in studies of socialization. *Psychological Review, 75*, 81–95.

Bellas, V. M., & Grolnick, W. S. (2007, March). *Emotion socialization in the classroom: An observational study of teach-child emotion interaction.* Paper presented at the Biennial Meeting of the Society for Research in Child Development, Boston, MA.

Belsky, J. (1984). The determinants of parenting: A process model. *Child Development, 55*, 83–96.

Boon, H. J. (2007). Low- and high-achieving Australian secondary school students: Their parenting, motivations, and academic achievement. *Australian Psychologist, 42*(3), 212–225.

Bronfenbrenner, U. (1986). Ecology of the family as a context for human development: Research perspectives. *Developmental Psychology, 22*, 723–742.

Bronstein, P., Ginsburg, G., & Herrera, I. (2005). Parental predictors of motivational orientation in early adolescence: A longitudinal study. *Journal of Youth and Adolescence, 34*(6), 559–575.

de Bruyn, E. H., Dekovic, M., & Meijnen, G. W. (2003). Parenting, goal orientations, classroom behavior, and social success in early adolescence. *Journal of Applied Developmental Psychology, 24*(4), 393–412.

Capaldi, D. M., Conger, R. D., Hops, H., & Thornbery, T. P. (2003). Introduction to special section on three-generational studies. *Journal of Abnormal Child Psychology, 31*, 123–125.

Chirkov, V., & Ryan, R. (2001). Parent and teacher autonomy-support in Russian and U. S. Adolescents: Common effects on well-being and academic motivation. *Journal of Cross-Cultural Psychology, 32*(5), 618–635.

Chavkin, N. F., & Williams, D. L. (1989). Low-income parents' attitudes toward parent involvement in education. *Journal of Sociology and Social Welfare, 16*, 17–28.

Chen, X., Dong, Q., & Zhou, H. (1997). Authoritative and authoritarian parenting practices and social and school performance in Chinese children. *International Journal of Behavioral Development, 5*, 81–94.

Christenson, S., Rounds, T., & Gorney, D. (1992). Family factors and student achievement: An avenue to increase students' success. *School Psychology Quarterly, 7*, 178–206.

Coleman, J. S., Campbell, H. Q., Hobson, C. J., McPartland, J., Mood, A. M., Weinfeld, F. D., & York, R. L. (1966). *Equality of educational opportunity*. Washington, DC: U.S. Office of Education.

Comer, J. (1984). Home-school relationships as they affect the academic performance of children. *Urban Society, 16,* 323–337.

Conger, R. D., & Conger, K. J. (2002). Resilience in Midwestern families: Selected findings from the first decade of a prospective, longitudinal study. *Journal of Marriage and Family, 64,* 361–373.

Conger, R. D., & Donnellan, M. B. (2007). An interactionist perspective on the socioeconomic context of human development. *Annual Review of Psychology, 58,* 175–199.

Connell, J. (1985). A new multidimensional measure of children's perceptions of control. *Child Development, 56*(4), 1018–1041.

Cooper, C. E., & Crosnoe, R. (2007). The engagement in schooling of economically disadvantaged parents and children. *Youth and Society, 38,* 372–391.

Cooper, H., Lindsay, J. J., & Nye, B. (2000). Homework in the home: How student, family and parenting-style differences relate to the homework process. *Contemporary Educational Psychology, 25,* 464–487.

Crnic, K., Greenberg, M., Ragozin, A., Robinson, N., & Basham, R. (1983). Effects of stress and social support on mothers of premature and full-term infants. *Child Development, 54,* 209–217.

Crocker, J., & Park, L. E. (2004). The costly pursuit of self-esteem. *Psychological Bulletin, 130,* 392–414.

Davis-Kean, P. E. (2005). The influence of parent education and family income on child achievement: The indirect role of parental expectations and the home environment. *Journal of Family Psychology, 19,* 294–304.

Dearing, E., McCartney, K., Weiss, H. B., Kreider, H., & Simpkins, S. (2004). The promotive effects of family educational involvement for low-income children's literacy. *Journal of School Psychology, 42,* 445–460.

Deci, E. L., Driver, R. E., Hotchkiss, L., Robbins, R. J., & Wilson, I. M. (1993). The relations of mothers' controlling vocalizations to children's intrinsic motivation. *Journal of Experimental Child Psychology, 55,* 151–162.

Deci, E. L., & Ryan, R. M. (1985). *Intrinsic motivation and self-determination in human behavior.* New York: Plenum.

Duncan, G. J., & Brooks-Gunn, J. (1997). Income effects across the life span: Integration and nterpretation. In G. J. Duncan & J. Brooks-Gunn (Eds.), *Consequences of growing up poor* (pp. 596–610). New York: Russell Sage Foundation.

Dweck, C. S., & Elliott, E. S. (1983). Achievement motivation. In P. H. Mussen (Ed.), *Handbook of child psychology* (3rd ed., Vol. 4, pp. 643–691).

Dweck, C. S., & Leggett, E. L. (1988). A social-cognitive approach to motivation and personality. *Psychological Review, 95,* 256–273.

Eaton, M. M., & Pomerantz, E. M. (2004). *Parental Contingent Self-Worth Scale.* Unpublished Manuscript, University of Illinois at Urbana-Champaign.

Eccles, J. S. (1984). Sex differences and achievement patterns. In T. Sonderegger (Ed.), *Nebraska Symposium on Motivation* (Vol. 32, pp. 97–1132). Lincoln: University of Nebraska Press.

Eccles, J. S. (2007). Families, schools, and developing achievement-related motivation and engagement. In J. E. Grusec & P. D. Hastings (Eds.), *Handbook of socialization: Theory and research* (pp. 665–691). New York: Guilford.

Eccles, J. S., & Harold, R.D. (1991). Gender differences in sport involvement: Applying the Eccles' expectancy-value model. *Journal of Applied Sport Psychology 3,* 7–35.

Eccles, J., & Harold R. D. (1996). Family involvement in children and adolescents' schooling. In A. Booth & J. F. Dunn (Eds.), *Family-school links: How do they affect educational outcomes* (pp. 3–33). Mahwah, NJ: Erlbaum.

Eccles-Parsons, J., Adler, T. F., Futterman, R., Goff, S. B., Kaczala, C. M., Meece, J. L., et al. (1983). Expectancies, values, and academic behaviors. In J. T. Spence (Ed.), *Achievement and achievement motivation* (pp. 75–146). San Francisco: Freeman.

Elliot, A. J. (1999). Approach and avoidance motivation and achievement goals. *Educational Psychologist, 34,* 169–189.

Elliot, A. J. (2005). A conceptual history of the achievement goal construct. In A. J. Elliot & C. S. Dweck (Eds.), *Handbook of competence and motivation,* (pp. 52–72). New York: Guilford.

Elliot, A. J., & Harackiewicz, J. M. (1996). Approach and avoidance goals and intrinsic motivation: A mediational analysis. *Journal of Personality and Social Psychology, 70,* 461–475.

Englund, M. M., Luckner, A. E., Whaley, G. J. L., & Egeland, B. (2004). Children's achievement in early elementary school: Longitudinal effects of parent involvement, expectations and quality of assistance. *Journal of Educational Psychology, 96,* 723–730.

Epstein, J. (2005). A case study of the Partnership Schools Comprehensive School Reform (CSR) model. *The Elementary School Journal, 106,* 151–170.

Epstein, J. L. (2001). *School, family and community partnerships: Preparing educators and improving schools.* Boulder, CO: Westview.

Fan, X., & Chen, M. (2001). Parental involvement and students' academic achievement: A meta-analysis. *Educational Psychology Review, 13,* 1–22.

Farkas, M. S., & Grolnick, W. S. (2006). *Toward a new model of parental structure.* Unpublished Manuscript, Clark University, Worcester, MA.

Feather, N. T., (1992). Values, valences, expectations, and actions. *Journal of Social Issues, 48,* 109–124.

Fredricks, J., & Eccles J. S. (2002). Children's' competence and value beliefs from childhood through adolescence: Growth trajectories in two male sex-typed domains. *Developmental Psychology, 38,* 519–533.

Fredricks, J., & Eccles J. S. (2005). Family socialization, gender, and sport motivation and involvement. *Journal of Sport and Exercise Psychology, 27,* 3–31.

Friendly, R. W., Grolnick, W. S., & Gurland, S. E. (2007, April). *The role of expectations in children's experience of novel events.* Paper presented at annual meeting of APA, San Francisco.

Frome, P. M., & Eccles J. S. (1998). Parents' influence on children's achievement related perceptions. *Journal of Personality and Social Psychology, 74,* 435–452.

Furrer, C., & Skinner, E. (2003). Sense of relatedness as a factor in children's academic engagement and performance. *Journal of Educational Psychology, 95,* 148–162.

Gardner, P., Riblatt, S., & Beatty, N., (2000). Academic achievement and parental involvement as a function of school size. *High School Journal, 83,* 21–27.

Gonzalez, A. L., & Wolters, C. A. (2006). The relation between perceived parenting practices and achievement motivation in mathematics. *Journal of Research in Childhood Education, 21*(2), 203–217.

Gonzalez-DeHass, A. R., Willems, P. P., & Holbein, M. D. (2005). Examining the relationship between parental involvement and student motivation. *Educational Psychology Review, 17*(2), 99–123.

Grolnick, W. S., Benjet, C., Kurowski, C. O., & Apostoleris, N. H. (1997). Predictors of parent involvement in children's schooling. *Journal of Educational Psychology, 89,* 538–548.

Grolnick, W., Frodi, A., & Bridges, L. (1984). Maternal control style and the mastery motivation of one-year-olds. *Infant Mental Health Journal, 5*(2), 72–82.

Grolnick, W. S., Gurland, S., DeCourcey, W., & Jacob, K. (2002). Antecedents and consequences of mothers' autonomy support: An experimental investigation. *Developmental Psychology, 38,* 143–155.

Grolnick, W. S., Kurowski, C.O., Dunlap, K. G., & Hevey, C. (2000). Parental resources and the transition to junior high. *Journal of Research on Adolescence, 10*(4), 465–488.

Grolnick, W. S., Price, C., E., Beiswenger, K. L., & Sauck, C. C. (2007). Evaluative pressure in mothers: Effects of situation, maternal and child characteristics on autonomy supportive versus controlling behavior. *Developmental Psychology, 43,* 991–1002.

Grolnick, W., & Ryan, R. (1989). Parent styles associated with children's self-regulation and competence in school. *Journal of Educational Psychology, 81*(2), 143–154.

Grolnick, W. S., Ryan, R. M., & Deci, E. L. (1991). Inner resources for school achievement: Motivational mediators of children's perceptions of their parents. *Journal of Educational Psychology, 83*(4), 508–517.

Grolnick, W. S., & Slowiaczek, M. (1994). Parents' involvement in their children's schooling: A multidimensional conceptualization and motivational model. *Child Development, 65,* 237–252.

Grolnick, W. S., Weiss, L., McKenzie, L., & Wrightman, J. (1996). Contextual, cognitive, and adolescent factors associated with parenting in adolescence. *Journal of Youth and Adolescence, 25,* 33–54.

Gurland, S. T., & Grolnick, W. S. (2003). Children's expectancies and perceptions of adults: Effects on rapport. *Child Development, 74,* 1212–1224.

Gurland, S. T., & Grolnick, W. S. (2005). Perceived threat, controlling parenting and children's achievement orientations. *Motivation and Emotion, 29,* 103–121.

Gutman, L. M. (2006). How student and parent goal orientations and classroom goal structures influence the math achievement of African Americans during the high school transition. *Contemporary Educational Psychology, 31*(1), 44–63.

Gutman, L. M., & Eccles, J. S. (1999). Financial strain, parenting behaviors, and adolescents' achievement: Testing model equivalence between African American and European American single- and two-parent families. *Child Development, 70,* 1464–1476.

Halle, T. G., Kurtz-Costes, B., & Mahoney, J. L. (1997). Family influences on school achievement in low-income African-American children. *Journal of Educational Psychology, 89,* 527–537.

Harackiewicz, J. M., Barron, K. E., Pintrich, P. R., Elliot, A. J., & Thrash, T. M. (2002). Revision of achievement goal theory: Necessary and illuminating. *Journal of Educational Psychology, 94,* 638–645.

Harter, S. (1982). The Perceived Competence Scale for Children. *Child Development, 53*(1), 87–97.

Heckhausen, H. (1977). Achievement motivation and its constructs: A cognitive model. *Motivation and Emotion, 1,* 283–329.

Hill, N. E. (2001). Parenting and academic socialization as they relate to school readiness: The roles of ethnicity and family income. *Journal of Educational Psychology, 93,* 686–697.

Hill, N. E., & Craft, S. A. (2003). Parent-school involvement and school performance: Mediated pathways among socioeconomically comparable African American and Euro-American families. *Journal of Educational Psychology, 95,* 74–83.

Hokoda, A., & Fincham, F. D. (1995). Origins of children's helpless and mastery achievement patterns in the family. *Journal of Educational Psychology, 87*(3), 375–385.

Howse, R. B., Calkins, S. D., Anastopoulos, A. D., Keane, S. P., & Shelton, T. L. (2003). Regulatory contributions to children's kindergarten achievement. *Early Education and Development, 14,* 101–119.

Jacobs, J., & Eccles, J. (1992).The impact of mothers' gender-role stereotypic beliefs on mothers' and children's ability perceptions. *Journal of Personality and Social Psychology, 63,* 932–944.

Jeynes, W. H. (2005). A meta-analysis of the relation between parental involvement to urban elementary school student academic achievement. *Urban Education, 40,* 237–269.

Jeynes, W. H. (2007). The relationship between parental involvement and secondary school student academic achievement. *Urban Education, 42,* 82–110.

Jodl, K. M., Michael, A., Malanchuk, O., Eccles, J. S., & Sameroff, A. (2001). Parents' roles in shaping early adolescents' occupational aspirations. *Child Development, 72,* 1247–1265.

Kerbow, D., & Bernhardt, A. (1993). Parental intervention in the school. In B. Schneider & J. Coleman (Eds.), *Parents, their children, and schools* (pp. 115–146). San Francisco: Westview.

Keating, D. P., & Hertzman, C. (1999). *Developmental health and the wealth of nations.* New York: Guilford.

Learner, D. G., & Kruger, L.J. (1997). Attachment, self-concept, and academic motivation in high-school students. *American Journal of Orthopsychiatry, 67,* 485–492.

Lee, J. S., & Bowen, N. K. (2006). Parent involvement, cultural capital, and the achievement gap among elementary school children. *American Educational Research Journal, 43,* 193–218.

Lollis, W., & Kuczynski, L. (1997). Beyond one-hand clapping: Seeing bidirectionality in parent-child relations. *Journal of Social and Personal Relationships, 14,* 441–461.

Markus, H., Kitayama, S., & Heiman, R. (1996). Culture and "basic" psychological principles. In E. T. Higgins & A. W. Kruglanski (Eds.), *Social psychology: Handbook of basic principles* (pp. 857–913). New York: Guilford Press.

Matos, L., Lens, W., & Vansteenkiste, M. (2007). Achievement goals, learning strategies, and language achievement among Peruvian high school students. *Psychologica Belgica, 47*(1-2), 51–70.

Mattanah, J. (2001). Parental psychological autonomy and children's academic competence and behavioral adjustment in late childhood: More than just limit-setting and warmth. *Merrill-Palmer Quarterly, 47*(3), 355–376.

McLoyd, V. C. (1990). The impact of economic hardship on Black families and children: Psychological distress, parenting, and socioemotional development. *Child Development, 61,* 311–346.

Meece, J. L., Wigfield, A., & Eccles J. S. (1990). Predictors of math anxiety and its consequences for young adolescents' course enrollment intentions and performances in mathematics. *Journal of Educational Psychology, 82,* 60–70.

Metropolitan Life Survey of the American Teacher (2001). *Key elements of quality schools.* Retrieved, June 20, 2007, from http://www.metlife.com/Companyinfo/Community/Found/Docs/2001ats.pdf

Midgley, C. (2002). *Goals, goal structures, and adaptive learning.* Mahwah, NJ: Erlbaum.

Miller, S. A., & Davis, T. L. (1992). Beliefs about children: A comparative study of mothers, teachers, peers and self. *Child Development, 63,* 1251–1265.

Mistry, R. S., Vandewater, E. A., Huston, A. C., & McLoyd, V. C. (2002). Economic well-being and children's social adjustment: The role of family process in an ethnically diverse low-income sample. *Child Development, 73,* 935–951.

Moss, E., & St. Laurent, D. (2001). Attachment at school age and academic performance. *Developmental Psychology, 37,* 863–874.

National Center for Educational Statistics. (1992). *National Education Longitudinal Study of 1988 First Follow-up: Student component data file user's manual.* Washington, DC: U.S. Department of Education, Office of Educational Research and Improvement.

Nelson, R. M., & DeBacker, T. K. (2008). Achievement motivation in adolescents: The role of peer climate and best friends. *Journal of Experimental Education, 76*(2), 170–189.

Nicholls, J. G. (1984). Achievement motivation: Conceptions of ability, subjective experience, task choice, and performance. *Psychological Review, 91,* 328–346.

Pallas, A. M., Entwisle, D. R. Alexander, K. L., & Stluka, M. F. (1994). Ability-group effects: Instructional, social, or institutional? *Sociology of Education 67,* 27–46.

Parsons, J. E., Adler, T. F., & Kaczala, C. M. (1982). Socialization of achievement attitudes and beliefs: Parental influences. *Child Development, 53,* 310–321.

Phillips, D. (1987). Socialization of perceived academic competence among highly competent children. *Child Development, 58,* 1308–1320.

Pianta, R. C., Nimetz, S. L., & Bennett, E. (1997). Mother-child relationships, teacher-child relationships, and school outcomes in preschool and kindergarten. *Early Childhood Research Quarterly, 12,* 263–280.

Pintrich, P. R. (2000). An achievement goal theory perspective on issues in motivation terminology, theory and research. *Contemporary Educational Psychology, 25,* 92–104.

Pomerantz, E. M., & Dong, W. (2006). Effects of mothers' perceptions of children's competence: The moderating role of mothers' theories of competence. *Developmental Psychology, 42,* 950–961.

Pomerantz, E. M., & Eaton, M. M. (2001). Maternal intrusive support in the academic context: Transactional socialization processes. *Developmental Psychology, 37,* 174–186.

Rich, D. (1987). *Schools and families: Issues and actions.* Washington, DC: National Education Association.

Roberts, W. L. (1989). Parents' stressful life events and social networks: Relations with parenting and children's competence. *Canadian Journal of Behavioral Science, 21,* 132–146.

Ryan, R. M., & Connell, J. P. (1989). Perceived locus of causality and internalization: Examining reasons for acting in two domains. *Journal of Personality and Social Psychology, 57,* 749–761.

Ryan, R., Connell, J., & Grolnick, W. (1992). When achievement is not intrinsically motivated: A theory of internalization and self-regulation in school. In A. K. Boggiano & T. S. Pittman (Eds.), *Achievement and motivation: A social-developmental perspective* (p. 167–188). New York: Cambridge University Press.

Ryan, R. M., Deci, E. L., Grolnick, W. S., & LaGuardia, J. G. (2006). The significance of autonomy and autonomy support in psychological development and psychopathology. In D. Cicchetti & D. J. Cohen (Eds.), *Developmental psycho-pathology, Vol 1: Theory and method* (2nd ed., pp. 795–849). Hoboken, NJ: Wiley.

Sanders, M. G., & Epstein, J. L. (2000). The National Network of Partnership Schools: How research influences educational practice. *Journal of Education for Students Placed at Risk, 5*, 61–76.

Sanders, M. G., & Simon, B. S. (2002). A comparison of program development at elementary, middle, and high schools in the National Network of Partnership Schools. *School Community Journal, 12*, 7–27.

Schaefer, E. S. (1965). Children's reports of parental behavior: An inventory. *Child Development, 36*, 413–424.

Sheldon, S. B., & Van Voorhis, F. L. (2004). Partnership programs in U.S. schools: Their development and relationship to family involvement outcomes. *School Effectiveness and School Improvement, 15*, 125–148.

Shields, A., Dickstein, S., Seifer, R., Guisti, L., Magee, K. D., & Spritz, B. (2001). Emotional competence and early school adjustment: A study of preschoolers at risk. *Early Education & Development, 12*, 73–96.

Simpkins, S. D., Fredricks, J. A., Davis-Kean, P. E., & Eccles, J. S. (2006). Healthy mind, healthy habits: The influence of activity involvement in middle childhood. In A. C. Huston & M. N. Ripke (Eds.), *Middle childhood: Contexts of development*. (pp. 283–302) New York: Cambridge University Press.

Skinner, E., Wellborn, J., & Connell, J. (1990). What it takes to do well in school and whether I've got it: A process model of perceived control and children's engagement and achievement in school. *Journal of Educational Psychology, 82*, 22–32.

Soenens, B., & Vansteenkiste, M. (2005). Antecedents and outcomes of self-determination in 3 life domains: The role of parents' and teachers' autonomy support. *Journal of Youth and Adolescence, 34*(6), 589–604.

Soenens, B., Elliot, A., Goossens, L., Vansteenkiste, M., Luyten, P., & Duriez, B. (2005). The intergenerational transmission of perfectionism: Parents' psychological control as an intervening variable. *Journal of Family Psychology, 19*(3), 358–366.

Stattin, H.. & Kerr, M. (2006). *Parents' reactions to and effects on adolescent development*. Paper presented at Autonomy Conference, Mitzpe Ramon, Israel.

Steinberg, L., Lamborn, S., Dornbusch, S., Darling, N. (1992). Impact of parenting practices on adolescent achievement: Authoritative parenting, school involvement, and encouragement to succeed. *Child Development, 63*(5), 1266–1281.

Stevenson, H. L., Chen, C., & Uttal, D. H. (1990). Beliefs and achievement: A study of Black White and Hispanic children. *Child Development, 61*, 508–523.

Stone, S. (2003). The transition to high school: Teacher and parent perspectives in a large, urban predominantly minority school system. *Journal of Ethnic and Cultural Diversity in Social Work, 12*, 47–67.

Stone, S. (2006). Correlates of change in student reported parent involvement in schooling: A new look at the National Education Longitudinal Study of 1988. *Journal of Orthopsychiatry, 76*, 518–530.

Turner, R., Irwin, C., Tschann, J., & Millstein, S. (1993). Autonomy, relatedness, and the initiation of health risk behaviors in early adolescence. *Health Psychology, 12*(3), 200–208.

U.S. Department of Health and Human Services (2005). Head Start Bureau. from http:///www.acf.hhs.gov/programs/hsb/

Vallerand, R. J., Fortier, M. S., & Guay, F. (1997). Self-determination and persistence in a real-life setting: Toward a motivational model of high school dropout. *Journal of Personality and Social Psychology, 72*, 1161–1176.

Wigfield, A. (1994). Expectancy-value theory of achievement motivation: A developmental perspective. *Educational Psychology Review, 6*, 49–78.

Wigfield, A., & Eccles, J. S. (2002). The development of competence beliefs and values from childhood through adolescence. In A. Wigfield & J. Eccles (Eds.), *Development of achievement motivation* (pp. 92–120). San Diego, CA: Academic Press.

Wigfield, A., Eccles, J. S., Schiefele, U., Roeser, R. W., & Davis-Kean, P. (2006). Development of achievement motivation. In W. Damon & R. Lerner (Series Eds.), & N. Eisenberg, W. Damon, R. M. Lerner (Vol. Eds.), *Handbook of child psychology: Vol. 3. Social, emotional, and personality development* (6th ed., pp. 933–1002). Hoboken, NJ: Wiley.

Zellman, G. L., & Waterman, J. M. (1998). Understanding the impact of parent school involvement on children's educational outcomes. *The Journal of Educational Research, 91*, 370–381.

15
Students' Relationships with Teachers as Motivational Contexts

Kathryn R. Wentzel

There is growing consensus that the nature and quality of children's relationships with their teachers play a critical and central role in motivating and engaging students to learn (Becker & Luthar, 2002; Pianta, Hamre, & Stuhlman, 2003; Stipek, 2004). Effective teachers are typically described as those who develop relationships with students that are emotionally close, safe, and trusting, that provide access to instrumental help, and that foster a more general ethos of community and caring in classrooms. These relationship qualities are believed to support the development of students' emotional well-being and positive sense of self, motivational orientations for social and academic outcomes, and actual social and academic skills. They also provide a context for communicating positive and high expectations for performance and teaching students what they need to know to become knowledgeable and productive citizens.

In light of this interest in teachers' relationships with students, a central question addressed in this chapter is how and why these relationships might be related to students' motivation to achieve academic and social outcomes at school. Toward this end, this chapter is organized around issues relevant for understanding the role that teacher-student relationships play in students' lives. First, the various theoretical perspectives that guide work in the field are described. Despite their common focus on the nature and functions of teachers' relationships with students, each of these perspectives provides unique assumptions concerning the causal role of teachers in promoting students' motivation and subsequent competence at school. Next, research on teacher-student relationships that informs questions of causal influence is reviewed. Measurement and design issues associated with this research also are raised. Finally, directions for future work in this area are offered.

Theoretical Perspectives

Researchers have documented significant relations between students' positive interactions and relationships with teachers and their academic and social accomplishments at school. To a lesser extent, significant associations between aspects of teacher-student relationships and students' motivation also have been reported. Why then, might students' relationships with teachers be associated with or even influence these school-related outcomes? The prevailing theoretical models that guide work in this area typically adopt a causal approach, with the affective quality of teacher-student relationships viewed as the central and critical motivator of student adjustment. The basic tenets of attachment theory (Bowlby, 1969; Bretherton, 1987), models of social support (e.g., Sarason, Sarason, & Pierce, 1990), and self-determination theory (Ryan & Deci, 2000) reflect this notion. Other perspectives that have contributed to this literature describe teacher-student relationships as socialization contexts that provide students with multiple motivational supports (Wentzel, 2004). In the following section, each of these approaches will be described.

The Affective Quality of Relationships

Attachment theory has provided the strongest impetus for work on teachers' relationships with young children. According to this perspective, the dyadic relationship between a child and care-giver (usually the mother) is a system in which children experience various levels of positive affect and responsiveness to their basic needs, with predictable and sensitive responses being associated with secure attachments, and more arbitrary and insensitive responses leading to insecure attachments (see Bowlby, 1969). Attachment theorists hypothesize qualitatively differ-ent outcomes associated with secure and insecure attachment systems. Secure relationships are believed to foster children's curiosity and exploration of the environment, positive coping skills, and a mental representation of one's self as being worthy of love and of others as being trustworthy. In contrast, insecure attachments are believed to result in either wary or inappropriately risky exploratory behavior, difficulty in regulating stress in new settings, and negative self-concepts. A basic tenet of attachment theory is that the primary attachment relationship results in children's mental representations of self and others, which are then used as a basis to interpret and judge the underlying intentions, reliability, and trustworthiness of others' actions in new relationships (Bretherton, 1987). Depending on the nature of primary attachments, children will expect new relationships to generate interactions marked by positive affect and trust, by conflict and rejection, or as anxiety-producing, overly-dependent or enmeshed.

Although teacher-student relationships are not typically viewed as primary attachment re-lationships, attachment theory principles imply that they would be fairly concordant with the quality of parent-child attachments and therefore, also related to children's functioning at school. Therefore, attachment theory has been used as a framework for generating predictions concern-ing children's relationships with their teachers, especially during the preschool and elementary school years. Hypothesizing connections between secure attachments and children's motivation for school-related activities is fairly straightforward. A positive sense of self, curiosity and will-ingness to explore, and trust in others can be viewed as central precursors to children's beliefs about their efficacy to learn and interact socially with others, beliefs about personal control, and intrinsic interest in classroom activities (e.g., Harter, 1978; Raider-Roth, 2005). To the extent that student-teacher attachments are positive, researchers assume that these same outcomes associated with secure parent-child attachments should occur.

Social support perspectives on teacher-student relationships also reflect the notion that teachers who are emotionally supportive can have a positive impact on students' adjustment to school. Similar to attachment theory, social support perspectives focus on students' mental rep-resentations of relationships, with perceived support serving as a buffer from stress and anxiety (Cohen & Wills, 1985; Sarason et al., 1990). Therefore, subjective appraisals of positive emotional support are believed to result in outcomes associated with secure attachments, such as perceived competence, social skills, and coping (Sarason et al., 1990). However, whereas attachment theory focuses on interpersonal relationships reflecting dyadic systems with fairly stable histories of interactions, social support perspectives typically consider relationships as personal resources that can range from highly familiar and stable (e.g., an elementary school teacher who has year-long daily contact with students), to relatively impersonal and fleeting (e.g., a high school counselor who meets with students once a year).

Finally, self-determination theory (Ryan & Deci, 2000) posits that students will engage positively in the social and academic tasks of the classroom when their needs for relatedness, competence, and autonomy are met. Contextual supports in the form of interpersonal involvement, structure, and provisions of autonomy and choice are believed to be essential to this process, with teacher involvement and students' corresponding sense of relatedness being most frequently associated with the study of teacher-student relationships. According to self-determination theory, involvement is expressed through teachers' demonstrations of interest in their students' personal well-being and provisions of emotional support. A resulting sense of relatedness, that is, feelings of emotional security and being socially connected to others, is believed to facilitate students' adoption of goals and interests valued by teachers, and desires to contribute in positive ways to the overall functioning of the social group. Teacher involvement has been studied most often in relation to aspects of motivational engagement (e.g., effort and interest; Connell & Wellborn, 1991; Skinner & Belmont, 1993).

Correlates of Emotionally Supportive Relationships As noted in the previous section, attachment theory, social support perspectives, and self-determination theory suggest that levels of emotional closeness and security associated with teacher-student relationships can play a causal role in the development of a range of positive social and academic outcomes in children. Although most of the research based on these perspectives is correlational, findings generally support this conclusion. In work on young children, teacher-student relationships typically are assessed by asking teachers about the affective quality of their relationships with students and relating their responses to academic outcomes such as school readiness and test scores, and to social competencies such as prosocial and antisocial forms of behavior and peer relationships (e.g., Howes & Hamilton, 1993; Peisner-Feinberg, et al. 2001; Pianta, Nimetz, & Bennett, 1997). In contrast, motivational outcomes have been studied less frequently, although in kindergarten, teacher-student relationships marked by emotional closeness have been related positively to students' reports of school liking (Birch & Ladd, 1997). In late elementary school, students' reports of negative relationships with teachers also have been related to anxiety and depression (Murray & Greenberg, 2000); secure relationships with teachers have been related to students' identification with teachers' values and positive social self-concept (Davis, 2001).

Perceived emotional support from teachers has been related significantly to students' academic performance and social functioning throughout the school-aged years (Blankemeyer, Flannery, & Vazsonyi, 2002; Chang, 2003; Crosnoe, Johnson, & Elder, 2004; Hughes, Cavell, & Jackson, 1999; Isakson & Jarvis, 1999; Murdock, Miller, & Kohlhardt, 2004; Wentzel, 1994, 1997). Motivational outcomes also have been studied frequently, especially during the adolescent years. For example, students' perceived support from teachers has been related to mastery and performance goal orientations, academic values, interest, and self-efficacy (Goodenow, 1993; Ibanez, Kuperminc, Jurkovic, & Perilla, 2004; Midgley, Feldlaufer, & Eccles, 1989; Mitchell-Copeland, Denham, & DeMulder, 1997; Murdock & Miller, 2003; Roeser, Midgley, & Urdan, 1996; A. M. Ryan & Patrick; Sanchez,

Colon, & Esparza, 2005; Valeski & Stipek, 2001; Wentzel, 1997, 1998, 2003). Midgley et al. found that young adolescents report declines in the nurturant qualities of teacher-student relationships after the transition to middle school that correspond to declines in academic motivation.

In direct support of a basic tenet of social support paradigms, perceptions of positive emotional support from teachers also have been related to emotional well-being (Wentzel, 1997, 1998), whereas a lack of perceived support has been related to internalizing problems such as depression and emotional distress (Mitchell-Copeland et al.; Reddy, Rhodes, & Mulhall, 2003; Wentzel, 1997). Students' appraisals of teacher emotional support also have been related to students' pursuit of goals to behave in prosocial and responsible ways (Wentzel, 1994, 1997, 1998, 2003). Similarly, reports of teacher involvement are strong predictors of elementary students' emotional functioning and engagement (e.g., effort) over time, especially when reports of relatedness and student functioning come from the same informant (student or teacher; Furrer, & Skinner, 2003). Finally, in middle school samples, the affective quality of relationships with teachers has been related to a range of motivational processes including perceived autonomy, perceived control, self-esteem, and positive self-regulatory skills (R.M. Ryan, Stiller, & Lynch, 1994; Zimmer-Gembeck & Locke, 2007).

Summary In general, the models used to guide research on the affective qualities of teacher-student relationships propose causal pathways by which affectively close and supportive relationships influence the development of children's school-related competence, primarily by promoting a positive sense of self and emotional well-being, and a willingness to engage with the environment. In line with attachment theory principles, evidence from correlational studies confirms that secure and close relationships with teachers are related positively to young children's motivation toward school and associated cognitive and social competencies. Similarly, work based on social support perspectives and self-determination theory provides evidence of associations between the affective quality of teacher-student relationships and older students' motivation and school-related outcomes. However, as will be discussed in a later section, the causal nature of these findings has yet to be determined.

An additional approach to the study of teacher-student relationships has been to consider relationships as serving a broader range of functions that contribute to students' competence at school. For the most part, scholars adopting this approach have focused on teachers as socialization agents who create interpersonal contexts that influence levels and quality of student motivation and engagement (see Connell & Wellborn, 1991; Wentzel, 2004). Although the affective tone of teacher-student interactions is a central focus of discussion, these perspectives propose that the contribution of teachers' relationships with students should be defined in terms of multiple dimensions that combine with emotional support to motivate students to engage in the social and academic life of school.

Similar to those described in models of effective parenting and parenting styles (e.g., Baumrind, 1971; Darling & Steinberg, 1993), these dimensions reflect levels of predictability and structure, instrumental resources, and concern with a student's emotional and physical well-being. These dimensions are believed to reflect necessary types of interpersonal resources that support a student's pursuit of personal goals but also their willingness to learn about and then actively pursue those social and academic goals that are valued by others at school. Moreover, as a set of interacting processes, these dimensions create a climate within which specific instructional practices and academic content is delivered. The degree to which these practices and content are learned depends on the quality of the relationship climate (Steinberg, 2001). In the following section, these additional dimensions are described.

Teacher-Student Relationships as Socialization Contexts

Models of socialization suggest several mechanisms whereby students' social interactions with teachers might influence motivation and goal-directed behavior. First, ongoing social interactions teach children what they need to do to become accepted and competent members of their social worlds. In addition, the quality of social interactions informs children about the degree to which they are valued and accepted by others. For example, children who enjoy interpersonal relationships with adults that are nurturant and supportive are more likely to adopt and internalize the expectations and goals that are valued by these adults than if their relationships are harsh and critical (see Grusec & Goodnow, 1994; R. Ryan, 1993). In general, these mechanisms correspond to parenting dimensions characterized by consistent enforcement of rules, expectations for self-reliance and self-control, solicitation of opinions and feelings, and concern for emotional and physical well-being (see Wentzel, 2002).

When applied to the social worlds of the classroom, these dimensions are reflected in opportunities for learning as reflected in teachers' communications of rules and expectations for behavior and performance, and openness to providing instrumental help. Models of socialization also imply that teachers are likely to have motivational significance for students if they create contexts in which children feel emotionally supported and safe, as described in the previous section. As evidenced in the family socialization literature, these mechanisms should be viable for all school-aged children. Moreover, just as parents interact with each of their children differently, it is believed that although teachers can establish classroom-level climates along these dimensions, they also create unique interpersonal contexts with students on an individual basis.

Wentzel (2004) describes more specifically how teacher-student interactions along these dimensions can promote student motivation and subsequent performance. Derived from theoretical perspectives on person-environment fit and personal goal setting (e.g., Bronfenbrenner, 1989; Eccles & Midgley, 1989), she argues that school-related competence is achieved to the extent that students are able to accomplish goals that have personal as well as social value, in a manner that supports continued psychological and emotional well-being. The ability to accomplish these goals, however, is contingent on opportunities and affordances of the school context that allow students to pursue their multiple goals.

Applying this perspective more specifically to the study of teacher-student relationships, Wentzel further suggests that students will come to value and subsequently pursue academic and social goals valued by teachers when they perceive their interactions and relationships with them as providing clear direction concerning goals that should be achieved; as facilitating the achievement of their goals by providing help, advice, and instruction; as being safe and responsive to their goal strivings; and as being emotionally supportive and nurturing (see also Ford, 1992). In this manner, students' school-based competencies are a product of social reciprocity between teachers and students. Just as students must behave in ways that meet teachers' expectations, so must teachers provide support for the achievement of students' goals. Students' motivation to achieve academic and social goals that are personally as well as socially valued should then serve as mediators between opportunities afforded by positive interactions with teachers and their academic and social accomplishments.

Empirical evidence supports the notion that positive interactions with teachers along these dimensions are related to various aspects of academic and social motivation at school. In the following sections, evidence that these dimensions of support can promote social and academic accomplishments by motivating students to display positive forms of social behavior and to engage in academic activities is reviewed.

Teacher Communications and Expectations It is reasonable to assume that the degree to which students pursue goals valued by teachers is dependent on whether teachers communicate clearly and consistently their values and expectations concerning classroom behavior and performance. As with parents, teachers vary in the degree to which they interact with their students in consistent and predictable ways (Wentzel, 2002). Moreover, clarity of communications and consistency of classroom management practices early in the academic year tends to predict positive academic and social outcomes in elementary and secondary level classrooms (see Gettinger & Kohler, 2006). Presumably, these practices promote a climate of interpersonal trust and fairness that promotes students' willingness to listen to teacher communications and adopt their behavioral and learning goals and values.

With respect to the content of these goals and values, researchers rarely have asked teachers directly about their specific goals for students. However, teachers' expectations for students can be gleaned from research on the characteristics of students that teachers tend to like. For example, Wentzel (2000) reports that middle school teachers' descriptions of "ideal" students reflect three general types of desired outcomes: social outcomes such as sharing, being helpful to others, and being responsive to rules; motivational qualities related to learning such as being persistent, hard-working, inquisitive, and intrinsically interested; and performance outcomes such as getting good grades and completing assignments. Similarly, elementary-school teachers have consistently reported preferences for students who are cooperative, conforming, cautious, and responsible (e.g., Brophy & Good, 1974). Researchers have documented that teachers continuously communicate these ideals directly to their students, regardless of their instructional goals, teaching styles, and ethnicity (Hargreaves, Hester, & Mellor, 1975).

Beyond communicating values and expectations for behavior and achievement at the classroom level, teachers also convey expectations about ability and performance to individual students. As part of ongoing interpersonal interactions, these communications have the potential to influence a student's beliefs about her own ability and goals to achieve academically. R. S. Weinstein (2002) describes these communications as part of a process of influence whereby teachers' expectations result in their differential treatment of students. These communications most often reflect beliefs that students are able to achieve more than previously demonstrated, or negative expectations reflecting underestimations of student ability. Teachers' negative expectations are often targeted toward minority students, with expectations for competent behavior and academic performance being lower for them than for other students (see e.g., Oates, 2003; Weinstein, Gregory, & Strambler, 2004).

Teachers' false expectations can become self-fulfilling prophecies, with student performance changing to conform to teacher expectations (see Weinstein, 2002), especially as students get older (Valeski & Stipek, 2001). Although the effects of these negative expectations appear to be fairly weak (e.g., Jussim, 1991; Jussim & Eccles, 1995), and short-lived (Jussim & Harber, 2005), self-fulfilling prophecies tend to have stronger effects on African-American students, students from low socioeconomic backgrounds, and low achievers (see Smith, Jussim, & Eccles, 1999). In addition, however, teachers' overestimations of ability seem to have a somewhat stronger effect in raising levels of achievement than teachers' underestimates have on lowering achievement, especially for low performing students (Madon, Jussim, & Eccles, 1997). Therefore, teachers who communicate high expectations for individual students can bring about positive changes in academic accomplishments. However, the direct impact of these expectations on student motivation has been examined infrequently (see Jussim, Robustelli, & Cain, this volume).

Willingness to Provide Help, Advice, and Instruction In the classroom, teachers play the central role of transmitting knowledge and training students in academic subject areas. In this role, teachers routinely provide children with resources that directly promote the development of social and academic competencies. These resources can take the form of information and advice, modeled behavior, or specific experiences that facilitate learning. The fact that teachers vary in the amount of help and instruction they offer to students is reflected in evidence that children's willingness to seek help from teachers is related to several factors, including the availability of emotional support, structure, and autonomy (Newman, 2000). Little is known about teacher characteristics that predict their willingness to help students. However, Brophy and Good (1974) documented the relevance of teachers' relationships with elementary-aged students for gaining access to academic resources. The teachers observed in their research reported that they were more appreciative and positive toward students who were cooperative and persistent (i.e., behaviorally competent) than toward students who were less cooperative but displayed high levels of creativity and achievement. Teachers also responded with help and encouragement to students about whom they were concerned when these students sought them out for help. In contrast, students toward whom they felt rejection were treated most often with criticism and typically were refused help.

Experimental work also suggests that the nature of teachers' responses to students' poor academic performance tends to vary as a function of their attributions for these outcomes (Reyna & Weiner, 2001). Specifically, teachers were prone to anger when students were perceived to fail for reasons that were under their control; when reasons for student failure were perceived to be uncontrollable, teachers tended to express sympathy. Of interest for understanding willingness to help, teachers in this study reported a greater likelihood to respond to controllable failures with punishment rather than with help. Given these findings, understanding why teachers like some students but not others, and identifying the reasons that teachers attribute to individual students' classroom behavior and academic performance is an important area of study that should not be ignored.

Emotional Support and Safety In conjunction with communicating clear expectations and providing instrumental help, teachers also create contexts characterized by levels of emotional support and personal safety (Connell & Wellborn, 1991; Isakson, & Jarvis, 1999). As evidenced by the work on affective qualities of teacher-student relationships, emotionally supportive interactions have the potential to provide strong incentives for students to engage in valued classroom activities. An additional aspect of teachers' emotional support is reflected in their efforts to protect students' physical well-being. Most frequently, issues of student safety are discussed with regard to peer interactions. National surveys indicate that large numbers of students are the targets of classmate aggression and take active measures to avoid being harmed physically as well as psychologically by peers (National Center for Educational Statistics, 1995). Although this literature implies that peers might be the primary source of threats to students' physical safety and well-being, of importance to understanding this process is that teachers can play a central role in creating classrooms that are free of peer harassment and in alleviating the negative effects of harassment once it has occurred (Olweus, 1993). Of special interest are findings that students are more likely to enjoy affectively positive relationships with teachers when they feel safe at school (Crosnoe et al., 2004).

Research on Multiple Dimensions of Support Describing teachers' relationships with students along multiple dimensions to include consistent communication of expectations, willingness to help, and protection of students' emotional and physical well-being expands understanding of ways that teachers can promote students' social and academic motivation and accomplishments. Support for this perspective is found in students' and teachers' qualitative descriptions of caring and supportive teachers, and from studies relating multiple types of support to student outcomes. Qualitative approaches have identified multiple types of teacher support by asking students and teachers what a supportive or caring teacher is like (see Hoy & Weinstein, 2006). For example, when asked to characterize teachers who care, middle school students describe teachers who demonstrate democratic and egalitarian communication styles designed to elicit student participation and input, who develop expectations for student behavior and performance in light of individual differences and abilities, who model a "caring" attitude and interest in their instruction and interpersonal dealings with students, and who provide constructive rather than harsh and critical feedback (Wentzel, 1998). Moreover, students who perceive their teachers as providing high levels of these multiple supports also tend to pursue appropriate social and academic classroom goals more frequently than students who do not (Wentzel, 2002).

Others have documented differences in middle school students' characterizations of supportive teachers as a function of student ability, with students from high ability tracks valuing teachers who challenge them, encourage class participation, and who express educational goals similar to theirs. In contrast, students from low ability tracks tend to value teachers who treat them with kindness, who are fair, explain subject matter clearly, and maintain control in the classroom (Daniels & Arapostathis, 2005). Ethnographic studies document that academically successful inner-city ethnic minority adolescents value instrumental help from teachers but also warmth and acceptance coupled with high academic expectations (Smokowski, Reynolds, & Bezrucko, 2000). Racially mixed groups of middle school students highlight the importance of teachers who are responsive to individual differences and needs, who provide students with autonomy and choice (Oldfather, 1993), who show interest in students as individuals, help with academics, encourage students to work up to their potential, and who teach well and make subject matter interesting (Hayes, Ryan, & Zseller, 1994).

Research on teachers' notions of what it means to be supportive and caring has been less frequent. However, C. S. Weinstein (1998) asked prospective elementary and secondary teachers about specific things they could do to demonstrate caring to their students. Almost two thirds of teachers' responses referred to affective qualities of interpersonal interactions such as establishing positive rapport, creating a climate of trust and respect, and fostering self-esteem, whereas specific teaching and classroom management strategies were mentioned less often. Ethnographic work also has documented teacher beliefs concerning the importance of making interpersonal connections, establishing rapport, and creating a classroom atmosphere of mutual respect and trust as important aspects of classroom instructional support (Moje, 1996). Similarly, middle school teachers have described their "ideal" students as sharing, helpful, responsive to rules, persistent, interested, and as earning high grades (Wentzel, 2003).

Additional evidence concerning multiple dimensions of teacher supports is provided in studies where a number of dimensions have been assessed simultaneously. This work has documented differential effects as a function of dimension and the outcome being studied (Isakson & Jarvis, 1999; Marchant, Paulson, & Rothlisberg, 2001; Skinner & Belmont, 1993; Wentzel, 2002; Wentzel, Battle & Looney, 2007; Wilson & Hughes, 2006). For example, Wentzel and her colleagues (Wentzel, Battle & Looney, 2007) documented unique relations of teachers' provisions of clear expectations, classroom safety, instrumental help, and emotional support to students' interest in class and efforts to behave appropriately. Skinner and Belmont also documented significant relations between teachers' provisions of involvement and structure (e.g., clear expectations, instrumental help) and students' engagement in class. Finally, classrooms characterized by high levels of observed emotional support (e.g., teacher sensitivity and warmth) and instrumental support (e.g., help, positive feedback) have been associated positively with first graders' social competencies to a greater extent than other configurations of emotional and instrumental support, especially for children previously identified as at-risk for social and academic problems in pre-school and Kindergarten (Wilson & Hughes).

Summary Models that examine multiple dimensions of student-teacher relationships provide a more complex and complete picture of the interpersonal contexts that teachers create for their students than those that focus exclusively on the affective quality of teacher-student relationships. Dimensions reflecting the communication of expectations and values, and provisions of help complement that of emotional support in explaining the potential influence of teachers on student accomplishments. Additional dimensions of support might also provide insights into the functions of teacher-student relationships. For instance, provisions of autonomy, as expressed in opportunities for choice and egalitarian decision making are likely to have a direct impact on students' own perceptions of autonomy and self-regulation (Grolnick, Gurland, Jacob, & Decourcey, 2002). In general, teacher provisions of autonomy along with structure and guidance have been related to a range of positive, motivational outcomes including students' perceptions of competence, self-determination, and relatedness to teachers (e.g., Grolnick & Ryan, 1989; Skinner & Belmont, 1993).

Conclusion

Researchers have documented significant relations between positive aspects of teacher-student relationships and students' social and academic motivation and accomplishments at school. At a general level, the theoretical perspectives used to guide this work are based on notions of causal influence, with the nature of teacher-student relationships resulting in student outcomes. In this regard, each acknowledges the importance of emotionally supportive relationships with teachers for students' success at school. Secure and emotionally supportive relationships and interactions are believed to result in a sense of belongingness and relatedness in children that in turn, support a positive sense of self, the adoption of socially desirable goals and values, and the development of social and academic competencies. Broader socialization perspectives based on the notion of person-environment fit complement this work by focusing on additional dimensions of teacher-student interactions, highlighting their independent as well as interdependent contributions to student outcomes.

In contrast to the prevailing assumption that teacher-student relationships have causal influence, it also is possible, however, that student competencies determine the nature and quality of teacher-student relationships or that significant correlations between qualities of teacher-student relationships and student outcomes are merely spurious. At the simplest level, it is possible that the nature of students' relationships with teachers and their social and academic accomplishments are correlated but not causally-related outcomes, and reflect the fact that many students who are highly competent in one domain of functioning also display high levels of functioning in other domains. These possibilities raise the important question as to whether the qualities of teacher-student relationships really matter when other factors are taken into account. In the following section, two bodies of evidence that address this question are reviewed. The first pertains to the relative impact of teacher-student relationships when relationships with parents and peers are taken into account. The second focuses on our ability to draw valid inferences from this work, as evidenced by the psychometric properties of measures and research designs employed in studies of teacher-student relationships.

Do Students' Relationships with Teachers Really Matter?

For the most part, when school-aged children rate the importance of their relationships with mothers, fathers, siblings, teachers, and friends, they typically report being very satisfied with their relationships with their teachers, and rank teachers as most important for providing instrumental aid and informational support at levels comparable to instrumental help from parents (Lempers & Clark-Lempers, 1992). In contrast, on dimensions such as intimacy, companionship, nurturance, and admiration, teachers are routinely ranked by children as the least likely source of support when compared to parents and peers (Furman & Buhrmester, 1985; Lempers & Clark-Lempers; Reid, Landesman, Treder, & Jaccard, 1989). Moreover, although these relative rankings remain stable from childhood into adolescence (Furman & Buhrmester), the overall importance of teachers for students appears to decline with age (Lempers & Clark-Lempers).

This literature provides fairly clear support for including provisions of instrumental help as a dimension of teacher-student relationships that is important to students at all ages, but calls into question the relative role of teachers' emotional support in most students' lives. Given these findings, it is important to ask if teacher-student relationships have a meaningful impact on students when other sources of support are taken into account. Indeed, most conclusions concerning the importance of teacher-student relationships and interactions are based on studies that have not taken into account the contribution of other relationships that might contribute to students' motivation and adjustment to school. The extant evidence is reviewed in the following section.

Teachers versus Parents and Peers

One of the enduring issues with respect to the influence of teacher-student relationships on student adjustment concerns the possibility that the quality of students' interactions with teachers simply duplicates the quality of their relationships at home. If so, then assessments of teacher-student relationships are merely proxies for those of parent-child relationships, with supports and continuity across home and school settings explaining student outcomes more so than students' experiences that are unique to teachers. In general, evidence that the effects of students' relationships with teachers on their functioning at school can be explained by the quality of parent-child relationship is mixed. As evidenced by research on the concordance of students' attachment relationships with parents and teachers, continuity across contexts is not always evident (Lynch & Cicchetti, 1997), and aspects of teacher-student relationships often predict academic and social outcomes over and above similar aspects of parent-child relationships (e.g., Brody, Dorsey, Forehand, & Armistead, 2002). The effects of teacher-student relationships on these outcomes appear to be strongest when parent-child relationships are less positive than teacher-student relationships (e.g., Hughes, Cavell, & Jackson, 1993), especially for ethnic minority students (Crosnoe et al., 2004).

Research that focuses specifically on motivational outcomes also has yielded complex results. For example, Furrer and Skinner (2003) reported that teacher involvement predicts classroom engagement and emotional functioning over and above involvement with parents and peers. In their study, teachers also appeared to play a compensatory role in that children who enjoyed high levels of relatedness to parents and peers but not to teachers demonstrated lower levels of school adjustment than did children who enjoyed high levels of relatedness across all three relationships. In addition, students who experienced low levels of relatedness in relationships with parents and peers but high levels in relationships with teachers also reported higher levels of positive engagement and emotion than did students who reported low levels of relatedness in all three relationships. Similarly, Zimmer-Gembeck & Locke (2007) found that positive relationships with teachers and parents were related to qualitatively different types of adolescents' self-regulatory strategies.

In addition, research on multiple sources of emotional support suggests that perceived teacher support remains a significant predictor of academic motivation in the form of self-efficacy, intrinsic value, and academic aspirations when support from parents and peers also is considered (Ibanez et al., 2004; Murdock, & Miller, 2003). Middle school students' perceptions of teacher emotional support have been related positively to students' perceived academic competence, and values and interest in academics, over and above the influence of perceived parental support (Marchant et al., 2001). In a study of perceived emotional support from teachers, parents, and peers, perceived support from teachers was unique in its relation to students' interest in class and pursuit of goals to adhere to classroom rules and norms; in contrast, perceived support from parents was related to students' motivational orientations toward achievement, and support from peers was related to students' pursuit of goals to be helpful and cooperative (Wentzel, 1998). Others have identified perceived teacher support as a mediator between adolescents' attachment relationships with their parents and their perceived academic efficacy (Duchesne & Larose, 2007).

Researchers also have examined the relative contribution of students' relationships with teachers and peers to their school-related outcomes. The notion that peers can serve as potentially powerful motivators of academic engagement is generally supported in the empirical literature (see Ladd et al., this volume; Wentzel, 2005). However, few of the studies on the quality of students' peer interactions and supports have also included assessments of the quality of teacher-student relationships. Indeed, positive peer relationships often are considered to be an outcome of positive relationships with teachers, at least for young children (e.g., Howes & Hamilton, 1993). In support of a conclusion that teacher-student relationships have unique influence relative to peer relationships, Ladd and Burgess (2001) reported teacher-child conflict and closeness to predict aspects of children's behavioral, psychological, and academic adjustment when taking into account levels of peer rejection and acceptance. A study of middle school students without friends (Wentzel & Asher, 1995) supports this finding in that students who had few friends and were neither well-liked or disliked by their peers (sociometrically neglected children), were the most well-liked by their teachers, the most highly motivated students, and were equally self-confident when compared to their average status peers. In contrast, Wentzel, Filisetti, and Looney (2007) reported that perceived peer (but not teacher) expectations for positive social behavior predicted middle school students' prosocial behavior. In this study, teacher and peer expectations both predicted students' reasons for behaving prosocially, however, peer expectations predicted internal reasons (e.g., it's important) and teachers' expectations predicted internal as well as external reasons (e.g. to stay out of trouble) for behavior.

In sum, findings from studies that included assessments of parent and teacher emotional support suggest that the effects of support from teachers might be domain and classroom specific, with teacher support being related most strongly to those outcomes to which teachers contribute most, such as subject matter interest and classroom behavior. Qualities of teacher-student relationships can moderate the effects of parent-child relationships on students' motivation at school, especially when parents are not supportive. In addition, students who enjoy positive emotional support from teachers in the absence of emotional support from parents might also demonstrate more positive levels of adjustment to school than students who have less positive relationships with both teachers and parents. The conjoint influence of teacher and peer relationships has been studied less frequently, although evidence suggests that each type of relationship has somewhat unique effects on student outcomes. Finally, understanding the significance of teacher-student relationships in students' lives is also dependent on careful examination of how these relationships are assessed and studied. Measurement and design issues that influence the ability to make valid inferences and causal conclusions are discussed next.

Measurement and Design Issues

Measuring Teacher-Student Relationships Most researchers who study the affective quality of teacher-student relationships typically assess attachment-related constructs of felt emotional close-ness and security, conflict, and over-dependency (e.g., Pianta et al., 2003), or levels of psychological proximity and affective qualities of relationships (e.g., Wellborn & Connell, 1987). However, assessment strategies differ with respect to the source of information about the relationship. The most widely used measure, the Student-Teacher Relationship Scale (STRS; Pianta & Steinberg, 1992), was developed to tap teachers' representations of their relationships with students (Lynch & Cicchetti, 1992). The STRS has been used almost exclusively to study the affective quality of teacher-child relationships in the preschool and early elementary school years. Therefore, a consideration of the psychometric properties of the STRS is essential for understanding the literature on teachers' relationships with young children.

On a positive note, STRS scale scores are reliable (Pianta & Stuhlman, 2004), and have demonstrated good predictive validity (e.g., Mantzicopoulos & Neuharth-Pritchett, 2003; Pianta & Steinberg, 1992; Valeski & Stipek, 2001). However, researchers also have reported a general lack of concordance between teacher and student reports of the quality of teacher-student relationships (Mantzicopoulos, 2005). Therefore, it is especially important to remember that studies using this measure rely on teachers' reports to assess the quality of teacher-student relationships. A sole reliance on information from teachers is problematic in several respects. First, teacher ratings of closeness and warmth tend to differ for boys and girls (e.g., Birch & Ladd, 1998; Hamre & Pianta, 2001; Silver, Measelle, Armstrong, & Essex, 2005) and for minority and majority children (Ladd & Burgess, 2001), with teachers reporting closer and less conflictual relationships with girls and majority (Caucasian) children. Moreover, teacher ethnicity and mismatch between the race/ethnicity of teachers and students is related (albeit weakly) to conflict and dependency in teacher-student relationships (O'Connor & McCartney, 2006; Saft & Pianta, 2001). These findings suggest that the role of specific teacher characteristics in creating biased reports cannot be discounted. Second, in many studies, teachers also tend to be the source of information about student outcomes (e.g., Birch & Ladd, 1997; Hughes & Kwok, 2006). Therefore, relationship quality and student adjustment scores rarely are independent; significant findings are likely to be inflated. Finally, the teachers who participate in these studies are female; it is unknown if male teachers would yield similar findings.

In research on middle school and high school students, researchers have typically employed student reports to assess the quality of teacher-student relationships. Most of the research on subjective appraisals of emotionally supportive teachers can be characterized by the assessment of students' general perceptions that teachers care about them, facilitate their emotional well-being, and demonstrate appreciation of them as individuals (see e.g., RAPS; Wellborn & Connell, 1987; IAA, Murray & Greenberg, 2000; Classroom Life Scale, Johnson, Johnson, Buckman, & Richards, 1985). Measurement issues also should inform interpretations of the research based on student reports. For instance, findings tend to differ depending on the characteristics of student informants. Students' positive perceptions of teacher support tend to decline with age and across school transitions (Blankemeyer et al., 2002; Reddy et al., 2003; Seidman, Allen, Aber, Mitchell, & Feinman, 1994), and are typically stronger for girls than for boys (Blankemeyer, et al.; Wentzel, 2002) and for Caucasian than for ethnic minority students (Wentzel). The degree to which these findings reflect differences in actual support received, or differences in the interpretation or relevance of items across different groups of students within different educational contexts remains an open question. Of note, a small number of researchers have assessed teacher emotional support from the perspective of teachers, asking them how much they like individual students personally or like having them in their classrooms. Results of these studies correspond closely to those obtained from researchers using student reports (Chang et al., 2004; Wentzel, 1994; Wentzel & Asher, 1995).

Design Issues Most conclusions concerning the importance of teacher-student relationships are based on correlational data. In contrast, studies of change in student outcomes as a result of changes in relationships with teachers are rare. However, when teachers are taught to provide students with warmth and support, clear expectations for behavior, and developmentally appropriate autonomy, their students tend to develop a stronger sense of community, increase displays of socially competent behavior, and show academic gains (Schaps, Battistich, & Solomon, 1997; Watson, Solomon, Battistich, Schaps, & Solomon, 1989). Many comprehensive school reform models also incorporate an explicit focus on teacher-student relationships as a strategy for improving student engagement and learning (Stipek, 2004). However, few of these efforts have documented the unique impact of these relationships on student motivation and academic improvements.

It is clear that establishing causal connections requires assessments of change in student outcomes as a function of changing perceptions of teachers from one year to the next (Wentzel, Williams, & Tomback, 2005), of changing perceptions and outcomes across multiple classrooms, or of interventions designed to change the quality of support from a particular teacher (see Pianta et al., 2003). An additional issue with respect to research design concerns the unit of analysis, and whether support is assessed at the level of the individual student, classroom, or school (Fraser & Fisher, 1982). Studies relating individual students' perceptions of support to student outcomes yield important information about the psychological impact of social support. For the most part, however, researchers that focus on individual differences typically disregard the fact that teacher or classroom effects might also explain student outcomes. For instance, class size has been related significantly and negatively to teachers' provisions of emotional support (Mashburn, Hamre, Downer, & Pianta, 2006; Pianta et al., 2003). Emotional support from teachers also appears to account for only a small amount of variance in observed climate in elementary classrooms (Pianta et al., 2003). Therefore, studies could profit from an examination of between-classroom effects by gathering information on a larger number of classrooms and a greater range of classroom characteristics. More complex designs that take into consideration the nested quality of social support at the level of student, classroom, and school are needed in this regard.

The moderating influence of students' and teachers' sex, race, and other background characteristics on the impact of teacher-student relationships also requires further examination. Indeed, research indicates that characteristics of students might enhance or detract from their tendency to establish supportive relationships with teachers and therefore, benefit from them. For example, in the elementary-school years, relations between close and secure teacher-student relationships and student adjustment tend to be stronger for ethnic minority and at-risk students than for Caucasian students (Burchinal, Peisner-Feinberg, Pianta, & Howes, 2002; Meehan, Hughes, & Cavell, 2003; cf., Ladd & Burgess, 2001). Relatedness with teachers also tends to be associated with student outcomes more strongly for special education students than for regular students (Little & Kobak, 2003), and more for boys than for girls (Furrer & Skinner, 2003).

Research on perceived emotional support also suggests that supportive relationships might be more important for some students than for others. In particular, relations between perceived emotional support from teachers and student adjustment are moderated by SES and race such that students from lower SES backgrounds (Dornbusch, Erickson, Laird, & Wong, 2001) and members of minority groups (Certo, Cauley, & Chafin, 2003; Crosnoe et al., 2004) tend to benefit more from close relationships with teachers than do other students; school-level factors such as safety, racial homogeneity, SES of the student body (Crosnoe et al.), and composition of instructional teams (Murdock & Miller, 2003) also appear to moderate relations between perceived teacher support and student outcomes. Finally, relatedness with teachers appears to differ as a function of students' age, with more elementary grade students reporting optimal or adequate relationships than middle school students (Lynch & Cicchetti, 1997). Most of these studies have focused on fairly objective outcomes such as grades, test scores, or delinquent and aggressive forms of behavior. The moderating impact of these characteristics on motivational processes is not well-understood.

Summary

Although research is mixed, there is some indication that students might form relationships with teachers that are different from those with parents and peers, and that these relationships can motivate positive student outcomes over and above other social influences. However, identifying specific ways in which these relationships can actively and directly promote the development of positive motivational orientations toward learning and academic competencies, independently of other relationship supports from parents and peers, remains a challenge for researchers in this area. Ways in which supports from multiple relationships interact to promote school success also need to be studied. Measurement and design issues also need to inform future work on students' relationships with teachers. In this regard, greater focus on individual differences and developmental trajectories and change over time is needed. Ideally, studies should be designed so that multiple and independent sources inform assessments. Work in this area also could benefit from more experimental approaches and observational techniques that capture supportive aspects of instructional practice.

Conclusions and Future Directions for the Field

I began this chapter by posing the question of how and why students' relationships with teachers might be related to their social and academic functioning at school. In general, the affective quality of teacher-student relationships has been associated with children's social and academic competencies as well as to motivational and affective functioning from the preschool years through adolescence. The research described in this chapter has established clear associations between the nature and quality of teacher-student relationships and students' social and academic motivation, behavioral competencies, and academic performance at school. These findings appear to be robust regardless of theoretical perspective, type of assessment, and student age.

Throughout this chapter, issues pertinent to the interpretation of research in this area have been raised. Although many of these findings are based on concurrent assessments of relationship quality and student outcomes, longitudinal findings indicate that the effects of teacher-student relationships might persist over time. However, the significance of the teacher-student relationship as a causal predictor of student adjustment is not yet clear. Although some evidence for causal influence has been reported, experimental work is rare. In addition, progress toward understanding the developmental significance of students' relationships with teachers requires more systematic attention to the construction of more complex theoretical models, further consideration of what might develop in students as a result of relationships with teachers, especially with respect to motivational processes, identification of individual differences in teachers that contribute to the nature and quality of their relationships, and students' motivational characteristics that contribute to the development of positive student-teacher relationships.

Theoretical Challenges

As noted at the beginning of this chapter, the predominant approach to the study of teacher-student relationships is to assume a causal connection such that the nature and quality of relationships and interactions influence student outcomes. A consideration of alternative pathways, however, would add critical and important insights to the discussion of these relationships. For instance, given the broad range of social and academic skills that students demonstrate at school, it is likely that the influence of student characteristics on the development of teacher-student relationships is as powerful as the reverse. Therefore, models that address the potential impact of children's motivation and engagement on teachers' behavior, and that identify motivational processes that lead to receptive as opposed to rejecting or neglectful behavior on the part of teachers need to be developed to inform this area of research. In fact, students' classroom behavior has been related to changes in teachers' provisions of supports over time (Marchand & Skinner, 2007). Similarly, models that identify factors that serve to maintain the cohesion and integrity of teacher-student relationships over time need to be developed. It also is important to consider the possibility that lack of concordance between teacher and student reports of supportive relationships does not always reflect methodological imprecision but rather the fact that relationships often function at a psychological level that is not necessarily reflected in reality. Therefore, examination of various ways in which students interpret teachers' behavior and of the degree to which they attribute their own successes and failures to this behavior is a critical next step in this area of research. Conversely, it also is reasonable to assume that students' social and academic achievements can elicit social approval and corresponding positive interactions with teachers.

A final issue with respect to model development is that although progress is being made, much of our current understanding of teacher-student relationships is based on studies of European American middle-class children. Therefore, models that take into account the diversity of student backgrounds also are needed in this area of research. Although it is likely that the underlying motivational processes that contribute to school adjustment are similar for all students regardless of race, ethnicity, gender, or other contextual and demographic variables, the degree to which these latter factors interact with motivation to influence adjustment is not known. To illustrate, self-regulation skills such as planning, monitoring, and regulation of behavior that support the development of efficacy beliefs and achievement of classroom goals might be more important for the adjustment of children from minority backgrounds than for children who come from families and communities whose goals and expectations are similar to those of the educational establishment (e.g., Fordham & Ogbu, 1986). Therefore, the specific role of teachers in supporting the development and use of these skills might be a particularly fruitful avenue of research. In addition, individual characteristics such as racial identity (Graham, Taylor, & Hudley, 1998), perceived discrimination, and the extent that students are oriented towards gaining social approval (Goetz & Dweck, 1980) are also likely to influence the degree to which students are open to forming relationships with teachers and being influenced by them.

What Develops?

Assuming that teacher-student relationships have a causal influence on student adjustment, what is it that develops or is changed on the part of students as a function of their relationships and interactions with teachers? As noted in this chapter, teacher-student relationships have been related positively to a range of students' social and academic competencies including peer relationships, behavioral styles, grades, and test scores. They also have been associated with a number of motivational outcomes such as students' goal pursuit, beliefs about competence and control, effort and persistence, and self-regulatory strategies. These findings, however, tell us little about how and why these relationships impact students' accomplishments at school. Therefore, an important remaining theoretical challenge is to articulate the various pathways and mechanisms by which teacher-student relationships have influence.

Of particular importance for this chapter is that several researchers have begun to explore specific motivational pathways by which teacher-student relationships influence students' social and academic functioning. For example, close and conflictual relationships with teachers appear to be related to academic achievement by way of young students' engagement in the form of effort, persistence, and attention (Hughes & Kwok, 2006; Ladd, Birch, & Buhs, 1999). Similarly, levels of teacher involvement have been related to elementary-aged students' academic and social outcomes by way of motivational processes such as effort (Zimmer-Gembeck & Locke, 2007), and their sense of relatedness, autonomy, and competence (Marchand & Skinner, 2007). In older students, relations between perceived emotional support from teachers and achievement appear to be mediated by students' mastery goal orientations and self-efficacy (Patrick, Ryan, & Kaplan, 2007), and their social goal pursuit tends to mediate relations between perceived teacher supports and students' prosocial behavior (Wentzel, 2002). Continued work in this area is essential if we are to understand fully the role of motivation in explaining the unique impact of teacher-student relationships on students' social and academic competencies at school. Identification of specific mechanisms that explain how certain qualities of these relationships (e.g., emotional closeness) lead to specific motivational outcomes (e.g., values, goal pursuit) at different ages also is needed.

Of additional importance for understanding "what develops" is a focus on the cumulative effects of having positive relationships with many teachers over time, and their contribution to a student's sense of school community and belongingness. School belongingness measures assess in part, students' perceptions of the quality of relationships with all of their teachers as a group (see Goodenow, 1993; Roeser & Eccles, 1998). The extent to which these more global beliefs develop out of interactions and relationships with single or multiple teachers, and reflect a student's ongoing history of relationships or a single but salient recent relationship are important remaining questions to address.

A Focus on Teachers

If teachers have influence by way of the relationships and interactions they have with students, it also becomes essential to understand those factors that contribute to teachers' ability and willingness to engage in these positive forms of social interaction. Research that examines factors that foster supportive and caring behavior on the part of teachers is relatively rare. However, teacher stress appears to contribute to the number of negative relationships that elementary school teachers report having with their students (Yoon, 2002), depression has been related to the sensitivity and responsiveness of preschool teachers (Hamre & Pianta, 2004), and a secure attachment style has been related to positive as opposed to conflictual interactions of elementary school teachers with their students (Morris-Rothschild & Brassard, 2006). Teachers' years of experience and sense of efficacy with regard to classroom management also have been related to positive relationships and interactions with pre-school and elementary-aged students (Mashburn et al., 2006; Morris-Rothschild & Brassard, 2006; Yoon, 2002). Therefore, the potential impact of teacher characteristics on their motivation and ability to develop positive relationships with students also needs to become a focus of research.

Research on characteristics of parents that predict effective parenting (see Grusec & Goodnow, 1994) might also be informative for understanding effective teachers. For example, it is clear that teachers communicate their expectations and goals to students on a daily basis. However, less is known about the nature of these communications that might predispose students to accept or reject them. The family socialization literature suggests that parental messages are more likely to be perceived accurately by children if they are clear and consistent, are framed in ways that are meaningful to the child, require decoding and processing, are perceived by the child to be of clear importance to the parent, and as being conveyed with positive intentions (Grusec & Goodnow). Adapting this work to the realm of the classroom might provide important insights into effective forms of teacher communication that lead to the development of positive teacher-student relationships and subsequent social and academic motivation.

Finally, school-level factors are likely to influence teachers' ability to create supportive classroom environments for their students. For example, job satisfaction, over and above gender, teacher education, and classroom management skills, has been related to high school teachers' provisions of instrumental help and challenge, especially with low ability students (Opdenakker & Van Damme, 2006). Other factors such as the quality of feedback given to teachers from administrators, teacher autonomy and participation in school decision making, opportunities for collaboration and development of positive relationships with peers, and instructional help and resources are likely to contribute to teachers' ability and willingness to provide similar kinds of supports for their students (see Firestone & Pennell, 1993). If provisions of positive supports contribute to students' successful functioning at school, provisions of similar supports to teachers are likely to improve their practice as well.

Student-Teacher Relationships and Student Characteristics

Aside from models that posit a direction of causal influence from teacher to student, the notion that establishing positive relationships with teachers is the result of students' motivational competencies has rarely been the focus of theoretical discussions, much less the focus of empirical study (cf., Skinner & Belmont, 1993). However, social-cognitive processes in the form of attributions of teacher intent (Wyatt & Haskett, 2001), social self-efficacy (Patrick, Hicks, & Ryan, 1997), beliefs about control (Wentzel, 1997) and accuracy of social-cognitive processing (O'Connor & Hirsch, 1999) explain at least in part, students' perceptions of teacher support. Other aspects of social-cognitive processing such as selective attention, attributions, and social biases and stereotypes (Lemerise & Arsenio, 2000), also can influence students' interpretations of social communications as well as teacher reactions to their behavior.

Students' metacognitive and self-regulatory processes also are likely to contribute to the development of positive relationships with teachers. Several theorists have posited goal-setting skills, emotion regulation, self-monitoring, attributions and means-end thinking, and other basic information-processing skills as factors that contribute to the ability to implement behavior that contributes to the formation of positive relationships (Lemerise & Arsenio, 2000). From a motivational perspective, goal networks and hierarchies based on students' beliefs about cause-effect relations also are likely to link the quality of relationships with teachers to performance in other domains. For instance, students might try to demonstrate academic competence to gain social approval from teachers or, they might behave in socially competent ways to earn the positive regard of their teachers (Wentzel, Filisetti, & Looney, 2007). The possibility that students' social and academic motivational characteristics contribute to the quality of their relationships with teachers and that forming positive relationships with teachers is an important competency in and of itself, should not be ignored in conceptualizations of teacher-student relationships.

References

Baumrind, D. (1971). Current patterns of parental authority. *Developmental Psychology Monograph, 4*(1, Pt.2).

Becker, B. E., & Luthar, S. S. (2002). Social-emotional factors affecting achievement outcomes among disadvantaged students: Closing the achievement gap. *Educationalist Psychologist, 37,* 197–214.

Birch, S. H., & Ladd, G. W. (1997). The teacher-child relationship and children's early school adjustment. *Journal of School Psychology, 35,* 61–79.

Birch, S. H., & Ladd, G. W. (1998). Children's interpersonal behaviors and the teacher-child relationship. *Developmental Psychology, 34,* 934–946.

Blankemeyer, M., Flannery, D. J., & Vazsonyi, A. T. (2002). The role of aggression and social competence in children's perceptions of the child-teacher relationship. *Psychology in the Schools, 39,* 293–304.

Bowlby, J. (1969). Attachment and loss. *Attachment vol. 1.* New York: Basic Books.

Bretherton, I. (1987). New perspectives on attachment relations: Security, communication and internal working models. In J. Osofsky (Ed.), *Handbook of infant development* (pp. 1061–1100). New York: Wiley.

Brody, G. H., Dorsey, S., Forehand, R., & Armistead, L. (2002). Unique and protective contributions of parenting and classroom processes to the adjustment of African American children living in single-parent families. *Child Development, 73,* 274–286.

Bronfenbrenner, U. (1989). Ecological systems theory. In R. Vasta (Ed.), *Annals of child development* (Vol. 6, pp. 187–250). Greenwich, CT: JAI.

Brophy, J. E., & Good, T. L. (1974). *Teacher-student relationships: Causes and consequences.* New York: Holt, Rinehart & Winston.

Burchinal, M.R., Peisner-Feinberg, E., Pianta, R., & Howes, C. (2002). Development of academic skills from preschool through second grade: Family and classroom predictors of developmental trajectories. *Journal of School Psychology, 40,* 415–436.

Certo, J. L., Cauley, K. M., & Chafin, C. (2003). Students' perspectives on their high school experience. *Adolescence, 38,* 705–724.

Chang, L. (2003). Variable effects of children's aggression, social withdrawal, and prosocial leadership as functions of teacher beliefs and behaviors. *Child Development, 74,* 535–548.

Chang, L., Liu, H. Y., Wen, Z. L., Fung, K. Y., Wang, Y., & Xu, Y. Y. (2004). Mediating teacher liking and moderating authoritative teaching on Chinese adolescents' perceptions of antisocial and prosocial behaviors. *Journal of Educational Psychology, 96,* 369–380.

Cohen, S., & Wills, T. A. (1985). Stress, social support, and the buffering hypothesis. *Psychological Bulletin, 98,* 310–357.

Connell, J. P., & Wellborn, J. G. (1991). Competence, autonomy, and relatedness: A motivational analysis of self-system processes. In M. R. Gunnar & L. A. Sroufe (Eds.), *Self processes and development: The Minnesota symposia on child development* (Vol. 23, pp. 43–78). Hillsdale, NJ: Erlbaum.

Crosnoe, R., Johnson, M. K., & Elder, G. H., Jr. (2004). Intergenerational bonding in school: The behavioral and contextual correlates of student-teacher relationships. *Sociology of Education, 77*, 60–81.

Daniels, E., & Arapostathis, M. (2005). What do they really want? Student voices and motivation research. *Urban Education, 40*, 34–59.

Darling, N., & Steinberg, L. (1993). Parenting style as context – An integrative model. *Psychological Bulletin, 113*, 487–496.

Davis, H. A. (2001). The quality and impact of relationships between elementary school students and teachers. *Contemporary Educational Psychology, 26*, 421–453.

Dornbusch, S. M., Erickson, K. G., Laird, J., & Wong, C.A . (2001). The relation of family and school attachment to adolescent deviance in diverse groups and communities. *Journal of Adolescent Research, 16*, 396–422.

Duchesne, S., & Larose, S. (2007). Adolescent parental attachment and academic motivation and performance in early adolescence. *Journal of Applied Social Psychology, 37*, 1501–1521.

Eccles, J. S., & Midgley, C. (1989). Stage-environment fit: Developmentally appropriate classrooms for young adolescents. In C. Ames & R. Ames (Eds.), *Research on motivation in education: Vol. 3* (pp. 139–186). New York: Academic Press.

Firestone, W. A., & Pennell, J. R. (1993). Teacher commitment, working conditions, and differential incentive policies. *Review of Educational Research, 63*, 498–525.

Ford, M. E. (1992). *Motivating humans: Goals, emotions, and personal agency beliefs.* Newbury Park, CA: Sage.

Fordham, S., & Ogbu, J. U. (1986). Black students' school success: Coping with "the burden of 'acting white." *The Urban Review, 18*, 176–206.

Fraser, B. J., & Fisher, D. L. (1982). Predicting students' outcomes from their perceptions of classroom psychosocial environment. *American Educational Research Journal, 19*, 498–518.

Furman, W., & Buhrmester, D. (1985). Children's perceptions of the personal relationships in their social networks. *Developmental Psychology, 21*, 1016–1024.

Furrer, C., & Skinner, E. (2003). Sense of relatedness as a factor in children's academic engagement and performance. *Journal of Educational Psychology, 95*, 148–162.

Gettinger, M., & Kohler, K. M. (2006). Process-outcome approaches to classroom management and effective teaching. In C. Evertson & C. Weinstein (Eds.), *Handbook of classroom management – Research, practice, and contemporary issues* (pg. 73–96). Mahwah, NJ: Erlbaum.

Goetz, T. S., & Dweck, C. S. (1980). Learned helplessness in social situations. *Journal of Personality and Social Psychology, 39*, 246–255.

Goodenow, C. (1993). The psychological sense of school membership among adolescents – Scale development and educational correlates. *Psychology in the Schools, 30*, 79–90.

Graham, S., Taylor, A., & Hudley, C. (1998). Exploring achievement values among ethnic minority early adolescents. *Journal of Educational Psychology, 90*, 606–620.

Grolnick, W. S., Gurland, S. T., Jacob, K. F., & Decourcey, W. (2002). The development of self-determination in middle childhood and adolescence. In A. Wigfield & J. Eccles (Eds.), *Development of achievement motivation* (pp. 148–174). San Diego: Academic Press.

Grolnick, W. S., & Ryan, R. M. (1989). Parent styles associated with children's self-regulation and competence in school. *Journal of Educational Psychology, 81*, 143–154.

Grusec, J. E., & Goodnow, J. J. (1994). Impact of parental discipline methods on the child's internalization of values: A reconceptualization of current points of view. *Developmental Psychology, 30*, 4–19.

Hamre, B. K., & Pianta, R. C. (2001). Early teacher-child relationships and the trajectory of children's school outcomes through eighth grade. *Child Development, 72*, 625–638.

Hamre, B. K., & Pianta, R. C. (2004). Self-reported depression in nonfamilial caregivers: prevalence and associations with caregiver behavior in child-care settings. *Early Childhood Research Quarterly, 19*, 297–318.

Hargreaves, D. H., Hester, S. K., & Mellor, F. J. (1975). *Deviance in classrooms.* London: Routledge & Kegan Paul.

Harter, S. (1978). Effectance motivation reconsidered toward a developmental model. *Human Development, 21*, 34–64.

Hayes, C. B., Ryan, A., & Zseller, E. B. (1994). The middle school child's perceptions of caring teachers. *American Journal of Education, 103*, 1–19.

Howes, C., & Hamilton, C. E. (1993). The changing experience of child care: Changes in teachers and in teacher-child relationships and children's social competence with peers. *Early Childhood Research Quarterly, 8*, 15–32.

Hoy, A. W., & Weinstein, C. S. (2006). Student and teacher perspectives on classroom management. In C. Evertson & C. Weinstein (Eds.), *Handbook of classroom management – Research, practice, and contemporary issues* (pp. 181–219). Mahwah, NJ: Erlbaum.

Hughes, J. N., & Kwok, O. M. (2006). Classroom engagement mediates the effect of teacher-student support on elementary students' peer acceptance: A prospective analysis. *Journal of School Psychology, 43*, 465–480.

Hughes, J. N., Cavell, T. A., & Jackson, T. (1999). Influence of the teacher-student relationship on childhood conduct problems: A prospective study. *Journal of Clinical Child Psychology, 28*, 173–184.

Hughes, J. N., Zhang, D., & Hill, C. R. (2006). Peer assessments of non-native and individual teacher-student support predict social acceptance and engagement among low-achieving children. *Journal of School Psychology, 43*, 447–463.

Ibanez, G. E., Kuperminc, G. P., Jurkovic, G., & Perilla, J. (2004). Cultural attributes and adaptations linked to achievement motivation among Latino adolescents. *Journal of Youth and Adolescence, 33*, 559–568.

Isakson, K., & Jarvis, P. (1999). The adjustment of adolescents during the transition into high school: A short-term longitudinal study. *Journal of Youth and Adolescence, 28*, 1–26.

Johnson, D. W., Johnson, R. T., Buckman, L. A. & Richards, P. S. (1985). The effect of prolonged implementation of cooperative learning on social support within the classroom. *The Journal of Psychology, 119,* 405–411.

Jussim, L. (1991). Social perception and social reality: A reflection-construction model. *Psychological Review, 98,* 9–34.

Jussim, L., & Eccles, J. (1995). Naturalistic studies of interpersonal expectancies. *Psychology, 63,* 947–961.

Jussim, L., & Harber, K. D. (2005). Teacher expectations and self-fulfilling prophecies: Knowns and unknowns, resolved, and unresolved controversies. *Personality and Social Psychology Review, 9,* 131–155.

Ladd, G. W., Birch, S. H., & Buhs, E. S. (1999). Children's social and scholastic lives in kindergarten: Related spheres of influence? *Child Development, 70,* 1373–1400.

Ladd, G. W., & Burgess, K. B. (2001). Do relational risks and protective factors moderate the linkages between childhood aggression and early psychological and school adjustment? *Child Development, 72,* 1579–1601.

Lemerise, E. A., & Arsenio, W. F. (2000). An integrated model of emotion processes and cognition in social information processing. *Child Development, 71,* 107–118.

Lempers, J. D., & Clark-Lempers, D. S. (1992). Young, middle and late adolescents' comparisons of the functional importance of five significant relationships. *Journal of Youth and Adolescence, 21,* 53–96.

Little M., & Kobak R. (2003). Emotional security with teachers and children's stress reactivity: A comparison of special-education and regular-education classrooms. *Journal of Clinical Child and Adolescent Psychology, 32,* 127–138.

Lynch, M., & Cicchetti, D. (1997). Children's relationships with adults and peers: An examination of elementary and junior high school students. *Journal of School Psychology, 35,* 81–99.

Madon, S., Jussim, L., & Eccles, J. (1997). In search of self-fulfilling prophecy. *Journal of Personality and Social Psychology, 72,* 791–809.

Mantzicopoulos, P. (2005). Conflictual relationships between kindergarten children and their teachers: Associations with child and classroom context variables. *Journal of School Psychology, 43,* 425–442.

Mantzicopoulos, P., & Neuharth-Pritchett, S. (2003). Development and validation of a measure to assess head start children's appraisals of teacher support. *Journal of School Psychology, 41,* 431–451.

Marchand, G., & Skinner, E. A. (2007). Motivational dynamics of children's academic help-seeking and concealment. *Journal of Educational Psychology, 99,* 65–82.

Marchant, G. J., Paulson, S. E., & Rothlisberg, B. A. (2001). Relations of middle school students' perceptions of family and school contexts with academic achievement. *Psychology in the Schools, 38,* 505–519.

Mashburn, A. J., Hamre, B. K., Downer, J. T., & Pianta, R. C. (2006). Teacher and classroom characteristics associated with teachers' ratings of prekindergartners' relationships and behaviors. *Journal of Psychoeducational Assessment, 24,* 367–380.

Meehan, B. T., Hughes, J. N., & Cavell, T. A. (2003). Teacher-student relationships as compensatory resources for aggressive children. *Child Development, 74,* 1145–1157.

Midgley, C., Feldlaufer, H., & Eccles, J. (1989). Student/teacher relations and attitudes toward mathematics before and after the transition to junior high school. *Child Development, 60,* 981–992.

Mitchell-Copeland, J., Denham, S. A., & DeMulder, E. K. (1997). Q-sort assessment of child-teacher attachment relationships and social competence in the preschool. *Early Education and Development, 8,* 27–39.

Moje, E. B. (1996). "I teach students, not subjects": Teacher-student relationships as contexts for secondary literacy. *Reading Research Quarterly, 31,* 172–195.

Morris-Rothschild, B. K., & Brassard, M. R. (2006). Teachers' conflict management styles: The role of attachment styles and classroom management efficacy. *Journal of School Psychology, 44,* 105–121.

Murdock, T. B., & Miller, A. (2003). Teachers as sources of middle school students' motivational identity: Variable-centered and person-centered analytic approaches. *Elementary School Journal, 103,* 383–399.

Murdock, T. B., Miller, A., & Kohlhardt, J. (2004). Effects of classroom context variables on high school students' judgments of the acceptability and likelihood of cheating. *Journal of Educational Psychology, 96,* 765–777.

Murray, C., & Greenberg, M. T. (2000). Children's relationship with teachers and bonds with school an investigation of patterns and correlates in middle childhood. *Journal of School Psychology, 38,* 423–445.

National Center for Educational Statistics. (1995). Student strategies to avoid harm at school. (NCES Publication No. NCES 95-203). Washington, DC: U.S. Government Printing Office.

Newman, R. S. (2000). Social influences on the development of children's adaptive help seeking: The role of parents, teachers, and peers. *Developmental Review, 20,* 350–404.

O'Connor, E., & McCartney, K. (2006). Testing associations between young children's relationships with mothers and teachers. *Journal of Educational Psychology, 98,* 87–98.

O'Connor, T. G., & Hirsch, N. (1999). Intra-individual differences and relationship-specificity of mentalising in early adolescence. *Social Development, 8,* 256–274.

Oates, G. L. (2003). Teacher-student racial congruence, teacher perceptions, and test performance. *Social Science Quarterly, 84,* 508–525.

Oldfather, P. (1993). What students say about motivating experiences in a whole language classroom. *The Reading Teacher, 46,* 672–681.

Olweus, D. (1993). Victimization by peers: Antecedents and long-term outcomes. In K. Rubin & J. B. Asendorf (Eds.), *Social withdrawal, inhibition, and shyness in childhood* (pp. 315–341). Chicago: University of Chicago Press.

Opdenakker, M. C., & Van Damme, J. (2006). Teacher characteristics and teaching styles as effectiveness enhancing factors or classroom practice. *Teaching and Teacher Education, 22,* 1–21.

Patrick H., Ryan, A. M., & Kaplan, A. (2007). Early adolescents' perceptions of the classroom social environment, motivational beliefs, and engagement. *Journal of Educational Psychology, 99*, 83–98.

Patrick, H., Hicks, L., & Ryan, A. M. (1997). Relations of perceived social efficacy and social goal pursuit to self-efficacy for academic work. *Journal of Early Adolescence, 17*, 109–128.

Peisner-Feinberg, E. S., Burchinal, M. R., Clifford, R.M., Culkin, M. L., Howes, C., Kagan, S. L., et al. (2001). The relation of preschool child-care quality to children's cognitive and social developmental trajectories through second grade. *Child Development, 72*, 1534–1553.

Pianta, R. C., & Steinberg, M. (1992). Teacher-child relationships and the process of adjusting to school. In W. Damon (Series Ed.) & R. C. Pianta (Vol. Ed.), *New directions for child development: Vol. 57. Beyond the parent: The role of other adults in children's lives* (pp. 61–80). San Francisco: Jossey-Bass.

Pianta, R. C., & Stuhlman, M. W. (2004). Teacher-child relationships and children's success in the first years of school. *School Psychology Review, 33*, 444–458.

Pianta, R. C., Hamre, B., & Stuhlman, M. (2003). Relationships between teachers and children. In W. Reynolds & G. Miller (Eds.), *Handbook of psychology, Vol. 7: Educational Psychology* (pp. 199–234). New York: Wiley.

Pianta, R. C., Nimetz, S. L., & Bennett, E. (1997). Mother-child relationships, teacher-child relationships, and school outcomes in preschool and kindergarten. *Early Childhood Research Quarterly, 12*, 263–280.

Raider-Roth, M. B. (2005). Trusting what you know: Negotiating the relational context of classroom life. *Teachers College Record, 107*, 587–628.

Research Assessment Package for Schools (RAPS). (1998). http://www.irre.org/publications/pdfs/RAPS_manual_entire_1998.pdf

Reddy, R., Rhodes, J. E., & Mulhall, P. (2003). The influence of teacher support on student adjustment in the middle school years: A latent growth curve study. *Development and Psychopathology, 15*, 119–138.

Reid, M., Landesman, S., Treder, R., & Jaccard, J. (1989). "My family and friends": Six-to twelve-year-old children's perceptions of social support. *Child Development, 60*, 896–910.

Reyna, C., & Weiner, B. (2001). Justice and utility in the classroom: An attributional analysis of the goals of teachers' punishment and intervention strategies. *Journal of Educational Psychology, 93*, 309–319.

Roeser, R. W., & Eccles, J. S. (1998). Adolescents' perceptions of middle school: Relation to longitudinal changes in academic and psychological adjustment. *Journal of Research on Adolescence, 8*, 123–158.

Roeser, R. W., Midgley, C., & Urdan, T. C. (1996). Perceptions of the school psychological environment and early adolescents' psychological and behavioral functioning in school: The mediating role of goals and belonging. *Journal of Educational Psychology, 88*, 408–422.

Ryan, R. M. (1993). Agency and organization: Intrinsic motivation, autonomy, and the self in psychological development. In J. Jacobs (Ed.), *Nebraska symposium on motivation, Vol 40* (pp. 1–56). Lincoln: University of Nebraska Press.

Ryan, R. M., & Deci, E. L. (2000). Self-determination theory and the facilitation of intrinsic motivation, social development, and well-being. *American Psychologist, 55*, 68–78.

Ryan, R. M., Stiller, J. D., & Lynch, J. H. (1994). Representations of relationships to teachers, parents, and friends as predictors of academic motivation and self-esteem. *Journal of Early Adolescence, 14*, 226–249.

Saft, E. W., & Pianta, R. C. (2001). Teachers' perceptions of their relationships with students: Effects of child age, gender, and ethnicity of teachers and children. *School Psychology Quarterly, 16*, 125–141.

Sanchez, B., Colon, Y., & Esparza, P. (2005). The role of sense of school belonging and gender in the academic adjustment of Latino adolescents. *Journal of Youth and Adolescence, 34*, 619–628.

Sarason, B. R., Sarason, I. G., & Pierce, G. R. (1990). Traditional views of social support and their impact on assessment. In B. R. Sarason, I. G. Sarason, & G. R. Sarason (Eds.), *Social support: An interactional view* (pp. 9–25). New York: Wiley.

Schaps, E., Battistich, V., & Solomon, D. (1997). School as a caring community: A key to character education. In A. Molnar (Ed.), *Ninety-sixth yearbook of the National Society for the Study of Education* (pp. 127–139). Chicago: University of Chicago Press.

Seidman, E., Allen, L., Aber, J. L., Mitchell, C., & Feinman, J. (1994). The impact of school transitions in early adolescence on the self-esteem and perceived social context of poor urban youth. *Child Development, 65*, 507–522.

Silver, R. B., Measelle, J. R., Armstrong, J. M., & Essex, M. J. (2005). Trajectories of classroom externalizing behavior: Contributions of child characteristics, family characteristics, and the teacher–child relationship during the school transition. *Journal of School Psychology, 43*, 39–60.

Skinner, E. A., & Belmont, M. J. (1993). Motivation in the classroom: Reciprocal effects of teacher behavior and student engagement across the school year. *Journal of Educational Psychology, 85*, 571–581.

Smith, A. E., Jussim., & Eccles, J. (1999). Do self-fulfilling prophecies accumulate, dissipate, or remain stable over time? *Journal of Personality and Social Psychology, 77*, 548–565.

Smokowski, P. R., Reynolds, A. J., & Bezrucko, N. (2000). Resilience and protective factors in adolescence: An autobiographical perspective from disadvantaged youth. *Journal of School Psychology, 37*, 425–448.

Steinberg, L. (2001). We know some things: Parent-adolescent relationships in retrospect and prospect. *Journal of Research on Adolescence, 11*, 1–19.

Stipek, D. (2004). *Engaging in schools: Fostering High school students' motivation to learn.* Committee on increasing high school students' engagement and motivation to learn. Division of Behavioral and Social Sciences and Education. Washington, DC: National Academy Press.

Valeski, T. N ., & Stipek, D. J. (2001). Young children's feelings about school. *Child Development, 72,* 1198–1213.

Watson, M., Solomon, D., Battistich, V., Schaps, E., & Solomon, J. (1989). The child development project: Combining traditional and developmental approaches to values education. In L. Nucci (Ed.), *Moral development and character education: A dialogue* (pp. 51–92). Berkeley: McCutchan.

Weinstein, C. S. (1998). "I want to be nice, but I have to be mean": Exploring prospective teachers' conceptions of caring and order. *Teaching and Teacher Education, 14,* 153–163.

Weinstein, R. S. (2002). *Reaching higher: The power of expectations in schooling.* Cambridge, MA: Harvard University Press.

Weinstein, R. S., Gregory, A., & Strambler, M. J. (2004). Intractable self-fulfilling prophecies: *Brown v. Board of Education. American Psychologist, 59,* 511–520.

Wentzel, K. R. (1994). Relations of social goal pursuit to social acceptance, classroom behavior, and perceived social support. *Journal of Educational Psychology, 86,* 173–182.

Wentzel, K. R. (1997). Student motivation in middle school: The role of perceived pedagogical caring. *Journal of Educational Psychology, 89,* 411–419.

Wentzel, K. R. (1998). Social support and adjustment in middle school: The role of parents, teachers, and peers. *Journal of Educational Psychology, 90,* 202–209.

Wentzel, K. R. (2000). What is it that I'm trying to achieve? Classroom goals from a content perspective. *Contemporary Educational Psychology, 25,* 105–115.

Wentzel, K. R. (2002). Are effective teachers like good parents? Interpersonal predictors of school adjustment in early adolescence. *Child Development, 73,* 287–301.

Wentzel, K. R. (2003). School adjustment. In W. Reynolds & G. Miller (Eds.), *Handbook of psychology, Vol. 7: Educational Psychology* (pp. 235–258). New York: Wiley.

Wentzel, K. R. (2004). Understanding classroom competence: The role of social-motivational and self-processes. In R. Kail (Ed.), *Advances in Child Development and Behavior, Vol. 32* (pp. 213–241). New York: Elsevier.

Wentzel, K. R. (2005). Peer relationships, motivation, and academic performance at school. In A. Elliot & C. Dweck (Eds.), *Handbook of Competence and Motivation* (pp. 279–296). New York: Guilford.

Wentzel, K. R., & Asher, S. R. (1995). Academic lives of neglected, rejected, popular, and controversial children. *Child Development, 66,* 754–763.

Wentzel, K. R., Battle, A., & Looney, L. (2007). *Teacher and peer contributions to classroom climate in middle school.* Unpublished manuscript.

Wentzel, K. R., Filisetti, L., & Looney, L. (2007). Adolescent prosocial behavior: The role of self-processes and contextual cues. *Child Development, 78,* 895–910.

Wentzel, K. R., Williams, A. Y., & Tomback, R. M. (2005, April). *Relations of Teacher and Peer Support to Classroom Behavior in Middle School,.* Paper presented at the annual meeting of the American Educational Research Association, Montreal, QC.

Wellborn, J. G., & Connell, J. P. (1987). *A Manual for the Rochester Assessment Package for Schools.* Unpublished manuscript, University of Rochester.

Wilson, V. L., & Hughes, J. N. (2006). Retention of Hispanic/Latino students in first grade: Child, parent, teacher, school, and peer predictors. *Journal of School Psychology, 44,* 31–49.

Wyatt, L. W., & Haskett, M. E. (2001). Aggressive and nonaggressive young adolescents' attributions of intent in teacher/student interactions. *Journal of Early Adolescence, 21,* 425–446.

Yoon, J. S. (2002). Teacher characteristics as predictors of teacher-student relationships: Stress, negative affect, and self-efficacy. *Social Behavior and Personality, 30,* 485–493.

Zimmer-Gembeck, M. J., & Locke, E. M. (2007). The socialization of adolescent coping behaviours: Relationships with families and teachers. *Journal of Adolescence, 30,* 1–16.

16
Peers and Motivation

Gary W. Ladd, Sarah L. Herald-Brown, and Karen P. Kochel

Problems such as declining academic motivation and achievement, increasing student alienation, and elevated school drop-out rates have spurred researchers to investigate why some children become more engaged in school than others. What has been learned thus far suggests that school engagement is an important indicator of children's motivation to learn and a pivotal predictor of their academic achievement (see Fredricks, Blumenfeld, & Paris, 2004). Thus, it can be argued that understanding the determinants of school engagement is an important scientific objective and one that deserves greater attention than it has received in past years. Although the origins of school engagement are probably diverse (see Fredricks et al., 2004; Ladd & Dinella, 2009; Perry & Weinstein, 1998), recent theory and evidence points to the importance of interpersonal factors, such as the types of relationships that children and adolescents form with classmates and teachers (see Ryan, 2000). Relations with classroom peers, in particular, have been increasingly linked with differing indicators of school engagement, suggesting that peers may play a critical, if not unique role in the behavioral, emotional, and cognitive orientations that children develop toward school.

Accordingly, the purposes of this chapter are to examine recent theory and evidence pertaining to the role of peers (i.e., classmates) in the socialization of children's school engagement and to critically appraise what has been learned thus far about the role of specific types of classroom peer relations in the development of children's participation in school-related tasks.

School Engagement as a Motivational Construct

The concept of motivation has received considerable attention because its indicators have been linked with school achievement, dropout rates, and success in the workplace (Fredricks et al., 2004). In the past, motivation has been operationalized in various ways, but current definitions typically emphasize the individuals' cognitions (i.e., attributions and goals) and values about learning and school (Eccles, Wigfield, & Schiefele, 1998). Brophy (1987), for example, describes a motivated student as one who values learning and strives for knowledge. Other researchers have advanced definitions of motivation that incorporate the concept of school engagement (i.e., an orientation on the part of a child that precedes and promotes learning and achievement; Fredricks et al., 2004). It may also be possible to construe school engagement in ways that subsume the construct of motivation. Simply by participating in classroom learning activities with peers, for example, children may develop specific perceptions and feelings about those activities which, in turn, affect their desire to engage in them.

A key hypothesis in the school engagement literature is that, for children to profit from schooling, they must do more than simply attend school or be present in classrooms. Rather, according to the school engagement hypothesis, children must engage the classroom environment in ways that promote learning. Research on this hypothesis identifies three forms of school engagement that may be determinants of learning and achievement: cognitive, behavioral, and emotional (see Fredricks et al., 2004).

Cognitive Engagement

Cognitive engagement is typically construed as the level of processing or intellectual effort that students devote to mastering learning tasks, and has been variously conceptualized as psychological investment in learning and skill mastery (Newmann, Wehlage, & Lamborn, 1992; Wehlage, Rutter, Smith, Lesko, & Fernandez, 1989), intentional task-specific thinking (Helme & Clarke, 2001), strategic thinking or learning (e.g., Lee & Anderson, 1993; Meece, Blumenfeld, & Hoyle, 1988), and preference for challenge, flexible problem solving, and positive coping in the face of failure (Connell & Wellborn, 1991). Beyond the debate about definitional considerations, one issue, in particular, complicates the study of cognitive engagement. Because cognitions are not readily observable, cognitive engagement is typically assessed via self-report measures, and children (depending on their ages and developmental levels) may lack the metacognitive abilities to provide accurate reports (Schneider & Pressley, 1997).

Accruing evidence substantiates the premise that cognitive engagement leads to higher levels of achievement (for a review, see Boekaerts, Pintrich, & Zeidner, 2000). For example, findings show that adolescents who effectively utilize cognitive strategies while studying (i.e., organization of material, elaboration and rehearsal) attain higher levels of achievement (Pintrich & DeGroot, 1990). Likewise, it has been reported that academically successful adolescents exhibit a greater degree of self-regulation of knowledge than their less-successful peers (Covington, 2000). In contrast, it has been discovered that low achieving students have difficulty judging their level of prior knowledge about a given task and, thus, often fail to utilize appropriate learning strategies (Borkowski & Thorpe, 1994).

Behavioral Engagement

The concept of behavioral engagement also has been defined in multiple ways. For example, some investigators have proposed that students who take initiative, are responsive, adopt classroom norms, and stay out of trouble are behaviorally engaged (Finn, 1989, 1993). Other investigators have interpreted behavioral engagement to mean that students exhibit constructive and cooperative participation, persistence, and attention in the classroom (Birch & Ladd, 1997; Buhs & Ladd, 2001; Skinner & Belmont, 1993).

Research on behavioral engagement has shown that many of these indicators correlate positively with achievement both concurrently (e.g., Connell, Spencer, & Aber, 1994; Skinner, Wellborn, & Connell, 1990) and prospectively (e.g., Alexander, Entwisle, & Dauber, 1993). Thus, although much more remains to be learned about this construct, there is support for the hypothesis that behavioral engagement (e.g., cooperative and active participation in the classroom) antecedes children's scholastic success in school.

Emotional Engagement

Emotional engagement, traditionally defined as students' attitudes or sentiments toward school, has been operationalized in terms of children's feelings about peers, teachers, schoolwork, or their affective reactions to the classroom or the larger school context (e.g., Ladd, Buhs, & Seid, 2000; Skinner & Belmont, 1993; Skinner et al., 1990; Stipek, 2002). Another, less common construal of emotional engagement has been termed "identification with school," which has been defined as the extent to which children feel that they value and belong in school (Finn, 1989).

This form of engagement, of the three types that have been proposed, has been investigated least because its indicators often have been combined with measures of behavioral or cognitive engagement (e.g., see Connell et al., 1994). As a consequence, it has been difficult for investigators to isolate its predictive contributions to achievement. Available evidence, however, suggests that measures of school identification correlate positively with achievement (e.g., Voelkl, 1997). Moreover, studies conducted with young school children (i.e., kindergartners) have shown that positive school attitudes and sentiments (e.g., liking school) correlate positively with early indicators of behavioral engagement (e.g., cooperative classroom participation) and achievement (e.g., school readiness; Ladd et al., 2000).

Although there is growing support for the engagement hypothesis, much remains to be learned about the social determinants of school engagement (see Fredricks et al. 2004; Ladd, Herald-Brown, & Reiser, 2008; Ladd & Dinella, 2009), and in particular, the role of children's classroom peer relations as antecedents of their cognitive, emotional, and behavioral engagement. In the sections that follow, we consider theory and evidence that reflects on the hypothesis that children's relations with their classmates facilitate, or in some cases impede, their school engagement. Toward this end, we consider the types of peer relationships that develop in classrooms, the processes that tend to occur within these relations (theoretically, or as empirically demonstrated), and the potential bearing that these processes have on children's learning and achievement in the school context.

Classroom Peer Relationships: Important Contributors to School Engagement and Adjustment?

Most of what has been discovered about the antecedents of children's classroom performance points to their cognitive and linguistic skills, their physical-motor skills, and their socioeconomic and ethnic backgrounds. Only recently have researchers systematically explored facets of children's classroom peer relations as predictors of their engagement and adjustment in the school context. This is surprising given that education is, in many respects, a social enterprise. Most modes of instruction require that teachers and students communicate and engage in social interaction. Likewise, educators have become increasingly reliant on peer-mediated activities (e.g., peer collaboration and tutoring, cooperative learning groups) to promote classroom learning and achievement (Furman & Gavin, 1989; Johnson & Johnson, 1998; O'Donnell, 2006).

Fortunately, recent theory and evidence on the interpersonal foundations of learning and achievement have elevated this topic's importance within the educational community (e.g., see Hamre & Pianta, 2001; Ladd, Herald, & Kochel, 2006; Perry & Weinstein, 1998). As a result, greater investigative attention has been devoted to the hypothesis that peer relations in the school context may influence multiple aspects of children's and adolescents' adjustment to school, including their school engagement.

The premise that children's relationships with classmates affect their school engagement represents an important investigative aim because, even though there is a growing body of research on the linkages between peer relationships and academic achievement, the potential impact of peer relationships on motivation has been relatively unexamined (Fredricks et al., 2004; Ryan, 2001). Further, it is conceivable that peers matter most (i.e., it is arguable that peers, as compared to teachers or parents, exert greater influence on children's engagement in school) given that school-aged youth spend the vast majority of their days immersed in a school context in which they are surrounded by and interacting with agemates (Hymel, Comfort, Schonert-Reichl, & McDougall, 1996).

Among the most promising lines of investigation are those predicated on the proposition that children's relationships with classmates immerse them in processes (e.g., participation vs. exclusion, support vs. conflict, receiving assistance vs. being ignored) that affect their ability to adapt to school challenges which, in turn, influences their development and achievement in this context (e.g., level of school engagement; amount of learning, increases or decreases in their sense of worth, academic competence, etc.; see Ladd, 2003, 2005). Because peer relationships bring different processes to bear upon children and confer different provisions, it is likely that they vary in adaptive significance for school-related demands (see Ladd, Kochenderfer, & Coleman, 1997). In the next three sections, the adaptive significance of several types of classroom peer relationships is considered. Within each of these sections we: (a) identify relationship processes that are hypothesized to affect children's motivation in school, and (b) review studies which yield empirical support for or against such processes.

Classroom Peer Acceptance and Rejection

A growing corpus of findings links children's acceptance or rejection by classroom peers with indicators of their school adjustment (see Ladd, 2005). Peer rejection is typically defined as how disliked (relative to how liked) a child is by members of his or her peer group (see Bukowski & Hoza, 1989). Early peer rejection—at school entry—has been shown to predict problems such as negative school attitudes, school avoidance, and underachievement during the first year of schooling and thereafter (Ladd, 1990; Ladd, Birch, & Buhs, 1999; Ladd & Burgess, 2001). Later, in the elementary years, peer acceptance has been linked with loneliness (Parker & Asher, 1993), conduct problems (Ladd, 2006), lower emotional well being (Ladd, 2006), and academic deficits (Ladd et al., 1997). Further, other studies suggest that exposure to classroom peer rejection may have long-term, negative educational consequences. Specifically, peer rejection during the school years has been linked with later-developing school adjustment problems, such as dropping out of school, truancy, and underachievement (see Cairns & Cairns, 1994; Ladd, 2005; Parker & Asher, 1987).

Thus, an important question for peer relations researchers is: How does peer group acceptance/rejection impact children's engagement in school? To date, investigators' attempts to answer this question have been guided by three principal "process" hypotheses. As is illustrated below, each of these hypotheses embodies differing, albeit related assumptions about the means (e.g., direct or intervening pathways of influence) through which peer group rejection affects children's school engagement and/or related aspects of their school adjustment.

Rejection Limits Engagement Opportunities It has been proposed that when peers dislike persons within their group, they tend to act in rejecting ways towards these children (e.g., ignoring, excluding them from activities), and these behaviors become observable indicators of rejection not only for rejected children, but also for the larger peer group (Buhs & Ladd, 2001; Coie, 1990; Hymel, Wagner, & Butler, 1990). A likely consequence is that, the more a child is recognized as rejected, the fewer opportunities he or she is likely to have for social engagement (i.e., interactions with peers). A related hypothesis is that peer rejection impairs children's school performance because, when individuals withdraw from or fail to engage in positive peer relationships, they are deprived of the interpersonal processes (e.g., peer affirmation and support, tutoring or mutual problem solving, being included in learning activities, study groups, etc.) that tend to facilitate learning and achievement (see Buhs et al., 2001; Buhs, Ladd, & Herald, 2006).

Examination of these hypotheses is incomplete, but the evidence obtained thus far has been consistent with researchers' expectations. Extant data show that rejected children often become marginalized from the mainstream of peer activities (Ladd, Price, & Hart, 1990), become disengaged from classroom activities (Buhs & Ladd, 2001), and are excluded from participation by classmates (Buhs et al., 2006). Further, findings from the latter two investigations (i.e., Buhs & Ladd, 2001; Buhs et al., 2006) buttress the contention that exclusion operates as an impediment to children's achievement.

Perhaps the most compelling support for the rejection-limits-engagement hypothesis comes from a recent investigation conducted by Ladd et al. (2008). These investigators traced children's movement in and out of classroom peer rejection across the grade school years and found that regardless of whether children were rejected during the early or later years of grade school, longer periods of rejection were accompanied by lesser growth in classroom participation. The most serious patterns of disengagement were found for children who were continuously rejected throughout grade school. In contrast, children who moved out of rejection and toward acceptance by their classmates were more likely to show gains in classroom participation.

Other data imply that the effects of peer rejection on children's engagement or opportunities for participation in peer activities may be fairly pervasive within the school context. Disliked or rejected children appear to exhibit higher levels of disengagement not only in relatively structured activities that occur in classrooms (e.g., cooperative learning groups; see Furman & Gavin, 1989; Johnson & Johnson, 1998), but also in relatively unstructured activities that occur outside the classroom (e.g., recess, playground periods; see Asher, Rose, & Garbriel, 2001; Ladd, Price, & Hart, 1990). For example, within the context of classroom peer activities (e.g., cooperative learning groups), disliked children are often the last to be chosen by peers for group work, and even when assigned to learning activities by teachers, these children sometimes remain isolated (Blumenfeld, Marx, Soloway, & Krajcik, 1996; Johnson & Johnson, 1981).

Rejection Leads to Negative Perceptions of Self and Peers Another hypothesis that has garnered considerable research attention is that classroom peer rejection affects children's attitudes and beliefs about themselves and others which, in turn, negatively impacts their school engagement or achievement. The importance of this premise is underscored by evidence indicating that children's attitudes and beliefs about themselves are powerful determinants of school success (e.g., Bandura, Barbaranelli, Caprara, & Pastorelli, 1996; Grolnick & Slowiaczek, 1994; Pierson & Connell, 1992; Zimmerman & Bandura, 1994). For example, Guay, Boivin, and Hodges (1999) found that children who perceived themselves as less academically competent had less growth in achievement over a 3-year period.

Investigators interested in this hypothesis have tended to study how peer group rejection is associated with specific aspects of children's social cognitions, including cognitive representations of the self and others (McDowell, Parke, & Spitzer, 2002). Another related domain of investigation has been focused on how children's perceptions of self and peers mediate their psychological and school adjustment (e.g., Andrews, Herald, & Ladd, 2005; Ladd & Troop-Gordon, 2003).

Evidence that reflects on these hypotheses indicates that grade-school children's exposure to peer group rejection was predictive of their propensity to see themselves as unlikable by others and as less competent socially and academically (Boivin & Begin, 1989; Boivin & Hymel, 1997). Further, there is some evidence that supports the hypothesis that 6- and 7-year-olds' belief systems (e.g., how they view themselves and others) are directly related to their adjustment in school (e.g., Betts & Rotenberg, 2007). For example, Betts and Rotenberg (2007) found that young grade-schoolers who viewed their peers as untrustworthy were less well adjusted in the classroom than were those who thought peers were generally trustworthy. These researchers also found that peer acceptance mediated the relationship between viewing peers as trustworthy and later adjustment such that children who viewed peers as untrustworthy tended to be less accepted by classmates and less well adjusted in the classroom.

Thus, research lends support for the idea that classroom peer rejection negatively affects children's perceptions of themselves and others, and these perceptions interfere with children's school engagement and adjustment. Evidence supports the notion that peer rejection impacts how children view their social world and that having a skewed perception of others may lead to negative consequences in the academic realm.

Rejection has Brain Consequences Very recently, researchers have begun to examine the neurobiology of peer rejection and have demonstrated that the pain a person experiences in negative social situations, such as peer rejection, elicits brain reactions similar to those activated when physical pain is encountered (Vaillancourt, Clinton, McDougall, Schmidt, & Hymel, in press). Vaillancourt and colleagues suggest that peer relations researchers should more carefully examine the role of biological influences (e.g., brain electrocortical activity, endocrinology, etc.) in the relation between peer rejection and school engagement. These researchers postulate that perhaps the reason rejected children do poorly in school is that they experience temporary or prolonged physiological states that interfere with learning. Although this hypothesis remains largely uninvestigated, it serves to illuminate another possible avenue through which classroom peer group rejection may influence children's school engagement and adjustment. It may be the case that peer group rejection has physiological as well as social and psychological effects on children.

Taken together, this evidence suggests that peer group rejection is an adverse classroom relationship that has consequences for children's motivation and engagement in school. Thus far, investigative efforts have been concentrated on three potential processes—limited engagement opportunities, social cognitive distortions, and neurobiological consequences—that may help to explain how rejection impacts children's engagement in school.

Besides peer group acceptance and rejection, most children participate in other types of peer relationships in classrooms. Considered within the next section is the role of classroom friendships in children's school engagement and adjustment.

Classroom Friendships

Establishing dyadic relationships—such as one or more friendships—with classmates represents another type of peer relationship that many, if not most, children develop in school. As early as preschool and kindergarten (see Howes, 1988; Ladd, 1988; Ladd, Price, & Hart, 1990), during grade school (see Berndt, & Hoyle, 1985; Ladd, 1983), and throughout the later school years (see Berndt, 1982; Hartup & Stevens, 1997), youth develop preferences for particular classmates, and they associate with these persons more frequently than they do with others. Sometimes these associations develop into friendships. Friendships differ from children's peer *group* relations (e.g., peer group acceptance, rejection) because they occur between *pairs* (i.e., dyads) of children, are created by mutual consent, and exist only as long as both participants choose to be in the relationship. This is in contrast to other types of peer relations that may be unilaterally defined and imposed on children by members of their group (e.g., peer group rejection).

Investigators have studied several aspects of classroom friendships including children's participation in a close friendship, the number of mutual friends they have in their classrooms, the duration of these relationships, and features that reflect the quality of a friendship (see Ladd, 2005). Another key objective has been to identify the types of processes that occur in friendships that influence children's school engagement and achievement. Included among the process hypotheses that researchers have investigated are premises about the effects of positive dynamics (e.g., the exchange of emotional and physical support between friends) and negative dynamics (e.g., the occurrence of conflict, rivalry, betrayal between friends). At present, there is a small but growing body of evidence linking one or more facets of friendship to children's school engagement.

Friendships Offer Emotional, Instrumental, and Physical Support One of the guiding premises in research on children's friendships has been that this form of relationship has the potential to provide children with assistance (e.g., help with social or scholastic problems) and a sense of emotional and/or physical security (Wentzel, 1998). It has also been argued that, in the school context, these forms of support may play an important role in promoting and sustaining children's classroom participation and other forms of school engagement (Berndt, Hawkins, & Jiao, 1999; Ladd, Kochenderfer, & Coleman, 1996).

Studies of classroom friendships provide evidence that is largely consistent with these assertions. Investigators have found that, as young children enter school, those who maintain preexisting friendships or form new friendships in their classrooms tend to develop favorable school perceptions and perform better academically than peers with fewer friends (Ladd, 1990). Ladd et al. (1996) detected variability in the quality of the friendships that children formed as they entered school and found that children who saw their friendships as offering higher levels of support and instrumental aid tended to view their classrooms as supportive interpersonal environments. Similarly, Wentzel (1998) found that children who felt supported by peers were more emotionally secure and engaged in the academic environment. The supportive nature of friends may also take a physical form. For example, children with friends are more likely than their friendless counterparts to report feeling physically safe and free from harassment in their school environment (Hodges, Boivin, Vitaro, & Bukowski, 1999).

A second theoretical assumption is that, as children progress through grade school, friendship status (i.e., the presence or absence of friends) and friendship features (e.g., friendship quality, processes) influence children's psychological adjustment. Findings from a study conducted with third- through fifth-graders showed that children with supportive friends felt less lonely in school (Parker & Asher, 1993). Along these lines, other researchers have found that young adolescents without friends are more lonely and depressed (Nangle, Erdley, Newman, Mason, & Carpenter, 2003) than those with friends. Further evidence indicates that young adolescents who have friends reported higher levels of emotional well-being (Berndt & Keefe, 1995) and that emotional well-being has been linked to positive classroom behavior and academic achievement (Connell

& Wellborn, 1991; Wentzel, 1998; Wentzel & McNamara, 1999). These investigations, when considered in the context of evidence that internalizing difficulties tend to interfere with several aspects of classroom engagement (e.g., participation), advance the argument that friendship (and subsequent emotional well-being) may serve as an impetus for the development or maintenance of motivation in school.

Friendships Are a Source of Conflict and Rivalry As investigators probed the features of children's friendships, it became apparent that not all of the processes that transpire between friends are supportive or positive. In studies where youth have been asked about the dynamics of their friendships, reports of interactions involving conflict, rivalry, and betrayal were not uncommon, and interactions of this type were mentioned by children and adolescents alike (e.g., see Berndt, 1986; Ladd et al., 1996; Parker & Asher, 1993; Youniss, 1980).

Only a few investigators have explored the relation between conflict processes in classroom friendships and children's school adjustment. The evidence assembled thus far implies that children who experience higher levels of discord in classroom friendships are at greater risk for school maladjustment, as reflected by indicators such as negative school attitudes, disaffection during the school day, and classroom disruptiveness. In one study conducted with kindergartners, it was discovered that children who reported higher levels of conflict in their classroom friendships were less prone to like school or experience positive emotions during the school day than children who experienced lesser conflict in their classroom friendships (Ladd et al., 1996). In studies conducted with adolescents, Berndt and colleagues (Berndt & Keefe, 1995; Berndt & Miller, 1993, as cited in Berndt, 1996) found that negative interactions between friends were associated with classroom disruptiveness. When this relation was examined longitudinally, it was discovered that participation in conflict-ridden friendships anteceded gains in disruptiveness over the course of a school year (Berndt & Keefe, 1995).

Friends Model Social Behavior Recently, researchers have argued that friends can be motivators of school success by modeling socially acceptable behavior (Berndt et al., 1999). There is some empirical evidence to corroborate this claim. For example, it has been found that children and preadolescents with friends engage in positive social interactions (Azmitia & Montgomery, 1993) and prosocial behaviors (McNamara-Barry & Wentzel, 2006) with greater frequency than their friendless counterparts. One possible explanation for these findings is that, in their attempt to develop intimacy (a feature vital to the establishment of close friendships; Hartup, 1996), children may inadvertently emulate (i.e., model) their friends' propensity to engage others in positive social interactions. It is conceivable that the prosocial behaviors associated with such positive social exchanges (e.g., sharing, helping, reciprocity) may help cultivate children's motivation in the classroom.

Or, it is possible that modeling may be more intentional, given the premise that children tend to align themselves with goals—academic or otherwise—that coincide with those of their friends. For example, in one study, preadolescents who viewed their friends as having high academic goals behaved in ways that helped promote their own academic achievement (Wentzel, Filisetti, & Looney, 2007). Thus, modeling represents one potential way in which friendship facilitates children's school engagement. Together these studies suggest that, in addition to peer group acceptance, the status and features of children's friendships are potential antecedents of school engagement.

A third relationship—peer victimization—has further implications for children's school adjustment. As explicated in the next section, victimization by schoolmates may have serious consequences for children's school engagement.

Peer Victimization

Findings indicate that many children encounter peer abuse as they enter school and progress through the primary grades, and these results have encouraged researchers to examine peer victimization as an antecedent of many forms of school maladjustment, including classroom disengagement. Although early findings characterized victimized children as emotionally anxious, physically weak, socially isolated, and low in self-esteem (Olweus, 1978, 1984), recent evidence implies that children who are frequently harassed by peers can be differentiated into two behavioral subtypes—*nonaggressive victims* and *aggressive victims* (i.e., also called passive or "provocative" victims, respectively; see Olweus, 1978). Empirically, more evidence has been gathered on passive than aggressive victims because more children belonging to the former subtype tend to be identified in research samples (Ladd & Kochenderfer-Ladd, 1998, 2001; Schwartz, Dodge, Pettit, & Bates, 1997; Schwartz, Proctor, & Chien, 2001). Findings suggest that whereas nonaggressive victims tend to exhibit solitary, reticent, and submissive behaviors (Coplan, Rubin, Fox, Calkins, & Stewart, 1994; Ladd & Kochenderfer-Ladd, 1998; Rubin, Burgess, & Hastings, 2002; Schwartz, Dodge, & Coie, 1993), aggressive victims more often display conduct problems and manifest over-reactive, negative emotional states (e.g., anger, impulsivity, irritability, dysregulated affect; see Kumpulainen et al., 1998; Perry, Hodges, & Egan, 2001; Schwartz, 2000; Schwartz et al., 1997; Schwartz, Proctor, & Chien, 2001).

Efforts to identify and study victimized children in school contexts have expanded exponentially in recent years, due to educators' and parents' concerns about school violence and children's safety in school (see Ladd, 2005). Accruing evidence suggests that peer harassment is a relatively age-invariant phenomena, occurring at all levels of schooling, including the earliest school years (e.g., kindergarten and the primary grades; see Kochenderfer-Ladd & Wardrop, 2001; Ladd & Kochenderfer-Ladd, 2002). Moreover, school-based harassment and victimization has been linked with many forms of school maladjustment, including absenteeism, low GPA, poor academic readiness and school avoidance (e.g., Juvonen, Nishina, & Graham, 2000; Kochenderfer & Ladd, 1996; Ladd et al., 1997; Lopez & DuBois, 2005; Schwartz, Gorman, Nakamoto, & Toblin, 2005).

In light of these findings, researchers have begun to generate process hypotheses to account for the relations observed between peer victimization and school disengagement. Of these perspectives, the two that follow have received the most empirical attention to date.

Peer Victimization Promotes Poor Mental Health It has been proposed that peer victimization produces psychological distress in children, and that the symptoms or dysfunctions that develop from these stressors are responsible for maladjustment in the school context. Thus, a key assumption within this process hypothesis is that the psychological problems that children develop as a result of peer victimization become the proximal causes of school disengagement.

The evidence gathered to address this hypothesis, although scant, has largely been consistent with researchers' expectations. For example, Ladd et al. (1997) found that young children who were exposed to high levels of peer victimization displayed increases in school avoidance and loneliness in school. It was reasoned that frequent harassment causes children to become preoccupied with feelings of social alienation and safety concerns to the extent that they have difficulty attending to school tasks, begin to dislike school, or seek to avoid school altogether. More recently, Schwartz et al. (2005) reported that, for a sample of third and fourth graders, victimization predicted increases in depression, which, in turn, forecasted gains in academic difficulties (i.e., GPA, achievement test scores) over a one year period. Consistent with these findings, evidence from two studies of middle school children suggest that the link between self-reported victimization and school adjustment (i.e., GPA, absenteeism) is mediated by psychological symptoms (e.g., self-worth, loneliness, depression; Juvonen et al., 2000; Lopez & DuBois, 2005). Taken together, the results of these studies suggest that victims of peer harassment are at high risk for school maladjustment and that psychological difficulties represent one mechanism underlying the relation between peer victimization and school maladjustment.

Peer Victimization Promotes Poor Physical Health Efforts to explicate the processes underlying the relations between peer victimization and school-related problems have primarily been devoted to examining the mediating role of various mental health difficulties. Alternate mechanisms have been proposed and investigated with comparatively less frequency but, nevertheless, warrant attention. For example, in recent years, investigators have begun to examine physical health as a process underlying the link between peer victimization and academic functioning. Results from one study indicated that the combination of peer victimization and chronic abdominal pain was predictive of poor academic competence (i.e., decreased cooperation, assertion, and self-control in the classroom setting; Greco, Freeman, & Dufton, 2006). Another investigation revealed that peer victimization forecasted gains in physical and psychological health problems, which, in turn, predicted school functioning (e.g., absences, poor GPA; Nishina, Juvonen, & Witkow, 2005). These findings imply that victimization has the potential to both provoke and exacerbate physical ailments and health-related behaviors that may detract from children's engagement in learning and achievement in school.

Overall, there is a growing support for the premises that classroom peer rejection, friendships and peer victimization bring different processes to bear upon children and have differing effects on their school adjustment. Because most children simultaneously participate in multiple forms of peer relationship within classrooms, it becomes important to consider the conjoint contributions of multiple forms of relationship to children's school engagement and adjustment.

Contributions of Multiple Classroom Relationships

In recent years, research on individual classroom relationships has been supplemented by studies in which investigators have gathered data on multiple relationships and examined the relative contributions of each relationship to children's school adjustment. Initial efforts to investigate differential relationship contributions were focused on peer rejection and victimization (see Perry, Kusel, & Perry, 1988) and peer rejection and friendship (Parker & Asher, 1993; Vandell & Hembree, 1994). In recent years, investigators have examined each of the three principal types of peer relationships that occur in school or classroom contexts (e.g., peer group rejection, friendships, and peer victimization; e.g., Ladd et al., 1997; 2003b).

Peer Group Rejection and Victimization The longstanding presumption that peer rejection and victimization are partially distinct forms of relationship (see Perry et al., 1988; Bukowski & Sippola, 2001) has been an impetus for investigations that are designed to test the hypothesis that these two forms of relationship contribute differentially to various forms of school maladjustment, including academic disengagement. Results from at least two studies lend support to this hypothesis. First, Buhs and Ladd (2001) found that many rejected elementary-aged children were also victimized by classmates, and that children who were maltreated eventually became less engaged in classroom activities and fell behind in their schoolwork. In a more recent study, Buhs and colleagues (2006) expanded upon these findings by showing that chronic peer abuse mediated the link between peer rejection and growth in school avoidance.

Together, findings suggest that peer group rejection forecasts gains in victimization, which, in turn, interferes with children's scholastic progress. Thus, extant evidence appears to suggest that rejection makes children more vulnerable to peer victimization, and that victimization (following exposure to rejection) becomes a distinct predictor (mediator) of increments in academic disengagement.

Peer Group Acceptance/Rejection and Friendship This line of inquiry has also been based on the premise that different relational experiences offer children distinct resources (e.g., provisions) or impediments (e.g., barriers, stressors) that impinge on their school adjustment. In this case, however, researchers have explored the hypothesis that classroom friendships and peer group acceptance make distinct contributions to children's scholastic engagement and progress. On the one hand, it has been reasoned that friendship features such as intimacy, validation and self-disclosure contribute to the development of children's self-esteem, which promotes initiative and engagement in the classroom. On the other hand, peer group acceptance has the potential to increase children's sense of inclusion and, thereby, enhance children's opportunities for engagement in academic tasks.

Much of the evidence obtained corroborates this logic. For example, it has been discovered that classroom friendship and peer acceptance uniquely predict changes in young children's school perceptions, school avoidance, and academic performance (Ladd, 1990). Likewise, Ladd et al. (1997) reported that classroom peer acceptance accounted for changes in kindergartners' classroom involvement and academic progress that could not be attributed to other relational predictors (i.e., victimization, friendship). Investigations of older grade-schoolers have yielded findings consistent with those obtained by Ladd and colleagues (1990, 1997; see also Wentzel & Caldwell, 1997). For example, Vandell and Hembree (1994) found that, even after controlling for friendships and family characteristics, children who were rejected by peers were prone to develop scholastic difficulties, as reflected in a composite measure containing indicators of children's grades, achievement, and intelligence.

This line of work extends earlier investigations in two key ways. First, the findings are consistent with the proposition that each form of relationship makes unique contributions to children's early scholastic adjustment, which insinuates that differing relational systems (e.g., peer acceptance, friendship) confer upon children some nonshared resources or impediments. Second, evidence indicates that peer group acceptance accounts for gains in children's academic adjustment that can not be attributed to friendship, which implies that relationships at the level of the peer group (i.e., peer group acceptance), as compared to dyadic relationships (i.e., friendship), may have greater implications for children's scholastic adaptation.

Peer Group Rejection, Friendship, and Victimization It has been rare for researchers to examine the contributions of peer group rejection, friendship and peer victimization to academic engagement within a single investigation. A few studies, though, offer compelling evidence that relationships vary in the extent to which they predict particular academic outcomes.

In one such study, the contributions of several types of peer relationships were examined after adjusting for shared predictive linkages, and some forms of relationship were found to be better predictors of children's school adjustment than others (Ladd et al., 1997). On the one hand, peer victimization predicted gains in children's school avoidance and loneliness in school, above and beyond associations that were attributable to friendship and peer group acceptance. On the other hand, peer group acceptance uniquely predicted improvements in children's achievement

Overall, these findings are consistent with the view that peer relationships are specialized in the types of resources or constraints they create for children (cf. Furman & Gavin, 1989; Ladd et al., 1997). More studies are needed to further clarify the unique and conjoint contributions of children's peer relationships to their subsequent engagement in school.

Empirical Status of Current Hypotheses and Future Research Directions

As has been illustrated in this review, theory and research point to a range of processes that may account for the association between peer relationships and school engagement. Moreover, in many cases, the implied linkages between peer relationships and school engagement tend to be circuitous (e.g., mediated through other intervening variables) rather than direct.

Given that much of the research on classroom peer processes, potential mediating mechanisms, and children's school engagement is at an early stage, it is important to appraise the extant knowledge base (i.e., consolidate what has been learned thus far), identify major limitations, and consider the types of studies and forms of evidence that are needed to substantiate (or falsify) and extend current hypotheses. Accordingly, our goals in the sections that follow are to: (a) review and evaluate the state of the evidence concerning the processes that have been implicated in the link between each form of peer relationship and school engagement, (b) specify relevant theoretical, methodological, and analytic challenges, and (c) consider some of the educational implications of extant findings.

Classroom Peer Group Acceptance and Rejection

There has been increasing empirical support for the hypothesis that classroom peer rejection limits or interferes with children's school engagement. Three relatively distinct "process hypotheses" have been proffered as potential explanations for this linkage.

Rejection Creates Interpersonal Barriers and Adverse Experiences that Interfere with School Engagement The first of these hypotheses is that, in classrooms, rejection by one's peers operates as an interpersonal barrier that prevents individuals (rejected children) from fully participating in classroom activities. Empirically, what has been established thus far is that rejected children often do exhibit lower levels of school engagement and classroom participation, and that children who suffer longer periods of rejection are at even greater risk for such outcomes. Unfortunately, however, evidence that would elucidate how this occurs—that is, shed light on the nature of the barriers that rejection creates for children, and how such barriers operate as detriments to learning and achievement, is currently in short supply.

Progress toward a better understanding of these relations is aided by the fact that researchers have identified several process hypotheses that warrant investigation. In nearly every case, however, these hypotheses remain theoretically underdeveloped and underspecified—that is, there is little conceptual specificity about the types of "barriers" that rejection creates for children, and how these barriers impact school engagement. Consider, for example, the premise that rejection signals to classmates that rejectees should be avoided, or more generally, sends the message that associating with rejected children will come at some "cost" to those who do so. It has yet to be articulated how this message is communicated, what children infer as costs when they realize that a peer is disliked, and what types of costs are sufficiently powerful to deter classmates from interacting or associating with rejected children.

Similarly, the hypothesis that peers' awareness of a child's rejected status serves as a trigger for abuse or maltreatment remains underspecified, even though there has been some attempt to link rejection with subsequent peer maltreatment (e.g., exclusion, victimization; see Buhs & Ladd, 2001; Buhs et al., 2006). In this case, we need to understand how, and under what conditions, consensual disliking in peer groups motivates children to perpetrate harsh or abusive behavior against classmates. While the logic of this hypothesis may seem obvious, the explicit social-psychological linkages between peer group attitudes and the ensuing treatment of disliked individuals have not been fully articulated for contexts such as classrooms (cf., Bukowski & Sippola, 2001).

Rejection Creates Self- and Interpersonal Perceptions that Hinder School Engagement The second "process hypothesis" is that rejection by one's classmates creates experiences that demean children's perceptions of self and others, and that such perceptions undermine children's school engagement and achievement. Of the various sub-premises that are embedded in this hypothesis, the assertion that negative *self* perceptions correlate with school disengagement and underachievement has received the most empirical support (e.g., see Marsh & Hau, 2003; Wigfield & Karpathian, 1991). There has been lesser corroboration of the tenet that peer group rejection causes children to see themselves and their classmates negatively. Of these two premises, there has been greater substantiation of the contention that rejection causes children to develop negative views of themselves or their abilities (Andrews et al., 2005; Boivin & Begin, 1989). However, much less is known about whether peer group rejection negatively skews children's perceptions of their classmates, and whether children who do develop negative perceptions of their classmates tend to become less engaged in classroom activities or schooling. Preliminary evidence suggests that children who are rejected, as compared to those who are accepted by classmates, do develop less positive views of their classmates (Andrews et al., 2005; Slutzky & Ladd, 2005), but whether such trajectories are associated with children's school engagement remains unclear.

Related to this investigative challenge is the theoretical task of specifying the types of peer perceptions that might operate as positive or negative influences on children's school engagement (e.g., participation in classroom activities), and the processes that might be responsible for such relations. Among the facets of children's peer perceptions that warrant further investigation are the several constructs that have garnered recent research attention (e.g., perceptions of peers' trustworthiness; supportiveness, inclinations to help vs. harm schoolmates, etc.; see Andrews et al., 2005; Betts & Rotenberg, 2007; Slutzky & Ladd, 2005). Unfortunately, however, these findings offer limited insight into how rejected children construe their classmates, and they say little or nothing about whether these perceptions predict rejected children's participation in the school environment, or mediate the link between classroom peer rejection and school engagement. This kind of knowledge, it seems, will require a stronger investment (theoretical and empirical) in research that examines peer perceptions as potential determinants of children's school engagement.

Rejection Activates Brain Mechanisms or Processes that Interfere with Learning and School Engagement The third process hypothesis is that rejection by one's classmates activates brain mechanisms or processes that make it difficult for children to engage in and learn from school-related activities. Clearly, of the premises posited as process explanations for the observed relations between classroom peer rejection and children's school performance, this is the most novel and least investigated. All of the caveats, criticisms, and recommendations raised in connection with the foregoing premises apply here as well.

A further assumption that is inherent within all of these process hypotheses is that rejection sets in motion certain intervening processes (e.g., rejection-induced peer avoidance, exclusion; altered self- or peer perceptions, physiological changes), all of which have the effect of undermining children's engagement and learning in school. Unfortunately, the conceptual explanations offered for how these intervening processes deter children's school engagement and achievement lack precision, or are poorly specified. In particular, many of the concepts that are included in these process hypotheses require greater theoretical elaboration.

As a starting point for hypothesis generation and testing, it might be of benefit to conduct descriptive research, or consider existing accounts of rejected children's peer interactions and experiences within classrooms or other types of school contexts (e.g., see Asher, Rose, & Gabriel, 2001). The information provided in these empirical accounts might aid hypothesis generation and inform critical research tasks such as model specification and development. For example, such accounts may help researchers discern whether (and to what extent) rejected children have experiences that: (a) function as interpersonal barriers to classroom participation, (b) color their perceptions of self and others, and (c) create emotional and physiological states or conditions that are likely to interfere with learning.

Classroom Friendships

Support has also been obtained for the hypothesis that classroom friendships are instrumental in shaping children's feelings about school and the nature of their participation in the school context. Insight into how classroom friendships might produce such effects has been advanced by the investigation of three process hypotheses, each of which has received some empirical substantiation.

Friendships as Resources that Support School Engagement and Achievement One of these process hypotheses characterizes friendship as an interpersonal resource—that is, a form of relationship that confers upon children certain "provisions" that help them adapt or adjust to school. Researchers who have worked from this perspective have considered three principal provisions by postulating that children may derive assistance, emotional support, and physical protection from their participation in classroom friendships.

As plausible as these premises are, they remain largely unsubstantiated because there has been little attempt to monitor the interactions of classroom friends to determine whether these or other resources are in fact exchanged. Currently, what is known about friends-as-resources in classrooms largely comes from efforts to study one partner's perceptions. That is, researchers have identified classmates who are friends and then asked one member of the relationship to report on the features of the friendship (i.e., as they see it; e.g., see Ladd et al., 1996; Parker & Asher, 1993). What these data tell is that many children think (perceive) that they are receiving assistance, support, or some other provision (e.g., affirmation, companionship) from their classroom friends, and that some children report higher levels of such provisions than others. For example, Parker and Asher found that, although rejected children reported receiving resources from their classroom friends, their estimations of the quality of specific friendship provisions were not as positive as those of nonrejected children.

As interesting as these findings are, they don't provide direct or unequivocal support for the friendship-as-resource hypothesis because these data are filtered through only one partner's perceptions. Until more direct and dyadic methods of assessment are utilized, insight into how friendships function in classrooms will remain limited. Important investigative priorities include examining how often children receive specific types of resources from their classroom friends, how mutual these exchange processes are, and whether the quality of the resources obtained are any better than what might be received from nonfriend classmates.

Another shortcoming is that current findings offer little insight into the contributions of particular friendship processes (e.g., instrumental vs. emotional support) to children's school engagement and performance. It is quite possible that friends regularly support and protect each other during the course of a school day, that these exchanges tend to be reciprocal within relationships, and that the receipt of such provisions empowers both members of the relationship to do well in school. It is also conceivable that classroom friends exchange other types of resources—provisions other than those hypothesized by researchers—that are important for children's school adjustment. Unfortunately, we cannot know whether our current suppositions about friendships as resources in the classroom are complete or valid, nor can we gauge the impact of these resources on children's school performance, until we conduct a much more extensive and encompassing analysis of the interactions that occur between friends versus nonfriends in everyday classroom environments.

Friendships as Stressors that Interfere with School Engagement and Achievement Rather than an interpersonal resource, the second process hypothesis depicts classroom friendships as a relationship that can distract children from productive engagement in schoolwork, or interfere with their participation in scholastic activities. It has long been known that friends quarrel (see Green, 1933), and it has been established that conflict in friendships can be stressful for children and disruptive of friendship satisfaction and stability (Ladd et al., 1996; Youniss, 1980). Thus, it is not surprising that processes such as conflict, rivalry, and betrayal—to the extent that they occur between friends in classrooms—have been linked with children's school adjustment problems.

Here again, however, knowledge about the friends-as-stressors hypothesis is incomplete because exemplary processes largely have been studied via one partner's perceptions rather than through observations of friends' dyadic interactions. With few exceptions (e.g., see Green, 1933), it has been rare for investigators to observe actual conflicts between friends in classroom settings either for the purpose of describing such interactions (e.g., frequency, intensity, mutuality of conflicts, etc.) or understanding how such processes are related to children's scholastic performance. Unless we supplement findings from studies of friends' perceptions with this kind of research, it will not be possible to achieve an accurate rendering of the types of discord that occur between friends in classrooms, or a fuller understanding of the role these interactions play in children's school engagement.

Friends as Models for School Engagement and Achievement The third process hypothesis portrays classroom friends as persons that children may choose to emulate. The premise that children imitate *friends* in their classrooms or schools is the least well researched of the three process hypotheses but one that clearly warrants further attention.

The premise that children imitate agemates, rather than classroom friends specifically, has been well substantiated. Early studies of observational learning indicated that children imitate many types of peer behaviors, including both positive (e.g., prosocial acts; see Cooke & Apolloni, 1976) and negative actions (e.g., aggression; see Bandura, Ross, & Ross, 1963). Also substantiated was the hypothesis that children are selective about the types of peers they imitate; findings showed that children and adolescents were most likely to emulate same-age and same-gender peers, dominant members of their peer group, and peers who were rewarded rather than punished for their actions (for reviews, see Ladd, 2007; Perry & Bussey, 1984).

Newer evidence suggests that support for the selective imitation hypothesis extends to peers that children and adolescents admire, respect, or wish to befriend in the school context (see Ladd, 2007). Existing findings have been interpreted to mean that children imitate friends' school-related behaviors and goals, and these actions and attitudes have the effect of encouraging or discouraging their participation in scholastic activities. The implication is that friends positively influence children's school engagement when they value schoolwork and participate willingly in classroom activities, but have the opposite effect when they disparage school and withdraw or rebel against the academic milieu.

Although it seems likely that these premises contain some truth, neither as of yet, has been convincingly substantiated. Evidence indicating that children's scholastic goals or classroom behaviors match those of a friend does not necessarily mean that they acquired them by imitating the friend. Children with similar aspirations and behavioral propensities may gravitate toward each other in school because they have attributes in common, or children may make friends with like-minded or like-acting peers because they are often placed together (deliberately or inadvertently) by school personnel (e.g., for academic tracking, reading groups, detentions, etc.).

Another challenge to this inference is the fact that children often have more than one school friend or are embedded in larger friendship networks, and it is likely that multiple friends or members of friendship groups differ in their school-related goals and behaviors. If this is the case, then children may be exposed to more than one model, and it is unclear how multiple and possibly discrepant friendship models might influence children's school engagement. Proving this hypothesis is also complicated by the fact that friendships are ongoing, and with the passage of time, friends have the opportunity to influence each other. As a result, the process by which children come to resemble their friends on school-related goals and behaviors may be one of reciprocal rather than unidirectional influence. It may be less the case that children imitate their friends than it is that friends' reciprocally influence each other's feelings and behaviors toward school.

If children's or adolescents' friends are members of larger peer networks, then the peer relationships they are exposed to may be influential at the level of the dyad *and* the group (Brown, 1989). That is, it is plausible that a child's academic motivation is influenced not only by the friend with whom the child most often interacts but, also, by an entire peer network (i.e., a network of peers who are also the child's friends, or a network of peers in which the child's friend is a member). It appears, for example, that children's membership in a social group facilitates positive school adaptation (e.g., high GPA; Wentzel & Caldwell, 1997), perhaps because positive socialization provides an ideal context for academic growth (Kindermann, 1993) or because children are likely to conform to norms (e.g., school engagement) espoused by their peer group (Brown, 1989). Although provocative, this premise has rarely been empirically examined and so it is not entirely clear whether social networks (of friends, or in which a friend is embedded) promote academic success or, conversely, whether "birds of a feather flock together" (i.e., youth with positive orientations toward school are drawn to one another, which results in the formation of cohesive groups of academically inclined children). This line of work, and elaborations and qualifications of the friends-as-models hypothesis, warrant attention in future studies.

Classroom Peer Victimization

The experience of being harassed or abused by schoolmates has been implicated as a precipitant of several forms of school disengagement and maladjustment and, thus far, efforts to account for these relations have focused on two process hypotheses. Both of these hypotheses imply that victimization negatively impacts children's health (mental or physical) and that ensuing forms of illness prevent children from fully or productively participating in school activities. Although the evidence obtained thus far has shed some light on these processes, a number of important questions remain.

Peer Victimization Promotes Poor Mental Health Extant evidence provides some support for hypothesis that victimization's effects on school adjustment are mediated through the development of mental health problems, particularly specific types of internalizing symptoms (i.e., depression, self-esteem, loneliness). For example, it has been shown that victimization is associated with depression, anxiety, and low self-esteem which, in turn, are associated with problems such as school disengagement and avoidance. Even though these findings are important, they offer limited insight into how victimization provokes psychological dysfunction and, moreover, how psychological dysfunction impedes academic engagement.

Progress toward an understanding of these relations has been impaired by underspecified and largely unexamined theoretical models. Consider, for example, the premise that children's exposure to negative peer experiences (i.e., peer victimization) decreases their opportunities for participation in interpersonal relations, which, in turn, prohibits a sense of belonging (Baumeister & Leary, 1995). An unmet need for belonging, which is acquired by most children through their engagement in multiple close peer relationships, presumably generates internalizing difficulties (e.g., depression, loneliness), which interfere with children's scholastic progress. This hypothesis is plausible but raises several questions. For example, what is it about victimization that decreases children's opportunities for interpersonal relations? Is it that peers shun victims for fear of also being targeted by bullies, or is it that peers do not find victimized youth likable? Moreover, why do internalizing difficulties interfere with academic success? Are youth with internalizing symptoms annoying and therefore ostracized during collaborative classroom activities, or, rather, do internalizing problems function to decrease children's drive to engage and achieve? This "belongingness hypothesis" is provocative but it is somewhat underdeveloped and has yet to be empirically validated.

Peer Victimization Promotes Poor Physical Health It has been rare for researchers to investigate the second process hypothesis—that peer victimization contributes to declines in physical health, which, in turn, provoke school difficulties—but this premise warrants further attention. Thus far, inquiries on these topics suggest that victims, as compared to nonvictims, are more likely to report somatic complaints (e.g., headache, stomachache, sore throat; Rigby, 1998). Furthermore, somatic symptoms and school related difficulties appear to be closely linked (Bernstein et al., 1997; Torsheim & Wold, 2001). These studies, although they do not establish causal relations, are consistent with the hypothesis that peer victimization and physical health—and physical health and academic difficulties—are interconnected. At least two investigations have employed a process-oriented approach as a means for examining the relation between peer victimization, physical health and academic achievement (Greco et al., 2006; Nishina et al., 2005). Together, these studies imply that physical health complaints play a role in the link between peer victimization and school success.

Unless, however, it is possible to shed light on several specific questions, it will be difficult to fully understand how victimization and physical health operate to bring about academic difficulties. For example, the processes through which somatic symptoms impede school success (e.g., absences from school) have yet to be understood. Moreover, it is unknown whether victimization provokes the onset of perceived or actual (i.e., diagnosed) physical symptoms and whether the former or latter is more likely to precipitate school difficulties. Future, process-oriented studies are needed to illuminate the means through which health problems (mental and physical) mediate the association between peer victimization and academic functioning.

Theoretical, Methodological, and Analytic Challenges

Even though the evidence reviewed thus far tends to corroborate the premise that classroom peer relations influence children's motivation and school engagement, it is also clear that this tenet requires further theoretical elaboration and empirical substantiation. Conceptually, more refined investigative models are needed. School engagement is a multifaceted construct, and some forms of engagement have been better investigated than others (see Ladd & Dinella, 2009). Likewise, children's classroom peer relations are complex and multifaceted, and there has been a propensity to investigate them separately rather than multiply or as simultaneously occurring forms of social relations. For example, it is not uncommon for children who have poor classroom peer relations to experience multiple peer adversities (Kochel, McConnell, & Ladd, 2007; Salmivalli & Isaacs, 2005) but little is known about how combinations of relationships or interpersonal experiences are associated with children's motivational or school engagement trajectories. Evidence also hints at the possibility that particular types of positive classroom peer relationship (e.g., friendships) might compensate for the effects of negative ones (e.g., peer group rejection). Parker and Asher (1993), for example, found that rejected children sometimes have supportive friends in the classroom. However, the consequences of these and other types of relational contingencies for school engagement remain to be explicated.

To address these shortcomings, it will be important to investigate when and how differing types of interpersonal processes and relations emerge in classrooms, how early- versus later-emerging relational developments shape short- and long-term engagement trajectories, and whether the observed relations or trajectories differ by gender and change in strength or direction across ages, grades, or transitions in schooling. Thus, in the near future, it will be important for investigators to: (a) construct richer characterizations of the types and timing of peer processes that occur in classrooms (e.g., the development and course of peer interactions; relationships; social roles, positions, or statuses; group dynamics; children's perceptions of classroom interpersonal and relational experiences, etc.), (b) create more detailed depictions of how these interpersonal processes and relations differ by gender, change with age, or are transformed by schooling (developmental process models), and (c) derive more nuanced and testable hypotheses about how classroom interpersonal processes and relations affect children's psychological states (e.g., motivation, attitudes toward school, etc.), behaviors, and learning/achievement in school.

Increments in the sophistication of developmental models should be accompanied by greater methodological and data-analytic rigor, including stronger approaches to model specification and evaluation. In future studies, greater emphasis should be placed on model testing and, in particular, the incorporation of designs and analyses that permit investigators to assess the extent to which their data conform to models that represent differing or competing theoretical positions. To illustrate, the premise that classroom peer relations influence children's motivation and school engagement remains undersubstantiated in part because most of today's evidence is correlational rather than experimental in nature, and more is known about concurrent than predictive linkages. These evidentiary circumstances limit what is understood about classroom peer relations as potential causes of children's motivation or school engagement. Necessarily, data-based inferences remain uncertain because it has not been possible to rule out competing hypotheses, such as the proposition that children's motivation or school engagement drives the development of their classroom peer relations (rather than vice versa).

To address questions about directions of effect (e.g., do classroom peer relations influence children's school engagement or vice versa?), investigators may find it difficult to experimentally manipulate children's classroom peer relations or school engagement, and so it will be necessary to invest in longitudinal studies and innovative assessment methodologies. It may be productive to make greater use of full-panel longitudinal designs, or studies in which investigators establish the temporal precedence of specific predictors (e.g., obtain measures of peer relations that precede those of school engagement as well as vice versa, for example, conduct repeated measures of both constructs across comparable and multiple time points), and statistically control and contrast differing pathways of influence (i.e., alternative predictor→ criterion, or predictor→ mediator/moderator→ criterion relations; for illustrations, see Ladd, 2003; 2006).

Educational Implications

Though the hypothesis that classroom peer relations influence children's school motivation and engagement has not been definitively "proven" (as a causal proposition), the support it has received suggests that it is not too early to contemplate its educational implications. As illustrated above, adverse relations with classmates (e.g., peer rejection, victimization, friendlessness), and associated processes (e.g., exclusion from learning activities, harassment), predict not only the inception of school adjustment problems (negative school attitudes, school disaffection/disengagement, underachievement; Buhs & Ladd, 2001; Ladd, 1990), but also the growth (e.g., Kochenderfer-Ladd & Wardrop, 2001; Ladd et al., 1997; Ladd & Burgess, 2001), and the long-term trajectories of these problems (see Buhs et al., 2006; Ladd, et al., in press).

Two inferences that can be drawn from these findings are that children who are experiencing classroom peer difficulties require assistance, and that there is a need to develop educational practices that will prevent or remediate peer problems in classrooms. Unfortunately, however, few classroom-based strategies for improving grade-schoolers' peer competence and relations have been developed (although for exceptions, see Ladd, Buhs, & Troop, 2002), most have not been tested empirically (see Gottfredson & Gottfredson, 2001), and existing programs are rarely implemented because teachers see them as: (a) usurping time needed for academic objectives, and (b) addressing goals (e.g., friendship formation, prosocial behavior) that appear irrelevant, or only indirectly germane to children's achievement.

Thus, creating feasible, realistic (useable), and effective practices for promoting positive classroom peer relations (or preventing/reducing adverse peer relations) constitutes important investigative objective. To achieve this objective, it will be necessary to work from the assumption that classroom peer processes are malleable and can be molded in ways that bring about positive developments for the majority of children who are members of classroom peer groups. The probability of achieving this objective, although difficult to estimate, appears favorable in light of evidence indicating that classroom peer group processes are responsive to environmental manipulations. Potential avenues for investigation include practices that incorporate specific instructional, organizational, and contextual manipulations (e.g., differential classroom/school policies, practices, programs, curricula).

Studies are needed, for example, on the relation between teachers' instructional behavior and management styles and classroom peer processes. Early studies of group leadership/instructional styles indicated that peer problems were less common in groups that were supervised by democratic rather than controlling, autocratic teachers or leaders (Lewin & Lippitt, 1938). Their findings showed that hostile interactions between peers were about 30 times more common under autocratic as compared to democratic conditions. Further, only in the autocratic group did children "scapegoat" others, or form alliances to bully certain individuals in the group. In contrast, children who worked under democratic conditions were more cooperative and friendly toward each other, and more often praised each other and offered assistance to peers. Results from other studies (e.g., Sherif, Harvey, White, Hood, & Sherif, 1961) suggest that environments in which adults encourage groups of children to compete against each other tend to produce similar, adverse effects on children's peer group interactions and relations.

The methods that teachers use to group classmates for learning activities appear to be a particularly promising avenue of investigation. Peer-mediated learning (PML) activities, such as investigative teams, peer collaboration and tutoring, and competitive and cooperative learning groups (Damon & Phelps, 1989; Johnson & Johnson, 2000; Maheady, Mallette, & Harper, 2006; Slavin, 1995) have become widely-used methods in American schools—nearly 80% of teachers use some form of cooperative or collaborative peer learning in their classrooms (Puma, Jones, Rock, & Fernandez, 1993).

However, after decades of research on PML, it is clear that more has been learned about the *academic* (e.g., cognitive learning) rather than the *social* processes and effects of these activities (see Blumenfeld et al., 1996; Bossert, 1988-1989; Furman & Gavin, 1989; O'Donnell, 2006). Proponents of PML have argued that peer processes (e.g., peer encouragement, helping, cooperation) are fundamental to many types of PML programs and activities and should, in theory, enhance not only children's academic learning but also their relations with classmates (e.g., improve friendships and peer group acceptance; Bossert, 1988–1989; Johnson & Johnson, 1985). However, empirical documentation of the actual peer *processes/influences* that occur within PML activities and the links between such processes and specific *social outcomes* (e.g., friendship making, gains in peer acceptance) remains limited (Bossert, 1988–1989; O'Donnell, 2006).

With respect to peer processes within PML, there is some evidence to suggest that children benefit from hearing peers provide explanations for academic tasks (Webb, 1985), and from teaching members of their groups (Peterson, Janicki, & Swing, 1981). Insight into the social effects of PML is also quite limited. There are some data to suggest that children become more prosocial as a result of participating in cooperative learning groups (Hertz-Lazarowitz, Sharan, & Steinberg, 1980; Johnson, Johnson, Johnson, & Anderson, 1976). However, other data suggest that peers do not always act prosocially toward or work to benefit members of their groups; during group activities, for example, some children attempt to dominate others, loaf instead of participate, ignore or exclude others from conversations, and so on (see Blumenfeld, et al., 1996). Evidence is also mixed on the effects of PML on children's broader classroom peer relations (e.g., peer group acceptance and friendships), but positive effects have been reported in the majority of studies in which investigators have examined these types of relational outcomes (for reviews, see Furman & Gavin, 1989; Slavin, 1983a). Findings from other studies imply that certain grouping strategies for PML (e.g., placing children from differing ethnic and racial backgrounds within the same groups) aids in the promotion of cross-ethnic/racial friendships (O'Donnell, 2006; Slavin, 1995). Here again, however, there is mixed rather than uniform support for this hypothesis (see Slavin, 1983b).

Thus, it appears that much remains to be learned about the peer processes that occur in PML and about the effects of PML on children's classroom peer relations and, ultimately, their school engagement. Toward this end, three wide-ranging investigative agendas can be identified. First, most of the research on the peer processes and outcomes that are associated with PML is outdated (O'Donnell, 2006) and should be updated and re-evaluated with modern PML variants and with 21st-century samples, classrooms, and schools. Second, as part of this re-evaluation, more detailed information should be gathered on the types of peer processes that occur in different types of PML activities, and on the classroom peer-relational outcomes that are associated with these processes and, more generally, children's involvement in specific PML programs. Third, those who evaluate the social processes and effects of PML should consider whether the extent to which children profit from CPL activities depends on the skills they bring to this context. It has been argued that "students must be taught the social skills required for high quality collaboration and be motivated to use them if cooperative groups are to be productive" (Johnson & Johnson, 1994). Further, some researchers contend that the effects of CPL on children's social competence tend to be weak and heterogeneous because these activities do not overcome impediments such as children's problem behaviors and lack of social skills (Dion, Fuchs, & Fuchs, 2005). Thus, to maximize the benefits learners derive from these instructional contexts it may be necessary to devise and implement classroom practices that will prepare children for the social demands CPL.

Finally, it may be important to experiment with classroom contextual and organizational designs, given that evidence suggests that fewer children fall at the extremes of peer group popularity distributions (i.e., fewer children are extremely popular or unpopular) in less as opposed to highly structured classrooms (e.g., open vs. traditional formats; see Hallinan, 1976, 1981). Clearly, determining how variations in classroom environments are associated with children's peer relations in those contexts should be a priority for future investigation.

Coda

In sum, investigation has progressed to the point where it is apparent that children's classroom peer relationships (i.e., peer group rejection, friendship, victimization), alone or in combination, are associated with an array of indicators of scholastic engagement or disengagement (e.g., school attitudes, classroom participation, school avoidance). As has been illustrated in this review, investigators have identified a range of processes that may account for the association between peer relationships and school engagement and, collectively, the assembled evidence lends support to the premise that children's relationships with classmates affects their ability to adapt to school challenges which, ultimately, affects their engagement and achievement in this context.

Movement beyond this point will require that researchers investigate more directly and thoroughly the processes that are presumed to account for the relations that have been observed between children's classroom peer relations and their school engagement. As illustrated in the foregoing sections, much remains to be learned about *how* children's relations with classmates are linked with their school engagement and performance. Even though some processes that might account for the linkages between classroom peer relationships and school engagement have been described, most remain theoretically underspecified and empirically underinvestigated. Further insight into the mechanisms that link classroom relationships with children's school performance will require a greater investment in model development and evaluation.

Acknowledgment

Portions of this manuscript, and many of the empirical articles cited herein that were published by the first author, have been prepared with support from the National Institutes of Health (1-RO1MH-49223, 2-RO1MH-49223, R01HD-045906) for the Pathways Project—a longitudinal investigation of children's social/psychological/scholastic adjustment in school contexts. Special appreciation is expressed to all the children and parents who made this study possible, and to members of the Pathways Project for assistance with data collection.

References

Alexander, K., & Entwisle, D. R., & Dauber, S. L. (1993). First grade classroom behavior: Its short- and long-term consequences for school performance. *Child Development, 64*, 801–814.

Andrews, R. K., Herald, S. L., & Ladd, G. W. (2005, April). *Chronic behavioral and relational risk factors as predictors of children's self and peer belief trajectories.* Poster presented at the biennial meeting of the Society for Research in Child Development, Atlanta, GA.

Asher, S. R., Rose, A. J., & Gabriel, S. W. (2001). Peer rejection in everyday life. In M. R. Laery (Ed.), *Interpersonal Rejection* (pp. 105–142). Oxford, England: Oxford University Press.

Azmitia, M., & Montgomery, R. (1993). Friendship, transactive dialogues, and the development of scientific reasoning. *Social Development, 2*, 202–221.

Bandura, A., Barbaranelli, C., Caprara, G. V., & Pastorelli, C. (1996). Multifaceted impact of self-efficacy beliefs on academic functioning. *Child Development, 67*, 1206–1222.

Bandura, A., Ross, D., & Ross, S. A. (1963). Imitation of film-mediated aggressive models. *Journal of Abnormal and Social Psychology, 66*, 3–11.

Baumeister, R. F., & Leary, M. R. (1995). The need to belong: Desire for interpersonal attachment as fundamental human motivation. *Psychological Bulletin, 117*, 497–529.

Berndt, T. J. (1982). The features and effects of friendship in early adolescence. *Child Development, 53*, 1447–1460.

Berndt, T. J. (1986). Children's comments about their friendships. In M Perlmutter (Ed.), *Cognitive perspectives on children's social and behavioral development* (pp. 189–212). Hillsdale, NJ: Erlbaum.

Berndt, T. J. (1996). Exploring the effects of friendship quality on social development. In W. M. Bukowski, W. M., A. F. Newcomb, & W. W. Hartup (Eds.), *The company they keep: Friendship in childhood and adolescence* (pp. 346–365). New York: Cambridge University Press.

Berndt, T. J., Hawkins, J. A., & Jiao, Z. (1999). Influences of friends and friendships on adjustment to junior high school. *Merrill-Palmer Quarterly, 45*, 13–41.

Berndt, T. J., & Hoyle, S. G. (1985). Stability and change in childhood and adolescent friendships. *Developmental Psychology, 21*, 1007–1015.

Berndt, T. J., & Keefe, K. (1995). Friends' influence on adolescent's adjustment to school. *Child Development, 66*, 1312–1319.

Bernstein, G. A., Massie, E. D., Thuras, P. D., Perwien, A. R., Borchardt, C. M., & Crosby, R. D. (1997). Somatic symptoms in anxious-depressed school refusers. *Journal of the American Academy of Child and Adolescent Psychiatry, 36*, 661–668.

Betts, L. R., & Rotenberg, K. J. (2007). Trustworthiness, friendships and self-control: Factors that contribute to young children's school adjustment. *Infant and Child Development, 16*, 491–508.

Birch, S. H., & Ladd, G. W. (1997). The teacher-child relationship and children's early school adjustment. *Journal of School Psychology, 35*, 61–79.

Blumenfeld, P. C., Marx, R. W., Soloway, E., & Krajcik, J. (1996). Learning with peers: From small group cooperation to collaborative communities. *Educational Researcher, 25*, 37–40.

Boekaerts, M., Pintrich, P. R., & Zeidner, M. (Eds.). (2000). *Handbook of self-regulation: Theory, research, and applications.* San Diego, CA: Academic Press.

Boivin, M., & Begin, G. (1989). Peer status and self-perception among early elementary school children: The case of the rejected children. *Child Development, 60*, 591–596.

Boivin, M., & Hymel, S. (1997). Peer experiences and social self-perceptions: A sequential model. *Developmental Psychology, 33*, 135–145.

Bossert, S. T. (1988–1989). Cooperative activities in the classroom. *Review of Research in Educaton, 15*, 225–250.

Borkowski, J. G., & Thorpe, P. K. (1994). Self-regulation and motivation: A life-span perspective on underachievement. In D. H. Schunk & B. J. Zimmerman (Eds.), *Self-regulation of learning and performance: Issues and educational applications* (pp. 45–73). Mahwah, NJ: Erlbaum.

Brophy J. E. (1987). Socializing students' motivation to learn. In M. L. Maehr & D Kleiber (Eds.), *Advances in motivation and achievement: Enhancing motivation* (pp. 181–210). Greenwich, CT: JAI.

Brown, B. B. (1989). The role of peer groups in adolescents' adjustment to secondary school. In T. J. Berndt & G. W. Ladd (Eds.), *Peer relationships in child development* (pp. 188–215). New York: Wiley.

Buhs, E. S., & Ladd, G. W. (2001). Peer rejection as antecedent of young children's school adjustment: An examination of mediating processes. *Developmental Psychology, 37,* 550–560.

Buhs, E. S., Ladd, G. W., & Herald, S. L. (2006). Peer exclusion and victimization: Processes that mediate the relation between peer group rejection and children's classroom engagement and achievement? *Journal of Educational Psychology,* 98, 1–13.

Bukowski, W. M., & Hoza, B. (1989). Popularity and friendship: Issues in theory, measurement, and outcome. In T. J. Berndt & G. W. Ladd (Eds.), *Peer relationships in child development* (pp. 15–45). New York: Wiley.

Bukowski, W. M., & Sippola, L. K. (2001). Groups, individuals, and victimization: A view of the peer system. In J. Juvonen & S. Graham (Eds.), *Peer harassment in school: The plight of the vulnerable and victimized* (pp. 355–377). New York: Guilford.

Cairns, R. B., & Cairns, B. D. (1994). *Lifelines and risks: Pathways of youth in our time.* New York: Cambridge University Press.

Coie, J. D. (1990). Toward a theory of peer rejection. In S. R. Asher & J. D. Coie (Eds.), *Peer rejection in childhood* (pp. 365–401). New York: Cambridge University Press.

Connell, J. P., Spencer, M. B., & Aber, J. L. (1994). Educational risk and resilience in African-American youth: Context, self, action, and outcomes in school. *Child Development, 65,* 493–506.

Connell, J. P., & Wellborn, J. G. (1991). Competence, autonomy, and relatedness: A motivational analysis of self-system processes. In M. R. Gunnar & et al. (Eds.), *Self processes and development. The Minnesota symposia on child psychology, Vol. 23* (pp. 43–77). Hillsdale, NJ: Erlbaum.

Cooke, T. & Apolloni, T (1976). Developing positive social-emotional behaviors: A study of training and generalization effects. *Journal of Applied Behavior Analysis, 9,* 65–78.

Covington, M. V. (2000). Goal theory, motivation, and school achievement: An integrative review. *Annual Review of Psychology, 51,* 171–200.

Damon, W., & Phelps, E. (1989). Strategic uses of peer learning in children's education. In Berndt, T. J., & Ladd, G. W. (1989). *Peer relationships in child development* (pp. 135–157). New York: Wiley.

Dion, E., Fuchs, D., & Fuchs, L. (2005). Differential effects of peer-assisted learning strategies on students' social preference and friendship making. *Behavioral Disorders, 30*(4), 421–429.

Eccles, J. S., Wigfield, A., & Schiefele, U. (1998). Motivation to succeed. In W. Damon & N. Eisenberg (Eds.), *Handbook of child psychology: Vol. 5.* (5th ed., pp. 1017–1095). New York: Wiley.

Finn, J. D. (1989). Withdrawing from school. *Review of Educational Research, 59,* 117–142.

Finn, J. D. (1993). *School engagement and students at risk.* Washington DC: Department of Education, National Center for Educational Statistics. (ERIC Document Reproduction Service No. ED 362 322).

Fredricks, J. A., Blumenfeld, P. C., & Paris, A. H. (2004). School engagement: Potential of the concept, state of the evidence. *Review of Educational Research, 74,* 59–109.

Furman, W., & Gavin, L. A. (1989). Peer's influence on adjustment and development: A view from the intervention literature. In T. J. Berndt & G.W. Ladd (Eds.), *Peer relationships in child development* (pp. 319–340). New York: Wiley.

Gottfredson, G., & Gottfredson, D. (2001). What schools do to prevent problem behavior and promote safe environments. *Journal of Educational and Psychological Consultation, 12*(4), 313–344.

Greco, L. A., Freeman, K. E., & Dufton, L. (2006). Overt and relational victimization among children with frequent abdominal pain: links to social skills, academic functioning, and health service use. *Journal of Pediatric Psychology, 32,* 319–329.

Green, E. (1933). Friendships and quarrels among preschool children. *Child Development, 4,* 237–252.

Grolnick, W. S., & Slowiaczek, M. L. (1994). Parents' involvement in children's schooling: A multidimensional conceptualization and motivational model. *Child Development, 65,* 237–252.

Guay, F., Boivin, M., & Hodges, E. V. E. (1999). Predicting changes in academic achievement: A model of peer experiences and self-system processes. *Journal of Education Psychology, 91,* 105–115.

Hallinan, M. T. (1976). Friendship patterns in open and traditional classrooms. *Sociology of Education, 49,* 245–265.

Hallinan, M. T. (1981). Recent advances in sociometry. In S. R. Asher & J. M. Gottman (Eds.), *The development of children's friendships* (pp. 91–115). New York: Cambridge University Press.

Hamre, B. K. & Pianta, R. C. (2001). Early teacher-child relationships and the trajectory of children's school outcomes through eighth grade. *Child Development, 72,* 625–638.

Hartup, W. W. (1996). The company they keep: Friendships and their developmental significance. *Child Development, 67,* 1–13.

Hartup, W. W., & Stevens, N. (1997). Friendships and adaptation in the life course. *Psychological Bulletin, 121,* 355–370.

Helme, S., & Clarke, D. (2001). Identifying cognitive engagement in the mathematics classroom. *Mathematics Education Research Journal, 13,* 133–153.

Hertz-Lazarowitz, R., Sharan, S., & Steinberg, R. (1980). Classroom learning style and cooperative behavior of elementary school children. *Journal of Educational Psychology, 72,* 99–106.

Hodges, E. V. E., Boivin, M., Vitaro, F., & Bukowski, W. M. (1999). The power of friendship: Protection against an escalating cycle of peer victimization. *Developmental Psychology, 35,* 94–101.

Howes, C. (1988). Peer interaction of young children. *Monographs of the Society for Research in Child Development, 53*(1, Serial No. 217).

Hymel, S., Comfort, C., Schonert-Reichel, K., & McDougall, P. (1996). Academic failure and school dropout: The influence on peers. In J. Juvonen & K. R. Wentzel (Eds.), *Social motivation: Understanding children's school adjustment. Cambridge studies in social and emotional development* (pp. 313–345). New York: Cambridge University Press.

Hymel, S., Wagner, E., & Butler, L. J. (1990). Reputational bias: View from the peer group. In S. R. Asher & J. D. Coie (Eds.), *Peer rejection in childhood. Cambridge studies in social and emotional development* (pp. 156–186). New York: Cambridge University Press.

Johnson, D., & Johnson, R. (1985). The internal dynamics of cooperative learning groups. In R. Slavin, S. Sharan, S. Kagan, R. Hertz-Lazarowitz, C. Webb, & R. Schmuck (Eds.), *Learning to cooperate, cooperating to learn* (pp. 103–124). New York: Plenum.

Johnson, D., & Johnson, R. (1994). *Leading the cooperative school* (2nd ed.). Edina, MN: Interaction Book Company.

Johnson, D., & Johnson, R. (1998). *Learning together and alone* (5th ed.). Boston: Allyn & Bacon.

Johnson, D., & Johnson, R. (2000). Cooperative learning, values, and culturally plural classrooms. In M. Leicester, C. Modgill, & S. Modgill (Eds.), *Values, the classroom, and cultural diversity* (pp. 15–28). London: Cassell PLC.

Johnson, D., Johnson, R., Johnson, J., & Anderson, D. (1976). Effects of cooperative versus individualistic instruction on student prosocial behavior, attitudes, toward learning, and achievement. *Journal of Educational Psychology, 68,* 446–452.

Juvonen, J., Nishina, A., & Graham, S. (2000). Peer harassment, psychological adjustment, and school functioning in early adolescence. *Journal of Educational Psychology, 92,* 349–359.

Kindermann, T. A. (1993). Natural peer groups as contexts for individual development: The case of children's motivation in school. *Developmental Psychology, 29,* 970–977.

Kochel, K. P., McConnell, E. M., & Ladd, G. W. (2007). *Do negative peer relationships provoke other peer adversities?* Poster presented at the biennial meetings of the Society for Research in Child Development, Boston, MA.

Kochenderfer, B. J., & Ladd, G. W. (1996). Peer victimization: Cause or consequence of school maladjustment? *Child Development, 67,* 1305–1317.

Kochenderfer-Ladd, B., & Ladd, G. W. (2001). Variations in peer victimization: Relations to children's maladjustment. In J. Juvonen & S. Graham (Eds.), *Peer harassment in school: The plight of the vulnerable and victimized* (pp. 25–48). New York: Guilford.

Kochenderfer-Ladd, B., & Wardrop, J. (2001). Chronicity and instability in children's peer victimization experiences as predictors of loneliness and social satisfaction trajectories. *Child Development, 72,* 134–151.

Kumpulainen, K., Rasanen, E., Henttonen, I., Almqvist, F., Kresanov, K., Linna, S. L., et al. (1998). Bullying and psychiatric symptoms among elementary school-age children. *Child Abuse and Neglect, 22,* 705–717.

Ladd, G. W. (1983). Social networks of popular, average, and rejected children in school settings. *Merrill- Palmer Quarterly, 29,* 283–307.

Ladd, G. W. (1988). Friendship patterns and peer status during early and middle childhood. *Journal of Developmental and Behavioral Pediatrics, 9,* 229–238.

Ladd, G. W. (1990). Having friends, keeping friends, making friends, and being liked by peers in the classroom: Predictors of children's early school adjustment? *Child Development, 61,* 1081–1100.

Ladd, G. W. (2003a). School transitions/school readiness: An outcome of early childhood development. In R. E. Tremblay, R. G. Barr, & RDeV Peters (Eds.), *Encyclopedia on early childhood development* (pp. 1–10). Montreal, Quebec: Center of Excellence for Early Childhood Development.

Ladd, G. W. (2003b). Probing the adaptive significance of children's behavior and relationships in the school context: A child by environment perspective. In R. Kail (Ed.), *Advances in Child Behavior and Development* (pp. 43–104). New York: Wiley.

Ladd, G. W. (2005). *Children's peer relations and social competence: A century of progress.* New Haven, CT: Yale University Press.

Ladd, G. W. (2006). Peer rejection, aggressive or withdrawn behavior, and psychological maladjustment from ages 5 to 12: An examination of four predictive models. *Child Development, 77,* 822–846.

Ladd, G. W. (2007). Social learning in the peer context. In O. Saracho & B. Spodek (Eds.), *Contemporary perspectives on research on social learning in early childhood education* (pp. 133–164), Charlotte, NC: Information Age.

Ladd, G. W., Birch, S. H., & Buhs, E. S. (1999). Children's social and scholastic lives in kindergarten: Related spheres of influence? *Child Development, 70,* 1373–1400.

Ladd, G. W., Buhs, E., & Seid, M. (2000). Children's initial sentiments about kindergarten: Is school liking an antecedent of early classroom participation and achievement? *Merrill-Palmer Quarterly, 46,* 255–279.

Ladd, G. W., Buhs, E. & Troop, W. (2002). Children's interpersonal skills and relationships in school settings: Adaptive significance and implications for school-based prevention and intervention programs. In P. K. Smith & C. H. Hart (Eds.), *Blackwell's handbook of childhood social development* (pp. 394–415). London: Blackwell.

Ladd, G. W., & Burgess, K. B. (2001). Do relational risks and protective factors moderate the linkages between childhood aggression and early psychological and school adjustment? *Child Development, 72,* 1579–1601.

Ladd, G. W. & Dinella, L. M. (2009). Continuity and change in early school engagement: Predictive of children's achievement trajectories from first to eighth grade? *Journal of Educational Psychology, 101,* 190–206.

Ladd, G. W., Herald, S. L., & Kochel, K. P. (2006). School readiness: Are there social prerequisites? *Early Education and Development, 17,* 115-150.

Ladd, G. W., Herald-Brown, S. L., & Reiser, M. (2008). Does chronic classroom peer rejection predict the development of children's classroom participation during the grade school years? *Child Development, 79,* 1001–1015.

Ladd, G. W., & Kochenderfer-Ladd, B. J. (1998). Parenting behaviors and the parent-child relationship: Correlates of peer victimization in kindergarten? *Developmental Psychology, 34,* 1450–1458.

Ladd, G. W., & Kochenderfer-Ladd, B. J. (2002). Identifying victims of peer aggression from early to middle childhood: Analysis of cross-informant data for concordance, estimation of relational adjustment, prevalence of victimization, and characteristics of identified victims. *Psychological Assessment, 14*, 74–96.

Ladd, G. W., Kochenderfer, B. J., & Coleman, C. C. (1996). Friendship quality as a predictor of young children's early school adjustment. *Child Development, 67*, 1103–1118.

Ladd, G. W., Kochenderfer, B. J., & Coleman, C. C. (1997). Classroom peer acceptance, friendship, and victimization: Distinct relational systems that contribute uniquely to children's school adjustment? *Child Development, 68*, 1181–1197.

Ladd, G. W., Price, J. M., & Hart, C. H. (1990). Preschoolers' behavioral orientations and patterns of peer contact: Predictive of peer status? In S. R. Asher & J. D. Coie (Eds.), *Peer rejection in childhood* (pp. 90–115). New York: Cambridge University Press.

Ladd, G. W., & Troop-Gordon, W. (2003). The role of chronic peer adversity in the development of children's psychological adjustment problems. *Child Development*, 74, 1325–1348.

Lee, O., & Anderson, C. W. (1993). Task engagement and conceptual change in middle school science classrooms. *American Educational Research Journal, 30*, 585–610.

Lewin, K., & Lippitt, R. (1938). An experimental approach to the study of autocracy and democracy: A preliminary note. *Sociometry, 1*, 292–300.

Lopez, C., & DuBois, D. L. (2005). Peer victimization and rejection: Investigation of an integrative model of effects on emotional, behavioral, and academic adjustment in early adolescence. *Journal of Clinical Child and Adolescent Psychology, 34*, 25–36.

Maheady, L., Mallette, B., & Harper, G. (2006). Four classwide peer tutoring models: Similarities, differences, and implications for research and practice. *Reading and writing quarterly, 22*, 65–89.

Marsh, H. W., & Hau, K. (2003). Big fish-little pond effect on academic self concept: A cross-cultural (26 country) test of the negative effects of academically selective schools. *American Psychologist, 58*, 364–376.

McDowell, D. J., Parke, R. D., & Spitzer, S. (2002). Parent and child cognitive representations of social situations and children's social competence. *Social Development, 11*, 469–486.

McNamara-Barry, C., & Wentzel, K. R. (2006). Friend influence on prosocial behavior: The role of motivational factors and friendship characteristics. *Developmental Psychology, 42*, 153–163.

Meece, J., Blumenfeld, P., & Hoyle, R. (1988). Students' goal orientations and cognitive engagement in classroom activities. *Journal of Educational Psychology, 80*, 514–523.

Nangle, D. W., Erdley, C. A., Newman, J. E., Mason, C. A., & Carpenter, E. M. (2003). Popularity, friendship quantity, and friendship quality: Interactive influences on children's loneliness and depression. *Journal of Clinical Child and Adolescent Psychology, 32*, 546–555.

Newmann, F., Wehlage, G. G., & Lamborn, S. D. (1992). The significance and sources of student engagement. In F. Newmann (Ed.), *Student engagement and achievement in American secondary schools* (pp. 11–39). New York: Teachers College Press.

Nishina, A., Juvonen, J., & Witkow, M. R. (2005). Sticks and stones may break my bones, but names will make me feel sick: The psychosocial, somatic, and scholastic consequences of peer harassment. *Journal of Clinical Child and Adolescent Psychology*, 34, 37–48.

O'Donnell, A. (2006). The role of peers and group learning. In P. Alexander & P. Winne (Eds.), *Handbook of educational psychology* (pp. 781–802). Mahwah, NJ: Erlbaum.

Olweus, D. (1978). *Aggression in the schools: Bullies and whipping boys.* Washington, DC: Hemisphere.

Olweus, D. (1984). Aggressors and their victims: Bullying at school. In N. Frude & H. Gault (Eds.), *Disruptive behavior in schools* (pp. 57–76). New York: Wiley.

Parker J. G., & Asher, S. R. (1987). Peer relations and later personal adjustment: Are low-accepted children "at risk"? *Psychological Bulletin, 102*, 357–389.

Parker, J. G., & Asher, S. R. (1993). Friendship and friendship quality in middle childhood: Links with peer group acceptance and feelings of loneliness and social dissatisfaction. *Developmental Psychology, 29*, 611–621.

Perry, D. G., & Bussey, K. (1984). *Social development.* Englewood Cliffs NJ: Prentice-Hall.

Perry, D. G., Kusel, S. J., & Perry, L. C. (1988). Victims of peer aggression. *Developmental Psychology, 24*, 807–814.

Perry, D. G., Hodges, E. V., & Egan, S. (2001). Determinants of chronic victimization by peers: A review and new model of family influence. In J. Juvonen & S. Graham (Eds.), *Peer harassment in school: The plight of the vulnerable and victimized* (pp. 73–104). New York: Guilford.

Perry, K. E., & Weinstein, R. S. (1998). The social context of early schooling and children's school adjustment. *Educational Psychologist, 33*, 177–194.

Peterson, P., Janicki, T., & Swing, S. (1981). Ability x treatment interaction effects on children's learning in large-group and small-group approaches. *American Educational Research Journal, 18*, 452–474.

Pierson, L. H., & Connell, J. P. (1992). Effect of grade retention in self-system processes, school engagement, and academic performance. *Journal of Educational Psychology, 84*, 300–307.

Pintrich, P. R., & DeGroot, E. V. (1990). Motivational and self-regulated learning components of classroom academic performance. *Journal of Educational Psychology, 82*, 33–40.

Puma, M., Jones, C., Rock, D., & Fernandez, R. (1993). *Prospects: The congressionally mandated study of educational growth and opportunity (Interim report).* Bethesda, MD: Abt Associates.

Rigby, K. (1998). The relationship between reported health and involvement in bully/victim problems among male and female secondary schoolchildren. *Journal of Health Psychology, 3,* 465–476.

Rubin, K. H., Burgess, K. B., & Hastings, P. D. (2002). Stability and social-behavioral consequences of toddlers' inhibited temperament and parenting behaviors. *Child Development, 73,* 483–495.

Ryan, A. (2000). Peer groups as a context for the socialization of adolescents' motivation, engagement, and achievement in school. *Educational Psychologist, 35,* 101–111.

Ryan, A. (2001). The peer group as a context for the development of young adolescent motivation and achievement. *Child Development, 72,* 1135–1150.

Salmivalli, C., & Isaacs, J. (2005). Prospective relations among victimization, rejection, friendlessness, and children's self and peer perceptions. *Child Development, 76,* 1161–1171.

Schneider, W., & Pressley, M. (1997). *Memory development between 2 and 20.* Mahwah, NJ: Erlbaum.

Sherif, M., Harvey, O. J., White, B. J., Hood, W. R., & Sherif, C. W. (1961). *Intergroup conflict and cooperation: The Robbers Cave experiment.* Norman: Univ. of Oklahoma Press.

Schwartz, D. (2000). Subtypes of victims and aggressors in children's peer groups. *Journal of Abnormal Child Psychology, 28,* 181–192.

Schwartz, D., Dodge, K. A., & Coie, J. D. (1993). The emergence of chronic peer victimization in boys' play groups. *Child Development, 64,* 1755–1772.

Schwartz, D., Dodge, K. A., Pettit, G. S., & Bates, J. E. (1997). The early socialization of aggressive victims of bullying. *Child Development, 68,* 665–675.

Schwartz, D., Gorman, A. H., Nakamoto, J., & Toblin, R. L. (2005). Victimization in the peer group and children's academic functioning. *Journal of Educational Psychology, 97,* 425–435.

Schwartz, D., Proctor, L. J., & Chien, H. (2001). The aggressive victim of bullying. In J. Juvonen & S. Graham (Eds.), *Peer harassment in school: The plight of the vulnerable and victimized* (pp. 147–174). New York: Guilford.

Skinner, E. A., & Belmont, M. J. (1993). Motivation in the classroom: Reciprocal effect of teacher behavior and student engagement across the school year. *Journal of Educational Psychology, 85,* 571–581.

Skinner, E. A., Wellborn, J. G., & Connell, J. P. (1990). What it takes to do well in school and whether I've got it: The role of perceived control in children's engagement and school achievement. *Journal of Educational Psychology, 82,* 22–32.

Slavin, R. E. (1983a). When does cooperative learning increase student achievement? *Psychological Bulletin, 94,* 429–445.

Slavin, R. E. (1983b). *Cooperative learning.* New York: Longman.

Slavin, R. (1995). *Cooperative Learning: Theory, research, and practice* (2nd ed.). Boston: Allyn & Bacon.

Slutzky, C., & Ladd, G. W. (2005, April). *The effects of chronic peer rejection on children's loneliness: Exploring peer trust as a mediating factor.* Paper presented at the biennial meetings of the Society for Research in Child Development, Atlanta GA.

Stipek, D. (2002). Good instruction is motivating. In A. Wigfield & J. Eccles (Eds.), *Development of achievement motivation* (pp. 310-334). San Diego, CA: Academic Press.

Torsheim, T., & Wold, B. (2001). School-related stress, support, and subjective health complaints among early adolescents: A multilevel approach. *Journal of Adolescence, 24,* 701–713.

Vaillancourt, T., Clinton, J., McDougall, P., Schmidt, L., & Hymel, S. (in press). The neurobiology of peer victimization and rejection. In S. R. Jimerson, S. M. Swearer, & D. L. Espelage (Eds.), *The international handbook of school bullying.* Mahwah, NJ: Erlbaum.

Vandell, D. L., & Hembree, S. E. (1994). Peer social status and friendship: Independent contributors to children's social and academic adjustment. *Merrill-Palmer Quarterly, 40,* 461–477.

Voelkl, K. E. (1997). Identification with school. *American Journal of Education, 105,* 204–319.

Webb, N. (1985). Student interaction and learning in small groups: A research summary. In R. Slavin, S. Sharan, S. Kagan, R. Hertz-Lazarowitz, C. Webb, & R. Schmuck (Eds.), *Learning to cooperate, cooperating to learn* (pp. 147–172). New York: Plenum.

Wehlage, G. G., Rutter, R. A., Smith, G. A., Lesko, N. L., & Fernandez, R. R. (1989). *Reducing the risk: Schools as communities of support.* Philadelphia: Farmer Press.

Wentzel, K. R. (1998). Social relationships and motivation in middle school: The role of parents, teachers, and peers. *Journal of Educational Psychology, 90,* 202–209.

Wentzel, K. R., Filisetti, L., & Looney, L. (2007). Adolescent prosocial behavior: The role of self-processes and contextual cues. *Child Development, 78,* 895–910.

Wentzel, K. R., & McNamara, C. (1999). Interpersonal relationships, emotional distress, and prosocial behavior in middle school. *Journal of Early Adolescence, 19,* 114–125.

Wentzel, K.R., & Caldwell, K. (1997). Friendships, peer acceptance, and group membership: Relations to academic achievement in middle school. *Child Development, 68,* 1198–1209.

Wigfield, A., & Karpathian, M. (1991). Who am I and what can I do? Children's self concepts and motivation in academic situations. *Educational Psychologist, 26,* 233–262.

Youniss, J. (1980). *Parents and peers in social development.* Chicago: University of Chicago Press.

Zimmerman, B. J., & Bandura, A. (1994). Imapct of self-regulatory influences on writing course attainment. *American Educational Research Journal, 29,* 663–676.

17
Teacher Expectations and Self-Fulfilling Prophecies

Lee Jussim, Stacy L. Robustelli, and Thomas R. Cain

Teacher expectations can create self-fulfilling prophecies. In general, self-fulfilling prophecies occur when false beliefs create their own reality (Merton, 1948). In the classroom, a self-fulfilling prophecy occurs when a teacher holds an initially erroneous expectation about a student, and who, through social interaction, causes the student to behave in such a manner as to confirm the originally false (but now true) expectation. The claim that teacher expectations create self-fulfilling prophecies in the classroom was once controversial; now, such a claim is supported by abundant evidence (see Jussim & Harber, 2005, for a review of the controversies and evidence).

This chapter has two main purposes: (a) to review the evidence that bears on some of the many controversies surrounding teacher expectations; (b) and to review the evidence regarding the educational, social, and psychological processes by which self-fulfilling prophecies in the classroom occur. Accordingly, this chapter is divided into two major sections.

In the first section, we take stock of the existing literature on the role of teacher expectations in producing self-fulfilling prophecies. This includes a review of the Pygmalion study (Rosenthal & Jacobson, 1968) that first demonstrated that teacher expectations may produce self-fulfilling prophecies; the research performed in the immediate aftermath of the controversies surrounding Pygmalion; research examining the conditions under which self-fulfilling prophecies in the classroom are stronger or weaker; and research on whether self-fulfilling prophecies accumulate or dissipate over time. We consider such a review important because, as shall be documented throughout this section, the self-fulfilling prophecy literature is frequently cited in support of conclusions that are not justified by the empirical scientific research.

In the second section, we review the process evidence. How do how self-fulfilling prophecies happen? How, when, and why do teachers develop erroneous expectations? How do teachers behave in such a manner as to increase or reduce the likelihood of producing self-fulfilling prophecies? How do students react to such teacher treatment? As shall be seen, far more is known about how and when teachers develop inaccurate expectations and about how they act on their expectations, than about how students react to expectancy-related forms of differential treatment. Therefore, our review of evidence regarding the role of students in the self-fulfilling prophecy draws heavily on work outside of that focusing on teacher expectation effects. Fortunately, a great deal of research over the last 20 years has addressed the teacher behaviors and practices that affect student motivation and learning. Our review suggests that this research may provide valuable insights, or, at minimum, testable hypotheses, regarding the ways in which student behavioral and psychological reactions to teacher treatment may mediate self-fulfilling prophecies.

Self-Fulfilling Prophecies in the Classroom: The State of the Literature

In this section of the chapter, we review the classic and controversial Pygmalion study (Rosenthal & Jacobson, 1968). One might wonder why it is necessary to review research that is 40 years old and that has been reviewed amply elsewhere. It is necessary for two reasons. First, Rosenthal and Jacobson's landmark Pygmalion in the Classroom study is still regularly cited in support of conclusions that their data did not actually support. Second, modern discussions of teacher expectations draw upon this literature to reach conclusions that are virtually all over the map, ranging from emphasizing their power to influence students (Gilbert, 1995; Schultz & Oskamp, 2000), to suggesting that such effects, while real, are minimal (Snow, 1995; Spitz, 1999), to denying their existence altogether (Roth, 1995; Rowe, 1995). Thus, in understanding their study, it is particularly important to stick close to the data in order to be quite clear regarding what it found, what it did not find, and what it did not even examine. After revisiting that study, we then review what has been found over the next several decades regarding the power and extent of self-fulfilling prophecies, the conditions under which they are stronger and weaker, and whether they accumulate or dissipate over time.

The Pygmalion Study

The innovative, influential, and highly controversial Pygmalion study (Rosenthal & Jacobson, 1968) raised the possibility that teacher expectations might create self-fulfilling prophecies. Rosenthal and Jacobson administered a nonverbal intelligence test to all of the children in Jacobson's elementary school (kindergarten through fifth grade). They did not, however, tell the teachers that this was an intelligence test. Instead, special test booklet covers labeled it as a "Test of Inflicted Acquisition," which, an information sheet explained, was a new test being developed at Harvard for identifying children likely to "bloom"—to show a sudden and dramatic intellectual spurt over the upcoming school year. After each test was supposedly graded, Rosenthal and Jacobson then informed each teacher which of his/her students had been identified as potential "late bloomers." These late bloomers (about 20% of the total in the school), however, were actually selected at random. As Rosenthal and Jacobson (1968, p. 70) stated, "The difference between the children earmarked for intellectual growth and the undesignated control children was in the mind of the teacher." They then administered the intelligence test again 1 year later and 2 years later.

Results: The Oversimplified Version

Teacher expectations created a self-fulfilling prophecy. One year later, the "late bloomers" gained more IQ points than did the control students (henceforth referred to as "bloomers" and "controls"). Even 2 years later, the bloomers' gains still exceeded those of the controls. Although the only initial systematic difference between bloomers and controls was in the teachers' minds, the late bloomers actually showed greater IQ gains relative to controls. The teachers' false beliefs had become true.

Rosenthal and Jacobson's (1968) results also showed that the more the control children gained in IQ, the less well adjusted, interesting, and affectionate they were seen by their teachers. Teachers seemed actively hostile toward the students showing unexpected intellectual growth. When described in this manner, these results seem dramatic. Inaccurate teacher expectations provided an undue advantage to some students. Additionally, when children unexpectedly exceeded teachers' expectations, rather than leading to support and reinforcement, this seemed to trigger oppressive teacher responses toward those students. These results seemed to explain how teachers' expectations, and by extension, expectations of managers, college admissions personnel, health professionals, etc., could be a major contributor to the social inequalities associated with race, sex, and social class (see Wineburg, 1987, for a review of perspectives reaching such conclusions; see Weinstein, Gregory, & Strambler, 2004, for a modern example).

Results: The Messier and Truer Version

There is nothing false in the above, oversimplified summary of Rosenthal and Jacobson (1968). It is a true synopsis, and to this day, the study is often described in this manner (Fiske & S. Taylor, 1991; Gilbert, 1995; Myers, 1999; Schultz & Oskamp, 2000). Nonetheless, Rosenthal and Jacobson's (1968) pattern of results was not quite as straightforward as the summary suggests.

One complication was that, on average, both groups of children—late bloomers and controls—showed dramatic IQ gains over the next year. On average, the late bloomers gained about 12 points and the controls gained about 8 points. This is important for at least two reasons. First, in this study, there was no IQ evidence of teachers' expectations decreasing students' level of achievement. Most students gained in IQ, regardless of experimental condition. The control group's average gain of 8 points is quite dramatic—it is about half of a standard deviation on a typical IQ test. Although the study's results did not preclude the possibility of teacher expectations actively harming students' achievement, there was no IQ evidence in this study indicating that such harm actually occurred.

Second, although the across-the-board IQ increases could be described as "dramatic," the differences between the gains of the late bloomers and the controls were not so dramatic. Averaging across all grade levels, that difference was about 4 points. This difference was statistically significant, but in most spheres of daily life, a 4 IQ point difference is not usually considered particularly dramatic.

Other ways to consider the size of the effect also yield a picture of a less than dramatic result. The difference between the experimental and control conditions corresponded to an effect size of d = .30 (difference between the experimental and control group in standard deviation units). Typically, effect sizes of d=.30 or less are considered small (Cohen, 1988). Or, we could simply correlate the manipulation with IQ scores. That correlation is r = .15 (Harris & Rosenthal, 1985). The size of the difference between bloomers and controls was something less than dramatic.

Although the average effect size was not dramatic, there was evidence of some dramatic effects. In the first grade, the bloomer's out-gained the control students by about 15 IQ points; in second grade the difference was about 10 points. In both grades, the control students gained IQ points, but such gains were not even close to those gained by the bloomers.

But the story again becomes more complicated. There was no difference between third-grade bloomers and controls. In fourth grade, bloomers gained more than controls, but the difference was not statistically significant. In fifth and sixth grade, bloomers actually gained fewer IQ points than did controls, but this difference was not statistically significant either. Thus, the overall effect averaged across all six grades was derived almost entirely from the effects in first and second grade.

A theoretically coherent and compelling account might be maintained by arguing that young children were more susceptible to teacher expectation effects. The ability of this explanation to account for Rosenthal and Jacobson's data, however, is more apparent than real.

After 2 years, the *oldest* children (then in sixth grade) showed the largest differences between bloomers and controls. If there was greater susceptibility among younger children, it did not last very long. What mechanism could explain why, among the older children, there was a complete absence of a teacher expectation effect in year 1 but the largest effects obtained in year 2? We cannot answer that question for two reasons—there remains no empirical evidence supporting any such explanation, and no follow-up research has replicated this pattern; as such, we will not discuss it further. Nonetheless, such patterns considerably muddied the interpretive waters surrounding the study.

Other oddities surrounding the original Pygmalion study led some researchers to doubt the credibility of the main self-fulfilling prophecy result. For example, Snow (1995) provided an intriguing re-analysis of the original Pygmalion data. This analysis showed that many of the first and second graders' scores (those among whom the expectancy effect was strongest), were quite bizarre: Some students had pre-test IQ scores near zero, and others had post-test IQ scores over 200. Obviously, however, the children were neither deceased nor geniuses.

Snow (1995) also pointed out that the intelligence test used in Pygmalion was only normed for scores between 60 and 160. If one excluded all scores outside this range, the expectancy effect disappeared. Moreover, there were five "bloomers" with wild IQ score gains: 17–110, 18–122, 133–202, 111–208, and 113–211. If one simply excluded these five bizarre gains, the difference between the bloomers and the controls evaporated.

What Can Be Concluded From The Pygmalion Study?

What can or cannot be concluded from Pygmalion is clearly a matter of scientific opinion and judgment. The harshest critics might say "nothing." The strongest advocates might say that it provides profound insight into social problems and inequality. Both reactions—uncritical acceptance and overgeneralization on one hand; vilifying criticism on the other—are probably too extreme. Therefore, in this section, we provide answers to questions regarding the Pygmalion study using the hard data from the original study.

Were self-fulfilling prophecies powerful and pervasive? They were not. The overall effect size equaled a correlation of .15. The mean difference in IQ gain scores between late bloomers and controls was four points. These are not powerful effects. Nor were they pervasive. Significant teacher expectation effects only occurred in two of six grades in year 1 and in one of five grades in year 2. Self-fulfilling prophecies did not occur in eight of eleven grades examined.

Were powerful expectancy effects ever found? Yes. The results in first and second grade in year 1 (15 and 10 point bloomer-control differences) were quite large. Were teacher expectations typically inaccurate? Rosenthal and Jacobson (1968) provided no information about the typical accuracy or inaccuracy of teacher expectations. Did demographic-based stereotypes unduly bias expectations and perceptions? Rosenthal and Jacobson did not assess the extent to which student demographics or social stereotypes influenced teacher expectations. Therefore, the study provided no data directly bearing on the issue of whether stereotypes bias teacher expectations.

Were self-fulfilling prophecies harmful? Rosenthal and Jacobson (1968) only manipulated positive expectations. They showed that false positive expectations could be self-fulfilling. It would have been unethical to instill false negative expectations. Therefore, they did not assess whether false negative expectations undermine student IQ or achievement. It is important to note that there was some evidence that the teachers acted negatively towards controls who gained; however, the self-fulfilling prophecies they found were beneficial—they *increased* student IQ scores.

Did the study show that more powerful self-fulfilling prophecies occur among younger children? There was no simple linear relationship between age and self-fulfilling prophecy effect size. Consistent with the age hypothesis, the largest effects in the first year of the study were for students in first and second grade. However, inconsistent with this hypothesis were results showing no significant effects in grades 3 through 6 in the first year of the study; and, in the second year of the study, the only significant effects occurred in sixth grade (among the oldest children).

The Scientific Contribution of Rosenthal and Jacobson

For all the drama and controversy, the study's actual findings ranged from nil (if one believes the critics) to quite modest, if taken at face value. This is clearly a case, however, where a study's contribution involved more than its specific results. Rosenthal and Jacobson's (1968) study opened up new areas of research in education and psychology (Brophy, 1983; Brophy & Good, 1974; Snyder, 1984). Nonetheless, given the controversy surrounding the study's actual results, the first order of business for many researchers was to evaluate the validity of the basic teacher expectation/ self-fulfilling prophecy phenomenon. That research is summarized next.

The Aftermath of Pygmalion

Given the controversies surrounding the Pygmalion study, numerous replications were attempted (see reviews by Brophy & Good, 1974; Rosenthal, 1974; Spitz, 1999). Because of the methodological criticisms of the study, many of the early replications focused not on the general question of whether teacher expectations can be self-fulfilling, but on narrow attempts to discover whether experimentally-induced erroneous teacher expectations actually had reliable self-fulfilling effects on student IQ and achievement.

Even these studies initially evoked considerable controversy. Only slightly over one third consistently demonstrated a statistically significant expectancy effect (Brophy, 1983; Rosenthal & Rubin, 1978). This pattern seemed to resolve nothing. It was often interpreted by the critics as demonstrating that the phenomenon did not exist because support was unreliable. Proponents interpreted this result as demonstrating the existence of self-fulfilling prophecies because, if only chance differences were occurring, replications would only succeed about 5% of the time.

This controversy was eventually resolved by Rosenthal and Rubin's (1978) meta-analysis of the first 345 experiments on interpersonal expectancy effects. The 345 studies were divided into eight categories. Z-scores representing the combined expectancy effect in all studies in each category were computed. The median of the eight combined Z-scores was 6.62, indicating that the self-fulfilling prophecy was real.

Experimentally-Induced versus Naturally-Occurring Self-Fulfilling Prophecies

Although the Rosenthal & Rubin (1978) meta-analysis settled the question of whether experimentally-induced inaccurate teacher expectations produced self-fulfilling prophecies, it left open the question of the extent to which self-fulfilling prophecies occur naturally. An answer to this question cannot be based on experimental research that intentionally misleads teachers to develop erroneous expectations, because teachers being intentionally misled by researchers is not a naturally-occurring process. Instead, conclusions regarding what happens under naturalistic conditions must be based on research that examines relations between naturally-occurring teacher expectations and student achievement.

Of course, the causal inferences reached on the basis of naturalistic research can rarely be as strong as those based on experimental research. Much naturalistic research on teacher expectations (see, e.g., reviews by Jussim & Eccles, 1995; Jussim & Harber, 2005), however, has gone to considerable methodological and statistical lengths to rule out alternative explanations for why teacher expectations predict student achievement. For example, most studies have used longitudinal designs in which teacher expectations are assessed early in the year and student achievement is assessed later in the year, or, sometimes, even in following years. Because the future cannot possibly cause the past, such designs eliminate the possibility that student achievement late in the year caused teacher expectations early in the year.

Longitudinal designs, however, still leave open third variable explanations. Perhaps some third variable or set of variables cause both teacher expectations and student achievement. If so, failing to include such variables in a naturalistic study of teacher expectations might lead to an overestimate of the power of self-fulfilling prophecies (which, by definition, involve teacher expectations *causing* student achievement). Nearly all naturalistic studies, however, have included many of the most likely potential third variables as controls (e.g., students' prior achievement, motivation, and demographic characteristics). This means that many of the most likely contenders for third variables have been ruled out in most naturalistic studies because they have been statistically controlled.

To what extent, then, do naturally-occurring teacher expectations create self-fulfilling prophecies? Table 17.1 presents the effect sizes obtained in every published naturalistic study that examined the effect of teacher expectations on student achievement within a school. Self-fulfilling prophecy effect sizes range from 0 to .4, with most falling between .10 and .20. Depending on how it is calculated, the overall mean effect size is between .07 and .17 (see Table 17.1 for more details).

Table 17.1 also highlights an extremely important aspect of the existing data. The larger the sample size, the smaller the self-fulfilling prophecy effect size (on average). Indeed, the correlation between sample size and effect size is –.72. This pattern strongly suggests that the larger effect sizes obtained in smaller scale studies may reflect the inherently greater variability of statistics based on small samples rather than any substantively generalizable evidence of larger self-fulfilling prophecies.

Effects of .07 to .17 are not very powerful by any standard. They would fall in the bottom third of effect sizes obtained in 380 meta-analyses covering a wide range of psychological phenomena (Hemphill, 2003). In fact, .17 is below the median of effect sizes found in social psychology, and .07 would be among the smallest effect sizes found in social psychology (Richard, Bond Jr., & Stokes-Zoota, 2003). In absolute terms, even an effect of .20 in a naturalistic study means that only 10% of students, on average, are substantially changed by self-fulfilling prophecy effects. This is, of course, the same thing as saying 90% are not substantially changed.

Nonetheless, self-fulfilling prophecies are not restricted to situations in which experimenters intentionally mislead teachers into developing false expectations. Nearly all naturalistic studies have found evidence of self-fulfilling prophecies. Indeed, the unweighted average effect size of r = .17 is very close to the overall effect size of r = .15 obtained in the original Rosenthal & Jacobson (1968) study and the r = .23 effect size obtained in experimental studies in which teacher

Table 17.1 Effect and Sample Sizes in Naturalistic Studies of the Self-Fulfilling Effects of Teacher Expectations

Study	Self-Fulfilling Prophecy Effect Size	Sample Size
Williams, 1976[a] Boys	.07	5,458
Williams, 1976[a] Girls	.00	5,072
Chapman & McCauley, 1993[b]	.03	4,308
West & Anderson, 1976[a]	.12	3,000
Jussim & Eccles, 1992[a]	.13	1,288
Jussim, 1989[a]	.13	443
Doyle et al (1972)[b]	.30	245
Brattesani et al (1984)[c]	.26	234
Trouilloud et al (2002)	.28	173
Kuklinski & Weinstein (2001), 5th Grade[a]	.19	140
Kuklinski & Weinstein (2001), 3rd Grade[a]	.20	124
Kuklinski & Weinstein (2001), 1st Grade[a]	.40	112
Palardy (1969)[b]	.14	107
Seaver (1973)[b]	.15	79

Note. The simple average of effect sizes, unweighted by sample size is .17. The sample weighted average is .07. For this table, the correlation between sample size and self-fulfilling prophecy effect size is -.72. Williams (1976) and Chapman & McCauley (1993) reported more than one self-fulfilling prophecy effect size. This table simply averaged them together. Williams (1976) performed analyses separately by student sex, and because these are two separate samples, are treated as two studies. Kuklinski & Weinstein (2001) is treated as three separate studies because they performed analyses separately for first, third, and fifth graders. They actually reported two separate effect sizes for each grade, which, for simplicity, we have averaged together for this table.
[a] Effect size reported as standardized regression coefficient.
[b] These were quasi-experiments. Effect sizes are therefore reported as correlations between quasi-experimental conditions (reflecting teacher expectations) and student achievement.
[c] Although this was a correlational study, path coefficients were not reported. Instead, they reported the r-squared increment obtained when adding teacher expectations to a model that included control variables. This table reports the square root of this value to more closely approximate a standardized regression coefficient.

expectations were induced within the first two weeks of the school year (Raudenbush, 1984). Even accounting for the possibility of publication bias (significant effects are more likely to be published), self-fulfilling prophecies have been found sufficiently often in naturalistic research that it currently seems reasonable to conclude that they are indeed very widespread. Naturally-occurring teacher expectations can be, and often are, self-fulfilling. On average, however, such effects are relatively modest.

Under What Conditions Do More Powerful Self-Fulfilling Prophecies Occur?

Although the evidence does not justify broad generalizations emphasizing the power of expectancies, there still may be some conditions where self-fulfilling prophecies are larger than usual. This section, therefore, reviews some of the evidence on moderators of self-fulfilling prophecies.

Timing of False Expectations

Experimental inductions of false teacher expectations early in the year produce stronger self-fulfilling prophecies than experimental inductions later in the year (Raudenbush, 1984). This meta-analysis showed that experimental studies produce a self-fulfilling prophecy effect on IQ of about r = .2 when false teacher expectations are induced within the first 2 weeks of the school year, and of 0 when false teacher expectations are induced thereafter.

Age and New Situations

Both Rosenthal and Jacobson's field experiment (1968) and Kuklinski and Weinstein's (2001) naturalistic study found that self-fulfilling prophecies were stronger in first grade than in subsequent elementary school grades. This might lead one to conclude that younger children are inherently more vulnerable to expectancy effects. In fact, however, neither Rosenthal and Jacobson's study (discussed previously) or Kuklinski and Weinstein's study (see Table 17.1) yield a linear relationship of age to size of expectancy effect.

Raudenbush's meta-analysis (1984) also found that the power of self-fulfilling prophecies varied by grade level. The strongest teacher expectation effects occurred in first, second, and seventh grades. A simple "younger children are more susceptible" hypothesis can account for the grades 1 and 2 effect, but not for the grade 7 effect. Another possibility is that people are most susceptible to self-fulfilling prophecies when they enter new situations—and people in general may be more vulnerable to all sorts of social influences in situations with which they are not familiar (see Jussim, Eccles, & Madon, 1996, for a review). This latter interpretation is also consistent with research showing that some of the most powerful self-fulfilling prophecies ever found have occurred among new military recruits (McNatt, 2000).

Student Stigmatization

Several naturalistic studies have examined the possibility that students who belong to a stigmatized group may be particularly vulnerable to self-fulfilling prophecies. One study examined whether self-fulfilling prophecies were stronger among students with prior histories of high or low achievement (Madon, Jussim, & Eccles, 1997). Consistent with this stigma vulnerability idea, erroneously high teacher expectations for previously low achieving students produced self-fulfilling prophecy effect sizes of .3–.4 (Madon et al., 1997), but self-fulfilling prophecy effect sizes of near zero among high achievers.

Another study examined whether teacher expectations produced stronger self-fulfilling prophecies among students from stigmatized demographic groups (Jussim et al., 1996). Although there was no consistent evidence of self-fulfilling prophecies among students from higher socioeconomic backgrounds, teacher expectations did produce self-fulfilling prophecy effects of .2–.3 among students from lower socio-economic backgrounds. There was also evidence that teacher expectations for low achieving students from lower social class backgrounds produced a self-fulfilling prophecy effect size of about .6. Furthermore, teacher expectations for African American students produced self-fulfilling prophecy effect sizes of .4 to .6. The self-fulfilling prophecies among lower achieving students from lower socioeconomic (SES) backgrounds and among African American students were large by any standard.

Do Negative Teacher Expectations Harm More than Positive Teacher Expectations Help?

There have been only four published teacher expectations studies on this issue, and they have yielded a decidedly mixed picture. Those studies are discussed next. In each case, "positive" self-fulfilling prophecy refers to high expectations improving student outcomes and "negative" self-fulfilling prophecy refers to low expectations harming student outcomes. A conclusion that "negative self-fulfilling prophecies were more powerful," therefore, means that negative teacher expectations harmed students' achievement more than positive ones helped students' achievement; a conclusion that "positive self-fulfilling prophecies were more powerful" means that positive teacher expectations helped students' achievement more than negative ones harmed students' achievement.

Do "High Bias" Teachers Produce More Negative Self-Fulfilling Prophecies in Gym? Babad, Inbar, and Rosenthal (1982) examined the power of negative and positive self-fulfilling prophecies among 26 teachers and 202 students in gym classes. They found no evidence of self-fulfilling prophecies at all among "low bias" teachers (those low in dogmatism and cognitive rigidity).

Among high bias teachers, there were: (a) more powerful negative self-fulfilling prophecies for one of three student outcomes (distance jumping); (b) more powerful positive self-fulfilling prophecies for sit-ups and pushups; (c) no evidence of self-fulfilling prophecy for running speed outcomes. Their results, therefore, did not provide clear evidence that either positive or negative self-fulfilling prophecies were more powerful.

Under- Versus Overestimating IQ Sutherland and Goldschmid (1974) assessed six first- and second-grade teachers' expectations 2 months into the school year. Ninety-three students were administered two intelligence tests at each of two time points: 2 months and 7 months into the school year. The relative power of positive versus negative self-fulfilling prophecies was tested among the subset of students for whom teacher expectations were discrepant from their actual IQ test scores. Discrepancies were identified in two ways: teacher "overestimates," which meant that the teacher's expectations were higher than the student's IQ score (e.g., a teacher describing a student with a below average IQ score as "average"), and teacher "underestimates," which meant that the teacher's expectation were lower than the student's IQ score (e.g., a teacher describing a student with above average scores as "average").

Sutherland and Goldschmid (1974) found stronger evidence of negative than of positive self-fulfilling prophecies. Teacher underestimates had an effect of about r = .5 on intelligence test scores, whereas teacher overestimates had effects of under r = .2. The interpretation of this difference is muddied, however, because the negative expectations probably more extremely underestimated students than the positive expectations overestimated them. Negative expectations consisted of rating students with IQ scores of 120–135 as "average." Positive expectations consisted of rating students with IQ scores of 80–95 as "average". An average IQ score is 100. Thus, an "average" rating probably underestimates a student with a score of 120–135 more (i.e., 20 to 35 points) than it overestimates a student with a score of 80–95 (i.e., 5 to 20 points). The greater power of negative versus positive self-fulfilling prophecies that emerged, therefore, may have reflected the greater inaccuracy of negative expectations as operationalized among their particular sample, rather than any generally greater power of negative expectations.

Under- vs. Overestimating Achievement in Math Classes The third study to address the relative power of positive vs. negative teacher expectations (Madon et al., 1997): (a) explicitly compared inaccurately low expectations to equally inaccurate high expectations, and (b) performed this comparison both overall and separately for students with histories of high and low achievement.

Polynomial regression (Judd & McClelland, 1989) was used to test whether teacher over- or underestimates more strongly predicted changes in students' math achievement. The slope of the relationship of teacher expectations to student achievement was about .3 among the most highly overestimated students and about .1 among the underestimated students. This pattern indicated greater power of positive than of negative self-fulfilling prophecies.

In addition, Madon et al. (1997) examined this pattern separately for students with prior records of high or low achievement. For high achievers, teacher underestimates had almost no self-fulfilling prophecy effect and teacher overestimates produced self-fulfilling prophecy effects of about .2. For low achievers, teacher underestimates produced self-fulfilling prophecy effects of about .1–.2 and teacher overestimates produced self-fulfilling prophecy effects of about .4. In sum, Madon et al. (1997) showed that positive expectancies tend to be more powerful than negative expectancies, especially for low-achieving students.

The Predictive Validity of Pre-school Teacher Expectations Alvidrez and Weinstein (1999) examined the extent to which pre-school teacher beliefs about student intelligence predicted the overall high school GPAs of 63 students (all of whom were 4 years old), in the context of a model that controlled for IQ and parental SES, both measured at age 4 (previous analyses showed that neither student gender nor ethnicity predicted GPA beyond the effects of IQ and SES). The results were quite striking: not only did the pre-school teacher expectations predict high school grades achievement (overall effect of nearly .4), polynomial regression showed that the largest effects occurred for negative expectations (underestimates) and that the effects of positive expectations were near zero.

Why did such a pattern occur? Several limitations to their study render its interpretation ambiguous. First, IQ tests among 4 year olds lack the reliability and validity of those administered to older people (e.g., Neisser et al, 1996). Furthermore, IQ tests have come a long way since the 1960s, which is when Alvidrez & Weinstein's (1999) data was collected (Neisser et al., 1996).

This raises the possibility that teacher perceptions at age 4 were sufficiently accurate to recognize student characteristics predictive of achievement that were not fully captured by the IQ test. Especially because student grades are often influenced by nonacademic aspects of behavior, such as cooperativeness, disruptiveness, and obedience (Jussim, Smith, Madon, & Palumbo, 1998), and because the personality characteristics underlying these behaviors are often strikingly consistent across the lifespan (e.g., Roberts, Kuncel, Shiner, Caspi, & Goldberg, 2007), it is possible that ratings provided by teachers of pre-schoolers had predictive validity not accounted for by the IQ tests.

Furthermore, Alvidrez and Weinstein (1999) acknowledged many of these issues and clearly stated that their study was not capable of distinguishing between accuracy and self-fulfilling prophecy as explanations for the patterns they observed. We agree, but would go further. They provided no data and little in the way of speculation regarding how the expectations held by pre-school teachers for 4-year-old children could actually cause achievement in high school (beyond a general reference to the potential for self-fulfilling prophecies). Far more long term, longitudinal research is needed before any conclusion that they identified a causal process could be justified (a point they themselves emphasized in their discussion section).

Conclusion: Are Positive or Negative Teacher Expectations More Powerful? It appears that Babad et al. (1982) found no clear and consistent pattern; Sutherland and Goldschmid's (1974) study was biased in the direction of finding stronger negative expectancy effects; and Alvidrez and Weinstein's (1999) study could not disentangle self-fulfilling prophecy from accuracy. Madon, et al. (1997) provided an unbiased test of the power of positive versus negative self-fulfilling prophecies, and examined this issue among a much larger sample than was included in any of these other prior studies (indeed, larger than in all of them combined). Whether the evidence from these four studies tilts in favor of the power of positive expectations or of negative expectations, therefore, is currently a matter of individual scientific judgment. Clearly, however, despite the frequency with which conclusions emphasizing the inordinate power of negative expectations appear in the literature (e.g., Darley & Fazio, 1980; Weinstein et al., 2004), it is premature to conclude that the main effect of self-fulfilling prophecies is to harm the achievement of low expectancy students.

Do Self-Fulfilling Prophecies Accumulate?

The Logic of Accumulating Self-Fulfilling Prophecies Many reviews and perspectives have suggested that empirical studies underestimate self-fulfilling prophecies, because expectancy effects may accumulate over time and/or over multiple perceivers (Claire & Fiske, 1998; Snyder, 1984; Weinstein & McKown, 1998). The logic of accumulation is straightforward:

1. Small effects are typically obtained in both short-term (1 hour) laboratory studies of self-fulfilling prophecies and teacher expectation studies conducted over a school year.
2. Although small in such contexts, many targets may be subjected to the same or similar erroneous expectations over and over again.
3. Effects that are only small in any one context will likely accumulate across multiple contexts to become quite large.

The Logic of Dissipation Despite the apparent compelling nature of this sort of analysis, there are equally good reasons to expect self-fulfilling prophecies to dissipate, rather than accumulate. Although an extended discussion of those reasons is beyond the scope of this chapter (but see, e.g., Jussim & Harber, 2005; Smith et al., 1999), two will be briefly discussed here. First, there is regression to the mean. A student whose achievement is enhanced or suppressed by a self-fulfilling prophecy effect is likely to return to their prior level of achievement, unless some process operates to maintain or increase the original self-fulfilling prophecy effect.

Second, there is self-verification (Swann, 1987), which refers to the idea that people are highly motivated to see themselves in a manner consistent with their own long-standing and deep-seated self-views, and to convince others to view them much as they view themselves. The self-verification motive may render many people resistant to confirming others' inaccurate expectations.

Thus, the bottom line is data, not argument. To what extent do the self-fulfilling effects of teacher expectations accumulate or dissipate?

The Data Supports Dissipation Four studies to date have addressed whether the self-fulfilling prophecy effects of teacher expectations accumulate or dissipate over time. All have provided more evidence of dissipation than accumulation. The first, Rosenthal and Jacobson's (1968) Pygmalion study, which has already been discussed, found about a 4 point IQ difference between bloomers and controls in the first year of the study, but less than a 3 point difference in the second year.

An observational study (Rist, 1970), which was interpreted at the time as demonstrating a "caste" system which creates and then exacerbates social class differences in achievement, actually failed to provide such evidence. The main "evidence" of self-fulfilling prophecy provided in this research was teacher seating patterns of children in kindergarten through second grade ("evidence" is in quotes here, because this constitutes teacher treatment, not student achievement;

a truly hardnosed critic might therefore conclude that the study provided no evidence whatsoever that directly bears on self-fulfilling prophecies). Regardless, there were fewer, not more, seating differences between social class groups over time, thereby providing no evidence of accumulation, and, instead, evidence suggesting dissipation.

Two quantitative studies (Smith et al., 1999; West & Anderson, 1976) also found dissipation. Smith et al. followed students for up to 6 years (from sixth through 12th grade) and found that, contrary to the accumulation hypothesis, the effects of sixth-grade teacher expectations on 12th grade achievement were smaller, not larger, than their effects on sixth- and seventh-grade achievement. West and Anderson followed students from ninth through 12th grades, and found essentially the same pattern (smaller, not larger, effects of ninth-grade teacher expectations on 12th-grade achievement than on ninth-grade achievement).

Conclusions About Accumulation and Dissipation The story one can tell on the basis of the idea that self-fulfilling prophecies accumulate is very appealing because it seems to provide a scientific basis for understanding many sorts of injustices and inequalities (e.g., Snyder, 1984; Weinstein et al., 2004). Unfortunately, regardless of how apparently compelling such stories may sound, they are not supported by the existing data. The evidence is quite clear that self-fulfilling prophecies in the classroom generally dissipate, not accumulate, over time.

Pattern and Extent of Self-Fulfilling Prophecies in the Classroom: Knowns and Unknowns

The first part of our review has, we hope, made clear what conclusions are and are not justified on the basis of existing teacher expectation research. Self-fulfilling prophecies do occur, but such effects are, in general, quite modest, corresponding, on average, to effect sizes of about .1 to .2. Even the original "dramatic" Rosenthal and Jacobson (1968) study only produced an average effect size of .15. In fact, given publication bias in favor of significant results, and the pattern clearly demonstrated in Table 17.1 showing that naturalistic studies with larger sample sizes produce smaller self-fulfilling prophecy effects, overall average effects in real classrooms are more likely to be near the lower end of our estimate.

Nonetheless, self-fulfilling prophecies sometimes exceed these average small effects. Effect sizes have been consistently larger among students in first and second grade. Whether such effects reflect a generally greater susceptibility to self-fulfilling prophecies among younger students, or a generally greater susceptibility to self-fulfilling prophecies among anyone in new situations, however, is unclear (and these possibilities are not necessarily mutually exclusive). Self-fulfilling prophecies are also considerably stronger among underachieving students and students from stigmatized social backgrounds.

Although considerable scholarship seems to take for granted the idea that self-fulfilling prophecies produce primarily negative effects (Darley & Fazio, 1980; Gilbert, 1995; Weinstein et al., 2004; Weinstein & McKown, 1998), the empirical evidence on this issue is decidedly mixed. Clearly, additional research on whether self-fulfilling prophecies tend to be mostly beneficial or mostly harmful is needed.

Another area in which the scholarship is mixed is on the topic of accumulation, with many articles emphasizing the power of accumulation (e.g., Claire & Fiske, 1998; Snyder, 1984; Weinstein et al., 2004; Weinstein & McKown, 1998), and a smaller number emphasizing dissipation (Smith et al., 1999; Jussim & Harber, 2005). Here, however, the data are quite clear. Narrative reviews notwithstanding, every study that has empirically examined the accumulation of self-fulfilling prophecies in the classroom has found that, rather than accumulating, they dissipate over time.

Self-Fulfilling Prophecy Processes

Based on the extant literature, it is clear that self-fulfilling prophecies do exist, and that they can occur in naturalistic settings. Therefore, in this section, we discuss how naturally-occurring self-fulfilling prophecies occur in the classroom. Many researchers have proposed models of the self-fulfilling prophecy process (Brophy & Good, 1974; Cooper, 1979; Cooper & Good, 1983; Darley & Fazio, 1980; Harris & Rosenthal, 1985; Jussim 1986; Rosenthal, 1974). Despite their differences, all agree on three main steps:

1. Teachers develop erroneous expectations.
2. Those expectations lead teachers to treat high expectancy students differently than they treat low expectancy students.
3. Students react to this differential treatment in such a manner as to confirm the originally erroneous expectation.

Step 1: Teachers Develop Erroneous Expectations

Because accurate expectations cannot be self-fulfilling (Jussim, 1991; Merton, 1948), self-fulfilling prophecies start with inaccurate expectations. Why do teachers' expectations go wrong?

Although this is a reasonable and necessary question to address, the bigger phenomenon is that teacher expectations are usually accurate. In this chapter, accuracy refers to teacher expectations predicting but not causing student achievement. Because teachers' expectations typically predict student achievement more often because they are accurate than because they are self-fulfilling (Brophy, 1983; Jussim & Harber, 2005), it is important to discuss some of the factors that contribute to teacher accuracy before understanding sources of inaccuracy.

Empirical Evidence of Accuracy

There are two ways that the existing research can provide information about the accuracy of teacher expectations. First, the results of naturalistic studies that simply correlated teacher expectations with student achievement can be compared with the effects of teacher expectations obtained in experimental studies. Such comparisons provide indirect evidence for high accuracy because the correlations were typically much higher (generally in the .4 to .8 range) than were the expectancy effect sizes (typically in the .1 to .2 range; see, e.g., Brophy, 1983; Jussim, 1991; Jussim & Harber, 2005, for reviews). The difference between the correlation and the effect size constitutes an indirect way to estimate the accuracy of teacher expectations, because this difference represents predictive accuracy without self-fulfilling influence (Jussim et al., 1996). By this metric, about 75% of the overall predictive validity of teacher expectations for standardized test scores reflects accuracy and the remaining 25% reflects self-fulfilling prophecy.

The second way of evaluating the accuracy of teacher expectations is to empirically assess it within a study (rather than compare results across studies). The basic methodology involves: (a) assessing teacher expectations (typically early in the school year); (b) assessing student achievement in the year prior to the assessment of teacher expectations; (c) assessing student outcomes at the end of the school year in which teacher expectations were assessed (most typically standardized test scores, but sometimes, grades, course selections, etc.); and (d) examining the extent to which teacher expectations predicted but did not cause student outcomes.

The logic here is straightforward. The correlation between teacher expectations early in the year and student achievement at the end of the school year represents the overall predictive validity of teacher expectations. That predictive validity can come from only two sources, which are both mutually exclusive and exhaustive: (a) teacher expectations cause student achievement (e.g., through self-fulfilling prophecies), and (b) teacher expectations predict, but do not cause, student achievement. To the extent that both teacher expectations and student achievement are caused by third variables, they will correlate without causing one another.

The standardized path coefficient (whether obtained in regression, latent variable models, hierchical linear models, or any structural equation technique) linking teacher expectations to student achievement in the context of a model that controls for plausible sources of accuracy (student prior grades and achievement, demographics, motivation, etc.) represents the best estimate of a naturally occurring self-fulfilling prophecy. It represents the best estimate of the extent to which teacher expectations early in the year predict *changes* in student achievement by the end of the school year (we know this because prior achievement is controlled). The difference between the overall predictive validity of teacher expectations (the correlation with achievement), and the standardized path coefficient estimating self-fulfilling prophecy, equals the extent to which teacher expectations predicted but did not cause student achievement. Prediction without causation is *exactly* how we define accuracy (see, e.g., Jussim, 1991, for a detailed example demonstrating how accuracy mathematically and statistically equals the correlation minus the path coefficient linking teacher expectations to students' future achievement).

The bottom line, however, has been that studies using this approach yielded essentially the same results as the cross-study comparisons (see reviews by Brophy, 1983; Jussim & Eccles, 1995). About 75% of the correlation between teacher expectations and student future achievement reflects accuracy, and about 25% reflects self-fulfilling prophecy.

Why Are Teachers' Expectations Typically Accurate?

Students' performance is so frequently evaluated, in such a variety of ways, that it should not be particularly surprising that teacher accuracy is quite high. Whether it is state-mandated standardized achievement tests, the SATs, or simply in-class assignments, tests, and quizzes, children's performance is so repeatedly evaluated and tested in school that teachers typically have abundant opportunities to obtain reasonably clear and objective information about students' achievement. Given this wealth of available information, it would be extraordinary if most teachers did not have at least a reasonably good idea of where most students stand with respect to their level of learning and achievement.

The Realistic Accuracy Model (RAM; Funder, 1995) provides one theoretical basis for understanding why teachers are so accurate in predicting student achievement. RAM specifies four steps as necessary to achieve accuracy. For one person's judgments about another's underlying attributes (in this case, academic competence) to become accurate, the underlying attribute must generate observable behavior. In most classrooms, where teachers give tests, quizzes, homework assignments, projects, and observe in-class participation, it does generate observable behavior. Second, that evidence has to be available to the (generic) perceiver (in this case, the teacher). Such performances are abundantly available to the teacher. Third, the perceiver/teacher must detect the evidence. In general, teachers detect student performance. Fourth, the perceiver/teacher has to actually use the detected evidence/cues (and weight them appropriately) for arriving at an accurate judgment. Although there may be some slippage here, teachers often have a highly organized system of weighting performances (e.g., homework is 10%, participation is 10%, quizzes are 30%, and tests are 50%), which helps them to assign a more accurate grade. Whether any particular weighting system is "appropriate" may be subject to debate, but, fortunately, the precise manner in which such different criteria are weighted rarely matters much anyway (Dawes, 1979).

Inaccuracy

So, why are teachers ever inaccurate? First, students change. They mature, their goals change, their home life changes, etc., in ways that can affect their performance. Therefore, even expectations based on clear, objective, and valid past information will not likely perfectly correspond to every student's future performance. Second, teachers' memories for students' past achievements may be imperfect. Their expectations may color and distort their interpretations of student achievement (Jussim, 1989; Jussim & Eccles, 1992; Williams, 1976). Like other people lacking specific training in statistics, logic, or decision-making, the ways in which they evaluate information, and especially make predictions, are subject to the same systematic errors and biases that characterize many laypeople (e.g., Kahneman, Slovic, & Tversky, 1982; Nisbett & Ross, 1980).

Third, social stereotypes may undermine the accuracy of teacher expectations. We do not want to overstate this, because the existing research strongly suggests that, for the most part, teachers' perceptions of differences between students from different demographic groups are quite accurate (Jussim et al., 1996; Madon et al., 1998; Williams, 1976). For example, two studies examined the accuracy of teacher expectations for African American students and for students from lower social class backgrounds (Jussim et al., 1996; Madon et al., 1998). They found that teachers perceived differences between different groups that closely corresponded to those groups' actual differences in prior grades and achievement tests, a pattern replicated in subsequent research. Although such findings appear to conflict with narrative reviews emphasizing the inaccuracy and biasing effects of stereotypes (APA, 1991; Aronson, 1999; Jones, 1986, 1990), they are consistent with a number of a meta-analyses all showing that biasing effects of stereotypes on person perception judgments tend to be quite small, typically averaging an r of about .1 (Davison & Burke, 2000; Kunda & Thagard, 1996; Mazella & Feingold, 1994; Sweeney & Haney, 1992; Swim, Borgida, Maruyama, & Myers, 1989).

Nonetheless, there is also evidence that, at least sometimes, social stereotypes and even diagnostic labels (e.g., "learning disabled") lead to inaccurate expectations for some students (Jussim et al., 1998; Jussim et al., 1996; Madon et al., 1998). For example, teachers often assume girls exert more effort than do boys, even though boys and girls exert similar effort (Jussim et al., 1998; Jussim et al., 1996, Madon et al., 1998). This turns out to be important because teachers often reward higher (perceived) effort with higher grades, which may seem reasonable until one keeps in mind that teacher perceptions of effort are themselves subject to bias and distortion. The common pattern of girls receiving higher grades than boys (on average) throughout their school years (e.g., Kimball, 1989; Pomerantz, Altermatt, & Saxon, 2002) may, therefore, be partially explained by the common pattern of sex stereotypes leading teachers to misperceive girls as trying harder than boys, and then rewarding them with higher grades. Whether erroneous perceptions of effort are also self-fulfilling (do erroneously high perceptions of effort actually cause greater effort?) is unknown because no research has addressed this question.

In summary, inaccurate expectations are the necessary starting point for self-fulfilling prophecies to occur. Although abundant research demonstrates moderate to high accuracy of teacher expectations, none demonstrates perfect accuracy. The relatively limited degree to which teacher expectations are usually inaccurate helps explain relatively modest overall self-fulfilling prophecy effects. At the same time, the pervasiveness of some degree of inaccuracy helps explain the pervasive occurrence of (modest) self-fulfilling prophecies.

Step 2: Teacher Expectations Lead to Differential Treatment

Four Major Types of Differential Treatment Teachers' expectations lead them to treat their students differently. Rosenthal (1974) identified four broad ways in which teachers treat high expectancy students differently than they treat low expectancy students (see Harris & Rosenthal, 1985 for a meta-analysis; Brophy, 1983; Brophy & Good, 1974; Jussim, 1986, for reviews). These different types of treatment, which are discussed next, are generally referred to as climate, feedback, input, and output.

First, teachers provide a more supportive emotional climate for high expectancy students. They are warmer, smile more, and offer them more encouragement. Second, teachers provide clearer and more favorable feedback to high expectancy students. Feedback (positive or negative) received by high expectancy students also tends to focus on performance. In contrast, low expectancy students receive considerably more feedback that is unrelated to achievement. Instead, feedback to low expectancy students is more likely to focus on behavior, cooperativeness, aggression, and so on. In addition, high expectancy students are praised more and criticized less than are low expectancy students.

Third, teachers often provide greater input into high expectancy students' education. They spend more time with and provide more attention to high expectancy students. They also may teach more material to high expectancy students. Fourth, teachers often provide high expectancy students with more opportunities for output. They call on high expectancy students more often; give high expectancy students more hints and prompts when they seem hesitant and unsure; provide high expectancy students with more time to respond to verbal questions; teach more difficult material to high expectancy students; and give high expectancy students more challenging class work and homework assignments.

Students' Perceptions of Differential Teacher Treatment

Are students aware of expectancy-triggered differential treatment? And if so, do such perceptions play a role in the self-fulfilling prophecy process? Questions such as these have been addressed by a very unique program of research.

Given that differential treatment is the behavioral means (on the part of teachers) by which self-fulfilling prophecies occur, Brattesani, Weinstein, and Marshall (1984) hypothesized that self-fulfilling prophecies would be larger in classrooms where students perceived their teachers as providing more preferential treatment to high expectancy students. Accordingly, Brattesani et al. asked students to indicate how much their teachers treated different students differently. They then split the teachers into two groups: Those whose students identified them as engaging in much differential treatment, and those whose students identified them as engaging in little differential treatment. Analyses then assessed the extent to which teacher expectations predicted student self-expectations and their future achievement, after controlling for achievement the prior year.

As predicted, teacher expectations most strongly predicted student expectations and achievement among classes in which the students perceived the greatest differential treatment. The effect sizes for teacher expectations predicting student expectations and achievement ranged from about 0 to .1 among the low differential treatment classes, and from about .3 to .4 among the high differential treatment classrooms.

Exactly what this means, however, is not completely clear, for two separate empirical reasons. First, a more recent study (Kuklinski & Weinstein, 2001) found that this pattern replicated in third grade, but not in first or fifth grade. Furthermore, both studies (Brattesani et al., 1984; Kuklinski & Weinstein, 2001) used relatively small sample sizes (see Table 17.1). Additional research is therefore needed before concluding that student perceptions of differential treatment are clear and consistent moderators of self-fulfilling prophecies.

In addition to the issue of replicability, the empirical status of student perceptions of differential treatment as a moderator versus epiphenomenon is unclear. One possibility is that the existing research can be taken at face value. In that case, student perception of differential treatment per se is indeed a moderator of self-fulfilling prophecy effects. This has an important implication: Student perceptions, *independent of actual teacher differential treatment,* moderate self-fulfilling prophecies. How such a process might actually work has never been articulated in the research on student perceptions of differential treatment.

Another possibility, however, is that student perceptions of differential treatment do not, by themselves, moderate self-fulfilling prophecies. Given that actual teacher differential treatment must occur in order to create a self-fulfilling prophecy, self-fulfilling prophecies, by definition, must be larger in classrooms with more actual differential treatment than in classrooms with no differential treatment (in which self-fulfilling prophecy effects would be zero). This should occur regardless of student perceptions. However, if students are not completely out of touch with the reality of teacher differential treatment, then their perceptions of differential treatment will correlate with actual differential treatment. Thus, student perceptions of differential treatment may appear to moderate self-fulfilling prophecies, even though they have no causal power to do so. Their apparent status as moderators could occur entirely because they are correlated with a necessary mediator of self-fulfilling prophecies—actual differential treatment.

Further complicating these issues is that much of the theorizing suggests that students' perceptions of differential treatment mediates rather than moderates self-fulfilling prophecies. The meditational model declares that differential treatment leads to perceptions of differential treatment which then influences students' self-expectancies, and these self-expectancies cause future achievement (e.g., Brattesani et al., 1984; Kuklinski & Weinstein, 2001; Weinstein, 1985). This implies a *mediating* (not moderating) role for student perceptions (the implicit model being something like: teacher expectations → differential treatment → perceptions of differential treatment → students' expectations → student achievement). The empirical research, however, has to date investigated student perceptions of differential treatment as moderators, not mediators, of self-fulfilling prophecies (Brattesani et al., 1984; Kuklinski & Weinstein, 2001). Greater clarity regarding the theoretical status of student perceptions of differential treatment as moderators versus mediators is clearly necessary to shed greater light on their causal role in achievement.

Regardless, research has found little or no evidence that student self-perceptions (of ability, self-expectations of performance, etc.) actually mediate self-fulfilling prophecies (e.g., Jussim, 1989; Kuklinski & Weinstein, 2001). This is because, in the context of models that include controls for prior achievement, standardized path coefficients relating self-perceptions to future achievement are typically between 0 and .10 (Jussim, 1989; Kuklinski & Weinstein, 2001). Even at .10, this means that mediational effects of student self-perceptions and expectations account for, at most, 1/10 of the self-fulfilling effects of teacher expectations on student achievement (this is because the mediated effect equals the product of the path coefficient relating teacher expectations to self-perceptions and the path coefficient relating student self-perceptions to achievement). Current evidence, therefore, has yet to identify a context in which student perceptions of differential treatment substantially account for self-fulfilling prophecies through the hypothesized mediator of student self-perceptions.

Step 3: Differential Treatment Affects Students

Given that teacher expectations create self-fulfilling prophecies and that teachers treat high expectancy students differently than they treat low expectancy students, expectancy-related differential treatment must somehow, therefore, be affecting students. Figuring out just how, however, has proven more difficult than it might have seemed. For example, the most obvious answer to how teacher expectations affect students (at least for many psychologists) was that it would affect students' motivation (e.g., Cooper, 1979; Cooper & Good, 1983; Eccles & Wigfield, 1985; Jussim, 1986; Weinstein, 1985). The motivational mediation idea is, at its core, quite simple: differential treatment affects student motivation which, in turn, affects student performance. To mediate self-fulfilling prophecies, this could mean that the treatment teachers accord high expectancy students generally increases motivation which improves their performance; and the treatment teachers accord low expectancy students generally undermines their motivation which harms their performance.

As simple as this core idea may be, and as common as it may be to theorizing about self-fulfilling prophecies (Cooper, 1979; Eccles & Wigfield, 1985; Jussim, 1986; Weinstein, 1985), it has proven difficult to demonstrate empirically. Although quite a few studies have examined effects of teacher expectations on a variety of student motivational variables (student self-expectancies, value placed on achievement, self-efficacy, etc.), none have ever shown that student motivation explains very much of the causal relationship between teacher expectations and student achievement (e.g., Brattesani et al., 1984; Cooper & Good, 1983; Jussim, 1989; Kuklinski & Weinstein, 2001). Effects on achievement of motivational variables assessed in such studies were often near zero, and rarely, if ever, exceeded .1 (in terms of standardized regression coefficients relating motivation to achievement, in the context of models that controlled for prior achievement and teacher expectations). Such effects, even when statistically significant, are just too small to account for very much of the relation between teacher expectations and student achievement.

Another, not mutually exclusive, route by which teacher treatment affects student achievement is by teacher expectations directly affecting student learning, independent of whatever effects they might have on motivation. Unfortunately, however, nor is there much evidence that teacher expectations create self-fulfilling prophecies because they directly cause students to learn more material, without mediation by student motivation. There is much evidence that teacher expectations influence student achievement, and that teachers treat high expectancy students differently than they treat low expectancy students. Exactly how that treatment translates into higher achievement, however, remains largely unknown.

There are only two broad categories of possible ways by which teacher treatment can affect students in such a manner as to result in self-fulfilling prophecies. It can affect their motivation, or it can affect something other than motivation. These two possibilities are mutually exclusive and exhaustive. This section addresses these possibilities in a largely speculative manner, because the existing research has yet to empirically identify the processes by which students' social and psychological responses to the types of differential treatment caused by teacher expectations ultimately manifest as self-fulfilling prophecies. In an attempt to identify some possible ways students' reactions to teacher treatment might mediate self-fulfilling prophecies, we must necessarily go beyond the traditional teacher expectation literature. We specifically review research on how teacher behavior and practices influence students' learning and motivation and we argue that many of those behaviors and practices map nicely on to what is known about teacher expectations and differential treatment. Absent direct empirical evidence, however, our review is necessarily speculative.

Direct Effects of Differential Treatment on Learning

Several of the types of differential treatment identified in Rosenthal's (1974; Harris & Rosenthal, 1985) four factor theory likely have direct effects on how much students learn, without necessarily influencing student motivation. For example, teachers often convey more and more difficult material to high expectancy students (the input factor from Rosenthal's theory). Often, this type of differential treatment will be appropriate and well-justified. It would be quite foolish indeed, for example, to try to teach calculus to a student who has not mastered algebra, whereas it is quite reasonable to teach calculus to a student who has mastered every math topic up through pre-calculus. Given the typically high accuracy of teacher expectations, many forms of differential treatment may reflect a well-justified attempt on the part of teachers to tailor their practices to individual students' needs.

We know, however, that self-fulfilling prophecies do occur, and that teachers are not always accurate. Therefore, when inaccurate, e.g., when a teacher erroneously believes Janie is more prepared for advanced work than is Johnny, this type of differential treatment may create a self-fulfilling prophecy. If Janie is given multiple opportunities to learn advanced material, whereas Johnny is given few or no such opportunities, by the end of the year, it is likely that Janie will have learned more material than did Johnny.

Rosenthal's (1974) output factor also may directly increase learning without influencing student motivation. The output factor refers to giving students opportunity to perform and demonstrate mastery of material. It includes everything from calling on students more frequently in class to allowing them to take on more difficult and challenging assignments. Although such differential treatment may have motivational effects (discussed later), independent of any such effects, it may also directly increase learning. When provided with an opportunity to work independently on complex projects, for example, students may learn more and more sophisticated material than when they are not given such opportunities. By giving students a chance to demonstrate mastery of a complex and partially independent project, teachers are creating opportunities for students to learn such material on their own. If teachers provide high expectancy students with more such opportunities, all other things being equal, again, they may simply learn more material than do low expectancy students who are not given such opportunities.

Clear and frequent feedback (Harris & Rosenthal, 1985; Rosenthal, 1974) also likely facilitates learning. Feedback provides useful information regarding how well one is learning a particular set of material or skills. Frequent and clear feedback, therefore, can be used by students to gauge their progress. In contrast, when such feedback is less frequently made available, it may be more difficult for students to determine how they stand with respect to the material. If students are not aware that they do not understand material, it may often be difficult to realize that they still need to learn that material. Thus, clear feedback may make it much easier for students to learn.

Direct Effects on Learning May be Synergistic with Motivational Effects

Direct effects of differential treatment on learning and achievement do not preclude the possibility that those effects also sustain or boost motivation. For example, after having succeeded at mastering difficult and complex material, students may more confidently take on difficult and challenging material in the future. Several lines of research are consistent with this. First, self-perceptions, self-efficacy, and expectations for one's own performance in an area are strongly affected by actual levels of accomplishment (Eccles & Wigfield, 1985). Second, students who were the beneficiaries of positive self-fulfilling prophecies in sixth grade math classes went on to take more advanced math classes in high school (Smith, Jussim & Eccles, 1999). Although this study did not examine motivational mediation, it raises the possibility that learning more early on leads to confidence that enhances students' willingness to tackle more difficult work at a later time. Thus, the direct effect of differential treatment (output) on learning may have further effects on motivation, which, in turn, influence future levels of achievement.

The effects of feedback on achievement may also be sustained, in part, through effects on motivation. Feedback can be used to regulate attention and effort. If one is succeeding at mastering the material, current levels of attention and effort are probably adequate. If not, increased attention and effort may be required. If such efforts prove successful, one has learned not only the material, but something about one's self—that one can achieve more highly by exerting greater effort. Consistent with this perspective, lack of clear performance feedback has been implicated in the underachievement of African American students (Crosby & Monin, 2007; Harber, 1998). Students (African American or not) who are not given clear information about where they stand with respect to mastering material are not given the chance to recognize and compensate for failures or difficulties in learning that material.

It seems likely, therefore, that some direct effects of differential treatment on learning also produce motivational effects, which, in turn, may further affect learning. In addition, differential treatment may not always directly affect learning. Instead, it may often affect motivation first, and it is only because of such motivational effects that differential treatment affects achievement. Such effects, therefore, are discussed next.

Motivational Mediation

Differential Treatment Revisited Understanding how students react to differential treatment starts with understanding differential treatment. Unfortunately, however, ever since Harris and Rosenthal's (1985) meta-analysis on differential treatment effects, relatively little research has been conducted on the ways in which teachers act on their expectations. One possible reason for this is that the meta-analysis was so clear and conclusive that researchers assumed that most or all of the interesting questions about differential treatment had been answered. Another possible reason is that the field simply lost interest.

Teacher behavior and instructional practices certainly include climate, feedback, input, and output, as indicated by Harris and Rosenthal's (1985) meta-analysis. Their meta-analysis was focused specifically on assessing the extent to which the literature, up to that point, supported the four factor theory of differential treatment (Rosenthal, 1974). Because they were focused on testing the four factor theory, however, they did not consider other forms of differential treatment. That, of course, does not necessarily mean that other forms of differential treatment do not occur.

Teacher behavior and instructional practices vary in many ways beyond climate, feedback, input, and output. For example, teachers may provide students with tasks that vary in how repetitive, complex or engaging they are. Such variability in tasks does not readily map on to Harris and Rosenthal's four factor meta-analysis. In addition, teachers may provide high expectancy students more autonomy to choose their own tasks and projects. This, too, does not readily map onto Harris and Rosenthal's (1985) four factor meta-analysis.

What, then, might be some types of differential treatment that are consistent with but also go beyond the four factor theory? And, particularly, what types of differential treatment might both reflect teacher expectations and also influence student motivation? Although there is no hard, direct empirical evidence that bears on these questions, there have been many advances in research on teacher practices that affect student motivation since the heyday of teacher expectation research in the 1970s and 1980s. Although a thorough review of that research is beyond the scope of the present chapter, one particular set of advances—the TARGET framework—appears to us to point to some strong contenders for teacher practices that both reflect expectations and influence motivation. Those practices are discussed next.

TARGET TARGET (advanced by Blumenfeld, 1992; Epstein, 1988) was introduced as a way of organizing the kinds of teacher practices and behaviors that increase or undermine students' motivation in the classroom. As such, the research on TARGET might help fill in some of the gaps with respect to how student motivation might mediate the relationship between expectancy-related teacher treatment and student achievement in such a manner as to help understand and explain self-fulfilling prophecies.

TARGET organizes these teacher practices along six dimensions: task, autonomy, recognition, goal structure/grouping, evaluation, and time. According to research on TARGET, a teacher who utilizes such practices enhances students' motivation by fostering the establishment of adaptive motivational patterns (e.g., Ames & Archer, 1988). Next, therefore, is a brief description of what constitutes adaptive motivational patterns, followed by a description of the six TARGET dimensions that produce such patterns.

Adaptive Motivational Patterns Adaptive motivational patterns refer to thoughts, feelings, and behaviors that contribute to students' learning in the classroom. Although a complete review of research on adaptive motivational patterns is beyond the scope of this chapter, abundant evidence testifies to the relationship between adaptive motivational patterns and positive outcomes in school (e.g., Church, Elliot, & Gable, 2001; Elliot & McGregor, 2001; Elliott & Dweck, 1988; Harackiewicz & Elliot, 1993; Pintrich, Conley, & Kempler, 2003; Smiley & Dweck, 1994). Next, therefore, we briefly describe adaptive motivational patterns and provide some examples.

Adaptive motivational patterns manifest in positive cognitions, affect, and behavior. Positive cognitions typically refer to higher-level thought processes. Deep level study strategies, for example, are higher-level thought processes that help information get from the working memory into the long-term memory. One example of a deep level study strategy is elaborative rehearsal. This involves connecting new information to existing, well-learned information. The opposite of elaborative rehearsal is rote memorization, which is a surface level study strategy. Self-regulatory strategies are also positive cognitions (setting goals for learning, monitoring and evaluating progress, and self-reinforcing for achieving goals). In contrast, students who do not set their own goals or monitor their own progress are not engaging in the type of positive cognitions that characterize adaptive motivational patterns.

Positive affect is also an important manifestation of adaptive motivational patterns. Examples of positive affect may include: (a) students who are excited by the prospect of learning and therefore seek out challenging academic situations to maximize learning and (b) students who feel confident about their ability to learn. These affects are viewed as part of an adaptive motivational pattern because they keep students engaged in school. The alternatives—students who are bored or disengaged and/or who lack confidence—are not likely to lead students to exert the type of effort necessary to maximize their achievement.

One reason positive cognitions and affects are so important is that they may lead to positive behaviors. Positive behaviors may include: (a) allowing more study time before an exam to learn the material on a deeper level, (b) taking in-depth notes during lectures, and (c) persisting at a task in the face of difficulty. Taken together, these three aspects of adaptive motivational patterns work in concert and can have reciprocal effects on each other and on motivation in general. For example, a student who focuses on improving test scores (adaptive thought) rather than earning the highest grade in the class (maladaptive thought) is more likely to spend more time to study for an exam (adaptive behavior) rather than cram the night before (maladaptive behavior), and will most likely feel more confident and excited by the prospect of learning (positive affect) rather than feeling stressed and overwhelmed (negative affect).

Teacher practices identified by TARGET may provide insights into how differential treatment alters student behavior in such a way as to produce self-fulfilling prophecies. The TARGET framework was created in order to characterize teacher practices that do, in fact, alter students' behavior in such a way as to sustain motivation to learn and increase achievement. Next, therefore, is a brief description of how each dimension of TARGET can produce adaptive motivational patterns.

Task The task dimension refers to the types of tasks that teachers assign their students. Tasks vary in a variety of ways that can affect student motivation (Ames, 1992; Blumenfeld, 1992). Tasks can differ in degree of difficulty and how they are structured or organized (essays, short answers, problem-solving, projects, etc.). They can also vary in how much students value them (see Eccles & Wigfield, 2002; Wigfield, Tonks, & Clauda, this volume, for more detailed discussions of the roles of values in motivation). According to TARGET, teachers should do their best to engage students in tasks that maximize how much those students value education and achievement.

Tasks can influence motivation in a variety of ways because students use information that is "…embedded in tasks…to make judgments about their ability, their willingness to apply effortful strategies, and their feelings of satisfaction" (Ames, 1992, p. 263). When tasks are varied, challenging, and applicable to real-world situations, they tend to foster sustained interest in and commitment to learning (Deemer, 2004). When tasks are repetitive and easy, students readily lose interest and commitment. Tasks that are too difficult, however, will likely evoke frustration and, if too frequently encountered, may be demotivating (Peterson, Maier, & Seligman, 1993).

Authority/Autonomy Autonomy refers to the degree of control students have in their classroom. Teachers who support autonomy in the classroom, as opposed to being controlling, tend to (a) offer choices to students with regard to tasks and other classroom activities, and (b) … "allow students to have a say in establishing priorities in task completion, method of learning, or pace of learning…" (Ames, 1992, p. 266). Because of these teacher practices, students are more likely to feel like valued members of the classroom community whose opinions matter, and to remain psychologically engaged in and committed to classroom activities (Ames, 1992; Blumenfeld, 1992; Deemer, 2004). When teachers fail to provide students with autonomy, it can be seriously demotivating for students. Under such circumstances, students may do what they are told, but when they engage in school activities entirely because they are under duress, there is less reason for them to become psychologically engaged in or committed to classroom activities.

Recognition Recognition refers to acknowledging and praising students for their effort, progress, and behavior in the classroom. The recognition factor in TARGET does not emphasize high performance. Although praising or publicly acknowledging high achieving students may be rewarding for those particular students, it may actually lead many other students in the same classroom to feel badly not just about their performance, but about education in general (Deemer, 2004). Furthermore, failing to recognize effort, progress, and constructive behaviors fails to encourage students to engage in those behaviors most likely to enhance their learning and achievement. In contrast, by praising students for effort, teachers encourage students to engage in a behavior that is crucial for maximizing their learning and achievement. In general, TARGET emphasizes the importance of teachers recognizing students for the behaviors that lead them to be as academically successful as they can be, rather than for meeting an external standard of success.

Grouping The ways in which teachers group their students for in-class activities (and whether they use grouping at all) can influence students' interest and engagement in an activity. In cooperative grouping, for example, students work together in face to face interactions to accomplish a shared goal, while individuals are still held accountable for their performance (e.g., Johnson & Johnson, 1991). Success, in particular, is determined by a focus on improvement rather than competition, as well as a shared responsibility and excitement for learning (Maehr & Anderman, 1993). When teachers utilize cooperative grouping, it provides opportunities for students to (a) enhance their social skills and social negotiation, (b) foster interdependence among one another, and (c) use more complex thinking strategies (Deemer, 2004). When teachers use no grouping at all, it may lead to boredom, lack of creativity, and isolation.

Evaluation The ways in which teachers evaluate their students' work is critical for the establishment of adaptive motivational patterns. Such patterns are most strongly sustained by evaluations that focus more on students' self-improvement and achievement of objective standards. Regardless of their rate of learning, or standing compared to other students, knowing that one has mastered a skill, technique, or a content domain that one previously had not mastered provides both a sense of accomplishment and feedback regarding one's progress. In contrast, evaluations that focus on social comparisons, which, unfortunately, is common practice in many classrooms, can be demotivating. For example, grading on a curve focuses quite explicitly on social comparisons. Such evaluations only inform students how their performance compares to other students. They provide little information about the extent to which students have mastered the required material (Deemer, 2004).

Time The amount of time teachers give their students to learn is critical to their success and motivation. Although unlimited time is not available (due to curriculum demands, for example), the more time they give students to learn, the better the chance students have to master the material. Furthermore, the more often topics are revisited in the classroom and the more flexible teachers are with time for learning, the more likely students are to master the material (Maehr & Anderman, 1993).

How TARGET Complements Existing Research on Differential Treatment The TARGET framework strongly suggests that certain specific teacher behaviors increase or decrease students' motivation. The behaviors previously identified as characterizing teacher treatment of high expectancy students (e.g., Harris & Rosenthal, 1985)—warmer climate, more feedback and more positive feedback, more teacher input, and more student opportunities for output—are all consistent with the TARGET framework. Nonetheless, the TARGET framework provides more specificity than most prior work on teacher treatment models of self-fulfilling prophecies.

For example, the positive interactions and teacher recognition factors of TARGET directly map onto the warmer climate and feedback factors in teacher expectation/differential treatment models. On the other hand, providing more meaningful and interesting tasks and greater autonomy (all identified by TARGET) also probably contribute to the warmer climate that teachers provide high expectancy students, but have not been specifically identified in prior work on self-fulfilling prophecies. Nonetheless, such practices are plausibly involved in differential treatment. Rote and repetitive tasks are often seen as necessary requirements for students performing below certain standards and teachers may be more likely to provide more freedom and autonomy to their high expectancy students. Undoubtedly, some aspects of such types of differential treatment may be appropriate for certain students under certain circumstances. Nonetheless, both TARGET and research on teacher expectations strongly suggests that, sometimes, teachers may provide too large a difference in autonomy and meaningful tasks to their high and low expectancy students (later in this chapter, we discuss the likely motivational effects of such differences).

A greater frequency of evaluations, especially positive ones involving recognition with a focus on improvement (as identified by TARGET), also fit the feedback dimension of the 4-factor theory of teacher treatment. The type of tasks and in-class groupings identified by TARGET correspond well with the input and output factors that are well-established in the research on expectancy-related differential treatment. Overall, therefore, the insights provided by TARGET with respect to improving student motivation are highly compatible with what is already known about the types of teacher behaviors that most heavily mediate self-fulfilling prophecies.

How TARGET Extends Beyond Existing Research on Differential Treatment The TARGET framework, however, does more than merely match up well with what is already known. It also provides additional, and more specific, guidance regarding ways in which teachers are likely to treat high expectancy students differently than low expectancy students—ways not well-recognized by existing theory or empirical research—and how such treatment might alter student motivation in such a way as to alter student achievement (and thus produce a self-fulfilling prophecy).

TARGET raises the possibility that self-fulfilling prophecies may occur, in part, because teachers evoke greater effort from their high expectancy students than from their low expectancy students. The hypothesis that teachers evoke greater effort from their high expectancy students, and may discourage effort among low expectancy students, has, as far as we know, never been directly tested. In business contexts, however, inspirational leaders often evoke extraordinary efforts from their followers, and such efforts are often a major part of what has made certain corporations extremely successful over the long term (Collins & Porras, 1997). Thus, the hypothesis that teachers evoke greater effort from their high expectancy students clearly warrants testing.

Another way in which TARGET extends beyond the four-factor theory is by suggesting that ability grouping practices might moderate self-fulfilling prophecies. Specifically, TARGET suggests that within class, same-ability grouping (e.g., having the high performing students work together and the low performing students work together) may undermine students' motivation. This may have little effect on the high expectancy students who typically will already be high achievers with high motivation. It is too easy, however, for such situations to undermine the motivation of the students in the low groups. If students realize they are in "low" groups, their own efficacy and performance expectations may decline, thereby undermining their achievement (Eccles & Wigfield, 1985; Steele, 1992). Among such students, therefore, teachers' expectations are likely to make the biggest difference.

For example, school tracking refers to the policy of segregating students into different classes according to their ability; that is, smart students may be assigned to one class, average students to another, and slow students to a third. Because tracking represents institutional justification for believing that some students are more able than others, some researchers have suggested that tracking may lead to the type of rigid teacher expectations that are most likely to evoke self-fulfilling prophecies (Oakes, 1986).

The one study to empirically investigate this hypothesis, however, failed to support it (Smith et al., 1998). Self-fulfilling prophecies among students grouped by ability between classes were no more powerful than those among students in heterogeneous classes—and both fell within the typically small range of 0–.2 (the results varied slightly by predictor and outcome, but not by between class groups).

There was, however, some evidence that *within class* grouping moderated self-fulfilling effects of teacher expectations (within class grouping refers to the practice of dividing students into two or more ability groups within a class). Although effects were near zero among students who were either not grouped at all, or who were in high groups, such effects were about .2 among those in low ability within class groups. Ability differences and group labels may be more salient to teachers who use within-class grouping. Students in low groups (within classes) are more vulnerable to confirming teachers' expectations. This is not necessarily bad. By adopting TARGET-like practices that involve encouraging and challenging low achieving students, teachers may disproportionately produce beneficial self-fulfilling prophecies. "I know that if you work at this, you can master this material" is likely to be particularly powerful among such students. When teachers communicate very low expectations for students in this group, it is likely to strengthen and reinforce the message of "you can't really do this."

Another way that TARGET contributes new insights into how teacher treatment alters student behavior includes the time they spend in the classroom, and the way in which they use that time. Teachers may sometimes just spend more time teaching, working with, assisting, and challenging high expectancy students. A simple tally of time spent with individual students might not capture this, to the extent that teachers also spend a fair amount of low quality time (disciplining, reprimanding, etc.) with low expectancy students. Indeed, such time is likely to be de-motivating. Instead, time spent on engaging and challenging topics (especially individual or small group time) is likely to encourage students to engage in adaptive motivational patterns. Little research has addressed the role of teachers spending different amounts of high quality intellectually challenging time, per se, with different students in creating self-fulfilling prophecies, although one observational study did find that teachers spent almost all of their time and attention teaching high expectancy students (Rist, 1970). This, too, was only a single study, and whether a similar pattern holds more generally is largely unknown.

Overall, TARGET contributes valuable information regarding additional ways in which teacher treatment likely alters student motivation and behavior. To what extent are such processes likely to mediate self-fulfilling prophecies? Unfortunately, there currently is no data that bears directly on this question. Thus, our analysis of the role of TARGET-like practices and student motivation in mediating self-fulfilling prophecies should be viewed more as hypothesis-generating ideas than as established empirical facts. The next section, therefore, considers the conditions under which such processes are more versus less likely to mediate self-fulfilling prophecies.

When Student Motivational Mediation Is Merely A Partial Explanation For A Modest Effect

Self-fulfilling prophecy effects, especially in real classes, are often not very large, averaging about .1–.2. And, undoubtedly, self-fulfilling prophecies do not occur exclusively because teachers raise or lower student motivation. So, this raises a "why bother" specter. Why bother trying to understand the role of student motivation in mediating the self-fulfilling effects of teacher expectations, if they merely constitute a partial explanation for a modest effect?

This is not an unreasonable or even cynical question. In fact, considering it seriously provides some important insights into what future research is and is not likely to find. Student motivation is a multi-faceted, multi-dimensional construct. There are many different aspects and types of motivation. Each one will likely provide only a partial contribution to the (itself) partial contribution that "student motivation" makes to the average modest self-fulfilling effect.

To get concrete, let us say that, in some context, self-fulfilling prophecies have an effect size of .20. Let us further say half of that is motivationally mediated. That means .10 of the effect of teacher expectations on student achievement comes via student motivation. If self-efficacy mediates part of that, and adaptive motivational patterns another part, and self-perceptions of ability another part, etc., each may only mediate a tiny fraction of a self-fulfilling prophecy—.02 here, .04 there. Such effects may be so small, that they may be difficult to detect with traditional analytic methods such as regression, ANOVA, or HLM. And failure to find "significant" evidence of motivational mediation may lead researchers to the pessimistic conclusion that motivation does not matter.

When Student Motivational Mediation May Be a Powerful Explanation for a Large Effect

A pessimistic conclusion that student motivational mediation of self-fulfilling prophecies does not matter would be at minimum premature, and most likely very wrong, at least in some very important circumstances. This section, therefore, discusses the contexts in which student motivation is likely to be a powerful mediator of a powerful expectancy effect.

The term "underachiever" is often used to refer to low performing students in much the same manner as "differently abled" is used to refer to people with handicaps. That is, it may often be a politically correct or diplomatic way to refer to students about whom one has very low expectations because their prior histories have demonstrated very low achievement. Nonetheless, there are theoretical, scientific, and real world reasons to think the term "underachiever" may have more than a grain of truth in it. That is, many low achieving students may be capable of achieving at much higher levels under the right conditions, and one of those conditions involves teacher expectations.

Abundant evidence suggests that school is often an unfriendly place for many African American and lower SES students (e.g., Condron & Roscigno, 2003; Lareau, 1987; Steele, 1992). When school is consistently a difficult place, students may often "disidentify" with achievement by devaluing the importance they place on school or by devaluing the particular subjects in which they feel devalued (e.g., Eccles & Wigfield, 1985; Jussim, 1986; Steele, 1992; Verkuyten & Thijs, 2004). Is this itself a self-fulfilling prophecy? Perhaps sometimes, but certainly not always. School can be difficult for students from stigmatized backgrounds for all sorts of reasons, many of which have nothing to do with teacher expectations. Poverty, one-parent or no-parent homes, cultural differences and many other factors probably contribute to the difficulties such children have in school. On the other hand, to the extent that teachers and administrators come to believe such students *cannot* do better, such beliefs probably do constitute self-fulfilling prophecies to the extent that they function to *prevent* students from doing better.

Regardless of the reasons for low achievement, however, disidentification and psychologically distancing one's self from school, in addition to undermining achievement, probably renders many such students more readily influenced by teacher expectations in several ways. When students with a history of negative school experiences find themselves faced with a supportive, encouraging teacher who also insists on high performance, it may feel like a breath of fresh air. Such a teacher may inspire some previously low achievers to engage in the efforts necessary to raise their achievement levels.

This perspective may not be as Pollyannaish as it sounds. In his influential article on Black disidentification with school, Steele (1992) describes academic programs in which previously low performing students (e.g., some with SATs in the 300s) take on difficult honors-level work and come to outperform their White and Asian classmates. Steele's (1992) description of these programs implies that the teachers often engage in behaviors much like those specified by TARGET and that lead to beneficial self-fulfilling prophecies in the classroom and workplace: They are challenging and supportive (e.g., Brophy & Good, 1974; Cooper, 1979; Eccles & Wigfield, 1985; Eden, 1984, 1986; Harris & Rosenthal, 1985; Jussim, 1986; Rosenthal, 1989; Wentzel, 1997). In addition, anecdotal evidence shows that charter schools serving impoverished ethnic minority communities in Boston and New York can dramatically improve student achievement, in large part, by holding students to high standards (high expectations) and by requiring and inspiring students to exert extraordinary levels of effort (*Boston Globe*, 2004; Sangree, 2000; Uncommon Schools, 2008).

In short, students suffering from some sort of stigma, whether demographic (race, class) or personal (handicap, disability, low achievement), may be particularly susceptible to self-fulfilling prophecies. However, because disproportionate numbers of such students often perform poorly, the main direction of their vulnerability to expectancy effects is up, not down. For students on a trajectory to drop out of high school, or even barely get by, there is far more potential to move up the academic achievement ladder than to move down. For a high achieving student, because there is less room to move up, an equally high teacher expectation has less potential to create a beneficial self-fulfilling prophecy.

Thus, positive teacher expectations are likely to have a disproportionately high effect on low achieving and stigmatized students. This perspective is entirely consistent with the research reviewed in the first major section of this chapter on the conditions under which powerful self-fulfilling prophecies occur. That section reviewed research showing that some of the largest self-fulfilling prophecies in the classroom ever obtained have been found among students from lower SES and low achieving backgrounds, and among students who are African American (Jussim et al., 1996; Madon et al., 1997).

Furthermore, there is also ample reason to believe that those self-fulfilling prophecies dispro-portionately increased students' achievement. Research based on the same data also found that teacher expectations that were erroneously high produced larger self-fulfilling prophecies (effect sizes of about .4) than did teacher expectations that were erroneously low (effect sizes of .1–.2), and that this difference between the power of positive and negative self-fulfilling prophecies was greater among low achieving than among high achieving students (Madon et al., 1997). Under the wrong conditions, negative teacher expectations can undoubtedly harm students; however, Madon et al's (1997) results are broadly consistent with the conclusion that underachieving students may be (fortunately) particularly susceptible to positive self-fulfilling prophecies.

Conclusion

This chapter had two major goals. First, we took stock of the existing research on teacher expecta-tions and self-fulfilling prophecies in order to provide a clearer picture regarding the power and prevalence of such effects, and the conditions that affect them. That review concluded that the actual findings of the original Rosenthal and Jacobson (1968) were quite modest and corresponded well with the similarly modest results of subsequent research. Nonetheless, self-fulfilling prophecies are not always so modest. Self-fulfilling prophecies are consistently larger than usual when people enter new situations (e.g., first and seventh grade; the military), among underachieving students, and among students who are African American or from lower socioeconomic backgrounds.

That review also highlighted two areas of divergence between narrative reviews and the em-pirical literature. Although many narrative reviews seem to emphasize the role of self-fulfilling prophecies in harming students, the evidence on whether self-fulfilling prophecies are primarily harmful or beneficial is mixed. Furthermore, although many narrative reviews emphasize the power of self-fulfilling prophecies to accumulate over time, the evidence shows that self-fulfilling prophecies in the classroom dissipate.

The second part of this chapter focused on self-fulfilling prophecy processes. It reviewed the well-established literature on how teachers act on their expectations, and then highlighted a major limitation to existing knowledge about how self-fulfilling prophecies occur. That is, little or no research has clearly demonstrated how differential teacher treatment of high and low expectancy students actually affects those students in such a manner as to ultimately produce changes in achievement consistent with a self-fulfilling prophecy.

Absent data, our review of the processes by which teacher treatment translates into expectancy-confirming achievement was necessarily indirect and speculative. On purely analytical grounds, we suggested that there are two potential routes by which this could occur. Teacher treatment could directly affect how much students learn, thereby altering their achievement; or, teacher treatment could alter student motivation, which, in turn, could affect their performance. Our review further pointed out that student motivation is often *not* likely to be a powerful mediator of self-fulfilling prophecies, in large part, because self-fulfilling prophecies themselves are often not a very powerful phenomenon. Nonetheless, the scientific research demonstrating that students from stigmatized backgrounds are more vulnerable to self-fulfilling prophecies suggests that, sometimes, student motivation may be a very powerful mediator of positive self-fulfilling prophecies.

Perhaps even more important, one of the primary potential benefits produced by the research on teacher expectations is that the potential power of self-fulfilling prophecies can be harnessed by knowledgeable administrators and teachers to help enhance the achievement of the students who need it the most (see also Eden, 1984, 1986). High expectations are not, by themselves, a solution for underachievement. However, when coupled with an understanding of the teaching practices well-established at enhancing student motivation, commitment, and involvement in school, high expectations can be one powerful tool for redressing some educational inequalities.

References

Alvidrez, J., & Weinstein, R. S. (1999). Early teacher perceptions and later student achievement. *Journal of Educational Psychology, 91*, 732–746.

American Psychological Association. (1991). In the Supreme Court of the United States: *Price-Waterhouse v. Ann B. Hopkins* (Amicus curiae brief). *American Psychologist, 46*, 1061–1070.

Ames, C. (1992). Classrooms: Goals, structures, and student motivation. *Journal of Educational Psychology, 84*, 261–271.

Ames, C., & Archer, J. (1988). Achievement goals in the classroom: Students' learning strategies and motivation processes. *Journal of Educational Psychology, 80*, 260–267.

Aronson, E. (1999). *The social animal* (8th ed.). New York: Worth Publishers.

Babad, E., Inbar, J., & Rosenthal, R. (1982). Pygmalion, Galatea, and the Golem: Investigations of biased and unbiased teachers. *Journal of Educational Psychology, 74*, 459–474.

Blumenfeld, P. C. (1992). Classroom learning and motivation: Clarifying and expanding goal theory. *Journal of Educational Psychology, 84*, 272–281.

Boston Globe. (2004, June 27). Retrieved March 17, 2009, from http://www.boston.com/news/local/massachusetts/articles/2004/06/27/closing_the_gap/

Brattesani, K. A., Weinstein, R. S., & Marshall, H. H. (1984). Student perceptions of differential teacher treatment as moderators of teacher expectation effects. *Journal of Educational Psychology, 76*, 236–247.

Brophy, J. (1983). Research on the self-fulfilling prophecy and teacher expectations. *Journal of Educational Psychology, 75*, 631–661.

Brophy, J., & Good, T. (1974). *Teacher-student relationships: Causes and consequences.* New York: Holt.

Chapman, G. B., & McCauley, C. (1993). Early career achievements of National Science Foundation (NSF) graduate applicants: Looking for Pygmalion and Galatea effects on NSF winners. *Journal of Applied Social Psychology, 54*, 428–438.

Church, M. A., Elliot, A. J., & Gable, S. L. (2001). Perceptions of classroom environment, achievement goals, and achievement outcomes. *Journal of Educational Psychology, 93*, 43–54.

Claire, T., & Fiske, S. (1998). A systemic view of behavioral confirmation: Counterpoint to the individualist view. In C. Sedikides, J. Schopler, & C. A. Insko (Eds.), *Intergroup cognition and intergroup behavior* (pp. 205–231). Mahwah, NJ: Erlbaum.

Cohen, J. (1988). *Statistical power analysis for the behavioral sciences* (2nd ed.). Hillsdale, NJ: Erlbaum.

Collins, J. C., & Porras, J. I. (1997). *Built to last: Successful habits of visionary companies.* New York: Harper-Collins.

Condron, D. J., & Roscigno, V. J. (2003). Disparities within: Spending inequality and achievement in an urban school district. *Sociology of Education, 76*, 18–36.

Cooper, H. M. (1979). Pygmalion grows up: A model for teacher expectation communication and performance influence. *Review of Educational Research, 49*, 389–410.

Cooper, H. M., & Good, T. (1983). *Pygmalion grows up: Studies in the expectation communication process.* New York: Longman.

Crosby, J. R., & Monin, B. (2007). Failure to warn: How student race affects warnings of potential academic difficulty. *Journal of Experimental Social Psychology, 43*, 663–670.

Darley, J. M., & Fazio, R. H. (1980). Expectancy-confirmation processes arising in the social interaction sequence. *American Psychologist, 35*, 867–881.

Davison, H. K., & Burke, M. J. (2000). Sex discrimination in simulated employment contexts: A meta-analytic investigation. *Journal of Vocational Behavior, 56*, 225–248.

Dawes, R. M. (1979). The robust beauty of improper linear models in decision making. *American Psychologist, 34*, 571–582.

Deemer, S. A. (2004). Classroom goal orientation in high school classrooms: Revealing links between teacher beliefs and classroom environment. *Educational Research, 46*, 73–90.

Doyle, W. J., Hancock, G., & Kifer, E. (1972). Teachers' perceptions: Do they make a difference? *Journal of the Association for the Study of Perception, 7*, 21–30.

Eccles, J. & Wigfield, A. (1985). Teacher expectations and student motivation. In J. Dusek (Ed.), *Teacher expectancies* (pp. 185–217). Hillsdale, NJ: Erlbaum.

Eccles, J. S., & Wigfield, A. (1995). In the mind of the achiever: The structure of adolescents' academic achievement related-beliefs and self-perceptions. *Personality and Social Psychology Bulletin, 21*, 215–225.

Eccles, J. S., & Wigfield, A. (2002). Motivational beliefs, values, and goals. *Annual Review of Psychology, 53*, 109–132.

Eden, D. (1984). Self-fulfilling prophecy as a management tool: Harnessing Pygmalion. *Academy of Management Review, 9*, 64–73.

Eden, D. (1986). OD and self-fulfilling prophecy: boosting productivity by raising expectations. *Journal of Applied Behavioral Science, 22*, 1–13.

Elliot, A. J., & McGregor, H. A. (2001). A 2 × 2 achievement goal framework. *Journal of Personality and Social Psychology, 80*, 501–519.

Elliott, E. S., & Dweck, C. S. (1988). Goals: An approach to motivation and achievement. *Journal of Personality and Social Psychology, 54*, 5–12.

Epstein, J. (1988). Effective schools or effective students: Dealing with diversity. In R. H. D. MacRae (Ed.), *Policies for America's public schools* (pp. 89–126). Norwood, NJ: Ablex.

Fiske, S. T., & Taylor, S. E. (1991). *Social cognition* (2nd ed.). New York: McGraw Hill.

Funder, D. C. (1995). On the accuracy of personality judgment: A realistic approach. *Psychological Review, 102*, 652–670.

Gilbert, D. T. (1995). Attribution and interpersonal perception. In A. Tesser (Ed.), *Advanced social psychology* (pp. 99–147). New York: McGraw-Hill.

Harackiewicz, J. M., & Elliot, A. J. (1993). Achievement goals and intrinsic motivation. *Journal of Personality and Social Psychology, 65*, 904–915.

Harber, K. D. (1998). Feedback to minorities: Evidence of a positive bias. *Journal of Personality and Social Psychology, 74*, 622–628.

Harris, M. J., & Rosenthal, R. (1985). Mediation of interpersonal expectancy effects: 31 meta-analyses. *Psychological Bulletin, 97*, 363–386.

Hemphill, J. F. (2003). Interpreting the magnitudes of correlation coefficients. *American Psychologist, 58*, 78-79.

Johnson, D. W., & Johnson, R. T. (1991). *Learning together and alone: Cooperative, competitive, and individualistic learning* (3rd ed.). Englewood Cliffs, NJ: Prentice Hall.

Jones, E. E. (1986). Interpreting interpersonal behavior: The effects of expectancies. *Science, 234*, 41–46.

Jones, E. E. (1990). *Interpersonal perception.* New York: W.H. Freeman.

Judd, C. M., & McClelland, G. H. (1989). *Data analysis: A model comparison approach.* New York: Harcourt Brace Jovanovich.

Jussim, L. (1986). Self-fulfilling prophecies: A theoretical and integrative review. *Psychological Review, 93*, 429–445.

Jussim, L. (1989). Teacher expectations: Self-fulfilling prophecies, perceptual biases, and accuracy. *Journal of Personality and Social Psychology, 57*, 469–480.

Jussim, L. (1991). Social perception and social reality: A reflection-construction model. *Psychological Review, 98*, 54–73.

Jussim, L., & Eccles, J. (1992). Teacher expectations II: Construction and reflection of student achievement. *Journal of Personality and Social Psychology, 63*, 947–961.

Jussim, L., & Eccles, J. (1995). Naturalistic studies of interpersonal expectancies. *Review of Personality and Social Psychology, 15*, 74–108.

Jussim, L., Eccles, J., & Madon, S. J. (1996). Social perception, social stereotypes, and teacher expectations: Accuracy and the quest for the powerful self-fulfilling prophecy. *Advances in Experimental Social Psychology, 29*, 281–388.

Jussim, L., & Harber, K. D. (2005). Teacher expectations and self-fulfilling prophecies: Knowns and unknowns, resolved and unresolved controversies. *Personality and Social Psychology Review, 9*, 131–155.

Jussim, L., Smith, A., Madon, S., & Palumbo, P. (1998). Teacher expectations. In J. Brophy (Ed.), *Advances in research on teaching* (Vol. 7, pp. 1–48). Greenwich, CT: JAI.

Kahneman, D., Slovic, P., & Tversky, A. (1982). *Judgment under uncertainty: Heuristics and biases.* New York: Cambridge University Press.

Kimball, M. M. (1989). A new perspective on women's math achievement. *Psychological Bulletin, 105*, 198–214.

Kuklinski, M. R., & Weinstein, R. S. (2001). Classroom developmental differences in a path model of teacher expectancy effects. *Child Development, 72*, 1554–1578.

Kunda, Z., Thagard, P. (1996). Forming impressions from stereotypes, traits, and behaviors: A parallel-constraint-satisfaction theory. *Psychological Review, 103*, 284-308.

Lareau, A. (1987). Social class differences in family-school relationships: The importance of cultural capital. *Sociology of Education, 60*, 73–85.

Madon, S. J., Jussim, L., & Eccles, J. (1997). In search of the powerful self-fulfilling prophecy. *Journal of Personality and Social Psychology, 72*, 791–809.

Madon, S. J., Jussim, L., Keiper, S., Eccles, J., Smith, A., & Palumbo, P. (1998). The accuracy and power of sex, social class and ethnic stereotypes: Naturalistic studies in person perception. *Personality and Social Psychology Bulletin, 24*, 1304–1318.

Maehr, M. L., & Anderman, E. M. (1993). Reinventing schools for early adolescents: Emphasizing task goals. *The Elementary School Journal, 93*, 593–610.

Mazella, R., & Feingold, A. (1994). The effects of physical attractiveness, race, socioeconomic status, and gender of defendants and victims on judgments of mock jurors: A meta-analysis. *Journal of Applied Social Psychology, 24*, 1315–1344.

McNatt, D. B. (2000). Ancient Pygmalion joins contemporary management: A meta-analysis of the result. *Journal of Applied Psychology, 85*, 314–322.

Merton, R. K. (1948). The self-fulfilling prophecy. *Antioch Review, 8*, 193–210.

Myers, D. G. (1999). *Social psychology* (6th ed.). New York: McGraw-Hill.

Neisser, U., Boodoo, G., Bouchard, T. J. Jr., Boykin, A. W., Brody, N., Ceci, S. J., et al. (1996). Intelligence: Knowns and unknowns. *American Psychologist, 51,* 77–101.

Nisbett, R. E., & Ross, L. (1980). *Human inference: Strategies and shortcomings of social judgment.* Englewood Cliffs, NJ: Prentice-Hall.

Oakes, J. (1986). Tracking, inequality, and the rhetoric of reform: Why schools don't change. *Journal of Education, 168,* 60–80.

Palardy, J. M. (1969). What teachers believe — what children achieve. *Elementary School Journal, 69,* 370–374.

Peterson, C., Maier, S. F., & Seligman, M. E. P. (1993). *Learned helplessness.* Oxford, England: Oxford University Press.

Pintrich, P. R., Conley, A., M., & Kempler, T. M. (2003). Current issues in achievement goal theory and research. *International Journal of Educational Research, 39,* 319–337.

Pomerantz, E. M., Altermatt, E. R., & Saxon, J. L. (2002). Making the grade but feeling distressed: Gender differences in academic performance and internal distress. *Journal of Educational Psychology, 94,* 396–404.

Raudenbush, S. W. (1984). Magnitude of teacher expectancy effects on pupil IQ as a function of the credibility of expectancy inductions: A synthesis of findings from 18 experiments. *Journal of Educational Psychology, 76,* 85-97.

Richard, F. D., Bond, C. F. Jr., Stokes-Zoota, J. J. (2003). One hundred years of social psychology quantitatively described. *Review of General Psychology, 7,* 331–363.

Rist, R. (1970). Student social class and teacher expectations: The self-fulfilling prophecy in ghetto education. *Harvard Educational Review, 40,* 411–451.

Roberts, B. W., Kuncel, N. R., Shiner, R., Caspi, A., & Goldberg, L. R. (2007). *Perspectives on Psychological Science, 2,* 313–345.

Rosenthal, R. (1989, August). *Experimenter expectancy, covert communication, & meta-analytic methods.* Paper presented at the 97th Annual Convention of the American Psychological Association, New Orleans, LA.

Rosenthal, R. (1974). *On the social psychology of the self-fulfilling prophecy: Further evidence for Pygmalion effects and their mediating mechanisms.* New York: MSS modular.

Rosenthal, R., & Jacobson, L. (1968). *Pygmalion in the classroom: Teacher expectations and student intellectual development.* New York: Holt.

Rosenthal, R., & Rubin, D. B. (1978). Interpersonal expectancy effects: The first 345 studies. *The Behavioral and Brain Sciences, 1,* 377–415.

Roth, B. M. (1995, January 2). We can throw teacher expectations on the IQ scrap heap. *New York Times,* p. A25.

Rowe, D. C. (1995, January 2). Intervention fables. *New York Times,* p. A25.

Sangree, H. (2000). *Charting a new course: Roxbury Prep redefines urban mission.* Retrieved March 17, 2009, from http://www.northeastern.edu/magazine/0005/charter.html

Schultz, P. W., & Oskamp, S. (2000). *Social psychology: An applied perspective.* Upper Saddle River, NJ: Prentice-Hall.

Seaver, W. B. (1973). Effects of naturally-induced teacher expectancies. *Journal of Personality and Social Psychology, 28,* 333–342.

Smiley, P. A., & Dweck, C. S. (1994). Individual differences in achievement goals among young children. *Child Development, 65,* 1723–1743.

Smith, A., Jussim, L., & Eccles, J. (1999). Do self-fulfilling prophecies accumulate, dissipate, or remain stable over time? *Journal of Personality and Social Psychology, 77,* 548–565.

Smith, A., Jussim, L., Eccles, J., Van Noy, M., Madon, S. J., & Palumbo, P. (1998). Self-fulfilling prophecies, perceptual biases, and accuracy at the individual and group level. *Journal of Experimental Social Psychology, 34,* 530–561.

Snow, R. E. (1995). Pygmalion and intelligence? *Current Directions in Psychological Science, 4,* 169–171.

Snyder, M. (1984). When belief creates reality. *Advances in Experimental Social Psychology, 18,* 247–305.

Spitz, H. H. (1999). Beleaguered Pygmalion: A history of the controversy over claims that teacher expectancy raises intelligence. *Intelligence, 27,* 199–234.

Steele, C. M. (1992, April). Race and the schooling of Black Americans. *The Atlantic Monthly, 269,* 68–78.

Sutherland, A. S. & Goldschmid, M. L. (1974). Negative teacher expectation and IQ change in children with superior intellectual potential. *Child Development, 45,* 852–856.

Swann, W. B., Jr. (1987). Identity negotiation: Where two roads meet. *Journal of Personality and Social Psychology, 53,* 1038–1051.

Sweeney, L. T., & Haney, C. (1992). The influence of race on sentencing: A meta-analytic review of experimental studies. *Behavioral Science and the Law, 10,* 179–195.

Swim, J., Borgida, E., Maruyama, G., & Myers, D. G. (1989). Joan McKay vs. John McKay: Do gender stereotypes bias evaluations? *Psychological Bulletin, 105,* 409–429.

Trouilloud, D., Sarrazin, P., Martinek, T., & Guillet, E. (2002). The influence of teacher expectations on students' achievement in physical education classes: Pygmalion revisited. *European Journal of Social Psychology, 32,* 591–607.

Uncommon Schools. (2008). Retieved March 17, 2009, from http://www.uncommonschools.org/usi/home/index.html.

Verkuyten, M., & Thijs, J. (2004). Global and ethnic self-esteem in school context: Minority and majority groups in the Netherlands. *Social Indicators Research, 67,* 235–281.

Weinstein, R. S. (1985). Student mediation of classroom expectancy effects. In J. B. Dusek (Ed.), *Teacher expectancies* (pp 329–350). Hillsdale, NJ: Erlbaum.

Weinstein, R. S., Gregory, A., & Strambler, M. J. (2004). Intractable self-fulfilling prophecies: 50 years after Brown v. Board of Education. *American Psychologist, 59,* 511–520.

Weinstein, R. S. & McKown, C. (1998). Expectancy effects in "context": Listening to the voices of students and teachers. In J. Brophy (Ed.), *Advances in research on teaching* (Vol. 7, pp. 215–242). Greenwich, CT: JAI..

Wentzel, K. R. (1997). Student motivation in middle school: The role of perceived pedagogical caring. *Journal of Educational Psychology, 89,* 411–419.

West, C., & Anderson, T. (1976). The question of preponderant causation in teacher expectancy research. *Review of Educational Research, 46,* 613–630.

Williams, T. (1976). Teacher prophecies and the inheritance of inequality. *Sociology of Education, 49,* 223–236.

Wineburg, S. S. (1987). The self-fulfillment of the self-fulfilling prophecy: A critical appraisal. *Educational Researcher, 16,* 28–40.

18

School as a Context of Student Motivation and Achievement

Robert W. Roeser, Timothy C. Urdan, and Jason M. Stephens

Schools hold a central place in the developmental agenda set forth for children and adolescents in nations throughout the world. As a consequence of their central and sustained presence in the lives of young people and their families, schools and educators play essential cultural functions with respect not only to the development of young peoples' subject-matter learning and educational attainments; but also with respect to the development of their curiosity and motivation to learn, their social-emotional skills and self-awareness, and their broader moral and civic role identities. It is this wider array of outcomes that transcends but includes academic learning that is important not only for young people's success in school, but for their lifelong love of learning, service to community, and well-being (Battistich, Watson, Solomon, Lewis, & Schaps, 1999; Comer, 1980; Damon, 2002; Eccles & Roeser, 1999; Greenberg et al., 2003; Rutter & Maughan, 2002; Wentzel & Wigfield, 1998). How schools can simultaneously address their academic missions *and* their broader social-emotional, moral, and civic missions in an age of increasing pressures for academic accountability is a challenge facing educators in many developed nations across the world today (Vanderwolf, Everaert, & Roeser, 2009).

In this chapter, we explore what constitutes a school context from an ecological perspective on human motivation and development, and how features of both the organizational context and culture of schools-as-a-whole can affect students' motivation to learn and achievement. Throughout the chapter, we highlight important connections between the social, moral, and academic cultures of schools and the related idea that acts of teaching and learning are inherently social-moral acts with consequences for the development of the whole person (e.g., Noddings, 2002). That is, we propose that the ways school contexts are organized for academic learning, and the ways teachers teach, implicitly engender social, emotional and moral messages that affect students' motivation to learn. We review selected research on how academic and social-moral features of school environments can affect students' motivation and behavior, and conclude with a discussion of future directions for research on schooling and motivation to learn during the primary and secondary school years. We propose that future research on schooling, motivation and achievement focus on issues of (a) the ethnic and racial diversity in the school-aged population today and issues of identity; (b) the geographically situated nature of schools and the challenges students and educators in different settings face today, and (c) the on-going need for school reforms that produce greater social equity through universal reforms that aim to enhance motivation, develop academic and social-emotional skills, and cultivate students' felt membership and participation in a school community.

Conceptualizing "School" and the School Environment

What constitutes a "school environment?" What are the ways scholars have conceptualized "school" in previous research? For purposes of this chapter, we distinguish between the school as an *organizational context*—discernible from third-person points of view, and the *organizational culture* of the school—discernible from first-person points of view (Anderson, 1982; Sarason, 1990). A significant body of interdisciplinary research now exists on how *third-person, objective features of the school context* such as sector (public vs. private), size, and administrative structure (e.g., degree of departmentalization) can affect both teacher motivation and teaching quality, and consequently, student engagement, achievement, and extracurricular activity participation (e.g., Barker & Gump, 1964; Bryk, Lee, & Holland, 1993; Lee, Bryk, & Smith, 1993). At the same time, work in educational and developmental psychology on motivation and schooling has offered numerous theoretical accounts of how and why specific *first person, subjective perceptions of the school culture,* such as the nature of a school's academic goal structures, authority structures and relationships, are motivationally and developmentally instigative with respect to behavioral engagement, behavioral choices, and achievement (see Deci & Ryan, 2000; Eccles & Roeser, 1999; Maehr, 1991; Midgley, 1993; Roeser & Galloway, 2002; Weinstein, 1989). This work places a central role on the active meaning-making tendencies of students by focusing on how students' appraisals of school environments in relation to personal and social goals, salient developmental needs, and cultural expectations play a major role in shaping their motivation and behavior in school and in relation to education.

One basic challenge in research on schools and motivation today is to bring together our understanding of how these two sets of factors—those third-person, *tangible* features of a school's organizational context (e.g., its level of resources, size, and administrative structure) as well as those *tacit* first-person perceptions of its organizational culture by students (e.g., its expressed mission, ideologies and norms, interpersonal climate) conjointly affect their motivation and achievement behavior in school. A second and related challenge in this area of research is the need for a new generation of theories about how school context features affect student school culture perceptions. A third challenge is to understand how, together, school context features and school culture perceptions synergistically affect student motivation, identity and achievement behavior over school transitions and across developmental time (e.g., Lee, 2000; Lee, Bryk & Smith, 1993; Eccles & Roeser, 1999; Maehr & Midgley, 1991; Midgley, 1993; Roeser & Galloway, 2002; Wigfield, Eccles, Schiefele, Roeser, & Kean, 2006).

Challenges [margin annotation]

The need for richer developmental-ecological accounts of schooling and its effects on students is evident in the fact that much of this research simplifies the "school environment" into a few summary variables and is cross-sectional in nature. Regarding the first issue, for example, because elementary school-aged children spend most of their school day in self-contained classrooms, whereas adolescents experience multiple classes, teachers, and groups of classmates on a daily basis, the focus on "school effects" at the elementary and secondary school levels represent two different kinds of conceptual simplification. In the case of children, the elementary school classroom is often treated as synonymous with "school." In the case of adolescents, the greater organizational complexity and differentiation of the secondary school environment makes it necessary to simplify and focus not on individual classes or myriad sequences of classes among different students, but on the school itself as an organizational unit of study (Lee, 2000). Both solutions are to some degree inadequate in capturing the complexity of young people's lives in school contexts. For example, one's "school experience," even in childhood, extends "beyond the classroom" to lunchrooms and gyms and playgrounds. In addition, during adolescence, one's "sequences of classes" (often within particular academic tracks) becomes a major part of one's "school experience" psychologically, socially, and even physically insofar as different groups of students are housed and taught in various parts of the overall school complex (e.g., Olson, 1997). This "spatial view" of "school" is one important perspective. We have also found a "temporal development view," in which researchers study how normative change in school environments across development affect individuals' life-paths is another useful perspective on "school effects over time" (Eccles & Roeser, 1999). How to integrate classroom experiences with wider perceptions and features of schools-as-a-whole; and how to think about classroom and school experience in ontogenetic time, are important conceptual issues researchers face when studying schools as contexts of motivation and achievement across development. New ways of addressing these challenges in research are needed.

In the work of the first author and his colleagues, both descriptive and prescriptive models of school environments, derived from a review of the sociological, developmental and motivational literatures, have been used to address some of the challenges inherent in studying schools as basic contexts of human development (Roeser & Galloway, 2002; Roeser, Peck, & Nasir, 2006). As presented in Figure 18.1, the Basic Levels of School Contexts (BLOSC) heuristic model conceptualizes schools as contexts that both consist of, and exist within, a system of embedded, multilevel contexts. These embedded contexts are depicted in Figure 18.1 from the perspective of a student and radiate out from the student "up to" the level of the school through the levels of tasks, classmates, teachers, classrooms; academic tracks, peers, and subject matter departments; and "out from" the level of the school to include the neighborhood, the community, the district, the state, and the nation (see also Cole, 1996; Eccles & Roeser, 1999; Talbert & McLaughlin, 1999). Each of the contexts that either envelope or are enveloped by the school-as-a-whole can be characterized by, and assessed in terms of, objective, third-person and subjective, first-person measures (Roeser & Galloway, 2002).

The left side of Figure 18.1 is meant to communicate the idea that, from one perspective, schools are *organizational contexts* comprised of tangible material and social features. These include things such as the physical environment of the classroom; the curricular content; the social background, qualifications, and practices of the teaching staff; the social background and school readiness of the student body; the number of different courses of study and actual courses offered; the degree of departmentalization; the size, grade-span, sector, the appearance of the physical plant and resources of the school; district, state, and federal educational policies; and the socioeconomic and demographic characteristics of the community of the school (Lee et al.,1993; Talbert & McLaughlin, 1999). These left-hand dimensions are apparent to outsiders and can be assessed from an "etic" or third-person perspective. The unit of analysis in studies of these kinds of features is often the school-as-a-whole, with a focus on how between-school differences in these features are associated with differences in student outcomes (Lee, 2000).

The right-hand side of Figure 18.1 is meant to communicate that from another perspective, schools are *organizational cultures* comprised of often tacit, social-symbolic, and social-relational features. These tacit features include the friendliness of the teacher and peers in the classroom;

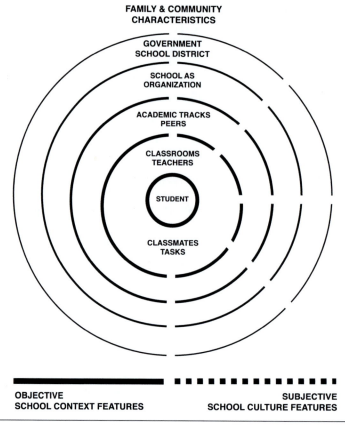

Figure 18.1 Embedded contexts model of school environments.

the challenge level and meaningfulness of the tasks and the sequence and scope of the different subject matter curricula; the discourse style, values, and goals of the teacher; the motivational attitudes and mental health of students and peer groups in "high" and "low" track classes; the culture of the school in terms of academic and social-moral norms, roles, rules; the culture of the district in terms of leadership style; the values of parents and the community; and the spirit of innovation or stagnation in the educational policies of the state and the nation (e.g., Lee et al., 1993; Maehr & Midgley, 1991; Stodolsky & Grossman, 1995). These more subjective dimensions of Figure 18.1 are not readily apparent to outsiders and are usually assessed via the perceptions of students, teachers, parents, educational leaders and other stakeholders who inhabit school and related settings on a daily basis (e.g., an "emic" or first-person perspective). Thus, the unit of analysis in studies of school organizational culture is often the individual, or some "consensus" (aggregate) measure of the "school culture as a whole" derived from a sample of individuals in the school (Anderson, 1982; Maehr, 1991).

Finally, the arrow of time at the bottom of Figure 18.1 is meant to indicate that these two features of school environments *develop* in historical and ontogenetic time. Regarding the former, for instance, with an increase in the size of the school-aged population, many schools now enroll more students (often in buildings of the same size) than they did previously. This means objective crowding in about one-quarter of the nation's schools is a condition of education today that students, teachers, and administrators experience that was not there previously (U.S. Department of Education, 2000). It addition, the arrow of time is meant to indicate that, from the perspective of the developing child moving through the school system, these contexts change over developmental time (Eccles & Roeser, 1999). For instance, from the perspective of the growing child, they generally are moving into larger schools over time as they transition from elementary to middle to high school.

School Effects Research

To understand how school level factors can affect students' motivation to learn, it is useful to draw upon and extend the decades old study of "school effects" on learning and achievement in the social and behavioral sciences (see Eccles & Roeser, 1999; Rutter & Maughan, 2002). Traditionally, school effects research has aimed to document school-contextual factors that could account for significant variation between schools in academic (e.g., attendance, rates of learning, school dropout, and educational attainment), social (e.g., participation in extra-curricular activities), and behavioral outcomes (e.g., delinquency) that could not solely be attributed to students' social backgrounds. The scientific challenges inherent in much of school effects research remain twofold. The first challenge is to identify and model school factors that exert a *socialization effect* on change in student outcomes above and beyond *selection effects* (e.g., the relevant background characteristics of school-aged children and their families who live in particular places and attend schools there). The second challenge is to identify how individuals' psychological construals of their schools over time, in addition to the more objective material and social features of these schools as experienced by the developing child over time, contribute to the prediction of change in motivation and achievement over time. In the next section, we explore some of the features of schools as organizational contexts and as organizational cultures that have proven important in understanding school effects on students, broadly construed. Though we separate our discussion of the more tangible material and social features of schools from that of the more tacit, social-psychological features of schools, these are clearly interdependent in that these factors exist as different dimensions of an overall school *system through* which young people develop over time and *within* which educators develop over time.

Features of the School as Organizational Context

School Sector and Grade Span Whether a school exists in the public or private (e.g., religious) sector is one feature of the organizational context of schools that has been related to students' motivation and achievement. Approximately 10% or about 5 million students attended private schools in the United States in 2004 (NCES, 2007). Various researchers have commented on the "religious schools effect" of private Catholic schools in terms of student achievement and educational attainments, especially among non-Catholics, those of lower socioeconomic status, and African Americans and Latinos living in urban areas (Bryk et al., 1993; Coleman, Hoffer, & Kilgore, 1982; Jeynes, 2002a, 2002b). In a meta-analysis of the effects of Catholic religious school attendance and personal religious commitment on academic achievement and school conduct, for instance, Jeynes (2002) found that, after accounting for socioeconomic status and gender, the effect sizes for religious school attendance were between .20 and .25 of a standard deviation for both academic achievement and school conduct. Although some suggest these effects are due to selection biases (i.e., either in the form of the schools selecting superior students or in the form of parental involvement—it takes certain level of parental commitment to education to move a child from a free public school to a private, parochial school), others have suggested that this claim is overdrawn and that the effects of a Catholic school education on achievement are quite robust (e.g., Bryk et al., 1993).

Several core features of Catholic schools have been highlighted as being instrumental in the reduction of inequality in these schools: smaller size and a communal organization, a philosophy of human dignity, and a restricted range of curricular offerings (Bryk et al., 1993). Catholic schools tend to be somewhat smaller than public schools, and this affords the possibility of their having a strong communal culture grounded in a rich array of rituals and activities outside of the classroom where teachers and students get to know one another. Smaller size and a greater sense of community, though not unique to private or parochial schools, can provide a social motivation for school learning—a set of caring relationships and a corresponding sense of community among faculty, staff and students—that fosters commitment and engagement. Second, Catholic schools communicate to all students that they can learn, and that they have a fundamental sense of personal dignity that is nonetheless independent of their ability to learn. To communicate the former message, these schools have what Bryk and colleagues (1993) call a "delimited technical core" (p. 297). Students in Catholic schools have many required classes and less electives, and therefore, all students are exposed to a common curriculum that the faculty expects them to learn. Although administrative sorting still occurs, there are less "tracks" and less differentiation of curricula by such tracks. The message to students is that every student is not only capable of, but is expected to learn the core curriculum. In short, the opportunity structure for learning is narrower and more focused on providing a basic education for all students. This approach is also viewed as having a moral purpose in that it reflects a certain kind of respect for a child's dignity and faith in every child's ability to learn.

The grade span of a school is another contextual feature that has been linked to student motivation and may help explain some of the "Catholic school effect." Eccles, Lord, and Midgley (1991) examined data from the NELS:88 dataset and noted that student outcomes among early adolescents, as rated by both teachers and students, were better in those attending K–8 schools than those who were attending a middle or junior high school during grades 6, 7, or 8. Students in K-8 schools were less likely to be truant, violent or to use substances at school; and were more likely to say they felt prepared for, and interested in, their class work compared to students in the middle or junior high schools. Furthermore, students in the K–8 schools reported higher self-concepts and greater locus of control, received higher grades, and did better on standardized achievement tests than those in the middle grades schools. These findings were consistent with other studies that showed K-8 schools were generally better for adolescents because, by their nature, they limited the number of school transitions students have to make during adolescence (see Simmons & Blyth, 1987). What is interesting in the Eccles et al. (1991) study is that the majority of the K–8 schools in the NEL:88 database that were found to be conducive to student motivation and achievement were also private religious schools (74%) and were smaller size than public middle and junior high schools.

School Size Consistent with this work, significant research has now documented that school size has significant implications for student motivation and achievement. The question of how much school size matters for overall student engagement and achievement was first asked during the 1960s. Barker and Gump (1964) proposed that smaller secondary schools afford young people various opportunities not available in larger schools, opportunities that foster engagement and *smaller schools =*

achievement. Such opportunities included (a) closer relationships between teachers and students, (b) greater adult monitoring of and responsibility for student progress; and (c) a particularly favorable roles-to-people ratio with respect to school extracurricular activities and the need for many students in the school to participate to fulfill those roles. By affecting these mediating processes, school size was hypothesized to affect student outcomes. Subsequent research has consistently verified these hypotheses.

For instance, in a national probability study of high school students, Crosnoe, Johnson, and Elder (2004) found that students' attachment to school in general and to their teachers in particular was significantly, negatively correlated with school size. Lee and Loeb (2000), in an urban Chicago sample of 264 (K–8) schools, found that in smaller schools (size < 400 students), teachers took greater responsibility for fostering students' learning and students showed greater 1-year gains in mathematics achievement. Schoggen and Schoggen (1988) counted student activity involvements from high school yearbook pictures of activity clubs and found that school size was strongly, negatively related to mean number of activity participations ($r = -.69$) and strongly, positively correlated with the percentage of students who participated in no school activities ($r = .77$; see also Crosnoe et al., 2004; Elder & Conger, 2000). Pittman and Haughwout (1987) found that school size had an indirect effect on school dropout rates through aspects of the school social climate, particularly the amount of opportunities for student participation in extracurricular activities

In sum, these studies show that positive relationships, opportunities to participate in the life of the school, and closer monitoring by teachers are key mechanisms in translating school size into greater student bonding with school, motivation to learn, engagement, and achievement (e.g., Hawkins, 1997; Hawkins, Kosterman, Catalano, Hill & Abbott, 2008). In a national study of high schools, Lee and Smith (1995) found that the greater the school size, the less positive were students' attitudes towards classes, investment of effort in school, and feelings of challenge. In summarizing the work of school size, Lee and Smith (1997) proposed that the most effective K–8 elementary schools with respect to student achievement gains are those that enroll 400 students or less, whereas the ideal 9–12 secondary school in this regard enrolls between 600–900 students. Students in elementary/middle schools that are larger than 400, and those in high schools smaller than 600 or larger than 1,200, learn less in reading and mathematics. Findings regarding optimal size were consistent regardless of the social class and racial composition of the school.

In sum, school size can affect students' motivation and achievement through various pathways. As size grows, student anonymity increases and teacher responsibility and efficacy decrease, leading to declines in student motivation and achievement (Eccles & Roeser, 1999). In addition, as school size increases, the number of available people grows more quickly than available roles do. This eventuates in fewer opportunities and less pressure for students in larger schools to participate in school activities and therefore, the life of the school beyond the classroom (Barker & Gump, 1964). From a motivational perspective, felt belonging, valuing of school and perceived interpersonal support and pedagogical care from teachers all are likely mediating psychological mechanisms between school size and student achievement outcomes.

School Resources and Physical Plant The level of economic resources and the appearance of the physical plant of a school may also affect student motivation and behavior through various causal pathways. Despite the common sense notion that more financial resources produces more educational success, the central question of how much school resources matter for raising achievement and reducing inequality in student outcomes raised by Coleman (1968) in his early work remains unresolved (Hanuschek, 1994; Hedges, Laine, & Greenwald, 1994). It may be, as some economists now argue, that return on social investments aimed at reducing achievement gaps are greatest when programs are targeted to the first 3 years of a child's life before school even begins (see Heckhausen & Masterov, 2007; Levin, 2008).

What is clear is that certain context features that are more common in low-income schools can make these under-resourced environments particularly un-motivating places for academic learning. For instance, low-income schools are staffed by disproportionately higher numbers of low-qualified teachers compared to affluent schools, and teacher turnover in these schools is high (Darling-Hammond, 1997). A key factor in these findings is teacher salary (Loeb, Darling-Hammond, & Luczak, 2005). In addition to lower qualifications in their content areas and greater turnover, some research shows that teachers in low-income schools may have a tendency towards exercising greater control over students, and to limit their use of constructivist teaching practices in part because they believe poor children lack the self-control necessary to motivate and regulate their own learning (see Evans, 2004; Solomon, Battistich, & Hom, 1996). Thus, candidate mechanisms by which school resources can affect student motivation and behavior are (a) teacher qualifications, (b) quality of teaching, and (c) the kinds of bonds that form or do not form in a school with a great deal of teacher turnover is present (Darling-Hammond, 1997).

Aspects of the physical plant of the school have also been discussed in relation to students' motivation and behavior, though few research studies been done on this topic. For instance, we know that schools with high concentrations of impoverished students are more likely to have metal detectors, bars on the windows and graffiti on the walls than wealthier schools (Planty & DeVoe, 2005). What message do such factors give rise to in students in terms of felt security, school belonging, and school pride? The "broken windows" theory of delinquency and crime (Wilson & Kelling, 1982), for instance, posits that unmaintained or abandoned physical spaces connote a message of a lack of ownership and, in a sense, a lack of moral structure. Such spaces therefore become tacit seedbeds for antisocial activity (Gladwell, 2000). Do schools that are physically neglected and uncared for give rise to a sense of unowned space and delinquent behavior on the part of particular students (Astor, 1998)? Do individuals who act out and misbehave in schools sometimes feel "neglected and uncared for" in a way that is mirrored in the physical environment of their school?

In a study of 12 London area secondary schools, Rutter and colleagues (1979) found that although the age of the school building was not significantly related to students' achievement or behavioral conduct, observer ratings of a building's cleanliness and of the presence of plants, pictures, and other decorations inside the building were significant predictors of student misconduct (after accounting for their social background characteristics). The less clean the school was, the less it had plants, and the less it had pictures and other decorations on the walls, the greater the misconduct of the students. In the future, motivational researchers might consider the effects of aspects of the objective physical plant of the school on student motivation, learning and behavior, especially when studying schools that are located in urban or rural areas where poverty is widespread, where the physical plants of school buildings may be decrepit and decaying, and where noise and pollution may be more prevalent. In a study of elementary school children attending schools near major European airports, for instance,, aircraft noise was associated with impaired reading comprehension after accounting for students' social background characteristics (Clark et al., 2005).

School Student Body Another fundamental feature of the organizational context of schools is the aggregate social background characteristics of the student body. The "mix" of socially disadvantaged students with those from families of greater means, or of those with significant emotional-behavioral difficulties and those without such problems in a school, has been associated with the educational outcomes of all students in a given school (Rutter & Maughan, 2002). In general, as the ratio of students who are socially disadvantaged goes up in a school, its aggregate achievement goes down. The aggregate behavioral histories of a school's student body also matter. LeBlanc, Swisher, Vitaro, & Tremblay (2007) found that between-school variation in the proportion of students with histories of disruptive problems predicted subsequent rates of classroom behavior problems among high school students. In sum, the composition of a school's student body has independent influences on the motivation and behavior of students in school. A variety of mechanisms, including peer influences and the concentration of alienated students in particular classes and schools, and relatedly, the development of maladaptive norms in a school given the prevalence of certain behaviors, have been proposed to account for these findings (e.g., Rutter & Maughan, 2002).

School Curricular Differentiation In the middle and high school years, between-classroom tracking becomes both more widespread and more broadly linked to the sequencing of specific courses for students bound for different post secondary school trajectories (college preparation, general education, and vocational education). As curriculum differentiation practices intensify during secondary years, students of different ability get exposed to (often very) different kinds of academic work, classmates, teachers, and teaching methods (e.g., Oakes, 2005).

A general consensus on the overall effects of curriculum differentiation as an educational practice remains elusive (Eccles & Roeser, 1999). Research suggests that students who are placed in high tracks evidence some educational benefits; whereas low tracks placements are associated with negative achievement outcomes (see Kao & Thompson, 2003; Oakes, 2005). As just one example, Hallinan and Kubitschek (1999) found that assignment to high track classes accelerated growth in school achievement, whereas assignment to a lower level or vocational track decelerated such growth. Studies have also demonstrated that lower-track students report being labeled "dumb" by teachers and peers (Persell, 1997), feel less committed to school, and feel less successful academically (Schafer & Olexa, 1971).

A persistent concern in research on tracking during both the primary and secondary school years is the fact that both poor students, and those who are African American, Latino, and Native American, are more likely than their wealthier and European or Asian American peers to be in low group and low track placements early and throughout their school careers (Oakes, 2005). Lucas (1999) explored the issue of mobility (i.e., student movement from one track to another) and found that track origins mattered most: those who started on the high and low tracks tended to stay on those tracks, whereas those who started on the middle tracks tended to move downward. These findings led Lucas to conclude that "wider social inequality continues to advantage those of more means... [and that] those of modest means are disadvantaged in high school placement...." (pp. 112–113).

Similarly, concerns have been raised about the marginalization and segregation of students who speak English as second language (ESL students) on middle and high school campuses (Valdez, 2001). There is also some evidence that students with limited English proficiency who are otherwise capable are placed in lower track classes (see Kao & Thompson, 2003). ESL programs are often housed on the periphery of regular school campuses and often fail to provide real opportunities for ESL students to interact with native English speakers. Furthermore, similar to the misassignment of African American and Latino students to and lack of mobility out of low academic tracks (e.g.,

Dornbush. 1994), there is some evidence that ESL students often get reassigned (downwardly) to ESL programs following school transition events even though they may have graduated from such programs into mainstream classes in their previous schools (Valdez, 2001). Although achievement gaps start prior to schooling (e.g., Ramey & Ramey, 2004), the stability of curricular placements once a child enters school is what is of most concern in these studies.

An interesting perspective on tracking comes from national studies using multilevel modeling analyses to examine how between-school differences in the extent of tracking and other reforms relates to student motivation and achievement. For instance, in a study of middle schools from NELS:88, Lee and Smith (1993) found that the greater the extent to which middle schools had engaged in restructuring practices (less departmentalization, more team teaching, more hetero-geneous grouping, etc.), the more students were engaged in learning, students in general learned more, and the school achieved a more equitable distribution of these outcomes across students from different social class backgrounds. Studies of religious schools and high schools have shown similar results—the more that all students in a school are expected to learn a core curriculum, the less inequality there is in student achievement by social background factors (Bryk et al., 1993; Lee & Bryk, 1989; Lee, Croninger, & Smith, 1997; Lee & Smith, 1993, 1995, 1997; Lee, Smith, & Croninger, 1997). Research on how curricular differentiation is related to both within and between-school differences in students' motivation to learn and achievement is rare, but could complement this existing body of work and further specify key psychological mediators for de-clines in inequality as curricular differentiation becomes narrower.

School Start and End Times Another subtle feature of the organizational context of schools that matters for students' motivation and achievement concerns the time school starts in the morning and ends in the afternoon. Carskadon (1997) has shown that as children progress through pu-berty they need more sleep and their natural sleep cycles shift such that adolescents want to go to sleep later in the evening and to wake up later in the morning. Unfortunately, secondary schools typically begin earlier in the morning than primary schools, necessitating earlier rise times for adolescents at the same time their biological sleep clock is resetting (Carskadon, 1997). In concert with these life changes that occur during adolescence, such as the later hours at which youth go to bed, the earlier start times of the middle and high school create a "developmental mismatch" that can both promote daytime sleepiness and undermine adolescents' ability to make it to school on time, alert, and ready to learn. A study of fifth-grade students in Israel, for example, compared two groups of students: those in a school that started at 7:10 am (early risers) and those in a school that started at 8:00 am (regular risers). Results showed that early risers slept less, reported more daytime fatigue and sleepiness, and reported greater attention and concentration difficulties in school compared to their later rising counterparts. The implication is that the time that schools begin can have a significant effect on mood, energy, attention, and therefore the motivation and learning of students.

The time at which school ends also has implications for students' motivation to learn and achievement. In communities where few structured opportunities for constructive after-school activities exist, young people are more likely to be involved in high-risk behaviors and less likely to be engaged in productive activities that can deepen academic motivation during the period between 2 and 8 p.m. (Eccles & Gootman, 2002).

School Transitions Early work suggested that the developmental configuration of schools a child attends across the course of her childhood and adolescence has implications for her motivation, achievement and attainments. The transition into a junior high school, rather than staying in a K–8 environment, for instance, is associated with poor psychosocial outcomes, especially among female adolescents (Eccles et al., 1991; Simmons & Blyth, 1987). Simmons, Black, and Zhou (1991) found that grades and liking of school declined more across the junior high school transitions for African-American compared to European American adolescents. These studies and others suggest that the more normative school transitions students undergo during their school careers, the greater their achievement loss (Alspaugh, 1998).

Several of the organizational context features discussed above also account for within-child changes in motivation and achievement across school transitions (Eccles & Midgley, 1989; Maehr & Anderman, 1993; Midgley, 1993; Simmons & Blyth, 1987). For instance, the increase in school size and decreases in felt belonging and close teacher-student relationships reported by students across the transition from elementary to secondary school are paralleled by teachers who have larger teaching loads, less ability to know their students, and less efficacy concerning their ability to reach all students. When teachers do not know how or feel able to effectively reach all their students, they may abandon the use of cooperative and autonomy-supportive practices in favor of extrinsic motivators and other forms of control (Eccles & Midgley, 1989). Whereas researchers have studied the transition into elementary and middle or junior high school (see Eccles & Roeser, 1999), more research is needed on the high school transition. Assessments of how changes in the organizational context and culture of feeder and receiver schools affect young people's motivation to learn as they transition from one school to another (e.g., Eccles & Roeser, 1999), as well as on how the loss or maintenance of peers across such transitions (e.g., Schiller, 1999) can condition the effects of school transitions on motivation and achievement is also needed.

Features of the School as Organizational Culture

In the history of school effects research, attention gradually shifted from a sole focus on organizational context features like size to a consideration of features linked to the organizational culture of the school as a whole (Brookover, Beady, Flood, Schweitzer, & Wisenbaker, 1979). Such features include things such as a school's leadership and work climate, academic and social climate, and everyday routines, norms and styles of interpersonal interaction among school staff and between staff and students. The hypothesis behind this line of "effective schools" research was that to the extent schools varied in their student outcomes, this variation would presumably be related to between school differences in features of the school organizational culture (Anderson, 1982). Differences in schools that were unusually effective or ineffective in terms of students' academic and behavioral outcomes after controlling for student intake characteristics were examined (e.g., Brookover et al., 1979; Rutter et al., 1979).

The effective schools research unequivocally established that features of the internal life of the school culture mattered for student outcomes above and beyond students' initial social background characteristics (Good & Weinstein, 1986; Rutter & Maughan, 2002). As Lee (2000) summarized it: "Effective schools have strong leadership focused on academic outcomes. They closely monitor student work. In such schools, teachers hold high expectations for all students. Their social environments are purposeful. Their climates are orderly" (p. 126). These were the findings derived from looking at aggregate perceptions of school contexts in relation to aggregate student achievement outcomes. In this section, we unpack these tacit features of the school organizational culture to emphasize that there are really several intersecting climates in a school—one having to do with academics and the purpose of learning, another with rules and discipline, and a more general social-moral climate derived from the organizational context of the school and the kinds of interactional patterns between and among teachers and students that such contexts facilitate and promote. In the research that we discuss below on school culture, it is important to note that the unit of analysis tends to shift to the individual.

School Academic Culture for Students Significant research on the organizational features of school cultures in psychology has come from motivational researchers espousing an Achievement Goal Theory perspective (Urdan, 1997). This work has utilized goal theory to describe the goal structure of the school as a whole in relation to students' motivation and learning (Maehr, 1991; Maehr & Fyans, 1989; Roeser, Midgley, & Urdan, 1996) and teachers' motivation and pedagogy (Maehr & Midgley, 1991; 1996; Roeser, Marachi, & Gelhbach, 2002).

Maehr and Midgley (1991, 1996) argued that there exist at least two kinds of school level *academic goal structures* with regard to student learning and achievement—a "performance-oriented" and a "mastery-oriented" goal structure. In a performance-oriented school culture, student's relative academic ability and status hierarchies based on such relative abilities are valued and recognized. Academic success is defined in terms of student's demonstration of superior ability and attainment of superior grades. Many students, by definition, fail in this kind of an environment. In a mastery-oriented school culture, effort, mastery, and improvement are valued and recognized. Academic success is defined in terms of student's effortful mastery of content, improvement of skills, and learning through trial, error, and social assistance. The meaning of failure is transformed in this situation from "not being smart" to "not trying" or "needing additional strategies and support." Midgley and Maehr (1991) suggested that school level decisions concerning the nature of the tasks to which students were exposed (e.g., textbook selection), norms associated with the empowerment of students (e.g., student government programs), means of recognizing students for various behaviors (e.g., honor rolls and public assemblies), approaches to grouping students (e.g., tracking policies), formats for formally evaluating students (e.g., portfolio assessments), and the use of time (e.g., block scheduling) could all eventuate in a culture at the school level that was more or less performance or mastery-oriented with regard to student learning and achievement.

This work grew out of the application of goal theory to changing classroom climates (e.g., Ames, 1992). Maehr and Midgley (1991, 1996) described their own experiences in which attempts to alter the achievement goal structures at the classroom level were undermined by school level policies, procedures, and practices. For example, a teacher's efforts to promote mastery goals and de-emphasize competition and social comparison (i.e., performance goals) in her classroom may be undermined by school-level policies and practices, such as publicly posting honor rolls to recognize students with the higher grade point averages or allowing only high achievers to participate in certain school activities or clubs. Because classrooms are situated within the larger social environment of schools, these authors argued that school-level efforts to alter the achievement goal structures are necessary to classroom reform.

Several correlational field studies have examined the associations of students' perceptions of school goal structures with motivation and achievement. Roeser et al. (1996) found that adolescent students' perceptions of the mastery goal structure in their middle school predicted their own personal mastery goals, which, in turn, positively predicted their academic self-efficacy beliefs and positive affect in school. Students' perceptions of the school performance goal structure were positively associated with their personal performance goal orientations, which in turn predicted their feelings of self-consciousness in school. Interestingly, students who perceived a strong performance-goal structure in their school were less likely to perceive that their teachers cared for them, whereas those perceiving a task goal structure in the school were more likely to see their teachers as caring.

In a second study, Roeser, Eccles, & Sameroff (1998) examined the relation of perceived middle school goal structures to longitudinal change in adolescent students' motivation to learn and well-being after controlling for their sex, race, parental education level, parental occupational prestige, and income. Adolescent students' perceptions of their school as performance-oriented were related to diminished feelings of academic competence and valuing of school, increased feelings of emotional distress, and decreased grades over time; whereas perceived school task goal structures were associated with increased valuing of school and diminished emotional distress over time after controlling for student background characteristics (Roeser et al., 1998). Similarly, Kaplan and Maehr (1999) reported that middle school students' perceptions of a mastery goal structure in their school were associated with greater sense of well-being and less misconduct whereas their perceptions of performance goal structure in their school were associated with greater misconduct.

Fiqueira-McDonough (1986) compared two high schools in the same community that were similar in student intake characteristics and achievement outcomes, but differed in their academic culture and rates of delinquent behavior. The high school characterized by a greater emphasis on competitive academic achievement (performance-oriented school culture) and unpredictable supervision had higher delinquency rates than the second school, and grades were the strongest predictor of delinquent behavior in this school. In contrast, the second high school took a greater interest in students' nonacademic needs, promoted a broader meaning of what it meant to be successful in school than out performing others, and had more predictable adult supervision of students. In this latter school, students reported higher levels of school attachment (valuing of school, liking teachers) and school attachment, not grades, was the primary (negative) predictor of delinquent activity. The authors concluded that the broader concern of the second school with the whole student and a noncompetitive view of success enhanced students' attachment to school, which, in turn, discouraged their involvement in delinquent behavior while in school. This latter school culture seems akin to what some have called a mastery goal structure.

A related set of issues involving the academic culture of middle and high schools concerns the equitable treatment of students not only regardless of their ability levels, but also regardless of their racial/ethnic backgrounds. Evidence is beginning to accrue that suggests that when ethnic minority students perceive that their ethnic group is seen as intellectually inferior by teachers and classmates from majority racial / ethnic backgrounds, their motivation to learn, well-being and achievement can suffer. Wong, Eccles, and Sameroff (2003), in a longitudinal study of approximately 600 African American 12–14 year-olds who were followed from the beginning of seventh to the end of eighth grade of middle school, found that perceived discrimination perpetrated by teachers, school staff, and classmates in school at eighth grade was associated with declines in their self-reported academic self-concept and teacher-rated grades, and increases in their self-reported psychological distress, from seventh to eight grade. Other research has documented that adolescents' perceptions of a school performance goal structure is positively correlated with perceptions of racial discrimination in school among African and Latin American youth (Roeser & Peck, 2003; Roeser, 2004). It may be that by adolescence, certain ethnic minority students become more aware of (a) differential reward structures and opportunities in the school, (b) who the primary benefactors of these structures and opportunities are, and (c) how such disparities in opportunities and outcomes mirror what youth see between racial/ethnic groups in the wider society. Focusing on task-oriented motivational strategies in schools may thereby reduce the salience and potentially debilitating effects of racial/ethnic stereotypes and relative ability-oriented rewards structures on the achievement of particular groups of students.

School Work Culture for Teachers Another important assumption of Achievement Goal Theory-guided research on school cultures is that not only can school-wide policies and practices influence students' motivation and achievement, but also teachers' professional identities and pedagogy. As many studies of "effective schools" have shown, competent leadership and a sense of mutual support among school staff are two important ingredients in effective schools (Good & Weinstein, 1986). However, not all schools have work environments in which there is equitable treatment of teachers, democratic decision-making processes, a spirit of innovation, and opportunities for the professional development of all teachers. From a goal theory perspective, it is hypothetically possible to describe the work environment of a school as emphasizing competition, social comparison, and differential treatment of teachers (e.g., a performance goal structure); cooperation, equity, and a spirit of innovation (e.g., a mastery goal structure); or to some degree, both.

Roeser et al. (2002), for instance, found that when elementary and middle school teachers perceived differential treatment of teachers by school leaders and a sense of competitiveness among their teacher colleagues in their school, they were also more likely to endorse classroom practices that highlighted competition and ability differences between students in the classroom. On the other hand, when teachers in elementary and middle schools perceived support for innovation and experimentation from school leaders and colleagues, they were more likely to emphasize these things in their own approaches to motivating and teaching students in the classroom. Together, these findings underscore the possibility that real change in students' motivation and learning through reform efforts may turn on whether or not a supportive work culture for teachers in which cooperation, innovation, and experimentation are valued exists in a school (Sarason, 1990). Reforms that are most likely to be successful and successfully integrated into the on-going life of a school are likely those that create a safe, supportive, and motivating climate for teachers and students alike (Deci & Ryan, 1985; Sarason, 1990).

Whole School Culture Change Efforts Work that attempts to change the whole school culture around learning provide a window into context and culture features and their relations at the school level. For instance, Maehr, Midgley and their colleagues attempted to alter the school goal structure of one elementary and one middle school over a 3-year period. They met regularly with the teachers, administrators, and parents of the two schools to discuss achievement goals and to develop strategies for promoting mastery goals, and de-emphasizing performance goals, in the two schools. Two comparison schools in the same districts were also included in this quasi-experimental study.

Empirical data generated from the Maehr and Midgley intervention project revealed that students in the elementary and middle school levels could reliably report on their perceptions of the school-level mastery and performance goal structures. For example, Midgley, Anderman, & Hicks (1995) reported that both students and teachers in middle level schools perceived stronger performance and weaker mastery goal structures at the school level than did teachers and students in elementary schools. This work was later extended by Roeser et al. (2002). They documented a linear increase from elementary to middle to high school in students' and teachers' perceptions of performance-oriented school cultures. Similarly, Harter and her colleagues (1992), in a study of middle school students retrospective reports on their school transition experience, found that "students who characterized the school environment as (increasingly) emphasizing and externally evaluating performance and competence relative to others had higher levels of extrinsic motivation and scholastic anxiety, and rated academic success as more important than did those not sharing these perceptions of the educational environment" (p. 797).

Although they did not assess students' perceptions of the school goal structure directly, Anderman, Maehr, and Midgley (1999) also presented evidence that Maehr and Midgley's attempts to alter the school-level goal structure in their school improvement work influenced the goal structures students perceived in their classrooms. Anderman and his colleagues (1999) found that when students moved from elementary schools into the treatment middle school (where efforts were underway to create a mastery goal structure), they reported a slight decrease in personal performance goals whereas students entering the control middle school reported an increase in performance goals. In addition, students moving to the treatment school reported no change in their perceptions of a performance goal structure in their classrooms whereas those moving into the comparison middle school reported increased emphasis on performance goals.

Other whole school change efforts also shed light on the nature of context-culture relations and reform efforts. One approach to school restructuring that focuses on both contextual and cultural features is the Accelerated Schools Project (ASP; Levin, 1988). The philosophy behind this approach is to view school as a democratic institution designed to promote the advancement of all students. Although most agree with this rhetoric, in practice most schools are organized according to a sorting and classification model. Even in the early grades, students are identified through testing and teacher observations as delayed, normal, or advanced in their academic abilities. Once the classification has been made, students are provided with different resources and opportunities, ranging from assignment to different reading groups within a classroom to placement in different programs, such as remedial classes or gifted and talented (GATE) programs. But if schools are truly viewed as organizations designed to help all students maximize their potential, less emphasis will be placed on classification and segregation and more on providing stimulating educational opportunities for all.

The ASP was developed in response to two separate but related developments in education in the mid-1980s. First, there was a growing recognition that programs designed to benefit at-risk (i.e., low-achieving students or those with risk factors, such as low socio-economic status) were doing little to shrink the achievement gap between higher-achieving and lower-achieving students and were actually further marginalizing at-risk students. These programs tended to provide at-risk students with remedial programs that had low expectations of students and tended to rely on drill-and-practice methods that failed to engage students. Another common approach was to simply raise standards and demand that students reach them. But this approach often failed to include the necessary support and changes in instructional practice necessary to help lower-achieving students actually meet the more demanding standards.

A second development in education that set lay the groundwork for the ASP was a new focus on the success of *all* students in school (Slavin, 1987). The leaders of this movement argued that for all students to have access to educational opportunities, such as advanced placement classes and, eventually, college attendance, they would need to accelerate their progress in the primary years (Hopfenberg, 1991). To accomplish this, schools could not simply identify at-risk students and offer them remedial instruction. Rather, the entire culture of the school would need to be transformed such that high expectations and standards for all students were articulated and all students were supported to reach these standards.

Levin and his colleagues (Levin, 1988; Hopfenber, 1991; Lee, Levin, & Soler, 2005) began with the proposal that the same approach used in GATE programs of providing an enriched, interesting, project-based curriculum should be used with all students in a given school, including at-risk students. For this to work on a school-wide level, all stakeholders in the school (parents, teachers, administrators, and other interested members of the school community) must buy into the program and share in the decision-making process. The curriculum in ASP schools should be interdisciplinary and thematic, with language and higher-order thinking skills emphasized across all subjects. Students should be provided with opportunities to explore topics in depth and instruction should promote active learning, cooperation among students, heterogeneous grouping, and authentic assessment.

Although there has been some effort to extend the ASP model to secondary schools (Hopfenberg, 1991), the vast majority of ASP schools are primary schools. It is one of the most widely adopted whole-school reform efforts with at least 50 schools and 3000 students participating in accelerated schools for at least 5 years (Lee et al., 2005). Although there is some evidence that student achievement in accelerated schools is enhanced, it is important to note that the ASP model is not particularly prescriptive, so the effects of ASP reform efforts varies widely across schools and even within classrooms of the same school. The ASP model provides a core set of guiding principles and values, but individual schools are encouraged to engage in a process of self-exploration that results in curricular reforms, instructional strategies, and governance structures that are unique to each school. Therefore, much of the research evidence for accelerated schools is in the form of case studies of one or two particular schools.

There are several important messages from the literature on accelerated schools. First, whole-school reform efforts require a commitment on the part of all interested parties to genuine transformation of the school. Such efforts must go beyond the development and implementation of small enrichment programs targeted at discreet groups of students. Because all students will be affected by truly whole-school reforms, the entire school culture, from the curriculum to the pedagogy to the mission to the governance structure, must change and require a shared vision and purpose among all of parties invested in the school. Second, whole-school reform efforts may be easier to accomplish at the primary school level than at the secondary school level. Secondary schools, with their separate departments, larger student bodies, and greater emphasis on achievement-level differences between students, are simply more resistant to the kinds of whole-school reform efforts found in the ASP. Although there have been attempts to extend the ASP to the secondary level, these efforts have not enjoyed nearly the success witnessed at the primary school level. Finally, even well designed whole-school reform efforts like the ASP are likely to produce widely varied results among classrooms within each school. In the final analysis, teachers still control much of the curriculum and instruction within their classrooms regardless of the reform efforts at the school level.

School Behavioral Climate Another key dimension of the school organizational culture concerns the rules governing appropriate behavior. In schools where teachers and administrators establish smoothly running and efficient procedures for monitoring student progress and behavior, providing feedback, enforcing accountability for work completion and rule-governed behavior, student achievement is improved and misconduct and anti-social behavior is reduced (Fiqueira-McDonough, 1986; Gottfredson, Gottfredson, & Hybl, 1993; Hawkins, 1997; Rutter et al., 1979). From a motivational perspective, providing orderly and predictable school-wide behavioral structure, where "structure" is defined as the presence of clear and fair expectations and rules, judicious use of rewards, informational forms of feedback, and consistency of rule enforcement, enhances children's and adolescents' rule-governed behavior because it affords information on how to be competent and successful in that environment (Connell & Wellborn, 1991; Deci & Ryan, 1985).

School Social Climate Supportive relationships between teachers and students are another critical part of a school's organizational culture for students' motivation and behavior in school. The quality of relationships between teachers and students can be affected by factors such as the school size, the nature of the work environment for teachers, and the qualities and qualifications of the teacher him or herself (e.g., Jennings & Greenberg, 2009). It is now widely acknowledged that relationships are the crucible in which learning and growth among teachers and students alike can flourish (e.g., Connell, 2003).

With regard to students, a significant body of experimental and field research has now demonstrated that perceptions of teacher social support and sense of belonging and membership in a learning community are important precursors to individuals' motivation to learn (Osterman, 2000; Wentzel, this volume). Sense of belonging is perhaps especially critical for young people who must traverse significant ethnic and racial, socioeconomic, and sociolinguistic borders to feel fully part of a school in which middle-class, majority cultural norms often predominate (Davidson & Phelan, 1999; Lucas, Henze, Donato, 1990; Garcia-Reid, Reid, & Peterson, 2005). Indeed, the importance of relationships for re-invigorating education and re-engaging disenfranchised students is at the heart of many of the most innovative approaches to school reform over the last decade (Brown, 1997; Connell, 2003; Schaps, 2003).

In addition to feeling emotionally supported as a person, perceptions that teachers care about what one is learning as a student, what Wentzel (1997) called "pedagogical caring," is also a critical aspect of a school's "social" climate. Indeed, this combination of interpersonal care and academic press seems particularly critical for insuring students' motivation *and* achievement (Lee & Smith, 1999). Here again, we see the line between "academic" and "social" features of school cultures and the relationships between teachers and students as overlapping significantly, with implications for students' motivation to learn.

With regard to teachers, Connell (2003) has shown how important creating supportive relationships among teachers and staff are in a school with regard to providing a firm foundation for school change efforts. In his reform called "First Things First," positive relationships among teachers in a school are the first things that are cultivated in preparation for whole school reform. Again, it appears that creating the conditions in schools that are conducive to teachers' well-being and growth is essential for teachers' motivation and ability to create those same conditions for their students in the classroom (Sarason, 1990).

School Moral Climate Another key dimension of the school organizational culture, one closely related to the social climate and particularly Wentzel's (1997) notion of pedagogical caring, is the moral climate of a school. Broadly defined, the school moral climate or atmosphere refers to how just and fair the rules and their enforcement are; whether or not school staff believe in and promote the learning and development of all students; the kind of role modeling enacted by adults in the school, and whether or not students are offered decision-making power and voice in the learning and in broader school affairs. The moral climate of a school in one sense permeates the entire school organizational culture and the acts of teaching and learning that occur in that culture (Noddings, 2002).

Kohlberg (1970), in his "just communities schools," pioneered a new approach in moral education that emphasized a whole school approach that apprenticed students in democracy and ethical reasoning (cf Power, Higgins, & Kohlberg, 1989). Central to the changes undertaken by just community schools was students' inclusion in school decision-making processes. The principle of one person-one vote was instituted in these schools—students and teachers had equal say and influence in the governance of their school community. As hypothesized, students in just community schools experienced significant gains in their moral reasoning ability (i.e., their ability to make principled judgments) and their tendency to feel obliged to act in accordance with reasoned judgments. They also reported greater honesty and service activity and less cheating, stealing and social exclusion. Kohlberg and his colleagues attributed these changes in judgment and behavior to changes in the moral climate of the school (Power et al., 1989).

Similar intervention work on fostering a moral climate in school has been done by the Child Development Project (CDP) in Oakland, California. The CDP project takes a school-level approach to fostering students' social and ethical development as well as their cognitive and academic development. Critically important to this approach are practices that directly engage students in cooperative and community-building activities at school. These include the use of cooperative learning techniques in classrooms, classroom management strategies that rely on student participation in norm-setting and decision making, teaching of conflict resolution skills, and curricula that focus students on themes of care. Research and intervention studies have shown that such practices foster a "community of care" that positively influences students' self-understanding, motivational beliefs and feelings of belonging, and in-school behavior (Battistich et al, 1996; Schaps, 2003).

In summary, school culture variables are important mediators and moderators for the influence of school context features on student outcomes. The "school culture" is not monolithic but has various dimensions that, in interdependent fashion, affect students' felt belonging, efficacy, goals, and values, well-being, achievement and behavioral choices. Understanding the combined and unique contributions of various aspects of the school culture for various student outcomes is a next step in this work.

Conceptualizing How Schools Influence Student Motivation

The strands of school effects research reviewed above reflect a descriptive taxonomy of the features of schools' organizational contexts and cultures that are consequential for students' motivation to learn and behavior. A third wave of research on schools that extends this earlier work on "school effects" in the educational and developmental sciences offers prescriptive accounts of how and why schools influence young people's motivation to learn within and over developmental time. Such approaches assume that students actively construct meaning from educational environments in terms of their material, mental and social affordances for meeting educationally and developmentally relevant needs and goals (Connell, 2002; Eccles et al., 1993; Ryan & Deci, 2000). In essence, motivational-developmental approaches have tended to view the school as a *psychological environment* that comes to have meaning for individuals, and treats this psychologically experienced context as an individual difference variable (Maehr & Fyans, 1989). An important assumption is that considerable variation in context perceptions may exist among inhabitants of the same setting.

The processes by which school settings influence students' context perceptions and therein their motivation, achievement and psychosocial development are described in rather similar ways by theorists with differing perspectives (e.g., Bronfenbrenner, 1993; Rogoff, 2003; Ryan & Deci,

2000). Social environments such as schools are conceptualized as catalysts for human motivation and healthy development insofar as these settings invite, permit, or inhibit movement from more peripheral to more central forms of participation in activities and responsibilities over time. Bronfenbrenner (1993), for instance, differentiated developmentally "constructive" from "destructive" environments according to their long-term consequences. Constructive environments were described in terms of people, practices, tasks, and resources that foster individuals' sense of safety and belonging, encourage their autonomous (but safe) exploration of the environment, scaffold their competence development, and invite them into increasingly more central forms of participation. Such environments foster positive patterns of motivation (Ryan & Deci, 2000). Destructive environments undermine individuals' sense of belonging and safety, overly-restrict autonomous exploration, forestall their competence development, and inhibit more central forms of participation. Such environments foster apathetic, resistant, or oppositional forms of motivation (Ryan & Deci, 2000).

Applied to schools, a number of motivational theorists have discussed how young people make appraisals of the constructive and destructive affordances in their schools in terms of their basic psychological needs for competence, autonomy and relatedness (Connell & Wellborn, 1991; Deci & Ryan, 1985; Eccles & Midgley, 1989; Skinner & Wellborn, 1994). The argument is rather straightforward: To the extent that school settings provide developmentally appropriate affordances for children/adolescents to actualize their competencies, exercise autonomy, and participate in caring, respectful relationships, children/adolescents will feel academically competent, value school, feel good about themselves, achieve, and act in pro-social ways. On the other hand, to the extent school environments undermine fulfillment of these needs, students may feel academically incompetent, devalue school, feel alienated, act out and fail.

Figure 18.2 presents a heuristic, motivational model of school effects. The top of the figure links features of the school organizational culture with students' appraisals of that culture and, consequently, their situationally relevant beliefs, goals and values, and feelings (see Connell &

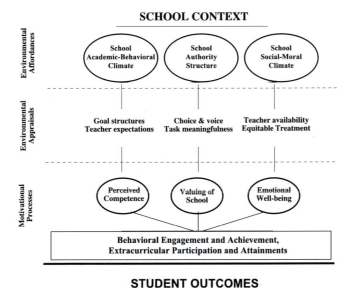

Figure 18.2 Motivational affordance model of school enviornments.

Wellborn, 1991; Deci & Ryan, 1985; Eccles & Midgley, 1989). Students' subjective perceptions of aspects of their school culture, as well as their beliefs, goals, values and well-being are hypothesized to mediate between the "actual" school context and their behavioral engagement, achievement, extra-curricular activity involvement, and educational attainments.

Perhaps students' subjective appraisals of their schools, from a motivational perspective, can best be captured by imagining students asking themselves several questions on a more or less regular basis about their experiences in school in relation to their stage-salient needs. For instance, in relation to the academic and behavioral climate of the school, students might wonder about motivationally relevant questions such as: "What is the purpose of learning in this school?" "Who gets rewarded and what counts as academic success here?" and, perhaps most importantly, "Can I succeed here and do I want to?" The school academic climate has direct implications for students' motivation to learn, specifically their need for competence and their achievement-related goals and values, emotions, and personal agency beliefs. In relation to the school behavioral climate, one could imagine students asking motivationally relevant questions such as: "What are the rules here?" "What is expected of me and how do I know?" "Do I care about and respect the rules of this place? Why or why not? The behavioral climate, we hypothesize, is most closely linked to needs for competence and autonomy, and students' conduct-related goals and values, emotions, and personal agency beliefs. Associated with the school social and moral climates, students' questions bearing on motivation might sound something like this: "Do I feel cared for and respected as a person in this school by classmates, teachers, and administrators? Do I view my teachers as role models and do I feel that I can go to them in times of need?" "Do my teachers care if I'm learning?" Finally, associated with themes of personal autonomy and authority as they play out in schools, questions young people might "ask" themselves in school bearing on motivation might include: "Am I given any sense of voice in and choice over the kinds of learning experiences I have in my classes? What am I asked to do in my classes and how do these activities fit with my own values, interests, and experiences?" By drawing attention to these salient questions, motivational theories provide a rich description of the psychological factors that mediate school context and culture effects on student outcomes.

Methodological Implications

By knowing what the features of a school context are, and how specific school features represent developmentally instigative phenomena based on their relation to basic human needs, the descriptive and prescriptive models presented in Figures 18.1 and 18.2 provide unique insights into schools as contexts of student motivation and achievement. Clearly, the best models for assessing school effects on motivation and achievement include both the organizational context of schools, and the psychological construal of these and the various dimensions of the school organizational culture by students and teachers who learn and work in these environments. That is, such models, by definition, are multilevel in nature (Lee, 2000). Traditionally, researchers have had to choose either the individual or the school level as the unit of analysis when modeling school effects. Often, one level of factors was ignored at the expense of the other, or both levels of analysis were used with statistical techniques not specifically designed to deal with such multilevel data (see Andersen, 1982; Lee & Bryk, 1989). These problems have been largely solved by multilevel statistical modeling tools (e.g., Lee, 2000; Rutter & Maughan, 2002).

Gradually, we are coming to a place in which, with appropriate tools, we can begin to address the effects of schooling on aspects of the "whole student" using statistical techniques and variable centered analyses. One of the main contributions that motivational researchers interested in learning and school can make to this research is a sophisticated analysis of the psychological factors, including context perceptions, and the motivational, ability, and volitional factors that mediate between the instigative features of the school setting and consequent patterns of behavioral engagement in learning or non-learning in school. Such a methodological model is depicted in Figure 18.3 and represents the fruit of a long history of work on school effects (Anderson, 1982; Lee, 2000).

Future Directions for Research on School Effects on Motivation

The school-aged population in the United States continues to grow and diversify ethnically, culturally, and linguistically. Within this context, several important directions for future research on schooling and motivational processes arise.

Race and Ethnicity Investigating how students' cultural, ethnic and racial, and social class backgrounds interact with the learning environment of the school, and thereby shape their educational

Traditional Hierarchical Model of School Effects

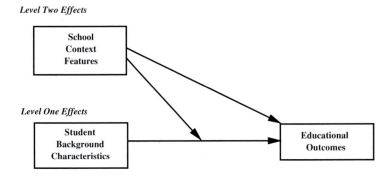

Hierarchical, Mediated Motivational Model of School Effects

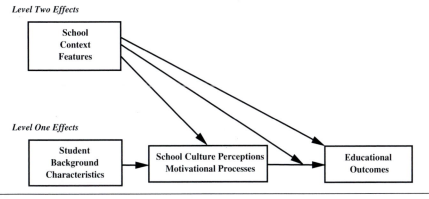

Figure 18.3 School effects model.

pathways through the school system, is an important direction for future research given on-going achievement gaps among school-aged children and youth from different backgrounds (Meece & Kurtz-Costes, 2001). One hypothesis is that for certain ethnic and language minority youth, the experience of moving into middle and high school may be particularly challenging (Tatum, 1997). These school transitions bring students into school settings that are larger, more stratified by class and race, and more performance-oriented compared to the elementary school environment (Roeser et al., 2002). As a consequence, status differences become more salient. Messages about who has the "right stuff" to succeed academically and who does not and are important issues that young people must manage as they form a sense of their identity and the place of school and education in it (Aronson & Steele, 2005). This collusion of ability stratification and societal stereotypes about intelligence may produce school cultures that are particularly unwelcoming and unfriendly for many ethnic minority youth during adolescence, especially those in low track or English-as-a-second-language classes. Thus, investigating the relation of school goal structures and perceptions of differential treatment by race, linguistic background and social class in schools represents an important future direction in this work, one with strong implications for educational equity (Aronson & Steele, 2005).

Geographical Context A related issue needing more investigation in the future concerns the challenges facing different kinds of schools and communities in urban, rural, and suburban settings today (Roscigno, Tomaskovic-Devey & Crowley, 2006). Approximately 30% of students attended school in cities in 2003–2004, with African American and Latinos overrepresented in urban schools. Approximately 40% attended schools in the suburbs, with European Americans over represented in these wealthier school districts. The final 30% of students are in rural schools, including an overrepresentation of European and Native Americans. Asian American youth are equally likely to attend schools in cities and suburbs, but are rarely found in rural areas. The point we wish to highlight here is that questions about school effects on students' motivation and achievement are situated in each different geographical locale (e.g., Lippmann, Burns & McArthur, 1996).

For instance, understanding the role of school factors in racial differences in academic engagement and achievement in youth, especially under-achieving African American and Mexican American students, is an issue that disproportionately involves city schools. As noted above, African American and Latino students are over-represented in such schools, schools that are often poorly resourced. In urban centers, approximately 20–25% of the population lives in poverty, and African American and Latino students are overrepresented in high poverty communities and schools that are segregated racially and linguistically (Orfield, 1999). In general, urban schools are larger than those in suburban or rural settings (Lippmann et al., 1996). Research has shown that students in large schools with high concentrations of poor and racial minority students show the least learning gains in reading and achievement over time (Lee & Smith, 1997). Large proportions of the staff in poor schools are made up of noncredentialed or unqualified teachers, substitutes regularly fill the places of full-time teachers, and there is little support for English language learners. Staff turn-over is also greatest in high poverty schools (Darling-Hammond, 1997). In terms of student experiences, high poverty urban schools are perceived as less safe than other schools (Lippmann, 1996). What are the motivational effects of this constellation of factors that characterize urban schools? How can staffs mobilize against these rather massive constraints to improve education in these centers? How can policy changes provide incentives for high-quality teachers to work in such environments? These are pressing issues in need of research attention.

The effects of schooling on students in rural America is also important to consider, perhaps especially because "the truth is that rural schools and communities are increasingly invisible in a mass society that is fundamentally preoccupied with its urban identity, its urban problems, and its urban future" (Johnson & Strange, 2005, p. vii). Indeed, some scholars have referred to rural youth as the "invisible poor" (Hodgkison & Obarakpor, 1994). Students living in rural areas show lower levels of achievement and higher rates of withdrawal from school prior to high school graduation on average compared to their nonrural peers (Roscigno & Crowley, 2001). Poverty is the major risk factor for educational outcomes across rural America.

In terms of motivation to learn, one issue facing rural youth concerns their conceptions of their futures, including their educational plans and related decisions about staying in rural communities or "moving to the big city" to find work in an increasingly urban world and global economy. This question of leaving home is likely to be a particularly important identity challenge facing students growing up in these environments, with implications for their motivation to learn in school (USDA, 2003). For instance, analyzing data from middle and high school students in three communities in Illinois, Hektner (1995) found that compared to nonrural youth, rural youth were more likely to feel emotionally conflicted over wanting to stay close to their families and wanting to stay close to their families and to move away from their community in the future. Youth who worried about this potential life choice reported feeling more empty, angry, and pessimistic about their future. Finally, compared to urban and suburban students, rural adolescents expressed more hesitancy about pursuing further education. This was particularly true for males in this study, highlighting the importance of attending to gendered identities and their development in research in such environments. Research has begun to examine sources of college attainment of this population, including the resilience of low-resource rural youth who nonetheless find a pathway to college (McGrath, Swisher, Elder & Conger, 2001).

Research in suburbs is common, but very important nonetheless in motivational studies. The relative affluence of the suburbs is often thought of as a place in which children and adolescents are at "low risk." However, recent psychological and educational research calls into question this stereotype and suggests considerable challenges confronting young people in their education and identity development in these settings as well (Luthar & Becker, 2002). In a series of studies, for instance, Luthar and her colleagues found significantly higher use of cigarettes, alcohol, marijuana and hard drugs among suburban teens compared to their urban peers, and that substance use and abuse was a form of self-medication for depression and anxiety. Many of the symptoms and problem behaviors seemed to arise in the period around the transition to secondary school (Luthar & Latendresse, 2005). Evidence is gathering that documents the achievement pressures that exist in many suburban families and schools that may be causing some of these substance use issues.

For example, Pope's (2001) book, *Doing School: How We Are Creating a Generation of Stressed Out, Materialistic, and Mis-educated Students*, documents the lives of five "successful" students attending a highly competitive suburban school in Northern California. The students represent an ethnically and economically diverse group, and Pope's description and analysis centers on the costs, pressures, and cynical strategies for what the students themselves call "doing school." As the expression suggests, "doing school" is a game of superficial, and even unethical, engagement in and approaches to academic learning. With the pursuit of high GPA's and admissions to the most elite colleges as the most pressing concern, the students come to regard genuine cognitive engagement and personal integrity as barriers to their "success."

In another study of an affluent high-achieving school in suburban Northern California, Stephens and Roeser (2003) found achievement pressures at work during 11th grade— the "crunch year" for getting high SAT scores and high GPAs so students can improve their chances for admissions to the best colleges. Comparative analyses of 10th and 11th graders showed that while almost all students reported some form of cheating in school (over 90% on homework and over 80% on a test), 11th graders reported significantly more test cheating. Specifically, all students perceived the classroom they cheated in most often as significantly more performance oriented and significantly less mastery oriented than the classroom in which they cheated least often—most frequently their math or science classroom (79%). Extreme group analyses further revealed that the students who reported cheating most frequently (the top tercile of the distribution) had a significantly lower sense of academic competence than students who reported cheating the least often (lowest tercile). In short, the configuration of being under pressure for high grades and feeling unable to *earn* those grades was associated with frequent cheating.

What are the school culture factors that may create high-pressure environments and potentiate academic dishonesty in wealthy suburban communities? Luthar (2003) offered the following hypothesis concerning such settings: "it is not the surfeit of riches in itself but rather an overemphasis on status and wealth that is likely to compromise well-being.... It is only when individuals become disproportionately invested in extrinsic rewards, concomitantly neglecting intrinsic rewards such as closeness in relationships, that there are likely to be ill-effects on their mental health outcomes" (p. 1589). Luthar & Latendresse (2005) summarize the need for research in the suburbs because, while "children rendered atypical by virtue of their parents' wealth are undoubtedly privileged in many respects, there is also, clearly, the potential for some nontrivial threats to their psychological well-being" (p. 49).

Moral Dimensions of Schooling Students' academic motivation is inextricably linked to their socio-moral motivation, and both are shaped by the interdependent spheres of the academic, social and moral climates in schools. The interconnection of these multiple domains has only infrequently been made explicit in the theoretical and empirical work on schooling and motivation (see Blumenfeld, Pintrich, & Hamilton, 1987; Nucci, 2001; Wentzel, 2003).

Social environments that emphasize the development of competence, provide support of autonomy, and attend the interpersonal needs of students are not only highly motivating environments, they are also highly moral ones as well insofar as they promote personal choice and personal responsibility. In the study of cheating cited above, Stephens and Roeser (2003) found significant relations between students' perceptions of classrooms goal structures and teacher qualities. Specifically, students' ratings of teacher fairness and caring were positively correlated with the mastery goal structure and negatively correlated with performance goal structure. Similarly, Murdock, Hale, and Weber (2001) found high correlations between classroom mastery goal structure and perceived teacher competence and commitment among middle school students. As Murdock et al. conclude in their study, "the academic climate and social climate of a classroom may not be independent of each other and raise some question about our conceptualization and measurement of these constructs" (p. 111). Further exploration of these interconnections at the level of the school, as well as there implications not only for motivation, achievement and cheating, but also pro-social behavior, are needed.

Excellence and Equity Finally, the question of school effects with respect to specific educational aims such as excellence or equity is also central to this entire area of research in the future and is a challenging scientific and social policy question. For many, it is clear that many public schools, especially but not exclusively those in poor urban environments, are underequipped and staffed to play a positive role in the educational progress of children and adolescents in their communities (e.g., Darling-Hammond, 1997; Pope, 2001). Indeed, it seems plausible that the long-standing and persistent achievement gap is, at least in part, a manifestation of a resource gap. On the other hand, other studies show that schools can be, and often are, an important part of the solution to the problem of social inequality and stratification in the United States, including in poor urban areas (Alexander, Entwistle, & Olson, 2001). Some of the most interesting findings to come out of sociology and developmental science during the past decade show that early childhood factors, including home stimulation and early childhood care and education (Heckhausen & Masterov, 2007; Levin, 2008), as well as summertime learning, may play equal, if not larger roles in achievement gaps between students of different social backgrounds than schools do (Entwistle, Alexander, & Olson, 1997; Ramey & Ramey, 2004). In fact, some of the evidence suggests that schools play an important role in redressing such inequality *during the time students are in school*, but that the progress schools accomplish with poor students cannot make up for differences that appear early in life before formal schooling begins, and that are exacerbated each summer when school is out of session (Alexander et al., 2001; Ramey & Ramey, 2004). Furthermore, religious schools and public schools that are smaller, have a strong sense of community, are less differentiated into "streams of study" such that all students are expected to learn a core curriculum, use team teaching and heterogeneous grouping more, and that have a fair and effective disciplinary climate have been shown to reduce inequality in student achievement by social background factors (Lee & Bryk, 1989; Lee, Croninger, & Smith, 1997; Lee & Smith, 1993,1995, 1997; Lee, Bryk & Smith, 1993). Thus, attending to both the aggregate level of overall student achievement attributable to school factors (educational effectiveness), as well as the social distribution of achievement across students from different social backgrounds (educational equity), are both important in the study of the effects of schooling and motivation on achievement.

Finally, it is important to inquire into how the testing movement in general, and the No Child Left Behind Act in particular, has influenced the motivational climate in schools. How has this law affected schools' missions? Teacher morale? Teacher-student relationships? The curriculum? These are also pressing questions for those interested in school effects on motivation and achievement (e.g., Ryan & LaGuardia, 1999).

Conclusion

In this chapter, we explored theoretical, conceptual, and methodological issues in the study of how schools as a whole can affect students' motivation and achievement. We began by describing our Basic Levels of School Contexts (BLOSC) model of schooling—a descriptive and prescriptive set of models of schooling based on extant sociological, educational, and motivational psychological research, respectively. In this context, we described several key school variables that may be of interest for educational psychologists interested in motivation and school effects in the future. We also discussed briefly how the advent of multilevel statistical modeling techniques has solved the "unit of analysis" problem in school research (Anderson, 1982; Lee, 2000), and articulated the need for more multilevel studies that draw upon ecological-motivational perspectives in modeling the contextual and individual determinants of educational outcomes. Nonetheless, because most school research represents a "simplification" of young people's actual school experience (Lee, 2000), we believe that the need for rich observational and ethnographic studies of schooling will continue to be important sources of knowledge in the field. We concluded by noting specific topics of schooling and motivation that are of concern in urban, rural, and suburban schools in the United States today.

In sum, schools, as central contexts of human development, play an integral cultural role in nurturing young people's learning and their motivation to learn. We hope that motivational researchers will contribute more to school effects research in the future. We believe motivational theories have much to contribute to this area of research in that these theories clearly lay out what the psychologically instigative features of school settings are with respect to students' and teachers' appraisals of those environment, their needs and goals, and their consequent patterns of motivation and behavior. As such, these theories provide unique and powerful social-ecological and psychological perspectives that policy makers and reformers can use to envision, design, enact, and assess efforts to motivate constructive change in educators, those being educated, and educational institutions writ large.

References

Alexander, K. L., Entwisle, D. R., & Olson. L. S. (2001). Schools, achievement and inequality: A seasonal perspective. *Educational Evaluation and Policy Analysis, 23*, 171–191.

Alspaugh, J. W. (1998). Achievement loss associated with the transition to middle school and high school. *Journal of Educational Research, 92*, 20-25.

Ames, C. (1992). Classrooms: Goals, structures, and student motivation. *Journal of Educational Psychology, 84*, 261–271.

Anderman, E. M., Maehr, M. L., & Midgley, C. (1999). Declining motivation after the transition to middle school: Schools can make a difference. *Journal of Research and Development in Education, 32*(3), 131–147.

Anderson, C. S. (1982). The search for school climate: A review of the research. *Review of Educational Research, 52*, 368–420.

Aronson, J., & Steele, C. M. (2005). Stereotypes and the fragility of academic competence, motivation, and self-concept. In A. J. Elliot & C. S. Dweck (Eds.), *Handbook of competence and motivation,* (pp. 436–456). New York: Guilford.

Astor, R. A. (1998). Moral reasoning about school violence: Informational assumptions about harm within school sub-contexts. *Educational Psychologist, 33*(4), 207–221.

Balfanz, R., & Legters, N. (2004). *Locating the dropout crisis.* Baltimore, MD: Center for Social Organization of Schools.

Barker, R., & Gump, P. (1964). *Big school, small school: High school size and student behavior.* Stanford, CA: Stanford University Press.

Battistich, V., Schaps, E., Watson, M., & Solomon, D. (1996). Prevention effects of the Child Development Project: Early findings from an on-going multisite demonstration trial. *Journal of Adolescent Research, 11*, 12–53.

Battistich, V., Watson, M., Solomon, D., Lewis, C. & Schaps, E. (1999). Beyond the three R's: A broader agenda for school reform. *Elementary School Journal, 99*, 415–432.

Blumenfeld, P. C., Pintrich, P. R. & Hamilton, V. L (1987). Teacher talk and students' reasoning about morals, conventions and achievement, *Child Development*, 58, 1389–1401.

Bronfenbrenner, U. (1993). The ecology of cognitive development: Research models and fugitive findings. In R. H. Wozniak and & K. W. Fischer (Eds.), *Development in context: Acting and thinking in specific environments: The Jean Piaget symposium series* (pp. 3–44). Hillsdale, NJ: Erlbaum.

Brookover, W., Beady, C., Flood, P., Schweitzer, J. & Wisenbaker, J. (1979*). School social systems and student achievement: Schools can make a difference.* New York: Praeger.

Brown, A. L. (1997). Transforming schools into communities of thinking and learning about serious matters. *American Psychologist, 52*, 399–413.

Bryk, A. S., Lee, V. E., & Holland P. B. (1993). *Catholic schools and the common good.* Cambridge, MA: Harvard University Press.

Carskadon, M.A. (1997, April, 21). *Adolescent sleep: Can we reconcile biological needs with societal demands?* Lecture given at Stanford University, Stanford, CA.

Clark, C., Martin, R., van Kempen, E., Alfred, T., Head, J., Davies, H. W., Haines, M. M., Barrio, I. L., Matheson, M. & Stansfeld, S. A. (2005). Exposure-effect relations between aircraft and road traffic noise exposure at school and reading comprehension. *American Journal of Epidemiology, 163*, 27–37.

Cole, M. (1996). *Cultural psychology: A once and future discipline.* Cambridge: Harvard University Press.

Coleman, J. S. (1968). *Equality of opportunity.* Washington, DC: U.S. Government Printing Office.

Coleman, J. S., Hoffer, T., & Kilgore, S. (1982). Cognitive outcomes in public and private schools. *Sociology of Education, 55*(2–3), 65–76.

Comer, J. (1980). *School power: Implications of an intervention project.* New York: Free Press.

Connell, J.P. (2003). Getting off the dime: Toward meaningful reform in secondary schools: Lessons on how model developers and school districts can facilitate the success of school reform. Retrieved January 2008, from http://www. irre.org/publications/pdfs/benchmarks_summer_2003.pdf

Connell, J. P., & Wellborn, J. G. (1991). Competence, autonomy and relatedness: A motivational analysis of self-system processes. In M. R. Gunnar, & L. A. Sroufe (Eds.), *Self-processes in development: Minnesota Symposium on Child Psychology* (Vol. 23, pp. 43–77). Hillsdale, NJ: Erlbaum.

Crosnoe, R., Johnson, M. K., & Elder, G. H. (2004). School size and the interpersonal side of education: An examination of race/ ethnicity and organizational context. *Social Science Quarterly, 85*(5), 1259–1274

Damon, W. (2002). *Bringing in a new era in character education.* Stanford, CA: Hoover Institution Press.

Darling-Hammond, L. (1997). *The right to learn: A blueprint for creating schools that work.* San Francisco: Jossey-Bass.

Davidson, A. L., & Phelan, P. (1999). Students' multiple worlds: An anthropological approach to understanding students' engagement with school. In T. C. Urdan (Ed.), *Advances in motivation: The role of context, Volume 11* (pp. 233–273). Stamford, CT: JAI.

Deci, E., & Ryan, R. (1985). *Intrinsic motivation and self-determination in human behavior.* New York: Academic Press.

Dornbush, S. M. (1994). *Off the track.* Presidential address at the biennial meeting of the Society for Research on Adolescence, San Diego, CA.

Eccles, J. S., & Gootman, J. A. (Eds.). (2002). *Community programs to promote youth development.* Washington, DC: National Academy Press.

Eccles, J. S., & Midgley, C. (1989). Stage/environment fit: Developmentally appropriate classrooms for early adolescents. In R. Ames & C. Ames (Eds.), *Research on motivation in education* (Vol. 3, pp. 139–181). New York: Academic Press.

Eccles, J. S., Lord, S., & Midgley, C. M. (1991). What are we doing to adolescents? The impact of educational contexts on early adolescents. *American Journal of Education, 99*, 521–542.

Eccles, J.S., Midgley, C., Wigfield, A., Buchanan, C.M., Reuman, D., Flanagan, C. & MacIver, D. (1993). Development during adolescence: The impact of stage-environment fit on adolescents' experiences in schools and families. *American Psychologist, 48*, 90–101.

Eccles. J. S., & Roeser, R. W. (1999). School and community influences on human development. In M. H. Boorstein & M. E. Lamb (Eds.), *Developmental psychology: An advanced textbook. Fourth edition* (pp. 503–554). Hillsdale, NJ: Erlbaum.

Elder, G. H., Jr., & Conger, R. D. (2000). *Children of the land: Adversity and success in rural America.* Chicago: University of Chicago Press.

Entwistle, D. R., Alexander, K. L. & Olson, L. S. (1997). *Children, schools and inequality.* Boulder, CO: Westview.

Evans, G. W. (2004). The environment of childhood poverty. *American Psychologist, 59*, 77–92.

Fiqueira-McDonough, J. (1986). School context, gender, and delinquency. *Journal of Youth and Adolescence, 15*, 79–98.

Garcia-Reid, P., Reid, R. J., & Peterson, N. A. (2005). School engagement among Latino youth in an urban middle school context: Valuing the role of social support. *Education and Urban Society, 37*(3), 257–275.

Gladwell, M. (2000). *The tipping point: How little things can make a big difference.* New York: Little, Brown.

Good, T. L., & Weinstein, R. S. (1986). Schools make a difference. *American Psychologist, 41*(10), 1090–1097.

Gottfredson, D. C., Gottfredson, G. D., & Hybl, L. G. (1993). Managing adolescent behavior A multiyear, multischool study. *American Educational Research Journal, 30*(1), 179–215.

Greenberg, M. T., Weissberg, R. P., Utne O'Brien, M., Zins, J. E., Fredericks, L., Resnik, H., & Elias, M. J. (2003). Enhancing school-based prevention and youth development through coordinated social, emotional, and academic learning. *American Psychologist, 58*, 466–474.

Hallihan, M.T. & Kubitschek, W.N. (1999). Curriculum differentiation and high school achievement. *Social Psychology of Education, 3*, 41–62.

Hanushek, E.A. (1994). Money might matter somewhere: A response to Hedges, Laine and Greenwald. *Educational Researcher, 23*, 5–8.

Harter, S., Whitesell, N. R., & Kowalski, P. (1992). Individual differences in the effects of educational transitions on young adolescents' perceptions of competence and motivational orientation. *American Educational Research Journal, 29*, 809–835

Hawkins, J. D. (1997). Academic performance and school success: Sources and consequences. In R. P. Weissberg, T. P. Gullotta, R. L. Hampton, B. A. Ryan, & G. R. Adams (Eds.), *Enhancing children's wellness, Volume 8, issues in children's and family's lives* (pp. 278–305). Thousand Oaks, CA: Sage.

Hawkins, J. D., Kosterman, R., Catalano, R. F., Kill, K. G., & Abbott, R. D. (2008). Effects of Social Development Intervention in childhood 15 years later. *Archives of Pediatrics and Adolescent Medicine, 162*, 1133–1141.

Heckman, J. J. & Masterov, D. V. (2007). The productivity argument for investing in young children. *Review of Agricultural Economics, 29*, 446–493.

Hedges, L. V., Laine, R. D., & Greenwald, R. (1994). An exchange: Part I: Does money matter? A meta-analysis of studies of the effects of differential school inputs on student outcomes. *Educational Researcher, 23*(3), 5–14.

Hektner, J. M. (1995). When moving up implies moving out: Rural adolescent conflict in the transition to adulthood. *Journal of Research in Rural Education 11*, 3–14.

Hodgkinson, H. & Obarakpor, A.M. (1994). *The invisible poor: Rural youth in America.* Washington, DC: Institute for Educational Leadership.

Hopfenberg, W. S. (1991, April). *The accelerated middle school: Moving from concept toward reality.* Paper presented at the Annual Meeting of the American Educational Research Association, Chicago, IL.

Jeynes, W. H. (2002a). A meta-analysis of the effects of attending religious schools and religiosity on Black and Hispanic academic achievement. *Education and Urban Society, 35*, 27–49.

Jeynes, W. H. (2002b). Educational policy and the effects of attending a religious school on the academic achievement of children. *Educational Policy, 16*, 406–424.

Kao, G. & Thompson, J.S. (2003). Racial and ethnic stratification in educational achievement and attainment. *Annual Review of Sociology, 29*, 417–442.

Kaplan, A., & Maehr, M. L. (1999). Achievement goals and student well-being. *Contemporary Educational Psychology, 24*(4), 330–358.

Kohlberg, L. (1970). Education for justice: A modern restatement of the Platonic view. In N. F. Sizer & T. R. Sizer (Eds.), *Moral education: Five lectures*. Cambridge, MA: Harvard University Press.

LeBlanc, L., Swisher, R., Vitaro, F., & Tremblay, R. E. (2007). School social climate and teachers' perceptions of classroom behavior problems: A ten-year longitudinal and multilevel study. *Social Psychology in Education, 10*, 429–442.

Lee, C. J., Levin, H., & Soler, P. (2005). Accelerated schools for quality education: A Hong Kong perspective. *Urban Review: Issues and Ideas in Public Education, 37*, 63–81.

Lee, V. E. (2000). Using hierarchical linear modeling to study social contexts: The case of school effects. *Educational Psychologist, 35*, 125–142.

Lee, V. E. & Bryk, A. S. (1989). A multilevel model of the social distribution of high school achievement. *Sociology of Education, 62*, 172–192.

Lee, V. E., & Loeb, S. (2000). School size in Chicago Elementary Schools: Effects on teacher attitudes and student achievement. *American Educational Research Journal, 37*, 3–31.

Lee, V. E., & Smith, J. B. (1993). Effects of restructuring on the achievement and engagement of midde-grade students. *Sociology of Education, 66*, 164–187.

Lee, V. E., & Smith, J. B. (1995). Effects of high school restructuring and size on early gains in achievement and engagement. *Sociology of Education, 68*, 241–270.

Lee, V. E., & Smith, J. B. (1997). High school size: Which works best for whom? *Educational Evaluation and Policy Analysis, 19*, 205–227.

Lee, V. E., & Smith, J. B. (1999). Social support and achievement for young adolescents in Chicago: The role of school academic press. *American Educational Research Journal, 36*, 907–945.

Lee, V. E., Bryk, A. S., & Smith, J. B. (1993). The organization of effective secondary schools. In L. Darling-Hammond (Ed.), *Review of research in education, Vol. 19* (pp. 171–267). Washington, DC: American Educational Research Association.

Lee, V. E., Croninger, R. G., & Smith, J. B. (1997). Course taking, equity, and mathematics learning: Testing the constrained curriculum hypothesis in U.S. secondary schools. *Educational Evaluation and Policy Analysis, 19*, 99–121.

Lee, V. E., Croninger, R. G., Linn, E., & Chen, X. (1996). The culture of sexual harassment in secondary schools. *American Educational Research Journal, 33*, 383–417.

Lee, V. E., Smith, J. B. & Croninger, R. G. (1997). How high school organization influences the equitable distribution of learning in mathematics and science. *Sociology of Education, 70*, 128–150.

Levin, H. M. (1988). Accelerated schools for at-risk students. CPRE Research Report Series RR-010. Center for Policy Research in Education, Eagleton Institute of Politics, Rutgers, The State University of New Jersey, New Brunswick.

Levin, H. M. (2009). The economic payoff to investing in educational justice. *Educational Researcher, 38*, 5-20.

Lippman, L., Burns, S., & McArthur, E. (1996). *Urban schools: The challenge of location and poverty* (NCES 94-184). Washington, DC: U.S. Department of Education.National Center for Education Statistics.

Loeb, S. Darling-Hammond, L., & Luczak, J. (2005). How teaching conditions predict teacher turnover in California schools. *Peabody Journal of Education, 80*, 44–70.

Lucas, S. R. (1999). *Tracking inequality: Stratification and mobility in American high schools*. New York: Teachers College Press.

Lucas, T., Henze, R., Donato, R. (1990). Promoting the Success of Latino Language-Minority Students: An Exploratory Study of Six High Schools. *Harvard Educational Review, 60*, 315–340.

Luthar, S. S. (2003). The culture of affluence: Psychological costs of material wealth. *Child Development, 74*(6), 1581–1593.

Luthar, S. S., & Becker, B. E. (2002). Privileged but pressured? A study of affluent youth. *Child Development, 73*(5), 1593–1610.

Luthar, S. S., & Latendresse, S. J. (2005). Children of the affluent: Challenges to well-being *Current Directions in Psychological Science, 14*(1), 49–53.

Maehr, M. L. (1991). The "Psychological Environment" of the school: A focus for school leadership. In P. Thurstone & P. Zodhiates (Eds.), *Advances in educational administration*. (Vol. 2, pp. 51–81). Greenwich, CT: JAI.

Maehr, M. L., & Anderman, E. M. (1993). Reinventing schools for early adolescents: Emphasizing task goals. *The Elementary School Journal, 93*, 593–610.

Maehr, M. L., & Fyans, L. J., Jr. (1989). School culture, motivation, and achievement. In M. L. Maehr & C. Ames (Eds.). *Advances in motivation and achievement: Motivation-enhancing environments* (Vol. 6, pp. 215–247). Greenwich, CT: JAI.

Maehr, M. L. & Midgley, C. (1991). Enhancing student motivation: A school-wide approach. *Educational Psychologist, 26*, 399–427.

Maehr, M. L., & Midgley, C. (1996). *Transforming school cultures to enhance student motivation and learning*. Boulder, CO: Westview.

McGrath, D. J., Swisher, R. R., Elder, G. H., & Conger, R. (2001). Breaking new ground: Diverse routes to college in rural America. *Rural Sociology, 66*, 244–267.

Meece, J. L. & Kurtz-Costes, B. (2001). Introduction: The schooling of ethnic minority children and youth. *Educational Psychologist, 36*, 1–7.

Midgley, C. (1993). Motivation and Middle Level Schools. In M. L. Maehr & P. Pintrich (Eds.) *Advances in motivation and achievement: Vol. 8: Motivation and adolescent development* (pp. 217–274). Greenwich, CT: JAI.

Midgley, C., Anderman, E., & Hicks, L. (1995). Differences between elementary and middle school teachers and students: A goal theory approach. *Journal of Early Adolescence, 15*, 90–113.

Murdock, T. B., Hale, N. M., & Weber, M. J. (2001). Predictors of cheating among early adolescents: Academic and social motivations. *Contemporary Educational Psychology, 96*(1), 96–115.

National Center for Education Statistics (2007). *The condition of education 2007* (NCES 2007-064), Special Analysis. Washington DC: U.S. Department of Education.

Noddings, N. (2002). *Educating moral people: A caring alternative to character education*. New York: Teachers College Press.

Nucci, L. P. (2001). *Education in the moral domain*. Cambridge: Cambridge University Press.

Oakes, J. (2005). *Keeping track: How schools structure inequality* (2nd ed.). New Haven, CT: Yale University Press.

Orfield, G. (1999). *Resegregation in American Schools*. Cambridge, MA: Harvard University Press.

Osterman, K. F. (2000). Students' need for belonging in the school community. *Review of Educational Research, 70*(3), 323–367.

Pittman, R. B., & Haughwout, P. (1987). Influence of high school size on dropout rate. *Educational Evaluation and Policy Analysis, 9*, 337–343.

Planty, M., & DeVoe, J. F. (2005). *An Examination of the Conditions of School Facilities Attended by 10th-Grade Students in 2002* (NCES 2006–302). U.S. Department of Education, National Center for Education Statistics. Washington, DC: U.S. Government Printing Office.

Pope, D. C. (2001). *Doing school: How we are creating a generation of stressed out, materialistic, and miseducated students*. New Haven, CT: Yale University Press.

Power, C., Higgins, A., & Kohlberg, L. (1989). *Lawrence Kohlberg's approach to moral education*. New York: Columbia University Press.

Roeser, R. W. (2004). Competing schools of thought in achievement goal theory? In M. L. Maehr & P. R. Pintrich (Eds.), *Advances in motivation and achievement, Vol. 13: Motivating students, improving schools* (pp. 265–299). New York: Elsevier.

Roeser, R. W., & Galloway, M. G. (2002). Studying motivation to learn in early adolescence: A holistic perspective. In F. Pajares & T. Urdan (Eds.), *Academic motivation of adolescents: Adolescence and education, Vol. II* (pp. 331–372). Greenwich, CT: Information Age.

Roeser, R. W., & Peck, S. C. (2003). Patterns and pathways of educational achievement across adolescence: A holistic-developmental perspective. In W. Damon (Series Ed.) & S. C. Peck & R. W. Roeser (Vol. Eds.), *New directions for child and adolescent development: Vol. 101. Person-centered approaches to studying human development in context* (pp. 39–62). San Francisco: Jossey-Bass.

Roeser, R. W., Marachi, R., & Gelhbach, H. (2002). A goal theory perspective on teachers' professional identities and the contexts of teaching. In C. M. Midgley (Ed.), *Goals, goal structures, and patterns of adaptive learning* (pp. 205–241). Mahwah, NJ: Erlbaum.

Roeser, R. W., Eccles, J. S., & Sameroff, A. J. (1998). Academic and emotional functioning in early adolescence: Longitudinal relations, patterns, and prediction by experience in middle school. *Development and Psychopathology, 10*, 321–352.

Roeser, R. W., Midgley, C. M., & Urdan, T. C. (1996). Perceptions of the school psychological environment and early adolescents' psychological and behavioral functioning in school: The mediating role of goals and belonging. *Journal of Educational Psychology, 88*, 408–422.

Roeser, R. W., Peck, S. C. & Nasir, N. S. (2006). Self and identity processes in school motivation, learning, and achievement. In P. A. Alexander & P. H. Winne (Eds.), *Handbook of educational psychology, 2nd ed.* (pp. 391–424). Mahwah, NJ: Erlbaum.

Rogoff, B. (2003). *The cultural nature of human development*. Oxford, England: Oxford University Press.

Roscigno, V. J., & Crowley, M. L. (2001). Rurality, institutional disadvantage, and achievement/attainment. *Rural Sociology, 66*, 268–293.

Roscigno, V. J., Tomaskovic-Devey, D., & Crowley, M. L. (2006). Education and the inequalities of place. *Social Forces, 84*, 2121–2145.

Rutter, M., & Maughan, B. (2002). School effectiveness findings 1979–2002. *Journal of School Psychology, 40*, 451–475.

Rutter, M., Maughan, B., Mortimore, P., & Ouston, J. (1979*). Fifteen thousand hours: Secondary schools and their effects on children*. Cambridge, MA: Harvard University Press.

Ryan, R. M., & Deci, E. L. (2000). Self-determination theory and the facilitation of intrinsic motivation, social development, and well-being. *American Psychologist, 55*, 68–78.

Ryan, R. M., & La Guardia, J. G. (1999). Achievement motivation within a pressured society: Intrinsic and extrinsic motivations to learn and the politics of school reform. In T. Urdan (Ed.), *Advances in motivation and achievement* (Vol 11, pp. 45–85). Greenwich, CT: JAI Press.

Sarason, S. B. (1990). *The predictable failure of educational reform: Can we change course before it's too late?* San Francisco: Jossey-Bass.

Schaps, E. (2003). The heart of a caring school. *Educational Leadership, 60*, 31–33.

Schafer, W. E., & Olexa, C. (1971). *Tracking and opportunity*. Scranton, PA: Chandler.

Schiller, K. S. (1999). Effects of feeder patterns on students' transition to high school. *Sociology of Education, 72*, 216–233.

Schoggen P., & Schoggen, M. (1988). Student voluntary participation and high school size. *Journal of Educational Research, 81*(5), 288–293.

Simmons, R. G., & Blyth, D. A. (1987). *Moving into adolescence: The impact of pubertal change and school context*. Hawthorn, NY: Aldine de Gruyler.

Simmons, R. G., Black, A., & Zhou, Y. (1991). African-American vs. White children and the transition to junior high school. *American Journal of Education, 99*, 481–520.

Skinner, E. A., & Wellborn, J. G. (1994). Coping during childhood and adolescence: A motivational perspective. In D. Featherman, R. Lerner, & M. Perlmutter (Eds.) *Life-span development and behavior* (Vol. 12, pp. 91–133). Hillsdale, NJ: Erlbaum.

Slavin, R. E. (1987, April). *Effective classroom programs for students at risk*. Paper presented at the Annual Meeting of the American Educational Research Association, Washington, DC.

Solomon, D., Battistich, V., & Hom, A. (1996). Teacher beliefs and practices in schools serving communities that differ in socioeconomic level. *Journal of Experimental Education, 64*, 327–347.

Stephens, J. M., & Roeser, R. W. (2003, April 25). *Quantity of motivation and qualities of classrooms: A person-centered comparative analysis of cheating in high school*. Paper presented at the Annual Meeting of the American Educational Research Association, Chicago, IL.

Stodolsky S. S., & Grossman, P. L., (1995). The impact of subject matter on curricular activity: An analysis of five academic subjects. *American Educational Research Journal, 32*, 227–249.

Talbert. J. E., & McLaughlin, M. W. (1999). Assessing the school environment: Embedded contexts and bottom-up research strategies. In American Psychological Association (Ed.), *Measuring environment across the life span: Emerging methods and concepts* (pp. 197–227). Washington DC: APA.

Tatum, B. D. (1997). *"Why are all the Black kids sitting together in the cafeteria?" and other conversations about race*. New York: Basic Books.

U.S. Department of Agriculture (2003, September). *Rural America at a Glance*. Retrieved July 3, 2007 from http://www.ers.usda.gov/publications/rdrr97-1/lowres_rdrr97-1.pdf

U.S. Department of Education, National Center for Education Statistics. (2000). *Condition of America's Public School Facilities: 1999*. NCES 2000-032, by Laurie Lewis, Kyle Snow, Elizabeth Farris, Becky Smerdon,Stephanie Cronen, and Jessica Kaplan. Bernie Greene, project officer. Washington, DC: 2000.

U.S. Department of Education, National Center for Education Statistics, Common Core of Data (CCD), "Public Elementary/Secondary School Universe Survey," 2004–05, Version 1a. Retrieved February 18, 2008, from http://nces.ed.gov/pubs2007/overview04/tables/table_2.asp

Urdan, T. C. (1997). Examining the relations among early adolescent students' goals and friends' orientation toward effort and achievement in school. *Contemporary Educational Psychology, 22*(2), 165–191.

Valdez, G. (2001). *Learning and not learning English: Latino students in American schools*. New York: Teachers College Press.

Vanderwolf, K.. Everaert, H. & Roeser, R. W. (in press). *Teacher stress in global perspective: The role of difficult students in 8 countries: Volume 6 – Research on stress and coping in education series*. Charlotte, NC: Information Age Publishing.

Weinstein, R. (1989). Perceptions of classroom processes and student motivation: Children's views of self-fulfilling prophecies. In C. Ames & R. Ames (Eds.), *Research on motivation in Education: Vol. 3. Goals and cognitions.* (pp. 13–44). New York: Academic Press.

Wentzel, K. A. (1997). Student motivation in middle school: The role of perceived pedagogical caring. *Journal of Educational Psychology, 89*(3), 411–420.

Wentzel, K. A. (2003). Motivating students to behave in socially competent ways. *Theory Into Practice, 42*(4), 319–326.

Wentzel, K. R. & Wigfield, A. (1998). Academic and social motivational influences on students' academic performance. *Educational Psychology Review, 10*, 155–175.

Wigfield, A. , Eccles, J. S., Schiefele, U., Roeser, R. W., & Kean, P. D. (2006). Development of achievement motivation. In W. Damon & R.M. Lerner (Series Eds.) & N. Eisenberg (Vol. Ed.), *Handbook of child psychology, 6th ed., Vol. 3, Social, emotional and personality development* (pp. 933–1002). New York: Wiley.

Wilson, J. Q., & Kelling, G. L. (1982, March). Broken windows, *Atlantic Monthly*. Retrieved May 2008, from http://www.theatlantic.com/doc/198203/broken-windows

Wong, C. A., Eccles, J. S., & Sameroff, A. J. (2003). The influence of ethnic discrimination and ethnic identification on African-Americans adolescents' school and socioemotional adjustment. *Journal of Personality, 71*, 1197–1232.

19
Gender and Motivation

Judith L. Meece, Beverly Bower Glienke, and Karyl Askew

The role of gender in shaping achievement motivation has a long history in psychological and educational research. Early studies drew on achievement motivation theories to explain why adult women and men differed in their educational and occupational pursuits. Prior to the 1970s, men were more likely than women to obtain a college degree, pursue advanced study, and enter high-paying occupations. Over the last three decades, unprecedented changes in women's level of educational participation and occupational status have been observed. Compared with boys, girls earn higher grades in elementary and secondary school, and they exceed boys in class ranks and academic honors (Downey & Yuan, 2005). Among secondary school students, large gender gaps in mathematics and science performance have decreased, and for basic skills, have been eliminated (Corbett, Hill, & Rose, 2008; National Center of Educational Statistics [NCES], 2005). Additionally, with the exception of physics, young women today are just as likely as men to take challenging mathematics and science coursework in high school (NCES, 2005).

While considerable progress has been made, important gender differences in educational achievement and occupational attainment remain. Girls continue to lag behind boys on tests of advanced mathematics competencies (Corbett et al., 2008), and college entrance exams (Corbett et al., 2008; Halpern, 2006). More high school girls today are enrolled in advanced high school mathematics and science classes, but they are less likely than boys to report liking these courses (NCES, 2004). Also, college women continue to be underrepresented in some fields of study, such as engineering, computer and information science, physical science, and chemistry, and women earn less than half of the professional degrees in business, law, dentistry, and medicine (NCES, 2004).

Other reports suggest that boys may have been left behind in school initiatives to address gender inequities in the last two decades (Sommers, 2000; Weaver-Hightower, 2003). Compared with gender trends for mathematics and science, there has been little change in NAEP reading and writing scores over the last 30 years (NCES, 2005). On average, girls enter school with stronger literacy skills than do boys, and gender gaps in literacy skills widen in the early elementary years (Ready, LoGerfo, Burkum, & Lee, 2005). Early reading skills are often important correlates, for both girls and boys, of schooling experiences that can ultimately place students on a pathway toward early school dropout (Alexander, Entwisle, & Kabbani, 2001; Ensminger & Slusarcick,

1992). Additionally, 38% of boys and 28% of girls, on average, leave school early (Swanson, 2002). Students' chances of dropping out of high school increase depending on their ethnic or socioeconomic background.

Within the last two decades of research on gender and motivation, the school population has become increasingly diverse. Current reports indicate that gender differences in academic achievement vary across ethnic and socioeconomic groups (e.g., American Association of Women, 1998; Corbett et al., 2008). For mathematics, the male advantage on national assessments is most consistently found for White samples. With regards to African American and Hispanic samples, there are small gender gaps favoring girls for mathematics achievement (Corbett et al., 2008).

This review will examine the role of motivation in explaining gender differences in academic achievement and attainment. The review will first focus on four theories of motivation that have been most frequently used in the last 30 years to explain such differences. The theories include expectancy-value, attribution, self-efficacy, and achievement goal theories. In keeping with the cognitive tradition in motivation research, these theories stress the importance of competency judgments, value beliefs, and goals. The review also includes a brief discussion of parental, school, and sociocultural influences on the development of gender differences in motivation. The final sections discuss methodological issues, directions for future research, and educational implications.

Early Psychological Theories of Achievement Motivation

Early theories of achievement motivation focused on differences in men's and women's motives for success. Achievement motives were viewed as personality dispositions that were acquired early and remained stable over the life course. McClelland, Atkinson, Clark, and Lowell (1953) used the Thematic Apperception Test (TAT) to assess achievement motives in college men and women. This measure depicted men and women in different ambiguous situations, and participants were asked to provide a description of the picture. Male students were shown pictures of two men at a machine and a man at a drafting table, whereas female students were shown pictures of two women in a laboratory and a woman upholstering a chair. The assumption of the TAT was that people would project their own motives and desires into the picture and stories, and highly success-oriented people would write stories that included a good deal of achievement imagery. In general, college men of the time responded to the TAT assessments with more achievement imagery than did their female counterparts. Accordingly, women were viewed as less success-oriented than men or as fearful of success. Horner (1975) concluded that "most women have a motive to avoid success, that is, a disposition to become anxious about achieving success because they expect negative consequences such as social rejection and/or feelings of being unfeminine" (p. 207). Fear of success, as a psychological barrier to women's achievement, generated a good deal of research in the 1970s.

Building on the work of McClelland et al., Atkinson (1957, 1964) introduced an expectancy-value model of achievement motivation. In this model, achievement motivation was a function of motives for success, expectations for success, the incentive value of success, and the motive to avoid failure. This model went beyond personality dispositions to include cognitive assessments represented by the person's subjective expectation for success at a particular task and for the anticipated outcomes or consequences of an outcome. Whereas achievement expectancies were defined as subjective probabilities of success, the incentive value of the task was defined in terms of its perceived difficulty level. According to Atkinson's theory, tasks that were more difficult and challenging would have more incentive value for the individual. Expectancies and values were inversely related so that highly valued tasks were those for which individuals had low expectations for success.

Like its predecessor, Atkinson's expectancy-value theory continued to emphasize gender differences related to the motives to approach or avoid success. Atkinson's research also indicated that men and women differ in their concerns about failure. For example, based on scores obtained from the *Test Anxiety Questionnaire* (Mandler & Sarason, 1952), female respondents, when compared with their male counterparts, scored higher on measures of test anxiety (Hill & Sarason, 1966; Maccoby & Jacklin, 1974). Finally, considerable research in the 1960s also documented that girls and women tend to have lower expectations for success than their male counterparts (Crandall, 1969; Feather, 1966; Veroff, 1969). Thus, according to the Atkinson expectancy-value theory, gender differences in motivation were related to motives to approach/avoid success, concerns about failure, and expectations for success.

By the late 1970s, much of the early research on achievement motives and fears of success had been refuted due to biases in research methodologies and inconsistent findings across studies (Frieze, Parsons, Johnson, Ruble, & Zellman, 1978). This research was also criticized because female achievement was often judged against a male standard that did not take into account gendered patterns of socialization and education that differentially shaped men's and women's academic and occupational choices (Eccles, 1994).

Attribution Theories of Motivation

During the 1970s and early 1980s, attribution theory was the predominant theory of motivation (Graham, this volume), and it was utilized to understand gender differences in achievement motivation (Dweck, 1986; Eccles et al., 1983; Frieze, 1975; Meece, Eccles, Kaczala, Goff, & Futterman, 1982). Research using an attribution framework identified gender differences in the ways that children and adults interpret their successes and failures. Early studies indicated that women were more likely to exhibit what has been labeled as a low-expectancy attribution pattern, and their achievement behavior has been found to suffer as a consequence. Specifically, men attributed their successes to internal stable causes (ability), whereas women attributed their failures, but not their successes, to these causes (Bar-Tal, 1978; Crandall, Katkovsky, & Crandall, 1965; Frieze, 1975; McMahan, 1973). However, these patterns were not consistently found across all studies and findings appeared to be more marked for achievement areas that were sex-typed as masculine or feminine domains (Frieze, Whitley, Hanusa, & McHugh, 1982). In mathematics, for example, girls are less likely than boys to attribute their successes to ability. Instead, girls attribute their successes to effort and hard work, which may undermine their expectations for success as mathematics increases in difficulty (Eccles et al., 1983; Parsons, Meece, Adler, & Kaczala, 1982; Wolleat, Pedro, Becker, & Fennema, 1980). Similar differences in causal attribution patterns have also been noted for successes and failures in science courses (Li & Adamson, 1995; Kahle & Meece, 1994). By contrast, few studies report gender differences for achievement tasks involving verbal and language abilities (Parsons, Adler, & Meece, 1984). Thus, gender differences in causal attribution patterns are evident but depend on the achievement domain. Studies also suggest that results vary depending on student ability and research methodology (e.g., open-ended vs. rank-order questions; Parsons et al., 1982).

Another prominent area of attribution research is the study of learned helplessness. Learned helplessness occurs when someone attributes failure to a lack of ability and gives up easily or shows a steady regression in problem-solving strategies when confronted with failure. Due to gender differences in attribution patterns, girls may be more prone to learned helplessness than boys, particularly with regards to mathematics and other male sex-typed domains (Dweck, 1986; Eccles et al., 1982; Farmer & Vispoel, 1990). Studies of children's attribution patterns in laboratory settings have identified gender differences in causal attribution and behavior patterns that are consistent with learned helplessness (Dweck & Bush, 1976). However, as with studies of causal attributions, findings are not consistent across studies. For example, Parsons (Eccles), Meece, Adler, and Kaczala (1982) used school-related learning tasks (number sequences and anagrams) to examine gender differences in learned helplessness patterns within a sample of adolescents (Grades 8–10). Although male and female students reported differential attributions to ability for successes and failures on the math problems, these causal attribution patterns did not translate into gender differences in behavioral responses (see also Kloosterman, 1990). Thus, attribution measures, rather behavioral responses to failure, tend to provide the strongest support for gender differences in learned helplessness. As discussed earlier, responses on attribution measures are influenced by many situational factors, including sex-role stereotypes and self-presentational concerns (Parsons et al., 1982; Parsons et al., 1984; Farmer & Vispoel, 1990 Frieze et al., 1982; McHugh, Frieze, & Hanusa, 1982).

In summary, early research on gender and motivation focused on differentiated patterns of causal attributions, with much of this research directed toward understanding the low expectancy patterns, achievement anxiety, and learned helplessness inhibiting female achievement. To date, research on gender differences in causal attributions and learned helplessness is inconclusive and equivocal. Patterns of gender differences depend on methodology used, academic domain, academic abilities, type of achievement task, and research setting (laboratory versus classroom). When gender differences are found, they tend to be small in magnitude and not a strong predictor of behavioral responses (Eccles et al., 1983; Parsons et al., 1982; Parsons et al., 1984). Additionally, few studies have examined when gender differences in attribution patterns begin to emerge. Evidence from a cross-cultural study suggests that girls as young as eight years of age may discount their academic abilities, even when they are doing as well, or better than, boys within a particular achievement domain (Stetsenko, Little, Gordeeva, Grasshof, & Oettingen, 2000). Future research needs to examine the socialization processes that explain the emergence of gender differences so early in development.

Contemporary Expectancy-Value Theories

As discussed previously, expectancy-value theories have been widely used to examine gender differences in motivation and achievement behavior. Building on the prior research of Atkinson (1957) and Weiner (1985, 1986), Eccles and her colleagues (1983) introduced a social cognitive model of academic choice that included a socialization component focused on the role of culture, parents, and teachers in shaping achievement-related beliefs, as well as identity development processes. The Eccles et al. (1983) model has been applied to different achievement domains (mathematics, science, and sports), as well as career choices and trajectories of young adults. In keeping with Atkinson, Eccles et al's model highlights the importance of expectancy and value beliefs (see Wigfield, Klauda, & Tonks, this volume).

Competency Beliefs Competency beliefs are defined as estimations of one's ability to perform or to succeed at an activity (Eccles et al., 1983). As early as first grade, children make distinct judgments about their abilities in different domains, including mathematics, reading, music, and sports (Eccles, Wigfield, Harold, & Blumenfeld, 1993). Also, small gender differences in children's competency beliefs also emerge in early elementary school (Eccles et al., 1993). Interestingly, the results follow gender norms and stereotypes with boys holding more positive competence beliefs for sports and mathematics than girls, and girls holding more positive competence beliefs for instrumental music than did boys (Eccles et al., 1993). These gender differences emerge even though boys and girls perform equally well in these domains (Eccles et al., 1993).

Additionally, cross-sectional and longitudinal research indicates that all children experience declines in their competency beliefs over the course of schooling (Wigfield & Eccles, 2000; Wigfield, Eccles, Yoon, & Harold, 1997). However, the rate of change differs by gender and by achievement domain. Girls' perceptions of their math abilities decline at a slower rate than boys, such that gender gaps in mathematics competence decrease over time (Fredericks & Eccles, 2002; Jacobs, Lanza, Osgood, Eccles, & Wigfield, 2002). For language arts, boys and girls begin elementary school with similar ability perceptions, but boys' perceptions rapidly decline in elementary school. By middle school, there are significant differences in boys' and girls' competency ratings for language arts. Like mathematics, gender gaps in language arts are somewhat smaller by high school (Jacobs et al., 2002). By contrast, gender differences in the sports domain, favoring boys, remain stable across all grades of school (Fredericks & Eccles, 2002; Jacobs et al., 2002).

Value Beliefs In Eccles et al.'s (1983) expectancy-value model, the influence of competency perceptions are moderated by the value attached to achievement activities. Task value is defined in terms of four components: (a) perceived importance of being good at an activity; (b) perceived usefulness of the activity for obtaining short- or long-term goals; (c) perceived interest or liking of the activity; and (d) perceived cost of engaging in the activity (e.g., time taken away from other activities, amount of effort needed to succeed, performance anxiety associated with the activity, etc.). Beginning with elementary school, gender differences are evident in the value children and adolescents attach to different academic domains.

As with competency beliefs, the patterns follow gender norms and stereotypes. In a longitudinal study of first- through fourth-grade students, Eccles and her colleagues (1993) defined task value as a composite score representing the perceived interest, enjoyment, importance, and usefulness of an academic domain. The results showed that boys placed a higher value on sports activities than girls, whereas girls placed a higher value than boys on musical and reading activities. Interestingly, there were no gender differences in the value attached to mathematics for elementary school children.

Studies with older children and adolescents also reveal similar patterns of gender differences in achievement task values. For example, Wigfield, Eccles, Mac Iver, and Reuman (1991) reported that students' perceptions of the value of mathematics, reading, and sports declined at the transition to junior high school (Grade 7). As with younger students, girls placed a greater value on English than did boys; whereas boys placed greater value than girls on sports. Expanding this research, Jacobs et al. (2002) used growth modeling procedures to examine changes in students' value perceptions from the first through the twelfth grade in three achievement domains. Over the course of schooling, students' value perceptions related to mathematics, language arts, and sports all declined, with the value of language arts declining most rapidly in elementary school and the value of mathematics declining most rapidly in high school. As expected, an examination of gender patterns revealed that boys placed a higher value on sports activities than girls, while the reverse was found for language arts. Similar to Eccles et al. (1993), no gender differences were found for the valuing of mathematics, nor for differences in the rate of change (see also Fredericks & Eccles, 2002). With respect to language arts, girls showed a more rapid decline in their value perceptions during elementary school than boys, but this direction reversed by the high school years (Jacobs et al., 2002).

In summary, research based on Eccles et al.'s (1983) expanded expectancy-value model of achievement behavior has provided many important insights into gender differences in motivation. This research has revealed that boys and girls begin school with different views of their abilities and interests (Eccles et al., 1993; Jacobs et al., 2002). Boys begin school with higher perceptions of their math abilities, whereas girls report higher perceptions of their language arts abilities. Gender gaps in these perceptions narrow for mathematics and increase for language arts over the course of schooling. When task values are defined as interest and importance, there appear to be no gender differences regarding the value of mathematics; however, gender differences are evident in students' valuing of language arts across the school years. Whereas previous research had suggested that gender differences would increase at the transition to adolescence or to new school environments (Wigfield et al., 1991), recent analyses using growth modeling procedures indicate that the most rapid period of decline in both competency and value perceptions occurs in the elementary school years (Jacobs et al., 2002).

Are gender differences in students' competency and value beliefs related to achievement behavior? Numerous studies have shown that children's and adolescents' competence beliefs are important predictors of their performance in different domains, even when the level of previous performance is controlled. In contrast, value perceptions are a stronger predictor of students' choice to participate or engage in an activity (see Wigfield et al., this volume). Further, relations for competency and value perceptions are found as early as first grade and the strength of these relations increase with age (Eccles et al., 1983, Eccles, 1994; Parsons et al., 1984; Wigfield & Eccles, 1992). Thus, if gender differences are evident in students' competency and value perceptions, these differences are likely to have an impact on their achievement-related activity choices, engagement, and performance.

Self-Efficacy Theory

Since its introduction almost 30 years ago (Bandura, 1977), the construct of self-efficacy has received increasing attention in educational research and studies of academic motivation and self-regulated learning. Self-efficacy refers to a person's judgment of their confidence to learn, perform academic tasks or succeed in academic endeavors (Bandura, 1986). Unlike more global beliefs such as self-concept, self-confidence and locus of control, self-efficacy involves judgments concerning one's ability to attain a certain level of performance in a particular activity or situation (Meece et al., 1990; Schunk, 1989). For example, respondents are asked to rate their level of confidence for solving a certain number of mathematics problems correctly, for obtaining a certain grade in a course, for comprehending reading passages of different levels of difficulty, or for learning technical terms in biology (Pajares, 1996). Research has consistently shown that self-efficacy beliefs are important mediators of all types of achievement-related behaviors (Bong & Skaalvik, 2003; Pajares, 1996; Pintrich & Schunk, 2002; Schunk & Pajares, 2002, this volume).

Self-efficacy theory has been widely used to understand gender differences in motivation and achievement patterns. Much of this research has focused on academic areas that are traditionally sex-typed as male or female domains of achievement. For example, numerous studies document that boys tend to report higher self-efficacy and expectancy beliefs than girls about their performance in math and science (Anderman & Young, 1994; Pajares, 1996, Pintrich & De Groot, 1990; Zimmerman & Martinez-Pons, 1990). The results of Whitley's (1997) meta-analysis of studies of gender differences in computer-related attitudes and behavior also revealed a similar pattern as men and boys exhibited higher computer self-efficacy than did their female counterparts. When the contexts were reading or writing, however, gender differences were reversed. For example, Pajares and Valiante (1997, 2001) reported that middle school girls had higher writing self-efficacy than boys, even though there were no gender differences in actual writing performance.

Research also suggests that gender differences in self-efficacy are linked to age or grade level (Schunk & Pajares, 2002), with differences beginning to emerge in the middle school years (Bandura, Barbaranelli, Caprara, & Pastorelli, 2001; Wigfield, Eccles, & Pintrich, 1996). In Whitley's (1997) meta-analysis of computer self-efficacy, mean effect sizes for gender differences varied depending on the age of the sample: .09 for grammar school (elementary and middle school/junior high), .66 for high school, .32 for college, and .49 for adult samples. Age-related gender differences in self-efficacy beliefs are generally attributed to increased concerns about conforming to gender-role stereotypes, which typically coincide with the entry into adolescence (Wigfield et al., 1996). However, research on gender differences in self-efficacy beliefs has not found a consistent pattern of gender differences among young adolescents (Pajares & Graham, 1999; Roeser, Midgley, & Urdan, 1996).

To summarize, a large body of research has examined gender differences in self-efficacy beliefs. This research is guided by Bandura's social cognitive theory (Bandura, 1986), which emphasizes the critical role of efficacy beliefs in human development and behavior. Compared to studies of academic competency beliefs, research on efficacy beliefs presents a more mixed pattern of results. One explanation for this discrepancy is the task specificity of efficacy beliefs. Gender differences may be more prevalent in measures that elicit group comparisons or evaluation of worth (e.g., "I am good at science."). In making these assessments, cultural stereotypes or gender expectations may lead to more biased assessments (Schunk & Meece, 2006). In fact, when gender role orientations are taken into account, gender differences in efficacy beliefs are no longer significant (Pajares & Valiante, 2001). Nevertheless, self-efficacy has been positively correlated with higher levels of academic achievement and participation across studies of different age levels (Schunk & Pajares, 2002, this volume). Given its positive influence on achievement and motivation, better understanding of gender and age-related differences in the development of self-efficacy beliefs is needed. Few studies to date have examined developmental changes by gender and content area in students' self-efficacy beliefs (Pajares & Viliante, 2001).

Goal Theories of Achievement Motivation

Achievement goal theory emphasizes the person's *reasons* for choosing, performing, and persisting at various learning activities. Two types of goal orientations have been mainly used to understand and to explain academic behaviors in school settings (see Ames, 1992; Dweck & Elliot, 1983; Meece, Anderman, & Anderman, 2006; Nicholls, 1984; Maehr & Zusho, this volume). Each goal type differs in terms of the standards used to judge performance and achievement. A *learning* or *mastery* goal orientation is defined as a desire to develop one's competencies, to master a task, or to improve intellectually, whereas a *performance* goal orientation is concerned with demonstrating high ability relative to others, competing for grades, or gaining recognition for ability. In recent years, *performance* goals have been further differentiated into *performance-approach* goals, which focus on the attainment of favorable judgments of competence, and *performance-*

avoidance goals, which focus on avoiding unfavorable judgments of ability (Elliot & Church, 1997; Elliot & Harackiewicz, 1996). As reviewed elsewhere (Ames, 1992; Anderman & Wolters, 2006; Maehr & Zusho, this volume; Meece et al., 2006), the goals individuals adopt in learning settings have important implications for a wide range of academic behaviors, including preference for challenging activities, task engagement and persistence, and reported use of learning strategies to enhance conceptual understanding and recall of information.

Compared with the other achievement theories discussed in this chapter, only a few studies have examined gender differences in achievement goal orientations. In a study of motivation and strategy use in elementary science, Anderman and Young (1994) reported that girls were more learning focused and less ability focused in science than were boys, even though girls reported lower levels of self-efficacy in science. In another study, Meece and Jones (1996) reported gender differences, favoring boys, in elementary school students' science-related efficacy beliefs; however, no main effects for gender were reported for mastery and performance goal scales. Gender effects were also moderated by the students' ability level. In the low ability group only, boys reported a stronger mastery goal orientation than did girls. In a third study based on a sample of ethnically and economically mixed sixth-grade students, Middleton and Midgley (1997) found that African American girls reported a stronger learning goal orientation than African American boys. No differences in goal orientations were found for European American students. In contrast to these findings, Greene and her colleagues (Greene, DeBacker, Ravindran, & Knows, 1999) reported no gender differences in high school students' learning and performance goals in mathematics. Taken together, these studies reveal no clear pattern of gender differences in students' achievement goal orientations. Differences are moderated by ability, race, and classroom context.

Sources of Gender Differences in Motivation

Socialization and achievement experiences play an important role in the development of gender differences in motivation. Because gender differences are found so early in development, the child's home environment plays an important role in the shaping of their competency beliefs and interests. At school, children have an opportunity to validate, refine, and enact their gender beliefs and behavior. According to the Eccles et al. (1983) model, both parents and teachers contribute to gender differences in motivation by (a) modeling sex-typed behavior, (b) communicating different expectations and goals for boys and girls, and (c) encouraging different activities and skills. This section reviews research on parental, school, and sociocultural influences on gender patterns of motivation.

Parental Influences

The Eccles et al. (1983) expanded expectancy-value model included a parental socialization component. According to this model, there are several important pathways by which parents influence their children's achievement motivation. Parents are important sources of information children draw on to form their ability and value perceptions. Parents also provide and encourage different recreational and learning activities that can support the development of specific skills and interests. Additionally, parents are important role models. They communicate information about their own abilities and skills, and what is valued and important, through their choice of work and leisure activities. With respect to gender differences in motivation, there is strong empirical support for the parental socialization component of the expectancy-value model (Eccles et al., 1983;

Parsons et al., 1982; Jacobs, 1991; Jacobs & Bleeker, 2004; Jacobs, Davis-Kean, Bleeker, Eccles, & Malanchuk, 2005; Jacobs & Eccles, 1992). Relevant findings are briefly summarized below.

Parental beliefs about their children's abilities have a strong influence on their children's own beliefs about their academic abilities (Bleeker & Jacobs, 2004; Eccles et al., 1998; Jacobs, 1991; Jacobs & Eccles, 1992). Research has shown that cultural stereotypes (e.g., men excel in mathematics and science) influence parents' perceptions of their children's abilities, leading parents to form different perceptions of their sons' and daughters' academic abilities. For example, Parsons, Adler, and Kaczala (1982) reported that parents, particularly fathers, thought that their daughters needed to work harder than their sons to do well in mathematics despite no differences in their children's mathematics achievement. In a separate study, Jacobs (1991) found that parents who held gender stereotypes about men's superior mathematical abilities reported less confidence in their children's mathematics abilities if they had daughters but more confidence if they had sons. Research has also shown that both mother's and fathers' perceptions of their children's abilities influence how children perceived their own abilities, even after controlling for differences in children's achievement (Jacobs & Eccles, 1992). Similar patterns are found for children's interests in mathematics and science (Jacobs et al., 2005)

Parental involvement in children's activities has also been found to differentially affect girls' and boys' choice of activities. For example, in a study of single-parent families, the amount of time mothers engaged in supportive activities with their children was positively related to their children's productive leisure activity during adolescence (Larson, Dworkin, & Gillman, 2001). Researchers have also found significant links between parents' gender stereotypes, children's gender stereotypes, and children's activity choice. In a two-year study of middle class girls and their parents, McHale, Shanahan, Updegraff, Crouter, and Booth (2004) investigated the amount of time girls spent in sex-typed leisure activities during middle childhood and adolescence. The researchers found that the more sex-typed beliefs parents and girls held, the more the girls were involved in sex-typed activities. Interestingly, while the parents' personality qualities (e.g., kindness and competitiveness) were strong predictors of girls' sex-typed activity, parental gender role attitudes were not. In addition, the mothers' personality qualities best predicted the sex-typed activities in middle childhood, while the fathers' qualities best predicted sex-typed activities in adolescence. This latter finding suggests that the paternal role ties children to the outside world and becomes more important as children age (McHale et al., 2004).

Combining the above areas of research, Bleeker and Jacobs (2004) examined ways parents promote positive attitudes and behaviors toward mathematics and science in their children. Their study examined information on (a) parental selection of math- or science-related toys, games, books and other activities, (b) parental involvement and participation in mathematics and science activities, and (c) parental perceptions of their children's math and science abilities. Parents' promotive activities were found to be dependent on the gender of both the child and the parent and were connected to children's later involvement in mathematics and science activities. More specifically, mothers were more likely to purchase mathematics and science items for boys than for girls, regardless of grade level; and six years later, analyses revealed an increase in children's mathematics and science interests related to the number of purchases made (Bleeker & Jacobs, 2004). However, both mothers and fathers were more likely to be involved in their daughters' mathematics and science activities than in those of their sons. This finding suggests that parents may think their daughters need more assistance with mathematics and science, and that unsolicited help can be deleterious to girls' self-perceptions (Graham, 1990).

Parental influence not only affects children's choice of activities and achievement beliefs but also impacts children's career interests and choices. Recent studies indicate that gender differences in mathematics and science course selection at the high school level have decreased since the 1980s (Coley, 2001). Despite this trend, occupation statistics continue to show gender differences in career choices, with men constituting the majority in science- and mathematics-related jobs (U.S. Census Bureau, 2003; Watt, 2006). Research has shown that parental beliefs and expectations can affect children's occupational choices. In one study, mother's beliefs about their children's abilities in mathematics in Grade 7 were related to adolescents' math and science career efficacy 12 years later (Bleeker & Jacobs, 2004). Another study revealed that parental expectations for their children at age 17 predicted their son's and daughters' career choices at age 28 (Jacobs, Chhin, & Bleeker, 2006). Thus, parental behaviors, beliefs, and expectations appear to have an enduring influence on young people's achievement attitudes and behaviors.

Schooling Influences

Schools also play a key role in shaping children's gender role conceptions, beliefs, and social identities. At school, children observe and learn about the adult world, and the adult images to which they are exposed may be more rigid and more polarized than those found in the larger society (Ruble & Martin, 1998). For example, women are more likely to perform traditional gender roles such as caring for young children, putting on Band-Aids, and preparing food, whereas men are more likely to manage the school and staff. Gender differences are also evident in staffing patterns at school. A majority of high school foreign language, humanities, business education, and English teachers are female, whereas only half the science teachers are female (Weiss, Banilower, McMahon, & Smith, 2001). Students also learn important gender role lessons from textbooks, videotapes, and computer software at school. Although textbooks are less gender biased than they were 30 years ago, male characters continue to outnumber female ones in basal readers, and representations of men have remained more stereotyped than those of women (Fleming, 2000).

Considerable research also has examined gender differences in teachers' perceptions of their students' abilities. Early studies suggested that teachers have higher achievement expectations for boys than for girls, especially in male sex-typed activities (for review, see Meece et al., 1982). However, subsequent studies of teacher expectations are mixed and equivocal (Dusek & Joseph, 1983; Parsons, Kaczala, & Meece, 1982; Jussim & Harber, 2005). Gender differences in teacher expectancies depend on grade level, student ability, subject matter, and schooling context. When student ethnicity is examined, research indicates that teachers hold lower expectations for urban, low-income African American males than they do for females. This finding holds even after researchers control for academic achievement, and patterns of gender differences for African American students can occur as early as six years of age (Wood, Kaplan, & McLoyd, 2007). Differences in teacher expectations are also a function of teacher characteristics. Their expectations of the opposite sex in teacher-student pairings had a greater impact on African American students' enrollment in higher-level mathematics courses beyond geometry than on other students (Klopfenstein, 2005).

A related area of research focuses on gender differences in classroom interaction patterns. Research suggests that teachers tend to be more supportive and warmer toward students for whom they hold high expectations. As a result, these students receive a disproportionately high number of opportunities to demonstrate mastery and to receive positive feedback in their abilities (Brophy & Good, 1974). The Brophy-Good Dyadic Child Interaction System (Brophy & Good,

1974) has been widely used to identify gendered differentiated patterns of classroom interactions. The system records teacher-interacted questions (direct questions, open questions, and call-outs), teacher-initiated feedback (criticism, praise, and neutral comments), student-initiated interactions (student questions, volunteering, spontaneous comments, etc.), and teacher-initiated interactions focused on behavioral management. Studies utilizing the Brophy-Good system have consistently documented that boys tend to have more interactions of all types than do girls (Altermatt, Jovanic, & Perry, 1998; Jones & Dindia, 2004; Meece, 1987; Parsons, Kaczala, & Meece, 1982). Results show that boys are called on more than girls to answer process, abstract, and complex questions, at both the elementary and secondary levels. Further, compared with girls, boys also receive more acknowledgement, approval, encouragement, criticism, and corrective feedback in response to their answers. These gender differences in classroom interaction patterns communicate different learning expectations for boys and girls (Brophy & Good, 1974).

Gender-differentiated classroom interaction patterns appear to be more pronounced in stereo-typically male sex-typed school subjects, such as mathematics and science, although these patterns are not consistently found across studies (Altermatt et al., 1998; Jones & Dindia, 2004; Kahle & Meece, 1994; Parsons, Kaczala, & Meece, 1982). Gender differences in classroom interactions are also moderated by children's ability levels and by classroom structures (Parsons, Kaczala, & Meece, 1982). For example, gender differences in interaction patterns are more pronounced in classrooms where whole-group instruction is the primary mode of instruction. Furthermore, evidence suggests gender differences in classroom interactions may be due to the fact that boys initiate more interactions with their teachers than do girls (Altermatt et al., 1998; Eccles & Blumenfeld, 1985). Whether or not these teacher-student interactions reflect teacher responsivity, the patterns serve to reinforce gender role stereotypes of male authority and competence.

Less is known about what role specific instructional and management practices may play in the development of gender differences in motivation. Eccles and Midgley (1989) maintain that children are maximally motivated to learn when classroom situations fit well with their needs, interests, and skill levels. In this regard, evidence suggests that the learning environment of elementary classrooms may favor girls more than boys (Kedar-Voivodas, 1983). For example, some researchers have speculated that curriculum activities and materials, particularly in literacy, tend to be better aligned with the learning interests and preferences of girls than those of boys (Brozo, 2002; Connell, 1996). Other evidence suggests that elementary school teachers tend to have more favorable attitudes and expectations for students who are cooperative, conforming, respectful, and orderly. Children who are assertive, independent, and difficult to manage are the least preferred by teachers (Brophy & Good, 1974; Feshbach, 1969). Given the nature of gender role socialization, girls are more likely than boys to exhibit the types of behaviors that enable them to adjust well to the elementary school environment (Kedar-Voivodas, 1983).

By the secondary school years, instructional activities and practices may have a different impact. Considerable research has demonstrated the negative influence of school transitions on adolescents. This research has shown that as students move from elementary school to middle/junior high schools, learning environments become more impersonal, structured, and teacher-controlled (Eccles & Midgley, 1989). As they make the transition to middle school, adolescents also perceive their classrooms as more focused on competition and ability differences (Anderman & Midgley, 1997; Urdan & Midgley, 2003). While these classroom environments can undermine the motivation of most students, there is some evidence to suggest that girls respond more negatively to competitive teaching conditions. For example, Tobin and Garnett (1987) report that whole-class lessons in science tend to be dominated by high-achieving boys. Other research suggests that girls initiate more interactions with teachers and report higher achievement expectations for mathematics in classes where individualized or cooperative learning is the primary mode of instruction (Parsons, Kaczala, & Meece, 1982; Kahle, 1990). Because secondary teachers tend to use whole-class lecture and discussion as the primary mode of instruction, boys are more likely than girls to take an active role in those classrooms. Additional research is needed to examine the role of different instructional practices in the development of gender differences in motivation during the secondary school years.

Sociocultural Influences

Identity processes play a central role in the development of motivation. According to Erikson (1963), a key aspect of identity development is to integrate self-conceptions with societal expectations and opportunities. Children begin to form gender role conceptions that influence their beliefs, attitudes, and behavior well before they enter school. By the preschool years, they prefer to engage in activities that are sex-typed as appropriate for their gender and react negatively to cross-gender behaviors (Ruble & Martin, 1998). As described earlier, gender stereotypes can permeate almost every aspect of children's daily experiences from activities in the home to staffing patterns at school. Eccles and colleagues (1983) have argued that socialization processes that lead children to internalize and accept these gender stereotypes are largely responsible for gender differences in motivation and achievement. However, the influence of gender stereotypes is moderated by the child's own sex-role identity. A masculine orientation is positively associated with self-perceptions of mathematics competence for both boys and girls (Eccles et al., 1983). Similarly, Pajares and Valiante (2001) have concluded that gender differences in writing motivation and achievement of middle school students may be more "a function of gender orientation rather than gender" (p. 376).

Despite the increasing cultural diversity of the school-aged population, little research has examined how gender differences in motivation differ by ethnicity, race, or socioeconomic status (SES; Eccles, Wong, & Peck, 2006; Graham & Taylor, 2002; Meece & Kurtz-Costes, 2001; Rowley, Kurtz-Costes, & Cooper, in press). Most studies compare girls and boys as if they represented homogeneous groups, and few studies have examined how race, socioeconomic status, and other cultural influences combine with gender to shape students' social identities and learning experiences at school. Yet there are several reasons to expect gender differences to vary across ethnic or socioeconomic groups. First, research indicates that gender socialization patterns are quite different for Hispanic, Asian, and African American youth. For example, parents of Latina and Asian girls generally expect their daughters to be obedient, responsible, dependent, and submissive, whereas African American girls are socialized to be self-reliant, resourceful, and assertive (Collins, 1998; Weiler, 2000). The socialization experiences of Latina and Asian girls are more consistent with the gendered expectations at school, and those girls may assimilate into school environments more easily than their African American peers. Along with gendered expectations, African American and Latina youth, as discussed below, must also cope with stereotypes of their intellectual inferiority and ethnic discrimination (Spencer, Swanson, & Cunningham, 1991; Steele, 1992). Considerable research has also documented the processes that lead ethnic minority youth to "disengage" from school environments that devalue their own cultural or racial heritage (Graham, Taylor, & Hudley, 1998; Fordham & Ogbu, 1986; Spencer et al., 1991)

Much of the available evidence on gender differences within ethnic groups is quite mixed. With respect to competency related beliefs, some studies report gender differences favoring girls among high ability African American adolescents (Kirst, 1993), while other studies report no gender differences (Alexander & Entwisle, 1988; Pollard, 1993). In a large-scale study using data from the National Educational Longitudinal Study of 1988 (NELS:88), Catsambis (1994) reported gender differences favoring eighth- and tenth-grade boys across African American, Latino, and White samples. Specifically, girls reported less confidence in their mathematical abilities than did their male counterparts. Gender differences for African American adolescents disappeared when differences in background characteristics (SES, prior achievement, amount of homework completion) were controlled.

A different gender pattern emerges when the focus is on achievement-related value beliefs. For example, Graham et al. (1998) reported more devaluing of academic achievement for African American boys than for girls of the same ethnic background. Further, African American girls nominated other girls of the same ethnicity and high achievers as the most respected and admired. Boys showed the same pattern when asked to nominate girls for the most admired and respected category. However, when nominating other males, African American boys selected low-achieving males as the most respected and admired. Overall, study results suggested a devaluing of academic achievement among African American and Latino males (Graham & Taylor, 2002).

In another line of research, Osborne (1995, 1997) examined relations between academic performance and self-esteem among boys and girls in a diverse sample. Consistent with the view that minority youth may devalue the importance of academic success, Osborne, using a large-scale educational database (NELS:88), found that academic performance was related to self-esteem for White and Hispanic students for both male and female participants. The same was true for African American girls; however, relations between self-esteem and academic performance decreased for African American boys from 8th to 12th grade. Thus, the devaluing of academic or school success may be more prevalent among non-White minority males than for girls of the same ethnic background.

Scholars are currently debating the prevalence and origins of the devaluing of academic success among ethnic minority youth. Some researchers argue that patterns of disengagement are more prevalent among youth who do not perceive the benefits of education for their futures due to racial discrimination or limited economic opportunities (Ogbu, 1994). Numerous studies have also examined the school-related experiences that can lead to gender-differentiated patterns of disengagement (Davis, 2003; Davis & Jordan, 1994; Eccles, Wong, & Peck, 2006; Phelan, Yu, & Davidson, 1994; Roderick, 2003; Rowley et al., in press; Wong, Eccles, & Sameroff, 2003). This body of research is examining the role of teacher beliefs, classroom interactions, curricular relevancy, academic problems, disciplinary actions, and daily experiences of racial discrimination for boys and girls within ethnic groups. Overall, findings suggest that ethnic minority boys are much more likely than their female counterparts to experience a negative classroom or school environment that would lead to lower academic engagement, lower participation in school activities, and lower school achievement.

Despite the gravity of these documented trends for boys of color, concerns have also been raised about the school experiences of non-White ethnic minority girls. Evidence suggests that girls of color are not receiving the types of supports they need to maintain high levels of academic motivation and school success (AAUW, 1998; Irvine, 1986; Philips, 1998). For example, both Grant (1984) and Irvine (1986) reported that African American girls received less attention and academic feedback from teachers than any other group. Moreover, a recent report indicated that a disproportionate number of girls who do not earn a high school diploma within a standard four-year period are African American, Latina, and Native American (National Women's Law

Center, 2007). Thus, there is still much to learn about the ways race and gender combine to influence academic motivation and school success.

Conclusions

Although there has been a recent decline in the gender gap in many achievement domains, it is clear that gender differences in achievement motivation still exist. Grounded in expectancy-value, attribution, self-efficacy, and achievement goal theories, today's motivation research uses improved methodologies to highlight specific areas where there are discrepancies between boys' and girls' achievement-related beliefs and values. Whereas early theories of motivation depicted women as underachievers, current research indicates that gender differences in causal attributions as well as in competency, value, and self-efficacy beliefs are domain-specific. In general, boys tend to have positive achievement-related beliefs in the areas of mathematics, science, and sports while girls report more favorable motivation patterns in language arts and reading. The gender gap in motivation related to mathematics and science tends to narrow with age, whereas differences in motivation related to language arts remains prominent throughout the school years. For these reasons, future research should pursue domain- or task-specific studies that try to understand children's motivation beliefs and behaviors at several different time intervals during their lives.

This review also emphasized the important role that the home and school environment play in shaping gendered patterns of motivation. Because children enter school with sex-typed views of their interests and abilities, the home environment clearly plays a critical role in this developmental process. Schools also impact children's gender role conceptions, beliefs, and academic values as children observe and imitate traditional gender roles and encounter racial or ethnic stereotypes in their classrooms. However, as discussed, much of the research presented in this chapter focused on the underachievement of girls. Much less is known about the ways schools shape boys' motivation and underachievement in the reading and language arts. Although a growing field of study, this review also documented the lack of research examining gender differences in motivation within ethnic and socioeconomic groups.

Methodological Issues for Future Research

There are a number of issues left unanswered in research on gender and motivation. First, as suggested throughout this chapter, gender differences in motivation depend on the academic domain assessed, specificity of the measures, ethnic and racial group, and age of assessments. In general, gender differences are larger when general measures of motivation are used (e.g., how well the student is expected to do in school, college, etc.). Also, gender differences are more consistently found when students are expected to give general assessments of their abilities within a specific domain such as mathematics, science, language arts, sports, and so on. Gender differences tend to be smaller in magnitude, or non-significant, when students are asked to provide task-specific ratings of their abilities, interests, and goals (e.g., a unit on writing narratives, proportional reasoning, or ecosystems). When questions are worded according to a general area of study (math, science, reading, etc.), gender and cultural stereotypes may be shaping students' assessments and interests. While not necessarily applying to research on gender and motivation alone, most studies rely on self-report measures of motivation. Perhaps due to the expense of such research, few studies have examined gender differences in behavioral measures of motivation, such as task persistence and choice. The exception are studies focusing on gender differences in learned helplessness (e.g., Dweck, Davidson, Nelson, & Enna, 1978; Eccles-Parsons, Adler, & Meece, 1984) and course enrollment patterns (e.g., Eccles, Vida, & Barber, 2004). Additionally, few studies use parallel assessments of student motivation from parents, teachers, and peers. Thus, most studies of gender differences in motivation rely on student assessments alone.

Other methodological issues concern data collection procedures and research designs. With rare exception, studies of gender differences are cross sectional, based on one time assessments during the school year. Research indicates that motivation changes during the school year (Meece & Miller, 2001; Eccles, Wigfield, Flanagan, Miller, Rueman, & Yee, 1989), and gender differences appear to be shaped by not only the subject matter domain (e.g., math, language arts) but also by aspects of the classroom context. For example, as described earlier, gender differences in math-related achievement expectancies seem to be more pronounced in mathematics classrooms that emphasize whole group instruction and normative assessments (Parsons et al., 1982). Multilevel analytic procedures are now available to examine the influence of classroom and school-level characteristics on gender differences in student achievement beliefs, motivation, and achievement (Lee, 2000; Raudenbush & Bryk, 2002).

Current research suggests that students' achievement-related beliefs may be shaped by gender and racial identities. As described earlier, Pajares and Valiente (2001) found that gender differences in self-efficacy beliefs for writing were moderated by middle school students' self-ratings of femininity-expressivity. Other research suggests that both boys and girls who view themselves as possessing masculine traits report greater efficacy or competency for learning mathematics (Eccles et al., 1983; Hackett, 1985). Similarly, research indicates that one's ethnic identity is associated with achievement related beliefs. In this case, minority students are more likely to report more positive motivation beliefs when they (a) perceive academic success as a valued trait of their ethnic group, and (b) perceive racial identity as central to their self-concept (Oysterman, Harrison, & Bybee, 2001; Chavous et al., 2003; Spencer & Markstrom-Adam, 1990). The role of social identities in the formation of achievement-related beliefs is a promising new area of motivation research. Evidence emerging from this research suggests that identity development processes, as well as perceptions of gender and racial traits are important for measuring and interpreting between- and within-group differences in achievement motivation.

Implications for School Professionals

The research discussed in this review has important implications for school professionals. First, it is important to recognize that gender differences in some subject areas (e.g., mathematics) have been inflated by popular media (Hyde, 2005). By reinforcing gender stereotypes and neglecting male areas of underachievement, the focus on gender inequities in mathematics has resulted in negative consequences for both boys and girls. However, gender differences in students' conceptions of their reading and athletic abilities emerge early and persist over the school years. School instructional and extracurricular activities may play an important role in reinforcing these patterns. Also, there is still much that can be done to change the feminine image of reading and writing and the masculine image of science and school athletics. Researchers have emphasized the important role that context plays in reinforcing, strengthening, or diminishing gender differences. Girls tend to respond more negatively than boys to competitive learning conditions (Eccles, 1994). In contrast, girls have more positive perceptions of their abilities and expectations for success in mathematics classrooms where individualized or cooperative learning is the primary mode of instruction (Parsons-Eccles et al., 1982).

In all schooling contexts, both boys and girls thrive when certain conditions are in place. Young people need school environments that (a) depict males and females from various cultures in a variety of roles, (b) provide opportunities of leadership for all students, (c) set high expectations for all students, (d) encourage awareness of cultural and gender issues, (e) provide meaningful learning opportunities, and (f) connect learning to their future and lives outside of school. Schools need counseling programs that encourage boys and girls to explore topics free of cultural norms and biases, and mentoring programs to help minority youth to cope with racism and discrimination. Schools need to collect and track academic achievement and course enrollment by gender, ethnicity, and socioeconomic status to identify gaps between and within gender groups. Moreover, it is critically important to examine the schooling processes that lead a high proportion of non-White ethnic minority students of both genders to lose confidence in their academic abilities and to devalue the importance of education for their futures. The especially low high school completion rates for poor and non-White ethnic minority students needs to be targeted and reduced. There is a growing body of research to guide school reform in this area (Hammond, Linton, Smink, & Drew, 2007; U.S. Department of Education, 2007).

Acknowledgments

The writing of this chapter was supported by a grant from the Spencer Foundation (200600132). The authors wish to thank Samantha Burg and Meredith Craver Walton for their research assistance.

References

Alexander, K. L., & Entwisle, D. R. (1988). Achievement in the first two years of school: Patterns and processes. *Monographs of the Society for Research in Child Development, 53*(2, Serial No. 218).

Alexander, K. L., Entwisle, D., & Kabbani, N. (2001). The dropout process in life course perspective. Early risk factors at home and school. *Teachers College Record, 103*, 760–822.

Altermatt, E. R., Jovanovic, J., & Perry, M. (1998). Bias or responsivity? Sex and achievement-level effects on teachers' classroom questioning practices. *Journal of Educational Psychology, 90*(3), 516–527.

American Association of University Women Educational Foundation (1998). *Gender gaps: Where schools still fail our children.* Washington, DC: Author.

Ames, C. (1992). Classrooms: Goals, structures, and student motivation. *Journal of Educational Psychology, 84*, 261–271.

Anderman, E. M., & Midgley, C. (1997). Changes in achievement goal orientations, perceived academic competence, and grades across the transition to middle-level schools. *Contemporary Educational Psychology, 22*(3), 269–298.

Anderman, E. M., & Wolters, C. (2006). Goals, values, and affect. In P. Alexander & P. Winne (Eds.), *Handbook of educational psychology* (2nd ed., pp. 369–390). Mahwah, NJ: Erlbaum.

Anderman, E. M., & Young, A. J. (1994). Motivation and strategy use in science: Individual differences and classroom effects. *Journal of Research in Science Teaching, 31*(8), 811–831.

Atkinson, J. W. (1964). *An introduction to motivation.* Oxford, England: Van Nostrand.

Atkinson, J. W. (1957). Motivational determinants of risk-taking behavior. *Psychological Review, 64*, 359–372.

Bandura, A. (1977). Self-efficacy: Toward a unifying theory of behavioral change. *Psychological Review, 84*, 191–215.

Bandura, A. (1986). *Social foundations of thought and action: A social cognitive theory.* Upper Saddle River, NJ: Prentice-Hall.

Bandura, A., Barbaranelli, C., Caprara, G. V., & Pastorelli, C. (2001). Self-efficacy beliefs as shapers of children's aspirations and career trajectories. *Child Development, 72*(1), 187–206.

Bar Tal, D. (1978). Attributional analysis of achievement-related behavior. *Review of Educational Research, 48*(2), 259–271.

Bleeker, M. M., & Jacobs, J. E. (2004). Achievement in math and science: Do mothers' beliefs matter 12 years later? *Journal of Educational Psychology, 96*(1), 97–109.

Bong, M., & Skaalvik, E. M. (2003). Academic self-concept and self-efficacy: How different are they really? *Educational Psychology Review, 15*, 1–40.

Brophy, J. E., & Good, T. L. (1974). *Teacher-student relationships: Causes and consequences.* Oxford, England: Holt, Rinehart and Winston.

Brozo, W. G. (2002). *To be a boy, to be a reader: Engaging teen and preteen boys in active literacy.* Newark, DE: International Reading Association.

Catsambis, S. (1994). The path to math: Gender and racial-ethnic differences in mathematics participation from middle school to high school. *Sociology of Education, 67*(3), 199–215.

Chavous, T. M., Bernat, D. H., Schmeelk-Cone, K., Caldwell, C. H., Kohn-Wood, L., & Zimmerman, M. A. (2003). Racial identity and academic attainment among African American adolescents. *Child Development, 74,* 1076–1090.

Coley, R. J. (2001). *Differences in the gender gap: Comparisons across racial/ethnic groups in education and work policy information report.* Princeton, NJ: Educational Testing Service.

Collins, P. H. (1998). *Fighting words: Black women and the search for justice.* Minneapolis: The University of Minnesota Press.

Connell, R. W. (1996). Teaching the boys: New research on masculinity, and gender strategies for schools. *Teachers College Record, 98*(2), 206–235.

Corbett, C., Hill, C., & Rose, A. (2008). *Where the girls are: The facts about gender equity in education.* Washington, DC: American Association of University Women.

Crandall, V. C., Katkovsky, W., & Crandall, V. J. (1965). Children's belief in their own control of reinforcement in intellectual-academic achievement situations. *Child Development, 36,* 91–109.

Crandall, V. C. (1969). Sex differences in expectancy of intellectual and academic reinforcement. In C. P. Smith (Ed.), *Achievement-related motives in children* (pp. 11–44). New York: Russell Sage Foundation.

Davis, J. E. (2003). Early schooling and academic achievement of African American males. *Urban Education, 38*(5), 515–537.

Davis, J. E., & Jordon, W. J. (1994). The effects of school context, structure, and experiences on African American males in middle and high school. *Journal of Negro Education, 63,* 570–587.

Diener, C. I., & Dweck, C. S. (1978). An analysis of learned helplessness: Continuous changes in performance, strategy, and achievement cognitions following failure. *Journal of Personality and Social Psychology, 36*(5), 451–462.

Downey, D., & Yuan, A. (2005). Sex differences in school performance during high school: Puzzling patterns and possible explanations. *Sociological Quarterly, 46,* 299–321.

Dusek, J. B., & Joseph, G. (1983). The bases of teacher expectancies: A meta-analysis. *Journal of Educational Psychology, 75*(3), 327–346.

Dweck, C. S. (1986). Motivational processes affecting learning. *American Psychologist, 41*(10), 1040–1048.

Dweck, C. S., & Bush, E. S. (1976) Sex differences in learned helplessness: (I) Differential debilitation with peer and adult evaluators. *Developmental Psychology, 12,* 147–156.

Dweck, C. S., & Elliot, E. S. (1983). Achievement motivation. In E. M. Hetherington (Ed.), *Handbook of child psychology. Vol. 4. Socialization, personality, and social development* (4th ed., pp. 643–691). New York: Wiley.

Dweck, C. S., Davidson, W., Nelson, S., & Enna, B. (1978). Sex differences in learned helplessness: II. The contingencies of evaluative feedback in the classroom. III. An experimental analysis. *Developmental Psychology, 14,* 268–276.

Dweck, C. S., & Reppucci, N. D. (1973). Learned helplessness and reinforcement responsibility in children. *Journal of Personality and Social Psychology, 25*(1), 109–116.

Eccles, J. S. (1994). Understanding women's educational and occupational choices: Applying the Eccles et al. model of achievement-related choices. *Psychology of Women Quarterly, 18,* 585–609.

Eccles, J. S., Adler, T. F., Futterman, R., Goff, S. B., Kaczala, C. M., & Meece, J. L. (1983). Expectancies, values and academic behaviors. In J. T. Spence (Ed.), *Achievement and achievement motives* (pp. 75–146). San Francisco: Freeman.

Eccles, J. S., & Blumenfeld, P. (1985). Classroom experiences and student gender: Are there differences and do they matter? In L. C. Wilkinson & C. B. Marrett (Eds.), *Gender influences in classroom interaction* (pp. 79–114). Orlando, FL: Academic Press.

Eccles, J. S., & Harold, R. D. (1991). Gender differences in sport involvement: Applying the Eccles' expectancy-value model. *Journal of Applied Sport Psychology, 3,* 7–35.

Eccles, J. S., & Midgley, C. M. (1989). Stage-environment fit: Developmentally appropriate classrooms for young adolescents. In C. Ames & R. Ames (Eds.), *Research on motivation in education* (Vol. 3, pp. 139–186) San Diego: Academic Press.

Eccles, J. S., & Wigfield, A. (2002). Motivational beliefs, values, and goals. *Annual Review of Psychology, 53*(1), 109.

Eccles, J. S., Wigfield, A., Flanagan, C., Miller, C., Rueman, D., & Yee, D. (1989). Self-concepts, domain values, and self-esteem: Relations and changes in early adolescence. *Journal of Personality and Social Psychology, 70,* 461–475.

Eccles, J. S., Wigfield, A., Harold, R. D., & Blumenfeld, P. (1993). Age and gender differences in children's self- and task perceptions during elementary school. *Child Development, 64,* 830–847.

Eccles, J. S., Wigfield, A., & Schiefele, U. (1998). Motivation to succeed. In W. Damon (Series Ed.) & N. Eisenberg (Vol. Ed.), *Handbook of child psychology: Vol. 3. Social, emotional, and personality development* (5th ed., pp. 1017–1095). New York: Wiley.

Eccles, J. S., Wong, C. A., & Peck, S. C. (2006). Ethnicity as a social context for the development of African-American adolescents. *Journal of School Psychology, 44*(5), 407–426.

Eccles, J.S., Vida, M. N., & Barber, B. L. (2004). The relation of early adolescents' college plans, and both academic and task value beliefs to subsequent college enrollment. *Journal of Early Adolescence, 24,* 215–225.

Eccles-Parsons, J., Adler, T. F., & Meece, J. L. (1984). Sex differences in achievement: A test of alternative theories. *Journal of Personality and Social Psychology, 46,* 26–43.

428 • Judith L. Meece, Beverly Bower Glienke, and Karyl Askew

Elliot, A. J., & Church, M. A. (1997). A hierarchical model of approach and avoidance achievement motivation. *Journal of Personality & Social Psychology, 72*(1), 218–232.

Elliot, A. J., & Harackiewicz, J. M. (1996). Approach and avoidance achievement goals and intrinsic motivation: A mediational analysis. *Journal of Personality & Social Psychology, 70*(3), 461–475.

Ensminger M., & Slusarcick, A. (1992). Paths to high school graduation or dropout: A longitudinal study of first-grade cohorts. *Sociology of Education, 65,* 95–113.

Erikson, E. H. (1963). *Childhood and society.* New York: Norton.

Farmer, H. S., & Vispoel, W. P. (1990). Attributions of female and male adolescents for real-life failure experiences. *Journal of Experimental Education, 58*(2), 127–140.

Feather, N. T. (1966). Effects of prior success and failure on expectations of success and subsequent performance. *Journal of Personality and Social Psychology, 3*(3), 287–298.

Fleming, P. (2000). Three decades of educational progress (and continuing barriers) for women and girls. *Equuity and Excellence in Education, 33,* 74–70.

Fordham, S., & Ogbu, J. U. (1986). Black students' school success: Coping with the "burden of acting white." *Urban Review, 18*(3), 176–206.

Fredricks, J. A., & Eccles, J. S. (2002). Children's competence and value beliefs from childhood through adolescence: Growth trajectories in two male-sex-typed domains. *Developmental Psychology, 38*(4), 519–533.

Frieze, I. H. (1975). Women's expectations for and causal attributions of success and failure. In T. Mednick, S. Tangi, & L. W. Hoffman (Eds.), *Women and achievement. Social and motivational analysis* (pp. 158–171). New York: Wiley.

Frieze, I. H., Parsons, J. E., Johnson, D., Ruble, D., & Zellman, P (1978). *Women and sex roles: A social psychological perspective.* New York: Norton.

Frieze, I. H., Whitley, B. E., Hanusa, B. H., & McHugh, M. C. (1982). Assessing the theoretical models for sex differences in causal attributions for success and failure. *Sex Roles, 8,* 333–343.

Graham, S. (1990). Communicating low ability in the classroom. Bad things good teachers sometimes do. In S. Graham & V. Folkes (Eds.), *Attribution theory: Applications to achievement, mental health, and interpersonal conflict* (pp. 17–36). Mahwah, NJ: Erlbaum.

Graham, S., & Taylor, A. Z. (2002). Ethnicity, gender, and the development of achievement values. In J. S. Eccles, & A. Wigfield (Eds.), *A volume in the educational psychology series* (pp. 121–146). San Diego, CA: Academic Press.

Graham, S., Taylor, A. Z., & Hudley, C. (1998). Exploring achievement values among ethnic minority early adolescents. *Journal of Educational Psychology, 90,* 606–620.

Grant, L. (1984). Black females "place" in desegregated classrooms. *Sociology of Education, 57,* 98–111.

Greene, B. A., DeBacker, T. K., Ravindran, B., & Krows, A. J. (1999). Goals, values, and beliefs as predictors of achievement and effort in high school mathematics classes. *Sex roles: A Journal of Research, 40,* 421–458.

Hackett, G. (1985). Role of mathematics self-efficacy in the choice of math-related majors of women and men: A path analysis. *Journal of Counseling Psychology, 32,* 47–56.

Halpern, D. (2006). Girls, boys, and academic success: Changing patterns of academic achievement. In J. Worrell & C. Goodheart (Eds.), *Handbook of girls' and women's psychological health* (pp. 272–282). New York: Oxford University Press.

Hammond, C., Linton, D., Smink, J., & Drew, S. (2007, May). Dropout risk factors and exemplary programs. A technical report. University of South Carolina, Clemson, SC: National Dropout Prevention Center/Network. Retrieved June 13, 2008, from http://www.dropoutprevention.org

Hill, K. T., & Sarason, S. B. (1966). The relation of test anxiety and defensiveness to test and school performance over the elementary-school years. *Monographs of the Society for Research in Child Development, 31*(2), 1–76.

Horner, M. S. (1975). Toward an understanding of achievement-related conflicts in women. In M. Ednick, S. Tangi & L. W. Hoffman (Eds.), *Women and achievement. social and motivational analyses* (pp. 206–220). New York: Wiley.

Hyde, J. S. (2005). The gender similarities hypothesis. *American Psychologist, 60,* 581–592.

Irvine, J. (1986). Teacher-student interactions: Effects of student race, sex, and grade level. *Journal of Educational Psychology, 78,* 14–21.

Jacobs, J. E. (1991). Influence of gender stereotypes on parent and child mathematics attitudes. *Journal of Educational Psychology, 83*(4), 518–527.

Jacobs, J. E., & Bleeker, M. M. (2004). Girls' and boys' developing interests in math and science: Do parents matter? *New Directions for Child and Adolescent Development, 106,* 5–21.

Jacobs, J. E., Chhin, C. S., & Bleeker, M. M. (2006). Enduring links: Parents' expectations and their young adult children's gender-typed occupational choices. *Educational Research and Evaluation, 12*(4), 395–407.

Jacobs, J. E., Davis-Kean, P., Bleeker, M., Eccles, J. E., Malanchuk, O. (2005). "I can but I don't want to": The impact of parents, interests, and activities on gender differences in math. In A. Gallagher & J. Kaufman (Eds.), *Gender differences in mathematics. An integrative psychological approach.* New York: Cambridge University Press.

Jacobs, J. E., & Eccles, J. S. (1992). The impact of mothers' gender-role stereotypic beliefs on mothers' and children's ability perceptions. *Journal of Personality and Social Psychology, 63*(6), 932–944.

Jacobs, J. E., Lanza, S., Osgood, D. W., Eccles, J. S., & Wigfield, A. (2002). Changes in children's self-competence and values: Gender and domain differences across grades one though twelve. *Child Development, 73*(2), 509–527.

Jones, S. M., & Dindia, K. (2004). A meta-analytic perspective on sex equity in the classroom. *Review of Educational Research, 74*(4), 443–471.

Jussim, L., & Harber, K. D. (2005). Teacher expectations and self-fulfilling prophecies: Knowns and unknowns, resolved and unresolved controversies. *Personality and Social Psychology Review, 9*(2), 131–155.

Kahle, J. B. (1990) Real students take chemistry and physics: Gender issues. In K. Tobin, J. B. Kahle, & B. J. Fraser (Eds.), *Windows into science classrooms: Problems associated with higher-cognitive learning* (pp. 92–134). New York: Falmer.

Kahle, J., & Meece, J. L. (1994). Research on gender issues in the classroom. In D. Gabel (Ed.), *Handbook of research in science teaching* (pp. 415–437). New York: MacMillian.

Kedar-Voivodas, G. (1983). The impact of elementary children's school roles and sex roles on teacher attitudes: An interactional analysis. *Review of Educational Research, 53*(3), 415–437.

Kirst, P. (1993). *Educational and career choices in math and science for high ability African American women.* Unpublished doctoral dissertation, University of North Carolina-Chapel Hill.

Kloosterman, P. (1990). Attributions, performance following failure, and motivation in mathematics. In E. Fennema, & G. C. Leder (Eds.), *Mathematics and gender* (pp. 96–127). New York: Teachers College Press.

Klopfenstein, K. (2005). Beyond test scores: The impact of black teacher role models on rigorous math taking. *Contemporary Economic Policy, 23*(3), 416–428.

Larson, R., Dworkin, J., & Gillman, S. (2001). Facilitating adolescents' constructive use of time in one-parent families. *Applied Developmental Science, 5*(3), 143–157.

Lee, V. (2000). Using hierarchical linear modeling to study social contexts: The case of school effects. *Educational Psychologist, 35,* 125–141.

Li, A. K. F., & Adamson, G. (1995). Motivational patterns related to gifted students' learning of mathematics, science and English: An examination of gender differences. *Journal for the Education of the Gifted, 18*(3), 284–297.

Maccoby, E. E., & Jacklin, C. N. (1974). *The psychology of sex differences.* Chicago: Stanford University Press.

Madon, S., Jussim, L., Keiper, S., Eccles, J., Smith, A., & Palumbo, P. (1998). The accuracy and power of sex, social class, and ethnic stereotypes: A naturalistic study in person perception. *Personality and Social Psychology Bulletin, 24*(12), 1304–1318.

Mandler, G., & Sarason, S. B. (1952). A study of anxiety and learning. *Journal of Abnormal and Social Psychology, 47,* 166–173.

McClelland, D., Atkinson, J. W., Clark, R. A., & Lowell, E. L. (1953). *The achievement motive.* New York: Appleton-Century-Crofts.

McHale, S. M., Shanahan, L., Updegraff, K. A., Crouter, A. C., & Booth, A. (2004). Developmental and individual differences in girls' sex-typed activities in middle childhood and adolescence. *Child Development, 75,* 1575–1593.

McHugh, M. C., Frieze, I. H., & Hanusa, B. H. (1982). Attributions and sex differences in achievement: Problems and new perspectives. *Sex Roles, 8*(4), 467–479.

McMahan, I. D. (1973). Relationships between causal attributions and expectancy of success. *Journal of Personality and Social Psychology, 28*(1), 108–114.

Meece, J. L. (1987). The influence of school experiences on the development of gender schemata. In L. S. Liben, & M. L. Signorella (Eds.), *Children's gender schemata. New directions for child development* (38th ed.). San Francisco: Jossey-Bass.

Meece, J. L., Anderman, E. M., & Anderman, L. H. (2006). Classroom goal structure, student motivation, and academic achievement. *Annual Review of Psychology, 57,* 487–503.

Meece, J. L., & Eccles (Parsons), J. S., Kaczala, C., Goff, S. B., & Futterman, R. (1982). Sex differences in math achievement: Toward a model of academic choice. *Psychology Bulletin, 91*(2), 324–348.

Meece, J. L., & Jones, M. G. (1996). Gender differences in motivation and strategy use in science: Are girls rote learners? *Journal of Research in Science Teaching, 33,* 393–404.

Meece, J. L., & Kurtz-Costes, B. (2001). Introduction: The schooling of ethnic minority children and youth. *Educational Psychologist, 36,* 1–7.

Meece, J. L. & Miller, S. D. (2001). A longitudinal analysis of elementary school students' achievement goals in literacy activities. *Contemporary Educational Psychology, 26,* 454–480.

Meece, J. L., Wigfield, A., & Eccles, J. S. (1990). Predictors of math anxiety and its influence on young adolescents' course enrollment intentions and performance in mathematics. *Journal of Educational Psychology, 82*(1), 60–70.

Middleton, M. J., & Midgley, C. (1997). Avoiding the demonstration of lack of ability: An underexplored aspect of goal theory. *Journal of Educational Psychology, 89,* 710–718.

National Center for Education Statistics (2004). *Trends in educational equity of girls and women.* Washington, DC: U.S. Department of Education.

National Center of Educational Statistics. (2005). *The condition of education 2004* (NCES 2004-077). Washington, DC: U.S. Government Printing Office.

National Women's Law Center (2007). When girls don't graduate, we all fail. Washington, DC: Author. Retrieved December 10, 2008, from http://www.nwlc.org

Nicholls, J. G. (1984). Achievement motivation: Conception of ability, subjective experience, task choice, and performance. *Psychological Review, 91,* 328–346.

Ogbu, J. (1992). Understanding cultural diversity and learning. *Educational Researcher, 21,* 5–14.

Osborne, J. W. (1995). Academics, self-esteem, and race – A look at the underlying assumptions of the disidentification hypothesis. *Personality and Social Psychology Bulletin, 21*(5), 449–455.

Osborne, J. W. (1997). Race and academic disidentification. *Journal of Educational Psychology, 89*(4), 728–735.

Osyerman, D., Harrison, K., & Bybee, D. (2001). Can racial identity be promotive of academic efficacy? *International Journal of Behavioral Development, 25,* 379–385.

Pajares, F. (1996). Self-efficacy beliefs in academic settings. *Review of Educational Research, 66*(4), 543–578.

Pajares, F. (2002). Gender and perceived self-efficacy in self-regulated learning. *Theory into Practice, 41*(2), 116–125.

Pajares, F., & Graham, L. (1999). Self-efficacy, motivation constructs, and mathematics performance of entering middle school students. *Contemporary Educational Psychology, 24*(2), 124–139.

Pajares, F., & Valiante, G. (1997). Influence of self-efficacy on elementary students' writing. *Journal of Educational Research, 90*(6), 353–360.

Pajares, F., & Valiante, G. (2001). Gender differences in writing motivation and achievement of middle school students: A function of gender orientation? *Contemporary Educational Psychology, 26*(3), 366–381.

Parsons, J. E., Adler, T., & Meece, J. L. (1984). Sex differences in achievement: A test of alternate theories. *Journal of Personality and Social Psychology, 46*(1), 26–43.

Parsons, J., Adler, T. F., & Kaczala, C. M. (1982). Socialization of achievement attitudes and beliefs: Parental influences. *Child Development, 53,* 310–321.

Parsons, J. E., Kaczala, C. M., & Meece, J. L. (1982). Socialization of achievement attitudes and beliefs: Classroom influences. Child Development, *53,* 322–339.

Parsons, J. E., Meece, J. L., Adler, T. F., & Kaczala, C. M. (1982). Sex differences in attributions and learned helplessness. *Sex Roles, 8*(4), 421–432.

Phelan, P., Yu, H. C., & Davidson, A. L. (1994). Navigating the psychosocial pressures of adolescence – The voices and experiences of high-school youth. *American Educational Research Journal, 31*(2), 415–447.

Phillips, L. (1998). *The girls report: What we know and need to know about growing up female.* New York: National Council for Research on Women.

Pintrich, P. R., & DeGroot, E. V. (1990). Motivational and self-regulated learning components of classroom academic performance. *Journal of Educational Psychology, 82,* 33–40.

Pintrich, P. R., & Schunk, D. H. (2002). *Motivation in education. Theory, research, and applications* (2nd ed.). Columbus, Ohio: Merrill Prentice Hall.

Pollard, D (1993). Gender, achievement, and African American students' perceptions of their school experience. *Educational Psychologist, 28,* 341–356.

Raudenbush, S. W., & Bryk, A. S. (2002). *Hierarchical linear models* (2nd ed.).Thousand Oaks, CA: Sage.

Ready, D. D., LoGerfo, L. F., Burkam, D. T., & Lee, V. E. (2005). Explaining girls' advantages in kindergarten literacy learning: Do Classroom behaviors make a difference? *The Elementary School Journal, 106,* 21–38.

Roderick., M. (2003). What's happening to the boys? Early high school experiences and school outcomes among African American male adolescents in Chicago. *Urban Education, 38,* 538–607.

Roeser, R. W., Midgley, C., & Urdan, T. C. (1996). Perceptions of the school psychological environment and early adolescents' psychological and behavioral functioning in school: The mediating role of goals and belonging. *Journal of Educational Psychology, 88*(3), 408–422.

Rowley, S. J., Krutz-Costes, B., & Cooper, S. M. (in press). The schooling of African American children. In J. Meece & J. Eccles (Eds.), *Handbook of research on schools, schooling, and human development.* New York: Erlbaum/Taylor & Francis Group.

Ruble, D. N., & Martin, C. L. (1998). Gender development. In N. Eisenberg (Ed.), *Handbook of child psychology: Vol 3. Social, emotional, and personality development* (5th ed., pp. 933–1016). New York: Wiley.

Schunk, D. H. (1989). Self-efficacy and achievement behaviors. *Educational Psychology Review, 57,* 149–174.

Schunk, D. H., & Meece, J. L. (2006). Self-efficacy development in adolescents. In F. Pajares, & T. Urdan (Eds.), Self-efficacy beliefs in adolescents (pp. 71–96). New York: Information Age.

Schunk, D. H., & Pajares, F. (2002). The development of academic self-efficacy. In A. Wigfield & J. S. Eccles (Eds.), Development of achievement motivation (pp. 16–31). New York: Academic Press.

Sommers, C. H. (2000). *The war against boys. How misguided feminism is harming our young men.* New York: Simon & Schuster.

Spencer, M. B., & Markstrom-Adams, C., (1990). Identity processes among racial and ethnic minority children in America. *Child Development, 61,* 290–310.

Spencer, M. B., Swanson, D. P., & Cunningham, M. (1991). Ethnicity, ethnic identity, and competence formation: Adolescent transition and cultural transformation. *The Journal of Negro Education, 60,* 366–387.

Steele, C. (1992, April). Race and the schooling of Black America. *Atlantic Monthly, 269*(4), 68–78.

Stetsenko, A., Little, T. D., Gordeeva, T., Grasshof, M., & Oettingen, G. (2000). Gender effects in children's beliefs about school performance: A cross-cultural study. *Child Development, 71,* 517–527.

Swanson, C. (2002). *Who graduates? Who doesn't? A statistical portrait of public high school graduation: Class of 2001.* Washington DC: The Urban Institute.

Tobin, K., & Garnett, P. (1987). Gender related differences in science activities. *Science Education, 71,* 91–103.

Urdan, T., & Midgley, C. (2003). Changes in the perceived classroom goal structure and pattern of adaptive learning during early adolescence. *Contemporary Educational Psychology, 28*(4), 524–551.

U.S. Department of Education, Institute of Education Sciences (2007, July). What Works Clearinghouse Topic Report. Dropout Prevention. Washington, DC: Author. Available at http://us.ed.gov/nces.wwc

U.S. Census Bureau (2003). *Facts on women workers.* Washington, DC: Author.

Veroff, J. (1969). Social comparison and the development of achievement motivation. In C. P. Smith (Ed.), *Achievement-related motives in children* (pp. 46–101). New York: Russell Sage Foundation.

Watt, F. M. (2006). Women in cell biology: Getting to the top. *Nature Reviews Molecular Cell Biology, 7*(4), 287–290.

Weaver-Hightower, M. (2003). The "boy turn" in research on gender and education. *Review of Educational Research, 73*(4), 471–498.

Weiler, J. (2000). Codes and contradictions: Race, gender, identity, and schooling. Albany: SUNY Press.

Weiner, B. (1985). An attributional theory of achievement motivation and emotion. *Psychological Review, 92*(4), 548–573.

Weiner, B. (1986). *An attributional theory of motivation and emotion.* New York: Springer-Verlag.

Weiss, I., Banilower, E., McMahon, K., & Smith, P. (2001). *Report of the 2000 national survey of science and mathematics education.* Chapel Hill, NC: Horizon Research, Inc.

Whitley, B. E. J. (1997). Gender differences in computer-related attitudes and behavior: A meta-analysis. *Computers in Human Behavior, 13*(1), 1–22.

Wigfield, A., & Eccles, J. S. (1992). The development of achievement values: A theoretical analysis. *Developmental Review, 12*, 265–310.

Wigfield, A., & Eccles, J. S. (1995). Middle grades schooling and early adolescent development, Part II: Interventions, practices, beliefs, and contexts. *Journal of Early Adolescence, 15*(1), 5–8.

Wigfield, A., & Eccles, J. S. (2000). Expectancy-value theory of achievement motivation. *Contemporary Educational Psychology, 25*(1), 68–81.

Wigfield, A., Eccles, J. S., MacIver, D., & Reuman, D. A. (1991). Transitions during early adolescence: Changes in children's domain-specific self-perceptions and general self-esteem across the transition to junior high school. *Developmental Psychology, 27*(4), 552–565.

Wigfield, A., Eccles, J. S., & Pintrich, P. R. (1996). Development between the ages of 11 and 25. In R. C. Calfee, & D. C. Berliner (Eds.), *Handbook of educational psychology* (pp. 148–185). New York: Prentice Hall.

Wigfield, A., Eccles, J. S., Yoon, K. S., & Harold, R. D. (1997). Change in children's competence beliefs and subjective task values across the elementary school years: A 3-year study. *Journal of Educational Psychology, 89*(3), 451–469.

Wolleat, P. L., Pedro, J. D., Becker, A. D., & Fennema, E. (1980). *Sex differences in cognitive functioning: Developmental issue.* New York: Academic Press.

Wong, C. A., Eccles, J. S., & Sameroff, A. (2003). The influence of ethnic discrimination and ethnic identification on African American adolescents' school and socioemotional adjustment. *Journal of Personality, 71*(6), 1197–1232.

Wood, D., Kaplan, R., & McLloyd V. C. (2007). Gender differences in the educational expectations of urban, low-income African American youth: The role of parents and the school. *Journal of Youth Adolescence, 36*, 417–427.

Zimmerman, B. J., & Martinez-Pons, M. (1990). Student differences in self-regulated learning: Relating grade, sex, and giftedness to self-efficacy and strategy use. *Journal of Educational Psychology, 82*(1), 51–59.

20
Achievement Motivation in Racial and Ethnic Context

Tamera B. Murdock

The underachievement of African American and Hispanic students relative to their Caucasian peers continues to be one of the most highlighted issues in any discussion of public education in the United States. In 2004–2005, the high school dropout rates for youth ages 16 to 24 were approximately 12% among African Americans and 24% for Hispanics compared with 7% for Caucasians (NCES, n.d.). These disparate patterns of school achievement begin as early as the fourth grade administration of the National Assessment of Educational Progress (NAEP) examinations, where African American and Hispanic students lag at least one standard deviation behind their Caucasian peers in math and reading (NCES, n.d.). At the same time, Asian Americans, academically outperform most other students. Fourth grade reading scores for this population on the NAEP equal those of Caucasians, their scores in mathematics are significantly better than all other groups and their rates of high school graduation are the highest in the nation at over 96%. Although variations in socioeconomic status (SES) account for some of these differences, they have not proven to be the entire story. Moreover, the repeated emphasis on between group differences also masks the large heterogeneity within racial and ethnic categories.

Scholars from educational, developmental, and social psychology have used the lens of achievement motivation theories as one mechanism to explore these unequal achievement outcomes, and more recently, to help better understand the factors influencing school engagement for an increasingly diverse population of children. Achievement motivation researchers study the factors contributing to students' effort, persistence, and task choice (Pintrich & Schunk, 2002). Historically, attempts to understand the school engagement of students from various racial and ethnic groups have applied constructs from the prevailing theories of achievement motivation in one of two ways: to examine racial or ethnic group differences in students' average levels of motivation, or to establish between group differences in the predictive value of the constructs (Graham, 1994; Weiner, 1986).

Until the mid 1960s, most scholarship in achievement motivation conceptualized motivation as an individual difference in personality or drive, most popularized in Atkinson's need for achievement (nAch) paradigm (Weiner, 1990). Accordingly, Graham's (1994) review of the literature on achievement motivation in European American and African American students focused on the prevailing motivational constructs of the time: need for achievement, locus of control, academic self-concept, and attributions. She reported few between-group differences, either in absolute scores on the various motivational constructs or in the relations among them. One reported exception was the relatively weaker association between self-concept variables and achievement among African American versus Caucasian youth. A later meta-analysis of the these same articles reached a generally similar conclusion; yet, the authors reported lower levels of need for achievement among African American than European American youth and these differences were more pronounced with younger children (Cooper & Dorr, 1995).

By the 1980s, research grounded in personality and drive constructs of motivation was largely replaced by social-cognitive approaches such as attribution theory (Weiner, 1986, 2005) expectancy-value theory (Eccles (Parsons) et al., 1983; Eccles, Wigfield, & Schiefele, 1998), self-efficacy theory (Bandura, 1997), and achievement goal theory (Ames & Archer, 1988; Elliot, 2005) that assume less stability in motivation and behavior across settings and emphasize students' beliefs, values, and goals as the main determinants of students' motivation. These perspectives focus on the psychological meaning of a situation as constructed through the eyes of the actor, and view motivated behavior as a reciprocal interaction between the individual and his or her environment. Motivation does not reside within people, but is a product of the person in context. Research on race and motivation was similarly broadened to not only include investigations of group differences in absolute levels of various motivation variables, but to include explorations of race and ethnicity as potential moderators of motivational processes (i.e., does self-efficacy predict behavior equally well across ethnic groups?).

Despite this increased emphasis on person-environment interactions, relatively few studies grounded in prevailing theories of achievement motivation have incorporated race or ethnicity, though theorists from these perspectives have all posited suggestions for this integration (McInerney & Van Etten, 2004). At the same time, there has been significant growth in research using culturally grounded approaches to student engagement and achievement that prioritize the unique social historical context of specific ethnic groups and incorporate constructs arising from these experiences into understandings of motivated behavior (e.g., Graham & Taylor, 2002; McCaslin, 2004, in press; Mickelson, 1990; Murdock, 1999, Steele, 1997). Within these frameworks, the larger societal dimensions of one's racial or ethnic status such as the prevailing cultural stereotypes, culturally specific values, experiences of discrimination, and lack of economic opportunity become key facets for understanding students' levels of engagement in academic tasks. Although some of the salient constructs from this work can be applied across populations, the impetus for their development has been to better represent the motivational context of historically understudied groups.

Constructs that have emerged from culturally grounded theories such as "stereotype threat" and "oppositional identity" have not often been explicitly tied to traditional theories of motivation. Many grow not from psychology per se but from related social science disciplines including anthropology and sociology. However, to a large extent, these perspectives significantly overlap with current motivation theories in as much as they can be seen as informing two central questions of motivation: (a) "Can I do this?" and (b) "Do I want to do this?" (i.e., "Do I value this?") (Wigfield & Eccles, 2002). Accordingly, the first two sections of this chapter summarize research which focuses on some specific experiences of racial and ethnic minority youth that may inform their answers to one of these two questions and hence influence their achievement motivation. Subsequently, in the third section of this chapter, I turn to the emerging scholarship on identity, a perspective which blends elements of both cognitive appraisals and emotional experiences, examining how people's constructed sense of who they are, how they want to be seen, and what they hope to become influences their school engagement. As used here, school engagement refers to arranging one's priorities and committing and managing one's resources to achieve academic outcomes. The chapter concludes with a discussion of the implications of this body of work for schools and classrooms and with suggestions for future scholarship.

Can I Do This?

Students' assessment of their abilities to perform a given task or achieve particular outcomes are seen as a driving force in achievement behavior within many prominent theories of achievement motivation, including expectancy-value theory (Eccles (Parsons) et al., 1983; Eccles et al., 1998) and self-efficacy theory (Bandura, 1997). Although the literature within these traditions recognizes that one's self beliefs develop through reciprocal interactions between the student and his or her environment such as parents, teachers and peers, to a large extent, research that is ancillary to these traditions more often explicitly looks at racially or ethnically specific experiences. Prevailing racial and ethnic intellectual stereotypes are an important aspect of this context and may influence student motivation via two mechanisms: teacher expectations and stereotype threat effects.

Stereotypes of Intellectual Abilities

A substantial body of scholarship suggests that various social groups are typed as being unmotivated, lazy, or low in ability, including African Americans, Hispanic Americans, and the poor (Cozzarelli, Tagler, & Wilkinson, 2002; Devine, 1995; Sorge, Newsom, & Hagerty, 2000) whereas Asian Americans are typecast as high-ability and hard-working individuals, particularly in math and science (Kao, 1995; Lee, 1994).

Children and adolescents of all ethnic groups are familiar with the stereotypes that are used to characterize them (Graham, 1994; Hudley & Graham, 2001; Kao, 1995, 2000; McKown & Weinstein, 2003). For some groups of students, stereotypes of intellectual abilities are so pervasive that they have been internalized, even when they are self-deprecating. In a series of studies by Hudley and Graham (2001), lower income African American seventh and eighth graders read descriptions of hypothetical students portrayed as either high or low achieving. When asked to select who from a group of 12 photos was most likely to match that description, male and female students disproportionately selected ethnic minority males as the low achiever: Latino males were overselected by everyone whereas African American males were overselected by other males. In contrast, stereotypes of high achievers were clearly female, with male respondents over selecting African American females and female respondents over selecting Caucasian females. In a replication study reported in this same manuscript, these results were found to largely generalize across African American, Caucasian, and Hispanic youth. Contrasting these findings, however, are the numerous studies showing that the self-reported academic self-assessments and self-esteem of African American and Hispanic youth are not significantly lower than Caucasians despite lower achievement (Fuligni, Witkow, & Garcia, 2005; Graham, 1994; Murdock, 1999).

As early as elementary school, some Asian American students have implicitly accepted the stereotype of their racial group as having superior capabilities in math: After hearing a story about a high-achieving math student, both males and females overwhelmingly chose a picture of a same-sex Asian versus Caucasian student as fitting that description (Ambady, Shih, Kim,

& Pittinsky, 2001). However, when explicitly asked whether Asians or Caucasians are better in math, most students reported that there are no differences between the two groups. Reports from Asian American adolescents confirm that while some students hold to the belief that their group is academically superior in some regards, that belief system is not universal. Many Asian students, particularly those who are not exceptional academically, find this stereotype to be a burden (Lee, 1994). Still others highlight the ethnic and socioeconomic heterogeneity within the Asian American population and the particular lack of relevance that stereotypes hold for many recent immigrants (Lee, 2006; Ngo, 2006).

Stereotypes and Teacher Behaviors

One motivational concern is that the pervasiveness of stereotypes of intellectual inferiority for African American and Latino youth become the basis for teachers' expectations, creating race-based expectation effects. Expectations are assumed to influence students' performance through both curricular and motivational mechanisms. At a curricular level, lower expectations can mean exposure to less challenging material. Motivationally, expectations are posited as potentially creating self-fulfilling prophecies (i.e., the Pygmalion effect; Rosenthal & Jacobson, 1968) if teachers communicate those expectancies to students though their attitudes and behaviors, and students perceive and respond congruently with those communications (Jussim, this volume).

Efforts to demonstrate the presence and impact of teachers' race-based expectations on student outcomes are quite complex. To begin with, as Ferguson (2003) notes, there is no shared consensus on how bias in expectations is defined. People who measure bias "unconditionally" argue that bias exists if teachers do not hold, on average, equally high expectations of students from all cultural groups, whereas those who propose a "race neutral" view define bias as holding varying expectations for students from different groups with the same level of observable accomplishments, as measured by grades or scores on standardized tests. Still others argue that bias occurs when there are race-based differences in expectations that are incongruent with a student's potential, or ability for future learning.

A recent meta-analysis of literature that used the unconditional, race-neutral approach suggests that there are small to moderate effects of race on teachers' expectations, and that these effects are strongest in more ecologically valid studies such as those that use simulated and actual teaching versus constructed vignettes (Tenenbaum & Ruck, 2007). Academic as well as social expectations were highest for Asian American students, consistent with the "model minority" stereotype and lowest for African American and Latino youth. In this same report, race-based differences were also documented for a variety of actual teacher behaviors (Tenenbaum & Ruck, 2007). African American students were referred more often for behavioral problems and special education placements, less often for gifted placements, and were less frequent recipients of positive or neutral interactions with teachers such as praise, requests for participation, or other types of attentive behaviors. No differences were revealed in the frequency of negative or discouraging interactions, such as yelling, criticizing, or ignoring.

Although these studies suggest that some groups of students may have more negative interactions with teachers than others, few studies have compared teacher expectations and behaviors after "conditioning" for current levels of achievement and even fewer have examined the extent to which teachers' expectations create self-fulfilling prophecies (Ferguson, 2003). For the most part, these studies have found little evidence of race-based expectancy effects. Although teachers in a large scale study of seventh grade math reported different expectations of students' performance, talent, and effort as a function of ethnicity (African American versus Caucasian) and social class, the differences were largely explained by actual disparities in prior behavior and achievement (Madon Jussim, Keiper, Eccles, Smith, & Palumbo, 1998). Similarly, in three studies reviewed by Ferguson (2003), the magnitude of the correlations between teacher ratings of students' academic performance and students' scores on standardized tests were the same across all ethnic groups.

For differential expectations to become self-fulfilling prophecies, they must be transmitted to students who must then adapt their behavior to the teachers' views. Longitudinal data underscore the complexity of teasing out race-based expectancy effects (Madon et al., 1998). In a large-scale sample of sixth-grade students, there were no significant differences in teachers' fall ratings of African American versus Caucasian students on performance, effort, or aptitude once a host of achievement (GPA and test scores) and motivational (self-rated effort and self-concept) variables were controlled for. However, when the same students were followed up at the end of the year, the effects of the teachers' fall expectations on spring achievement were much greater for African American youth, suggesting they were more responsive to teachers' communicated beliefs. Ethnicity also was found to moderate teacher expectancy effects in a study of younger children in grades one, three, and five (McKown & Weinstein, 2002). Specifically, the effects of expectations were largest among the subgroup of African American students in grades three to five whose abilities were most underestimated by their teachers.

Personal Consequences of Stereotypes: Stereotype Threat

Claude Steele (1997) advanced the notion of stereotype threat as a mechanism for explaining certain patterns of racial differences in achievement and achievement motivation, particularly among African Americans. According to the perspective, the achievement of historically discriminated minorities must be understood in the larger societal context where stereotypes of poor intellectual functioning abound and concomitant low expectations enforce those stereotypes (Steele, 1997). He argues that while some students protect themselves from these threats by disengaging their self-worth from their success in academic endeavors (discussed later in the chapter), for those students who are identified with school, the fear of conforming to the stereotypes in performance situations might threaten their egos thereby undermining performance.

Classic studies of stereotype threat conducted with Stanford University students found that stereotype threats are indeed relevant for high achieving (identified) youth, and can be rather easily activated in performance situations (Steele & Aronson, 1995). African American and Caucasian participants completed a test comprised of difficult GRE (Graduate Record Examination) verbal items after having been primed or not primed for intellectual stereotypes. In study one, the priming was achieved based on how the task was described (test of ability versus laboratory problem solving tasks) and in the second, the priming was via a demographic form that half the participants completed prior to the task, assumedly making race salient to the participants. After controlling for entry level verbal ability, African American students performed worse than Caucasian students in both of the stereotype primed conditions, but equally well in the conditions where stereotypes were not assumed to be activated.

Since these initial studies, other research has consistently documented the occurrence of stereotype threat effects for African American college students (Blascovich, Spencer, Quinn, & Steele, 2001; Cadinu, Maass, Frigerio, Impagliazzo, & Latinotti, 2003; McKay, Doverspike, Bowen-Hilton, & Martin, 2002). Moreover, recent work suggests that stereotype threat effects can occur during intellectual tests, even without explicit priming of intellectual stereotypes. For example,

African American students performed as well as Caucasian students on the Raven's Advanced Progressive Matrices when they were told it was a nondiagnostic lab task, but underperformed compared too Caucasian students when they were specifically told it was a test of ability as well as when they were given the standard administration instructions which make no reference to ability (Brown & Day, 2006).

Stereotype threat responses have also been found with other social and cultural groups for whom stereotypes of intellectual functioning exist. Low-socioeconomic students performed worse on a task when they were told it was an ability diagnostic versus not (Croizet & Claire, 1998; Croizet, Desert, Dutrevis, & Leyens, 2001), or were given instructions indicating that the task was one on which low-income youth typically did more poorly than middle and higher income youth (Harrison, Stevens, Monty, & Coakley, 2006). Hispanic students responded to stereotype activation in the same way (Gonzales, Blanton, & Williams, 2002; Schmader & Johns, 2003). Women, typically stereotyped as low performing in math, have also been found to exhibit stereotype threat effects in this domain (Schmader, 2002; Spencer, Steele, & Quinn, 1999) even as early as middle school (Muzzatti & Agnoli, 2007).

Stereotypes of Asian Americans may also implicitly influence performance. High-performing undergraduate Asian female students attending an elite university outperformed a control group on a mathematics task when they were primed to think about their Asian identity; in contrast, those who were primed to think of themselves as females performed more poorly than the control group (Shih, Pittinsky, & Ambady, 1999). More recently, these same effects were demonstrated among Asian American females in early elementary and middle school, with a female prime leading to lower performance and an Asian prime to higher performance (Ambady et al., 2001). For Asian American males in these same age groups, both ethnicity and gender primes were associated with improved performance. Making ethnicity salient is not always beneficial for this "model minority;" however, as Cheryan (2000) found performance declines following priming of ethnicity for Asian American females when the prime stressed the high standards that others expected of them.

Stereotype Threat Mechanisms: How Is Motivation Effected? Educational psychologists hypothesize that stereotype threat might influence achievement through several motivational mechanisms (Ryan & Ryan, 2005; Smith, 2004) which mediate between the experience of threat and achievement outcomes. However, although there are data suggesting that various affective and cognitive variables mediate stereotype threat effects, the evidence is not very robust (Wheeler & Petty, 2001) in terms of magnitude or consistency across studies. Those mediators with the strongest support include anxiety, performance expectations, and cognitive load (Aronson & Steele, 2005). Two of the mediators, anxiety, a key influence on self-efficacy judgments (Bandura, 1986) and performance expectations, are consistent with the idea that stereotype threat may undermine motivation.

Other scholars have argued that stereotype threat influences motivation by affecting the goals student strive for. For example, Ryan and Ryan (2005) proposed that in situations where stereotype threat is activated, students are likely to be less mastery or task focused and more focused on performance or ego goals, particularly on performance avoidance goals, or the desire to protect one's ability. Smith (2004) argued, however, that not all people who are in "threatening" achievement situations adopt performance-avoidance goals. In fact, some students adopt performance approach goals. In a series of recent studies with female college undergraduates, she and her colleagues (Smith, Sansone, & White, 2007) found that among those who were higher in a need to achieve, a stereotype threat manipulation resulted in them rating a computer task as less interesting than without the threat (Study 1) and they were more likely to adopt performance–avoidance goals (Study 2). Among those who were lower in need for achievement, stereotype threat conditions led to higher interest and more performance-approach responses. This work reminds us that students will vary widely in their understanding of what it means to "be successful," not only providing some insight into why the logical mediators of stereotype threat do not always pan out, but underscoring the importance of considering individual differences within groups that we often treat as homogenous. It may also explain why public primes of ethnicity, that focus the participants' attentions on others' positive expectations of Asians (Cheryan, 2000) might undermine rather than improve performance by facilitating the adoption of performance-avoidance goals.

Summary: Can I Do This?

One mechanism that appears to have some influence on the motivation of various ethnic groups are the prevailing intellectual stereotypes that become associated with that group, creating the potential for both differential treatment by others, but also for unconscious integration of those beliefs into one's self-schema of intellectual competence. What is perhaps most thought-provoking about the findings reviewed in this section is the attention they bring to the role of unconscious processes and emotions, supporting current questions by some scholars in the field about the usefulness of theories that are completely grounded in rationale, decision-making models of human behavior (see McCaslin, in press). At the same time, these findings continue to support the importance of attending to phenomenological understandings of people's lived experiences. Although ethnicity is clearly part of the context that delineates one's opportunities and experiences, work such as that by Smith (2004) underscores the range of interpretations and responses among people with apparent shared objective realities.

Do I Want to Do This?

Having the confidence in one's skills to carry out a given task or accomplish a specific goal is only part of the motivational picture. To a large extent, students' decision of what they choose to do versus not do are determined by the extent to which they value either the task itself (interest or intrinsic value) or the outcomes associated with achieving the task (extrinsic or utility value). Both expectancy-value (Eccles (Parsons) et al., 1983) and interest theories (Hidi, 2000; Renninger, 2000) of motivation reflect the importance of this value dimension of engagement. In contrast, goal theorists emphasize the different reasons that people might have for pursuing a given task.

The sections below address several bodies of work that have sought to pinpoint socialization experiences potentially undergirding the development of goals and values for ethnic minority youth. The review begins with a brief examination of cultural differences in students' achievement goals, and then focuses on the development of students' school-related values.

Goals, Goal Theory, and Ethnicity

Goal theorists focus on the meaning that students ascribe to their academic tasks (Ames, 1992; Pintrich, 2000; Pintrich & Schunk, 1996). Pursing learning for its own sake, valuing effort and improvement, and seeking to master a task are described as characteristics of students who have mastery or task orientations, whereas students whose focus is more on demonstrating that one is smart and capable (or not incapable) are said to have performance or ego orientations. Some people further divide these orientations into approach and avoidance components, describing people's tendency to approach success versus avoid failure. Approach motivation is generally considered more adaptive than avoidance motivation, and mastery goals are associated with more persistence and engagement than performance goals (Elliot, 2005).

Several scholars have investigated the moderating influence of ethnicity on students' goal and/ or approach–avoidance orientations and their consequences. Freeman, Gutmann, and Midgley (2002) examined the role of personal, parental, and classroom goal orientations on self-efficacy and achievement in mathematics across the transition from eighth grade to high school among lower to lower-middle African American students attending school in an urban district with a large percentage of African American and low-income students. Consistent with predictions from goal theory research, students with higher mastery goals in Grade 9 also had higher self-efficacy and achievement, after controlling for eighth grade scores on the same measures. With regard to perceived classroom context, higher levels of ninth-grade mastery goal focus and lower levels of performance goal focus predicted increased self-efficacy in Grade 9 after controlling for Grade 8 self-efficacy. However, when eighth-grade goal structures were added to the model, the effects of Grade 9 goal structures were no longer significant. These results provide little support for ethnic group differences in the motivational consequences of students' goals or classroom goal structures.

Elliot, Chircov, Kim, and Sheldon (2001) argue that it is not mastery or performance goals per se that vary with cultural norms, but rather the relative adoption of avoidance versus approach goals. Specifically, they argue that students who come from cultures that emphasize interdependent selves (i.e., more collectivistic culture) are more likely to adopt avoidance goals than those from less collectivist cultures which see the self as an isolated being. They further posit that avoidance goals should have less of a negative effect on various outcomes in more collectivist societies. Data from a series of studies with adults supports their hypotheses: Asian Americans adopted more avoidance goals that non-Asian Americans; people having a more interdependent sense of self adopted more avoidance goals, and avoidance goals were inversely related to subjective well-being among people from individualistic but not collectivist societies (Elliot et al., 2001)

At least two studies have examined how approach and avoidance orientations and goals differently influence achievement and indicators of achievement motivation among Asian American versus Caucasian youth. In a sample of ninth-grade students, Eaton and Dembo (1997) reported higher levels of fear of failure, lower self-efficacy, and higher performance among Asian American versus European Americans engaged in a word task. More important, fear of failure was a positive predictor of achievement among Asians only, consistent with the notion that avoidance orientations may be differentially predictive across cultures. More recently, Zusho, Pintrich, and Cortina (2004) examined the relations among achievement orientations (fear of failure, need for achievement), goals, and various indicators of motivation such as anxiety, and found no evidence for the differential benefits of avoidance orientations. Among very high-achieving college students, Asian Americans reported more avoidance motivation that European Americans, but the relations between avoidance, anxiety, and achievement were not ethnically moderated. Together, results from these studies suggest that the influence of goal valence (approach vs. avoidance) rather than goal context may be moderated by ethnicity, explaining some differences between individuals from highly collectivist cultures, such as Asians or Asian Americans and their White, European American peers.

Ethnicity and Values

Although most motivation research emphasizes task-specific valuing, a growing body of literature on racial and ethnic minority students focuses on their assessments of the more general value of schooling. There are at least three reasons why one might assume that the perceived value of education might vary across racial and ethnic groups. First, as Steele (1997) hypothesized, repeated exposure to stereotypes might encourage some racial minority groups to uncouple their sense of self-worth from their academic performance, by devaluing academics. Such a strategy might be viewed as minimizing their costs. Second, students from some racial and ethnic minority groups cope with a burden of discrimination (i.e., less favorable treatment) within their schools and awareness of the future discrimination they may face in the future job market. Finally, the social segregation of our nations' schools means that many African American and Hispanic students, particularly the large percentage who live in urban areas, are attending schools with consistently low levels of academic achievement (Lee & Bryk, 1998a, 1998b), reinforcing school and peer norms that are not consistent with academic excellence.

Disidentification: Devaluing of Academics and Academic Feedback

Stereotype threat is one potential response to pervasive negative stereotypes about one's group, but only for those whose academic accomplishments play some central role in their self-definition (Steele & Aronson, 1995). For many other students, it has been suggested that these stereotypes may have a more debilitating consequence of encouraging them to disidentify with academics altogether as a way to protect their self-concept or self-evaluation (Osborne, 1995, 1997). Disidentification has been defined as a "defensive detachment of self esteem from one's outcomes in a domain such that self esteem is not contingent on one's outcomes in that domain" (Schmader, Major, & Gramzow, 2001, p. 94). In short, performance in the domain is devalued.

The disidentification of intellectual accomplishments from self-esteem has been found in laboratory situations, with African American college students' self-esteem being less affected by negative feedback about their performance on a supposed intelligence test than their Caucasian peers (Major, Spencer, Schmader, Wolfe, & Crocker, 1998). Using the nationally representative National Educational Longitudinal Study (NELS) data set, (Osborne, 1995, 1997) reported support for disidentification by showing that correlations between grades, tests scores, and self-esteem plummeted dramatically for African American males across grades 8, 10, and 12.

More recently, social psychologists have suggested further nuances to tests of disidentification. Two different mechanisms have been proposed for explaining disidentification effects: devaluing of educational achievement and disregarding (or devaluing) the feedback as biased. A reanalysis of the NELS data focusing on both aspects of disidentification and with more careful attention to the statistical analyses yielded different results than Osborne's studies (Morgan & Mehta, 2004). Discounting was tested by examining the relations between academic achievement and self-assessments, whereas the devaluing hypothesis was assessed by examining the extent to which academic achievement and academic self-concept judgments predicted overall self-esteem. Although the links between grades, tests scores, and academic self-concept were significantly weaker for African Americans, supporting the discounting hypothesis, the data did not suggest race or race by gender interactions in the centrality of academic accomplishments to self-esteem: Academic self-concept and measures of achievement were equally predictive of self-esteem across groups. Similarly, Saunders, Davis, Williams, and Williams (2004) found evidence that African American males may rely less on judgments of others when forming their own academic self-evaluations: African American males had lower GPAs and less academic self-efficacy than their same race female peers, but the predictive value of GPA for their self-assessed efficacy was smaller. Arguably, in both these studies, the interpretation that feedback is discounted is also suspect. Students most likely make judgments about their academic competence based not only on objective criterion itself, but also by comparison to their social reference group. Given that African American and Hispanic youth are more likely to attend schools with average lower-levels of achievement, the "miscalibration" may reflect nothing more than differences in local norms.

Schmader and her colleagues hypothesized that devaluing and discounting might be adaptive strategies by racial minority individuals who believe their group is discriminated against in a given area versus simply a self-protection of one's esteem (Schmader et al., 2001). In a test of this hypothesis with African American, Hispanic, and Caucasian college students, they looked at relations between achievement, academic devaluing, perceived test bias (discounting), and two measures of perceived discrimination: general beliefs in ethnic discrimination and beliefs that one's own group is personally discriminated against. Among African Americans there was no relationship between doing poorly in school and either devaluing or discounting, whereas devaluing increased among both Hispanic and Caucasian low-achievers. More interestingly, the level of both discounting and devaluing increased in relation to perceived racial discrimination: among African Americans and Hispanic students who reported more discrimination also were more apt to discount the test feedback.

Differential Treatment in Schools

Several key motivational theorists have emphasized the important role that positive teacher-student relationships may play in supporting the development of values, goals, and behaviors that are congruent with academic engagement (Connell &Wellborn, 1991; Ford, 1992; Wentzel, 1998). According to these scholars, when teachers behave in ways that respect and value students and/ or make them feel like they belong in the school community, they are more apt to internalize the values of those individuals (Ryan, 1993). At present, there is evidence both that feeling valued and respected supports motivation, and that, some groups of ethnic minority student may be likely to perceive poorer treatment from their teachers than Caucasians and outward discrimination.

Teacher-Student Relationships In her pioneering work on school belonging, Goodenow (1993) demonstrated how multiple aspects of psychological school membership including subjective feelings of belonging, teacher support and respect, and peer support related to motivational beliefs and behaviors. Among students in sixth through eighth grades, perceived teacher support was consistently the strongest predictor of motivation as measured by intrinsic interest, perceived value and expectancies for success. More recently, Wentzel (1998) reported positive associations between teachers' communicated social and academic support and several indicators of positive school values: intrinsic interest, pursuit of prosocial goals (e.g., help others in the class), and pursuit of social responsibility goals (e.g., pays attentions to the teacher's requests); whereas Murdock and Miller (2003) found that perceived teacher caring predicted change in motivation as measured by self-reported effort, self-efficacy, and intrinsic valuing across grades 7 and 8, after controlling for motivational influences from parents and peers. Other studies suggest that teacher support may be differentially perceived/received by members of different racial and ethnic groups, accounting for some of the motivational and achievement disparities between those groups. For example,

Murdock (1999) found that among seventh- and eighth-grade students, perceived teacher treatment partially mediated the relations between ethnicity (African American vs. Caucasian), poverty status (free lunch vs. not), and two teacher rated indicators of school commitment: engagement and discipline problems. Low-income, African American youth were more apt than their peer to perceive teachers as disinterested and critical, which partially explained their higher rates of noncompliance with teacher expectations.

Whereas all of the above studies rely on students' reported classroom experiences, there is a large, emerging body of work within pre-k and kindergarten classrooms that assesses student-teacher relations using teacher reports or objective observation. Although these studies do not examine the impact of teacher treatment on values per se, they do document important links between the quality of teacher support and students' behaviors that suggest more and less engagement, such as compliance with school norms and on task behavior. Moreover, they underscore potential ethnic differences in students' experiences with their teachers.

Saft and Pianta (2001) asked teachers to report on their perceptions of the quality of their relationships with their students and found higher reported amounts of child-teacher conflict when the student was of a different race than the teacher. Given that the majority of teachers in this country continue to be Caucasian, this means that ethnic minority youth may be more apt to have relationships with teachers that are perceived as conflict-ridden. Observational studies of classrooms also document the teacher's important role in creating a positive social-emotional climate. Pianta, la Paro, Payne, Cox, and Bradley (2002) studied the relationship between observers' ratings of social and instructional environment created by teachers, the social-emotional quality of their interaction with one child in that classroom, and various aspects of that target child's adaptation including observer ratings of school competence, on-task behavior, and teacher ratings of students' social and academic competence. Results revealed that classroom-level measures of child-centered interactions (social-emotional climate) and instructional quality as well as the observed level of positive interaction between the teacher and the target child predicted scores on each of the student outcome measures. Moreover, the behaviors that teachers exhibited were related to the demographic make-up of the classrooms, with more child-centered and positive interactions occurring in those with higher average income and higher levels of maternal education, classrooms where a disproportionately low number of African American and Latino youth spend their school years.

A second study of pre-K classrooms focused specifically on determining the prevalence of various profiles of classroom characteristics using similar observation assessments as described above to measure five aspects of social-emotional climate (e.g., high positive emotional climate, low over control, low negative climate) and four aspects of instructional support (e.g., use of instructional conversation, interactive assessment, etc.; LoCasale-Crouch et al., 2007). Five clusters emerged: two with very high (cluster 1) or high (cluster 2) scores on all scales, one with high social-emotional but average instructional scores, one with average social-emotional scores and poor instructional scores, and a fifth with low scores across the board. Classrooms with the highest concentrations of either non-White youth or youth who met the poverty criteria were under-represented in the cluster of highest quality classrooms and over-represented in the lowest-quality classrooms, however the effect sizes were quite small.

Perceived Discrimination in School Students' experiences with school-based discrimination have been linked to various indices of the value they ascribe to schooling or specific educational tasks. For example, in a study of African American middle school youth, Wong, Eccles, and Sameroff

(2003) reported moderate relations between perceived discriminatory behaviors from their teachers and peers during the eighth grade and declines in the perceived utility value of school between the start of Grade 7 and the end of Grade 8. Smaller, but significant associations with intrinsic value and academic expectancies were also documented. This study also revealed how experiences at a given point in time can shift the context of students' lives for some time to come: increased perceived discrimination over that one period was predictive of an increased likelihood for associating with peers who display negative school attitudes and behaviors. Similar relations between perceived discrimination and broader school valuing have been aptly documented in qualitative investigations of minority youth (Fine, 1991; Phelan, Yu, & Davidson, 1994).

Economic Discrimination

Still other scholars focus not on discrimination within schools, but on students' understanding of larger societal race-based inequalities. Mickelson (1990) observed that although most students are raised to believe in the Protestant work ethic, and would in fact, both repeat and endorse it when asked, many ethnic minority and low-income youth have concrete experiences in their lives which are in staunch contrast to these values, such as seeing people work hard every day and not get ahead, facing discrimination because of who they are, and having the highest paid workers in their neighborhoods be high school drop-outs (Mickelson, 1990). Moreover, she argued that these lived experiences and measures that tap these experiences are more apt to predict low-income and minority students' academic engagement and achievement than are abstract measures of Protestant values. A test of her hypothesis, Mickelson confirmed that that while students across racial and income groups believed in the "abstract value" of education, low-income and African American students simultaneously reported more negative attitudes on a concrete values scale than did their middle class and/or Caucasian peers. More importantly, school achievement was more strongly predicted by students' concrete than abstract values.

Since that time, several other scholars have documented similar ethnic differences in students' concrete attitudes as well as links between these attitudes and various indices of motivation and achievement (Ford, 1992; Murdock, 1999; Murdock, Anderman, & Hodge, 2000; Steinberg, Dornbusch, & Brown, 1992; Taylor et al., 1994). For example, in large scale study of high school students, Steinberg et al. (1992) found that whereas Asian American, Hispanic, African American and Caucasian students equally endorsed an item about the benefits of schooling, there were significant group differences in students' views about the negative consequences of not getting an education. Asian Americans were the most fearful about the consequences of not achieving in school, followed by Caucasians, and then African Americans and Hispanics. These same patterns of ethnic group differences were noted in achievement, with Asian Americans having the highest achievement outcomes. The more doubts students had about the consequences of not being educated, the less adaptive their motivation profiles as evidenced by lower levels of both effort and attributions of school success to hard work.

In our own research, higher and lower income African American middle school students also reported having more doubts about the value of education than did higher income Caucasian youth, but not lower income Caucasian youth (Murdock, 1999). Although doubts about the value of education were not uniquely related to current levels of engagement or disengagement from school, 2 years later, these eighth-grade attitudes were one of the strongest predictors of whether or not the students had plans to continue their education beyond high school, even after controlling for standardized achievement and academic self-concept (Murdock et al., 2000). More recently,

Irving & Hudley (2005) examined the motivational consequences of minority distrust of Whites and White authority (i.e., cultural mistrust). Lower to lower-middle income African American high school students rated education in terms of its potential to facilitate twenty occupational outcomes and the value they ascribed to each of those outcomes. The more doubts students have about Whites' willingness to provide fair treatment to non-whites, the lower their occupational expectancies for education and the less they reported valuing those outcomes.

Finally, Taylor and Graham (2007) explicitly examined the links between perceived educational and occupational barriers and adolescent students' school values, as measured by a peer nomination technique. Students nominated peers in their school who they held in the most esteem as measured by "most admire," "most respect" and "most want to be like" as well as those who they view as being high and low in level of effort, achievement, and obedience. Values were captured implicitly by examining the attributes of the students who they most esteem. However, their data did not support the hypothesis that the development of nonacademic values was related to perceived job and school discrimination. The discrepancy between these findings and those described above may be attributable to differences in how values were measured.

Ethnic Differences in School and Peer Norms

An additional influence on students' developing school values are the large racial differences is students' school-wide socioeconomic status, and the concomitant norms that students are exposed to in these settings. Although some race-comparative studies try to tease out influences of individual SES from race-related effects, rates of poverty at the school level are much more strongly associated with school outcomes than is personal SES and these differences appear to be largely mediated by the quality of the curriculum that students are exposed to (Lee & Bryk, 1998a, 1998b).

Students in underserved schools typically recognize their disadvantage relative to other social groups in the country (Fine, 1991, 2003; O'Connor, 1999; Weis & Fine, 1993) and many express helplessness as well as anger at this situation. Not only does the concentration of some racial and ethnic minority groups in low-achieving schools limit their exposure to higher level curriculum, it also circumscribes the other students they are exposed to. Recent work by Graham and her colleagues suggests that within schools with large concentrations of low-income minority youth, academic accomplishments may not be uniformly valued (Graham & Taylor, 2002; Graham, Taylor, & Hudley, 1998a, 1998b; Taylor & Graham, 2007). This work, which uses the peer nomination technique described in the previous section focuses on the accomplishments and behaviors that youth most admire, and provides an exciting bridge between traditional motivation research and the growing scholarship on identities, reviewed below.

Findings suggest that academic values are influenced by the combination of race and gender. Among African American middle school students, females admired female students with high grade-point averages whereas the males over nominated their low achieving peers (Graham et al., 1998a). Nominations for effortful and compliant behavior were disproportionately made to high achieving females whereas low-achieving males were overrepresented in the nominations of the effortless and disobedient. A follow-up study of African American, Latino, and Caucasian middle school youth suggests that these findings are not simply a function of gender, but are related to students' minority status. Among females of all three ethnic groups and among Caucasian males, high and average achievers were nominated with a greater frequency than low achievers.

In contrast, African American and Latino males admired low achieving males from their own ethnic group more so than the average and high achievers.

More recently, Taylor and Graham (2007) took a developmental look at these gendered academic values. Among both females and males, second- and fourth-grade African American and Latino students disproportionately nominated high or average achieving students as those they esteemed and under nominated low achieving students. By Grade 7, however, only the females of both ethnic groups continued to over nominate high achievers and under nominate low achievers, whereas the pattern for males had changed. Among African American males, there were no significant preferences across categories, and seventh-grade low achievers received disproportionately more nominations than did second and fourth graders. This pattern was even more extreme among the Latino males.

There are several possible interpretations of the above studies, one being that school achievement is not seen as desirable or valuable for minority males. However, the results of these studies may in fact reflect the described demographics of the schools where the research was conducted. In all situations, schools were described as predominantly lower income. As such, the value patterns displayed by these students may be more a reflection of the achievement norms within the studied schools than they are of minority males in general. To test this hypothesis, we collected similar data on low-income African American adolescents attending a public college preparatory charter school in an urban school district. Although any student could attend the school, and the full range of achievement levels were represented (Murdock & Miller, 2002), high educational standards were the norm and students were routinely held back if they did not meet the standards. Within this setting, we found no evidence that African American males preferred low-achievers (Jahnke & Murdock, 2002).

Summary: Do I Want to Do This?

Scholarship on racial and ethnic minorities has helped to elucidate a multitude of ways that one can think about how valuing influences motivation. As seen in the above research, the development of one's self-assessments and one's values do not develop orthogonally to one another but have reciprocal connections. Students are exposed to a wide range of information that they can use to make inferences about their capabilities, and they may frame that information as something that reflects on themselves, or, alternatively, discount the self-relevance of the feedback, which devalues what teachers and schools have to offer. Similarly, it appears that the feeling valued and respected by one's teachers increases the likelihood that one will adopt the teachers' communicated values, but that opportunities for positive teacher-student interactions may not be equally distributed across racial and ethnic line. Beyond teachers, however, the opportunities we provide to students in school (i.e., curriculum quality), and their experiences of how their schooling will or will not provide future opportunities, are all part of the larger socialization context in which students are constructing their understanding of the value of academic accomplishment.

Who Am I?

Among the newest theoretical perspectives on motivation are those that posit identity as central to understanding students' engagement, persistence and choices (McCaslin, 2004, in press). Identity perspectives blur the distinction between expectations and values by asking questions about what is central to a given person's construction of who they are. Identity, according to McCaslin "is based, in part, on what we do, why, and our own and other's beliefs about what that means both now and for the future" (p. 6). For members of minority groups in this country, these identities are constructed within a larger social context where stereotypes and discrimination still pervade. Moreover, race, like gender, is a strong filter through which we view ourselves and others, as social-cognition theorists have repeatedly shown these two attributes of people to be the fastest, most automatically processed (Brewer & Hewstone, 2004). In this section, the focus is on three bodies of identity work that have been explicitly applied to understanding student motivation of ethnic minority youth: oppositional identity, ethnic identity, and possible selves.

Oppositional Identity

Oppositional identity theory, as put forth by Ogbu (1978), asserts that members of involuntary caste minorities (i.e., minority groups who were brought to the United Sates without their consent and who are typically looked down upon) such as African Americans who have been subject to continuous discrimination and denial of opportunity, develop identities directly in opposition to those of the mainstream culture as a coping response to being shut out. These oppositional identities include the stereotyping of academic achievement as something that is a "White" behavior, or evidence that the person has sold out or bought into an unjust system. Reinforcing these identities are the norms of the same-race peer group.

Ethnographic studies of African American youth in both low-income (Fordham & Ogbu, 1986) and middle-class (Ogbu, 2003) communities provide some support for the oppositional identity theory. Among the high school students who were academically successful, many spoke of being verbally harassed and degraded by their peers for their display of academic interest and accomplishment. Reports of similar behaviors were documented in an ethnography of Mexican American youth (Matute-Bianchi, 1986), and other scholars have reported that being academically inclined and in honors courses are seen by non-Caucasian youth as "acting White" (Bergin & Cooks, 2002).

Although the theory has gained wide-spread popularity across numerous academic disciplines as well as in the popular press, evidence for the "acting White" hypothesis as the cause of racial disparities in achievement is actually quite tenuous. Specific tenants of the theory were clearly rejected in two large-scale studies (Ainsworth-Darnell & Downey, 1998; Cook & Ludwig, 1997) that used data from the National Educational Longitudinal Study (NELS). For example, Ainsworth-Darnell and Downey (1998) found that African American students more strongly endorsed items pertaining to both the importance of education for future job success and to their engagement in behaviors that demonstrate positive school attitudes than did Caucasian students. The only support for an "oppositional culture" came from racial disparities in teachers' reports of students' behaviors. Moreover, perceived popularity among one's peers was more strongly associated with high achievement for African American than Caucasian students, and between group achievement differences could not be explained by "oppositional" attitudes or behaviors. Although the African American students in some of my own research indicated that their peers' had lower educational aspirations than the Caucasian students from the same middle school, they reported similar levels of peer support for engaging in academic behaviors (Murdock, 1999; Murdock & Miller, 2003).

Disparities between the original formulation of the "acting White" hypothesis and the contradictory findings might best be understood by recognizing the heterogeneity in beliefs, responses and circumstances of the youth being studied (Carter, 2006). Academically successful African

American and Mexican American high school students in Bergin and Cooke's (2002) study admitted that they had been accused of "acting White" by some of their same race peers; however, their responses to these taunts were anger and indignation rather than the hypothesized conformity. Still other scholars point to the role of institutional values in determining the prevalence of oppositional norms. For example, African Americans relied on their peers for positive support as they negotiated academic identities within a predominantly White elite private school with strong academic norms (Datnow & Cooper, 1998).

Tyson, Darity, and Castellino (2005) found that racialized peer pressure against academic success in eight North Carolina high schools was highly dependent on the composition of the schools. In most of schools, such pressures were uncommon and more students than not reported having peer support for their achievement. Moreover, as in the Bergin and Cooks (2002) study, African American students who did experience harassment seemed to disregard any criticism they received about false racial identities and socialized with peers who supported their success. This study also raises questions about the extent to which the devaluing of academics is a race-specific strategy. Teasing and harassment of high-achieving students (e.g., nerds) was evident across racial groups and was largely a function of the level of tension between low and high achievers within the school. One Caucasian woman in this situation reported managing her identity by accentuating other nonacademic aspects of herself. In short, these students are typical of other adolescents in that they are aware of and utilize impression management techniques to try to minimize the status consequences that can be the price for high effort and achievement (Juvonen & Murdock, 1993, 1995), and these responses may not be racially or ethnically specific.

The Tyson et al. (2005) study also highlights the ways in which course placement policies can lead to isolation of minority students in integrated schools where low concentrations of racial and ethnic minority students are in advanced classes. Indeed, the level of integration in the school may adversely affect the social integration of some ethnic minority students. Based on an analysis of the adolescent health data, Fryer and Torrelli (2005) concluded that popularity of African American students among same-ethnic peers is unaffected by having a high GPA in all Black schools, but is detrimental in schools that are predominantly Caucasian.

Racial and Ethnic Identity

In contrast to theories of oppositional identity, theories of racial identity development emphasize individuals' identification with their racial or ethnic group and the characteristics they personally ascribe to that group (e.g., Phinney, 1990; Sellers & Shelton, 2003). Some theoretical models posit a stage-like progression with an ideal endpoint (Cross, 1971; Parham & Helms, 1985), whereas others view racial identity as a multidimensional construct (Sellers & Shelton, 2003; Thomas, Townsend, & Belgrave, 2003) with multiple configurations that can be adaptive depending on one's context. Both perspectives assume, however, that a strong, positive racial identity provides strength and support in a society where negative stereotypes and discrimination abound.

Stage Theories of Racial and Ethnic Identity

According to stage theories of identity development, members of minority groups move through stages of increasing self-acceptance and integration of ethnicity into one's identity. Parham and Helms (1985) delineate four stages of African American racial identity development ranging from pre-encounter, where African Americans adopt White attitudes and accept societal stereotypes of their own group, through internalization, which represents a positive identification with being African American as well as an appreciation of individual differences. Based on this theoretical perspective, one would anticipate that a stronger identity with one's racial or ethnic group rather than with the dominant majority provides the vision and the support necessary for setting and achieving high achievement goals. Indeed, in a challenge to Ogbu's hypothesis, Spencer, Noll, Stoltzfus, and Harpalani (2001) showed that high levels of achievement and self-esteem among inner-city African American youth were associated with internalization (Afrocentric identity), whereas more Eurocentric identities were associated with lower achievement and poorer self-evaluations. Similarly, Oyserman, Kemnelmeier, Fryberg, Brosh, and Hart-Johnson (2003) found that African American, Hispanic, and Native American middle school students whose racial self-schemas include both attributes of their own ethnic group (termed "in group" schema) as well as of their ethnic group in the larger society, performed better in school and improved more over the course the year than those who did not think of themselves in terms of ethnicity (a-schematic) or whose identities were only in terms of the "in-group."

Links between attitudes, achievement, and stages of racial identity of African American youth have also been found among intellectually gifted youth (Ford & Harris, 1997). Gifted African American high school students had higher rates of internalization than either their potentially gifted or general education peers. Males who were underachieving also had significantly lower levels of internalization compared to appropriately achieving males and females or underachieving females. Finally, there is some evidence that when stereotype threat is low, such as on a classroom task where race or ability are not specifically primed, higher levels of internalized identity might be associated with improved performance (Davis, Aronson, & Moises, 2006).

Studies based on dimensional theories of racial identity development also support the protective role of a positive racial identity at least for African American youth. Sellers and Shelton (2003) conceptualize racial identity as comprised of various components including centrality of race to one's self-definition, private regard, one's personal feelings about one's group and public regard, or one's perception of the larger public's view of one group. A large scale longitudinal study based on this method focused on how the combination of these components of identity related to student motivation (Chavous, Bernat, Schmeelk-Cone, Caldwell, Kohn-Wood, & Zimmerman, 2003). School attachment and self-efficacy were lowest among the "alienated group," who had low race centrality as well as low public and private regard. More important, the alienated group had the largest percentage of students who had not remained in school until 12th grade and the lowest records of college attendance 2 years later. Students with the highest probability of continuing their education into college were those they labeled defensive/buffering: they had a strong connection to and high private regard for their racial group but recognized that others may not. Other evidence for motivational consequences of racial identity comes from findings of relations between positive identity, self-efficacy, and achievement in an African American high school sample (Witherspoon, Speight, & Thomas, 1997) and links between racial identity and academic achievement at the college level (Sellers, Chavous, & Cooke, 1998). Better school adjustment as measured by both teacher and self-reports was associated with more positive assessments of one's group and stronger belief in Afrocentric values among African American fourth graders (Thomas et al., 2003).

Longitudinal data on African American middle school students intimate that a more positive ethnic identify may protect achievement motivation in the face of perceived discrimination in school (Wong et al., 2003). Although perceived discrimination was generally inversely related to adolescents' academic self-concept and their beliefs about the importance and utility of school, the relation to self-concept was moderated by ethnic identity. Among those with more positive identities, the effects of perceived discrimination were significantly less.

A strong sense of ethnic identity is advantageous for other minority groups as well. Among ninth-grade adolescents from Mexican, Chinese, and European backgrounds, those who had higher levels of positive regard and ethnic centrality also reported an increased valuing and identifying with school as well as a more positive academic self-concept (Fuligni et al., 2005). On most measures of motivation, the Chinese and Mexican students scored higher than the Caucasians. Moreover, the strength of identification among Mexican and Chinese students accounted for between 20 and 71% of the differences in the level of motivation for their groups versus Caucasians.

Identity Content Theories

Oyserman's model of identity development incorporates not only students' feelings about being a member of their racial group, but also their assessments of the extent to which being academically engaged is part of that racial identity. Specifically, she conceptualizes identity as incorporating feelings of connectedness to members of their own group, level of perceived discrimination directed at one's group, and the centrality of academic achievement to one's group identity. Among African American females, having a positive value of one's group actually predicted declines in self-efficacy when coupled with beliefs that African Americans were discriminated against and academic achievement was not part of ethnic identity (Oyserman, Harrison, & Bybee, 2001). In contrast, when academic achievement was part of the racial identity, high connection to one's group was associated with strong academic self-efficacy in the face of high levels of perceived discrimination. A longitudinal study of African American and Latino adolescents also suggests that connection to one's group alone is not necessarily protective of academic achievement. Across males and females in both ethnic groups, an increased sense of connection was only related to increased achievement for those students who saw academic achievement as a strong element of their ethnic identity; similar levels of strong connection coupled with low endorsement of academic identity actually led to declining performance (Altschul, Oyserman, & Bybee, 2006).

Possible Selves

Possible selves theories emphasize constructed future selves as a key component of motivation that focuses goal setting, task choices and persistence (Markus & Nurius, 1986). These future-directed self-concepts include a hoped for self, an expected self, and a feared self, thus mirroring the approach and avoidance aspects of many theories of achievement motivation (Pintrich & Schunk, 2002; Weiner, 1986). Hoped for selves are presumed to be akin to abstract values (Mickelson, 1990); they are internalized dreams of what one should hope for, but are not necessarily believed by those who report them, and therefore not strong predictors of behavior (see Yowell, 1999). In contrast, expected and feared selves are presumed to be more strongly rooted in the students' lived experiences, and therefore better behavioral predictors. Yowell's (1999) study of low-income Hispanic youth revealed some support for these propositions: students' hoped for selves were largely as highly educated professionals (e.g., doctors, lawyers) whereas their anticipated selves required less education, such as being a police officer or teacher. In addition, neither hoped for not anticipated selves predicted school achievement, but there was a moderate inverse relationship between feared for selves and attainments.

In depth interviews with high students from various racial and ethnic backgrounds revealed that while all groups of students generated the same number of possible selves, the content of these selves was strongly influenced by prevailing school and societal stereotypes as was the balance between hoped for, expected and feared images (Kao, 2000). Possible selves of African American youth were dominated by avoidance of stereotypical images of being unintelligent and low-achieving whereas Hispanics were determined not to become low-paid manual workers. In contrast, to these negative images, narratives of Asian American students reflected a strong concern with not being able to live up to the high standards that typified stereotypical expectations. Positive hoped for images were most abundant among the Caucasian students. Kao concludes that these prevailing stereotypes and the racial and ethnic based standards for success they generate help explain the paradox between self-views of accomplishment and actual levels of achievement. If one's goal is simply not to fail, then anything beyond that is good; whereas if one's goal is to be in the top of the class, then B and C grades are not adequate.

Oyserman and her associates also stress the societal backdrop against which African Americans meet the task of developing positive identities that balance feared for and desired academic possible selves (Oyserman, Bybee, & Terry, 2006; Oyserman, Gant, & Ager, 1995). Positive selves provide the impetuous for setting and maintaining goals, whereas awareness of the feared-for selves is posited to help maintain persistence in the face of setbacks and circumscribe some behaviors as unacceptable, even if they might be expedient ways of achieving one's goals. Findings from African American middle school students confirm that balance is an important predictor of school engagement as measured by both teacher and student reports, particularly for males (Oyserman et al., 1995). Beyond balance, however, students must also have strategies to attain their possible selves.

Summary: Who Am I?

Work on identity illustrates how racial, ethnic, and gender categories, so salient in our society, influence students' construction of who they are and who they can be. Environments that provide opportunities for racial minority students to develop positive images of themselves as a member of their ethnic group as well as to see academic achievement as something that can be a meaningful and realistic part of that identity may help to foster students' school engagement.

Implications for Classrooms and Schools

What is clear from the vast literature that sheds light on motivation of racial and ethnic minority youth is that the construction of a student's academic identity takes place in a complex ecological context that includes many racially, economically, and culturally specific experiences. Many students are developing their values, goals, and self-assessments within the constraints of racially and gender based stereotypes, low-achieving schools, unsafe communities, and job discrimination. Despite these barriers, many students remain motivated and committed to school. The research reviewed for this chapter not only underscores some of the mechanisms that contribute to the development of students' motivation, it also illuminates several potential ways that school might better serve racial and ethnic minority youth.

Targeting Stereotypes and Identity

Laboratory and field-based interventions designed to reduce the effects of stereotype threat have proven efficacious. As a group, these interventions aim at weakening the link between an individual's personal identity and a negative stereotype, and/or broadening the focus of their identity. For example, by priming aspects of women's identities that reinforced their accomplishments, such as getting accepted at a private college versus simply priming their gender, the effects of stereotype threat were eliminated on a measure of spatial reasoning (McGlone & Aronson, 2006). Having students engage in writing tasks that focused on something positive about themselves or providing self-affirmations resulted in reduced stereotype threat in both African American (Cohen, Garcia, Apfel, & Master, 2006) and female (Martens, Johns, Greenberg, & Schimel, 2006) students. Other effective interventions aimed at broadening the self-concept of stigmatized group members include having participants identify the similarities they share with others who are members of a different social reference group (Rosenthal & Crisp, 2006), reading stories about members of their group who had been successful (McIntyre, Paulson, & Lord, 2003), and drawing self-concept maps with many nodes, to represent a multi-faceted self-view (Gresky, Ten Eyck, Lord, & McIntyre, 2005).

Although the above interventions have been explicitly used for stereotype threat, implying that students are involved and already identified with academics, reinforcing multiple aspects of identity seems like an appropriate intervention for all students and fits with many models of multicultural education that stress exposure to the accomplishments of members of one's group. Social learning theory (Bandura, 1977) also reminds us that successful role models need to be people who students see as enough like themselves that they represent an attainable outcome. Broadening students' possible identities has been the focus of a successful intervention program aimed at improving the motivation and achievement of low-income, African American and Hispanic youth (Oyserman et al., 2006; Oysterman, Terry, & Bybee, 2002). The program helps students develop balance in their possible selves, encourages them to see these selves as attainable and provides strategies to move towards these selves and to deal with setbacks along the way. An experimental evaluation of the program showed declines in discipline problems, increases in attendance, and improvement in grades and test scores that were maintained for 2 years (Oyserman et al., 2006).

Targeting Attributions

Attributions refer to the reasons one uses to explain a particular event; in the context of achievement, various dimensions of one's attributions for success and failure are considered to have motivational implications. In failure situations, attributions to internal, controllable causes such as lack of effort, or selection of a poor strategy are considered most adaptive, because, from a motivational perspective, it gives the student the power to change the outcome in the future. In contrast, attributions to stable causes, such as ability, or external causes, such as an unfair teacher, suggest there is little to be gained from continuing to persevere.

Targeting students' performance attributions may also be a viable mechanism for reducing stereotype threat effects. After demonstrating in a laboratory setting that manipulating information about the malleability or fixedness of intelligence, thereby defining intellect as something that is controllable rather than uncontrollable), stereotype threat effects were eliminated for African American college students (Aronson, Fried, & Good, 2002). Good, Aronson, and Inzlicht (2003) applied those findings to developing a field based intervention. Low-income, minority females who were just beginning middle school were assigned to a college mentor over the course of an academic year. This mentor either encouraged them to view their intelligence as malleable or to attribute any problems in the school to the difficulties inherent in the middle school transition. At the end of the year, the students who had been in either of the intervention groups achieved higher standardized test scores in math and reading than those in the control condition. Making teachers aware of both intentional and unintentional ways that their own behavior communicates attributions to students (Graham, 1984) should help not only reduce stereotype threat effects, but more generally improve students' outcome expectations and persistence.

Targeting Expectations and Teacher Development

Changing expectations of academic outcomes may be a viable strategy for improving the motivation and achievement of minority youth, but only if such changes are coupled with improved curriculum, instructional skills, and decreased use of academic tracking. Teachers' understandings of the causes of the racial- and socioeconomic-based educational disparities might determine how they respond in their classrooms to students struggling to learn. In case studies of two teachers working with low-income, low-achieving minority youth, Hudley (1997) found that between-class differences in students' motivation and competence beliefs could be linked to teachers' attitudes and instructional practices. In the classroom where students were more intrinsically interested, the instructor framed the students' educational problems in terms of the larger contexts of their lives, developed curricula tied to students' own interests, and used instructional strategies that allowed for interaction and engagement. However, where instructors' attributions of poor performance were characterized by lower levels of motivation and the students' lack of ability, few efforts were made at instructional innovation.

These case studies reveal that it is not expectations in isolation, but the expectation-based practices and curriculum that students get exposed to which need addressing. Similarly, Ferguson (2003) reports that the Great Expectations program developed by Marva Collins was successful in raising achievement of low-income children by providing teachers with the knowledge, strategies, and support to actually teach differently in their classroom rather than simply telling them that all students can learn. At a school-wide level, students from underserved groups need the opportunities, encouragement and instructional support to take more advanced level courses. Without closing the gap in course-taking practices that exist between racial and ethnic groups, the disparities in achievements outcomes will never disappear (Lee & Bryk, 1988a, 1988b).

Limitations and Suggestions for Future Research

One of the most frequently noted limitations of research on race and ethnicity is its failure to tease out social class influences. Moreover, many of the methods used to statistically uncouple these variables (e.g., controlling for SES) create groups with little ecological validity (Murdock, 2000). Living in poverty, having parents with limited education and low status jobs (i.e., SES) are realities for a disproportionate number of African American and Latino youth in this country, and we need to continue to strive to incorporate into research the elements of these realities that impinge on the development of their motivational identities. This includes recognizing that racial groups not only tend to vary in terms of students' personal socioeconomic status, but also in the larger socioeconomic context in which they live such as their schools and neighborhoods Students who are African American, Hispanic, or from recent immigrant families are far more likely to attend schools with high concentrations of poverty than are other students, a factor that has been repeatedly linked to the safety of the school environment, the quality of the curriculum and teaching, and not surprisingly, the average level of achievement. Understanding the psychological impact of these differences in school context will require more large-scale collaborative studies to model classroom and school effects on individual outcomes (Lee, 2002). Other sources of contextual variation also likely contribute to the lack of consistency in findings across studies. For example, some studies draw conclusions about the extent to which groups of students identify with academic achievement based on relationships between one's achievement and one's self-concept using data from national surveys (Osborne, 1995, 1997). However, these studies do not account for the wide variation in school-level achievement norms, which presumably would influence students' views of themselves more so than an abstract national criterion.

Moderator variables that deserve increased attention include age, developmental and grade level and gender. Developmental researchers have consistently demonstrated age-related changes in the complexity of children's self-concepts and achievement values, as well as their understanding of the malleability of intelligence and the interrelations among effort, intelligence and achievement (see Wigfield, Eccles, Schiefele, Roeser, & Davis-Keene, 2005, for review). However, there has been limited systematic attention to developmental changes in much of the literature reviewed for this chapter and there is an overall dearth of studies focusing on children in elementary and middle school as compared to older students.

As seen throughout the literature reviewed, many of the findings are not consistent across gender. This is not surprising given that stereotypes of men and women are not the same, and for some ethnic minorities, particularly African American and Hispanics, males elicit stronger negative stereotyping than females. In addition, while much of the discussion throughout this chapter was on people described by researchers as either Caucasian, African American, or Hispanic, these pan ethnic labels are neither accurate indicators of how many students define themselves, nor reflective of the unique experiences of being a member of one ethnic group or another. Kao (2000) provides an excellent discussion of the multitude of different "Asian" groups within one school, the varying ways they define themselves and each other, and their heterogeneous experiences as part of that school community.

Construct and measurement clarity are also key areas that need to be addressed to improve the quality of our future research. For example, measurement issues cloud many of the conclusions about the role of anxiety as a mediator of stereotype threat effects. Heightened anxiety was clearly implicated in studies that used physiological indicators of arousal such as blood pressure (Blascovich et al., 2001) and heart-rate variability (Croizet et al., 2004), or behavioral observations of anxious behavior (Bosson, Haymovitz, & Pinel, 2004). Yet, when participants report on their own anxiety, it often does not mediate stereotype threat effects (Oswald & Harvey, 2001; Schmader, 2002), or, these effects appear to depend on the timing of the anxiety assessment.

The limitations of self-report measures more generally should also be given more scrutiny. In several cases throughout this review, there were notable differences between conclusions based on survey questions and those that were found using other methodologies. For example, several studies revealed that students seemed to have internalized stereotypes of their own group's academic abilities when implicit methods of tapping these stereotypes were used, such as selecting a photo (Ambady et al., 2001; Hudley & Graham, 2001). When more explicit methods are used, such as asking about one group or another or asking a student about herself, these differences were not found (Ambady et al., 2001).

Findings in many areas are either inconsistent or yield effect sizes that are minimal, suggesting they would not offer a lot of promise for intervention. Recall that two (Eaton & Dembo, 1997; Elliot et al., 2001) of three studies found avoidance goals were differentially adaptive for Asian versus non-Asian populations, but the third (Zusho et al., 2004) did not; meta-analyses of teacher expectation effects (Tenenbaum & Ruck, 2007) do not consistently demonstrate differential expectations to be a consistent source of differential outcomes. Making sense of this variation is quite difficult, because, as noted above, there is often little cross-study consistency in construct measurement and few studies designed to replicate previously documented findings are conducted. Although the literature on ethnic identity and stereotype threats appears to provide more consistent findings that in some other arenas, in most cases, the effect sizes for these finds are quite small affording little hope of practical significance. In addition, many of the studies reviewed in this chapter, particularly those on stereotype threat, were conducted in experimental settings, where the control over extraneous variables greatly exceeds what is possible in field settings where classroom learning takes place.

Finally, minimal research was found that focused on curriculum, pedagogy or other types of instructional interventions which might be used to improve student engagement or to help close the existing achievement gaps. As noted above, however, there are some data to suggest that the findings from various literatures including stereotype threat and possible selves' theory might inform testable interventions and evidence for the efficacy of those interventions.

Implications for Theories of Motivation

Although situated within a volume on classroom motivation, most of the work reviewed in this chapter does not draw from classic theories of achievement motivation, largely because there is not one identifiable literature to turn to. This raises questions with respect to the usefulness of our current theories for contributing to the national dialog about the achievement gap, or for providing teachers with information about how to promote engagement of a continually increasingly diverse student population. As with many fields of psychology, educational psychologists who study achievement motivation continue to highlight the importance of broadening our theories and research to account for the experiences and behaviors of individuals from a range of racial of ethnic backgrounds (McInerney & Van Etten, 2004). At the same time, however, it is important to remember that theories we currently rely on were themselves developed in a racial and ethnic context, a context that was largely European and White. As such, while many of our current perspectives such as expectancy-value models of motivation (Eccles (Parson) et al., 1983), clearly specify the importance of delineating the social-cultural determinants of the experiences and interpretations of experiences that influence the psychological processes constituting motivation, less work has been done to explicitly expand the constructs in our theories based on research with culturally diverse groups. The work highlighted in this chapter illustrates the importance of such considerations.

Another essential point for consideration is the extent to which motivational theorists should concern themselves with between- versus within-group motivation. Some of the constructs that have provided interesting insights into motivation of specific racial groups such as racial identity are not useful for thinking about how groups differ from one another but may be applicable for exploring within group variation for some students. In addition, the limited ability of current motivation theories to describe racial differences in performance should probably not be surprising given the generally small relations between our cognitive motivational constructs and behavioral outcomes. As McCaslin (in press) reminds us, the outward display of people's motivational dispositions (i.e., their values, expectancies, etc.) are highly dependent on available opportunities. This includes the differential quality of teaching and curriculum as a function of the school's average socio-economic status but also, constraints or costs associated with all kinds of choices. For example, although I may strongly value education, there may be more people in my immediate environment who can provide acceptance and validation for my athleticism or sense of humor than my academic skills, encouraging me to focus my limited energies in those directions. Similarly, the cost of not holding a part-time job that may compete with the ability to do well in school, is probably highly variable depending on the economic need of the family as well as the cultural and personal value that one attaches to money and the ability to demonstrate having money. As motivational theorists strive to explain behavioral choices and persistence among a broader population that they have typically studied, it will be imperative to continually consider the unique affordances and constraints circumscribing students' displays of achievement motivation.

References

Ainsworth-Darnell, J. W., & Downey, D. B. (1998). Assessing the oppositional culture explanation for racial/ethnic differences in school performance. *American Sociological Review, 63,* 536–553.

Altschul, I., Oyserman, D., & Bybee, D. (2006). Racial-ethnic identity in mid-adolescence: Content and change as predictors of academic achievement. *Child Development, 77*(5), 1155–1169.

Ambady, N., Shih, M., Kim, A., & Pittinsky, T. L. (2001). Stereotype susceptibility in children: Effects of identity activation on quantitative performance. *Psychological Science, 12,* 385–390.

Ames, C. (1992). Classrooms: Goals, structures, and student motivation. *Journal of Educational Psychology, 84*(3), 261–271.

Ames, C., & Archer, J. (1988). Achievement goals in the classroom: Students' learning strategies and motivation processes: *Journal of Educational Psychology, 80,* 260–267.

Aronson, J,, Fried, C., & Good, C. (2002). Reducing the effects of stereotype threat on African American college students by shaping theories of intelligence. *Journal of Experimental Social Psychology, 38,* 113–125.

Aronson, J., & Steele, C. M. (2005). Stereotypes and the fragility of academic competence, motivation, and self-concept. In A. J. Elliot & C. S. Dweck (Eds.), *Handbook of Competence and Motivation* (pp. 436–456). New York: Guilford.

Bandura, A. (1977). *Social learning theory.* Englewood Cliffs, NJ: Prentice Hall.

Bandura, A. (1986). *Social foundations of thought and action: A social cognitive theory.* Englewood Cliffs, NJ: Prentice Hall.

Bandura, A. (1997). *Self-efficacy: The exercise of control.* New York: W.H. Freeman.

Bergin, D. A., & Cooke, H. C. (2002). High school students of color talk about accusations of "acting white." *The Urban Review, 34,* 113–134.

Blascovich, J., Spencer, S. J., Quinn, D., & Steele, C. (2001). African Americans and high blood pressure: The role of stereotype threat. *Psychological Science, 12,* 225–229.

Bosson, J. K., Haymovitz, E. L., & Pinel, E. C. (2004). When saying and doing diverge: The effects of stereotype threat on self-reported versus non-verbal anxiety. *Journal of Experimental Social Psychology, 40*(2), 247–255.

Brewer, M., & Hewstone, M. (Eds.). (2004). *Social cognition.* Blackwell.

Brown, R. P., & Day, E. A. (2006). The difference Iin't Black and White: Stereotype threat and the race gap on Raven's advanced progressive matrices. *Journal of Applied Psychology, 91,* 979–985.

Cadinu, M., Maass, A., Frigerio, S., Impagliazzo, L., & Latinotti, S. (2003). Stereotype threat: The effect of expectancy on performance. *European Journal of Social Psychology 33,* 267–285.

Carter, P. L. (2006). Straddling boundaries: Identity, culture and school. *Sociology of Education, 79,* 304–328.

Chavous, T. M., Bernat, D. H., Schmeelk-Cone, K., Caldwell, C. H., Kohn-Wood, L., & Zimmerman, M. A. (2003). Racial identity and academic attainment among African American adolescents. *Child Development, 74,* 1076–1090.

Cheryan, S. (2000). When positive stereotypes threaten intellectual performance: The psychological hazards of "model minority" status. *Psychological Science, 11,* 399–402.

Cohen, G. L., Garcia, J., Apfel, N., & Master, A. (2006). Reducing the racial achievement gap: A social-psychological Intervention. *Science 137,* 1307–1310.

Connell, J. P., & Wellborn, J. G. (1991). Competence, autonomy, and relatedness: A motivational analysis of self-system processes. In M. R. Gunnar & L. A. Sroufe (Eds.), *Self processes and development: The Minnesota symposia on child development* (Vol. 23, pp. 43–78). Hillsdale, NJ: Erlbaum.

Cook, P., & Ludwig, J. (1997). Weighing the "burden of 'acting White'": Are there race differences in attitudes toward education? *Journal of Policy Analysis and Management, 16,* 256–278.

Cooper, H, & Dorr, N. (1995). Race comparisons and need for achievement: A meta-analytic alternative to Graham's narrative review. *Review of Educational Research, 65,* 483–495.

Cozzarelli, C., Tagler, M. J., & Wilkinson, A. V. (2002). Do middle-class students perceive poor women and poor men differently? *Sex Roles, 47,* 519–529.

Croizet, J., Despres, G., Gauzins, M., Huguet, P., Leyens, J., & Meot, A. (2004). Stereotype threat undermines intellectual performance by triggering a disruptive mental load. *Personality and Social Psychology Bulletin, 30*(6), 721–731.

Croizet, J.-C., & Claire, T. (1998). Extending the concept of stereotype and threat to social class: The intellectual underperformance of students from low socioeconomic backgrounds. *Personality and Social Psychology Bulletin 24,* 588–594.

Croizet, J.-C., Desert, M., Dutrevis, M., & Leyens, J.-P. (2001). Stereotype threat, social class, gender, and academic underachievement: When our reputation catches up to us and takes over: *Social Psychology of Education, 4,* 295–310.

Cross, W. E. (1971). The negro-to-black conversion experience. *Black World, 20*(9), 13–27.

Datnow, A., & Cooper, R. (1998). Peer networks of African American students in independent schools: Affirming academic success and racial identity. *Journal of Negro Education, 66,* 56–72.

Davis III, C., Aronson, J., & Moises, S. (2006). Shades of threat: Racial identity as a moderator of stereotype threat. *Journal of Black Psychology, 32,* 399–417.

Devine, P. G. (1995). Are racial stereotypes really fading? The Princeton trilogy revisited. *Personality and Social Psychology Bulletin, 21,* 1139–1150.

Eaton, M., & Dembo, M. (1997). Differences in the motivational beliefs of Asian Americans and non-Asian students. *Journal of Educational Psychology, 89,* 433–440.

Eccles (Parsons), J., Adler, T. F., Futterman, R., Goff, S., Kaczala, C. M., Meece, J. L., et al. (1983). Expectations, values and academic behaviors. In J. T. Spence (Ed.), *Perspectives on achievement and achievement motivation* (pp. 75–146). San Fransisco: Freeman.

Eccles, J. S., Wigfield, A., & Schiefele, U. (1998). Motivation. In N. Eisnenberg (Ed.), *Handbook of child psychology, 5th edition* (Vol. 3, pp. 1017–1095). New York: Wiley.

Elliot, A. J. (2005). A conceptual history of the achievement goal construct. In A. J. Elliot & C. S. Dweck (Eds.), *Handbook of competence and motivation* (pp. 52–72). New York: Guilford.

Elliot, A. J., Chirkov, V. I., Kim, Y., & Sheldon, K. M. (2001). A cross-cultural analysis of avoidance (relative to approach) personal goals. *Psychological Science, 12*(6), 505–510.

Ferguson, R. F. (2003). Teacher's perceptions and expectations and the black-white test score gap. *Urban Education, 38,* 460–507.

Ferguson, R. F. (2003). Teachers' perceptions and expectations and the black-white test score gap. *Urban Education, 38*(4), 460–507.

Fine, M. (1991). *Framing dropouts: Notes on the politics of an urban public high school.* Albany: State University of New York Press.

Fine, M. (2003). Silencing and nurturing voice in an improbable context: Urban adolescents in public school. In M. Fine & L. Weis (Eds.), *Silenced voices and extraordinary conversations: Re-imagining schools* (pp. 13–37). New York: Teachers College Press.

Ford, D. Y. (1992). Self-perceptions of underachievement and support for the achievement ideology among early adolescent African-Americans. *Journal of Early Adolescence, 12,* 228–252.

Ford, D. Y., & Harris, J. J. (1997). A study of the racial identity and achievement of black males and females. *Roeper Review, 20,* 105–110.

Ford, M. E. (1992). *Motivating humans: Goals, emotions, and personal agency beliefs.* Newbury Park, CA: Sage.

Fordham, S., & Ogbu, J. U. (1986). Black student's school success: Coping with the "burden of 'acting White.'" *Urban Review, 18,* 176–206.

Freeman, K. E., Gutman, L. M., & Midgley, C. (2002). Can achievement goal theory enhance our understanding of the motivation and performance of African American young adolescents? In C. Midgley (Ed), *Goals, goal structures, and patterns of adaptive learning* (pp. 175–204). Mahwah, NJ: Erlbaum.

Fryer, R., & Torelli, P. (2005). *An empirical analysis of "acting White"* (Working Paper No. 11334). Cambridge, MA: National Bureau of Economic Research.

Fuligni, A. J., Witkow, M., & Garcia, C. (2005). Ethnic identity and the academic adjustment of adolescents from Mexican, Chinese, and European backgrounds. *Developmental Psychology, 41,* 799–811.

Gonzales, P. M., Blanton, H., & Williams, K. J. (2002). The effects of stereotype threat and double-minority status on the test performance of Latino women. *Personality and Social Psychology Bulletin, 28,* 659–670.

Good, C., Aronson, J., & Inzlicht, M. (2003). Improving adolescents' standardized test performance: An intervention to reduce the effects of stereotype threat. *Journal of Applied Developmental Psychology, 24*(6), 645–662.

Goodenow, C. (1993). Classroom belonging among early adolescent students: Relationships to motivation and achievement. *Journal of Early Adolescence, 13,* 21–43.

Graham, S. (1984). Teacher feelings and student thoughts: An atttributional approach to affect in the classroom. *Elementary School Journal, 85,* 91–104.

Graham, S. (1994). Motivation in African Americans. *Review of Educational Research, 64,* 55–117.

Graham, S., & Hudley, C. (2005). Race and ethnicity in the study of motivation and competence. In A. J. Elliot & C. S. Dweck (Eds.), *Handbook of competence and motivation* (pp. 392–413). New York: Guilford.

Graham, S., & Taylor, A. Z. (2002). Ethnicity, gender, and the development of achievement values. In A. Wigfield & J. Eccles (Eds.), *Development of achievement motivation* (pp. 121–146). San Diego, CA: Academic Press.

Graham, S., Taylor, A. Z., & Hudley, C. (1998a). Exploring achievement values among ethnic minority early adolescents. *Journal of Educational Psychology, 90,* 606–620.

Graham, S., Taylor, A. Z., & Hudley, C. (1998b). Exploring achievement values among ethnic minority early adolescents. *Journal of Educational Psychology, 90,* 606–620.

Gresky, D. M., Ten Eyck, L. L., Lord, Charles, G., & McIntyre, R. B. (2005). Effects of salient multiple identites on women's performance under mathematics stereotype threat. *Sex Roles, 53,* 703–716.

Harrison, L. A., Stevens, C. M., Monty, A. N., & Coakley, C. A. (2006). The consequences of stereotype threat on the academic performance of White and non-White lower income college students. *Social Psychology of Education, 9,* 341–357.

Hidi, S. (2000). An interest researcher's perspective: The effects of extrinsic and intrinsic factors on motivation. In C. Sansone & J. M. Harackiewicz (Eds.), *Intrinsic and extrinsic Motivation: The search for optimal motivation and performance* (pp. 309–339). San Diego: Academic Press.

Hudley, C. (1997). Supporting achievement beliefs among ethnic minority adolescents: Two case examples. *Journal of Research on Adolescence, 7,* 133–152.

Hudley, C., & Graham, S. (2001). Stereotypes of achievement striving among early adolescents. *Social Psychology of Education, 5*(2), 201–224.

Irving, M. A., & Hudley, C. (2005). Cultural mistrust: Academic outcome expectations, and outcomes values among African-American adolescent men. *Urban Education, 40,* 476–496.

Jahnke, S. & Murdock, T.B. (2002). *Achievement norms among African-American students in a college preparatory high school program.* Paper completed in partial fulfillment of the requirement for the doctoral degree in Counseling Psychology, University of Missouri-Kansas City.

Juvonen, J., & Murdock, T. B. (1993). How to promote social approval: Effects of audience and achievement outcome on publicly communicated attributions. *Journal of Educational Psychology, 85,* 365–376.

Juvonen, J., & Murdock, T. B. (1995). Grade-level differences in the social value of effort: Implications for self-presentation tactics of early adolescents. *Child Development, 87* 1694–1705.

Kao, G. (1995). Asian Americans as model minorities?: A look at their academic performance. *American Journal of Education, 103,* 121–159.

Kao, G. (2000). Group images and possible selves among adolescents: Linking stereotypes to expectations by race and ethnicity. *Sociological Forum, 15,* 407–431.

Lee, S. J. (1994). Behind the model-minority stereotype: Voices of high- and low-achieving Asian American students. *Anthropology and Education Quarterly, 25,* 413–429.

Lee, S. J. (2006). Additional complexities: Social class, ethnicity, generation, and gender in Asian American student experiences. *Race Ethnicity and Education, 9,* 17–28.

Lee, S. J. (2002). Learning "America": Among American high school students. *Education and Urban Society 34*(2), 233–246.

Lee, V. E., & Bryk, A. S. (1998a). Curriculum tracking as mediating the social distribution of high school achievement. *Sociology of Education, 61,* 78–94.

Lee, V. E., & Bryk, A. S. (1998b). A multilevel model of the social distribution of high school achievement. *Sociology of Education, 62,* 172–192.

LoCasale-Crouch, J., Konold, T., Pianta, R., Howes, C. Burchinal, M., Bryant, D., et al. (2007). Observed classroom quality profiles in state-funded pre-kindergarten programs and associations with teacher, program, and classroom characteristics. *Early Childhood Research Quarterly, 22,* 3–17.

Madon, S., Jussim, L., Keiper, S., Eccles, J., Smith, A., & Palumbo, P. (1998). The accuracy and power of sex, social class, and ethnic stereotypes: A naturalistic study in person perception. *Personality and Social Psychology Bulletin, 24,* 1304–1318.

Major, B., Spencer, S., Schmader, T., Wolfe, C., & Crocker, J. (1998). Coping with negative stereotypes about intellectual performance: The role of psychological disengagement. *Personality of Social Psychology Bulletin, 24*(1), 34–50.

Markus, H., & Nurius, P. (1986). Possible selves. *American Psychologist, 41*(9), 954–969.

Martens, A., Johns, M., Greenberg, J., & Schimel, J. (2006). Combating stereotype threat: The effect of self-affirmation on women's intellectual performance. *Journal of Experimental Social Psychology, 42,* 236–243.

Matute-Bianchi, M. (1986). Ethnic identities and patterns of school success and failure among Mexican-descent and Japanese American students in a California high school: An ethnographic analysis. *American Journal of Education, 95,* 233–255.

McCaslin, M. (2004). Co-regulation of opportunity, activity, and identity in student motivation: Elaborations on Vygotskian themes. In S. M. McInerney & S. Van Etten (Eds.), *Big theories revisited: Research on sociocultural influences on motivation and learning* (Vol. 4, pp. 249–274). Greenwich, CT: Information Age.

McCaslin, M. (in press). Co-regulation of student motivation and emergent identity. *Educational Psychologist*

McGlone, M. S., & Aronson, J. (2006). Stereotype threat, identity salience, and spatial reasoning. *Journal of Applied Developmental Psychology, 27,* 486–493.

McInerney, S. M. &Van Etten, S. (Eds.). (2004). *Big theories revisited: Research on sociocultural influences on motivation and learning.* Greenwich, CT: Information Age.

McIntyre, R. B., Paulson, R. M., & Lord, C. G. (2003). Alleviating women's mathematics stereotype threat through salience of group achievements. *Journal of Experimental Social Psychology, 30*(1), 83–90.

McKay, P. F., Doverspike, D., Bowen-Hilton, D., & Martin, Q. D. (2002). Stereotype threat effects on the Raven Advanced Progressive Matrices scores of African-Americans. *Journal of Applied Social Psychology*, 32, 767–787.

McKown, C., & Weinstein, R. S. (2002). Modeling the role of child ethnicity and gender in children's differential response to teacher expectations. *Journal of Applied Social Psychology, 32*, 159–184.

McKown, C., & Weinstein, R. S. (2003). The development and consequences of stereotype consciousness in middle childhood. *Child Development, 7*, 498–515.

Mickelson, R. A. (1990). The attitude-achievement paradox among Black adolescents. *Sociology of Education, 63*, 44–61.

Morgan, S. L., & Mehta, J. D. (2004). Beyond the laboratory: Evaluating the survey evidence for the disidentification explanation of black-white differences in achievement. *Sociology of Education, 77*, 82–101.

Murdock, T. B. (1999). The social context of risk: Status and motivational predictors of alienation in middle school. *Journal of Educational Psychology, 91*, 62–75.

Murdock, T. B. (2000). Incorporating economic context into educational psychology: Methodological and conceptual challenges. *Educational Psychologist*, 35, 113–124.

Murdock, T. B., & Miller, A. (2003). Teachers as sources of middle school students' motivational identity: Variable-centered and person-centered analytic approaches. *Elementary School Journal* 103, 383–399.

Murdock, T. B., & Miller, A. D. (2002). *Evaluation of University Academy*. Kansas City.

Murdock, T. B., Anderman, L. H., & Hodge, S. A. (2000). Middle-grade predictors of students' motivation and behavior in high school. *Journal of Adolescent Research, 15*, 327–351.

Muzzatti, B., & Agnoli, F. (2007). Gender and mathematics: Attitudes and stereotype threat susceptibility in Italian children. *Developmental Psychology, 43*, 747–759.

National Center for Education Statistics, Common Core Data. (n.d.). Dropout rates in the United States: 2004. Documents NCES-2007-024. Retrieved from http://nces.ed.gov/ccd/pub_dropouts.asp

National Center for Education Statistics, National Assesment of Educations Progress Data Explorer. (n.d.). Retrieved June 7, from http://nces.ed.gov/nationsreportcard/nde/criteria.as

Ngo, B. (2006). Learning from the margins: The education of Southeast and South Asian Americans in context. *Race, Ethnicity and Education, 9*, 51–65.

O'Connor, C. (1999). Race, class and gender in America: Narratives of opportunity among low-income African-American youths. *Sociology of Education, 72*, 137–157.

Ogbu, J. U. (1978). *Minority education and caste: the American system in cross-cultural perspective*. New York: Academic Press.

Ogbu, J. U. (2003). *Black students in an affluent suburb: A study of academic disengagement*. Mahwah, NJ: Erlbaum.

Osborne, J. W. (1995). Academic, self-esteem, and race: A look at the underlying assumptions of the disidentification hypothesis. *Personality and Social Psychology Bulletin, 21*, 441–455.

Osborne, J. W. (1997). Race and academic disidentification. *Journal of Educational Psychology, 89*, 728–735.

Oswald, D. L., & Harvey, R. D. (2001). Hostile environments, stereotype threat, and math performance among undergraduate women. *Current Psychology: Developmental, Learning, Personality, Social, 19*, 338–356.

Oyserman, D., Bybee, D., & Terry, K. (2006). Possible selves and academic outcomes: How and when possible selves impel action. *Journal of Personality and Social Psychology, 91*, 188–204.

Oyserman, D., Gant, L., & Ager, J. (1995). A socially contextualized model of African American identity: Possible selves and school persistence. *Journal of Personality and Social Psychology, 69*, 1216–1232.

Oyserman, D., Harrison, K., & Bybee, D. (2001). Can racial identity be promotive of academic efficacy? *International Journal of Behavioral Development, 25*, 379–385.

Oyserman, D., Kemmelmeier, M., Fryberg, S., Brosh, H., & Hart-Johnson, T. (2003). Racial-ethnic self-schemas. *Social Psychology Quarterly, 66*(4), 333–347.

Oyserman, D., Terry, K., & Bybee, D. (2002). A possible selves intervention to enhance school involvement. *Journal of Adolescence, 25*, 313–326.

Parham, T. A., & Helms, J. E. (1985). Relation of racial identity attitudes to self-actualization and affective states of black students. *Journal of Counseling Psychology, 32*(2), 431–440.

Phelan, P., Yu, H. C., & Davidson, A. L. (1994). Navigating the psychosocial pressures of adolescence: The voices and experiences of high school youth. *American Educational Research Journal, 31*(2), 415–447.

Phinney, J. (1990). Ethnic identity in adolescents and adults: A review of research. *Psychologcial Bulletin, 108*, 498–514.

Pianta, R. C., la Paro, K. M., Payne, C., Cox, M. J., Bradley, R. (2002). The Relation of kindergarten classroom environment to teacher, family, and school characteristics and child outcomes. *The Elementary School Journal, 102*, 225–238.

Pintrich, P. (2000). Multiple goals, multiple pathways: The role of goal orientation in learning and achievement. *Journal of Educational Psychology, 92*(3), 544–555.

Pintrich, P. R., & Schunk, D. H. (2002). *Motivation in education: Theory, research and application*. Upper Saddle River: Merrill Prentice Hall.

Pintrich, P., & Schunk, D. (1996). *Motivation in education: theory, research, and applications*. Englewood Cliffs, NJ: Prentice Hall.

Renninger, K. A. (2000). Individual interest and its implications for understanding intrinsic motivation. In C. Sansone

& J. M. Harackiewicz (Eds.), *Intrinsic and extrinsic motivation: The search for optimal motivation and performance* (pp. 373–404). San Diego: Academic Press.

Rosenthal, H. E. S., & Crisp, R. J. (2006). Reducing stereotype threat by blurring intergroup boundaries. *Personality and Social Psychology Bulletin, 32*(4), 501–511.

Rosenthal, R., & Jacobson, L. (1968). *Pygmalion in the classroom: Teacher expectation and pupils' intellectual development.* New York: Holt, Rinehart, and Winston.

Ryan, K. E., & Ryan, A. M. (2005). Psychological processes underlying stereotype threat and standardized math test performance. *Educational Psychologist, 40*, 53–63.

Ryan, R. M. (1993). Agency and organization: Intrinsic motivation, autonomy, and the self in psychological development. In J. Jacobs (Ed.), *Nebraska symposium on motivation, 1990* (Vol. 40, pp. 1–56). Lincoln: University of Nebraska Press.

Saft, E. W., & Pianta, R. C. (2001). Teachers' perceptions of their relationships with student: Effects of child age, gender, and ethnicity of teachers and children. *School Psychology.*

Saunders, J., Davis, L., Williams, T., & Williams, J. H. (2004). Gender differences in self-perceptions and academic outcomes: A study of African American high school students. *Journal of Youth and Adolescence, 33*, 81–90.

Schmader, T. (2002). Gender identification moderates stereotype threat effects on women's math performance. *Journal of Experimental Social Psychology, 38*, 194–201.

Schmader, T., & Johns, M. (2003). Converging evidence that stereotype threat reduces working memory capacity. *Journal of Personality and Social Psychology, 85*, 440–452.

Schmader, T., Major, B., & Gramzow, R. H. (2001). Coping with ethnic stereotypes in the academic domain: Perceived injustice and psychological disengagement. *Journal of Social Issues, 57*, 93–111.

Sellers, R. M., Chavous, T. M., & Cooke, D. Y. (1998). Racial ideology and racial centrality as predictor's of African American college student's academic performance. *Journal of Black Psychology, 24*, 8–27.

Sellers, R. M., & Shelton, J. N. (2003). The role of racial identity in perceived racial discrimination. *Journal of personality and social psychology, 84*(5), 1079–1092.

Shih, M., Pittinsky, T. L., & Ambady, N. (1999). Stereotype susceptibility: Identity salience and shifts in quantitative performance. *Psychological Science, 10*, 80–83.

Smith, J. L. (2004). Understanding the process of stereotype threat: A review of mediational variables and new performance goal directions. *Educational Psychology Review, 16*, 177–206.

Smith, J. L., Sansone, C., & White, P. H. (2007). The stereotyped task engagement process: The role of interest and achievement motivation. *Journal of Educational Psychology, 99*, 99–114.

Sorge, C., Newsom, H. E., & Hagerty, J. J. (2000). Fun is not enough: Attitudes of Hispanic middle school students toward science and scientists. *Hispanic Journal of Behavioral Sciences 22*, 322–345.

Spencer, M. B., Noll, E., Stoltzfus, J., & Harpalani, V. (2001). Identity and school adjustment: Revisiting the "action white" assumption. *Educational Psychologist, 36*(1), 21–30.

Spencer, S. J., Steele, C. M., & Quinn, D. M. (1999). Stereotype threat and women's math performance. *Journal of Experimental Social Psychology, 35*, 4–28.

Steele, C. M. (1997). A threat in the air: How stereotypes shape intellectual identity and performance. *American Psychologist, 52*, 613–629.

Steele, C. M., & Aronson, J. (1995). Stereotype threat and the intellectual performance of African Americans. *Journal of Personality and Social Psychology, 69*, 797–811.

Steinberg, L., Dornbusch, S. M., & Brown, B. B. (1992). Ethnic differences in adolescent achievement: An ecological perspective. *American Psychologist, 47*, 723–729.

Taylor, A. Z., & Graham, S. (2007). An examination of the relationship between achievement values and perceptions of barriers among low-SES African American and Latino Students. *Journal of Educational Psychology, 99*, 52–64.

Taylor, R. D., Casten, R., Flickinger, S. M., Roberts, D., et al. (1994). Explaining the school performance of African-American adolescents. *Journal of Research on Adolescence, 4*, 21–44.

Tenenbaum, H. R., & Ruck, M., D. (2007). Are teachers' expectations different for racial minority than for European-American students? A meta analysis. *Journal of Educational Psychology, 99*, 253–273.

Thomas, D. E., Townsend, T. G., & Belgrave, F. Z. (2003). The influence of cultural and racial identification on the psychological adjustment of inner-city African American children in school. *American Journal of Community Psychology, 32*, 217–228.

Tyson, K., Darity Jr., W., & Castellino, D. R. (2005). It's not "a Black thing": Understanding the burden of acting White and other dilemmas of high achievement. *American Sociological Review, 70*, 582–605.

Weiner, B. (1986). *An attributional theory of motivation and emotion.* New York: Springer-Verlag.

Weiner, B. (1990). History of motivational research in education. *Journal of Educational Psychology, 82*, 616–622.

Weiner, B. (2005). Motivation from an attributional perspective and the social psychology of perceived competence. In A. J. Elliot & C. S. Dweck (Eds.), *Handbook of competence and motivation* (pp. 73–84). New York: Guilford.

Weis, L., & Fine, M. (1993). *Beyond silenced voices: Class, race, and gender in United States schools.* Albany, NY: State University of New York Press.

Wentzel, K. R. (1998). Social relationships and motivation in middle school: The role of parents, teachers, and peers. *Journal of Educational Psychology, 90*, 202–209.

Wheeler, S. C., & Petty, R. E. (2001). The effects of stereotype activation on behavior: A review of possible mechanisms. *Psychological Bulletin 127*, 797–826.

Wigfield, A. & Eccles, J. (Eds.) (2002). Development of achievement motivation. San Diego: Academic Press.

Wigfield, A., Eccles, J. S., Schiefele, U., Roeser, R. W., & Davis-Keene, P. (2005). Development of achievement motivation. In W. Damon & N. Eisenberg (Eds.), *Handbook of child psychology* (Vol 3, pp. 933–1002). New York: Wiley.

Witherspoon, K. M., Speight, S. L., & Thomas, A. J. (1997). Racial identity attitudes, school achievement, and academic self-efficacy among African American high school students. *Journal of Black Psychology, 23*, 344–357.

Wong, C. A., Eccles, J. S., & Sameroff, A. (2003). The influence of ethnic discrimination and ethnic identification on African American adolescents' school and socio-emotional adjustment. *Journal of Personality and Social Psychology, 71*, 1197–1232.

Yowell, C. (1999). The role of the future in meeting the challenge of Latino school dropouts. *Educational Foundations, 13*, 5–28.

Zusho, A., Pintrich, P. S., & Cortina, K. S. (2004). Motives, goals, and adaptive patterns of performance in Asian American and Anglo American students. *Learning and Individual Differences, 15*(2), 141–158.

21

Commentary: The Role of Environment in Contextual and Social Influences on Motivation
Generalities, Specificities, and Causality

Adele Eskeles Gottfried

In considering the context within which academic motivation is embedded, the role of environment is primary in discerning the variables that either moderate or mediate motivation. A pertinent aspect of understanding the role of context concerns determining the contributions of distal and proximal environment that impact academic motivation. Across the 20th century, studies of environment have investigated both distal and proximal variables with an increasingly large emphasis on the proximal environment to determine the specific experiences that directly impinge on the child (A.W. Gottfried, 1984; Hunt, 1961; Skodak, 1939; Van Alstyne, 1929; Wachs & Gruen, 1982; Walberg & Marjoribanks, 1976). Distal environmental variables (also referred to as macroenvironmental) comprise background factors such as socioeconomic status (SES), maternal employment status, gender, race, and the like, whereas proximal variables (also referred to as microenvironmental) provide an analysis of the specific environmental processes that directly impinge on the child (Bradley, 2002; A. E. Gottfried, Gottfried, & Bathurst, 1988; A. W. Gottfried, 1984; A. W. Gottfried, & Gottfried, 1984; A. W. Gottfried, Gottfried, Bathurst, & Guerin, 1994; Wachs, 1991). Whereas distal variables may be related to children's development in reliable ways, they, by themselves, do not comprise the specific environmental processes to which children are exposed. Rather, the proximal environment provides information as to the cognitive, social-emotional, family, peer, and physical environment impinging on children. Research in developmental and educational psychology has proliferated to explore and investigate the influence of proximal environment on children's development and academic outcomes (e.g., Bronfenbrenner, 1979; A. E. Gottfried, 2008b; A. E. Gottfried, Fleming, Gottfried, 1994, 1998; A. W. Gottfried, 1984; Hunt, 1971; Kellaghan, Sloane, Alvarez, & Bloom, 1993; Wachs, 1992).

The chapters in this section on Contextual and Social Influences on Motivation continue this rich tradition of considering the role of environmental variables when focusing on academic motivation, and relate such factors to aspects of the distal (macro) and proximal (micro) environment. The roles of different socialization agents, such as parents, peers, teachers, and a range of other educators are incorporated in determining the pathways between distal and proximal variables. Collectively, the chapters contribute to understanding academic motivation as conveyed through differing levels of distal environment including ecology, organizational structures, culture, gender, and race, for example. The chapters also broaden our knowledge concerning the role of specific environmental processes (i.e., proximal) within these contexts that impinge on the child as conveyed by socialization agents as well as characteristics of the classroom.

Adding to this complexity, academic motivation theories and research have also proliferated from early conceptions considering achievement motivation as a need, to contemporary perspectives comprising a myriad of specific theories, approaches, and influences. Each chapter adds to deepening our understanding of the evolution of theory and research through discussions of the history of academic motivation, reviews of contemporary research concerning the specifics of environmental context from childhood through adolescence; demographic factors such as socioeconomic status, race and gender; and social development as integral to the development of academic motivation.

In reflecting on these chapters, one is struck by the proliferation of research which provides a great wealth of knowledge concerning specific conditions and variables affecting the manner of and degree to which academic motivation plays a role in student competency. We can agree that we can never go back to a conception of academic motivation without due consideration of these specificities. On the other hand, detailing specific, and sometimes causal, relations between context and academic motivation raises the issue as to whether there continues to exist any generalities regarding academic motivation and relations to academic competency. Without such general principles, theory development and research are limited.

In this chapter, I focus on the role of both distal and proximal environments in elucidating the ways in which varying contexts influence academic motivation. I consider both the generalities and specificities across constructs and findings and implications for establishing causality. My discussion integrates across the chapters, and, as requested, incorporates perspectives on academic motivation which have emanated from my own research to frame and elaborate on the issues. I conclude with the concept of motivational school culture as an overall explanatory construct.

I began my research program on academic intrinsic motivation by considering the balance between generality and specificity. As I pondered how best to assess this construct, there was a burgeoning literature on intrinsic motivation in education (Berlyne, 1965, 1971; Deci, 1975; Harter, 1981; Lepper, 1983; White, 1959). At the time, whereas some of the literature had addressed dimensions of intrinsic motivation (e.g., perceptual, internal vs. external influences, self-determination, challenge orientation), none had considered whether there would be a distinction in intrinsic motivation across different subject areas. With regard to academic intrinsic motivation, defined as enjoyment of school learning characterized by an orientation toward mastery; curiosity; persistence; task-endogeny; and the learning of challenging, difficult, and novel tasks (A. E. Gottfried, 1985), I deemed that subject area specificity was important to address. Individual students' experiences and successes would be expected to vary according to subject areas, and further, such specificity would be expected to relate to academic performance differentially depending on the subject area of the outcome. Stronger relations were predicted within corresponding compared to noncorresponding subject areas (A. E. Gottfried, 1985). Hence, I set out to develop a method for studying academic intrinsic motivation that distinguished between major subject areas in school, including reading, math, social studies and science (A. E. Gottfried, 1985). Nevertheless,

I wasn't willing to completely give up on the possibility that there is also a general orientation for academic intrinsic motivation that emerges from a student's overall school experience not specific to subject area, and I therefore included a "school in general" subscale in addition to the subject area subscales. To measure academic intrinsic motivation both as a construct differentiated into specific subject areas and for school in general, I developed the Children's Academic Intrinsic Motivation Inventory (CAIMI; A. E. Gottfried, 1985, 1986) as no such instrument existed. This instrument has also become integral to my research program as well as being used nationally and internationally and translated into several languages.

My research program has provided evidence of the roles of distal and proximal environments in academic intrinsic motivation, and has also obtained data indicating generalities, specificities, and causality. This research has been conducted both in schools and as part of the Fullerton Longitudinal Study, a contemporary study of development from infancy through adulthood (e.g., A. E. Gottfried, 1985; A. E. Gottfried, Fleming, & Gottfried, 2001; A. W. Gottfried, Gottfried, & Guerin, 2006). The following provide examples of the findings.

Subject area differentiation has been validated by findings showing that academic intrinsic motivation yields higher relations within corresponding subject areas, rather than across noncorresponding subject areas, with academic achievement, perceptions of competence, and academic anxiety (A. E. Gottfried, 1985, 1990). Findings have also supported the general orientation in academic intrinsic motivation to account for overall school experience not defined by subject area, or related to outcome criteria that are not subject area specific (e.g., A. E. Gottfried, Gottfried, Morris, & Cook, 2008; A. W. Gottfried, Gottfried, Cook, & Morris, 2005).

In addition to subject area specificity, this research program has included examination of the generalizability and specificity of academic intrinsic motivation. Findings indicating generalities include positive relations between academic intrinsic motivation and performance contemporaneously and across age; an increase in motivational stability with advancing development from childhood through adolescence; and developmental declines in academic intrinsic motivation from childhood through late adolescence (A. E. Gottfried, 1985, 1990; A. E. Gottfried et al., 2001; A. E. Gottfried, Marcoulides, Gottfried, Oliver, & Guerin, 2007; Marcoulides, Gottfried, Gottfried, & Oliver, 2008). These findings have been corroborated in the research literature as well.

A propos contextual specificity, the following results have been obtained in this research. For example, parental task-intrinsic and task-extrinsic motivational practices were investigated to determine their impact on children's academic intrinsic motivation (A. E. Gottfried, Fleming, & Gottfried, 1994). Task-intrinsic practices, such as "I encourage my child to enjoy school learning," were found to be facilitative; whereas task-extrinsic practices, such as, "When my child does well at school, I usually reward him/her with money," were found to be adverse with regard to the development of children's academic intrinsic motivation (A. E. Gottfried et al., 1994). In another study, the proximal environment comprising cognitive home stimulation (e.g., provision of educational and intellectual activities such as lessons, political and social discussions, and visits to libraries and museums), was found to positively impact academic intrinsic motivation beyond SES, a distal variable, across time (A. E. Gottfried, Fleming, & Gottfried, 1998). This supported the view that specific environmental processes influence intrinsic motivation beyond distal variables.

Regarding group differences, children evidencing consistently high or low academic intrinsic motivation, were designated as motivationally gifted and at-risk, respectively (A. E. Gottfried et al., 2008; A. W. Gottfried et al., 2005; Marcoulides et al., 2008). Motivationally gifted and at-risk children were found to be exposed to different parental motivation practices. The motivationally gifted were exposed to more task-intrinsic practices, whereas the motivationally at-risk were exposed to more task-extrinsic practices (A. E. Gottfried & Gottfried, 2008) suggesting that parents' use of such practices may influence their children's development of academic intrinsic motivation. Additionally, since motivationally gifted and at-risk children also evidence consistently different histories of academic performance and competence across childhood through adulthood favoring the motivationally gifted (A. E. Gottfried et al., 2008; A. W. Gottfried et al., 2005), the influence of parental motivational practice is essential to determine. This research therefore shows that considering motivation in its extremes provides another aspect of context to consider.

In sum, aspects of context that I have studied within this research program include distinguishing between distal (e.g., socioeconomic status) and proximal (e.g., provision of cognitive stimulation) environments as influences on academic intrinsic motivation, and discerning generalities, specificities, and causality across these findings. These dimensions provide the framework with which I address these chapters concerning context and social influences on motivation.

Generalities emerging across the chapters included a focus on endogenous aspects of academic motivation emphasizing mastery orientation, self-competence, self-determination, self-efficacy, task-endogeny and intrinsic rather than extrinsic motivation; the role of student perceptions as mediators of the associations between context and motivation; and the associations between organizational aspects of schools and how they relate to processes driving motivation. Specificities concern the roles and impact of different socialization agents both within and outside of the school setting on children's academic motivation; role of specific group membership (e.g., gender, race, culture, SES) and the socialization experiences, perceptions, and opportunities that are associated with such membership; and the broader societal culture, and school organization, and their roles in moderating and mediating the impact of context on children's academic motivation. Each chapter is considered regarding its contribution to informing these generalities and specificities, albeit some chapters emphasize more of one or the other. The research comprising this section of the handbook also delineates distal and proximal environment as contributing to the impact of context, and generalities and specificities may occur with regard to both aspects of environment. Further, the chapters directly and indirectly raise the issue of causal relations between context and academic motivation. Examples from each are provided as pertinent.

Grolnick, Friendly, and Bellas provide an overview of research regarding parental involvement in children's academic progress, and relate parenting processes to three motivational theories: self-determination, expectancy-value, and goal orientation. Findings across these three orientations, and across different research groups and methods, converge on a number of generalizations. First, positive parental supportiveness is facilitative of children's academic competency, albeit this finding is interpreted differently through the lens of each of these three motivational orientations. With regard to self-determination theory, parental supportiveness is interpreted as providing autonomy support. With regard to expectancy-value theory, positive parental influences are viewed as facilitating children's perceptions of their future successes in various domains, as well as placing different values (e.g., instrumental vs. intrinsic) on certain tasks. Parental beliefs about student motivation and success, teaching strategies, expectations of their children's success, and the degree to which they themselves emphasize and value the importance of such activities for their children are seen as playing a role in children's development of motivation for academic competency. Regarding goal-orientation theory, parents' encouragement of mastery rather than performance goals, through specific behaviors such as responsiveness and sensitivity to requests for help, and authoritativeness, would encourage mastery goals in children. The authors themselves identify certain convergences across these theoretical orientations, such as involvement, warmth, autonomy support, and the translation of parental beliefs into practice.

Many of these parental processes are viewed as mediated through children's own cognitions, perceptions, and values.

The authors also discuss areas of specificity that may serve to both moderate and mediate parental inputs to children. Regarding moderation, if parents' culture and socioeconomic background provide values and practices that differ from those cited above, then parental involvement with children and their schooling may differ in both kind and amount. For example, not all cultural groups value autonomy support as pointed out in their chapter, and instead may focus on more collectivistic values rather than on individual achievement. Other specificities concern the role of socioeconomic status of parents and their access to the educational system; parents' gender stereotypes that determine the kinds of experiences to which children are exposed; parental emphases on specific academic domains such as math for boys and English/language arts for girls; teacher and school encouragement of parental involvement; parental stress; and the role of child characteristics. Such factors may serve to alter the degree of supportiveness parents provide to their children, the types of role models and values to which children are exposed, and the processes that mediate between parental and child characteristics on the one hand and child motivation and academic competence on the other.

Wentzel's chapter focuses on teacher-student relationships and their role in student academic motivation and competency. The chapter begins with a generality that cuts across theoretical perspectives, that the affective nature of teacher-student relationships motivates student adjustment, and this issue is framed within attachment, self-determination, and social support theories. Processes that emerge from these theories are applied to teacher-student relationships in the classroom. For example, with regard to attachment theory, the constructs of secure and insecure attachment, and sensitive responsiveness of the parent to the child, are applied to representing teacher-pupil relationship processes in the classroom. With regard to self-determination theory, core processes of the need for relatedness, competence, and autonomy are applied to teachers being emotionally supportive and actively interested in the well-being and accomplishments of their students. Social support theories advance the views that teachers are an emotional resource in the classroom by providing emotional support to buffer students from stress and anxiety.

Interestingly, these three theories converge on similar constructs inasmuch as all of them rely on conceptions of teacher emotional support that serves to enhance students' attachment security, curiosity, intrinsic motivation, school engagement, emotional security in the classroom, and reduction of stress. These processes are seen to begin with the teacher and transmitted to the student, with the result that students are more emotionally secure and, hence, able to be engaged, motivated, and competent. Teachers are viewed as socialization agents who create the contexts in which students may be more or less motivated and engaged. Hence, a causal direction is invoked, which Wentzel clearly points out at the beginning of the chapter. Wentzel reviews much research that supports these constructs and processes of teacher supportiveness as related to students' positive school motivation, engagement, adjustment, and performance. These findings generalize across age from preschool through adolescence.

A number of specific relationships appear in this literature. Wentzel cites evidence regarding the impact of continuity between teacher-student and parent-child contexts on children's school functioning. The impact of teacher-student relationships may depend on how positive the child's relationships are with both teachers and parents. When parent-child relationships are less positive than the child's relationship with the teacher, the child's relationship with the teacher has a greater impact. Perhaps the teacher's relationship with the child compensates for a less positive relationship with the parent, and when parent-child relationships are more positive, the teachers' emotional supportiveness play a less important role. This example of specificity is important because it emphasizes that the different contexts in which the child is embedded may simultaneously influence the child. The child's relationship with other domains of the classroom context, such as the peer group, may provide another arena that impacts the child's relationship with the teacher.

Throughout the chapter, Wentzel indicates the complexity of influences on the teacher-pupil relationship. Specificity of processes also emerges from the methodologies used to assess teacher-student relationships, as well as gender and ethnic differences. An interesting aspect of specificity concerns the difference in middle school students' views of supportive teachers which were related to their ability. Students in high ability tracks valued teachers who challenged and stimulated them, whereas students in low ability tracks valued teachers who treated them with kindness, were fair, explained clearly, and maintained control. Hence, students' values and perceptions of what is a supportive teacher are likely to differ depending on their ability, which might be proxies for motivational variables such as goal orientations, expectancies of success, and intrinsic motivation, these would be expected to be stronger in the high achieving group. Overall, this complex literature conveys that more positive teacher-student relationships are associated with more academically engaged and motivated students. However, there are many specific factors that can be expected to influence the security of that relationship, as well as their expected causal effects.

Jussim, Robustelli, and Cain's chapter also concerns teachers' classroom processes. They begin with an overview of the initial research on teacher expectations in the classroom conducted by Rosenthal and Jacobson (1968). Teacher expectations are defined as those that develop from erroneous information which cause teachers to treat students differently resulting in students' reacting in accord with this falsely developed expectation, or self-fulfilling prophecies. Whereas Jussim et al. point out the limits of teacher expectation effects, their review nevertheless shows that teacher expectation effects do exist. Hence, the substantiation of teacher expectation effects, and self-fulfilling prophecies, form a generalization and foundation on which to frame research issues to delineate specificities regarding this effect.

The authors provide conceptual analyses and review empirical data showing limitations of the robustness of teacher expectation effects. For example, they consider the longevity of teacher expectation effects. The evidence reviewed indicates that the impact of teacher expectations is not permanent and appears to dissipate over the child's school years. With academic advancement, perhaps the child's exposure to other peers, teachers, and different histories of success, alter the role of the initial teacher expectation. In view of Wentzel's chapter, teacher-student relationships in subsequent years could diminish the teacher-expectation effect, especially if the relationship is warm and emotionally supportive.

A particularly intriguing finding discussed is the tendency for teacher expectation effects to be larger when children are new to a situation, or are making a school transition, such as entry into first grade and middle school. These trends raise a number of intriguing possibilities regarding the specific role of context. The authors suggest that when students enter new situations, they are more susceptible to teacher expectations. Could it be that teachers' lack of direct knowledge about children new to a school contributes to the development of erroneously based expectations, perhaps based on pre-existing beliefs? The authors also explore other contextual conditions such as being a member of a stigmatized group, or being a student of low socioeconomic status, that may increase such students' vulnerability to the impact of teacher expectations.

Jussim et al. explore the role of motivation as mediating between teacher expectations and child outcome. They discuss possible classroom and school interventions to raise expectations, and provide a case study of a high school which employs procedures designed to raise the expectations of students. They conclude that high teacher expectations are likely to have more positive effects on low achieving and stigmatized students. Finally, whereas causal directions are assumed to proceed from teacher expectation to student, research is needed to verify and delineate the processes.

Ladd, Herald-Brown, and Kochel's chapter contributes to understanding the extant nature of research on the role of peer relationships in children's school engagement. This chapter provides hypotheses regarding specificities of peer relationships and their roles in facilitating or impeding students' school engagement or competency. The many findings cited by the authors provide a potential generalization about peer acceptance being positively associated with processes that are likely to augment students' school competence and engagement, whereas peer rejection is associated with more adverse outcomes. The potential roles of variables that might be associated with these overall relationships are complex and examples comprise peer relationships that facilitate or impede access to classroom resources, inclusion in cooperative peer groups, mental health, and self-esteem. It is through such processes that the impact of peer acceptance on child outcomes is hypothesized to operate, and the authors remind us throughout the chapter that such pathways remain to be elucidated.

Determining such specificities will augment our general conception of how various components of the classroom and school context combine and interact. In this regard, Ladd et al. identify several possible specific paths of influence between peer relationships on the one hand and student engagement or motivation, on the other. Salient constructs in these possible pathways include peer acceptance vs. rejection, development of classroom friendships, and peer aggression and victimization. They hypothesize about several linkages between processes that may account for the relationship between peer relations and student competence and engagement. For example, peer rejection may result in students' negative school attitudes and self-beliefs, and these in turn could affect school engagement and achievement. The reasons for the onset of peer rejection, the timing and length of such rejection, and the role of parents and teachers in being able to moderate or mediate such rejection may also play a role in this complex interweave of processes.

The chapters by Meece and Glienke regarding gender, and by Murdock on race and ethnicity, show convergences in a number of ways. Both chapters identify cultural stereotypes affecting the experiences of children differing in race, ethnicity, and gender, and both also address possible interactions between race and gender that may affect academic motivation. Both chapters also indicate that negative stereotypes have adverse effects on various aspects of motivation such as causal attributions, expectations, persistence, values, and perceptions of competency, and discuss how stereotypes adversely impact academic motivation. Subject area specificity plays a particular role with regard to gender, in that encouragement is often gender biased, with boys receiving more opportunity, exposure, positive expectations, and encouragement in math, science, and technology related areas, whereas girls receive these positive emphases in the language arts and the arts.

Supporting the points raised across both chapters, and providing an illustration of gender-culture relationships in each, are the results of a recent study addressing the role of gender equality on math and reading gender gaps in achievement cross-nationally (Guiso, Monte, Sapienza, & Zingales, 2008), which expands the role of context to the societal and international level. Using a World Economic Forum Gender Gap Index to assess the degree women's well-being, economic and political opportunities, and education, findings indicated that the gender gap in math, which favors boys, disappears in countries higher in gender equality whereas the math gender gap favoring boys remains in countries with less gender equality. Interestingly, across all countries, a gender gap in reading favoring girls also increased in countries with greater gender equality. It was shown that the gender gap in math is eliminated in more gender-equal societies, whereas the gender gap in reading, which favors girls, increases in gender-equal countries. These authors concluded that within more gender equal countries, girls become better in both math and reading. Hence, the gender gap in math is eliminated, but the gender gap in reading favoring girls increases.

This study is particularly pertinent to the Meece and Glienke, and Murdock, chapters, and interesting because it emphasizes the point that cultural context on a societal level plays a role in achievement patterns across diverse groups. It might be speculated that all achievement gaps between different demographic groups are due to both distal processes in which social values are structured at the societal level, and which are transmitted to students by parents, teachers, and peers through the opportunities and experiences in the proximal environment. The resulting academic motivation can be considered to have been shaped by all levels of context. This explanation relates well to Bronfenbrenner's (1979) ecological model in which proximal environment is transmitted to the child in the microsystem through higher order and more distal levels of culture and society, i.e., the macrosystem, exosystem, and mesosystem. Such an explanation emphasizes the importance of distal and proximal environments.

Across the theories that Meece and Glienke review, it is interesting to note generality with regard to the processes described. For example, expectancy-value, self-efficacy, and goal orientation theories all examine motivational processes that result in achievement related choices, persistence, engagement, and performance. All three theories also discuss the important role of socialization agents, self-judgments and perceptions, and efficacy beliefs, and all three tend toward emphasizing the importance of inherent task values, self-efficacy, and mastery orientations. Hence, there are many important linkages between these theories that would explain gender differences with reference to the impact of role models, exposure, encouragement, and cognitive and self-evaluative processes. Specific findings are cited as well. For example, the degree of developmental declines in competency perceptions vary by gender according to subject area with greater achievement gaps in gender-typed areas occurring in earlier years rather than high school. These intriguing developmental findings may relate to the concept of gender equality in society (Guiso et al., 2008). Could these differences in developmental trends be related to more general societal changes toward gender equality that happen to coincide with children's development? This intriguing hypothesis would need data to elucidate whether these differences in developmental change are due to the impact of social values, school experience, achievement history, or interactions of all.

The theme of parental provision of sex-typed activities and experiences is also raised as an influence on gender and motivation, bringing continuity across chapters by linking it to the themes of Grolnick et al.'s chapter. Meece and Glienke point out that links between parental beliefs and expectations may affect career choice in gendered ways as well and also discuss teachers' roles in perpetuating gender differences in students. Finally, the authors caution that more data is needed as to how gender differences might be affected by culture, SES, and race.

Murdock's chapter relates constructs emerging from social psychological studies of race with theories of motivation, and by so doing provides a nuanced integration of important issues pertinent to the intersection and overlaps, as well as distinctions, in these domains. Murdock first discusses the differential emphases in cultural stereotypes pertaining to groups including African Americans, Hispanic Americans, and Asian Americans. Not only are such stereotypes known to children and adolescents, but they are often the foundation for development of teacher expectations which may be influential for children's motivation and achievement outcomes, with more positive stereotypes applying to Asian Americans and more negative stereotypes to African Americans and Hispanic Americans. This discussion provides continuity with Jussim et al.'s chapter on teacher expectations inasmuch as they both discuss the likelihood that teacher expectations have greater impact on more vulnerable students. Murdock also discusses stereotype threat and its links to achievement through motivation including such processes as anxiety, performance expectations, and cognitive load; and devaluation of schooling, and disidentification with school, as a student's protection of self-worth in the context of environments that are discriminatory and adverse. Hence, one would expect that devaluation of schooling, and disidentification, serve to disengage the student from academic performance. However, as Murdock points out, data do not usually show a complete absence of academic engagement in stigmatized students, and, hence, complex relationships exist between devaluation, motivational processes, and academic engagement.

Another issue discussed in this chapter pertains to teacher respect and inclusion of students as valuable members of the school community, emphasizing teacher-student relationships and student perceptions. This ties well with Wentzel's chapter in which it was found that students' academic motivation is more positive when they perceive their teachers as being emotionally supportive of them. Hence, these contextual specificities play an important role in refining motivational constructs to account for the proximal environmental variables teachers convey. In addition, economic status plays a role in student values as pointed out in a study in which African American students of lower and higher SES had more doubts about the value of education than higher, but not lower, SES European American students. Specificities of ethnic identity and possible selves are further discussed as being influenced by societal background and also having a mediating role on motivation and achievement.

The chapter by Roeser, Urdan, and Stephens is considered last because it provides a structure that relates to many themes presented in the other chapters. The Basic Levels of School Contexts model that the authors propose is consistent with a conceptualization of distal and proximal environmental variables and also includes developmental change. The figure depicting the descriptive embedded contexts model presents the outer layers of concentric circles as comprising broader family and community characteristics. This can be aligned with the macrosystem presented in Bronfenbrenner's model, and also can include the distal variables, such as SES, race, ethnicity, and gender, that provide a broader environmental context that eventually is experienced by the child in the proximal environment. The inner layers concern features of schools that proceed from distal to proximal from the district level, through the school, down to the academic programs, involvement of teachers and students, and finally to the environment that ultimately impinges on the child within the classroom itself and also considering the impact of subject areas. The authors present a time line at the bottom of the figure. Many of the themes and findings presented in the chapters in this section can be represented in some portion of the model.

The depiction of the prescriptive motivational model of school presents three aspects of school context (school academic and behavioral structure, school authority structure, and school social climate), their relationships to characteristics of tasks, goal structures and teacher expectations, and teacher availability, which ultimately relates to aspects of achievement motivation (perceived competence, valuing of school, and emotional well-being). Again, the movement of environmental influences in this model is from distal to proximal, with school context influences ultimately relating more specifically to school and classroom processes and motivational outcomes. Finally, the depiction of school effects identifies how hierarchical models may be able to tease out the role of school factors from student characteristics leading to motivational mediating processes and educational outcomes, as nested under school effects. Throughout the chapter, the authors flesh out various aspects of their models in referring to theory and research which vary in their placement depending on whether they are more distal or more proximal. They discuss a wide array of topics including school, student, curriculum, and organizational school contexts and culture, and developmental and motivational processes primarily with regard to achievement goal theory. This chapter provides a conceptualization which aids in organizing various contexts in their influence on students' motivation and academic performance.

The issue of causality deserves special attention as the chapters converge on the conclusion that whereas much data have been collected showing relations between contexts and motivation, a great deal more needs to be done to establish directionality and causal links. In many of the chapters, bidirectional hypotheses are offered, and mediating processes are speculated upon, but virtually all of the authors acknowledge the difficulty of establishing causality, and the need for longitudinal and multivariate studies that would permit this.

Across chapters, the authors caution us not to misinterpret correlational findings as causal. For example, it is appealing to assume causality proceeds from parent to child, from teacher to student, from peer to peer, and logic might lead us to conclude that these variables are causal. However, determining the possibilities of transactions between variables, multiplicity of influences, and identifying uniqueness of variables is essential. Timing of influence and developmental trajectories may also play a role. And so, each chapter has provided an important piece to the puzzle of suggesting paths of influence by reviewing pertinent literature, suggesting hypotheses, delineating possible causal pathways, and by also showing us how far we still need to go. It is laudatory for these chapters to have covered this much ground and also forged new hypotheses.

Longitudinal studies are considered to be the best alternative for assessing causal influences (Card, Little, & Bovaird, 2007). Multivariate modeling methods are recommended for analyses (Card et al., 2007; Raykov & Marcoulides, 2006), and to study the role of context on development in longitudinal studies (Little, Bovaird, & Card, 2007). As an example, in a study using longitudinal multivariate latent change modeling (e.g., A. E. Gottfried et al., 2007), we investigated the dual developmental declines of intrinsic math motivation and math achievement from ages 9 through 17. We found that both motivation and achievement were significant contributors to these dual developmental declines; directly in the case of the contribution of achievement to these developmental declines, whereas motivation contributed to the declines indirectly through its relationship with achievement. We concluded that poorer initial levels of math achievement place the child at-risk for long-term declines in both intrinsic math motivation and achievement. Therefore, the role of early achievement on both contemporaneous and subsequent intrinsic math motivation and achievement may be examined with regard to developing causal hypotheses.

In their overview on academic motivation, Wigfield, Eccles, Schiefele, Roeser, & Davis-Kean (2006) noted the need to employ multivariate methods emphasizing processes related to developmental change going beyond the documentation of mean level, or normative, decline. This suggestion is in harmony with our research program investigating developmental pathways contributing to developmental decline in academic intrinsic motivation beyond the documentation of normative decline itself (e.g., A. E. Gottfried et al., 2007; A. E. Gottfried, Marcoulides, Gottfried, & Oliver, in press).

Additonally, Wentzel (2008) urged that research be framed to elucidate the mechanisms and underlying psychological processes linking social contexts with academic motivation and competence. She recommended incorporating longitudinal experimental research to plan social reform.

The mandate for future research on the contexts of academic motivation is clear. There is a need to continue to discern relations between distal and proximal environmental processes as to their direct and indirect impact on academic motivation within longitudinal research. This may be accomplished within nonexperimental and experimental research using statistical modeling techniques to discern plausible causal pathways. Integration of findings across different studies, research groups, and methods is essential to determine robustness of findings and for developing hypotheses for testing causality.

Conclusion: Motivational School Culture

Motivational school culture has been a construct conceptualized as pertaining to individual differences between group members regarding their perceptions of the motivational academic environment (Maehr & Fyans, 1989). In their recent volume focusing on academic motivation and the culture of school, Hudley and Gottfried (A. E. Gottfried, 2008a; Hudley, 2008; Hudley & Gottfried, 2008) put forth a conceptualization of motivational school culture going beyond the normative organizational settings in which students are embedded to examining the contributions of students' specific experiences and perceptions which shape each individual's motivational school culture. Motivational school culture is viewed as emanating from an interplay of factors including students' competencies, their self views, their conceptions of society's views of them, and the matches or mismatches between student characteristics, perceptions and the school context including the roles of teachers, peers, and parents. Hudley (2008) and Gottfried (2008a) concluded that motivational culture of the school does not comprise a uniform set of norms, values, and expected behaviors, but rather is unique as related to the specific perceptions resulting from complex interplays of factors. Motivational school culture is also seen as playing a potentially causal role in the academic competence of diverse students.

The chapters on context in this section of the handbook fit well with Hudley and Gottfried's view of motivational school culture, and as such may provide an overall explanatory construct regarding the associations between contexts and academic motivation. This conception of motivational school culture helps to expand our knowledge base and theories to propose increasingly nuanced theories of academic motivation while also examining the degree of generalizeability and robustness within and across theories. By showing generalities across contexts, and also delineating limits of theories by showing divergences and specific relations, theory and research will be advanced. The research challenge is to incorporate both the generalities and specificities into more refined theories.

This section on contexts and social influences clearly shows the important and needed direction of the contemporary research focus in academic motivation, which has been predominantly on delineating specificities. It is important to now judge the integrity of the original theories that spawned this trend. How might these theories be modified given the moderators and mediators of specific contexts, and what refinements to existing and potentially new theories are now needed? The chapters herein contribute to advancement of knowledge about academic motivation, and to helping to determine what modifications to the theories, as well as new theories, are needed, including how they should be investigated.

Finally, this knowledge base must inform educational practice. Several chapters discussed educational and intervention programs. In order to develop intervention programs that enhance all students' academic motivation and competency, a scientific base that includes generalities, specificities, and causality, and incorporates an understanding of contextual and social influences, must be incorporated into and made available to education professionals (e.g., Gottfried, 2008a;

Hudley, 2008). These chapters provide important directions in this regard as they contribute to understanding the roles of context and social influences in academic motivation on the general and specific levels, with regard to distal and proximal environment, the need to investigate causality, and to planning motivationally driven educational programs and interventions.

References

Berlyne, D. E. (1965). Curiosity and education. In J. D. Krumboltz (Ed.), *Learning and the educational process* (pp. 67–89). Chicago: Rand McNally.

Berlyne, D. E. (1971). What next? Concluding summary. In H. I. Day, D. E. Berlyne, & D. E. Hunt (Eds.), *Intrinsic motivation: A new direction in education* (pp. 186–196). Toronto: Holt, Rinehart & Winston of Canada.

Bradley, R. H. (2002). Environment and parenting. In M. H. Bornstein (Ed.), *Handbook of parenting, Vol. 2, 2nd ed.* (pp. 281–314). Mahwah, NJ: Erlbaum.

Bronfenbrenner, U. (1979). *The ecology of human development.* Cambridge, MA: Harvard University Press.

Card, N. A., Little, T. D., & Bovaird, J. A. (2007). Modeling ecological and contextual effects in longitudinal studies of human development In T. D. Little, J. A. Bovaird,& N. A. Card (Eds.), *Modeling contextual effects in longitudinal studies* (pp. 1–11). Mahwah, NJ: Erlbaum.

Deci, E. L. (1975). *Intrinsic motivation.* New York: Plenum.

Gottfried, A. E. (1985). Academic intrinsic motivation in elementary and junior high school students. *Journal of Educational Psychology, 77,* 631–635.

Gottfried, A. E. (1986). *Children's Academic Intrinsic Motivation Inventory.* Lutz, FL: Psychological Assessment Resources.

Gottfried, A. E. (1990). Academic intrinsic motivation in young elementary school children. *Journal of Educational Psychology, 82,* 525–538.

Gottfried, A. E. (2008a). Academic motivation and the culture of schooling: Integration of findings. In C. Hudley & A. E. Gottfried (Eds.), *Academic motivation and the culture of school in childhood and adolescence* (pp. 286–296). New York: Oxford University Press.

Gottfried, A. E. (2008b). Home environment and academic intrinsic motivation. In N. Salkind (Ed.), *Encyclopedia of educational psychology, Vol. 1* (pp. 485–490). Thousand Oaks, CA: Sage.

Gottfried, A. E., Fleming, J. S., & Gottfried, A. W. (1994). Role of parental motivational practices in children's academic intrinsic motivation and achievement. *Journal of Educational Psychology, 86,* 104–113.

Gottfried, A. E., Fleming, J. S., & Gottfried, A. W. (1998). Role of cognitively stimulating home environment in children's academic intrinsic motivation: A longitudinal study. *Child Development, 69,* 1448–1460.

Gottfried, A. E., Fleming, J. S., & Gottfried, A. W. (2001). Continuity of academic intrinsic motivation from childhood through late adolescence: A longitudinal study. *Journal of Educational Psychology, 93,* 3–13.

Gottfried, A. E., & Gottfried, A. W. (2008, March). *Parental motivational strategies differ for motivationally gifted and at-risk children: A longitudinal study.* Paper presented at the annual meeting of the American Educational Research Association, New York.

Gottfried, A. E., Gottfried, A. W., & Bathurst, K. (1988). Maternal employment, family environment, and children's development: Infancy through the school years. In A. E. Gottfried & A. W. Gottfried (Eds.), *Maternal employment and children's development: Longitudinal research* (pp. 11–58). New York: Plenum.

Gottfried, A. E., Gottfried, A. W., Morris, P., & Cook, C. (2008). Low academic intrinsic motivation as a risk factor for adverse educational outcomes: A longitudinal study from early childhood through early adulthood. In C. Hudley & A. E. Gottfried (Eds.), *Academic motivation and the culture of school in childhood and adolescence* (pp. 36–69). New York: Oxford University Press.

Gottfried, A. E., Marcoulides, G. A., Gottfried, A. W., Oliver, P., & Guerin, D. (2007). Multivariate latent change modeling of developmental decline in academic intrinsic math motivation and achievement: Childhood through adolescence. *International Journal of Behavioral Development, 31,* 317–327.

Gottfried, A. E., Marcoulides, G. A., Gottfried, A. W., & Oliver, P. H. (in press). A latent curve model of parental motivational practices and developmental decline in math and science academic intrinsic motivation. *Journal of Educational Psychology.*

Gottfried, A. W. (Ed.). (1984). *Home environment and early cognitive development: Longitudinal research.* New York: Academic Press.

Gottfried, A. W., & Gottfried, A. E. (1984). Home environment and cognitive development in young children of middle-socioeconomic-status families. In A. W. Gottfried (Ed.), *Home environment and early cognitive development: Longitudinal research* (pp. 57–115). New York: Academic Press.

Gottfried, A. W., Gottfried, A. E., Bathurst, K., & Guerin, D. (1994). *Gifted IQ: Early developmental aspects.* New York: Plenum.

Gottfried, A. W., Gottfried, A. E., Cook, C. R., & Morris, P. E. (2005). Educational characteristics of adolescents with gifted academic intrinsic motivation: A longitudinal study from school entry through early adulthood. *Gifted Child Quarterly, 49,* 172–186.

Gottfried, A. W., Gottfried, A. E., & Guerin, D. W. (2006). The Fullerton Longitudinal Study: A long-term investigation of intellectual and motivational giftedness. *Journal for the Education of the Gifted, 29,* 430–450.

Guiso, L., Monte, F., Sapienza, P., & Zingales, L. (2008). Culture, gender, and math. *Science, 320,* 1164–1165.

Harter, S. (1981). A model of mastery motivation in children: Individual differences and developmental change. In W. A. Collins (Ed.), *Aspects of the development of competence* (pp. 215–255). Hillsdale, NJ: Erlbaum.

Hudley, C. (2008). Academic motivation and the culture of school: Thematic integration. In C. Hudley & A. E. Gottfried (Eds.), *Academic motivation and the culture of school in childhood and adolescence* (pp. 277–285). New York: Oxford University Press.

Hudley, C., & Gottfried, A. E. (Eds.). (2008). *Academic motivation and the culture of school in childhood and adolescence.* New York: Oxford Uinversity Press.

Hunt, J. McV. (1961). *Intelligence and experience.* New York: The Ronald Press Company.

Hunt, J. McV. (1971). Intrinsic motivation and psychological development. In H. M. Schroder & P. Suedfeld (Eds.), *Personality theory and information processing* (pp. 131–177). New York: The Ronald Press Company.

Kellaghan, T., Sloane, K., Alvarez, B., & Bloom, B. S. (1993). *The home environment and school learning: Promoting parental involvement in the education of children.* San Francisco: Jossey-Bass.

Lepper, M. R., (1983). Extrinsic and intrinsic reward: Implications for the classroom. In J. M. Levine & M. C. Wang (Eds.), *Teacher and student perceptions: Implications for learning* (pp. 281–317). Hillsdale, NJ: Erlbaum.

Little, T. D., Bovaird, J. A., & Card, N. A. (Eds.). (2007). Modeling contextual effects in longitudinal studies. Mahwah, NJ: Erlbaum.

Maehr, M. L., & Fyans, L. J., Jr. (1989). School culture, motivation, and achievement. In M. L. Maehr & C. Ames (Eds.), *Advances in motivation and achievement: A research annual. Vol. 6.* (pp. 215–247), Greenwich, CT: JAI.

Marcoulides, G. A., Gottfried, A. E., Gottfried, A. W., Oliver, P. (in press). Latent transition analysis of academic intrinsic motivation from childhood through adolescence. *Educational Research and Evaluation: An International Journal on Theory and Practice.*

Raykov, T., & Marcoulides, G. A. (2006). *A first course in structural equation modeling, 2nd ed.* Mahwah, NJ: Erlbaum.

Rosenthal, R., & Jacobson, L. (1968). *Pygmalion in the classroom: Teacher expectations and student intellectual development.* New York: Holt.

Skodak, M. (1939). Children in foster homes: A study of mental development. Iowa: University of Iowa City.

Van Alstyne, D. (1929). *The environment of three-year-old children: Factors related to intelligence and vocabulary tests.* New York: Columbia University, Bureau of Publications.

Wachs, T. D. (1991). Environmental considerations in studies with nonextreme groups. In T. D. Wachs & R. Plomin (Eds.), *Conceptualization and measurement of organism-environment interaction* (pp. 44–67). Washington, DC: American Psychological Association.

Wachs, T. D. (1992). *The nature of nurture.* Newbury Park, CA: Sage.

Wachs, T. D., & Gruen, G. E. (1982). *Early experience and human development.* New York: Plenum.

Walberg, H. J., & Marjoribanks, K. (1976). Family environment and cognitive development: Twelve analytic models. *Review of Educational Research, 46,* 527–551.

Wentzel, K. R. (2008). Social competence, sociocultural contexts, and school success. In C. Hudley & A. E. Gottfried (Eds.), *Academic motivation and the culture of School in childhood and adolescence* (pp. 297–310). New York: Oxford University Press.

White, R. W. (1959). Motivation reconsidered: The concept of competence. *Psychological Review, 66,* 297–333.

Wigfield, A., Eccles, J. S., Schiefele, U., Roeser, R. W., & Davis-Kean, P. (2006). Development of achievement motivation. In Eisenberg, N. (Ed.), *Handbook of Child Psychology: Vol. 3. Social, Emotional, and Personality Development* (6th ed., pp. 933–1002). New York: Wiley.

Section III
Teaching, Learning, and Motivation

22
Beliefs About Learning in Academic Domains

Michelle M. Buehl and Patricia A. Alexander

Beliefs matter. This statement seems so simple, so basic. However, beliefs are such an intricate part of who we are and what we do that they often go overlooked and unexamined. This is unfortunate. The influence and power of beliefs should neither be underestimated nor ignored. Indeed, medical doctors and researchers recognize the power of the placebo effect and the patient *believing* a treatment may work. Wars are fought; boundaries and alliances are formed, based in part on religious and ideological beliefs. But as educational researchers and practitioners, we do not need to look outside the classroom or the school to see the power of beliefs at work.

One of the outcomes of the cognitive revolution within psychology and education has been greater attention on understanding individuals' beliefs, as well as how those beliefs relate to human learning and development. For instance, various belief constructs have been explored and discussed in empirical research and in reviews of the literature, including self-efficacy beliefs (e.g., Bandura, 1997; Pajares, 2003), beliefs about ability (e.g., Dweck, 2002), and beliefs about knowledge and knowing (i.e., epistemic beliefs; Hofer & Pintrich, 1997). This corpus highlights the connection between teachers' and students' beliefs and academic behaviors and serves as a reminder that there can be strong resistance to belief change, even in the face of compelling evidence (e.g., Chinn & Brewer, 1993; Chinn & Malhotra, 2002). Here, we examine beliefs about learning in academic domains and discuss these beliefs in relation to motivation in school.

Motivation is generally defined as desire to act or move toward a particular activity or task (e.g., Pintrich, 2000a; Weiner, 1992). However, as evidenced by the chapters in this volume, motivation is multifaceted and manifested in a variety of constructs including self-efficacy and competency beliefs, task value and interest, self-determination, and goal orientations. Additionally, motivation can be viewed as movement toward any goal. Within the school context academic performance and achievement goals are particularly salient and have been the primary focus of study. However, individuals may also possess other goals (e.g., social goals; Ford, 1992; Wentzel, 2000) that direct and energize their behavior in school. Thus, we use the term *motivation in school* to refer to the various motivational constructs that may be at work in educational settings. Further, because schools are complex social settings the include students as well as teachers, we view motivation in schools as including the motivations of both students and teachers.

The relation of beliefs about learning in academic domains to motivation in school deserves consideration for several reasons. First, beliefs are at the core of the current motivation literature. That is, instead of focusing on inner drives or extrinsic reinforcement, many current motivation theories focus on individuals' beliefs (e.g., self-efficacy beliefs). These motivation beliefs and beliefs about learning co-exist in an interconnected network or system of beliefs and, as we will discuss, interact and influence each other in various ways that need to be recognized and taken into consideration.

Second, teachers and students possess fundamental beliefs about the very nature of academic domains (e.g., "What is science?"). Such ontological beliefs shape conceptions about what is necessary to perform well in that domain (i.e., task analysis) and form the basis for the evaluations individuals make of themselves and others. For instance, students make judgments about their capabilities to perform well in a domain (i.e., academic self-beliefs), while teachers form conceptions about what it would take to guide the learning of others within that domain (i.e., sense of teaching efficacy beliefs). Certainly, individuals' judgments about their likelihood of successfully performing a specific domain task or mastering a body of domain content would seem predicated, in part, on what they believe the domain to be, as well as what knowledge they consider central to that domain.

Third, whether they are aware of it or not, students and teachers possess broad conceptions of what constitutes knowledge and what it means to know academically (e.g., Perry, 1970; Schommer, 1990, 2004). Generic epistemic beliefs take on a particular character when they are framed in terms of academic domains (e.g., science or history) or domain-specific tasks (e.g., conducting an experiment or resolving conflicting historical accounts) and can influence prevailing notions as to what it means to be a "good" student (Sternberg, 2003). Moreover, epistemic beliefs can trigger judgments about strategic processing needed to master domain topics or tasks (e.g., Kardash & Howell, 2000; Schommer, Crouse, & Rhodes, 1992).

In this chapter, we briefly discuss what constitutes an academic domain and define beliefs. We then provide a model of how beliefs about learning in academic domains may promote or hinder students' academic development and motivation in schools. This model is discussed in light of two domains (i.e., science and history/social studies). Our purpose here is not to provide an exhaustive review of beliefs related to academic domains but to offer an overview of the beliefs that have been investigated and their potential connections to motivation in school. Finally, we briefly discuss methodological issues and implications for the study and domain beliefs and motivation in school.

Academic Domains: What Are They and Why Do They Matter?

Humans exhibit the tendency to divide up and organize their world. Academic domains are one mechanism by which that organization is achieved. Although domains are contemporary educational structures, throughout history (e.g., Durant, 1954–1975) educational researchers and theorists have debated whether they exist in nature or are merely human contrivances devised by societies (Bereiter, 1994; VanSledright, 2002a). Whether real or contrived, domains are prevalent features of educational institutions and exert significant influence on those who populate those institutions.

Internationally, education is organized around specific subjects or academic domains representing bodies of knowledge acquired over time and through formal training (Alexander, 2006). Mathematics, science, history or social studies, reading, and writing serve as examples. In turn, bodies of relevant knowledge are organized around core concepts and principles recognized by domain experts and around common procedures or rituals that mark one as a member of the community of practice (e.g., Matthews, 1994; Stahl, Hynd, Glynn, & Carr, 1996). Beyond these similarities, academic domains can be differentiated by the modes of encryption used to represent ideas (e.g., numbers or letters), the typical tasks undertaken, the underlying processes in which individuals engage, and pedagogical practices used to apprentice others into that domain. Indeed, many teachers hold strong views about the nature of academic domains and organize their instruction accordingly (Graham, 2006; Pressley, 2006). Nor are students immune to the influence of academic domains. Even young elementary students talk about school in terms of academic domains and judge themselves and their peers accordingly (Buehl & Alexander, 2000; Wigfield & Eccles, 2002).

Despite the potency and ubiquity of domains, they have not consistently been the focus of empirical study (Shulman & Quinlan, 1996). For instance, interest in domains at the turn of the 20th century (e.g., Dewey, 1897/1972; Judd, 1915) waned as psychologists sought to identify general principles of learning and development. Recently, there has been a movement away from such grand theories and a greater appreciation for the contextualized nature of learning, motivation, and teaching (e.g., Alexander & Winne, 2006; Pintrich, 2000b). Yet, just as Shulman and Quilan (1996) noted, "any discourse on learning and teaching of mathematics must first attend to the nature of mathematics itself" (p. 413), discussion of specific domains must attend not only to the nature of domains but also to individuals' *beliefs* about knowledge and the process of knowing within those domains.

What Do We Mean by Beliefs?

How beliefs are defined and distinguished from other constructs (e.g., knowledge or opinions) is a thorny issue (e.g., Pajares, 1992). For example, considerable theoretical debate and discussion as well as empirical studies have addressed the relations between beliefs and knowledge (e.g., Nespor, 1987; Nisbett & Ross, 1980; Rokeach, 1968). Although there is some conceptual overlap, there are also distinctions between these constructs (e.g., Alexander & Dochy, 1995). For instance, both refer to individuals' thoughts and ideas. However, knowledge is often viewed as having a "truth" dimension in that it can be externally verified or confirmed. This is in line with the more formal philosophical definition of knowledge as justified true belief. Beliefs, in contrast, are more subjective claims that the individual accepts as true but which may not be verified or confirmed by others (Nespor, 1987) and may persist even when confronted with conflicting evidence (Murphy & Mason, 2006).

For our purposes, we view beliefs as "psychologically held understandings, premises, and propositions about the world that are felt to be true" (Richardson, 1996, p. 103). Even though beliefs may not be internally consistent, individuals still view them as important and meaningful enough to act upon (e.g., Murphy & Mason, 2006). Further, while beliefs, attitudes, and opinions have an affective component, beliefs represent what one holds true *about* an issue, whereas attitudes and opinions are more indicative of whether one is *for* or *against* that particular issue.

Beliefs in Relation to Schooling and Academic Development

Given our general definition of beliefs, there are several points about beliefs in academic contexts to highlight before we consider them in relation to motivation in school. As noted, beliefs are related to individuals' thoughts, intentions, and behaviors and can be quite resistant to change. Additionally, beliefs can be defined and assessed with varying levels of specificity (e.g., Limón, 2006). For instance, one could address beliefs about knowledge and knowing *in general*, as Schommer-Aikins (e.g., 1990) and others (e.g., Baxter Magolda, 1992; Schraw, Bendixen, & Dunkle, 2002) have done. However, a finer grained analysis of beliefs is provided by studying beliefs at domain-specific (e.g., Buehl, Alexander, & Murphy, 2002; Muis, Bendixen, & Haerle, 2006) and topic specific levels (e.g., Estes, Chandler, Horvath, & Backus, 2003; Hammer, & Elby, 2002). For the purpose of this chapter, we focus discussion primarily at the level of the domain, but also draw from relevant findings based on domain-general beliefs.

As a case in point, considerable discussion and research has focused on the development of individuals' general beliefs about knowledge and knowing over time (e.g., Baxter Magolda, 1992; Cano, 2005; Perry, 1970). For instance, King and Kitchener's (1994, 2004) Reflective Judgment Model depicts a developmental progression in individuals' views of knowledge and their conceptions of justification and argumentation. In the proposed stages, individuals progress from believing that knowledge is certain and that there is a correct answer that can be verified by an authority (i.e., pre-reflective thinking) to recognizing the uncertainty and construction of knowledge but questioning the basis for judging the validity of a claim or perspective (i.e., quasi-reflective thinking) to finally understanding that knowledge is uncertain and constructed and that it is possible to evaluate the competing positions with reasoned judgment of the evidence and context (i.e., reflective thinking).

Such general models of belief development are a reminder that individuals may possess general patterns of thinking, which may be related to their level of cognitive development (Perry, 1970), and that such beliefs may constrain or contribute to individuals' beliefs about learning in specific academic domains (e.g., Buehl & Alexander, 2006). Further, individuals' beliefs about knowledge and learning in specific academic domains may also undergo developmental changes. Depending on the domain, students' educational exposures may be naturally broad and integrated or, conversely, highly specified or particularized. Shifts in the breadth and organization of domain content over the course of schooling, combined with the changing structures of schools and classroom themselves, are likely mirrored in the beliefs that students hold about those domains.

Additionally, beliefs about academic domains may be implicitly conveyed or formed such that individuals may not be fully aware of their beliefs nor possess the language to communicate them to others. Moreover, beliefs about academic domains are reflective of individuals' perspectives and may not be reflective of how any domain is viewed or conceptualized by experts in the field. For instance, research has documented how domain experts and students may conceptualize academic domains differently (e.g., Sandoval, 2005; VanSledright, 2002a) and how naïve misconceptions may impede students' progress within a domain. Thus, we consider the spectrum of beliefs that individuals may hold about learning in academic domains (i.e., expert and naïve perspectives).

Academic learning typically occurs within classrooms and involves various interactions between and among teachers and students. In reviewing research related to beliefs about learning in academic domains, we felt it was important to consider not just student beliefs but also teacher beliefs. Specifically, students are influenced by their teachers and the beliefs expressed by teachers may be indicative of the types of beliefs that students come to hold. Also, much of teacher education is structured around domains and associated pedagogical practices. Issues of domain ontology and domain epistemology are thus intertwined with teacher development (e.g., Calderhead, 1996; Richardson, 1996).

We identified numerous investigations examining the beliefs of teachers and students. Some studies focused directly on individuals' beliefs (e.g., "What do students or teachers believe about _____?"), whereas others examined how ontological or epistemic beliefs were related to other constructs or outcome variables (e.g., instructional practices, strategy use). Still other studies investigated belief change, or lack thereof, and the conditions that might account for the modifiability or immutability of those beliefs.

We not only attempted to unearth the trends in beliefs across academic content but also to speculate on the processes by which such beliefs are co-constructed and related to motivation in school. Toward that end, we developed the organizational model presented in Figure 22.1 based on the research in educational psychology and teacher education (e.g., Murphy & Mason, 2006; Woolfolk-Hoy, Davis, & Pape, 2006; Richardson, 1996). This model situates academic learning in the classroom environment and encompasses teachers' and their students' beliefs. Teachers' beliefs about knowledge and knowing are depicted as influencing their instructional practices. Those instructional practices, in turn, affect students' perceptions of domains and the beliefs about self (e.g., self-efficacy beliefs and competency beliefs), which then play a role in the students' goals, interests and values, feelings of self-determination, and, ultimately, their learning.

The model also recognizes the role of forces outside of the immediate classroom. For instance, the professional preparation of teachers, as well as their prior experiences, knowledge, and beliefs influence subsequent beliefs about knowledge and knowing in academic domains. Of course, teachers' enactments in the classroom are not simply the product of their ontological and epistemic beliefs, but are also determined by other factors such as organizational resources and constraints (e.g., time or school administration), state or national standards and assessment practices, and school curricula. Similarly, students' beliefs are not solely based on the practices of *one* teacher but are informed by all collective experiences in and out of school. These forces are depicted in Figure 22.1 as being on the periphery of the classroom context but affecting, either directly or indirectly, the learning environment and those who populate that environment.

In the model, we shaded the boxes that represent teachers' and students' beliefs and included bidirectional arrows between beliefs and other components. The shading is meant to signify how teachers' and students' experiences are filtered through their pre-existing beliefs. In effect, teachers' and students' beliefs are not only the product of their prior experiences but also determinants of how individuals perceive and learn in new situations (Murphy & Mason, 2006; Woolfolk-Hoy et al., 2006). The bidirectional arrows thus depict the continuous and reciprocal relations between individuals' beliefs, experiences, and motivations.

Domain-Specific Beliefs about Knowledge and Learning in Relation to Motivation

Empirical works addressing how teacher and student domain beliefs are related to motivation in school are limited. Additionally, much of the research is correlational, making it difficult, if not impossible, to draw strong conclusions about the direction of the relations between ontological and epistemic beliefs and specific motivation constructs. Thus, additional research is needed to more fully understand *how* and *why* beliefs about knowledge and knowing are related to individuals' motivation in school. As that research takes shape, it will be important to consider the specific character of domains as they are experienced during formal education and to ascertain

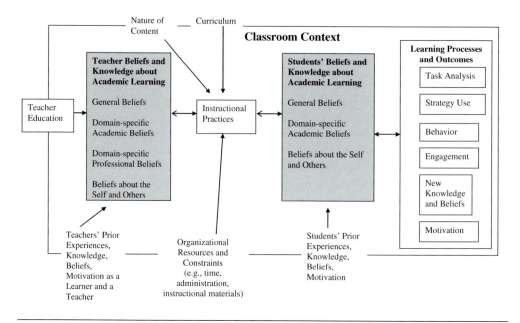

Figure 22.1 Relations among beliefs in academic contexts.

how the nature of domains and the knowledge and processes associated with them influence motivation in school.

As depicted in Figure 22.1, teachers' and students' beliefs and motivation in school exist in an interconnected system. We propose that there are several avenues by which beliefs about academic domains and motivation are related. For instance, beliefs about academic domains may serve as a source of information up on which motivation beliefs are based. Additionally, beliefs about domains as well as motivation beliefs may together motivate teachers and students toward or away from specific instructional practices or courses of action. Further, as discussed in the conceptual change and persuasion literatures, motivation is an important component to belief change. That is, individuals must be motivated to alter and modify their current beliefs and willing to invest persistent effort in order for modification to occur.. Thus, motivation may be a prerequisite for beliefs about academic domains to undergo major shifts and minor modifications. Finally, we cannot overlook the possibility that some domain beliefs and aspects of motivation may be correlated but not causally related.

Academic Domain Beliefs as a Source of Information for Motivation Beliefs

The perceptions that individuals hold about what it means "to know," "to do," or "to learn" a specific domain are likely to contribute to various aspects of individuals' motivation in school. Here we explicate some of the potential linkages between academic domain beliefs and self-efficacy and competency beliefs, value and interest, self-determination, and goal orientations. This is by no means meant to be exhaustive, merely those that we see as particularly salient and or supported by previous research.

Self-Efficacy and Competency Beliefs Beliefs about the nature of the domain (i.e., ontological beliefs) as well as the nature of knowledge (i.e., epistemic beliefs) and learning within that domain may be used as a standard for forming beliefs about one's capability to succeed in the domain in general or at a specific task. That is, analyzing the task at hand and understanding its demands are important to the formation of self-efficacy and competency beliefs (e.g., Eccles et al., 1983; Tschannen-Moran & Woolfolk-Hoy, 2001; Wigfield & Eccles, 2000). Thus, when individuals make judgments about their self-efficacy and competency beliefs, they may compare their capabilities to their beliefs about what the domain involves.

These proposed relations are supported by the empirical research conducted to date. Across several studies, self-efficacy and competency beliefs were significantly related to beliefs about: (a) the isolation and simplicity of knowledge (Hofer, 1999; Paulsen & Feldman, 1999a); (b) the personal construction of knowledge (Bråten & Strømsø, 2005; Buehl, 2003); (c) the certainty of knowledge (Bråten & Strømsø, 2005; Buehl, 2003); (d) the speed of learning or the effort required to learn (Neber & Schommer-Aikins, 2002; Schommer-Aikens, Duell, & Hutter, 2005); and (e) fixed ability (Paulsen & Feldman, 1999a). Also, knowledge and learning beliefs typically viewed as more constructivist (i.e., knowledge is complex, interrelated, uncertain, and constructed; learning occurs gradually over time with effort) were related to higher levels of self-efficacy and competency beliefs. An exception to this trend was a study by Buehl (2003) in which beliefs about the certainty of knowledge were positively related to competency beliefs (i.e., the more knowledge was viewed as static and unchanging, the more confident students felt in their ability to succeed in history and mathematics). We suspect this finding may reflect assessment practices as well as students feeling more confident when they can "know the facts."

Value and Interest Individuals' valuing and interest in a specific academic domain are also likely predicated on their beliefs about the domain. In our view, beliefs about the isolation or integration of knowledge within the domain and across other domains may be particularly salient in that individuals may place greater value on domains in which the knowledge is viewed as more connected and integrated with other aspects of their lives. Moreover, beliefs about the certainty of knowledge may also play into whether individuals value learning the content associated with a particular domain. That is, if individuals believe that domain knowledge will soon change or if they view all perspectives as equally valid (i.e., a more multiplist stance; D. Kuhn, 1990), they may not value the domain or be interested in learning material (e.g., "why bother, it will soon change anyway").

Additionally, beliefs about the source of knowledge may contribute to the value and interest individuals have for specific classroom activities. Specifically, teachers and students who view the textbook as the source of knowledge may not value or see a need for class discussion or the development of reasoning skills. Instead, teachers may choose to take a more didactic approach and students may prefer to learn from a textbook or from a lecture in with which the teacher (i.e., a source of authority) tells them what they need to know.

Research examining knowledge beliefs in relation to value and interest support these proposed links. For example, task value and interest were significantly related to beliefs about: (a) the isolation and simplicity of knowledge (Hofer, 1999; Paulsen & Feldman, 1999a); (b) the personal construction of knowledge (Bråten & Strømsø, 2005; Buehl, 2003); (c) the certainty of knowledge (Bråten & Strømsø, 2005; Buehl, 2003); (d) the speed of learning or the effort required to learn

(Neber & Schommer-Aikins, 2002; Schommer-Aikins et al., 2005); and (e) fixed ability (Paulsen & Feldman, 1999a).

Self-Determination Self-determination (i.e., individuals' need to experience choice and control; Ryan & Deci, 2000) is an aspect of motivation that has not been explored in relation to individuals' beliefs about domains or the knowledge within domains. However, individuals' beliefs about academic domains may influence their experience of self-determination to the extent that their beliefs facilitate or hinder the satisfaction of the three needs that are necessary for self-determination (i.e., competency, autonomy, and relatedness; Ryan & Deci, 2000). We have already discussed the potential role of domain beliefs with respect to self-efficacy and competency beliefs. However, we also believe that domain beliefs may contribute to individuals' feelings of autonomy, or the lack thereof.

With respect to autonomy, beliefs about the certainty and simplicity of knowledge as well as the source and justification for knowing may be particularly salient. Individuals who believe that there are multiple possible answers or at least multiple ways to reach an appropriate outcome are more likely to feel autonomous than individuals who perceive there is only one right answer or correct path to a response. Additionally, if individuals view themselves as a source of knowledge, through their own reasoning, construction and modification of knowledge, they may feel less controlled than individuals who perceive knowledge as coming from an authority figure who holds all of the answers and who will judge the correctness of the one's performance.

Goal Orientations One area that has proven fertile in the empirical study of beliefs and motivation is the work on goal orientations. As Dweck documents in this volume, individuals' implicit theories of intelligence have been examined and the implications of these theories for learning discussed. In particular, individuals who believe that intelligence is malleable and open to development are more likely to adopt mastery goals and attribute poor performance to the task demands or personal effort, but not ability, whereas individuals who view intelligence as static and fixed are more likely to adopt performance goals and demonstrate learned helpless behaviors (e.g., Dweck & Leggett, 1988). In recent studies, students' perceptions of a fixed or innate ability to learn have been positively related to performance goals (e.g., Qian & Burrus, 1996; Ravindran, Greene, & Debacker, 2005) and negatively related to intrinsic, mastery, or task goals (e.g., Neber & Schommer-Aikins, 2002; Paulsen & Feldman, 1999a).

Relations have also been identified between other aspects of students' beliefs and goal orientations. For one, beliefs about simplicity of knowledge have been positively related to performance or extrinsic goals (Paulsen & Feldman, 1999a; Qian & Burrus, 1996; Ravindran et al., 2005) and negatively related to intrinsic goals (Hofer, 1999; Paulsen & Feldman, 1999a). That is, students who viewed knowledge as more simplistic and isolated tended to achieve in order to receive external praise and rewards, whereas students who viewed knowledge as complex and interrelated engaged in tasks in order to satisfy their own interests and desires. Also, Bråten and Strømsø (2005) found that beliefs about the speed of learning and the certainty of knowledge were negatively related to mastery goals.

Academic Domain and Motivation Beliefs as Motivating Specific Behaviors

In addition to beliefs about academic domains promoting self-efficacy and competency beliefs, task value and interest, self-determination, and goal orientations, domain beliefs may work with these motivation constructs to move individuals toward or away from specific behaviors or activities (e.g., Graham & Weiner, 1996). Because the behaviors individuals choose to engage in may be viewed as a measure of motivation, the relations between specific beliefs and behaviors offer insight into how beliefs move individuals to action.

From a teacher perspective, there are implications for the types of instructional practices teachers are motivated to implement in the classroom. That is, teachers may be motivated toward or away from specific instructional and assessment practices, depending on their beliefs about the domain and their sense of efficacy for implementing those practices. For instance, Yadav and Koehler (2007) found that preservice teachers who viewed knowledge as more simplistic preferred teaching practices in which they maintained control within the classroom. In contrast, those who viewed knowledge as more complex favored instructional practices that provided opportunities for class discussion in which the integration of concepts was emphasized. Others have also identified consistencies between teachers' beliefs and instructional practices (e.g., Kang & Wallace, 2004; Tsai, 2007) and recognize beliefs about the domain must change before instructional practices will be implemented (e.g., Ragland, 2007).

Teachers' beliefs may also influence their assessment practices and the feedback provided to students. In the same study by Yadav and Koehler (2007), preservice teachers who viewed knowledge as certain and unambiguous focused more on identifying mistakes and correcting errors in student work whereas those who viewed knowledge as more complex and integrated provided opportunities for students to revise their work. Thus, differences in teachers' instructional practices across domains may be attributable, at least in part, to differences in their beliefs about the domains themselves.

The role of teachers' sense of efficacy beliefs for implementing the practices associated with the domain also cannot be overlooked. That is, teachers' teaching efficacy beliefs are related to the instructional practices they value and enact (Cantrell & Callaway, in press; Cousins & Walker, 2000; Guskey, 1988). For instance, teachers with higher levels of teacher efficacy were more likely to implement mastery-oriented and reform-oriented teaching practices than teachers with lower levels of efficacy (e.g., Deemer, 2004; Ghaith & Yaghi, 1997).

Because the beliefs of teachers influence the practices they implement, these beliefs have an indirect influence on students in their classrooms (Figure 22.1). Specifically, teachers' words and actions within the classroom influence how the students experience the domain, including what the students come to learn and believe (e.g., Warren, 2002). Indeed, studies have documented that students' beliefs about learning in general and in specific domains may change in response to types of instruction they receive (e.g., Tsai, 2007; Valanides & Angeli, 2005).

The beliefs that students hold about academic domains have implications for the types of tasks they choose as well as how they engage in those tasks. Further, when students choose to engage in a domain-specific task, their domain beliefs in combination with aspects of their motivation (e.g., efficacy beliefs, interest, and value relative to the domain) may influence the goals and standards they use to judge success (e.g., knowing the right answers vs. understanding the process), the strategies they employ, the effort they invest, the sources of information that they consult, and how they respond to mistakes and difficult content. These connections are supported by research that has identified relations between students' epistemic beliefs and their help-seeking, self-regulation, metacognition, and strategy use.

More specifically, beliefs about the simplicity or isolation of knowledge as well as the certainty of knowledge were related to the use of more rehearsal strategies, fewer elaborative strategies, and surface-level processing (e.g., Cano, 2005; Dal, Bals, & Tuir, 2005; Paulsen & Feldman, 1999b;

Ravindran et al., 2005; Ryan, 1984), and less overall strategy use (e.g., Bräten & Strømsø, 2006). Beliefs about the speed of learning and knowledge acquisition were related to: the number and quality of strategies used; the conclusions drawn from inconclusive text; and distortions of textual information (e.g., Cano, 2005; Kardash & Howell, 2000; Paulsen & Feldman, 1999b; Schommer, 1990; Schommer et al., 1992). In recent studies, beliefs about the speed of knowledge acquisition were related to how students searched the Internet (e.g., Bräten & Strømsø, 2006), while beliefs about the construction and modification of knowledge were related to help-seeking and use of online communication to support students' learning (e.g., Bartholome, Stahl, Pieschl, & Bromme, 2006; Bräten & Strømsø, 2006; Hofer, 2004).

There has also been theoretical discussion of how and why individuals' beliefs are related to their behavior (e.g., Hofer, 2004; Kitchener, 1983). For instance, Muis (2007) recently proposed that epistemic beliefs are a key element in self-regulation to the extent that beliefs influence (a) the analysis and definition of a task, (b) the standards individuals use to set goals for learning, (c) the strategies and courses of action individuals selected to pursue their goals, and (d) the metacognitive standards and processing individuals use while engaged in the learning task.

Additionally, for both teachers and students, domain and motivation beliefs may amplify or interfere with the intended outcomes of specific instructional practices. For instance, teachers may modify recommended instructional practices (e.g., inquiry learning) based on their domain beliefs as well as their sense of efficacy for using the practices. Students may also distort classroom activities based on their beliefs (e.g., viewing class discussion as a waste of time). Consequently, changing one aspect of the classroom context alone (e.g., requiring specific modes of instruction) is not enough to alter the way a domain is perceived, taught, or learned (e.g., Khishfe & Abd-El-Khalick, 2002). Instead, changes to instructional practices must include scaffolding and support for the development of beliefs that are congruent with the new instructional methods.

Role of Motivation in Belief Change

The potential need to change individuals' beliefs about domains highlights a third avenue by which beliefs about academic domains and motivation in school are related. Specifically, previous research indicates that teachers' and students' beliefs about knowledge can be changed through specific instruction and intervention (e.g., Jacobson & Spiro, 1995; Marra, 2005; Mason & Scrivani, 2004). However, the literature on conceptual change and persuasion recognizes that for meaningful change to occur and endure, individuals must be motivated and recognize the need for change (e.g., Murphy & Mason, 2006; Pintrich, Marx, & Boyle, 1993; Sinatra & Pintrich, 2003). Thus, just as motivation is implicated in individuals' understanding of concepts within a domain, motivation is also involved in changing beliefs about the domain itself.

Further, the level of individuals' motivation in school will likely predict their level of belief change. For instance, low levels of self-efficacy toward the tasks in a domain, low levels of value for the domain, and or low levels of a desire to master and understand the domain more deeply may result in a lack of belief change and the persistence of more naïve perspectives about knowledge and knowing within the domain. Such resistance can occur at both the level of the teacher and the student. However, in our view, resistance from teachers is perhaps more concerning given their role in creating the learning environments that contribute to the development of students' beliefs, understandings, and motivations.

Academic Domain Beliefs and Motivation Beliefs May Not Be Causally Related

Finally, in exploring the relations between beliefs about academic domains and motivation, we must recognize that domain beliefs and some aspects of motivation in school may not necessarily be causally related. Instead, they may be related by virtue of another variable. For instance, individuals' level of cognitive development or life experience may account for relations between domain beliefs and their valuing of domain knowledge. Alternatively, perhaps knowledge beliefs are related to mastery goals due to a shared relation with self-efficacy. The possibility for the lack of a causal relation must be considered as research in this area progresses.

Domain Beliefs and Motivation in School: Examples from Two Academic Domains

As a means to illustrate some of the relations just articulated, we discuss beliefs related to two academic domains: science and history/social studies. We chose these domains for several reasons. First, we wanted to highlight core academic domains that also complemented the other chapters in this volume. Second, we wanted to select domains that differed in terms of the content, typical tasks, and pedagogical approaches often employed. Third, our examination of the literature revealed that all domains are not represented equally. For example, electronic searches of the PsychInfo and ERIC databases, using term strings such as "belief* about DOMAIN," "belief* about DOMAIN, student," "belief* about learning, DOMAIN," identified more works addressing mathematics, science, reading, and writing than history or social studies. Others have also noted the disproportionate attention given to history and social studies (e.g., Levstik, 2002; Wineburg, 1996). Thus, our choice of science and social studies/history allows us to consider one school subject (i.e., science) that has been more frequently studied and that tends to be treated as a more well-structured domain (i.e., characterized by well-specified problems, more algorithmic procedures, and generally agreed-upon "correct" solutions) and one subject (i.e., history/social studies) that has been less frequently studied and is approached as a more ill-structured domain (i.e., characterized by more open-ended problems, more heuristic procedures, and a greater range of acceptable responses or outcomes).

For each domain, we provide a brief description of the domain's perceived nature, contrasting the beliefs of experts with those of teachers and students. More specifically, beliefs more aligned with the philosophical question of "what *is* X?" are positioned these under the heading of ontological beliefs (Table 22.1). Beliefs professed about knowledge and knowing as well as learning and instruction in the domains are positioned under the heading epistemic and learning beliefs. Throughout the discussion of beliefs related to the two domains, we address the linkages between beliefs and teachers' and students' motivation in school. Some of these connections have been documented in prior investigations, whereas others are more speculative.

Science

Ontological Beliefs Although experts debate the exact definition of science, there are points of general agreement (e.g., Driver, Leach, Miller, & Scott, 1996; Matthews, 1994). Broadly defined, science pertains to the systematic understanding of the physical, biological, psychological, and social world in which we live (Rutherford & Ahlgren, 1990) and is viewed as a dynamic, social, and sometimes controversial enterprise in which understandings about the world are constructed

Table 22.1 Summary of Ontological and Epistemic Beliefs and Beliefs Trends by Domain

	Ontological Beliefs		Epistemic Beliefs:	
	Experts Views	**Teachers and Students**	**Expert Views**	**Teachers and Students**
Science	Systematic revision of what is known about the world; achieved through gathering, analyzing, and interpreting data; evidence obtained through accepted methodology	Collection of findings about the world; finding out what is "fact" or "true" about the physical world	Tentative and constructed nature of science is at the core of teaching and learning in the domain	Distinct views about how scientists come to learn about the world and how non-scientists learn science; doing science is different than teaching and learning science
History/ Social Studies	Interpretation of primary and secondary sources to study the past and changes over time due to human activity	Collection of information about the past; memorization of significant names, dates, and places	Various forms of history knowledge acquired through complex cognitive processes and discussion	Knowledge acquired from books or authority figures (e.g., teachers) with some recognition of the role of discussion

through the use of diverse procedures and methods (Lederman, Abd-El-Khalick, Bell, & Schwartz, 2002; Osborne Collins, Ratcliffe, Millar, & Duschl, 2003; Thagard, 1994). Various forms of knowledge are recognized (e.g., theories, laws, or models) and, although tentative and open to revision, within science, knowledge claims can be evaluated based on available evidence (T. Kuhn, 1970; Sandoval, 2005). Moreover, individuals' understanding of the nature of science has long been viewed as essential for participation and functioning in modern society due to its implications for daily life and public policy (e.g., American Association for the Advancement of Science [AAAS], 1993; Dewey, 1900/1990; Hogan, 2000).

Perhaps more than any other domain, researchers have attended to teachers' and students' views of the nature of science. A considerable body of research reveals that while some teachers and students express views similar to the experts, many do not. Instead, science is often viewed as a discrete set of relatively static facts that are to be learned, but that are not particularly relevant to everyday life (Gallagher, 1991; Hashweh, 1996; Linn & Songer, 1993). Such conceptions of science may vary depending on the specific content, scientific discipline, or topic under consideration (e.g., Estes et al., 2003; Hammer & Elby, 2002).

These beliefs about the nature of science as a domain may influence self-efficacy and competency beliefs via the standards used to judge mastery of the domain. That is, if science is viewed as a dynamic process of revising what is known about the world through the use of accepted methodology, the criteria by which individuals determine whether they can learn or know science may include the ability to make inferences and reason from evidence as well as the ability to implement the accepted methodology. In contrast, individuals who view science as a collection of findings about the world would more likely base their self-efficacy and competency beliefs for learning and knowing science on the ability to memorize and recall factual information. Further, the extent to which science as a domain is viewed as an integral part of daily life, as experts purport, the more likely individuals will value and be interested in scientific endeavors. If science is viewed as unrelated to other areas of study or aspects of daily living, teachers and students are less likely to value or be interested in science as a field of study.

Teachers' perceptions of science as a domain may also influence students' beliefs, motivations, and learning via the practices that are implemented in the classroom. Specifically, teachers' beliefs about science influence the teaching goals that they set and the practices that they implement (Kang, 2008). In addition to domain beliefs, teachers' actions are also predicted by their feelings of efficacy for implementing specific science practices as well as the teachers' need for control (e.g., Mulholland & Wallace, 2004). Thus, if science teachers do not endorse a dynamic view of science or are not efficacious, students may not experience teaching practices that reflected the constructed nature of science, thereby limiting the development of students' beliefs about science. Moreover, students' perceptions of teachers' practices have been related to students' motivation in science. Specifically, perceptions of teachers' autonomy supportive practices (e.g., asking for student opinions about science related material) were positively related to self-determine science motivation and intentions to engage in science activities (Lavigne, Vallerand, & Miquelon, 2007). These relations were mediated by students' feeling of competence and autonomy.

Epistemic and Learning Beliefs Elements associated with knowing science include understanding the nature of science and its substantive concepts, logical reasoning, procedures, and metacognitive awareness (Linn, Songer, & Eylon, 1996). In the 1960s, Schwab (1962) articulated the concept of inquiry-based science teaching as a method to engage students in the scientific process. Inquiry is broadly defined as a "process of asking questions, generating and pursuing strategies to investigate those questions by generating data, analyzing and interpreting those data, drawing conclusions from them, communicating the conclusions, applying the conclusions back to the original question, and perhaps following up with new questions as they arise" (Sandoval, 2005, p. 636). The implementation of inquiry-based instruction is viewed as a means to "do science," develop more sophisticated views about the nature of science, and understand scientific concepts at a deeper level. Support for the use of inquiry, while not unanimous, is reflected in the National Science Education Standards' call for inquiry as the "central strategy for teaching science" (National Research Council [NRC], 1996, p. 31).

However, the ultimate benefits of inquiry rest in part on the beliefs and actions of individual teachers and students (Hogan, 2000). Examinations of teachers' and students' views about science reveal that some individuals make distinctions between the "doing" of science and the "learning" of science (e.g., Kang & Wallace, 2004; Tsai, 2002). That is, individuals differ in their conceptions of how scientists come to know science in their professional lives and how non-scientists come to know science in schooled settings (e.g., Hogan, 2000; Sandoval, 2005).

Further, teachers' and students' views influence the instructional practices that are implemented and individuals' motivation in the classroom (Gallagher, 1991; Hashweh, 1996; Wallace & Kang, 2004). For instance, Kang and Wallace (2004) found that teachers modified practices intended to reflect an inquiry approach to science instruction, based to their beliefs about science and science learning. Specifically, a teacher who viewed science knowledge as factual information to be learned used laboratory experiments with students to verify scientific "truths." In contrast, another with more complex beliefs about scientific knowledge used laboratory experiments as an opportunity for students to explore and test their hypotheses. Even if teachers' implementations of practices reflect an inquiry approach, students may distort the inquiry activities based on their beliefs. For instance, Tsai (1999) found that students with more naïve scientific epistemological views believed experiments as a way to memorize scientific truths instead of a means to test competing hypotheses and reason scientifically.

Additionally, if individuals perceive that knowledge within science is to be acquired quickly with little effort or that the acquisition of scientific knowledge is due to innate abilities, depending on individuals' success and rate of learning, such beliefs may contribute to or undermine a sense of self-efficacy and competency. Alternatively, belief in the gradual acquisition of knowledge, effortful learning, and malleable ability may have a different effect on self-efficacy and competency beliefs, particularly when obstacles are encountered. Neber and Schommer-Aikins (2002) found that students who believed that success does not require hard work had lower levels of self-efficacy, task value, and task goal orientations in science.

Beliefs about the certainty and source of science knowledge also have implications for feelings of self-determination. As an example, consider a student working on a science laboratory experiment. If this student views scientific knowledge as tentative and evolving based on evidence and reasoning, she may not feel that she is completing the experiment merely to replicate what is in the textbook or to give the "right" answer to the teacher. In contrast, another student, who views science as more static and based on what experts deem as "true," may feel more controlled while completing the same experiment.

History

Ontological Beliefs History has often been described as the study of change over time (e.g., Stearns, 1998), with that change arising from "human activities and events" that can be "social, cultural, political, and economic in nature" (Voss, 1999, p. 163). There is a general agreement that history is tied to the past. However, from this point there can be significant departure between experts and the larger educational community. To experts, the nature of history is one of interpreting the past based on evidence that is valid and reliable to the degree possible. Thus, the historical narrative is not singular and unchanging but can be framed from diverse vantage points. Although there are anchoring events or "facts" for these narratives, history is certainly not a matter of memorizing a given set of names, dates, and places.

However, for too many teachers and students, history is about the memorization of historical information that should be simply accepted as true without question or deeper analysis (VanSledright, 2004). Because too few educators are equipped to engage in meaningful analysis of primary and secondary sources of evidence, and because current assessments treat history as facts to be memorized, this ontological disconnect between experts and others is apt to persist. Also, what counts as history becomes confounded in educational practice within the American education system where history is subsumed under social studies at the elementary school level (VanSledright, 2002a) and used as the content through which other skills are taught (e.g., reading; Brophy & Alleman, 2006; Levstik, 2002).

Teachers' and students' perceptions of history have serious implications for students' valuing of the domain and their interest in it. Specifically, if history is viewed as an isolated collection of discrete facts about the past that are not connected with other areas of study or aspects of students' lives, it is likely students will not see a purpose for history, as a field of study, nor value or be interested in learning history, on a personal level. Indeed, students (e.g., fifth grade) often do not recognize the value of learning history for their lives outside school and have difficulty articulating a reason why history is important (VanSledright, 1997; VanSledright & Brophy, 1992). Although studies with middle school and high school students suggest students make some progress in appreciating the value of learning history (e.g., reasons for studying history included to learn from the past and about the world; VanSledright, 1997; Yeager, Foster, & Greer, 2002), they rarely referred to the benefits of learning history from the perspective of supporting participatory citizenship or fostering the development of argumentation and reasoning skills (VanSledright, 1997). Buehl (2003) also found evidence with college students that expressed belief in the isolation of history knowledge was associated with less of an intention to engage in history related activities.

Epistemic and Learning Beliefs In education, the goals of history instruction can typically be classified into one of two broad categories: (a) to develop students' appreciation and awareness of history and the perspectives of others, or (b) to support students in their development of other concepts and skills that have both more domain-general (e.g., cultural literacy or argumentation) or domain-specific (e.g., sourcing) character (VanSledright, 2002a; Voss, 1999). Since the cognitive revolution, the cognitive processes involved in learning history have received greater attention (e.g., Maggioni & Alexander, in press; VanSledright, 2002a). That is, although knowing and understanding historical facts are aspects of history (e.g., Spoehr & Spoehr, 1994; Wineburg, 1991), historians and educators also recognize the key processes—such as understanding time and causality, locating and evaluating evidence, making interpretations, and formulating explanations—that are essential to components of knowing history (e.g., Leinhardt, Stainton, & Virji, 1994; VanSledright, 2004). Additionally, researchers distinguish between first-order substantive knowledge (i.e., knowledge of past events, historical figures, contexts), second-order substantive knowledge (i.e., knowledge of concepts and ideas used to interpret and make meaning of the past), and strategic knowledge (i.e., knowledge of how to implement historical thinking in order to create first-order knowledge; Limón, 2002; VanSledright & Limón, 2006).

However, many teachers and students do not share these views and instead view historical knowledge as isolated facts to be memorized (Gabella, 1994). Whereas some teachers work to counter this perception and focus on the interpretive nature of history (e.g., VanSledright, 2002a), others do not, or do so only for students with above average ability (e.g., Wilson & Wineburg, 1993). Thus, such beliefs are likely to endure, thereby influencing teachers' and students' motivations for specific activities and practices.

For instance, Stodolsky, Salk, and Glaessner (1991) examined fifth-grade students' beliefs about how they learn social studies and mathematics. Overall, students tended to believe that they could learn social studies on their own but needed someone to teach them mathematics. Further, students indicated that they learn social studies primarily from reading textbook or other books, thus downplaying the role of interpretation and social interaction. In another study, Yeager et al. (2002) found that American students reported learning more about history inside school than outside school, whereas British students believed that their knowledge of history came more from outside school (e.g., family, television, and the Internet) rather than inside the school environment. Such beliefs may influence the extent to which both teachers students value classroom activities or engage with specific sources of information or processes of knowing (e.g., class discussion; Sosniak & Perlman, 1990).

Beliefs about the processes and sources of history knowledge as well as justification for knowing also have potential implications for students' feelings of self-determination and social motivation. That is, a belief that events can be interpreted in multiple ways will provide more autonomy support by allowing students the freedom to develop their perspective and support their reasoning rather than a belief that history is only about giving a correct accounting of the facts. Students' feelings of relatedness and social motivation may be addressed to the extent they perceive opportunities for collaboration and social interaction as they develop and defend their perspectives. Empirical research is needed to explore these potential connections.

However, even once such relations are substantiated, attempts to address students' beliefs about the interpretive and tentative nature of historical knowledge may be thwarted by difficulties involved in changing beliefs. That is, researchers committed to the study of historical analysis and historical thinking have found that attempts to teach teachers and students to engage in viable historical thinking can have the undesired consequence of replacing the naïve belief that history is about the memorization of factual information with the equally naïve perspective that any interpretation of the historical evidence is equally as valid as the next (Maggioni, Riconscente, & Alexander, 2006). VanSledright (2002b) called this the movement from "naïve trust to widespread suspicion" (p. 49). Individuals with widespread suspicion are not likely to value or be interested in learning historical information, highlighting how teachers and students need assistance in realizing that historical knowledge is not completely tentative and uncertain (i.e., a multiplistic stance). Instead, individuals need to recognize that there are more or less valid interpretations of history based on the quality of available evidence (i.e., an evaluativist stance). The need to develop such a position is also discussed in the general epistemic belief literature (e.g., King & Kitchener, 1994; D. Kuhn, 1990).

Continuing Concerns and Future Directions

To bring this discussion of domain beliefs and motivation in school to closure, we want to consider three broad areas of concern that have significant implications for educational research and instructional practice: assessment, development, and instruction. Even though we will address these topics individually, their interactive nature is undeniable.

Assessment Conundrums

Aspects of assessment related to domain beliefs and motivation in school remain formidable barriers to educational research and instructional practice including the psychometric quality of current measures, elusive constructs, over-reliance on self-report data, and an absence of guiding theoretical models.

Psychometric Quality of Current Measures The data reported for domain beliefs and learner motivations are only as good as the instruments and procedures used to gather those data. Many of the measures used to examine students' and teachers' beliefs about knowledge and knowing come with warnings as to the validity and reliability of resulting data. For instance, the best known and most widely used measure of epistemic beliefs, the Schommer Epistemological Questionnaire or SEQ (Schommer, 1990), is routinely criticized for scales that seem outside the scope of epistemology (Hofer & Pintrich, 1997) and for scale reliabilities that are hard to confirm and of questionable strength. There have been efforts to produce better epistemic belief measures (e.g., Hofer, 2000; Wood & Kardash, 2002), including our own (Buehl et al., 2002), but none of those valiant attempts have proven satisfactory to date.

Elusive Constructs Part of the problem in crafting measures with sound psychometric properties is that the constructs under investigation are abstract and elusive. For example, there is nothing clean or simple about the philosophical study of ontology and epistemology. It is no surprise that educational researchers confront serious questions of validity in measurement conception and construction when ontology and epistemology are the focus. Likewise, the diversity and complexity of motivation constructs have only expanded over the last decade, along with questions about the quality of their measurement.

There are also lingering concerns as to the level of domain or task specificity required at the item level for domain beliefs and motivation constructs. Are general epistemic or goal orientation measures sufficient, or should questions focus on such constructs at the level of the domain? For instance, are students to be consistently mastery oriented regardless of the domain or the specific educational context in which that domain is studied? Or, are there meaningful variations in goal orientations based on learner, content, and context interactions?

Over-reliance on Self-Report Data In some programs of inquiry (e.g., teacher knowledge), researchers have turned to proxy measures (e.g., years of experience, advanced degrees) as more practical and concrete substitutes for elusive constructs. The use of proxies addresses the over-reliance on self-report data. However, the use of proxy indicators is less viable in the study of domain beliefs and motivation as well-accepted proxy measures are equally elusive.

Nonetheless, any time one must rely on self-reports, there is reason for concern. If students cannot be trusted to report their past academic performance accurately or honestly (e.g., GPA), then how likely are they to call to mind the feelings and perceptions underlying such performance? Even when the perceptions about domain learning and motivation are honestly conceived and unambiguous, individuals may find the language required to communicate them elusive or the social consequence of expressing a particular stance too great. Thus, the words uttered are limited or stilted and the ideas articulated are censured or distorted.

Absence of Guiding Theoretical Models The issues we have identified to this point have focused more at the level of the instrument. But the assessment problems for the study of domain beliefs and motivation in school are much broader. Specifically, even if researchers could devise psychometrically-sound measures of ontological and epistemic beliefs or of domain-specific motivations, they would be still operating largely in the dark when it comes to positioning those measures in a meaningful theoretical framework. Theory must guide measurement and data interpretation. Yet, we are sadly short on theory when it comes to the alignment of domain beliefs and motivations. So, speculation abounds. How should the interplay of domain beliefs and motivations be configured? How would that configuration change across domains and for those at differing levels of maturation or expertise? Further, what theoretical differences would be anticipated when the outcome variables are less about school achievement and more about learning (Alexander & Riconscente, 2005)?

Developmental Dilemmas

The literature pertaining to domain beliefs and motivation in school focus largely on older or more mature students and has been predominately cross-sectional in nature. We feel that these trends reflect two methodological issues that must be addressed in the future.

Linguistic and Cognitive Confounds The assessment difficulties just described permeate the literature on domain beliefs and motivations. Yet there are particular linguistic and cognitive issues that come into play when the focus of the research is young children and those less able to communicate their beliefs and motivations. On the one hand, how do you find the words that will be understandable when asking the young, less experienced, or cognitively challenged about ontological or epistemic beliefs and motivations? On the other hand, will those individuals have the words (or mental ability) to reflect on their beliefs and motivations or the language required to share those with others? Is their language up to the task of comprehending questions on written measures? As this myriad of questions suggests, there is simply no easy way around the linguistic and cognitive demands that come with the study of domain beliefs and motivations.

Longitudinal Data If we are to understand the nature of domain beliefs and motivations and the relations between them, it is essential to move beyond the cross-sectional studies that have dominated the literature. Without longitudinal data, we will not understand how domain beliefs and motivations initially form and how experiences in school and out of school change those constructs and their relations over time. We appreciate the difficulties in conducting longitudinal studies. However, we believe that these are challenges must be confronted if this area of research is to improve.

Instructional Paradoxes

Continuing concerns are also reflected in instructional practice. Here we briefly touch on two instructionally-related issues with significant implications for the study of domain beliefs and motivations, the question of societal and scholastic values, and curricular constraints.

Societal and Scholastic Values One reason for tackling the complex issues of domain beliefs and motivation in school is that, as educators, we hope to contribute to the learning and development of children and youth. Yet, in the arena of domain beliefs and motivation, it is difficult to know *how*, *when*, and even *if* we should intercede. For instance, even though there is the tendency to characterize particular beliefs about domains or about knowledge and knowing in those domains as more or less sophisticated or naïve, such characterizations are premature and controversial. Thus, even if we are able to relate particular instructional practices or teacher actions with certain beliefs about domains or knowledge in those domains, is there valid reason to push for instructional change?

Similarly, students, particularly in the middle-school and high-school years, are depicted as declining in their motivations (Alexander & Fox, in press; Ryan & Patrick, 2001; Wigfield, Eccles, & Rodriguez, 1998). Is this a fair assessment? Or, is it more accurate to say that students are just not motivated by the conditions that we, as educators, desire for them? For instance, if students do not report a high level of valuing for school in general or certain academic subjects in particular, is the problem with the student, the teacher, or the learning environment?

Curricular Constraints Finally, it is important to remember that there is a broader instructional context to weigh as we explore domain beliefs and motivation in school. Whether the actual beliefs and motivations of teachers and students can be enacted in classrooms depends on the degrees of freedom they experience within the educational system. Regrettably, the pervasive testing mentality and the push toward accountability in schools may be coloring the beliefs of teachers and students. Further, even if teachers and students retain beliefs about domains and about themselves correspond with those advocated in the literature, there are no assurances that teachers and students can manifest those beliefs in ways that will be valued or rewarded. Moreover, the pervasive testing mentality may well diminish the natural differences that exist across domains or disciplines and, therefore, unduly constrain or distort the beliefs and motivations that students and teachers may form about those domains. That is, on multiple-choice tests with definitely right and wrong answers, history begins to look more like science and their instruction may become less differentiated as well.

In essence, we conclude at the same point we began. Beliefs matter. As we have discussed, there are various ways by which teachers' and students' beliefs about academic domains may be related to their motivations, instructional practices and learning behaviors, as well as learning outcomes and belief change. However, additional research is needed to understand the mechanisms and processes by which beliefs about academic domains are related to students' academic development within the school environment. Only then can we confidently plot a course to harness the power of beliefs to improve student learning and motivation.

References

Alexander, P. A. (2006). The path to competence: A lifespan developmental perspective on reading. *Journal of Literacy Research, 37*, 413–436.

Alexander, P. A., & Dochy, F. J. R. C. (1995). Conceptions of knowledge and beliefs: A comparison across varying cultural and educational communities. *American Educational Research Journal, 32*, 413–442.

Alexander, P. A., & Fox, E. (in press). Adolescent reading. In M. L. Kamil, P. D. Pearson, E. B. Moje, & P. Afflerbach (Eds.), *Handbook of reading research, Vol. IV*. New York: Routledge.

Alexander, P. A., & Riconscente, M. M. (2005). A matter of proof: Why achievement ≠ learning. In J. S. Carlson & J. R. Levin (Eds.), *The No Child Left Behind legislation: Educational research and federal funding* (pp. 27–36). Greenwich, CT: Information Age.

Alexander, P., A., & Winne, P. H. (2006). *Handbook of educational psychology*. Mahwah, NJ: Erlbaum.

American Association for the Advancement of Science (AAAS). (1993). *Benchmarks for science literacy*. New York: Oxford University Press.

Bandura, A. (1997). *Self-efficacy: The exercise of control*. New York: W. H. Freeman.

Bartholome, T., Stahl, E., Pieschl, S., & Bromme, R. (2006). What matters in help-seeking?: A study of help effectiveness and learner-related factors. *Computers in Human Behavior, 22*, 113–129.

Baxter Magolda, M. B. (1992). *Knowing and reasoning in college: Gender-related patterns in students' intellectual development*. San Francisco: Jossey-Bass.

Bereiter, C. (1994). Constructivism, socioculturalism, and Popper's World 3. *Educational Researcher, 23*(7), 21–23.

Bråten, I., & Strømsø, H. (2005). The relationship between epistemological beliefs, implicit theories of intelligence, and self-regulated learning among Norwegian postsecondary students. *British Journal of Educational Psychology, 75*(4), 539–565.

Brophy, J., & Alleman, J. (2006). *Children's thinking about cultural universals*. Mahwah, NJ: Erlbaum.

Buehl, M. M. (2003). *At the crossroads of cognition and motivation: Modeling the relationships between students' domain-specific epistemological beliefs, achievement motivation, and task performance*. Unpublished doctoral dissertation, University of Maryland, College Park, Maryland.

Buehl, M. M., & Alexander, P. A. (2000, August). *Children's beliefs about knowledge and learning*. Paper presented at the annual meeting of the American Psychological Association, Washington, DC.

Buehl, M. M., & Alexander, P. A. (2006). Examining the dual nature of epistemological beliefs. *International Journal of Educational Research, 45*, 28–42.

Buehl, M. M., Alexander, P. A., & Murphy, P. K. (2002). Beliefs about schooled knowledge: Domain general or domain specific? *Contemporary Educational Psychology, 27*, 415–449.

Calderhead, J. (1996). Teachers: Beliefs and knowledge. In D. C. Berliner & R. C. Calfee (Eds.), *Handbook of educational psychology* (pp. 709–725): New York: Macmillan.

Cano, F. (2005). Epistemological beliefs and approaches to learning: Their change through secondary school and their influence on academic performance. *British Journal of Educational Psychology, 75*(2), 203–221.

Cantrell, S. C., & Callaway, P. (in press). High and low implementaters of content literacy instruction: Portraits of teacher efficacy. *Teaching and Teacher Education*.

Chinn, C. A., & Brewer, W. F. (1993). The role of anomalous data in knowledge acquisition: A theoretical framework and implications for science instruction. *Review of Educational Research, 63*, 1–49.

Chinn, C. A., & Malhotra, B. A. (2002). Children's responses to anomalous scientific data: How is conceptual change impeded? *Journal of Educational Psychology, 94*(2), 327–343.

Cousins, J. B., & Walker, C. A. (2000). Predictors of educators' valuing of systematic inquiry in schools [Special issue]. *Canadian Journal of Program Evaluation*, 25–53.

Dal, T. I., Bals, M., & Turi, A. L. (2005). Are students' beliefs about knowledge and learning associated with their reported use of learning strategies? *British Journal of Educational Psychology, 75,* 257–273.

Deemer, S. (2004). Classroom goal orientation in high school classrooms: Revealing links between teacher beliefs and classroom environments. *Educational Research, 46*(1), 73–90.

Dewey, J. (1897/1972). The psychological aspect of the school curriculum. In J. A. Boydston & F. Bowers (Eds.), *The early works of John Dewey 1882–1903: Vol. 5 1885–1898.* Carbondale: Southern Illinois University Press.

Dewey, J. (1900/1990). *The school and society.* Chicago: University of Chicago Press.

Driver, R., Leach, J., Miller, R., & Scott, P. (1996). *Young people's images of science.* Buckingham, England: Open University Press.

Durant, W. (1954–1975). *Story of civilization: Parts I–XI.* New York: Simon & Schuster.

Dweck, C. (2002). The development of ability conceptions. In A. Wigfield & J. Eccles (Eds.), *The development of achievement motivation* (pp. 57–91). San Diego, CA: Academic Press.

Dweck, C. S., & Leggett, E. L. (1988). A social-cognitive approach to motivation and personality. *Psychologist Review, 95,* 56–73.

Eccles, J. S., Adler, T. F., Futterman, R., Goff, S. B., Kaczala, C. M., Meece, J. L., & Midgley, C. (1983). Expectancies, values, and academic behaviors. In J. T. Spence (Ed.), *Achievement and achievement motives* (pp. 75–146). San Francisco: W. H. Freeman.

Estes, D., Chandler, M., Horvath, K. J., & Backus, D. W. (2003). American and British college students' epistemological beliefs about research on psychological and biological development. *Applied Developmental Psychology, 23,* 625–642.

Ford, M. (1992). *Motivating humans: Goals, emotions, and personal agency beliefs.* Newbury Park, CA: Sage.

Gabella, M. S. (1994). Beyond the looking glass: Bringing students into the conversation of historical inquiry. *Theory and Research in Social Education, 22*(3), 340–363.

Gallagher, J. J. (1991). Prospective and practicing secondary school science teachers' knowledge and beliefs about the nature of science. *Science Education, 75,* 121–134.

Ghaith, G., & Yaghi, H. (1997). Relationships among experience, teacher efficacy, and attitudes toward the implementation of instructional innovation. *Teaching and Teacher Education, 13*(4), 451–458.

Graham, S. (2006). *Writing.* In P. A. Alexander & P. H. Winne (Eds.), *Handbook of educational psychology* (2nd ed., pp. 457–478). Mahwah, NJ: Erlbaum.

Graham, S., & Weiner, B. (1996). Theories and principles of motivation. In D. C. Berliner & R. C. Calfee (Eds.), *Handbook of educational psychology* (pp. 63–84). New York: Macmillan.

Guskey, T. (1988). Teacher efficacy, self-concept, and attitudes toward the implementation of instructional innovation. *Teaching and Teacher Education, 4*(1), 63–69.

Hammer, D., & Elby, A. (2002). On the form of personal epistemology. In B. K. Hofer & P. R. Pintrich (Eds.), *Personal epistemology: The psychology of beliefs about knowledge and knowing* (pp 169–190). Mahwah, NJ: Erlbaum.

Hashweh, M. Z. (1996). Effects of science teachers' epistemological beliefs in teaching. *Journal of Research in Science Teaching, 33,* 47–63.

Hofer, B. K. (1999). Instructional context in the college mathematics classroom: Epistemological beliefs and student motivation. *Journal of Staff, Program, and Organization Development, 16,* 73–82.

Hofer, B. K. (2004). Epistemological understanding as a metacognitive process: Thinking aloud during online searching. *Educational Psychologist, 39,* 43–56.

Hofer, B. K., & Pintrich, P. R. (1997). The development of epistemological theories: Beliefs about knowledge and knowing and their relation to learning. *Review of Educational Research, 67,* 88–140.

Hogan, K. (2000). Exploring a process view of students' knowledge of about the nature of science. *Science Education, 84,* 51–70.

Jacobson, M. J., & Spiro, R. J. (1995). Hypertext learning environments, cognitive flexibility, and the transfer of complex knowledge: An empirical investigation. *Journal of Educational Computing Research, 12*(4), 301–333.

Judd, C. H. (1915). *The psychology of high school students.* Boston: Ginn.

Kang, N. (2008). Learning to teach science: Personal epistemologies, teaching goals, and practices of teaching. *Teaching and Teacher Education, 24,* 478–498.

Kang, N., & Wallace, C. (2004). Secondary science teachers' use of laboratory activities: Linking epistemological beliefs, goals, and practices. *Science Education, 89*(1), 140–165.

Kardash, C. M., & Howell, K. L. (2000). Effects of epistemological beliefs and topic-specific beliefs on undergraduates' cognitive and strategic processing of dual-positional text. *Journal Educational Psychology, 92(2),* 524–535.

Khishfe, R., & Abd-El-Khalick, F. (2002). Influence of explicit and reflective versus implicit inquiry-oriented instruction on sixth graders views of nature of science. *Journal of Research in Science Teaching, 39,* 551–578.

King, P. M., & Kitchener, K. S. (1994). *Developing reflective judgment: Understanding and promoting intellectual growth and critical thinking in adolescents and adults.* San Francisco: Jossey-Bass.

King, P. M., & Kitchener, K. S. (2004). Reflective judgment: Theory and research on the development of epistemic assumptions through adulthood. *Educational Psychologist, 39,* 5–18.

Kitchener, K. S. (1983). Cognition, metacognition and epistemic cognition. A three level model of cognitive processing. *Human Development, 26,* 222–232.

Kuhn, D. (1990). *The skill of argument.* Cambridge, England: Cambridge University Press.

Kuhn, T. (1970). *The structure of scientific revolutions* (2nd ed.). Chicago: Chicago University Press.

Lavigne, G., Vallerand, R., & Miquelon, P. (2007). A motivational model of persistence in science and education: A self-determination theory approach. *European Journal of Psychology of Education, 22*(3), 351–369.

Lederman, N. G., Abd-El-Khalick, F., Bell, R. L., & Schwartz, R. S. (2002). Views of nature of science questionnaire: Toward valid and meaningful assessment of learners' conceptions of nature of science. *Journal of Research on Science Teaching, 39*, 497–521.

Leinhardt, G., Stainton, C., & Virji, S. M. (1994). A sense of history. *Educational Psychologist, 29*(2), 79–88.

Levstik, L. S. (2002). Introduction. *The Elementary School Journal, 103*(2), 93–97.

Limón, M. (2002). Conceptual change in history. In Limón, M. & Mason, L. (Eds.), *Reconsidering conceptual change: Issues in theory and practice* (pp. 259–289). Dordretch, The Netherlands: Kluwer Academic Press.

Limón, M. (2006). The domain generality-specificity of epistemological beliefs: A theoretical problem, a methodological problem, or both? *International Journal of Educational Research, 45*, 7–27.

Linn, M. C., & Songer, N. (1993). How do students make sense of science? *Merrill-Palmer Quarterly, 39*(1), 47–73.

Linn, M. C., Songer, N. B., & Eylon, B., S. (1996). *Shifts and convergences in science learning and instruction.* In R. Calfee & D. Berliner (Eds.), *Handbook of educational psychology* (pp. 438–490). Riverside, NJ: Macmillan.

Maggioni, L., & Alexander, P. A. (in press). Knowledge domains and domain learning. In B. McGaw, P. L. Peterson, & E. Baker (Eds.), *International encyclopedia of education* (3rd ed.). Amsterdam, Netherlands: Elsevier.

Maggioni, L., Riconscente, M., & Alexander, P. A. (2006) Perceptions of knowledge and beliefs among undergraduate students in Italy and in the United States. *Learning and Instruction 16*(5), 467–491.

Marra, R. M. (2005). The impact of the design of constructivist learning environments on faculty teaching epistemologies. *Learning Environments Research, 8*(2), 135–155.

Mason, L., & Scrivani, L. (2004). Enhancing students' mathematical beliefs: An intervention study. *Learning and Instruction, 14*(2), 153–176.

Matthews, M. R. (1994). *Science teaching: The role of history and philosophy of science.* New York: Routledge.

Muis, K. R. (2007). The role of epistemic beliefs in self-regulated learning. *Educational Psychologist, 42*(3), 173–190.

Muis, K. R., Bendixen, L. D., & Haerle, F. C. (2006). Domain-generality and domain-specificity in personal epistemology research: Philosophical and empirical reflections in the development of a theoretical framework. *Educational Psychology Review, 18*(3), 3–54.

Mulholland, J., & Wallace, J. (2004). Teaching induction and elementary science teaching: Enhancing self-efficacy. *Teaching and Teacher Education, 17*, 243–261.

Murphy, P. K., & Mason, L. (2006). *Changing knowledge and beliefs.* In P. A. Alexander & P. H. Winne (Eds.), *Handbook of educational psychology* (2nd ed., pp. 305–324). Mahwah, NJ: Erlbaum.

National Research Council [NRC]. (1996). *The national science education standards.* Washington, DC: National Academy Press.

Neber, H., & Schommer-Aikins, M. (2002). Self-regulated science learning with highly gifted students: The role of cognitive, motivational, epistemological, and environmental variables. *High Ability Studies, 13*(1), 59–74.

Nespor, J. (1987). The role of beliefs in the practice of teaching. *Journal of Curriculum Studies, 19*, 317–328.

Nisbett, R., & Ross, L. (1980). *Human inference: Strategies and shortcomings of social judgment.* Englewood Cliffs, NJ: Prentice-Hall.

Osborne, J., Collins, S., Ratcliffe, M., Millar, R., & Duschl, R. A. (2003). What "ideas-about-science" should be taught in school science? A Delphi study of the expert community. *Journal of Research in Science Teaching, 40*, 692–720.

Pajares, F. (1992). Teachers' beliefs and educational research: Cleaning up a messy construct. *Review of Educational Research, 62*, 307–332.

Pajares, F. (2003). Self-efficacy beliefs, motivation, and achievement in writing: A review of the literature. *Reading & Writing Quarterly, 19*, 139–158.

Paulsen, M. B., & Feldman, K. A. (1999a).Student motivation and epistemological beliefs. *New Directions for Teaching and Learning, 78*, 17–25.

Paulsen, M. B., & Feldman, K. A. (1999b). Epistemological beliefs and self-regulated learning. *Journal of Staff, Program, & Organizational Development, 16*(2), 83–91.

Perry, W. G. (1970). *Forms of intellectual and ethical development in the college years: A scheme.* New York: Holt, Rinehart, and Winston.

Pintrich, P. R. (2000a). A motivational science perspective on the role of student motivation in learning and teaching contexts. *Journal of Educational Psychology, 95*, 667–686.

Pintrich, P. R. (2000b). Educational psychology at the millennium: A look back and a look forward. *Educational Psychologist, 35*(4), 221–226.

Pintrich, P. R., Marx, R. W., & Boyle, R. A. (1993). Beyond cold conceptual change: The role of motivational beliefs and classroom contextual factors in the process of conceptual change. *Review of Educational Research, 63*(2), 167–199.

Pressley, M. (2006). *Reading instruction that works.* New York: Guilford.

Qian, G., & Burrus, B. M. (1996). The role of epistemological beliefs and motivational goal in ethnically diverse high school students' learning from science texts. In D. J. Leu, C. K. Kinzer, & K. A. Hinchman (Eds.), *Literacies for the 21st Century* (pp. 159–169). Chicago: National Reading Conference.

Ragland, R. G. (2007). Changing secondary teachers' views of teaching American history. *The History Teacher, 40*(2), 219–246.

Ravindran, B., Greene, B. A., & Debacker, T. K. (2005). Predicting preservice teachers' cognitive engagement with goals and epistemological beliefs. *Journal of Educational Research, 98*(4), 222–232.

Richardson, V. (1996). The role of attitudes and beliefs in learning to teach. In J. Sikula (Ed.), *Handbook of research on teacher education* (pp. 102–119). New York: Macmillian.

Rokeach, M. (1968). *Beliefs, attitudes, and values: A theory of organization and change.* San Francisco: Jossey-Bass.

Rutherford, F. J., & Ahlgren, A. (1990). *Science for all Americans.* New York: Oxford University Press.

Ryan, A. M., & Patrick, H. (2001). The classroom social environment and changes in adolescents' motivation and engagement during middle school. *American Educational Research Journal, 38,* 437–460.

Ryan, M. (1984). Monitoring text comprehension: Individual differences in epistemological standards. *Journal of Educational Psychology, 76*(2), 248–258.

Ryan, R. M., & Deci, E. (2000). Intrinsic and extrinsic motivations: Classic definitions and new directions. *Contemporary Education Psychology, 25,* 54–67.

Sandoval, W.A. (2005). Understanding students' practical epistemologies and their influence on learning through inquiry. *Science Education, 89*(4), 345–372.

Schommer-Aikins, M. (2004). Explaining the epistemological belief system: Introducing the embedded systematic model and coordinated research approach. *Educational Psychologist, 39,* 19–29.

Schommer, M. (1990). Effects of beliefs about the nature of knowledge on comprehension. *Journal of Educational Psychology, 82,* 498–504.

Schommer, M., Crouse, A., & Rhodes, N. (1992). Epistemological beliefs and math text comprehension: Believing it is simple does not make it so. *Journal of Educational Psychology, 84,* 435–443.

Schommer-Aikins, M., Duell, O., & Hutter, R. (2005). Epistemological beliefs, mathematical problem-solving beliefs, and academic performance of middle school students. *Elementary School Journal, 105*(3), 289–304.

Schraw, G., Bendixen, L. D., & Dunkle, M. E. (2002). Development and validation of the Epistemic Belief Inventory (EBI). In B. K. Hofer & P. R. Pintrich (Eds.), *Personal epistemology: The psychology of beliefs about knowledge and knowing* (pp 261–275). Mahwah, NJ: Erlbaum.

Schwab, J. J. (1962). *The teaching of science: The teaching of science as inquiry.* Cambridge, MA: Harvard University Press.

Shulman, L. S., & Quinlan, K. (1996). The comparative psychology of school subjects. In R. Calfee & D. Berliner (Eds.), *Handbook of educational psychology* (pp. 399–422). New York: Macmillan.

Sinatra, G. M., & Pintrich, P. R. (2003). The role of intentions in conceptual change. In G. M. Sinatra & P. R. Pintrich (Eds.), *Intentional conceptual change* (pp. 1–18). Mahwah, NJ: Erlbaum.

Sosniak, L., & Perlman, C. (1990). Secondary education by the book. *Journal of Curriculum Studies, 22*(5), 427–442.

Spoehr, K. T., & Spoehr, L. W. (1994). Learning to think historically. *Educational Psychologist, 29*(2), 71–77.

Stahl, S., Hynd, C., Glynn, S., & Carr, M. (1996). *Beyond reading to learn: Developing content and disciplinary knowledge through texts.* Hillsdale, NJ: Erlbaum.

Stearns, P. N. (1998). Goals in teaching history. In J. F. Voss & M. Carretero (Eds.), *International review of history. Vol. 2. Learning and reasoning in history* (pp. 138–161). London: Woburn.

Sternberg, R. J. (2003). Who is an expert student? *Educational Researcher, 32*(8), 5–9.

Stodolsky, S. S., Salk, S., & Glaessner, B. (1991). Student views about learning math and social studies. *American Educational Research Journal, 28*(1), 89–116.

Thagard, P. (1994). Mind, society, and the growth of knowledge. *Philosophy of Science, 61,* 629–645.

Tsai, C. (1999). Laboratory exercises help me memorize the scientific truths: A study of eighth graders' epistemological views and learning in laboratory activities. *Science Education, 83,* 654–674.

Tsai, C. (2002). Nested epistemologies: Science teachers' beliefs of teaching, learning, and science. *International Journal of Science Education, 24,* 771–783.

Tsai, C. (2007). Teachers' scientific epistemological views: The coherence of instruction and students' views. *Science Education, 91,* 222–243.

Valanides, N., & Angeli, C. (2005). Effects of instruction on changes in epistemological beliefs. *Contemporary Educational Psychology, 30,* 314–330.

Vansledright, B. A. (1997). And Santayana lives on: Students' views on the purposes for studying American history. *Curriculum Studies, 29*(5), 529–557.

VanSledright, B. A. (2002a). Confronting history's interpretive paradox while teaching fifth graders to investigate the past. *American Educational Research Journal, 39*(4), 1089–1115.

VanSledright, B. (2002b). *In search of America's past: Learning to read history in elementary school.* New York: Teachers College Press.

VanSledright, B. A. (2004). What does it mean to think historically and how do you teach it? *Social Education, 68,* 230–233.

VanSledright, B., & Brophy, J. (1992). Storytelling, imagination, and fanciful elaboration in children's historical reconstructions. *American Educational Research Journal, 29*(4), 837–859.

VanSledright, B. A., & Limón, M. (2006). Learning and teaching social studies: A review of cognitive research in history and geography. In P. A. Alexander & P. H. Winne (Eds.), *Handbook of educational psychology* (2nd ed., pp. 545–570). Mahwah, NJ: Erlbaum.

Voss, J. F. (1999). Issues in the learning of history. *Issues in Education, 4*(2), 163–209.

Wallace, C. S., & Kang, N. H. (2004). An investigation of experienced secondary science teachers' beliefs about inquiry: An examination of competing beliefs. *Journal of Research in science teaching, 41,* 936–960.

Warren, D. (2002). Curriculum design in a context of widening participation in higher education. *Arts and Humanities in Higher Education, 1*(1), 85–99.

Weiner, B. (1992). *Human motivation: Metaphors, theories, and research.* Newbury Park, CA: Sage.

Wentzel, K. R. (2000). What is it that I'm trying to achieve? Classroom goals from a content perspective. *Contemporary Educational Psychology, 25,* 105–115.

Wigfield, A., & Eccles, J. S. (2000). Expectancy-value theory of achievement motivation. *Contemporary Educational Psychology, 25,* 68–81.

Wigfield, A., & Eccles, J. S. (2002). The development of competence beliefs, expectancies for success, and achievement values from childhood through adolescence. In A. Wigfield & J. S. Eccles (Eds.), *The development of achievement motivation* (pp. 92–122). New York: Academic Press.

Wigfield, A., Eccles, J. S., & Rodriguez, D. (1998). The development of children's motivation in school contexts. *Review of Research in Education, 23,* 73–118.

Wilson, S. M., & Wineburg, S. S. (1993). Wrinkles in time and place: Using performance assessments to understand the knowledge of history teachers. *American Educational Research Journal, 30*(4), 729–779.

Wineburg, S. S. (1991). Historical problem solving: A study of the cognitive processes used in the evaluation of documentary and pictorial evidence. *Journal of Educational Psychology, 83,* 73–87.

Wineburg, S. S. (1996). The psychology of learning and teaching history. In D. C. Berliner & R. C. Calfee (Eds.), *The handbook of educational psychology* (pp. 423–437). New York: Simon Schuster Macmillan.

Wood, P., & Kardash, C. (2002). Critical elements in the design and analysis of studies of epistemology. In B. K. Hofer & P. R. Pintrich (Eds.), *Personal epistemology: The psychology of beliefs about knowledge and knowing* (pp 231–260). Mahwah, NJ; Erlbaum.

Woolfolk Hoy, A., Davis, H., & Pape, S. J. (2006). Teacher knowledge and beliefs. In P. A. Alexander & P. H. Winne (Eds.), *Handbook of educational psychology* (2nd ed., pp. 715–737). Mahwah, NJ: Erlbaum.

Yadav, A., & Koehler, M. J. (2007). The role of epistemological beliefs in preservice teachers? Interpretation of video cases of early-grade literacy instruction. *Journal of Technology and Teacher Education, 15*(3), 335–361.

Yeager, E. A., Foster, S. J., & Greer, J. (2002). How eighth graders in England and the United States view historical significance. *The Elementary School Journal, 103,* 199–219.

23
Reading Motivation

John T. Guthrie and Cassandra S. Coddington

Introduction and Background

Purposes

The purposes of this chapter are to discuss reading motivation as an educational phenomenon and to integrate the research bearing on educational conditions that influence students' reading motivations. We propose a framework to synthesize the variables and educational conditions that account for these phenomena in school-age students. This chapter begins with the diverse values, goals, reasons, dispositions, and affects and behaviors surrounding reading.

Pertinent to the challenge of explaining motivations for reading is the importance of reading in the contemporary schooling and culture of the United States and other Western economies. It goes without saying that reading magazines, books, and myriad documents is highly pervasive in the United States, and competency in reading is highly associated with income and placement in desirable occupations (Kirsch, Braun, Yamamoto, & Sum, 2007). Within schooling, reading is self-evidently the pathway for success in English, science, history, geography, health, math, and the arts (Bean & Readance, 2002), and predictive of high school completion (Finn & Rock, 1997).

A previous review proposed that reading motivation is multifaceted (Guthrie & Wigfield, 2000), including constructs of intrinsic motivation, self-efficacy, extrinsic motivation, and social motivation all of which correlate positively with reading achievement. Since that review, new research has revealed that performance-avoidance, referring to students' desire to avoid appearing incompetent (Elliot, 1999), and investigations of amotivation within self-determination theory, referring to students' belief that stronger forces beyond themselves determine their behavior (Otis, Grouzet, & Pelletier, 2005; Ryan & Deci, 2006), correlate negatively and uniquely with school achievement. We refer to these motivations of performance avoidance and amotivation as undermining because they are likely to reduce achievement and decrease students' amount and breadth of school-relevant reading activities. While performance-avoidance undermines reading, a construct such as intrinsic motivation is affirming for reading because it is likely to increase achievement and expand students' amount of reading activity. We propose, however, that undermining motivations are not mere opposites of affirming motivations because a low score on the affirming motivation may or may not be associated with the undermining motivation.

Reading motivations may be expected to be diverse because students may have interests in poems, songs, history, science, biographies, and multiple languages, as well as stories, fiction, fantasies, novels, and literature. Because a broad array of interests and knowledge may connect to reading, we can anticipate that a broad array of motivations may be integral to reading motivations and behaviors. This accounts partially for the decrease in correlation between reading motivation and math motivation from grades 1–6 (Chapman & Tunmer, 1995; Gottfried, 1990). Since reading is integral to one's identity as a distinctive individual or a member of a subculture (Guthrie et al., 2007; McCarthey & Moje, 2002), it is reasonable that a diverse set of variables will be needed to fully explain the spectrum of reading motivation phenomena.

Following the suggestion that reading motivation is multifaceted is the view that multiple motivations may reside within one individual. Although motivations in reading are diverse, they may be moderately and positively correlated either in their affirming or undermining forms. To represent these sets of moderate correlations we recommend the framework of reading profiles. A profile is a set of reading motivations that characterizes a group of individuals. Previous studies have identified motivational profiles qualitatively (Levy, Kaplan, & Patrick, 2004) or quantitatively (Pastor, Barron, Miller, & Davis, 2007), but these have not been related to reading motivation among K-12 students. Proceeding from the view that reading motivations may be affirming (positive in form such as intrinsic motivation) or undermining (negative in form such as performance avoidance), we propose four profiles. These are groups of readers consisting of the following:

- avid: high levels of multiple affirming motivations
- ambivalent: some high affirming and some high undermining motivations
- apathetic: low levels of affirming or undermining motivations
- averse: high levels of undermining motivations with few affirming motivations

These profiles draw on existing motivational constructs and theories to characterize the reading motivational phenomena represented in a diverse array of students. Researchers are enabled to predict achievement and the educational conditions that increase achievement more effectively than the use of any single construct or any solitary, theoretical viewpoint.

This review relates the profiles of reading motivation to four prevalent theories including self-determination theory (Ryan & Deci, 2006), goal theory (Meece, Anderman, & Anderman, 2006), social cognitive theory (Schunk, 2003a), and interest development theory (Hidi & Renninger, 2006). It is organized to follow these four questions:

1. What affirming motivational processes are positively correlated with reading achievement?
2. What experiences, events, and environmental factors in schooling are associated with these affirming motivations for reading?
3. What undermining motivational processes are negatively associated with reading achievement, and what experiences, events, and environmental factors in schooling are associated with these undermining motivations for reading?
4. To what extent are reading motivations correlated with each other to form composites that characterize students' profiles as readers who may be avid, ambivalent, apathetic, or avoidant?

What Affirming Motivational Processes are Positively Correlated with Reading Achievement?

Intrinsic Motivation Conceptually, intrinsic motivation has been characterized by behaviors in which "the reward is the satisfaction of the activity itself" (Vansteenkiste, Lens, & Deci, 2006, p. 20). Intrinsic motivation for reading refers to a student's desire to read for the sake of reading without extrinsic rewards. Sharing many characteristics with the construct of interest, which is described as positive emotions accompanying engagement (Hidi & Renninger, 2006), intrinsic motivation has been shown to correlate significantly with reading achievement in several studies (Gottfried, 1990; Unrau & Schlackman, 2006; Wang & Guthrie, 2004). This correlation has also been observed with ethnically diverse populations of Asian students, using a measure of intrinsic motivation for reading (Unrau & Schlackman, 2006; Wang & Guthrie, 2004). In a longitudinal study, academic intrinsic motivation was found to be positively associated with reading achievement for students in grades 4–12 (Gottfried, Fleming, & Gottfried 2001). Thus, in diverse populations, research has revealed that intrinsic motivation for reading has a positive association with performance on measures of reading achievement.

Perceived Autonomy Conceptually defined within self-determination theory (SDT), "autonomous motivation involves the experience of preference and choice" (Vansteenkiste et al., 2006, p. 19). It is important to note that autonomous motivation is not limited to actions or choices of the individual's own creation, but refers to the perception of control. Consistent with Harter (1992), we will refer to autonomous motivation as perceived autonomy. In this discussion, perceived autonomy for reading refers to the value of choosing books and the self-direction of reading behaviors (Guthrie et al., 2007).

Relations between perceived autonomy and achievement in reading have been documented for elementary school students. Students' perceived autonomy in the forms of valuing book selection and book ownership predicted their growth in reading comprehension across 4 months of school from September to December (Guthrie et al., 2007). In a path model, students' perceived autonomy directly predicted achievement test scores in reading and math combined, as well as combined grades. In this model, perceived autonomy contributed to academic outcomes indirectly by increasing students' positive engagement in classroom activities (Skinner, Wellborn, & Connell, 1990).

Self-Efficacy Within social cognitive theory (Bandura, 1977), "self-efficacy refers to beliefs about an individual's capabilities to learn or execute behaviors at identified levels" (Schunk, 2003b, p. 161). Successful students participate more readily, work harder, and persevere longer in the face of difficulties, and achieve at a higher level. Thus, efficacious readers believe they are capable of performing reading activities and are willing to attempt more challenging texts. However, students with high efficacy may not perform well on tasks if their actual abilities do not match their perceptions and beliefs.

Self-efficacy for reading has been operationalized as students' perceptions of competence in reading, which refer to beliefs regarding ability and skill in reading tasks (Chapman & Tunmer, 1995). Research on student perceptions of competence in reading has revealed a positive association with reading comprehension for fourth- and fifth-grade students (Chapman & Tunmer, 1995). In addition, students reporting higher levels of perceived competence obtained higher reading comprehension scores than those students with lower levels of perceived competence (Chapman & Tunmer, 1995; Wigfield & Guthrie, 1997).

Task Mastery Task mastery goals are conceptually defined as "a desire to improve ability in mastering a skill, and comprehending learning material" (Meece & Miller, 2001, p. 490). A central tenant of goal theory is that students who possess mastery goals view success in terms of self-improvement (Meece et al., 2006). Students with mastery goal orientations persevere through reading tasks, because they have a desire to master the material and gain a deeper understanding and knowledge. These students also gain satisfaction from the inherent qualities of the task, such as its interest and challenge.

Researchers have studied the impact of mastery goals on reading comprehension experimentally (van den Broek, Lorch, Linderholm, & Gustafson, 2001). Mastery goals were experimentally induced by asking students to read material for the purpose of studying (as opposed to entertainment). Students with mastery goals made more metacognitive comments, paraphrased text more often, and made more connecting inferences than those students who were told to read texts for the purpose of entertainment (Linderholm & van den Broek, 2002). Students who read the texts for the purpose of studying utilized the goal of mastering the reading material, which enabled them to comprehend the text at a deeper level (van den Broek et al., 2001).

Performance Goals Performance goals refer to students' concerns for their ability and performance relative to others (Pintrich, 2000). In addition, performance-approach goals encourage peer comparisons and the display of competence relative to others (Elliot, 1999). Performance goals can also be viewed as extrinsic motivations for achieving reading tasks. Extrinsic motivation refers to participation in an activity based on external criteria and incentives such as recognition, grades, and competition, and (Wang & Guthrie, 2004).

Performance goals have been found to have a positive association with students' reading performance. In a multicultural study, Chinese and American students' extrinsic motivations were found to be positively associated with past reading achievement (Wang & Guthrie, 2004). The performance goals of reading for the purposes of recognition and high grades had a lower correlation than intrinsic motivations of curiosity and involvement with a measure of text comprehension. However, with grades as the indicator of achievement, the performance goals correlated higher than intrinsic motivations (Wang & Guthrie, 2004). The performance goals of recognition and competition correlated lower than intrinsic motivations of curiosity and involvement for a measure of the extent that students used complex reading strategies to understand their texts during school learning. In all of these findings, the performance goals correlated at a low level, or not significantly different from zero, whereas the intrinsic measures correlated at a statistically significant level (Guthrie, Wigfield, & VonSecker, 2000). These findings are similar to the report of Pintrich (2000), whose literature review showed that performance goals correlated lower with achievement for high school and college students than mastery goals in several studies. These correlations are much lower than intrinsic motivation to reading achievement, and are often zero.

Social Motivation Perceptions of social support from important others has been shown to correlate with academic achievement (Furrer & Skinner, 2003; Wentzel, 1996). Specifically, relatedness refers to the "perceived availability of trusted others act[ing] as a buffer, allowing people to show more self-reliance, vigor, and tenacity in the face of obstacles" (Furrer & Skinner, 2003, p. 149). This concept is important in the domain of reading, where perceptions of social support can promote more perseverance and persistence when tackling challenging words or books. Linked to perceived social support are social goals defined as a measure of students' perceived efforts to assist peers with personal and academic difficulties (Wentzel, 2002; Wentzel, Barry, & Caldwell,

2004). Students who value relatedness and hold prosocial goals are likely to collaborate in reading, that is communicating with others orally or in writing about reading (Guthrie et al., 2007).

Prosocial goals and compliance goals relevant for engaging in academic activities in sixth grade have been shown to be associated with effort in English class and English grades in both sixth and eighth grades (Wentzel, 1996). Students who reported efforts to be more prosocial in class and willing to help others on assignments, put forth more effort in English class and had higher grades than those who reported being less social in class. Social goal pursuit has also been found to be a statistically significant predictor of the amount of effort sixth-grade students put forth in English classes (Wentzel, 1996). Collaboration in reading has been shown to correlate with teacher assigned grades in reading (Sweet, Guthrie, & Ng., 1998).

Value in Reading Value has been conceptually defined in motivation literature as a multidimensional motivational construct. Specifically, researchers have discussed four basic components of task value: attainment value, intrinsic value, utility value, and cost (Eccles & Wigfield, 2002). Among these, utility value pertains to the extent that "a task can have positive value to a person because it facilitates important future goals, even if he or she is not interested in the task for its own sake" (p. 120). Valuing is highly related to identified regulation in self-determination theory, representing the student's belief in the importance of schooling or reading. This is a strong form of internal motivation, which correlates as highly as intrinsic motivation for some school activities, such as doing the reading for homework (Otis et al., 2005).

In a study of the longitudinal development of intrinsic value and importance of reading in 4th and 10th grade students, researchers found several significant associations. Intrinsic value for reading in 4th and 10th grades was associated with time spent reading for leisure (Durik, Vida, & Eccles, 2006), while in 10th grade, importance of reading was additionally associated with reading for career aspirations (Durik et al., 2006). Identified regulation correlated with completing homework, attending classes, and holding positive expectations for high school completion (Otis et al., 2005). Thus, students' beliefs in the intrinsic value of reading and the importance they place on reading activities influence reading activities and achievements of students in primary and secondary grades.

What Experiences, Events, and Environmental Factors in Schooling are Associated with the Affirming Motivations for Reading?

Intrinsic Motivation and Interest As described in the previous section, there is some evidence that students' reading achievement is positively associated with their affirming motivations for reading including the following constructs: (a) intrinsic motivation, (b) perceived autonomy, (c) self-efficacy, (d) task mastery, (e) performance approach, (f) social motivation, and (g) value for reading. These are affirmative in the sense that they contribute to success in school. We next address instructional interventions, or classroom characteristics that are associated with these motivations for reading beginning with intrinsic motivation, which refers to reading for enjoyment or reading as an end in itself. As indicated previously, for this review, reading interest is not distinguished from intrinsic motivation, as they both are associated with positive affect, enjoyment, high amounts of reading, and disposition to behave favorably toward reading. We make this association for purposes of economy in this review, although interest is often defined as more task specific (Hidi & Renninger, 2006; Schiefele, 1991) than intrinsic motivation (Ryan & Deci, 2000).

Classroom studies have found that instructional practices of providing relevance in the texts and tasks of reading are associated with students' intrinsic motivation for reading and learning activities. For example, Assor, Kaplan, and Roth (2002) reported that when students viewed classroom activities as related to their goals and experiences, the students at two levels, including grades 3–5 and 6–8, reported "comfort, enjoyment, and interest" (p. 267). In a field experiment, classrooms with a relatively high amount of hands-on activities related to book reading showed higher intrinsic motivation for reading than classrooms with fewer relevance-producing, hands-on activities (Guthrie, Wigfield, Humenick, Perencevich, Taboada, & Barbosa, 2006). Furthermore, teacher questioning that enables students to find relevance by linking their experiences to stories and texts they are reading, increased students' interests as measured by on-task behaviors in reading (Taylor, Pearson, & Peterson, 2003).

In controlled laboratory conditions, Vansteenkiste, Simons, Lens, Sheldon, and Deci (2004) experimentally manipulated the extent that reading tasks were intrinsically or extrinsically motivating. In the intrinsic condition, adolescents who were at least mildly obese were given nutrition texts and instructed to "read for your own interest," and students in the extrinsic condition were instructed to read the same materials to get the highest possible score on a test. Students in the intrinsic condition showed more involvement and gained higher conceptual knowledge than students in the extrinsic condition. Students in the extrinsic condition showed higher levels of verbatim memorizing. In experimental studies, it is shown that when students rate a segment of text (either a sentence or a section of a textbook) as relevant to their purpose for reading, they show increased interest and higher recall for the content (Schraw & Dennison, 1994; Wade, Buxton, & Kelly, 1999). In many experiments, Schiefele (1999) reported that when students rate a text as highly interesting, they report higher positive affect and recall higher amounts of content than students who rate text as less interesting, even when prior knowledge is controlled.

Although interestingness of text is well-correlated with intrinsic motivation for reading and with knowledge gained from text interactions, a practical problem is that students seldom find school texts to be interesting. In surveys of middle school students (Ivey & Broaddus, 2001) and elementary-age children (Worthy, Patterson, Salas, Prater, & Turner, 2002), children at all levels of reading achievement typically reported that there were few classroom books, or even school library books, that they would choose to read on their own initiative. Because teachers cannot necessarily supply intrinsically motivating texts for school reading, instruction should explicitly include conditions that foster interest.

Perceived Autonomy One of the main ways to foster perceived autonomy is to afford students choices about their reading activities. This may include choice of text (which page or which book to read), choice of task (how to read), or choice of display (how to show one's knowledge gained from reading). Such experiences are highly associated with students' commitment and sense of control over classroom reading (Assor et al., 2002). Support for student autonomy is increased by allowing students to express opinions about texts, and give input into sequences of reading and instructional activities. Teacher autonomy support can be taught relatively easily. Reeve, Jang, and Reeve (2006) and Reeve, Jang, Carrell, Jeon, and Barch (2004) showed that one informational session with high school teachers on supporting students' autonomy increased their observed autonomy-supportive behaviors and students' engagement in a learning task. Additionally, teacher support for student engagement in school reading tasks in the form of allowing students to work in their own ways increased students' commitment and persistence in completing complex reading tasks (Skinner & Belmont, 1993).

Experiments have documented the effects of affording students significant academic choices in reading tasks on their perceived autonomy in reading. For example, Reynolds and Symons (2001) enabled students to select from a menu of texts to answer questions they had composed. They reported that student time spent and quality of text interactions were increased by the instructional choice conditions in comparison to control conditions. Grolnick and Ryan (1987) showed that allowing students to read for the purpose of teaching another student increased the students' perceived autonomy more than a condition in which students were asked to read with the goal of scoring well on a test. Based on interviews with teachers, Flowerday and Schraw (2000) enumerated a broad spectrum of academic choices that secondary teachers may provide to students. Many of these instructional actions increase perceived autonomy, which refers to students' sense that they are in charge of their reading, that they can make significant decisions within the approved classroom goal structure, and that the teacher is partly dedicated to their self-direction as students who learn from text. Although Assor et al. (2002) suggested that relevance was more related to student engagement and feelings about school than autonomy, the measurement, scaling, and variance on scales did not permit a conclusive comparison among constructs. While Flowerday, Schraw, and Stevens (2004) suggested that choice had little impact on academic performance, they only examined conditions of test-taking, which are not generalizable to classroom instruction or teaching situations.

Self-Efficacy Student self-efficacy in reading has been systematically increased by a procedure of modeling by an expert (such as a teacher) with feedback about progress in task performance. In several experiments, Schunk and his colleagues have shown that self-efficacy can be increased for several reading skills, including word recognition (Schunk & Rice, 1991), gaining the main idea from text (Schunk & Rice, 1993), and revising text to increase coherence (Zimmerman & Kitsantas, 2002). The procedure begins by having learners observe and attempt to emulate an expert model who performs the task flawlessly. Next, students set goals for performing and receive feedback about their task success. Based on this information, students observe new models and set new goals, which generate self-regulation of task performance. Under these conditions, self-efficacy is often excessively high and inaccurate at the outset of instruction. Informative feedback leads to initial decreases for some students to align their task performance with their self-efficacy. Modeling and feedback have positive effects and self-efficacy is highly associated with reading skill at the close of the interventions. It should be noted that simply improving reading skill is insufficient to improve efficacy (Nelson, Stage, Epstein, & Pierce, 2005) because students' self-confidence may not necessarily increase unless the feedback about their success is fully processed.

Self-efficacy is integral to the self-regulation of reading strategies necessary for reading comprehension activities. Integrated models that support self-efficacy development and reading strategy acquisition simultaneously increase self-efficacy more than models that include either the strategy support or motivational support alone (Rozendaal, Minnaert, & Boekaerts, 2005; Souvignier & Mokhlesgerami, 2006).

Task Mastery Goals It is well documented that teachers' use of mastery goals in the classroom is associated with students' report of mastery goals in their reading and text interactions (Anderman, 1999; Pintrich & de Groot, 1990). When teachers emphasize that grasping the themes and integrating the knowledge base across separate segments is the highest priority, students invest in making connections and building internal causal models (van den Broek et al., 2001) as their purposes for reading. For elementary school students, task mastery goals are often implemented by emphasizing optimal challenge of reading of texts for students. In contrast, some teachers emphasize simple sentence-level activities with a large volume of easy, right and wrong answers. However, these tasks do not motivate students for task mastery, and are more likely to increase performance goals (Meece & Miller, 1999).

Across a range of ages and classroom environments, teachers who emphasize understanding text content enable students to become oriented to deep comprehension. In contrast, teachers who emphasize grades and extrinsic incentives increase students' attention to their performance and their standing relative to peers, which represent extrinsic motivations for reading. Under these conditions, students often use surface strategies in reading which reduce, rather than increase, their tested reading achievement. At the secondary level, students are capable of perceiving changes in goal structure across tasks within one classroom. If a teacher emphasizes mastery goals for reading a novel but performance goals for learning vocabulary, students will adjust their learning goals accordingly to be consistent with the teacher and aligned with the classroom demands (Greene, Miller, Crowson, Duke, & Akey, 2004). Thus, mastery goals for reading are task sensitive, as well as teacher sensitive, across a range of variations within and across classrooms. This contextual sensitivity for task mastery goals in reading co-exists with a broader motivational orientation across mastery goals and performance goals for secondary students (Pintrich, 2000).

Performance-Approach Goals This refers to giving students external incentives such as grades, rewards, or recognition, as a motivational support for reading. Although every school gives grades, honor roll recognition, and other rewards for success, there appears to be little empirical evidence that students who seek to attain these rewards are consistently higher achievers than those who are indifferent toward them (Pintrich, 2000; Wang & Guthrie, 2004; Wigfield & Guthrie, 1997).

In light of this low correlation, it may seem unnecessary to address the issue of whether classroom conditions enhance performance-approach goals. However, there seems to be no more frequent motivational practice than awarding grades or threatening to give tests for attaining short-term control of students' attention and effort in school reading tasks. One literature review of 10 experimental studies reported no overall effect of giving an external incentive on reading comprehension, vocabulary, or reading practices (McQuillan, 1997).

Conversely, rigorous experiments with college students showed a positive impact of performance-contingent rewards on motivational outcomes. The task consisted of nonverbal games (playing pinball machines) and the reward consisted of information about success and failure. Under these conditions, performance-contingent rewards increased students' perceived competence, valuing of confidence, and task involvement. However, the rewards did not increase students' desire for the rewards, thus providing no evidence immediately pertinent to the issue of whether classroom conditions influence the extrinsic goals of learners (Sansone & Harackiewicz, 2000). While the potentially undermining effect of providing extrinsic incentives for an intrinsically motivating activity such as reading has been hotly contested (Lepper & Henderlong, 2000), there is little evidence on this point with respect to reading in schools. Thus, the scientific jury is out about whether the most widely used motivational practice in education, consisting of evaluating, testing, and grading students is positive, negative, or indifferent as an influence on students' motivations for reading achievement. In addition, the school practice of offering pizzas, gold stars, or bracelets for reading books has not been evaluated experimentally for its effects on reading achievement or reading motivation.

Social Motivation Our use of this construct with regard to reading is relatively broad, including feelings of connectedness or belonging (Furrer & Skinner, 2003), pursuit of prosocial goals (Wentzel, 2005), and interpersonal relationships with a social group (Davis, 2003). Substantial evidence from research utilizing hierarchical multiple regression and structural equation modeling shows that students who possess strong positive relationships with teachers and students are likely to report higher social motivation, such as feelings of acceptance within the classroom. While it is not clear whether these social motivations relate directly to reading for students beyond elementary school, students in the primary grades who enjoy a positive relationship with teachers were more socially interactive with peers and more highly engaged in reading activities than others (Hughes & Kwok, 2007). Furthermore, students in the later elementary grades who perceive the classroom structure to be interactionally supportive are likely to be more intrinsically motivated in their reading than others (Ng, Guthrie, Van Meter, McCann, & Alao, 1998), and students who frequently share books with friends are more likely than others to be higher achievers on standardized tests (Guthrie, Schafer, Wang, & Afflerbach, 1995).

Can teachers construct classroom environments or enact practices that increase social motivation and subsequent reading achievement? While limited, the experimental evidence on this question is promising. At the secondary level, Applebee, Langer, Nystrand, and Gamoran (2003) showed that holding "open discussions," in which students actively participate directly with each other in English classes, increased commitment to venturing risky viewpoints and listening deferentially to peers, which imply a measure of social acceptance. These conversational literary discussions led to higher achievements in literature interpretation by enabling students to perceive characters from multiple perspectives and gain a more nuanced understanding of literary themes. Although the studies are limited to correlational data, and are not focused on reading, a range of evidence shows the association of positive teacher-student relationships and academic achievement (Furrer & Skinner, 2003; Wentzel, 2002).

In parallel form, a large experiment at the elementary level showed that students could be taught to collaborate in literature discussions by expressing opinions, listening politely, building on others' viewpoints, and taking diverse perspectives. Students in the collaborative conditions gained the ability to perceive literature from multiple perspectives, and increased their social responsiveness (Almasi, 1995). Furthermore, Isaac, Sansone, and Smith (1999) found that when students across a wide range of ages were assigned to work collaboratively on a one-hour activity of designing a school campus, they found the task interesting and wanted to continue the social activity, even after it was completed. In contrast, students who were assigned to work on the same task individually, without interaction or conversation with other students, were less likely to rate the task as interesting, and not at all keen to pursue the activity after the experimental study was completed. In conclusion, collaborative structures appear to increase the disposition for social interaction in reading and interpersonal involvement with text.

Value in Reading Value in reading correlates with reading achievement and engagement in school reading tasks at the secondary level (Greene et al., 2004). As described previously, valuing reading is closely allied with the construct of "identified motivation" in self-determination theory (Ryan & Deci, 2000). A reader with identified motivation believes that "being a good reader is important for me." This motivation is associated with completing homework, which ties it closely to reading, and to being engaged in education through attending classes and completing high school (Otis et al., 2005). However, there appears to be little evidence on whether classroom conditions or instructional practices are associated with valuing reading.

Integrated Classroom Practices Supporting Multiple Motivations It is likely that many of the motivations including intrinsic motivation, self-efficacy, mastery goals, and others may be correlated with one another. If so, classroom structures with multiple supports for motivations might impact students substantially. Several studies verify this expectation. Hamre and Pianta (2005) conducted a study with 1,364 Grade 1 students from 827 classrooms in 747 schools from 295 districts in 32 states. Based on 80 minutes of classroom observation during one day, it was found that teachers' motivational support for students varied substantially. Teachers ranged in (a) sensitivity to students' needs and interests, (b) climate of laughter and warmth, (c) use of flexible routines, (d) being student centered, (e) showing anger, and (f) over-controlling students. In these terms, motivation support was positively associated with students' achievement in reading for individuals who were at risk (needing motivation support), but not individuals who were in a no-risk category. Remarkably, motivation support had as much impact on reading achievement as the quality of literacy instruction.

At grade levels 3–5, integrated support for multiple motivations has been shown to increase both motivation and achievement in reading. In one approach, Concept-Oriented Reading Instruction (CORI) includes classroom practices of relevance, choice, success, collaboration, and thematic units that are intended to support students' intrinsic motivation, perceived autonomy, self-efficacy, social motivation, and mastery goals respectively. A meta-analysis of 11 experimental studies showed that CORI has an effect size on individual motivations of curiosity, self-efficacy, and social motivation of about .30. The effect size on a composite representing intrinsic motivation was 1.26. The mean effect size on a measure of teacher ratings of student engagement in reading was 1.00, illustrating that the multiple support system impacted students' diverse motivations for reading (Guthrie, McRae, & Klauda, 2007). In a related experimental study, integrated motivational support of social studies for Grade 3 students from The Netherlands contained the practices of relevance, choice, success, collaboration, and a thematic unit which were highly similar to CORI. Students in a multiple motivation group were higher in reading motivation and reading strategies than students in control groups (Aarnoutse & Schellings, 2003). It appears that the classroom characteristics and instructional practices presented in this section may be integrated into educational programs that are likely to generate increases in several internal motivations for reading achievement.

What Undermining Motivational Processes are Negatively Associated with Reading Achievement, and What Experiences, Events, and Environmental Factors in Schooling are Associated with these Undermining Motivations for Reading?

Statement of Perspective We propose that undermining motivations in reading are important due to their pervasiveness in the population of secondary school students and their relative uniqueness in predicting reading achievement. We define undermining motivations as associated with negative affect in reading (dislike or discomfort in reading activities) and negative behaviors toward reading (low frequency of reading, procrastination, and self-handicapping). We suggest there are multiple undermining motivations including: (a) the sense of being controlled (coerced) during reading activities, (b) perceived difficulty of reading tasks, (c) meaninglessness of texts, (d) performance goals in the classroom and school structure, and (e) identity formation that opposes reading or conflicts with values favoring reading. Limited but distinctive evidence indicates that classroom conditions and instruction may increase each of these sources of reading avoidance.

Rationale for a Focus on Undermining Motivations in Reading

When investigators interview or observe students in classrooms and naturalistic environments to characterize the students' affects and behaviors toward reading, the predominant outcome of their observations is that students avoid school reading (Alvermann et al., 2007; Dowson & McInerney, 2003; Franzak, 2006; Smith & Wilhelm, 2002). In interviews, students claim that: (a) the texts are not interesting (Ivey & Broaddus, 2001), (b) their friends do not read school materials frequently (Moje & Young, 2000), (c) the tasks are irrelevant to them (Smith & Wilhelm, 2002), (d) peers they identify with are not proficient readers (Taylor & Graham, 2007), and (e) reading conflicts with their social goals and norms (Dowson & McInerney, 2003). Remarkably, however, the salience of these undermining reading motivations has not been fully addressed in quantitative investigations.

A large majority of quantitative studies of reading motivation measure such constructs as intrinsic motivation and self-efficacy. These constructs are affirming in the sense that agreement with a statement such as "I enjoy reading long books" implies a high level of intrinsic motivation. Likewise, the statement "I read daily" is an affirming behavioral indicator of intrinsic motivation. Low scores on a scale with items such as these denote a lack of intrinsic motivation. Students who disagree with these statements are failing to affirm their intrinsic motivation. However, students who are low on intrinsic motivation do not necessarily avoid reading. Disagreeing with "I enjoy reading." is very different from agreeing with "I hate reading." Thus, students who are low in intrinsic motivation are heterogeneous with respect to avoidance. Some are avoidant, others may be apathetic or externally regulated, and therefore not completely avoidant of reading.

In these conditions, a scale that measures avoidance of reading will contribute uniquely beyond a scale measuring intrinsic motivation to the prediction of reading achievement. It appears that the undermining motivations of dislike or perceived difficulty are not the mere inverse of affirming motivation such as intrinsic, efficacy, mastery, or social reading motivations. Undermining motivations contain their own affects and behaviors, and thus, are not merely on the opposite end of a bipolar scale with affirming motivations.

After interviewing middle school students ages 12–15, Dowson and McInerney (2003) reported a variety of sources of work avoidance in school tasks such as history or English that inevitably required reading. Their students reported frequent off-task behavior, "tuning out" of complex reading activities, and feigning incompetence or misunderstanding of texts. Students reported boredom and even anger toward the teachers and homework tasks that were excessively difficult. Prominent was students' attempt to minimize effort by finding shortcuts and reducing cognitive demands. When students experienced social isolation or rejection in school, they often retreated from the reading and academic tasks associated with those experiences. In quantitative studies of work-avoidant goal orientation, Meece and Miller (2001) focused on minimizing effort to complete required tasks with items such as, "I wanted to do as little as possible on this assignment." However, this meaning for the 'avoid' construct is less pervasive and extreme than the meanings emerging from interviews of Dowson and McInerney (2003).

Brophy (2004) contributes to the discussion of avoidance by saying that "Apathetic students are uninterested, or even alienated, from school learning," [which represents] "the ultimate motivational problem facing teachers" (p. 307). In Brophy's view, there are two sources of reading avoidance: lack of interest and alienation. We suggest, however, these represent independent constructs. A student may be apathetic, with the attributes of indifference or disinterest. On the other hand, an avoidant student who is "alienated" will be averse, strategically evasive, and hostile toward texts and reading activities related to school.

Earlier, Wigfield and Guthrie (1997) investigated the construct of reading work avoidance, consisting of four reasons for not reading such as "complicated stories are no fun to read," which correlated negatively with achievement (Baker & Wigfield, 1999). However, to update that view, we propose that avoidant motivation consists of a diverse set of negative affects and negative behaviors toward texts and reading activities. We believe there are multiple emotions, feelings, and motivational constructs that may operate to undermine reading.

Motivational Sources of Reading Aversion

We view reading avoidance as heterogeneous in the sense that it is influenced by diverse affects and represented by a range of behaviors. These motivations consist of task avoidance, perceived lack of control, perceived task difficulty, meaninglessness of texts, performance avoidance, social isolation, and dis-identity. We next address each of these briefly.

Task Avoidance Reading achievement is the most prominent correlate of reading avoidance in the empirical literature. According to a variety of definitions, reading avoidance is negatively associated with reading achievement. For children in the later elementary grades, Wigfield and Guthrie (1997) reported that reading work avoidance correlated negatively with amount of reading. Confirming and extending this, Baker and Wigfield (1999) found that reading work avoidance was especially predictive for African American students, and was more highly predictive of achievement for them than a measure of intrinsic motivation. Meece and Holt (1993) reported that work avoidant students (who are also low on mastery orientations) had low achievement test scores (usually reading comprehension tests) and superficial engagement in reading activities (such as copying work from a friend). Students with negative perceived autonomy (believing they were externally controlled by the teacher) showed lower academic achievement than students with positive perceived autonomy (Skinner, Wellborn, & Connell, 1990).

Beyond the correlation of reading avoidance and reading achievement, several investigations report reciprocal determination between these variables. For primary students ages 6–7, Onatsu-Arvilommi and Nurmi (2000), using structural equation modeling across four points in time, found that high levels of task avoidance in reading predicted low levels of reading skills at two points in time. Additionally, a low level of reading skill respectively predicted a high level of task-avoidant behaviors at one point in time. These findings occurred in models that controlled the counterpart constructs, suggesting there is a downward spiral, with lower achievement resulting from higher task avoidance progressively across time. In a similar finding, Chapman and Tunmer (2003) reported that the perceived difficulty of reading tasks (which is an undermining reading motivation) was associated with lower achievement in word reading tasks in year 1 of schooling, and perceived difficulty was associated with lower achievement in reading comprehension tasks in year 4 of schooling, with the correlation increasing across time. Thus, perceived difficulty and reading achievement become more highly aligned across time in elementary school.

Perceived Lack of Control In a recent paper, Ryan and Deci (2006) emphasized the contrast between autonomy (internal sources of control) and heteronomy (external sources of control) of one's behaviors and values. We suggest that a student who feels controlled believes that he is not directing his activities, not making decisions about his reading strategies, and not selecting texts relevant to his goals or interests. Assor, Kaplan, Kanat-Maymon, and Roth (2005) reported that students who feel controlled in these ways are disengaged from classroom reading activities. They do not participate in reading tasks, do not put forth effort to comprehend complex materials, and disrupt classroom routines. Similarly, Seifert and O'Keefe (2001) reported that students who felt controlled were relatively high in their avoidance of schoolwork and attempted to minimize their effort to complete tasks required by the educational program. Finally, Skinner, Wellborn, and Connell (1990) found that their construct of negative perceived control, which reflected students' amotivation for school activities, was associated with disengagement in schoolwork, as shown by low levels of participation, inattention, and lack of persistence. Thus, feeling controlled is associated with reading avoidance and explicit evasion of academic literacy.

Perceived Task Difficulty In several studies, Chapman and Tunmer (1995) illustrated that when students believe that reading is difficult, they are likely to have negative attitudes and aversive feelings toward reading, which in turn, are likely to lead to reading avoidance. In a complementary finding, Seifert and O'Keefe (2001) reported that students who perceived tasks to be difficult were likely to be work avoidant in the sense of minimizing effort and reducing the necessary activities to maintain a minimally acceptable grade. Therefore, when students believe that reading tasks are troublesome and difficult to handle, they are likely to exhibit avoidant motivations.

Meaninglessness of Texts When a student sees a reading task as meaningless, she finds it irrelevant to her interests, needs, or knowledge. In this sense, meaninglessness was associated with disengagement from classwork (Assor et al., 2002). In a scale representing "forced meaningless activities," students reported that they tended to rebel against tasks that were meaningless (such as homework that did not help them), and answering questions that seemed useless. Confirming this, Seifert and O'Keefe (2001) reported that when students described their reading as meaningless, they were likely to work as little as possible (becoming work avoidant), rather than enjoying learning new things (displaying intrinsic motivation).

Performance Avoidance It has been shown that work avoidant goals are negatively associated with task mastery goals and performance goals (Meece & Holt, 1993). As students' performance goals increase in the transition from elementary to middle school, and their mastery goals decline during this period (Meece et al., 2006), it is plausible that work avoidance increases as a consequence.

Social Isolation A child's sense of isolation can stem from several sources. Furrer and Skinner (2003) suggest that relatedness derives from "a history of interactions with specific social partners" (p. 148). Students who do not establish trusting relationships with significant partners tend to hold views about themselves as "unlovable" and about the social world in general as "hostile" (p. 148). Students who have a sense of unrelatedness or lack of belonging in the classroom environment, either from teachers or peers, may disengage from the classroom context (Furrer & Skinner, 2003).

More directly, peer rejection has been found to have a statistically significant relationship with achievement scores for elementary aged students in kindergarten through fifth grade (Buhs, Ladd, & Herald, 2006). Peer rejection can detrimentally affect both a child's willingness to engage in the classroom and their overall performance in that classroom. In this context, peer rejection has been characterized as the "extent to which individuals [are] disliked by classroom peers" (Buhs et al., 2006, p. 3). Also isolating is mistrust which refers to "inattention, carelessness, and lack of willingness to work out difficulties in relationships with friends" (Levy-Tossman, Kaplan, & Assor, 2007). Students who have a general sense of mistrust of their peers and classmates have been shown to report lower levels of self-efficacy and higher levels of performance avoidance. Mistrust of one's peers is associated with detrimental self-perceptions, which have in turn been connected with negative achievement outcomes.

Dis-Identity A range of quantitative (Taylor & Graham, 2007) and qualitative (Guthrie, Hoa, Wigfield, Tonks, & Perencevich, 2006; McCarthey & Moje, 2002) studies suggest that students' identity formation, especially during adolescence, may undermine their reading motivations and generate opposition to school reading. In some cases, students may value popularity (Taylor & Graham, 2007), social relationships (Davis, 2003), or topical interests of pop culture (McCarthey & Moje, 2002) that conflict with their affirmative motivations for school reading. As students embrace out-of-school literacies, they often reject school reading. While this appears to be especially true for those struggling with reading, and those whose cultural backgrounds may not mesh well with school, quantitative studies are needed on the demographic scope of these undermining motivations. While some students in early adolescence (Guthrie, Hoa, et al., 2006) and later adolescence (Otis et al., 2005) are self-regulating readers who are intrinsically motivated to read a wide range of literature and informational books, these students are a minority of less than 20% of the U. S. school-age population (Kirsch, de Jong, Lafontaine, Medelovits, & Monseur, 2002). The force of reading avoidance accumulates during the secondary school years.

Classroom Experiences That Exacerbate Undermining Motivations

Teacher Over-Control Excessive teacher control refers to teachers being domineering in their management, rigid in the use of routines, insensitive to students' interests, and rejecting of students' requests or needs to express opinions. According to several investigators, this teacher behavior of over-controlling reading and writing activities in the classroom leads to low perceived autonomy. Such teacher over-control is associated with reading avoidance and low reading achievement in Grade 1 (Hamre & Pianta, 2005), grades 3–5 (Assor et al., 2002), and grades 6–8 (Assor et al., 2002; Skinner et al., 1990). Beyond these correlations, experimental studies show that teacher autonomy support can be increased with suitable, professional development. Teachers in comparison conditions used highly procedural, over-controlling practices and the students showed low engagement with reduced achievement (Reeve et al., 2004). This finding indicates that the variable of teacher over-control is causally related to students' negative affects of being controlled (coercion), with the probable consequence of reading avoidance.

Difficulty of Texts and Reading Tasks In an interview study with children in the middle elementary grades, investigators recorded the extent to which specific books, and books in general, were easy or too hard to read. Students who reported that classroom books were too difficult for them were highly likely to be nonreaders, saying that they had no favorite books or authors, did not read frequently, and avoided books when possible (Guthrie et al., 2007). Likewise, students who reported that they could not read words, did not know vocabulary, and were unable to read easily were most likely to be oppositional to school reading (Guthrie et al., 2007; Smith & Wilhelm, 2002). It is quite rational to avoid reading activities in circumstances where reading well is highly prized, such as a classroom, and one's reading competence is doubtful.

Content Irrelevance Evidence suggests that when students find text irrelevant to their goals, interests, and needs, they become avoidant. In a construct termed "fostering relevance," students reported their perception of the teacher with such items as: "The teacher explains why it is important to study certain topics in school" and "The teacher talks about the connection between what we study in school and what happens in real life." A low score on items such as these reflect the perception of irrelevance in school tasks and reading materials. Low perceived relevance was associated with low behavioral and cognitive engagement in classrooms for students in grades 3–5, as well as in grades 6–8 (Assor et al., 2002). Consistent with the effects on engagement, students who perceived low relevance in classroom activities had negative feelings of stress, anger, and boredom, and rarely had the positive feelings of comfort, enjoyment, and interest in schoolwork (Assor et al., 2005). Irrelevance of school reading is a central theme of qualitative research that attempts to investigate the alignment between students' quest for social identity and their adjustment to school reading requirements (Bean & Readance, 2002). Students who find that school reading is irrelevant to their needs soon become avoidant (O'Brien & Stewart, 1995).

Social Isolation Although evidence supports the association of socially affirming motivations such as need for relatedness, prosocial goals, and social popularity with academic achievement in reading (Furrer & Skinner, 2003; Hamre & Pianta, 2005; Hughes & Kwok, 2007; Wentzel, 2005), there are relatively few cases in which negative classroom characteristics that may lead to isolation or rejection have been related to reading motivation or reading achievement. If teachers approach the textbook by emphasizing solitary work, avoiding group discussions, restricting opinion sharing, and de-emphasizing student input into classroom management, students may feel socially disconnected, and thus become reading avoidant. However, this has not been investigated empirically with respect to reading and remains to be explored with new conceptualizations and measures in the reading domain.

Profiles of Reading Motivation

To What Extent Are Reading Motivations Correlated with Each Other to Form Composites that Characterize Students' Profiles as Readers Who May be Avid, Ambivalent, Apathetic, or Averse?

Background to this Section We have documented that reading motivations of intrinsic motivation, perceived autonomy, self-efficacy, social interaction, and mastery goals are all positively associated with reading achievement, and many are positively correlated with amount and breadth of reading activities. In contrast, several reading motivations are noteworthy for their undermining qualities including: meaninglessness, lack of perceived control, perceived difficulty, performance avoidance, and social isolation. Many of these are associated with low achievement and avoidance of reading in empirical literature. Complementing these correlations of reading motivation and achievement, the empirical literature shows that classroom practices and teacher-student interactions are associated with both the affirmative and undermining motivations, indicating that classroom practices are a source of influence on these motivations.

Profiles of Reading Motivation: A Proposal

In this section, we present initial evidence that many of the affirming motivations are substantially correlated with each other. For example, intrinsic motivation for reading and self-efficacy in reading are positively associated in numerous studies, although the theoretical origins of these motivational constructs were quite different. Likewise, we suggest that all of the affirming motivations, including intrinsic motivation, perceived autonomy, self-efficacy, social interaction, task mastery goals, and value in reading are positively associated for a diverse population of students in grades 4–12. We further suggest that the undermining motivations of meaninglessness, perceived control, perceived difficulty, devaluing reading, and possibly social isolation are also positively associated with each other, and we offer initial empirical evidence of this pattern.

Building on this pattern of associations, we propose that there are four profiles of students including the following:

1. *Avid readers* are those who have high levels of affirming motivations and low levels of undermining motivations for reading. These students are typically the highest achievers in reading.
2. *Ambivalent readers* are those with an uneven profile with some high affirming motivations and some high avoidant motivations for reading. For example, these students may be efficacious for school reading (believing they can do it), but uninterested, with low intrinsic motivation. This group may be expected to be intermediate in reading achievement and school success.
3. *Apathetic readers* are those who have medium levels of affirming and medium levels of undermining motivations for reading. Their achievement may be expected to be intermediate between the avid and averse readers.
4. *Averse readers* are those who exhibit high levels of undermining motivations and low levels of affirming motivations for reading. These students are typically low in reading achievement.

There are likely to be important variations of these profiles across achievement levels, age groups, and contexts. For example, struggling readers are more likely to be averse than avid, but high achievers may also be apathetic in high proportions. In the transition from elementary to middle school, students are likely to become more ambivalent, with strong likes and dislikes in reading. This may include rejection of school homework reading but an embrace of pop magazines. Most important, averse students may have various, multiple undermining motivations, all of which may need to be addressed to re-engage students in school reading. A student with low social acceptance, but adequate self-efficacy, and interest in reading, needs different support than a student with low self-efficacy, but adequate social interactions and interests in reading.

We suggest that the proposed set of four profiles represents the phenomena of reading motivation more comprehensively than it can be represented in any single, prevailing motivational theory, including self-determination theory, goal theory, social cognitive theory, and interest theory. In other words, explaining reading motivation fully requires multiple theories, rather than a single one. Consequences of the profile framework for reading motivation are that it can provide a relatively comprehensive accounting of motivation phenomenon, offer stronger predictions of reading achievement than otherwise possible, and can supply a framework for adapting classroom instruction and schooling to students' motivational characteristics.

Associations Among Affirming Motivations for Reading

The profile of avid readers is characterized by multiple, associated affirming motivations. We provide a sample of evidence documenting the positive correlations among motivational constructs that are central to prominent theoretical formulations. The construct of intrinsic motivation is central to self-determination theory and represents the highest level of autonomous behavior (Ryan & Deci, 2006). At a similar level of prominence is the construct of self-efficacy within the theoretical framework of social cognitive theory (Bandura, 1977; Schunk, 2003a). Referring to belief in one's capacity to perform tasks well, self-efficacy is viewed as the enabler of students' successful performance and well-being. For the domain of reading, intrinsic motivation and self-efficacy for reading have been found to be positively correlated, based on evidence from interviews with students and self-report questionnaires (Guthrie et al., 2007). It is reasonable that students who profess to enjoy reading for its own sake should also be relatively assured of their abilities to read proficiently. Thus, these two motivational constructs at the center of two prominent theoretical formulations pertinent to reading development are shown to be well-connected empirically.

Another major theoretical framework pertinent to reading motivation is goal theory. In this framework, mastery goals refer to students' desire to comprehend deeply and understand schoolwork, including texts. Such mastery goals are substantially positively correlated with self-efficacy for high school students (Greene et al., 2004). Students who claim to seek deep understanding in their reading and schoolwork are relatively confident about their capacity to understand their school texts. In addition, task mastery goals have been associated with social goals related to maintaining good relationships and supporting students interpersonally within classroom learning situations that involve reading and writing activities (Wentzel, 2005). It appears that desire for deep understanding and content mastery from reading is accompanied by relatively high self-confidence and positive social dispositions.

In the theoretical formulation of expectancy value theory, the construct of valuing is integral (Eccles & Wigfield, 2002). Valuing reading refers to the belief that reading is beneficial, important for the future, and will contribute to success in valued endeavors, such as higher education. Especially for high school students, valuing reading is associated with task mastery goals, which refers to the quest for fully understanding texts, and self-efficacy, representing positive belief in the capacity to succeed in reading situations (Greene et al., 2004). For elementary school students, valuing reading as measured by rated importance of reading as a skill was associated with intrinsic motivations of involvement and curiosity in reading (Wigfield & Guthrie, 1997).

In brief, each of the constructs we have identified as affirming, including intrinsic motivation (interest), perceived autonomy, self-efficacy, task mastery goals, valuing reading, and socially interacting around reading, are positively associated with at least one other construct in this set of constructs. This supports our expectation that an important subset of students will likely possess an array of multiple affirming motivations for reading. For these students, reading motivation will be multifaceted.

Associations Among Undermining Motivations for Reading

The profile of averse readers shows multiple undermining motivations, although the number of studies addressed to the undermining motivations reading is substantially fewer than those addressing affirming motivations. Conceptually, these motivations are intended to represent the inverse of the affirming ones previously presented. In that light, we suggest that meaninglessness (boredom) is the inverse of intrinsic reading motivation. This is justified by the fact that meaninglessness is associated with nonreading, whereas intrinsic motivation is a disposition to read for its own sake (Seifert & O'Keefe, 2001). For high school students, Legault, Green-Demers, and Pelletier (2006) reported that students who found studying (inevitably including reading) to be boring, repetitive, and meaningless also reported low self-efficacy for succeeding in schoolwork and meeting the text demands of the classroom. In an interview study, elementary school students who disliked reading because it was meaningless (boring) were unlikely to value choice in reading, and believed that powerful others, such as teachers and parents, were in control of the decisions surrounding their reading and learning activities (Guthrie et al., 2007). Thus, meaninglessness was associated with relatively low self-efficacy, devaluing reading, and perceived external control in reading.

A relatively well-investigated construct is perceived difficulty, referring to students' belief that many reading tasks are impossible for them to perform. At the elementary school level, perceived difficulty is associated with meaninglessness (Guthrie et al., 2007). At the high school level, students who experience difficulty in completing their reading tasks for schoolwork, and believe they do not have the ability to be successful, are likely to devalue school and believe that reading and schooling are not important for them (Legault et al., 2006).

When students believe they are externally controlled in reading (feeling coerced), they are likely to find reading aversive (Guthrie et al., 2007), and report high levels of work avoidance for reading and other school activities (Assor et al., 2005). In extreme forms of perceived external control, students report anger and hostility toward the teacher and the tasks associated with the classes (Assor et al., 2005). Additionally, students who believe they are externally controlled in reading rarely interact with other students by sharing books or talking about the content of their reading (Guthrie et al., 2007). When reading is not something the individual initiates and directs, it is improbable that a reading behavior can foster interpersonal relationships.

Evidently, the undermining motivational constructs of meaninglessness, perceived difficulty, perceived external control, and devaluing of reading are empirically associated with each other in many instances. The current evidence suggests that an important subset of students will possess multiple undermining reading motivations. At least some students will find reading to be meaningless, extremely difficult, externally imposed, and worthless to their futures. Such a subset of students may be expected to show a high commitment to avoiding reading, as suggested in several studies (Assor et al., 2005; Legault et al., 2006; Seifert & O'Keefe, 2001). These students would exhibit the avoidant profile within our proposed framework.

Relation of Reading Profiles to Theoretical Frameworks

In summary, we suggest that the four profiles include subsets of students consisting of: (a) *avid readers*, (b) *ambivalent readers*, (c) *apathetic readers*, and (d) *averse readers*. It is evident that the multiple motivational constructs, drawn from four major theoretical perspectives, including intrinsic motivation, mastery goals, self-efficacy, social motivation, and value in reading, contribute to each profile. Because these profiles are not fully explained by any single, extant motivational theory, we suggest it will be fruitful for reading motivation to investigate the affective, cognitive, and social attributes of each profile and generate potential explanations (theories) for the profiles in relation to each other.

Using a person-centered analytical perspective, a few researchers have proposed to relate profiles of motivation to social or achievement variables. Investigators have reported that a motivational profile consisting of relatively high mastery orientation and relatively low performance orientation is associated with high levels of friendship among seventh graders (Levy-Tossman et al. 2007). A descriptive qualitative study suggested that fifth graders with this profile of high mastery-low performance collaborated with other students based on their peers' productive contributions to the group irrespective of their social standing, whereas students with other profiles collaborated based on their peers' social standing (Levy et al., 2004). At the university level, students with the high mastery-low performance profile used deep-level learning strategies more than other students (Braten & Olaussen, 2005). From a self-determination perspective, investigators reported that high school and college students with a profile that combined high perceived autonomy together with high perceived control were the highest achievers with the least distraction and most school satisfaction (Ratelle, Guay, Vallerand, Larose, & Senecal, 2007). Thus, although motivational profiles have been associated with social and academic characteristics, motivation profiles have not been formed for reading or related to reading achievement in the grades 4–12 population.

Practical Consequences of a Profile Framework

To the extent that the proposed profile framework is valid, the potential for predicting achievement is increased. If the undermining motivations are not mere opposites of the affirming motivations, then both sets will contribute substantially to predicting achievement. In other words, in a multiple regression with a large sample, the undermining motivations will add significantly beyond the affirming motivations to explain variance in reading achievement. The same may be expected to occur for reading practices such as the types and amounts of reading that people do. A motivational frame, with undermining as well as affirming explicitly measured and entered, should be more predictive of the diverse practices in and out of school, across a variety of media, than any single set of motivational constructs.

If there are students who may be considered avoidant readers, it may be beneficial to adapt instruction to the multiple motivational sources of their resistance to reading. For example, if averse readers find that reading is meaningless, impossibly difficult, coerced, irrelevant, and socially conflicting, the processes of classroom instruction and schooling may be improved by addressing these issues. For low-achieving students, especially in middle and high school, it seems highly likely that multiple, undermining reading motivations prevail. To increase the reading achievement of these students, classrooms will need to adapt to these motivational attributes, as well as attend to cognitive issues. Although teaching reading strategies is the most popular approach to improving reading achievement in secondary schools, this approach is futile for students who will not open a book, do not believe they can read successfully, and possess social values that conflict with reading. The experimental question is whether instruction that is adapted to the undermining motivations of averse readers is more successful in boosting achievement than instruction that does not attempt to adapt to the undermining motivations.

Finally, it may be valuable to examine whether students from different minorities, such as second language learners or ethnic minority groups, show different profiles of affirming and undermining motivations for reading (Kaplan & Maehr, 1999). For example, African American males and Hispanic males appear to devalue achievement as they enter middle school (Taylor & Graham, 2006). Furthermore, African American males show a substantially lower correlation of intrinsic motivation and reading achievement than other ethnic-gender combinations (Osbourne, 1997). If such diversity of profiles occurs, an important schooling issue is how to adapt the educational environment to the profiles of minority groups in ways that are productive to achievement and reading success for the highest proportion of students.

References

Aarnoutse, C., & Schellings, G. (2003). Learning reading strategies by triggering reading motivation. *Educational Studies, 29*, 387–409.

Almasi, J. F. (1995). The nature of fourth graders' sociocognitive conflicts in peer-led and teacher-led discussions of literature. *Reading Research Quarterly, 30*, 314–351.

Alvermann, D. E., Hagood, M. C., Heron-Hruby, A., Hughes, P., Williams, K. B., & Yoon, J.-C. (2007). Telling themselves who they are: What one out-of-school time study revealed about underachieving readers. *Reading Psychology, 28*, 31–50.

Anderman, L. H. (1999). Classroom goal orientation, school belonging and social goals as predictors of students' positive and negative affect following the transition to middle school. *Journal of Research & Development in Education, 32*, 89–103.

Applebee, A. N., Langer, J. A., Nystrand, M., & Gamoran, A. (2003). Discussion-based approaches to developing understanding: Classroom instruction and student performance in middle and high school English. *American Educational Research Journal, 40*, 685–730.

Assor, A., Kaplan, H., Kanat-Maymon, Y., & Roth, G. (2005). Directly controlling teacher behaviors as predictors of poor motivation and engagement in girls and boys: The role of anger and anxiety. *Learning and Instruction, 15*, 397–413.

Assor, A., Kaplan, H., & Roth, G. (2002). Choice is good, but relevance is excellent: Autonomy-enhancing and suppressing teacher behaviours predicting students' engagement in schoolwork. *British Journal of Educational Psychology, 72*, 261–278.

Baker, L., & Wigfield, A. (1999). Dimensions of children's motivation for reading and their relations to reading activity and reading achievement. *Reading Research Quarterly, 34*, 452–477.

Bandura, A. (1977). *Social learning theory.* Oxford, England: Prentice-Hall.

Bean, T. W., & Readence, J. E. (2002). Adolescent literacy: Charting a course for successful futures as lifelong learners. *Reading Research and Instruction, 41*, 203–210.

Braten, I., & Olaussen, B. S. (2005). Profiling individual differences in student motivation: A longitudinal cluster-analytic study in different academic contexts. *Contemporary Educational Psychology, 30*, 359–396.

Brophy, J. (2004). *Motivating students to learn.* Mahwah, NJ: Erlbaum.

Buhs, E. S., Ladd, G. W., & Herald, S. L. (2006). Peer exclusion and victimization: Processes that mediate the relation between peer group rejection and children's classroom engagement and achievement? *Journal of Educational Psychology, 98*, 1–13.

Chapman, J. W., & Tunmer, W. E. (1995). Development of young children's reading self-concepts: An examination of emerging subcomponents and their relationship with reading achievement. *Journal of Educational Psychology, 87*, 154–167.

Chapman, J. W., & Tunmer, W. E. (2003). Reading difficulties, reading-related self-perceptions, and strategies for overcoming negative self-beliefs. *Reading & Writing Quarterly: Overcoming Learning Difficulties, 19*, 5–24.

Davis, H. A. (2003). Conceptualizing the role and influence of student-teacher relationships on children's social and cognitive development. *Educational Psychologist, 38*, 207–234.

Dowson, M., & McInerney, D. M. (2003). What do students say about their motivational goals?: Towards a more complex and dynamic perspective on student motivation. *Contemporary Educational Psychology, 28*, 91–113.

Durik, A. M., Vida, M., & Eccles, J. S. (2006). Task values and ability beliefs as predictors of high school literacy choices: A developmental analysis. *Journal of Educational Psychology, 98*, 382–393.

Eccles, J. S., & Wigfield, A. (2002). Motivational beliefs, values, and goals. *Annual Review of Psychology, 53*, 109–132.

Elliot, A. J. (1999). Approach and avoidance motivation and achievement goals. *Educational Psychologist* (Vol. 34, p. 169). Mahwah, NJ: Erlbaum.

Finn, J. D., & Rock, D. A. (1997). Academic success among students at risk for school failure. *Journal of Applied Psychology, 82*, 221–234.

Flowerday, T., & Schraw, G. (2000). Teacher beliefs about instructional choice: A phenomenological study. *Journal of Educational Psychology, 92*, 634–645.

Flowerday, T., Schraw, & G., Stevens, J. (2004). The role of choice and interest in reader engagement. *Journal of Experimental Education, 72*, 93–114.

Franzak, J. K. (2006). *Zoom*: A review of the literature on marginalized adolescent readers, literacy theory, and policy implications. *Review of Educational Research, 76*, 209–248.

Furrer, C., & Skinner, E. (2003). Sense of relatedness as a factor in children's academic engagement and performance. *Journal of Educational Psychology, 95*, 148–162.

Gottfried, A. E. (1990). Academic intrinsic motivation in young elementary school children. *Journal of Educational Psychology, 82*, 525–538.

Gottfried, A. E., Fleming, J. S., & Gottfried, A. W. (2001). Continuity of academic intrinsic motivation from childhood through late adolescence: A longitudinal study. *Journal of Educational Psychology, 93*, 3–13.

Greene, B. A., Miller, R. B., Crowson, H. M., Duke, B. L., & Akey, K. L. (2004). Predicting high school students' cognitive engagement and achievement: Contributions of classroom perceptions and motivation. *Contemporary Educational Psychology, 29*, 462–482.

Grolnick, W. S., & Ryan, R. M. (1987). Autonomy in children's learning: An experimental and individual difference investigation. *Journal of Personality and Social Psychology, 52*, 890–898.

Guthrie, J. T., Hoa, A. L. W., Wigfield, A., Tonks, S. M., Humenick, N. M., & Littles, E. (2007). Reading motivation and reading comprehension growth in the later elementary years. *Contemporary Educational Psychology, 32*, 282–313.

Guthrie, J. T., Hoa, L. W., Wigfield, A., Tonks, S. M., & Perencevich, K. C. (2006). From spark to fire: Can situational reading interest lead to long-term reading motivation? *Reading Research and Instruction, 45*, 91–117.

Guthrie, J. T., McRae, A. C., & Klauda, S. L. (2007). Contributions of Concept-Oriented Reading Instruction to knowledge about interventions for motivations in reading. *Educational Psychologist, 42*, 237–250.

Guthrie, J. T., Schafer, W., Wang, Y. Y., & Afflerbach, P. (1995). Relationships of instruction to amount of reading: An exploration of social, cognitive, and instructional connections. *Reading Research Quarterly, 30*, 8–25.

Guthrie, J. T.; Wigfield, A. (2000) Engagement and motivation in reading. In M. L. Kamil & P. B. Mosenthal (Eds.), *Handbook of reading research, Vol. III.* (pp. 403–422). Mahwah, NJ: Erlbaum.

Guthrie, J. T., Wigfield, A., Humenick, N. M., Perencevich, K. C., Taboada, A., & Barbosa, P. (2006). Influences of stimulating tasks on reading motivation and comprehension. *Journal of Educational Research, 99*, 232–245.

Guthrie, J. T., Wigfield, A., & VonSecker, C. (2000). Effects of integrated instruction on motivation and strategy use in reading. *Journal of Educational Psychology, 92*, 331–341.

Hamre, B. K., & Pianta, R. C. (2005). Can instructional and emotional support in the first-grade classroom make a difference for children at risk of school failure? *Child Development, 76*, 949–967.

Harter, S. (1992). The relationship between perceived competence, affect, and motivational orientation within the classroom: Processes and patterns of change. In A. K. Boggiano, & T. S. Pittman (Eds.), *Achievement and motivation: A social-developmental perspective* (pp. 77–114). New York: Cambridge University Press.

Hidi, S., & Renninger, K. A. (2006). The four-phase model of interest development. *Educational Psychologist, 41*, 111–127.

Hughes, J., & Kwok, O.-m. (2007). Influence of student-teacher and parent-teacher relationships on lower achieving readers' engagement and achievement in the primary grades. *Journal of Educational Psychology, 99*, 39–51.

Isaac, J. D., Sansone, C., & Smith, J. L. (1999). Other people as a source of interest in an activity. *Journal of Experimental Social Psychology, 35*, 239–265.

Ivey, G., & Broaddus, K. (2001). 'Just plain reading': A survey of what makes students want to read in middle school classrooms. *Reading Research Quarterly, 36*, 350–377.

Kaplan, A., & Maehr, M. L. (1999). Enhancing the motivation of African American students: An achievement goal theory perspective. *The Journal of Negro Education, 68*, 23–41.

Kirsch, I., Braun, H., Yamamoto, K., & Sum, A. (2007, January). *America's perfect storm: Three forces changing our nation's future.* Retrieved April 20, 2008, from Educational Testing Service Web site http://www.ets.org/Media/Education_Topics/pdf/AmericasPerfectStorm.pdf

Kirsch, I., de Jong, J., Lafontaine, D., Medelovits, J., & Monseur, C. (2002). *Reading for change: Performance and engagement across countries – Results from PISA 2000.* Danvers, MA: OECD Publications.

Legault, L., Green-Demers, I., & Pelletier, L. (2006). Why do high school students lack motivation in the classroom? Toward an understanding of academic amotivation and the role of social support. *Journal of Educational Psychology, 98*, 567–580.

Lepper, M. R., & Henderlong, J. (2000). Turning 'play' into 'work' and 'work' into 'play': 25 years of research on intrinsic versus extrinsic motivation. In C. Sansone, & J. M. Harackiewicz (Eds.), *Intrinsic and extrinsic motivation: The search for optimal motivation and performance* (pp. 257–307). San Diego, CA: Academic Press.

Levy, I., Kaplan, A., & Patrick, H. (2004). Early adolescents' achievement goals, social status, and attitudes towards cooperation with peers. *Social Psychology of Education, 7*, 127–159.

Levy-Tossman, I., Kaplan, A., & Assor, A. (2007). Academic goal orientations, multiple goal profiles, and friendship intimacy among early adolescents. *Contemporary Educational Psychology, 32*, 231–252.

Linderholm, T., & van den Broek, P. (2002). The effects of reading purpose and working memory capacity on the processing of expository text. *Journal of Educational Psychology, 94*, 778–784.

McCarthey, S. J., & Moje, E. B. (2002). Identity matters. *Reading Research Quarterly, 37*, 228–238.

McQuillan, J. (1997). The effects of incentives on reading. *Reading Research and Instruction, 36*, 111–125.

Meece, J. L., Anderman, E. M., & Anderman, L. H. (2006). Classroom goal structure, student motivation, and academic achievement. *Annual Review of Psychology, 57*, 487–503.

Meece, J. L., & Holt, K. (1993). A pattern analysis of students' achievement goals. *Journal of Educational Psychology, 85*, 582–590.

Meece, J. L., & Miller, S. D. (2001). A longitudinal analysis of elementary school students' achievement goals in literacy activities. *Contemporary Educational Psychology, 26*, 454–480.

Meece, J. L., & Miller, S. D. (1999). Changes in elementary school children's achievement goals for reading and writing: Results of a longitudinal and an intervention study. *Scientific Studies of Reading, 3,* 207–229.

Moje, E. B., & Young, J. P. (2000). Reinventing adolescent literacy for new times: Perennial and millennial issues. *Journal of Adolescent & Adult Literacy, 43,* 400.

Nelson, J. R., Stage, S. A., Epstein, M. H., & Pierce, C. D. (2005). Effects of a rereading intervention on the literacy and social skills of children. *Exceptional Children, 72,* 29–45.

Ng, M. M., Guthrie, J. T., Van Meter, P., McCann, A., & Alao, S. (1998). How do classroom characteristics influence intrinsic motivations for literacy? *Reading Psychology, 19,* 319–398.

O'Brien, D. G., & Stewart, R. A. (1995). Why content literacy is difficult to infuse into the secondary school: Complexities of curriculum, pedagogy, and school culture. *Reading Research Quarterly, 30,* 442–463.

Onatsu-Arvilommi, T., & Nurmi, J. E. (2000). The role of task-avoidant and task-focused behaviors in the development of reading and mathematical skills during the first school year: A cross-lagged study. *Journal of Educational Psychology, 92,* 478–491.

Osbourne, J. W. (1997). Race and academic disidentification. *Journal of Educational Psychology, 89,* 728–735.

Otis, N., Grouzet, F. M. E., & Pelletier, L. G. (2005). Latent motivational change in an academic setting: A 3-year longitudinal study. *Journal of Educational Psychology, 97,* 170–183.

Pastor, D. A., Barron, K. E., Miller, B. J., & Davis, S. L. (2007). A latent profile analysis of college students' achievement goal orientation. *Contemporary Educational Psychology, 32,* 8–47.

Pintrich, P. R. (2000). Multiple goals, multiple pathways: The role of goal orientation in learning and achievement. *Journal of Educational Psychology, 92,* 544–555.

Pintrich, P. R., & de Groot, E. V. (1990). Motivational and self-regulated learning components of classroom academic performance. *Journal of Educational Psychology, 82,* 33–40.

Ratelle, C. F., Guay, F., Vallerand, R. J., Larose, S & Senecal, C. (2007). Autonomous, controlled, and amotivated types of academic motivation: A person-oriented analysis. *Journal of Educational Psychology, 99,* 734–736.

Reeve, J., & Jang, H. (2006). What teachers say and do to support students' autonomy during a learning activity. *Journal of Educational Psychology, 98,* 209–218.

Reeve, J., Jang, H., Carrell, D., Jeon, S., & Barch, J. (2004). Enhancing students' engagement by increasing teachers' autonomy support. *Motivation and Emotion, 28,* 147–169.

Reynolds, P. L., & Symons, S. (2001). Motivational variables and children's text search. *Journal of Educational Psychology, 93,* 14–22.

Rozendaal, J. S., Minnaert, A., & Boekaerts, M. (2005). The influence of teacher perceived administration of self-regulated learning on students' motivation and information-processing. *Learning and Instruction, 15,* 141–160.

Ryan, R. M., & Deci, E. L. (2000). Self-determination theory and the facilitation of intrinsic motivation, social development, and well-being. *American Psychologist, 55,* 68–78.

Ryan, R. M., & Deci, E. L. (2006). Self-regulation and the problem of human autonomy: Does psychology need choice, self-determination, and will? *Journal of Personality, 74,* 1557–1586.

Sansone, C., & Harackiewicz, J. M. (2000). Rewarding competence: The importance of goals in the study of intrinsic motivation. In C. Sansone & J. M. Harackiewicz (Eds.), *Intrinsic and extrinsic motivation: The search for optimal motivation and performance.* San Diego, CA: Academic Press.

Schiefele, U. (1991). Interest, learning, and motivation. *Educational Psychologist, 26,* 299–323.

Schiefele, U. (1999). Interest and learning from text. *Scientific Studies of Reading, 3,* 257–279.

Schraw, G., & Dennison, R. S. (1994). The effect of reader purpose on interest and recall. *Journal of Reading Behavior, 26,* 1–18.

Schunk, D. H. (2003a). Self-efficacy for reading and writing: Influence of modeling, goal setting, and self-evaluation. *Reading & Writing Quarterly: Overcoming Learning Difficulties, 19,* 159–172.

Schunk, D. H. (2003b). Self-efficacy for reading and writing: Influence of modeling, goal setting, and self-evaluation. *Reading & Writing Quarterly, 19,* 159–172.

Schunk, D. H., & Rice, J. M. (1991). Learning goals and progress feedback during reading comprehension instruction. *Journal of Reading Behavior, 23,* 351–364.

Schunk, D. H., & Rice, J. M. (1993). Strategy fading and progress feedback: Effects on self-efficacy and comprehension among students receiving remedial reading services. *The Journal of Special Education, 27,* 257–276.

Seifert, T. L., & O'Keefe, B. A. (2001). The relationship of work avoidance and learning goals to perceived competence, externality and meaning. *British Journal of Educational Psychology, 71,* 81–92.

Skinner, E. A., & Belmont, M. J. (1993). Motivation in the classroom: Reciprocal effects of teacher behavior and student engagement across the school year. *Journal of Educational Psychology, 85,* 571–58.

Skinner, E. A., Wellborn, J. G., & Connell, J. P. (1990). What it takes to do well in school and whether I've got it: A process model of perceived control and children's engagement and achievement in school. *Journal of Educational Psychology, 82,* 22–32.

Smith, T. L., & Wilhelm, J. D. (2002). *"Reading don't fix no chevys": Literacy in the lives of young men.* Portsmouth, NH: Heinemann.

Souvignier, E., & Mokhlesgerami, J. (2006). Using self-regulation as a framework for implementing strategy instruction to foster reading comprehension. *Learning and Instruction, 16,* 57–71.

Sweet, A. P., Guthrie, J. T., & Ng, M. (1998). Teacher perceptions and student reading motivation. *Journal of Educational Psychology, 90*, 210–224.

Taylor, B. M., Pearson, P. D., & Peterson, D. S. (2003). Reading growth in high-poverty classrooms: The influence of teacher practices that encourage cognitive engagement in literacy learning. *The Elementary School Journal, 104*, 3–28.

Taylor, A. Z., & Graham, S. (2007). An examination of the relationship between achievement values and perceptions of barriers among low-SES African American and Latino students. *Journal of Educational Psychology, 99*, 52–64.

Unrau, N., & Schlackman, J. (2006). Motivation and its relationship with reading achievement in an urban middle school. *Journal of Educational Research, 100*, 81–101.

van den Broek, P., Lorch, R. F. J., Linderholm, T., & Gustafson, M. (2001). The effects of readers' goals on inference generation and memory for texts. *Memory & Cognition, 29*, 1081–1087.

Vansteenkiste, M., Lens, W., & Deci, E. L. (2006). Intrinsic versus extrinsic goal contents in self-determination theory: Another look at the quality of academic motivation. *Educational Psychologist, 41*, 19–31.

Vansteenkiste, M., Simons, J., Lens, W., Sheldon, K. M., & Deci, E. L. (2004). Motivating learning, performance, and persistence: The synergistic effects of intrinsic goal contents and autonomy-supportive contexts. *Journal of Personality and Social Psychology, 87*, 246–260.

Wade, S. E., Buxton, W. M., & Kelly, M. (1999). Using think-alouds to examine reader-text interest. *Reading Research Quarterly, 34*, 194–216.

Wang, J. H.-Y., & Guthrie, J. T. (2004). Modeling the effects of intrinsic motivation, extrinsic motivation, amount of reading, and past reading achievement on text comprehension between U.S. and Chinese students. *Reading Research Quarterly, 39*, 162–186.

Wentzel, K. R. (1996). Social and academic motivation in middle school: Concurrent and long-term relations to academic effort. *Journal of Early Adolescence, 16*, 390–406.

Wentzel, K. R. (2005). Peer relationships, motivation, and academic performance at school. In A. J. Elliot & C. S. Dweck (Eds.), *Handbook of competence and motivation* (pp. 279–296). New York: Guilford.

Wentzel, K. R. (2002). The contribution of social goal setting to children's school adjustment. In A. Wigfield & J. Eccles (Eds.), *Development of achievement motivation* (pp. 221–246). New York: Academic Press.

Wentzel, K. R., Barry, C. M., & Caldwell, K. A. (2004). Friendships in Middle School: Influences on Motivation and School Adjustment. *Journal of Educational Psychology, 96*, 195–203.

Wigfield, A., & Guthrie, J. T. (1997). Relations of children's motivation for reading to the amount and breadth or their reading. *Journal of Educational Psychology, 89*, 420–432.

Worthy, J., Patterson, E., Salas, R., Prater, S., & Turner, M. (2002). 'More than just reading': The human factor in reaching resistant readers. *Reading Research and Instruction, 41*, 177–202.

Zimmerman, B. J., & Kitsantas, A. (2002). Acquiring writing revision and self-regulatory skill through observation and emulation. *Journal of Educational Psychology, 94*, 660–668.

24
Understanding Motivation in Mathematics
What is Happening in Classrooms?

Julianne C. Turner and Debra K. Meyer

What is it about mathematics that prompts strong reactions in so many children and adults? If asked to do a free association with "mathematics," the first thing to spring to many minds would be "math anxiety." Math anxiety appears to be a learned behavior, and it is associated with experiences in school. School experience may help explain why many Americans think that only some students will be successful in learning math, whereas everyone will learn to read and write (Grouws & Lemke, 1996). Accordingly, students' positive attitudes and motivation toward math decline through the middle school years and into high school (Stipek, 2002; Wigfield, Byrnes, & Eccles, 2006), including their enjoyment and valuing of mathematics (Middleton & Spanias, 1999; Wigfield et al., 1997). This "motivational" characterization of a discipline has linked mathematics and motivation in a way not often found in studies of motivation and learning in other subject areas. The longevity of math anxiety, both in popular lore and in research, indicates that the linkage of motivation and mathematics is a compelling argument for considering how mathematics teaching, learning and motivation are negotiated in the classroom.

Motivation is a theoretical construct used to explain the initiation, direction, intensity, persistence and quality of goal-directed behavior (Maehr & Meyer, 1997). Motivation is evident in beliefs, behaviors, and affect, processes that co-occur and are probably reciprocal. We are especially concerned with motivation to learn mathematics in this chapter. Therefore, we will examine research in both mathematics and in motivation that bears on their relationship. We say "mathematics *and* motivation" because our review of the literatures suggests that the two topics have remained somewhat distinct with few exceptions (e.g., Stipek, Salmon, Givvin, Kazemi, Saxe, & MacGyvers, 1998; see Carr, 1996a, and Middleton & Spanias, 1999, for reviews). Therefore, we have organized the chapter to reconsider what we know from the perspectives of researchers in both areas. We conclude with a call to integrate the valuable perspectives and methods of these researchers to generate a more comprehensive literature of "motivation to learn mathematics."

We have identified three different literatures that can be organized conceptually by considering their relative focus on motivation or mathematics. Educational psychology and mathematics education specifically focus within their respective research traditions on motivation *or* mathematics. These literatures are complex and distinct. For example, they each address student learning, methods of teaching, and curriculum issues from preschool through college. In the educational psychology literature, the research is more focused on students and individual differences regarding their achievement goals, values, and efficacy for mathematics. In the mathematics education literature, the research questions are more likely to examine the processes through which students acquire mathematical understanding and problem solving skills. A third, smaller, literature has emerged from these two larger literatures to apply motivation theory to mathematics classrooms.

We have chosen to provide a targeted review of these three distinct literatures by selecting the work of those who have contributed a line of research concentrated in K-12 mathematics classrooms as opposed to synthesizing separate studies. We suggest that each of the three literatures could benefit from employing the strengths of the others, with a goal of studying motivation and mathematics not as separate or complementary, but as integrated, mutually constituted, and situated. From our examination of these literatures we assert that *what* students learn (i.e., mathematical knowledge and processes), *how* they learn it (i.e., instruction, interaction), and *where* they learn it (i.e., classroom culture) are essential components of understanding motivation to learn mathematics. Our goal is to illustrate how research could be more effective in explaining how motivation to learn mathematics develops and changes and what teachers could do to promote positive dispositions and learning outcomes for their students across the school years.

Mathematics: A Special Case?

Throughout this chapter, we assume that mathematics presents a special case for studying motivation. This assumption goes back at least as far as Duncan and Biddle's (1974) model of teaching, which included subject matter as part of the setting or context. The disciplines taught in schools have distinct traditions and specific ideas of what counts as learning, which can change over time and create conflicting expectations, as the mathematics reform movement has demonstrated. Nickson (1992) argued that "mathematics exerts a unique influence on the context in the classroom" (p. 101). Furthermore, as Stodolsky (1988) illustrated, instructional formats in different content areas vary and these subject-matter contexts differentially affect students' ideas about how to learn a school subject such as math or social studies. Stodolsky (1988) was among the first to call attention to how subject matter has been largely ignored in psychological theory and research (see also Sheull, 1996; Shulman & Quinlan, 1996, Wineburg, 1996). Without considering content as part of our research findings, important influences on motivation and differences in motivation across contexts may be unnecessarily lost.

Specifically, math presents a special case for two major reasons—individual beliefs about mathematics and characteristics of mathematics classrooms. First, personal beliefs about mathematics have unique influences on motivation to learn mathematics. Kloosterman (1996) interviewed 29 first- through fourth-grade students each year for 3 years about how their beliefs about mathematics influenced their motivation, and, in turn, their mathematics achievement. He outlined four types of beliefs, describing how they reflected motivational constructs found in expectancy-value and goal theory. The first set of beliefs is related to what "math is." For example, math is useful, math requires computation and proof, and math has clearly defined problems with right answers. A second type of beliefs includes "self" beliefs about oneself as a mathematics learner. Kloosterman discussed how self-confidence in mathematics varies by the mathematics activity.

For example, self-efficacy may vary depending on whether or not the activity is routine and what math topic is being learned (e.g., fractions, geometry, or algebra). Third, Kloosterman illustrated how students' beliefs about the role of the teacher in a mathematics classroom (e.g., teacher as transmitter or as the source of answers) also are important for understanding student motivation to learn mathematics. Finally, Kloosterman discussed beliefs about how mathematics is learned, such as mathematics is a discipline that only a few can learn, that errors are to be avoided, that there is one best approach, and that math is an individual endeavor. In addition, Kloosterman emphasized that researchers needed to explore how these beliefs are formed, how they change developmentally, and how instruction might change beliefs that negatively influence student motivation to learn mathematics. It is worth noting that such beliefs were evident as young as the primary grades.

Second, contextual features of mathematics classrooms shape motivation to learn mathematics. These can include societal views of mathematics, classroom instructional characteristics, as well as features of mathematical tasks. Grouws and Lembke (1996) illustrated how understanding intrinsic motivation is essential to understanding mathematics learning. They discussed Good and Brophy's (1987) four preconditions—supportive environment, appropriate challenge, learning goals, and motivational strategies—in terms of the classroom culture of mathematics. At a general level, these preconditions seem to apply to all learning situations; however the ways in which they apply are discipline-specific (e.g., Nickson, 1992). Thus mathematics in school can either match or mismatch students' expectations. Issues of *authority* (one approach-one correct answer vs. multiple strategies), *control* (self- and co-regulation vs. reliance on teacher), *task involvement* (mastery vs. completion), and *instructional organization* (cooperative vs. competitive) become highly salient in the mathematics classroom. Moreover, mathematics is organized as a "spiral curriculum," and students typically revisit areas of math at increasingly more abstract levels of understanding as they move through the grade levels. In addition, as students enter upper-elementary and middle school they are increasingly grouped by ability, and then "officially" tracked in high school mathematics courses. These curriculum features present additional discipline-specific challenges to motivating students to learn mathematics and continue their engagement in this school subject.

Motivation Research in Educational Psychology

Motivation research in the educational psychology literature uses mathematics classrooms primarily as one of its sites for data collection, ignoring discipline-specific influences on motivation. That is, this literature is mostly concerned with theoretical constructs, predictions, and relationships among motivational variables such as expectancy, value, achievement goals, self-efficacy, and interest. Furthermore, most of these data are self-reported by the students and do not detail the classroom interactions or issues of mathematical practices and learning that are reflected in students' reports of motivation. To illustrate this body of literature, we will review two programs of research done primarily from the perspectives of Expectancy-Value theory by Jacquelynne Eccles and colleagues and Achievement Goal theory, using our research.

Using Theoretical and Developmental Models of Motivation

Eccles and her colleagues have conducted extensive studies of motivation in mathematics classrooms from the perspective of Expectancy-Value theory. Their findings have contributed significantly to understanding developmental trajectories and gender differences in expectancy for success and task value, and have documented the synergistic nature of expectancy and value. We present a brief chronological summary of some contributions of this extensive research program particularly in mathematics.

The disparity between male and female career paths in mathematics prompted an early study (Eccles, 1983) that examined how students' expectancies and values predicted their course-taking in mathematics. Another goal of the study was to test the efficacy of the expectancy-value model to predict individual differences (a "psychological model") as well as social influences (a "developmental model") in achievement and course taking. Eccles and her colleagues surveyed 668 students in 5th through 12th grade in a cross-lagged panel design. In addition, they surveyed their parents and teachers and conducted classroom observations in mathematics classes.

The Eccles expectancy-value model was fruitful in illuminating both individual differences and developmental trends. Expectancy for success predicted math achievement and perceptions of the value of math predicted intentions to take more math courses. In particular, sex-differentiated course enrollment was a joint function of perceived task difficulty, self-concept of ability, and the subjective value of math. The effects of the students' sex and past academic histories were mediated almost completely by the *interpretation of these events* made by parents and teachers and by the students themselves. Parents' views of the difficulty of math for their children were the most highly correlated in students' expectancies and values. Teachers' expectancies for student success predicted students' expectancies, but classroom observation measures did not predict or mediate students' achievement-related attitudes. To see if teacher behaviors were related to students' expectancies, Eccles (1983) selected the five classrooms with the most and the five classrooms with the least differences in the self-reported expectancies between males and females. She reasoned that teacher and student "style" (e.g., use of praise, initiating dyadic interaction) might explain the differences. Eccles found that the number of response opportunities and the number of open questions were positively and consistently related to how much female students liked math, but not to expectancies. This work gave early indications of the importance of instructional interactions in mathematics, especially of questioning, in providing affordances and constraints for the development of competence and value. Also relevant to educational outcomes, this study was important in establishing an age-related downward trajectory in expectancy and value for mathematics.

The Childhood and Beyond studies followed students in several cohorts from 1989 to 1999 and measured students' competence and value beliefs in math and other domains (Eccles et al., 1993; Jacobs, Lanza, Osgood, Eccles, & Wigfield 2002; Wigfield et al., 1997) from 1st through 12th grades in a predominantly European American, middle-class sample. As previewed in earlier studies, both competence and task value beliefs in math declined significantly across the 12 grades for both males and females. Although males reported higher competence beliefs in math initially, this gap narrowed over time, with boys' perceptions of competence declining at a faster rate than did girls'. Even after controlling for competence, value beliefs were similar for males and females throughout the school years and girls valued math more by the end of high school. In addition, this longitudinal study demonstrated that changes in competence beliefs in mathematics had a large effect on changes in task values, explaining most of the gender differences and change over time. These studies have made further theoretical contributions by demonstrating why expectancy beliefs and values should be studied together. In terms of classroom instruction in mathematics, Eccles' research underscores the importance of fostering understanding and competence in mathematics, as it is highly correlated with students' interests and values in mathematics. However, *how* these goals are accomplished during mathematics instruction across grade levels and mathematical topics cannot be gleaned from these findings.

In a 2-year, four-wave panel study (the Transitions at Early Adolescence Project), Eccles and her colleagues (e.g., Eccles et al., 1993) focused attention on the rapid decline of students' expectancies and values in math across the transition to junior high school. The sample was drawn from 12 school districts located in middle-income communities in southeastern Michigan and included 1,500 students moving from sixth grade in elementary school to seventh grade in junior high school. The researchers argued that a misfit between the developmental needs of early adolescents and their educational environments (i.e., the "stage-environment fit") predicted negative motivational consequences. This research was specific about classroom organizational, instructional, and climate variables in mathematics classes that might be inconsistent with developmental needs. The researchers proposed that fewer opportunities for decision-making, poorer teacher-student relationships, and increased public evaluation practices, among others, might help explain negative motivational consequences. Most analyses used student and teacher self-reports although trained observers completed parallel self-report "surveys," which were also collected in a subset of classrooms (Feldlaufer, Midgley, & Eccles, 1988; Midgley, Eccles, & Feldlaufer, 1991). Analyses demonstrated that when students moved from more developmentally appropriate sixth-grade classrooms to less developmentally appropriate seventh-grade classrooms, students reported decrements in perceptions of competence in and value for mathematics (e.g., Midgley & Feldlaufer, 1987; Midgley, Feldlaufer, & Eccles, 1989a, 1989b).

The contribution of this research program lies in its elegant theoretical formulations and extensive longitudinal and cross-sectional data analyses. Eccles' enduring interest in mathematics as a domain for achievement has yielded important developmental and gender-related findings specific to expectancy for success and task value. Nevertheless, despite the fact that the data were collected in mathematics classrooms, there is no information about the nature of the mathematics itself or of the mathematics instruction. Observers rated generic classroom features such as competition, teacher control, student input, and teacher disposition (e.g., "unfair," "unfriendly") rather than behaviors and interactions specific to the subject area. Therefore, it is impossible to say if and how the documented declines might be related to features of students' beliefs about mathematics as a discipline and the mathematics classroom environments.

Examining Motivational Theory Through Self-Reports

A major reason that psychological studies of motivation may be disconnected from mathematics as a discipline is the reliance on self-reports. As an illustration, we collected survey data from 160 fifth and sixth graders in their mathematics classrooms to investigate the relation among negative affect and students' reports of achievement goals and self-regulatory beliefs and behaviors (Turner, Thorpe, & Meyer, 1998). Like many researchers, we modified our survey instruments to be specific to mathematics class (e.g., "I like to do math work that is difficult for me" from *The School Failure Tolerance Scale*, Clifford, 1988; "Even if the work in math is hard, I can learn it" adapted from *The Patterns of Adaptive Learning Survey*, PALS; Midgley & Maehr, 1991). From these student survey responses, we reported that negative affect mediated performance goals and self-regulatory beliefs and behaviors, including strategy use, preference for difficulty, and self-efficacy. Similar to many "generic" research studies in motivation (i.e., research that ignores discipline-specific beliefs and practices), our results had theoretical implications; we could not (and did not) say much about the role of mathematics content or achievement in our findings. Our reference to mathematics was broad and we do not know how the students interpreted "math" in the survey items. For example, did they report to us about their beliefs of: (a) mathematics in general, which is more of a measure of their academic self-concept in mathematics, (b) as the current topic being studied in math, which we did not report, or (c) as the particular math class, which would include attributes of the mathematics culture or of the teacher? In hindsight, we probably received self-reports that spanned all these possibilities and some that we have not yet considered. It remains an empirical question as to whether more focused self-reports could provide better information about students' beliefs, but the question persists about how development and change can be measured adequately with self-reports (e.g., Turner & Patrick, 2008).

Furthermore, we discussed our findings in relation to the discipline of mathematics only tangentially, by connecting our findings regarding tolerance of error and negative affect after failure to Carr's (1996b) caution that right answers, speed, and correctness emphases in mathematics may encourage concerns about relative ability rather than individual progress and learning. Although we acknowledged that results from mathematics might be different than those of other content areas, we did not use the mathematics discipline as part of the context in which to situate our theoretical framework, our methods, or our interpretations. However, we did assume that making mistakes might be more readily apparent and perhaps more meaningful in mathematics learning. This study focused on motivation, asking students to limit their responses to a broad content area on surveys. So little "mathematics" was involved in our investigation, we can only wonder if the students' responses would have been any different had we simply asked about school in general (e.g., "I like to do school work that is difficult for me" or "Even if the work in school is hard, I can learn it").

Much of the research in educational psychology involving math and motivation has inquired into the *why* of motivation, generating or looking for support for various theories related to constructs such as competence, value, interest, goals and relatedness. To that end, this body of research contributes mostly to theory instantiation, and much less to understanding motivation *in* mathematics. Although valuable, theories do not lead directly to explaining *how* learners' motivation develops and changes in learning situations. As diSessa (1991) has noted, grand theory lacks orientation to particular situational events and tends to miss important details. We conclude that the much of the research on motivation theory has not yet elucidated the mathematical "situational events" to enable us to understand motivation to learn mathematics.

Connecting Self-Reports with Classroom Instructional Characteristics

Another strand of motivation research in educational psychology is framed within motivational theory perspectives and incorporates mathematics into studies at the classroom level of analysis through teachers' instructional approaches and by investigating students' beliefs about their mathematics classes. The classroom motivation research informs us about the classroom-level processes (e.g., instructional practices, social norms) that might be underlying the correlations found among motivational variables and moves us closer to understanding these mathematics classes, although the focus remains quite motivational. It differs from the motivation theory research in that it adopts a situated view of educational psychology (Bredo, 2006).

Almost all of our work in upper-elementary and middle school mathematics classrooms illustrates this type of research (Meyer, Turner, & Spencer, 1997; Patrick, Turner, Meyer, & Midgley, 2003; Turner & Patrick, 2004; Schweinle, Turner, & Meyer, 2006; Turner, Meyer, Midgley, & Patrick, 2003; Turner, Meyer, et al., 1998; Turner, et al. 2002). In our classroom studies we typically combined self-report methods with qualitative methods by coding classroom discourse during teacher-student interactions. Our coding scheme described general instructional discourse patterns, although it did seem sensitive to several ubiquitous characteristics of mathematics instruction, such as a focus on correct answers and procedures versus understanding and justification (cf., Boaler, 2002, and Kazemi & Stipek, 2001). Similarly, the discourse reflected the mathematics topics, such as factoring, fractions, decimals and percents and geometry, but we did not consider how the difference in topics might be related to students' motivation. Consequently, we described what teachers said (and did) in classrooms in which students reported different goals, avoidance strategies, emotions, risk-taking behaviors, and flow. Classroom learning environments that supported or undermined student motivation were our foci, but the quality of the mathematical learning environments was left unexamined.

Given our focus on motivational constructs and combination of survey research and classroom research, this body of work contributed several worthwhile findings about how well motivational theory did and did not apply in mathematics classrooms. In most cases we used multiple methods and therefore our findings could be connected to the motivation theory research. For example, in one study we classified classrooms as high or low involvement (i.e., relative match of challenge and skill) using constructs from Flow Theory (Turner et al., 1998). Using students' reports of flow in combination with our classroom observations, we were able to test theoretical predictions in the classrooms. In the three "low involvement" classrooms the students reported more "non-flow experiences," such as apathy or boredom, which would be theoretically predicted. Also, in one "high involvement" classroom, the students reported "low flow." From our qualitative data we concluded that this teacher's instructional practices were consistently challenging and highly conceptual, but perhaps too challenging, as students reported higher levels of anxiety (i.e., more experiences in which challenges exceeded skills) than their peers in other classes (cf. Kazemi & Stipek's study of "press," 2001, discussed below). One counter-theoretical finding was that students reported high levels of happiness, but low levels of pride, during boring experiences (i.e., when their skills were higher than the mathematical challenges). These research findings highlighted how the social context of the experiences (e.g., levels of challenge in a classroom activity, teachers' instructional practices) might influence the appraisal and experiences of students within a particular classroom. Studying the instructional interactions in those classrooms helped us understand the students' responses, but not in ways that were specific to mathematics.

An overarching finding from our classroom research has been that teacher-student patterns of interactions generically create and sustain qualities of classroom contexts. We believe that understanding these contexts is critical to explaining *why* students report particular motivational beliefs and perceptions (Meyer, Turner, & Spencer, 1997; Patrick, Turner, Meyer, & Midgley, 2003; Turner & Patrick, 2004; Turner et al., 2002). Furthermore, by focusing on the positive features of instructional interactions, our findings corroborated those of other researchers who also have examined how teachers' instructional strategies help to explain the relationships among motivational constructs (e.g., Stipek, Salmon et al., 1998; Urdan, Kneisel, & Mason, 1999; Vermunt & Verloop, 1999). At the same time, our research in mathematics classrooms has described some unexpected characteristics of classrooms that support or do not support student motivation. For example, we found that even cognitively supportive instruction, as would be investigated in mathematics research, is inadequate for motivation without affective supports such as encouraging persistence, showing enthusiasm, reducing anxiety, and encouraging peer collaboration (Turner et al., 2003). Thus our research findings on supportive instructional characteristics also corroborated those of other motivational researchers who had documented how teachers' affective support is important at the cognitive level *and* interpersonal levels (e.g., Lepper & Woolverton, 2002; Patrick,

Anderman, Ryan, Edelin, & Midgley, 2001; Skinner & Belmont, 1993; Wentzel, 1997). Common positive instructional characteristics found across all of these studies have been the teachers' enthusiasm, humor, and passion for learning. In other words, teachers' demonstrations of positive affect and intrinsic motivation appear to be critical features of instructional interactions that correlate with student reports of motivation to learn. Humor and enthusiasm appear to be less common in mathematics instruction (e.g., Boaler, 2002; Kaput, 1989), and this may explain why these factors were particularly salient in the classrooms we studied.

Our findings illustrate how motivation research can be situated in classroom instruction but not in *mathematics*. We did not determine how teacher-student interaction or teachers' instructional behaviors created contexts for mathematics learning in particular. Furthermore, although our studies have been located in mathematics classrooms, it is difficult to return to our articles and discern what mathematics students were learning and any changes in their mathematical understanding or attitudes toward mathematics. In addition, our studies are agnostic about how teachers and students constructed notions of mathematics, what counted as mathematical explanations, whether mathematics was meaningful, and how students thought about themselves as mathematical learners. In short, mathematical beliefs, norms, and practices were *implicit* in our research methods and analyses in contrast to the research literatures that follow.

In summary, motivation research from psychological perspectives has not typically reported contextualized and discipline-specific understandings of motivation in classrooms. Although many motivation researchers have chosen to examine theoretical constructs specifically in mathematics, this research has largely ignored *what* is taught and learned and *how* and *why* students are learning about mathematics. Viewing this approach as too narrow, Blumenfeld (1992) called on educational psychologists to integrate motivation with instruction and learning, which implied that content ways of knowing and teaching are essential. In contrast, as we will describe later in this chapter, mathematics education research has focused specifically on mathematics learning and instruction, but with little reference to motivation theory. Thus, Middleton and Spanias (1999) echoed Blumenfeld's call with specific reference to motivation in mathematics: "In particular, researchers interested in studying motivation in the content domain of school mathematics need to examine the relationship that exists between mathematics as a socially constructed field and students' desire to achieve" (p. 65). Fortunately, there has been a small group of researchers who have taken up the challenge of examining "motivation in mathematics," as we discuss in the next section.

Motivation in Mathematics Research

Motivation *in* mathematics research explicitly integrates motivation constructs, such as students' valuing of mathematics and their goals for learning mathematics, with explicit characteristics of mathematics classrooms. We have chosen two lines of research to illustrate how motivation theory has been applied: (a) one that emphasized student beliefs about mathematics, and (b) one that focused on the instructional practices in mathematics and explicitly connected mathematical dispositions and learning to motivational constructs and theories.

Examining Student Beliefs about Mathematics

Although most motivation in mathematics research has focused on teachers' instructional strategies to examine mathematics-reform practices, Kloosterman and his colleagues examined student beliefs about mathematics (Kloosterman, 1996) and their change over time (Kloosterman, Raymond, & Emenaker, 1996). Kloosterman et al.'s (1996) research study concentrated on domain-specific characteristics of mathematics in examining student beliefs about knowing and doing mathematics within grades 4, 5, and 6 across a 3-year span. Students were asked in interviews to discuss their attitudes and beliefs about mathematics and these responses were compared across time and connected to teacher interviews and observations of classroom practices. Kloosterman et al. defined *beliefs* as "personal assumptions from which individuals make decisions about the actions they will undertake" (p. 39). Adapting a synthesis by McLeod (1992), they applied a mathematics-specific framework for examining four types of beliefs: (a) *beliefs about mathematics* (e.g., its utility value, its difficulty); (b) *beliefs about self* (e.g., confidence, attributions), (c) *beliefs about teaching* (e.g., teacher support, instructional grouping for learning), and (d) *beliefs about the social context* (e.g., competition, parental influences). For example, as Kloosterman and colleagues found, students' attitudes about working independently versus in a small group could readily be connected to teachers' perceptions of and practices involving student grouping in mathematics—the more the teacher successfully promoted group work, the more value students attributed to it in learning mathematics. In fact, although the authors reported relative stability in students' views of the importance of mathematics and their competence in mathematics, these findings may have had more to do with being in classrooms with similar mathematics practices across all 3 years because all the teachers were in the same school and participating in a reform-based project on improving mathematical teaching through the use of problem solving. The students, who represented a low-income, at-risk population, had been recommended by their teachers as representing a "range of abilities in mathematics" (p. 42). Regardless of ability, one of the most interesting findings from this 3-year investigation was that "most students grew to like mathematics as it became harder" (p. 53), suggesting that the instructional context of teachers using problem-solving approaches to learning mathematics may have had a very positive impact on student learning and mathematical dispositions. The influence of "challenge" in mathematics remains understudied, especially at higher grade levels.

Linking Student Motivation to Instructional Practices

Stipek and her colleagues have contributed to the study of motivation research in mathematics classrooms by focusing on teacher instructional practices. Moreover, they have examined classroom climate, including positive teacher support, explicitly linking motivation theory to reform practices in mathematics. For example, Stipek, Salmon et al. (1998) integrated the literatures on achievement motivation and reform practices in mathematics education around five motivational constructs: a focus on learning, self-confidence in mathematics, risk taking, enjoyment, and positive feelings (e.g., pride). They used the literature from achievement goal theory to examine how teacher practices might foster student engagement in learning fractions. Twenty-four fourth- through sixth-grade teachers participated in the study, which involved an ethically diverse, urban population of 624 students. Approximately two thirds of the teachers had participated in professional development workshops on implementing mathematics reforms in teaching fractions and half of these teachers also had been involved in a year-long intervention to help them implement these practices in their classrooms. These teachers were matched with peers who had not participated in any of the professional development. The researchers videotaped and then rated teachers interacting during whole class and independent instruction on fractions using a variety of variables that classified motivational practices (e.g., emphasizing effort, learning, performance, autonomy) and constructs (e.g., interest in mathematics, speed in completion).

Stipek, Salmon, et al. (1998) found that teacher practices rarely changed and that the affective climate was the best predictor of students' reports of motivation. Furthermore, they concluded that mastery-focused mathematics practices had a positive effect on students' conceptual understanding, but no effect on rote or procedural knowledge, thus linking motivation directly to mathematics learning. Their findings distinguished between two types of mathematics classrooms: those in which students were engaged in understanding fractions and those in which the focus was on completion of fraction problems with ease and accuracy. For example, common teacher practices such as indicating the number correct on papers were correlated with lower student reports of positive emotions whereas written teacher comments on papers were associated with higher reports of mastery goals and positive emotions while working on fractions.

In one of the few mathematics studies to take a motivationally explicit perspective while also being mathematically focused, Kazemi and Stipek (2001; see also Cobb et al., 1991, later in the chapter) examined four teachers who exhibited high positive affect but differed in their "press for learning" (two high in press, two moderate in press) during mathematics instruction. Press was judged based on whether teachers encouraged students to solve difficult problems, required them to justify answers, encouraged students to be autonomous thinkers, and de-emphasized "right answers." By differentiating between social norms and sociomathematical norms (e.g., Yackel & Cobb, 1996), Kazemi and Stipek examined two types of instructional strategies—classroom and mathematical. Whereas all four classrooms shared classroom-level social norms such as students were expected to (a) describe their thinking, (b) seek multiple ways to solve problems, (c) view mistakes as constructive, and (d) collaborate to find solutions, they differed when it came to sociomathematical norms. The two teachers with higher "press" applied these standards to mathematics in more rigorous ways. For example, describing a strategy meant giving a mathematical argument not the procedural steps, which was acceptable in the low press classes. Similarly, sharing strategies and comparing them meant understanding the relationships among the strategies. Errors were not just acceptable but they were opportunities to re-conceptualize a problem, examine contractions, and look for an alternative approach. Finally, collaboration meant more than working together in high press classrooms; it meant reaching a mathematical consensus and involved being individually accountable for understanding. From a motivational perspective, "press" encouraged challenge seeking, effort, and autonomy. It emphasized mastery goals (meaningful learning) and it deemphasized performance goals, or the desire to demonstrate competence with little effort. Thus, the motivational construct of "press" was integrated with mathematics teaching and learning. The researchers described how social norms helped establish a climate for inquiry and how more specific sociomathematical norms were needed to promote conceptual understanding and the students' engagement in mathematics.

These researchers are among a small group of scholars who have explicitly brought motivation theory and mathematics education together in meaningful ways. Kloosterman's work on attribution theory and self-confidence in mathematics (Kloosterman & Gorman, 1990; Kloosterman, 1984, 1988) and Stipek and colleagues' research on reform-based mathematics (Givvin, Stipek, & Salmon, 2001; Stipek, Givvin, Salmon, & MacGyvers, 1998; Stipek, Salmon, et al., 1998) were also among the first studies to illustrate how motivation theory and mathematics education research could complement each other. In addition, Middleton's work (1995, 1999) has examined attributions (e.g., locus of control) and intrinsic motivators within mathematics (e.g., utility value of mathematics). By integrating mathematical beliefs and understandings into their classroom research on motivation, these researchers showed us how understanding the classroom context can explain student motivation in important, and more nuanced, ways that are characteristic of mathematics (e.g., the tolerance for errors, the emphasis on accuracy, the importance of speed of completion). However, unlike most research in mathematics teaching and learning, these studies foreground motivational constructs and theory, which also challenged motivation theory for explanations. Research that situates motivation in mathematics asks us to explain how teacher practices and classroom norms influence not only the classroom environment, but also mathematics learning specifically. Furthermore, these researchers seek to explain what might promote higher-level mathematical understanding through the development of and changes in teacher practices and student beliefs while investigating these simultaneously.

Examining Teacher Perceptions of Student Motivation to Learn Mathematics

Motivation in mathematics research also reminds motivation and mathematics researchers that students' beliefs about *why* they are motivated to learn mathematics are intricately connected to *what* they are learning, *how* they are learning, and *where* they are learning it. These researchers have been explicit about the mathematics curriculum and instruction in their studies, seeking to inform mathematics education researchers about the importance of understanding motivation. A few studies involving mathematics motivation have examined teachers' perceptions of student motivation and their beliefs about what motivates students to learn mathematics (Givvin et al., 2001; Middleton, 1995), which is vital for understanding why teachers make instructional decisions and how they interact in mathematics activities. For example, through videotape and interviews, Middleton (1995) examined teachers' and students' beliefs about what makes mathematics intrinsically motivating. He asked five middle-school mathematics teachers (grades 6 to 8) to rank their students' motivation for mathematics and then examined the congruence between the two perspectives. The students chosen from each classroom were similar in ability, although their teachers perceived them as different in their intrinsic motivation for mathematics. Like Givvin et al. (2001), Middleton found that teachers and students did not report completely congruent perceptions of student motivation. Moreover, he reported that teachers generally lacked knowledge about motivation theory, often admitting this openly, and relied on extrinsic reinforcers to "motivate" their students. Finally, motivational constructs did not always promote intrinsic motivation as hypothesized. For example, although both teachers and students reported believing that mathematics was important and useful for students' lives, these intrinsic reasons for mathematics did not appear to be sufficient motivators for the students.

Generally, the *motivation-in-mathematics* studies were published for a mathematics education audience, in essence bringing motivation theory to mathematics research, which is rare. Middleton and Spanias (1999) were very explicit about the need for integrating achievement motivation and mathematics education research in their literature review and they delineated several areas for improvement of mathematics motivation research, which are still relevant today. They argued that theories of motivation have not been adequately tested in mathematics classrooms, in part because motivation theories need to be more accurate, precise, and applicable. A common finding across the educational psychology research and this body of research is that classroom norms with consistently supportive learning environments are critical to motivation in mathematics. However, as we highlighted at the beginning of this chapter, the mathematics classroom offers a unique context for examining motivation because both teachers and students tend to see it as a "right/wrong" discipline with curriculum materials, teaching methods, and evaluation practices that highlight student competence in very public ways. Similarly, Stipek, Salmon, et al. (1998) concluded that "[e]xtant motivation theories do not explain why a positive motivational climate would foster a mastery orientation" (p. 483). In sum, students' views of their efficacy, competence, and identity are intricately tied to their mathematical experiences, which are always a part of our data whether we analyze it or not. Just as these researchers brought motivation theory to mathematics education, in the next section we attempt to bring mathematics education research to motivation researchers. Our goal is to illustrate different and more complex ways to understand student and teacher interactions and interrelationships in mathematics.

Mathematics Education Research

Mathematics education research represents a third literature that is relevant to motivation in mathematics. This literature has been influenced by the National Council for Teachers of Mathematics Standards (NCTM, 1989, 2000), which consider motivation an integral part of mathematics instruction and learning. The NCTM (2000) stated that *in addition to* focusing on problem solving and higher order thinking (e.g., Henningsen & Stein, 1997), teachers also need to promote the valuing of mathematics and confidence in one's own ability as two of the foremost goals for their students. Below we discuss two lines of research consistent with these twin goals of mathematics instruction.

Mathematics as Meaningful Thinking and Problem Solving

Meaningfulness has been a central goal of reform mathematics (NCTM, 2000) because, sadly, there is consensus that students perceive much mathematics instruction as meaningless. As Kaput (1989) eloquently explained:

> … the experience of meaningfulness of the mathematics [is neglected].… Few now deny that school mathematics as experienced by most students is compartmentalized into meaningless pieces that are isolated from one another and from the students' wider world. Symbols are manipulated without regard to the meanings that might be carried, either by referents of the symbols or by actions on them. Theorems are 'proved' without the slightest attempt to generate the statement to be proved or to justify the need for proof. This *experienced meaninglessness* of school mathematics devastates the motivation to learn or use mathematics and is entirely incompatible with a view of mathematics as a tool of personal insight and problem solving. This core problem of alienation is compounded by the difficulties inherent in dealing with formal symbols (e.g., algebra, isolated from other knowledge). (pp. 99–100)

Similarly, Blumenfeld (1992) noted the importance to motivation when she argued that achievement goal theory needed to take account of meaningfulness, "… the quality of student engagement may diminish if what is being improved is not perceived as meaningful or valued by the student….and can be used in an out-of-school situation" (p. 273). She concluded that new research on "teaching for understanding can provide additional light on task meaningfulness" (p. 273).

Cognitive Engagement in Mathematics

Henningsen and Stein's (1997) research is one example of the largest proportion of mathematics research that investigates how classroom factors such as tasks support or obstruct high-level mathematical thinking and cognitive engagement. Their research was part of the Qualitative Understanding: Amplifying Student Achievement and Reasoning (QUASAR) project based at the Learning Research and Development Center at the University of Pittsburgh and conducted in middle schools in economically disadvantaged communities. This qualitative investigation of four mathematics classrooms is rich with descriptions of student engagement in a variety of high-level mathematical tasks. The authors examined 58 tasks in mathematics classrooms of which 22 tasks were coded as demonstrating active student engagement in mathematical understanding and 36 tasks were not (e.g., 8 focused on procedures, 11 were unsystematic exploration, and 10 had no mathematical focus). Yet, the conceptual framework for studying the teacher-student interactions was one that focused on the cognitive qualities of the tasks; high-level thinking was presumed to be "engaging" and to foster motivation. The authors' analysis of motivation is generic, similar to mathematics references in most motivational research. For example, when high-level mathematical tasks declined into ineffective mathematical exploration, the authors concluded, "teachers must know their students well in order to make intelligent choices regarding the *motivational appeal*, difficulty level, and degree of task explicitness needed to move students into the right cognitive and affective space so that high-level thinking can occur and progress can be made on the task" (Henningsen & Stein, 1997, p. 537, emphasis added). Although it is not apparent what "motivational appeal" means, the authors discussed how high-level tasks that require self-monitoring promote student control and competence, resulting in students staying engaged in a difficult task. They suggested that there are several common reasons why students disengage from a task or might find the task unappealing, citing the "lack of alignment between tasks and students' prior knowledge, interests, and motivation" (p. 526) or the lack of clear task goals.

Henningsen and Stein's (1997) findings exemplify a line of research in which motivation is often implied in the use of the terms such as "engagement," "affective," or "mathematical dispositions;" defined not by what students report rather by what they do. Therefore, in this body of research, the focus on mathematics and the methods for studying student perspectives often differ from motivation research (i.e., observation rather than self-report). For example, Henningsen and Stein characterized a mathematical disposition as actions that can be observed by a teacher (e.g., seeking understanding, using resources, making sense, thinking and reasoning flexibly, and evaluating results). Motivational constructs are implicit throughout such fine-grained studies of engagement in high-level mathematical tasks, but they are rarely defined, except as a general process that might explain the quality of the tasks or the engagement and disengagement of the students in these activities. However, motivational researchers can easily glean multiple theoretical connections to achievement goals, self-regulation, situational interest, and so forth from these studies. In summary, this study is but one example among many to illustrate how research in mathematics that focuses on mathematical concepts and learning processes provides a potential for testing motivational theory *in* mathematics classrooms. It also serves as an example of the types of mathematics instruction and learning issues that are central to motivation in mathematics.

Mathematical Norms, Social Processes, and Identity

In contrast to the larger mathematics classroom research, there is a distinct body of mathematics *situative* research that explains what students and teachers do, how they interact, and how they feel about mathematics learning. These research programs also have motivational relevance because they reveal the culturally and instructionally relevant activity that helps explain *why* and *how* classrooms support or discourage motivation to learn. Using examples primarily from the work of Jo Boaler, Paul Cobb, James Greeno, and their colleagues, we have organized the research examples into three subcategories. Each category represents a different vantage point for viewing motivation in mathematics. First, we discuss the implication of mathematics classroom cultures, norms and meaning making for motivation. Next, we review motivational implications of social and instructional interactions in mathematics. Finally, we present students' views of participation in mathematics classrooms as sources of motivation to learn.

Classroom Culture, Norms, and Meaning-making

Classroom Culture Nickson (1992) defined culture as the "invisible and apparently shared meanings that teachers and students bring to the mathematics classroom and that govern their interaction in it" (p. 102). Nickson's statement carries several implications for the study of mathematics classrooms, learning, and motivation. First, every classroom has a "culture," regardless of whether it is recognized by the researcher, and it directs the meanings and norms developed within (see Kloosterman, 1996). Second, mathematics classrooms are unique, having developed distinct epistemologies over time. As we noted earlier, they are not easily compared to English, the natural sciences, or social sciences. Third, mathematics classrooms differ from each other depending on the shared meanings developed. Just as motivation researchers speak of cognitive, affective, and behavioral correlates of mastery and performance goal structures (e.g., Ames, 1992), so mathematics researchers identify differences in knowledge, norms, and values in distinct classroom cultures. Norms, or taken-as-shared meanings, goals, beliefs and assumptions of classroom participants, are central to a mathematics classroom culture at all grade levels (Grouws & Lembke, 1996; Kloosterman, 1996). Interestingly, epistemological assumptions about *what math is* do not seem to be related to the developmental levels of students. Primary grade classrooms resemble middle and high school classrooms in their emphasis on procedures, recall, speed and accuracy (e.g., Boaler, 2002; Cobb, Wood, Yackel, & McNeal, 1992).

Norms Yackel and Cobb (1996) described both *social* and *sociomathematical* norms that supported mathematical activity (and engagement) in the primary grade classrooms they studied. Social norms applied both to small group work and to whole-class discussions. For small groups, social norms included persisting to solve challenging problems, explaining to a partner, trying to make sense of a partner's explanation, and attempting to achieve consensus. Social norms in whole class discussions included explaining and justifying solutions, trying to understand solutions posed by others, indicating agreement or disagreement, and questioning alternatives when there was more than one. These norms require students to expend effort and to persist, to focus on mastering the concepts, and to collaborate with others, hallmarks of what might be called a mastery goal structure.

Sociomathematical norms, while also motivationally relevant, are particular to the mathematics culture. These norms sustain the standards of the discipline that "mathematical activity should be explainable, justifiable, and rationally grounded" (Cobb, Yackel, & Wood, 1989, p. 128). They included normative understandings of what counts as a "different" solution, and what is mathematically "sophisticated," "efficient," or "elegant." While the social norm was an expectation that students would explain their thinking, the sociomathematical norm governed what counted as an "acceptable" mathematical explanation. For example, in accepting solutions for the problem $16 + 14 + 8 = $ ___, the teacher called on students by querying, "Different [solution]?" Students learned that the teacher accepted different solutions, but not those that were little more than "restatements" of previous solutions, as in this teacher's comment, "[Your solution is] almost similar to…" (Yackel & Cobb, 1996, p. 463). This emphasis on higher order thinking demonstrates how, from a motivational perspective, students who want to learn are more inclined to use deep processing. Yet, deep processing is not seen as an individual attribute, but related to the affordances of the classroom norms.

In addition, these norms contribute to intellectual autonomy, a motivational as well as a mathematical goal. Yet, distinct from the notion of "autonomy as a context-free characteristic of the individual," the authors argue that "autonomy is defined with respect to students' participation in the practices of the classroom community.... [these students are] aware of, and draw on, their own intellectual capabilities when making mathematical decisions...." (Yackel & Cobb, 1996, p. 473). Social and sociomathematical norms, together, mediated teacher and student behavior such that they helped sustain a high level of mathematical engagement and served to support the dispositions of valuing mathematics and feeling confident about one's knowledge. In addition, the classroom observations were essential in understanding why students reported positive perceptions in a classroom where the instruction was mechanical, where learning was rote, and where support for autonomous thinking was absent (e.g., Turner, 2001). Such a close analysis of classroom mathematical activity provides us with explanations of both motivationally relevant instruction and student participation. It highlights how motivation and mathematics are mutually constituted.

Mathematics as Meaningful vs. Procedural Boaler and Greeno (2000) investigated the motivational implications of meaningful mathematics instruction in interviews with 48 students from six California high schools. All the students were enrolled in advanced placement (AP) calculus. In two classes, the students worked collaboratively and teachers encouraged discussion. These students did find mathematics meaningful, as in these comments: "I can get more into it ... why is this the way you do it?" And "Yeah, you want to figure out the problem, you want to understand the concept" (Boaler & Greeno, 2000, p. 182). In contrast, students in the other four classes perceived them as "solitary" environments in which their task was to practice and repeat demonstrated procedures. Students in the "didactic" classrooms described them as predictable (e.g., reviewing homework and doing exercises) and procedural.

> It's all about the formulas. If you know how to use it, then you've got it made. Even if you don't quite understand the concept, if you're able to figure out all the parts of the formulas, if you have the formula, then you can do it. (Boaler & Greeno, 2000, p. 180)

Some students found security in this instructional approach. As one student said, "I always like subjects where there is a definite right or wrong answer.... Because I don't really think about how or why something is the way it is. I just like math because it is or it isn't" (Boaler & Greeno, 2000, p. 185). In contrast, other students in the didactic classes who disliked math used words like "obedience," "frustration," and "ridiculous." They made comments like this one: "We knew HOW to do it. But we didn't know WHY we were doing it.... And I think that's what I really struggle with is—I can get the answer, I just don't understand why (Boaler & Greeno, 2000, p. 184).

It is important to remember that all these students were quite successful math students. Therefore, it was not low self-efficacy or perceptions of competence that alienated some in didactic classes; it was the emphasis on "received knowledge" and the perceived denial of options for self-expression and application to life—the sense of being controlled (Assor, Kaplan, & Roth, 2002). One student commented, "I care more about science and English, stuff that makes sense to me where I think I'm learning morals and lessons ..." (Boaler & Greeno, 2000, p. 187). Interestingly, many fewer of the students in the didactic classes said that they intended to continue studying mathematics, contributing to the analyses of how students' value for mathematics influences future course taking (e.g., Eccles, 1983). Boaler and Greeno (2000) concluded:

> Mathematics classrooms discourage most from pursuing mathematics. [They are] unusually narrow and ritualistic, leading able students to reject the discipline.... Traditional pedagogies and procedural views of mathematics combine to produce environments in which most students must surrender agency and thought in order to follow predetermined routines. (p.171)

Meaningfulness, then, is related to aspects of the classroom culture and the norms for what mathematics is. These research findings demonstrated *how* and *why* students view certain kinds of mathematics instruction as meaningful or meaningless, and how that might be related to their liking of math as well as their continuing to study math. This study contributes to the evidence that mathematics, because of its traditional emphases on procedural correctness and lack of conceptual relevance, has negative motivational connotations for many students (i.e., Kaput, 1989). It extends motivation research on goals, values, interest, and autonomy and how they can be promoted in classrooms.

Social Processes in Learning Mathematics

Another key aspect of classroom cultures is their social nature, prompting researchers like Boaler, Cobb, and Greeno to conclude that analyses of teaching and learning (and motivation) should no longer rely solely on "psychological representations of the mind at work… [but focus on how] learners function as part of broader worlds that are socially and culturally constituted" (Boaler, 2000a, p. 2). Taking a more situated view, the research question becomes not only *what* beliefs are, but also *how* they have developed and *how* they guide actions.

Social Interaction Boaler (2000b) noted that mathematics research has paid scant attention to student relationships. Motivation researchers have emphasized the importance of social goals (e.g., Wentzel, 1997, 1999), but have not related them to interactions with specific content in mathematics classes. Students repeatedly mention the importance of social relationships to their learning and motivation. Nickson (1992) reported that students disliked mathematics because it was *asocial,* because it "emphasize[d] the abstractness of mathematics to be done individually and more or less in silence…" (p 105). Boaler (2000b) explained that students developed alienation from learning partly because mathematics instruction was disassociated from human interaction, and thus not from their world, but from "another world."

In an interview study with 76 ninth-grade students in England, Boaler (2000b) asked students about their views of their mathematics environments. These students participated in "traditional" mathematics instruction for the U.K. (and the U.S.), meaning that it mostly consisted of demonstration and practice, with students working through short, closed questions or books for most of the class period in all the curriculum topics for students aged 12–16. One student likened being a mathematics learner to acting like a "robot"—someone "who could abandon natural human desires to attain meaning and to interact socially with others" (Boaler, 2000b, p. 392). Also, many students objected to the practice, customary at this grade, to being removed from their familiar heterogeneous groups to be placed in homogeneous math groups. Being with their familiar classmates influenced their attitude toward mathematics. One student commented: "Like, if you know that's like your group of people you don't feel shy to do anything in front of them" (p. 388). Furthermore, students overwhelmingly reported preferring to ask for help from a peer rather than a teacher.

Students in Boaler's (2000b) study also placed importance on relationships with the teacher, which is important in understanding motivation (e.g., Anderman, 1999; Wentzel, 1997, 1999), as in the following observation: "Miss Barley (mathematics teacher), I know you are not meant to be familiar with teachers, but she keeps it *so* far away. Mr. Hughes sort of, not becomes your friend, but becomes, well, and he explains everything, you know? "(p. 388). Support for the importance of social relationships comes also from American students in California who participated in collaborative, discussion-based classes.

S: Ms. Green works really hard on making it social and not just by yourself.
S: Yeah, this is my favorite class this year because the environment is so like family and you can just go there and talk about math or any problems …
S: Yeah, we always socialize about math. Weird but it happens. (Boaler & Greeno, 2000, p. 178)

Boaler (2000b) concluded that "relationships with others and the interactions they experienced are central to their learning of mathematics" (p. 389) and they contrast with the notion that mathematics, more than other subjects, is perceived and taught as an individual and solitary activity (Kloosterman, 1996). Boaler (2000b) further noted that there are motivational consequences for students of ignoring the importance of social relationships in learning: "For while educators have been focusing upon individual cognitive development, students have been living through communities and the nature of the practices and relationships they have encountered there may well have inhibited their agency, affiliation, and knowing " (p. 393). These findings support research in motivation about the importance of social relationships (Anderman, 1999; Wentzel, 1997, 1999) by specifying how beliefs and practices specific to mathematics are related to motivation.

Instructional Interactions.   The kinds of social relationships that students develop in mathematics also are closely related to instructional practices, including the goals of instruction, questioning, and grouping. In a comparison of "traditional" and "reform-oriented" algebra instruction in two different high schools[1] in California, Boaler and Staples (2008) analyzed teacher questions and the time spent in instructional activities. At Hilltop, teachers talked or asked procedural questions about one third of the time, and students almost never presented their work (0.2% of class time). At Railside, teachers posed longer, conceptual questions and combined student presentations with whole group teacher questioning. For example, when students found the perimeter of a figure with side lengths represented algebraically as $10x + 10$, the teacher probed, asking each student in the group, "Where's the 10?" requiring the students to relate the equation to the figure. Also, teachers presented "open" problems, allowing students to use different methods and solution paths, and enabling more students to "contribute ideas and feel valued" (Boaler & Staples, 2008, p. 20). Students reported many opportunities for participation, including asking good questions, being logical, using manipulatives, and asking for justification. In contrast, students at Hilltop said that to be successful, they needed to pay attention and to concentrate (cf. Kloosterman, 1996).

A reason that students at Railside reported enjoying math more may have been because there were many ways to *be successful*, and, as a result, many more students *were successful*. They learned more, enjoyed mathematics more, and progressed to higher mathematical levels. Although the instructional environment at Railside offered opportunities for students to interact, the interaction was facilitated by the creation of "groupworthy" problems. These problems provided affordances for learning and for motivation (Horn, 2006) and help explain *how* instructional interactions fostered increased competence among Railside students. The way group work was structured also related to teachers' explicit goals for teaching students how to be responsible for each other's learning, fostering relatedness (e.g., cf. Furrer & Skinner, 2003). One student commented: "… people that doesn't know how to understand it, I want to help them…. [and] I want them to be good at it" (p. 25). Boaler and Staples (2008) also provide examples of how the mathematics instruction fostered motivation through respect for others, high cognitive demand, the emphasis on effort over ability, and persistence, all familiar motivation constructs (see also, Empson, 2003).

We interpret this research as suggesting how motivation researchers can move beyond reporting and analyzing the kinds of beliefs (mastery, performance, social goals, expectancies, values) students self-report to investigating the kinds of "practices and relationships" that help constitute such beliefs. We need to better understand how students co-construct their beliefs and identities in mathematics and how they differ depending on relationships, norms, and disciplinary epistemologies. Close studies of the interrelationships of teacher-student and student-student interactions during instruction help us understand how motivation develops and changes in mathematics as a distinct disciplinary case. This research provides explicit examples of how certain classroom practices in mathematics co-produce effort, persistence, value, and other expressions of motivation to learn. Although the motivational constructs are familiar, how such beliefs and behaviors develop differ in mathematics because of its distinct epistemology and disciplinary traditions (e.g., Kloosterman, 1996; Nickson, 1992).

Students' Views of Themselves as Mathematics Learners

In this section we further discuss how the mathematics situative literature has captured motivational implications of students' feelings about mathematics learning. We begin with a brief examination of math anxiety, then focus on two approaches in the mathematics literature that illuminate the sources of math anxiety, beyond those explored in the psychological literature: (a) that of affect in relation to mathematics instruction and (b) that of constructing identities as mathematics learners.

Math Anxiety Although Goetz, Frenzel, and Pekrun (2006) recently reported that very little work as been done on the domain specificity of emotional experiences, mathematics continues to be popularly associated with anxiety. Burns (1998), a prominent mathematics educator and author of many books on teaching mathematics, cites reports that two thirds of American adults "fear and loathe" mathematics. Why is mathematics, rather than other disciplines, associated with anxiety? Middleton and Spanias (1999) speculated, "In mathematics, perhaps because it is viewed as a difficult and important subject, students tend to internalize their experiences into their self-concept more than in other subject areas" (p. 78). Shields (2006), in interviews with college students about math anxiety, found that 61% of the students attributed math anxiety to the teacher, that 51% experienced math anxiety in algebra class, and that 45% began to feel anxious about math during grades 7–9, when algebra is usually introduced. More than 60% said that they had been told math was important to their future, but they did not realize how. The timing of the mathematics anxiety appears at the same time that students are first being grouped into higher and lower achieving mathematics classrooms and as they begin to study the complex and abstract area of algebra, as we described at the beginning of this chapter. The psychological literature has mostly investigated the cognitive and affective mechanisms and motivation- and achievement-related results of anxiety (e.g., Hembree, 1990; McLeod & Adams, 1989; Wigfield & Meece, 1988). Furthermore, Goetz et al. (2006) found that the empirical literature on anxiety suggested that it was domain-specific, although the literature on other academic emotions was lacking. In their study of anxiety, boredom, and enjoyment in mathematics and three language courses (Latin, German, and English) in 7th, 8th, 9th, and 10th grades in Germany, they found that all three emotions were domain-specific for each subject area, even though three of the areas were the study of languages. Interestingly, they reported that the highest correlation between a domain-specific factor (all emotions within a subject area) and achievement in that subject were found in mathematics: mathematics, .48; Latin, .32; English, .30; and German, .28. The mathematics situative literature approaches the study of negative affect, such as anxiety, as well as enjoyment of mathematics from the perspective of how affective climates are cultivated and how students develop identities as mathematics learners.

The co-construction of Affect in Mathematics Classrooms   Cobb et al. (1989) described a second-grade classroom in which the teacher specifically cultivated a climate focused on honoring student thinking and on helping children experience and recognize the enjoyment of problem solving. The teacher characterized students' views of problem solving as an interesting and rewarding endeavor and fostered tolerance of error. For example, the teacher took a non-evaluative stance when students offered solutions by asking, "how did you discover that?" in contrast to the standard Initiation-Response-Evaluation (IRE) discourse that stresses evaluations of correctness (Mehan, 1979). Similarly, she directly addressed children's reactions of embarrassment when they made a mistake by reiterating the classroom norms: "Boys and girls, even if your answer is not correct, I am most interested in having you think. That's the important part." Furthermore, she helped establish positive emotions about mathematics. She helped students identify their feelings when they had solved a problem, asking, "How did you feel when you finally got your solution?" prompting the students to reply "Good!" (p. 129). She encouraged pride and excitement about mathematics by urging children who had found solutions to let other children "get the enjoyment out of figuring it [the problem] out for themselves." She banned certain responses in the classroom that could cause negative affect: "It hurts my feelings when someone says, 'Oh, that's easy!' When I am struggling and trying so hard, it makes me feel kind of dumb and stupid" (p. 131). Thus, it became acceptable for a student to smile and admit his mistake to the class with "I disagree with my [first] answer" (p. 135). Cobb and his colleagues noted that because many students related mathematics to negative emotion (e.g., McLeod & Adams, 1989), it is important to clarify that "positive emotional acts [in this classroom] were not reactions to extraneous factors, such as receiving extrinsic rewards … but stemmed directly from mathematical activity" (Cobb et al., 1989, p. 138.) Other researchers have noted how teachers develop caring relationships through mathematics-related interactions (Cobb et al., 1992; Gresalfi, Fiori, Boaler, & Cobb, 2004; Hackenberg, 2005).

Developing Mathematical Identities   A key concept in the mathematics situative literature is the development of student identity. Boaler and Greeno (2000) describe "identity" as the position or role one adopts in reference to how mathematics is defined in the classroom. Students' might portray their identities as "receivers," "negotiators," or "oppositional" figures in their classrooms depending on how they understand "knowing and learning mathematics" in those settings.

Researchers demonstrate that learners do not just learn knowledge and processes in mathematics classrooms, they learn to "*be* mathematics learners [who] cannot be separated from their interactional engagement in the classroom" (Boaler, 2000b, p. 380). They assert that students develop "self-understandings … about their relationships to the subject of mathematics, which are co-constructed through their experiences in the social world" (Horn, 2006, pp. 5–6), and that these *experiences* must be understood to explain motivation. A key aspect of these interpretations lies in the concept of "relationship." Even successful mathematics learners (e.g., Boaler & Greeno, 2000) may dis-identify with mathematics because their experience of "mathematics" is not consistent with the kind of person they want to be. That is, they do not want to play the kind of "role" that is offered to them.

Boaler and Greeno (2000) demonstrated that "mathematics" for many signifies loss of agency (or control over what one is doing). When asked what it took to be successful in mathematics, students did not mention the obvious—effort, ability, or interest. Instead, they mentioned patience and obedience, signaling that to be successful, they were expected to forfeit opportunities to think, be creative, or even be active. One exasperated student noted: "[It's about] obedience…I just can't follow directions when I see people doing something completely irrational" (p. 184). A young woman complained that "math is so 'it's that and that's it'.… Women … want to explore stuff … I'm more interested in phenomena and nature … I'm not interested in just you give me a formula, I'm supposed to memorize the answer, apply it and that's it" (pp. 186–187).

From these accounts we learn not only *that* students felt controlled, but also *why*—certain features of classroom instruction caused them to reject the role of "mathematics learner." Mathematical identity emerges from students' mathematical experiences in different mathematics classrooms. Thus, it is essential to understand the pedagogical practices that students related to the nature of mathematics. This literature is useful in distinguishing the particulars (Pajares, 2007) that put "flesh" on the bones of our theoretical constructs and generalizations. Although the situative mathematics research is theoretically consistent with motivational research on negative and positive affect (Turner et al., 1998) and on autonomy (e.g., Assor, Kaplan & Roth, 2002), it is more holistic in that it merges cognitive and affective components; it describes the person (e.g., identity), not just beliefs; and it focuses on how feelings are co-constructed in relationships as opposed to viewing them mostly as individual differences. Therefore, this literature is complementary to the theoretical research in motivation. It relies on constructs theorized in the motivation literature and attempts to demonstrate how motivation (e.g., beliefs, goals, affects) develops in particular situations to explain the special case of mathematics.

Conclusion

In this chapter, we targeted three distinct literatures that each study motivation and mathematics, but from different perspectives, using different methodologies, and with different emphases on and integration of motivation and mathematics. We conclude that, while each literature makes a specific contribution, no one body of work adequately addresses motivated mathematics learning and teaching. We believe that researchers in these areas have much to learn from each other. From our viewpoint as motivation researchers, we propose several recommendations for the future study of motivation in mathematics.

First, situate motivational theories. There is growing sense among some critics of psychological and motivational research that our questions and methods are ill suited to our objects of study.

Pajares (2007) warns that "research findings and generalizations drawn from educational psychology broadly, and motivation theory and research in particular, cannot be taken as general rules that are independent of contextual variation" (p. 19). Although motivation researchers have begun to move in this direction (e.g., Turner & Meyer, 2000; Urdan, et al., 1999), they have not yet attended to the particulars of classroom and disciplinary cultures that make motivation in mathematics unique. The attempt to address contextual features in motivation research in classrooms is still in its infancy and struggles with definitions and methods (Nolen & Ward, 2008; Perry, Turner, & Meyer, 2006). Motivation researchers bring explanatory theories and provide the opportunity for theory testing and building. On the other hand, mathematics researchers contribute nuanced, disciplinary-focused understandings of teaching and learning in mathematics classrooms. Both are essential. Learning from each other can be mutually informative. As we have tried to demonstrate, the goals of mathematics research and motivation research in classrooms are inherently intertwined, regardless of how explicitly they have been connected in research. For example, an overarching goal of the National Council of Teachers of Mathematics' (NCTM, 2000) principles and standards is to provide the richest mathematical learning experience possible— an environment in which students learn with understanding, and value, and engage in mathematics.

Understanding motivation is essential to mathematics because it provides the reasons for engagement or disengagement in learning. Through more explicitly synthesizing motivation theory and mathematics research (e.g., Kazemi & Stipek, 2001), mathematics researchers can provide frameworks not only for investigating mathematics classrooms, but also for sharing their rich findings with researchers outside of mathematics and with teachers in classrooms. As we described, mathematics researchers have just begun to take advantage of an extensive body of work in classroom motivation, yet their understanding of motivation lacks appreciation of the contribution of theory. Furthermore, as the National Research Council and the Institute of Medicine (2004) has reported, classroom context or the educational learning environment continuously influences engagement in multiple and significant ways: (a) perceptions of competence and control, (b) academic values and goals (e.g., higher-order thinking, collaboration, active participation), and (c) meaningful connections to students' cultures and lives (e.g., creating a sense of belonging). These are all critically important in supporting students as motivated learners of mathematics. We see these paths converging, to the benefit of each.

Second, study the particulars, not just the abstractions. We need to explain not only *what* motivates students and teachers, but also *how* and *why*. Motivation is not instructionally neutral. Answers to *how* and *why* will come from the affordances and constraints of mathematics classrooms. Students do not develop interest in and value for mathematics if instruction is meaningless and rote or denies them opportunities to think and interact. Furthermore, teachers' efficacy for teaching mathematics to students with lower achievement in mathematics declines as students get older and has significant implications for mathematics instruction (Eccles et al., 1993; Kloosterman, Raymond, & Emenaker, 1996). Yet most studies of motivation have focused on student beliefs without attention to their sources or outcomes. Clearly, "mathematics" is inadequate to describe what teachers and students are doing in classrooms. The microcultures of the classroom, with their social and sociomathematical norms, the mathematical topics "taught" and "learned," the "ways of being" mathematics learners, the attitudes, fears and joys—all of these are essential to understanding motivation in mathematics. We cannot dissect the cognitive, affective, motivational, and social in human experience the way we do psychological constructs. Furthermore, as with academic emotions (Goetz et al., 2006), we have very little research regarding how the different areas within mathematics (e.g., arithmetic, algebra, geometry, calculus, probability, etc.) might differ from each other in terms of student learning and motivation.

Third, integrate inquiry approaches rather than segregate them. We need to develop approaches to studying the *co-construction* of mathematics motivation and learning in classrooms. This likely involves multiple methods to capture the personal meanings, the social interactions, and the community norms and practices that together inform motivation to learn mathematics. Methods might include observations, interviews, discourse analyses and self-reports, as well as analyses of curriculum and instruction, teacher-student interactions and group processes, achievement outcomes, and political and social pressures (e.g., No Child Left Behind). Methods should consider personal, interpersonal, and community levels of analysis, though researchers might foreground one area while backgrounding others (e.g., Rogoff, 1997). The methodological challenges are so great that collaboration of motivation researchers and mathematics education researchers is essential. Collaboration in conducting studies and adapting multimethod approaches with teams of researchers focusing on the same interactions, but acknowledging their very different lenses would allow integration of the unique perspectives each brings. The collaboration may be in the form of disseminating research findings (e.g., co-presentations at conferences, multiple-perspective edited volumes, or special journal issues) and other forms of research syntheses or in testing specific motivation theories and sociomathematical norms (e.g., Kazemi & Stipek, 2001).

Concluding Thoughts

Understanding motivated mathematics learning and teaching requires a far greater synthesis of motivation theory and mathematics research than the current literatures provide. As Zurawsky (2006) makes clear, mathematics education and achievement has been left to assume its natural course—the more successful a student is in math, the more math courses they take, the higher their mathematics achievement. Thus, in the United States, raising the expectations for all students in mathematics is a "relatively new idea" for "[e]ven in the 1960's movement to improve U.S. mathematics education, which was based on the argument that an excellent scientific education was necessary for a strong economy and national defense, largely was limited to 'college-capable' students" (p. 1). The potential contributions are enormous if researchers can help all stakeholders (e.g., students, parents, teachers, administrators, politicians) understand that motivated mathematics teaching and learning is necessary for achieving better mathematical understanding and positive dispositions. As researchers we must remember that there are multiple influences on the classroom as well—families, school communities, and broader societal values and expectations. But in the end, the shared goal of all inquiry perspectives and research traditions is to provide the best research possible that not simply has implications for practice and theory, but actually contributes equally to the improvement of mathematical practices and learning and to theory development (Schoenfeld, 2006).

Note

1. "Hilltop" school (traditional approach) is rural, with a population of half Latino and half White. "Railside" school (reform approach) is urban and poor, with students of many ethnicities. Students entered with significantly lower mathematics achievement than did those at Hilltop. The percentage of students receiving free/reduced lunch was 23% at Hilltop and 31% at Railside.

References

Ames, C. (1992). Classrooms: Goals, structures, and student motivation. *Journal of Educational Psychology, 84,* 261–271.

Anderman, L. (1999). Classroom goal orientation, school belonging and social goals as predictors of students' positive and negative affect following the transition to middle school. *Journal of Research and Development in Education, 32,* 89–103.

Assor, A., Kaplan, H., & Roth, G. (2002). Choice is good, but relevance is excellent: Autonomy-enhancing and suppressing teacher behaviours predicting students' engagement in schoolwork. *British Journal of Educational Psychology, 72,* 261–278.

Blumenfeld, P. C. (1992). Classroom learning and motivation: Clarifying and expanding goal theory. *Journal of Educational Psychology, 84,* 272–281.

Boaler, J. (2000a). Introduction: Intricacies of knowledge, practice, and theory. In J. Boaler (Ed.), *Multiple perspectives on mathematics learning and teaching* (pp. 1–17). Westport, CT: Ablex.

Boaler, J. (2000b). Mathematics from another world: Traditional communities and the alienation of learners. *Journal of mathematics behavior, 18,* 379–397.

Boaler, J. (2002). *Experiencing school mathematics: Traditional and reform approaches to teaching and their impact on student learning.* Mahwah, NJ: Erlbaum.

Boaler, J., & Greeno, J. (2000). Identity, agency, and knowing in mathematics worlds. In J. Boaler (Ed.), *Multiple perspectives on mathematics learning and teaching* (pp. 171–200). Westport, CT: Ablex.

Boaler, J. & Staples, M. (2008). Transforming students' lives through an equitable mathematics approach: The case of Railside School. *Teachers College Record, 110,* 608–645.

Bredo, E. (2006). Conceptual Confusion and Educational Psychology. In P. H. Winne & P. A. Alexander P. (Eds.), *Handbook of educational psychology* (pp. 43–57). Mahwah, NJ: Erlbaum.

Burns, M. (1998). *Math: Facing an American phobia.* Sausalito, CA: Math Solutions Publications.

Carr, M. (Ed.). (1996a). *Motivation in mathematics.* Cresskill, NJ: Hampton Press.

Carr, M. (1996b). Metacognitive, motivational, and social influences on mathematics strategy use. In M. Carr (Ed.), *Motivation in mathematics* (pp. 89–111). Cresskill, NJ: Hampton Press.

Clifford, M. M. (1988). Failure tolerance and academic risk-taking in ten- to twelve-year-old students. *British Journal of Educational Psychology, 58,* 15–27.

Cobb, P., Wood, T., Yackel, E., & McNeal (1992). Characteristics of classroom mathematics traditions: An interactional analysis. *American Educational Research Journal, 29,* 573–604.

Cobb, P., Wood, T., Yackel, E., Nicholls, J., Wheatley, G. Trigatti, B., & Perlwitz, M. (1991). Assessment of a problem-centered second-grade mathematics project. *Journal for Research in Mathematics Education, 22,* 3–29.

Cobb, P., Yackel, E., & Wood, T. (1989). Young children's emotional acts while engaged in mathematical problem solving. In D. B. McLeod & V.M. Adams, (Eds.), *Affect and mathematical problem solving* (pp. 117–148). New York: Springer-Verlag.

diSessa, A. (1991). Local sciences: Viewing the design of human-computer systems as cognitive science. In J. M. Carroll (Ed.), *Designing interaction: Psychology at the human-computer interface* (pp. 162–202). New York: Cambridge University Press.

Duncan, M., & Biddle, B. (1974). *The study of teaching.* New York: Holt, Rinehart, & Winston.

Eccles (Parsons), J. (1983). Expectancies, values, and academic behavior. In J. T. Spence (Ed.), *Achievement and achievement motives* (pp. 75–137). New York: Freeman.

Eccles, J. S., Wigfield, A., Midgley, C., Reuman, D., MacIver, D., & Feldlaufer, H. (1993). Negative effects of traditional middle schools on students' motivation. *Elementary School Journal, 93,* 552–574.

Empson, S. B. (2003). Low-performing students and teaching fractions for understanding: An interactional analysis. *Journal for Research in Mathematics Education, 34,* 305–343.

Feldlaufer, H., Midgley, C., & Eccles, J. S. (1988). Student, teacher, and observer perceptions of the classroom environment before and after the transition to junior high school. *Journal of Early Adolescence, 8,* 133–156.

Furrer, C., & Skinner, E. (2003). Sense of Relatedness as a Factor in Children's Academic Engagement and Performance. *Journal of Educational Psychology, 95,* 148–162.

Givvin, K. B., Stipek, D. J, Salmon, J. M., & MacGyvers, V. I. (2001). In the eyes of the beholder: Students' and teachers' judgments of students' motivation. *Teaching and Teacher Education, 17,* 321–331.

Goetz, T., Frenzel, A. C., & Pekrun, R. (2006). The domain specificity of academic emotional experiences. *The Journal of Experimental Education, 25,* 5–29.

Good, T. L., & Brophy, J. E. (1987). *Looking in classrooms* (4th ed.). New York: Harper & Row.

Gresalfi, M. S., Fiori, N., Jo, B. and Cobb, P. (2004, Oct). *Exploring an elusive link between knowledge and practice.* Paper presented at the annual meeting of the North American Chapter of the International Group for the Psychology of Mathematics Education, Toronto, Ontario, Canada Retrieved April 12, 2008, from http://www.allacademic.com/meta/p117506_index.html

Grouws, D. A., & Lembke, L. O. (1996). Influential factors in student motivation to learn mathematics: The teacher and classroom culture. In M. Carr (Ed.), *Motivation in mathematics* (pp. 39–62). Cresskill, NJ: Hampton Press.

Hackenberg, A. (2005). *Mathematical caring relations as a framework for supporting research and learning.* Paper presented at the Proceedings of the 27th annual meeting of the North American Chapter of the International Group for the Psychology of Mathematics Education, Roanoke, VA. Retrieved February 5, 2009, from http://www.allacademic.com/meta/p24575_index.html

Hembree, R. (1990). The nature, effects, and relief of mathematics anxiety. *Journal for Research in Mathematics Education, 21*, 33–46.

Henningsen, M., & Stein, M. K. (1997). Mathematical tasks and student cognition: Classroom-based factors that support and inhibit high-level mathematical thinking and reasoning. *Journal for Research in Mathematics Education, 28*, 524–549.

Horn, I. (2006, April). *"Turnaround" students in high school mathematics: The department's role in student persistence and identity construction.* Paper presented at the annual meeting of the American Educational Research Association, San Francisco.

Jacobs, J. E., Lanza, S., Osgood, W., Eccles, J. S., & Wigfield, A. (2002). Changes in children's self-competence and values: Gender and domain differences across grades one through twelve. *Child Development, 73*, 509–527.

Kaput, J. (1989). Information technologies and affect in mathematics experiences. In D. B. McLeod & V. M. Adams (Eds.), *Affect and mathematical problem solving* (pp. 89–103). New York: Springer-Verlag.

Kazemi, E. & Stipek, D. (2001). Promoting conceptual thinking in four upper-elementary mathematics classrooms. *Elementary School Journal, 102*, 59–80.

Kloosterman, P. (1984, April). Attribution theory and mathematics education. Paper presented at the American Educational Research Association, New Orleans, LA. (ERIC Document Reproduction Service No. ED244830).

Kloosterman, P. (1988). Self-confidence and motivation in mathematics. *Journal of Educational Psychology, 80*, 345–351.

Kloosterman, P. (1996). Students' beliefs about knowing and learning mathematics: Implications for motivation. In M. Carr (Ed.), *Motivation in mathematics* (pp. 131–156). Cresskill, NJ: Hampton Press.

Kloosterman, P., & Gorman, J. (1990). Building motivation in the elementary mathematics classroom. School Science and Mathematics, *90*(5), 375–382.

Kloosterman, P., Raymond, A. M., & Emenaker, C. (1996). Students' beliefs about mathematics: A three-year study. *Elementary School Journal, 97*, 39–56.

Lepper, M. R., & Woolverton, M. (2002). The wisdom of practice: Lessons learned from the study of highly effective tutors. In J. Aronson (Ed.), *Improving academic achievement: Impact of psychological factors on education* (pp. 135–158). San Diego: Academic Press.

Maehr, M. L., & Meyer, H. (1997). Understanding motivation and schooling: Where we've been, where we are, and where we need to go. *Educational Psychology Review, 9*, 371–409.

McLeod, D. B. (1992). Research on affect in mathematics education: A reconceptualization. In D. Grouws (Ed.), *Handbook of research on mathematics teaching and learning* (pp. 575–596). New York: Macmillan.

McLeod, D. B., & Adams, V. M. (1989). *Affect and mathematical problem solving: A new perspective.* New York: Springer-Verlag.

Mehan, H. (1979). *Learning lessons: Social organization in the classroom.* Cambridge, MA: Harvard University Press.

Meyer, D. K., Turner, J. C., & Spencer, C. A. (1997). Challenge in a mathematics classroom: Students' motivation and strategies in project-based learning. *Elementary School Journal, 97*, 501–521.

Middleton, J. A. (1995). A study of intrinsic motivation in mathematics classrooms: A personal constructs approach. *Journal for Research in Mathematics Education, 26*, 254–279.

Middleton, J. A. (1999). Curricular influences on the motivational beliefs and practices of two middle school mathematics teachers: A follow-up study. *Journal for Research in Mathematics Education, 30*, 349–358.

Middleton, J. A., & Spanias, P. A. (1999). Motivation for achievement in mathematics: Findings, generalizations, and criticisms of the research. *Journal for Research in Mathematics Education, 30*, 65–89.

Midgley, C., & Feldlaufer, H. (1987). Students' and teachers' decision-making fit before and after the transition to junior high school. *Journal of Early Adolescence, 7*, 225–241.

Midgley, C., Feldlaufer, H., & Eccles, J. S. (1989a). Change in teacher efficacy and student self- and task-related beliefs in mathematics during the transition to junior high school. *Journal of Educational Psychology, 81*, 247–258.

Midgley, C., Feldlaufer, H., & Eccles, J. S. (1989b). Student/teacher relations and attitudes toward mathematics before and after the transition to junior high school. *Child Development, 60*, 981–992.

Midgley, C., & Maehr, M. (1991). *Patterns of Adaptive Learning Survey.* Ann Arbor: University of Michigan.

Midgley, C., Eccles, J. S., & Feldlaufer, H. (1991). Classroom environment and the transition to junior high school. In H. J. Walberg & B. J. Fraser (Eds.), *Educational environments: Evaluation, antecedents and consequences* (pp. 113–139). Elmsford, NY: Pergamon Press.

National Council of Teachers of Mathematics. (1989). *Curriculum and evaluation standards for school mathematics.* Reston, VA: Author.

National Council of Teachers of Mathematics. (2000). *Principles and standards for school mathematics.* Reston, VA: Author.

National Research Council and the Institute of Medicine. (2004). *Engaging schools: Fostering high school students' motivation to learn.* Committee on Increasing High School Students' Engagement and Motivation to Learn. Board on Children, Youth, and Families, Division of Behavioral and Social Sciences and Education. Washington, DC: The National Academies Press.

Nickson, M. (1992) The culture of the mathematics classroom: an unknown quantity. In D. A. Grouws, (Ed.), *Handbook of research on mathematics Teaching and learning* (pp. 100–114). New York: Macmillan.

Nolen, S. B., & Ward, C. (2008). Sociocultural and situative approaches to studying motivation. In M. Maehr, S. Karabenik, & T. Urdan (Eds.), *Social psychological perspective on motivation and achievement: Advances in motivation and achievement* (Vol. 15, pp. 428–460). Bingley, UK: Emerald Group.

Pajares, F. (2007). Culturalizing educational psychology. In F. Salili & R. Hoosain (Eds.), *Culture, motivation and learning: A multicultural perspective* (pp. 19–42). Charlotte, NC: Information Age.

Patrick, H., Anderman, L. H., Ryan, A. M., Edelin, K. C., & Midgley, C. (2001). Teachers' communication of goal orientations in four fifth-grade classrooms. *Elementary School Journal, 102*, 35–58.

Patrick, H., Turner, J. C. Meyer, D. K., & Midgley, C. (2003). How teachers establish psychological environments during the first days of school: Associations with avoidance in mathematics. *Teachers College Record, 105*, 1521–1558.

Perry, N., Turner, J. C., & Meyer, D. K. (2006). Student Engagement in the classroom. In P. Alexander & P. Winne (Eds.), *Handbook of Educational Psychology* (pp. 327–348). Mahwah, NJ: Erlbaum.

Rogoff, B. (1997). Evaluating development in the process of participation: Theory, methods, and practice building on each other. In E. Amsel & K. A. Renninger (Eds.), *Change and development: Issues of theory, method, and application* (pp. 265–285). Mahwah, NJ: Erlbaum.

Schoenfeld, A. H. (2006). Mathematics teaching and learning. In P. A. Alexander & P. H. Winne (Eds.), *Handbook of educational psychology* (2nd ed., pp. 479–510). Mahwah, NJ: Erlbaum.

Schweinle, A., Turner, J. C., & Meyer, D. K. (2006). Striking the right balance: Students' motivational experiences and affect in upper elementary mathematics classes, *Journal of Educational Research, 99*, 271–293.

Shields, D. (2006). *Causes of math anxiety: The student perspective.* Unpublished doctoral dissertation, Indiana University of Pennsylvania.

Sheull, T. J. (1996). Teaching and learning in a classroom context. In D. C. Berliner & R. C. Calfee (Eds.), *Handbook of educational psychology* (pp. 726–764). New York: Simon and Schuster Macmillan.

Shulman, L. S, & Quinlan, K. M. (1996). The comparative psychology of school subjects. In D. C. Berliner & R. C. Calfee (Eds.), *Handbook of educational psychology* (pp. 399–422). New York: Simon and Schuster Macmillan

Skinner, E. A., & Belmont, M. J. (1993). Motivation in the classroom: Reciprocal effects of teacher behavior and student engagement across the school year. *Journal of Educational Psychology, 85*, 571–581.

Stipek, D. (2002) *Motivation to learn: Integrating theory into practice (4th ed.).* Boston, MA: Allyn & Bacon.

Stipek, D., Givven, K. B., Salmon, J. M., & MacGyvers, V. L. (1998). Can a teacher intervention improve classroom practices and student motivation in mathematics? *Journal of Experimental Education, 66*, 319–337.

Stipek, D., Salmon, J. M., Givvin, K. B., Kazemi, E, Saxe, G., & MacGyvers, V. L. (1998). The value (and convergence) of practices suggested by motivation research and promoted by mathematics education reformers. *Journal for Research in Mathematics Education, 29*, 465–488.

Stodolsky, S. (1988). *The subject matters: Classroom activity in mathematics and social studies.* Chicago: University of Chicago Press.

Turner, J. C. (2001). Using context to enrich and challenge our understanding of motivational theory. In Volet, S. & Järvelä, S. (Eds.), *Motivation in learning contexts: Theoretical and methodological implications* (pp. 85–104). Amsterdam: Pergamon Press.

Turner, J. C., & Meyer, D. K. (2000). Studying and understanding the instructional contexts of classrooms: Using our past to forge our future. *Educational Psychologist, 35*, 69–85.

Turner, J. C., & Patrick, H. (2004). Motivational influences on student participation in classroom learning activities. *Teachers College Record, 106*, 1759–1785.

Turner, J. C., & Patrick, H. (2008). How does motivation develop and why does it change? Reframing Motivation Research. *Educational Psychologist, 43*. 1–13.

Turner, J. C., Meyer, D. K., Cox, K. E., Logan, C., DiCintio, M. & Thomas, C. (1998). Creating contexts for involvement in mathematics. *Journal of Educational Psychology, 90*, 730–745.

Turner, J. C., Meyer, D. K., Midgley, C., & Patrick, H. (2003). Teacher discourse and students' affect and achievement-related behaviors in two high mastery/high performance classrooms. *Elementary School Journal, 103*, 357–382.

Turner, J. C., Midgley, C., Meyer, D. K., Gheen, M., Anderman, E., Kang, Y., & Patrick, H. (2002). The classroom environment and students' reports of avoidance strategies in mathematics: A multi-method study. *Journal of Educational Psychology, 94*, 88–106.

Turner, J. C., Thorpe, P. K., & Meyer, D. K. (1998). Students' reports of motivation and negative affect: A theoretical and empirical analysis. *Journal of Educational Psychology, 90*, 758–771.

Urdan, T. C., Kneisel, L., & Mason V. (1999). Interpreting messages about motivation in the classroom: Examining the effects of achievement goal structures. In T. C. Urdan (Ed.), *Advances in motivation and achievement: The role of context* (Vol. 11, pp. 123–158). Stamford, CT: JAI.

Vermunt, J. D., & Verloop, N. (1999). Congruence and friction between learning and teaching. *Learning and Instruction, 9*, 257–280.

Wentzel, K. (1997). Student motivation in middle school: The role of perceived pedagogical caring. *Journal of Educational Psychology, 89*, 411–419.

Wentzel, K. R. (1999). Social-motivational processes and interpersonal relationships: Implications for understanding motivation at school. *Journal of Educational Psychology, 91*, 76–97.

Wigfield, A., & Meece, J. (1988). Math anxiety in elementary and secondary school students. *Journal of Educational Psychology*, *80*, 210–216.

Wigfield, A., Byrnes, J. P., & Eccles, J. S. (2006). Development during early and middle adolescence. In P. A. Alexander & P. H. Winne (Eds.), *Handbook of educational psychology* (2nd ed., pp. 87–113). Mahwah, NJ: Erlbaum.

Wigfield, A., Eccles, J. S., Yoon, K. S., Harold, R. D., Arbreton, A. J. A., & Blumenfeld, P. C. (1997). Changes in children's competence beliefs and subjective task values across the elementary school years: A three-year study. *Journal of Educational Psychology, 89*, 451–469.

Wineburg, S. S. (1996). The psychology of learning and teaching history. In D. C. Berliner & R. C. Calfee (Eds.), *Handbook of educational psychology* (pp. 423–437). New York: Simon and Schuster Macmillan.

Yackel, E., & Cobb, P. (1996). Sociomathematical norms, argumentation, and autonomy in mathematics. *Journal for Research in Mathematics Education, 27*, 458–77

Zurawsky, C. (2006, Fall). Do the math: Cognitive demand makes a difference. *Research Points, 4*(2), 1–4.

25
Motivation and Achievement in Physical Education

Ang Chen and Catherine D. Ennis

Theories of achievement and motivation in physical education have experienced a significant transformation during the past two decades. Learning achievement in physical education, traditionally characterized by proficiency in playing sports and developing sport-related skills, is being replaced gradually by a demonstrated mastery of knowledge and skills related to healthful living. Similar to the study of motivation in learning academic subject matter, learner motivation in physical education has been viewed through multiple theoretical lenses beyond the behaviorist perspective (e.g., using win/loss as rewards for motivation). Currently, researchers are examining how achievement and motivation strategies can be used to help learners achieve the goals of developing and sustaining a physically active lifestyle.

In this chapter, we will frame our discussion of learners' achievement and motivation in physical education in the broad context of curriculum and student learning to explore the critical relationships among content, motivation, and learning achievement. We will (a) discuss the impact of major achievement motivation theories on research in physical education, (b) review and critique major research findings, and (c) discuss possible challenges for future research in physical education.

We have focused this review on research conducted with K-12 students in physical education, rather than physical activity associated with sport or recess. Although all three are beneficial to students in school, the meaningfulness of achievement in sport is limited to a small group of highly skilled students, while recess does not represent a meaningful achievement setting. The emphasis on physical education allows us to examine achievement in physical education learning environments within a domain specific context. Thus, the studies reviewed in this chapter were conducted in physical education settings, rather than in youth sport or recess. For sport-related motivation issues, we refer the reader to an excellent collection of reviews on motivation edited by Roberts (2001).

An Overview of Achievement in Physical Education

Physical education as a school subject has been around as long as education itself. In fact, education *through the physical* was central to Greek and Roman philosophy and is one of the oldest forms of education (Hackensmith, 1966). In the United States, contemporary physical education began in the 19th century, notably in schools, such as Amherst College directed by Dr. Edward Hitchcock and Harvard University by Dr. Dudley Sargent. Initially, gymnastics programs such as those imported from Germany and Sweden were designed to involve *all* students and achievement was defined in terms of improvement in anthropometric measurements (Hackensmith, 1966). By the mid-19th century, however, physicians and scholars began to argue that these programs' narrow gymnastics-only focus was not meeting the needs of American youth (Weston, 1962). In the mid-1800s, physical education was expanded to include programs in elementary and secondary schooling in large cities such as Boston, St. Louis, and Cincinnati. Although physical education was flourishing by the turn of the 20th century at all school levels, achievement outcomes were aimed at bodily hygiene from a preventive medicine perspective. The medical and public health advocates' influence on purpose and curriculum seemed to have limited physical education's contribution to the education of the whole child.

The medical focus of physical education curricula continued into the 20th century and confined students' learning experiences to calisthenics and large group military drills. In his infamous report on the function of physical education and assessment of achievement, Dr. Thomas Wood (1913), Teachers College, Columbia University, criticized then popular mass-exercise programs as too narrow in focus and too isolated from the mission of education. Wood (1913) suggested that achievement goals in physical education should be as broad as education itself to encompass children's needs for physical, cognitive, and social development. Wood and Cassidy's (1930) perspective on physical education, described as *The New Physical Education*, emphasized the role of biology, physiology, and sociology in a "naturalized" program of movement and physical skill development in games. In this type of curricula, students were encouraged to study and think about movement in physical education as they increased their health and vitality, posture and bearing, bodily functions, agility, quickness, strength, and endurance (Wood & Cassidy, 1930, p. 293). Influenced by John Dewey, Wood and Cassidy's (1930) perspective was a dramatic change in physical education curriculum that greatly influenced physical education programming through the first half of the 20th century. Following their work, physical education began a long journey addressing student needs and incorporating achievement goals valued in education. Learning goals became central to most curriculum models that evolved during the 20th century.

Physical education has undergone a substantial transformation during the last 60 years. Changes have reflected the evolution of societal perspectives on all forms of physical movement. Specifically, in schools, physical activity or human movement was perceived as the core content in physical education and viewed in terms of three general functions or purposes: physical/movement education, sport/athletics, and recreation/leisure activities. In modern schools, these three physical activity programs were organized as (a) formal curriculum—physical education, (b) interscholastic athletics—physical training for sport competitions, and (c) recess—voluntary recreational physical activities. Currently, each serves a particular purpose and gives children unique physically-oriented experiences.

Physical Education

Today, physical education serves the mission of schooling by providing structured learning opportunities for *all* children in school. It helps the child to learn about the body, mechanisms of body movement, and the relationship between body movement and its consequences (e.g., physical activity and health). Professional organizations such as the National Association for Sport and Physical Education [NASPE] (2004) have approved student content standards that have become central to physical education curriculum design at state and local levels. Further, during the past 15 years, educators and researchers have realized that physical education can provide an effective learning environment for children to apply classroom-based content, such as mathematics (DeFrancesco & Casas, 2004), science (Hatch & Smith, 2004), and language (Rattigan, 2006). When physical education content is structured to reflect natural connections between science and movement (e.g., acceleration, power, force) and health (e.g., body system responses to stress; psychological aspects of exercise adherence; caloric balance), physical education can become a meaningful part of schooling that contributes directly to the academic mission of schools.

Sport

Sport flourishes in the United States and around the world because it provides socially sanctioned outlets for athletic competition. Reflecting competitive values espoused in society, sport/athletics has become an organized venue for interscholastic competition in most secondary schools across the United States. Competitive sport functions to provide opportunities for physically gifted children to perform in specialized sports and entertainment events and receive recognition for their skill and prowess within the community. Sport programs typically promote goals of physical dominance or winning in competition and may espouse goals of character development, although with mixed results. Achievement in school sports programs, then, is often defined by win/loss records. Achievement for the individual student, especially at the high school level, is manifested through selection into a higher level sport entity, such as college or professional teams.

Recess

School-based recreational activity programs are often described as recess. The main purpose of recess is to provide children with a short break (usually 20 minutes or less) during the school day to refresh their body and mind. Recess typically is a time for students to participate in voluntary activities that are not structured by adults, although children do organize and interact in small and large group games and fantasy activities (e.g., playing horses; pretending to be NBA basketball players). Although there is strong social involvement in recess activities, the recreational nature does not provide well defined achievement goals. In this sense, achievement is usually absent in school-based recreational activities characterized by recess.

Standards, Achievement, and Student Engagement

Physical education provides a unique setting in which achievement encompasses a broad spectrum of mastery standards (NASPE, 2004). A student who achieves these standards is considered by professional organizations to be "physically educated." The NASPE Student Content Standards for Physical Education (NASPE, 2004) state that the physically educated child:

- Demonstrates competency in motor skills and movement patterns needed to perform a variety of physical activities (Standard 1),
- Demonstrates understanding of movement concepts, principles, strategies, and tactics as they apply to the learning and performance of physical activities (Standard 2),
- Participates regularly in physical activity (Standard 3),
- Achieves and maintains a health-enhancing level of physical fitness (Standard 4),
- Exhibits responsible personal and social behavior that respects self and others in physical activity settings (Standard 5), and
- Values physical activity for health, enjoyment, challenge, self-expression, and/or social interaction (Standard 6; NASPE, 2004, p. 4).

Thus, the standards are focused on three components: content-related competences (Standards 1, 2, and 4), expected behaviors (Standards 3 and 5), and dispositions (Standard 6). The standards can be conceptualized both as competence-based, such as standards 1, 2, 4, and noncompetence-based as in standards 3, 5, and 6. The multiple aims embedded in the standards encourage students both to achieve the goal of learning knowledge and skill and to develop a positive disposition, central to the enjoyment and appreciation of learning physical activity. The standards elevate educational physical education above the recreational need for "fun" experiences and directly address criticisms of low educational value inherent in recreational physical education (Goodlad, 2004).

Many students perceive educational physical education as both enjoyable and educational. They like participating in physical activities and engage wholeheartedly in skill and concept development within tasks and activities (Goodlad, 2004). Engagement is typically defined as students' involvement with school (Finn, 1993). Marks (2000) argued that engagement is a "psychological process that includes attention, interest, investment, and effort students expend in the work of learning" (p. 155). Finn (1993) reported that existing studies consistently demonstrate a strong positive relationship between engagement and performance across diverse populations. In physical education, students demonstrate engagement when they listen and contribute respectfully to group activity, demonstrate effort in physical tasks, and participate with interest and enthusiasm. In physical education research, student engagement is operationalized in many forms ranging from general instructional time on task (e.g., ALT-PE, see Metzler, 1989), to time spent in fitness development activities (e.g., SOFIT, see McKenzie, 1991) and physiological intensity (e.g., calorie expenditure, see Chen, Martin, Sun, & Ennis, 2007).

Research indicates, however, that as some students progress through school their intrinsic motivation level decreases, and they become disengaged from learning. In physical education, disengagement has been described on a continuum from mild forms such as "going through the motions" and "giving the teacher what he/she wants" (Hastie & Pickwell, 1996), to resisting and refusing to participate in the content (Ennis, Cothran, & Davidson, 1997), and to choosing not to enroll in physical education beyond the graduation requirement (National Center for Education Statistics [NCES], 1996).

Disengagement is characterized by lack of motivation. Researchers (e.g., Marks, 2000) attribute disengagement to personal and social factors, including learner maladaptive goal orientations, inadequate development of self-efficacy, problematic perceptions of competence, ill-structured learning environments, unnecessary peer competition, and dull and boring content and instruction. These characteristics have been documented in physical education research as contributing factors to student disengagement (Chen & Ennis, 2004) and recently have become the focus of motivation research in physical education. Theory-guided motivation research in physical education has provided key research findings influential in an understanding of motivation in physical education settings.

Theoretical Foundations for Motivation Research in Physical Education

Achievement motivation research in physical education has been based primarily on several motivational constructs delineated in previous chapters of this volume. These include goal orientations, self-efficacy, expectancies and values, interests, and, recently, self-determination. In physical education research, these theoretical frameworks and their associated constructs have been adapted to address important issues central to physical activity. These issues include motivational function of competitiveness and task completion (goal orientations), perceived physical competence (self-efficacy, expectancies), the fun element (interests), contribution to life (values), and behavior regulation and change (self-determination). Because research on motivation in physical education has been viewed as part of the larger paradigm of psychological studies, rather than content-centered inquiry, physical education researchers have not hypothesized and developed unique theoretical constructs. Recently, however, some researchers (e.g., Chen & Ennis, 2004) have begun to challenge this view, arguing for physical education content specificity within the examination of learner motivation (Chen et al., 2007).

Theoretical perspectives on motivation share a strong social cognitive focus that considers learner motivation dependent on both the learning environment and individual dispositions. Applied in physical education, most theories seem to share a common premise that achievement motivation relies largely on the interaction between perceived competence and achievement outcomes defined in the curriculum. The theoretical perspectives mentioned in the above paragraph should not be considered an exhaustive list of theories that researchers use in physical education research.

For example, consistent with society's current emphasis on combating childhood obesity, NASPE Standard 3 encourages K-12 students to participate regularly in physical activity and has become a pervasive goal of most physical education programs. From this perspective, a central task of physical education is to induce and sustain students' physically active behaviors. To meet this goal, alternative theoretical perspectives are emerging in physical education research. For instance, Martin, Tipler, Marsh, Richards, and Williams (2006) examined a model encompassing both cognitive and behavioral determinants of motivation, including perceived flow and physical self-concept as well as adaptive and maladaptive behavior indicators (e.g., planning for action, persistence, avoidance, disengagement). The researchers hypothesized that behavioral change is multidimensional with either adaptive or impeding cognitive (self-concept) and behavioral (planning for action) determinants. Thus, behavior change might rely on the interaction between behavioral and cognitive determinants. Data from 171 Australian high school students support the hypothesized dimensional structure and revealed various relationships between motivation derived from the interaction of correlates in the two dimensions and actual physical activity behavior patterns. A theoretical ramification of this study for motivation research in high school physical education is to suggest a motivation approach consisting of both behavioral and cognitive components that may be effective to enhance adolescents' motivation for physical activity.

The research on the impact of extrinsic reward on intrinsic motivation has influenced physical education curricula design. After an extensive review of the literature, Deci, Koestner, and Ryan (1999) concluded that once extrinsic reward is withdrawn, the motivation derived from receiving extrinsic rewards is likely to disappear. In sport-based physical education curricula, students often demonstrate their physical and cognitive abilities publicly when completing sport-like learning tasks and receive extrinsic rewards from the teacher in the form of learning performance contingencies (e.g., praises, stickers, publicly posted rankings) meant to enhance their motivation. Conversely, physical educators also may choose to include enjoyable learning tasks long considered an important source of intrinsic motivation. Thus, it is not unusual for extrinsic reward-based motivation and enjoyable experience solicited intrinsic motivation to co-exist in the process of performing learning tasks. Learning in physical education can be situationally interesting (Chen, Darst, & Pangrazi, 1999) and, therefore, intrinsically motivating. Thus, extrinsic rewards, such as winning/losing records, or losing/controlling body weight, may produce the effect of overjustification (Greene, Sternberg, & Lepper, 1976) and may not be needed in physical education.

Physical educators frequently emphasize the motivational nature of the physical context. For instance, curriculum developers typically are more sensitive to the salience of cooperative contexts and to the situational interest inherent in physical education environments than they are to students' mental dispositions and the actual impact of the context or situational interest on knowledge/skill acquisition or behavioral change (Shen, McCaughtry, Martin, & Dillion, 2006). In some cases, motivation effects might be compromised by weaknesses of a particular theoretical construct and its hidden side effects. For example, the high school physical education curriculum *Looking Good, Feeling Good* (Williams, Harageones, Johnson, & Smith, 1993) is based on positive effects of self-concept in motivating students to participate in physical activity. However, the curricular emphasis on and promise of a "trim and sculptured" body and the hidden message of *a-good-looking-body-is-lean* becomes an extrinsic reward. The demotivation impact of extrinsic reward withdrawal (i.e., when students do not experience these effects) is given little consideration in the curriculum (Deci et al., 1999).

Measuring Motivation Constructs

Achievement motivation is defined as an internal process in which "goal-directed activity is instigated and sustained" (Pintrich & Schunk, 1996, p. 4). Motivation consists of energy and direction and can only be inferred through observable indicators such as choice decisions, persistence, effort, achievement, and verbalization. In research, these indicators and actual achievement are often used to represent motivation or outcomes of motivated learning behavior, depending on the role of the measure in particular studies. Achievement goal orientation/climate, self-efficacy, expectancy beliefs and task values, interests, and extrinsic rewards and regulations are considered sources of motivation. These constructs represent different motivation mechanisms through which learners adopt adaptive or maladaptive approaches to motivation.

In classroom-based research, these indicators usually are measured using learner self-reports that tap into learners' cognitive elaboration of motivation. The self-report approach is appropriate in these research settings where behaviors relevant to cognitive engagement are difficult to detect. In physical education, however, movement is the vehicle through which the content is experienced, learning is accomplished, and achievement is demonstrated. The motivation indicators are usually observable in the actual instructional setting. For instance, physical effort can be coded with direct observation instruments or electronic devices that record physiological data (e.g., heart rate, calorie expenditure). In addition to the overt behavioral display observed in actual learning settings, self-reports also are needed to obtain information about the cognitive processes of motivation. Due to difficulties in taking actual behavioral measures reliably, most researchers in physical education have adopted self-report as the primary choice of measurement of motivation. For example, effort is usually measured using "perceived effort" survey questions adapted from classroom research rather than using accelerometers or direct observation to measure physical intensity that may represent effort in the physical education setting. Similar measurement practices are used in assessing achievement. In 36 data-based reports we sampled, only 16 employed nonself-report motivation measures, including actual achievement on knowledge and skill or participation behavior (e.g., steps, physiological intensity).

In general, in both classroom and physical education research, motivation sources are measured using self-report scales. In most instances, scholars who advance innovative theories develop and validate psychometric scales to examine and confirm the presence of theoretical constructs central to the new theory. For example, Nicholls' Motivation Orientation Scale was developed as Nicholls and his colleagues proposed and examined achievement goal orientation theory (Nicholls, Cheung, Lauer, & Pastashnick, 1989). Likewise, Eccles and her colleagues designed and validated the Expectancy-Value Questionnaire to investigate the role of expectancy value in relevant settings (e.g., Eccles, Adler, & Meece, 1984). These instruments later were revised into parallel versions for physical education research. For example, Duda and Nicholls (1992) developed the Goal Orientation Scale – Sport Questionnaire, and Xiang and her colleagues (e.g., Xiang, McBride, Guan, & Solmon 2003) adapted the Expectancy-Value Questionnaire (Eccles et al., 1984; Eccles & Wigfield, 1995) for their research in elementary school physical education. More recently, instruments, such as the Situational Interest Scale (Chen et al., 1999), were designed to measure the situational interest construct in specific movement tasks, while a separate instrument was developed to measure students' social goals in physical activity/education settings (Guan, Xiang, & McBride, 2006).

Researchers are very cognizant about maintaining validity and reliability of these measures. Most researchers pilot instruments and procedures prior to data collection and, when necessary, design sophisticated instrument development studies to validate and ensure high quality instruments. For example, Chen and his colleagues (1999) designed multisample, dual-stimuli experiments to develop the Situational Interest Scale. Researchers commonly examine instrument construct validity using the confirmatory factor analysis approach to ensure that the structural integrity of a measure is maintained.

The validity of measurement in physical education motivation research is based on the measure of constructs within a specific context. Thus, measurement validity is less an issue of measurement theory and statistical procedures, than it is one of motivation research design. It has become clear that student motivation often is a *contextualized* construct associated with the content and task in which students engage. Although there is some evidence that achievement goal orientation may be a global disposition that *crosses* different content areas (Bong, 2001; Duda & Nicholls, 1992), other constructs have been found to be content and domain specific (Bong, 2001; Jacobs, Lanza, Osgood, Eccles, & Wigfield, 2002). Because school-based sport and physical education reflect different purposes, competencies, and dispositions, it is likely that they also represent two distinct domains. Motivation in one may not transfer to another. Thus, a central measurement issue is to what extent each motivation construct reflects a global disposition or an activity-specific entity? Globally identified constructs might be measured with a few generic instruments, while activity or domain specific constructs require specifically designed instruments to maintain construct integrity/validity within the context of interest.

Certainly, motivation research must go beyond merely identifying and describing learner motivation in order to inform actual learning behavior change and achievement. Currently, most motivation studies have not reached this goal from a measurement perspective. In these instances, motivation is rarely measured in relation to behavior or achievement indicators.

Although self-reports provide reliable measures of learner motivation, other forms of data can contribute useful information to explain the relationship between motivation and achievement. For example, Shen et al. (2006) reported that physical education students can be motivated by seductive details, reflecting a form of situational interest in physical education. Seductive details are attention-attracting factors such as colorful balls or obstacle courses that, although exciting, may not contribute directly to learning achievement. Thus, in a recreational physical education program where there is little learning goal and instruction, situational interest-based motivation represents motivation for recreation rather than learning. In short, measuring achievement motivation constructs without concomitant examinations of context leads to misinterpretation. Research conducted in physical education settings with little emphasis on learning or behavioral indicators may confound the findings, making it difficult to know whether students are motivated for learning or for other purposes, such as socializing (Hastie & Pickwell, 1996).

Motivation research in physical education has clarified confusion and eliminated myths for both researchers and practitioners (Corbin, 2002). The research effort has become integrated into curriculum reform initiatives that purposefully integrate motivation strategies into the curriculum (Ennis & Lindsay, in press). Consistent with other school subject areas, physical education is expected to help students learn knowledge and skills beneficial for life. It is toward that goal that we have framed our summary and critique of the findings. In the following sections we first summarize the findings by their theoretical traditions, and then comment on their ramifications for student learning.

Research Examining Achievement Goal Theory

Similar to definitions of the achievement goal construct in classroom-based research, achievement goals are defined in physical education research as the purpose or reason a student becomes motivated to achieve what they *want* to achieve (Urdan, 1997). Achievement goals can be understood as learner mental dispositions, namely, ego- and task-oriented or instructional climate with a mastery or performance focus. Within the research programs mentioned earlier (Duda & Nicholls, 1992), physical education researchers began to adopt an extended conceptualization with the approach-avoidance dimensions of the goals. A trichotomous (i.e., mastery, performance-approach, performance-avoidance) model was adopted in several recent studies (Elliot, Cury, Fryer, & Huguet, 2006; Xiang, McBride, & Bruene, 2004; Xiang, McBride, & Bruene, 2006). Recently, a 2×2+1 model, mastery and performance with approach-avoidance dimensions plus social goals, was examined for its tenability (Guan et al., 2006).

Achievement goal research findings reflect the theoretical development process. From the dual-goal orientation perspective, research findings have demonstrated with strong evidence that learners with high task-oriented goals perceive success and failure as associated with effort, report a high likelihood to select more challenging learning tasks, and enjoy learning experiences more frequently. Conversely, learners with a high ego-orientation tend to avoid difficult learning tasks and attribute success or failure to genetic ability. They are more likely to be motivated when they predict that their performance will be superior to that of others' than when they predict it will be inferior. Based on student self-report of goal-orientations and motivation levels, these findings have been observed among learners in elementary schools (Xiang & Lee, 1998), secondary schools (Xiang & Lee, 2002), and college (Spray, Biddle, & Fox, 1999). Further, Wang, Chatzisarantis,

Spray, and Biddle (2002) reported that a high task goal orientation coupled with high perceived competence is a viable predictor of motivation for physical activity participation. Students with strong task goal orientation tend to become intrinsically motivated (by the tasks), value learning experiences, and often are able to regulate their own learning behavior.

Within the trichotomous framework, Elliot et al.'s (2006) recent experiment showed that students with either a mastery or performance-approach orientation demonstrated similar performance in skill tests. Their test performances exceeded those of students with a performance-avoidance orientation. Furthermore, students with the performance-avoidance orientation were found more likely than those with other orientations to engage in self-handicapping in learning motor skills. Self-handicapping is characterized by creating reasons or excuses not to engage in a task to avoid failure. It also may be described as actively seeking "inhibitory factors that interfere with performance" to establish a causal explanation for failure (Arkin & Baumgardner, 1985, p. 170). Although learning achievement was not measured in the study, the findings do provide evidence showing that performance-approach orientation is associated with learner motivation and increased performance (Hidi & Harackiewicz, 2000).

Since the mid-1990s, physical education research on instructional climate has gained increased attention. Researchers often employ the TARGET system (Ames, 1992; Epstein, 1988) to manipulate instruction to represent a mastery or performance climate. The findings generally support the premise that a mastery climate is more likely than a performance climate to nurture student motivation. Further, learners taught in a mastery climate are more likely than those taught in a performance climate to choose challenging tasks (Solmon, 1996), perceive themselves having high intrinsic motivation (Goudas, Biddle, Fox, & Underwood, 1995), and report a high level of perceived satisfaction (Treasure, 1997). Todorovich and Curtner-Smith (2003) also found that each of the distinctive instructional climates may strengthen the respective goal orientation that is consistent with the climate. These findings suggest that the motivational effect of these goals is context-dependent and that motivation to learn motor skills and physical activity is likely to be enhanced in a mastery instructional climate (Solmon, 1996).

There is little evidence, however, regarding the influence of the achievement goal-based motivation on enhanced learning achievement. In most studies, actual learning behavior and outcomes have been rarely measured. The researchers' intent to establish a direct link from the achievement goals to motivated learning behavior and further to learning achievement seems to be weak. In the few studies in which the attempt was made, findings show that achievement goals may have limited direct impact on learning outcomes. For example, in Berlant and Weiss' (1997) study, college students ($n = 30$) with different goal orientations viewed several videotaped demonstrations of a correctly performed tennis forehand stroke and then were assessed on visual recognition accuracy and verbal recall of key skill characteristics. The canonical correlation analysis indicated no correlation between goal orientations and the initial phase (visualization of a skill sequence) of learning this motor skill. Further, Solmon and Boone's (1993) research with college students ($n = 90$) confirmed that achievement goal orientations were not predictive of skill achievement. Additional research in middle school physical education also failed to establish the link between the goal orientations and learning achievement measured using knowledge and skill tests (Chen & Shen, 2004).

There is evidence, however, suggesting that the link between the instructional climate and learning may depend on whether the climate measured was *perceived* or *actual*. Using a random, experimental design, Solmon (1996) found that *actual* motivation climates measured by direct and objective observations were valid predictors for the number of trials students performed on challenging tasks. Conversely, when students were asked to imagine a climate (i.e., students' *perceived* climate), their perceptions did not appear to be a valid predictor. Solmon (1996) concluded that actual situational influences rather than perceptions of the learning climate account for major variations in learning behavior. These findings seem to suggest limited impact of the goal orientations on learning behavior and achievement in physical education.

Research Examining Self-Efficacy Theory

Self-efficacy has been a dominant framework in motivation studies in youth sport (see a review by Feltz, 1992) and youth and adult habitual exercise behavior (see a review by McAuley, Peña, & Jerom, 2001). Compared to these domains, research in physical education is scarce and scattered. A limited number of studies focusing on efficacious information sources for self-efficacy (Chase, 1998) examined its role in learning behavior change (Cardinal & Kosma, 2004), skill achievement (Harrison, Fellingham, & Buck, 1995), transfer from one physical activity to others (Samuels & Gibb, 2002), predictability on choice decisions (Vincent-Morin & Lafont, 2005), and teacher self-efficacy about teaching physically active lessons (Martin & Kulinna, 2005).

Self-efficacy is an activity-specific construct (Bandura, 1997). Its formation depends on efficacious information one receives from various sources. Based on in-depth interviews of 24 children (8–14 years old), Chase (1998) found different sources of efficacy information for children. Subjective perception of successful performance, comparison with others, and practicing effort were three critical sources of information children relied on to form their efficacious beliefs. Younger children primarily relied on their own subjective definition of success, while older children began to rely on others' or objective assessment information to define success. Social comparison and practicing effort contributed to the development of self-efficacy. Children tended to be "happy … because I can do that and most people couldn't" (Chase, 1998; p. 83). Practicing effort helped increase the children's confidence. Most children believed working hard lead to competence and success.

The association of self-efficacy with learning behavior change, skill achievement, and transfer to other activities was studied with college student samples. When adopted as part of cognitive strategies to help college students in weight training classes to move through behavior change stages based on a transtheoretical framework (Prochaska & Velicer, 1997), Cardinal and Kosma (2004) found that self-efficacy is an important factor that helped students move from a low stage (not thinking about behavior change) to a high stage (overt positive behavior change and maintenance). Self-efficacy is particularly important for individuals at a low stage where they need positive efficacious information to confirm their competence to endure the behavior change. In Harrison et al.'s study (1995), self-efficacy was found to co-vary with skill improvement. College students studying volleyball improved their serving skills along with self-efficacy for the skill. In addition, self-efficacy was reported (Samuels & Gibb, 2002) to transfer from a boxing course to other physical activity courses, but not from a swimming course. The researchers speculated that only self-efficacy developed in conditions requiring strong physicality could transfer.

Research examining self-efficacy with younger learners in physical education has been rare. One study (Vincent-Morin & Lafont, 2005) revealed that sixth graders' self-efficacy could predict their choice of instructional methods. Those with strong self-efficacy were likely to prefer methods with strong autonomy. When exploring the impact of certain instructional methods on self-efficacy in learning volleyball in secondary school students, Harrison et al. (1999) found that both mastery learning (incremental acquisition of skills) and direct skill instruction (skill practice leading to modified game play) could improve self-efficacy.

Few scholars have directly examined the relationship between self-efficacy and learning behavior and achievement in physical education. As a construct, self-efficacy may be viewed similarly to perceived competence or expectancy beliefs in physical education research, despite the subtle conceptual differences among them (see Wigfield, 1994). It is clear that more research is needed to clarify the role of self-efficacy in physical education learning.

Research Examining Expectancy-Value Theory

Studies based on expectancy-value theory in physical education share the same fundamental assumption guiding this line of research in classrooms. Specifically, the assumption posits that students' willingness to engage in learning and to achieve is dependent on, or at least can be explained by, their beliefs about success and the extent to which they value the content to be learned (Wigfield & Eccles, 2002). Motivated learning behavior and achievement are based on two parallel and related constructs: expectancy beliefs and subjective task values. According to Wigfield and Eccles (1992), *expectancy for success* is defined as students' beliefs about how well they will perform on upcoming activities.

Subjective task values represent students' perceptions of the extent to which the value in a particular task attracts them to the task. Eccles and her colleagues (e.g., Eccles & Wigfield, 1995) have identified three common values that can be perceived in any content area. Briefly, *attainment value* refers to the personal importance of success in an activity, while *intrinsic value* refers to the enjoyment the individual gains from the activity. *Utility value* is the perception of the activity's perceived worth in relation to current and future life goals. A critical component in this construct is *cost* which refers to the negative aspects of engaging in a task, such as fear of failure or lost opportunities associated with choosing one activity over others (Wigfield, 1994).

Current research in physical education (Chen & Liu, 2009; Chen et al., 2007; Xiang et al., 2003, 2004) has documented the presence of expectancy beliefs and attainment, intrinsic, and utility values in students as young as elementary school. Limited interview data suggest that physical discomfort, boredom, content dislike, and perceived incompetence are among the perceived costs for elementary school students (Xiang et al., 2006), while lack of learning goals, unfriendly curriculum context, and irresponsible teachers are among the costs for college students in China (Chen & Liu, 2009).

Most expectancy-value studies did involve measures of learning behavior or achievement as motivation indicators. For example, Xiang et al. (2003) measured persistence and effort in a year-round running task and found that running performance was predicted by expectancy beliefs. A unique finding in physical education research is that expectancy-value is content-specific. As Chen, Martin, Ennis, and Sun (2008) reported, no significant differences were found with elementary school students between intrinsic interest value and cardio-respiratory fitness, muscular capacity, flexibility and exercise principles. Significantly higher expectancy beliefs, attainment value, and utility values were reported for the cardio-respiratory fitness unit. Correlations among the expectancy-value components were differentiated among the content conditions, providing further evidence of content specificity in the expectancy-value motivation process. In addition, Xiang et al (2004) reported that expectancy beliefs for current competence and future success in running are strong predictors of running test scores, while intrinsic value predicts the intention for practicing running in the future. The evidence suggests that the expectancy beliefs and task values should be incorporated in theoretical platforms for curriculum development to help identify tasks that enhance expectancy beliefs and task values for optimal motivation.

For college and elementary school students, alike, expectancy beliefs and task values were found to be associated with choice decisions. The data from a random sample of 368 university students in China (Chen & Liu, 2009) showed that daily self-initiated after-school physical activity was motivated by attainment value, while the decision to take physical education was determined by intrinsic and utility value. Conversely, elementary school students indicated that they liked to attend physical education regardless of any potential cost (Chen, Ennis, Martin, & Sun, 2006a). The findings strongly suggest that the physical education content is a potential motivation source in itself. Other findings on the expectancy beliefs and task values indicate parents' competence beliefs are related to their children's persistence/effort and performance on a running test (Xiang et al., 2003) and after-school physical activity participation (Dempsey, Kimiecik, & Horn, 1993).

In the limited number of studies in which variables associated with learning were measured, persistence and effort were predicted by task values, and performance was correlated with the expectancy beliefs (e.g., Xiang et al., 2004). In another study, Chen et al. (2006a) examined the effects of situational interest and the expectancy-value components on learning in a concept-based physical education curriculum. The researchers found that the effect of the expectancy-value components on student fitness knowledge gain was overridden by the effect of situational interest. Additional research is needed to understand contributions of the expectancy beliefs and task values to learning.

The development of expectancy beliefs and task values in the physical movement domain has developed concomitantly with research in other subject domains (Jacobs et al., 2002). A common characteristic observed across various content domains is the decline of the expectancy-task value induced motivation during early adolescent years. A 10-year longitudinal analysis (Jacobs et al., 2002) on children-adolescents' motivation for different school subjects and sport revealed that children's perceived competence and task values decline steadily from elementary to high school. Similar motivational declines also were observed with cross-sectional data on motivation to learn in physical education (Xiang et al., 2003). It is believed (Chen & Liu, 2009) that instilling and sustaining expectancy beliefs and task values in physical education can be a mechanism to be built into physical education curriculum to enhance students' motivation to learn and participate in physical education.

Research Examining Interest-Based Theory

In physical education, the individual-situational conceptualization of interest is the most viable construct identified to date to explain the motivational impact of interest in physical education (Chen & Ennis, 2004). Individual interest influences learning behavior and achievement by placing the individual in an information surplus environment where he/she can rely on acquired knowledge to self-motivate and self-regulate learning behavior. Situational interest, on the other hand, is triggered by contextual conditions in which an information deficiency is created. The individual in a situationally interesting environment is constantly being prompted by salient task characteristics, such as novelty, uniqueness, and surprise, to initiate and maintain focused attention and a positive affective reaction to the task outcome (Hidi, 2000). Situational interest, therefore, operates in a learning setting where learners rely on stimuli external to them that motivate and regulate their behavior.

Hidi and Anderson (1992) argue that, because individual interest is stable and difficult to change while situational interest can be manipulated, situational interest provides more potential than individual interest to motivate students to learn through explicit curricular designs. Research in physical education has been influenced by this assumption and has focused on the motivation effects of situational interest (Chen & Ennis, 2004). An important goal in earlier studies was to examine the tenability of the construct. In this effort, Chen et al. (1999) conducted a four-stage study analyzing the dimensional sources of situational interest using a multisample design. A dual measurement environment was constructed to contrast a situationally interesting activity with a situationally boring, but identical, activity. Through exploratory and confirmatory factor analyses on four data sets from 674 middle school students, the researchers examined situational interest and its relationship with five dimensional sources: novelty, challenge, exploration opportunity, instant enjoyment, and attention demand of the activity. Chen et al. (1999) proposed that these dimensions represent features of physical activities that may contribute to situational interest.

Chen, Darst, and Pangrazi (2001) further examined the hypothesis that the five dimensional sources predicted situational interest. Middle school students ($n = 281$) responded to the Situational Interest Scale after viewing a video-recorded jogging task (low situational interest activity) and gymnastic stunts (high situational interest activity), and then performing a basketball stationary chest pass task (low situational interest activity) and a pass-shoot task (high situational interest activity). Path analyses revealed that instant enjoyment and exploration contributed strongly to situational interest, while novelty and attention demand partially contributed as well. An important finding from this research is that challenge contributed little to situational interest in physical activities. Thus, middle school teachers should be cautious when attempting to motivate learners by challenging them with difficult tasks. Additional research further revealed that discrepancies in situational interest between boys and girls are likely due to lack of skill rather than gender (Chen & Darst, 2002). When skill level was controlled, there was no significant difference between boys and girls' situational interest, suggesting all can be motivated by highly situationally interesting tasks.

Because situational interest presumably can be controlled by the teacher, it is imperative to explore the potential of designing situationally interesting learning tasks to enhance student motivation. Using performance on mathematics tasks as the dependent variable, Mitchell (1993) demonstrated that situational interest relies on those task components that can instantly "catch" learner's intense cognitive attention to induce learner motivation. In an experiment, Chen and Darst (2001) hypothesized that the cognitive demand of a physical activity might play a similar "catching" role as it did in Mitchell's puzzle-based learning tasks in mathematics (Mitchell, 1993). In their study, Chen and Darst (2001) manipulated learning conditions by controlling the cognitive and physical demand of physical education learning tasks. Data from middle school students ($n = 242$) who experienced similar learning tasks with different combinations of cognitive and physical demands consistently rated the tasks with high cognitive demand significantly higher in situational interest than those with low cognitive demand. The results demonstrate that situational interest can be controlled by adjusting the level of cognitive demand in physical activities.

The pedagogical significance of situational interest lies in the observable effects on the improvement of learning behavior and achievement. Chen et al. (2002) examined the relationship between situational interest and learning by following a random sample of middle school students ($n = 104$) studying six content units during a 17-week observation. Situational interest was measured as the source of motivation, while individual interest was measured as a control variable. Physiological intensity was measured as the indicator of learning behavior using pedometers with concurrent validation using heart rate monitors. Learning achievement was measured using performance scores on summative skill and knowledge tests. Correlation analysis revealed that individual interest had a low, but positive and significant relationship with physiological intensity ($r = .35, p < .01$)

and achievement ($r = .24, p < .01$), while situational interest (alone) demonstrated a highly positive correlation with physiological intensity ($r = 67, p < .01$). Regression and path analyses confirmed the relationship, suggesting low predictability of individual interest for the two outcomes and high predictability of situational interest for physiological intensity.

In a replication of the above study in a dance unit, Chen, Shen, Scrabis, and Tolley (2003) reported a higher correlation between individual interest and achievement outcomes for girls ($r = .62, p < .01$) than for boys ($r = .26, p > .05$). Both boys and girls considered the unit to be highly situationally interesting. The correlation between situational interest and in-class physiological intensity was similar between boys ($r = .69, p < .01$) and girls ($r = .73, p < .01$). The researchers did not find a meaningful correlation between situational interest and achievement. The findings seem to support the assumption that the motivation effect of situational interest may be short-lived, but can have an immediate effect of engaging students in the learning process (Hidi & Harackiewicz, 2000).

In a large-scale curriculum intervention study, situational interest was incorporated in the curriculum design conceptual framework (Ennis & Lindsay, in press). The motivation effect of situational interest on learning fitness-related knowledge was examined in this randomized, controlled experimental study involving approximately 6,000 students in 30 elementary schools (Chen, Ennis, Martin, & Sun, 2006b). The findings demonstrated that alone, situational interest was highly correlated with knowledge gain ($r = .83, p < .01$) as were the dimensional sources of exploration intention ($r = .59, p < .01$) and novelty ($r = .60, p < .01$). However, when placed in a hierarchical regression model along with the curriculum conditions, situational interest and its five dimensional sources accounted for 27% of variance in knowledge gain, while the curriculum condition alone accounted for 24% of knowledge gain. Instant enjoyment accounted for 37% of variance in calorie expenditure.

The findings have strong curricular implications. We now can conclude that motivating children *to learn* demands more than "fun." Situational interest, alone, may have limited impact on learning. Nevertheless, when incorporated as an integral component of the curriculum, its contribution to learning can be sizeable. The findings imply that the functions of situational interest should be emphasized in developing a coherent curriculum.

Recently, situational interest researchers have focused on its negative impact, described as seductive details. Situational interest achieved through seductive details is based on materials irrelevant to learning (Garner, Gillingham, & White, 1989). For example, physical education teachers may include activities or equipment irrelevant to learning in an attempt to create enthusiasm and excitement to engage students in the lesson content. When these constitute seductive details unrelated to the content, they are not conducive to learning. In a controlled, experimental study, Shen et al. (2006) found that seductive details interfered with learning knowledge and motor skills. The findings challenge researchers and curriculum developers to distinguish situational interest from seductive details before incorporating materials or tasks in the curriculum.

Research Examining Self-Determination Theory

In the research based on the above theoretical perspectives, motivation is viewed as a process that an individual adopts to meet the challenges in external environments. As an innate mental process, motivation should also be conceptualized as a drive residing within a person that can be called upon in need (Hidi & Harackiewicz, 2000). In articulating the self-determination theory, Deci and Ryan (2000) repeatedly remind researchers that motivation must be conceptualized as a desire to meet the need for competence, autonomy, and relatedness. In physical education, examinations of self-determination theory currently represent a limited, but well planned, systematic research program (e.g., Ntoumanis, 2001, 2005).

Based on a hierarchical model (Vallerand, 1997), Ntoumanis (2001, 2005) conceptualized and tested the relationships among the need for competence, autonomy, and relatedness and social environmental factors supporting these needs. The results have led to a conceptual model with operationalized factors that can be measured in physical education using student self-report methods. The relationship between student behavior regulation choices within different achievement goal climates was also examined. Ntoumanis (2001, 2005) hypothesized that a mastery environment and opportunities to make choice decisions would better satisfy individuals' needs for competence, autonomy, and relatedness than a performance-based context. Using a structural equation modeling analysis of the responses from 424 British middle school students, Ntoumanis (2001) found that the mastery goal climate strongly supported the satisfaction of the three innate needs of relatedness, competence, and autonomy. Despite the relationship, he also found that the mean rating on autonomy was low (mean < 3 on the 5-point scale). Ntoumanis (2001) attributed the low autonomy finding to the British mandatory national curriculum that gave students few opportunities to experience autonomy. In this controlled environment, Ntoumanis speculated, teachers were reluctant to nurture autonomy.

Thus, the research on the relationship between needs satisfaction and self-regulated motivation has presented a complex picture. For example, autonomy was found to contribute little to self-regulation (Ntoumanis, 2001), but significantly to introjected regulation (Standage, Duda, & Ntoumanis, 2003), identified regulation, and intrinsic motivation (Hagger, Chatzisarantis, Barkoukis, Wang, & Baranowski, 2005). The need for competence was positively related to identified and introjected regulation (Ntoumanis, 2001), while predictive for intrinsic motivation (Ntoumanis, 2001; Standage et al., 2003).

The self-determination theory postulates that a consequence component should be included in the model to represent the outcome of regulated motivation. Depending on the research context, the nature of the consequence may vary. In a learning context, for example, the consequence can be competence-based achievement or noncompetence-based outcomes such as enjoyment. In physical education research, only noncompetence-based outcomes were used exclusively as the consequence. They include self-reported concentration level (Standage, Duda, & Ntoumanis, 2005), preference to attempt challenging tasks, positive or negative affect (e.g., happiness, satisfaction, disappointment, boredom), intention for physically active living (Ntoumanis, 2001, 2005; Standage et al., 2003, 2005), and effort (Ntoumanis, 2001).

In physical education research, the absence of learning achievement as a variable has, again, left a void in researchers' understanding of this construct. Scholars do not yet understand the significance of self-determination findings in informing curriculum and instruction or to what extent self-determination will lead the learner "explicitly to ways of knowing, understanding, and constructing meaning" manifested in learning achievement (Oldfather & Dahl, 1994, p. 139).

Research examining self-determination theory in physical education is still in its infancy. It has tremendous potential because learning in physical education is a unique process in which engagement and achievement are often demonstrated in an observable setting. Consequently, the display of extrinsic and intrinsic motivation is explicit and observable and can be examined reliably by researchers. Learning achievement may be a viable path through which to employ the four self-regulations, helping physical education students (and teachers alike) move from externally regulated motivation to intrinsic motivation as they achieve competence-based learning goals.

Challenges in Motivation Research in Physical Education

Achievement motivation research in physical education has advanced our knowledge about motivation and its function. Collectively, the research evidence supports the premise that students can report whether they are motivated in physical education and researchers can identify the relevant motivation sources in a given learning setting. The findings also suggest that as an internal process, motivation can be observed in learning, either in the form of self-perceptions, actual physical movement patterns, choice decisions on tasks, or physiological responses to physical activity. It is encouraging that the research has begun to address the critical issues linking motivation to learning achievement.

The findings also present great challenges. As Chen and Ennis (2004) argued, it is necessary to reframe motivation research for a better understanding of motivation's impact on competence-based achievement. The fundamental challenge for future researchers is to search for optimal motivators that lead to learning outcomes that are not only desired by the learner (e.g., enjoyment), but also expected by the public (e.g., a physically educated person). Below, we elaborate the demands that derive from this fundamental challenge.

The Future Is Now

The continued concern regarding increases in obesity in children and adolescents has raised public awareness of the health benefits stemming from physical activity. It is clear that a successful physical education curriculum can contribute to child and adolescent health by helping them develop a healthy, physically active lifestyle (Weir, 2000). At a time when the knowledge and skills taught in physical education are increasingly valued, however, physical education has not been allocated sufficient instructional time and resources to meet minimal activity requirements (NASPE, 2006) in the current educational atmosphere in which all subject areas are competing for resources. Physical education continues to suffer from the "high need, low demand" dilemma (Ennis, 2001, 2006). Although the society needs physical educators to teach knowledge and skills for healthful, active living, the opportunity to address the obesity epidemic through quality physical education is limited by inadequate instructional time, staffing, facilities, and equipment resources.

The curricular change from the traditional team sport content to the content focusing on health behaviors can be instrumental in students' lifestyle decisions. The change can be realized through cross-disciplinary content integrating disciplinary content knowledge both in the cultural-humanities and in the kinesiological, biological-medical, and sociopsychological sciences. Motivation research can advance our understanding of the process students use to acquire knowledge and skills. In this effort, the focus should be placed on studying curricular and instructional approaches that motivate students for competence-based achievement without sacrificing noncompetence benefits.

There is an immediate need to pursue this research effort to take advantage of the policy and political initiatives that have focused both public support and funding on issues associated with physical health and child obesity intervention. In a recent 5-year longitudinal study, Ennis and her colleagues (Ennis, Lindsay, & Chen, 2005) designed and field-tested a health-science based physical education curriculum, *Be Active Pals! Science-based Physical Education Curriculum*, in elementary schools. The curriculum was designed following principles that focus on mastery goals, used high cognitively engaging physical activity tasks, and emphasized the simultaneous acquisition of cognitive knowledge and physical activity benefits (Ennis & Lindsay, in press). The study involved approximately 6,000 third- through fifth-grade students in 30 schools randomly assigned to experimental (the curriculum) and control (traditional) conditions. The motivation constructs measured included situational interest (Chen et al., 1999), expectancy beliefs, and subjective task values (Eccles & Wigfield, 1995). Learning behavior was monitored using both student workbook journaling and accelerometers to record calorie expenditure, while learning achievement was measured using standardized knowledge tests.

The initial findings indicated that this curriculum (Ennis et al., 2006) significantly enhanced elementary school students' knowledge about physical activity. Students' knowledge growth measured in the *Be Active Pals! Curriculum* was approximately 20% greater than student knowledge growth in the traditional physical education curriculum (Chen et al., 2006b). In addition, the curriculum presented a learning environment as situationally interesting to the students as that of the traditional curriculum (Chen et al., 2006b). Despite the cognitive tasks involved in the learning process, the students in the *Be Active Pals! Curriculum* were as physically active as those in the traditional curriculum (Chen et al. 2007). The findings also confirmed that situational interest is a functional motivator in the learning process (Sun, Chen, Ennis, Shen, & Martin, 2008), although the function of task values may depend on the nature of the content focus (i.e., cardio-respiratory fitness, muscular capacity, or functional flexibility; Chen et al., 2008). This in-depth analysis further indicated that learning achievement is better facilitated when the curriculum and situational interest are designed purposefully to mutually support student engagement and learning.

In most achievement motivation studies in physical education, the direct link between motivation sources and learning achievement rarely has been documented. When observed, the impact of motivation sources on achievement is often small (Shen et al., 2003; Shen & Chen, 2006). The findings from the *Be Active Pals!* research, however, suggest that for motivation sources to contribute directly to learning achievement, they should be designed as an integral part of the curriculum, rather than supplemental add-ons. This reflects an important step in which researchers have successfully integrated findings from motivation research into a curriculum reform initiative in physical education. To integrate motivation approaches in the curriculum, we believe that the two following issues should be addressed in research. First, it is necessary to define achievement and the achievement setting in physical education so that learning motivation can be studied in relation to learning achievement. Second, an open-minded approach to the adoption of different theoretical frameworks should be used to understand the function of motivation from various sources in learning in physical education. Each is discussed further below.

Defining Achievement and Achievement Settings Motivation, in short, consists of energy and direction. Although children and adolescents can be full of energy, at times they may lack direction or purpose in their efforts (Schneider & Stevenson, 1999). Thus, whether the direction is extrinsic or intrinsic might have a different impact on achievement. For example, losing weight and learning to enjoy physical activity are extrinsic and intrinsic motivators, respectively. For a student who wants to control weight, losing or gaining weight/muscle can be an effective motivator. If a curriculum is successful, the student can internalize the enjoyable value of physical activity while working intensely to achieve the weight control goal. In this scenario, the challenge becomes how to instill diverse goals, while helping students internalize the intrinsic value of an activity acknowledged by others into his/her own belief system.

Many motivation researchers operate on the assumption that the physical education context is an achievement-oriented setting with unquestionable learning goals that students effectively achieve. Further, they assume that students understand the nature of this setting and have internalized their participation as necessary in order to learn. In other words, it is assumed that students have understood and answered the question, "why should I learn and achieve in physical education." Logically, the internal and external validity of motivation research relies on the extent to which these assumptions are met in each research setting. In other words, for the results to be valid, students must perceive that the setting resembles a knowledge and skill-oriented learning environment consistent with the curriculum; not athletics or recess.

Unfortunately, these assumptions are not always met in many physical education settings. For example, Goodlad (1984, 2004) reported that many physical education settings do not appear to have learning goals for students to achieve. Although students like physical education and are willing to participate, some curricula do not provide a standard of excellence that specifies criteria for student achievement. Unfortunately, some recreational and sport-oriented physical education programs continue to focus on recreational and athletic goals that emphasize behavioral compliance rather than learning achievement. These programs may focus on controlling management objectives and assess students on attendance, dressing in the prescribed uniform, and following directions (Siedentop, Doutis, Tsangaridou, Ward, & Rauschenbach, 1994). In these contexts, there is little to energize or inspire student learning and it follows that examining student achievement motivation in these recreational settings will be fruitless.

Multiple Approaches to Educational Motivation   Many studies in physical education on *achievement* motivation are limited to a simplistic search for *the* perfect motivator, namely, enjoyment. The premise is that enjoyment will lead physical education students to become *intrinsically* motivated to participate regularly in physical activity throughout their lives. That is, for them to engage in physical activity because they enjoy the activity, rather than to lose weight, prevent heart disease, become a skillful professional athlete, or any purpose other than for the pure enjoyment of the activity itself. Although this is the Holy Grail for many motivation researchers, it may be unrealistic in the complex world of schools.

In analyzing interest-based and goal oriented motivation, Hidi and Harackiewicz (2000) acknowledged the complexity of motivating each individual student, separately, and cautioned researchers not to limit their efforts to only one strategy. They explain:

> All children have interests, motivation to explore, to engage, but not all children have academic interests and motivation to learn to the best of their abilities in school. For example, some children find physical activities much more enjoyable than mental ones. These children's interests may orient them towards sports, and their mastery goals couple with their physical interests can drive them to practice swinging their bats thousands of times to perfect their hitting. It is noteworthy that they often practice skills with an eye toward ultimately winning games and competitions. Many children seem able to effectively combine mastery goals (improving their skills and striving for "personal best") with performance goals (trying to outperform others and win), and both are probably necessary to achieve athletic excellence. (p. 168)

After contrasting a sport-loving child with a television-loving child, Hidi and Harackiewicz (2000) raised the question, "… what can educators do about children who would rather be outside the classroom playing ball or at home watching their favorite shows?" (p. 168). In response to Hidi and Harackiewicz, we believe that educators should not be discouraged by the diversity of dispositional motivators, including goal orientations, self-efficacy, expectancy beliefs, perceived task values, and expectations for rewards. Instead, we urge educators and scholars to generate curricular alternatives and create multiple research-proven opportunities to *engage* children deeply and meaningfully in the physical education learning process. As Hidi and Harackiewicz suggested, "As the first step, we need to get children engaged in activities.… Situational interests and performance goals may contribute to the triggering and maintenance of such activities. Once these activities are maintained, individuals may become personally involved, interested, and develop mastery goals" (p. 168).

Physical education is taught in a very public environment. Displaying physical competence is an inevitable part of learning. Physical education is replete with opportunities for the learner to develop inner strength and nurture persistence to meet the challenges and obstacles in competitive and noncompetitive tasks. It is likely that a task or an event can be interpreted in different ways by students with different motivation dispositions. Their diverse interpretations may lead to a range of task reactions and diverse motivational states in that particular learning context. To further our understanding of achievement motivation in physical education, we need to reconceptualize motivation research questions and develop collaborations with curriculum and instruction, educational policy, and educational sociology scholars as well as psychologists (Burke, 1995; Hidi & Carackiewicz, 2000; Urdan, Midgley, & Wood, 1995). From this integrated perspective, we can study achievement motivation issues within authentic achievement settings defined by the curricular context and the learning goals that students are expected to achieve.

References

Ames, C. (1992). Classrooms: Goals, structures, and student motivation. *Journal of Educational Psychology, 84*, 261–271.

Arkin, R. M., & Baumgardner, A. H. (1985). Self-handicapping. In J. Harvey & G. Weary (Eds.), *Attribution: Basic issues and applications* (pp. 169–202). Orlando, FL: Academic Press.

Bandura, A. (1997). *Self-efficacy: The exercise of control*. New York: Freeman.

Berlant, A. R., & Weiss, M. R. (1997). Goal orientation and the modeling process: An individual's focus on form and outcome. *Research Quarterly for Exercise and Sport, 68*, 317–330.

Bong, M. (2001). Between and within-domain relations of academic motivation among middle and high school students: Self-efficacy, task value, and achievement goals. *Journal of Educational Psychology, 93*, 23–34.

Burke, D. J. (1995). Connecting content and motivation: Education's missing link. *Peabody Journal of Education, 70*, 66–81.

Cardinal, B. J., & Kosma, M. (2004). Self-efficacy and the stages and processes of change associated with adopting and maintaining muscular fitness-promoting behaviors. *Research Quarterly for Exercise and Sport, 75*, 186–196.

Chase, M. A. (1998). Sources of self-efficacy in physical education and sport. *Journal of Teaching in Physical Education, 18*, 76–89.

Chen, A., & Darst, P. W. (2001). Situational interest in physical education: A function of learning task design. *Research Quarterly for Exercise and Sport, 72*, 150–164.

Chen, A., & Darst, P. W. (2002). Individual and situational interest: The role of gender and skill. *Contemporary Educational Psychology, 27*, 250–269.

Chen, A., & Ennis, C. D. (2004). Searching for optimal motivators: Goals, interests, and learning in physical education. *The Journal of Educational Research, 97*(6), 329–338.

Chen, A., & Liu, X. (2009). Task values, cost, and choice decisions in physical education. *Journal of Teaching in Physical Education, 28*, 191–213.

Chen, A., & Shen, B. (2004). A web of achieving in physical education: Goals, interest, outside-school activity and learning. *Learning and Individual Differences, 14*(3), 169–182.

Chen, A., Darst, P. W., & Pangrazi, R. P. (1999). What constitutes situational interest? Validating a construct in physical education. *Measurement in Physical Education and Exercise Science, 3*, 157–180.

Chen, A., Darst, P. W., & Pangrazi, R. P. (2001). An examination of situational interest and its sources in physical education. *British Journal of Educational Psychology, 71*, 383–400.

Chen, A., Ennis, C. D., Martin, R., & Sun, H. (2006a). Exploring motivation sources in elementary school physical education: Situational interest and expectancy-values. *Research Quarterly for Exercise and Sport, 77*(supplement), 52.

Chen, A., Ennis, C. D., Martin, R., & Sun, H. (2006b). Situational interest – A curriculum component enhancing motivation to learn. In S. N. Hogan (Ed.), *New developments in learning research* (pp. 235–261). Hauppauge, NY: Nova Science Publishers.

Chen, A., Martin, R., Ennis, C. D., & Sun, H. (2008). Content specificity of expectancy beliefs and task values in elementary physical education. *Research Quarterly for Exercise and Sport, 79,* 195–208.

Chen, A., Martin, R., Sun, H., & Ennis, C. D. (2007) Is physical activity at risk in constructivist physical education? *Research Quarterly for Exercise and Sport, 78,* 500–509.

Chen, A., & Shen, B. (2004). A web of achieving in physical education: Goals, interest, outside-school activity and learning. *Learning and Individual Differences, 14*(3), 169–182.

Corbin, C. B. (2002). Physical activity for everyone: What every physical educator should know about promoting lifelong physical activity. *Journal of Teaching in Physical Education, 21,* 128–144.

Deci, E. L., Koestner, R., & Ryan, R. M. (1999). A meta-analytic review of experiments examining the effects of extrinsic rewards on intrinsic motivation. *Psychological Bulletin, 125,* 627–668.

Deci, E. L., & Ryan, R. M. (2000). The "what" and "why" of goal pursuits: Human needs and the self-determination of behavior. *Psychological Inquiry, 11,* 227–268.

DeFrancesco, C., & Casas, B. (2004). Elementary physical education and math skill development. *Strategies: A Journal for Physical and Sport Educators, 18*(2), 21–23.

Dempsey, J. M., Kimiecik, J. C., & Horn, T. S. (1993). Parental influence on children's moderate to vigorous physical activity participation: An expectancy-value approach. *Pediatric Exercise Science, 5,* 151–167.

Duda, J. L., & Nicholls, J. G. (1992). Dimensions of achievement motivation in schoolwork and sport. *Journal of Educational Psychology, 84,* 290–299.

Eccles, J., & Wigfield, A. (1995). In the mind of the actor: The structure of adolescents' achievement task value and expectancy-related beliefs. *Personality and Social Psychology Bulletin, 21,* 215–225.

Eccles, J., Adler, T. F., & Meece, J. L. (1984). Sex differences in achievement: A test of alternative theories. *Journal of Personality and Social Psychology, 46,* 26–43.

Elliot, A. J., Cury, F., Fryer, J. W., & Huguet, P. (2006). Achievement goals, self-handicapping, and performance attainment: A mediational analysis. *Journal of Sport & Exercise Psychology, 28,* 344–361.

Ennis, C. D. (2001). Addressing the "high need, low demand" status of physical education. In P. Ward & P. Doutis (Eds.), *Physical education in the 21st century* (pp. 199–213). Lincoln: University of Nebraska Press.

Ennis, C. D. (2006). Curriculum: Forming and reshaping the vision of physical education in a high need, low demand world of schools. *Quest, 58,* 41–59.

Ennis, C. D., & Lindsay, E.L. (in press). *The Be Active Pals! Science-enriched physical education curriculum.* Champaign, IL: Human Kinetics.

Ennis, C. D., Cothran, D. J., & Davidson, K. S. (1997). Implementing curriculum within a context of fear and disengagement. *Journal of Teaching in Physical Education, 17,* 52–71.

Ennis, C. D., Lindsay, E., & Chen, A. (2005, November). *Science and physical education: The perfect partnership.* Paper presented at the National Science Teachers Association annual meeting, Chicago.

Epstein, J. L. (1988). Effective schools or effective students: Dealing with diversity. In R. Haskins & D. J. MacRae (Eds.), *Policies for America's public schools: Teachers, equity, and indicators* (pp. 89–126). Westport, CT: Ablex.

Feltz, D. L. (1992). Understanding motivation in sport: A self-efficacy perspective. In G. C. Roberts (Ed.), *Motivation in sport and exercise* (pp. 93–105). Champaign, IL: Human Kinetics.

Finn, J. D. (1993). *School engagement and students at risk.* Washington, DC: National Center for Education Statistics.

Garner, R., Gillingham, M. G., & White, C. S. (1989). Effects of "seductive details" on macroprocessing and microprocessing in adults and children. *Cognition and Instruction, 6,* 41–57.

Goodlad, J. I. (1984). *A place called school: Prospects for the future.* New York: McGraw-Hill.

Goodlad, J. I. (2004). *A place called school: Twentieth anniversary edition.* New York: McGraw-Hill.

Goudas, M., Biddle, S. J. H., Fox, K. R., & Underwood, M. (1995). It ain't what you do, it's the way that you do it! Teaching style affects children's motivation in track and field lessons. *The Sport Psychologist, 9,* 254–264.

Greene, D., Sternberg, B., & Lepper, M. R. (1976). Overjustification in a token economy. *Journal of Personality and Social Psychology, 34,* 1219–1234.

Guan, J., Xiang, P., & McBride, R. (2006). Achievement goals, social goals, and students' reported persistence and effort in high school physical education. *Journal of Teaching in Physical Education, 23,* 58–74.

Hackensmith, C. W. (1966). *History of physical education.* New York: Harper & Row.

Hagger, M. S., Chatzisarantis, N. L. D., Barkoukis, V., Wang, C. K. J., & Baranowski, J. (2005). Perceived autonomy support in physical education and leisure-time physical activity: A cross-cultural evaluation of the trans-contextual model. *Journal of Educational Psychology, 97,* 376–390.

Harrison, J. M., Fellingham, G. W., & Buck, M. M. (1995). Self-efficacy, attribution, and volleyball achievement. *International Journal of Physical Education, 32*(4), 4–10.

Harrison, J. M., Preece, L. A., Blakemore, C. L., Rechards, R. P., Wilkinson, C., & Fellingham, G. W. (1999). Effects of two instructional models – skill teaching and mastery learning – on skill development, knowledge, self-efficacy, and game play in volleyball. *Journal of Teaching in Physical Education, 19,* 34–57.

Hastie, P. A., & Pickwell, A. (1996). Take your partners: A description of a student social system in a secondary school dance class. *Journal of Teaching in Physical Education, 15,* 171–187.

Hatch, G. M., & Smith, D. R. (2004). Integrating physical education, math, and physics. *Journal of Physical Education, Recreation and Dance, 75*(1), 42–51.

Hidi, S. (2000). An interest researcher's perspective: The effects of extrinsic and extrinsic factors on motivation. In C.

Sansone & J. M. Harackiewicz (Eds.), *Intrinsic and extrinsic motivation: The search for optimal motivation and performance* (pp. 309–339). San Diego, CA: Academic Press.

Hidi, S., & Anderson, V. (1992). Situational interest and its impact on reading and expository writing. In K. A. Renninger, S. Hidi, & A. Krapp (Eds.), *The role of interest in learning and development* (pp. 215–238). Hillsdale, NJ: Erlbaum.

Hidi, S., & Harackiewicz, J. M. (2000). Motivating the academically unmotivated: A critical issue for the 21st century. *Review of Educational Research, 70,* 151–179.

Jacobs, J. E., Lanza, S., Osgood, E. W., Eccles, J. S., & Wigfield, A. (2002). Changes in childrens' self-competence and values: Gender and domain differences across grades one through twelve. *Child Development, 73,* 509–527.

Marks, H. M. (2000). Student engagement in instructional activity: Patterns in the elementary, middle, and high school years. *American Educational Research Journal, 37,* 153–184.

Martin, A. J., Tipler, D. V., Marsh, H. W., Richards, G. E., & Williams, M. R. (2006). Assessing multidimensional physical activity motivation: A construct validity study of high school students. *Journal of Sport & Exercise Psychology, 28,* 171–192.

Martin, J. J., & Kulinna, P. H. (2005). A social cognitive perspective of physical activity related behavior in physical education. *Journal of Teaching in Physical Education, 24,* 265–281.

McAuley, E., Peña, M. M., & Jerom, G. J. (2001). Sefl-efficacy as a determinant and an outcome of exercise. In G. C. Roberts (Ed.). *Advances in motivation in sport and exercise* (pp. 235–262). Champaign, IL: Human Kinetics.

McKenzie, T. L. (1991). Observational measures of children's physical activity. *Journal of School Health, 61,* 224–227.

Metzler, M. (1989). A review of research on time in sport pedagogy. *Journal of Teaching in Physical Education, 8,* 87–103.

Mitchell, M. (1993). Situational interest: Its multifaceted structure in the secondary school mathematics classroom. *Journal of Educational Psychology, 85,* 424–436.

National Association for Sport and Physical Education [NASPE]. (2004). *Moving into the future: National standards for physical education. A guide to content and assessment.* St. Louis: MO: Mosby.

NASPE (2006). *Shape of the nation: Status of physical education in the U.S.A.* Reston, VA: Author.

National Center for Education Statistics [NCES]. (1996). *National Education Longitudinal Study: 1988–1994.* Washington, D. C.: Office of Educational Research and Improvement, U. S. Department of Education.

Nicholls, J. G., Cheung, P. C., Lauer, J., & Pastashnick, M. (1989). Individual differences in academic motivation: Perceived ability, goals, beliefs, and values. *Learning and Individual Differences, 1,* 63–84.

Ntoumanis, N. (2001). A self-determination approach to the understanding of motivation in physical education. *British Journal of Educational Psychology, 71,* 225–242.

Ntoumanis, N. (2005). Aprospective study of participation in optional school physical education using a self-determination theory framework. *Journal of Educational Psychology, 97,* 444–453.

Oldfather, P., & Dahl, K. (1994). Toward a social constructivist reconceptualization of intrinsic motivation for literacy learning. *Journal of Reading Behavior, 26,* 139–158.

Pintrich, P. R., & Schunk, D. H. (1996). *Motivation in education: Theory, research and applications.* Englewood Cliffs, NJ: Prentice-Hall.

Prochaska, J. O., & Velicer, W. F. (1997). The transtheoretical model of behavior change. *American Journal of Health Promotion, 12,* 38–48.

Rattigan, P. (2006). An interdisciplinary twist on traditional games. *Teaching Elementary Physical Education, 17,* 63–66.

Roberts, G. C. (Ed.) (2001). *Advances in motivation in sport and exercise.* Champaign, IL: Human Kinetics.

Samuels, S. M., & Gibb, R. W. (2002). Self-efficacy assessment and generalization in physical education courses. *Journal of Applied Social Psychology, 32,* 1314–1327.

Schneider, B., & Stevenson, D. (1999). *The ambitious generation: America's teenagers – motivated but directionless.* New Haven, CT: Yale University Press.

Shen, B., & Chen, A. (2006). Examining the interrelations among knowledge, interests, and learning strategies. *Journal of Teaching in Physical Education, 25,* 182–199.

Shen, B., Chen, A., Scrabis, K., & Tolley, H. (2003). Gender and interest-based motivation in learning dance. *Journal of Teaching in Physical Education, 22,* 396–409.

Shen, B., McCaughtry, N., Martin, J., & Dillion, S. (2006). Does "sneaky fox" facilitate learning? Examining the effects of seductive details in physical education. *Research Quarterly for Exercise and Sport, 77,* 498–506.

Siedentop, D., Doutis, P., Tsangaridou, N., Ward, P., & Rauschenbach, J. (1994). Don't sweat gym! An analysis of curriculum and instruction. *Journal of Teaching in Physical Education, 13,* 375–394.

Solmon, M. A. (1996). Impact of motivational climate on students' behaviors and perceptions in a physical education setting. *Journal of Educational Psychology, 88,* 731–738.

Solmon, M. A., & Boone, J. (1993). The impact of student goal orientation in physical education classes. *Research Quarterly for Exercise and Sport, 64,* 418–424.

Spray, C. M., Biddle, S. J. H., & Fox, K. R. (1999). Achievement goals, beliefs about the cause of success and reported emotion in post-16 physical education. *Journal of Sports Sciences, 17,* 213–219.

Standage, M., Duda, J. L., & Ntoumanis, N. (2003). Using constructs from self-determination and achievement goal theories to predict physical activity intentions. *Journal of Educational Psychology, 95,* 97–110.

Standage, M., Duda, J. L., & Ntoumanis, N. (2005). A test of self-determination theory in school physical education. *British Journal of Educational Psychology, 75,* 411–433.

Sun, H., Chen, A., Ennis, C. D., Shen, B., & Martin, R. (2008). An examination of the multidimentionality of situational interest in elementary school physical education. *Research Quarterly for Exercise and Sport, 79,* 62–70.

Todorovich, J. R., & Curtner-Smith, M. D. (2003). Influence of the motivational climate in physical education on third grade students' task and ego orientations. *Journal of Classroom Interaction, 38,* 36–46.

Treasure, D. C. (1997). Perceptions of the motivational climate and elementary school children's cognitive and affective response. *Journal of Sport & Exercise Psychology, 19,* 278–290.

Urdan, T. C. (1997). Achievement goal theory: Past results, future directions. In M. L. Maehr & P. R. Pintrich (Eds.), *Advances in motivation and achievement* (Vol. 10, pp. 99–141). Greenwich, CT: JAI.

Urdan, T., Midgley, C., & Wood, S. (1995). Special issues in reforming middle level schools. *Journal of Early Adolescence, 15,* 9–37.

Vallerand, R. J. (1997). Toward a hierachical model of intrinsic and extrinsic motivation. In M. P. Zanna (Ed.), *Advances in experimental social psychology* (Vol. 29, pp. 271–360). New York: Academic Press.

Vincent-Morin, M., & Lafont, L. (2005). Learning-method choices and personal characteristics in solving a physical education problem. *Journal of Teaching in Physical Education, 24,* 226–242.

Weir, T. (2000, May 2). The new PE. *USA Today,* p. C1.

Wang, C. K. J., Chatzisarantis, N. L. D., Spray, C. M., & Biddle, S. J. H. (2002). Achievement goal profiles in school physical education: Differences in self-determination, sport ability beliefs, and physical activity. *British Journal of Educational Psychology, 72,* 433–445.

Weston, A. (1962). *The making of American physical education.* New York: Appleton-Century-Crofts.

Wigfield, A. (1994). Expectancy-value theory of achievement motivation: A developmental perspective. *Educational Psychology Review, 6,* 49–78.

Wigfield, A., & Eccles, J. S. (1992). The development of achievement task values: A theoretical analysis. *Developmental Review, 12,* 265–310.

Wigfield, A., & Eccles, J. S. (2002). The development of competence beliefs, expectancies for success, and achievement values from childhood through adolescence. In A. Wigfield & J. S. Eccles (Eds.), *Development of achievement motivation* (pp. 1–10). San Diego, CA: Academic Press.

Williams, C. S., Harageones, E. G., Johnson, D. J., & Smith, C. D. (1993). *Personal fitness: Looking good, feeling good.* Dubuque, Iowa: Kendal-Hunt Publishing.

Wood, T. D. (1913). *The ninth yearbook of the national society for the study of education* (Part I). Chicago: University of Chicago Press.

Wood, T. D., & Cassidy, R. F. (1930). *The new physical education: A program of naturalized activities for education toward citizenship.* New York: Macmillan.

Xiang, P., & Lee, A. (1998). The development of self-perceptions of ability and achievement goals and their relations in physical education. *Research Quarterly for Exercise and Sport, 69,* 231–241.

Xiang, P., & Lee., A. (2002). Achievement goals, perceived motivational climate, and students' self-reported mastery behaviors. *Research Quarterly for Exercise and Sport, 73,* 58–65.

Xiang, P., McBride, R., & Bruene, A. (2003). Relations of parents' beliefs to children's motivation in an elementary physical education running program. *Journal of Teaching in Physical Education, 22,* 410–425.

Xiang, P., McBride, R., & Bruene, A. (2004). Fourth graders' motivation in an elementary physical education running program. *The Elementary School Journal, 104,* 253–266.

Xiang, P., McBride, R., & Bruene, A. (2006). Fourth graders' motivational changes in an elementary physical education running program. *Research Quarterly for Exercise and Sport, 77,* 195–207.

Xiang, P., McBride, R., Guan, J., & Solmon, M. (2003). Children's motivation in elementary physical education: An expectancy-value model of achievement choice. *Research Quarterly for Exercise and Sport, 74,* 25–35.

26
Emotions at School

Reinhard Pekrun

Emotions are ubiquitous in school settings. Learning and achievement are of fundamental importance for students' educational careers, implying that achievement-related emotions such as enjoyment of learning, hope, pride, anger, anxiety, or boredom are frequent, pervasive, manifold, and often intense in academic situations. The social nature of these situations also contributes to the emotional character of school settings; emotions such as admiration, contempt, or envy likely play a major role in these settings as well (Weiner, 2007). Furthermore, adding to their relevance, emotions are functionally important for students' motivation, cognitive performance, and personality development. Adaptive emotions like enjoyment of learning help to envision goals and challenges, open the mind to creative problem-solving, and lay the groundwork for self-regulation (Ashby, Isen, & Turken, 1999; Pekrun, Goetz, Titz, & Perry, 2002a). Maladaptive emotions like excessive anxiety, hopelessness, or boredom, on the other hand, are detrimental to academic attainment, induce students to drop out of school, and impact negatively on their psychological and physical health (Zeidner, 1998).

In spite of their clear relevance, however, emotions have been neglected by educational research, including research on motivation at school (Pekrun, Goetz, Titz, & Perry, 2002b; Schutz & Pekrun, 2007). On a theoretical level, the achievement emotions pride and shame were regarded as central to the instigation of achievement behavior in traditional achievement motivation theories (Heckhausen, 1991). Empirically, however, emotions were not studied as phenomena in their own right by classical achievement motivation research. Rather, they were regarded as being subcomponents of global, summary constructs of achievement motives, with the exception of test anxiety that was often equated with the fear of failure motive. Also, the recent boom of emotion research in basic disciplines of psychology and in the neurosciences was just ignored by the mainstream of educational research.

There are two notable exceptions to this inattention to achievement-related emotions. One is research on students' test anxiety that originated in the 1930s (e.g., Brown, 1938), started to flourish in the 1950s, and has continued to be a highly active field of research since then (Zeidner, 1998, 2007). Whereas achievement emotions other than anxiety attracted few researchers, test anxiety has been analyzed in more than 1,000 empirical studies to date. The second exception is research on the attributional antecedents of emotions following success and failure, largely originating in Bernard Weiner's attributional theory of achievement motivation and emotion (Weiner, 1985, 2007; see Graham & Williams, this volume).

As a consequence of neglecting emotional processes, we still lack empirical knowledge on students' emotions. Over the past 10 years, there has been a discernable increase in the number of studies dealing with students' emotions, as evidenced in three recent special issues and one edited volume on this topic (Efklides & Volet, 2005; Linnenbrink, 2006; Schutz & Pekrun, 2007; Schutz & Lanehart, 2002). These studies have produced initial findings on a number of emotions. To date, however, this evidence is still too scant to warrant firm conclusions, research on test anxiety being the predominant exception.

In the following sections, I will first discuss basic conceptual issues concerning emotion, including the relations between emotion, motivation, and cognition. Second, the diversity of emotions in school settings and their assessment will be addressed. In the third and fourth sections, I will discuss origins and development of students' emotions, as well as their functional relevance for motivation, learning, and achievement. Next, I will outline basic assumptions and corollaries of the control-value theory of achievement emotions (Pekrun, 2000, 2006) which makes an attempt to reconcile diverging approaches on students' emotions. In concluding, I will discuss implications for educational practice and directions for future research.

Constructs of Emotion

Conceptual Paradigms and Definition of Emotion

Emotions function as reactions to significant events and objects. They serve the preparation and adaptive organization of subsequent processes of perception, cognition, and action. Different approaches to emotion have emphasized different components of this process and have offered different definitions of the concept emotion (Kleinginna & Kleinginna, 1981). In the tradition of 19th century evolutionary biology, early theories focusing on *emotion expression* addressed the importance of emotion for adaptation to the environment by decoupling fixed associations between stimulus and reaction, and by communicating with others. Assumptions on the importance of facial feedback for emotions, and emotion definitions based on facial expression, were central to these approaches (Keltner & Ekman, 2000). In contrast, *psychoanalytical approaches*, which became prominent during the first decades of the 20th century, focused on emotions such as anxiety as resulting from intrapsychic, unconscious conflicts, and on their maladaptive consequences in terms of psychopathological problems.

Since the 1960s, *cognitive approaches* to emotion emphasized the qualitative differences between emotions that are implied by cognitive appraisals of the self and the environment. In these approaches, appraisals are regarded as main determinants and components of emotion (Scherer, Schorr, & Johnstone, 2001). Prominent examples are the transactional model proposed by Lazarus (Lazarus & Folkman, 1984) and Weiner's (1985) attributional theory. Both of these theories have also been used to explain students' emotions at school (see below). Finally, throughout the 20th century, a number of theorists attempted to define and explain emotion by patterns of *physiological activation*. Before the advent of brain imaging techniques, research in this tradition had to rely on measures of peripheral activation that are of limited value for assessing emotions. Today, a number of techniques are available that allow to analyze emotion-related patterns of brain activation (such as EEG and fMRI). By providing insights into the brain mechanisms constituting emotion, these techniques lay the foundations for current advances in neuroscientific research on emotion ("neuroaffective science"; Davidson & Sutton, 1995).

These different approaches focus on different facets of emotion, and some theorists define emotion by referring to specific facets only. For example, some emotion scientists define emotion as physiological and behavioral reactions, but do not regard feelings and cognitive appraisals as being part of emotion (see Davidson, Scherer, & Goldsmith, 2003). However, most researchers likely would agree today that emotions also comprise subjective representations. From this more comprehensive view, emotions consist of multiple coordinated processes, important components being the following (e.g., Scherer, 2000): (a) *affective components* referring to the activation or disinhibition of cortical and subcortical systems (like the amygdala) that is subjectively represented as emotional feelings (e.g., uneasy, nervous feelings in anxiety); (b) *cognitive components* involving emotion-specific thoughts (such as worry cognitions in anxiety); (c) *physiological components* serving the preparation of action (e.g., peripheral physiological activation in anxiety); (d) *motivational components* comprising behavioral impulses and wishes (e.g., avoidance motivation in anxiety); and (e) *expressive components* including facial, postural, and vocal expression of emotion.

In spite of consensus on important components of emotion, a largely unresolved issue is how the conceptual boundaries of the construct emotion should be defined. While it seems clear that prototypical cases like the "primary" emotions joy, anger, anxiety, etc. are members of the family of emotion constructs, this is less clear for other concepts relating to students' feelings and affect, such as mood, interest, curiosity, or metacognitive feelings. For example, whereas some researchers regard interest being an emotion (see Ainley, 2007), others define interest as a more complex construct involving enjoyment, values, and knowledge (Schiefele, this volume).

Relation of Emotion to Motivation and Cognition

There seems to be agreement that emotion, motivation, and cognition are neighboring constructs that are overlapping and closely linked in many cases (Pekrun, 2006). This may be especially true for emotion and motivation that are so closely related that one may be tempted to regard them as being inseparable. More specifically, emotion and motivation can be linked in three different ways. First, as noted above, emotion-specific motivational impulses are regarded as an integral part of emotions by most emotion theorists. This may be especially true for negative emotions which are strongly coupled with evolutionary-based, specific behavioral tendencies (such as flight and fight in anxiety and anger, respectively). Second, motivational processes can precede, trigger, and modulate emotions. Two examples detailed below are students' achievement goals and their perceived values of achievement. Third, emotions do not only include motivational components themselves, but can also influence subsequent motivational processes. For example, enjoyment of learning can positively influence students' motivation to engage with learning material in creative, exploratory ways.

Motivation and emotion, on the one hand, and cognition, on the other, are closely related as well. For example, the anxious wish of a student to escape from an exam situation can be regarded as cognition (since wishes are cognitive representations of desired states), but at the same time, it is an emotion (anxiety) and a motivation (escape motivation). By implication, while it is possible to separate these three constructs at an analytical level, it often is difficult to separate them empirically.

Classification of Emotions

Two different approaches are used to classify emotions. In the *discrete emotions approach*, different positive and negative emotions such as joy, pride, anger, anxiety, or shame are regarded as distinct phenomena. As such, each of these emotions is supposed to involve a unique pattern of emotion components and to serve specific cognitive, behavioral, and social functions. In contrast, in the *dimensional approach*, it is assumed that using a small number of affective dimensions is sufficient to describe human affect. Valence and activation have been proposed as the two most important dimensions (e.g., Feldman Barrett-Russell, 1998). However, the two approaches are not mutually exclusive. Rather, they can be integrated by regarding discrete emotions as lower-level factors, and affective dimensions as higher-order factors describing their common properties.

The two dimensions valence (positive/negative) and activation (activating/deactivating) can also been used to classify students' achievement emotions (Pekrun, 2006; see Table 26.1). The two dimensions render four broad categories of emotions: (a) *Activating positive* emotions (e.g., joy, hope, pride); (b) *deactivating positive* emotions (e.g., relief, relaxation); (c) *activating negative* emotions (e.g., anger, anxiety, shame); and (d) *deactivating negative* emotions (e.g., hopelessness, boredom). In addition, achievement emotions are characterized by a specific object focus, relating either to *achievement activities*, or to the *success and failure outcomes* of these activities (see Table 26.1). Traditionally, research on achievement emotions has focused on outcome-related achievement emotions like anxiety, pride, and shame (Weiner, 1985; Zeidner 1998). Activity-related achievement emotions such as enjoyment of learning or boredom experienced during classroom instruction, however, are likely no less important for students' motivation and academic agency.

Variety and Assessment of Emotions in School Settings

Exploratory Research on Emotional Variety

As noted, academic situations can be assumed to frequently induce emotions. Empirically, however, there is a lack of evidence on the occurrence, frequency, and intensity of different emotions as experienced by students in academic settings. Test anxiety is a unique exception, as this emotion has consistently been found to be experienced by many students before and during test taking (Zeidner, 1998). In our own research, we conducted exploratory studies to analyze the different emotions occuring in K-12 and university students. Using semistructured interviews and questionnaires, these studies explored emotional experiences in academic situations of attending class, studying, and taking test and exams (Pekrun, 1992a; Pekrun, Goetz, Titz, & Perry, 2002b;

Table 26.1 A Three-Dimensional Taxonomy of Achievement Emotions

Object Focus	Positive [a]		Negative [b]	
	Activating	Deactivating	Activating	Deactivating
Activity Focus	Enjoyment	Relaxation	Anger Frustration	Boredom
Outcome Focus	Joy Hope Pride Gratitude	Contentment Relief	Anger Anxiety Shame	Sadness Disappointment Hopelessness

[a] Positive = pleasant emotion.
[b] Negative = unpleasant emotion.

Spangler, Pekrun, Kramer, & Hofmann, 2002; Titz, 2001). In each of the interviews and questionnaires, students were asked a series of fixed questions and could give open-ended answers, thus providing qualitative narratives of emotional episodes.

As expected, the results showed that students experience a wide variety of emotions in academic settings. There was no major human emotion that was not reported in the students' narratives, disgust being an exception. Anxiety proved to be the emotion that was reported most frequently, accounting for 15–27% of all emotional episodes reported in these studies. Anxiety was mentioned with regard to all three types of academic situations (attending class, studying, and taking tests). This prevalence of anxiety corroborates the importance of test anxiety research. Also, the anxiety problems reported by many students imply that they are faced with a "workplace" at school that can pose a serious threat to their psychological health. Achievement pressure and expectancies of failure were reported as major determinants of anxiety, indicating that a reduction of excessive demands and an increase in opportunities for success might benefit students' psychological health.

However, our findings on relative frequencies also imply that the vast majority of emotions reported pertained to emotion categories other than anxiety. Overall, positive emotions were mentioned no less frequently than negative emotions. Enjoyment, satisfaction, hope, pride, and relief were reported as being experienced often in academic settings, as were anger, shame, and boredom. Furthermore, there were many accounts of less frequently experienced emotions, including hopelessness as well as social emotions like gratitude, admiration, contempt, and envy. The relative frequencies of emotions differed across the three types of academic situations specified. In the classroom setting and during studying, positive emotions typically accounted for slightly more than 50% of the emotions reported, whereas negative emotions outweighed positive emotions when taking tests and exams. Typically, attending class and studying involves less pressure for achievement and more autonomy for self-regulation than writing an exam, which may explain these differential frequencies.

Assessment of Student Emotions by Self-Report Scales

The findings of our exploratory research confirm assumptions on the diversity of emotions experienced in academic settings. By implication, any more comprehensive assessment of students' emotions should attend to diversity by providing multidimensional measures of emotion. To date, however, most instruments available focus on measuring students' test anxiety, since test anxiety has been the one emotion that has attracted educational researchers' interest universally. Over the past seven decades, considerable progress has been made in the development of measures of test anxiety, making it amenable to scientific investigation (Brown, 1938; Pekrun, Goetz, Perry, Kramer, & Hochstadt, 2004; Zeidner, 1998). Self-report instruments asking students to report about their anxiety experienced prior to or during exams are the method used most frequently (Zeidner, 1998). Self-report scales can be employed to assess students' momentary emotional reactions to tests and exams (*state* test anxiety), as well as their habitual tendency to react, typically, by experiencing anxiety when being confronted with tests or exams (*trait* test anxiety).

In the early stages of test anxiety research, measurement instruments conceived the construct as being one-dimensional (e.g., the Test Anxiety Questionnaire, TAQ; Mandler & Sarason, 1952). Following the proposal put forward by Liebert and Morris (1967) to distinguish affective and physiological components (*emotionality*) from cognitive components (*worry*) of test anxiety, more recent measures take the multicomponent nature of this emotion into account (e.g., the Test Anxiety Inventory, TAI; Spielberger, 1980). Today, most of the available test anxiety scales possess good psychometric properties. Coefficients of internal reliability typically are above Alpha = .85. Structural validity is ensured by use of confirmatory factor analysis, and external construct validity by correlations with measures of academic learning and performance (Zeidner, 1998). The sophistication achieved in the measurement of test anxiety was instrumental for the success of test anxiety research in analyzing functions, development, and remediation of this emotion.

Measures for students' emotions other than test anxiety are still largely lacking. Based on the findings of our exploratory research cited above, we therefore constructed a multidimensional instrument measuring a variety of major achievement emotions experienced by students, including test anxiety, but assessing other achievement emotions as well (Achievement Emotions Questionnaire, AEQ; Pekrun et al., 2002b; Pekrun, Goetz, & Perry, 2005). The original version of the AEQ measures emotions as experienced by university students. We also constructed domain-specific variants of the AEQ assessing elementary, middle, and high school students' emotions relating to specific school subjects (such as mathematics; Pekrun, Goetz, & Frenzel, 2005).

The AEQ measures a number of discrete emotions for each of the three main categories of academic achievement situations; that is, attending class, studying, and writing tests and exams. These situations differ in terms of functions and social structures, implying that emotions regarding these situations can differ as well. For example, enjoyment of classroom instruction may be different from enjoying the challenge of an exam—some students may be excited when going to class, others when taking exams. Therefore, the AEQ provides separate scales for learning-related, class-related, and test-related emotions. In its current version, the AEQ can be used to assess eight different achievement emotions within each of these categories (see Table 26.2). These emotions were selected because they are experienced frequently by students (see above). In addition, hopelessness was included because of its theoretical relevance (Pekrun et al., 2002b). Using the consensual multicomponent definition of "emotion" cited above, the items of each of the scales pertain to affective, cognitive, motivational, physiological, and expressive components of the emotion to be measured.

Reliability coefficients confirm the psychometric quality of the AEQ scales (Alpha = .84 to .94). The structural validity of the AEQ scales has been tested by confirmatory factor analysis

Table 26.2 Achievement Emotions Questionnaire (AEQ): Scales and Reliabilities

| Emotions | Scales | | | | | |
| | Learning-Related Emotions | | Class-Related Emotions | | Test Emotions | |
	α	Items	α	Items	α	Items
Enjoyment	.90	14	.89	15	.90	23
Hope	.86	9	.84	9	.89	16
Pride	.84	9	.86	9	.92	16
Relief	—	[a]—	—	—	.89	14
Anger	.89	14	.85	11	.89	17
Anxiety	.92	18	.89	13	.94	31
Hopelessness	.93	13	.88	10	.94	21
Shame	.90	14	.91	15	.93	19
Boredom	.93	17	.93	14	—[b]	—

[a] Relief scale for test emotions only.
[b] Boredom scale for learning-related and class-related emotions only.

(e.g., Pekrun et al., 2004). As to external validity, the AEQ has been shown to be predictive for students' academic achievement, course enrollment, and dropout rates (e.g., Pekrun et al., 2002b). Also, achievement emotions as assessed by the AEQ relate to components of students' learning processes such as achievement goals (Pekrun, Elliot, & Maier, 2006), study interest, intrinsic and extrinsic motivation to learn, effort, strategies of learning, and the self-regulation of learning (e.g., Pekrun et al., 2002a, b; Pekrun et al., 2004; Perry, Hladkyj, Pekrun, Clifton, & Chipperfield, 2005). Gender (Frenzel, Pekrun, & Goetz, 2007a), teachers' instructional behavior (Frenzel, Goetz, Lüdtke, Pekrun, & Sutton, 2008; Pekrun et al., 2007), the composition and social climate of classrooms (Frenzel, Pekrun, & Goetz, 2007b), and the cultural context (Frenzel, Thrash, Pekrun, & Goetz, 2007) have been shown to be further important correlates of the achievement emotions assessed by the AEQ.

Alternative Types of Assessment

Self-report methods for assessing emotions are easy to administer, and there is clear evidence for their validity. However, they also share a number of limitations. Specifically, self-report may be subject to biases (e.g., responding according to social desirability), cannot cover subconscious processes, and is not well suited to analyze rapid emotional processes with sufficient temporal resolution. Fortunately, given the diversity of emotion components that can be used to assess emotions, there are alternative methods that could be employed for measuring students' emotions. These methods include neuroimaging techniques (fMRI, EEG), analysis of peripheral physiological processes, and observation of nonverbal behavior such as facial, gestural and postural expression, and prosodic features of verbal speech.

To date, all of these alternative methods are still underused in educational research. For example, while video-based research on classroom interaction flourishes, this research has yet to attempt to analyze the emotional processes that characterize interactions between instructors and students. This could be done by adapting methods developed in emotion research for use in classroom observation (e.g., the Facial Action Coding System, FACS; Ekman & Rosenberg, 1997). Similarly, neuroimaging methods could be employed to analyze brain indicators of students' emotional reactions when confronted with academic tasks, and an assessment of peripheral physiological processes could be used to analyze students' emotional activation in academic settings (recording of heart rate, skin resistance, cortisol levels, etc.; see e.g., Spangler et al., 2002).

Origins and Development of Students' Emotions

Since test anxiety has been the one student emotion that attracted researchers' interest, a number of theoretical accounts explaining its antecedents have been put forward, including early (neo-) behavioristic accounts as well as cognitive theories (Zeidner, 1998). There also have been attempts, however, to explain achievement emotions other than anxiety. Most notably, Weiner's (1985) attributional theory addresses the appraisal antecedents of various outcome-related achievement emotions. In addition, recent research on students' achievement goals also addressed the importance of students' goals for their affective experiences. Beyond these three specific research agendas, studies are rare, with few exceptions pertaining to the antecedents of activity-related emotions like enjoyment of learning and boredom (Pekrun et al., 2002b; Watt & Vodanovich, 1999).

Contemporary test anxiety theories, attributional theories, and goal research share the assumption that cognitive processes are central to the instigation of emotion. It should be noted, however, that affective preferences and dislikes do not always need elaborate cognitive inferences, as noted early by Zajonc (1980). Additional factors include genetic dispositions, neurohormonal processes, evolutionary-based features of stimuli (e.g., color; Elliot, Maier, Moller, Friedman, & Meinhardt, 2007), as well as schema-based elicitation of emotion resulting from habitualization of appraisal-driven emotions (Reisenzein, 2001). Studies on the importance of such factors for students' emotions are still largely lacking. Most research on these emotions is based on the reasonable assumption that cognitive mediation is most important for achievement emotions, since these emotions depend on perceptions and cognitive evaluations that are shaped by socialization and cultural processes.

In the following sections, anxiety-related appraisals, causal attributions, and achievement goals will be discussed in turn. Next, the role of classroom instruction and social environments will be addressed, and evidence on the development of students' emotions across the school years will be summarized.

Threat Appraisals, Expectancies, and Values as Antecedents of Test Anxiety

Test anxiety is a prospective emotion relating to threat of failure in an upcoming or ongoing exam. Therefore, threat-related appraisals have been regarded as main proximal determinants of test anxiety by many authors. Specifically, the *transactional stress model* provided by Lazarus has often been used to explain test anxiety (Lazarus & Folkman, 1984). In this model, *stress* is defined as any situation involving demands that tax or exceed the individual's resources. In a *primary appraisal* of the situation, an evaluation in terms of potential threat, challenge, harm, or benefit implied by the situation is made. This appraisal pertains to the evaluation of the situation or its outcomes as being subjectively relevant to the individuals' needs and goals. In a *secondary appraisal*, possibilities to cope with the situation are explored cognitively. Depending on the combined result of the two appraisals, different emotions can be aroused. In the case of threat and insufficient control over the threatening event, anxiety is assumed to be instigated.

Lazarus' analysis implies that achievement-related anxiety is aroused when two conditions are met. First, there has to be an anticipation of failure that can happen and is sufficiently important to the individual to imply subjective threat. Second, the individual has to doubt whether it will be possible to control the situation such that failure is avoided. In an *expectancy-value model* of test anxiety, and of anxiety more generally, I have made an attempt to reconceptualize these two assumptions in formalized ways (Pekrun, 1984, 1992b). In this model, it is assumed that test anxiety is a function of (a) the expectancy of failure (specifically, its subjective probability), and (b) the subjective value of failure. Both components are assumed to be necessary for test anxiety to be instigated (if one is sure that failure can't happen, there is no need to be afraid of an exam; the same applies if one doesn't care). Anxiety is assumed to be a curvilinear function of expectancy, being replaced by hopelessness if failure is subjectively certain. The subjective value of failure is seen to be a function of both the intrinsic importance of achievement per se, and of its extrinsic, instrumental relevance in terms of producing further outcomes. For example, failing an exam may be threatening for a student because failure is inherently negative for him or her, because positive outcomes like the students' career prospects are compromised, or because negative consequences like contempt by peers can result.

Situational appraisals can relate to objective characteristics of the setting (e.g., the relative difficulty of exam material), but they are also influenced by individual beliefs. These beliefs can take "irrational" forms (Ellis, 1962) implying that failures are appraised as being likely in spite of high individual ability, or as undermining self-worth and peer recognition even if pertaining to unimportant fields of achievement. Irrational beliefs can make students highly vulnerable to experiencing anxiety and related negative achievement emotions, like shame and hopelessness ("I am not allowed to fail—if I fail, I am a worthless person").

The available empirical evidence is in line with these assumptions. Test anxiety has been found to correlate positively with students' expectancies of failure, and negatively with their self-concepts of ability, self-efficacy expectations, and control beliefs (Hembree, 1988; Pekrun et al., 2004; Zeidner, 1998). Also, in research on linkages between achievement goals and test anxiety, it has consistently been found that students' performance avoidance goals (implying high subjective relevance of failure) relate positively to their test anxiety scores (Linnenbrink & Pintrich, 2002; Pekrun, Elliot, & Maier, 2006).

Causal Attributions as Antecedents of Achievement Emotions

Extending the perspective beyond the single emotion anxiety, Weiner proposed an attributional approach to the appraisal antecedents of emotions following success and failure (Weiner, 1985, 2007). In Weiner's theory, causal attributions of success and failure are held to be the primary determinants of many of these emotions. More specifically, it is assumed that achievement outcomes are first evaluated subjectively as success or failure. This outcome appraisal immediately leads to "primitive," cognitively less elaborated, attribution-independent emotions, including happiness after success, and frustration and sadness after failure. Following outcome appraisal and the immediate emotional reaction, causal ascriptions are sought that lead to cognitively more differentiated, attribution-dependent emotions.

Three dimensions of causal attributions are assumed to play a key role in determining attribution-dependent emotions: (a) the perceived *locus* of causes (differentiating internal vs. external causes of achievement, such as ability and effort vs. environmental circumstances or chance); (b) the perceived *controllability* of causes (differentiating, for example, subjectively controllable effort from uncontrollable ability); and (c) the perceived *stability* of causes (differentiating, for example, stable ability from unstable chance). *Pride* is assumed to be linked to the locus dimension, being aroused by attributions of achievement to internal causes. *Shame, guilt, gratitude,* and *anger* are deemed to depend on both the locus and the controllability of causes. Weiner posits that shame and guilt are instigated by failure that is attributed to internal, controllable causes such as lack of effort, and gratitude and anger by attributions of success or failure to external causes that are under control by others.

Weiner's attributional theory focuses primarily on retrospective emotions following success and failure that occur to the student, in line with the retrospective nature of causal attributions seeking to explain the causes of experienced events. However, some predictions for prospective, future-related emotions are made as well. Specifically, hopefulness and hopelessness are expected to be linked to attributions of success and failure, respectively, to stable causes (like stable ability, or lack of ability). Furthermore, Weiner (2007) recently extended his theory by also speculating about the causal attributional antecedents of "moral" emotions such as envy, scorn, sympathy, admiration, regret, and *schadenfreude*.

Much of the evidence on the validity of these assumptions was gained by scenario studies asking students how they, or others, might react to success and failure. In such studies, participants' subjective theories about links between achievement outcomes, attributions, and emotions following achievement are tested. Findings support the congruence between attributional theory and students' subjective theories. However, there also are experimental and field studies corroborating the validity of many of Weiner's assumptions (Heckhausen, 1991).

Other approaches to the affective relevance of causal attributions have also found evidence that attributions can play a role in students' emotional reactions. Specifically, studies on the *reformulated helplessness and hopelessness theories* of depression have demonstrated that students' emotions can be explained, in part, by their attributional styles. In this research tradition, the perceived *globality* of causes, that is, their degree of generalization across situations, is held to be an additional important dimension of causal attributions (e.g., Metalsky, Halberstadt, & Abramson, 1987).

Goals as Antecedents of Achievement Emotions

A few studies have analyzed relations between students' achievement goals and their positive vs. negative affect (see Linnenbrink & Pintrich, 2002; Pekrun et al., 2006). Most of these studies used the dichotomous model of achievement goals differentiating between mastery goals and performance goals (see Maehr & Zusho, this volume). The findings of studies using dichotomous conceptions of goals, as well as dichotomous conceptions of positive vs. negative affect, are inconsistent, with the exception of a positive relation between mastery goals and positive affect.

As argued by Pekrun et al. (2006), this lack of consistency may have been due to insufficient differentiation between different types of goals and between different emotions (see also Maehr & Zusho, this volume). Specifically, regarding goals, approach goals and avoidance goals may have quite different effects on students' emotions. In the studies reported by Pekrun et al. (2006), college students' achievement goals were assessed early in the semester, and their course-related achievement emotions later in the semester. Mastery approach goals were positive predictors of course-related enjoyment of learning, hope, and pride, and negative predictors of boredom and anger. Performance-approach goals were positive predictors of pride, whereas performance-avoidance goals were positive predictors of anxiety, hopelessness, and shame. These findings corroborate that value-related cognitions such as achievement goals can be important for students' emotions.

The Role of Classroom Composition, Classroom Instruction, and Social Environments

To date, educational research has focused on the individual antecedents of students' emotions, whereas the role of classrooms and social environments remains largely unexplored. Again, research on students' test anxiety is a major exception. Classroom composition, the design of instruction and exams, as well as achievement-related expectancies and reactions in students' social environments have been found to play a significant role in the development of students' emotion (summaries for anxiety in Zeidner, 1998, 2007; also see the section on implications for educational practice).

Classroom Composition The ability level of the classroom determines the likelihood of performing well relative to one's classmates. Other things being equal, chances for performing well in the classroom are higher in low-ability classrooms, as compared to high-ability classrooms. Therefore, other things being equal, students' self-concepts of ability tend to be higher in low-ability classrooms, as compared to high-ability classrooms. By implication, it may be preferable to be a "big fish in a little pond" rather than being member of a classroom of gifted students (Marsh, 1987). Since negative self-evaluations of competence can trigger anxiety of failure, the "big-fish-little-pond" effect of classroom ability level on self-concept can entail similar effects on students' anxiety. Other things being equal, anxiety has, in fact, been found to be higher in high-ability classrooms than in low-ability classrooms (e.g., Pekrun, Frenzel, Goetz, & Perry, 2006; Preckel, Zeidner, Goetz, & Schleyer, 2008).

Classroom Instruction and Design of Exams Lack of structure and clarity in classroom instruction as well as excessive task demands relate positively to students' test anxiety (Zeidner, 1998, 2007). The effects of these factors are likely mediated by students' expectancies of failure (Pekrun, 1992b). With exams as well, lack of structure and transparency has been shown to contribute to students' anxiety (e.g., lack of information on demands, materials, and grading practices). Furthermore, the format of items has been found to be relevant, with open-ended formats inducing more anxiety than multiple-choice formats. Open-ended formats require more working memory capacity which may be less available in states of anxiety due to the consumption of cognitive resources by worrying and task-irrelevant thinking, thus inducing more threat and debilitating performance in anxious students. The use of multiple-choice formats can reduce these effects. In addition, giving students the choice between items, relaxing time constraints, and giving them second chances in terms of retaking tests has been found to reduce test anxiety, presumably so because perceived control and achievement expectancies are enhanced under these conditions.

Beyond anxiety, a few studies have investigated relationships between classroom instruction and students' positive emotions. Teacher-centered instruction emphasizing rigid drill and exercise related negatively to students' general positive emotional attitudes toward school and enjoyment of task accomplishment in studies by Stipek, Feiler, Daniels, and Milburn (1995), and Valeski and Stipek (2001). In contrast, the cognitive quality of instruction and tasks oriented towards creative mental modeling rather than algorithmic routine procedures correlated positively with students' enjoyment of learning mathematics in a recent longitudinal study (Pekrun et al., 2007). In addition, support for students' autonomy at learning also correlated positively with students' enjoyment in this study. Finally, teachers' own enjoyment and enthusiasm during teaching has been found to relate positively to students' enjoyment, suggesting transmission of positive emotions from teachers to students (Frenzel, Goetz, Ludtke, Pekrun, & Sutton, 2008; Stipek et al., in press).

Social Environments at School and in the Family High achievement expectancies from significant others, negative feedback after achievement, and negative consequences of failure were found to correlate positively with students' test anxiety. Also, competition in classrooms is positively related to students' test anxiety, probably because competition reduces expectancies for success and increases the importance of avoiding failure. In contrast, a cooperative classroom climate and social support by parents and teachers often fail to correlate with students' test anxiety scores (Hembree, 1988). This surprising lack of correlation may be due to coercive components of teachers' and parents' efforts to support students which can counteract beneficial effects of support per se. A second explanation would be negative feedback loops between support and anxiety implying that social support alleviates anxiety (negative effect of support on anxiety; also see Sarason, 1981), but that anxiety provokes support in the first place (positive effect of anxiety on demanding support; e.g., Stoeber, 2004), thus yielding an overall zero correlation.

Development of Emotions Across the School Years

At the age of 2 to 3 years, children are able to express pride and shame when successfully solving tasks or failing to do so, suggesting that they are able to differentiate internal vs. external causation of success and failure. During the early elementary school years, they additionally acquire capabilities to distinguish between different types of internal and external causes, such as ability and effort, to develop related causal expectancies, and to cognitively combine expectancies, attributions, and value-related information (Heckhausen, 1991). By implication, it can be assumed that students have developed the cognitive competencies to experience all major types of achievement emotions early in their academic career.

Empirical evidence on the development of these emotions at school is scarce, with the exception of test anxiety studies. These studies have shown that average scores for test anxiety are low at the beginning of elementary school, but increase substantially during the elementary school years (Hembree, 1988). This development is congruent to the decline of academic self-concepts of ability during this period, and is likely due to increasing realism in academic self-perceptions, and to the cumulative failure feedback many students receive across the years in many schools today. After elementary school, average anxiety scores stabilize and remain at high levels throughout middle school, high school, and college. However, stability at the group level notwithstanding, anxiety can change in individual students. One important source for individual dynamics is the change of reference groups implied by transitions between schools and classrooms (Zeidner, 1998). As noted above, other things being equal, the likelihood of low achievement relative to peers is higher in high-ability classrooms, and lower in low-ability classrooms. Therefore, changing from a low-ability to a high-ability classroom can increase anxiety, while the reverse can happen when entering a low-ability classroom.

While anxiety increases in the average student, positive emotions such as enjoyment of learning seem to decrease across the elementary school years (Helmke, 1993). The decrease of enjoyment can continue through the middle school years (Pekrun et al., 2007), which is consistent with the decline of average scores for subject-matter interest and general attitudes toward school (e.g., Fredricks & Eccles, 2002; Watt, 2004). Important factors responsible for this development may be an increase of teacher-centered instruction and academic demands in middle school, the competition between academic and nonacademic interests in adolescence, and the stronger selectivity of subject-matter interest that is part of adolescent identity formation. However, to date these assumptions are speculative since empirical studies testing their validity for emotions are largely lacking.

Conclusions

In sum, theories on achievement emotions and related empirical evidence imply that failure expectancies and perceived lack of competence are primary individual determinants of students' test anxiety. Furthermore, research has shown that causal attributions of achievement are important antecedents of emotions following success and failure, and that students' achievement goals can also influence their emotions. Research on the social origins of these emotions suggests that classroom composition, classroom instruction, and achievement-related expectancies and reactions by significant others are important antecedents of students' test anxiety. Finally, there is evidence showing that average test anxiety scores increase during the elementary school years and tend to remain at relatively high levels thereafter. Beyond these specific bodies of research, the evidence on determinants and development of students' emotions is too scarce to allow generalizable conclusions. Perhaps most importantly, more research on the origins of students' activity-related emotions such as enjoyment or boredom experienced during learning is clearly needed.

Functions of Emotions for Motivation, Learning, and Achievement

Are students' emotions functionally important by influencing their academic motivation, learning, and achievement? Two lines of research provide evidence bearing on this question. First, in experimental research, mood and emotions have been found to influence a wide range of cognitive processes, including attention, memory storage and retrieval, social judgment, decision making, problem solving, and creative thinking (Lewis & Haviland-Jones, 2000). Typically, studies in this tradition used laboratory settings and did not care about the ecological validity of findings for real-life classroom situations. In contrast, educational research on emotions directly analyzed the effects of emotions on students' academic agency. Most of this research focused on test anxiety, but a few studies analyzed emotions other than test anxiety as well.

Findings from Mood Research

Three important findings from experimental mood research are the following. First, it has been shown that emotional states consume *cognitive resources* by focusing attention on the object of emotion (Ellis & Ashbrook, 1988). Consumption of cognitive resources for task-irrelevant purposes implies that less resources are available for task completion, thereby reducing performance (Meinhardt & Pekrun, 2003). Second, mood can enhance *mood-congruent memory recall* (e.g., Levine & Burgess, 1997). Positive mood can facilitate the retrieval of positive self- and task-related information, whereas negative mood sustains the retrieval of negative information (e.g., Olafson & Ferraro, 2001). Mood-congruent recall thus contributes to positive cycles of positive mood, enhanced motivation, and improved performance, and to vicious cycles of negative mood, reduced motivation, and failure.

Third, positive and negative mood have been shown to influence *cognitive problem solving*. Positive mood can be beneficial for flexible, creative, and holistic ways of solving problems, and for a reliance on generalized, heuristic knowledge structures. Negative mood can help more focused, detail-oriented, and analytical ways of thinking. A number of theoretical explanations have been proffered for these findings. For example, in mood-as-information approaches, it is assumed that positive affective states signal that "all is well," whereas negative states imply that something is going wrong (e.g., Bless et al., 1996). "All is well" conditions imply safety and the discretion to creatively explore the environment, broaden one's cognitive horizon, and build new actions, as addressed by Fredrickson's (2001) "broaden-and-build" metaphor of the effects of positive emotions. In contrast, if there are problems threatening well-being and agency, it may be wise to focus on these problems in analytical, cognitively cautious ways.

However, it is open to question as to whether the findings of experimental mood research are generalizable to real-life field settings and to the more intense emotions experienced in these settings. It may be that different mechanisms are operating under natural conditions, or that these mechanisms interact in different ways. For example, in experimental mood research, it has often been assumed that positive emotions are detrimental to motivation and cognitive performance (see Aspinwall, 1998). In contrast, laypersons' everyday experiences, as well as more recent empirical evidence, indicate that positive emotions, typically, exert positive effects on motivation and performance in academic settings (see below). Laboratory research may be useful for generating hypotheses, but that it cannot replace an ecologically valid analysis of students' real-life emotions.

Effects of Test Anxiety

The effects of test anxiety on academic learning and performance have been analyzed in several hundreds of studies (Hembree, 1988; Zeidner, 1998, 2007). These studies have shown that test anxiety impairs performance on complex or difficult tasks that demand cognitive resources (e.g., difficult intelligence test items). Performance on easy, less complex, and repetitive tasks need not suffer, or is even enhanced. Attempting to explain this finding, *interference* and *attentional deficit* models of test anxiety assume that anxiety produces task-irrelevant thinking that reduces on-task attention, and, therefore, interferes with performance on tasks requiring cognitive resources in terms of working memory capacity (e.g., Wine, 1971). An extension of interference models is Eysenck's (1997) *processing efficiency* model proposing that anxiety can reduce the efficiency of cognitive processing due to the working memory load imposed by anxiety. Finally, an alternative hypothesis is put forward by *skills-deficit models* (Zeidner, 1998). Skills-deficit models hypothesize that test anxious students suffer from a lack of competence in the first place, implying an increased probability of failure on complex or difficult tasks, as well as increased anxiety induced by appraisals of these deficits.

These different models can be regarded as complementary rather than mutually exclusive. Empirically, test anxiety has been shown to be accompanied by task-irrelevant thinking distracting attention away from cognitive tasks, and the available evidence also shows that low-ability students are more prone to experience exam-related anxiety. Furthermore, it seems reasonable to assume that competence, anxiety, and performance are often linked by reciprocal causation over time: Lack of competence can induce anxiety of failure, anxiety can impair the quality of learning and performance, and poor-quality learning leads to a lack of competence.

In line with the findings of experimental research, field studies have shown that self-report measures of test anxiety correlate moderately negatively with students' academic performance. The results of meta-analyses indicate that, typically, 5–10% of the variance in students' achievement scores is explained by self-reported anxiety (Hembree, 1988; Zeidner, 1998). However, caution should be exerted in interpreting these correlations. It may be that relations between test anxiety and achievement are primarily caused by effects of success and failure on the development of test anxiety, rather than by effects of anxiety on academic performance. The little longitudinal evidence available to date suggests that test anxiety and students' achievement are linked by reciprocal causation across school years, but this evidence also seems to suggest that the effects of achievement on anxiety are stronger than effects of anxiety on achievement (e.g., Meece, Wigfield, & Eccles, 1990). Furthermore, correlations with performance variables have not been uniformly negative across studies. Zero and positive correlations have sometimes been found, pointing to the complexity of anxiety-achievement relationships. Anxiety likely has deleterious effects on many students, but it may induce motivation to study harder, and thus facilitate overall performance, in those who are more resilient to the devastating aspects of anxiety (Pekrun & Hofmann, 1996).

From an educator's perspective, however, any benefits of anxiety in resilient, highly motivated students are certainly outweighed by the negative effects of anxiety on motivation and performance in the vast majority of students, particularly those experiencing excessive anxiety. Also, beyond effects on academic learning, test anxiety can have severe consequences for students' long-term psychological well-being, social adaptation, and physical health (Zeidner, 1998), thus indicating an urgent need to ameliorate students' fear of failing in their academic careers.

Effects of Negative Emotions other than Anxiety

Few studies have addressed the effects of students' negative emotions other than anxiety. Most of these studies pertained to students' anger, shame, boredom, or hopelessness. *Anger* is an activating negative emotions implying physiological arousal, being similar to anxiety in this respect. The available evidence suggests that students' anger at school correlates positively with task-irrelevant thinking, and negatively with academic self-efficacy, interest, self-regulation of learning, and performance (Boekaerts, 1993; Pekrun et al., 2004). However, as with anxiety, the underlying pattern of functional mechanisms may be complex and imply more than just negative effects. For example, in a study reported by Lane, Whyte, Terry, and Nevill (2005), depressed mood interacted with anger experienced before an academic exam such that anger was related to *improved* performance in students who did not feel depressed. Likely, anger is detrimental for motivation under many conditions, can contribute to aggressive behavior at school, but can also translate into increased task motivation when expectancies for success are favorable.

The emotion of *shame* is at the core of negative feelings of self-worth, often implying devastating, pervasive feelings of self-debasement (Covington, this volume; Covington & Beery, 1976). Students' achievement-related shame as measured by the AEQ shame scales shows negative overall correlations with students' effort and academic achievement (Pekrun et al., 2004; Titz, 2001). However, as with anxiety and anger, shame seems to exert motivational effects that can be variable. For example, Turner and Schallert (2001) showed that students experiencing shame following negative exam feedback increased their motivation when continuing to be committed to academic goals and holding positive expectancies to reach these goals.

Boredom and *hopelessness* are deactivating emotions that, typically, are characterized by reduced levels of physiological activation. These two emotions can be assumed to reduce both intrinsic and extrinsic motivation, and to be detrimental for any kind of cognitive performance. However, in spite of the frequency of boredom experienced by students, this emotion has received scant attention, as has the less frequent, but devastating emotion of achievement-related hopelessness. Boredom at work was researched early as being induced by monotonous assembly-line work (e.g., Wyatt, 1930), and boredom at school was discussed as being experienced by gifted students in recent years. In our own studies using the AEQ boredom and hopelessness scales, these two emotions correlated negatively with measures of motivation, study behavior, and achievement (Pekrun et al., 2004; Titz, 2001).

Effects of Positive Emotions

In traditional approaches to human emotions, it was often assumed that positive emotions are maladaptive by inducing unrealistic appraisals, fostering superficial information processing, and reducing motivation to pursuit challenging goals (Aspinwall, 1998; Pekrun et al., 2002a). Much of the available experimental, laboratory-based evidence seems to support such a view. As aptly summarized by Aspinwall (1998, p. 7), traditional approaches to positive emotions imply that "our primary goal is to feel good, and feeling good makes us lazy thinkers who are oblivious to potentially useful negative information and unresponsive to meaningful variations in information and situation." However, as noted above, educators' experiences as well as more recent evidence contradict views that positive emotions are uniformly detrimental for motivation and cognitive performance. Specifically, as noted, experimental research has shown that positive mood can enhance divergent thinking and flexible problem solving.

Direct empirical evidence on the effects of students' positive emotions is scarce, but supports the view that positive emotions can enhance academic motivation and performance. Specifically, enjoyment of learning, hope, and pride have been found to correlate positively with students' interest, effort, elaboration of learning material, self-regulation of learning, and academic achievement, thus corroborating that these emotions can be beneficial for students' academic motivation and agency (Pekrun et al., 2002a, b).

Implications

In sum, the available evidence suggests that emotions exert profound effects on students' motivation, learning, and achievement. However, these effects can be complex, and the contradictions between some of the theoretical accounts trying to explain these effects are not easy to reconcile. Three general implications are the following: (a) It would seem insufficient to simply distinguish positive vs. negative affect (or mood) for explaining the effects of students' emotions. For example, the findings imply that activating negative emotions such as anxiety and anger can exert ambiguous motivational effects, in contrast to deactivating negative emotions like hopelessness and boredom. Therefore, differentiated conceptions of emotions are needed to explain their effects on motivation and achievement. (b) Similarly, it would be insufficient to assume uniformly positive or negative effects for specific emotions. Rather, the effects on different kinds of motivation and cognitive processes may diverge. (c) In theory and empirical research, it would be important to untangle when emotions do, in fact, causally impact motivation and learning, and when they are effects of motivation and learning (e.g., effects of students' achievement goals as outlined above). An attempt to use these three conclusions to derive a more coherent set of assumptions on the functions of students' emotions is presented as part of the next section.

The Control-Value Theory of Achievement Emotions: An Integrative Approach to Students' Emotions at School

As outlined in the previous sections, various theoretical accounts for students' emotions have evolved, but have operated in relative isolation to date. As such, research on emotions in education, and on achievement emotions more generally, is in a state of fragmentation today. More integrative frameworks seem to be largely lacking, which hampers theoretical and empirical progress. The control-value theory of achievement emotions (Pekrun, 2000, 2006; Pekrun, Frenzel, Goetz, & Perry, 2007) aims to provide such an integrative framework. It is based on the fact that current approaches to achievement emotions share a number of common basic assumptions and can be regarded as complementary rather than mutually exclusive. More specifically, the theory builds on assumptions from expectancy-value models of emotions (Pekrun, 1984, 1988, 1992b; Turner & Schallert, 2001), transactional theories of stress-related emotions (Folkman & Lazarus, 1985), attributional theories of achievement emotions (Weiner, 1985), and models addressing the effects of emotions on learning and performance (Fredrickson, 2001; Pekrun et al., 2002b). It goes beyond these views by integrating propositions from different theories, and by explicitly focusing on both outcome-related and activity-related achievement emotions, thus addressing all major variants of achievement emotions.

In this section, I first address the propositions of the theory on the appraisal antecedents of students' achievement emotions. Next, conceptual corollaries and extensions of the theory are outlined. Specifically, I discuss implications for the multiplicity of students' emotions; their more distal individual and social antecedents; their effects on motivation, learning, and performance;

the reciprocal relations between emotions, antecedents, and effects; and the relative universality of achievement emotions across sociohistorical contexts, genders, and individuals.

Control and Value as Determinants of Achievement Emotions

Propositions regarding the arousal of achievement emotions are at the heart of the theory. It is assumed that students' appraisals of ongoing achievement activities, and of their past and future outcomes, are of primary importance in this respect (link 1 in Figure 26.1). Succinctly stated, this central part of the theory can be summarized by the proposition that students experience emotions when they feel being in control of, or out of control of, achievement-related activities

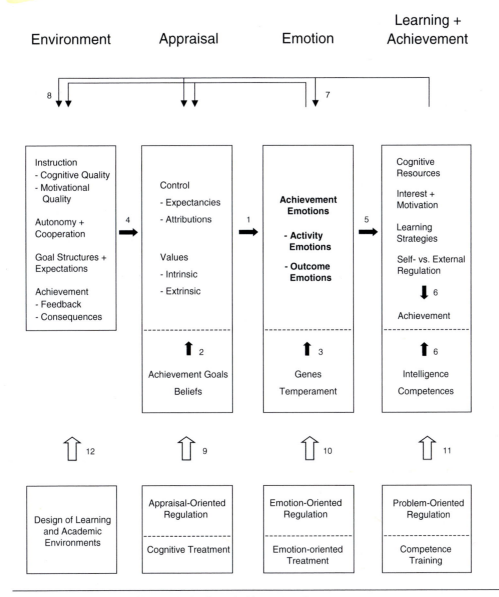

Figure 26.1 Basic propositions of the control-value theory of achievement emotions.

and outcomes that are subjectively important to them—implying that *control appraisals* and *value appraisals* are the proximal determinants of their achievement emotions.

Control appraisals pertain to the perceived controllability of achievement-related actions and outcomes. The controllability of causes of achievement as addressed by Weiner's (1985) theory is assumed to be relevant by contributing to perceived control over actions and outcomes, as are the locus and the stability of causes. Appraisals of control, or of factors contributing to control, are seen as being implied by causal expectations (self-efficacy expectations and outcome expectancies), causal attributions of achievement, and students' competence appraisals (e.g., self-concepts of ability). *Value appraisals* relate to the subjective importance of achievement activities and their outcomes. Value appraisals are part of students' subject matter interest, and of their achievement goals implying the desire to attain success or to avoid failure.

Different kinds of control and value appraisals are expected to instigate different kinds of achievement emotions. For outcome emotions, expectancies and attributions are held to be main determinants, in addition to value appraisals. More specifically, causal expectancies are assumed to influence prospective outcome emotions like hope, anticipatory joy, anxiety, and hopelessness, and causal attributions retrospective outcome emotions like pride and shame. For activity emotions, competence appraisals and value appraisals are posited to be important.

Prospective Outcome Emotions Prospective, anticipatory *joy* and *hopelessness* are seen to be triggered when there is high perceived control (joy), or a complete lack of perceived control (hopelessness). *Hope* and *anxiety* are expected to be instigated when there is uncertainty about control, the attentional focus being on the positive valences of anticipated success in the case of hope, and on the negative valences of anticipated failure in the case of anxiety.

Retrospective Outcome Emotions As for retrospective outcome emotions induced by the experience of success or failure, *joy* and *sadness* about achievement outcomes are seen as immediately following perceived success and failure, without any more elaborate cognitive mediation (in line with Weiner's (1985) assumptions cited above). In contrast, *disappointment* and *relief* are assumed to depend on appraisals of the match between previous expectations and the actual outcome, disappointment being induced when anticipated success did not occur, and relief when anticipated failure did not occur. The emotions *pride*, *shame*, *gratitude*, and *anger* are seen to be induced by attributions of success and failure as being caused by oneself or other persons, respectively. In contrast to Weiner's assumptions, the perceived controllability of success and failure *themselves* is assumed to be of critical importance for these emotions, rather than the controllability of the *causes* of success and failure (Pekrun, 2006).

Activity Emotions As noted, activity emotions have been neglected by previous theories of achievement emotions, in spite of their importance for students' learning and academic agency. These emotions are also posited to depend on appraisals of control and values. *Enjoyment* of achievement activities (e.g., enjoyment of learning) is seen to depend on a combination of positive competence appraisals, and positive appraisals of the intrinsic qualities of the action (e.g., studying) and its objects (e.g., learning material). *Anger* and *frustration* are expected to be aroused when the incentive values of the activity are negative (e.g., when studying difficult problems takes too much effort experienced as being aversive). Finally, *boredom* is experienced when the activity lacks any incentive values. Specifically, this may be the case with tasks involving demands that are far below one's own competences, as suggested by Cszikszentmihalyi (1975).

Implications: I. Subconscious Appraisals and Habitualized Achievement Emotions

The control-value theory does not suggest that students' achievement emotions are always mediated by conscious appraisals. Rather, it is assumed that recurring appraisal-based induction of emotions can habitualize over time. When academic experiences are repeated over and over again, appraisals and the induction of emotions can become routinized to the extent that there is no longer any conscious mediation of emotions, or no longer any cognitive mediation at all (Pekrun, 1988; Reisenzein, 2001).

Implications: II. Multiplicity and Domain Specificity of Achievement Emotions

The theory positis that qualitatively different achievement emotions are characterized by different combinations of appraisal antecedents. By implication, a full account of these emotions presupposes to acknowledge their multiplicity. Furthermore, since variables of control and value have been shown to be organized in domain-specific ways (Bong, 2001), it follows from the theory that the emotions determined by control and values should be domain-specific as well, in contrast to more traditional conceptions regarding achievement emotions as generalized personality traits (e.g., test anxiety; Zeidner, 1998). Hypotheses on the domain specificity of students' emotions were corroborated in recent studies (e.g., Goetz, Frenzel, Pekrun, Hall, & Lüdtke, 2007).

Implications: III. Distal Individual Antecedents: Temperament, Beliefs, and Goals

To the extent that control and value appraisals are proximal determinants of students' emotions, more distal individual antecedents should affect these emotions by influencing control and value appraisals in the first place (link 2 in Figure 26.1). Examples of such antecedents are students' achievement goals and their achievement-related control and value beliefs. However, the theory acknowledges that emotions are influenced by non-cognitive factors like physiologically bound temperament as well (link 3). Specifically, positive and negative affectivity (Watson, 2002) may predispose individuals to experience positive and negative achievement emotions, respectively. Regarding achievement goals, it is expected that mastery approach goals focus attention on the controllability and positive values of achievement activities, thus fostering positive activity emotions like enjoyment of learning, and reducing negative activity emotions such as boredom. In contrast, performance-approach goals should focus attention on positive outcome-related appraisals, and performance-avoidance goals on negative outcome-related appraisals, thus facilitating positive or negative outcome emotions, respectively (Pekrun et al., 2006).

Implications: IV. Classroom Instruction and Social Antecedents

In line with assumptions of social-cognitive learning theories, the control-value theory implies that the impact of environments on students' emotions is also largely mediated by individual appraisals (link 4 in Figure 26.1). By implication, environmental factors affecting students' appraisals should be important for their emotions. As all of these factors are of immediate practical relevance, they are discussed in the section on implications for educational practice (see below).

Implications: V. Effects of Emotions on Learning and Achievement

In addition to the determinants of achievement emotions, the theory also addresses their functions for learning and achievement. Specifically, it is posited that emotions influence cognitive resources, interest and motivation, use of strategies, and self- vs. external regulation of learning (link 5 in Figure 26.1). The effects of emotions on students' achievement are posited to be mediated by these processes (link 6). Using the taxonomy of achievement emotions described above (Table 26.1), the following is assumed.

Cognitive Resources Enlarging assumptions of the resource allocation model by Ellis and Ashbrook (1988), it is proposed that positive activity emotions such as enjoyment of learning help focus attention on ongoing learning activities. These emotions foster experiences of flow in which attention is fully absorbed by task activities (Csikszentmihalyi, 1975). Emotions not relating to the activity, on the other hand, distract attention away, implying that they reduce cognitive resources available for task purposes, and impair performance needing such resources. For example, if a student is angry about failure, or worries about an upcoming exam, task-related attention will be impaired (Pekrun et al., 2004).

Interest and Motivation Positive activating emotions such as enjoyment of learning are posited to increase interest and strengthen motivation, and negative deactivating emotions such as hopelessness and boredom are held to be detrimental for any kinds of motivation. In contrast, the effects of positive deactivating emotions like relief, as well as negative activating emotions like anger, anxiety, and shame, are posited to be more complex. For example, failure-related anxiety can reduce interest and intrinsic motivation, but can, at the same time, strengthen motivation to invest effort in order to avoid failure. If a student is afraid of failing an upcoming exam, intrinsic motivation to learn the material will be reduced, while motivation to avoid failure can be increased. In line with these assumptions, we found that students' enjoyment of learning and instruction related positively to their intrinsic and extrinsic motivation, whereas relations for hopelessness and boredom were negative, and relations for anxiety and shame ambiguous (e.g., Pekrun et al., 2002b; Pekrun et al., 2004).

Strategies of Learning In line with the findings of mood research cited above, it is expected that positive activating emotions help using flexible strategies such as elaboration of learning material, whereas negative activating emotions can facilitate the use of more rigid strategies like simple rehearsal. Furthermore, it is assumed that deactivating emotions are detrimental to any more elaborate processing of task-related information.

Self-Regulation vs. External Regulation of Learning Self-regulation requires flexible use of meta-cognitive, meta-motivational, and meta-emotional strategies (Wolters, 2003) making it possible to adapt behavior to goals and environmental demands. It is assumed that positive activating emotions such as enjoyment of learning enhance self-regulation, whereas negative emotions like anxiety or shame facilitate students' reliance on external guidance.

Academic Achievement The effects of emotions on students' achievement are seen to be a joint product of the four mechanisms described above, and any interactions between these mechanisms and the task demands of learning. For most task conditions, however, it can be assumed that positive activating emotions such as learning-related enjoyment exert positive overall effects, and negative deactivating emotions such as hopelessness and boredom negative effects. The effects of positive deactivating emotions like relaxation, and of negative activating emotions like anger, anxiety, and shame, can be assumed to be more ambiguous, due to the complex effects of these emotions on motivation and cognitive processing. If a student is able, for example, to use the motivational energy implied by exam-related anxiety to increase his or her efforts, and if task demands are congruent to a more rigid processing of information as facilitated by anxiety, exam performance can be enhanced instead of being impaired (see Turner & Waugh, 2007, for related assumptions on shame).

In line with these propositions, enjoyment, hope, and pride as assessed by scales of the AEQ related positively, and hopelessness as well as boredom negatively, to students' academic achievement (Pekrun et al., 2002b). For anger, anxiety, and shame, overall sample correlations were negative as well, suggesting that negative effects of these emotions outweigh positive effects across individuals. However, as expected, we also found that there are individual students who can profit, in terms of motivation and achievement, from their anxiety. Specifically, in a diary study investigating individual trajectories of achievement emotions experienced before and during final university exams in a sample of student teachers, we found that exam anxiety correlated negatively with achievement-related agency over time in many students, but showed positive correlations in others (Pekrun & Hofmann, 1996).

Implications: VI. Feedback Loops of Emotions, Antecedents, and Effects

Emotions are posited to influence motivation and achievement, but achievement outcomes are expected to act back on students' emotions (Figure 26.1, link 7), and on the environment within, and outside of, the classroom (link 8). By implication, antecedents, emotions, and their effects are thought to be linked by reciprocal causation over time (see the chain of links 1 to 8), including reciprocal causation of emotions, motivational antecedents, and motivational effects. In line with perspectives of dynamical systems theory (Turner & Waugh, 2007), it is assumed that reciprocal causation can take different forms and can extend over fractions of seconds (e.g., in linkages between appraisals and emotions), days, weeks, months, or years. Positive feedback loops likely are typical (e.g., teachers' and students' anger reciprocally reinforcing each other), but negative feedback loops can also be important (e.g., failure inducing anxiety in a student, and anxiety motivating the student to successfully avoid failure on the next exam). Assumptions on reciprocity have implications for the regulation and treatment of achievement emotions (links 9 to 11), and for the design of "emotionally sound" (Astleitner, 2000) learning environments (link 12).

In our empirical studies, we found evidence for feedback loops within students, and preliminary evidence for relations between teachers' and students' affect (Frenzel et al., in press). Specifically, in structural equations modeling of longitudinal data on students' academic development through grades 5 to 10, we found that students' emotions and their academic achievement were reciprocally linked over the years, implying that success and failure were important antecedents of students' emotional development, and that their emotions reciprocally affected their achievement (e.g., Pekrun, 1992b). Typically, these feedback loops were positive, with success and positive emotions, as well as failure and negative emotions, reinforcing each other over the years.

Implications: VII. Sociocultural Context, Gender, and the Individual: Relative Universality of Achievement Emotions

In the control-value theory, it is assumed that the functional mechanisms of human emotion are bound to universal, species-specific characteristics of our mind. In contrast, the contents of emotions, as well as specific values of process parameters such as the intensity of emotions, may be specific to different individuals, genders, and cultures. For example, it follows from the theory that relations between control and value appraisals, on the one hand, and achievement emotions, on the other, should be structurally equivalent for male and female students, even if mean values for these variables differ between genders. Similarly, relations between appraisals and emotions are assumed to be structurally equivalent across countries and cultures (for evidence corroborating these propositions, see Frenzel et al., 2007a; Frenzel, Thrash, Pekrun, & Goetz, 2006; Pekrun, in press).

Implications for Educational Practice

The evidence on social determinants of students' test anxiety cited above, and the propositions of the control-value theory, imply that environmental factors play a major role in shaping students' emotions. Specifically, it follows from the control-value theory that teachers and parents can influence students' emotional development by influencing their perceived control and academic values. By implication, educators likely have a major impact on students' emotions and can attempt to foster the development of adaptive emotions. Throughout students' academic careers, the following factors may be especially important.

(1) Cognitive Quality of Learning Environments and Tasks The cognitive quality of classroom instruction and assignments should have positive effects on students' perceived competence and control, and of their valuing of instruction and academic contents, thus positively influencing their emotions. The relative difficulty of instruction and tasks may be important as well. Difficulty can influence perceived control, and the match between task demands and students' competences can influence the subjective value of tasks. If demands are too high or too low, the incentive value of tasks may be reduced to the extent that boredom is experienced.

(2) Motivational Quality of Learning Environments and Tasks Teachers and peers deliver direct messages conveying academic values, as well as more indirect messages implied by their behavior. Two ways of inducing emotionally relevant values in indirect ways may be most important. First, if instruction, learning environments and assignments are shaped such that they meet the needs of students, positive activity-related emotions should be fostered. For example, learning environments that support cooperative student learning should help students to fulfill needs for social relatedness, thus making learning in such environments subjectively more valuable. Second, teachers' own enthusiasm in dealing with academic material can facilitate students' adoption of academic values. Observational learning and emotional contagion may be primary mechanisms mediating the effects of teachers' enthusiasm on students' values (Hatfield, Cacioppo, & Rapson, 1994).

(3) Support of Autonomy and Self-Regulated Learning Learning environments supporting students' self-regulated learning can be assumed to increase their sense of control. In addition, meeting needs for autonomy, such environments can increase academic values. However, these

beneficial effects likely depend on the match between students' competence and individual need for academic autonomy, on the one hand, and the affordances of these environments, on the other. In case of a mismatch, loss of control and negative emotions can result.

(4) Goal Structures and Achievement Expectations Academic achievement can be defined by standards of individual mastery pertaining to absolute criteria or intraindividual competence gain, by normative standards based on competitive social comparison between students, or by standards pertaining to cooperative group performance instead of individual performance. These different standards imply individualistic (mastery), competitive (normative), or cooperative goal structures in the classroom (Johnson & Johnson, 1974; see Maehr & Zusho, this volume). Goal structures probably influence students' emotions in two ways. First, to the extent that these structures are adopted by students, they influence their achievement goals and any emotions mediated by these goals as outlined above. Second, goal structures and grading practices determine students' relative opportunities for experiencing success and perceiving control, thus influencing expectancy-dependent emotions. Specifically, competitive goal structures imply, by definition, that some students experience success, whereas others have to experience failure. It can be assumed that students' average achievement expectancies are lower under these conditions, such that average values of negative prospective outcome emotions like anxiety and hopelessness are increased. Similarly, the demands implied by excessively high achievement expectancies of significant others can lead to lowered expectancies by the student, and to all of the negative emotions resulting from reduced subjective control.

(5) Feedback and Consequences of Achievement Cumulative success can strengthen students' perceived control, and cumulative failure can undermine subjective control. In systems involving frequent testing, test feedback is likely one primary mechanism determining students' outcome-related achievement emotions. In addition, the perceived consequences of success and failure are important, since consequences affect the instrumental values of achievement outcomes. Positive outcome emotions like hope for success can be increased if a student appraises academic success to produce beneficial long-term outcomes (e.g., in terms of future occupational chances), and perceives sufficient contingencies between own efforts, success, and these outcomes. Negative outcomes of academic failure, on the other hand, may increase students' achievement-related anxiety and hopelessness.

(6) Treatment of Appraisals and Emotions Appraisal theories like the control-value theory imply that educators and therapists can attempt to change students' emotions by directly addressing the appraisals underlying these emotions (cognitive treatment). One way of doing this would be through attributional retraining that has proved to be successful for improving students' motivation and achievement, and might also prove helpful for changing emotions (e.g., Ruthig, Perry, Hall, & Hladkyj, 2004). Alternatively, treatment of achievement emotions can focus on directly changing the target emotion (emotion-oriented treatment), or on developing students' problem-solving skills and academic agency influencing their emotions (competence training; see Figure 26.1, links 9 to 11).

(7) Fostering Students' Self-Regulation of Emotions The control-value theory implies that regulating control and value appraisals is one important mechanism for emotional self-regulation (Figure 26.1, link 9). Educators can assist students in developing regulatory skills and in self-regulating

their appraisals and achievement emotions, thereby indirectly fostering their emotional development (Goetz, Frenzel, Pekrun, & Hall, 2006).

Directions for Future Research

As outlined in this chapter, research on emotions in school settings has been slow to emerge. While students' test anxiety has been researched since the 1930s, emotions other than anxiety have been neglected, with the exception of attributional research on emotions following success and failure. During the past 10 years, however, there has been an increase of studies into the nature of emotions experienced by students (Schutz & Pekrun, 2007). These studies have produced new insights. The findings demonstrate that emotions profoundly affect students' engagement, performance, and personality development, which also implies that they are of critical importance for the agency of educational institutions and of society of large.

At the same time, however, the studies conducted so far seem to pose more new, challenging questions than they can answer. Theories, strategies, and measures for analyzing these emotions are yet to be fully developed. Also, to date studies are too scarce to allow any meta-analytic synthesis based on cumulative evidence, or any firm conclusions informing educational practitioners in validated ways how to deal with emotions, evidence on test anxiety being an exception. The progress made so far is promising, but much more has to be done if educational research on emotions is to evolve over the next years in ways benefiting education and society. Important challenges for future research are the following (see Pekrun & Schutz, 2007, for a more comprehensive analysis).

Constructing More Integrative Theories

Different traditions of research on emotions have been working in relative isolation, in spite of often sharing basic assumptions. As in other fields of research on affect and motivation, and of psychology and the social sciences more generally, there seems to be a proliferation of small constructs and theories in the study of human emotions (see Lewis & Haviland-Jones, 2000). As a result, there is a lack of theoretical integration that has to be overcome if cumulative progress is to be made. Specifically, there is a need to find more of a consensus on constructs of emotions, and to integrate theoretical models that share assumptions on the functions of emotions. For example, as noted above, there is a need for a more precise conceptualization of educationally relevant constructs that might, or might not, be considered as belonging to the domain of emotions (such as interest, mood, or metacognitive feelings). A second important case in point is experimental vs. field-based traditions of research on the functions of emotions. As noted, these research traditions differ in terms of theoretical approaches, methodology, and practical implications, meaning that there is a clear need to reconcile these different paradigms.

Making Use of Neuroscientific Perspectives

Emotions are coordinated psychological processes that are deeply embedded in the human brain. Neuroscientific research has made substantial progress in analyzing relevant brain structures during the past 20 years. The limbic system (specifically, the amygdala and hippocampus) and its connections to other parts of the brain (e.g., the frontal lobe responsible for executive control processes) have been identified as being central to emotion, the regulation of emotion, and the effects of emotion on thinking, decision making, learning, and memory (Davidson, Pizzagalli,

Nitschke, & Kalin, 2003). Educational research on emotions, however, has virtually ignored the progress made in this field.

Neuroscientific approaches can be used by educational emotion research in several ways. First, neuroscientific research provides information about basic processes of emotion that have important implications for conceptualizing and assessing emotion at school. For example, affective neuroscience has provided evidence corroborating that emotional processes are often implicit and can occur without awareness (e.g., Ohman & Soares, 1998), suggesting that self-report assessment of emotion needs to be complemented by measures of implicit emotional processes. Second, neuroscientific research provides indicators suitable to assess the effects of emotions on cognitive processes and learning. For example, neuroimaging methods such as EEG and fMRI help tracking the effects of emotional states on attention and cognitive problem solving during learning. Finally, affective neuroscience also allows analyzing the physiological mechanisms of individual emotional problems such as excessive anxiety experienced in achievement settings.

By implication, there is a clear need to integrate neuroaffective perspectives into educational research. However, when doing so, the limitations of these perspectives should be kept in mind as well. Learning at school involves the formal acquisition of culturally defined, systematic knowledge. Formal learning follows its own logic and cannot simply be explained by brain mechanisms based on biological evolution; rather, the contents and contexts of learning also have to be taken into account (Blakemore & Frith, 2005). By implication, for explaining the role of emotions in school learning, an analysis of the contents of students' emotions, their cognitive and social antecedents, and their functions for formal learning and performance is needed, which cannot be provided by perspectives from neuroaffective science alone.

Analyzing the Dynamics of Emotions over Time

With few exceptions (e.g., Ainley, 2007), research on emotions in school settings has not yet attempted to fully capture the multifaceted, dynamic nature of emotional processes in these settings. To do so would require the construction of dynamic theories and the use of real-time estimates of emotion processes. For modeling affective processes, Atkinson and Birch's (1970) dynamic action theory represented a major step forward. With few exceptions, however, this theory was never tested empirically, probably due to the lack of precise measures of process parameters. In view of the significant advances in real-time assessment, it would be useful to pursue Atkinson and Birch's approach as well as more recent computational process approaches to emotions (Wehrle & Scherer, 2001), and to construct suitable dynamic models for emotional processes in school settings.

Taking Multiple Levels of Educational Institutions and Sociohistorical Contexts into Account

In education, the individual, typically, is part of an educational setting such as the classroom. In turn, classrooms are nested within schools or universities, and schools within educational systems, societies, and cultures. To date, research on emotions in school settings mainly addressed the individual level of emotions. Future research should take the level of educational institutions, and of different cultural and sociohistorical contexts, into account as well. Specifically, *multilevel classroom studies* are needed that analyze students' and teachers' emotions from a multilevel perspective, addressing the variation of emotions between individuals as well as classrooms, schools, and educational systems, in order to answer questions about the social origins of these emotions. Answers to such questions are of critical importance for adequately designing educational interventions. Furthermore, *cross-cultural* and *sociohistorical studies* are needed that analyze the variation of emotions across different cultures and historical epochs that involve different values and practices of education.

The Need for Intervention Research on Emotions in School Settings

To date, practical considerations on how to enhance students' emotions can be deduced from theoretical assumptions as presented above. Related empirical evidence, however, is still largely lacking, with the single exception of research on the prevention and treatment of students' test anxiety. This research provides evidence-based principles on how to alleviate test anxiety (Zeidner, 1998), and cognitive-behavioral ways of modifying this emotion are among the most successful methods of psychotherapy available today (effect sizes of $d > 1$; Zeidner, 1998). However, what can be done to reduce students' boredom, anger, shame, or hopelessness, and to foster their hope, pride, and enjoyment of learning?

Concerning these emotions, empirical research cannot yet provide firm, evidence-based conclusions on how to design classroom instruction, learning environments, and educational systems in "emotionally sound" (Astleitner, 2000) ways. By implication, we need more educational intervention studies demonstrating in which ways educators, parents, and the organization of schooling can influence students' emotions. To date, the few available intervention studies on emotions other than test anxiety have met with only partial success (e.g., Glaeser-Zikuda, Fuss, Laukenmann, Metz, & Randler, 2005), meaning that creating affectively sound environments will not be an easy task. The success story of test anxiety research, however, suggests that it will be possible to generate useable knowledge for emotions other than anxiety as well. Most likely, it will prove to be possible to design emotionally effective learning environments and interventions targeting these emotions, such that educational emotion research will be able to inform educational practice in validated ways in the near future.

Conclusion

In the concluding chapter of their 2000 *Handbook of Self-Regulation* that covered the state of the art in research on self-regulation, Boekaerts, Pintrich, and Zeidner (2000, p. 754) posed the question, "How should we deal with emotions or affect?" The review provided by the present chapter has shown that research on emotions at school has started to search for answers. Theoretical considerations and the evidence that has been accumulated so far suggest that the emotions experienced in academic settings are critical to students' motivation, learning and achievement. Furthermore, emotions likely are no less important for students' overall personality development, social behavior, and health. By implication, education research would be well advised to pay more attention to the affective sides of students' scholastic development. With the advent of broader conceptions of human psychological functioning replacing an exclusive focus on cognitive processes by including neuropsychological, emotion-oriented, and sociocultural perspectives as well, chances may, in fact, have increased that researchers analyze the emotional aspects of students' learning, personality development, and well-being.

References

Ainley, M. (2007). Being and feeling interested: Transient state, mood, and disposition. In P. A. Schutz & R. Pekrun (Eds.), *Emotion in education* (pp. 147–163). San Diego, CA: Academic Press.

Ashby, F. G., Isen, A. M., & Turken, A. U. (1999). A neuropsychological theory of positive affect and its influence on cognition. *Psychological Review, 106,* 529–550.

Aspinwall, L. (1998). Rethinking the role of positive affect in self-regulation. *Motivation and Emotion, 22,* 1–32.

Astleitner, H. (2000). Designing emotionally sound instruction: The FEASP-approach. *Instructional Science, 28,* 169–198.

Atkinson, J. W., & Birch, D. (1970). *A dynamic theory of action.* New York: Wiley.

Blakemore, S.-J., & Frith, U. (2005). *The learning brain: lessons for education.* Oxford, England: Blackwell.

Bless, H., Clore, G. L., Schwarz, N., Golisano, V., Rabe, C., & Wölk, M. (1996). Mood and the use of scripts: Does a happy mood really lead to mindlessness? *Journal of Personality and Social Psychology, 71,* 665–679.

Boekaerts, M. (1993). Anger in relation to school learning. *Learning and Instruction, 3,* 269–280.

Boekaerts, M., Pintrich, P., & Zeidner, M. (Eds.). (2000). *Handbook of self-regulation.* San Diego: Academic Press.

Bong, M. (2001). Between- and within-domain relations of motivation among middle and high school students: Self-efficacy, task value and achievement goals. *Journal of Educational Psychology, 93,* 23–34.

Brown, C. H. (1938). Emotional reactions before examinations: II. Results of a questionnaire. *Journal of Psychology, 5,* 11–26.

Covington, M. V., & Beery, R. G. (1976). *Self-worth and school learning.* Oxford, England: Holt, Rinehart & Winston.

Csikszentmihalyi, M. (1975). *Beyond boredom and anxiety.* San Francisco: Jossey-Bass.

Davidson, R. J., Pizzagalli, D., Nitschke, J. B., & Kalin, N. H. (2003). Parsing the subcomponents of emotion and disorders of emotion: Perspectives from affective neuroscience. In R. J. Davidson, K. R. Scherer, & H. H. Goldsmith (Eds.), *Handbook of affective sciences* (pp. 8–24). Oxford, England: Oxford University Press.

Davidson, R. J., Scherer, K. R., & Goldsmith, H. H. (2003). Introduction. In R. J. Davidson, K. R. Scherer, & H. H. Goldsmith (Eds.), *Handbook of affective sciences* (pp. xii–xvii). Oxford, England: Oxford University Press.

Davidson, R. J., & Sutton, S. K. (1995). Affective neuroscience: The emergence of a discipline. *Current Opinion in Neurobiology, 5,* 217–224.

Efklides, A., & Volet, S. (Eds.). (2005). Feelings and emotions in the learning process [Special issue]. *Learning and Instruction, 15,* 377–515.

Ekman, P., & Rosenberg, E. L. (Eds.). (1997). *What the face reveals: Basic and applied studies of spontaneous expression using the Facial Action Coding System (FACS).* New York: Oxford University Press.

Elliot, A. J., Maier, M. A., Moller, A. C., Friedman, R., & Meinhardt, J. (2007). Color and psychological functioning: The effect of red on performance in achievement contexts. *Journal of Experimental Psychology: General, 136,* 154–168.

Ellis, A. (1962). *Reason and emotion in psychotherapy.* New York: Lyle Stuart.

Ellis, H. C., & Ashbrook, P. W. (1988). Resource allocation model of the effect of depressed mood states on memory. In K. Fiedler & J. Forgas (Eds.), *Affect, cognition, and social behavior* (pp. 213–236). Toronto: Hogrefe International.

Eysenck, M. W. (1997). *Anxiety and cognition.* Hove, East Sussex, England: Psychology Press.

Feldman Barrett, L., & Russell, J. A. (1998). Independence and bipolarity in the structure of current affect. *Journal of Personality and Social Psychology, 74,* 967–984.

Folkman, S., & Lazarus, R. S. (1985). If it changes it must be process: Study of emotion and coping during three phases of a college examination. *Journal of Personality and Social Psychology, 40,* 150–170.

Fredricks, J. A., & Eccles, J. (2002). Children's competence and value beliefs from childhood through adolescence: Growth trajectories in two male-sex-typed domains. *Developmental Psychology, 38,* 519–533.

Fredrickson, B. L. (2001). The role of positive emotions in positive psychology: The broaden-and-build theory of positive emotions. *American Psychologist, 56,* 218–226.

Frenzel, A. C., Goetz, T., Lüdtke, O., Pekrun, R., & Sutton, R. E. (in press). Emotional transmission in the classroom: Exploring the relationship between teacher and student enjoyment. *Journal of Educational Psychology.*

Frenzel, A. C., Pekrun, R., & Goetz, T. (2007a). Girls and mathematics — a "hopeless" issue? A control-value approach to gender differences in emotions towards mathematics. *European Journal of Psychology of Education, 22,* 497–514.

Frenzel, A. C., Pekrun, R., & Goetz, T. (2007b). Perceived learning environments and students' emotional experiences: A multilevel analysis of mathematics classrooms. *Learning and Instruction, 17,* 478–493.

Frenzel, A. C., Thrash, T. M., Pekrun, R., Goetz, T. (2007). Achievement emotions in Germany and China: A cross-cultural validation of the Academic Emotions Questionnaire-Mathematics (AEQ-M). *Journal of Cross-Cultural Psychology, 38,* 302–309.

Glaeser-Zikuda, M., Fuss, S., Laukenmann, M., Metz, K., & Randler, C. (2005). Promoting students' emotions and achievement — Instructional design and evaluation of the ECOLE-approach. *Learning and Instruction, 15,* 481–495.

Goetz, T., Frenzel, A., Pekrun, R., & Hall, N. (2006). Emotional intelligence in the context of learning and achievement. In R. Schulze & R. D. Roberts (Eds.), *Emotional intelligence: An international handbook* (pp. 233–253). Cambridge, MA: Hogrefe & Hubers.

Goetz, T., Frenzel, A. C., Pekrun, R., Hall, N. C., & Lüdtke, O. (2007). Between- and within-domain relations of students' academic emotions. *Journal of Educational Psychology.*

Hatfield, E., Cacioppo, J. T. & Rapson, R. L. (1994). *Emotional contagion.* New York: Cambridge University Press.

Heckhausen, H. (1991). *Motivation and action.* New York: Springer.

Helmke, A. (1993). Die Entwicklung der Lernfreude vom Kindergarten bis zur 5. Klassenstufe [Development of enjoyment of learning from kindergarten to grade 5]. *Zeitschrift für Pädagogische Psychologie, 7,* 77–86.

Hembree, R. (1988). Correlates, causes, effects, and treatment of test anxiety. *Review of Educational Research, 58,* 47–77.

Johnson, D. W., & Johnson, R. T. (1974). Instructional goal structure: Cooperative, competitive or individualistic. *Review of Educational Research, 4*, 213–240.

Keltner, D., & Ekman, P. (2000). Facial expression of emotion. In M. Lewis & J. M. Haviland-Jones (Eds.), *Handbook of emotions* (pp. 236–264). New York: Guilford.

Kleinginna, P. R., & Kleinginna, A. M. (1981). A categorized list of emotion definitions, with suggestions for a consensual definition. *Motivation and Emotion, 5*, 345–379.

Lane, A. M., Whyte, G. P., Terry, P. C., & Nevill, A. M. (2005). Mood, self-set goals and examination performance: The moderating effect of depressed mood. *Personality and Individual Differences, 39*, 143–153.

Lazarus, R. S., & Folkman, S. (1984). *Stress, appraisal, and coping.* New York: Springer.

Levine, L. J., & Burgess, S. L. (1997). Beyond general arousal: Effect of specific emotions on memory. *Social Cognition, 15*, 157–181.

Lewis, M., & Haviland-Jones, J. M. (Eds.). (2000). *Handbook of emotions.* New York: Guilford.

Liebert, R.M., & Morris, L.W. (1967). Cognitive and emotional components of test anxiety: A distinction and some initial data. *Psychological Reports, 20*, 975–978.

Linnenbrink, E. A. (Ed.). (2006). Emotion research in education: Theoretical and methodological perspectives on the integration of affect, motivation, and cognition [Special issue]. *Educational Psychology Review, 18*(4), 315–341.

Linnenbrink, E. A., & Pintrich, P. R. (2002). Achievement goal theory and affect: An asymmetrical bidirectional model. *Educational Psychologist, 37*, 69–78.

Mandler, G., and Sarason, S. B. (1952). A study of anxiety and learning. *Journal of Abnormal and Social Psychology, 47*, 166–173.

Marsh, H. W. (1987). The big-fish-little-pond effect on academic self-concept. *Journal of Educational Psychology, 79*, 280–295.

Meece, J. L., Wigfield, A., & Eccles, J. S. (1990). Predictors of math anxiety and its influence on young adolescents course enrollment intentions and performance in mathematics. *Journal of Educational Psychology, 82*, 60–70.

Meinhardt, J., & Pekrun, R. (2003). Attentional resource allocation to emotional events: An ERP study. *Cognition and Emotion, 17*, 477–500.

Metalsky, G. I., Halberstadt, L. J., & Abramson, L. Y. (1987). Vulnerability to depressive mood reactions: Toward a more powerful test of the diathesis-stress and causal mediation components of the reformulated theory of depression. *Journal of Personality and Social Psychology, 52*, 386–393.

Ohman, A., & Soares, J. J. F. (1998). Emotional conditioning to masked stimuli: Expectancies for aversive outcomes following nonrecognized fear-relevant stimuli. *Journal of Experimental Psychology: General, 127*, 69–82.

Olafson, K. M., & Ferraro, F. R. (2001). Effects of emotional state on lexical decision performance. *Brain and Cognition, 45*, 15–20.

Pekrun, R. (1984). An expectancy-value model of anxiety. In H. M. van der Ploeg, R. Schwarzer, & C. D. Spielberger (Eds.), *Advances in Test Anxiety Research* (Vol. 3, pp. 53–72). Lisse, The Netherlands: Swets & Zeitlinger.

Pekrun, R. (1988). *Emotion, Motivation und Persönlichkeit* [Emotion, motivation and personality]. Munich, Germany: Psychologie Verlags Union.

Pekrun, R. (1992a). Kognition und Emotion in studienbezogenen Lern- und Leistungssituationen: Explorative Analysen [Cognition and emotion in academic learning and achievement: An exploratory analysis]. *Unterrichtswissenschaft, 20*, 308–324.

Pekrun, R. (1992b). Expectancy-value theory of anxiety: Overview and implications. In D. G. Forgays, T. Sosnowski, & K. Wrzesniewski (Eds.), *Anxiety: Recent developments in self-appraisal, psychophysiological and health research* (pp. 23–41). Washington, DC: Hemisphere.

Pekrun, R. (2000). A social cognitive, control-value theory of achievement emotions. In J. Heckhausen (Ed.), *Motivational psychology of human development* (pp. 143–163). Oxford, England: Elsevier.

Pekrun, R. (2006). The control-value theory of achievement emotions: Assumptions, corollaries, and implications for educational research and practice. *Educational Psychology Review, 18*, 315–341.

Pekrun, R. (in press). Global and local perspectives on human affect: Implications of the control-value theory of achievement emotions. In M. Wosnitza, S. A. Karabenick, A. Efklides, & P. Nenninger (Eds.), *Contemporary motivation research: From global to local perspectives.* Toronto: Hogrefe.

Pekrun, R., Elliot, A. J., & Maier, M. A. (2006). Achievement goals and discrete achievement emotions: A theoretical model and prospective test. *Journal of Educational Psychology, 98*, 583–597.

Pekrun, R., Frenzel, A., Goetz, T., & Perry, R. P. (2006, April). *Control-value theory of academic emotions: How classroom and individual factors shape students' affect.* Paper presented at the annual meeting of the American Educational Research Association, San Francisco, CA.

Pekrun, R., Frenzel, A., Goetz, T., & Perry, R. P. (2007). The control-value theory of achievement emotions: An integrative approach to emotions in education. In P. A. Schutz & R. Pekrun (Eds.), *Emotions in education* (pp. 13–36). San Diego, CA: Academic Press.

Pekrun, R., Goetz, T., & Frenzel, A. C. (2005). *Achievement Emotions Questionnaire–Mathematics (AEQ-M). User's manual.* Department of Psychology, University of Munich, Munich, Germany.

Pekrun, R., Goetz, T., & Perry, R. P. (2005). *Achievement Emotions Questionnaire (AEQ). User's manual.* Department of Psychology, University of Munich, Munich, Germany.

Pekrun, R., Goetz, T., Perry, R. P., Kramer, K., & Hochstadt, M. (2004). Beyond test anxiety: Development and validation of the Test Emotions Questionnaire (TEQ). *Anxiety, Stress and Coping, 17*, 287–316.

Pekrun, R., Goetz, T., Titz, W., & Perry, R. P. (2002a). Positive emotions in education. In E. Frydenberg (Ed.), *Beyond coping: Meeting goals, visions, and challenges* (pp. 149–174). Oxford, England: Elsevier.

Pekrun, R., Goetz, T., Titz, W., & Perry, R. P. (2002b). Academic emotions in students' self-regulated learning and achievement: A program of quantitative and qualitative research. *Educational Psychologist, 37*, 91–106.

Pekrun, R., vom Hofe, R., Blum, W., Frenzel, A. C., Goetz, T. & Wartha, S. (2007). Development of mathematical competencies in adolescence: The PALMA longitudinal study. In M. Prenzel (Ed.), *Studies on the educational quality of schools* (pp. 17–37). Muenster, Germany: Waxmann.

Pekrun, R., & Hofmann, H. (1996, April). *Affective and motivational processes: Contrasting interindividual and intraindividual perspectives.* Paper presented at the annual meeting of the American Educational Research Association, New York.

Pekrun, R., & Schutz, P. A. (2007). Where do we go from here? Implications and future directions for inquiry on emotions in education. In P. A. Schutz & R. Pekrun (Eds.), *Emotions in education* (pp. 313–331). San Diego, CA: Academic Press.

Perry, R. P., Hladkyj, S., Pekrun, R. H., Clifton, R. A., & Chipperfield, J. G. (2005). Perceived academic control and failure in college students: A three-year study of scholastic attainment. *Research in Higher Education, 46*, 535–569.

Preckel, F., Zeidner, M., Goetz, T., & Schleyer, E. (2008). Female 'big fish' swimming against the tide: The 'big-fish-little-pond effect' and gender ratio in special gifted classes. *Contemporary Educational Psychology, 33*, 78–96.

Reisenzein, R. (2001). Appraisal processes conceptualized from a schema-theoretic perspective. In K. R. Scherer, A. Schorr, & T. Johnstone, T. (Eds.), *Appraisal processes in emotion* (pp. 187–201). Oxford, England: Oxford University Press.

Ruthig, J. C., Perry, R. P., Hall, N. C., & Hladkyj, S. (2004). Optimism and attributional retraining: Longitudinal effects on academic achievement, test anxiety, and voluntary course withdrawal in college students. *Journal of Applied Social Psychology, 34*, 709–730.

Sarason, I. G. (1981). Test anxiety, stress, and social support. *Journal of Personality, 49*, 101–114.

Scherer, K. R. (2000). Emotions as episodes of subsystems synchronization driven by nonlinear appraisal processes. In I. Granic & M. D. Lewis (Eds.), *Emotion, development, and self-organization: Dynamic systems approaches to emotional development* (pp. 70–99). New York: Cambridge University Press.

Scherer, K. R., Schorr, A., & Johnstone, T. (Eds.). (2001). *Appraisal processes in emotion.* Oxford, England: Oxford University Press.

Schutz, P. A., & Lanehart, S. L. (2002) (Eds.), Emotion in education [Special issue]. *Educational Psychologist, 37*, 67–134.

Schutz, P. A., & Pekrun, R. (Eds.). (2007). *Emotions in education.* San Diego, CA: Academic Press.

Spangler, G., Pekrun, R., Kramer, K., & Hofmann, H. (2002). Students' emotions, physiological reactions, and coping in academic exams. *Anxiety, Stress and Coping, 15*, 413–432.

Spielberger, C. D. (1980). *Test Anxiety Inventory: Preliminary professional manual.* Palo Alto, CA: Consulting Psychologist Press.

Stipek, D., Feiler, R., Daniels, D., & Milburn, S. (1995). Effects of different instructional approaches on young children's achievement and motivation. *Child Development, 66*, 209–223.

Stipek, D., Salmon, J. M., Givvin, K. B., Kazemi, E., Saxe, G., & MacGyvers, V. L. (1998). The value (and convergence) of practices suggested by motivation research and promoted by mathematics education reformers. *Journal of Research in Mathematics Education, 29*, 465–488.

Stoeber, J. (2004). Dimensions of test anxiety: Relations to ways of coping with pre-exam anxiety and uncertainty. *Anxiety, Stress and Coping, 17*, 213–226.

Titz, W. (2001). *Emotionen von Studierenden in Lernsituationen* [Students' emotions at studying]. Münster, Germany: Waxmann.

Turner, J. E., & Schallert, D. L. (2001). Expectancy-value relationships of shame reactions and shame resiliency. *Journal of Educational Psychology, 93*, 320–329.

Turner, J. E., & Waugh, R. M. (2007). A dynamical systems perspective regarding students' learning processes: Shame reactions and emergent self-organizations. In P. A. Schutz & R. Pekrun (Eds.), *Emotions in education* (pp. 125–145). San Diego, CA: Academic Press.

Valeski, T. N., & Stipek, D. J. (2001). Young children's feelings about school. *Child Development, 72*, 1198–1213.

Watson, D. (2002). Positive affectivity: The disposition to experience pleasurable emotional states. In C. R. Snyder & S. J. Lopez (Eds.), *Handbook of positive psychology* (pp. 106–119). New York: Oxford University Press.

Watt, H. M. G. (2004). Development of adolescents' self-perceptions, values, and task perceptions according to gender and domain in 7th- through 11-th grade Australian students. *Child Development, 75*, 1556–1574.

Watt, J. D., & Vodanovich, S. J. (1999). Boredom proneness and psychosocial development. *Journal of Psychology: Interdisciplinary and Applied, 133*, 303–314.

Wehrle, T., & Scherer, K. R. (2001). Toward computational modeling of appraisal theories. In K. R. Scherer, A. Schorr, & T. Johnstone (Eds.), *Appraisal processes in emotion* (pp. 350–365). New York: Oxford University Press.

Weiner, B. (1985). An attributional theory of achievement motivation and emotion. *Psychological Review, 92*, 548–573.

Weiner, B. (2007). Examining emotional diversity on the classroom: An attribution theorist considers the moral emotions. In P. A. Schutz & R. Pekrun (Eds.), *Emotions in education* (pp. 73–88). San Diego, CA: Academic Press.

Wine, J. D. (1971). Test anxiety and the direction of attention. *Psychological Bulletin, 76,* 92–104.

Wolters, C. A. (2003). Regulation of motivation: Evaluating an underemphasized aspect of self-regulation. *Educational Psychologist, 38,* 189–205.

Wyatt, S. (1930). The problem of monotony and boredom in industrial work. *Industrielle Psychotechnik, 7,* 114–123.

Zajonc, R. B. (1980). Feeling and thinking: Preferences need no inferences. *American Psychologist, 35,* 151–175.

Zeidner, M. (1998). *Test anxiety: the state of the art.* New York: Plenum.

Zeidner, M. (2007). Test anxiety in educational contexts: What I have learned so far. In P. A. Schutz & R. Pekrun (Eds.), *Emotions in education* (pp. 165–184). San Diego, CA: Academic Press.

27
Motivation and Learning Disabilities
Past, Present, and Future

Georgios D. Sideridis

If the LD field is to make important breakthroughs in coming years, it must avoid becoming insular and parochial. Individuals outside the LD field can bring fresh perspectives that allow us to see beyond the boundaries of our current frameworks and procedures. A key element missing in most works [that deal with definition, etiology, prevention, and treatment] is a sophisticated and systematic concept of human motivation. (Deci, 1986, p. 587)

In a recent report by the U.S. Department of Education (July, 2007), 4.1% of the kindergartners in the United States received some sort of special education services. As these students moved to higher grades the percentage receiving special education services increased to 5.4% (in Grade 1), 9.4% (in Grade 3), and 11.9% (in Grade 5). Learning disabilities (LD) affects about 10–15% of the general population, and represents one of the most important challenges in schooling today. The percentages are higher for boys, small town schools, and poorer schools. If the numbers of students with LD continues to grow, and the evaluation and intervention practices remain as they are today, how are these students going to meet the standards of high-stakes testing? Are we leading these students to failure?

Importance of Motivation for the Field of Learning Disabilities

There is ample empirical evidence that motivation strongly predicts students' with and without LD achievement (Adelman & Taylor, 1983, 1986), either in the form of antecedent forces that operate prior to and during an achievement situation (e.g., Antoniou & Sideridis, 2008) or as intervention elements that are built in specific interventions (e.g., Antoniou & Souvignier, 2007). As Wigfield and Guthrie (1997) pointed out in regard to reading: "…cold cognitive models cannot explain fully individuals' participation in activities such as reading" (p. 57) because reading is an effortful activity that involves the element of choice. They added that motivation and cognition need to be tied together in a unified theoretical framework (Eccles, Wigfield, & Shiefele, 1998; Wigfield, Eccles, Schiefele, Roeser, & Davis-Kean, 2006). In that regard, Wigfield (1997) presented a multidimensional approach to reading motivation that came out of quantitative and qualitative evidence with students. In Wigfield's work, motivation addresses three salient questions without which there can be literally no goal attainment: (a) "Can I do well?" which involves students' self-system (e.g., esteem and competence beliefs), (b) "Do I want to do well?" which reflects a motivational focus on the self (intrinsic motivation) or external causes (extrinsic motivation), and (c) "Why do I want to do well?" which captures students' achievement goals. Baker, Scher, and Mackler (1997) extended the motivational model of reading in students' homes by pointing to the fact that enjoyable reading activities increase students' motivation and ability and further added the moderating role of parents' beliefs and interest about reading. Others have attempted to examine how instructional contexts may be accountable for student's motivation and achievement (e.g., Guthrie et al., 1996; Karabenick, 2004; Linnenbrink, 2005). Research studies that examined the above three questions, across various settings, and for students with LD, are the primary focus of the present chapter.

Purpose

The purpose of the present chapter is to review the literature with regard to motivation and learning disabilities across various theoretical schemata, critique the relevant research works, and propose recommendations for the future. The chapter is organized along three axes. First, the disorder (LD) is defined and described using empirical means. Then, a review of the literature on motivation and learning disabilities for each theoretical view of motivation is presented. Last, methodological issues with regard to conducting research in learning disabilities are discussed along with relevant recommendations for future research.

Definitions, Conceptual Issues, and Challenges in Describing Learning Disabilities

With the origination of U.S. public law 94-142, also known as the Education of All Handicapped Children Act, in 1975, a law stating that students with disabilities should be educated in the least restrictive environment, the door was opened for the concepts of inclusion/integration/mainstreaming of students with disabilities in general education settings. This law also stated guidelines on how to provide the best services for students who needed them by use of a multi-disciplinary team who would plan an appropriate course of action for every student with a need. By that time, several definitions of learning disabilities had come out (Hammill, 1990), but the most prevalent one stated that: "The term 'specific learning disability' means those children who have a disorder in one or more of the basic psychological processes involved in understanding or using language, spoken or written, which disorder may manifest itself in imperfect ability to listen, think, speak, read, write, spell or perform mathematical computations. The term includes such conditions as perceptual handicaps, brain injury, minimal brain dysfunction, dyslexia and developmental aphasia. The term does not include a learning problem which is primarily the result of visual, hearing, or motor handicaps, of mental retardation, of emotional disturbance, or environmental, cultural, or economic disadvantage" (p.65083, PL 105-17; Federal Register, 1997). This definition has had its criticisms as it is deficient in at least two areas: (a) the absence of specific criteria regarding the discrepancy between a students' potential and his/her achievement, and (b) the absence of details on what causes the disorder (the definition describes what are not causes of learning disabilities).

From the above definition, it also is obvious that there is no mention of the contribution of motivational and emotional factors, although these characteristics have represented salient discriminating variables in a number of classification studies, and, at times, were more effective into classifying correctly students with LD compared to cognitive and metacognitive variables alone (Sideridis, Morgan, Botsas, Padeliadu, & Fuchs, 2006; Sideridis, Mouzaki, Simos, & Protopapas, 2006; Watkins, 2005). In fact, out of the more than 60 definitions of learning disabilities (Hammill, 1972) not one mentions motivation (Sabatino & Miller, 1979). Recently, experts from five countries, in addition to the United States, mentioned motivation and emotions as core features of learning disabilities (Sideridis, 2007a). The view that motivational and emotional factors are salient and core characteristics of learning disabilities is based on empirical findings as, by definition, learning disabilities *cannot* be the cause of low motivation or emotional factors (both represent exclusionary criteria). It is, however, a view that is shared among few researchers in the field of LD (e.g., Deci & Chandler, 1986; Sideridis et al., 2006). For example, as early as 1986, Deci and Chandler stated that: "What seems to us to be missing from the former (more theoretical) approach is the possibility that emotional and motivational variables are central to some (if not all) learning disabilities either as initial causes or as factors that exacerbate problems that are based in neurological deficits" (p. 587). Thus, there is also the view that learning disabilities may be better defined by inclusion of motivational and emotional factors, particularly given high misclassification rates when using the discrepancy model (i.e., discrepancy between potential as measured by an IQ test) and achievement (domain specific achievement, e.g., on reading).

To illustrate this point, Deci and Chandler (1986) reported results in which student comparisons between typical students ($n \sim 460$) and students with identified LD ($n = 40$) showed that the latter group had, on average, 14 points lower IQ. This finding certainly challenges the criteria employed by that school district, given that the definition of the disorder precludes low IQ as an identifying factor. Not only that, but at the beginning of the field, experts disagreed with regard to the criteria employed in defining learning disabilities. For example, Kirk, Senf, and Larsen, (1981) presented data from 1,250 experts on the field (teachers, psychologists, etc.) and the diversity of opinion was striking. Similar variability in responding about the attributes of the disorder was reported by Tucker, Stevens, and Ysseldyke (1983) in two studies involving a sample of 79 professionals in 1979 and 250 experts in 1981. Concerns in both studies were raised with regard to what constitutes discrepancy in functioning, the absence of empirical evidence regarding the viability of the criteria proposed in the definition, vagueness, and political correctness, among others.

The above concerns have been with the field of LD until today. For example, from early on, Frankenberger and Harper (1987) reported that states used different guidelines and, although in their second survey (1985/86) more states were using the discrepancy model (compared to 1981/82 results), 43% of states were not using any discrepancy criteria. That would be problematic had the discrepancy model been valid. However, Fletcher et al. (2001) reported that there was no difference in reading ability (as measured by CBM tests) between poor readers and LD students who demonstrated a significant discrepancy between potential and achievement. Thus, they questioned the validity of the discrepancy model, the only criterion mandated by the state (see also Elksnin et al., 2001; Morris, 1988). As if this was not the only problem, Schultz (1997) reported that use of the WJ-R IQ test resulted in a classification of 86% of a sample as having LD (based on 15 points of discrepancy), but the respective percentage when WISC-III was employed was only 48%. This finding puts into question the concurrent validity of the most widely used measures of potential, that of the WISC and W-J. Obviously, different measures would be associated with positive (by using the WISC) or negative (by using the W-J) biases in the identification of students as having LD, depending on the measure.

The identification of LD becomes even more complicated when dealing with specific learning disabilities, e.g., those related with math. For example, Fuchs et al. (2005) reported that attention problems contributed significantly more heavily in the identification of math disabilities compared to other, well-accepted, cognitive variables (similarly, Sideridis, in press, linked cognitive failures to the presence of attention problems). More problems were put forth by Watkins and his colleagues (Watkins, 1996, 2005; Watkins, Kush, & Glutting, 1997; Watkins, Kush, & Schaefer, 2002; Watkins & Worrell, 2000) who reported that various well-known and valid measures of students' potential (i.e., IQ) possessed little or no discriminatory power in differentiating students with LD from typical students (see also Ward, Ward, Glutting, & Hatt, 1999).

From the above, it is apparent that the field of LD is at a turning point. The existing definition of LD does not seem to work and research evidence suggests the need for a different, more enriched and more specific taxonomy. Additional deficits of individuals with LD reported in the empirical literature have been with regard to the presence of psychopathology (Gregg, Hoy, King, Moreland, & Jagota, 1992), social skills deficits (Kavale & Forness, 1996), psychosocial adjustment (Sorensen et al., 2003), behavioral and emotional problems (Handwerk, & Marshall, 1998), and family characteristics (e.g., Margalit and Heiman, 1986 reported high levels in parental anxiety and a more controlling home environment for children with LD compared to typical children). Two potential propositions may involve (a) expanding the range of inclusionary criteria for identification, and, (b) using multiple methods for identification (Sofie & Riccio, 2002). Large percentages of false positive or false negative cases have serious implications for students' lives as, assessments of learning disabilities start at an early age (first grades in elementary school) and the potential of stigma from misclassification is tremendous.

Motivation and Learning Disabilities: Review of the Literature

This section presents a review of the literature on studies that examined how motivation operates in the population of students with learning problems/disabilities. These studies stem from different theoretical perspectives on motivation, and thus, this section is organized by "theory." Initially a framework is described and it is followed by a review of the literature, specifically with regard to students with LD.

Rotter's Social Learning Theory and Weiner's Attribution Theory and Learning Disabilities Rotter's (1966) theory stated that thoughts and beliefs about the cause of success or reward can explain human behavior. He considered individuals as having *internal locus of control* if they thought that their own actions are responsible for specific outcomes and others as having an *external locus of control* if they thought that events and outcomes are non-contingent (and thus uncontrollable). Similarly, attribution theory originated in the work of Weiner (1985) who described a comprehensive framework based upon attributions of causality for success and failure. The theory mainly answers the question: "Why did I succeed or fail?" (Weiner, 1979, p. 3). Such attributional questions are the soul of the theoretical framework. These attributions relate strongly to Rotter's (1966) earlier concept of *locus of control*, which Weiner termed *locus of causality*. Weiner distinguished two types of causality, internal (e.g., ability) and external (e.g., luck). Within this dichotomy, Weiner added the concept of stability by distinguishing stable (e.g., typical effort) from unstable (e.g., mood) and controllable (e.g., effort) versus uncontrollable attributions (e.g., ability). This section will summarize research in the area of locus of causality and locus of control based on both the works of Rotter and Weiner, and both terms will be used interchangeably as they both convey very similar, conceptually, behaviors. Although there is a strong relationship between these two schemes and learned helplessness, the latter framework will be described independently in the next section.

The results regarding the causal attributions and locus of control of individuals with LD have been pretty clear and consistent, with a few exceptions. In a recent meta-analysis, Mamlin, Harris, and Case (2001) reported that in 19 out of the 22 studies reviewed between 1980 and 1996, students with LD had significantly elevated scores on external locus of control, compared to typical groups, with most studies being conducted with elementary school students. Thus, from that literature review the findings are compelling that students with LD tend to attribute their success to luck and their failure to lack of ability. Subsequent findings have confirmed these earlier findings. For example, Tabassam and Grainger (2002) classified attributions as positive or negative and reported that students with LD and with combined LD/ADHD had significantly lower scores on positive attributions and higher scores on negative attributions. Anderman (1998) used data from the National Education Longitudinal Study and reported significantly lower levels of perceived control (a related construct; see Skinner, 1995), for students with LD compared to a typical comparison group. Similar findings linking students with LD with external perceptions of control, low expectations and negative perceptions of ability have been reported by Chapman (1988a). Ring and Reetz (2002) reported that students with LD had significantly elevated scores on external attributions such as "luck," "teacher likes student," and "easy class" but also higher scores on internal attributions such as "skills," "effort," and "student likes subject." Thus, students with LD had higher scores across most constructs, both positive and negative. The conflicting findings across studies could be attributed to at least two reasons (a) heterogeneity in the population of students with LD and existence of subgroups (Kavale & Forness, 1987), and (b) invalidity of self-reports for students with LD (Graham & Harris, 1989). The latter cause is discussed in detail in the "methodological issues" section of this chapter. The former is discussed in the next paragraphs because it relates directly to research on locus of control.

Durrant (1993) investigated whether the presence of subgroups of elementary students with LD moderates the findings regarding locus of control and locus of causality. She compared the attribution of students with LD, students with LD that also had externalizing problems, and students with LD who had both internalizing and externalizing problems. Results indicated that students with LD plus internalizing and externalizing problems had significantly higher attributions regarding bad luck, compared to the LD only group. Also, the LD externalizing group made more external attributions compared to the LD only group. Thus, this study supports the "heterogeneity hypothesis" (Hallahan, Gajar, Cohen, & Tarver, 1978; Kavale & Forness, 1987) in that the LD population should be treated as several distinct groups rather than a large heterogeneous group.

Interestingly, compared to Rotter's (1966) view of the stable nature of locus of control, Weiner (1985) perceived attributions as characteristics that can change. For that purpose, based on the notion that attributions are malleable, several interventions have been targeted at modifying attributions with the hope that outcomes and behaviors will change. In an experimental study, Borkowski, Weyhing, and Carr (1988) taught LD students reading strategies with the addition of complex attributions, which involved student-experimenter dialogues about effort and the causes of academic failure. Results indicated that the experimental group, which was taught strategy instruction plus was trained on attributions, improved 50% more based on ratio scores in paragraph summarizing compared to only 15% of the participants in the strategy only condition. These effects are compelling with regard to the additional role of attributions and motivation in general in enhancing academic achievement outcomes.

The issue of changing attributions may be particularly important given research findings that pointed to the fact that attributions of students with LD were not different compared to the attributions of their parents (Kane-Lewis & Lawrence-Patterson, 1989). Thus, in addition to the explanation that causal attributions may reflect continuous failures and may be the outcome of a vicious cycle of failure and eventual helplessness, the findings from the Kane-Lewis and Lawrence-Patterson study suggest that a path that originates in the family may be accountable for the maladaptive attributions of students with LD. Consequently, interventions might be more effective if focused on changing the attributions of students at both the classroom level and at home.

An additional issue regarding attributions of students with LD comes from Seligman, Abramson, Semmel, and von Baeyer (1979). They suggested the presence of a depressive attributional style in which a generalized lack of control may lead to helplessness and then depression, because depression-prone individuals tend to attribute negative outcomes to stable and internal factors. The authors further demonstrated that the attributions of depressed people were unstable and external for good outcomes and stable and global for negative outcomes. Of relevance for understanding learning disabilities is that students with LD have reportedly high levels of depression (see meta-analysis by Maag & Reid, 2006; Sideridis, 2006a). For example, in the Sideridis (2006a) meta-analysis, elevated depression (at clinical or statistical levels) was reported in 88% of the reviewed studies. Thus, if students with LD have depression, they may also have an external locus of causality, which is clearly maladaptive with regard to motivation and achievement. If, on the other hand, students with LD hold external attributions, these attributions are likely associated with poor motivational and achievement outcomes and may be linked to helplessness and/or depression (Dykman, 1998; Sideridis, 2005a). Thus, causal attributions and external locus of control are strongly related to helplessness, which is the topic of the next section.

Learned Helplessness Theory and Learning Disabilities The concept of learned helplessness originated in the work of Seligman and his colleagues using animals (Diener & Dweck, 1978; Overmier, & Seligman, 1967) and later on humans (Klein, Fencil-Morse, & Seligman, 1976). Learned helplessness represents the inability to learn when one perceives that there is no relationship between his/her behavior and reinforcement (Overmier & Seligman, 1967). In other words, whenever a person feels that he/she has no control over a situation, motivational withdrawal is likely to lead to helpless responding (i.e., disengagement and task withdrawal). Klein et al. (1976) added that it is "the expectancy that responding will be ineffective [that] reduces the incentive to initiate instrumental responses and disrupts later learning of response-reinforcement contingencies" (p. 508). From the above, it is apparent that the relationship between causal attributions and helplessness is strong, which is why the original framework (Seligman, 1975) was modified and termed the attributional reformulation of learned helplessness (Abramson, Seligman, & Teasdale, 1978; Martin, Seligman, Abramson, Semmel, & Baeyer, 1979).

Given that helplessness results in the lack of initiating behaviors because of repeated failures, it makes inherent sense to test the existence of this phenomenon with students with LD who have failed repeatedly. Thomas (1979) suggested that the findings on learned helplessness parallel the findings in research in special education, as students with LD tend to no longer believe that they can learn and therefore, to not attempt to engage in problem solving. Swartz, Purdy, and Fullingim (1983) presented a list of 23 features of learned helplessness (e.g., passivity, withdrawal, defeatism, disorganization, lowered response initiation, etc.), which corresponded to empirical findings in the literature on characteristics of students with LD.

Wilgosh (1984) systematically examined the phenomenon of learned helplessness in elementary school girls with and without LD. Students were administered a failure task, which involved two solvable and six unsolvable puzzles. Students had to trace all lines without lifting their pencil. Results indicated that the girls with LD gave up significantly earlier compared to girls without LD as indicated by the overall amount of time spent with the puzzle. Nevertheless, although they spent less time overall, they attempted more puzzles than did the girls without LD, indicating that they spend less time with each puzzle. Following an experimental manipulation that involved training, differences between groups disappeared with the exception that girls with LD attempted fewer puzzles compared to the typical female group. Thus, this study reported encouraging findings from application of a training programme.

Cullen and Boersma (1982) also conducted an experimental study to alleviate the negative effects of helplessness following failure. Two groups of elementary students with and without LD were initially subjected to failure. Outcome measures involved performance but also attributions. Results indicated that in two out of the three conditions, the typical student group persisted significantly longer compared to the LD group. Salient between-group differences were observed with regard to attributions as well. With regard to attributions for failures and responses to the question "Why did you give up early?" 57% of the typical student group gave personal strategy reasons and the respective percentage for students with LD was only 27%. Similar responses to the question "Why did you have trouble solving the puzzle?" were reported, with responses reflecting personal strategy reasons mounting to 54% for the typical student group and only 19% for students with LD. In success attributions, typical students endorsed personal strategies and students with LD mentioned task difficulty as the main reason for that outcome.

Similarly, Butkowsky, and Willows (1980) examined differences between elementary students with and without LD across perceptions and attributions related to learned helplessness following administration of success and failure conditions. Results indicated that students of low reading ability had lower expectations for success, they persisted significantly less compared to typical students, and they attributed their failure to stable factors such as lack of ability. Valas (2001) took this line of research one step further by linking helplessness and attributions to depression (as suggested by the revised framework, Seligman et al., 1979) in a large sample of students with LD. Results, using a complex structural equation model, indicated that helplessness was predicted negatively by internal attributions and expectations. Depression was predicted directly from expectations (negatively) and self-esteem, and indirectly from helplessness (through its effects on self-esteem). This was the first study to present a multivariate test of the learned-helplessness model for students with LD. As in previous studies, the effects of gender were salient, with boys showing greater levels of helplessness. Similar findings that demonstrate helplessness in students with LD compared to typical student samples have been reported earlier (e.g., Thomas, 1979).

Nevertheless, different findings have been observed by Swartz et al. (1983) who also induced helplessness in two groups of students with and without LD. The results were unequivocal: Helplessness affected equally students with and without LD within the helpless group (the one that encountered an unsolvable task) showing significant deficits in motivation. Failure to find differences in the attributions or helpless responses of students with LD compared to typical students have been reported in several more instances (e.g., Aponik & Dembo, 1983; Hill & Hill, 1982; Pintrich, Anderman, & Klobucar, 1994). Why is the empirical literature less conclusive? Two obvious explanations may relate to the methodology of self-reported assessments and their validity, as students with LD may have inflated their judgments of competence and self (Graham, Harris, & Saddler, in press). Another explanation may be associated with the quality of engagement in achievement tasks. For example, effort withdrawal would be an indicator of helplessness or hopelessness and, at times, has been an attribute of students with LD. However, in a recent study, Sideridis (2006b) reported that students with LD felt obliged to engage in an academic activity (and they did engage as much as the typical students) but achieved much less because the quality of their engagement with the task was very questionable. Thus, there are several reasons (usually methodological) that likely account for the differences observed in the empirical literature.

In summary, several studies have demonstrated the presence of learned helplessness in students with LD, more so, than the absence of helplessness with this population. However, there are some inconsistencies in results across the different studies. Now let's turn to the application of self-determination theory to the study of the motivation in learning disabilities.

Self-Determination Theory and Learning Disabilities Self-determination theory (Deci & Ryan, 1985, 2000, this volume) originated in the 1970s as a humanistic approach to understanding human behavior. It was influenced by the classical motivational dichotomy of intrinsic versus extrinsic motivation but also the achievement motive from which some of the basic psychological needs were incorporated (need for autonomy, competence, and relatedness). The theory briefly posits that three basic psychological needs are the causal determinants of human action. These needs in turn guide behavior which can range from amotivated to intrinsically motivated, which in turn leads to self-determined actions. Specifically, Deci and Ryan (2000) described four processes that affect motivated behavior in unique ways which originate in extrinsic or intrinsic motivation (called organismic integration theory, Deci & Ryan, 1985). Four motivational processes originate in extrinsic motivation, namely: delete italics: (a) *external regulation* (b) *introjected regulation*, (c) *identified regulation*, and, (d) *integrated regulation*. *External regulation* occurs when an individual is engaged with an activity to gain rewards or avoid punishment. It is considered a maladaptive form of motivation being far from intrinsic motivation. *Introjected regulation* reflects voluntary involvement with an activity in which the person identifies its value, but doesn't fully accept its value. *Identified regulation*, on the other hand, occurs when an individual finds value in an activity but still is engaged with it for external reasons (important for parents, peers, etc.). The last form of external regulation, *integrated regulation*, involves full assimilation of the value of the activity with the self and thus, this type of regulation resembles intrinsic motivation. At the extreme of what constitutes adaptive regulation is *intrinsic motivation*, which involves engagement with an activity out of interest, enjoyment, inherent satisfaction, and the identification of value. Intrinsic regulation has been considered the most adaptive form of motivation.

There have not been a lot of studies stemming from this theory that have included LD students. In the studies that have been done, self-determination has been defined as a "...combination of knowledge skills and beliefs that enable a person to engage in goal directed, self-regulated, autonomous behaviour" (Field, Martin, Miller, Ward, & Wehmeyer, 1998, p. 2). Others have added the concepts of self-actualization, assertiveness, creativity, pride, and self-advocacy (Ward, 1992). In one study, Sands, Spencer, Gliner, and Swaim (1999) investigated the role of students' self-determination in predicting students' actions with a sample of 237 middle and high school individuals that predominantly had learning disabilities (60.8%) but also other handicapping conditions. The dependent variable comprised action taking which involved students' planning of goals, self-evaluation and self-adjustment. Self-determination was defined as students' sense of self-determination, autonomy, self-regulation empowerment, self-realization, self-worth and locus of control. Results indicated that the theoretical link between self-determination and action taking was not strongly supported with their sample. Although that link was significant, the authors chose to move to a statistically more parsimonious model, by constraining that parameter to have no contribution to action taking. Thus, self-determination was not predictive of action taking.

In another study, Durlak, Rose, and Bursuck (1994) used direct instruction to teach self-determination skills to adolescents with LD during transitions to middle school. Using a pre-post multiple-baseline design with eight adolescents, results showed that individuals acquired some aspects of self-determination, such as assertiveness and self-concept but not others such as self-awareness. No improvements in self-advocacy were observed. Similarly, Karvonen, Test, Wood, Browder, and Algozzine (2004) evaluated the effectiveness of six interventional programs that aimed to improve self-determination in students with and without learning and other disabilities. They found several instances in which students became autonomous, confident, and were able to self-regulate but several other negative instances in which training for self-determination was not effective. These findings, however, may have been a reflection of the implementation of the studies rather than the actual importance of the construct itself as issues of treatment fidelity and degree of student involvement were not dealt with systematically by all authors. The researchers suggested that more research is needed to evaluate both the outcomes of self-determination but also the processes that may lead to more successful self-determination.

Another explanation for this finding may lie on the fact that perceptions of self-determination may be distorted in LD students (as well as other self-perceptions in learning disabilities; see section on Methodological Issues). As Traynor (2007) reported from a qualitative study, females with LD perceived themselves as being self-determined, although they were missing from their descriptions some salient aspects of self-determination. For example, their self-knowledge was general and at times vague, and they had some difficulty in connecting their knowledge and skills with their goals. Nevertheless, self-determination in students with LD is at higher levels compared to other disability groups such as students with emotional disturbances (Carter, Lane, Pierson, & Glaeser, 2006).

An additional finding is that individuals with LD tend to perceive the school environment to dampen rather than foster self-determination. Traynor (2005) reported findings from a qualitative study in which students with LD cited instances of humiliation and embarrassment, which clearly lower feelings of self-determination. That study also highlighted the presence of psychopathology (such as depression), which also can be a strong negative predictor of self-determination but also achievement and adjustment at school (Maag & Reid, 2006).

Other outcomes also have been associated with autonomy in students with LD. Earlier work also looked at beliefs about autonomy in students with LD and confirmed its predictive validity with regard to academic achievement (Deci, Hodges, Pierson, & Tomassone, 1992). Deci et al. (1992) reported strong associations between LD students' autonomy and teacher's warmth. Furthermore, maternal support of autonomy was predictive of students' reading comprehension ability. Margalit and Shulman (1986) compared sixth and seventh graders with and without LD on their perceptions of autonomy. Results showed lower levels of autonomy for students with LD compared to typical peers, with accompanied high levels in anxiety. With regard to autonomy, students with LD had lower perceptions in 3 out of 4 autonomy scenaria (parent pressure, peer pressure, trauma pressure, but not obstacle pressure).

In summary, most of the self-determination theory-based research on learning disabilities has focused on the construct of self-reported self-determination, particularly during students' transition to adolescence. Thus, how self-determination theory and its broader range of constructs are predictive of the behaviour of individuals with LD still remains unanswered and is a direction for future research. More on issues of the "self" follows in the next section on self-efficacy as defined in Bandura's (1977) social learning theory.

Self-Efficacy, Self-Concept, and Learning Disabilities In Bandura's (1977) social learning theory the concept of self-efficacy plays a prominent role. Self-efficacy is defined as one's sense of capability to perform a skill (see also Harter, 1982; Harter, Whitesell, & Junkin, 1998; Smith & Nagle, 1995 for a similar conception). Bandura (1977) presented a model in which self-efficacy expectations create the conditions under which a human being will achieve his or her goals. He concluded that "Given appropriate skills and adequate incentives, efficacy expectations are a major determinant of people's choice of activities, how much effort they will expend, and of how long they will sustain effort in dealing with stressful situations" (p. 194).

Self-concept refers to a more global evaluation of the self (Shavelson, Hubner, & Stanton, 1976). In discussing self-concept, Shavelson et al. (1976) presented a multifaceted approach to self-concept by assessing self-perceptions across domains (e.g., math, language, social skills, etc.). Numerous studies confirmed Marsh's predictions with samples of students with and without learning disabilities (Baker & Wigfield, 1999; Cooley & Ayres, 1988; Bryan, 1986; Grolnick & Ryan, 1990; Lincoln & Chazan, 1979; Schunk, 1989).

With regard to perceptions of self-efficacy, Klassen (2002) conducted a meta-analysis in comparative and intervention studies that involved students with and without LD. Results indicated that, with some exceptions (e.g., Tabassam & Grainger, 2002), students with LD did not hold lower self-efficacy beliefs compared to their typical counterparts. They attributed this puzzling finding to the presence of overestimation of the self by students with LD and the miscalibration of the instruments used. For example, Alvarez and Adelman (1986) reported that perceptions of efficacy by elementary students with LD were inflated in 30% of the participants. They attributed this finding to the function of "self-protection" by students with LD who attempt to hide their difficulties from the public. Similar findings have been reported in various academic domains (e.g., Graham & Harris, 1989).

Two major meta-analyses were conducted on the issue of self-concept in students with LD by Chapman (1988a) and Bear, Minke, and Manning (2002) across two time points. They both concluded that students with LD perceive their academic ability less favorably compared to typical peers. Chapman (1988a) conducted a developmental analysis of students' with LD self-concepts and compared that to normative estimates. He concluded that students with LD hold stable perceptions of low competence by Grade 3, and those perceptions likely persist through adolescence, given that subsequent performance evaluations will likely be consistently negative. The difference between typical groups and students with LD were around 20% in terms of the general self concept (typical students were in the 50th percentile and students with LD at the 30th). Chapman concluded that although the students with LD held lower self-concepts compared to typical students, across scales, their mean scores were around the average in some of the scales. Thus, based on normative scores (e.g., in the Piers-Harris scale), the self-concepts of students with LD were not low, but just average. Furthermore, there were no significant differences in the self-concepts of students who were educated in general versus mainstreamed settings, although students with LD who were receiving remedial services held higher self-concepts compared to the same students who did not receive remedial instruction.

Bear et al. (2002) conducted a meta-analysis by excluding the studies involved in the Chapman (1988a) analysis, which resulted in a pool of 282 studies. Out of the 61 studies which were eventually included, the authors concluded that students with LD held significantly lower self concepts. All comparisons were significant in within-study contrasts, and ranged between –.22 and –.96 in effect size metric (in global self-worth and in spelling, respectively). The respective estimates when using normative evaluative standards ranged between –.03 and –.94 (in global self-worth and in reading, respectively). As in the Chapman (1998b) study, the authors failed to find any differences with regard to placement. With regard to age, younger students with LD held less favorable perceptions about themselves compared to older students with LD. Last, there were no differential effects for gender.

Interestingly, a number of researchers have attempted to modify the self-perceptions of LD students, such as their self-concepts and self-efficacy beliefs. Garcia and de Caso (2006) conducted an experimental study in which they trained students with LD to be more self-efficacious about their writing ability; consequently, their program was targeted at improving writing ability first. Using a 10-session program, the authors demonstrated significant gains in writing self-efficacy and in writing, as demonstrated by higher scores in 24 out of 28 indicators of writing success, compared to the comparison group students who followed the general education curriculum for their grade. Similar results were reported by Schunk and Rice (1993) with regard to reading. The latter authors applied a cognitive strategy program with feedback to students with reading deficits and were able to improve their reading comprehension and reading efficacy significantly. In the same domain, Nelson and Manset-Williamson (2006) employed an explicit self-regulatory strategy programme to students with reading disabilities from grades 4 through 8 and compared it to a guided reading programme. Results indicated improvements in students' self-efficacy using the guided reading programme. All three studies were successful in changing feelings of self-efficacy by first changing students' skills, which is the obvious key to changing perceptions of efficacy (see also Metlzer, Katzir, Miller, Reddy, & Roditi, 2004). For an excellent model on enhancing the reading ability of at-risk students using goal setting and guided practice, see Margolis and McCabe (2004). The discussion of goal setting continues below with the description of achievement goal theory and goal orientations.

Achievement Goal Theory and Learning Disabilities Achievement goal theory involves constructs from various theoretical frameworks. Initially it was influenced from the "achievement motive" tradition (MacClelland, Atkinson, Clark, & Lowell, 1953; Atkinson, 1974), helplessness theory (Seligman, 1975) and attributions theory (Weiner, 1979). In the dual motive form (Dweck & Leggett, 1988), two goal orientations were described that were associated with unique patterns of self-regulation, experiential, and achievement outcomes (see also Wentzel, 1989). Performance goals in which the focus was extrinsic, (i.e., reinforcement came from outperforming others) and mastery goals with an intrinsic focus (i.e., reinforcement came from within—intrinsic motivation), in which individuals engaged in an activity out of interest and enjoyment. When individuals held the belief that intelligence was a fixed entity (i.e., one is either smart or not smart) and they adopted performance goals, the end result was self-regulation failure, negative affectivity, and low achievement (which is why Dweck termed these individuals as "helpless"). On the contrary, individuals who thought that intelligence was a malleable entity usually adopted mastery goals, and the associated outcomes were effective self-regulation and positive achievement gains with collaterally positive affect. Achievement goal theory has since then adopted performance avoidance goals, in which the focus is on avoiding demonstrating low ability compared to others (Elliot & Harackiewicz, 1996).

Results, with regard to the application of achievement goal theory in learning disabilities, have been inconclusive. For example, Fulk, Brigham, and Lohman (1998) reported that there were no differences between students with and without LD across mastery and performance goals. The only differences observed were with regard to task avoidance goals in favor of the LD group (similar findings with regard to task avoidance goals were reported by Bouffard & Couture, 2003). Others have reported significant between-groups differences. For example, Carlson, Booth, Shin, and Canu (2002) and Sideridis (2005b) reported significantly lower levels in mastery goals for elementary students with LD/ADHD compared to typical students across four measures of goals, and significantly elevated scores in performance goals. Higher percentages of students with ADHD reporting performance goals were also reported in Dunn and Shapiro (1999) and the opposite was observed by Barron, Evans, Baranik, Serpell, and Buvinger (2006), and Botsas and Padeliadu (2003). On the contrary, Bouffard and Couture (2003) reported higher levels in performance goals for the high achieving, typical student group, compared to medium and low achieving groups of students. Thus, with regard to one adoption of goals, students with LD have endorsed all possible combinations of goals. What may be of more interest, however, is how these goals have influenced specific processes.

Sideridis (2005b) examined the relationship between goal orientations and constructs from the theory of planned behaviour, a social cognitive model in which attitudes, subjective norms and perceived control are predictive of intentions to achieve and, then in turn, intentions are predictive of actual behavior. Results indicated that the b-weights linking performance-approach goals to attitudes were positive and significant for both groups, but more pronounced for the LD group (Study 1). Similar significant positive effects were reported in the relationship between performance goals and the "intention to achieve," and these effects were again more pronounced for the LD group. Thus, performance approach goals appeared to have positive effects with regard to the regulation of students' with LD behavior in achievement situations. Positive effects of mastery approach goals and academic achievement, positive affect, engagement, have also been reported in other studies (Sideridis, 2003, 2007b).

Recently, achievement goal theory took an interesting turn towards exploring goal-oriented environments that may be accelerators of students' motivation and achievement. As Lepola, Salonen, Vauras, and Poskiparta (2004) stated it is fruitless to look for underachievement in students' dispositions and motivation only. One needs to look at those characteristics within the educational context "in which they are interactively formed" (p. 181). Thus, the mastery/performance dichotomy has been "transferred" to the classroom level and evaluations of classrooms now involve elements of the two goal constructs (Ames, 1992; Karabenick, 2004; Wolters, 2004; Urdan, 2004a). With regard to students with LD, Sideridis (2005c) presented a three-level hierarchical model in which students' behavior over time was nested between group characteristics (typical vs. LD), and those latter attributes were nested within classroom climates. Results indicated that performance goal structures were particularly maladaptive for students with LD with regard to positive affect and active engagement in their classroom (in Study 1). A mastery goal structure was particularly adaptive with regard to reinforcement (i.e., can you give an example of what is meant by reinforcement?) across both groups of students (Study 2). Given the interactionist perspective of goal orientations presented by Barron and Harackiewicz (2001), a combined mastery and performance motivational discourse was associated with significantly more positive effects, compared to the effects of each linear term, with regard to positive affect, negative affect, and engagement.

Sideridis (2007c) replicated the 2005 findings with regard to the positive relationship between a mastery goal structure and positive affect and extended this work to evaluate the "matching hypothesis" (Linnenbrink, 2005). According to the "matching" (vs. buffering hypothesis), when one's goal orientation "meets" the respective goal structure in the classroom (i.e., a student with a mastery goal meeting a mastery goal structure), the effects of that matching on students' motivation and achievement are expected to be more pronounced. Results for students with LD indicated that matching mastery goals with a mastery goal structure was associated positively with positive affect, perceptions of reinforcement, and engagement and negatively with boredom. Similar effects were reported for the typical student group. In a recent study (Sideridis, Protopapas, Mouzaki, & Simos, 2008), comparisons were made between the two matched terms (mastery goals/mastery goal structure vs. performance goals/performance goal structure). Results indicated that the matching of mastery goals with a mastery goal structure was associated with significantly improved academic gains compared to the matching of performance goals with performance goal structures. Thus, it is not the matching per se, but the quality of the motives that are matched. It is suggested that this line of research is interesting and may provide valuable suggestions on how to intervene and elevate the achievement and motivation of students with learning problems.

From the above it is apparent that motivation plays a significant role in the academic experience of students with LD. In most studies, motivational constructs play a salient role in learning disabilities (either by differentiating students with LD from other students or in predictions) and at times (with regard to prediction) are more significant determinants of academic achievement. Thus, it is important to work on how to incorporate this knowledge base into instructional programs? in order to enhance the academic achievement of students with LD.

Methodological Issues in Research on Motivation and Learning Disabilities

There are conceptual, methodological, and statistical considerations in motivational research on learning disabilities that have implications for the quality and validity of our research reports. These issues are described in detail below.

Conceptual Issues: Linear versus Curvilinear Relationships In at least two theoretical schemes, namely the achievement motive and achievement goal theory, the relationship between specific motives and achievement is expected to be curvilinear. As Atkinson (1974) nicely put it with regard to achievement motivation: "I believe it is rather nonsensical routinely to run product-moment correlations (which tell us only the degree of linear relationship) between every possible measure of motivation and/or performance ... The solution will most probably involve a triple interaction involving the nature of the task, the motives of the individual, and the incentive character of the work situation" (p. 217). This theoretical expectation has rarely been tested in current empirical studies in the context of achievement goal theory. For example, Sideridis (2003) examined the curvilinear hypothesis in samples of students with and without LD with regard to the relationship between performance goals and achievement using a path model and reported that curvilinear effects were present, statistically significant, and larger in magnitude compared to linear effects. However, it may be important to capture that change using dynamic designs in which change in motivation and achievement are assessed concurrently and in real time. Sideridis (2007d), using a typical student sample, assessed how physiological arousal would change over time as a function of different goal orientations. By applying quadratic models (as suggested by the achievement motive literature), results pointed to significant quadratic effects across all goal orientations, with the most prominent being with regard to mastery avoidance goals. Other types of non-linear models (e.g., Rasch, 1980) have also been applied to examine the regulation that is the outcome of adopting performance goals (Sideridis, 2007e) and may aid our understanding of the functioning of these motives.

Methodological Issues: Inflated or Distorted Participant Responding The fact that students with LD report exaggerated or invalid judgements of their efficacy and other perceptions has been a major concern in this line of research (Kistner, Haskett, White, & Robbins, 1987). For example, Kistner et al. (1987) compared teacher and student ratings and concluded that some students with LD had unrealistically positive perceptions of themselves. Such inflated judgements are likely responsible for the lack in finding significant differences between students with LD and typical students, in occasions when that was expected (e.g., on judgments about self-efficacy). For example, Graham, Schwartz, and MacArthur (1993) reported that students with LD were overconfident with regard to their ability in writing. When assessing the self-efficacy of students aged 10–14 years, the authors reported that students with LD had similar perceptions of self-efficacy across various writing tasks when compared with their peers who had higher ability in writing. If this finding is true, then one would expect positive effects (e.g., enhanced persistence) for students high on self-efficacy, unless this overconfidence leads to the allocation of fewer resources (Graham et al., in press).

Another scenario with regard to presenting inflated judgements about the self may be rooted to students' unwillingness to accept their incapability (Sawyer, Graham, & Harris, 1992), and thus, this inflation may serve a "self-protective" function. Similarly, positive biases on students' with LD self-reports have been evidenced earlier (Bear & Minke, 1996). Furthermore, Sideridis, Ageriadis, Irakleous, Siakalli, and Georgiou (2006) reported that students with LD distorted reality as their perception of their classroom's motivational discourse was significantly different (actually on the opposite direction) from that rated by independent observers. For example, a mastery goal structure was rated as being performance and the opposite. This finding did not hold for typical students. Such effects likely distort the research literature and we have literally no way of knowing which findings represent valid reports and which reflect exaggerated ones. The employment of qualitative methods, in addition to quantitative measurements, may help researchers improve the validity of their samples' ratings, along with the employment of multiple methods (Urdan, 2004b).

Other methodological concerns in studies assessing motivational constructs with students with LD were put forth by Mamlin et al. (2001). The authors attempted to meta-analyse all studies related to locus of control with this specific population. Among methodological errors, the authors reported: (a) absence of description of participants (e.g., as having specific reading disabilities), which makes generality of the findings to the respective population impossible; (b) existence of variable identification criteria; (c) the presence of comorbidity; (d) the lack in reporting reliability of the measures; (e) the absence of normative data to allow direct comparisons with the population; (f) absence of descriptive statistics of the measures; and (g) absence in reporting administration conditions. Given that these methodological shortcomings were present in a large number of studies (e.g., reliability of the measures was reported in only one study), the effects reported in those studies are, the least to say, questionable. Chapman (1988a) also presented concerns with the assessment of self-concepts as it related to the validity of the scales used, whereas Bear et al. (2002) presented some concerns regarding the positive bias induced by some measures of the self.

Statistical Issues: Power of the Statistical Tests with Small Samples As is evident with this specific population, studies involving students with LD often involve small samples. Small samples are associated with large standard error estimates and, given that standard errors comprise the denominator of fractions that are associated with statistics, large denominators are linked to small effects for a given numerator. Small statistical estimates are linked to large p-values and, likely, Type-II errors. Type-II errors are a function of low power, which reflects the probability of identifying significant effects when these exist in the population (Cohen, 1992; Onwuegbuzie, Levin, & Leach, 2003). The effects of low power can be devastating. For example, Sideridis (1999) conducted a power analysis for a study which concluded that there were no differences between students with dyslexia and typical students in reading, spelling and phonological tasks. Power analysis indicated that the probability to identify significant effects of medium size ranged between 1% and 63%. Thus, no comparison had adequate levels of power. An analysis of the actual difference between groups indicated that in 5 out of the 6 comparisons, effect sizes were larger than medium, given Cohen's suggestions. Power analysis may become particularly cumbersome for analyses involving latent variables or hierarchical models, because estimation of the respective parameter is more difficult. However, it is an important necessity in our research. Alternatives to statistical significance given low power are available as they are unaffected by sample size (e.g., Good, 2005; Killeen, 2005).

Other statistical problems encountered when reviewing the literature on motivation and learning disabilities were related to: (a) analyses in which no adjustment was made for family-wise error rates, (b) decisions on the efficiency of modelling based on number of iterations for convergence, and (c) cyclical thinking in that independent and dependent variables were, in some form, related. Those judgements may have had serious effects on the "behavior" of the statistical estimates, plus the fact that most findings could likely be Type-II errors. Certainly, attention to the internal validity of study designs? is needed in order to avoid errors of the past and improve the way we conduct research in the future.

Summary

One conclusion of the present synthesis is that in some cases, the research findings are inconclusive. For example, there is overwhelming evidence regarding the presence of external locus of control in students with LD, but not the presence of helplessness. Inconsistency appears also with regard to goal orientations. Nevertheless, if we try to summarize these research findings, we would rather take the stand that students with LD have external locus of control and are low on self-efficacy and, whenever they are motivated, they do so using maladaptive motivational means.

An interesting question that evolves from this synthesis is: "What does a student with LD face at school?" Figure 27.1 presents a hypothetical scenario of a student with a need for competence (a basic psychological need), who approaches a task having a performance approach or performance avoidance goal orientation, holds external attributions for success but internal and stable attributions for failure, has low self-esteem, lacks persistence, and eventually fails. If we think of this hypothetical cycle being repeated again and again, we may think that helplessness is a property of students with learning disabilities. Any person who would experience repeated failures, as the students with LD experience, will most likely have the same behaviors and outcomes. The purpose here is not to provide a pessimistic picture of students with LD but to put into perspective a likely experience that may take place every day for this population. Another implication from the research synthesis above is that, in most cases, researchers did not conduct a full evaluation of the theoretical frameworks but tested some aspects of these theories. Thus, there is great need to inform practice by testing these theories as a whole and even integrate them

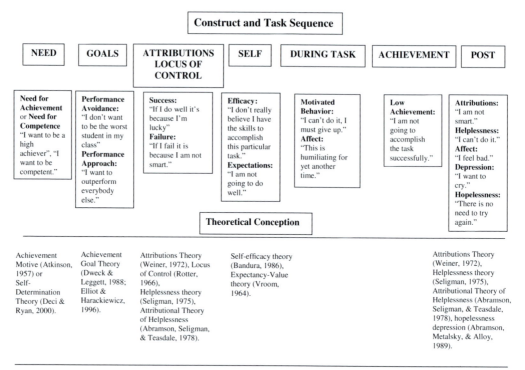

Figure 27.1 Hypothetical thoughts of what goes through the mind of a student with learning disabilities during an achievement situation.

to enrich our understanding of functional relationships between students' behaviors, classroom environments, and achievement.

Recommendations for Future Research

The above research synthesis also points to the fact that most research in learning disabilities involving motivation is descriptive and correlational. Although there is a good deal of information regarding the role and function of several motivational constructs, very little or no research has been developed to change, modify, or alter motivation with the aim of enhancing academic achievement. This is not specific to the LD field, however. For example, a great amount of research has been published on achievement goal theory, yet, there is no specific intervention designed to change students' goal orientations. Although research on classroom environments adds knowledge concerning the relationship between various classroom settings and students' engagement and achievement, we still don't have a specific set of interventions from those findings. I can only hope that the next years of research will put an emphasis on interventions that will improve the learning conditions of students with LD.

Conclusions

What has been most striking from the above research synthesis is the fact that experts in the field of learning disabilities have been long advocating for a stronger consideration of the role of motivation in LD students' functioning at school. Research evidence suggests that whenever interventions involve elements of motivation, improvements are tremendous (e.g., Garcia & de Caso, 2004). For example, in a recent meta-analysis of the single-subject literature involving students with LD, the two most effective interventions with regard to improving fluency were based on motivation (goal setting, plus feedback, and reinforcement/goal setting plus feedback; Morgan & Sideridis, 2006). Nevertheless, we are still at the same point we were 20 years ago, still advocating for the importance of motivation in learning disabilities. Let's just hope that 20 more years will not go by before the field acknowledges and incorporates motivation into the curriculum.

References

Abramson, L. Y., Metalsky, G. I., & Alloy, L. B. (1989). Hopelessness depression: A theory-based subtype of depression. *Psychological Review, 96,* 358–372.

Abramson, L., Y., Seligman, M. E. P., & Teasdale, J. D. (1978). Learned helplessness in humans: Critique and reformulation. *Journal of Abnormal Psychology, 87,* 49–74.

Adelman, H. S., & Taylor, L. (1986). The problems of definition and differentiation and the need for a classification schema. *Journal of Learning Disabilities, 19,* 514–520.

Alvarez, A., & Adelman, H. S. (1986). Overstatements of self-evaluations by students with psychoeducational problems. *Journal of Learning Disabilities, 19,* 567–571.

Ames, C. (1992). Classrooms: Goals, structures, and student motivation. *Journal of Educational Psychology, 84,* 261–271.

Anderman, E.M. (1998). The middle school experience: Effects on the math and science achievement of learning disabled adolescents. *Journal of Learning Disabilities. 31,* 128–138.

Antoniou, F., & Sideridis, G. D. (2008). Prediction of reading comprehension, reading interest and reading efficacy from teaching styles and classroom climate: A multilevel random coefficient modeling analysis for students with learning disabilities. *Advances in Learning and Behavioral Disabilities, 21,* 223–251.

Antoniou, F., & Souvignier, E. (2007). Strategy instruction in reading comprehension: An intervention study for students with learning disabilities. *Learning Disabilities: A Contemporary Journal, 5,* 41–57.

Aponik, D. A., & Dembo, M. H. (1983). LD and normal adolescents' causal attributions of success and failure at different levels of task difficulty. *Learning Disability Quarterly, 6,* 31–39.

Atkinson, J. W. (1974). The mainsprings of achievement oriented activity. In J. Atkinson & J. Raynor (Eds.), *Motivation and achievement* (pp. 13–41). New York: Wiley.

Baker, L., Scher, D., & Mackler, K. (1997). Home and family influences on motivations for reading. *Educational Psychologist, 32,* 69–82.

Baker, L., & Wigfield, A. (1999). Dimensions of children's motivation for reading and their relations to reading activity and reading achievement. *Reading Research Quarterly, 34,* 452–457.

Bandura, A., (1977). Self-efficacy: Toward a unifying theory of behavioral change. *Psychological Review, 84,* 191–215.

Bandura, A. (1986). *Social foundations of thought and action: A social cognitive theory.* Englewood Cliffs, NJ: Prentice Hall.

Barron, K., Evans, S. W., Baranik, L. E., Serpell, Z. N., & Buvinger, E. (2006). Achievement goals of students with ADHD. *Learning Disability Quarterly, 29,* 137–158.

Barron, K., & Harackiewicz, J. (2001). Achievement goals and optimal motivation: Testing multiple goal models. *Journal of Personality and Social Psychology, 80,* 706–722.

Bear, G. G., & Minke, K. M. (1996). Positive bias in maintenance of self-worth among children with LD. *Learning Disability Quarterly, 19,* 23–32.

Bear, G. G., & Minke, K. M., & Manning, M. A. (2002). Self-concept of students with learning disabilities: A meta-analysis. *School Psychology Review, 31,* 405–427.

Borkowski, J. G., Weyhing, R. S., & Carr, M. (1988). Effects of attributional retraining on strategy-based reading comprehension in learning-disabled students. *Journal of Educational Psychology, 80,* 46–53.

Botsas, G., & Padeliadu, S. (2003). Goal orientation and reading comprehension strategy use among students with and without reading difficulties. *International Journal of Educational Research, 39,* 477–495.

Bouffard, T., & Couture, N. (2003). Motivational profile and academic achievement among students enrolled in different schooling tracks. *Educational Studies, 29,* 19–38.

Bryan, T. H. (1986). Self-concept and attributions of the learning disabled. *Learning Disabilities Focus, 1,* 82–89.

Butkowsky, I. S. & Willows, D. M. (1980). Cognitive-motivational characteristics of children varying in reading ability: Evidence for learned helplessness in poor readers. *Journal of Educational Psychology, 72,* 408–422.

Carlson, C. L., Booth, J. E., Shin, M., & Canu, W. H. (2002). Parent-, teacher-, and self-rated motivational styles in ADHD subtypes. *Journal of Learning Disabilities, 35,* 104–113.

Carter, E. W., Lane, K. L., Pierson, M. R., & Glaeser, B. (2006). Self-determination skills and opportunities of transition-age youth with emotional disturbance and learning disabilities. *Exceptional Children, 72,* 333–346.

Chapman, J. W. (1988a). Learning disabled children's self-concepts. *Review of Educational Research, 58,* 347–371.

Chapman, J. W. (1988b). Cognitive-motivational characteristics and academic achievement of learning disabled children: A longitudinal analysis. *Journal of Educational Psychology, 80,* 357–365.

Cohen, J. (1992). A power primer. *Psychological Bulletin, 112,* 155–159.

Cooley, E. J., & Ayres, R. R. (1988). Self-concept and success-failure attributions of nonhandicapped students and students with learning disabilities. *Journal of Learning Disabilities, 21,* 174–178.

Cullen, J. L., & Boersma, F. J. (1982). The influence of coping strategies on the manifestation of learned helplessness. *Contemporary Educational Psychology, 7,* 346–356.

Deci, E. L., & Chandler, C. L. (1986). The importance of motivation for the future of the LD field. *Journal of Learning Disabilities, 19,* 587–594.

Deci, E. L., Hodges, R., Pierson, L., & Tomassone, J. (1992). Autonomy and competence as motivational factors in students with learning disabilities and emotional handicaps. *Journal of Learning Disabilities, 25,* 457–471.

Deci, E. L., & Ryan, R. M. (1985). *Intrinsic motivation and self-determination in human behavior.* New York: Plenum.

Deci, E. L., & Ryan, R. M. (2000). The 'what' and 'why' of goal pursuits: Human needs and the self-determination of behavior. *Psychological Inquiry, 11,* 227–268.

Diener, C. I., & Dweck, C. S. (1978). An analysis of learned helplessness: Continuous changes in performance, strategy, and achievement cognitions following failure. *Journal of Personality and Social Psychology, 36,* 451–462.

Dunn, P. B., & Shapiro, S. K. (1999). Gender differences in the achievement goal orientations of ADHD children. *Cognitive Therapy and Research, 23,* 327–344.

Durlak, C., Rose, E., & Bursuck, W. (1994). Preparing high school students with learning disabilities for the transition to postsecondary education. *Journal of Learning Disabilities, 27,* 51–60.

Durrant, J. E. (1993). Attributions for achievement outcomes among behavioral subgroups of students with learning disabilities. *Journal of Special Education, 27,* 306–320.

Dweck, C. S. (1986). Motivational processes affecting learning. *American Psychologist, 41,* 1040–1048.

Dweck, C. S., & Leggett, E. L. (1988). A social-cognitive approach to motivation and personality. *Psychological Review, 95,* 256–273.

Dykman, B. M. (1998). Integrating cognitive and motivational factors in depression: Initial tests of a goalorientation approach. *Journal of Personality and Social Psychology, 74,* 139–158.

Eccles, J. S., Wigfield, A., & Schiefele, U. (1998). Motivation to succeed. In W. Damon (Series Ed.) & N. Eisenberg (Vol. Ed.), *Handbook of child psychology* (5th ed., Vol. III, pp. 1017–1095). New York: Wiley.

Elksnin, L. K., Bryant, D., Gartland, D., King-Sears, M., Ronseberg, M., Scanlon, D., et al. (2001). LD summit: Important issues for the field of learning disabilities. *Learning Disability Quarterly, 24,* 297–305.

Elliot, A. J., & Harackiewicz, J. M. (1996). Approach and avoidance achievement goals and intrinsic motivation: A mediational analysis. *Journal of Personality and Social Psychology, 70,* 461–475.

Elliot, A. J. (1999). Approach and avoidance motivation and achievement goals. *Educational Psychologist, 34,* 169–189.

Federal Register. (1977). Washington, DC: U. S. Government Printing Office.

Field, S., Martin, J., Miller, R., Ward, M., & Wehmeyer, M. (1998). *A practical guide for teaching self-determination.* Reston, VA: Council for Exceptional Children.

Fletcher, J. M., Lyon, G. R., Barnes, M., Stuebing, K. K., Francis, D. J., Olson, R. K., et al. (2001). *Classification of learning disabilities: An evidence-based evaluation.* Paper presented at the 2001 Learning Disabilities Summit-Building a Foundation for the Future. Executive summary retrieved October 2, 2001, from http://www.air.org/ldsummit

Frankenberger, W., & Harper, J. (1987). States' criteria and procedures for identifying learning disabled children: A comparison of 1981/82 and 1985/86 guidelines. *Journal of Learning Disabilities, 20,* 118–121.

Fuchs, L. S., Compton, D. L., Fuchs, D., Paulsen, K., Bryan, J. D., & Hamlett, G. L. (2005). The prevention, identification and cognitive determinants of math difficulty. *Journal of Educational Psychology, 97,* 493–513.

Fulk, B. M., Brigham, F. J., & Lohman, D. A. (1998). Motivation and self-regulation: A comparison of students with learning and behavior problems. *Remedial and Special Education, 19,* 300–309.

Garcia, J. J., & de Caso, A. M. (2004). Effects of a motivational intervention for improving the writing of children with learning disabilities. *Learning Disability Quarterly, 27,* 141–159.

Garcia, J. J., & de Caso, A. M. (2006). Changes in writing self-efficacy and writing products and processes through specific training in the self efficacy beliefs of students with learning disabilities. *Learning Disabilities: A Contemporary Journal, 4,* 1–27.

Good, P. I. (2005). *Introduction to statistics through resampling methods and microsoft excel.* Hoboken, NJ: Wiley.

Graham, S., & Harris, K. (1989). Components analysis of cognitive strategy instruction: Effects on learning disabled students' compositions and self-efficacy. *Journal of Educational Psychology, 81,* 353–361.

Graham, S., Harris, K., & Saddler, B. (in press). Teaching students with learning disabilities to be smarter writers: Self-regulated strategy development. In G. D. Sideridis & T. A. Citro (Eds.), *Classroom management and learning strategies for struggling learners.* Lanham, MD: Rowman & Littlefield.

Graham, S., Schwartz, S., & MacArthur, C. (1993). Knowledge of writing and the composing process, attitude toward writing, and self-efficacy for students with and without learning disabilities. *Journal of Learning Disabilities, 26,* 237–249.

Gregg, N., Hoy, C., King, M., Moreland, C., & Jagota, M. (1992). The MMPI-2 profile of adults with learning disabilities in university and rehabilitation settings. *Journal of Learning Disabilities, 20,* 386–395.

Grolnick, W. S., & Ryan, R. M. (1990). Self-perceptions, motivation, and adjustment in children with learning disabilities: A multigroup group comparison study. *Journal of Learning Disabilities, 23,* 177–184.

Guthrie, J. T., Van Meter, P., McCann, A., Wigfield, A., Bennett, L., Poundstone, C., et al. (1996). Growth of literacy engagement: Changes in motivations and strategies during concept-oriented reading instruction. *Reading Research Quarterly, 31*, 306–333.

Hallahan, D. P., Gajar, A. H., Cohen, S. B., & Tarver, S. G. (1978). Selective attention and locus of control in learning disabled and normal children, *Journal of Learning Disabilities, 11*, 47–52.

Hammill, D. (1972). Training visual perception processes. *Journal of Learning Disabilities, 5*, 552–559.

Hammill, D. D. (1990). On defining learning disabilities: An emerging consensus. *Journal of Learning Disabilities, 23*, 74–84.

Handwerk, M. L., & Marshall, R. M. (1998). Behavioral and emotional problems of students with learning disabilities, serious emotional disturbance, or both conditions. *Journal of Learning Disabilities, 31*, 327–338.

Harter, S. (1982). The perceived competence scale for children. *Child Development, 53*, 87–97.

Harter, S., Whitesell, N. R., & Junkin, L. J. (1998). Similarities and differences in domain-specific global self-evaluations of learning-disabled, behaviorally disordered, and normally achieving adolescents. *American Educational Research Journal, 35*, 653–680.

Hill, C., & Hill, K. (1982). Achievement attributions of learning-disabled boys. *Psychological Reports, 51*, 979–982.

Kane-Lewis, S., & Lawrence-Peterson, E. (1989). Locus of control of control of children with learning disabilities and perceived locus of control by significant others. *Journal of Learning Disabilities, 22*, 255-257.

Karabenick, S. A. (2004). Perceived achievement, goal structure and college student help-seeking. *Journal of Educational Psychology, 96*, 569–581.

Karvonen, M., Test, D. W., Wood, W. M., Browder, D., & Algozzine, B. (2004). Putting self-determination into practice. *Exceptional Children, 71*, 23–41.

Kavale, K. A., & Forness, S. R. (1987). The far side of heterogeneity: A critical analysis of empirical subtyping research in learning disabilities. *Journal of Learning Disabilities, 20*, 374–382.

Kavale, K. A., & Forness, S. R. (1996). Social skill deficits and learning disabilities: A meta analysis. *Journal of Learning Disabilities, 29*, 226–237.

Killeen, P. R. (2005). An alternative to null-hypothesis significance tests. *Psychological Science, 16*, 345–353.

Kirk, S. A., Berry, P. B., & Senf, G. M. (1979) A survey of attitudes concerning learning disabilities. *Journal of Learning Disabilities, 12*, 239-245.

Kistner, J., Haskett, M., White, K., & Robbins, F. (1987). Perceived competence and self-worth of ld and normally achieving students. *Learning Disability Quarterly, 10*, 37–44.

Klassen, R. (2002). A question of calibration: A review of the self-efficacy beliefs of students with learning disabilities. *Learning Disability Quarterly, 25*, 88–102.

Klein, D. C., Fencil-Morse, E., & Seligman, M. E. P. (1976). Depression, learned helplessness, and the attribution of failure. *Journal of Personality and Social Psychology, 85*, 11–26.

Lepola J., Salonen, P., Vauras, M., & Poskiparta, E. (2004). Understanding the development of subnormal performance in children from a motivational-interactionist perspective. *International Review of Research in Mental Retardation, 28*, 145–189.

Lincoln, A., & Chazan, S. (1979). Perceived competence and intrinsic motivation in learning disability children. *Journal of Clinical Child Psychology, 8*, 213–216.

Linnenbrink, E. A. (2005). The dilemma of performance-approach goals: The use of multiple goal contexts to promote students' motivation and learning. *Journal of Educational Psychology, 97*, 197–213.

MacClelland, D. C., Atkinson, J. W., Clark, R. A., & Lowell, E. L. (1953). *The achievement motive.* Princeton, NJ: Van Nostrand.

Maag, J. W., & Reid, R. (2006). Depression among students with learning disabilities: Assessing the risk. *Journal of Learning Disabilities, 39*, 3–10.

Mamlin, N., Harris, K., & Case, L. (2001). A methodological analysis of research on locus of control and learning disabilities. *Journal of Special Education, 34*, 214-225.

Margalit, M., & Heiman, T. (1986). Learning-disabled boys' anxiety, parental anxiety, and family climate. *Journal of Clinical Child Psychology, 15*, 248–253.

Margalit, M., & Shulman, S. (1986). Autonomy perceptions and anxiety expressions of learning disabled adolescents. *Journal of Learning Disabilities, 19*, 291–293.

Margolis, H., & McCabe, P. P. (2004). Self-efficacy: A key to improving the motivation of struggling learners. *The Clearing House, 77*, 241–249.

Martin, E. P., Seligman, M. E. P., Abramson, L. Y., Semmel, A., & von Baeyer, C. (1979). Depressive attributional style. *Journal of Abnormal Psychology, 88*, 242–247.

Meltzer, L., Katzir, T., Miller, L., Reddy, R., & Roditi, B. (2004). Academic self-perceptions, effort, and strategy use in students with learning disabilities: Changes over time. *Learning Disabilities Research & Practice, 19*, 99–108.

Morgan, P., & Sideridis, G. D. (2006). Contrasting the effectiveness of fluency interventions for students with or at risk for learning disabilities: A multilevel random coefficient modeling meta analysis. *Learning Disabilities: Research and Practice, 21*, 191–210.

Morris, R. D. (1988). Classification of learning disabilities: Old problems and new approaches. *Journal of Consulting and Clinical Psychology, 56*, 789–794.

Nelson, J. M., & Manset-Williamson, G. (2006). The impact of explicit, self-regulatory reading comprehension strategy instruction on the reading-specific self-efficacy, attributions, and affect of students with reading disabilities. *Learning Disability Quarterly, 29*, 213–230.

Onwuegbuzie, A., Levin, J. R., & Leach, N. L. (2003). Do effect sizes measure up? A brief assessment. *Learning Disabilities: A Contemporary Journal, 1*, 37–40.

Overmier, J. B., & Seligman, M. E. P. (1967). Effects of inescapable shock upon subsequent escape and avoidance learning. *Journal of Comparative and Physiological Psychology, 63*, 28–33.

Pintrich, P. R., Anderman, E. M., & Klobucar, C. (1994). Intraindividual differences in motivation and cognition in students with and without learning disabilities. *Journal of Learning Disabilities, 27*, 360–370.

Rasch, G. (1980). *Probabilistic models for some intelligence and attainment tests.* Chicago: University of Chicago Press.

Ring, M. M., & Reetz, L. (2000). Modification effects on attributions of middle school students with learning disabilities. *Learning Disabilities Research and Practice, 15*(1), 34–42.

Rotter, J. B. (1966). Generalized expectancies for internal versus external control of reinforcement. *Psychological Monographs, 80*(Whole No. 609), 1–28.

Sabatino, D. A., & Miller, T. L. (1979). *Describing learner characteristics of handicapped children and youth.* New York: Grune and Stratton.

Sands, D. J, Spencer, K. C., Gliner, J. A., & Swaim, R. (1999). Structural equation modelling of student involvement in transition-related actions: The path of least resistance. *Focus on Autism and Other Developmental Disabilities, 14*, 17–27.

Sawyer, R., Graham, S., & Harris, K. R. (1992). Direct teaching, strategy instruction, and strategy instruction with explicit self-regulation: Effects on the composition skills and self-efficacy of students with learning disabilities. *Journal of Educational Psychology, 84*, 340–352.

Schultz, M. K. (1997). WISC-III and WJ-R tests of achievement: Concurrent validity and learning disability identification. *Journal of Special Education, 31*, 377–386.

Schunk, D. H. (1989). Self-efficacy and cognitive achievement: Implications for students with learning problems. *Journal of Learning Disabilities, 22*, 14–22.

Schunk, D. H., & Rice, J. M. (1993). Strategy fading and progress feedback: Effects on self-efficacy and comprehension among students receiving remedial reading services. *Journal of Special Education, 27*, 257–276.

Seligman, M. E. P. (1975). *Helplessness: On depression, development and death.* San Francisco: W. H. Freeman.

Seligman, M. E. P., Abramson, L. Y., Semmel, A., & von Baeyer, C. (1979). Depressive attributional style. *Journal of Abnormal Psychology, 88*, 242–247.

Shavelson, R. J., Hubner, J. J., & Stanton, G. C. (1976). Self-concept: Validation of construct interpretations. *Review of Educational Research, 46*, 407–441.

Sideridis, G. D. (1999). On establishing non-significance. *Dyslexia, 5*, 47–52.

Sideridis, G. D. (2003). On the origins of helpless behavior of students with learning disabilities: Avoidance motivation? *International Journal of Educational Research, 39*, 497–517.

Sideridis, G. D. (2005a). Goal orientations, academic achievement, and depression: Evidence in favor of revised goal theory. *Journal of Educational Psychology, 97*, 366–375.

Sideridis, G. D. (2005b). Performance approach-avoidance motivation and planned behavior theory: Model stability with Greek students with and without learning disabilities. *Reading and Writing Quarterly, 21*, 331–359.

Sideridis, G. D. (2005c). Classroom goal structures and hopelessness as predictors of day-to-day experience at school: Differences between students with and without learning disabilities. *International Journal of Educational Research, 43*, 308–328.

Sideridis, G. D. (2006a). Understanding low achievement and depression in children with learning disabilities: A goal orientation approach. *International Review of Research in Mental Retardation, 31*, 163–203.

Sideridis, G. D. (2006b). Goal orientations and strong oughts: Adaptive or maladaptive forms of motivation for students with and without suspected learning disabilities? *Learning and Individual Differences, 16*, 61–77.

Sideridis, G. D. (2007a). International approaches to learning disabilities: More alike or more different? *Learning Disabilities Research & Practice, 22*, 211–216.

Sideridis, G. D. (2007b). Why are students with learning disabilities depressed? A goal orientation model of depression vulnerability. *Journal of Learning Disabilities, 40*, 526–539.

Sideridis, G. D. (2007c). Goal orientations and classroom goal structures as predictors of classroom student behaviors for Greek students with and without learning difficulties: Clarifying the differential role of motivational orientations. *Advances in Learning and Behavioral Disabilities, 20*, 101–138.

Sideridis, G. D. (2007d). The regulation of affect, anxiety, and stressful arousal from adopting mastery avoidance goal orientations. *Stress and Health, 24*, 55–69.

Sideridis, G. D. (2007e). Persistence of performance approach individuals in achievement situations: An application of the Rasch model. *Educational Psychology, 27*, 753–770.

Sideridis, G. D. (in press). Assessing cognitive interference using the emotional stroop task in students with and without attention problems. *European Journal of Psychological Assessment.*

Sideridis, G. D., Ageriadis, T., Irakleous, I., Siakali, M., & Georgiou, M. (2006). Do students with and without learning difficulties have accurate perceptions of their classrooms' motivational climate? *Insights on Learning Disabilities, 3*, 9–23.

Sideridis, G. D., Mouzaki, A., Simos, P., & Protopapas, A. (2006). Classification of students with reading comprehension difficulties: The roles of motivation, affect, and psychopathology. *Learning Disability Quarterly, 29*, 159–180.

Sideridis, G. D., Protopapas, A., Mouzaki, A., & Simos, P. (2008, April). *Matching goal orientations with classroom goal structures: Predicting reading comprehension growth in elementary school students.* Poster Presented at the American Educational Research Association, New York.

Skinner, H. (1995). *Perceived control, motivation, and coping: Individual differences and development.* Thousand Oaks, CA: Sage.

Sofie, C. A., & Riccio, C. A. (2002). A comparison of multiple methods for the identification of children with reading disabilities. *Journal of Learning Disabilities, 35,* 234–244.

Sorensen, L. G., Forbes, P. W., Bernstein, J. H., Weiler, M. D., Mitchell, W. M., & Waber, D. P. (2003). Psychosocial adjustment over a two-year period in children referred for learning problems: Risk, resilience, and adaptation. *Learning Disabilities Research & Practice, 18,* 10–24.

Smith, D. S., & Nagle, R. J. (1995). Self-perceptions and social comparisons among children with LD. *Journal of Learning Disabilities, 28,* 364–371.

Swartz, J. D., Purdy, J. E., & Fullingim, B. G. (1983). Learned helplessness in normal and learning disabled children: Emerging issues and explanations. *Advances in Learning and Behavioral Disabilities, 2,* 265–280.

Tabassam, W., & Grainger, J. (2002). Self-concept, attributional style and self-efficacy beliefs of students with learning disabilities with and without attention deficit hyperactivity disorder. *Learning Disability Quarterly, 25,* 141–151.

Thomas, A. (1979). Learned helplessness and expectancy factors: Implications for research in learning disabilities. *Review of Educational Research, 49,* 208–221.

Traynor, A. A. (2007). Perceptions of adolescent girls with LD regarding self-determination and post-secondary transition planning. *Learning Disability Quarterly, 30,* 31–45.

Traynor, A. A. (2005). Self-determination perceptions and behaviors of diverse students with LD during the transition planning process. *Journal of Learning Disabilities, 38,* 233–249.

Tucker, J., Stevens, L. J., & Ysseldyke, J. E. (1983). Learning disabilities: The experts speak out. *Journal of Learning Disabilities, 16,* 6–14.

Urdan, T. C. (2004a). Predictors of academic self-handicapping and achievement: Examining achievement goals, classroom goal structures, and culture. *Journal of Educational Psychology, 96,* 251–264.

Urdan, T. C. (2004b). Using multiple methods to assess students' perceptions of classroom goal structures. *European Psychologist, 9,* 222–231.

U.S. Department of Education (2007). *Demographic and school characteristics of students receiving special education in the elementary grades.* Institute of Education Sciences, National Center for Education Statistics (NCES 2007-005).

Valas, H. (2001). Learned helplessness and psychological adjustment. *Scandinavian Journal of Educational Research, 45,* 101-125.

Vroom, V. (1964). *Work and Motivation.* New York: Wiley.

Ward, M. J. (1992). Introduction to secondary special education and transition issues. In F. Rusch, L. DeStefano, J. Chadsey-Rusch, L. A. Phelps & E. Szymanski (Eds.), *Transition from school to adult life: Models, linkages and policy* (pp. 387–389). Sycamore, IL: Sycamore.

Ward, T. J., Ward, S. B., Glutting, J. J., & Hatt, C. V. (1999). Exceptional LD profile types for the WISC-III and WIAT. *School Psychology Review, 28,* 629–643.

Watkins, M. W. (1996). Diagnostic utility of the WISC-III developmental index as a predictor of learning disabilities. *Journal of Learning Disabilities, 29,* 305–312.

Watkins, M. W. (2005). Diagnostic validity of Wechsler subtest scatter. *Learning Disabilities: A Contemporary Journal, 3,* 20–29.

Watkins, M. W., Kush, J. C., & Glutting, J. J. (1997). Discriminant and predictive validity of the WISC-III acid profile among children with learning disabilities. *Psychology in the Schools, 34,* 309–319.

Watkins, M. W., Kush, J. C., & Schaefer, B. A. (2002). Diagnostic utility of the learning disability index. *Journal of Learning Disabilities, 35,* 98–103.

Watkins, M. W., & Worrel, F. C. (2000). Diagnostic utility of the number of WISC-III subtests deviating from mean performance among students with learning disabilities. *Psychology in the Schools, 37,* 303–309.

Weiner, B, (1979). A theory of motivation for some classroom experience. *Journal of Educational Psychology, 71,* 3–25.

Weiner, B. (1985). An attributional theory of achievement motivation and emotion. *Psychological Review, 2,* 543–571.

Wentzel, K. (1989). Adolescent classroom goals, standards for performance, and academic achievement: An interactionist perspective. *Journal of Educational Psychology, 81,* 131–142.

Wigfield, A. (1997). Reading motivation: A domain-specific approach to motivation. *Educational Psychologist, 32,* 59–68.

Wigfield, A., Eccles, J. S., Schiefele, U., Roeser, R., & Davis-Kean, P. (2006). Development of achievement motivation. In W. Damon & N. Eisenberg (Eds.), *Handbook of child psychology* (6th ed., pp. 933–1002). New York: Wiley.

Wigfield, A., & Guthrie, J. T. (1997). Relations of children's motivation for reading to the amount and breadth of their reading. *Journal of Educational Psychology, 89,* 420–432.

Wigfield, A., & Guthrie, J. T. (1997). Motivation for reading: An overview. *Educational Psychologist, 32,* 57–58.

Wilgosh, L. (1984). Learned helplessness in normally achieving and learning disabled girls. *Mental Retardation and Learning Disability Bulletin, 12,* 64–70.

Wolters, C. A. (2004). Advancing achievement goal theory: Using goal structures and goal orientations to predict students' motivation, cognition, and achievement. *Journal of Educational Psychology, 96,* 236–250.

28
Teachers' Self-Efficacy Beliefs

Anita Woolfolk Hoy, Wayne K. Hoy, and Heather A. Davis

Teachers' beliefs serve as cognitive filters that screen their experiences and thus shape their thoughts and actions. Beliefs about students, teaching, and learning drive teachers' planning and their moment-to-moment decisions about class management, teaching strategies, relationships with students, and assessment (Calderhead, 1996; Gregoire, Ashton, & Algina, 2004; Pajares, 1993, 1996; Woolfolk Hoy, Davis, & Pape, 2006; Woolfolk Hoy & Weinstein, 2006).

In this chapter, we suggest that among the many beliefs teachers might hold, few are as powerful as their self-efficacy for teaching—a belief that can trump others in the complex process of navigating classroom life. In fact, Gregoire (2003) suggests even when teachers understand that a given method may be more effective, their efficacy beliefs for enacting the new method will drive their implementation decisions.

The focus of this chapter is teachers' sense of efficacy at the individual and collective levels. The chapter begins with a conceptual framework for understanding teachers' efficacy and the critical issues related to its measurement. We then review findings on teachers' efficacy judgments in specific academic subjects and the relationships of those judgments to student and teacher outcomes. Some of this research focuses on teachers' efficacy for the content they teach (efficacy for doing mathematics, for example). We also examine emergent research on teachers' sense of efficacy in relation to the some of the current challenges they face: classroom management; using, implementing, and integrating technology; and working with children with disabilities. We then turn to the organizational context and collective efficacy, exploring possible effects on teachers, especially beginning teachers. We end the chapter with a discussion of criticisms of the teacher efficacy construct and recommendations for future research.

Teachers' Sense of Efficacy: Conceptualization and Measurement

Over 30 years ago, Albert Bandura (1977) introduced the concept of self-efficacy as an important factor in human motivation. More recently, Bandura's efforts and the work of many other researchers have focused on the role self-efficacy in *human agency*, which involves "not only the deliberate ability to make choices and action plans, but the ability to give shape to appropriate courses of action and to motivate and regulate their execution" (2006b, p. 165). Newer definitions of self-efficacy such as "people's beliefs about their capabilities to produce designated levels of performance that exercise influence over events that affect their lives" (Bandura, 1994, p. 71) reflect the important role of self-efficacy in human agency.

Self-Efficacy, Self-Concept, and Responsibility

Before examining self-efficacy in teaching, it is useful to make some distinctions between teachers' sense of efficacy, self-concept, self-esteem, and sense of personal responsibility. These constructs are frequently used interchangeably and, often, inappropriately throughout the literature (see the chapter by Schunk and Pajares in this volume for a further discussion). Self-efficacy is a context-specific assessment of competence to do something specific; self-concept is a more global construct that contains many perceptions about the self, including self-efficacy. Compared to self-esteem, self-efficacy is concerned with judgments of personal capabilities; self-esteem is concerned with judgments of self-worth. Self-efficacy beliefs are stronger predictors of behavior than self-concept or self-esteem (Bandura, 1997). Finally, teachers' responsibility is teachers' beliefs about whether they can or should be held accountable for student outcomes (Guskey, 1981; Kozel, 2007).

Thus self-efficacy for teaching is a future-oriented, task-specific judgment. Tschannen-Moran, Woolfolk Hoy, and Hoy's (1998) definition emphasized the situation specific nature of efficacy: "Teacher efficacy is the teacher's belief in her and his ability to organize and execute the courses of action required to successfully accomplish a specific teaching task in a particular context" (p. 233).

A Model of Teachers' Efficacy Beliefs

Recently, researchers have refined conceptions of teachers' sense of efficacy and called for both clarification and broadening of the construct (Labone, 2004; Wheatley, 2005). The model of teacher efficacy presented by Tschannen-Moran et al. (1998, see Figure 28.1) suggests that teachers' efficacy judgments are the result of an interaction between (a) a personal appraisal of the factors that make accomplishing a specific teaching task easy or difficult (analysis of teaching task in context) and (b) a self-assessment of personal teaching capabilities and limitations specific to the task (analysis of teaching competence). The resultant efficacy judgments impact the goals teachers set for themselves, the effort they invest in reaching these goals, and their persistence when facing difficulties. These decisions and behaviors lead to outcomes that themselves become the basis for future efficacy judgments. The model is intended to be appropriate for all levels of teaching, though most research using the model has been with preservice and practicing teachers in K-12 classrooms.

As shown in Figure 28.1, the major influences on efficacy beliefs about teaching are assumed to be cognitive interpretation of the four sources of efficacy information described by Bandura (1997)—mastery experience, physiological arousal, vicarious experience, and verbal persuasion. However, like all self-efficacy judgments, teachers' efficacy beliefs are context-specific. Teachers can be expected to feel more or less efficacious under different circumstances. A teacher, for example, who feels highly efficacious about instructing her honors literature class may feel less efficacious about teaching freshman composition or vice versa. Reviewing the literature about contextual effects on efficacy, Ross (1998) concluded that teacher efficacy generally is higher in settings with high ability, orderly students; when teachers are working in the area of their expertise; when teacher workloads are moderate; and when the school culture is collaborative.

By conceptualizing teacher efficacy in terms of the confluence of judgments about personal teaching competence and the teaching task, both competence and contingency (i.e., both agent-means and means-ends relations as described by Skinner, 1996) are considered in an explanation of resultant teacher efficacy. In addition, the model highlights the situational and developmental nature of teaching task analysis. For example, the analysis of the task likely will be more salient in shaping efficacy beliefs when tasks are novel or when teachers lack experience.

One of the factors that makes teachers' efficacy judgments so powerful is the cyclical nature of the process. As noted in Figure 28.1, the performances and outcomes create a new mastery experience, which provides new information that will be processed to shape future efficacy beliefs. Greater efficacy leads to greater effort and persistence, which leads to better performance, which, in turn, leads to greater efficacy. The reverse is also true. Lower efficacy leads to less effort and giving up easily, which leads to poor teaching outcomes, which then produce decreased efficacy.

The Measurement of Teachers Sense of Efficacy

Measurement issues have dominated much of the research attempting to conceptualize teachers' efficacy beliefs, perhaps because the first measure, two items added at the last minute to Rand Corporation evaluations of innovative educational programs, proved so successful (Armor et al., 1976; Berman, McLaughlin, Bass, Pauly, Zellman, 1977). In these studies, teachers' level of efficacy was determined by computing a total score for their responses to two Likert scale items: (a) "When it comes right down to it, a teacher really can't do much because most of a student's motivation and performance depends on his or her home environment," and (b) "If I try really hard, I can get

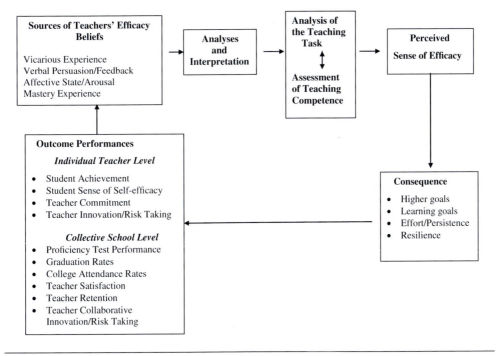

Figure 28.1 The cycle of teachers' efficacy judgments. Adapted from Tshcannen-Moran, Woolfolk Hoy, & Hoy, 1998 and Goddard, Hoy, and Woolfolk Hoy, 2005

through to even the most difficult or unmotivated students." A two-item scale invited questions about reliability and validity, and the quest for better measures commenced.

Teacher Efficacy Scale (TES)

In an attempt to improve on the validity and reliability of the Rand two-item scale, Gibson and Dembo (1984) developed the Teacher Efficacy Scale (TES), a 30-item scale (later reduced to 16 items) that yields two factors consistent with the Rand items. Whereas the Rand items were grounded in Rotter's (1966) locus of control theory, Gibson and Dembo turned to Bandura's social cognitive theory to interpret the two factors. They labeled their first factor *personal teaching efficacy* and assumed this factor assessed Bandura's efficacy expectations. The second factor, *teaching efficacy*, was assumed to capture Bandura's notions of outcome expectancy (for an alternative view of the meaning of these two factors, see Woolfolk & Hoy, 1990). Studies of both preservice and inservice teachers have found that from 18% to 30% of the variance between teachers is explained by these two factors (Hoy & Woolfolk, 1993; Soodak & Podell, 1993).

Even though the TES has been used in hundreds of studies and translated into several languages, some researchers have raised questions about the meaning of the scale, particularly the second outcome expectancy factor, often called "general teaching efficacy" or GTE (Guskey & Passaro, 1994; Henson, Kogan, & Vacha-Haase, 2001; Soodak & Podell, 1996). Reliability coefficients for the scales vary considerably across studies (Henson et al., 2001). Other researchers suggest the TES is best represented by three or even four subscales (Brouwers, Tomic, & Stijnen, 2002; Denzine, Cooney, & McKenzie, 2005), but confirmatory factor analyses failed to support a two-, three-, or four-factor model of the TES. Even though Denzine et al. (2005) were able to modify a version of the TES (Woolfolk & Hoy, 1990) to adequately fit a three-factor model to their data, they question the use of the TES; an opinion shared by Brouwers et al. (2002) who concluded that "the *Teacher Efficacy Scale* in its current state does not provide precise and valid information about teacher efficacy beliefs" (p. 211).

Teacher Sense of Efficacy Scale (TSES)

Drawing on earlier versions of Bandura's (2006a) guide to creating self-efficacy scales, Tschannen-Moran and Woolfolk Hoy (2001) developed the Teachers' Sense of Efficacy Scale (TSES) to incorporate items that describe the types of tasks representative of frequent teaching activities. With in-service and preservice teachers as participants, they reported three dimensions of teaching efficacy: efficacy for instructional strategies, efficacy for classroom management, and efficacy for student engagement. Confirmatory factor analyses have generally supported the three scales, with the efficacy for student engagement being the least stable scale (Henson, 2002; Moore, 2007; Wolters & Daugherty, 2007).

Labone (2004), in her critical analysis of research on teachers' sense of efficacy, encouraged researchers to expand conceptions of efficacy to include insights from interpretivist and critical theory perspectives (see also Hebert, Lee, & Williamson, 1998; Wheatley, 2005). Qualitative approaches (Fishler & Firestone, 2006; Milner & Woolfolk Hoy, 2003; Mulholland & Wallace, 2001; Shore, 2004) and mixed method (Gerges, 2001) studies of teachers' efficacy beliefs are appearing and likely will increase. Improved efficacy beliefs instruments may be used to identify teachers with interesting profiles for case studies or ethnographic research. Results from case studies and interviews could be used to improve the language and content of efficacy scales.

Criticisms of Efficacy Measures: Global

The global scores provided by most efficacy measures have been a source of concern for many researchers, especially given the specific and context dependent nature of self-efficacy constructs (Henson, 2002; Wheatley, 2005). When teachers are asked, "How well can you implement alternative strategies in your classroom?" or "How much can you do to calm a student who is disruptive or noisy?" which strategy or student do they have in mind as they answer? Middle and high school teachers are responsible for many different classes and students. Which classes and students are the foci of the efficacy questions, if these are not specified in the scale? Because efficacy varies within teachers across classes and contexts (Ross, Cousins, & Gadalla, 1996), the notion of one "efficacy level" for a given teacher is inconsistent with both the empirical findings and self-efficacy theory. Subject and task specific measures of efficacy have addressed but not eliminated this criticism.

Ceiling Effects and Calibration

A persistent problem with teacher efficacy beliefs scales is that virtually all teachers, novice or experienced, rate themselves above average. Thus average scores on the 9-point TSES generally are above 6 and average scores on 5- or 6-point scales also are above the midrange. Based on Bandura's (2006a) guidelines for designing self-efficacy scales, this could mean that the survey items do not present difficult tasks to challenge respondents—every task is easy enough to be assigned a number at the high end of the scale. There is some evidence for this possibility in Benton-Borghi's (2006) research on efficacy for using assistive technologies and for teaching students with disabilities. Where specific and challenging tasks were described, teachers' responses indicated lower efficacy on average than is usually found in research on teachers' efficacy judgments. It also is possible that respondents in many studies are overestimating or intentionally inflating their judgments. When efficacy scores are used in selection or screening processes, as in Praxis II, social desirability in responding is a possibility (Wheatley, 2005).

As measures of teachers' efficacy beliefs developed, many researchers confronted the issue of task and context specificity in efficacy judgments.

Teachers' Efficacy Beliefs: General and Specific Efficacy Judgments

One of the unresolved issues in the measurement of teacher efficacy is determining the optimal level of specificity. For example, is efficacy specific to teaching mathematics, or more specific to teaching algebra, or even more specific to teaching quadratic equations? Are distinct measures needed to assess efficacy beliefs about different aspects of teaching such as managing classrooms, instructing students with special needs, or using technology? Teachers' sense of efficacy for subject matter understanding and subject teaching may become increasingly important during the middle grades. This is because academic content grows more complex and difficult. Adolescents in middle school may be working with teachers who are responsible for several subjects and who may not be as deeply grounded in one of the subjects they teach. Thus, teachers' sense of efficacy for knowing and teaching the subject may be increasingly important in the middle school years and beyond. What has been learned about teachers' efficacy beliefs in specific contexts?

Science and Mathematics

With Gibson and Dembo's (1984) TES as a guide, researchers have developed the Science Teaching Efficacy Belief Instrument (STEBI, Riggs & Enochs, 1990), the Mathematics Teaching Efficacy Beliefs Instrument (MTEBI; Enochs, Smith, & Huinker, 2000), and the Self-Efficacy Teaching and Knowledge Instrument for Science Teachers (SETAKIST; Henson, 2002). Research with these and other instruments relates science teachers' sense of efficacy to their instructional goals and strategies (Tobin, 1998). For example, compared to the goals of lower efficacy teachers, high efficacy science teachers include students' problem solving and logical thinking skills for real life situations, depend less on curriculum guides, use themes to integrate science into other subjects, and emphasize hands-on science experiences. Lower efficacy teachers preferred prescriptive materials that provided step-by-step guidance and answers to problems (De Laat & Watters, 1995; Ramey-Gassert, Shroyer, & Staver, 1996). Preservice teachers who lack confidence in their knowledge of science content and pedagogy tend to deemphasize or avoid science teaching or teach using transmissive as opposed to inquiry methods (Cantrell, Young, & Moore, 2003; Mulholland & Wallace, 2001; Palmer, 2006; Plourde, 2002; Rice & Roychoudhury, 2003; Tosun, 2000).

Language and Literacy

Using an adaptation of the TES (Gibson & Dembo, 1984) to assess efficacy for teaching writing, Graham, Harris, and Fink (2001) found the same two factors of personal and general teaching efficacy identified in previous research. In addition, the instructional practices of teachers characterized as high in self-efficacy for teaching writing (top 20%) differed from the practices of teachers characterized as low in self-efficacy (bottom 20%). Higher efficacy teachers spent significantly more time teaching grammar, usage, and basic composition and their students spent more time composing.

In a mixed methods study of English as a foreign language (EFL) middle school teachers in Venezuela, Chacón (2005) found no obvious differences between high and low efficacy teachers in regards to the use of communication-oriented strategies and grammar-oriented strategies. However, high efficacy teachers were more likely to use group work activities and choose more challenging tasks and mastery experiences for their students. Further, high efficacy teachers were more likely to pursue self-directed learning through planning courses of action to improve their English proficiency (see also Sercu, 2005).

Diversity and Inclusion

To study the likelihood of referral to special education in the Netherlands, Meijer and Foster (1988) developed the Dutch Teacher Self-Efficacy Scales to assess personal teaching efficacy beliefs (see also Coladarci & Breton, 1997). They found that high efficacy teachers working with special education populations were more likely to feel that a student with disabilities was appropriately placed in the regular classroom. More recently, Benton-Borghi (2006) adapted the TSES to ask about efficacy for teaching, managing, and motivating students with disabilities and for specific applications of assistive technologies. For teachers in the study, self-efficacy for working with students in general was higher than self-efficacy for working with disabled students or for using assistive technology.

Similarly, Kozel (2007) found preservice teachers' sense of efficacy may vary as a function of their conception of diversity and inclusion. Kozel (2007) developed a measure of efficacy, using Bandura's (2006a) guidelines, to capture teacher's perceived capability to enact culturally relevant pedagogy. She found preservice teachers tended to report lower sense of responsibility and efficacy for teaching some populations of students, specifically gay, lesbian, and bisexual students and students of non-Christian faith. Her findings suggest that even though preservice teachers may report higher sense of efficacy for addressing multicultural issues in their classrooms, examining their efficacy for working with specific populations of students may provide researchers and teacher educators with some insight as to why teachers may not enact culturally relevant pedagogy in their classroom.

Technology

With increasing pressure to both integrate technology instruction into existing curriculum and subsequently train and support new and practicing teachers in their integration, researchers have begun to explore the role of teachers' sense of efficacy for technology (Ropp, 1999). Common among studies of teachers' sense of efficacy are examinations of teachers' judgments of their specific knowledge of the technology (e.g., subject matter efficacy) and their experience of comfort/anxiety with the technology (e.g., arousal; see Pierson, 2001). Fewer studies have explored teachers' sense of efficacy for teaching about technology (Davis, Ring, & Ferdig, 2002; Straub, 2007) or their efficacy for managing classrooms with technology.

Computer efficacy has been measured in terms of perceived ease of use (Davis, 1989), computing autonomy and control (Charlton, 2005), as well as specific task-related judgments (see Straub, in press, for review.) Straub describes how perceived self-efficacy in a particular computer-based task may, in turn, influence the perceived ease-of-use (Agarwal, Sambamurthy, & Stair, 2000; Davis, 1989). Perceived ease-of-use may be an important factor in determining whether a teacher will ultimately adopt a particular piece of technology in her classroom. On the other hand, individuals who believe in their own abilities to complete a task do not necessarily need to rely on computer technology (de Vries, Midden, & Bouwhuis, 2003). Thus, more research is needed to identify the ways in which globally efficacious teachers, who lack confidence in their specific abilities to use technology, approach the increasingly 'technological' tasks of classroom life (e.g., submitting and posting grades).

Beyond the obvious social and verbal persuasion preservice and practicing teachers may be receiving from their classes and districts, to develop a sense of efficacy for integrating technology into their teaching, they must have opportunities for mastery experiences with technology; opportunities to experience pleasant emotions, and cope with unpleasant emotions surrounding technology use; and opportunities to learn vicariously from a credible model who successfully evidences technology use/integration in her classroom (Straub, 2007). Moreover, successful teacher education and professional development programs may need to think beyond developing efficacy for using and teaching technology, to supporting preservice and practicing teachers in developing a sense of efficacy for how to manage a classroom in which the dynamics of instruction have been changed by the integration of a new piece of technology (i.e., management of resources—single computer vs. multiple computer classroom—and the management of student behavior) as well as efficacy for developing student motivation and engagement with the new technology.

Classroom Management

Emmer and Hickman (1991) adapted the Gibson and Dembo instrument to better assess classroom management beliefs, yielding a 36-item measure with three efficacy subscales: efficacy for classroom management and discipline, external influences, and personal teaching efficacy. Among a sample of preservice teachers, the efficacy subscales were correlated with preferences for using positive strategies for classroom management, that is, strategies aimed at increasing or encouraging desirable student responses through praise, encouragement, attention, and rewards. More recent research with practicing teachers by Morris-Rothschild and Brassard (2006) reached similar conclusions using structural equation modeling methods. Teachers with more teaching experience and higher self-efficacy for classroom management reported greater use of integrating, compromising, and obliging styles management strategies.

A Process Approach to Research on Teacher and Student Outcomes

Even though research over the past 30 years has documented relationships between teachers' sense of efficacy and both teacher and student outcomes, there has been little work on the processes through which efficacy beliefs might impact teachers' decisions and actions and how these teacher effects might influence student learning. One exception is Ross's (1998) review of 88 teacher efficacy studies. Ross identified potential links between teachers' sense of efficacy and their behaviors. He suggested that teachers with higher levels of efficacy are more likely to (a) learn and use new approaches and strategies for teaching, (b) use management techniques that enhance student autonomy and diminish student control, (c) provide special assistance to low achieving students, (d) build students' self-perceptions of their academic skills, (e) set attainable goals, and (f) persist in the face of student failure. Even with these findings, few studies have attempted to model the processes by which beliefs may differentially shape teacher behavior and, in their enactment, affect student behavior and outcomes.

Beginning with Ross's (1998) conclusions, Woolfolk Hoy and Davis (2006) developed a framework to link teachers' efficacy beliefs to adolescent students' outcomes. They outlined two types of potential consequences of teachers' efficacy beliefs: Consequences for Teaching Beliefs and Behaviors and Consequences for Students' Beliefs and Behaviors, as shown in Figure 28.2.

Teachers' Decision, Actions, and Communications

Woolfolk Hoy and Davis (2006) argued, as did Ross (1998), that teachers' behaviors in the classroom, such as their planning and curricular decisions; their attention, monitoring, and verbalizations; and their interactions with students, are shaped in part by their sense of efficacy. In turn, these efficacy-influenced teacher behaviors and decisions may have direct, indirect, and relational consequences for students' behaviors, emotions, and decisions. Direct consequences involve instructional decisions and actions such as how much time to allocate to a topic. Indirect consequences involve communications (verbal and nonverbal) about behavioral and attitudinal expectations, values, motivation, and management. Relational consequences involve the interpersonal and emotional dynamics of the classroom and the relationships among the participants. Of course, these categories are not mutually exclusive, but making the distinctions is useful in organizing the research. Because little research has investigated these direct, indirect, and relational consequences, the arrows in Figure 28.2 are simply suggestive of likely and plausible relationships that could be investigated in future research.

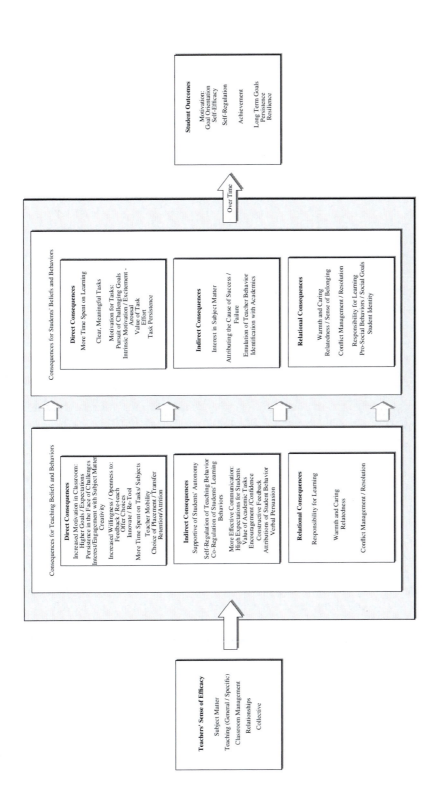

Figure 28.2 A model of possible relationships between teachers' self-efficacy and student outcomes. Adapted from Woolfolk hoy & Davis, 2005.

Direct Teacher Outcomes In terms of direct instructional effects, teachers with a strong sense of efficacy tend to exhibit greater levels of planning, organization, direct teaching, and enthusiasm (Allinder, 1994; Muijs & Reynolds, 2001), and spend more time teaching in subject areas where their sense of efficacy is higher (Graham et al., 2001; Riggs & Enochs, 1990), whereas teachers tend to avoid subjects when efficacy is lower. Teachers with higher efficacy judgments tend to be more open to new ideas, more willing to experiment with new methods to better meet the needs of their students, and more persistent if innovations falter initially (Cousins & Walker, 2000; Guskey, 1988; Hani, Czerniak, & Lumpe, 1996), more likely to use powerful but potentially difficult-to-manage methods such as inquiry and small group work (Chacón, 2005; De Laat & Watters, 1995; Riggs & Enochs, 1990), and less likely to use easy-to-adopt but weaker methods such as lecture (Ashton & Webb, 1986). Higher efficacy teachers are less likely to criticize students, are more persistent in following up on student wrong answers (Ashton & Webb, 1986, Gibson & Dembo, 1984), and more likely to select strategies that support student learning rather than strategies that simply cover the curriculum (Ashton, Webb, & Doda, 1983). Higher efficacy teachers tend to be more active in monitoring seatwork and maintaining academic focus, respond quickly to student misbehavior by redirecting attention without showing anger or becoming threatened, and generally evidence greater "withitness" (Ashton & Webb, 1986, Gibson & Dembo, 1984).

Based on the above findings, we suggest that higher efficacy teachers in many ways fit descriptions of active teaching or direct instruction associated with greater student learning of basic skills (Brophy & Good, 1986). In fact, Muijs and Reynolds (2001) found some evidence for a connection between sense of efficacy for teaching mathematics and the use of effective direct instruction practices.

Indirect Influences Moving to indirect influences on student learning, higher efficacy teachers are more likely to confront management problems and seek solutions (Chacón, 2005; Woolfolk & Hoy, 1990), work longer with struggling students (Gibson & Dembo, 1984), attend to the special needs of exceptional students, and work with parents (Hoover-Dempsey, Bassler, & Brissie, 1992), and are less likely to refer a difficult student to special education (Meijer & Foster, 1988; Soodak & Podell, 1993). In their study of elementary and middle school teachers' assessments of case descriptions of students, Tournaki and Podell (2005) concluded that higher efficacy teachers "make less negative predictions about students, and seem to adjust their predictions when student characteristics change, while low efficacy teachers seem to be paying attention to a single characteristic when making their predictions" (p. 299). Higher efficacy teachers are more likely to offer students choices (Midgley, Feldlaufer, & Eccles, 1989) perhaps because they have confidence that they can manage students who are working on different tasks or projects. Higher efficacy teachers also are more likely to set learning rather than performance goals (Wolters & Daugherty, 2007). By persistently moving toward learning rather than performance goals, teachers with a higher sense of efficacy effectively have higher expectations for all their students. In fact, one definition of efficacy is a teacher's belief that she or he can reach even the most difficult students. The body of research on teacher expectation effects documents many ways that teachers' expectations are translated into instructional and interpersonal processes (Good & Brophy, 2008).

Though research does not speak to this, having a higher sense of efficacy may cause teachers to make controllable attributions for their own successes and failures, and those of their students. Believing in themselves and their students, higher efficacy teachers look to controllable factors such as increased effort, improved teaching or learning strategies, better explanations or instructional activities, or improved help and support. Thus, these teachers may not only directly teach their students better strategies, they may also model for the students an active, strategic, and effortful (agentic) approach to overcoming leaning problems.

Relational Outcomes Turning to relational teacher outcomes, it is possible that teachers who judge themselves competent with regard to content and pedagogical knowledge, as well as classroom management, may be more likely to assume responsibility for working with "problem" students (Brophy, 1996). If teachers' sense of efficacy is not threatened by the challenges and confrontations of their students, the teachers may be less likely to feel the need for control (Hoy, 2001) and more likely to listen to students. If these teachers are confident in their teaching and managerial capabilities, they may be less ego-involved, angered, or insulted by the students' behaviors and more willing to solve the problem rather than punish the student.

Delpit (1995) argued that teachers' decisions to assume responsibility for developing rapport have important consequences for working with students of diverse backgrounds. Specifically, she found commitment on the part of teachers to establishing and maintaining relationships with students had a transformative effect on students' attitudes and achievement patterns. This was particularly true for negotiating conflict and helping students to regulate negative emotions in the classroom (e.g., frustration, apathy). Further, efficacious teachers may feel freer to respond with warmth instead of hostility when students express frustration. In brief, a sense of efficacy may free teachers to care about their students without being overwhelmed by student behaviors they cannot understand or control (Newberry & Davis, 2008).

Student Outcomes Related to Teachers Decisions, Actions, and Communications

In addition to being related to student achievement (Ashton & Webb, 1986; Muijs & Reynolds, 2001; Ross, 1998), teachers' sense of efficacy has been associated with other student outcomes (Ross, Hogaboam-Gray, & Hannay, 2001).

Direct Outcomes: Time to Learn In terms of direct student outcomes, one of the consequences of teachers who are active and organized; set clear, high learning goals; and persistently reteach when necessary, is increased academic learning time. Almost every study examining time and learning has found a significant relationship between time spent on content and student learning (Weinstein, & Mignano 2007). In addition, when teachers set challenging and proximal goals, students are more likely to be motivated to reach the goals because the target is clear. Decades of research on goals attest to the value of challenging, attainable goals (Locke & Latham, 2002, 2004).

Indirect Influences: Motivation and Engagement Turning to indirect student outcomes, when teachers set higher goals and are persistent and resilient in moving toward them, students may be more willing to cooperate in class activities and value learning. Students who hear controllable attributions from their teachers and see teachers act in keeping with those attributions may be more likely to make controllable attributions themselves, especially if their teacher is persuasive and confident. Intrinsic motivation to learn is also encouraged when students are given choices and when they are provided informational rather than controlling communications (Ryan & Deci, 2000).

Relational Influences Little research has been completed examining the relationship between teachers' sense of efficacy and its connection to relational consequences for students. Summers,

Davis, and Woolfolk Hoy (2006) found that middle school students reported feeling less close and experiencing more conflict with teachers who reported a higher sense of personal efficacy at the beginning of the academic year but not at the end of the academic year. Could this be a sign that teachers who feel more also efficacious feel more confident in their ability to set boundaries, push students towards more challenging goals, and to confront classroom issues?

In a qualitative case study of changes in teaching efficacy experienced by 12 preservice interns during student-teaching, Rushton (2000) found preservice teachers' perspectives on relationships change as a function of their increasing efficacy in their classroom. Consistent with Summers et al. (2006), novice teachers reported greater ease with setting and maintaining boundaries as a function of increased efficacy in the classroom.

Perhaps, when interpreting these findings, we can turn to the more abundant research on students' perceptions of their teachers as caring. Woolfolk Hoy and Weinstein (2006) document the value that students place on teachers' willingness to "be there" for them, to listen, and to show concern—in short, to *care* (Cothran, Kulinna, & Garrahy, 2003; Ferreira & Bosworth, 2001; Wentzel, 1998). But caring may not be enough to foster student learning. For example, Katz (1999; see also Bischoff, 2007) found that high expectations for academic achievement combined with caring and support are the essential components of a productive teacher-student relationship, especially for students who have been marginalized.

These findings suggest a critical dimension of being perceived as a caring teacher includes having the confidence (efficacy) to press students towards high standards (see also Davis, 2006). Few studies have explored the relationship between teachers' efficacy beliefs and their students' perceptions of high challenge and support—high standards and caring—but this is a question that might yield valuable findings.

Research on the Development and Support of Teachers' Efficacy Beliefs

Because a strong sense of efficacy can support higher motivation, greater effort, persistence, and resilience across the span of a teaching career, the development and support of efficacy beliefs has become another focus of teacher efficacy research. We begin our consideration of this research with a look at the sources of efficacy and then examine the relationship of teaching experience to teachers' efficacy beliefs and studies of how efficacy beliefs develop over the career.

The Sources of Efficacy

Researchers have examined the sources that contribute to the development of self-efficacy for teaching, although the findings on this question are not extensive. Mastery is usually considered the most important source of efficacy. Labone (2004) argued that experiencing mastery by critically analyzing teaching is a source of efficacy. Likewise, Henson (2001) found that engaging teachers in action research—implementing interventions and reflecting on the results—enhanced efficacy. For all teachers, but especially for beginning teachers, content knowledge may be a part of mastery experiences. For example, Ross, Cousins, Gadalla, and Hannay (1999) examined the self-efficacy of teachers after they were given courses to teach outside their subject. These individuals had significantly lower self-efficacy scores for the courses taught outside their field. For many beginning students in fields such as science and mathematics, understanding content is a significant challenge (Schoon & Boone, 1998). Thus, Palmer (2006) suggests, for prospective teachers at least, understanding science content is a form of mastery experience that is "distinct from enactive mastery because it involves success in understanding something rather than success in doing something. It could therefore be referred to as 'cognitive content mastery'" (p. 339).

The level of arousal, either of anxiety or excitement, adds to the feeling of mastery or incompetence, depending on how the arousal is interpreted. Even though a lower sense of efficacy has been related to teacher burnout and attrition (Evers, Brouwers, & Tomic, 2002; Friedman & Farber, 1992), few studies have examined the role of teachers' interpretations of arousal in promoting a sense of efficacy. However, individual differences in teachers' interpretations (e.g., feelings of tension reflecting anxiety and fear that failure is immanent vs. excitement or being "psyched" for a good class) may play an important role in teachers' judgments of confidence.

Vicarious experiences are those in which changes in teachers' behavior or beliefs occur as the result of observing a model. The degree to which the observer identifies with the model moderates the efficacy effect on the observer (Bandura, 1997). Opportunities to observe credible models or mentors, those who teach well, during internships or induction years may play an important role in promoting preservice teachers' sense of efficacy for attempting complex teaching tasks not easily replicated in the teacher education classroom. For preservice and beginning teachers, opportunities to observe even videotapes and classroom simulations that provide models of teaching may be sources of vicarious experiences in support of efficacy (Posnanski, 2002; Rice & Roychoudhury, 2003).

Social or verbal persuasion may entail a "pep talk" or specific performance feedback from a supervisor, colleague, or students. Social persuasion, though limited in its impact, may provide an "efficacy boost" to counter occasional setbacks that might have instilled enough self-doubt to interrupt persistence. The potency of persuasion depends on the credibility, trustworthiness, and expertise of the persuader (Bandura, 1997). The opportunity to collaborate with other teachers may provide both social persuasion and vicarious experiences. Research shows that increases in teacher efficacy are related to increased opportunities to work with other teachers toward common goals, discuss professional issues, plan, and solve problems (Henson, 2001; Puchner & Taylor, 2006; Tschannen-Moran, Uline, Woolfolk Hoy, & Mackley, 2000).

Sources of efficacy may vary, depending on the experience level of the teacher. For example, Tschannen-Moran and Woolfolk Hoy (2007) found that the availability of resources and support from colleagues and the community were significant predictors of support for novice, but not for experienced teachers. Mastery experience (assessed as satisfaction with teaching performance this year) was related to self-efficacy judgments for both novice and experienced teachers, but made a larger contribution to predicting self-efficacy for novices. As mastery experiences accumulate, the other three sources may be less influential as efficacy increasingly is based on memories and reflections about past mastery. Efficacy beliefs are considered to be most malleable early in learning (Bandura, 1997). Once self-efficacy beliefs have been firmly established, Bandura suggested that it would take a shock of some kind to provoke a reassessment. Thus the early years may be the most important in shaping a teacher's efficacy beliefs.

Although all four sources of information play roles in the creation of efficacy beliefs, it is the interpretation of this information that is critical. Cognitive processing determines how the sources of information will be weighed as well as how they will influence the analysis of the teaching task in context and the assessment of personal teaching competence. What is attended to, what is considered important or credible, and what is remembered influence the impact of experience on efficacy beliefs. The standards the teacher holds for what constitutes good teaching also will influence how sources of information are interpreted and weighed (Labone, 2004; Wheatley, 2005).

The development of efficacy beliefs among teachers has generated a great deal of research interest because once established, the beliefs appear to be resistant to change. But results are mixed on the relationship between time teaching in schools and teacher efficacy. Because patterns of change in efficacy appear to vary, depending on the teacher's career stage, we examine the different stages separately.

Teacher Education and Student Teaching

There is some evidence that course work and practice have differential impacts on sense of efficacy. General teaching efficacy (GTE) beliefs are more likely to change when students are exposed to vicarious learning experiences or social persuasion, such as college course work whereas actual teaching experiences during student teaching practica have a greater impact on PTE or personal teaching efficacy (Housego, 1992; Hoy & Woolfolk, 1990). GTE has remained the same or shown a decline after field experiences or student teaching (Hoy & Woolfolk, 1990; Li & Zhang, 2000) suggesting that the optimism of young teachers may be somewhat tarnished when confronted with the realities and complexities of the teaching task. However, PTE increased in all three of these studies. Assessed using Tschannen-Moran and Woolfolk Hoy's (2001) measure or Bandura's (1997) instrument, teachers' sense of efficacy increased after student teaching (Knoblauch & Woolfolk Hoy, 2008; Woolfolk Hoy & Burke-Spero, 2005). Knoblauch and Woolfolk Hoy also found that student teachers' perceptions of their cooperating teachers' efficacy were predictive of and positively related to the student teachers' TSES scores at the end of their student teaching experience.

Some researchers have examined the relationships between teacher preparation and prospective teacher self-efficacy by looking at the outcomes of specific courses, particularly methods classes. For example, using a mixed method design with the STEBI-B (Riggs & Enochs 1990) as the quantitative measure of efficacy beliefs, Bleicher and Lindgren (2005) identified increases in science teaching self-efficacy and outcome expectancy at the end of a science methods course that modeled constructivist, hands-on teaching. Findings from focus group interviews and analysis of student journals also revealed increased confidence in ability to teach science. Conceptual knowledge in science also increased significantly. Also using mixed-methods, Shore (2004) concluded that participating in courses based on multiple-intelligence theory led to increases in sense of efficacy for graduate-level teacher preparation students.

Teacher Induction

Using Gibson and Dembo's (1984) measure, studies have found declines in general teaching efficacy (GTE) after the first year of teaching (e.g., Housego, 1992; Hoy & Woolfolk, 1990). In addition, Woolfolk, Rosoff, and Hoy (1990) found that lower GTE was a significant predictor of being more controlling and mistrustful of students and less supportive of student autonomy. These changes in GTE can be interpreted as reflecting an increased sense of the difficulty of the teaching task in general and a growing pessimism about the overpowering negative external constraints that can undermine the teacher's efforts.

Using multiple instruments for assessing efficacy, Woolfolk Hoy and Burke-Spero (2005) found that efficacy increased during teacher preparation and student teaching, but then decreased during the first year of teaching. One explanation for possible initial declines in efficacy with early teaching experience is that the social support available during preparation and student teaching diminishes as teachers move to the public school settings (Cantrell et al., 2003). Also, when novice teachers enter the teaching force, they frequently encounter a reality shock as they confront the complexity of the teaching task. There is a tempering of the unrealistic optimism they held as prospective teachers (Weinstein, 1989). A get tough attitude may result for those teachers who conclude that the constraints of teaching are formidable and resources for dealing with the problems are weak.

There is some evidence to suggest that context variables may be particularly salient among novice teachers and teachers who move into a new setting. For novice and experienced teachers beginning their first year in an urban school, increased opportunities for collaboration with other adults were associated with a greater sense of efficacy (Chester & Beaudin, 1996). Capa (2005) found that first-year teachers' efficacy was related to their ratings of the support of their principals as well as the quality of their preparation programs. Beginning teachers who perceived that they had received higher levels of support in general also reported higher self-efficacy for teaching at the end of their first year (Woolfolk Hoy & Burke-Spero, 2005). A recent study of first year teachers found that weekly contact of at least 1 hour with a mentor was related to the teacher's perception of being helped, but not to the teacher's sense of efficacy (Moore, 2007). Teachers in these studies represented the full range of grades, preschool through high school. In fact, Capa's target population included every first-year teacher who began teaching in Ohio in 2003–2004 and Moore's initial target population included every first year teacher in elementary school buildings in Ohio in 2004–2005.

Efficacy and Experienced Teachers

The trajectory of teachers' efficacy beliefs after the early years is not clear. For example, in a case study of science teaching efficacy, Mulholland and Wallace (2001) found that efficacy increased with experience as the teacher in their case study grew better able to manage the students' behaviors and the science inquiry activities. Some survey studies of larger samples also have found that efficacy increases with experience (de la Torre Cruz & Arias, 2007; Morris-Rothschild & Brassard, 2006). But several studies have found very little correlation at all between experience and teaching efficacy (Cantrell et al., 2003; Plourde, 2002), whereas other research has reported that teacher efficacy decreased with time teaching (Ghaith & Yaghi, 1997; Soodak & Podell, 1996).

Very discouraged teachers with diminished efficacy may leave the profession, and the higher efficacy scores of those who remain may give the appearance that efficacy increases with experience. In one of the largest studies (1,024 prekindergarten through 12th grade teachers across an entire school district), Wolters and Daugherty (2007) used a revised version of the TSES (Tschannen-Moran & Woolfolk Hoy, 2001) and concluded: "Although the effects were modest, … teachers with additional years of experience felt more confident in their ability to employ instructional and assessment practices that would benefit even their most difficult-to-reach students" (p. 188). The same conclusion held for classroom management efficacy, but not for efficacy in motivating students. After 10 years, however, the association between increasing years of experience and increasing efficacy ended. There were no interactions between experience and the academic level of the teacher (elementary, middle, high school), although elementary teachers reported significantly higher efficacy for motivating students than either middle or high school teachers

Once established, efficacy beliefs resist change, even when teachers are exposed to workshops and new teaching methods (Ross, 1995). For example, teachers who attended an "Efficacy Seminar" designed to increase their sense of efficacy had higher efficacy scores immediately following the seminar but, when the scores were measured again 6 weeks later, the increases had disappeared (Ohmart, 1992). Bandura (1997) suggested that when people gain new skills and experiences that challenge their low estimates of their capabilities, they "hold their efficacy beliefs in a provisional status, testing their newly acquired knowledge and skills before raising their judgments of what they are able to do" (p. 83).

Practicing teachers' efficacy can be enhanced through participation in action research (Henson, 2001) or lesson study work (Puchner & Taylor, 2006), regular feedback that focuses on the successful accomplishment of goals (Labone, 2004), and self-reflection that interprets mastery experiences and develops self-regulation skills (Schunk & Zimmerman, 1998).

Teachers' sense of efficacy also appears to be associated with other aspects of teachers' professional lives. Teacher graduates with a higher sense of efficacy are more committed to the teaching profession and efficacy is related, through professional commitment, to entering teaching (Rots, Aelterman, Vlerick, & Vermeulen, 2007). Higher efficacy practicing teachers are more committed to and satisfied with their profession (Caprara, Barbaranelli, Borgogni, & Steca, 2003; Coladarci, 1992). They are more likely to participate in extra-role behaviors such as volunteering for school committees or helping others during free time (Somech & Drach-Zahavy, 2000). Higher efficacy teachers are absent less often, experience less stress, are less likely to experience burn out, and are rated as more competent by their supervisors (Brouwers & Tomic, 2000; Egyed & Short, 2006).

Collective Efficacy

Thus far, we have examined teachers' sense of efficacy as an individual teacher variable. But human behavior is socially situated and teaching is no exception. Teaching is achieved in organizational structures, usually schools, through collective effort (Bandura, 2006b). Teachers often depend upon each other in performing their tasks as they implement complementary roles. Group success necessitates effective interdependent connections of tasks, skills, and roles (Bandura, 1997).

Collective teacher efficacy is *the perception of teachers in a school that the efforts of the faculty as a whole will have a positive effect on students*. Within a school, perceived collective efficacy represents the shared beliefs of group members concerning "the performance capability of a social system as a whole" (Bandura, 1997, p. 469). Collective teacher efficacy is an emergent group-level attribute—the product of the interactive dynamics of the group members; thus, it is more than the sum of the individual parts. It is "the group's shared belief in its conjoint capabilities to organize and execute courses of action required to produce given levels of attainments" (Bandura, 1997, p. 477). For a discussion of the measurement of collective teacher efficacy, see Goddard, Hoy, and Woolfolk Hoy (2000), Goddard and Goddard (2001), and Goddard (2002).

A school's system of shared beliefs provides social cohesion and gives a school a distinctive identity often termed its *organizational culture*. Hence, it should not be surprising that collective efficacy is a salient cultural aspect of schools. In a school, teachers acting on their common beliefs contribute to the transactional dynamics that promote group achievement of goals. In fact, a meta-analysis of research on collective efficacy supports the conclusion that the more extensive interdependence within a social system, the higher the predictiveness of the perceived collective efficacy of the system (Bandura, 2006b). Similar to self-efficacy, collective efficacy is associated with the tasks, level of effort, persistence, shared thoughts, stress levels, and achievement of groups.

Sources of Collective Efficacy

Organizational functioning depends on the knowledge, vicarious learning, self-reflection, and self-regulation of teachers and students. Just as mastery experience, vicarious experience, social persuasion, and emotional arousal are critical for individual sense of efficacy, they are also basic in the development of collective teaching efficacy.

Mastery experiences are important for organizations; in fact, they are the most powerful source of efficacy information (Goddard, 2001; Goddard, 2003). A resilient sense of collective efficacy requires overcoming difficulties through persistent effort. Organizations learn by experience and thus are likely to succeed in attaining their goals (Huber, 1996; Levitt & March, 1996). Consistent with Huber's analysis of learning organizations, schools, like individuals, "tend to learn well what they do, and tend to do what they learn well" (p. 152).

Just as *vicarious experience* and *modeling* serve as effective sources of personal teacher efficacy, they also promote collective teacher efficacy. Teachers listen to stories about the accomplishments of their colleagues as well as success stories of other schools. Organizations learn by observing other organizations (Huber, 1996). For example, a school that reacts to declining achievement scores by using a curricular reform that was effective in a neighboring district is engaged in a self-regulatory process informed by the vicarious learning of its members.

Verbal persuasion and socialization are other means of strengthening a faculty's conviction that it has the capability to achieve what it seeks. Teachers can be changed by talks, workshops, professional development activities, and feedback about achievement; however, the more cohesive the faculty, the more likely the group as a whole can be persuaded by sound argument. Persuasion can promote extra effort and persistence, both of which are critical in problem solving. New teachers are also *socialized* by the organization (Hoy & Woolfolk, 1990) and quickly begin to accept the efficacy perspective of schools that have a strong culture of efficacy. New teachers learn that extra effort and success are the norm.

Organizations also have *affective states*. Just as individuals react to stress, so do organizations. Efficacious organizations learn to tolerate pressure, manage crises, and continue to function effectively; they learn to adapt and cope with disruptive forces. Less efficacious organizations often react in dysfunctional ways when confronted with problems, which, in turn, reinforces their basic acceptance of and dispositions toward failure. The affective state of an organization is critical in how it interprets challenges.

In addition to these four basic sources of collective efficacy, a variety of *contextual variables* such as socioeconomic status (SES) can influence the formation collective efficacy (Goddard, Hoy & Woolfolk Hoy 2004; Hoy, Sweetland, & Smith, 2002). Adams and Forsyth (2006) found that two other contextual variables, enabling school structure and school level are sources of collective efficacy. For example, developing enabling structures means the principal organizes the work to enhance and support teacher professional judgments based on their expertise and experience rather than enforcement of rigid bureaucratic rules. In enabling structures principals manifest leadership that keeps a school running smoothly and makes it a pleasant and productive place for teachers to learn and teach (McGuigan & Hoy, 2006).

Formation of Collective Efficacy

Although all of these sources of information are pivotal in the formation of collective efficacy, processing and interpreting the information are critical. Teachers assess what they need to teach;

they analyze the teaching task. At the school level, such reflection produces inferences about the challenges of teaching in that particular school, that is, what it would take for the institution to be successful. Such venues might include regular faculty meetings, informal meetings, professional development activities, and collaborative projects among schools. Teachers consider the means needed to make the school successful, including the available resources and limitations and barriers to be overcome, and evaluate the teaching task in conjunction with assessments of the teaching competency of the faculty. At the school level, the analysis of teaching competence leads to inferences about the faculty's teaching skills, methods, training, and expertise. As with individual teacher efficacy, analyses of task and competence occur simultaneously, and interact as collective teacher efficacy emerges.

Power of the Collective

School cultures develop norms and shared beliefs that give teachers some control over the actions of others when those actions have consequences for the group (Coleman, 1990). For example, when a teacher's actions are inconsistent with the shared beliefs of the group, group members sanction those actions. Thus, in schools with strong cultures of efficacy, the normative and cultural environments constrain teachers to persist in their educational efforts and sanction those who do not.

The consequences of strong collective teacher efficacy are the acceptance of challenging goals, strong organizational effort, and a persistence that leads to better performance. Of course, the opposite is also true. Lower collective efficacy yields less effort, the propensity to give up, and a lower performance. The process and components of collective teacher efficacy are similar to those of individual teacher efficacy and are illustrated in Figure 28.1. Once established, a school culture of efficacy is a relatively stable property that requires substantial effort to change.

Collective Efficacy and Achievement

Not surprisingly, Bandura (1993, 1997) concludes that collective teacher efficacy is an important school property because it is a key the link between teacher efficacy and student achievement (Ross, 1992, 1995). When compared with the impact of a number of powerful and common school contextual properties such as socioeconomic status, proportion of minority students, school size, and past achievement, collective efficacy is the aspect of school context most strongly related to teacher's sense of personal efficacy. Self-efficacy of teachers is reinforced and made even more potent by the positive power of a culture of efficacy (Goddard & Goddard, 2001; Goddard et al., 2004).

Before the year 2000, a few researchers had examined collective teacher efficacy by aggregating individual teacher efficacy scores to obtain a school score (e. g., Hoover-Dempsey et al., 1992), but we found only one study that assessed teacher perceptions of the collective faculty as a whole (Bandura, 1993). In this groundbreaking study, Bandura reached two important conclusions: (a) student achievement (aggregated to the school level) was significantly and positively related to collective efficacy, and (b) collective efficacy had a greater effect on student achievement than did student socioeconomic status (aggregated to the school level).

With our students, we began a line of inquiry to assess collective efficacy and its relationship to student achievement. Consistent with Bandura (1993), but using hierarchal linear modeling, we found that collective efficacy of the school had a greater positive impact on student achievement than that of any one of the demographic controls for the achievement variables (Goddard, Hoy, & Woolfolk Hoy, 2000). Subsequent research has demonstrated the significant relationship between collective efficacy and school achievement in rural schools (Hoy et al., 2002), elementary schools (Cybulski, Hoy, & Sweetland, 2005; Goddard, Tschannen-Moran, & Hoy, 2001), and high schools (Goddard, LoGerfo, & Hoy, 2004). The last study is arguably the most comprehensive because it examined a diverse sample of high schools using structural equation modeling, controlling for urbanicity, socioeconomic status, prior achievement and other demographic characteristics, and incorporated multiple measures of achievement, including standardized test measures of math, science, reading, and writing. In all cases, collective efficacy was a significant predictor of school achievement.

In brief, research to date supports the strong linkage between perceived collective efficacy and school achievement while controlling for a host of demographic variables including socioeconomic status, thus extending Bandura's social cognitive theory of self-efficacy to the organizational level to explain how the social context of the school interacts with personal attributes of teachers to motivate them to exert strong effort, to persist, and to rebound with resilience when there is not initial success.

Criticisms of Efficacy Research

Henson (2002), Wheatley (2002, 2005), and Labone (2004) have critically analyzed the conceptual foundations and empirical research on teachers' efficacy beliefs. In spite of the large body of literature describing positive outcomes associated with higher levels of individual and collective efficacy, Wheatley (2005) suggested that several forms of teacher self-efficacy might be problematic. One is the "unrealistic optimism" of beginning teachers (described earlier) that interferes with their ability to accurately judge their own effectiveness, particularly their ability to manage classes (Emmer & Hickman, 1991; Weinstein, 1989). Another problematic consequence of higher efficacy is resistance to learning new knowledge and skills and a tendency to "stick with what works"—with the ways of teaching that have provided the sense of mastery in the past. Overconfident efficacy may quickly be followed by giving up if the task proves more difficult than first thought.

Wheatley (2002) identified a number of benefits for teacher learning that might follow from having doubts about one's efficacy. These include the possibility that doubts might foster reflection, motivation to learn, greater responsiveness to diversity, productive collaboration, and change-provoking disequilibrium. We believe a sense of efficacy for learning would be necessary to respond to doubts in such positive ways, but the point is well taken that persistent high efficacy perceptions in the face of poor performance can produce avoidance rather than positive action. It seems likely that teachers are best served by a balance of confidence and openness to learning based on a realistic assessment of personal strengths and weaknesses.

Another criticism is that the findings from efficacy research, because they are correlational and global in nature, provide no guidance for teacher education or professional development. More recent work using confirmatory factor analysis and structural equation modeling speaks to concerns about correlations, but it is true that very few intervention studies have examined efficacy change or the mechanisms through which teachers' efficacy beliefs might influence student outcomes. The Woolfolk Hoy and Davis (2006) model (Figure 28.2) is a beginning in mapping possible connections, but remains to be tested.

Because experimental studies are lacking, it is difficult to determine whether efficacy leads to or is a consequence of positive outcomes, which themselves could be caused by other factors.

Even though causal connections have not been established, much of the writing on teachers' efficacy beliefs seems to assume causality. Wheatley (2005) noted "teacher efficacy researchers regularly slip into causal language to describe the relationships between teachers' efficacy beliefs and other variables of interest. Claims about the 'effect,' 'influence' and 'power' of teacher efficacy appear frequently throughout the literature" (p. 755). Our integrated model of teacher efficacy (Tschannen-Moran, Woolfolk Hoy, & Hoy, 1998) assumes reciprocal causality, in keeping with Bandura's (1997) social cognitive theory. Clearly, more longitudinal, quasi-experimental, and qualitative work is needed to better understand the sources, antecedents, interrelationships, and consequences of teachers' efficacy beliefs at individual and collective levels.

A Look to the Future

It is likely that work will continue to develop better ways of assessing teachers' efficacy beliefs. For example, we are working with students who have adapted the TSES to assess teachers' efficacy beliefs about inclusion and technology (Benton-Borghi, 2006), English as a foreign language in Venezuela (Chacón, 2005), English language teaching in Korean elementary schools (Jeong-Ah, 2007), and multicultural education (Kozel, 2007). The TES and the TSES have been translated into a number of languages including Spanish, Chinese, Korean, and Turkish. With translations come challenges to make items not only subject and student specific, but also culturally appropriate.

Kozel (2007) has suggested that a third factor be considered—teachers' sense of responsibility for outcomes. Kozel noted that even if a teacher knows that particular behaviors will likely lead to certain outcomes and also feels a sense of efficacy for accomplishing those behaviors, the teacher may not act unless he or she feels a sense of personal responsibility for the outcomes. Specifically, Kozel assessed preservice teachers on their efficacy for multicultural education, their advocacy for social justice outcomes, and their sense of responsibility for those outcomes. She found that their sense of responsibility was significantly lower than their advocacy and that efficacy was related to, but not the same as responsibility. She suggested that responsibility may be a better predictor of teachers' engagement in multicultural education.

Efficacy Beliefs about Relationships with Students

Using items from several measures of teacher efficacy (Emmer & Hickman, 1991; Gibson & Dembo, 1984; Woolfolk, Rosoff, & Hoy, 1990) Ho and Hau (2004) found three factors in their Australian and Chinese teacher samples: instruction, discipline/management, and personal guidance (fostering students' personal social adjustment). Even though the factors of instruction and management are consistent with the TSES, these finding suggest there may exist cultural differences with regard to teachers' beliefs about their responsibility towards personal guidance. It also is possible that the role of teachers in motivating and maintaining relationships with students is an interpersonal aspect of teachers' self-efficacy not well captured by current instruments (see Labone, 2004).

In the classrooms, the majority of teachers' successes and failures depend on their ability to cope with the "in-the-moment" decision-making problems of managing their classrooms and interacting with their students. To be successful, teachers must feel confident in their abilities to read and interpret students' verbal and nonverbal communications; to identify, express, and cope with their own emotions; and to help their students to learn to manage and cope with the emotions they experience in the classroom. Yet, to our knowledge, with the exception of Ho and Hau (2004), few researchers have explored teachers' sense of efficacy for developing relationships with students and its potential role in shaping both the academic and socioemotional climates of the classroom, the affective tenor of the classroom, students' learning behaviors, and subsequently students' motivation and achievement. Because relationships with teachers may prove central to students' development (Davis, 2006; Pianta, Belsky, Vandergrift, Houts, & Morrison 2008; Wentzel, 1998), future research needs to explore the roles that efficacy for developing relationships with students may play in supporting students' achievement. For example, do teachers' efficacy for teaching as well as for relationships predict relational and academic outcomes in the classroom?

Beyond Efficacy to Academic Optimism

A sense of efficacy is by its very nature an optimistic perspective (Bandura, 2006b); it focuses on a "can do" attitude. In an attempt to capture this feature of optimism in the school workplace, Hoy and his colleagues (Hoy, Tarter, & Woolfolk Hoy, 2006a, b) have extended the notion of teachers' sense of efficacy to the more general construct of *academic optimism*. Academic optimism weds three influential characteristics of teachers (teachers' efficacy expectations, teachers' trust in students, and academic emphasis) into an overarching latent construct; all three component concepts reflect a sense of the possible and all three are positively related to student achievement. Teachers' sense of efficacy is a belief; it is *cognitive*. Teachers' trust in students and parents is an *affective* response. Teacher academic emphasis is the press for particular *behaviors* in the classroom. Consequently, a teacher's sense of academic optimism paints a rich picture of human agency that explains teacher behavior in terms of cognitive, affective, and behavioral dimensions.

The concept of academic optimism, like efficacy, can be examined at both the individual and collective levels. There have been only a few studies exploring academic optimism and most have been at the collective level. The first study (Hoy et al., 2006a) was a confirmatory factor analysis that demonstrated the structure and composition of the construct of academic optimism with elementary schools. Next, Hoy et al. (2006b) examined high schools and once again, a confirmatory factor analysis supported the nature and meaning of academic optimism. But this study went one step further; it also demonstrated that academic optimism had a positive and direct effect on school student achievement in both math and science controlling for numerous demographic factors, including SES. A study of urban elementary schools (Smith & Hoy, 2007) also replicated the link between academic optimism and school achievement.

A fourth study on academic optimism (McGuigan & Hoy, 2006) pushed the research even further by examining what principals can do to cultivate a culture of academic optimism in secondary schools. The researchers concluded that principals who were able to develop school structures in which the rules, policies, and procedures enabled the basic teaching and learning mission of the schools had cultures of academic optimism. The authors theorized that enabling school structures captured the outcomes of what effective leaders do—they enable the key work of the school and they create a culture of optimism.

To date, only one study has examined the concept of academic optimism at the individual level (Woolfolk Hoy, Hoy, & Kurz, 2008). It suggests the viability of individual academic optimism as a general constellation of beliefs that is theoretically and conceptually united into a single construct. In addition, humanistic classroom management, student-centered beliefs and practices, and organizational citizenship behavior were individually and collectively related to the teacher's sense of academic optimism, controlling for student SES.

Much more remains to be done, especially at the individual level, to explore and to refine this latent construct and to examine the relationships between individual teacher academic optimism and student outcomes. Both antecedents and consequences of academic optimism at both the collective and individual levels offer researchers a rich and heuristic set of research agendas that have both practical and theoretical implications for student learning.

References

Adams, C. M., & Forsyth, P. A. (2006). Proximate sources of collective teacher efficacy. *Journal of Educational Administration, 44,* 625–642.

Agarwal, R., Sambamurthy, V., & Stair, R. (2000). Research report: The evolving relationship between general and specific computer self-efficacy — an empirical assessment. *Information Systems Research, 11*(4), 418–430.

Allinder, R. M. (1994). The relationship between efficacy and the instructional practices of special education teachers and consultants. *Teacher Education and Special Education, 17,* 86–95.

Armor, D., Conroy-Oseguera, P., Cox M., King, N., McDonnell, L., Pascal, A., et al. (1976). *Analysis of the school preferred reading programs in selected Los Angeles minority schools.* (REPORT NO. R-2007-LAUSD). Santa Monica, CA: Rand Corporation. (ERIC Document Reproduction Service No. 130 243)

Ashton, P.T., & Webb, R. B., (1986). *Making a difference: Teachers' sense of efficacy and student achievement.* New York: Longman.

Ashton, P. T., Webb, R. B., & Doda, N. (1983). *A study of teacher sense of efficacy.* Final Report. Gainesville: University of Florida. (ERIC EDRS# ED231833)

Bandura, A., (1977). Self-efficacy: Toward a unifying theory of behavioral change. *Psychological Review 84,* 191–215.

Bandura. A. (1982). Self-efficacy mechanism in human agency. *American Psychologist, 37,* 122-147.

Bandura, A. (1993). Perceived self-efficacy in cognitive development and functioning. *Educational Psychologist, 28,* 117–148.

Bandura, A. (1994). Self-efficacy. In V. S. Ramachaudran (Ed.), *Encyclopedia of human behavior* (Vol. 4, pp. 71–81). New York: Academic Press.

Bandura, A. (1997). *Self-efficacy: The exercise of control.* New York: W. H. Freeman and Company.

Bandura, A. (2006a). Guide to the construction of self-efficacy scales. In F. Pajares & T. Urdan (Eds.). *Self-efficacy beliefs of adolescents* (Vol. 5., pp. 307–337). Greenwich, CT: Information Age.

Bandura, A. (2006b). Toward a psychology of human agency. *Perspectives on Psychological Science, 1,* 164–180.

Benton-Borghi, B. N. (2006) *Teaching every student in the 21st century: Teacher efficacy and technology.* Unpublished doctoral dissertation, The Ohio State University, Columbus.

Berman, P., McLaughlin, M., Bass, G., Pauly, E., & Zellman, G. (1977). *Federal Programs supporting educational change. Vol. VII Factors affecting implementation and continuation* (Report No. R-1589/7-HEW). Santa Monica, CA: The Rand Corporation. (ERIC Document Reproduction Service No. 140 432)

Bischoff, A. E. (2007). Exploring connections among teacher expectation, student-teacher relationships, intrinsic motivation and self-efficacy. Unpublished master's thesis, The Ohio State University, Columbus.

Bleicher, R. E., & Lindgren, J. (2005). Success in science learning and preservice teaching self-efficacy. *Journal of Science Teacher Education, 16,* 205–225.

Bohning, G., Hale, L., & Chowning, F. (1999). Change-of-career preservice elementary teachers: Their concerns about teaching science. *Education, 120*(1), 143-148.

Brophy, J. (1996). *Teaching problem students.* New York: Guilford.

Brophy, J. E., & Good, T. (1986). Teacher behavior and student achievement. In M. Wittrock (Ed.), *Handbook of research on teaching* (3rd ed., pp. 328–375). New York: Macmillan.

Brouwers, A., & Tomic, W. (2000). A longitudinal study of teacher burnout and perceived self-efficacy in classroom management. *Teaching and Teacher Education, 16,* 239–253.

Brouwers, A., Tomic, W., & Stijnen, S. (2002). A confirmatory factor analysis of scores on the teacher efficacy scale. *Swiss Journal of Psychology, 61,* 211–219.

Calderhead, J. (1996). Teachers: Beliefs and knowledge. In D. Berliner & R. Calfee (Eds.), *Handbook of educational psychology* (pp. 709–725). New York: Macmillan.

Cantrell, P., Young, S., & Moore, A. (2003). Factors affecting science teaching efficacy of preservice elementary teachers. *Journal of Science Teacher Education, 14*(3), 177–192.

Capa, Y. (2005). *Factors influencing first-year teachers' sense of efficacy.* Unpublished doctoral dissertation, The Ohio State University, Columbus.

Caprara, G. V., Barbaranelli, C., Borgogni, L., & Steca, P. (2003). Efficacy beliefs as determinants of teachers" job satisfaction. *Journal of Educational Psychology, 95,* 821–832.

Chacón, C. T. (2005). Teachers' perceived efficacy among English as a foreign language teachers in middle schools in Venezuela. *Teaching and Teacher Education 21,* 257–272.

Charlton, J. P. (2005). Measuring perceptual and motivational facets of computer control: The development and validation of the computing control scale. *Computers in Human Behavior, 21,* 791–815.

Chester, M., & Beaudin, B. Q. (1996). Efficacy beliefs of newly hired teachers in urban schools. *American Educational Research Journal, 33,* 233–257.

Coladarci, T., & Breton, W. (1997). Teacher efficacy, supervision, and the special education resource-room teacher. *Journal of Educational Research, 90*, 230–239.

Coleman, J. S. (1990). *Foundations of social theory.* Cambridge, MA: Harvard University Press.

Cothran, D. J., Kulinna, P. H., & Garrahy, D. A. (2003). "This is kind of giving a secret away...": Students' perspectives on effective class management. *Teaching and Teacher Education, 19*, 435–444.

Cousins, J. B., & Walker, C. A. (2000). Predictors of educators' valuing of systemic inquiry in schools [Special issue]. *Canadian Journal of Program Evaluation*, 25–53.

Cybulski, T., Hoy, W. K., & Sweetland, S. R. (2005). The roles of collective efficacy and fiscal efficiency in school achievement. *The Journal of Educational Administration, 43*, 439–461.

Davis, F. (1989). Perceived usefulness, perceived ease of use, and user acceptance of information technology. *MIS Quarterly, 13*, 319–340.

Davis, H. A. (2006). Exploring the contexts of relationship quality between middle school students and teachers. *The Elementary School Journal: Special Issue on the Interpersonal Contexts of Motivation and Learning, 106*, 193–223.

Davis, H. A., Ring, G., & Ferdig, R. E. (2002, March). Integrating Technology into the Study of Teaching and Learning. In Willis, D. A., Price, J., & Davis, N. E. (Eds.), *2002 Information Technology and Teacher Education Annual: Proceedings of SITE2002* (pp. 1306–1307). Norfolk, VA: Association for the Advancement of Computing in Education (AACE).

De Laat, J., & Watters, J. (1995). Science teaching self-efficacy in a primary school: A case study. *Research in Science Education, 25*(4), 453–464.

de la Torre Cruz, M. J., & Casanova Arias, P. F. (2007). Comparative analysis of expectancies of efficacy in in-service and prospective teachers. *Teaching and Teacher Education, 23*, 641–652.

Delpit, L. (1995). *Other people's children: Cultural conflict in the classroom.* New York: The New Press.

De Vries, P., Midden, C., & Bouwhuis, D. (2003). The effects of errors on system trust, self-confidence, and the allocation of control in route planning. *International Journal of Human-Computer Studies, 58*, 719–735.

Denzine, G. M., Cooney, J. B., & McKenzie, R. (2005). Confirmatory factor analysis of the Teacher Efficacy Scale for prospective teachers. *British Journal of Educational Psychology, 75*, 689–708.

Egyed, C. J., & Short, R. J. (2006). Teacher self-efficacy, burnout, experience and decision to refer a disruptive student. *School Psychology International, 74*, 462–474.

Emmer, E., & Hickman, J. (1991). Teacher efficacy in classroom management. *Educational and Psychological Measurement, 51*, 755–765.

Enochs, L. G., Smith, P. L., & Huinker, D. (2000). Establishing factorial validity of the mathematics teaching efficacy beliefs instrument. *School Science and Mathematics, 100*(4), 194–202.

Evers, W. J. G., Brouwers, A., & Tomic, W. (2002). Burnout and self-efficacy: A study on teachers' beliefs when implementing an innovative educational system in the Netherlands. *British Journal of Educational Psychology, 72*, 227–245.

Ferreira, M. M., & Bosworth, K. (2001). Defining caring teachers: Adolescents' perspective. *Journal of Classroom Interaction, 36*(1), 24–30.

Fishler, J., & Firestone, W. A. (2006). Teacher learning in a school–university partnership: Exploring the role of social trust and teaching efficacy beliefs. *Teachers College Record, 108*, 1155–1185.

Friedman, I. A., & Farber, B. A. (1992). Professional self-concept as a predictor of teacher burnout. *Journal of Educational Research, 86*, 28–36.

Gerges, G. (2001). Factors influencing preservice teachers' variation in use of instructional methods: Why is teacher efficacy is not a significant contributor? *Teacher Education Quarterly, 28*(4), 71–88.

Ghaith, G., & Yaghi, H. (1997). Relationships among experience, teacher efficacy, and attitudes toward the implementation of instructional innovation. *Teaching and Teacher Education, 13*(4), 451–458.

Gibson, S., & Dembo, M., (1984). Teacher efficacy: A construct validation. *Journal of Educational Psychology, 76*(4), 569–582.

Goddard, R. D. (2001). Collective efficacy: A neglected construct in the study of schools and student achievement. *Journal of Educational Psychology, 93*(3), 467–476.

Goddard, R. D. (2002). Collective efficacy and school organization: A multilevel analysis of teacher influence in schools. *Theory and Research in Educational Administration, 1*, 169–184.

Goddard, R. D. (2003). The impact of schools on teacher beliefs, influence, and student achievement: The role of collective efficacy. In J. Raths & A. McAninch (Eds.), *Advances in teacher education* (Vol. 6, pp. 183–204). Westport, CT: Information Age.

Goddard, R. D., & Goddard, Y. L. (2001). A multilevel analysis of teacher and collective efficacy. *Teaching and Teacher Education, 17*, 807–818.

Goddard, R. G., Hoy, W. K., & Woolfolk Hoy, A. (2000). Collective teacher efficacy: Its meaning, measure, and impact on student achievement. *American Educational Research Journal, 37*, 479–508.

Goddard, R. D., Hoy, W. K., & Woolfolk Hoy, A. (2004). Collective efficacy: Theoretical developments, empirical evidence, and future directions. *Educational Researcher, 33*(3), 3–13.

Goddard, R. G., LoGerfo, L., & Hoy, W. K. (2004). High school accountability: The role of collective efficacy. *Educational Policy, 18*(30), 403–425.

Goddard, R. G., Sweetland, S. R., & Hoy, W. K. (2000). Academic emphasis of urban elementary schools and student achievement: a multi-level analysis. *Educational Administration Quarterly, 36*, 692–701.

Goddard, R. D., Tschannen-Moran, M., & Hoy, W. K. (2001). Teacher trust in students and parents: A multilevel examination of the distribution and effects of teacher trust in urban elementary schools. *Elementary School Journal,* *102*(1), 3–17.

Good, T., & Brophy, J. (2008). *Looking in classrooms* (10th ed.). Boston, MA: Allyn & Bacon.

Graham, S., Harris, K. R., Fink, & McArthur, C. A. (2001). Teacher efficacy in writing: A construct validation with primary grade teachers. *Scientific Studies of Reading, 5*, 177–202.

Gregoire, M. (2003). Is it a challenge of a threat? A dual process model of teachers' cognition and appraisal processes during conceptual change. *Educational Psychology Review, 15*, 147–179.

Gregoire, M., Ashton, P., & Algina, J. (2004). Changing preservice teachers' beliefs about teaching and learning in mathematics: An intervention study. *Contemporary Educational Psychology, 29*, 164–186.

Guskey, T. R. (1981). Measurement of responsibility teachers assume for academic successes and failures in the classroom. *Journal of Teacher Education, 32*, 44–51.

Guskey, T. R. (1988). Teacher efficacy, self-concept, and attitudes toward the implementation of instructional innovation. *Teaching and Teacher Education, 4*(1), 63–69.

Guskey, T., & Passaro, P. (1994). Teacher efficacy: A study of construct dimensions. *American Educational Research Journal, 31*, 627–643.

Hani, J., Czerniak, C., & Lumpe, A. (1996). Teacher beliefs and intentions regarding the implementation of science education reform strands. *Journal of Research in Science Teaching, 33*, 971–993.

Hebert, E., Lee, A., & Williamson, L. (1998). Teachers' and teacher education students' sense of efficacy: Quantitative and qualitative comparisons. *Journal of Research and Development in Education, 31*(4), 214–225.

Henson, R. K. (2001). Effect of participation in teacher research on teacher efficacy. *Teaching and Teacher Education, 17*, 819–836.

Henson, R. K. (2002). From adolescent angst to adulthood: Substantive implications and measurement dilemmas in the development of teacher efficacy research. *Educational Psychologist, 37,* 137–150.

Henson, R. K., Kogan, L., & Vacha-Haase, T. (2001). A reliability generalization study of the Teacher Efficacy Scale and related instruments. *Educational and Psychological Measurement, 61*, 404–420.

Ho, I. T., & Hau, K. T. (2004). Australian and Chinese teachers efficacy: Similarities and differences in personal instruction, discipline, guidance efficacy and beliefs in external determinants. *Teaching and Teacher Education, 20,* 313–323.

Hoover-Dempsey, K. V., Bassler, O. C., & Brissie, J. S. (1992). Explorations in parent-school relations. *Journal of Educational Research, 85*, 287–294.

Housego, B. (1992). Monitoring student teachers' feelings of preparedness to teach and teacher efficacy in a new elementary teacher education program. *Journal of Education for Teaching, 18*(3), 259–272.

Hoy, W. K. (2001). The pupil control studies: A historical, theoretical, and empirical analysis. *Journal of Educational Administration, 39,* 424–442.

Hoy, W. K., Sweetland, S. R., & Smith, P. A. (2002). Toward an organizational model of achievement in high schools: The significance of collective efficacy. *Educational Administration Quarterly, 38*, 77–93.

Hoy, W. K. & Woolfolk, A. E. (1990). Socialization of student teachers. *American Educational Research Journal, 27,* 279–300.

Hoy, W. K., & Woolfolk, A. E. (1993). Teachers' sense of efficacy and the organizational health of schools. *The Elementary School Journal, 93*, 356–372.

Hoy, W. K., Tarter, C. J., & Woolfolk Hoy, A. (2006a). Academic optimism of schools. In W. K. Hoy & C. Miskel (Eds.), *Contemporary issues in educational policy and school outcomes* (pp. 135–156). Greenwich, CT: Information Age.

Hoy, W. K., Tarter, C. J., & Woolfolk Hoy, A. (2006b). Academic optimism of schools: A force for student achievement. *American Educational Research Journal, 43*, 425–446.

Huber, G. P. (1996). *Organizational learning: The contributing processes and literatures.* In M. D. Cohen & L. S. Sproull (Eds.), *Organizational learning* (pp. 124–162). Thousand Oaks, CA: Sage.

Jeong-Ah, (2007). *Teachers' sense of efficacy in teaching English, perceived English proficiency, and attitudes toward the English language: A case of Korean public elementary school teachers.* Unpublished doctoral dissertation proposal, Ohio State University, Columbus.

Katz, S. R. (1999). Teaching in tensions: Latino immigrant youth, their teachers, and the structures of schooling. *Teachers College Record, 100*(4), 809–840.

Knoblauch, D., & Woolfolk Hoy, A. (2008). "Maybe I can teach *those* kids." The influence of contextual factors on student teachers' sense of efficacy. *Teaching and Teacher Education, 24,* 166–179.

Kozel, S. (2007). *Exploring pre-service teachers' sense of responsibility for multiculturalism and diversity: Scale construction and construct validation.* Unpublished master's thesis, The Ohio State University, Columbus.

Kurz, N., Woolfolk Hoy, A., & Hoy, W. K. (2007, April). *Predictors of academic optimism: Teachers' instructional beliefs and professional commitment.* Paper presented at the annual meeting of the American Educational Research Association, Chicago, IL.

Labone, E. (2004). Teacher efficacy: Maturing the construct through research in alternative paradigms. *Teaching and Teacher Education, 20,* 341–359.

Levitt, B. L., & March, J. G. (1996). In M. D. Cohen & L. S. Sproull (Eds.), *Organizational learning* (pp. 516–540). Thousand Oaks, CA: Sage.

Li, X., & Zhang, M. (2000). *Effects of early field experiences on preservice teachers' efficacy beliefs – a pilot study.* (ERIC Document Reproductive Service No. ED 444973)

Locke, E. A., &Latham, G. P. (2002). Building a practically useful theory of goal setting and task motivation: A 35-year odyssey. *American Psychologist, 57,* 705–717.

Locke, E. A., & Latham, G. P. (2004). What should we do about motivation theory? Six recommendations for the twenty-first century. *Academy of Management Review, 29,* 388–403.

McGuigan, L. & Hoy, W. K. (2006). Principal Leadership: Creating a culture of academic optimism to improve achievement for all students. *Leadership and Policy in Schools, 5*(3), 203–229.

Meijer, C., & Foster, S. (1988) The effect of teacher self-efficacy on referral chance. *Journal of Special Education, 22,* 378–385.

Midgley, C., Feldlaufer, H., & Eccles, J., (1989). Change in teacher efficacy and student self- and task-related beliefs in mathematics during the transition to junior high school. *Journal of Educational Psychology, 81,* 247–258.

Milner, H. R., & Hoy, A. W. (2003). A case study of an African American Teacher's self-efficacy, stereotype threat, and persistence. *Teaching and Teacher Education, 19,* 263–276.

Moore, R. (2007). *Relating 2004–2005 and 2005–2006 beginning, public, elementary, teachers' perceptions of support, efficacy beliefs, and performance on Praxis III.* Unpublished doctoral dissertation, The Ohio State University, Columbus.

Morris-Rothschild, B. K., & Brassard, M. R. (2006). Teachers' conflict management styles: The role of attachment styles and classroom management efficacy. *Journal of School Psychology, 44,* 105–121.

Muijs, D., & Reynolds, D. (2001). Teachers' beliefs and behaviors: What really matters. *Journal of Classroom Interaction, 37,* 3–15.

Mulholland, J., & Wallace, J. (2001). Teacher induction and elementary science teaching: Enhancing self-efficacy. *Teaching and Teacher Education, 17,* 243–261.

Newberry, M. & Davis, H. A. (2008). The role of elementary teachers' conceptions of closeness to students on their differential behavior in the classroom. *Teaching and Teacher Education, 24, 1965–1985.*

Ohmart, H. (1992). *The effects of an efficacy intervention on teachers' efficacy feelings.* Unpublished doctoral dissertation, University of Kansas, Lawrence. UMI 9313150.

Pajares, F. (1993). Preservice teachers' beliefs: A focus for teacher education. *Action in Teacher Education, 15*(2), 45–54.

Pajares, F. (1996). Self-efficacy beliefs in academic settings. *Review of Educational Research, 66,* 533–578.

Palmer, D. H. (2006). Sources of self-efficacy in a science methods course for primary teacher. *Research in Science Education, 36,* 337–353.

Pianta, R. C., Belsky, J., Vandergrift, N., Houts, R., & Morrison, F. J. (2008). Classroom effects on children's achievement trajectories in elementary school. *American Educational Research Journal, 45,* 365–397.

Pierson, M. E. (2001). Technology integration practice as a function of pedagogical expertise. *Journal of Research on Computing in Education, 33,* 413–430.

Plourde, L. A. (2002). The influence of student teaching on preservice elementary teachers' science self-efficacy and outcome expectancy beliefs. *Journal of Instructional Psychology, 29*(4), 245–253.

Posnanski, T. J. (2002). Professional development programs for elementary science teachers: An analysis of teacher self-efficacy beliefs and a professional development model. *Journal of Science Teacher Education, 13,* 189–220.

Puchner, L. D., & Taylor, A. R. (2006). Lesson study, collaboration and teacher efficacy: Stories from two school-based math lesson study groups. *Teaching and Teacher Education, 22,* 922–934.

Ramey-Gassert, L., Shroyer, L., & Staver, J. (1996). A qualitative study of factors influencing science teaching self-efficacy of elementary level teachers. *Science Teacher Education, 80*(3), 283–315.

Rice, D. C., & Roychoudhury, A. (2003). Preparing more confident preservice elementary science teachers: One elementary science methods teacher's self-study. *Journal of Science Teacher Education, 14*(2), 97–126.

Riggs, I., & Enochs, L. (1990). Toward the development of an elementary teacher's science teaching efficacy belief instrument. *Science Education, 74*(6), 625–638.

Ropp, M. M. (1999). Exploring individual characteristics associated with learning to use computers in preservice teacher preparation. *Journal of Computing in Education, 31,* 402–424.

Ross, J. A. (1992). Teacher efficacy and the effects of coaching on student achievement. *Canadian Journal of Education, 17*(1), 51–65.

Ross, J. A. (1995). Strategies for enhancing teachers' beliefs in their effectiveness: Research on a school improvement hypothesis. *Teachers College Record, 97,* 227–251.

Ross, J. A. (1998). The antecedents and consequences of teacher efficacy. In J. Brophy (Ed.), *Advances in research on teaching* (Vol. 7, pp. 49–73). Greenwich, CT: JAI.

Ross, J. A., Cousins, J. B., & Gadalla, T. (1996). Within-teacher predictors of teacher efficacy. *Teaching and Teacher Education, 12,* 385–400.

Ross, J. A., Cousins, J. B., Gadalla, T., & Hannay, L. (1999). Administrative assignment of teachers in restructuring secondary schools: The effect of out-of-field course responsibility on teacher efficacy. *Educational Administration Quarterly, 35,* 782–804.

Ross, J. A., & Gray, P. (2004, April). *Transformational leadership and teacher commitment to organizational values: The mediating effects of collective teacher efficacy.* Paper presented at the annual meeting of the American Educational Research Association, San Diego.

Ross, J. A., Hogaboam-Gray, A., & Hannay, L. (2001). Effects of teacher efficacy on computer skills and computer cognitions of K-3 students. *Elementary School Journal, 102*(2), 141–156.

Rots, I., Aelterman, A., Vlerick, P., & Vermeulen, K. (2007). Teacher education, graduates' teaching commitment and entrance into the teaching profession. *Teaching and Teacher Education, 23,* 543–556.

Rotter, J. B. (1966). Generalized expectancies for internal versus external control of reinforcement. *Psychological Monographs, 80,* 1–28.

Rushton, S. P. (2000). Student teacher efficacy in inner-city schools. *Urban Review, 32,* 365–383.

Ryan, R. M., & Deci, E. L. (2000). Intrinsic and extrinsic motivation: Classic definitions and new directions. *Contemporary Educational Psychology, 25,* 54–67.

Schoon, K. J., & Boone, W. J. (1998). Self-efficacy and alternative conceptions of science of elementary teachers. *Science Education, 82,* 553–568.

Schunk, D. H., & Zimmerman, B. J. (1998). *Self-regulated learning: From teaching to self-reflective practice.* New York: Guilford.

Sercu, L. (2005). Foreign language teachers and the implementation of intercultural education: a comparative investigation of the professional self-concepts and teaching practices of Belgian teachers of English, French and German. *European Journal of Teacher Education, 28,* 87–105.

Shore, J. R. (2004). Teacher education and multiple intelligences: A case study of multiple intelligences and teacher efficacy in two teacher preparation courses. *Teachers College Record, 106,* 112–139.

Skinner, E. A. (1996). A guide to constructs of control. *Journal of Personality and Social and Personality Psychology, 71,* 549–570.

Smith, P. A., & Hoy, W. K. (2007). Academic optimism and student achievement in urban elementary schools. *Journal of Educational Administration, 45,* 556–568.

Somech, A., & Drach-Zahavy, A. (2000). Understanding extra-role behavior in schools: the relationship between job satisfaction, sense of efficacy, and teachers' extra-role behavior. *Teaching and Teacher Education, 16,* 649–659.

Soodak, L., & Podell, D. (1993). Teacher efficacy and student problem as factors in special education referral. *Journal of Special Education, 27,* 66–81.

Soodak, L., & Podell, D. (1996). Teaching efficacy: Toward the understanding of a multi-faceted construct. *Teaching and Teacher Education, 12,* 401–412.

Straub, E. (2007, April). *Multidimensional appraisals and emotional responses in technology-based scenarios.* Presented at Annual Conference of the American Educational Research Association, Chicago, IL.

Straub, E. (2009).Understanding technology adoption: Theory and future implications for informal education. *Review of Educational Research*

Summers, J. E., Davis, H. A., & Woolfolk Hoy, A. (2006, July) *The effects of teaching efficacy on students' motivation, perceptions of relationship quality, and academic achievement.* Paper presented as part of the symposia on the Interpersonal Contexts of Teaching Selves: Where Have We Been and Where Are We Going? at the Fourth Biennial International SELF Conference, Ann Arbor, MI.

Tobin, K. G. (1998). Issues and trends in the teaching of science. In B. J. Fraser & K. G. Tobin (Eds.), *International handbook of science education* (pp. 129–151). Dordrecht, The Netherlands: Kluwer.

Tosun, T. (2000). The beliefs of preservice elementary teachers toward science and science teaching. *School Science and Mathematics, 100*(7), 374–379.

Tournaki, N., & Podell, D. M. (2005). The impact of student characteristics and teacher efficacy on teachers' predictions of student success. *Teaching and Teacher Education 21,* 299–314.

Tschannen-Moran, M., Uline, C., Woolfolk Hoy, A., & Mackley, T. (2000). Creating smarter schools through collaboration. *Journal of Educational Administration, 38,* 247–271.

Tschannen-Moran, M., & Woolfolk Hoy, A. (2001). Teacher efficacy: Capturing and elusive construct. *Teaching and Teacher Education, 17,* 783–805.

Tschannen-Moran, M., & Woolfolk Hoy, A. (2007). The differential antecedents of self-efficacy beliefs of novice and experienced teachers. *Teaching and Teacher Education, 23,* 944–956

Tschannen-Moran, M., Woolfolk Hoy, A., & Hoy, W. K. (1998). Teacher efficacy: Its meaning and measure. *Review of Educational Research, 68,* 202–248.

Weinstein, C. (1989). Teacher education students' perceptions of teaching. *Journal of Teacher Education, 40*(2), 53–60.

Weinstein, C. S., & Mignano, A. (2007). *Elementary classroom management: Lessons from research and practice* (4th ed.). New York: McGraw-Hill.

Wentzel, K. R. (1998). Social relationships and motivation in middle school: The role of parents, teachers, and peers. *Journal of Educational Psychology, 90*(2), 202–209.

Wheatley, K. F. (2005). The case for reconceptualizing teacher efficacy research, *Teaching and Teacher Education, 21,* 747–766.

Wheatley, K. F. (2002). The potential benefits of teacher efficacy doubts for educational reform. *Teaching and Teacher Education, 18,* 5–22.

Wolters, C. A., & Daugherty, S. G. (2007). Goal structures and teachers' sense of efficacy: Their relation and association to teaching experience and academic level. *Journal of Educational Psychology, 99,* 181–193.

Woolfolk, A. E., & Hoy, W. K. (1990). Prospective teachers' sense of efficacy and beliefs about control, *Journal of Educational Psychology, 82,* 81–91.

Woolfolk, A. E., Rosoff, B., & Hoy, W. K. (1990). Teachers' sense of efficacy and their beliefs about managing students. *Teaching and Teacher Education, 6,* 137–148.

Woolfolk Hoy, A., & Burke-Spero, R. (2005). Changes in teacher efficacy during the early years of teaching: A Comparison of four measures. *Teaching and Teacher Education, 21,* 343–356.

Woolfolk Hoy, A., & Davis, H. (2006). Teachers' sense of efficacy and adolescent achievement. In T. Urdan & F. Pajares (Eds.), *Adolescence and education: Volume V: Self-efficacy beliefs during adolescence* (pp. 117–137). Greenwich, CT: Information Age Publishing.

Woolfolk Hoy, A., Davis, H., & Pape, S. (2006). Teachers' knowledge, beliefs, and thinking. In P. A. Alexander & P. H. Winne (Eds.), *Handbook of educational psychology* (2nd ed., pp. 715–737). Mahwah, NJ: Erlbaum.

Woolfolk Hoy, A. Hoy, W. K., & Kurz, N. M. (2008). Teacher's academic optimism: The development and test of a new construct. *Teaching and Teacher Education, 24,* 821–835.

Woolfolk Hoy, A., & Weinstein, C. S. (2006). Students' and teachers' perspectives about classroom management. In C. Evertson & C. S. Weinstein (Eds.), *Handbook for classroom management: Research, practice, and contemporary issues* (pp. 181–220). Mahwah, NJ: Erlbaum.

29

Commentary: What Can We Learn from a Synthesis of Research on Teaching, Learning, and Motivation?

Barbara L. McCombs

It is an honor and a privilege to be invited to give a commentary on this wonderful collection of chapters. The authors of these chapters are my friends and have been my colleagues for quite a number of years. We have struggled with a field that was ignored for many years and has finally come into its own. These authors, with the wisdom and empirical results they contribute, represent a hope for the future of our field as well as the future of education. Results from the fields of teaching, learning, and motivation—as an integrated and inclusive body of research and practice—now have a chance to influence education and its paradigm in innovative and transformative ways.

That said, I want to begin by acknowledging that the field is still in its infancy in so many ways. During my professional lifetime that spans about 35 to 40 years, I have seen the field move from the behaviorist constructs of Skinnerian's in the 1960s that put motivation outside the learner, to early cognitive psychology in the late 1960s by giants in the field such as David Ausabel, Daniel Berlyne, John Bruner, Art Combs, and others who put motivation in the hands of learners. I then saw the field focus on information processing theories, perceptual psychology and humanistic theories, and then learning and motivational strategies in the 1970s. It wasn't until the mid 1980s that educational, cognitive, or social psychologists began to acknowledge that motivation might be as important, or even more so, to student learning, achievement, and development as cognitive and intellectual processes. So, this has been an exciting journey for me.

Before commenting on the chapters in this section, I begin by laying out my assumptions about learning, motivation, and teaching. These assumptions are fairly simple, but deliberately so. Over the years of my study and experience with learners of all ages, including my children and now four young grandchildren, I have learned the truth of the following assumptions:

- *What we learn about teaching, learning, and motivation from researchers is not necessarily what common sense would tell us.* By this I mean that researchers can "discover truth(s)" that match what we intuitively believe or they can run counter to these intuitive and experiential understandings (our tacit knowledge).

- *When research findings run counter-intuitive to our tacit knowledge, we must discover where the error lies.* The error may lie in our tacit knowledge or in the assumptions and methodology that underlies the research findings.

- *Learners of all ages, from cradle to grave, naturally learn in self-organizing ways that are holistic and unending.* All learners come into life with an insatiable curiosity and motivation to learn. In fact, learning is self-organizing by its nature.

- *What happens to learners in school is that they begin to engage in unnatural learning in unnatural contexts and with unnaturally organized and fragmented curriculum and content divisions.* It is no surprise to me that learners quickly become disengaged in school and display disengagement or compliance (depending on their parentally or otherwise externally imposed orientations to please others or rebel against such external or controlling demands).

- *Choice and the permission to be a natural learner are essential to lifelong learning dispositions.* Without choice and some level of control, too many of the students in our schools, both in the United States and internationally, see schools as unwelcoming places, as places where they don't want to be or don't want to learn. Too many of our students of all genders, races, ethnic groups, and socioeconomic levels are increasingly finding schools to be places where they have to go (or not) and the real-world outside of school as where they want to learn and do learn what they are most interested in or have to learn to survive.

- *The way we think about motivation, learning, and teaching must change if we are to change the current state of affairs for students and those that teach them.* This means that assumptions about human capacity, learning, teaching, and motivation must be changed so that a transformational paradigm for education can emerge.

I will say more about each of these assumptions as I move into my comments about each chapter. But finally, I want to take another liberty. I want to discuss the chapters in the order in which I read them. This order was of my choosing, and I began with the chapter that interested me the most and ended with the chapter *that I thought* would interest me least, but, in fact, was one of the most interesting in its novelty. What I learned as I read the seven chapters surprised me. For that reason, in the proverbial sense (from Proverbs to Job to Ecclesiastics), "The first shall be last, and the last shall be first." Following my brief comments about each chapter, I will conclude with some suggestions for where the field can go and how we can move from the increased complexity of motivational studies to a simpler, more integrative, and holistic view that I hope will lead us into greater knowledge and wisdom. With this knowledge and wisdom, it is my dream that we can achieve an increasingly united and global community of learners—including the students themselves and their teachers—who become dynamic, self-organizing members of an interconnected and interrelated social network and collaborative learning community. That is now my work as well as my dream for the future of us all.

Commentary on Each Chapter in this Section

I want to make clear that the order of this commentary should in no way reflect on the quality or importance of each chapter. It is simply my order of choice when I read the chapters in preparation for this commentary. It is also an example of how I and most of us learn naturally. We start with what interests us most and move on from there. And many times we are surprised, and our interests change as we learn.

Chen and Ennis Chapter

I read the chapter by Ang Chen and Catherine Ennis, entitled "Motivation and Achievement in Physical Education" last because it is an area that I have studied the least, other than my personal contact with Joel Kirsch, PhD, president of the American Sports Institute in Mill Valley, California, and a former sports psychologist for the San Francisco Giants. From working with Joel, however, I have learned that sports teaches us lessons for reuniting mind, body, and spirit and that these lead to high student achievement in all areas of schooling. The impact of his approach was verified in our evaluation of his work (McCombs & Lauer, 1997). Joel's highly effective *Promoting Achievement in School through Sport* (PASS) program for schools has also taught me that in these lessons are further lessons for school reform that move us beyond testing and standardization to schooling that integrates the whole human being and that respects and honors the diversity of abilities and talents of each learner. This is a similar view to what I found in the Chen and Ennis chapter.

From Chen and Ennis I learned that in the last 60 years there has been transformation in the field of physical education. This field now provides structured learning opportunities for all children—opportunities that teach them about not only their bodies and physical activities, but also about their health and activities for healthy living throughout their lives. The authors argue that the best approaches are those that integrate sports and recess activities with the total educational curriculum so that physical education is not just an "add-on" but an anchor to the motivation and engagement of students in all of school learning. Research evidence is convincingly presented to confirm this point. What was further intriguing was Chen and Ennis's review of research findings showing that although there are similar findings related to engagement, learning, and performance in physical education as in other areas of schooling, there are also some clear differences that qualify for more in-depth studies that are situated in the settings of physical education and that take into account the performance and goal differences for diverse student populations.

Although Chen and Ennis acknowledge that the same set of motivational constructs come into play (e.g., choice, persistence, effort, self-efficacy, expectancy beliefs and task values, interests, extrinsic rewards and regulations), not enough research is available to know how they operate specifically in physical education for specific student populations. Another concern is that the measurement issues are different in that both self-report and physical activities can be used, with the later often being more reliable and valid indicators of student motivation.

What I also found interesting is that the link between instructional climate and learning has both actual and perceived relationships that are different than those found in studies of motivation in other domains. That is, whereas student perceptions of climate normally correlate more with performance measures than direct and objective observations, in the physical education research arena, perceived climate is a less valid predictor. Similarly, Chen and Ennis report that an individual-situational conceptualization of interest is more appropriate and viable in explaining the motivational impact of interest in physical education. They argue that this is because the features (e.g., novelty, challenge, exploration opportunity, etc.) of physical activity tasks have been found to contribute to situational interest which can be manipulated in contrast to more stable individual interest that is difficult to change. For teachers and other practitioners this is a key finding that can help them design more situationally interesting learning tasks that enhance student motivation and engagement. What is also important from a theoretical perspective is that it brings us back to the prior state-trait anxiety research showing differential predictability of this motivational construct under a variety of different situations (Spielberger, 2006). This allows the field to circle back to earlier important findings that might usefully be applied in current research to simplify the complexity of cognitive and motivational phenomena.

A final important point from the Chen and Ennis chapter is their argument that it is necessary to reframe motivation research in order to better understand how motivation impacts competence-based achievement. They also point out that this challenge can be addressed by designing a more holistic curriculum that is integrated based on both empirical results and theoretical truths or principles related to motivation. I would suggest we take this a step further, however, and ground *all* motivation related research—whether it is more general or situated—in these research-validated principles and timeless truths about human capacities, individual differences, social and interpersonal needs, motivation, learning, and development (see McCombs, 2004a, for further discussion). It is vital to learners that they be at the center of the educational process *from their perspective as whole learners with social, emotional, physical, motivational, intellectual, and spiritual capacities and needs* during any learning process. It is essential that the assumptions and principles of education are aligned with and respect the learner as agent with natural learning and motivational capacities (cf. McCombs & Miller, 2007, 2008).

Guthrie and Coddington Chapter

Since my interests in motivation and self-regulated learning have been more generalized, this chapter was second to last. As I read it, however, I found myself once again impressed with the quality of thinking in the approach to studying motivation in the content area of reading. What Guthrie and Coddington have accomplished in this chapter is an excellent example of how the field can put the learner holistically in the center of the learning process while still acknowledging that humans as complex systems requires an integrated approach to studying motivation. What these authors accomplish is also noteworthy in that they take the broader living systems view. They offer an integrated, multitheoretical view of motivation that is situated in the content domain of reading. This allows the field to rethink current teaching practices in reading instruction that may inappropriately profile students and further alienate them from the pursuit, engagement, and enjoyment of reading throughout their lifetimes.

As I learned from this chapter's research review, I also found myself rethinking some of my current notions about what has been learned recently in this field. Although I found myself initially concerned about the possibility of a four-dimensional learning profile system for describing readers being dangerous in terms of how it might be misused to label or track students and not fully capture the self-directing and organizing capacities of human learners, I later saw how Guthrie and Coddington were able to rationally and empirically justify this approach. My initial concerns that this approach might not call practitioner or researcher attention to the central role of the self as agent in the learning process were suspended. The further I read, the more I became convinced that these authors understood the role of the individual learner and groups of learners in directing how best they learned to read, based on their perceptions of the complex personal (efficacy beliefs, goals, values, need for autonomy), interpersonal (peer and teacher relationship issues), contextual (teacher practices and climate) variables operating in their specific reading experiences.

Further important points in this chapter that are vital to the field are that research has documented the dynamic nature of student perceptions, how individualized these perceptions are, and how sensitive they are to varying personal and contextual and instructional practice variables. Understanding these findings suggests the need to consistently identify individual and developmental and cultural factors that may impact reading motivation as we suggested in my earlier work in how to motivate secondary students to read their textbooks (McCombs, 1995, 1997; McCombs & Barton, 1998). This chapter also suggests that other content areas such as math can benefit by considering how individual differences in motivational and psychological processes contribute to student performance on high-stakes math assessments as demonstrated recently in research by Ryan, Ryan, Arbuthnot, & Samuels (2007).

Guthrie and Coddington advance the field of reading motivation by making key points that build from the theoretical to the practical, thus reinforcing the need for integrated approaches to research and practice in this field. With integrated approaches, particularly those that support self-efficacy development and reading strategy acquisition at the same time, research finds that self-efficacy is increased more than with models that include either strategy support or motivational support alone. Similarly, the authors wisely suggest that researchers and practitioners need to be concerned with the current practice of reward-giving, particularly in our culture of testing and accountability (cf. McCombs, 2007, for further motivational issues with our testing policies in schools). The issue is that students will become either withdrawn (literally or psychologically) and avoid reading (or learning in general) or become compliant (shallow learners that do not engage in deep processing of information) with such policies that do not value them as self-motivated and self-directed learners when the conditions that support motivation and engagement are present. Guthrie and Coddington's points about various undermining motivations also suggest that educators at all levels of our educational system must consider not only positive motivations for learning but also factors that may increase reading avoidance.

I also found myself drawn to points made in this chapter about the importance of social motivation for learning. After being involved as a member of a new APA (American Psychological Association) Task Force that is developing evidence-based Web-based modules for teachers in a variety of content areas, I was privileged (McCombs, 2005, 2006) to learn about important new research by colleagues in multiple psychological fields in the practice areas of (a) Using practice effectively, (b) Formative assessment—giving feedback to students, (c) Using praise to enhance student learning, (d) Dealing with bullies effectively, (e) Managing students' disruptive behaviors, (6) Students' knowledge that affects learning, (f) Students' pre-instructional misconceptions, (g) Developing more autonomous learners (my module, McCombs, 2008), (h) Improving students' relationships with teachers, and (i) Capitalizing on research in brain function and learning.[1] This research to practice is important and relevant to the Guthrie and Coddington points about the developmentally-related importance of student perceptions, also reiterated in research by Harter (2006) and Combs (1991), even for young children (Daniels, Kalkman, & McCombs, 2001; McCombs, Daniels, & Perry, 2008).

Pekrun Chapter

This chapter was intriguing because it dealt with an ageless psychological concept: emotions at school. Pekrun's treatment of the topic provides further insights into the importance of emotions for student motivation as well as academic success and personality development. As he points out, however, in spite of the centrality of emotions to motivation, they have been neglected by educational research on school-aged children.[2] Pekrun also points out that even though there has been a recent boom of emotion research in the basic disciplines of psychology, the mainstream of educational research has ignored these findings. The exceptions have been research on anxiety during learning and test taking as well as Weiner's attribution theory of achievement motivation and emotion (see Graham, this volume). To rectify this problem, Pekrun provides a nice review of the constructs of emotion and the conceptual paradigms, definitions of emotion, and how these relate emotion to motivation and cognition. He also provides two approaches to the classification of emotions (discrete and dimensional), followed by an interesting discussion of diversity and assessment of emotions in school settings. Emotions such as disgust and anxiety were found to be the predominant negative emotions when taking exams or tests, while positive emotions accounted slightly more than half of the emotions reported by his own exploratory studies of K–12 and university students regarding attending class and studying.

What I found of additional interest was Pekrun's discussion of how best to assess student emotions by self-report scales. The field has moved in important ways from one-dimensional measurement of emotional constructs such as test anxiety to multidimensional measures such as those of Spielberger (2006). Pekrun's own development of the AEQ measures of discrete emotions while attending class, studying, and taking tests and exams provides a good example of how self-reports of emotions in school can be advanced through multidimensional approaches. It is important that he acknowledges that although self-report measures are easy to administer and there is clear evidence for their validity, there are limitations in terms of a number of well-known biases. Pekrun then discusses alternative types of assessment such as neuroimaging techniques and observations of nonverbal behavior that show promise for this field.

I was impressed with his in-depth discussion of the origins and development of students' emotions. This has been a long-neglected area in terms of understanding the areas reviewed relative to test anxiety, achievement emotions from a causal attributional and goals perspective, and the role of classroom composition, instruction, and social environments. Our own research has confirmed many of these findings in terms of learner-centered practices and their impact on motivation and emotions (curiosity and interest) at different developmental stages (cf. McCombs, 1999 ; Meece, Herman, & McCombs, 2003). Our work with learner-centered practices also confirms studies of the impact of teacher-centered instruction on positive students' and teachers' positive emotions in school settings (McCombs & Whisler, 1997 ; McCombs & Miller, 2007).

Finally, I appreciated Pekrun's point that laboratory research can help in generating hypotheses regarding student emotions in school, but real-life emotions must be studied in ecologically valid ways. I also learned that we should be studying a range of other emotions impacting student learning in schools. These include negative emotions such as anger, shame, boredom, hopelessness. We should also be spending more time studying positive emotions that relate to academic motivation and agency such as hope and pride that correlate with interest, effort, elaboration of learning material, self-regulation of learning and academic achievement. My challenge is to extend the control-value theory of achievement emotions to emphasize learner or person centered approaches (cf. Cornelius-White, 2007), developmental diversities (Harter, 2006), the research on social and emotional learning (Zins, Weissberg, Wang, & Walberg, 2004), or emotions such as curiosity (McCombs & Miller, 2007; McCombs & Whisler, 1997).

Buehl and Alexander Chapter

Knowing both of these scholars, it was such a pleasure reading what they have learned regarding how beliefs about learning in different academic domains can influence learning and motivation. Although we have disagreed at times in our views of students' motivation and learning, I greatly appreciate the work they have done in these areas. I read with great interest their review of the research that led to the development of a quality model of the role of beliefs (both teacher's and their students') in producing desired motivational outcomes in different content domains. My only issue with this model is that it does not deal sufficiently, in my opinion, with social relationships and emotions, except to the extent that they are related to motivation (which, of course, they are). Where we strongly agree is that there is an essential link between student and teacher beliefs and academic behaviors. This link is essential because, without it, the social dimensions of learning and the necessary social and emotional supports would be missing (cf. Zins et al., 2004). Differences in student and teacher beliefs provide the "space" for change on either side. By "space" I mean the context in which both, when the differences in beliefs are articulated or otherwise made known to the other, generates the *will to change*. The will to change is the necessary first step but certainly not the last (see McCombs & Marzano, 1989).

How all of this relates to the Buehl and Alexander discussion of content domains is fairly simple and creatively constructed in this chapter. When a model begins with the learner (self as agent), there are an infinite set of possibilities that can emerge. The challenge is to structure this ill-structured problem in such a way that one can separate factors important to motivation and academic achievement so as to define the field(s) of influence on that single self-organizing system who is itself engaged in a process of self-organized learning. This very complex and unpredictable phenomena can *only* be understood in terms of the domains of influence and the factors within each of those domains. The model presented in Buehl and Alexander (see Figure 22.1 in their chapter) is right on if one sees the self as a metacognitive domain prior to content. Their model implicitly implies the presence of self and the influence of the learner's or teacher's beliefs.[3]

The other point that should not be missed in the Buehl and Alexander chapter is that beliefs about academic domains by either teachers or their students may not fit at all with what experts in the field think or have found in their own research. That is because the complexity and multivariate nature of individual beliefs cannot possibly be mapped in any predictable way. That may sound pessimistic but that is not my perspective. I find it hopeful and empowering. The problem is differentiating, for research purposes, how complex human systems are related and interrelated in different content domains, different contexts, and with a host of individual and developmental differences. To bring simplicity to the challenges and complexities, we must, as Buehl and Alexander suggest, have an integrative and systemic approach. This approach must capture the best of what we know from practical, intuitive, and empirical sources about the role of beliefs on learner motivation and learning. I use the term "learner" here to refer to both students and teachers in their dynamic and interconnected relationship(s).

Buehl and Alexander's review of the research on the interplay between general and content domain beliefs is fascinating. It is helpful to see the differentiation of kinds of beliefs spelled out in the chapter as it furthers our understanding of how these beliefs can operate in practice. Buehl and Alexander's model recognizes that teacher practices in the classroom influence how students experience a given academic content domain and they further contribute to the students' own beliefs about that domain.

A final noteworthy insight provided by this chapter is that in any given academic content domain, beliefs and motivation may not be causally related. That surprised me at first but upon reflection, it made perfect sense. The complexity of both human constructs could not possibly allow for the disentanglement of person (beliefs) vs. outcome (motivation) variables. And should they? That is a key question for the field and one on which I weigh down heavily on the side of "should we even bother if we have the goal of releasing natural learning and motivation in all learners and all teachers as learners?"

Woolfolk Hoy, Hoy, and Davis Chapter

Following the same focus on beliefs related to motivation, the Woolfolk Hoy, Hoy, and Davis chapter provided many key insights and findings. Their focus was teacher beliefs as separate from student beliefs, and thus theirs was necessarily a less holistic and systemic view than that presented in the Buehl and Alexander chapter. Given the importance of the area of teacher beliefs, this chapter's treatment of the topic is outstanding in furthering knowledge of this field.

As Woolfolk Hoy, Hoy, and Davis so aptly point out, teacher self-efficacy beliefs are among the most powerful for teaching. This is true at an intuitive level. When one thinks about him- or herself in any given situation, it is impossible to imagine how we would handle it if we didn't feel we were competent, likely to be successful, had some control or choice in the decisions related to that situation, or weren't connected to some form of social support in order for us to make the hard choices that impact other people. In a nutshell, that is what the jobs of teachers entail—on a daily, hourly, and moment-to-moment basis. It is no small wonder that so many teachers—young and old, experienced and inexperienced, leave the profession when these needs are stifled or ignored. Our own research found this to be repeatedly true in a wide range of school settings from rural to urban to suburban, with diverse samples of teachers and students at different developmental stages and grade levels (cf. McCombs & Miller, 2007, 2008; McCombs & Whisler, 1997).

The treatment of teachers' sense of self-efficacy in this chapter is insightful and thorough. The authors guide the reader through a discussion of research on how teachers' sense of efficacy is conceptualized and measured, including how these efficacy beliefs are individuated into self-schemas. We learn about how these beliefs are both general and specific (the old trait-state distinction á la Spielberger, 2006), and how a process approach can be used to study these efficacy beliefs and their impact on teacher and student outcomes. In this part of Woolfolk Hoy, Hoy, and Davis' discussion, I was struck with the significance of several key research findings: (a) high efficacy teachers use more learner-centered, hands-on approaches to teaching a variety of subjects; (b) high efficacy teachers are more likely to be self-directed in their own learning; (c) levels of teacher efficacy can predispose them to feel less responsibility for teaching some populations of students (e.g., gays, certain cultural and ethnic groups); and (d) without mastery experiences in integrating technology into classroom curricula and experiences, at both the pre- and inservice levels, teachers cannot provide students with adequate and much needed technology literacy skills.

In their review of research on teacher efficacy beliefs, Woolfolk Hoy, Hoy, and Davis confirm the teacher as learner notion and force us to acknowledge that preservice teacher education programs need to explicitly and expertly provide the kind of early mastery experiences that can help young teachers develop the efficacy they need. This efficacy is particularly important when young or inexperienced teachers enter settings where they may not believe they are competent or may not feel that they belong (Deci & Ryan, 1991). Another important point Woolfolk Hoy et al. make is the value of supporting teachers in collaborative groups or learning communities. They can work with other teachers, share ideas, be mentored in trying out new approaches, and primarily gain in efficacy and self-confidence in mutually interdependent and supportive relations. This is in keeping with work by many motivational theorists.

Research in this area, however, must be designed to distinguish between expert and novice teachers in their analyses of results. It must also be able to capture collective teacher efficacy that emerges, as the authors point out, as the group-level product of interactive group dynamics. These dynamics allow change at higher systems levels and help create, foster, and sustain a new school culture. This phenomenon has been shown as the research presented in this chapter reveals to increase the predictiveness of perceived collective teacher efficacy of valued student outcomes—including not only student learning and achievement variables but also student attendance and disruptive behaviors—as we have found in our own research (McCombs & Quiat, 2002).

But also as we have repeatedly found, enhanced organizational functioning (functioning that supports meaningful learning and engages students in lifelong learning processes) *requires* a supportive environment in schools—one that gives teachers time to reflect, discuss, share experiences, and receive social and emotional support (Deakin-Crick, McCombs, Haddon, Broadfoot, & Tew, 2007; McCombs, 2004a). This is what allows teachers to be able to deal with aversive, nonlearner-centered school policies and requirements as well as how to deal with negative student reactions to these policies (McCombs & Miller, 2007, 2008). As Woolfolk Hoy, Hoy, and Davis discuss in their chapter, teacher individual and collective efficacy beliefs are at the center of them being able to assume the shared leadership roles than can transform aversive systems into self-enhancing and empowering systems that support natural learning and motivation.

Sideridis Chapter

This chapter spoke to issues near and dear to me—how best to study motivation with learners who have special learning needs and challenges. Sideridis brilliantly addresses this issue, and I was particularly taken with his attempt to address the beginning of his chapter's challenge of taking a sophisticated, integrative, and systematic approach. My earlier work in this area came to mind, particularly a project for the Office of Special Education programs in 1985–89. In this project we studied how simulation technology could be used to promote social competence in high school students who were classified as mildly retarded, learning disabled, and behaviorally disturbed. What we learned was the validity of the model so clearly presented in the Sideridis chapter (see McCombs, 2004b, for more detail).

Other noteworthy aspects of this chapter are the review of recent literature suggesting the complexity of issues surrounding the identification, diagnosis, and treatment of students classified as "learning disabled" at different developmental stages. This research clearly indicates the complex array of family, individual, and classroom-school context variables that must be taken into account in studying motivation with this population. Sideridis' Figure 27.1 that lays out the important constructs and their theoretical roots is a vital contribution to the field. It highlights the importance of taking an integrative and systemic approach to research and practice in this area, much as we discovered (McCombs, 2004b). For high school students, in particular, it is important to their engagement and sense of self as a learner that they know they can "think, know, and do" whatever is required in any learning situation. We learned that they are helped with integrated metacognitive, cognitive, motivational, and behavioral approaches. As researchers in the field, we cannot ignore the need for whole person assumptions with *any* population of learners.

The review of research on depressive, learned helplessness, self-efficacy/self-concept, lower levels of self-determination, and lower achievement goals aspects of many students classified with the label of "learning disabled" and the resultant treatment in too many schools is compellingly presented in this chapter. This research points us to the importance of seeing the learner's perspective and expectations for success as well as the learning challenges that are present for this population. The fact that training interventions can be highly effective provides clear evidence as well as hope that motivational, metacognitive, cognitive, emotional, social, and behavioral issues can be successfully addressed. Sideridis also fairly points out that research is mixed, particularly when it comes to gender differences and to whether differences in research findings between LD populations and normal students may be more methodological than real.

Sideridis' own research was particularly interesting in that it provided some hope for the field from an intervention, motivation and learning outcomes, and methodological perspective. That means we are making progress for both practice and research in understanding how best to motivate and improve the achievement of students with special learning needs. From a research perspective, using nonlinear hierarchical models and both quantitative and qualitative designs shows much promise. From a practice perspective, this chapter clearly suggests that motivation variables lie at the heart of any work on interventions—a phenomenon all too clear to today's teachers.

Turner and Meyer Chapter

Now we come to the end of my journey in reviewing the chapters in this section of the handbook. I read this chapter first because I have known and admired the work of these researchers for a number of years. I've also been personally curious for all of my life it seems about how the general research-validated Learner-Centered Psychological Principles (LCPs; APA, 1993, 1997) can be applied in a content area that is more well-defined (maybe) than other academic domains such as social studies. The ontological and epistemological assumptions that seem to undergird instructional practices in mathematics have long been a hindrance to not only my aversion to pursuing academic success in this area, but have also to, as Turner and Meyer show, many other females and diverse cultural or ethnic groups in America and other parts of the world. The research reviewed in this section helps us all better understand, from a motivational perspective, why this problem lingers in our schools and how it is related to particular ways of thinking about mathematics and practices in the classroom for students at all developmental levels that derive from these assumptions and practices.

In this chapter, we learn that a more holistic synergy is needed in our understanding of mathematics *and* motivation. This is consistent with the review of research that led to the development of the LCPs (McCombs, 1994) as well as consistent with the research reviewed in this chapter. My recent review of much of this same literature in preparing my module for the new APA task force in the area of self-regulated learning and motivation struck home to me how far we have yet to go in helping both researchers and practitioners understand the new underlying assumptions about learning and learners that are needed if we truly want the kind of educational systems and instructional practices that engage all learners in the learning of mathematical principles and processes. Mathematics is a dynamic and nonlinear field where scientists and educational researchers are increasingly recognizing that except at the computational level, there are no truly right or wrong answers. It is also being recognized that mathematics provides a way of framing and thinking about phenomena in our world that can simplify complexities and help us understand the relativity of many things we experience (e.g., time, space, connections between and among objects).[4]

Turner and Meyer help us understand that many things in our realities are not "either-or," general vs. specific, trait vs. trait, or content-driven vs. generalizable. Just as in the fields of mathematics and mathematics education, we must recognize that black and white thinking, nonsystemic thinking, and nonrelational thinking is outdated and erroneous given recent scientific discoveries relative to principles operating at universal and global levels (cf. Scharmer, 2004;

Wheatley, 2007). As Turner and Meyer persuasively argue, not only do reviews of at least three distinct literatures need to be synthesized to advance the field, but instructional practice in K–12 mathematics classrooms needs to reflect this synthesis instead of fragmenting curriculum into separate studies.

Natural learning and motivational principles clearly dictate a new approach that can more effectively explain how motivation to learn mathematics develops and changes for both students and teachers. If we are to promote positive dispositions and learning outcomes, we must change research and practice to a new paradigm that honors and respects this holistic, learner-centered perspective (McCombs, 2008; McCombs & Miller, 2008). At the same time, as these authors argue, we must consider content as part of the research findings in motivation or we will loose important synergistic influences of content on motivation and differences in motivation across a variety of contexts and for different diverse individuals and groups of students. A growing number of other researchers agree (e.g., d'Ailly, 2003, 2004; Graham, 1994; Graham, Taylor, & Hudley, 1998; Heine, Lehman, Markus, & Kitayama, 1999; Holloway, 1988; Nisbett, Peng, Choi, & Norenzayan, 2001; Pressley, Raphael, Gallagher, & DiBella, 2004; Walker, Pressick-Kilborn, Arnold, & Sainsbury, 2004). It has certainly been a point research colleagues and I have urged over recent decades (e.g., Kanfer & McCombs, 2000; McCombs, 2000, McCombs, 2003a, 2003b, 2007; McCombs & Pope, 1994).

Turner and Meyer importantly suggest that we need a new set of assumptions about the research that should be done in the fields of mathematics and mathematics education. It is time to move beyond labor intensive methodologies that "lose the forest for the trees." Without taking advantage of new technological and statistical approaches such as hierarchical linear modeling, we will miss the truths in our data. We will continue to be bogged down in the details and will not build on the knowledge and experience of our best motivation and learning researchers in specific academic discipline areas and in general motivation theory. And, without larger and more integrative concepts and measurable constructs, we will never be able to reduce complexity to simplicity for either researchers or practitioners.

Finally, Turner and Meyer convincingly state that there are micro cultures in every classroom that promote "ways of being" mathematical learners and we can and should not dissect the learner the way we do psychological constructs. They wisely counsel us to study in new ways the teacher-student patterns of interacting that create and sustain either high or low quality classroom contexts in general and for mathematics in particular. Without understanding these contexts, they argue (and I wholeheartedly agree), we will not be able to explain *why* (emphasis theirs and mine) students report particular beliefs, perceptions, and feelings about a subject or discipline.

Emotions or feelings are a critical part of the puzzle, as we also saw in the Pekrun chapter, if we are to understand motivation and learning performance and achievement in any school discipline. Turner and Meyer also stress that we need to understand the role of student beliefs about mathematics (or any subject areas for that matter) and their change over time as we examine and try to influence mathematics reform practices. With appropriate, learner-centered and evidence-based practices, students will and do grow to like mathematics even as it becomes harder. This I know from personal experience, the observations and experiments I have been part of with a wide variety of K–12 and college students, and the excellent research review in this chapter and the urgings of Turner and Meyer to take a holistic, integrative, and synthetic approach to research and practice.

Now that the individual chapter review is over, I hope you as readers see the underlying integrative and synthetic structure that has emerged. I didn't plan it deliberately that way—it emerged from my natural motivation and learning just as it does for all learners. So, now I am ready to provide you with my suggestions for the field.

Suggestions for the Field

As the reader(s) can surmise at this point, my early assumptions have shown through and my goal of being transparent has been accomplished. I stated at the onset of this commentary that my six assumptions about human capacity, learning, motivation, development and their implications for teaching would frame my remarks. Even in writing this commentary, I found that I now have a seventh assumption:

- *We must keep our research and suggestions for practitioners simple if we are to have an impact on the field and on practice.* By keeping it simple but sophisticated based on current and ancient research, we speak back to our intuition and common sense. When we do that we have a chance of influencing policymakers who live in different worlds and realities than ours. They need to hear our results as stories that are motivational, engaging, easy to read and understand, and easy to implement. They simply do not have the time or the background to read long technical reports or research studies. And, if we are to make the difference in transforming our educational system that the research presented in this section strongly implies, we must bridge that gap and soon if we are to remain committed to and actively involved in holistic, integrative, and inclusive educational systems that match the known truths and research-validated principles and practices that *do engage* all learners in natural, self-organizing learning for a lifetime.

I now want to conclude by sharing briefly my own recent work. In so doing, I hope to inspire you to pursue new and innovative research and practice that moves us beyond the current assumptions and methodologies in the field of motivation.

Examples from My Own Research and New Projects

As I have developed in my thinking and research based on what I have learned about motivation and learning, I have been involved with the APA in developing the Learner-Centered Psychological Principles[5] (APA, 1993, 1997), the Learner-Centered Model (LCM), and a set of research-validated learner-centered self-assessment and reflection tools for students and teachers in grades K–3, 4–8, 9–12, and college. Research-validated findings with the ALCP surveys have provided evidence for the ALCP Model (see McCombs & Miller, 2007, 2008, for complete descriptions of the model and its research basis).

Purpose The purpose of this project was to provide a research-based foundation that could inform decision making about the systemic reforms necessary in instruction, curriculum, assessment, school management, parent and community involvement, and policy such that current problems of student alienation, boredom, and perceptions of irrelevancy could be addressed.

Assumptions An assumption of the effort was that the *psychological* knowledge base (as well as relevant knowledge from the fields of education, sociology, anthropology, and cultural studies) on learners and learning was the appropriate focus for this foundational knowledge base in that learning is essentially a socially-mediated psychological process. It was further assumed that focusing on individual learner needs and learning capacities will provide a perspective for educational decision making that directly addresses reported student issues and problems with traditional models of schooling which focus on administrative, curricular, or instructional concerns. Although a constructivist and social constructivist theoretical framework guided much of the research review, it was also later acknowledge by Alexander and Murphy (1998), and by the APA Task Force directors, that application of these assumptions required a broader view that included a situated and content focus (cf. Lambert & McCombs, 1998).

These efforts, since the early 1990s, have generated data from diverse groups of students and teachers in urban, rural, and suburban schools across America (more than 30,000 students and their 7,000 teachers, cf. McCombs & Miller, 2007, 2008). We are also increasingly obtaining requests and data from our self-assessment tools from many countries around the world (e.g., Deakin-Crick et al., 2007). Through collaboration with Judith Meece, these variables encompass the list of those mentioned throughout this section, from self-efficacy and perceived competence, to goal orientation, to self-regulatory strategies, to curiosity and interest, to values orientation, to knowledge-seeking curiosity (cf. Meece, Herman, & McCombs, 2003)

The direct relevance of this work for my commentary is that the model is a self-assessment combined with deep reflection and a respectful consultancy approach. This Learner-Centered Model has the aim of situating the responses of both teachers and students at all school levels in the important motivational context. That context can include the content being taught, the specific instructional and/or motivational practices a particular classroom teacher is demonstrating from both the students' and their teacher's perspective, or any other variable of importance in a given research project. The system is invitational because we know people will come when they are ready. They will be ready when they trust self-assessment results, based on discrepancies between teacher and student perceptions, are confidential and will be in no way used against them individually or collectively.

Thus, issues raised by many of the chapter authors in this section about the number of challenges to the field (e.g., the importance of *both* generalized motivation constructions and specific areas in which these constructs are expected to vary are examined) do have a more transformative and parsimonious person-driven set of solutions. We must trust that these will emerge in the natural way of learning and change. When this happens, I will know that the field is starting to make a difference to those people in the system that we value. And it will be in a way that simplifies some of the methodological as well as theoretical concerns that have been raised in the chapters reviewed in this section.

A Concluding Challenge and Opportunity

As I have done in many of my recent books, book chapters, and articles—I will leave you with a challenge and an opportunity to help change the future of education and educational research: Will you join me and a growing host of other national and international researchers and practitioners in creating the vision we need based on the timeless truths that have been continually revalidated? Will we create the schools and forms of schooling that we all need for a lifetime? I hope and believe so.

Notes

1. Readers interested in following the activities of this APA Task Force can visit the APA Web site:http://www.apa.org/ed/cpse/cpseinit.html
2. One exception was research on computer-based training (CBT) effects on anxiety while learning, and the effects of advance organizers and memory support in reducing anxiety and increasing knowledge-seeking state (epistemic) curiosity during CBT (Leherissey-McCombs, 1971a, 1971b; Leherissey-McCombs, O'Neil, & Hanson, 1971, 1973). Our later research examined what motivational variables were important in school and military settings, particularly those settings using technology, including the emotional and motivational variables impacting achievement and performance during learning (McCombs, Bruce, & Lockhart, 1986; McCombs, Doll, Baltzley, & Kennedy, 1987; McCombs & Dobrovolny, 1982; McCombs, Lockhart, Bruce, & Smith, 1986).
3. See McCombs and Miller (2007, 2008) for a discussion of how this works in a living systems framework such as those posed by Scharmer, Senge, and Wheatley (Scharmer, 2004; Senge, Scharmer, Jaworksi, & Flowers, 2004; Wheatley, 2006, 2007).
4. Supported by the research of Tom Carpenter and Tom Romberg (e.g., at the University of Wisconsin-Madison's U.S. Department of Education National Center for Research in Mathematics Education and Research in Mathematics and Science Education (1987–1995) and, more recently, the Department of Education National Center for Improving Student Learning and Achievement in Mathematics and Science (1995–2004)., and others (deBruno, 1985; Pietsch, Walker, & Chapman, 2003).
5. A complete version of these principles can be found at the APA Web site: http://www.apa.org/ed/lcp2/lcp14.html

References

Alexander, P. A., & Murphy, P. K. (1998). The research base for APA's Learner-Centered Psychological Principles. In N. Lambert & B. L. McCombs (Eds.), *How students learn: Reforming schools through learner-centered education* (pp. 25–60). Washington, DC: American Psychological Association.

APA Task Force on Psychology in Education (1993, January). *Learner-centered psychological principles: Guidelines for school redesign and reform*. Washington, DC: American Psychological Association and Mid-Continent Regional Educational Laboratory.

APA Work Group of the Board of Educational Affairs (1997, November). *Learner-centered psychological principles: A framework for school reform and redesign*. Washington, DC: American Psychological Association.

deBuno, E. (1985). The CORT thinking program. In J. W. Segal, S. F. Chipman, & R. Glasen (Eds.), *Thinking and learning skills* (Vol. 1, pp. 363–388). Hillsdale, NJ: Erlbaum.

Combs, A. W. (1991). *The schools we need: New assumptions for educational reform*. Lanham, MD: University Press of America.

Cornelius-White, J. (2007). Teachers who care are more effective: A meta-analysis of learner-centered relationships. *Review of Educational Research, 77*(1), 113–143.

d'Ailly, H. (2003). Children's autonomy and perceived control in learning: A model of motivation and achievement in Taiwan. *Journal of Educational Psychology, 95*(1), 84–96.

d'Ailly, H. (2004). The role of choice in children's learning: A distinctive cultural and gender difference in efficacy, interest, and effort. *Canadian Journal of Behavioural Science, 36*(1), 17–29.

Daniels, D. H., Kalkman, D. L., & McCombs, B. L. (2001). Individual differences in young children's perspectives on learning and teacher practices: Effects of learner-centered contexts on motivation. *Early Education and Development, 12*(2) 253–273.

Deci, E. L., & Ryan, R. M. (1991). A motivational approach to self: Integration in personality. In R. Dienstbier (Ed.), *Nebraska symposium on motivation. Vol. 38. Perspectives on motivation* (pp. 237–288). Lincoln: University of Nebraska Press.

Deakin-Crick, R., McCombs, B., Haddon, A., Broadfoot, P., & Tew, M. (2007). The ecology of learning: Factors contributing to learner-centred classroom cultures. *Research Papers in Education, 22*(3), 267–307.

Graham, S. (1994). Motivation in African Americans. *Review of Educational Research, 64*, 55–117.

Graham, S., Taylor, A. Z., & Hudley, C. (1998). Exploring achievement values among ethnic and minority early adolescents. *Journal of Educational Psychology, 90*, 606–620.

Harter, S. (2006). *The cognitive and social construction of the developing self*. New York: Guilford.

Heine, S. Lehman, D., Markus, H., & Kitayama, S. (1999). Is there a universal need for positive self regard? *Psychological Review, 106*, 766–794.

Holloway, S. (1988). Concepts of ability and effort in Japan and the United States. *Review of Educational Research, 58*, 327–345.

Kanfer, R., & McCombs, B. L. (2000). Motivation. In H. F. O'Neil, Jr., & S. Tobias (Eds.), *Handbook on training* (pp. 85–108). New York: Macmillan.

Lambert, N., & McCombs, B. L. (Eds.). (1998). *How students learn: Reforming schools through learner-centered education*. Washington, DC: APA Books.

Leherissey-McCombs, B. L. (1971a, May). *The development of a measure of state epistemic curiosity* (Tech. Memo No. 34). Tallahassee: Florida State University.

Leherissey-McCombs, B. L. (1971b, December). *The effects of stimulating state epistemic curiosity on state anxiety and performance in a complex computer-assisted learning task* (Report No. 23). Tallahassee: Florida State University.

Leherissey-McCombs, B. L., O'Neil, H. F., Jr., & Hansen, D. N. (1971a). Effects of memory support on state anxiety and performance in computer-assisted learning. *Journal of Educational Psychology, 62,* 413–420.

Leherissey-McCombs, B. L., O'Neil, H. F., Jr., & Hansen, D. N. (1971b, July). *Effect on anxiety, response mode, and subject matter familiarity on achievement in computer-assisted learning* (Tech. Memo No. 41). Tallahassee: Florida State University.

McCombs, B. L. (1995). Alternative perspectives for motivation. In L. Baker, O. Afflerbach, & D. Reinking (Eds.), *Developing engaged readers in school and home communities* (pp. 67–87). Hillsdale, NJ: Erlbaum.

McCombs, B. L. (1997). Commentary: Reflections on motivations for reading — through the looking glass of theory, practice, and reader experiences. *Educational Psychologist, 32*(2), 125–134.

McCombs, B. L. (1999). What role does perceptual psychology play in educational reform today? (pp. 148–157) In H. J. Freiberg (Ed.), *Perceiving, behaving, becoming: Lessons learned.* Alexandria, VA: Association for Supervision and Curriculum Development.

McCombs, B. L. (2000). Reducing the achievement gap. *Society, 37*(5), 29–36.

McCombs, B. L. (2003a). What really happens in school reform in the new economy: It's more than simply changing classes. Review of "Changing Classes" by Martin Packer. *Contemporary Psychology, 48*(6), 796–800.

McCombs, B. L. (2003b). From credible research to policy for guiding educational reform. In W. M. Reynolds & G. E. Miller (Eds.), *Comprehensive handbook of psychology, volume 7: Educational psychology* (pp. 583–607). New York: Wiley.

McCombs, B. L. (2004a). The Learner-Centered Psychological Principles: A framework for balancing a focus on academic achievement with a focus on social and emotional learning needs. In J. E. Zins, R. P. Weissberg, M. C. Wang, & H. J. Walberg (Eds.), *Building academic success on social and emotional learning: What does the research say?* (pp. 23–39). New York: Teachers College Press.

McCombs, B. L. (2004b). Learner-centered principles and practices: Enhancing motivation and achievement for children with learning challenges and disabilities. *International Review of Research in Mental Retardation, 28,* 85–120.

McCombs, B. L. (2005, August). *History of the APA Learner-Centered Psychological Principles.* Paper presented in the Symposium, "Building a Toolbox for Evaluating School Improvement Designs," Annual Meeting of the American Psychological Association, Washington, DC.

McCombs, B. L. (2006, April). *Applying the Science of Learning to Teaching PreK-12 Student.* Invited session of the American Psychological Association Task Force on the work of the APA *Learner-Centered Psychological Principles.* Panel session at the Annual Meeting of the American Educational Research Association, San Francisco.

McCombs, B. L. (2007). Balancing accountability demands with research-validated, learner-centered teaching and learning practices. In C. E. Sleeter (Ed.), *Educating for democracy and equity in an era of accountability* (pp. 41–60). New York: Teachers College Press.

McCombs, B. L. (2008, April). From one-size-fits-all to personalized learner-centered learning: The evidence. *The F. M. Duffy Reports, 13*(2), 1–12.

McCombs, B. L., & Barton, M. L. (1998). Motivating secondary school students to read their textbooks. *NASSP Bulletin, 82*(600), 24–33.

McCombs, B. L., Bruce, K. L., & Lockhart, K. A. (1986). *Enhancements to motivational skill training for military technical training students: Phase I evaluation study report.* Alexandria, VA: Army Research Institute for the Behavioral and Social Sciences.

McCombs, B. L., Daniels, D. H., & Perry, K. E. (2008). Understanding children's and teachers' perceptions of learner centered practices: Implications for early schooling. *Elementary School Journal, 109,* 16–35.

McCombs, B. L., & Dobrovolny, J. L. (1982, December). *Student motivational skill training package: Evaluation for Air Force technical training* (AFHRL-TP-82-31). Lowry AFB, CO: Air Force Human Resources Laboratory, Technical Training Division.

McCombs, B. L., Doll, R. E., Baltzley, D. R. & Kennedy, R. S. (1987). *Predictive validates of primary motivation scales for reenlistment decision-making.* (ARI Final Report). Alexandria, VA: Army Research Institute for the Behavioral and Social Sciences.

McCombs, B. L. & Lauer, P. A. (1997). *Promoting academic success through sports (PASS): The PASS Program passes the learner-centered test.* Unpublished report. Aurora, CO: Mid-continent Regional Educational Laboratory.

McCombs, B. L., Lockhart, K. A., Bruce, K. L., & Smith, G. A. (1986). *Enhancements to motivational skill training for military technical training students: Phase II evaluation study report.* Alexandria, VA: Army Research Institute for the Behavioral and Social Sciences.

McCombs, B. L., & Marzano, R. J. (1989). Integrating skill and will in self-regulation: Putting the self as agent in strategies training. *Teaching Thinking and Problem Solving, 11*(5), 1–4.

McCombs, B. L., & Miller, L. (2007). *Learner-centered classroom practices and assessments: Maximizing student motivation, learning, and achievement.* Thousand Oaks, CA: Corwin Press.

McCombs, B. L., & Miller, L. (2008). *The school leader's guide to learner-centered education: From complexity to simplicity.* Thousand Oaks, CA: Corwin Press.

McCombs, B. L., O'Neil, H. F., Jr., Heinrich, D. L., & Hansen, D. N. (1973). Effect of anxiety, response mode, subject matter familiarity, and program length on achievement in computer-assisted learning. *Journal of Educational Psychology, 64,* 310–324.

McCombs, B. L., & Quiat, M. A. (2002). What makes a comprehensive school reform model learner-centered? *Urban Education, 37*(4), 476–496.

McCombs, B. L., & Whisler, J. S. (1997). *The learner-centered classroom and school: Strategies for enhancing student motivation and achievement.* San Francisco: Jossey-Bass.

McCombs, B. L. & Pope, James E. (1994). Motivating hard to reach students. In B. L. McCombs & S. McNeely (Eds.), *Psychology in the classroom: A mini-series on applied educational psychology.* Washington, DC: American Psychological Association.

Meece, J. L., Herman, P., & McCombs, B. L. (2003). Relations of learner-centered teaching practices to adolescents' achievement goals. *International Journal of Educational Research, 39*(4–5), 457–475.

Nisbett, R., Peng, K., Choi, I., & Norenzayan, A. (2001). Culture and systems of thought: Holistic versus analytic cognition. *Psychological Review, 108*, 291–310.

Otis, N., Grouzet, F. M. E., & Pelletier, L. G. (2005). Latent Motivational Change in an Academic Setting: A 3-Year Longitudinal Study. *Journal of Educational Psychology, 97*(2), 170–183.

Pietsch, J., Walker, R., & Chapman, E. (2003, September). The relationship among self-concept, self-efficacy, and performance in mathematics during secondary school. *Journal of Educational Psychology, 95*(3), 589–603.

Pressley, M., Raphael, L., Gallagher, J. D., & DiBella, J. (2004). Providence-St. Mel School: How a school that works for African American students works. *Journal of Educational Psychology, 96*(2), 216–235.

Ryan, K. E., Ryan, A. M., Arbuthnot, K., & Samuels, M. (2007). Students' motivation for standardized math exams. *Educational Researcher, 36*(1), 5–13.

Scharmer, C. O. (2004, May). *Theory U: Leading profound innovation and change by presencing emerging futures.* Cambridge, MA: Massachusetts Institute of Technology.

Senge, P. M., Scharmer, C. O., Jaworksi, J., & Flowers, B. S. (2004). Awakening faith in an alternative Future: A consideration of *Precence: Human purpose and the field of the future. Reflection, 5*(7), 1–16.

Spielberger, C. D. (2006). Cross-cultural assessment of emotional states and personality traits. *European Psychologist, 11*(4), 297–303.

Walker, R. A., Pressick-Kilborn, K., Arnold, L. S., & Sainsbury, E. J. (2004). Investigating motivation in context: Developing sociocultural perspectives. *European Psychologist, 9*(4), 245–256.

Wheatley, M. (2006). Relationships: The basic building blocks of life. Retrieved June 28, 2007, from http://www.margaretwheatley.com/articles/relationships.html

Wheatley, M. (2007). *Core practices of life-affirming leaders.* Retrieved July 6, 2007, from http://www.berkana.org/articles/core_practices.htm

Zins, J. E., Weissberg, R. P., Wang, M. C., & Walberg, H. J. (Eds.). (2004). *Building academic success on social and emotional learning: What does the research say?* New York: Teachers College Press.

Index

Page numbers in italic refer to figures or tables

A

Ability
  characterized, 130
  how students judge, 130–132
  self-efficacy, 131–132
  self-esteem, 131–132
Ability belief constructs
  cross-cultural research, 68–70
    meaning, 70
  expectancy-value theory, 57–58
    cultural influences, 69–70
    development, 59–60
    measurement, 58–59
  relations, 60–61
Ability praise, 134
Academic achievement, purposes of middle school
    students, 112–113
Academic choices, interest, 213–214
Academic domains, *See* Domains
Acceptance, peers, 326–330, 334–336
  classroom friendships, 328–330
Achievement anxiety, 148–150
Achievement emotions
  causal attributions as antecedents, 583–584
  control-value theory, 590–592, *591*
    activity emotions, 592
    control appraisals, 592
    prospective outcome emotions, 592
    retrospective outcome emotions, 592
    value appraisals, 592
  domain specificity, 593
  gender, 596
  goals as antecedents, 584
  multiplicity, 593
  sociocultural context, 596
  universality, 596
Achievement expectancies, value, 228
Achievement gap, 2
Achievement goal theory, 77–100
  approach and avoidance goals, 86–91, *88*
  in classroom, 91–94
  competence, 79–80
  conceptual history, 81–91
  construct definition, 77–79
  developmental issues, 93–94

future directions, 98–100
gender, 417–418
goals and self-related processes intertwined, 80–81
goals create motivational systems, 80
goal source, 82–85, *83*
goal theory perspectives, 82–91, *83*
learning disabilities, 615–617
mastery goals, 79–80
methodological issues, 97–98
motivation as process, 79
multiple goal endorsement, 90
orientations, 230
origins, 81–82
performance goals, 79–80
physical education motivation, 560–562
practical issues, 94–95
theoretical assumptions, 79–81
theoretical issues, 95–96
valence, 87, *88*
Achievement motivation
  early psychological theories, 412–418
  ethnicity
    devaluing of academics and academic feedback,
      441–442
    differential treatment in schools, 442–444
    disidentification, 441–442
    economic discrimination, 444–445
    ethnic identity, 448–450
    ethnic identity stage theories, 448–450
    future research, 453–455
    goals, 439–440
    goal theory, 439–440
    history, 433–435
    identity content theories, 450
    oppositional identity, 434, 447–448
    peers, 445–446
    perceived discrimination in school, 443–444
    possible selves theories, 450–451
    stereotype and teacher behaviors, 436–437
    stereotype of intellectual abilities, 435–436
    stereotype personal consequences, 437–439
    stereotype threat, 434, 437–439
    stereotype threat mechanisms, 438–439
    targeting attributions, 452–453
    targeting expectations, 453

Achievement motivation (*continued*)
    targeting stereotypes and identity, 452
    targeting teacher development, 453
    teacher-to-student relationships, 442–443
    values, 441
  race
    devaluing of academics and academic feedback, 441–442
    differential treatment in schools, 442–444
    disidentification, 441–442
    economic discrimination, 444–445
    future research, 453–455
    goals, 439–440
    goal theory, 439–440
    history, 433–435
    identity content theories, 450
    oppositional identity, 434, 447–448
    peers, 445–446
    perceived discrimination in school, 443–444
    possible selves theories, 450–451
    racial identity, 448–450
    racial identity stage theories, 448–450
    stereotype and teacher behaviors, 436–437
    stereotype of intellectual abilities, 435–436
    stereotype personal consequences, 437–439
    stereotype threat, 434, 437–439
    stereotype threat mechanisms, 438–439
    targeting attributions, 452–453
    targeting expectations, 453
    targeting stereotypes and identity, 452
    targeting teacher development, 453
    teacher-to-student relationships, 442–443
    values, 441
Action
  concept, 225–226
  disaffection, 233–234
  engagement, 225–226, 233–234
Activity emotions, 592
Affect, mathematics motivation, co-construction, 545
Affective states, 643
African Americans, *See* Ethnicity; Race
Age, parents, 290–295
Aggression, 24–25
Alienation, 226
Analysis, self-efficacy, 50–51
Anxiety, achievement process, 148–150
Applicability, self-worth theory, 165
Applied research, 2
Approach and avoidance goals, achievement goal theory, 86–91, *88*
Aspirations, self-determination theory, 182–183
Attachment theory, student-teacher relationship, 302–304
Attribution theory, 11–30, *See also* Causal attributions
  achievement domain, 12, *13*
  attribution retraining, 20–22
  causal controllability
    achievement evaluation, 23

  attributional antecedents, 14–18
  attributional consequences, 18–26
  attribution retraining, 20–22
  causal attributions, individual differences, 16–17
  causal controllability, 22–25
  causal stability, 20–22
  controllability, 13
  development, 11
  dimensions of causes, 12–14
  discrimination among stigmatized groups, 19–20
  entity *vs.* incremental theories of intelligence, 17
  expectancy of success, 20–22
  explanatory style, 16–17
  failure, 15
  hedonic bias, 18
  history, 11
  indirect attributional cues, 14–16
  interpersonal theory of motivation, 11, 12–14, *13, 22–25*
  intrapersonal theory of motivation, 11, 12–14, *13*
  locus, 13
  locus of causality, 18–20
  peer-directed aggression, 24–25
  self-esteem, 18–20
  self-handicapping, 18–19
  spontaneous causal thinking, 12
  stability, 13
  stereotypes, 23–24
  teacher feedback, 15–16
ethnicity, 29–30
gender, 413–414
learning disabilities, 609–610
motivation
  dependent variables, 26–27
  developmental perspective, 27–28
  mediation, 28
  methods, 26–27
  moderation, 28
race, 29–30
unconscious motivation, 29
Authority, 370–371
Autonomy, 180–181, 215, 283–284, 370–371
  cross-cultural aspects, 189–190
  reading motivation, 505, 508–509
  self-determination theory, 173–174
    continuum, 176–177, *177*
    delayed students, 181–182
    gifted students, 181–182
    special populations, 181–182
  testing, 184–186
Autonomy-supportive teaching
  self-determination theory, 183–184
  teachers, 183–184

B

Behavioral engagement, school engagement, 324–325
Beliefs

belief constructs
    experiential influences, 61–65
    psychological influences, 61–65
  characterized, 481–483
  competency, 485
  defined, 481
  domain, 660–662
    academic domain beliefs as source of information
      for motivation beliefs, 484–486
    assessment conundrums, 494–495
    developmental dilemmas, 495–496
    future directions, 494–497
    history, 492–494
    instructional paradoxes, 496–497
    knowledge and learning in relation to motivation,
      483–489, *484*
    as motivating specific behaviors, 486–488
    motivation beliefs may not be causally related, 489
    science, 489–492
  education, 482–483
  emotion, 593
  goal orientations, 486
  importance, 479
  interest, 485–486
  mathematics motivation, student beliefs about
    mathematics, 534–545
  motivation role in belief change, 488
  self-determination, 486
  self-efficacy, 485
  teachers, self-efficacy, 627–648, 662–663
  value, 485–486
Belonging, 2–3
Benevolent sexism, 15–16
Big-fish-little-pond effect, 39

C
Calibration, self-efficacy, 41–42
  performance, 47–48
  social cultures of schools, 42
Catch facets, 216–217
Causal attributions, 12–14, *13*, *See also* Attribution
  theory
  self-regulated learning, 254
Causal controllability
  attribution theory, 22–25
    achievement evaluation, 23
    peer-directed aggression, 24–25
    stereotypes, 23–24
  interpersonal theory of motivation, 22–25
Causality, 228, 472–473
Causal stability
  attribution theory, 20–22
  expectancy of success, 20–22
Choice, expectancy-value theory, 59
Classroom composition, emotion, 584–585
Classroom culture, mathematics motivation, 540
Classroom instruction, emotion, 593

Classroom management, 634
Cognition, emotion, relationship, 577
Cognitive engagement, school engagement, 324
Coherence, self-worth theory, 157–158
Collective efficacy, 642–645
  achievement, 644–645
  contextual variables, 643
  formation, 643–644
  power, 644
  sources, 643
Collective self-efficacy, 38
Collective teacher self-efficacy, 38
Communication, self-theories, 134–136
Competence, 99–100
  achievement goal theory, 79–80
  beliefs, 485
    gender, 414–415
  motivation, 214–215
  self-determination theory, 173–174
Concept Oriented Reading Instruction (CORI), 66,
  67–68
Constructs
  evolution, 6
  integration, 6
Content, motivational development, 232–233
Content goals
  Ford and Nichols' proposed taxonomy, 109–110
  student goals, 111–112
    relationship between different goals, 113–115, *114*
    students espouse distinctive purposes, 112–115
Content irrelevance, reading motivation, 515, 517
Contextual influences
  environment, 463–474
  self-efficacy, 48–49
Control
  reading motivation, 514–515
  self-regulation, 248
Control appraisals, 592
Controllability, attribution theory, 13
Control-value theory, achievement emotions, 590–592,
  591
  activity emotions, 592
  control appraisals, 592
  prospective outcome emotions, 592
  retrospective outcome emotions, 592
  value appraisals, 592
Criterion-referenced grading, 159–161
Criticism, self-theories, 135
Cross-cultural aspects
  autonomy, 189–190
  self-determination theory, 189–190
Cross-cultural research
  ability beliefs, 68–69, 68–70
    meaning, 70
  expectancy beliefs, 68–69
  expectancy constructs, 68–70
    meaning, 70

Cross-cultural research (*continued*)
  self-efficacy theory, 49–50
  task values, 69–70
  value constructs, 68–70
    meaning, 70
Cultural background, parents, 290–295
Cultural influences, self-efficacy, 43

D
Decision making, motivation
  action alternatives, 99
  relationship, 99–100
  role of goals, 100
  sense of competence, 99–100
Decision theory framework, motivation, 98–100
Dependent variables, 26–27
Developmental issues
  achievement goal theory, 93–94
  self-determination theory, social development needs,
    188–189
Developmental psychology, expectancy-value theory,
    56–57
  Eccles et al. Expectancy-Value Model, 56–57, *57*
Disaffection
  action, 233–234
  common motivational theory constructs, 227–231, *229*
  conceptualizations, 238
  definitions, 224–225
  as key motivational system components, 231–234
  motivational conceptualization, *227*
  motivational dynamics, *237*
  motivational perspective, 224–227
  as organizational constructs, 223–241
  as proximal processes, 234–235
  self, 233
Discrimination among stigmatized groups, attribution
    theory, 19–20
Disengagement, 226
  physical education, 556–557
Dis-identity, reading motivation, 516
Diversity, 632–633
  parents, 290–295
Domain
  beliefs, 660–662
    academic domain beliefs as source of information
      for motivation beliefs, 484–486
    assessment conundrums, 494–495
    developmental dilemmas, 495–496
    future directions, 494–497
    history, 492–494
    instructional paradoxes, 496–497
    knowledge and learning in relation to motivation,
      483–489, *484*
    as motivating specific behaviors, 486–488
    motivation beliefs may not be causally related, 489
    science, 489–492
  beliefs about learning, 479–497

characterized importance, 480–481
Dyadic relationships, 328–330

E
Eccles et al. Expectancy-Value Model, 56–57, *57*
Economic discrimination, 444–445
Education, *see also* School
  beliefs, 482–483
Educational context, expectancy-value theory,
    development of expectancies and values, 65–70
Educational influences, self-efficacy, 43–44
Educational policy, 2
Educational psychology
  expectancy-value theory, 56–57
    Eccles et al. Expectancy-Value Model, 56–57, *57*
  motivation research, 529–534
Efficacy, 228
Effort, self-theories, 127–128
Effort praise, 134
Emotion, 575–600, 659–660, *See also* Specific type
  achievement effects, 594–595
  assessment, 580–581
    alternative types, 581
  beliefs, 593
  classification, 578, *578*
  classroom composition, 584–585
  classroom instruction, 593
  cognition, relationship, 577
  conceptual paradigms, 576–577
  constructs, 576–578
  definition, 576–577
  development, 581–587
    across school years, 585–586
  distal individual antecedents, 593
  effects of negative emotions other than anxiety, 589
  effects of positive emotions, 589–590
  exam design, 585
  exploratory research on emotional variety, 578–579
  failure, attributional antecedents, 575–576
  feedback loops, 595
  functions, 587–593
  future research, 598–600
  goals, 593
  habitualized achievement emotions, 593
  implications for educational practice, 596–598
  instruction, 584–585
  learning effects, 594–595
  mood research, 587
  motivation, relationship, 577
  origins, 581–587
  parents, 585
  self-report, 579–581, *580*
  social antecedents, 593
  social environment, 584–585
  subconscious appraisals, 593
  success, attributional antecedents, 575–576
  temperament, 593

variety, 578–579
Emotional conflict, self-worth theory, 141–142
Emotional engagement, school engagement, 325
Emotional support, student-teacher relationship, 307
Engagement, 6, 150–152, 171–191, 230–231
    academic work, 230–231
    action, 225–226, 233–234
    behavioral engagement, 324–325
    classroom peer relationships, 325–334
    cognitive engagement, 324
    common motivational theory constructs, 227–231, *229*
    conceptualizations, 238
    definitions, 224–225
    as diagnostic tool, 239
    dynamics, 240
    emotional engagement, 325
    episodes, 240
    intrinsic/extrinsic dichotomy, 151–152
    as key motivational system components, 231–234
    as mediator of motivational processes effects, 235
    motivational conceptualizations, 226, *227*
    as motivational construct, 225, 323–325
    motivational dynamics, *237*
    motivational perspective, 224–227
    opposite of, 226–227
    as organizational constructs, 223–241
    physical education, 555–557
    process, 240
    as proximal processes, 234–235
    reactions of social partners, 235
    self, 233
Entity theory
    intelligence, 124
    praising, 134
    self-theories, 124
Environment
    contextual influences, 463–474
    social influences, 463–474
Environmental control, self-regulated learning, 253
Environmental structuring, self-regulated learning, 251
Epistemic beliefs
    history, *490*, 493–494
    science, *490*, 491–492
Equity, school, 404–405
Ethnicity
    achievement motivation
        devaluing of academics and academic feedback, 441–442
        differential treatment in schools, 442–444
        disidentification, 441–442
        economic discrimination, 444–445
        ethnic identity, 448–450
        ethnic identity stage theories, 448–450
        future research, 453–455
        goals, 439–440
        goal theory, 439–440
        history, 433–435

identity content theories, 450
        implications for theories of motivation, 455–456
        oppositional identity, 434, 447–448
        peers, 445–446
        perceived discrimination in school, 443–444
        possible selves theories, 450–451
        stereotype and teacher behaviors, 436–437
        stereotype of intellectual abilities, 435–436
        stereotype personal consequences, 437–439
        stereotype threat, 434, 437–439
        stereotype threat mechanisms, 438–439
        targeting attributions, 452–453
        targeting expectations, 453
        targeting stereotypes and identity, 452
        targeting teacher development, 453
        teacher-to-student relationships, 442–443
        values, 441
    attribution theory, 29–30
    peers, 445–446
    school, 401–402, 442–444
Evolutionary theory, motivational theorizing, 265–269
Exam design, emotion, 585
Excellence, school, 404–405
Excuses, self-worth theory, 145–146
Expectancy, test anxiety, 582–583
Expectancy beliefs, cross-cultural research, 68–69
Expectancy constructs
    cross-cultural research, 68–70
        meaning, 70
    expectancy-value theory, 57–58
        cultural influences, 69–70
        development, 59–60
        measurement, 58–59
    experiential influences, 61–65
    psychological influences, 61–65
    relations, 60–61
Expectancy of success
    attribution theory, 20–22
    causal stability, 20–22
Expectancy-value models of achievement, 228
Expectancy-value theory, 55–71
    ability belief constructs, 57–58
        cultural influences, 69–70
        development, 59–60
        measurement, 58–59
    choice, 59
    developmental psychology, 56–57
        Eccles et al. Expectancy-Value Model, 56–57, *57*
    educational context, development of expectancies and values, 65–70
    educational psychology, 56–57
        Eccles et al. Expectancy-Value Model, 56–57, *57*
    expectancy constructs, 57–58
        cultural influences, 69–70
        development, 59–60
        measurement, 58–59
    gender, 414–416

Expectancy-value theory (*continued*)
  history, 55–56
  parents, 286–288
  performance, 59
  physical education motivation, 563–564
  research findings, 59–61
  value constructs, 57–58
    cultural influences, 69–70
    development, 59–60
    measurement, 58–59
Experiential influences
  belief constructs, 61–65
  expectancy constructs, 61–65
  value constructs, 61–65
Explanatory style, attribution theory, 16–17
Extrinsic goals, self-determination theory, 182
Extrinsic motivation
  internalization, continuum, 176–181
  self-determination theory, 173–174
    ego-involvement, 176–177, *177*
    externally regulated, 176–177, *177*
    identified regulation, 176–177, *177*
    integrated regulation, 176–177, *177*
    introjected regulation, 176–177, *177*
    measuring, 177–178
    types, 177–178

F
Failure
  attribution theory, 15
  emotion, attributional antecedents, 575–576
  quadripolar model of individual differences, 146–148, *147*
  self-theories, 128–129
Family, *See also* Parents
  self-efficacy, 42–43
Fear of failure
  Hidden Agenda, 153–154
  self-worth theory, 153–154
Feedback loops, emotion, 595
First Things First, 187
Friendships, peers, 328–330, 336–338
  emotional, instrumental, and physical support, 329–330
  friends model social behavior, 330
  peer group acceptance/rejection, 333
  source of conflict and rivalry, 330

G
Gender, 411–426
  achievement emotions, 596
  achievement goal theory, 417–418
  attribution theory, 413–414
  competency beliefs, 414–415
  differences in educational achievement, 411–412
  expectancy-value theories, 414–416
  implications for school professionals, 425–426
  mastery goal orientation, 417–418

  methodological issues for future research, 424–425
  occupational attainment, 411–412
  parents, motivation differences, 418–420
  performance goal orientation, 417–418
  schools, 419–422
  self-efficacy theory, 416–417
  self-theories, 136
  sociocultural influences, 422–424
  sources of gender differences in motivation, 418–424
  value beliefs, 415–416
Generality, self-efficacy, 47
Generalizability, self-worth theory, 164–165
Goal-directed behavior, in classroom, 105–120
Goal orientations, 230
  beliefs, 486
Goal orientation theory, *See also* Achievement goal theory
  parents, 288–289
Goals, 105–120, *See also* Achievement goal theory; Specific type
  competing, 115–119
  defined, 77–78
  distinguished, 77–78
  emotion, 593
  Ford and Nichols' taxonomy of 24 content goals, 109–110
  future research, 119
  hierarchical model, *78,* 78–79, 110–111
  multiple goals, 105–106
    classroom interaction, 116–117
    managing simultaneous pursuit, 115–119
    vs. single goal, 106–107
  nonprimed goal pursuit, 117–118
  person-centered view, 82–84
  primed goal pursuit, 117–118
  Schwartz's theory of human values, *108,* 108–109
  self-determination theory, 182–183
  situated perspective, 84–85
  source, 82–85, *83*
  student goal content, 107–112
  students processing cues from multiple sources, 107
Grades, self-worth theory, 156
  criterion-referenced grading, 159–161
  effort/outcome linkage, 160
  perceived equity, 160
  positive alliances, 160

H
Hands-on activities, 66–67
Harassment, student-teacher relationship, 307
Hedonic bias, attribution theory, 18
Hidden Agenda, fear of failure, 153–154
High school dropouts, 180
High-stakes testing movement, undermining student and teacher autonomy, 184–186
Hispanic students, *See* Ethnicity; Race
History, 492–494

epistemic beliefs, *490*, 493–494
learning beliefs, *490*, 493–494
ontological beliefs, *490*, 492–493
Hold facets, 216–217

I
Identification, 231
Identity
  developing mathematical identities, 545–546
  mathematics education research, 539–540
Identity content theories, 450
Imagery, self-regulated learning, 251
Inclusion, 632–633
Incremental theory
  intelligence, 124
  self-theories, 124
Individual interest
  as affective-evaluative orientation, 201–203
  changes of interest in school subjects, 205–206
  as combination of knowledge and value, 203–204
  conceptualized, 198, 201–204
  development, 206–214
  intrinsic motivation, relationship, *204*, 204–205
  measurement, 205–206
  situational interest, relationship, *204*, 204–205
  from situational to individual interest, 208–209
Instruction, emotion, 584–585
Instructional self-efficacy, 38
Integration, self-determination theory, 171–172
Intellectual development issues, self-determination
    theory, social development needs, 188–189
Intelligence
  entity theorists, 17
  entity theory, 124
  incremental theorists, 17
  incremental theory, 124
  self-efficacy, 131–132
  self-esteem, 131–132
  students' belief, 123–138
  theories about, 17
Intelligence praise, 134
Interest, *See also* Specific type
  academic choices, 213–214
  beliefs, 485–486
  contextual influences, 214–217
  defined, 197
  learning, 209–213
  measurement, 205–206
  motivation, distinguished, 197
  reading motivation, 507–508
  as relational construct, 197
  school achievement, 213–214
  text learning, 209–213
Interest-based theory, physical education motivation,
    564–566
Interest enhancement, self-regulated learning, 253
Internalization

extrinsic motivation, continuum, 176–181
  self-determination theory, 172, 178–180
Interpersonal theory of motivation
  attribution theory, 11, 12–14, *13*, 22–25
  causal controllability, 22–25
Intervention, 2
Intrapersonal theory of motivation, attribution theory,
    11, 12–14, *13*
Intrinsic goals, self-determination theory, 182
Intrinsic motivation
  individual differences, 230
  individual interest, relationship, *204*, 204–205
  learning, 175–176
  motivation, 174–175
  reading motivation, 505, 507–508
  self-determination theory, 171–172, 173–174
  situational interest, relationship, *204*, 204–205
IQ, 357

J
Judgment, self-regulation, 248

L
Latino students, *See* Ethnicity; Race
Learned drives, self-worth theory, 141–142
Learned helplessness, 228
  learning disabilities, 610–612
Learner-Centered Model, 666
Learner-Centered Psychological Principles, 666
Learning
  assumptions, 655–656
  interest, 209–213
  intrinsic motivation, 175–176
  self-efficacy, 44–46
    correlational research, 44–45
    experimental research, *45*, 45–46
Learning beliefs
  history, *490*, 493–494
  science, *490*, 491–492
Learning disabilities, 605–621, 663–664
  achievement goal theory, 615–617
  attribution theory, 609–610
  challenges in describing, 606–608
  conceptual issues, 606–608
  definitions, 606–608
  future research, 620
  importance of motivation, 605–606
  learned helplessness, 610–612
  linear *vs.* curvilinear relationships, 617–618
  methodological issues, 617–620
  motivation, literature review, 606–617
  self-determination theory, 612–614
  self-efficacy, 614–615
  social learning theory, 608–609
Learning goal orientation, self-regulated learning, 252
Locus, attribution theory, 13
Locus of causality, attribution theory, 18–20

M

Mastery-approach goals, *88,* 89
Mastery-avoidance goals, 87–88, *88,* 89
Mastery experiences, 643
Mastery goal orientation, gender, 417–418
Mastery goals, achievement goal theory, 79–80
Mastery orientation, parents, 288–289
Math anxiety, 527
Mathematics, 632
    special case for studying motivation, 528–529
Mathematics education research, 538–546
    cognitive engagement in mathematics, 538–539
    identity, 539–540
    mathematical norms, 539–540
    mathematics as meaningful thinking and problem
        solving, 538
    social processes, 539–540
Mathematics motivation, 527–548, 664–666
    affect, co-construction, 545
    classroom culture, 540
    linking student motivation to instructional practices,
        535–537
    mathematics as meaningful *vs.* procedural, 541–542
    motivation in mathematics research, 534–548
    norms, 540–541
    social processes, 542–544
    students
        beliefs about mathematics, 534–545
        developing mathematical identities, 545–546
        students' views of themselves as mathematics
            learners, 544–546
    teachers, perceptions of student mathematics
        motivation, 537–538
Meaningfulness, subject content, 215–216
Measurement
    individual interest, 205–206
    interest, 205–206
    self-efficacy, 50–51
    self-theories, 124–130
    situational interest, 205–206
    tools, 7
Mediation, 28
Metacognitive monitoring, self-regulated learning,
    249–251
Methodological tools, 7
Modeling, 643
Moderation, 28
Mood research, emotion, 587
Moral dimensions of schooling, 404
Motivation, *See also* Specific type
    assumptions, 655–656
    attribution theory, 11–30
        dependent variables, 26–27
        developmental perspective, 27–28
        mediation, 28
        methods, 26–27
        moderation, 28

competence perceptions, 214–215
current state of theory and research, 1–2
decision making
    action alternatives, 99
    relationship, 99–100
    role of goals, 100
    sense of competence, 99–100
decision theory framework, 98–100
defined, 1, 77–79, 197, 479
developmental models, 529–531
emotion, relationship, 577
future research, 666–667
general process model, *232,* 234
history of scholarship, 1
importance, 1
interactions of individual and contextual factors, 1
interest, distinguished, 197
intrinsic motivation, 174–175
learning disabilities, literature review, 606–617
other domains, 7
self-efficacy, 44–46
    correlational research, 44–45
    experimental research, *45,* 45–46
social aspects, 2–3
Motivational affordance model, school environment, *399,*
    399–400
Motivational development
    content, 232–233
    trends, 240
Motivational pluralism, 272–273
Motivational systems
    differential development, 235–237, *237,* 237–238
    dynamics, 234–235
    identification of common construct, 238–239
    motivational resources and liabilities, 236–237
    research challenges, 237–240
Motivational theorizing, 265–274
    evolutionary theory, 265–269
    motivational pluralism, 272–273
    personal goals, 269–270
    social purpose hypothesis, 270–272
    theoretical integration, 273–274
    theoretical models, 529–531
    theoretical traditions, 1
Motivation research, educational psychology, 529–534

N

Need achievement, quadripolar model, 146–148, *147*
Needs
    definition, 182
    self-determination theory, 182
Need satisfaction, self-determination theory, 178–180
Norms, mathematics motivation, 540–541

O

Ontological beliefs
    history, *490,* 492–493

science, 489–491, *490*
Oppositional identity, 447–448
Outcome expectations
    self-efficacy, contrasted, 40–41
    self-regulated learning, 252

P
Parents, 279–296, *See also* Family
    age, 290–295
    child characteristics, 294–295
    cultural background, 290–295
    diversity, 290–295
    emotion, 585
    expectancy-value theories, 286–288
    external stresses, 291–292
    gender, motivation differences, 418–420
    goal orientation theory, 288–289
    internal pressure, 293–294
    mastery orientation, 288–289
    parent education, 280
    performance orientation, 288–289
    resources, 291–292
    school factors, 292–293
    self-determination theory, 281–285
        autonomy, 283–284
        involvement, 281–283
        structure, 285–286
        support *vs.* control, 283–284
    socioeconomic status, 280, 290–295
    student-teacher relationship, contrasted, 310–312
Participation, 231
Peer-mediated learning, 342–343
Peers, 323–343
    acceptance, 326–330, 334–336
        classroom friendships, 328–330
    empirical status of current hypotheses, 334–343
    ethnicity, 445–446
    friendships, 328–330, 336–338
        emotional, instrumental, and physical support, 329–330
        friends model social behavior, 330
        peer group acceptance/rejection, 333
        source of conflict and rivalry, 330
    future research directions, 334–343
    importance, educational implications, 341–343
    multiple classroom relationships, 332–334
    race, 445–446
    rejection, 326–330, 334–336
        brain consequences, 328
        limits engagement opportunities, 327
        negative perceptions of self and peers, 327–328
    school engagement, classroom peer relationships, 325–334
    student-teacher relationship, contrasted, 310–312
    victimization, 331–332, 338–340
        mental health, 331–332
        peer group rejection, 332–334

physical health, 332
Perceived autonomy, reading motivation, 505, 508–509
Perceived control, 228
    self-efficacy, contrasted, 40–41
Perceived lack of control, reading motivation, 514–515
Perceived noncontingency, 228
Performance
    expectancy-value theory, 59
    self-theories, 129–130
Performance-approach goals, *88,* 89
    reading motivation, 510
Performance avoidance, reading motivation, 515
Performance-avoidance goals, 88, *88*
Performance goal orientation, self-regulated learning, 252
Performance goals
    achievement goal theory, 79–80
    differing views of role of, 85–86
    reading motivation, 506
Performance orientation, parents, 288–289
Personal agency, self-efficacy, contrasted, 40–41
Personal feedback, self-regulated learning, 249–251
Personal goals
    defined, 105
    motivational theorizing, 269–270
    strategy use, 118–119
Physical education
    achievement, 555–557
    characterized, 555
    disengagement, 556–557
    engagement, 555–557
    history, 554
    overview of achievement, 554
    standards, 555–557
Physical education motivation, 553–571, 657–658
    achievement goal theory, 560–562
    achievement settings, 569–570
    defining achievement, 569–570
    expectancy-value theory, 563–564
    interest-based theory, 564–566
    measuring motivation constructs, 558–560
    multiple educational motivation approaches, 570–571
    research challenges, 568–571
    self-determination theory, 566–567
    self-efficacy theory, 562–563
    theoretical foundations, 557–567
Physical safety, student-teacher relationship, 307
Possible selves theories, 450–451
Praise
    entity theory, 134
    self-theories, 134–135
Prospective outcome emotions, 592
Psychological influences
    belief constructs, 61–65
    expectancy constructs, 61–65
    value constructs, 61–65

R

Race
  achievement motivation
    devaluing of academics and academic feedback,
      441–442
    differential treatment in schools, 442–444
    disidentification, 441–442
    economic discrimination, 444–445
    future research, 453–455
    goals, 439–440
    goal theory, 439–440
    history, 433–435
    identity content theories, 450
    implications for theories of motivation, 455–456
    oppositional identity, 434, 447–448
    peers, 445–446
    perceived discrimination in school, 443–444
    possible selves theories, 450–451
    racial identity, 448–450
    racial identity stage theories, 448–450
    stereotype personal consequences, 437–439
    stereotypes and teacher behaviors, 436–437
    stereotypes of intellectual abilities, 435–436
    stereotype threat, 434, 437–439
    stereotype threat mechanisms, 438–439
    targeting attributions, 452–453
    targeting expectations, 453
    targeting stereotypes and identity, 452
    targeting teacher development, 453
    teacher-to-student relationships, 442–443
    values, 441
  attribution theory, 29–30
  peers, 445–446
  school, 401–402, 442–444
Reading motivation, 503–522, 658–659
  affirming motivations, 507–512
  associations among affirming motivations, 519
  associations among undermining motivations,
    519–520
  autonomy, 505, 508–509
  background, 503–504
  classroom experiences exacerbating undermining
    motivations, 516–517
  content irrelevance, 515, 517
  control, 514–515
  dis-identity, 516
  integrated classroom practices supporting multiple
    motivations, 512
  interest, 507–508
  intrinsic motivation, 505, 507–508
  motivational sources of reading aversion, 514–516
  multifaceted, 503
  perceived autonomy, 505, 508–509
  perceived lack of control, 514–515
  performance-approach goals, 510
  performance avoidance, 515
  performance goals, 506

reader profiles, 504
  relation of reading profiles to theoretical frameworks,
    520–521
  self-efficacy, 505, 509
  situational interest, text-based interest sources,
    199–200
  social isolation, 515, 517
  social motivation, 506–507, 511
  student profiles, 517–522
  task avoidance, 514
  task difficulty, 515
  task mastery, 506, 509–510
  undermining motivational processes, 512–514
  value in reading, 507, 511
Recess, *See also* Physical education motivation
  characterized, 555
Reciprocal determinism, 35
Rejection, peers, 326–330, 334–336
  brain consequences, 328
  limiting engagement opportunities, 327
  negative perceptions of self and peers, 327–328
Relatedness, 2–3, 215
Relatedness, self-determination theory, 172
Relationships
  affective quality, 302–304
  emotionally supportive relationship correlates,
    303–304
Research methodologies, 3
Retrospective outcome emotions, 592

S

School, 381–406
  academic culture for students, 392–394
  behavioral climate, 396–397
  conceptualizing, 382–385, *384*
  curricular differentiation, 389–390
  equity, 404–405
  ethnicity, 401–402, 442–444
  excellence, 404–405
  gender, 419–422
  geographical context, 402–404
  grade span, 385–386
  moral climate, 397–398
  moral dimensions of schooling, 404
  motivational school culture, 473–474
  as organizational context, 385–391
  as organizational culture, 391–398
  physical plant, 387–388
  race, 401–402, 442–444
  resources, 387–388
  school effects model, 400–401, *401*
  school effects research, 385–398
  school sector, 385–386
  school transitions, 390–391
  size, 386–387
  social climate, 397
  start and end times, 390

structures and controls, 172
student body background characteristics, 388–389
student motivation conceptualization, 398–401, *399*, *401*
whole school culture change efforts, 394–396
work culture for teachers, 394
School achievement, interest, 213–214
School culture, motivational school culture, 473–474
School dropouts, 180
School environment
  conceptualizing, 382–385, *384*
  motivational affordance model, *399*, 399–400
Schooling, mission, 1
School reform, self-determination theory, 186–187
  First Things First, 187
  top-down approach, 187
Science, 489–492, 632
  epistemic beliefs, *490*, 491–492
  learning beliefs, *490*, 491–492
  ontological beliefs, 489–491, *490*
Self
  disaffection, 233
  engagement, 233
Self-concept
  learning disabilities, 614–615
  self-efficacy, contrasted, 39
  teachers, 628
Self-confidence, self-efficacy, contrasted, 40–41
Self-consequences, self-regulated learning, 253
Self-determination theory, 171–191, 215, 230
  aspirations, 182–183
  autonomy, 173–174
    continuum, 176–177, *177*
    delayed students, 181–182
    gifted students, 181–182
    special populations, 181–182
  autonomy-supportive teaching, 183–184
  beliefs, 486
  competence, 173–174
  cross-cultural aspects, 189–190
  developmental issues, social development needs, 188–189
  extrinsic goals, 182
  extrinsic motivation, 173–174
    ego-involvement, 176–177, *177*
    externally regulated, 176–177, *177*
    identified regulation, 176–177, *177*
    integrated regulation, 176–177, *177*
    introjected regulation, 176–177, *177*
    measuring, 177–178
    types, 177–178
  goals, 182–183
  integration, 171–172
  intellectual development issues, social development needs, 188–189
  internalization, 172, 178–180
  intrinsic goals, 182

intrinsic motivation, 171–172, 173–174
  learning disabilities, 612–614
  needs, 182
  need satisfaction, 178–180
  parents, 281–285
    autonomy, 283–284
    involvement, 281–283
    structure, 285–286
    support *vs.* control, 283–284
  physical education motivation, 566–567
  relatedness, 172
  school reform, 186–187
    bottom-up approach, 186–187
    First Things First, 187
    top-down approach, 187
  social environment, 172
  student-teacher relationship, 303
  universality, 188–190
Self-efficacy, 35–61, 228
  ability, 131–132
  analysis, 50–51
  beliefs, 485
  calibration, 41–42
    performance, 47–48
    social cultures of schools, 42
  contextual influences, 48–49
  cross-cultural research, 49–50
  cultural influences, 43
  defined, 35, 36
  development, 42–44
  distinctions with other variables, 39–41
  educational influences, 43–44
  in educational settings, 41–42
  effective schools, 50
  effects, 36–38, *38*
  family, 42–43
  future research directions, 49–51
  gender, 416–417
  generality, 47
  intelligence, 131–132
  learning, 44–46
    correlational research, 44–45
    experimental research, *45*, 45–46
  learning disabilities, 614–615
  for learning skills, 38
  measurement, 50–51
  motivation, 44–46
    correlational research, 44–45
    experimental research, *45*, 45–46
  outcome expectations, contrasted, 40–41
  perceived control, contrasted, 40–41
  for performance, 38
  personal agency, contrasted, 40–41
  physical education motivation, 562–563
  predictive power, 46
  reading motivation, 505, 509
  self-concept, contrasted, 39

Self-efficacy (*continued*)
   self-confidence, contrasted, 40–41
   self-esteem, contrasted, 40–41
   self-regulated learning, 251–252
   self-regulation, 44–46
      correlational research, 44–45
      experimental research, *45*, 45–46
   skill possession, contrasted, 39
   social influences, 43
   sources, *36*, 36–38
   teachers, 627–648, *628*, 662–663
      beyond efficacy to academic optimism, 647–648
      calibration, 631
      ceiling effects, 631
      classroom management, 634
      collective efficacy, 642–645
      development and support research, 638–642
      direct outcomes, 637
      direct teacher outcomes, 636
      diversity, 632–633
      efficacy beliefs about relationships with students, 646–647
      efficacy judgments, 631–634
      efficacy measure criticisms, 631
      efficacy research criticisms, 645–646
      efficacy sources, 638–640
      engagement, 637
      future research, 646–648
      inclusion, 632–633
      indirect influences, 636–637
      language, 632
      literacy, 632
      mathematics, 632
      measurement of teachers' sense of efficacy, 629–630
      model of teachers' efficacy beliefs, 628–631, *629*
      motivation, 637
      process approach on teacher and student outcomes research, 634–638, *635*
      relational influences, 637–638
      relational outcomes, 637
      science, 632
      student outcomes, 637–638
      student teaching, 640
      teacher education, 640
      Teacher Efficacy Scale, 630
      teacher experience, 641–642
      teacher induction, 640–641
      teachers' decisions, actions, and communications, 634–637
      Teachers' Sense of Efficacy Scale, 630
      technology, 633
   types, 38
Self-esteem
   ability, 131–132
   attribution theory, 18–20
   defined, 40
   intelligence, 131–132

   self-efficacy, contrasted, 40–41
   teachers, 628
Self-evaluative judgments, self-regulated learning, self-reflection phase sources of motivation, 253–254
Self-fulfilling prophecies, teacher expectations, 349–377
   accumulating self-fulfilling prophecies, 359, 360
   accuracy of teacher expectations, 361–364
   adaptive motivational patterns, 369–370
   age, 356
   authority, 370–371
   autonomy, 370–371
   conditions, 355
   differential teacher treatment, 364–366
   differential treatment affects students, 366–374
   differential treatment direct effects, 367–368
   dissipation of self-fulfilling prophecies, 359–360
   experimentally-induced *vs.* naturally-occurring self-fulfilling prophecies, 353–361, *355*
   extent, 360–361
   harm *vs.* help, 356–359
   motivational mediation, 368–374
   new situations, 356
   pattern, 360–361
   power of positive *vs.* negative teacher expectations, 356–359
   predictive validity of pre-school teacher expectations, 358
   Pygmalion study, 350–353
   Rosenthal and Jacobson, 353
   self-fulfilling prophecy processes, 361–374
   state of the literature, 350–353
   student motivational mediation as partial explanation for modest effect, 374
   student motivational mediation as powerful explanation for large effect, 374–376
   students' perceptions of differential teacher treatment, 364–366
   student stigmatization, 356
   synergistic with motivational effects, 368
   TARGET, 369, 372–374
   timing of false expectations, 355–356
   under- *vs.* overestimating achievement in math classes, 357–358
   under- *vs.* overestimating IQ, 357
Self-handicapping, attribution theory, 18–19
Self-instruction, self-regulated learning, 251
Self-observation, self-regulation, 248
Self-reaction, self-regulation, 248
Self-recording, self-regulated learning, 250
Self-reflection phase sources of motivation, 253–254
Self-regulated learning, 247–261
   causal attribution judgments, 254
   cyclical phase model, 248–254, *249*
   defining, 247–248
   developing, 256–258, *258*
   empowering students with self-regulation and motivation deficiencies, 258–260, *260*

environmental control, 253
environmental structuring, 251
event measures, 255–256
forethought phase sources of motivation, 251–252
imagery, 251
interest enhancement, 253
metacognitive monitoring, 249–251
microanalytic measures, 255–256
outcome expectations, 252
performance goal orientation, 252
performance phase sources of motivation, 252
personal feedback, 249–251
self-consequences, 253
self-efficacy, 251–252
self-evaluative judgments, self-reflection phase sources
    of motivation, 253–254
self-instruction, 251
self-recording, 250
self-satisfaction, 254
social learning, 256–258, *258*
strategic planning, 250
task interest, 252
task strategy, 250
time management, 251
Self-regulation
    control, 248
    judgment, 248
    self-efficacy, 44–46
        correlational research, 44–45
        experimental research, *45,* 45–46
    self-observation, 248
    self-reaction, 248
    social cognitive perspective, 248
Self-Regulation Empowerment Program, 258–260, *260*
Self-reports
    classroom instructional characteristics connection,
        532–534
    emotion, 579–581, *580*
    examining motivational theory through, 531–532
Self-satisfaction, self-regulated learning, 254
Self-System Model of Motivational Development, 231
Self-theories, 123–138
    changing, 136–137
    communication, 134–136
    criticism, 135
    development, 133–136
    effort, 127–128
    entity theory, 124
    failure, 128–129
    future directions, 137–138
    gender, 136
    incremental theory, 124
    leading to different goals, 125–126
    measurement, 124–130
    patterns of responses, 123–124
    performance, 129–130
    praise, 134–135

stereotype threat, 132–133
Self-worth theory, 40, 141–167
    applicability, 165
    coherence, 157–158
    emotional conflict, 141–142
    excuses, 145–146
    fear of failure, 153–154
    generalizability, 164–165
    grades, 156
        criterion-referenced grading, 159–161
        effort/outcome linkage, 160
        perceived equity, 160
        positive alliances, 160
    instructor/student mismatches, 155–156
    learned drives, 141–142
    perspective, 164–167
    reinventing teaching/learning process, 156–161
    roles and responsibilities mismatch, 155–156, 158–159
    self-worth reformulation, 161–164
    solutions as goals, 156–161
    students, 144–145
    student/teacher value conflict, 144
    systematic research agenda, 145–152
    theoretical overview, 142–145
    timing, 165–167
    transparency, 157–158
Sense of personal responsibility, teachers, 628
Situational interest
    definitions, 197–199, *198*–199
    individual interest, relationship, *204,* 204–205
    intrinsic motivation, relationship, *204,* 204–205
    measurement, 205–206
    reading, text-based interest sources, 199–200
    from situational to individual interest, 208–209
    text learning, 209–210
    triggered *vs.* maintained, 200–201
    two-phase model, 200
Skill possession, self-efficacy, contrasted, 39
Social antecedents, emotion, 593
Social cognitive theory, 1, 35–36
Social environment
    emotion, 584–585
    self-determination theory, 172
Social influences
    environment, 463–474
    self-efficacy, 43
Social isolation, reading motivation, 515, 517
Socialization, 643
Social learning, self-regulated learning, 256–258, *258*
Social learning theory, learning disabilities, 608–609
Social motivation, reading motivation, 506–507, 511
Social processes
    mathematics education research, 539–540
    mathematics motivation, 542–544
Social purpose hypothesis, motivational theorizing,
    270–272
Social relatedness, 2–3, 215

Social support, student-teacher relationship, 302–303
Sociocultural context, achievement emotions, 596
Sociocultural influences, gender, 422–424
Sport, *See also* Physical education motivation
    characterized, 555
Stability, attribution theory, 13
Statistics, small sample size, 618–619
Stereotype threat, 437–439
    defined, 132
    mechanisms, 438–439
    self-theories, 132–133
Strategic planning, self-regulated learning, 250
Student beliefs
    intelligence, 123–138
Student characteristics, student-teacher relationship,
        317–318
Student goals, 105–120
    content goals, 111–112
        relationship between different goals, 113–115, *114*
        students espouse distinctive purposes, 112–115
    Ford and Nichols' taxonomy of 24 content goals,
        109–110
    future research, 119
    hierarchical organization of goals, 110–111
    multiple goals, 105–106
        classroom interaction, 116–117
        managing simultaneous pursuit, 115–119
        vs. single goal, 106–107
    nonprimed goal pursuit, 117–118
    primed goal pursuit, 117–118
    Schwartz's theory of human values, *108,* 108–109
    student goal content, 107–112
    students processing cues from multiple sources, 107
Students
    mathematics motivation
        developing mathematical identities, 545–546
        students' views of themselves as mathematics
            learners, 544–546
    self-worth theory, 144–145
Student stigmatization, 356
Student-teacher relationship, 301–318, 442–443
    attachment theory, 302–304
    design issues, 313–314
    emotionally supportive relationship correlates,
        303–304
    emotional support, 307
    focus on teachers, 317
    harassment, 307
    importance, 310–314, 316
    measuring, 312–313
    multiple dimensions of support, 307–309
    parents, contrasted, 310–312
    peers, contrasted, 310–312
    physical safety, 307
    self-determination theory, 303
    as socialization contexts, 305–309
    social support, 302–303

student characteristics, 317–318
    teacher communications, 306
    teacher expectations, 306
    teacher willingness to provide help, 307
    theoretical challenges, 315–316
    theoretical perspectives, 301–310
Student teaching, 640
Subject content
    meaningfulness, 215–216
    value, 215–216
Success
    emotion, attributional antecedents, 575–576
    quadripolar model of individual differences, 146–148,
        147
Support *vs.* control, 283–284

T
TARGET, 91, 369, 372–374
Task avoidance, reading motivation, 514
Task difficulty, reading motivation, 515
Task interest, self-regulated learning, 252
Task mastery, reading motivation, 506, 509–510
Task strategy, self-regulated learning, 250
Task values, cross-cultural research, 69–70
Teacher education, 640
Teacher Efficacy Scale, 630
Teacher expectations
    self-fulfilling prophecies, 349–377
        accumulating self-fulfilling prophecies, 359, 360
        accuracy of teacher expectations, 361–364
        adaptive motivational patterns, 369–370
        age, 356
        authority, 370–371
        autonomy, 370–371
        conditions, 355
        differential teacher treatment, 364–366
        differential treatment affects students, 366–374
        differential treatment direct effects, 367–368
        dissipation of self-fulfilling prophecies, 359–360
        experimentally-induced *vs.* naturally-occurring self-
            fulfilling prophecies, 353–361, *355*
        extent, 360–361
        harm *vs.* help, 356–359
        motivational mediation, 368–374
        new situations, 356
        pattern, 360–361
        power of positive *vs.* negative teacher expectations,
            356–359
        predictive validity of pre-school teacher
            expectations, 358
        Pygmalion study, 350–353
        Rosenthal and Jacobson, 353
        self-fulfilling prophecy processes, 361–374
        state of the literature, 350–353
        student motivational mediation as partial
            explanation for modest effect, 374
        student motivational mediation as powerful

explanation for large effect, 374–376
students' perceptions of differential teacher
    treatment, 364–366
student stigmatization, 356
synergistic with motivational effects, 368
TARGET, 369, 372–374
timing of false expectations, 355–356
under- *vs.* overestimating achievement in math
    classes, 357–358
under- *vs.* overestimating IQ, 357
student-teacher relationship, 306
Teacher feedback, attribution theory, 15–16
Teacher induction, 640–641
Teachers, *see also* Student-teacher relationship
autonomy-supportive teaching, 183–184
beliefs, self-efficacy, 627–648, 662–663
communication, 306
instructor/student mismatches, 155–156
mathematics motivation, 537–538
    student perceptions, 537–538
school work culture for teachers, 394
self-concept, 628
self-efficacy, 38, 627–648, 628, 662–663
    beyond efficacy to academic optimism, 647–648
    calibration, 631
    ceiling effects, 631
    classroom management, 634
    collective efficacy, 642–645
    development and support research, 638–642
    direct outcomes, 637
    direct teacher outcomes, 636
    diversity, 632–633
    efficacy beliefs about relationships with students,
        646–647
    efficacy judgments, 631–634
    efficacy measure criticisms, 631
    efficacy research criticisms, 645–646
    efficacy sources, 638–640
    engagement, 637
    future research, 646–648
    inclusion, 632–633
    indirect influences, 636–637
    language, 632
    literacy, 632
    mathematics, 632
    measurement of teachers' sense of efficacy, 629–630
    model of teachers' efficacy beliefs, 628–631, 629
    motivation, 637
    process approach on teacher and student outcomes
        research, 634–638, 635
    relational influences, 637–638
    relational outcomes, 637
    science, 632
    student outcomes, 637–638
    student teaching, 640
    teacher education, 640
    Teacher Efficacy Scale, 630

teacher experience, 641–642
teacher induction, 640–641
teachers' decision, actions, and communications,
    634–637
Teachers' Sense of Efficacy Scale, 630
technology, 633
self-esteem, 628
sense of personal responsibility, 628
Teachers' Sense of Efficacy Scale, 630
Teaching, assumptions, 655–656
Technology, 633
Temperament, emotion, 593
Test anxiety, 575–578
    effects, 588
    expectancy, 582–583
    threat appraisal, 582–583
    values, 582–583
Testing, 2
    undermining student and teacher autonomy, 184–186
Text learning
    interest, 209–213
    situational interest, 209–210
    topic interest, 210–213
Theory of basic human values, *108,* 108–109
Threat appraisal, test anxiety, 582–583
Time management, self-regulated learning, 251
Timing, self-worth theory, 165–167
Topic interest, text learning, 210–213
Transforming School Cultures (Maehr and Midgley),
    92–93
Transparency, self-worth theory, 157–158

U
Unconscious motivation, attribution theory, 29
Universality, self-determination theory, 188–190

V
Valence, achievement goal theory, 87, *88*
Value
    achievement expectancies, 228
    beliefs, 485–486
    sources, 63–64
        developmental considerations, 64–65
    subject content, 215–216
Value appraisals, 592
Value beliefs, gender, 415–416
Value constructs
    cross-cultural research, 68–70
        meaning, 70
    expectancy-value theory, 57–58
        cultural influences, 69–70
        development, 59–60
        measurement, 58–59
    experiential influences, 61–65
    psychological influences, 61–65
    relations, 60–61
Value in reading, reading motivation, 507, 511

Values, test anxiety, 582–583
Verbal persuasion, 643
Vicarious experience, 643
Victimization, peers, 331–332, 338–340
    mental health, 331–332

peer group rejection, 332–334
physical health, 332

W
Will to learn, 150–152
    intrinsic/extrinsic dichotomy, 151–152